Morrill

Rienzi Overture -
Wagner   get

DIZIONARIO TASCABILE

ITALIANO-INGLESE & INGLESE-ITALIANO

DI

J. E. WESSELY

INTERAMENTE RIFATTA

DA

G. RIGUTINI E G. PAYN

———————

HANDY DICTIONARY

ITALIAN-ENGLISH & ENGLISH-ITALIAN

BY

J. E. WESSELY

THOROUGHLY REVISED AND RE-WRITTEN

BY

G. RIGUTINI AND G. PAYN

PHILADELPHIA

DAVID McKAY COMPANY

WASHINGTON SQUARE

1942

Trasposizione della Pronunzia Inglese.

ă = *e* in *pera.*
ā = *a* in *casa.*
â = *o* in *cuôre* (vocale essenzialmente inglese, partecipando
insieme ad *a* e ad *o*).
ĕ = *e* in *pero.*
ĭ = *i* in *vino.*
ẽ = *e* in *mente.*
ī = *ai* in *Cairo.*
ĭ = *i* in *ritto.*
ŏ = *o* in *no.*
ō = *u* in *cura.*
ŏ = *o* in *cuôre* (partecipando insieme ad *o* e ad *a*).
ŏ = *o* in *orbe.*
ŭ = *iu* in *iure.*
ũ = *eu* francese in *neuf* (vocale
essenzialmente inglese, partecipando ad *e* e ad *u*).

ŭ = *u* in *tutto.*
ŏŭ = *au* in *aura.*

j = *g* in *gettare, giro.*
ch = *cc* in *caccia.*
g = *gh* in *ghirlanda,* o *g* in *gamba;*
seguita da *e* o *i,* qualquevolta
= *g* in *gettare, giro.*
gl = *gl* in *glossario.*
k = *c* in *cane.*
y = *i* in *iambo.*
s = *s* in *stante.*
z = *s* in *rosa.*
sh = *sc* in *lasciare.*
th }
th } consonanti bisbiglianti proprie
dell' inglese; el *th* pronunzian-
dosi più acutamente del *th.*

Transposition of Italian Pronunciation.

ā = *a* in *fate.*
ā = *a* in *far.*
ī = *ee* in *meet.*
ẽ = *e* in *met*
ĭ = *i* in *hit.*
ō = *o* in *pole.*
ŏ = *o* in *prove.*
ŏ = *o* in *hot.*
ŭ = *u* in *full.*

j = *j* in *jar.*

dj = *dg* in *hedge.*
dsh = *ch* in *reach.*
tsh = *ch* in *church.*
ŝ (soft) = *s* in *rose.*
s (sharp) = *s* in *stand.*
ssh = *sh* in *shall.*
dż (soft) = *ds* in *goods.*
tz (sharp) = *ts* in *its.*
ly = *lli* in *million.*
ny = *ni* in *onion* (or *gn* French,
as in *agneau*).

Abbreviature.

Abbreviations.

a. = adjective, *aggettivo*.
ad. = adverb, *avverbio*.
(am.) = americanism, *americanismo*.
(ar.) = arithmetic, *aritmetica*.
art. = article, *articolo*.
(bibl.) = biblical, *biblico*.
(bot.) = botany, *botanica*.
c. = conjunction, *congiunzione*.
(cant) = cant term, *espressione di gergo*.
(chem.) = chemistry, *chimica*.
(com.) = commerce, *commercio*.
(cont.) = contraction, *abbreviazione*.
f. = feminine gender, *genere femminino*.
(fam.) = familiarly, *familiarmente*.
(fig.) = figuratively, *figuratamente*.
(gr.) = grammar, *grammatica*.
i. = interjection, *interiezione*.
(in comp.) = in compounds, *in voci composte*.   [*prudenza*.
(jur.) = jurisprudence (law term), *giuris-*

m. = masculine gender, *genere mascolino*.
(mar.) = marine, *marina*.
(med.) = medicine, *medicina*.
(mil.) = military term, *termine militare*.
(mus.) = music, *musica*.
p. = participle, *participio*.
pl. = plural, *plurale*.
(poet.) = poetry, *poetica*.
pn. = pronoun, *pronome*.
pr. = preposition, *preposizione*.
(rail.) = railway, *strada ferrata*.
s. = substantive, *sostantivo*.
v. a. = verb active, *verbo transitivo*.
v. def. = verb defective, *verbo defettivo*.
v. imp. = verb impersonal, *verbo impersonale*.
v. ir. = verb irregular, *verbo irregolare*.
v. n. = verb neuter, *verbo intransitivo*.
v. r. = verb reflective, *verbo riflessivo*.
(vulg.) = vulgar(ly), *volgare, volgarmente*.

ITALIAN-ENGLISH DICTIONARY

A.

a, ă, pr. at, to, by, in, on, for, with, under.
abaco, ă' băkŏ, m. abacus, plinth; multiplication-table.
abantico, –bănt'kŏ, ad. formerly.
abâte, –bă'tĕ, m. abbot.
abazia, –bātz'ă ă, f. abbey.
abbacare, –bbăkă'rĕ, v. a. to examine closely; –, v. n. to puzzle oneself.
abbacchiare, –kĭă'rĕ, v. a. to beat down with a pole (fruit).
abbacchiatura, –tŭ'ră, f. the beating down of fruit from trees with a pole.
abbachista, –kĭs'tă, m. arithmetician.
abbacinamento, –dshĭnămĕn'tŏ, m. dazzling. [cloud.
abbacinare, –dshĭnă'rĕ, v. a. to dazzle, to delay. [to delay.
abbaco, ăb'băkŏ, m. arithmetic.
abbadare, –bădă'rĕ, v. a. to stand trifling.
abbadessa, –bădĕs'să, f. abbess.
abbadia, –bădĭ'ă, f. abbey.
abbagliamento, –bălyămĕn'tŏ, m. dimness of sight; mistake. [liant.
abbagliante, –lyăn'tĕ, a. dazzling, brilliant.
abbaglianza, –lyăn'tză, m. dimness of sight; mistake; (fig.) shortsightedness.
abbagliare, –lyă'rĕ, v. a. to dazzle; (fig.) to beguile, to bewitch; to impose upon; –, v. n. to be dazzled. [fusedly.
abbagliatamente, –tămĕn'tĕ, ad. confusedly.
abbaglio, –băl'yŏ, m. dazzling; mistake.
abbaiamento, –bălămĕn'tŏ, m. barking, yelping. [to boast, to brag.
abbaiare, –bălă'rĕ, v. n. to bark, to yelp; to brag.
abbaiatore, –tŏ'rĕ, m. barker; slanderer.
abbaiatrice, –trĭ'dshĕ, f. censorious woman, detractress.
abbaino, –bă'ĭnŏ, m. dormer-window.
abbaione, –bă'ĭŏ'nĕ, m. a noisy fellow.
abballare, –băllă'rĕ, v. a. to embale.
abbalordire, –bălŏrdĭ'rĕ, v. a. to stun, to bother. [with cotton.
abbambagiare, –bămbăjă'rĕ, v. a. to stuff with cotton.
abbandonamento, –băndŏnămĕn'tŏ, m. abandoning, abandonment.
abbandonare, –dŏnă'rĕ, v. a. to abandon, to forsake, to give over; to quit; to leave; abbandonarsi, –năr'sĭ, to give oneself up to. [perately.
abbandonatamente, –tămĕn'tĕ, ad. desperately.
abbandono, –dŏ'nŏ, m. forsaking, desertion; in –, in confusion; at random.

abbarbagliamento, –bărbălyămĕn'tŏ, m. dazzling. [to stupefy.
abbarbagliare, –yă'rĕ, v. a. to dazzle, to stupefy.
abbarbicare, –bĭkă'rĕ, v. n. to take root.
abbarcare, –kă'rĕ, v. a. to heap up, to pile.
abbarrare, –ră'rĕ, v. a. to bar, to stop up.
abbaruffamento, –rŭffămĕn'tŏ, m. scuffle, quarrel. [fusion.
abbaruffare, –fă'rĕ, v. a. to put in confusion.
abbassamento, –băssămĕn'tŏ, m. abasement; diminution.
abbassare, –să'rĕ, v. a. to abase, to cast down; to lower; to diminish; to humble; –, v. n. to come down; to decline; abbassarsi, –săr'sĭ, to fall, to sink; to humble oneself.
abbasso, –băs'sŏ, ad. below, down.
abbastanza, –băstăn'tză, ad. enough.
abbattere, –băt'tĕrĕ, v. a. to overthrow; to subdue; to abate; to humble; abbattersi, –tĕrsĭ, to meet with.
abbattimento, –tĭmĕn'tŏ, m. overthrow; conflict, battle; accident, chance.
abbattitore, –tŏ'rĕ, m. feller; destroyer; bully. [pressed.
abbattuto, –băttŭ'tŏ, a. cast down, depressed.
abbatuffolare, –ffŏlă'rĕ, v. a. to throw into confusion.
abbazia, –bătzĕ'ă, f. abbey. [rian.
abbecedario, –bĕdshĕdă'rĭŏ, m. abecedarian.
abbellare, –bĕllă'rĕ, v. a. to embellish; –, v. n. to grow handsome. [ment.
abbellimento, –lĭmĕn'tŏ, m. embellishment.
abbellire, –lĕ'rĕ, v. a. to beautify, to adorn.
abbenché, –bĕnkĕ', c. although.
abbendare, –dă'rĕ, v. a. to bind, to tie; to bend. [with battlements.
abbertescare, –bĕrtĕskă'rĕ, v. a. to fortify with battlements.
abbeverare, –bĕvĕră'rĕ, v. a. to give drink; to cause a profound sleep, to stupefy.
abbeveratoio, –tŏ'ĭŏ, m. horse pond.
abbiadare, –bĭădă'rĕ, v. a. to give a feed of oats. [of oats.
abbicci, –bĭtshĭ', m. alphabet.
abbigliamento, –bĭlyămĕn'tŏ, m. dress, finery, attire.
abbigliare, –yă'rĕ, v. a. to dress, to trim up; abbigliarsi, –yăr'sĭ, to adorn oneself.
abbindolamento, –bĭndŏlămĕn'tŏ, m. cheat, trick. [cheat.
abbindolare, –dŏlă'rĕ, v. a. to deceive, to

abbiosciare, –bĭŏsshă´rĕ, v. n. to get disheartened; **abbiosciarsi,** –shăr´sĭ, to
lose courage.   [to be necessary.
abbisognare, –bĭsŏnyă´rĕ, v. n. to want;
abboccamento, –bŏkkămĕn´tŏ, m. conference, interview.
atboccare, –kă´rĕ, v. a. to fill to the
brim; to seize with the teeth; **abboc-
carsi,** –kăr´sĭ, to have an interview with.
abboccato, –kă´tŏ, a. delicate.   [furnace.
abboccatoio, –tŏ´ĭŏ, m. mouth of a
abboccatura, –tŏ´ră, f. brim.
abbocconare, –kŏnă´rĕ, v. a. to cut into
morsels, to mince.
abbonacciamento, –bŏnătshămĕn´tŏ, m.
calm.   [to pacify.
abbonacciare, –nătshă´rĕ, v. a. to calm,
abbonamento, –mĕn´tŏ, m. subscription.
abbonare, –nă´rĕ, v. a. to meliorate; to
admit (an account); **abbonarsi,** –năr´sĭ,
to subscribe (for).   [copious.
abbondante, –bŏndăn´tĕ, a. abundant,
abbondantemente, –tĕmĕn´tĕ, ad. abundantly.   [plenty.
abbondanza, –dăn´tză, f. abundance.
abbondanziere, –tzĭĕ´rĕ, m. city-vic-
tualler (at Florence).
abbondare, –dă´rĕ, v. a. to abound with.
abbondevole, –dĕ´vŏlĕ, a. abundant.
abbondevolmente, –vŏlmĕn´tĕ, ad. abundantly.
abbondevolezza, –vŏlĕt´ză, f. abundance.
abbonire, –bŏnĕ´rĕ, v. a. to perfect; to
soften, to calm.   [ship.
abbordaggio, –bŏrdăd´jŏ, m. boarding a
abbordare, –dă´rĕ, v. a. to board (a ship);
to accost.   [landing.
abbordo, –bŏr´dŏ, m. approach, access;
abborracciare, –bŏrrătshă´rĕ, v. a. to
bungle, to huddle to botch.   [stuff.
abborrare, –ră´rĕ, v. a. to go astray; to
abbottinarsi, –bŏttĭnăr´sĭ, v. r. to mutiny.
abbottonare, –tŏnă´rĕ, v. a. to button.
abbottonatura, –nătŏ´ră, f. button-holes,
pl.   [draft, sketch.
abbozzamento, –bŏtzămĕn´tŏ, m. rough
abbozzare, –tză´rĕ, v. a. to sketch; to
trace.   [half-ripe.
abbozzaticcio, –tă´tshŏ, a. half-sketched;
abbozzo, –bŏt´zŏ, sm. sketch, rough draft.
abbozzolarsi, –lăr´sĭ, v. r. to form its
cocoon (of caterpillars).   [honey-suckle.
abbracciaboschi, –brătshăbŏs´kĭ, m. (bot.)
abbracciamento, –mĕn´tŏ, m. embrace.
abbracciare, –tshă´rĕ, v. a. to embrace.
abbracciata, –tshă´tă, f. embrace; acco-
lade.   [grasp; to hold fast.
abbrancare, –brănkă´rĕ, v. a. to gripe, to
abbreviamento, –brĕvĭămĕn´tŏ, m. abridgment.
abbreviare, –vĭă´rĕ, v. a. to abridge; to
abbreviate; to shorten.
abbreviatore, –tŏ´rĕ, sm. abbreviator,
abridger.   [a word).
abbreviatura, –tŏ´ră, f. abbreviation (of
abbreviazione, –tzĭŏ´nĕ, f. shortening.
abbrezzare, –brĕtză´rĕ, v. a. to shrink,
to shudder.

abbriccare, –brĭkkă´rĕ, v. a. to fling, to
cast, to throw, to hurl, to lance.
abbrivare, –brĭvă´rĕ, v. a. (mar.) to un-
moor.   [cold.
abbrividire, –vĭdĕ´rĕ, v. n. to shiver with
abbrivo, –brĕ´vŏ, m. (mar.) sea-way, run,
course, headway.   [burning.
abbronzamento, –brŏndzămĕn´tŏ, m. sun-
abbronzare, –dză´rĕ, v. a. to tan; to sun-
burn.   [scorch superficially, to singe.
abbruciacchiare, –brŭdshăkĭă´rĕ, v. a. to
abbruciamento, –mĕn´tŏ, m. burning.
abbruciare, –dshă´rĕ, v. a. to burn, to consume; **abruciato di denaro,** penniless.   [ing.
abbrunamento, –brŭnămĕn´tŏ, m. darken-
abbrunare, –nă´rĕ, abbrunire, –nĕ´rĕ,
v. a. to make brown; **abbrunarsi,** –năr´-
sĭ, to put on mourning.   [to scorch.
abbrustiare, –brŭstĭă´rĕ, v. a. to singe;
abbrustolire, –tŏlĕ´rĕ, v. a. to toast, to
crisp; to scorch.
abbrutire, –brŭtĕ´rĕ, v. a. to brutify.
abbuiare, –bŭĭă´rĕ, v. a. to hide; to darken.
abbuono, –bŭŏ´nŏ, m. improvement.
abburattamento, –bŭrăttămĕn´tŏ, m.
sifting; bolting.   [to abuse.
abburattare, –tă´rĕ, v. a. to bolt; to sift;
abdicare, –dĭkă´rĕ, v. a. to abdicate.
abdicazione, –kătzĭŏ´nĕ, f. abdication.
abduttore, –dŭttŏ´rĕ, m. (an.) abductor.
abduzione, –dŭtzĭŏ´nĕ, f. abduction.
aberrazione, –ĕrrătzĭŏ´nĕ, f. aberration.
abesperto, –ĕspĕr´tŏ, ad. by experience.
abetaia, –bĕtă´ĭă, f. fir-plantation.
abete, ăbĕ´tĕ, **abeto,** –tŏ, m. fir-tree; pine.
abetino, ăbĕtĕ´nŏ, a, or like a fir-tree.
abiettamente, ăbĭĕttămĕn´tĕ, ad. abjectly.
abiettezza, –tĕt´ză, f. abjectness.
abietto, ăbĭĕt´tŏ, a. abject.
abiezione, –tzĭŏ´nĕ, f. abjection.
abigeato, ăbĭjĕă´tŏ, m. cattle-stealing.
abigeo, –jĕ´ŏ, m. cattle-stealer.
abile, ă´bĭlĕ, a. able, clever.
abilità, ăbĭlĭtă´, f. ability, dexterity.
abilitare, –tă´rĕ, v. a. to enable, to qualify.
abilitativo, –tăĭ´vŏ, a. qualifying.
abilitazione, –tătzĭŏ´nĕ, f. enabling.
abilmente, –mĕn´tĕ, ad. ably.   [to ruin.
abissare, ăbĭssă´rĕ, v. a. to precipitate;
abisso, ăbĭs´sŏ, m. abyss, gulf; hell.
abitabile, ăbĭtă´bĭlĕ, a. habitable.
abitacolo, –tă´kŏlŏ, m. dwelling; (mar.)
binnacle.
abitante, –tăn´tĕ, m. dweller, inhabitant.
abitare, –tă´rĕ, v. a. to dwell.
abitatore, –tŏ´rĕ, m. dweller, inhabitant.
abitatrice, –trĕ´dshĕ, f. female dweller.
abitazioncella, –tzĭŏndshĕl´lă, f. small
lodging or house.   [tion, residence.
abitazione, –tzĭŏ´nĕ, f. dwelling, habita-
abito, ă´bĭtŏ, m. habit, custom, use; dress,
clothes; temperament.
abituale, ăbĭtŭă´lĕ, a. habitual, customary.
abitualmente, –tŭălmĕn´tĕ, ad. habitually.
abituare, –tŭă´rĕ, v. a. to use, to accustom;
abituarsi, –tŭăr´sĭ, to accustom oneself.

abituatezza, –tĕ'ză, f. custom.
abitudine, –tŏ'dĭnĕ, f. habitude.
abituro, –tŏ'rŏ, m. humble abode.
abiurare, –tŭrā'rĕ, v. a. to abjure; to renounce.
abiurazione, –tzĭŏ'nĕ, f. abjuration.
ablativo, –lătĕ'vŏ, m. (gr.) ablative case.
abluzione, –lŭtzĭŏ'nĕ, f. ablution.
abolire, ăbŏlē'rĕ, v. a. to abolish, to annul.
abolizione, –lĭtzĭŏ'nĕ, f. abolition.
abominabile, ăbŏmĭnā'bĭlĕ, a. abominable, execrable. [to hate, to abhor.
abominare, –nā'rĕ, v. a. to abominate.
abominazione, –nătzĭŏ'nĕ, f. abomination, detestation. [execrable.
abominevole, –nă'vŏlĕ, a. abominable.
abominio, –mĕ'nĭŏ, m. abomination.
abominoso, –mĭnŏ'sŏ, a. detestable.
aborrimento, ăbŏrrĭmĕn'tŏ, m. abhorrence, aversion. [to detest.
aborrire, –ŏrrē'rĕ, v. a. to abhor, to loathe,
aborritore, –rĭtŏ'rĕ, m. hater, detester.
abortire, ăbŏrtē'rĕ, v. n. to miscarry.
abortivo, –tē'vŏ, a. abortive. [child.
aborto, ăbŏr'tŏ, m. abortion, abortive
abosina, ăbŏsē'nă, f. plum.
abosino, –nŏ, m. plum-tree.
abrogare, –rŏgā'rĕ, v. a. to abrogate.
abrogazione, –tzĭŏ'nĕ, f. abrogation.
abrotano, –tŏ'tănŏ, m. southernwood.
abusare, –ŭsā'rĕ, v. a. & n. to abuse.
abusivamente, –sĭvāmēn'tĕ, ad.abusively.
abusivo, –sē'vŏ, a. abusive.
abuso, –ŏ'sŏ, m. abuse, disuse.
acca, ăk'kă, f. the letter H. [sity.
accademia, –ăd'mĭă, f. academy, university.
accademico, –mĭkŏ, a. & ad. academical; academician. [befall.
accadere, –dā'rĕ, v. n. ir. to happen, to
accaffare, –kăffā'rĕ, v. a. to snatch away.
accagionamento, –kăjŏnămĕn'tŏ, m. imputation. [accuse of.
accagionare, –nā'rĕ, v. a. to impute; to
accagionatore, –nătŏ'rĕ, m. accuser.
accalappiare, –kălăppĭā'rĕ, v. a. to inveigle, to befool, to delude.
accalorare, –tŏrā'rĕ, v. a. to warm; to incite. [campment.
accampamento, –kămpămĕn'tŏ, m. encampment.
accampare, –pā'rĕ, v. n. to encamp; accamparsi, –păr'sĭ, to pitch one's camp.
accanalare, –kănălā'rĕ, v. a. to channel, to chamfer. [irritate.
accanare, –nā'rĕ, v. a. to uncouple; to
accanato, –nā'tŏ, a. furious; very angry.
accanire, –nē'rĕ, v. a. to irritate.
accanitamente, –nĭtămēn'tĕ, ad.furiously.
accannellare, –nĕllā'rĕ, v. a. to wind upon
accanto, –kăn'tŏ, ad. aside. [bobbins.
accaparrare, –pārā'rĕ, v. a. to make a bargain, to give or receive earnest-money.
accapezzare, –pĕtză'rĕ, v. a. to finish.
accapigliarsi, –pĭlyăr'sĭ, v. r. to take one another by the hair.
accappatoio, –pătŏ', m. combing-cloth.
accappiare, –pĭā'rĕ, v. a. to insnare.

accappiatura, –tŏ'ră, f. running knot; snare. [capons.
accapponare, –pŏnā'rĕ, v. a. to make
accaprettare, –prĕttā'rĕ, v. a. to tie an animal by the four legs.
accapricciare, –prĭtshā'rĕ, v. n., accapricciarsi, –tshăr'sĭ, to shudder, to shiver. [caressing.
accarezzamento, –kărĕtzămĕn'tŏ, m.
accarezzare, –tză'rĕ, v. a. to caress, to fondle. [into the flesh.
accarnare, –kărnā'rĕ, v. a. to dash deep
accartocciare, –tŏtshā'rĕ, v. a. to wrap up in a cornet. [wedding.
accasamento, –kăsămĕn'tŏ, m. marriage,
accasare, –sā'rĕ, v. a. to build houses; –, v. n. to take a wife; accasarsi, –săr'sĭ, to marry; to begin house-keeping. [tude.
accasciamento, –sshămĕn'tŏ, m. decrepitude.
accasciare, –sshā'rĕ, v. a. to weaken; –, v. n., accasciarsi, –sshăr'sĭ, to become feeble through age.
accasermare, –kăsermā'rĕ, v. a. (mil.) to place into barracks.
accastellato, –kăstĕllā'tŏ, a. (mar.) having a fore- and hind-castle. [catarrh.
accatarramento, –tărrāmĕn'tŏ, m. cold,
accatarrare, –rā'rĕ, v. n. to catch a cold.
accatastare, –tăstā'rĕ, v. a. to heap up.
accattabrighe, –tăbrē'ghĕ, m. quarrelsome fellow. [ging.
accattamento, –mĕn'tŏ, m. beggary, begging.
accattapane, –pă'nĕ, m. beggar.
accattare, –kăttā'rĕ, v. a. to borrow; to beg, to request; to impetrate.
accattatore, –tŏ'rĕ, m. borrower; beggar.
accattatozzi see accattapane.
accatteria, –tĕr'ĭă, f. borrowing; begging.
accatto, –kăt'tŏ, m. borrowing; begging.
accattone, –tŏ'nĕ, m. vile beggar, blackguard; impostor. [upon.
accavalcare, –kăvălkā'rĕ, v. a. to mount
accavalciare, –tshā'rĕ, v. a. to ride or sit astraddle. [another.
accavallare, –lā'rĕ, v. a. to pile one upon
accavigliare, –vĭlyā'rĕ, v. a. to wind on bobbins. [ness; error.
accecamento, ătshĕkămĕn'tŏ, m. blindness.
accecare, –kā'rĕ, v. a. to blind.
accecatoio, –kătŏ'ĭ, m. ruff.
accecatore, –tŏ'rĕ, m. deceiver, cheat.
accecatura, –tŏ'ră, f. wimble.
accedere, ătshĕ'dĕrĕ, v. n. to approach.
acceffare, ătshĕffā'rĕ, v. a. to catch with the teeth.
acceggia, ătshĕd'jă, f. wood-cock.
acceleramento, –lĕrămĕn'tŏ, m. acceleration, hastening, speed. [to speed.
accelerare, –rā'rĕ, v. a. to accelerate,
acceleratamente, –tămĕn'tĕ, ad. in a hurry.
accelerativo, –tē'vŏ, a. accelerating.
accelerazione, –tzĭŏ'nĕ, f. acceleration.
accendere, ătshĕn'dĕrĕ, v. a. ir. to kindle; to set on fire. [combustible.
accendibile, –dē'bĭlĕ, a. inflammable,

accendimento, -ātmĕn'tŏ, m. setting on fire; kindling.

accenditoio, -dĭtŏ'ŏ, m. lighting-stick.

accenditore, -tŏ'rĕ, m. kindler; inflamer.

accennamento, -nămĕn'tŏ, m. nod, wink, hint, sign. [to advise.

accennare, -nā'rĕ, y. a. to hint; to feign; to advise.

accennatore, -tŏ'rĕ, m. beckoner.

accenno, ātshĕn'nŏ, m. advertisement.

accensibile, -sĕ'bĭlĕ, a. inflammable.

accensione, -stŏ'nĕ, f. conflagration.

accentare, -tā'rĕ, v. a. to place the accents on words, to accent.

accento, ātshĕn'tŏ, m. accent; pronunciation; voice; word. [oneself.

accentrarsi, -trăr'sĭ, v. r. to concentrate

accentuare, -tŭā'rĕ, v. a. to accentuate.

accerchiamento, ātshĕrkĭāmĕn'tŏ, m. encircling, encompassing. [to encircle.

accerchiare, -kĭā'rĕ, v. a. to encompass,

accerchiellare, -kĭĕllā'rĕ, v. a. to hoop.

accercinare, ātshĕrdshĭnā'rĕ, v. a. to shape like a porter's knot.

accertamento, -tămĕn'tŏ, m. confirmation; certainty.

accertare, -tā'rĕ, v. a. to ascertain, to assure.

accertatamente, -tămĕn'tĕ, ad. surely.

accertazione, -tzĭŏ'nĕ, f. assertion, affirmation, ascertaining.

accesamente, ātshĕsămĕn'tĕ, ad. ardently.

acceso, ātshā'sŏ, a. kindled, lighted; inflamed; flashing.

accessibile, ātshĕssĕ'bĭlĕ, a. approachable.

accessione, -stŏ'nĕ, f. accession; access.

accesso, ātshĕs'sŏ, m. fit, paroxysm. [fit.

accessoriamente, -sŏrĭămĕn'tĕ, ad. accessorily.

accessorio, -sŏ'rĭŏ, a. accessory.

accestire, ātshĕstŏ'rĕ, v. n. (bot.) to become bushy.

accetta, ātshĕt'tă, f. hatchet. [able.

accettabile, -tā'bĭlĕ, a. acceptable; agreeable.

accettante, -tăn'tĕ, m. (com.) accepter.

accettare, -tā'rĕ, y. a. to accept.

accettatore, -tŏ'rĕ, m. acceptor.

accettazione, -tzĭŏ'nĕ, f. acceptation.

accettevole, -tā'vŏlĕ, a. pleasant.

accettevolmente, -tĕvŏlmĕn'tĕ, ad. with pleasure.

accetto, ātshĕt'tŏ, a. acceptable, agreeable.

acchetare, ăkkĕtā'rĕ, v. a. to calm, to appease; acchetarsi, -tār'sĭ, v. to become calm. [to seize.

acchiappare, -kĭāppā'rĕ, v. a. to catch,

acchiocciolarsi, -kĭŏtshŏlār'sĭ, v. r. to sit cowering.

acchitarsi, -kĭtār'sĭ, v. r. to play the first stroke at billiards.

acchito, ăkkĕ'tŏ, m. the position of the ball when played.

acchiudere, -kĭŏ'dĕrĕ, v. a. ir. to enclose (said chiefly of letters).

acchiuso, -kĭŏ'sŏ, a. included.

accia, ăt'shă, f. thread; axe.

acciabattare, -băttā'rĕ, v. a. to botch.

acciaccare, -kā'rĕ, v. a. to bruise, to pound, to squash.

acciaccatura, -kātŏ'ră, f. (mus.) a kind of arpeggio. [indisposition.

acciacco, ātshăk'kŏ, m. outrage, affront;

acciaiare, ātshāīā'rĕ, v. a. to harden (steel).

acciaio, ātshā'ĭŏ, m. steel.

acciaiuolo, -ĭāŏ'lŏ, m. fire-steel.

acciarino, -rĕ'nŏ, m. fire-steel.

acciaro, ātshā'rŏ, m. (poet.) sword.

acciarpare, ātshārpā'rĕ, v. a. to botch, to bungle, to huddle.

acciarpatore, -tŏ'rĕ, m. bungler.

acciarpone, ātshārpŏ'nĕ, m. continual bungler.

accidentale, -tā'lĕ, a. accidental, casual.

accidentalità, -tālĭtā', f. accident.

accidentalmente, -tālmĕn'tĕ, ad. accidentally.

accidentario, -tā'rĭŏ, accidentoso, -tŏ'sŏ, a. accidental, unlucky.

accidentato, ātshĭdĕntā'tŏ, a. uneven, not level. [fortune; apopletic fit.

accidente, -dĕn'tĕ, m. chance; hap; mis-

accidia, ātshĕ'dĭă, f. idleness, indolence.

accidiosamente, ātshĭdĭŏsămĕn'tĕ, ad.

accidioso, -dĭŏ'sŏ, a. idle, lazy. [lazily.

acciecare, ātshĕkā'rĕ, v. a. to blind.

accigliamento, ātshĭlyămĕn'tŏ, m. sadness, sorrow. [brows.

accigliarsi, -lyăr'sĭ, v. r. to knit one's

accigliato, -lyā'tŏ, ad. gloomy, sullen; reserved.

accileccare, -lĕkkā'rĕ, v. a. to nestle.

accincignare, ātshĭndshĭnyā'rĕ, v. a. to tuck up. [pare oneself.

accingersi, ātshĭn'jĕrsĭ, v. r. ir. to pre-

accinto, ātshĕn'tŏ, a. girt; prepared, ready.

acciò, ātshŏ', acciocchè, -kĕ', c. in order that, so that. [pebbles.

acciottolare, -tŏlā'rĕ, v. a. to pave with

acciottolio, -tŏlĕ'ŏ, m. the sound made by plates struck together.

accismare, ātshĭsmā'rĕ, v. a to cut asunder.

acciuffare, ātshŭffā'rĕ, v. a. to take by the hair

acciuga, ātshŏ'gă, f. anchovy. [the hair

acciugata, ātshŏgā'tă, f. anchovy sauce.

accivettare, ātshĭvĕttā'rĕ, v. a. to flirt.

accivettato, -tā'tŏ, a. cautious, wise.

accivimento, ātshĭvĭmĕn'tŏ, m. provision, storing, victualling.

accivire, -vĕ'rĕ, v. a. to provide.

acclamare, ăkklāmā'rĕ, v. a. to acclaim; to applaud. [tion, applause.

acclamazione, -mătzĭŏ'nĕ, f. acclamation.

acclimare, -klĕmā'rĕ, v. a. to acclimatize.

acclimazione, -mătzĭŏ'nĕ, f. acclimation.

acclive, ăkklĕ'vĕ, a. sloping, steep.

acclività, ăkklĕvĭtā', f. acclivity, steepness.

accoccare, ăkkŏkkā'rĕ, v. a. to play a trick upon.

accoccolarsi, -kŏlār'sĭ, v. r. to sit squat.

accodarsi, -dār'sĭ, v. r. to follow close at one's heels.

accoglienza, -kŏlyĕn'tză, f. kind reception.

accogliere, -kŏl'yĕrĕ, v. a. ir. to gather; to welcome; accogliersi, -kŏl'yĕrsĭ, to meet, to assemble. [kind reception.

accoglimento, -lyĭmĕn'tŏ, m. assemblage;

accogliticcio, –tŭt'shŏ, a. hastily gathered up.   [ceiver.
accoglitore, –tŏ'rĕ, m. gatherer; re-
accolito, –kŏ'lŭtŏ, m. acolyte.
accollare, –kŏllä'rĕ, v. a. to yoke; to join;
accollarsi, –lär'sĭ, to take charge of.
accollo, äkkŏl'lŏ, m. job-work.
accolta, –kŏl'tä, f. assembly.   [a knife.
accoltellare, –lĕllä'rĕ, v. a. to stab with
accomandare, –dä'rĕ, v. a. to recommend.
accomandatario, –dätä'rĭŏ, m. trustee,
agent, mandatory, assignee.   [ship.
accomandita, –dĕ'tä, f. (com.) partner-
accomandolare, –dŏlä'rĕ, v. a. to join
broken threads (in weaving).
accomiatare, –mĭätä'rĕ, v. a. to dismiss,
to disband; accomiatarsi, –tär'sĭ, to
take one's leave.   [modable.
accomodabile, –mŏdä'bĭlĕ, a. accom-
accomodamento, –dämen'tŏ, m. adjustment, agreement.
accomodare, –dä'rĕ, v. a. to accommodate; to adjust, to arrange; to procure;
accomodarsi, –där'sĭ, to accommodate
oneself; to sit down.   [suitably, justly.
accomodatamente, –dätämen'tĕ, ad.
accomodatizio, –tĭ'dzĭŏ, a. pliant, supple.
accomodato, –dä'tŏ, a. adapted; proper.
accomodatrice, –dätrĭ'dshĕ, f. milliner.
accomodatura, –tŏ'rä, f. adjustment;
agreement.   [accompaniment; suite.
accompagnamento, –pänyämen'tŏ, m.
accompagnare, –yä'rĕ, v. a. to accompany; accompagnarsi, –yär'sĭ, to
marry.   [accompanies; companion.
accompagnatore, –yätŏ'rĕ, m. one that
accompagnatrice, –trĕ'dshĕ, f. she that
accompanies.
accompagnatura, see accompagna-
mento.   [munity.
accomunamento, –mŭnämen'tŏ, m. com-
accomunare, –mŭnä'rĕ, v. a. & n. to put
in common; to live in a community;
accomunarsi, –när'sĭ, to familiarise
oneself.   [finery, dress.
acconcezza, –kŏndshĕt'zä, f. convenience;
acconciamente, –dshämen'tĕ, ad. properly.   [ment; amends.
acconciamento, –men'tŏ, m. adjust-
acconciare, –dshä'rĕ, v. a. to fit; to prepare; to adorn; acconciarsi, –dshär'sĭ,
to agree; to settle oneself.
acconciatore, –tŏ'rĕ, m.adjuster; mender;
hair-dresser; attirer.
acconciatura, –tŏ'rä, f. head-dress.
acconcime, –dshĕ'mĕ, m. repairing (of a
house or farm).
acconcio, –kŏnd'shŏ, a. fitted, suitable;
–, m. advantage; gain.
acconigliare, –nĭlyä'rĕ, v. a. (mar.) to
ship oars.   [sent.
acconsentimento, –sĕntĭmen'tŏ, m. con-
acconsentire, –tĕ'rĕ, v. a. to consent.
acconto, äkkŏn'tŏ, m. correspondent.
accoppare, –kŏppä'rĕ, v.a. to knock down.
accoppiabile, –pĭä'bĭlĕ, a. matchable.
accoppiamento, –pämen'tŏ, m. coupling.
accoppiare, –pĭä'rĕ, v. a. to accouple.

accoppiatura, –tŏ'rä, f. coupling, union.
accoramento, –kŏrämen'tŏ, m. sorrow,
grief.   [to encourage.
accorare, –rä'rĕ, v. a. to afflict deeply;
accorato, –rä'tŏ, a. afflicted, sad.
accoratoio, –rätŏ'iŏ, m. misfortune; –, a.
heart-rending.
accorciamento, –kŏrdshämen'to, m.
shortening, contraction.   [to abridge.
accorciare, –dshä'rĕ, v. a. to contract,
accorciatamente, –tämen'tĕ, ad. briefly.
accorciativo, –tĕ'vŏ, a. shortening.
accordamento, –kŏrdämen'tŏ, m., ac-
cordanza, –dän'tzä, f. accord; harmony;
agreement.
accordare, –dä'rĕ, v. a. & n. to tune
(instruments); to agree; accordarsi,
–där'sĭ, to agree together.
accordatamente, –tämen'tĕ, ad. unanimously.   [suitable.
accordevole, –dĕ'vŏlĕ, a. reconcileable;
accordo, –kŏr'dŏ, m. agreement, harmony;
accord, conformity.
accorgere, –kŏr'jĕrĕ, v. n. ir. to perceive,
to discover; accorgersi, –kŏr'jĕrsĭ, to
observe.   [tion, prudence.
accorgimento, –jĭmen'tŏ, m. circumspec-
accorrere, –kŏr'rĕrĕ, v. n. ir. to run
after; to help.   [ningly.
accortamente, –kŏrtämen'tĕ, ad. cun-
accortezza, –tĕt'zä, f. cunning, sagacity.
accorto, –kŏr'tŏ, a. circumspect, prudent.
accosciarsi, –kŏsshär'sĭ, v. r. to squat,
to sit down cowering.   [access.
accostamento, –kŏstämen'tŏ, m. approach.
accostante, –stän'tĕ, a. pliant, supple.
accostare, –stä'rĕ, v. a. to approach.
accostatura, –tŏ'rä, f. connexion.
accostevole, –stĕ'vŏlĕ, a. of easy approach or access, affable.
accosto, –kŏs'tŏ, ad. beside, near.
accostumare, –kŏstŭmä'rĕ, v. a. & n. to
accustom; to be accustomed.   [nap.
accotonare, –kŏtŏnä'rĕ, v. a. to raise the
accovacciarsi, –kŏvätshär'sĭ, v. r. to
cower down, to hide.
accozzamento, –kŏtzämen'tŏ, m. gathering, collection, mass.
accozzare, –tzä'rĕ, v.a. to gather, to amass.
accreditare, –krĕdĭtä'rĕ, v. a. to give
credit to.   [rized; estimable; worthy.
accreditato, –dä'tŏ, a. accredited, autho-
accrescere, –krĕssh'ĕrĕ, v. a. & n. ir. to
increase, to augment.   [augmentation.
accrescimento, –sshĭmen'tŏ, m. increase,
accrescitore, –sshĭtŏ'rĕ, m. increaser;
amplifier.
accucciarsi, –kŭtshär'sĭ, v. r. to lie down
in the kennel; (vulg.) to go to bed.
accudire, –kŭdĕ'rĕ, v. n. to apply oneself to.
accularsi, –kŭlär'sĭ, v. r. to sit at one's
ease or lazily.
accumulamento, –kŭmŭlämen'tĕ, m. accumulation, heap.
accumulare, –mŭlä'rĕ, v. a. to heap up.
accumulazione, see accumulamento.
accuratamente, –kŭrätämen'tĕ, ad. ac-
curately.

accuratezza, –tĕt'zā, f. accuracy, care.
accurato, –rā'tŏ, a. accurate, careful.
accusa, –kŏ'sā, f. accusation.
accusabile, –sā'bĭlĕ, a. accusable.
accusare, –sā'rĕ, v. a. to accuse, to reproach, to impeach.   [case.
accusativo, –sătĕ'vŏ, m. (gr.) accusative
accusatore, –tŏ'rĕ, m. accuser.   [cuses.
accusatrice, –trĕ'dshĕ, f. she that ac-
accusazione, –tsĭŏ'nĕ, f. accusation.
acefalo, ādshĕ'fălŏ, a. acephalous, headless.
aceraia, ādshĕrā'ĭ ā, f. wood of maple-trees.
acerbamente, –bāmĕn'tĕ, ad. prematurely,
   unseasonably ; pertinaciously.
acerbetto, –bĕt'tŏ, a. tartish, sourish;
   coy, shy.   [f. acerbity.
acerbezza, ādshĕrbĕt'zā, acerbita, –bĭtā',
acerbità, ādshĕrbĭtā', f. acerbity, harshness, asperity.
acerbo, ādshĕr'bŏ, a. sour, tart; hard, severe.
acero, ā'dshĕrŏ, m. maple-tree.
acérrimo, ādshĕr'rĭmŏ, a. very sour.
acervo, ādshĕr'vŏ, m. (poet.) heap, pile.
acetire, ādshĕtĕ'rĕ, v. n. to become acid.
aceto, ādshĕ'tŏ, m. vinegar.
acetosa, –tŏ'sā, f. sorrel.
acetosità, –tŏsĭtā', f. acidity.
acetoso, –tŏ'sŏ, a. sourish.
acetume, –tŏ'mĕ, m. pickles.
acidezza, ādshĭdĕt'zā, f. acidity.
acido, ā'dshĭdŏ, a. acid, tart.
acidulo, ādshĕ'dŭlŏ, a. acidulated.
acino, ā'dshĭnŏ, m. grape-stone.
acidume, ādshĭdŭ'mĕ, m. any acid fruit.
aconito, ākŏ'nĭtŏ, m. (bot.) aconite.
acori, ākŏ'rĭ, m. pl. running ulcers on
   the face.
acqua, āk'kŭā, f. water; (fig.) rain; – cedrata, lemonade; – concia, sugared
   water; – di latte, whey; – dolce, fresh
   water; – di mare, sea-water; – nanfa,
   orange-flower water; a fiore d'–, at
   water's level.
acquaccia, ākkŭā'shā, f. muddy water.
acquaforte, –kŭāfŏr'tĕ, f. aquafortis.
acquaio, –kŭā'ĭŏ, m. gutter.
acquaiuolo, ŭŏ'lŏ, a. aquatic, watery.
acquapendente, –pĕndĕn'tĕ, m. water-
acquare, –kŭā'rĕ, v. a. to water.   [shed.
acquartierarsi, –kŭārtĕrār'sĭ, v. r. to
   take rooms, to rent a lodging.
acquarzente, –tzĕn'tĕ, f. brandy.
acquata, ākkŭā'tā, f. (mar.) supply of
acquatico, see acquatico.   [fresh water.
acquattarsi, –tār'sĭ, v. r. to squat, to
acquavite, –vĕ'tĕ, f. brandy.   [cower.
acquazzone, –tzŏ'nĕ, m. sudden and heavy
   shower of rain.
acquedotto, –kŭĕdŏt'tŏ, m. aqueduct.
acqueo, āk'kŭĕŏ, a. watery, aqueous.
acquerellare, –kŭĕrĕllā'rĕ, v. a. to paint
   in water-colours.   [watery wine.
acquerello, –rĕl'lŏ, m. water-colour.
acquerugiola, –rŏ'jŏlā, f. drizzling rain.
acquetare, –tā'rĕ, v. a. to appease, to quiet.
acquetta, –kŭĕt'tā, f. drizzling or fine rain.
acquicella, –kŭĭdshĕl'lā, f. rivulet.

acquidoso, –dŏ'sŏ, a. humid, moist.
acquidoccio, –dŏt'shŏ, s. aqueduct.
acquiescenza, –ĕsshĕn'tzā, f. acquiescence;
   quiet, quietness.
acquietare, –ĕtā'rĕ, v. a. to appease.
acquisizione, –sĭzĭŏ'nĕ, f. acquisition,
   purchase.
acquistare, –stā'rĕ, v. a. to acquire.
acquistatore, –tŏ'rĕ, m. purchaser.
acquisto, ākkŭĭs'tŏ, m. acquisition.
acquitrino, –trĕ'nŏ, m. marsh, bog.
acquoso, –kŭŏ'sŏ, a. aqueous, watery.
acre, ā'krĕ, a. sharp, sour; harsh.
acre(mente), –(mĕn'tĕ), a. (& ad.) sharp(ly),
   harsh(ly).   [ness.
acrimonia, ākrĭmŏ'nĭā, f. acrimony, sharp-
acrobata, ākrŏ'bătā, m. acrobat, rope-
   dancer, funambulist.
acromatico, ākrŏmā'tĭkŏ, a. achromatic.
acrostico, ākrŏs'tĭkŏ, m. acrostic.
acuire, ākŭĕ'rĕ, v. a. to edge, to whet.
aculeo, ākŏ'lĕŏ, m. sting, goad; spur,
   stimulus.   [of wit, acumen.
acume, ākŏ'mĕ, m. sharp point; sharpness
acuminato, ākŭmĭnā'tŏ, a. pointed.
acustica, ākŭs'tĭkā, f. acoustics.
acutamente, ākŭtāmĕn'tĕ, ad. acutely,
   sharply.
acutezza, –tĕt'zā, f. acuteness; wit.
acuto, ākŏ'tŏ, a. acute, sharp, pointed;
   piercing.   [one.
ad, ād, pr. to, at; – uno – uno, one by
adacquare, –ākkŭā'rĕ, v. a. to water.
adagiare, –ājā'rĕ, v. a. to supply with the
   conveniencies of life; adagiarsi, –jār'sĭ,
   to take one's ease.
adagio, –ā'jŏ, m. (mus.) adagio; proverb;
   –, ad. slowly, softly.
adamante, –āmān'tĕ, m. diamond.
adamantino, –tĕ'nŏ, a. adamantine; hard.
adastiare, –āstĕ'rĕ, v. a. to envy.
adattabile, –āttā'bĭlĕ, a. applicable.
adattabilità, –tābĭlĭtā', f. aptitude, suitableness, suitability.
adattamento, –tāmĕn'tŏ, m. adaptation.
adattare, –āttā'rĕ, v. a. to adapt, to fit,
   to adjust; to apply.
adattazione, –tātsĭŏ'nĕ, f. adaptation.
adatto, ādāt'tŏ, a. adapted; fit, proper,
   suitable.   [to.
addarsi, āddār'sĭ, v. r. to addict oneself
addaziare, –dātzĭā'rĕ, v. a. to tax, to levy
   duty on.   [ness.
addebolimento, –dĕbŏlĭmĕn'tŏ, m. feeble-
addebitare, –dĕbĭtā'rĕ, v. a. to debit, to
   charge to one's account.
addebito, –dā'bĭtŏ, m. debit.
addecimare, –dĕdshĭmā'rĕ, v. a. to tithe.
addensare, –dĕnsā'rĕ, v. a. to make dense.
addentare, –tā'rĕ, v. a. to bite.
addentellato, –tĕllā'tŏ, m. toothing-
   stone.
addentro, –dĕn'trŏ, ad. within, inwardly.
addestramento, –dĕstrāmĕn'tŏ, m. instruction.
addestrare, –trā'rĕ, v. a. to prepare; to
   drill; to instruct.
addetto, –dĕt'tŏ, a. dedicated, attached.

addicare &c., see abdicare.
addietro, –dĭd´trŏ, ad. behind.
addiettivo, –ĕttĭ´vŏ, m. adjective.
addimandare, –dĭmändĭ´rĕ, v. a. to ask.
addimesticare, –mĕstĭkä´rĕ, v. a. to tame.
addio, –dĕ´ŏ, ad. farewell.
addirizzare, –dĭrĭtzämĕn´tŏ, m. direction, instruction.
addirizzare, –tzä´rĕ, v. a. to put in the right way; to correct; to reform; to instruct.
addirsi, –dĭr´sĭ, v. r. to suit, to become.
additamento, –dĭtämĕn´tŏ, m. indication.
additare, –dĭtä´rĕ, v. a. to show, to indicate.
addivenire, see divenire.
addizionale, –dĭtzĭŏnä´lĕ, a. additional.
addizionare, –nä´rĕ, v. a. to addition.
addizione, –dĭtzĭŏ´nĕ, f. addition; supplement.
addobbamento, –dŏbbämĕn´tŏ, m. ornament, attire.
addobbare, –bä´rĕ, v. a. to embellish, to adorn.
addobbo, –dŏb´bŏ, m. (ornamental) furniture.
addolcimento, –dŏldshĭmĕn´tŏ, m. softening; mitigation.
addolcire, –dshĭ´rĕ, v. a. to sweeten, to soften.
addolcitivo, –dshĭtĭ´vŏ, m. lenitive.
addolorare, –dŏlŏrä´rĕ, v. a. to afflict, to vex; addolorarsi, –rär´sĭ, to grieve.
addomandare, –dŏmändä´rĕ, v. a. to demand.
addome, –dŏ´mĕ, m. abdomen.
addomesticamento, –mĕstĭkämĕn´tŏ, m. taming, familiarise.
addomesticare, –kä´rĕ, v. a. to tame, to adomesticate.
addomesticatore, –tŏ´rĕ, m. tamer.
addopparsi, –dŏppär´sĭ, v. r. to hide behind, fold.
addoppiare, –pĭä´rĕ, v. a. to double, to redouble.
addoppiatura, –tŏ´rä, f. doubling.
addormentare, –dŏrmĕntä´rĕ, v. a. to lull asleep, burden.
addossamento, –dŏssämĕn´tŏ, m. charge.
addossare, –sä´rĕ, v. a. to lay upon one's back, to charge; to intrust.
addosso, –dŏs´sŏ, ad. upon one's back; on, about; metter le mani – a uno, to lay hold of one.
addottorare, –dŏttŏrä´rĕ, v. a. to confer a doctor's degree.
addottorato, –rä´tŏ, a. certified doctor.
addottrinare, –dŏttrĭnä´rĕ, v. a. to teach, to instruct.
addurre, –dŭr´rĕ, v. a. ir. to bring in, to adduce, to allege, balance.
adeguare, –dĕgŭä´rĕ, v. a. to equalize; to adeguatamente, –tämĕn´tĕ, ad. equally.
adempiere, –dĕm´pĭĕrĕ, adempire, –pĕ´rĕ, v. a. ir. to fulfil, to effect.
adempimento, –pĭmĕn´tŏ, m. execution.
adempitore, –tŏ´rĕ, m. executor.
adepto, –dĕp´tŏ, m. adept.
adequazione, –dĕkŭätzĭŏ´nĕ, f. adequation.
aderente, –rĕn´tĕ, m. adherer, ment.
aderenza, –rĕn´tzä, f. adherence, attachment.
adergersi, –ĕr´jĕrsĭ, v. r. to rise.
aderire, –rĕ´rĕ, v. n. to adhere.
adescare, –ĕskä´rĕ, v. a. to bait; to allure.

adesione, –zĭŏ´nĕ, f. adherence.
adespoto, –dĕs´pŏtŏ, a. anonymous (of writings).
adesso, –ĕs´sŏ, ad. now, this instant.
adiacente, –tädshĕn´tĕ, a. adjacent, contiguous, adjoining.
adiacenza, –dshĕn´tzä, f. adjacency.
adiettivo, –ĕttĭ´vŏ, m. adjective.
adipe, ä´dĭpĕ, m. grease, fat.
adiposo, –pŏ´sŏ, a. adipose; plump, fat.
adiramento, –rämĕn´tŏ, m. anger, wrath.
adirare, –rä´rĕ, v. a. to make angry, to irritate; adirarsi, –rär´sĭ, to get angry.
adire, ädĕ´rĕ, v. r. to take possession of an inheritance, inheritance.
adizione, –ĭtzĭŏ´nĕ, f. entering into an adnata, –nä´tä, f. (an.) conjunctiva, fat.
adocchiare, –ŏkkĭä´rĕ, v. a. to eye, to stare.
adolescente, ädŏlĕsshĕn´tĕ, m. young man, youth, adolescent.
adolescenza, –sshĕn´tzä, f. adolescence.
adombramento, –ŏmbrämĕn´tŏ, m. shading, shade, to sketch.
adombrare, –brä´rĕ, v. a. to overshadow; adombrazione, –brätzĭŏ´nĕ, f. shade; adumbration, to disguise.
adonestare, –ŏnĕstä´rĕ, v. a. to palliate; adonide, ädŏ´nĭdĕ, f. (bot.) adonis.
adontare, –ŏntä´rĕ, v. a. to affront; adontarsi, –tär´sĭ, to get angry.
adoperabile, –ŏpĕrä´bĭlĕ, a. employable.
adoperamento, –rämĕn´tŏ, m. using, employment.
adoperare, –rä´rĕ, v. a. to employ; to operate; adoperarsi, –rär´sĭ, to exert oneself; to speak for, tion; employ.
adoperazione, –rätzĭŏ´nĕ, f. use, exercise.
adorabile, ädŏrä´bĭlĕ, a. adorable.
adorare, –rä´rĕ, v. a. to adore, to worship.
adoratore, –tŏ´rĕ, m. adorer, worshipper.
adorazione, –tzĭŏ´nĕ, f. adoration, worship, attire.
adornamento, –ŏrnämĕn´tŏ, m. ornament, adornare, –ŏrnä´rĕ, v. a. to adorn.
adorno, ädŏr´nŏ, m. ornament, attire.
adottare, ädŏttä´rĕ, v. a. to adopt.
adottativo, see adottivo.
adottatore, –tŏ´rĕ, m., adottatrice, –trĕ´dshĕ, f. adopter.
adottazione, –tzĭŏ´nĕ, f. adoption.
adottivo, –ĭĕ´vŏ, a. adoptive, adopted.
adozione, –tzĭŏ´nĕ, f. adoption.
aduggiamento, –djämĕn´tŏ, m. blighting shade.
aduggiare, –djä´rĕ, v. a. to shadow in a hurtful manner, to bewitch.
adulante, ädŭlän´tĕ, a. flattering.
adulare, –lä´rĕ, v. a. to flatter.
adulatore, –tŏ´rĕ, m., adulatrice, –trĕ´dshĕ, f. flatterer, teringly.
adulatoriamente, –tŏrĭämĕn´tĕ, ad. flatteringly.
adulatorio, –tŏ´rĭŏ, a. flattering.
adulazione, –tzĭŏ´nĕ, f. flattery.
adulterare, –ältĕrä´rĕ, v. n. to commit adultery; to adulterate.
adulteratore, –rätŏ´rĕ, m. adulterer.
adulteratrice, –trĕ´dshĕ, f. adulteress.

adulterazione, –tzĭŏ′nĕ, f. adulteration; corruption, forgery. [terfeit, corrupted.

adulterino, –tĕrĭ′nŏ, a. adulterine; coun-

adulterio, –ŭltĕ′rĭŏ, m. adultery.

adultero, –ŭl′tĕrŏ, **adulteroso,** –rŏ′sŏ, a. adulterous.

adunamento, –ŭnămĕn′tŏ, m. uniting, as-sembling; meeting.

adunanza, –năn′tză, f. meeting, assembly.

adunare, –nă′rĕ, v. a. to assemble, to con-voke; **adunarsi,** –năr′sĭ, to come to-gether, to assemble.

adunco, –ŭn′kŏ, a. crooked. [the claws.

adunghiare, –ghlă′rĕ, v. a. to seize with

adunque, –ŭn′kŭĕ, ad. then, therefore.

adusto, –ŭs′tŏ, a. scorched, burnt up.

aere, ă′ĕrĕ, m. air, wind.

aereo, ă′ĕrĕŏ, a. aerial.

aeriforme, –rĭfŏr′mĕ, a. aeriform.

aerometro, –rŏ′mĕtrŏ, m. aerometer.

aeronauta, –rŏnă′ŭtă, m. aeronaut.

aerostatica, –stă′tĭkă, f. aerostatic.

aescare, ăĕskă′rĕ, v. a. to bait; to allure.

afa, ă′fă, f. suffocating heat.

afato, ăfă′tŏ, a. faded.

afelio, ăfĕ′lĭŏ, m. aphelion.

aferesi, ăfĕ′rĕsĭ, f. aphaeresis.

affabile, ăffă′bĭlĕ, a. affable; civil.

affabilità, –bĭlĭtă′, f. affability.

affaccendarsi, –tshĕndăr′sĭ, v. r. to be very busy. [cupied.

affaccendato, –dă′tŏ, a. very busy, oc-

affaccettare, –tshĕttă′rĕ, v. a. to cut in facets.

affacchinarsi, –kĭnăr′sĭ, v. r. to drudge.

affacciare, –tshă′rĕ, v. a. to smoothe, to plane; **affacciarsi,** –tshăr′sĭ, to show oneself. [up, to fardel.

affagottare, –făgŏttă′rĕ, v. a. to bundle

affaldare, –făldă′rĕ, v. a. to plait; to double.

affamare, –fămă′rĕ, v. a. to famish.

affamato, –mă′tŏ, a. starved, famished.

affangare, –făngă′rĕ, v. a. & n. to soil; to get muddy.

affannamento, –fănnămĕn′tŏ, m. anxiety.

affannante, –năn′tĕ, a. grievous, vexatious.

affannare, –nă′rĕ, v. a. to grieve, to vex; to perplex; **affannarsi,** –năr′sĭ, to fret.

affanno, –făn′nŏ, m. anxiety, trouble.

affannone, –nŏ′nĕ, m. busybody.

affannosamente, –nŏsămĕn′tĕ, ad. an-xiously, restlessly.

affannoso, –nŏ′sŏ, a. grievous, vexatious.

affardellare, –fărdĕllă′rĕ, v. a. to make up into a bundle, to bundle up.

affare, –fă′rĕ, m. affair, business; rank.

affarsi, –făr′sĭ, v. n. ir. to suit, to become.

affascinamento, –sshĭnămĕn′tŏ, m. fasci-nation.

affascinare, –nă′rĕ, v. a. to bewitch.

affascinazione, –nătzĭŏ′nĕ, f. bewitching.

affaticante, –tĭkăn′tĕ, a. fatiguing.

affaticare, –kă′rĕ, v. a. to fatigue.

affatto, –fă′tŏ, ad. quite, entirely.

affatturare, –tŭră′rĕ, v. a. to bewitch.

affatturazione, –răzĭŏnĕ, f. bewitching.

affazzonamento, –tzŏnămĕn′tŏ, m. em-bellishment. [embellish.

affazzonare, –nă′rĕ, v. a. to adorn, to

afrazzonare, –nă′rĕ, v. a. to adorn, .to

affè, –fĕ′, ad. upon my faith.

affermare, –fĕrmă′rĕ, v. a. to affirm.

affermativamente, –tĭvămĕn′tĕ, ad. af-firmatively.

affermativo, –tĕ′vŏ, a. affirmative.

affermazione, –tzĭŏ′nĕ, f. affirmation.

afferrare, –fĕrră′rĕ, v. a. to lay hold of, to seize, to grasp.

affertilire, –fĕrtĭlĭ′rĕ, v. a. to fertilize.

affettare, –fĕttă′rĕ, v. a. to cut to pieces; —, v. n. to aim at; to affect; to fold or plait.

affettato, –tă′tŏ, a. affected. [plait.

affettazione, –tzĭŏ′nĕ, f. affectation.

affettivo, –tĕ′vŏ, a. affecting, touching; pathetic.

affetto, –fĕt′tŏ, a. & m. affected; inclined; affection, passion; inclination; love.

affettuosamente, –tŭŏsămĕn′tĕ, ad. af-fectionately. [affable.

affettuoso, –tŭŏ′sŏ, a. affectionate, kind,

affezionare –tzĭŏnă′rĕ, v. a. to enamour;

affezionarsi, –tzĭŏnăr′sĭ, to get fond of, to delight in; to become attached to.

affezione, –tzĭŏ′nĕ, f. affection, tenderness.

affiatarsi, –fĭătăr′sĭ, v. r. to become in-timate with one. [clasp.

affibbiare, –fĭbbĭă′rĕ, v. a. to buckle, to

affibbiatoio, –tŏ′ĭŏ, m. button-hole.

affibbiatura, –tŏ′ră, f. buckling; hooks and eyes. [trust to.

affidare, –fĭdă′rĕ, v. a. to confide in, to

affievolire, –fĭĕvŏlĭ′rĕ, v. a. to weaken, to enfeeble; **affievolirse,** –lĭr′sĕ, to weaken, to get feeble. [stick up.

affiggere, –fĭdj′ĕrĕ, v. a. ir. to fasten, to

affiguramento, –fĭgŭrămĕn′tŏ, m. recog-nition, recollection. [recollect.

affigurare, –ră′rĕ, v. a. to recognize, to

affilare, –fĭlă′rĕ, v. a. to whet, to sharpen; to excite.

affilato, –lă′tŏ, a. sharp, pointed.

affilatura, –tŏ′ră, f. sharp edge.

affilettare, –lĕttă′rĕ, v. a. to lay snares; to catch in a net.

affinamento, –nămĕn′tŏ, m. refinement.

affinare, –nă′rĕ, v. a. to refine, to purify (by fire).

affinatoio, –tŏ′ĭŏ, m. crucible.

affinatore, –tŏ′rĕ, m. refiner.

affinchè, –fĭnkĕ′, c. to the end that.

affinità, –fĭnĭtă′, f. affinity, kindred, al-liance. [ness.

affiocamento, –fĭŏkămĕn′tŏ, m. hoarse-

affiochire, –kĕ′rĕ, v. n. to get hoarse.

affissamento, –fĭssămĕn′tŏ, m. fixed look.

affissare, –să′rĕ, v. a. to fix one's eyes upon. [(gr.) affix.

affisso, –fĭs′sŏ, a. & m. fixed, fastened;

affittaiuolo, –fĭttăĭŭŏ′lŏ, m. farmer.

affittare, –tă′rĕ, v. a. to let, to hire, to

affitto, –fĭt′tŏ, m. rent. [farm.

affliggere, –flĭdj′ĕrĕ, v. a. ir. to afflict.

afflittare, –flĭttă′rĕ, v. a. to afflict.

afflittivo, –tĕ′vŏ, a. afflictive.

afflitto, –flīt'tō, a. afflicted, sad.

afflizione, –tziō'nĕ, f. affliction, grief.

affluente, –flŭĕn'tĕ, a. abundant.

affluenza, –ĕn'tzā, f. abundance.

afflusso, –flŭs'sō, m. afflux; increase.

affocare, –fōkā'rĕ, v. a. to set on fire.

affocato, –kā'tō, a. of a fiery colour, burnt.

affogaggine, –gād'jĭnĕ,f., affogamento, –gāmĕn'tō, m. suffocation, choking.

affogare, –gā'rĕ, v. a. to stifle, to choke, to suffocate; to drown.

affollare, –fōllā'rĕ, v. a. to crowd together.

affoltare, –tā'rĕ,v.n., affoltarsi, –tār'sĭ, to rush upon. [sion, sinking.

affondamento, –fōndāmĕn'tō, m. submersion, sinking.

affondare, –dā'rĕ, v. a. & n. to sink; to be swallowed up.

afforestierare, –fōrĕstĕrā'rĕ, v. n. to give a strange appearance to.

affortificare, –fōrtĭfĭkā'rĕ,v.a. to fortify.

afforzare, –fōrtzā'rĕ, v. a. to strengthen; afforzarsi, –tzār'sĭ, to strengthen oneself. [ditch.

affossare, –fōssā'rĕ, v. a. to intrench, to

affralire, –frālē'rĕ, v. a. to weaken, to enervate.

affrancare, –frānkā'rĕ, v. a. to free; affrancarsi, –kār'sĭ, to get freed; to become vigorous.

affrancato, –kā'tō, a. freed. [harass.

affrangere, –frān'jĕrĕ, v. a. to break, to

affranto, –frān'tō, a. fatigued.

affratellarsi, –frātĕllār'sĭ, v. r. to live like brothers. [straint.

affrenamento, –frĕnāmĕn'tō, m. check, restraint.

affrenare, –nā'rĕ, v. a. to restrain.

affrettare, –frĕttā'rĕ, v. a. to hasten, to speed. [to cut in pieces.

affrittellare,–frĭttĕllā'rĕ,v.a.to fry (eggs);

affrontare, –frōntā'rĕ, v. a. to attack; (mil.) to engage in front; to confront.

affronto, –frōn'tō, m. affront, insult.

affumato, –fūmā'tō, a. smoked, smoky.

affumicare, –mĭkā'rĕ, v. a. to smoke-dry.

aforismo, āfōrĭs'mō, m. aphorism.

afretto, –frĕt'tō, a. sourish.

afrezza, –frĕt'zā, f. sourness.

afro, ā'frō, a. sour, sharp; rough.

agape, ā'gāpĕ, f. love-feast.

agarico, āgā'rĭkō, m. (bot.) agarick.

agata, ā'gātā, f. agate.

agente, ājĕn'tĕ, m. agent, manager.

agenzia, ājĕntzĭā', f. agency.

agevole, ājā'vōlĕ, a. easy; manageable.

agevolezza, ājĕvōlĕt'zā, f. facility; easiness.

agevolmente, –mĕn'tĕ, ad. easily; readily.

aggavignare, āggāvĭnyā'rĕ, v. a. to grip, to seize. [teel; to embellish.

aggentilire,āddjĕntĭlē'rĕ,v.a.to render genteel;

aggettare, āddjĕttā'rĕ, v. n. to project, to jut out.

aggettivo, –tē'vō, s. adjective. [jut out.

aggetto, āddjĕt'tō, m. projection, prominence. [frost, congealment.

agghiacciamento, āgghiātshāmĕn'tō, m.

agghiacciare, –tshā'rĕ, v. a. to freeze.

agghiadamento, –dāmĕn'tō, m. numbness. [with cold.

agghiadare, –dā'rĕ, v. n. to be benumbed

aggiacere, āddjādshā'rĕ, v. n. ir. to confine; to be convenient.

aggio, ād'jō, m. exchange, discount.

aggiogare, –gā'rĕ, v. a. to yoke (cattle).

aggiornamento, āddjōrnāmĕn'tō, m. adjournment.

aggiornare, āddjōrnā'rĕ, v. a. to adjourn; aggiornarsi, –nār'sĭ, to dawn.

aggiramento, –djrāmĕn'tō, m. circumventing; fraud; surprise.

aggirare, –djrā'rĕ, v. a. & n. to surround; to go about; aggirarsi, –rār'sĭ, to ramble, to straggle.

aggiratore, –rātō'rĕ, m., aggiratrice, –trē'dshĕ, f. rambler; vagabond; deceiver.

aggiudicare, –djūdĭkā'rĕ,v.a. to adjudge.

aggiudicazione, –kātzĭō'nĕ, f. adjudication. [to join; to reach.

aggiungere, –djŭn'jĕrĕ, v. a. ir. to add;

aggiunta, –djŭn'tā, f. addition, increase.

aggiuntare, –tā'rĕ, v. a. to add, to adjoin.

aggiuntivo, –tē'vō, a. additional.

aggiunto, –djŭn'tō, a. added, united.

aggiustamento, –djĭustāmĕn'tō, m. adjustment; agreement.

aggiustare, –tā'rĕ, v. a. to adjust, to settle; to adapt; – fede, to believe; aggiustarsi, –tār'sĭ, to adjust oneself; to come to a settlement.

aggiustatezza, –tĕt'zā, f. justness, exactness; propriety. [hunch-backed

aggobbire, āggōbbē'rĕ, v. n. to become

aggomitolare, –mĭtōlā'rĕ, v. a. to wind up; to make into a clew.

aggottare, –gōttā'rĕ, v. a. (mar.) to pump.

aggradevole, –grādĕ'vōlĕ, a. agreeable.

aggradimento, –dĭmĕn'tō, m. agreement.

aggradire, –dē'rĕ, v. a. to receive kindly; to like. [stiffen with cold.

aggranchiarsi, –grānkiār'sĭ, v. r. to

aggrancire, –dshē'rĕ, v. a. to seize with a hook. [dizement.

aggrandimento, –dĭmĕn'tō, m. aggrandizement;

aggrandire, –dē'rĕ, v. a. to enlarge, to aggrandize; aggrandirsi, –dēr'sĭ, to become large; to grow; to raise oneself.

aggrappare, –grāppā'rĕ, v. a. to grapple, to grasp.

aggraticciare, –tĭtshā'rĕ,v.a. to entwine; aggraticciarsi, –tshār'sĭ, to become interwoven.

aggravamento, –vāmĕn'tō, m. surcharge.

aggravare, –vā'rĕ, v. a. to aggravate; aggravarsi, –vār'sĭ, to grow heavy; to feel aggrieved. [damage.

aggravio, –grā'vĭō, m. injury; impost;

aggraziare, –tzĭā'rĕ, v. a. to grace, to favour. [gracefully.

aggraziatamente, –tzātāmĕn'tĕ, ad.

aggraziato, –tzĭā'tō, a. graceful, genteel.

aggredire, āggrĕdē'rĕ, v. a. to attack; to give offence. [assemble.

aggregare, –gā'rĕ, v. a. to aggregate; to

aggregato, *–gā′ tŏ,* m. aggregate; assemblage.   [association.

aggregazione, *–tzĭŏ′ nĕ,* m. aggregation;

aggreggiare, *–djā′ rĕ,* v. a. to assemble in herds.

aggressione, *–grĕssĭŏ′ nĕ,* f. aggression.

aggressore, *–sŏ′ rĕ,* m. aggressor.

aggrinzare, *–grīntzā′ rĕ,* v. n. to wrinkle.

aggrottare, *–grŏttā′ rĕ,* v. a. to knit one's brows.

aggrovigliare, *–grŏvĭlyā′ rĕ,* v. n., **aggrovigliarsi,** *–yār′ sĭ,* to shrink up.

aggrumato, *–grūmā′ tŏ,* a. curdled.

aggrumolare, *–mŏlā′ rĕ,* v. a. to hoard up.

aggruppamento, *–grūppāmĕn′ tŏ,* m. forming a knot.   [ing equal.

aguagliamento, *–gŭālyāmĕn′ tŏ,* m. making

aguagliare, *–yā′ rĕ,* v. a. to equalise; to level; to compare; **aguagliarsi,** *–yār′ sĭ,* to compare oneself with.

aguantare, *–gŭāntā′ rĕ,* v. a. to seize suddenly, to catch, to snatch.

aguerrire, *–gŭĕrrē′ rĕ,* v. a. to train up to war.

aguindolare, *–gŭīndŏlā′ rĕ,* v. a. to reel off, to wind up; (fig.) to lead by the nose.

aghetto, *āghĕt′ tŏ,* m. lace, tag.

aghirone, *āghīrŏ′ nĕ,* m. heron.

agiatamente, *ājātāmĕn′ tĕ,* ad. with ease, commodiously.   [comfort.

agiatezza, *–tĕt′ zā,* f. easy circumstances;

agiato, *ājā′ tŏ,* a. wealthy; convenient;

agibile, *ājĕ′ bĭlĕ,* a. feasible.   [gentle.

agile, *ā′ jĭlĕ,* a. agile, nimble.

agilità, *ājĭlĭtā′,* f. agility, nimbleness.

agio, *ā′ jĭŏ,* m. ease, comfort.

agire, *ājē′ rĕ,* v. a. to act, to operate.

agitamento, *ājĭtāmĕn′ tŏ,* m. agitation.

agitare, *–tā′ rĕ,* v. a. to agitate, to disquiet; to vex; **agitarsi,** *–tār′ sĭ,* to be alarmed.

agitatore, *–tā′ rĕ,* m. inciter, caballer.

agitazione, *–tzĭŏ′ nĕ,* f. agitation; political excitement.

agliata, *ālyā′ tā,* f. garlic-sauce.

aglio, *ā′ lyŏ,* m. (bot.) garlic.

agna, *ăn′ yā,* f. (poet.) ewe-lamb.

agnato, *–yā′ tŏ,* m. agnate, kinsman by the male line.

agnazione, *–tzĭŏ′ nĕ,* f. agnation, kindred by the father's side.

agnella, *ānyĕl′ tā,* f. little ewe-lamb.

agnello, *–yĕl′ tŏ,* m. lambkin.

agnizione, *ānyĭtzĭŏ′ nĕ,* f. recognition.

Agnus dei, *ānyŭs dā′ ĭ,* m. Agnus Dei.

ago, *ā′ gŏ,* m. needle; hand (of a clock); stile (of a sundial); sting (of a bee, &c.); compass.   [to aspire.

agognare, *āgŏnyā′ rĕ,* v. n. to covet eagerly,

agone, *āgŏ′ nĕ,* m. packing-needle; combat; wrestling-ground.

agonia, *–nē ā,* f. agony; anguish; intensity.

agonizzare, *–nītzā′ rĕ,* v. n. to agonize.

agoraio, *–rā′ ŏ,* m. needle-maker; needle-case.

agostino, *āgŏstē′ nŏ,* a. born in August.

agosto, *āgŏs′ tŏ,* m. August.

agramente, *āgrāmĕn′ tĕ,* ad. sourly; severely.   [verely.

agrario, *āgrā′ rĭŏ,* a. agrarian.

agreste, *āgrĕs′ tĕ,* a. rural; clownish, rude; sharp, sour.

agrestino, *–tē′ nŏ,* a. sourish.

agresto, *āgrĕs′ tŏ,* m. verjuice.

agretto, *āgrĕt′ tŏ,* m. (bot.) sorrel.

agrezza, *āgrĕt′ zā,* f. acidity.   [man.

agricoltore, *āgrĭkŏltŏ′ rĕ,* m. husband-

agricoltura, *–tŏ′ rā,* f. agriculture.

agrigno, *āgrēn′ yŏ,* a. sourish, harsh.

agrimensore, *–mĕnsŏ′ rĕ,* m. land-surveyor.

agrimensura, *–sŏ′ rā,* f. land-surveying.

agro, *ā′ grŏ,* a. sour, acid; sharp, rough; severe.

agrodolce, *–dŏl′ dshĕ,* a. sweet and sour.

agronomia, *–nŏmē ā,* f. agronomy.

agronomo, *āgrŏ′ nŏmŏ,* m. agriculturist.

agrume, *āgrŏ′ mĕ,* m. acid fruits.

agucchiare, *āgŭkkĭā′ rĕ,* v. a. to sew, to stitch.

aguato, *āgŭā′ tŏ,* m. ambuscade.

aguglia, *āgŭl′ yā,* f. steeple, obelisk; magnetic needle.

aguzzare, *–tzā′ rĕ,* v. a. to whet, to sharpen, to edge; to set a razor.

aguzzatore, *–tŏ′ rĕ,* m. grinder.

aguzzatura, *–tŏ′ rā,* f. sharpening.

aguzzino, *–tzĭ′ nŏ,* m. convict overseer.

aguzzo, *āgŏt′ zŏ,* a. acute, sharp, pointed.

ahi! *ā′ ĭ,* oh! alas!

ahibò! *āĭbŏ′,* i. fie! humph!

ahimè, *āĭmĕ′,* i. alas!

aia, *ā′ ā,* f. thrashing-floor; governess.

aietta, *āĕt′ tā,* f. hot-bed.

aio, *ā′ ŏ,* m. preceptor, governor.

aita, *āĭ′ tā,* f. &c., see **aiuto,** &c.

aiuola, *āĭŏ′ lā,* f. small barn-floor; trench.

aitare, see **aiutare.**

aiutante, *āĭŭtān′ tĕ,* m. helper, assistant; **– di campo,** m. aide-de-camp.

aiutare, *–tā′ rĕ,* v. a. to help, to assist.

aiuto, *āĭŭ′ tŏ,* m. help, assistance.

aizzare, *–tŏ′ rĕ,* v. a. to stir up, to irritate; to set on dogs.

aizzatore, *–tŏ′ rĕ,* m. provoker, instigator.

ala, *ā′ lā,* f. wing; (fig.) protection.

alabarda, *–bār′ dā,* f. halberd.

alabardiere, *–dĭā′ rĕ,* m. halberdier.

alabastro, *–bās′ trŏ,* m. alabaster.

alacre, *ā′ lākrĕ,* a. cheerful, gay, merry.

alacrità, *–krĭtā′,* f. alacrity, liveliness.

alano, *ālā′ nŏ,* m. boar-hound.

alare, *ālā′ rĕ,* m. andiron.

alaterno, *ālātĕr′ nŏ,* m. (bot.) privet.

alato, *ālā′ tŏ,* a. winged.

alba, *āl′ bā,* f. break of day.

albagia, *–jē ā,* f. self-conceit.

albagioso, *–jŏ′ sŏ,* a. conceited, proud.

albeggiamento, *–bĕdjāmĕn′ tŏ,* m. whiteness; brightness.   [whitish; to dawn.

albeggiare, *–jā′ rĕ,* v. n. to become

alberare, *–bĕrā′ rĕ,* v. a. to plant; to set up.

alberella, *–bĕrĕl′ lā,* f. aspen-tree.   [dwell.

albergare, *–gā′ rĕ,* v. a. & n. to lodge; to

albergatore, –tŏ'rĕ, m. inn-keeper, host.
albergo, –bĕr'gŏ, m. inn, tavern.
albero, ăl'bĕrŏ, m. tree; mast; pedigree.
albicante, –bĭkăn'tĕ, a. whitish.
albicocca, –kŏk'kă, f. apricot.
albicocco, –kŏk'kŏ, m. apricot-tree.
albino, –bĕ'nŏ, m. albino; –, a. whitish.
albo, ăl'bŏ, a. white.
albore, –bŏ'rĕ, m. dawn; lustre.
albume, –bŏ'mĕ, m. white of an egg.
alcali, ăl'kălĭ, m. fossil salt; alkali.
alchermes, ălkĕr'mĕs, m. kermes, al-
  kermes.
alchimia, –kĭnĭ'ă, f. alchemy.
alchimista, –mĭs'tă, m. alchemist.
alcione, –dshŏ'nĕ, halcyon, king-fisher.
alcool, ălkŏŏl, m. alcohol, proof-spirit.
alcorano, –kŏră'nŏ, m. Alcoran.
alcova, –kŏ'vă, f. alcove.
alcuno, –kŏ'nŏ, pn. somebody; none;
  alcuna volta, sometimes.
aleatico, ălĕă'tĭkŏ, m. Leatico wine, a delicious wine.   [flutter.
aleggiare, –dja'rĕ, v. n. to try to fly, to
alena, ăld'nă, f. breath.
alenare, –nă'rĕ, v. n. to breathe.
aletta, ălĕt'tă, f. pinion; fin (of a fish.)
alfabetico, –făbĕ'tĭkŏ, a. alphabetic.
alfabeto, –bĕ'tŏ, alphabet.
alfiere, –fĭĕ'rĕ, m. ensign-bearer; bishop
alga, ăl'gă, f. sea-weed.   [(at chess.)
algebra, ăl'jĕbră, f. algebra.
algebrico, –jĕ'brĭkŏ, a. algebrical.
algore, –gŏ'rĕ, m. chillness.
alice, ălĭ'dshĕ, f. anchovy.
alido, ă'lĭdŏ, see arido.
alienabile, ălĭĕnă'bĭlĕ, a. alienable.
alienare, –nă'rĕ, v. a. to alienate.
alienato, –nă'tŏ, a. alienated, estranged,
  unkind, unfriendly.
alienazione, –tzĭŏ'nĕ, f. alienation.
alieno, ălĭĕ'nŏ, a. foreign; averse.
aligero, ălĭ'jĕrŏ, a. winged.
alimentare, ălĭmĕntă'rĕ, v. a. to nourish,
  to feed, to maintain.
alimentario, –tă'rĭŏ, a. alimentary.
alimento, –mĕn'tŏ, m. nourishment.
alimentoso, –tŏ'sŏ, a. alimental, nutri-
alitare, –tă'rĕ, v. n. to pant.   [tive.
alito, ă'lĭtŏ, m. breath; breeze.
alitoso, –tŏ'sŏ, a. odorous.
allacciamento, –tshămĕn'tŏ, m. lacing.
allacciare, –tshă'rĕ, v. a. to lace; to
  ensnare, to entrap.
allagagione, –găjŏ'nĕ, f. allagamento,
  –mĕn'tŏ, m. inundation, deluge.
allagare, –gă'rĕ, v. a. to overflow.
allargamento, –lărgămĕn'tŏ, m. en-
  larging, ampliation.
allargare, –gă'rĕ, v. a. to enlarge.
allarme, –lăr'mĕ, m. alarm.
allato, –lă'tŏ, ad. beside, by.
allattamento, –lăttămĕn'tŏ, m. giving
  suck, suckling.
allattare, –tă'rĕ, v. a. to suckle.
alleanza, –lĕăn'tză, f. alliance, league.

alleato, –lĕă'tŏ, a. allied.
alleficarsi, –fĭkăr'sĕ, v. r. to take root.
allegare, –gă'rĕ, v. a. to allege, to cite;
  allegarsi, –găr'sĕ, to enter into a league
  with.   [relief.
alleggerimento, –djĕrĭmĕn'tŏ, m. easing,
alleggerire, –djĕrĭ'rĕ, v. a. to mitigate, to
  relieve; alleggerirsi, –rĭr'sĕ, to take off
  one's clothes, to undress.
allegoria, –gŏrĭ'ă, f. allegory.
allegorico, –gŏ'rĭkŏ, a. allegorical.
allegorizzare, –rĭtză'rĕ, v. a. to allego-
  rize.   [cheerily; readily.
allegramente, –grămĕn'tĕ, adv. gaily.
allegrare, –gră'rĕ, v. a. to cheer, to
  delight.   [f. gladness, joyousness.
allegrezza, –grĕt'ză, allegria, –grĭ'ă,
allegro, –lă'grŏ, a. cheerful, gay, merry,
  mirthful; brisk, quick.
allenamento, –lĕnămĕn'tŏ, m. delay.
allenare, –lĕnă'rĕ, v. n. to decay.
allentamento, –tămĕn'tŏ, m. relaxation;
  mitigation.   [stop; to relax.
allentare, –tă'rĕ, v. a. & n. to loosen, to
allestare, –lĕstă'rĕ, allestire, –tĕ'rĕ, v.
  a. to prepare.   [ment; charm.
allettamento, –lĕttămĕn'tŏ, m. allure-
allettare, –tă'rĕ, v. a. to allure; to charm.
allettevole, –tĕ'vŏlĕ, a. attractive, seductive.   [education.
allevamento, –ngămĕn'tŏ, m. bringing up,
allevare, –vă'rĕ, v. a. to bring up, to
  educate.
allevatore, –tŏ'rĕ, m. foster-father.
alleviare, –vĭă'rĕ, v. a. to alleviate, to
allezzare, –tză'rĕ, v. n. to stink.   [ease.
allibbrare, –lĭbbră'rĕ, v. a. to book, to
  down.   [rejoice.
allietare, –lĕtă'rĕ, v. a. to gladden, to
allievo, –lĭĕ'vŏ, m. pupil, scholar.
alligata, –lĭgă'tă, f. enclosure in a letter.
alligatore, –tŏ'rĕ, m. alligator.
allignare, –lĭnyă'rĕ, v. a. to take root.
allindare, –dă'rĕ, allindire, –dĭ'rĕ, v. a.
  to make spruce; to adorn.   [into lines.
allineare, –nĕă'rĕ, v. a. (mil.) to form
allividire, –lĭvĭdĕ'rĕ, v. n. to grow black
  and blue, to get pale as death.
allocco, –lŏk'kŏ, m. screech-owl.
allodola, –lŏ'dŏlă, f. sky-lark.
allogagione, –lŏgăjŏ'nĕ, f. alloga-
  mento, –mĕn'tŏ, m. lease.   [to farm.
allogare, –gă'rĕ, v. a. to place, to settle;
alloggiamento, –lŏdjămĕn'tŏ, m. lodging.   [to dwell.
alloggiare, –djă'rĕ, v. a. & n. to lodge;
alloggio, –lŏ'djŏ, m. lodging-house,
  lodging-rooms.
allogliato, –lŏlyă'tŏ, a. stupid, dull.
allontanamento, –lŏntămĕn'tŏ, m. distance, remoteness.
allontanare, –nă'rĕ, v. a. to remove.
allora, –lŏ'ră, ad. then, at that time.
alloro, –lŏ'rŏ, m. laurel-tree.
alluciare, –lădshŭ'ă'rĕ, v. a. (poet.) to
  eye, to stare at.   [twist.
allucignolare, –dshĭnyŏlă'rĕ, v. a. to

allucinazione, -nåtzĭŏ'nĕ, f. hallucina-
alluda, -lŏ'dă, m. sheep's skin. [tion.
alludere, -lŏ'dĕrĕ, v. a. ir. to allude.
allumare, -lŭmă'rĕ, v. a. to kindle; to
allume, -lŏ'mĕ, m. alum. [set fire to.
alluminare, -lŭmĭnă'rĕ, v. a. to enlighten.
allungamento, -lŭngămĕn'tŏ, m. lengthen-
ing; distance. [prolong.
allungare, -gă'rĕ, v. a. to lengthen; to
allupare, -lŭpă'rĕ, v. n. to starve.
allusione, -sĭŏ'nĕ, f. allusion.
allusivo, -sĭ'vŏ, a. allusive.
alluvione, -vĭŏ'nĕ, f. alluvion.
alma, ăl'mă, f. (poet.) soul.
almanaccare, -nåkkă'rĕ, v. n. to build
castles in the air.
almanacco, -nåk'kŏ, m. almanac.
almanco, -măn'kŏ, almeno, -mă'nŏ, ad.
at least.
almo, ăl'mŏ, a. (poet.) nourishing; benign.
aloè, ălŏ'ĕ, m. aloes. [excellent.
alpestre, -pĕs'trĕ, a. mountainous; rough,
wild. [of the Alps.
alpigiano, -pĭjă'nŏ, a. & m. inhabitant
alquanto, -kŭăn'tŏ, ad. somewhat, in some
altalena, -tălĕ'nă, f. see-saw. [degree.
altamente, -mĕn'tĕ, ad. highly; greatly,
deeply; nobly; remarkably.
altana, -tă'nă, f. balcony; turret.
altare, -tă'rĕ, m. altar.
alterabile, -tĕră'bĭlĕ, a. alterable.
alterare, -ră'rĕ, v. a. to change; to debase.
alterazione, -tzĭŏ'nĕ, f. alteration.
altercare, -tĕrkă'rĕ, v. n. to dispute, to
quarrel.
altercazione, -tzĭŏ'nĕ, f. altercation.
alterco, -tĕr'kŏ, m. dispute, quarrel.
alterezza, -rĕt'ză, alterigia, -rĕ'jă, f.
arrogance; ostentation.
alternare, -nă'rĕ, v. a. to alternate.
alternativa, -nătĭ'vă, f. alternative.
alternativo, -tĭ'vŏ, a. alternate by turns.
altero, -tă'rŏ, a. haughty.
altezza, -tĕt'ză, f. height; sublimity;
alticcio, -tĭt'shŏ, a. tipsy. [highness.
altiero, -tĭă'rŏ, a. haughty, lofty; noble.
altimetria, -mĕtrĕ'ă, f. altimetry.
alto, ăl'tŏ, a. high; tall; loud; deep; -,
ad. loud; -, m. high sea.
altresì, -trĕsĭ', ad. also, likewise, too.
altrettanto, -tăn'tŏ, ad. as much.
altri, ăl'trĭ, pn. another; some, others.
altrieri, -trĭă'rĭ, m. the day before
yesterday.
altrimenti, -trĭmĕn'tĭ, ad. otherwise.
altro, ăl'trŏ, a. other, another.
altrochè, -kĕ', ad. except, unless, but.
altronde, -trŏn'dĕ, ad. from elsewhere.
altrove, -trŏ'vĕ, ad. somewhere else.
altrui, -trŭ'ĭ, pn. others, other people.
altura, -tŏ'ră, f. height.
alunno, ălŭn'nŏ, m. pupil, scholar.
alveare, -vĕă'rĕ, m. bee-hive.
alveo, ăl'vĕŏ, m. bed of a river.
alveolo, -vĕ'ŏlŏ, m. alveole.
alvo, ăl'vŏ, m. (poet.) belly, womb.
alzaia, -tză'ă, f. cable.

alzamento, -tzămĕn'tŏ, m. lifting up.
alzare, -tză'rĕ, v. a. to raise, to lift up;
alzarsi, -tză'rsĭ, to get up, to rise.
amabile, ămă'bĭlĕ, a. amiable.
amabiltà, -bĭltă', f. amiability.
amabilmente, -mĕn'tĕ, ad. kindly, in
an amiable manner.
amalgama, ămăl'gămă, f. amalgam.
amalgamare, -gămă'rĕ, v. a. to amalga-
amante, ămăn'tĕ, m. lover, gallant; [mate.
amanuense, -nŭĕn'sĕ, m. amanuensis,
secretary.
amaranto, -răn'tŏ, m. amaranth.
amarasca, -răs'kă, f. egriot. [tree.
amarasco, -răs'kŏ, m. black hard cherry-
amare, ămă'rĕ, v. a. to love; to like;
- meglio, to like better, to have rather,
to prefer.
amareggiare, -rĕdjă'rĕ, v. a. & n. to
embitter; to have a bitter taste.
amarezza, -rĕt'ză, f. bitterness; grief.
amaritudine, -rĭtŭ'dĭnĕ, f. bitterness;
grief.
amaro, ămă'rŏ, a. bitter; grievous, cruel.
amarulento, -rŭlĕn'tŏ, a. rather bitter.
amatore, -tŏ'rĕ, m. lover; admirer.
amaurosi, -ăŭrŏ'sĭ, f. amaurosis, drop
serene.
amazzone, -tzŏ'nĕ, f. amazon.
ambasceria, -băshĕrĕ'ă, f. embassy.
ambascia, -băssh'tă, f. shortness of breath;
anxiety. [grieve.
ambasciare, -sshă'rĕ, v. n. to pant; to
ambasciata, -sshă'tă, f. embassy; message, commission.
ambasciatore, -tŏ'rĕ, m. ambassador.
ambascioso, -sshŏ'sŏ, a. sorrowful.
ambedue, ămbĕdŭ'ĕ, pn. both.
ambiante (cavallo), -bĭăn'tĕ, m. ambler.
ambiare, -bĭă'rĕ, v. n. to amble.
ambiente, -bĭĕn'tĕ, m. surrounding air,
atmosphere; circumference. [guously.
ambiguamente, -bĭgŭămĕn'tĕ, ad. ambi-
ambiguità, -gŭĭtă', f. ambiguity.
ambiguo, -bĕ'gŭŏ, a. ambiguous.
ambire, ămbĭ'rĕ, v. a. to desire ardently.
ambito, ăm'bĭtŏ, m. cabal, intrigue.
ambizione, -tzĭŏ'nĕ, f. ambition.
ambizioso, -tzĭŏ'sŏ, a. ambitious.
ambo, ăm'bŏ, pn. both.
ambra, ăm'bră, f. amber. [amber.
ambrare, -bră'rĕ, v. a. to perfume with
ambrosia, -brŏ'stă, f. ambrosia. [fly.
ambulare, -bŭlă'rĕ, v. n. to run away, to
ambulatorio, -lătŏ'rĕŏ, m. ambulatory;
itinerant.
amenità, ămĕnĭtă', f. agreeableness.
ameno, ămă'nŏ, a. pleasing, agreeable.
ametista, ămĕtĭs'tă, f. amethyst. [sweet.
amica, ămĕ'kă, f. female friend.
amicarsi, ămĭkă'rsĭ, v. r. to form a friendship. [gentle.
amichevole, -kĕ'vŏlĕ, a. amiable, affable,
amicizia, -dshĕ'tzĭă, f. friendship.
amico, ămĕ'kŏ, m. friend.
amido, ă'mĭdŏ, m. starch.
amistà, ămĭstă', f. friendship

ammaccamento,—*måkkåmĕn'tŏ*,m. bruise, contusion. [crush.
ammaccare, —*kå'rĕ*, v. a. to bruise; to
ammaccatura, —*kåtŏ'rå*, f. bruise, contusion. [instruction; education.
ammaestramento,—*måĕstråmĕn'tŏ*, m.
ammaestrare, —*trå'rĕ*, v. a. to teach, to instruct. [structor.
ammaestratore,—*tŏ'rĕ*, m. teacher, instructor.
ammagliare, —*mâlyå'rĕ*, v. a. to bind with meshes. [to fall away.
ammagrire, —*mågrĕ'rĕ*, v. n. to get lean.
ammainare, —*måinå'rĕ*, v. a. (mar.) to lower the sails.
ammalare, —*lå'rĕ*, v. n. to fall sick.
ammalato, —*lå'tŏ*, a. sick, ill.
ammaliamento,—*liåmĕn'tŏ*, m. witchcraft.
ammaliare, —*liå'rĕ*, v. a. to bewitch, to charm. [cious.
ammalizito, —*litzi'tŏ*, a. grown malicious.
ammanettare, —*mănĕttå'rĕ*, v. a. to fetter.
ammanierare, —*mănĕrå'rĕ*, v. a. to embellish with ornaments, to adorn.
ammansare, —*så'rĕ*, ammansire, —*sĕ'rĕ*, v. a. to tame, to domesticate, to break in.
ammantare, —*tå'rĕ*, ammantellare, —*tĕllå'rĕ*, v. a. to cloak, to palliate.
ammanto, —*mån'tŏ*, m. cloak, mantle.
ammassare, —*måsså'rĕ*, v. a. to heap up.
ammassicciarsi, —*sitshår'si*, v. r. to get compact, to grow hard. [cumulation.
ammasso, *åmmås'sŏ*, m. heap, mass; accumulation.
ammatassare, —*tåsså'rĕ*, v. a. to wind into skeins. [to go mad.
ammattire,—*tĕ'rĕ*, v. a. & n. to drive mad;
ammattonare, —*tŏnå'rĕ*, v. a. to pave with bricks. [ter; massacre.
ammazzamento,—*tzåmĕn'tŏ*, m. slaughter.
ammazzare, —*tzå'rĕ*, v. a. to murder, to massacre. [gerer.
ammazzasette, —*sĕt'tĕ*, m. bully, swaggerer.
ammazzatoio,—*tŏi'ŏ*, m. slaughter-house; slaughtering bench.
ammazzatore, —*tŏ'rĕ*, m. murderer.
ammazzolare, —*tzŏlå'rĕ*, v. a. to make nosegays.
ammelmare, —*mĕlmå'rĕ*, ammemmare, —*mĕmmå'rĕ*, v. n. to sink in the mire, to get entangled.
ammen, *åmmĕn'*, j. amen! so be it!
ammenare, —*mĕnå'rĕ*, v. a. to swing; to brandish; to give a blow. [reform.
ammenda, —*mĕn'då*, f. amends; punition;
ammendare, —*då'rĕ*, v. a. to amend, to reform; to indemnify. [to receive.
ammettere, —*mĕt'tĕrĕ*, v. a. ir. to admit, to
ammezzare, —*mĕtzå'rĕ*, v. a. & n. to divide in two; to grow overripe. [beckon.
ammiccare, —*mikkå'rĕ*, v. a. to wink, to
amminicolo, —*nĕ'kŏlŏ*, m. adminicle, help.
amministrare, —*nistrå'rĕ*, v. a. to administer, to govern. [tor, manager.
amministratore, —*tŏ'rĕ*, m. administrator.
amministrazione, —*tzĭŏ'nĕ*, f. administration, government.
ammirabile, —*mirå'bilĕ*, a. admirable.
ammiragliato, —*rålyå'tŏ*, f. admiralty, admiralship.

ammiraglio, —*rål'yŏ*, m. admiral; flagship; looking-glass.
ammirando, —*rån'dŏ*, a. wonderful.
ammirare, —*rå'rĕ*, v. a. to admire.
ammirativo, —*tĕ'vŏ*, a. wonderstruck.
ammiratore, —*tŏ'rĕ*, m. admirer.
ammirazione, —*tzĭŏ'nĕ*, f. admiration.
ammissibile, —*missĭ'bilĕ*, a. admissible.
ammissione,—*siŏ'nĕ*, f. admission; access.
ammodernare, —*mŏdĕrnå'rĕ*, v. a. to modernize.
ammogliare, —*mŏlyå'rĕ*, v. a. to marry (a son); ammogliarsi, —*yår'si*, to marry, to get married.
ammollamento,—*mŏllåmĕn'tŏ*, ammollimento, —*limĕn'tŏ*, m. steeping, soaking; softening. [lify, to soften.
ammollare, —*lå'rĕ*, v. a. to steep, to mollify.
ammoniaca, —*mŏnĕ'åkå*, f. ammoniac.
ammonire, —*nĕ'rĕ*, v. a. to admonish, to warn; to advise. [advice.
ammonizione, —*tzĭŏ'nĕ*, f. admonition.
ammontare, —*mŏntå'rĕ*, v. a. to heap up.
ammorbare, —*mŏrbå'rĕ*, v. a. & n. to infect; to smell strong. [ness, effeminacy.
ammorbidimento,—*bidĭmĕn'tŏ*, m. softness.
ammorbidire, —*bidĕ'rĕ*, v. a. to soften; to render effeminate. [meat.
ammorsellato,—*sĕllå'tŏ*, m. hash, mincemeat.
ammortare, —*tå'rĕ*, v. a. to quench, to stifle; to cool. [to deaden.
ammorzare, —*tzå'rĕ*, v. a. to extinguish, to deaden.
ammoscire, —*mŏsshĕ'rĕ*, v. n. to fade, to languish. [grapes.
ammostare, —*mŏstå'rĕ*, v. a. to press grapes.
ammostatoio, —*tŏi'ŏ*, wine-press.
ammottare, —*mŏttå'rĕ*, v. n. to roll down.
ammucchiare, —*måkkĭå'rĕ*, v. a. to heap up, to pile up.
ammuffare, —*måffå'rĕ*, v. n. to get musty.
ammusarsi, —*sår'si*, v. r. to meet face to face. [tiny.
ammutinamento, —*tĭnåmĕn'tŏ*, m. mutiny.
ammutinarsi, —*tĭnår'si*, v. r. to mutiny.
ammutinatore, —*tŏ'rĕ*, m. mutineer.
ammutire, —*tĕ'rĕ*, ammutolire, —*tŏlĕ'rĕ*, v. n. to grow mute.
amnistia, —*nisti'å*, f. amnesty.
amo, *å'mŏ*, m. angle, fishing-hook.
amore, *åmŏ'rĕ*, m. love; affection; charity;
- di se, self-love; - proprio, self-love.
amoreggiare, —*rĕdjå'rĕ*, v. a. to make love to.
amorevole, —*rĕ'vŏlĕ*, a. kind, amorous.
amorevolmente, —*mĕn'tĕ*, ad. with kindness, kindly. [fection, lovingly.
amorosamente,—*rŏsåmĕn'tĕ*, ad. with affection.
amorosità, —*rŏsĭtå'*, f. amorousness.
amoroso, —*rŏ'sŏ*, m. lover; gallant; —, a. amorous, enamoured, in love.
amovibile, —*vĕ'bilĕ*, a. removeable.
ampiezza, *åmpiĕt'zå*, f. largeness, extenampio, *åm'piŏ*, a. ample, spacious. [sion.
amplesso, —*plĕs'sŏ*, m. embrace. [tend.
ampliare, —*pliå'rĕ*, v. a. to enlarge, to extend.
ampliazione, —*tzĭŏ'nĕ*, f. ampliation, enlargement.

amplificare, –plĭfĭkă′rĕ, v. a. to amplify; to exaggerate.
amplitudine, –tŏ′ dĭnĕ, f. amplitude.
ampolla, –pŏl′lă, f. phial, glass vessel.
ampollosità, –lŏsĭtă′, f. bombast.
ampolloso, –lŏ′sŏ, a. bombastic.
amuleto, ămŭlĕ′tŏ, m. amulet.
anabattista, ănăbăttĭs′tă, m. anabaptist.
anace, ă′năshĕ, m. anise-seed, aniseed.
anacoreta, ănăkŏrĕ′tă, m. anchorite.
anacronismo, –krŏnĭs′mŏ, m. anachronism.
anagogia, –gŏjĭ′ă, f. mystical sense.
anagogico, –gŏ′jĭkŏ, a. mystical.
anagramma, –grăm′mă, m. anagram.
analisi, ănă′lĭsĭ, f. analysis.
analitico, –lĭ′tĭkŏ, a. analytical.
analizzare, –lĭzză′rĕ, v. a. to analyse.
analogia, –lŏjĭ′ă, f. analogy.
analogico, –lŏ′jĭkŏ, analogo, ănă′lŏgŏ, a. analogical.
ananasse, –năs′sĕ, m. ananas, pine-apple.
anarchia, ănărkĭ′ă, f. anarchy.
anarchico, ănă′rkĭkŏ, a. anarchical.
anatema, ănătĕ′mă, f. anathema, excommunication.
anatomia, –tŏmĭ′ă, f. anatomy.
anatomico, –tŏ′mĭkŏ, a. anatomical.
anatomista, –tŏmĭs′tă, m. anatomist.
anatomizzare, –mĭtză′rĕ, v. a. to anatomatra, ă′nătră, f. duck. [tomise.
anca, ăn′kă, f. hip, hip-bone, haunch.
ancella, –dshĕl′lă, f. maid-servant.
anche, ăn′kĕ, ad. also, too, likewise, even.
ancheggiare, –djă′rĕ, v. n. to wag one's legs.
anco, ăn′kŏ, ad. also, yet, still. [legs.
ancona, ăn′kŏnă, f. large altar-piece.
ancona, ănkŏ′nă, f. thigh.
ancora, ăn′kŏră, f. anchor. [again.
ancora, –kŏ′ră, ad. also, yet, still, even,
ancorachè, –kĕ′, c. although, even though.
ancoraggio, –ră′jŏ, m. anchorage.
ancorare, –ră′rĕ, v. n. to cast anchor.
ancorchè, see ancorachè.
ancudine, –kŏ′dĭnĕ, f. anvil.
andamento, –dămĕn′tŏ, m. gait, step, proceeding; carriage. [andante.
andante, –dăn′tĕ, a. going; –, m. (mus.)
andare, –dă′rĕ, v. n. ir. to go; to march; andarsene, –dăr′sĕnĕ, to go away; to disappear; – a cavallo, to go on horseback.
andata, –dă′tă, f. step, walk; (med.) evacuation, stool.
andatura, –tŏ′ră, f. manner of walking.
andazzo, –dăt′zŏ, m. passing fashion.
andirivieni, –dĭrĭvĭ′nĭ, m. pl. windings; incoherent discourse.
andito, ăn′dĭtŏ, m. passage, entrance.
androgino, –drŏ′jĭnŏ, m. hermaphrodite.
androne, –drŏ′nĕ, m. corridor; antechamber.
aneddoto, ănĕd′dŏtŏ, m. anecdote.
anelare, –lă′rĕ, v. n. to pant, to be out of breath.
anello, ănĕl′lŏ, m. ring. [breath.
anemone, ănĕmŏ′nĕ, f. (bot.) anemony.

anfanare, –fănă′rĕ, v. n. to prate; to ramble.
anfanatore, –tŏ′rĕ, m. prater.
anfibio, –fĭ′bĭŏ, a. amphibious.
anfiteatro, –tĕă′trŏ, m. amphitheatre.
anfora, ăn′fŏră, f. pitcher, mug.
anfratto, –frăt′tŏ, m. narrow dark place.
angariare, –gărĭă′rĕ, v. a. to overtax, to extort tyrannically.
angela, ăn′jĕlă, f. angel (of a woman).
angelico, –jĕ′lĭkŏ, a. angelic.
angelo, ăn′jĕlŏ, m. angel.
angheria, –ghĕrĭ′ă, f. extortion, vexation; compulsion.
angina, –jĕ′nă, f. quinsy.
angiporto, –jĕpŏr′tŏ, m. blind alley.
anglicismo, –glĭjĭs′mŏ, anglicanismo, –kănĭs′mŏ, m. anglicism.
angolare, –gŏlă′rĕ, a. angular.
angolo, ăn′gŏlŏ, m. angle; corner.
angore, –gŏ′rĕ, m. anguish, grief.
angoscia, –gŏssh′tă, f. anguish, affliction.
angosciare, –sshă′rĕ, v. a. to grieve, to vex; to anger.
angoscioso, –sshŏ′sŏ, a. anxious.
angue, ăn′gŭĕ, m. (poet.) snake, serpent.
anguilla, –gŭĭl′lă, f. eel. [want.
angustia, –gŭs′tĭă, f. narrowness; distress;
angustiare, –tĭă′rĕ, v. a. to press; to distress, to vex.
angustioso, –tĭŏ′sŏ, a. afflicted, anxious.
angusto, –gŭs′tŏ, a. narrow; hampered.
anice, ă′nĭdshĕ, m. anise-seed, aniseed.
anile, ănĕ′lĭ, a. (poet.) aged, old.
anima, ă′nĭmă, f. soul; life; person.
animalaccio, –mălăt′shŏ, m. great ugly animal; (fig.) stupid fellow.
animale, –mă′lĕ, m. animal.
animaletto, –lĕt′tŏ, m. animalcule.
animalità, –lĭtă′, f. animality.
animante, –măn′tĕ, m. living being; animated creature. [courage.
animare, –mă′rĕ, v. a. to animate, to enanimavversione, –vĕrsĭŏ′nĕ, f. animadversion, punishment. [courage.
animazione, –tzĭŏ′nĕ, f. animation.
aninella, –mĕl′lă, f. sweet-bread; sucker (of a pump). [courage.
animo, ă′nĭmŏ, m. understanding, mind;
animosità, –mŏsĭtă′, f. animosity.
animoso, –mŏ′sŏ, a. courageous; averse.
anitra, ă′nĭtră, f. duck. [with water.
annacquare, ănnăkkŭă′rĕ, v. a. to mix
annacquaticcio, –tĭt′shŏ, a. mixed with a little water.
annaffiare, –fĭă′rĕ, v. a. to water.
annale, –nă′lĕ, a. annual, yearly.
annali, –nă′lĭ, m. pl. annals, pl.
annasare, –să′rĕ, v. a. to smell.
annebbiamento, –nĕbbĭămĕn′tŏ, m. cloudiness, dark weather.
annebbiare, –bĭă′rĕ, v. a. to cloud.
annegare, –nĕgă′rĕ, v. a. to drown; to deny.
annegazione, –tzĭŏ′nĕ, f. self-denial.
anneghittire, –ghĭttĭ′rĕ, v. n. to grow lazy. [tura, –rĭtŏ′ră, f. blackness.
anneramento, –rắmĕn′tŏ, m. anneri-

annerare, _–rā′ rĕ_, annerire, _–rē′ rĕ_, v. a. to blacken; to tarnish; to defame.

annesso, _–nĕs′ sŏ_, a. annexed.

annestamento, _–nĕstāmĕn′ tŏ_, m.grafting, ingraftment. [sert; to unite.

annestare, _–tā′ rĕ_, v. a. to graft; to in-

annichilare, _–nīkĭlā′ rĕ_, annichilire, _–lē′ rĕ_, v. a. to annihilate.

annidare, _–nīdā′ rĕ_, v. a. to nestle; annidarsi, _–dăr′ sī_, to nestle; to settle oneself.

annientare, _–nīĕntā′ rĕ_, v. a. to annihilate.

anniversario, _–vērsā′ rĭŏ_, m. anniversary.

anno, _ăn′ nŏ_, m. year.

annobilitare, see nobilitare.

annodamento, _–dāmĕn′ tŏ_, m.tying; knot.

annodare, _–dā′ rĕ_, v. a. to tie, to knot.

annoiare, _–nŏā′ rĕ_, v. a. to annoy, to tease.

annona, _–nŏ′ nā_, f. victuals, stores, pl.

annonario, _–nŏnā′ rĭŏ_, a belonging to provisions.

annoso, _–nŏ′ sŏ_, a. old, ancient.

annotare, _–tā′ rĕ_, y. a. to annotate.

annotatore, _–tŏ′ rĕ_, m. annotator.

annotazione, _–tzĭŏ′ nĕ_, f. annotation.

annoveramento, _–vērāmĕn′ tŏ_, m. enumeration. [to number, to count.

annoverare, _–rā′ rĕ_, v. a. to enumerate.

annuale, _–nŭā′ lĕ_, annuario, _–nŭā′ rĭŏ_, a. annual, yearly. [yearly.

annualmente, _–mĕn′ tĕ_, ad. annually,

annullamento, _–nŭllāmĕn′ tŏ_, m. annulling, repeal. [repeal; to abolish.

annullare, _–lā′ rĕ_, v. a. to annul, to

annullazione, _–tzĭŏ′ nĕ_, f. annulling, abolition, repeal. [to predict.

annunziare, _–nūntzĭā′ rĕ_, v. a to announce,

annunziazione, _–tzĭŏ′ nĕ_, f. annunciation; Lady-day. [news, prognostic.

annunzio, _–nūn′ tzĭŏ_, m. announcing;

annuo, _ăn′ nŭŏ_, a. yearly. [cloudy.

annuvolare, _–nŭvŏlā′ rĕ_, v. a. to grow

ano, _ă′ nŏ_, m. anus; arse, back-side.

anodino, _–dē′ nŏ_, a. (med.) anodyne.

anomalia, _–mālē′ ā_, f. anomaly.

anomalo, _ănŏ′ mălŏ_, a. anomalous.

anonimo, _ănŏ′ nĭmŏ_, a. anonymous.

ansamento, _–sāmĕn′ tŏ_, m. shortness of breath. [short.

ansare, _–sā′ rĕ_, v. n. to pant, to breathe

ansietà, _–sĭĕtā′_, f. anxiety.

ansio, _ăn′ sĭŏ_, ansioso, _–sĭŏ′ sŏ_, a.anxious.

ansiosamente, _–mĕn′ tĕ_, ad. anxiously.

ansioso, _ănsĭŏ′ sŏ_, a. anxious. [nism.

antagonismo, _–tāgŏnēs′ mŏ_, m. antago-

antagonista, _–tāgŏnēs′ tā_, m. antagonist.

antartico, _–ār′ tĭkŏ_, a. antarctic.

antecedere, _ăntĕdshā′ dĕrĕ_, v. a. ir. to go before, to precede.

antecessore, _–tshĕssŏ′ rĕ_, m. predecessor.

antelucano, _–lŭkā′ nŏ_, a. before day-break.

antenato, _–nā′ tŏ_, m. forefather, ancestor.

antenna, _–tĕn′ nā_, f. feeler; sail-yard.

anteporre, _–pŏr′ rĕ_, v. a. ir. to prefer.

anteposizione, _–pŏsĭtzĭŏ′ nĕ_, f. preference.

anteposto, _–pŏs′ tŏ_, a. preferred. [mer.

anteriore, _–rĭŏ′ rĕ_, a. anterior, prior, for-

anteriorità, _–rĭŏrĭtā′_, f. priority.

anteriormente. _–mĕn′ tĕ_, ad. previously, before.

antescritto, _–skrĭt′ tŏ_, a. above written.

anticaglia, _ăntĭkāl′ yā_, f. antiquities, pl.

anticamente, _–kāmĕn′ tĕ_. ad. anciently, formerly.

anticamera, _–kăm′ ĕrā_, f. antechamber.

anticato, _–kā′ tŏ_, a. used; antiquated.

antichità, _–kĭtā′_, f. antiquity; ancients, pl.

anticipare, _–dshĭpā′ rĕ_, v. a. to anticipate.

anticipazione, _–tzĭŏ′ nĕ_, f. anticipation.

anticonoscere, _–kŏnŏssh′ ĕrĕ_, v. a. ir. to foresee, to foreknow.

anticorrere, _–kŏr′ rĕrĕ_, v. a. ir. to outrun, to run before.

anticorriere, _–rā′ rĕ_, m. forerunner.

anticorte, _–kŏr′ tĕ_, f. forecourt.

anticristo, _–krĭs′ tŏ_, m. antichrist.

anticursore, _–kŭrsŏ′ rĕ_, m. forerunner.

antidetto, _–dĕt′ tŏ_, a. aforesaid.

antidire, _–dē′ rĕ_, v. a. ir. to predict, to foretell. [poison.

antidoto, _ăntē′ dŏtŏ_, m. antidote, counter-

antifona, _–fŏnā_, f. anthem. [guard.

antiguardia, _ăntĭgŭār′ dĭā_, f. (mil.) van-

antimettere, _–mĕt′ tĕrĕ_, v. a. ir. to prefer.

antimonio, _–mŏ′ nĭŏ_, m. antimony.

antipapa, _–pā′ pā_, m. antipope.

antipasto, _–pās′ tŏ_, m. spoon-meat.

antipatia, _–pātē′ ā_, f. antipathy.

antipatico, _–pā′ tĭkŏ_, a. antipathetic.

antipodi, _ăntē′ pŏdĭ_, m. pl. antipodes, pl.

antisapere, _ăntĭsāpā′ rĕ_, v. a. ir. to foreknow.

antitesi, _ăntē′ tĕsĭ_, f. antithesis. [see.

antivedere, _ăntĭvĕdā′ rĕ_, v. a. ir. to fore-

antivenire, _–vĕnē′ rĕ_, v. n. ir. to prevent.

antivigilia, _–vĭjĭl′ yā_, f. day before the eve.

antologia, _ăntŏlŭjē′ ā_, f. anthology.

antonomasia, _–nŏmā′ sĭā_, f. antonomasia.

antrace, _ăntrā′ dshĕ_, m. (med.) carbuncle.

antro, _ăn′ trŏ_, m. cave, grotto.

antropologia, _–pŏlŭjē′ ā_, f. anthropology.

anulare, _ănŭlā′ rĕ_, m. ring-finger.

anzi, _ăn′ tzĭ_, pr. before; –, ad. rather; even; also; on the contrary.

anzianità, _–tzĭānĭtā′_, f. seniority.

anziano, _–tzĭā′ nŏ_, a. ancient; –, m. elder, senior.

anziché, _–tzĭkē′_, ad. & c. before that.

anzi che no, _–kē nŏ′_, ad. rather, sooner.

anzinato, _–nā′ tŏ_, a. eldest, first-born.

aoliato, _āŏlĭā′ tŏ_, a. oily, greasy.

apatia, _āpătē′ ā_, f. apathy.

apatico, _āpă′ tĭkŏ_, a. insensible.

ape, _ā′ pĕ_, f. bee.

aperta, _āpĕr′ tā_, f. hole, aperture.

apertamente, _–mĕn′ tĕ_,ad.openly,publicly.

aperto, _–tŏ_, a. opened, open; clear,evident, plain.

apertura, _–tŏ′ rā_, f. aperture; hole.

apice, _ā′ pĭdshĕ_, m. peak, top, summit.

Apocalisse, _ăpŏkālēs′ sĕ_, Apocalissi, _–lēs′ sĭ_, f. Apocalypse. [ful.

apocrifo, _āpŏ′ krĭfŏ_, a. apocryphal; doubt-

apogeo, _–jā′ ŏ_, m. apogee. [palliative.

apologetico, _–lŏjĕ′ tĭkŏ_, a. apologetic;

apologia, –lŏjĕ'ă, f. apology.
apologo, ăpŏ'lŏgŏ, m. apologue; allegory.
apoplessia, ăpŏplĕssĕ'ă, f. apoplexy.
apoplettico, –plĕt'tĭkŏ, a. apoplectic.
apostasia, –stăsĕ'ă, f. apostasy.
apostata, ăpŏs'tătă, m. apostate, renegade.
apostatare, –tătă'rĕ, v. n. to apostatise.
apostema, –id'mă, m. tumour, abscess.
apostolato, –tŏlă'tŏ, m. apostleship.
apostolico, –tŏ'lĭkŏ, a. apostolic.
apostolo, –tŏlŏ, m. apostle.
apostrofare, –trŏfă'rĕ, v. a. to insert an apostrophe; to apostrophise.
apostrofe, –trŏfĕ, a. apostrophe.
apoteosi, ăpŏtĕŏ'sĭ, a. apotheosis.

appaciare, ăppădshă'rĕ, v. a. to pacify; to appease.   [pitch a tent, to encamp.
appadiglionare, –pădĭlyŏnă'rĕ, v. a. to
appagare, –păgă'rĕ, v. a. to satisfy, to please.   [couple, to pair.
appaiare, –păiă'rĕ, v. a. to match, to
appalesare, –pălĕsă'rĕ, v. a. to discover, to declare.   [farm.
appaltare, –păltă'rĕ, v. a. to let out, to
appaltatore, –tŏ'rĕ, m. farmer.
appalto, –păl'tŏ, m. farm.
appaltone, –tŏ'nĕ, m. intriguer, impostor.
appannaggio, –pănăd'jŏ, m. appanage.
appannamento, –mĕn'tŏ, m., appannatura, –tŏ'ră, f. dimness, tarnish.
appannare, –nă'rĕ, v.a. to dim, to tarnish.
appannato, –nă'tŏ, a. dull; caught in a snare.   [learn; to provide.
apparare, –pără'rĕ, v. a. to prepare; to
apparato, –ră'tŏ, m. apparatus; preparation.
apparecchiare, –rĕkkĭă'rĕ, v. a. to prepare, to treat; apparecchiarsi, –kĭăr'sĭ, to prepare oneself; to get ready.
apparente, –rĕn'tĕ, a. apparent, visible.
apparentemente, –mĕn'tĕ, ad. apparently.
apparenza, –rĕn'tză, f. appearance.
apparimento, –rĭmĕn'tŏ, m. apparition.
apparire, –rĕ'rĕ, v. n. ir. to appear, to come forth.   [appearance.
appariscenza, –rĭsshĕn'tză, f. splendid
apparitore, –tŏ'rĕ, m. sergeant, constable.
apparizione, –tzĭŏ'nĕ, apparsione, –sĭŏ'nĕ, f. apparition, vision.
appartamento, –părtămĕn'tŏ, a. apartment; suite of chambers.   [self.
appartarsi, –tăr'sĭ, v. r. to withdraw oneself.
appartato, –tă'tŏ, a. separated, set apart.
appartenenza, –tĕnĕn'tză, f. appurtenance.
appartenere, –tĕnĕ'rĕ, v. n. ir. to belong, to concern, to become.   [passion; love.
appassimento, –păssĭmĕn'tŏ, m. ardour.
appassionarsi, –stŏnăr'sĭ, v. r. to have a strong passion for.
appassionato, –nă'tŏ, a. passionate.
appassire, –sĕ'rĕ, v. n. to fade, to wither.
appastare, –tă'rĕ, v. a. to paste, to stick.
appellante, –pĕllăn'tĕ, m. appellant.
appellare, –lă'rĕ, v. a. to call; to cite, –, v. n. to appeal.
appellativo, –lătĕ'vŏ, m. (gr.) appellative.
appello, –pĕl'lŏ, m. call, appeal; challenge.

appena, –pă'nă, ad. hardly, scarcely.
appenare, –pĕnă'rĕ, v. n. to suffer.
appendere, –pĕn'dĕrĕ, v. a. ir. to hang on.
appendice, –pĕn'dĭshĕ, m. appendix.
appensatamente, –sătămĕn'tĕ, ad. designedly, purposedly.
appestare, –pĕstă'rĕ, v. a. to infect.
appetente, –pĕtĕn'tĕ, a. desirous.
appetibile, –tĕ'bĭlĕ, a. desirable.
appetire, –tĕ'rĕ, v. n. to long for.
appetitivo, –tĭtĕ'vŏ, a. desirable.   [sire.
appetito, –tĕ'tŏ, m. appetite; ardent desire.
appetitoso, –tŏ'sŏ, a. appetising.
appetizione, –tzĭŏ'nĕ, f. appetency, desire.
appettare, –tă'rĕ, v. a. to have at heart.
appetto, –pĕt'tŏ, pr. in comparison.
appiacevolire, –păsshĕvŏlĕ'rĕ, v. a. to mitigate, to soften.   [level.
appianare, –nă'rĕ, v. a. to smooth, to
appiastrare, –stră'rĕ, appiastricciare, –strĕtshă'rĕ, v. a. to stick, to fix.
appiattare, –tă'rĕ, v. a. to hide.
appiattatamente, –mĕn'tĕ, ad. secretly.
appiccagnolo, –pĭkkăn'yŏlŏ, m. hook, crook.   [stick together.
appiccare, –kă'rĕ, v. a. to hang up, to
appiccatoio, –tŏ'yŏ, m. hook; hold-fast.
appicciare, –tshă'rĕ, v. a. to stick to.
appiccinire, –tshĭnĕ'rĕ, v. a. to diminish.
appicciolire, –tshŏlĕ'rĕ, v. a. to lessen.
appicco, –pĭk'kŏ, m. adhesion, junction.
appiè, –pĭĕ', appiede, –pĭĕ'dĕ, ad. at the foot, at the bottom.
appieno, –pĭĕ'nŏ, ad. completely, quite.
appigionare, –pĭjŏnă'rĕ, v. a. to let out, to lease, to hire out.
appigliare, –pĭlyă'rĕ, v. a. to stick; to adhere; to follow; appigliarsi, –yăr'sĭ, to be caught.
appigrirsi, –pĭgrĕr'sĭ, v. r. to grow idle.
appillottarsi, –pĭllŏttăr'sĭ, v. r. to linger.
appio, ăp'pĭŏ, m. (bot.) parsley.   [to loiter.
applaudire, –plădĕ'rĕ, v. a. to applaud.
applauso, –plă'ŭsŏ, m. applause.
applicabile, –plĭkă'bĭlĕ, a. applicable.
applicare, –kă'rĕ, v. a. to apply, to assign; applicarsi, –kăr'sĭ, to apply oneself to.
applicazione, –tzĭŏ'nĕ, f. application.
appo, see appresso.
appoggiare, –pŏdjă'rĕ, v. a. to lean, to prop; to support.
appoggiatoio, –tŏ'yŏ, m., appoggiatura, –tŏ'ră, f., appoggio, –pŏd'jŏ, m. prop, support.   [favour, protection.
appoggio, –pŏd'jŏ, m. support, prop;
apporre, –pŏr'rĕ, v. a. ir. to appose; to blame; apporsi, –pŏr'sĭ, to guess.
apportare, –tă'rĕ, v. a. to bring; to convey; to breed.
apportatore, –tŏ'rĕ, m. messenger.
apposizione, –pŏsĭtzĭŏ'nĕ, f. (gr.) apposition.   [snare.
appostamento, –pŏstămĕn'tŏ, m. ambush;
appostare, –tă'rĕ, v. a. to watch, to spy.
appostatamente, –tămĕn'tĕ, ad. purposely, on purpose.

apprendente, –prĕndĕn'tĕ, m. scholar; apprentice.

apprendere, –prĕn'dĕrĕ, v. a. ir. to learn; to conceive; to teach. [study.

apprendimento, –dīmĕn'tŏ, m. learning.

apprensibile, –sĕ'bīlĕ, a. conceivable, intelligible, comprehensible.

apprensione, –stŏ'nĕ, f. apprehension.

apprensivo, –sĕ'vŏ, a. apt to learn; fearful. [to represent.

appresentare, –prĕsĕntā'rĕ, v. a. to show;

appreso, –prā'sŏ, a. learned; thickened; taken. [near; to approach.

appressare, –prĕssā'rĕ, v. a. & n. to draw

appresso, –prĕs'sŏ, pr. near, hard by, by, about; –. ad. after, afterwards.

apprestare, –prĕstā'rĕ, v. a. to prepare, to make ready. [valuable.

apprezzabile, –prĕtzā'bīlĕ, a. appreciable,

apprezzamento, –mĕn'tŏ, m. estimate, appraising. [to esteem.

apprezzare, –tzā'rĕ, v. a. to value, to rate;

apprezzativo, –tĕ'vŏ, a. commendable.

apprezzatore, –tŏ'rĕ, m. valuer.

approccio, –prŏt'shŏ, m. approach; (mil.) approaches, pl.

approdare, –prŏdā'rĕ, v. n. to land; to be useful.

approdo, –prŏ'dŏ, m. landing.

approfittare, –fīttā'rĕ, v. n. to profit.

approfondare, –fŏndā'rĕ, approfondire, –dē'rĕ, v. a. to dig, to deepen.

approntare, –prŏntā'rĕ, v. a. to prepare, to make ready.

appropinquarsi, –prŏpīnkŭār'st, v. r. to approach. [priate.

appropriare, –prĭā'rĕ, v. a. to appropriate.

appropriazione, –tzīŏ'nĕ, f. appropriation.

approssimare, –prŏssīmā'rĕ, v. a. & n. approssimarsi, –mār'st, v. r. to approach; to come near. [mation.

approssimazione, –tzĭŏ'nĕ, f. approximation.

approvabile, –prŏvā'bīlĕ, a. approvable.

approvare, –vā'rĕ, v. a. to approve, to confirm. [probation, approvingly.

approvatamente, –tāmĕn'tĕ, ad. with approbation.

approvazione, –tzĭŏ'nĕ, f. approbation, liking. [ment; convention.

appuntamento, –pŭntāmĕn'tŏ, m.appointment.

appuntare, –tā'rĕ, v. a. to point, to sharpen; to sew; to blame.

appuntatura, –tŏ'rā, f. blame; mark.

appuntellare, –tĕllā'rĕ, v. a. to prop, to support, to stay.

appunto, –pŭn'tŏ, ad. precisely.

appurare, –pŭrā'rĕ, v. a. to purify; to write a fair copy.

appuzzare, –pŭtzā'rĕ, v. n. to emit an offensive smell.

aprico, āprē'kŏ, a. sunny; sun-burnt.

aprile, āprē'lĕ, m. April.

aprire, āprē'rĕ, v. a. ir. to open, to discover; aprirsi, –rēr'st, to burst.

aquatico, ākŭā'tīkŏ, a. aquatic; watery.

aquila, ā'kŭīlā, f. eagle.

aquilino, –lē'nŏ, a. aquiline.

aquilonare, –lŏnā'rĕ, a. northerly, boreal;

aquilone, –lŏ'nĕ, m. northwind. [stormy.

ara, ā'rā, f. (poet.) altar.

arabesco, –bĕs'kŏ, m. arabesque.

arabico, ā'rā'bīkŏ, a. strange.

aragna, ārān'yā, f. spider.

araldica, ārāl'dīkā, f. heraldry.

araldico, –dīkŏ, a. belonging to heraldry.

araldo, ārāl'dŏ, m. herald.

arancia, ārān'dshā, f. orange.

aranciata, –dshā'tā, f. orangeade.

aranciato, –dshā'tŏ, a. orange-coloured.

arancio, –dshŏ, m. orange-tree.

arare, ārā'rĕ, v. a. to plough, to till; to cultivate.

aratore, –tŏ'rĕ, m. ploughman.

aratro, ārā'trŏ, m. plough.

aratura, –tŏ'rā, f. ploughing, tillage.

arazziere, –tzĭā'rĕ, m. tapestry-maker; tapestry-seller.

arazzo, ārāt'zŏ, m. tapestry. [judge.

arbitrare, ārbītrā'rĕ, v. a. to arbitrate, to

arbitrario, –trā'rĭŏ, a. arbitrary.

arbitratore, –tŏ'rĕ, m. arbitrator, umpire.

arbitrio, ārbē'trĭŏ, m. free-will; absolute power.

arbitro, ār'bītrŏ, m. arbiter, umpire.

arbore, ār'bŏrĕ, m. tree; (mar.) mast.

arboscello, –bŏsshĕl'lŏ, arbuscello, –bŭsshĕl'lŏ, m. little tree, shrub. [tomb.

arca, ār'kā, f. chest, coffer; coffin; urn,

arcaico, –kā'īkŏ, a. antique.

arcaismo, –kāīs'mŏ, m. archaism; ancient or obsolete phrase.

arcale, –kā'lĕ, m. arch (of a door).

arcano, –kā'nŏ, m. arcanum, mystery.

arcare, –kā'rĕ, v. a. to shoot with a bow;

arcata, –kā'tā, f. bow-shot. [to cheat.

archeggiare, –kĕdjā'rĕ, v. a. to bend like an arch.

archeologia, –kĕŏlŏjē'ā, f. archeology.

archetipo, –kĕtē'pŏ, m. archetype.

archetto, –kĕt'tŏ, m. violin-bow.

archibugiare, –kībūjā'rĕ, v. n. to shoot with an arquebuse.

archibugio, see archibuso.

archibusiere, –būsĭā'rĕ, m. arquebusier; gun-smith. [buse.

archibuso, –bŏ'sŏ, m. hand-gun, arquebuse.

archipenzolo, –pĕn'tzŏlŏ, m. lead-plummet. [contrive.

architettare, –tĕttā'rĕ, v. a. to build; to

architetto, –tĕt'tŏ, m. architect.

architettonico, –tĕ'nīkŏ, a. architectural.

architettura, –tŏ'rā, f. architecture.

architrave, –trā'vĕ, m. architrave, frieze.

archivio, ārkē'vĭŏ, m. archives, old records-office.

archivista, –vīs'tā, m. recorder.

arcidiacono, ārdshīdīā'kŏnŏ, m. archdeacon.

arciducato, –dŭkā'tŏ, m. archdukedom.

arciduca, –dŏ'kā, m. archduke. [deacon.

arciduchessa, –dŭkĕs'sā, f. archduchess.

arciere, ārdshīā'rĕ, arciero, –rŏ, m. archer, bowman.

arcigno, ārdshīn'yŏ, a. sharp, harsh, gruff.

arcimaestro, –māĕs'trŏ, m. head-master.

arcionato, *–dshŏnă'tŏ,* a. saddled.
arcione, *–dshŏ'nĕ,* m. saddle-bow.
arcivescovado, *–vĕskŏvă'dŏ,* m. archbishopric.   [copal.
arcivescovile, *–vĕskŏvĕ'lĕ,* a. archiepiscopal.
arcivescovo, *–vĕs'kŏvŏ,* m. archbishop.
arco, *ăr'kŏ,* m. bow, arch.
arcobaleno, *–bălă'nŏ,* m. rainbow.
arcolaio, *–lā'ŏ,* m. reel, winder.
arcoreggiare, *–rĕdjă'rĕ,* v. n. to belch.
arcuato, *–kŭă'tŏ,* a. crooked, curved.
ardente, *–dĕn'tĕ,* a. ardent, hot, fiery; eager.
ardenza, *–dĕn'tză,* f. ardour, heat; burning desire.   [be on fire; to be bright.
ardere, *ăr'dĕrĕ,* v. n. to burn, to glow, to
ardesia, *ărdă'siă,* f. slate.   [buckle.
ardiglione, *–dĭlyŏ'nĕ,* m. tongue of a
ardimento, *–dĭmĕn'tŏ,* m. boldness, impudence, daring, sauciness.
ardire, *–dĕ'rĕ,* v. n. to dare, to be bold.
ardito, *–dĕ'tŏ,* a. bold, daring; valiant.
ardore, *–dŏ'rĕ,* m. ardour, passion.
arduità, *–dŭĭtă',* f. steepness; difficulty.
arduo, *ăr'dŭŏ,* a. difficult, perilous.
arena, *ără'nă,* f. sand, gravel; wrestling-place.
arenoso, *ărĕnŏ'sŏ,* a. sandy.   [place.
arfasatto, *–făsăt'tŏ,* m. lowborn fellow.
argano, *ăr'gănŏ,* m. windlass; crane; (mar.) capstan.
argentaio, *ărjĕntā'ŏ,* m. silver-smith.
argentato, *–tă'tŏ,* a. silver-plated.
argenteo, *–jĕn'tĕŏ,* a. silver; silvered.
argenteria, *–tĕrĕ'ă,* f. silver-plate.
argentiera, *–tĭă'ră,* f. silver-mine.
argentiere, *–tĭă'rĕ,* m. silver-smith.
argentino, *–tĕ'nŏ,* a. silver-coloured.
argento, *–jĕn'tŏ,* m. silver; **– vivo,** quick-silver.
argilla, *ărjĭl'lă,* f. potter's clay.
argilloso, *–jĭl'sŏ,* a. clayey.
arginare, *–jĭnă'rĕ,* v. a. to fortify, to make ramparts.
argine, *ăr'jĭnĕ,* m. causeway, bank, mole.
argomentare, *–gŏmĕntă'rĕ,* v. n. to argue, to reason.   [tation.
argomentazione, *–tzĭŏ'nĕ,* f. argumen-
argomento, *–mĕn'tŏ,* m. argument, reason.
arguire, *–gŭĕ'rĕ,* v. a. to argue, to conclude; to reprimand.
argutamente, *–gŭtămĕn'tĕ,* ad. cunningly.
argutezza, *–tĕt'ză,* f. quibble; smartness.
arguto, *–gŏ'tŏ,* a. subtle; witty.
arguzia, *–gŏ'tzĭă,* f. subtility, piquancy; smartness.
aria, *ă'rĭă,* f. air; mien; (mus.) air, song.
aridità, *ărĭdĭtă',* f. aridity, barrenness; (fig.) tiresomeness.   [(fig.) tiresome.
arido, *ă'rĭdŏ,* a. dry; poor; wretched;
arieggiare, *ărĭĕdjă'rĕ,* v. n. to resemble.
ariete, *ărĭĕ'tĕ,* m. battering-ram.
Ariete, *–,* m. Aries.   [little air.
arietta, *ărĭĕt'tă,* **ariettina,** *–tĕ'nă,* f.
aringa, *ărĭn'gă,* f. herring.
ariolo, *ărĕ'ŏlŏ,* m. diviner, soothsayer.
arioso, *ărĭŏ'sŏ,* a. airy; lightsome, handsome; graceful.
aristarco, *ărĭstăr'kŏ,* m. severe critic.

aristocratico, *–tŏkră'tĭkŏ,* a. aristocratic.
aristocrazia, *–tzĕ'ă,* f. aristocracy.
aritmetica, *ărĭtmă'tĭkă,* f. arithmetic.
arlecchino, *ărlĕkĕ'nŏ,* m. harlequin, buffoon.
ariotto, *–lŏt'tŏ,* m. glutton, devourer.
arma, *ăr'mă* (poet.), *see* **arme.**   [board.
armadio, *–mă'dĭŏ,* m. clothes-press, cupboard.
armaiuolo, *–mălŭŏ'lŏ,* m. armourer, gunsmith.
armamentario, *–mĕntă'rĭŏ,* m. arsenal.
armamento, *–mĕn'tŏ,* m. arming, armament.   [armour.
armare, *–mă'rĕ,* v. a. to arm; to put on
armario, *see* **armadio.**
armata, *–mă'tă,* f. navy; army.
armatore, *–tŏ'rĕ,* m. (mar.) privateer.
armatura, *–tŏ'ră,* f. armour; prop.
arme, *ăr'mĕ,* f. arms, weapons, pl., armour; **all' armi !** to arms.   [tilt.
armeggiare, *–mĕdjă'rĕ,* v. n. to joust; to
armentario, *–mĕn'tă'rĭŏ,* m. herdsman.
armento, *–mĕn'tŏ,* m. herd of cattle.
armeria, *–mĕrĕ'ă,* f. arsenal, armoury.
armigero, *–mĕ'jĕrŏ,* a. warlike.
armillare, *–mĭllă'rĕ,* a. armillary.
armistizio, *–mĭstĕ'tzĭŏ,* m. armistice.
armonia, *–mŏnĕ'ă,* f. harmony.
armonico, *–mŏ'nĭkŏ,* **armonioso,** *–mŏnĕ'ŏsŏ,* a. harmonious, melodious.
armonizzare, *–mŏnĭtză'rĕ,* v. n. to harmonise.   [ture.
arnese, *–nă'sĕ,* m. harness; utensils, furniture.
arnia, *ăr'nĭă,* f. bee-hive.
arnione, *–nĭŏ'nĕ,* m. kidney.
aroma, *ărŏ'mă,* m. aroma.
aroma, *–,* m. aromatics, spices, pl.
aromatario, *ărŏmătă'rĭŏ,* m. druggist.
aromatico, *–mă'tĭkŏ,* a. aromatic.
arpa, *ăr'pă,* f. harp.
arpeggiare, *–pĕdjă'rĕ,* v. n. to play on the harp; (mus.) to arpeggiate.
arpeggio, *–pĕd'jŏ,* m. harping; (mus.) arpeggto.
arpia, *–pĕ'ă,* f. harpy; quarrelsome wench.
arpione, *–pĭŏ'nĕ,* m. hinge, hook; tenter.
arra, *ăr'ră,* f. earnest-money.
arrabbiare, *–bĭă'rĕ,* v. n. to get furious; **arrabbiarsi,** *–bĭăr'sĭ,* to get into a rage, to fly into a passion.
arrabiamento, *–bĭămĕn'tŏ,* m. rage, madness.   [snatch.
arraffare, *–fă'rĕ,* v. a. to grapple, to
arramacciare, *–mătshă'rĕ,* v. a. to drive in a sledge.   [limp.
arrancare, *–rănkă'rĕ,* v. n. to go lame, to
arrandellare, *–dĕllă'rĕ,* v. a. to tie; to hurl.   [some; to grow angry.
arrangolare, *–gŏlă'rĕ,* v. n. to be mettle-
arrantolato, *–tŏlă'tŏ,* a. hoarse.
arrapinato, *–răpĭnă'tŏ,* a. peevish, tedious.
arrappare, *see* **arraffare.**
arrecare, *–rĕkă'rĕ,* v. a. to bring; to convey; **arrecarsi,** *–kăr'sĭ,* to make shift.
arredo, *–ră'dŏ,* m. rigging, furniture.
arrembaggio, *–rĕmbăd'jŏ,* m. (mar.) boarding a ship.

arrembare, –bår'rĕ, v. a. (mar.) to board a ship. [aground; to desist.
arrenare, –rĕnå'rĕ, v. a. (mar.) to run aground; to desist.
arrendersi, –rĕn'dĕrsĭ, v. r. to surrender.
arrendevole, –då'võlĕ, a. flexible, supple.
arrendevolezza, –dĕvõlĕt'zå, f. flexibility, pliantness, suppleness; docility.
arrendimento, –dĭmĕn'tŏ, m. surrender.
arrestare, –rĕstå'rĕ, v. a. to arrest, to seize, to detain; arrestarsi, –tår'sĭ, to stop; to tarry.
arresto, –rĕs'tŏ, arrestamento, –tåmĕn'tŏ, m. arrest; delay; decree, sentence.
arreticare, –rĕtĭkå'rĕ, v. a. to take in a net.
arretrarsi, –trår'sĭ, v. r. to go back, to recoil, to recede. [adorn.
arricchire, –rĭkkĕ'rĕ, v. a. to enrich; to
arricciamento, –tshåmĕn'tŏ, m. fright, horror, shivering.
arricciare, –tshå'rĕ, v. n. & a. to bristle up, to stand on end; to curl. [to favour.
arridere, –rĕ'dĕrĕ, v. a. ir. to smile upon;
arringa, –rĭn'gå, f. discourse; herring.
arringare, –rĭngå'rĕ, v. n. to harangue.
arringhiera, –ghĭå'rå, f. chair; bar, hustings. [harangue.
arringo, årrĭn'gŏ, m. lists; bar, pulpit;
arrischiamento, –rĭskĭåmĕn'tŏ, m. risk.
arrischiante, –kĭån'tĕ, a. daring, venturous. [hazard.
arrischiare, –kĭå'rĕ, v. a. to risk, to
arrischio, –rĭs'kĭŏ, m. risk, peril.
arrisicare, –rĕsĭkå'rĕ, v. a. to risk, to hazard.
arrivare, –rĭvå'rĕ, v. n. to arrive, to reach.
arrivo, –rĕ'vŏ, m. arrival, coming.
arrocare, –rŏkå'rĕ, arrochire, –kĕ'rĕ, v. n. to grow hoarse. [pieces, to cobble.
arrocchiare, –kĭå'rĕ, v. a. to cut in pieces, to cobble.
arrogante, –gån'tĕ, a. arrogant, proud.
arrogantemente, –mĕn'tĕ, ad. arrogantly.
arroganza, –gån'tzå, f. arrogance, pride.
arrogare, –gå'rĕ, v. n. to arrogate.
arrogere, –rŏ'jĕrĕ, v. a. ir. to add, to give to boot, to give into the bargain.
arrolare, –rŏlå'rĕ, v. a. to enrol, to register.
arrompere, –rŏm'pĕrĕ, v. a. ir. to break; to go off. [out.
arroncare, –rŏnkå'rĕ, v. a. to weed, to root out; to twist, to strive.
arrostarsi, –rŏstår'sĭ, v. r. to struggle, to twist, to strive.
arrostire, –rŏstĕ'rĕ, v. a. to roast, to toast.
arrosto, –rŏs'tŏ, m. roast meat.
arrotare, –rŏtå'rĕ, v. a. to whet, to grind; arrotarsi, –tår'sĭ, to be restless.
arrotino, –tĕ'nŏ, m. knife-grinder.
arrotolare, –tŏlå'rĕ, v. a. to make up into a ball. [tate; to get angry.
arrovellare, –vĕllå'rĕ, v. a. & n. to irritate; to get angry.
arroventimento, –vĕntĭmĕn'tŏ, m. making red-hot. [hot.
arroventire, –tĕ'rĕ, v. n. to grow red-hot.
arrovesciamento, –vĕsshåmĕn'tŏ, m. overthrow, ruin. [to destroy.
arrovesciare, –sshå'rĕ, v. a. to overthrow,
arrovesciatura, –tŏ'rå, see arrovesciamento.

arrozzire, –tzĕ'rĕ, v. a. to make rough.
arruffare, –rŭffå'rĕ, v. a. to ruffle the hair. [to pimp.
arruffianare, –fĭånå'rĕ, v. a. to couple,
arru(g)ginire, –rŭ(d)jĭnĕ'rĕ, v. n. to rust, to grow rusty. [or stiff.
arruvidire, –vĭdĕ'rĕ, v. n. to grow rough
arsenale, –sĕnå'lĕ, m. arsenal.
arsenico, –sĕ'nĭkŏ, m. arsenic.
arsibile, –sĕ'bĭlĕ, a. combustible. [sun.
arsicciare, –sĭtshå'rĕ, v. a. to dry in the
arsiccio, –sĕt'shŏ, a. scorched, burnt.
arsione, –sĭõ'nĕ, f. excessive heat; thirst.
arso, år'sŏ, a. burnt; consumed; wretched.
arsura, –sõ'rå, f. burning heat; extreme misery. [ingeniously.
artatamente, –tåtåmĕn'tĕ, ad. artfully.
arte, år'tĕ, f. art; artifice; skill; craft,
artefatto, –fåt'tŏ, a. artificial. [deceit.
artefice, –tå'fĭdshĕ, m. artificer; workman.
arteria, –tå'rĭå, f. artery. [man.
articella, –tĭdshĕl'lå, f. poor business.
articina, –dshĕ'nå, f. industry.
artico, år'tĭkŏ, a. arctic, northern.
articolare, –kŏlå'rĕ, v. a. to articulate, to pronounce distinctly; –, a. articular.
articolo, –tĕ'kŏlŏ, m. article; point, clause; – di fondo, leading article (of a journal).
artificiale, –fĭdshĭå'lĕ, a. artificial, artful.
artificialmente, –mĕn'tĕ, ad. artificially.
artificio, –fĕ'dshĭŏ, m. artifice; industry; fraud. [sly.
artificioso, –fĭdshĭõ'sŏ, a. artful; crafty,
artigiano, –jå'nŏ, m. artisan; workman.
artigliere, –tĭlyå'rĕ, m. cannonier, gunner.
artiglieria, –yĕrĕ'å, f. artillery.
artiglio, –tĕl'yŏ, m. claw, talon; clutch.
artimone, –mŏ'nĕ, m. (mar.) mizzen-sail.
artista, –tĕs'tå, m. artist. [artistically.
artisticamente, –mĕn'tĕ, ad. skilfully,
artistico, –tĕs'tĭkŏ, a. artistic.
arto, år'tŏ, a. narrow, strait.
aruspice, årŏ'spĭdshĕ, m. augur, diviner.
arzigogolo, årtzĭgŏ'gŏlŏ, m. fancy, chimera, conceit, fad, crotchet.
arzillo, –tzĕl'lŏ, a. sprightly; bold.
asbesto, åsbĕs'tŏ, m. asbestos.
asce, åssh'ĕ, ascia, åssh'å, f. axe.
ascella, åsshĕl'lå, f. arm-pit.
ascendente, åsshĕndĕn'tĕ, a. & m. ascending; ascendant; horoscope.
ascendenza, –dĕn'tzå, f. ascent; rise.
ascendere, –sshĕn'dĕrĕ, v. a. ir. to ascend, to mount. [sion-day.
ascensione, –sĭõ'nĕ, f. ascension; Ascension-day.
ascetico, åsshå'tĭkŏ, a. & m. ascetic.
asciare, åsshå'rĕ, v. a. to square with a hatchet, to smoothe. [fast; to breakfast.
asciolvere, åsshŏl'vĕrĕ, v. a. & v. n. to break-fast; to breakfast.
asciugare, åsshĭgå'rĕ, v. a. to dry; to wipe.
asciugatoio, –tŏ'iŏ, m. towel.
asciuttamente, –tåmĕn'tĕ, ad. dryly.
asciuttezza, –tĕt'zå, f. dryness.
asciutto, åsshūt'tŏ, a. & m. arid, dry; dryness.
ascolta, åskŏl'tå, f. listening. [dryness.
ascoltare, –tå'rĕ, v. a. to listen, to mind.

ascoltatore, -tŏ'rĕ, m. hearer, listener.
ascolto, -kŏl'tŏ, m. hearing. listening.
ascondere, &c., see nascondere, &c.
ascosamente, -kŏsămĕn'tĕ, ad. secretly.
ascrivere, ăskrē'vĕrĕ, v. a. ir. to ascribe.
asfalto, -făl'tŏ, m. asphaltum.
asfissia, -fĭssē'ā, f. asphyxia.
asilo, ăsē'lŏ, m. asylum, refuge.
asina, ā'sĭnā, f. she-ass, jenny-ass.
asinaccio, -năt'shŏ, m. great ass; very
    stupid fellow.
asinaggine, -năd'jĭnĕ, f. stupidity.
asinaio, -nāī'ŏ, m. ass-driver.
asineria, -nĕrē'ā, f. stubbornness.
asinesco, -nĕs'kŏ, a. stupid, dull.
asinino, -nē'nŏ, a. asinine; stupid.
asinità, -nĭtā', f. stupidity.   [ass.
asino, ā'sĭnŏ, m. ass; — salvatico, wild
asma, ăs'mā, f. asthma.
asmatico, -mā'tĭkŏ, a. asthmatic.
asolare, ăsŏlā'rĕ, v. n. to pant; to take
    an airing; to ramble about.
asolo, ā'sŏlŏ, m. breath, open air; ease;
    button-hole.
asparago, ăspā'răgŏ, m. asparagus.
asperare, -pĕrā'rĕ, v. a. to exasperate,
    to provoke.
aspergere, -pĕr'jĕrĕ, v. a. ir. to sprinkle.
aspergine, -pĕr'jĭnĕ, f. aspersion.
asperità, -pĕrĭtā', f. roughness; severity.
aspersione, -sĭŏ'nĕ, f. aspersion, sprink-
    ling.
aspersorio, -sŏ'rĭŏ, m. sprinkling with
    holy-water.   [notable.
aspettabile, -pĕttā'bĭlĕ, a. remarkable,
aspettante, -tăn'tĕ, a. waiting, expect-
    ing; —, m. spectator, bystander.
aspettare, -tā'rĕ, v. a. [to expect, to wait
    for.   [pectance, hope.
aspettativa, -tē'vā, f. expectation, ex-
aspettazione, -tzĭŏ'nĕ, f. expectation.
aspetto, -pĕt'tŏ, m. aspect; countenance.
aspide, ăs'pĭdĕ, m. aspic.
aspirante, -pērăn'tĕ, a. aspiring to;
    tromba-, f. suction-pump; —, m. can-
    didate.
aspirare, -rā'rĕ, v. a. to aspire; to be a
    candidate for; (gr.) to aspirate.   [ated.
aspirativo, -tē'vŏ, a. that must be aspir-
aspirazione, -tzĭŏ'nĕ, f. aspiration, aspir-
    aspo, ăs'pŏ, m. reel.   [ing.
asportare, -pŏrtā'rĕ, v. a. to export, to
    carry away.   [irritation, exasperation.
aspreggiamento, -prĕdjămĕn'tŏ, m.
aspreggiare, -djā'rĕ, v. a. to exasperate,
    to exacerbate, to irritate.
aspretto, -prĕt'tŏ, a. a little harsh.
asprezza, -prĕt'zā, f. harshness, asperity.
asprigno, -prĭn'yŏ, a. sourish.
aspro, ăs'prŏ, a. sour, sharp, harsh; rough.
assaggiare, -sādjā'rĕ, v. a. to taste; to
    try, to assay.
assaggiatore, -tŏ'rĕ, m. taster; assayer.
assai, ăssā'ī, ad. enough, much, very;
    richly.   [tack.
assalimento, -sālĭmĕn'tŏ, m. assault, at-

assalire, -lē'rĕ, v. a. to assail, to assault.
assalitore, -tŏ'rĕ, m. assailer.
assalto, -săl'tŏ, m. assault, onset.
assannare, see azzannare.
assaporamento, -săpŏrămĕn'tŏ, m.
    tasting.
assaporare, -pŏrā'rĕ, v. a. to taste; to
    essay.   [sination.
assassinamento, -sĭnămĕn'tŏ, m. assas-
assassinare, -sĭnā'rĕ, v. a. to assassinate.
assassinio, -sē'nĭŏ, m. assassination.
assassino, -sē'nŏ, m. assassin.
asse, ăs'sĕ, f. board, shelf; axis.
assecchire, -kē'rĕ, see seccare.
assecondare, -kŏn'dārĕ, v. a. to second,
    to assist.
assediante, -sĕdĭăn'tĕ, m. besieger.
assediare, -dĭā'rĕ, v. a. to besiege.
assediatore, -tŏ'rĕ, m. besieger.
assedio, -sĕ'dĭŏ, m. siege, blockade.
assegnare, -sĕnyā'rĕ, v. a. to assign, to
    settle.
assegnatezza, -tĕt'zā, f. sparingness.
assegnazione, -tzĭŏ'nĕ, f., assegno,
    -sĕn'yŏ, m. assignment; income.
asseguimento, -sĕgŭĭmĕn'tŏ, m. getting,
    acquisition,   [obtain.
asseguire, -gŭē'rĕ, v. a. to execute; to
assemblea, -sĕmblā'ā, f. assembly, meet-
    ing.   [shock; combat.
assembramento, -brămĕn'tŏ, m. clash,
assennare, -sĕnnā'rĕ, v. a. to warn, to
    advise.   [tion.
assenso, -sĕn'sŏ, m. consent, approba-
assentare, -tā'rĕ, v. a. to send away;
    assentarsi, -tăr'sī, to absent oneself.
assente, -sĕn'tĕ, a. absent; distant.
assentimento, -tĭmĕn'tŏ, m. assent, con-
    sent.   [assent.
assentire, -tē'rĕ, v. n. to approve, to
assentito, -tē'tŏ, a. skilful, prudent,
    cunning.
assenza, -sĕn'tzā, f. absence.   [sinthe-
assenzio, -sĕn'tzĭŏ, m. worm-wood; ab-
asserenare, -sĕrĕnā'rĕ, v. a. to clear up;
    to cheer; asserinarsi, -năr'sī, to be-
    come clear.
asserire, -rē'rĕ, v. a. to assert, to affirm,
    to assure.   [cade.
asserragliare, -rălyā'rĕ, v. a. to barri-
assertorio, -tŏ'rĭŏ, a. affirmative.
asserzione, -tzĭŏ'nĕ, f. assertion.
assessore, -sĕssŏ'rĕ, m. assessor.
assestare, -sĕstā'rĕ, v. a. to adjust; to
    agree; assestarsi, -tăr'sī, to accom-
    modate oneself.
assestatore, -tŏ'rĕ, m. (mar.) stower.
assetare, -sĕtā'rĕ, v. a. to make thirsty.
assettare, -sĕttā'rĕ, v. a. to adjust, to
    arrange.
assettatore, -tŏ'rĕ, m. regulator; at-
    tirer; follower.
assettatura, -tŏ'rā, f. staidness; pro-
    priety; accommodation; ornament.
asseveramento, -vĕrămĕn'tŏ, m., asse-

veranza', –răn' tză, f. assurance, as-sertion. |swear.

asseverare, –verā' rĕ, v. a. to assure, to

asseverazione, –tzǐŏ' nĕ, f. asseveration, assurance.

assicella, –sĭdshĕl' lă, f. thin shingle.

assicuramento, –kǐrămĕn' tŏ, m., **assi-curanza,** –răn' tză, f. assurance.

assicurare, –kǐrā' rĕ, v. a. to secure, to guarantee, to insure.

assicuratore, –tŏ' rĕ, m. insurer.

assicurazione, –tzǐŏ' nĕ, f. insurance; **società d'** –, f. insurance-company.

assiderare, –derā' rĕ, v. a. to chill, to quake.

assidersi, –sĕ' dĕrsĭ, v. r. ir. to sit down.

assiduità, –sǐdǔǐtă', f. assiduity.

assiduo, –sĕ' dǔŏ, a. assiduous.

assieme, –sǐĕ' mĕ, ad. together.

assiepare, –sǐĕpā' rĕ, v. a. to hedge in.

assillare, –sĭllā' rĕ, v. a. to smart; to rage.

assillo, –sĭl' lŏ, m. horse-fly; stinging of a horse-fly. |to counterfeit.

assimilare, –sǐmǐlā' rĕ, v. a. to assimilate.

assimilazione, –tzǐŏ' nĕ, f. assimilation.

assioma, –sǐŏ' mă, **assiomate,** –sǐŏ' mătĕ, m. axiom. |assizes, pl.

assisa, –sĕ' să, f. livery; duty; **assise,** pl.

assiso, –sĕ' sŏ, a. sitting.

assistente, –sǐstĕn' tĕ, m. assistant, helper.

assistenza, –tĕn' tză, f. aid, help.

assistere, –sǐs' tĕrĕ, v. a. ir. to assist; to

assito, –sĕ' tŏ, m. board-partition. |help.

asso, ăs' sŏ, m. ace (at cards or dice).

associare, –dshā' rĕ, v. a. to accompany.

associatore, –tŏ' rĕ, m. associator.

associazione, –tzǐŏ' nĕ, f. association, partnership, commercial union; funeral procession. |settle.

assodare, –dā' rĕ, v. a. to consolidate, to

assoggettare, –djĕttā' rĕ, v. a. to subdue.

assoggettamento, –mĕn' tŏ, m. sub-jection, subduing.

assolato, –lā' tŏ, a. exposed to the sun.

assoldare, –sŏldā' rĕ, v. a. to enlist, to raise troops. |to discharge, to finish.

assolvere, –sŏl' vĕrĕ, v. a. ir. to absolve,

assolutamente, –lǔtămĕn' tĕ, ad. abso-lutely.

assoluto, –lǔ' tŏ, a. absolute, arbitrary.

assolutorio, –tŏ' rǐŏ, a. absolutory.

assoluzione, –tzǐŏ' nĕ, f. absolution; for-giveness.

assomigliamento, –sŏmǐlyămĕn' tŏ, m., **assomiglianza,** –ylăn' tză, f. resem-blance. |pare; to resemble.

assomigliare, –ylǐā' rĕ, v. a. & n. to com-

assommare, –mā' rĕ, v. a. to finish; to perfect, to accomplish.

assonante, –nān' tĕ, a. harmonious.

assonanza, –năn' tză, f. assonance.

assonnare, –nā' rĕ, v. a. & n. to lull asleep; to get drowsy.

assopire, –pē' rĕ, v. a. to lull asleep.

assorbere, –sŏr' bĕrĕ, **assorbire,** –bē' rĕ, v. a. ir. to absorb, to swallow up.

assordamento, –dāmĕn' tŏ, m. stunning, dumbfounding; giddiness.

assordare, –dā' rĕ, **assordire,** –dē' rĕ, v. a. & n. to deafen; to grow deaf.

assorgere, –sŏr' jĕrĕ, v. a. to rise.

assortimento, –tǐmĕn' tŏ, m. lot; assort-ment, suit. |sort.

assortire, –tē' rĕ, v. a. to draw lots; to

assottigliare, –sŏttǐlyā' rĕ, v. a. to make thin; to sharpen.

assuefare, –sǔĕfā' rĕ, v. a. to accustom;

assuefarsi, –făr' sǐ, to accustom oneself.

assuefatto, –făt' tŏ, **assueto,** –sǔĕ' tŏ, a. accustomed, used. |tice.

assuetudine, –tŏ' dǐnĕ, f. custom; prac-

assumere, –sŏ' mĕrĕ, v. a. ir. to assume, to undertake.

assunto, –sǔn' tŏ, m. undertaking; charge.

assunzione, –tzǐŏ' nĕ, f. Assumption of the Virgin Mary.

assurdità, –sǔrdǐtă', f. absurdity.

assurdo, –sǔr' dŏ, a. absurd.

assurgere, see **sorgere.**

asta, ăs' tă, f. pole, staff; lance.

astante, ăstăn' tĕ, a. & m. standing by, present; assistant; keeper of an infirmary.

astata, –lă' tă, f. blow with a lance.

astemio, –tĕ' mǐŏ, a. abstemious.

astenersi, –tĕnĕr' sǐ, v. r. ir. to abstain from. |stergent, cleansing.

astergente, –tĕrjĕn' tĕ, a. (med.) ab-

astergere, –tĕr' jĕrĕ, v. a. ir. to cleanse.

asterisco, –rǐs' kŏ, m. asterisk.

asterismo, –rǐs' mŏ, m. constellation.

astersione, –sǐŏ' nĕ, f. cleansing, purging.

astersivo, –sĕ' vŏ, a. cleansing.

astiare, –tǐā' rĕ, v. a. to envy, to grudge.

astinente, –tǐnĕn' tĕ, a. abstinent.

astinenza, –nĕn' tză, f. abstinence.

astio, ăs' tǐŏ, m. envy, rancour.

astioso, –tǐ' ŏsŏ, a. envious.

astore, –tŏ' rĕ, m. goshawk. |separate.

astraere, –trā' ĕrĕ, v. a. ir. to abstract; to

astrale, –trā' lĕ, a. astral, starry.

astrarre, see **astraere.**

astratto, –trăt' tŏ, a. abstracted.

astrazione, –tzǐŏ' nĕ, f. abstraction.

astretto, –trĕt' tŏ, p. & a. constrained.

astrignere, –trǐn' yĕrĕ, **astringere,** –jĕrĕ, v. a. ir. to force, to compel.

astringente, –jĕn' tĕ, a. astringent, binding.

astro, ăs' trŏ, m. star.

astrologia, –lŏjē' ă, m. astrology.

astrologo, –trŏ' lŏgŏ, m. astrologer.

astronomia, –nŏmē' ă, f. astronomy.

astronomico, –nŏ' mǐkŏ, a. astronomical.

astronomo, –trŏ' nŏmŏ, m. astronomer.

astruso, –trŏ' sŏ, a. abstruse, obscure.

astuccio, –tǔt' shŏ, m. case, box.

astutezza, –tĕt' ză, f. cunning, artifice.

astuto, –tǔ' tŏ, a. crafty, cunning.

astuzia, –tŏ' tzǐă, f. craftiness, cunning, art.

ateismo, ătĕ' smŏ, m. atheism.

ateista, –ǐs' tă, **ateo,** ă' tĕŏ, m. atheist.

ateo, ă' tĕŏ, a. atheistical.

atlante, ătlăn' tĕ, m. atlas.

atleta, –lā' tă, m. wrestler.

atletico, –lā' tǐkŏ, a. athletic, vigorous.

atmosfera, –mŏsfā' ră, f. atmosphere.

atmosferico, –fä′rĭkŏ, a. atmospheric.
atomo, ä′tŏmŏ, m. atom.
atonia, –nĕ′ä, f. weakness.
atrabile, äträ′bĭlĕ, f. black bile, spleen.
atrabiliare, –bĭlĭä′rĕ, a. splenetic.
atrio, ä′trĭŏ, m. porch, vestibule; railway-
atro, ä′trŏ, a. black; dreadful. [station.
atroce, ätrŏ′dshĕ, a. atrocious.
atrocemente, –mĕn′tĕ, ad. atrociously.
atrocità, –dshĭtä′, f. atrocity.
atrofia, –fĕ′ä, f. consumption. [ment.
attaccamento, –täkkämĕn′tŏ, m. attach-
attaccare, –kä′rĕ, v. a. to fasten; to attach: **attaccarsi,** –kär′sĭ, to addict oneself (to).
attaccaticcio, –tät′shŏ, a. viscous, sticky.
attacco, –täk′kŏ, m. sticking; attack.
attagliarsi, –tälyär′sĭ, v. r. to suit, to
comply with. [to content.
attalentare, –tälĕntä′rĕ, v. a. to please,
attapinarsi, –pĭnär′sĭ, v. r. to complain,
to groan.
attastare, see **tastare.** [thrive.
attecchire, –tĕkkĭ′rĕ, v. n. to grow; to
attediare, –dĭä′rĕ, v. a. to tease, to weary.
atteggiare, –tĕdjä′rĕ, v. a. to animate a
statue; –, v. n. to gesticulate.
attemparsi, –tĕmpär′sĭ, v. n. to grow old.
attempato, –pä′tŏ, a. aged.
attendare, –tĕndä′rĕ, v. a. to encamp;
attendarsi, –där′sĭ, (mil.) to pitch a
camp. [to mind.
attendere, –tĕn′dĕrĕ, v. n. ir. to await;
attenente, –tĕnĕn′tĕ, a. belonging to.
attenenza, –nĕn′tzä, f. appurtenance.
attenere, –nĕ′rĕ, v. n. ir. to keep one's
word; **attenersi,** –nĕr′sĭ, to hold fast,
to stick; to abstain.
attentare, –tĕntä′rĕ, v. a. to attempt; **at-
tentarsi,** –tär′sĭ, to expose oneself to.
attentato, –tä′tŏ, m. criminal action;
enterprise. [to weaken.
attenuare, –tĕnŭä′rĕ, v. a. to make thin,
attenzione, –tztŏ′nĕ, f. attention; application. [to withdraw.
attergare, –tĕrgä′rĕ, v. a. to place behind;
atterramento, –rämĕn′tŏ, m. overthrow.
atterrare, –rä′rĕ, v. a. to cast down, to
overthrow; **atterrarsi,** –rär′sĭ, to prostrate oneself.
atterrimento, –rĭmĕn′tŏ, m. terror, dread.
atterrire, –rĕ′rĕ, v. a. to terrify, to alarm.
attesa, –tĕ′sä, f. attention.
atteso, tĕ′sŏ, pr. (**–che**) with regard to.
attestare, –tĕstä′rĕ, v. a. to attest.
attestato, –tä′tŏ, m., **attestazione,**
–tztŏ′nĕ, f. attestation, testimony.
atti, ät′tĭ, m. pl. behaviour.
atticciato, –tshä′tŏ, a. strong-limbed, thick.
attignere, –tĭn′yĕrĕ, v. a. ir. to draw up;
to perceive.
attiguo, –tĕ′gŭŏ, a. adjacent.
attillarsi, –tĭllär′sĭ, v. r. to dress in an
affected manner.
attimo, ät′tĭmŏ, m. moment, instant.
attingere, –tĭn′jĕrĕ, v. a. ir. to draw up.
attiraglio, –tĭrä′lyŏ, m. luggage, imple-
ments, pl.

attirare, –rä′rĕ, v. a. to draw; to attract.
attitare, –tä′rĕ, v. a. to plead.
attitudine, –tŏ′dĭnĕ, f. skill; attitude.
attivamente, –vämĕn′tĕ, ad. actively.
attività, –vĭtä′, f. activity.
attivo, –tĕ′vŏ, a. active; quick.
attizzare, –tzä′rĕ, v. a. to poke the fire;
to irritate. [–, a. proper, fit.
atto, ät′tŏ, m. act; action; deed; sign;
attonito, –tŏ′nĭtŏ, a. astonished.
attorcere, –tŏr′dshĕrĕ, v. a. & ir. to twist,
to wring. [factor; plaintiff.
attore, –tŏ′rĕ, m. actor, player; agent,
attorniare, –nĭä′rĕ, v. a. to enclose.
attorno, –tŏr′nŏ, pr. & ad. round about.
attortigliare, –tĭlyä′rĕ, v. a. to twist, to
attorto, –tŏr′tŏ, a. twisted. [wrap round.
attoscare, –tŏskä′rĕ, v. a. to poison.
attossicamento, –sĭkämĕn′tŏ, m. poison-
ing.
attossicare, –kä′rĕ, v. a. to poison.
attossicatore, –tŏ′rĕ, m. poisoner.
attraente, –trän′tĕ, a. attractive.
attraere, see **attrarre.** [reach.
attrappare, –pä′rĕ, v. a. to catch, to over-
attrarre, –trär′rĕ, v. a. ir. to attract, to
entice, to allure.
attrattiva, –tĕ′vä, f. attraction; charm.
attrattivo, –tĕ′vŏ, a. attractive.
attraversare, –vĕrsä′rĕ, v. a. to traverse,
to cross.
attraverso, –vĕr′sŏ, ad. across, through.
attrazione, –tztŏ′nĕ, f. attraction.
attrazzo, –trät′zŏ, **attrezzo,** –trĕt′zŏ, m.
tool, instrument. [to ascribe.
attribuire, –trĭbŭĕ′rĕ, v. a. to attribute,
attributo, –bŏ′tŏ, m. attribute.
attrice, –trĕ′dshĕ, f. actress. [affliction.
attristamento, –trĭstämĕn′tŏ, m. sadness,
attristare, –tä′rĕ, **attristire,** –tĕ′rĕ, v. a.
to grieve, to sadden.
attrizione, –tztŏ′nĕ, f. attrition.
attrupparsi, –trŭppär′sĭ, v. r. to band
together.
attuale, –tŭä′lĕ, a. actual, real.
attualità, –lĭtä′, f. actuality.
attualmente, –mĕn′tĕ, ad. actually, at
this moment; really, indeed.
attuare, –tŭä′rĕ, v. a. to perform.
attuario, –tŭä′rĭŏ, m. notary.
attuccio, –tŭ′tshŏ, m. childish action.
attuffare, –fä′rĕ, v. a. to plunge.
attuoso, –tŭä′sŏ, a. active, efficacious.
attutare, –tä′rĕ, **attutire,** –tĕ′rĕ, v. a.
to quench; to soften.
audace, äŭdä′dshĕ, a. audacious, bold.
audacia, –dä′dshĭä, f. audacity, boldness.
augurare, –gŭrä′rĕ, v. a. & n. to augur,
to foretell; to wish. [soothsayer.
auguratore, –tŏ′rĕ, **augure,** ä′ŭgŭrĕ, m.
augurio, –gŏ′rĭŏ, m. augury, omen.
augusto, –gŭs′tŏ, a. august; royal.
aula, ä′ŭlä, f. royal palace.
aulico, ä′ŭlĭkŏ, a. of the court.
aumentare, –mĕntä′rĕ, v. a. to augment.
auna, ä′ŭnä, f. ell, yard. [plause.
aura, ä′ŭrä, f. (poet.) gentle breeze; ap-

aurato, _–rä´tõ_, a. gilded; bright.
aureo, _ä´ŭrĕõ_, a. golden; gilded.
aureola, _–rä´õlä_, f. glory.
auricolare, _–rĭkõlä´rĕ_, a. auricular, secret.
auro, _ä´ŭrõ_, m. (poet.) gold.
aurora, _–rõ´rä_, f. dawn, break of day.
ausiliare, _–sĭlĭä´rĕ_, ausiliario, _–lĭä´rĭõ_, a. auxiliary, helpful.
ausilio, _–sĕ´lĭõ_, m. help, assistance.
auspice, _ä´ŭspĭshĕ_, m. protector.
auspicio, _–spĕ´dshõ_, auspizio, _–tzĭõ_, m. omen; protection.
austerità, _–stĕrĭtä´_, f. severity, roughness.
austero, _–stä´rõ_, a. severe; sour.
autenticità, _–tĕntĭshĭtä´_, f. authenticity.
autentico, _–tĕn´tĭkõ_, a. authentic.
autografo, _–tõ´grä´põ_, m. autograph; –, a. autographic.
automa, _–tõ´mä_, m. automaton.
autore, _–tõ´rĕ_, m. author; maker, inventor; cause.
autorità, _–rĭtä´_, f. authority.
autorizzare, _–tzä´rĕ_, v. a. to authorize.
autrice, _–trĕ´dshĕ_, f. authoress; female writer.
autunnale, _–tŭnnä´lĕ_, a. autumnal.
autunno, _–tŭn´nõ_, m. autumn.
avacciare, _ävätshä´rĕ_, v. a. to hasten.
avaccio, _–vät´shõ_, ad. in haste.
avania, _–nĕ´ä_, f. exaction; affront.
avanti, _ävän´tĭ_, pr. & ad. before, forward.
avantichè, _–kĕ´_, c. before that. [rather.
avanguardia, see vanguardia.
avanzare, _–tzä´rĕ_, v. a. to advance; to augment, to improve; avanzarsi, _–tzär´sĭ_, to take courage.
avanzaticcio, _–tĭt´shõ_, m. remnant, scrap.
avanzo, _–vän´tzõ_, m. remainder, residue; profit; d'avanzo, over and above.
avanzuglio, _–tzŭl´yõ_, m. remnant; scrap.
avaramente, _ävärämĕn´tĕ_ ad. avariciously, sordidly.
avaria, _–värĕ´ä_, f. average.
avarizia, _–rĕ´tzĭä_, f. avarice.
avaro, _–vä´rõ_, a. avaricious.
ave, _ä´vĕ_, aye! all hail!
avellana, _ävĕllä´nä_, f. filbert, hazel-nut.
avello, _ävĕl´lõ_, m. (poet.) tomb, sepulchre.
avena, _ävä´nä_, f. oats; pastoral pipe.
avere, _ävä´rĕ_, v. a. ir. to have, to possess.
averno, _ävĕr´nõ_, m. (poet.) hell, inferno.
avidità, _ävĭdĭtä´_, f. avidity.
avido, _ä´vĭdõ_, a. greedy.
avo, _ä´võ_, m. grandfather.
avocare, _–kä´rĕ_, v. a. to carry a law-suit, to appeal.
avola, _ä´võlä_, f. grandmother.
avolo, _ä´võlõ_, m. grandfather.
avorio, _ävõ´rĭõ_, m. ivory.
avunculo, _ävŭn´kŭlõ_, m. uncle.
avvallare, _–vällä´rĕ_, v. a. to let down; to abase. [to animate.
avvalorare, _–lõrä´rĕ_, v. a. to strengthen.
avvampare, _–vämpä´rĕ_, v. a. to burn; to singe. [advantage; gain.
avvantaggiamento, _–mäntädjämĕn´tõ_, m.

avvantaggiare, _–djä´rĕ_, v. a. to advantage; avvantaggiarsi, _–djär´sĭ_, to derive advantage, to have the better of.
avvantaggio, _–täd´jõ_, m. advantage, profit, benefit, gain.
avvedimento, _–vĕdĭmĕn´tõ_, m. foresight.
avveduto, _–dŭ´tõ_, a. cautious, provident.
avvegnachè, _–vēnyäkĕ´_, avvegnadiochè, _–dĭõkä´_, c. though.
avvelenare, _–vĕlĕnä´rĕ_, v. a. to poison; avvelenarsi, _–när´sĭ_, to poison oneself.
avvenente, _–nĕn´tĕ_, a. agreeable, genteel; charming.
avvenevole, _–nä´võlĕ_, a. handsome, genteel, charming, dainty.
avvenire, _–nĕ´rĕ_, v. n. ir. to happen; –, m. future, futurity; per l'–, henceforth, in future, for the future.
avventare, _–tä´rĕ_, v. a. to shoot, to dart.
avventataggine, _–täd´jĕnĕ_, f. imprudence, rashness, inconsiderateness.
avventato, _–tä´tõ_, a. hasty, thoughtless.
avventizio, _–tĕ´tzĭõ_, a. adventitious.
avvento, _–vĕn´tõ_, m. event; arrival; Advent.
avventore, _–tõ´rĕ_, m. customer. [vent.
avventura, _–tõ´rä_, f. accident, adventure.
avventurare, _–tŭrä´rĕ_, v. a. to hazard; avventurarsi, _–rär´sĭ_, to run the risk.
avventurato, _–rä´tõ_, a. fortunate, lucky.
avventuriere, _–rĭĕ´rĕ_, m. adventurer.
avverare, _–vĕrä´rĕ_, v. a. to aver, to verify; avverarsi, _–rär´sĭ_, to prove true.
avverbio, _–vĕr´bĭõ_, m. adverb.
avverdire, _–dĕ´rĕ_, v. a. to make verdant.
avversario, _–sä´rĭõ_, m. adversary.
avversione, _–sĭõ´nĕ_, f. aversion.
avversità, _–sĭtä´_ f. adversity.
avverso, _–vĕr´sõ_, a. adverse, inimical; –, pr. against. [attention.
avvertenza, _–tĕn´tzä_, f. circumspection, warning. [to warn; to take care.
avvertimento, _–tĭmĕn´tõ_, m. advice; warning. [to warn; to take care.
avvertire, _–tĕ´rĕ_, v. a. & n. to advise, to instruct; to guess, to contrive, to perceive.
avvezzare, _–vĕtzä´rĕ_, v. a. to accustom; avvezzarsi, _–tzär´sĭ_, to accustom oneself to.
avviare, _–vĭä´rĕ_, v. a. to begin, to set agoing; avviarsi, _–vĭär´sĭ_, to set out, to go forward. [nate, to go in turns.
avvicendare, _–dshĕn´dä´rĕ_, v. n. to alternate.
avvicinamento, _–dshĭnämĕn´tõ_, m., avvicinanza, _–nän´tza_, f. approach.
avvicinare, _–nä´rĕ_, v. n. to approach.
avvilimento, _–lĭmĕn´tõ_, m. humiliation.
avvilire, _–lĕ´rĕ_, v. a. to vilify.
avviluppare, _–lŭppä´rĕ_, v. a. to entangle; to wrap up.
avvinare, _–nä´rĕ_, v. a. to mix with wine.
avvinazzarsi, _–tzär´sĭ_, v. r. to get tipsy.
avvincere, _–vĕn´dshĕrĕ_, v. a. to tie; av- vinchiare, _–kĭä´rĕ_, avvincigliare, _–dshĭlyä´rĕ_, v. a. to fasten, to tie up, to bind with twigs.
avvisare, _–vĭzä´rĕ_, v. a. to advise, to warn; to instruct; to guess, to contrive, to perceive.
avviso, _–vĕ´sõ_, m. advice; news.

avvistare, –vīstā'rē, v. a. to observe intently. [to twine.
avviticchiare, vītīkkiā'rē, v. a. to twist,
avvivare, –vīvā'rē, v. a. to enliven.
avvizzire, –vītzē'rē, v. n. to fade away.
avvocare, –vōkā'rē, v. a. to plead.
avvocatura, –tō'rā, f. advocate's office.
avvocato, –kā'tō, m. advocate.
avvolgere, –vōl'jērē, v. a. ir. to wrap round; **avvolgersi**, –vōl'jērsī, to wander.
avvolontato, –lōntā'tō, a. rash, headstrong.
avvolpacchiare, –pākkiā'rē, v.a. to wrap up; to turn round. [to dupe.
avvolpinare, –pīnā'rē, v. a. to deceive,
avvoltare, –tā'rē, v. a. to wrap up; to turn round.
avvoltoio, –vōltōi'ō, **avvoltore**, –tō'rē, m. vulture.
azienda, ātzīěn'dā, f. domestic economy.
azionista, ātzīōnī'stā, m. stock or shareholder. [share.
azione, ātzīō'nē, f. action, deed; right;
azoto, ātzō'tō, m. azot [the teeth.
azzannare, ātzānnā'rē, v. a. to seize with
azzardare, ādzārdā'rē, v. a. to hazard, to risk; **azzardarsi**, –dār'sī, to venture.
azzardo, –zār'dō, m. hazard, danger.
azzardoso, –dō'sō, a. hazardous, dangerous. [move.
azzicare, –zūkā'rē, v. a. to stir; to re-
azzimarsi, –mār'sī, v. r. to adorn oneself.
azzimella, –měl'lā, f. unleavened bread.
azzimo, ād'zīmō, a. unleavened.
azzoppare, –zōppā'rē, v. a. to limp, to hobble.
azzuffarsi, –zūffār'sī, v. r. to come to blows; to drink like a fish.
azzurro, –zūr'rō, m. azure.

B.

babbo, bāb'bō, m. papa, dad (for father,)
babbuasso, –bāās'sō, a. foolish, stupid, awkward.
babbuino, –bū'nō, f. baboon.
bacalare, bākālā'rē,m.great wit(ironically).
bacare, –kā'rē, v. n. to be worm-eaten.
baccalà, –kālā', **baccalare**, –lā'rē, m. stock-fish.
baccanale, –kānā'lē, m. bacchanals, pl.
baccano, –kā'nō, m. great noise.
baccante, –kān'tē,m. priestess of Bacchus.
baccellaio, bātshēllāi'ō, m. bachelor's degree.
baccelliere, –līā'rē, m. bachelor of arts.
baccello, –tshěl'lō, m. husk.
bacchetta, –kět'tā, f. rod, staff.
bacchettona, –tō'nā, f., **bacchettone**, –tō'nē, m. devotee, hypocrite.
bacchio, bāk'kīō, m. pole, cudgel.
bacheca, bākē'kā, f. glass-case; (fig.) man of fine appearance.

baciabasso, bādshābās'sō, m. bow. reverence. [pliment.
baciamano, –mā'nō, m. hand-kiss; compliment.
baciare, –dshā'rē, v. a. to kiss; to salute.
bacile, –dshē'lē, m. basin.
bacio, bā'dshō, m. kiss; salute; place exposed to the northwind.
baciozzo, –dshōt'zō, m. hearty kiss.
baciucchiare, –dshūkkiā'rē, v. a. to kiss repeatedly, to buss.
baco, bā'kō, m. silk-worm; mite.
bada, bā'dā, ad. trifling.
badalona, –lō'nā, f. plump jolly woman.
badalone, –lō'nē, m. great trifler; dunce.
badaluccare, –lākkā'rē, v. n. to skirmish; to lounge, to idle.
badalucco, –lāk'kō, m. skirmish.
badare, –dā'rē, v. a. to stand trifling; to
badessa, –děs'sā, f. abbess. [take care of.
badia, –dē'ā, f. abbey.
badiale, –dīā'lē. a. great, large.
badile, –dē'lē, m. shovel.
baffo, bāf'fō, m. mustachios, whiskers, pl.
bagaglio, bāgāl'yō, m. baggage, luggage.
bagaglione, –yō'nē, m. soldier's boy.
bagascia, –gāshā'ā, f. strumpet.
bagascione, –eshō'nē, m. strumpet's man.
bagattella, –tēl'lā, f. trifle, bauble.
bagattelliere, –līā'rē, m. juggler, trifler.
bagattino, –tī'nō, m. farthing (smallest piece of money). [ness.
baggianata, –gjānā'tā, f. silly act, foolish-
baggiano, –gjā'nō, m. simpleton, dullard.
bagliore, bālyō'rē, m. flash of light.
bagnaiuolo, bānyāiū'lō, m. bath-keeper.
bagnare, –yā'rē, v. a. to wet, to wash; **bagnarsi**, –yār'sī, to bathe.
bagnatore, –tō'rē, m. bather.
bagno, bān'yō, m. bath.
baia, bā'ā, f. joke, banter.
baiata, bāā'tā, f. joke, raillery.
baietta, bāět'tā, f. small bay; estuary.
baio, bā'ō, a. chestnut-coloured.
baiocco, bāōk'kō,m bajocco (Roman coin).
baione, bāō'nē, m. great joker.
baionetta, –ět'tā, f. bayonet.
bainca, –bāā'kā, f. trifle, bagatelle.
balaustrata, bālāāstrā'tā, f. balustrade.
balbettare, bālbēttā'rē, v.a. to stammer.
balbuzzare, –tzā'rē, v. n. to stammer.
balbo, bāl'bō, a. stammering.
balcone, –kō'nē, m. balcony.
baldacchino, –dākkē'nō,m.canopy; tester.
baldanza, –dān'tzā, f. boldness.
baldanzoso, –tzō'sō, a. bold, valiant.
baldo, bāl'dō, a. bold; haughty.
baldoria, –dō'rīā, f. bonfire.
balena, –lē'nā, f. whale. [tate.
balenare, –nā'rē, v. n. to lighten; to hesi-
baleno, –lē'nō, m. lightning; in un –, instantly.
balestra, –lěs'trā, f. cross-bow.
balestrare, –trā'rē,v.a.&n.to vex; to dart.
balestrata, –trā'tā, f. bow-shot. [sure.
balestriera, –trīā'rā, f. loop-hole, embra-
balestriere, –trīā'rē, m. bow-man.

balestro, –lĕs'trŏ, m. cross-bow.
balia, bä'lïä, f. wet-nurse; balia, –lï'ä, power, authority.
baliaggio, –lïäǵ'jŏ, m. bailiwick.
balio, bä'lïŏ, m. foster-father.
balioso, –lï'ŏsŏ, a. vigorous.
balla, bäl'lä, f. bale, pack.   [steady.
ballare, –lä'rĕ, v. n. to dance; to be un-
ballata, –lä'tä, f. dancing-song, ballad.
ballatoio, –tŏ'ŏ, m. gallery, platform.
ballerino, –lĕrë'nŏ, m. opera-dancer; dancing-master.
balletto, –lĕt'tŏ, m. ballet; interlude.
ballo, bäl'lŏ, m. ball, assembly of dancers.
ballotta, –lŏt'tä, f. boiled chestnut; vote.
ballottare, –lä'rĕ, v. a. to ballot, to vote.
baloccare, bälŏkkä'rĕ, v. a. to amuse; to detain, to stop.
balocco, –lŏk'kŏ, m. booby, ninny.
baloccone, –kŏ'nĕ, ad. foolishly, heedlessly.   [–dĕr'ä, f. stupidity.
balordaggine, –lŏrdäd'jïnĕ, balorderia,
balordo, –lŏr'dŏ, a. & m. silly; logger-head.
balsamico, –sä'mïkŏ, a. balmy; [head.
balsamo, bäl'sämŏ, m. balm.
balteo, bäl'tĕŏ, m. belt, cincture.
baluardo, –bär'dŏ, m. bulwark.
balza, bäl'tsä, f. rock, cliff.
balzano, –tsä'nŏ, a. piebalded (of horses); giddy-brained.
balzare, –tsä'rĕ, v. n. to climb, to jump.
balzatore, –tŏ'rĕ, m. leaper, jumper.
balzello, –tsĕl'lŏ, m. additional tax.
balzo, bäl'tsŏ, m. bound, jump.
bambagia, bämbä'jä, f. cotton.
bambagioso, –jŏ'sŏ, a. soft as cotton.
bambino, –bë'nŏ, m. little boy, babe.
bambola, bäm'bŏlä, f. doll, puppet; looking-glass.
bamboleggiare, –lĕdjä'rĕ, v. n. to behave childishly, to do childish things.
banca, bän'kä, f. soldier's pay-office.
banchettare, –kĕttä'rĕ, v. a. to banquet.
banchetto, –kĕt'tŏ, m. banquet. [to feast.
banchiere, –kïä'rĕ, banchiero,–kïä'rŏ, m. banker.
banco, bän'kŏ, m. bench; shop-counter.
banda, bän'dä, f. side, band; troop.
bandeggiare, –dĕdjä'rĕ, v. a. to banish.
banderaio, –dĕrä'ŏ, m. ensign-bearer.
bandiera, –dïä'rä, f. banner; ensign; whore, strumpet.
bandinella, –dïnĕl'lä, f. towel; bed-curtain.
bandito, –dë'tŏ, m. outlaw; assassin.
banditore, –tŏ'rĕ, m. public crier.
bando, bän'dŏ, m. ban, banishment.
bandoliera, –lïä'rä, f. bandolier, shoulder-belt.
bara, bä'rä, f. bier, litter, coffin.   [belt.
barabuffa, –bŭf'fä, f. riot, noise.
baracca, –räk'kä, f. barrack, hut.
barare, –rä'rĕ, v. n. to cheat, to overreach.
barat(r)o, –rä't(r)ŏ, m. abyss, gulf.
barattare, –rättä'rĕ, v. a. to exchange, to truck; to cheat, to deceive.
baratto, –rät'tŏ, m. exchange, truck; cheat; (rail.) macchina di –, f. sliding-rail.
barba, bär'bä, f. beard; root, origin; far la –, farsi la –, to shave.

barbabietola, –bïä'tŏlä, f. beet-root.
barbagianni, –jän'nï, m. owl; simpleton.
barbaglio, –bäl'yŏ, m. dimness of sight.
barbare, –bä'rĕ, v. n. to take root.
barbarico, –bä'rïkŏ, a. barbarous, cruel.
barbarie, –bä'rïĕ, f. barbarity.
barbata, –bä'tä, f. small roots, pl.
barbatella, –tĕl'lä, f. layer, sprig.
barbato, –bä'tŏ, a. bearded, rooted.
barbazzale, –tzä'lĕ, m. curb; check.
barbicare, –bïkä'rĕ, v. n. to take root.
barbiere, –bïĕ'rĕ, m. barber.
barbieria, –bïĕrë'ä, f. barber's shop.
barbino, –bë'nŏ, m. miser, pinch-penny; poodle-dog, poodle.
barbio, bär'bïŏ, m. barbel (fish).
barbugliare, –bŭlyä'rĕ, v. a. to stammer.
barbuto, –bŭ'tŏ, a. bearded; rooted.
barca, bär'kä, f. bark, ferry-boat.
barcaiuolo, –kälŭŏ'lŏ, barcaruolo, –rŭŏ'lŏ, m. boatman.
barcata, –kä'tä, m. boat-full.
barco, bär'kŏ, m. park.   [to stagger.
barcollare, –lä'rĕ, v. n. to waver, to totter,
bardatura, –dätŭ'rä, f. horse-trappings, pl.
bardella, –dĕl'lä, f. pack-saddle.
bardosso (a –), –dŏs'sŏ, ad. without saddle.
barella, –rĕl'lä, f. hand-barrow.
barellare, –lä'rĕ, v. a. to carry on a hand-barrow.
bargello, –jĕl'lŏ, m. sheriff.
bargigli, –jïl'yï, m. pl. cock's wattles.
barile, –rë'lĕ, m. hogshead, barrel.
bariletto, bärïlĕt'tŏ, m. dram-bottle; little cask.
barlettaio, –lĕttä'ŏ, m. cooper.
baro, bä'rŏ, m. cheat, knave.
barocco, –rŏk'kŏ, baroccolo, –kŏlŏ, m. extortion; usury.
barometrico, –mä'trïkŏ, a. barometrical.
barometro, –rŏ'mĕtrŏ, m. barometer.
baroncio, –rŏn'dshŏ, m. slovenly boy.
barone, –rŏ'nĕ, m. baron; vagabond.
baronessa, –nĕs'sä, f. baroness.
baronia, –në'ä, f. barony.
barra, bär'rä, f. bar; gag.   [to cheat.
barrare, –rä'rĕ, v. a. & n. to bar, to stop;
barretta, –rĕt'tä, f. artifice, deceit, trick.
barricata, –rïkä'tä, f. barricade.
barriera, –rïĕ'rä, f. palisade; turn-pike.
baruffa, bärŭf'fä, f. baruffo, –fŏ, m. fray, altercation.
barullo, –rŭl'lŏ, m. retailer.
barzelletta, –tzĕllĕt'tä, f. joke, banter.
basalte, bäsäl'tĕ, m. basalt.   [trick.
base, bä'sĕ, f. base, basis, ground; card-
basetta, –sĕt'tä, f. moustache, whisker.
basilica, –së'lïkä, f. cathedral; hall.
basilico, –së'lïkŏ, m. (bot.) sweet basil.
basilisc(h)o, –sës'k(ï)ŏ, m. basilisk.
bassare, bässä'rĕ, v. a. to abate; to humble.
bassetta, –sĕt'tä, f. basset (card-game).
bassezza, –sĕt'zä, f. meanness, lowness.
basso, bäs'sŏ, a. low; mean, base, abject; –, m. profundity, depth; bottom; (mus.) base, base-viol.
bassorilievo, –rïlïä'vŏ, m. bas-relief.
bassotto, –sŏt'tŏ, a. short and thick; –, m. terrier.

basta, *băs'tă*, ad. enough, stop.
bastabile, *-tă'bĭlĕ*, a. sufficient.
bastalena (a.-), *-lă'nă*, ad. with all one's
bastante, *-tăn'tĕ*, a. sufficient.   [might.
bastanza, *-tăn'tză*, f. sufficiency; a –,
  enough.
bastardire, *-tărdĕ'rĕ*, v. n. to degenerate.
bastardo, *-tăr'dŏ*, a. & m. bastard.
bastare, *-tă'rĕ*, v. n. to be sufficient.
bastia, *-tĕ'ă*, f. bastione, bulwark.
bastimento, *-tēmĕn'tŏ*, m. ship, vessel.
bastionare, *-tŏnă'rĕ*, v. a. to fortify with
  bastions; to strengthen.
bastione, *-tŏ'nĕ*, m. bastion, rampart.
basto, *băs'tŏ*, m. pack-saddle.
bastonare, *-nă'rĕ*, v. a. to cudgel.
bastonata, *-nă'tă*, f. bastinade, cudgelling.
bastone, *-tŏ'nĕ*, m. staff, truncheon.
batacchiare, *bătăkkĭă'rĕ*, v. a. to cudgel.
batacchio, *-tăk'kĭŏ*, m. cudgel.
batista, *-tĭs'tă*, f. cambric, lawn.
batocchio, *-ŏk'kĭŏ*, m. blindman's staff;
  bell-clapper, clapper.
batolo, *bă'tŏlŏ*, m. cap, hood.
batosta, *-tŏs'tă*, f. quarrel, dispute.
battaglia, *băttăl'yă*, f. battle.   [combat.
battagliare, *-yă'rĕ*, v. a. to fight, to
battagliero, *-yĕ'rŏ*, m. combatant.
battaglio, *-tăl'yŏ*, m. bell-clapper.
battaglione, *-yŏ'nĕ*, m. battalion.
battello, *-tĕl'lŏ*, m. skiff, canoe; - a vapore, steamer.   [to thrash.
battere, *băt'tĕrĕ*, v. a. to beat; to knock;
batteria, *-tĕrĕ'ă*, f. battery.
battesimale, *-tĕsĭmă'lĕ*, a. baptismal.
battesimo, *-tă'sĭmŏ*, m. baptism.
battezzare, *-tĕdză'rĕ*, v. a. to baptize.
batticuore, *-tĭkŭŏ'rĕ*, m. palpitation.
battifuoco, *-fŭŏ'kŏ*, m. steel (to strike a
  light with).
battigia, *-tĭ'jă*, f. falling-sickness.
battiloro, *-tĭlŏ'rŏ*, m. gold-beater.
battiporto, *-pŏr'tŏ*, m. plank (on to a
  ship), gangway.
battisoffia, *-sŏf'fĭă*, f. fright.
battistero, *-stĕ'rŏ*, battisterio, *-tĕ'rĭŏ*,
  m. font, baptistery.
battitoio, *-tŏ'ŏ*, m. rabbet of a door.
battuta, *-tŭ'tă*, f. time (in music).
battuto, *-tŭ'tŏ*, a. beaten, struck.
batuffolo, *bătŭf'fŏlŏ*, m. heap, hoard, crowd.
baule, *bă'ŭ'lĕ*, m. trunk, travelling-chest.
bava, *bă'vă*, f. slaver, foam.
bavaglio, *-văl'yŏ*, m. slabbering-bib.
bavero, *bă'vĕrŏ*, m. collar of a cloak.
bazza, *băd'ză*, f. good luck.
bazzana, *-dză'nă*, f. tanned sheep-skin.
bazzica, *băt'zĭkă*, f. conversation; intimacy; a card game.
bazzicare, *-zĭkă'rĕ*, v. a. to frequent.
bazzicature, *-tŏ'rĕ*, f. pl. trifles.
bazzotto, *-dzŏt'tŏ*, a. half done.
beare, *bĕă'rĕ*, v. a. (poet.) to bless, to beatify.
beatificare, *-tĭfĭkă'rĕ*, v. a. to beatify.
beatificazione, *-tzĭŏ'nĕ*, f. beatification.
beatitudine, *-tŏ'dĭnĕ*, f. beatitude, bliss.

beato, *bĕă'tŏ*, a. blessed.
beccaccia, *bĕkkăt'shă*, f. wood-cock.
beccaccino, *-tshĕ'nŏ*, m. snipe.
beccafico, *-fĕ'kŏ*, m. fig-pecker.
beccaio, *-kă'ŏ*, m. butcher.
beccaliti, *-lĕ'tĭ*, m. chicaner, litigious
                   [man.
beccamorti, *-mŏr'tĭ*, m. grave-digger.
beccare, *-kă'rĕ*, v. a. to peck.
beccaro, see beccaio.   [bill-full.
beccata, *-kă'tă*, f. stroke with the bill;
beccatello, *-tĕl'lŏ*, m. bracket, corbel.
beccheria, *-kĕrĕ'ă*, f. butchery.
becchino, *-kĕ'nŏ*, m. sexton, grave-digger.
becco, *bĕk'kŏ*, m. beak; prow; he-goat.
beccone, *-kŏ'nĕ*, m. large he-goat, ram.
beccuccio, *-kŭt'shŏ*, m. gullet, spout.
befana, *bĕfă'nă*, f. puppet, goblin.
beffa, *bĕf'fă*, f. trick, joke.
beffardo, *-făr'dŏ*, m. jester, banterer.
beffare, *-fă'rĕ*, v. a. to laugh at, to ridicule.
beffatore, *-tŏ'rĕ*, m. jeerer, mocker.
belare, *bĕlă'rĕ*, v. n. to bleat; to talk non-
belato, *-lă'tŏ*, m. bleating.   [sense.
belletta, *bĕllĕt'tă*, f. mud, filth.
belletto, *-tŏ*, m. paint, cheek-varnish.
bellezza, *-lĕt'ză*, f. beauty.
bellico, *bĕl'lĭkŏ*, m. navel; middle.
bellicoso, *-ĭkŏ'tŏ*, belligero, *-lĕ'jĕrŏ*, a.
  martial, warlike.   [prettily, finely.
bello, *bĕl'lŏ*, a. beautiful, handsome; –, ad.
bellone, *-lŏ'nĕ*, a. very handsome.
bellumore, *-ŭmŏ'rĕ*, a. facetious, merry.
belo, *bĕ'lŏ*, m. bleating.
beltà, *bĕltă'*, f. beauty.
belva, *bĕl'vă*, f. (poet.) wild beast.
bembè, *bĕmbĕ'*, ad. well, well!
benavventurato, *bĕnăvvĕntŭră'tŏ*, a. lucky.
benchè, *-kĕ'*, c. although.
bencreato, *-krĕă'tŏ*, a. well brought up.
benda, *bĕn'dă*, f. band.
bendare, *-dă'rĕ*, v. a. to bind, to tie with
  a fillet.   [chief.
benduccio, *-dŭt'shŏ*, m. child's handker-
bene, *bĕ'nĕ*, m. good; advantage; property,
  wealth; –, ad. well, justly, right.
benedetto, *-dĕt'tŏ*, a. blessed.
benedetto, *-dĕt'tŏ*, m. falling-sickness.
benedire, *bĕnĕdĕ'rĕ*, v. a. to bless; to consecrate.   [dinner.
benedicite, *-dĕ'dshĭtĕ*, m. grace before
benefattore, *-făttŏ'rĕ*, m. benefactor.
benefattrice, *-trĕ'dshĕ*, f. benefactress.
beneficare, *-fĭkă'rĕ*, v. a. to benefit, to
  do good to.
beneficiata, *-dshă'tă*, f. beneficiary.
beneficio, *-fĕ'dshŏ*, benefizio, *-fĕ'dzĭŏ*,
  m. benefice; advantage; living.
benefico, *bĕnĕ'fĭkŏ*, a. beneficent.
benemerenza, *-mĕrĕn'tză*, f. merit.
benemerito, *-mĕ'rĭtŏ*, a. well deserving,
  well merited.   [sure, convenience.
beneplacito, *-plă'dshĭtŏ*, m. option, plea-
benestante, *bĕnĕstăn'tĕ*, a. healthy; in
  good circumstances.
benevogliente, *-vŏlyĕn'tĕ*, a. benevolent.
benevolenza, *-lĕn'tză*, f. benevolence,
  kindness.

benignità, –nĭn'yĭtä', f. benignity.
benigno, –nēn'yŏ, a. benign.
bennato, –nä'tŏ, a. well-born; lucky.
benservito, –sĕrvī'tŏ, m. testimonial; character.
beone, bĕŏ'nĕ, m. tippler, drunkard.
bere, bā'rĕ, v. a. ir. to drink.
bergolinare, bĕrgŏlĭnä'rĕ, v. a. to pun, to rally, to joke. [able.
bergolo, bĕr'gŏlŏ, a. fickle; lively, change-
berlina, –lē'nä, f. berlin.
Berlingaccio, –lĭngät'shŏ, m. Shrove-Tuesday. [sweet biscuit.
berlingozzo, –gŏt'zŏ, m. puff-pastry.
bernesco, –nĕs'kŏ, a. burlesque.
bernoccolo, –nŏk'kŏlŏ, m. boss, knob.
bernoccoluto, –tū'tŏ, a. knobby.
berretta, –rĕt'tä, f. bonnet, cap.
berrettaio, –tä'ŏ, m. cap-maker.
berroviere, –rŏvĭā'rĕ, m. highwayman; bailiff. [a mark.
bersagliare, –sälyä'rĕ, v. a. to shoot at
bersagliere, –yā'rĕ, m. sharp-shooter.
bersaglio, –säl'yŏ, m. mark, target; laughing-stock, butt. [woman.
berta, bĕr'tä, f. trifle; foppery; gossiping
berteggiare, –tĕdjä'rĕ, v. a. to mock, to ridicule, to rally.
bertolotto, –tŏlŏt'tŏ, a. scot-free.
bertone, –tŏ'nĕ, m. cropped horse.
bertovello, –vĕl'lŏ, m. bow-net.
bertuccia, –tūt'shä, f., bertuccio, –tshŏ, m. monkey. [awkwardness.
bessaggine, bĕssä'djĭnĕ, f. foolishness.
bestemmia, bĕstĕm'mĭä, f. blasphemy.
bestemmiare, –mĭä'rĕ, v.n. to blaspheme.
bestemmiatore, –tŏ'rĕ, m. blasphemer.
bestia, bĕs'tĭä, f. beast; entrare in –, to fly into a passion.
bestiale, –tĭä'lĕ, a. bestial, brutal.
bestialità, –tĭä', f. bestiality; brutish stupidity, sottishness. [bestially.
bestialmente, –mĕn'tĕ, ad. brutally,
bestiame, –tĭä'mĕ, m. cattle; herd.
bettola, bĕt'tŏlä, f. ale-house, tavern.
bettoliere, –lĭā'rĕ, m. tavern-keeper.
bettonica, –tŏ'nĭkä, f. betony; (fig.) an excellent thing.
betulla, –tŭl'lä, f. birch-tree.
beveraggio, bĕvĕräd'jŏ, m. beverage; tip, pourboire. [ing-vessel.
beveratoio, –tŏ'ŏ, m. horse-pond; drink-
bevere, bā'vĕrĕ, v. a. to drink.
bevibile, bĕvē'bĭlĕ, a. drinkable.
bevitore, bĕvĭtŏ'rĕ, m. drinker; tippler.
bezzicare, bĕzzĭkä'rĕ, v. a. to peck; to
biacca, bĭäk'kä, f. white-lead. [dispute.
biada, bĭä'dä, f. standing corn; oats, pl.
biadaiuolo, –dä'ŏ'lŏ, m. corn-chandler.
biancastro, bĭänkäs'trŏ, a. whitish.
biancheggiare, –kĕdjä'rĕ, v. a. & n. to whiten; to grow white. [linen.
biancheria, –kĕrĭä', f. linen-clothes, pl.
bianchezza, –kĕt'zä, f. whiteness.
bianchimento, –kĭmĕn'tŏ, m. bleaching.
bianchire, –kē'rĕ, v. a. to bleach, to whiten; –, v. n. to grow white or hoary.

bianco, bĭän'kŏ, a. white; pale; hoary; –, m. whiteness.
biancospino, –spē'nŏ, m. hawthorn.
biasciare, bĭässhä'rĕ, v. a. to munch, to chew. [censure.
biasimare, –sĭmä'rĕ, v. a. to blame, to
biasimevole, –mā'vŏlĕ, a. blamable.
biasimo, bĭä'sĭmŏ, m. blame, reproof.
Bibbia, bĭb'bĭä, f. Bible.
bibita, bē'bĭtä, f. draught; cup, glass.
biblico, bē'blĭkŏ, a. biblical.
bibliografia, bĭblĭŏgräfē'ä, f. bibliography.
bibliografo, –blĭŏ'gräfŏ, m. biblio-grapher.
biblioteca, –tā'kä, f. library.
bibliotecario, –tēkä'rĭŏ, m. librarian.
bica, bē'kä, f. rick, heap, pile.
bicchiere, bĭkkĭā'rĕ, m. drinking-glass.
bicipite, bĭdshē'pĭtĕ, a. bicipitous.
bicocca, –kŏk'kä, f. hamlet; hot, cottage.
bicorno, –kŏr'nŏ, a. two-horned.
bidello, –dĕl'lŏ, m. beadle.
bieco, bĭā'kŏ, a. squinting, grim.
biennio, bĭĕn'nĭŏ, m. space of two years.
bietola, bĭā'tŏlä, f. beet; –, m. booby, simpleton. [herd.
bifolco, bĭfŏl'kŏ, m. ploughman; cow-
biforcarsi, –fŏrkär'sĭ, v.r. to become forked.
bifronte, –frŏn'tĕ, a. double-faced.
biga, bē'gä, f. two-wheeled carriage.
bigamia, bĭgämē'ä, f. bigamy.
bigamo, –gä'mŏ, m. bigamist.
bigio, bē'jŏ, m. grey colour; heretic.
biglietto, bĭlyĕt'tŏ, m. bill, ticket.
bigoncia, bĭgŏn'dshä, f. large tub. [lance.
bilancia, –län'dshä, f. pair of scales, ba-
bilanciare, –dshä'rĕ, v. a. to weigh, to ponder; to examine. [clock.
bilanciere, –dshĭā'rĕ, m. pendulum of a
bilancino, –dshē'nŏ, m. small scales; spring-bar; postilion's horse; driver, leader. [counts; ledger.
bilancio, –län'dshŏ, m. balance of ac-
bile, bē'lĕ, f. bile; wrath, choler.
bilia, bē'lĭä, f. billard-ball.
biliardo, –lĭär'dŏ, m. billiards.
bilicare, bĭlĭkä'rĕ, v. a. to counterpoise; to examine.
bilico, bē'lĭkŏ, m. equipoise, hinge.
bilione, bĭlĭŏ'nĕ, m. billion.
bilioso, –lĭŏ'sŏ, a. bilious.
bilottato, –lŏt'tŏ, a. speckled.
bilustre, –lŭs'trĕ, a. ten years old.
bimbo, bĭm'bŏ, m. baby.
bimembre, –mĕm'brĕ, a. two-membered.
binario, –nä'rĭŏ, m. (rail.) track.
binato, –nä'tŏ, a. & m. twin-born; twin.
bindoleria, bĭndŏlĕrī'ä, f. cunning, artifice.
bindolo, bĕn'dŏlŏ, m. swing; cheater.
bioccolo, bĭŏk'kŏlŏ, m. fleece of wool.
biografia, bĭŏgräfē'ä, f. biography.
biografo, bĭŏ'gräfŏ, m. biographer.
biondo, bĭŏn'dŏ, a. flaxen, fair.
bioscio, bĭŏssh'ŏ, a. awry.
bipede, bē'pĕdĕ, a. two-footed.
birbante, bĭrbän'tĕ, m. rogue, idle beggar.
birbone, –bŏ'nĕ, m. vagrant, cheat.

birboneria, –nĕrĕ'ă, f. knavery, fraud.
bircio, bĭr'dshŏ, a. short-sighted.
birilli, –rē'lĭ, m. pl. nine-pins; bowling-green.
birra, bĭr'ră, f. beer.
birraio, –răĭ'ŏ, m. brewer.
birreria, –rĕrĕ'ă, f. brewery; body of bailiffs.
birresco, –rĕs'kŏ, a. bold.
birro, bĭr'rŏ, m. bailiff, serjeant.
bisaccia, bĭsät'shă, f. wallet, knapsack.
bisava, –ä'vă, **bisavola,** –ä'vŏlă, f. great-grandmother.
bisavo, –ä'vŏ, **bisavolo,** –ä'vŏlŏ, m. great-grandfather.
bisbigliare, –bĭlyä'rĕ, v. n. to whisper.
bisbiglio, –bēl'yŏ, m. whisper.
bisca, bĭs'kă, f. gaming-house.
biscazzare, –kätzä'rĕ, v. n. to gamble extravagantly.
biscazziere, –tzĭä'rĕ, m. gamester.
bischero, bĭs'kĕrŏ, m. peg (of a stringed instrument); penis.
biscia, bĭs'shă, f. snake, adder.
biscotto, –kŏt'tŏ, m. biscuit, sugar-cake.
bisestile, –sĕstē'lĕ, a. bisextile; **anno –,** m. leap-year.
bisesto, –sĕs'tŏ, m. odd day in a leap-year.
bisillabo, –sēl'läbŏ, a. dissyllabic.
bislungo, bĭslŭn'gŏ, a. oblong.
bisogna, –sŏn'yă, f. business.
bisognare, –yä'rĕ, v. imp. to want, to need; to be necessary. [cessary.
bisognevole, –yä'vŏlĕ, a. needful, ne-
bisogno, bĭsŏn'yŏ, m. want; exigency.
bisognoso, –yŏ'sŏ, a. needy; necessitous.
bistecca, bĭstĕk'kă, f. beef-steak.
bisticciare, –tĭtshä'rĕ, v. n. to dispute.
bisticcio, –tĭt'shŏ, m. quibble.
bistorto, –tŏr'tŏ, a. crooked; deceitful.
bitume, bĭtŏ'mĕ, m. bitumen.
bivio, bĭ'vĭŏ, m. cross-way.
bizza, bĭt'ză, f. wrath, choler. [ness.
bizzarria, –dzärrē'ă, f. whim, fantastical-
bizzarro, –dzär'rŏ, a. odd, whimsical.
bizzoco, –dzŏ'kŏ, m. hypocrite. [ment.
blandimento, blándĭmĕn'tŏ, m. blandish-
blandire, –dē'rĕ, v. a. to flatter.
blando, blän'dŏ, a. bland, soft; affable.
blasfemo, bläsfĕ'mŏ, m. blasphemer.
blasone, –sŏ'nĕ, m. blazonry.
bleso, blĕ'sŏ, a. stammering.
bloccare, blŏkkä'rĕ, v. a. to block up.
blocco, blŏk'kŏ, m. blockade.
boaro, bŏä'rŏ, m. cow-herd.
bocca, bŏk'kă, f. mouth; taste; aperture.
boccale, –kä'lĕ, m. decanter, mug. [face).
boccata, –kä'tă, f. mouthful; slap (on the
boccetta, bŏtshĕt'tă, f. burgeon, bud, gem; decanter. [pant.
boccheggiare, –kĕdjä'rĕ, v. n. to gasp, to
boccia, bŏtsh'ă, f. bud, button; matrass.
boccino, –tshē'nŏ, a. belonging to black-cattle.
boccone, –kŏ'nĕ, m. mouthful, bit.
bofonchiare, –fŏnkiä'rĕ, v. n. to grumble,
boia, bŏĭ'ă, m. hangman. [to mutter.
bolcione, bŏldshŏ'nĕ, m. battering-ram.
bolgetta, –jĕt'tă, f. small valise.

bolgia, bŏl'jă, f. valise, budget, portmanteau; pit, hole. [letter).
bolla, bŏl'lă, f. bubble, blister; bull (pope's
bollare, –lä'rĕ, v. a. to seal, to stamp; to brand a malefactor.
bolletta, –lĕt'tă, f. certificate of health.
bollire, –lē'rĕ, v. n. to boil, to bubble up.
bollitura, –lĭtŏ'ră, f. ebullition; boiling liquor, decoction.
bollo, bŏl'lŏ, m. seal, stamp.
bollore, –lŏ'rĕ, m. ebullition.
bolso, bŏl'sŏ, a. asthmatic.
bomba, bŏm'bă, f. butt, mark; bomb.
bombarda, –bär'dă, f. (mar.) bomb-ketch.
bombardamento, –mĕn'tŏ, m. (mil.) bombardment. [bard.
bombardare, –dä'rĕ, v. a. (mil.) to bomb-
bombardiere, –dĭä'rĕ, m. (mil.) bombardier. [happiness.
bonaccia, bŏnät'shă, f. calm (at sea);
bonarietà, –rĭĕtä', f. good-nature.
bonario, –nä'rĭŏ, a. good-natured. [mend.
bonificare, –nĭfĭkä'rĕ, v. a. to better, to
borbottare, bŏrbŏttä'rĕ, v. n. to grumble, to mutter. [to lace.
bordare, –dä'rĕ, v. a. to cudgel; to border,
bordeggiare, –dĕdjä'rĕ, v. n. (mar.) to veer, to tack about.
bordello, –dĕl'lŏ, m. brothel.
bordo, bŏr'dŏ, m. border; (mar.) board.
borgata, –gä'tă, f. borough.
borghese, –ghĕ'sĕ, f. burgess, citizen.
borgo, bŏr'gŏ, m. borough, market-town.
borgomastro, –mä'strŏ, m. burgomaster, mayor, magistrate.
boria, bŏ'rĭă, f. arrogance, vainglory.
boriare, –rĭä'rĕ, v. n., **boriarsi,** –är'sĭ, to be proud.
borsa, bŏr'să, f. purse; exchange.
borsaio, –säĭ'ŏ, m. purse-maker.
borsaiuolo, –säĭŏ'lŏ, m. cut-purse.
borzacchino, –tzäkkē'nŏ, m. buskin.
boscaglia, bŏskäl'yă, f. woods, grove.
boschetto, –kĕt'tŏ, m. grove.
bosco, bŏs'kŏ, m. wood, forest.
boscoso, –kŏ'sŏ, a. woody, full of woods.
bosso, bŏs'sŏ, m. box-tree.
bossolo, bŏs'sŏlŏ, m. box, dice-box.
botanica, bŏtä'nĭkă, f. botany.
botanico, –tä'nĭkŏ, m. botanist; –, a. botanical.
botta, bŏt'tă, f. toad; blow, thrust.
bottaccino, –tätshē'nŏ, m. small flagon.
bottaio, –täĭ'ŏ, m. cooper.
bottega, –tĕ'gă, f. shop.
bottegaio, –tĕgäĭ'ŏ, m. shop-keeper.
bottiglia, –tĭl'yă, f. bottle.
bottigliere, –yä'rĕ, m. butler, steward.
bottiglieria, –yĕrē'ă, f. butler's office.
bottino, –tē'nŏ, m. booty, pillage.
botto, bŏt'tŏ, m. blow; toll (of a bell).
bottone, –tŏ'nĕ, m. button; bud.
bottoniera, –nĭä'ră, f. button-hole; bouquet.
bove, bŏ'vĕ, m. (poet.) ox.
bovile, bŏvē'lĕ, m. ox-stall.
bovino, –vē'nŏ, a. of oxen.
bozza, bŏä'ză, f. swelling; rough draught.
bozzetto, –zĕt'tŏ, m. bud; rough sketch.

[handwritten marginalia: >braggadocio? American word pretending to be Italian? or outdated (1942 v 2016) dic? 74 yrs behind]

bozzo, *bŏd′zŏ*, m. rough stone, free-stone; cuckold. [up.

bozzolare, *–lā′rĕ*, v. a. to taste; to pick

braccare, *brăkkā′rĕ*, v. a. to scent, to smell; to quest. [cuff.

bracciale, *–tshā′lĕ*, m. armlet; leather

braccialetto, *–tshālĕt′tŏ* m. bracelet.

bracciata, *–tshā′tă*, f. armful; embrace.

braccio, *brăt′shŏ*, m. arm; cubit, fathom.

bracciuolo, *–shŏd′lŏ*, m. elbow-prop; arm of a chair.

bracco, *brăk′kŏ*, m. settler (dog).

brace, *brā′tshĕ*, f. burning cinders, pl.

brache, *brā′kĕ*, **brachesse**, *–kĕs′sĕ*, f. pl. small-clothes, breeches, pl.

brachiere, *–kĭā′rĕ*, m. truss; suspensory.

braciere, *–tshā′rĕ*, m. brazier.

bracino, *–tshĭ′nŏ*, m. retail charcoal-seller.

braciuola, *–tshŏd′lă*, f. chop, steak, cutlet.

brachuolo, *–tshŏd′lŏ*, m. coke-seller.

bracone, *–kŏ′nĕ*, m. boaster; great coward; breeches, trousers, inexpressibles, pl.

brado, *brā′dŏ*, a. unsubdued, wild.

brage, *brā′jĕ*, f. burning coal.

braghesse, *–ghĕs′sĕ*, f. pl. breeches pl

brago, *brā′gŏ*, m. mud, mire, marsh.

brama, *brā′mă*, f. strong desire, eagerness.

bramare, *–mā′rĕ*, v. a. to wish, to desire.

bramoso, *–mŏ′sŏ*, a. desirous, eager, greedy.

branca, *brăn′kă*, f. claw, gripe, paw.

brancare, *–kā′rĕ*, v. a. to gripe, to claw.

brancata, *–kā′tă*, f. handful. [feel.

brancicare, *–tshĭkā′rĕ*, v.a. to handle, to

branco, *brăn′kŏ*, m. flock, herd.

brancolare, *–kŏlā′rĕ*, v. n. to grope along, to fumble.

branda, *brăn′dă*, f. hammock.

brandire, *–dĭ′rĕ*, v. a. to brandish; to

brando, *brăn′dŏ*, m. sword. [shake.

brano, *brā′nŏ*, m. bit, piece, rag.

brasca, *brās′kă*, f. cabbage.

bravaccio, *–vāt′shŏ*, m. bully.

bravare, *–vā′rĕ*, v. a. to brave, to defy; to affront.

bravata, *–vā′tă*, f. bravado; insult.

bravazzone, *–tsŏ′nĕ*, m. bully.

braveria, *–vĕrĭ′ă*, f. valour.

bravo, *brā′vŏ*, m. & a. cut-throat, assassin; brave, courageous; –, i. bravo, very well.

bravura, *–vŏ′ră*, f. bravery.

breccia, *brĕtsh′ă*, f. breach.

breve, *brā′vĕ*, a. & ad. brief(ly), short(ly); –, m. short inscription; brief.

brevemente, *–mĕn′tĕ*, ad. briefly, in short.

brevetto, *brĕvĕt′tŏ*, m. brevet.

breviale, *–vĭā′lĕ*, **breviario**, *–vĭā′rĭŏ*, m. breviary.

brevità, *–vĭtā′*, f. brevity, conciseness.

brezza, *brĕ′dză*, f. lightbr eeze.

briaco, *brĭā′kŏ*, a. tipsy.

briccone, *–kŏ′nĕ*, m. knave, vagabond.

bricconeria, *–nĕrĭ′ă*, f. knavery.

brieve, *brĭā′vĕ*, a. brief, short.

briga, *brĭ′gă*, f. trouble, uneasiness.

brigadiere, *brĭgădĭĕ′rĕ*, m. brigadier.

brigante, *–găn′tĕ*, a. intriguing; officious; industrious; –, m. rogue. [to shift.

brigare, *–gā′rĕ*, v. a. to solicit, to strive;

brigata, *–gā′tă*, f. troop brigade.

briglia, *brĭl′yă*, f. bridle.

brigliaio, *–yā′ŏ*, m. bridle-maker.

brillante, *–lăn′tĕ*, a. brilliant, bright.

brillare, *–lā′rĕ*, v. n. to glitter, to sparkle.

brillo, *brĭl′lŏ*, a. tipsy; merry.

brina, *brĕ′nă*, **brinata**, *brĭnā′tă*, f. white-frost, rime.

brindisi, *brĭn′dĭsĭ*, m. toast, health.

brinoso, *–nŏ′sŏ*, a. hoary.

brio, *brĕ′ŏ*, m. vivacity, fire.

brioso, *brĭŏ′sŏ*, a. lively, brisk, spirited.

brivido, *brĕ′vĭdŏ*, m. piercing cold; (fig.) goose-flesh.

brizzolato, *–tzŏlā′tŏ*, a. speckled, spotted.

brocca, *brŏk′kă*, f. pitcher, jar.

broccare, *–kā′rĕ*, v. a. to spur.

broccata, *–kā′tă*, f. blow, attack, fight.

brocco, *brŏk′kŏ*, **broccolo**, *–kŏlŏ*, m. peg; sprout, tendril; brocoli.

broda, *brŏ′dă*, f. hog-wash, dirt.

brodetto, *brŏdĕt′tŏ*, m. fine soup.

brodo, *brŏ′dŏ*, m. broth, soup.

brodoso, *–dŏ′sŏ*, a. dirty, slovenly.

brogliare, *brŏlyā′rĕ*, v. n. to embroil; to

broglio, *brŏl′yŏ*, m. tumult. [revolt.

broncio, *brŏn′tshŏ*, m. anger, passion.

bronco, *brŏn′kŏ*, m. trunk, stem.

brontolare, *–tŏlā′rĕ*, v. a. to grumble.

bronzino, *–dzĭ′nŏ*, a. bronzed; sun-burnt.

bronzista, *–dzĭs′tă*, m. smelter, founder.

bronzo, *brŏn′dzŏ*, m. bronze, brass.

brucare, *brŭkā′rĕ*, v. a. & n. to strip off leaves; to go away.

bruciare, *–dshā′rĕ*, v. a. to burn.

bruciatura, *–tŏ′ră*, f. burning, scorching.

bruco, *brŏ′kŏ*, m. caterpillar; –, a. tattered.

brullo, *brŭl′lŏ*, a. ragged; naked.

brulotto, *brŭlŏt′tŏ*, m. fire-ship.

bruma, *brŏ′mă*, f. mid-winter; cabin-boy.

brumale, *brŭmā′lĕ*, a. wintry.

brunazzo, *–nāt′zŏ*, **brunetto**, *–nĕt′tŏ*, a. brownish.

brunezza, *–nĕt′ză*, f. swarthiness.

brunire, *–nĭ′rĕ*, v. a. to burnish; to polish.

brunitoio, *–nĭtŏ′ŏ*, m. burnishing-tool.

bruno, *brŏ′nŏ*, a. brown; dark; –, m. mourning.

brusco, *brŭs′kŏ*, a. sour; rough, rude.

bruscolo, *–kŏlŏ*, m. whisp of straw.

brustolare, *–tŏlā′rĕ*, v. a. to grill, to fry, to toast.

brutale, *brŭtā′lĕ*, a. brutal, brutish.

brutalità, *–tālĭtā′*, f. brutality.

bruto, *brŏ′tŏ*, m. brute, beast. [dirty.

bruttare, *–tā′rĕ*, v. a. to soil, to stain, to

bruttezza, *brŭttĕt′ză*, f. ugliness.

brutto, *brŭt′tŏ*, a. ugly, filthy; –, m. gross-weight. [cheat.

bubbolare, *bŭbbŏlā′rĕ*, v. a. to bubble; to

bubbone, *–bŏ′nĕ*, m. bubo.

bubulca, *–bŭl′kă*, f. acre of land.

buca, *bŏ′kă*, f. hole, cave.

bucare, *–kā′rĕ*, v. a. to pierce, to bore.

bucato, *–kā′tŏ*, m. wash; washing.

buccia, *bŭt′shă*, f. bark, peel, skin.

buccina, *–shĕ′nă*, f. trumpet. [proclaim.

buccinare, *–nā′rĕ*, v. a. to trumpet; to

bucherare, *băkĕrä′ rĕ,* v. a. to pierce.
bucinare, *–dshĭnä′ rĕ,* v. n. to whisper, to
budello, *–dĕl′ lō,* m. gut, bowels.   [buzz.
bue, *bō′ĕ,* m. (pl. **buoi**) ox; dunce.
bufalo, *bū′fălō,* m. wild ox, buffalo.
buffa, *băf′fä,* f. blast; idle story; trifle,
   nonsense, joke.   [trifle.
buffare, *–fä′ rĕ,* v. a. to rally, to mock, to
buffetto, *–fĕt′ tō,* m. fillip; cupboard.
buffo, *băf′fō,* m. whiff; comic actor ; –, a.
   comic, comical.
buffone, *–fō′ nĕ,* m. buffoon, jester.
buffoneria, *–nĕrē′ ä,* f. buffoonery.
buffonesco, *–nĕs′ kō,* a. droll, ludicrous,
   humorous, odd, facetious.
bufolo, *bū′fŏlō,* m. buffalo, wild ox.
bugia, *–jē′ä,* f. lie; flat candlestick.
bugiardo, *–jăr′ dō,* m. liar.   [to fib.
bugiare, *–jä′ rĕ,* v. a. & n. to pierce; to lie,
bugigattolo, *–găt′ tŏlō,* m. small hole.
buglinolo, *būlyăb′ tŏlō,* m. small barrel,
bugno, *băn′ yō,* m. bee-hive.   [bucket.
bugnola, *–yŏlä,* f. straw-basket.
buio, *bū′ō,* a.dark, obscure; –, m. darkness.
bulbo, *băl′ bō,* m. bulb, onion.   [bubble.
bulicare, *–lĭkä′ rĕ,* v. n. to boil, to
bulima, *bō′lĭmä,* f. crowd, press.
bulimo, *–lĭmō,* m. canine hunger.
bulino, *bălĭ′ nō,* m. burin ; graver.
bulletta, *băllĕt′ tä,* f. passport; lottery-
   ticket.
bullettino, *–tē′ nō,* m. safe-conduct; billet.
buonaccordo, *băōnăkkŏr′ dō,* m. harp-
   sichord.   [tip, pourboire.
buonamano, *băōnămä′ nō,* f. drinkmoney,
buonavoglia, *–vŏl′ yä,* m. volunteer.
buondì, *băōndē′,* m. good-morning!
buono, *băō′ nō,* a. good, kind; fit, proper.
buratto, *būrăt′ tō,* m. bombasin; bolter.
burbanzare, *–bănzä′ rĕ,* v. n. to boast.
burbanzoso, *–tzō′ sō,* a. proud, vain, lofty.
burbero, *būr′ bĕrō,* a. crabbed.
burchiello, *–kĭĕl′ lō,* m. wherry, ferry.
burchio, *băr′ kĭō,* m. bark, lighter.
burla, *băr′ lä,* f. trick, waggery.
burlare, *–lä′ rĕ,* v. a. to jest, to ridicule.
burlesco, *–lĕs′ kō,* a. ludicrous, burlesque.
burletta, *–lĕt′ tä,* f. comic opera.
burlone, *–lō′ nĕ,* m. jester.
burrasca, *–răs′ kä,* f. tempest, hurricane.
burro, *see* **butirro.**
burrone, *–rō′ nĕ,* m. precipice.
burroso, *–rō′ sō,* a. buttery.
busbaccare, *băsbăkkä′ rĕ,* v. a. to cheat.
busbacco, *–băk′ kō,* m. cheat.
busca, *băs′ kä,* f. search, inquest.   [self.
buscarsi, *–kär′ sĭ,* v. r. to procure for one-
busecchia, *–sĕk′ kĭä,* f., **busecchio,** *–sĕk′–
   kĭō,* m. entrails, pl.
buso, *bō′ sō,* a. pierced, empty.   [business.
bussa, *băs′ sä,* f. stroke; trouble; fatiguing
bussare, *–sä′ rĕ,* v. a. to beat, to knock.
busso, *băs′ sō,* m. bustle; noise.
bussola, *băs′ sŏlä,* f. mariner's compass;
busta, *băs′ tä,* f. book-case.   [sedan-chair.
busto, *băs′ tō,* m. bust; stays, pl.
butirro, *bătĭr′ rō,* m. butter.   [thrust out.
buttare, *băttä′ rĕ,* v.a. to fling, to throw, to

butterato, *–tĕrä′ tō,* a. pock-marked.
buttero, *băttĕ′ rō,* m. pock-mark.
buzzo, *băd′ zō,* m. pin-cushion; belly.
buzzone, *–zō′ nĕ,* m. big-bellied person.

C.

cabala, *kä′ bălä,* f. cabal.   [end of a piece.
cabaletta, *–lĕt′ tä,* f. musical phrase at the
cabalista, *–lĭs′ tä,* m. cabalist.
cabottaggio, *kăbŏttäd′ jō,* m. coasting.
cacaiuola, *–kăĭŭō′ lä,* f. flux of the belly.
cacare, *–kä′ rĕ,* v. a. to evacuate, to shite.
cacazibetto, *–zĭbĕt′ tō,* m. fop, spark,
   dandy, masher, beau.   [pursuit.
caccia, *kät′ shä,* f. hunting; game; sport;
cacciare, *–tshä′ rĕ,* v.n. to chase, to hunt;
   to pursue; to banish.
cacciatore, *–tō′ rĕ,* m. hunter, sportsman.
caccole, *kăk′ kŏlĕ,* f. pl. rheum, blearedness.
caccoloso, *–lō′ sō,* a. blear-eyed.
cacio, *kä′ dshō,* m. cheese.
cadavere, *–dä′ vĕrĕ,* m. corpse.
cadente, *–dĕn′ tĕ,* a. falling; weak, frail.
cadenza, *–dĕn′ tzä,* f. fall; (mus.) cadence,
   pause.
cadere, *–dĕ′ rĕ,* v. n. ir. to fall; to happen.
cadetto, *–dĕt′ tō,* m. cadet; younger brother.
cadevole, *–dä′ vŏlĕ,* a. transient; frail.
cadimento, *–dĭmĕn′ tō,* m. fall, ruin fault.
caducità, *–dădshĭtä′,* f. frailty.
caduco, *–dä′ kō,* a. frail, infirm.
caduta, *–dä′ tä,* f. fall, ruin; disgrace.
caffè, *kăffĕ′,* m. coffee; coffee-house.
caffettiera, *–tĭä′ rä,* f. coffee-pot.
caffettiere, *–tĭä′ rĕ,* m. coffee-house keeper.
caffo, *kăf′ fō,* a. odd (of numbers); singular.
cagionare, *–jŏnä′ rĕ,* v. a. to occasion; to
   impute.
cagione, *–jō′ nĕ,* f. cause, reason.
cagionevole, *–nä′ vŏlĕ,* a. sickly, weak.
cagna, *kăn′ yä,* f. bitch.
cagnazzo, *–nät′ zō,* a. dog-like, ugly.
cagneggiare, *–nĕdjä′ rĕ,* v. a. to snarl, to
cala, *kä′ lä,* f. bay; keelhauling.   [gnash.
calafatare, *–fătä′ rĕ,* v. a. to caulk.
calafato, *–fä′ tō,* m. oakum; caulker.
calamaio, *–mä′ ō,* m. ink-stand.
calamita, *–mĭ′ tä,* f. loadstone.
calamità, *–mĭtä′,* f. calamity, misfortune.
calamitare, *–tä′ rĕ,* v. a. to magnetize.
calamitoso, *–tō′ sō,* a. calamitous, miser-
calamo, *kä′ lämō,* m. reed, cane.   [able.
calandra, *–lăn′ drä,* f. wood-lark.
calappio, *–lăp′ pĭō,* m. snare, trap.
calare, *–lä′ rĕ,* v. a. to lower; –, v. n. to
   go down, to decrease.   [falling off.
calata, *–lä′ tä,* f. descent, declivity ; (mar.)
calca, *kăl′ kä,* f. crowd, press.
calcagnare, *–kănyä′ rĕ,* v. n. to run away.
calcagno, *–kän′ yō,* m. heel.
calcare, *–kä′ rĕ,* v. a. to tread upon, to
   crush ; to oppress.
calce, *kăl′ dshĕ,* f. chalk, lime.
calcestruzzo, *–strät′ zō,* m. cement.

calcetto, –dshĕt'tŏ, m. sock, pump.
calcina, –dshē'nā, f. lime, mortar.
calcinare, –nā'rĕ, v. a. to calcine.
calcinazione, –tziŏ'nĕ, f. calcination.
calcio, kăl'dshŏ, m. kick : blow with the foot, kick.   [resist.
calcitrare, –dshītrā'rĕ, v. n. to kick ; to calco, kăl'kŏ, m. slight sketch ; chalking.
calcolare, –lā'rĕ, v. a. to calculate.
calcolatore, –tŏ'rĕ, m. accountant, computer.   [tion.
calcolo, kăl'kŏlŏ, m. calculation, computa-
caldaia, –dā'ā, f. small boiler, kettle.
caldana, –dā'nā, f. meridian heat.
caldano, –dā'nŏ, m. brazier.
caldeggiare, –dēdjā'rĕ, v. a. to protect, to favour.   [tea-kettle.
calderotto, –dĕr'ŏt'tŏ, m. seething-pot ;
caldezza, –dĕt'zā, caldità, –dūā', f. heat ; zeal ; affection, good will.
caldo, kăl'dŏ, a. hot ; ardent, fervent ; caldo caldo, immediately ; –, m. heat ; ardour ; vigour.
calduccio, –dūt'shŏ, a. luke-warm.
calendario, kălēndā'rĕŏ, calendaro, –dā'rŏ, m. calendar.
Dalepino, kālĕpē'nŏ, m. collectaneous notes.
calere, –lā'rĕ, v. imp. ir. to care, to take an calesse, –lĕs'sĕ, m. calash.   [interest in.
calettare, –lĕttā'rĕ, v. a. to enchase, to mortise, to rabbet.
calia, kāli'ā, f. gold-filings ; nothing, jot.
calibro, –lē'brŏ, m. calibre.
calice, kā'līdshĕ, m. chalice ; calix.
calido, kā'līdŏ, a. warm, hot.
caligine, –lē'jīnĕ, f. darkness ; ignorance.
caliginoso, –lījīnŏ'sŏ, a. caliginous ; dim.
calla, kāl'lā, callaia, –lā'ā, f. breach, passage, entrance, entry.
calle, kāl'lĕ, f. (poet.) way, path.
calligrafia, –līgrāfī'ā, caligraphy.
calligrafo, –lē'grāfŏ, m. writing-master.
callo, kăl'lŏ, m. bunion, corn.
callosità, –lŏsītā', f. callosity, hardness.
calloso, –lŏ'sŏ, a. callous, full of corns.
calma, kăl'mā, f. calm, coolness.
calmante, –mān'tĕ, a. lenient.
calmare, –mā'rĕ, v. a. to calm, to appease.
calmo, kăl'mŏ, m. twig, layer, graft.
calo, kā'lŏ, m. descent, diminution.
calore, –lŏ'rĕ, m. heat ; affection.
caloria, –lŏrē'ā, f. manure.
caloroso, –rŏ'sŏ, a. hot, fiery.
calpestare, kălpĕstā'rĕ, v. n. to trample upon ; to scorn.   [feet.
calpestio, –pĕstē'ŏ, m. stamping with the
calunnia, –lūn'nīā, f. calumny.
calunniare, –nīā'rĕ, v. a. to calumniate.
calunniatore, –tŏ'rĕ, m., calunniatrice, trē'dshĕ, f. slanderer.   [derous.
calunnioso, –nīŏ'sŏ, a. calumnious, slan-
calvario, –vā'rīŏ, m. calvary.
calvinismo, –vīnīs'mŏ, m. Calvinism.
calvinista, –nīs'tā, m. Calvinist.
calvizie, –vē'tzīĕ, f. baldness.
calvo, kăl'vŏ, a. bald, hairless.
calza, kăl'tzā, f. stocking ; clyster-pipe.

calzare, –tzā'rĕ, v. a. to put on shoes and stockings.
calzatura, –tŏ'rā, f. shoes and stockings.
calzetta, –tzĕt'tā, f. fine stocking.
calzo, kăl'tzŏ, m. shoe, stocking.
calzolaio, –lāē'ŏ, m. shoemaker.
calzoleria, –lĕrē'ā, f. shoemaker's shop.
calzoni, –tzŏ'nī, m. pl. breeches, pl.
camaglio, kămā'lyŏ, m. coat of mail.
camaleonte, –lēŏn'tĕ, m. chameleon.
camarlingo, –mārlīn'gŏ, m. chamberlain.
camato, kămā'tŏ, m. switch, stick.
cambiabile, –bīā'bīlĕ, a. fickle, volatile.
cambiale, –bīā'lĕ, f. bill of exchange.
cambiare, –bīā'rĕ, v. a. to change ; to truck, to draw upon for money.
cambiatore, –tŏ'rĕ, m., cambia-valute, kăm'bīā vālū'tĕ, m. banker, exchanger.
cambio, kăm'bīŏ, m. change, exchange.
cambista, –bīs'tā, m. banker.
camera, kā'mērā, f. chamber.
camerata, –rā'tā, f. roomful, society.
cameretta, –rĕt'tā, f. small room, closet ; water-closet.   [ber-maid.
cameriera, –rī'ā, f. lady's-maid, cham-
cameriere, –rī'ĕ'rĕ, m. waiter ; valet, gentleman's servant.
camerista, –rīs'tā, f. maid of honour.
camicia, –mē'dshā, f. shirt, shift.
camiciotto, –dshŏt'tŏ, m. under-waistcoat.
camiciuola, –mīdshūŏ'lā, f. flannel-waist-coat.
caminetto, –nĕt'tŏ, m. little chimney.
camino, –mē'nŏ, m. chimney.
cammello, –mĕl'lŏ, m. camel.
cammeo, –mā'ŏ, m. cameo.   [walk.
camminare, –mīnā'rĕ, v. n. to travel, to
camminata, –nā'tā, f. walk, journey ; hall.
cammino, –mē'nŏ, m. way ; journey ; chimney ; – a vapore, (rail.) steam-chimney.
camomilla, –mŏmīl'lā, f. camomile.
camoscio, –mŏssh'ŏ, m. chamois ; shammy ; –, a. flat-nosed.
camozza, –mŏd'zā, m. wild she-goat.
campagna, kāmpān'yā, f. country, campaign.   [man.
campagnuolo, –pānyūŏ'lŏ, m. country-
campale, –pā'lĕ, a. arrayed ; battaglia –, f. pitched battle.   [ment.
campamento, –mĕn tŏ, m. (mil.) encamp-
campana, –pā'nā, f. bell ; curfew.
campanaio, –nāĕ'ŏ, m. bell-ringer ; bell-founder.   [blue-bell.
campanella, –nĕl'lā, f. small bell ; (bot.)
campanello, –nĕl'lŏ, m. little bell, hand-campanile, –nē'lĕ, m. belfry.   [bell.
campare, –pā'rĕ, v. a. to save, to deliver ; camparsi, –pār'sī, to escape, to live.
campeggiare, –pĕdjā'rĕ, v. n. to encamp.
campeggio, –pĕd'jŏ, m. log-wood.
campestre, –pĕs'trĕ, campestro, –trŏ, a. rural, savage.   [Rome].
campidoglio, –pīdŏl'yŏ, m. Capitol (at
campione, –pīŏ'nĕ, m. champion.
campo, kăm'pŏ, m. field, plain ; camp ; (fig.) opportunity ; – santo, churchyard.

camuffare, –mǐlffü'rě, v. n. to disguise.
camuso, –mŏ'sŏ, a. flat-nosed.
canaglia, –nǎl'yǎ, f. rabble, canaille.
canale, –nǎ'lě, m. canal, channel, strait.
canaletto, –lět'tŏ, m. little canal.
canapa, kǎ'nǎpǎ, m. hemp.
canape, kǎ'nǎpě, m. hemp-twist; rope.
canapino, –pǐ'nŏ, a. hempen.
canapo, kǎ'nǎpŏ, m. (mar.) cable; tackle, cordage; –, kǎnǎ'pŏ, m. miner.
canarino, –rě'nŏ, m. canary-bird.
canata, –nǎ'tǎ, f. scolding, reprimand.
canatteria, –nǎttěrě'ǎ, f. pack of dogs.
canattiere, –tǐd'rě, m. dog-keeper.
canavaccio, –vǎt'shŏ, m. canvass; towel.
cancellare, kǎndshěllǎ'rě, v. a. to cancel; to enclose with rails – , v. n. to give way, to vacillate. [or used in chancery.
cancelleresco, –lěrěs'kŏ, a. belonging to
cancelleria, –lěrě'ǎ, f. chancery.
cancelliere, –lǐd'rě, m. chancellor.
cancello, –dshěl'lŏ, m. lattice; ballustrade; court-bar.
canceroso, –dshěrŏ'sŏ, a. cancerous.
canchero, kǎn'kěrŏ, m. canker.
cancrena, –krǎ'nǎ, f. gangrene.
cancro, kǎn'krŏ, m. cancer; crab.
candela, –dǎ'lǎ, f. candle.
candelabro, –lǎ'brŏ, m. chandelier.
candeliere, –lǐd'rě, m. candlestick.
candente, –děn'tě, a. burning, shining.
candi(zucchero), kǎn'dǐ(tzŭk'kěrŏ), m. sugar-candy.
candidato, –dǎ'tŏ, m. candidate.
candidezza, –dět'zǎ, f. whiteness; purity.
candido, kǎn'dǐdŏ, a. white; fair; sincere, open. frank, ingenuous, upright.
candire, –dǐ'rě, v. a. to candy, to preserve.
candito, –dǐ'tŏ, m. candied fruits.
candore, –dŏ'rě, m. whiteness; purity; sincerity.
cane, kǎ'ně, m. dog; cock (of a gun); Tartar prince; – da caccia, hound, harrier, pointer.
canestro, –něs'trŏ, m. basket.
canfora, kǎn'fŏrǎ, f. camphor.
cangiante, –jǎn'tě, a. varying colours.
cangiare, –jǎ'rě, v. a. to change; to shift.
cangio, kǎn'jŏ, a. changing.
cangrena, –grǎ'nǎ, f. gangrene.
canicola, –ně'kŏlǎ, f., dog-star; dog-days, pl.
canicolare, –nǐkŏlǎ'rě, a. canicular.
canile, –ně'lě, m. dog-kennel; miserable [bed.
canino, –ně'nŏ, a. canine, currish.
canna, kǎn'nǎ, f. cane; reed-pipe.
cannamele, –mǎ'lě, f. sugar-cane.
cannata, –nǎ'tǎ, f. blow with a stick.
cannella, něl'lǎ, f. switch; cinnamon.
cannetta, –nět'tǎ, f. soldering-pipe.
cannibale, –nǐbǎ'lě, m. cannibal.
canniccio, –nǐt'shŏ, m. hurdle.
cannocchiale, –nŏkkǐǎ'lě, m. telescope.
cannonata, –nǎ'tǎ, f. cannonade.
cannone, –nŏ'ně, m. great tube; cannon.
cannoneggiare, –nědjǎ'rě, v. a. to cannonade.
cannoniera, –nǐd'rǎ, f. embrasure.

cannoniere, –nǐd'rě, m. artillery-man.
canone, –nŏ'ně, m. canon, church-law.
canonica, –nŏ'nǐkǎ, f. chapter-house; canoness. [canonical.
canonico, –nŏ'nǐkŏ, m. canon; –, a.
canonizzare, –dzǎ'rě, v. a. to canonize.
canonizzazione, –tziŏ'ně, f. canonization.
canoro, kǎnŏ'rŏ, a. canorous, harmonious.
canotto, –nŏt'tŏ, m. canoe.
canova, kǎ'nŏvǎ, f. cellar; tavern.
canovaccio, –vǎt'shŏ, m. canvass; towel.
canovaio, –vǎ'ŏ, butler, store-keeper.
cansare, –sǎ'rě, v. a. to remove; to shelter; cansarsi, –sǎr'sǐ, to retire.
cantabile, kǎntǎ'bǐlě, a. that may be sung.
cantambanca, –tǎmbǎn'kǎ, f. enchantress.
cantambanco, –bǎn'kŏ, m. impostor.
cantare, –tǎ'rě, v. a. to sing; to praise.
cantaride, –tǎ'rǐdě, f. cantharides, pl.
cantaro, –tǎ'rŏ, m. quintal; close-stool pan.
cantata, –tǎ'tǎ, f. song with a recitative.
cantatore, –tŏ'rě, m. singer, songster.
cantatrice, –trě'dshě, f. songstress.
canterella, –těrěl'lǎ, f. Spanish-fly.
canterina, –rě'nǎ, f. songstress.
cantero, kǎn'těrŏ, m. quintal.
cantica, –tě'kǎ, f., cantico, –kŏ, m. canticle; hymn. [song.
cantilena, –tǐlě'nǎ, f. little song; love-
cantimplora, –tǐmplŏ'rǎ, f. ice-pail.
cantina, –tě'nǎ, f. cellar, cave.
cantiniere, –nǐd'rě, cantiniero, –rŏ, m. butler, vintner.
canto, kǎn'tŏ, m. singing; song; side, part; corner; dal – mio, as for me.
cantonare, –nǎ'rě, v. n. to retire.
cantonata, –nǎ'tǎ, f. corner, angle.
cantone, –tŏ'ně, m. corner-stone; canton.
cantoniera, –nǐd'rǎ, f. strumpet.
cantore, –tŏ'rě, m. chorister, singer.
cantoria, –tŏrě'ǎ, f. singing-gallery.
canutezza, –nǔtět'zǎ, f. hoariness, gray hair. [cold.
canuto, –nǔ'tŏ, a. hoary, gray-headed,
canzonare, –tzŏnǎ'rě, v. a. to sing; to celebrate; to quiz.
canzone, –tzŏ'ně, f. song, ballad.
canzoniere, –nǐd'rě, m. song-book, collection of lyric poems.
caos, kǎ'ŏs, m. chaos, confusion.
capace, –pǎ'dshě, a. capable, fit.
capacità, –dshǐtǎ', f. capacity; extent.
capacitare, –tǎ'rě, v. a. to enable, to qualify.
capanna, –pǎn'nǎ, f. cottage; barn.
caparbietà, –pǎrbǐětǎ', f. obstinacy, stubbornness, headiness.
caparbio, –pǎr'bǐŏ, a. obstinate, stubborn.
caparra, –pǎr'rǎ, f. earnest-money; pledge.
caparrare, –rǎ'rě, v. a. to give earnest.
capata, –pǎ'tǎ, f. blow with the head.
capecchio, –pěk'kǐŏ, m. coarse tow; trash.
capellizio, –lǐt'dztŏ, m. hair (of the head).
capello, –pěl'lŏ, m. hair. [hair.
capelvenere, –vě'něrě, m. (bot.) maiden-
capere, –pǎ'rě, v. a. & n. to contain, to understand.

capestreria, -pĕstrĕr'ĕ'ä, f. oddness.

capestro, -pĕs'trŏ, m. halter, rope; villain.

capezzale, -pĕtzä'lĕ, m. handkerchief;

capezzolo, -pĕt'zŏlŏ, m. nipple. [pillow.

capillare, -pĭllä'rĕ, a. hair-like, hairy.

capillato, -lä'tŏ, a. haired.

capire, -pĕ'rĕ, v. a. & n. to contain; to comprehend; to understand.

capitale, -pĭtä'lĕ, a. capital; chief, main; -, m. capital, stock, principal; -, f. capital, metropolis. [man.

capitalista, -lĭs'tä, m. capitalist, monied

capitana, -tä'nä, f. flag-ship.

capitanare, -nä'rĕ, v. a. & n. to appoint chiefs or commanders; to command.

capitano, -tä'nŏ, m. captain. [arrive at.

capitare, -tä'rĕ, v. a. & n. to finish; to

capitello, -tĕl'lŏ, m. capital of a column.

capitolare, -tŏlä'rĕ, v. n. & a. to capitulate; to divide into chapters.

capitolazione, -tziŏ'nĕ, f. capitulation.

capitolo, -pĭ'tŏlŏ, m. chapter; matter.

capitombolare, -tŏmbŏlä'rĕ, v. n. to tumble, to fall headlong.

capitombolo, -tŏm'bŏlŏ, m. tumble.

capo, kä'pŏ, m. head; chief; beginning; origin; summit; promontory; commander, governor; fancy, idea; da -, over again; - per -, point by point.

capocchia, -pŏk'kĭä, f. knob; thick end.

capocchio, -pŏk'kĭŏ, a. dull, heavy, silly.

capofila, -fĕ'lä, m. file-leader. [pl.

capogatto, -gät'tŏ, m. vertigo, staggers,

capogiro, -jĕ'rŏ, m. dizziness, giddiness.

capolavoro, -lävŏ'rŏ, m. master-piece.

caponaggine, -näd'jĭnĕ, f. headiness, obstinacy. [person.

capone, -pŏ'nĕ, m. large head; headstrong

capoparte, -pär'tĕ, m. head of a faction.

capopiè, -pĭĕ', capopiede, -pĭĕ'dĕ, ad. topsy-turvy.

caporale, -rä'lĕ, m. corporal.

caposquadra, -skuä'drä, m. (mar.) commodore. [verse.

capoverso, -vĕr'sŏ, m. beginning of a

capovolgere, -vŏl'jĕrĕ, v. a. to overturn; to turn upside down. [verted.

capovolto, -vŏl'tŏ, a. upside down; in-

cappa, käp'pä, f. cloak; hood, cape.

cappare, -pä'rĕ, v. a. to pick out.

cappella, -pĕl'lä, f. chapel; choir; maestro di -, leader of the choir.

cappellaio, -läi'ŏ, m. hatter.

cappellania, -länĭ'ä, f. chaplainship.

cappellano, -lä'nŏ, m. chaplain; almoner.

cappellata, -lä'tä, f. cap in hand, bow.

cappelliera, -lĭ'rä, f. hat-box.

capperi, käp'pĕrĭ, i. heyday!

cappero, käp'pĕrŏ, m. caper; caper-bush.

capperone, -rŏ'nĕ, m. hood; carrier's

cappio, käp'pĭŏ, m. running-knot. [cloak.

capponata, -pŏnä'tä, f. christening-meal.

cappone, -pŏ'nĕ, m. capon. [monk.

cappuccino, -pätshĕ'nŏ, m. capuchin

cappuccio, -pät'shŏ, m. cowl, hood; cabbage.

capra, kä'prä, f. she-goat. [bage.

capraio, -prä'ĭ'ŏ, capraro, -prä'rŏ, m. goat-herd. [whim.

capriccio, -prĕt'shŏ, m. shivering; caprice,

capriccioso, -tshŏ'sŏ, a. capricious.

capricorno, -kŏr'nŏ, m. capricorn.

caprifico, -fĕ'kŏ, m. wild-fig-tree.

caprifoglio, -fŏl'yŏ, m. honey-suckle.

caprigno, -prĭn'yŏ, caprino, -prĕ'nŏ, a. goatish. [goats.

caprile, -prĕ'lĕ, m. goat-house, pen for

capriola, -prĭŏ'lä, f. caper, capriole.

capriolare, -lä'rĕ, v. n. to cut capers.

capriolo, -prĭŏ'lŏ, m. roe-buck, wild-goat; tendril.

capriuola, -prĭäŏ'lä, f. doe, roe.

caprizzante, -prĭtzän'tĕ, a. irregular (of the pulse).

capro, kä'prŏ, m. roe-buck, wild-goat.

carabina, -räbĕ'nä, f. carabine.

carabiniere, -nĭĕ'rĕ, m. carabinier.

caracollare, -räkŏllä'rĕ, v. n. to caracol, to wheel about.

caracollo, -kŏl'lŏ, m. wheeling about.

caraffa, -räf'fä, f. decanter.

caratare, -rätä'rĕ, v. a. to ponder; to deliberate carefully.

carato, -rä'tŏ, m. carat.

carattere, -rät'tĕrĕ, m. character; dignity; quality; style.

caratteristica, -tĕrĭs'tĭkä, f. characteristic.

caratteristico, -tĭkŏ, a. characteristic.

caratterizzare, -rĭdzä'rĕ, v. a. to characterize. [ditch; coal-woman.

carbonaia, kärbŏnäi'ä, f. coal-pit; dungeon;

carbonaio, -näi'ŏ, m. coal-man.

carbonata, -nä'tä, f. carbonado, grillade.

carbonchio, -bŏn'kĭŏ, carboncolo, -kŏlŏ, m. carbuncle (tumour and gem).

carbone, -bŏ'nĕ, m. coal; carbuncle.

carcare, -kä'rĕ, v. a. (poet.) to charge, to burden.

carcassa, -käs'sä, f. quiver.

carcerare, -dshĕrä'rĕ, v. a. to imprison.

carcere, kär'dshĕrĕ, m. prison, jail.

carceriere, -rĭä'rĕ, m. jailer.

carcinoma, -dshĭnŏ'mä, f. cancer.

carciofaia, -dshŏfäi'ä, f. field planted with artichokes.

carciofo, -dshŏ'fŏ, m. artichoke.

carco, kär'kŏ, m. charge, burden.

cardare, -dä'rĕ, v. a. to card (wool); to slander.

cardellino, -dĕllĕ'nŏ, m. gold-finch.

cardinale, -dĭnä'lĕ, a. & m. cardinal.

cardine, kär'dĭnĕ, m. hinge, pole.

cardo, kär'dŏ, m. thistle; carder's comb.

careggiare, -rĕdjä'rĕ, v. a. to caress; to value, to esteem.

carena, -rä'nä, f. keel (of a ship).

carestia, -rĕstĕ'ä, f. dearth; scarcity.

carezza, -rĕt'zä, f. caress, fondness.

carezzare, -tzä'rĕ, v. a. to caress, to flatter.

carezzevole, -tzä'vŏlĕ, a. flattering.

cariare, -rĭä'rĕ, v. n. n. to gangrene.

carica, kä'rĭkä, f. charge, load; care.

caricare, -kä'rĕ, v. a. to charge, to load; to exaggerate.

Italian and English.

caricatura, –tŏo'rä, f. caricature.
carico, kä'rĭkŏ, a. loaded, charged.
carie, kä'rĭĕ, f. rottenness.
cariello, –rĭĕl'lŏ, m. cushion, pillow; pillow of the stool.
carisma, –rĭs'mä, f. favour, present.
carità, –rĭtä', f. charity; affection; alms.
caritativo, –tätĕ'vŏ, a. charitable, kind.
carlino, –lē'nŏ, m. a silver coin.
carme, kär'mĕ, m. poem, strain.
carmelitano, –tä'nŏ, m. carmelite-monk.
carminativo, –mĭnätĕ'vŏ, a. carminative.
carminio, –mē'nĭŏ, m. carmine.
carnaggio, –näd'jŏ, m. slaughter, carnage.
carnagione, –jŏ'nĕ, f. carnation, flesh-colour.
carnale, –nä'lĕ, a. carnal; sensual.
carne, kär'nĕ, f. flesh; meat; pulp of fruit; carnal lust.
carnefice, –nä'fēdshĕ, m. hangman.
carneo, kär'nĕŏ, a. carneous; fleshy.
carnevale, –nĕvä'lĕ, m. carnival.
barniera, –nĭä'rä, f. game-pouch.
carnivoro, –nē'vŏrŏ, a. carnivorous.
carnoso, –nŏ'sŏ, a. fleshy, muscular.
caro, kä'rŏ, a. dear, costly; beloved; agreeable; –, ad. dearly, dear, at a high price; –, m. dearness (of provisions), scarcity.
carogna, –rŏn'yä, f. carrion; jade.
carosello, –rŏsĕl'lŏ, m. carousal.
carota, –rŏ'tä, f. carrot.
carotide, –rŏ'tĭdĕ, f. carotid-artery.
carovana, –rŏvä'nä, f. caravan; convoy.
carpare, see carpire.
carpentiere, –pĕntĭä'rĕ, m. carpenter.
carpine, kär'pĭnĕ, m. horn-beam.
carpione, –pĭŏ'nĕ, m. carp (fish).
carpire, –pē'rĕ, v. a. to snatch, to seize; to steal, to rob.   [man.
carradore, –rädŏ'rĕ, m. cartwright; cart-
carratello, –tĕl'lŏ, m. hogshead, barrel.
carreggiata, –djä'tä, f. cart-road.
carretta, –rĕt'tä, f. carriage (of a cannon); carriage with two wheels.
carriaggio, –rĭäd'jŏ, m. baggage, luggage.
carriera, –rĭä'rä, f. carreer; race; life.
carro, kär'rŏ, m. car; cart-load; Greater Bear.
carrozza, –rŏt'zä, f. carriage, coach.
carrozzabile, –tzä'bĭlĕ, a. practicable, fit for passage.   [cock.
carrucola, –rŏo'kŏlä, f. pulley; weather-
carta, kär'tä, f. paper; sheet of paper; card; bill, bond; – geografica, map; – marezzata, marble paper; – da navigare, sea-chart; – pecora, parchment; – sugante, blotting paper.
cartaceo, –tä'dshĕŏ, a. paper, of paper.
cartaio, –tä'ŏ, m. paper-maker; paper-seller, dealer in paper, stationer.
cartapesta, –tä'pĕs'tä, f. papier-maché.
carteggiare, –tĕdjä'rĕ, v. a. to glance over a book; to correspond; to play at cards.
carteggio, –tĕd'jŏ, m. correspondence.
cartello, –tĕl'lŏ, m. bill, manifesto.
cartellone, –lŏ'nĕ, m, placard.

cartiera, –tĭä'rä, f. paper-mill.
cartilagine, –tĭlä'jĭnĕ, f. cartilage, gristle.
carcoccio, –tŏt'shŏ, m. paper-cup, cornet; cartouch.   [stationer.
cartolaio, –lä'ŏ, m. paper-merchant;
cartolaro, –lä'rŏ, m. journal, diary; (mar.) log-book.
cartoleria, –lĕrĭ'ä, f. stationery.
cartone, –tŏ'nĕ, m. paste-board.
casa, kä'sä, f. house; family; – di campagna, country-house.   [–, by chance.
casaccio, –sät'shŏ, m. strange accident; a
casale, –sä'lĕ, m. hamlet, village.
casalingo, –lēn'gŏ, a. domestic; sedentary; pane –, m. household-bread.
casamatta, –mät'tä, f. casemate.
casato, –sä'tŏ, m. family, race; surname.
cascare, –kä'rĕ, v. n. to fall; to lose courage.
cascata, käs'kätä, f. fall; cascade.
caschetto, –kĕt'tŏ, m. helmet, head-piece.
cascina, –shē'nä, f. dairy, cow-park.
casella, –sĕl'lä, f. small house, cell.
caserma, –sĕr'mä, f. (mil.) barrack.
casino, –sē'nŏ, m. small country-box; summer-house; pleasure-house.
caso, kä'sŏ, m. case, accident, chance; a –, per –, by chance; –che, in case that.
casolare, –lä'rĕ, m. den, hovel, hut.
cassa, käs'sä, f. chest, coffer, trunk; treasury; money-box.   [with back.
cassapanca, –pän'kä, f. wooden bench
cassare, –sä'rĕ, v. a. to annul, to abolish.
cassazione, –tzĭŏ'nĕ, f. cassation, annul-
casserola, –sĕrŏ'lä, f. saucepan.   [ling.
cassetta, –sĕt'tä, f. casket; alms-box.
cassettone, –tŏ'nĕ, m. chest of drawers; escritoire, bureau.
cassone, –sŏ'nĕ, m. great trunk, coffer.
castagna, –tän'yä, f. chestnut.   [trees.
castagneto, –yĕ'tŏ, m. grove of chestnut-
castagno, –tän'yŏ, m. chestnut-tree.
castellano, –tĕllä'nŏ, m. castellain; lord of a manor.
castello, –tĕl'lŏ, m. castle; (mar.) capstan.
castità, –tĭtä', f. chastity.
casto, käs'tŏ, a. chaste.
castoro, kästŏ'rŏ, m. beaver; castor-hat.
castrare, –trä'rĕ, v. a. to castrate, to geld.
castrato, –trä'tŏ, m. mutton; eunuch.
castroneria, –trŏnĕrĭ'ä, f. tattle, silliness.
casuale, käsŭä'lĕ, a. casual, accidental.
casualità, –lĭtä', f. casualty, chance.
catacomba, –täkŏm'bä, f. catacombs, pl.
catafalco, –fäl'kŏ, m. scaffold, funeral canopy.
catalessia, –lĕssĭ'ä, f. catalepsy, coma.
cataletto, –lĕt'tŏ, m. coffin, bier, litter.
catalogo, –tä'lŏgŏ, m. catalogue, list.
catapecchia, –pĕk'kĭä, f. wilderness.
catarrale, –tärrä'lĕ, a. catarrhal.
catarro, –tär'rŏ, m. catarrh, rheum, cold.
catarroso, –rŏ'sŏ, a. catarrhous.
catasta, –täs'tä, f. pile of wood; funeral pile.   [or ground-rent.
catastare, –tä'rĕ, v. a. to impose a tax
catasto, –täs'tŏ, m. rent-roll.
catastrofe, –täs'trŏfĕ, f. catastrophe.

catechismo, _těkĭs'mŏ_, m. catechism.
catechista, _kĭs'tă_, m. catechist.
catechizzare, _kĭt'zărĕ_, v. a. to catechise.
catecumeno, _kŏ'mēnŏ_, m. catechumen.
categoria, _gŏrē'ă_, f. category.'
categorico, _gŏ'rĭkŏ_, a. categorical.
catena, _tā'nă_, f. chain, fetter; ridge.
catenaccio, _těnăt'shŏ_, m. padlock.
catenare, _nā'rĕ_, v. a. to chain, to shackle.
cateratta, _rāt'tă_, f. sluice, flood-gate.
caterva, _těr'vă_, f. crowd, multitude; band.
catino, _tē'nŏ_, m. basin; kitchen-vessel.
catrame, _trā'mĕ_, m. tar.   [see.
cattedra, _kăt'tēdră_, f. public chair; papal
cattedrale, _drā'lĕ_, f. cathedral, head-
church.   [subdue, to master.
cattivare, _tĭvā'rĕ_, v. a. to captivate; to
cattività, _vĭtă'_, f. captivity; wickedness.
cattivo, _tē'vŏ_, a. a wretched, wicked;
miserable.   [cism.
cattolicismo, _tŏlĭdshĭs'mŏ_, m. Catholi-
cattolico, _tŏ'lĭkŏ_, a. catholic; pious.
cattura, _tŏ'rā_, f. seizure, apprehension.
catturare, _rā'rĕ_, v. a. to seize, to apprehend.
causa, _kāŭ'să_, f. cause, reason, origin;
law-suit, action; a – che, because.
causalità, _sălĭtă'_, f. causality.
causare, _sā'rĕ_, v. a. to cause, to occasion; to produce.
causidico, _sē'dĭkŏ_, m. pleader, advocate.
caustico, _kāŭs'tĭkŏ_, a. & m. caustic.
cautela, _tā'lă_, f. caution; precaution;
(jur.) security, bail.   [to bail.
cautelare, _lā'rĕ_, v. a. to answer for,
cauterio, _tā'rĭŏ_, m. cautery.
cauto, _kā'tŏ_, a. cautious, wary, prudent.
cauzione, _tzĭŏ'nĕ_, f. caution; security.
cava, _kā'vă_, f. cave, hole; quarry.   [bail.
cavalcare, _vălkā'rĕ_, v. n. to ride; to
domineer.
cavalcata, _kā'tă_, f. cavalcade.
cavaliere, _vālĭā'rĕ_, m. cavalier, knight;
horseman; da –, like a gentleman, nobly;
– d'industria, m. fortune-hunter.
cavalla, _văl'lă_, f. mare.
cavalleresco, _lěrēs'kŏ_, a. noble, gallant.
cavalleria, _lěrē'ă_, f. knighthood; horse,
cavalry.
cavallo, _văl'lŏ_, m. horse; horseman;
knight (at chess); sand-bank; – d'affitto,
cab-horse; – di corsa, race-horse; –
marino, sea-horse; – da sella, saddle-
horse; – verde, grass-hopper.
cavalocchio, _ŏk'kĭŏ_, m. wasp; exactor.
cavare, _vā'rĕ_, v. a. to take off; to dig.
cavata, _vā'tă_, f. ditch, pit; digging; –
di sangue, bleeding.
cavatina, _tē'nă_, f. (mus.) short air, arietta.
caverna, _věr'nă_, f. cavern, den, cave.
cavernoso, _nŏ'sŏ_, a. cavernous.
cavezza, _vět'ză_, f. halter; bridle.
cavezzone, _tzŏ'nĕ_, m. cavesson.
caviale, _vĭā'lĕ_, m. caviar.
caviglia, _vĭl'yă_, f. peg; ankle.
cavillare, _vĭllā'rĕ_, v. n. to cavil, to
wrangle.

cavità, _vĭtă'_, f. cavity, hole; pit.
cavo, _kā'vŏ_, a. hollow; concave; dug.
cavolo, _kā'vŏlŏ_, m. cabbage, colewort; –
fiore, m. cauliflower.
ce, _dshĕ'_, ad. here, there.
cecaggine, _kād'jĭnĕ_, f. blindness.
cecca, _dshĕk'kă_, f. magpie.
cece, _dshĕ'dshĕ_, m. chick-pease; vetch.
cecità, _dshĭtă'_, f. blindness; infatuation.
cedere, _dshā'dĕrĕ_, v. a. & n. reg. & ir. to
yield, to give up.
cedevole, _dshědă'vŏlĕ_, a. flexible; docile.
cedola, _dshā'dŏlă_, f. bill, bond.   [lemon.
cedrare, _drā'rĕ_, v. a. to season with
cedrato, _drā'tŏ_, m. lime; lime-tree; lime-
water.   [citron-coloured.
cedrino, _drē'nŏ_, a. made of cedar;
cedriuolo, _drĭāŏ'lŏ_, m. cucumber.
cedro, _dshā'drŏ_, m. cedar; citron; lime-tree.
ceduo, _dshā'dăŏ_, a. fit to be cut down.
ceffata, _fā'tă_, f. box on the ear, slap.
ceffo, _dshĕf'fŏ_, m. snout, muzzle.
ceffone, _fŏ'nĕ_, m. slap on the mouth.
celabro, see cervello.   [guise.
celare, _dshĕlā'rĕ_, v. a. to conceal, to dis-
celata, _lā'tă_, f. ambuscade; casket.
celato, _lā'tŏ_, a. concealed; latent.
celeberrimo, _lěbĕr'rĭmŏ_, a. very famous.
celebrante, _brăn'tĕ_, m. officiating
priest.   [to praise.
celebrare, _brā'rĕ_, v. a. to celebrate;
celebrazione, _tzĭŏ'nĕ_, f. celebration;
glory, praise.
celebre, _dshā'lěbrĕ_, a. famous, illustrious.
celebrità, _dshĕlěbrĭtă'_, f. celebrity.
celere, _dshā'lěrĕ_, a. swift, nimble.
celerità, _lěrĭtă'_, f. celerity, swiftness.
celeste, _lěs'tĕ_, a. celestial, heavenly.
cella, _dshā'lă_, f. joke, playfulness; trick.
cellare, _dshĕlā'rĕ_, v. a. & n. to jest, to
joke, to banter, to sport.
celibato, _lĭbā'tŏ_, m. celibacy.
celibe, _dshā'lĭbĕ_, a. single, unmarried.
cella, _dshĕl'lă_, f. cell; cellar, cave.
cellula, _dshĕl'lŭlă_, f. small cellar.
cellulare, _lā'rĕ_, celluloso, _lŏ'sŏ_, a.
cellular.
cembalo, _dshĕm'bălŏ_, m. cymbal, tabour.
cementare, _měntā'rĕ_, v. a. to cement,
to calcine.
cemento, _měn'tŏ_, m. cement.
cena, _dshā'nă_, f. supper.
cenacolo, _dshěnā'kŏlŏ_, m. supper-room.
cenare, _nā'rĕ_, v. n. to sup.
cenciaiuolo, _dshěndshāĭŭŏ'lŏ_, m. rag.
cencio, _dshěn'dshŏ_, m. rag, dish-clout.
cencioso, _dshŏ'sŏ_, a. ragged, in tatters.
cenere, _dshěn'ěrĕ_, m. & f. ashes, cinders,
pl.; remains, pl.; giorno delle ceneri,
m. Ash-Wednesday.
cenerino, _rē'nŏ_, a. ash-coloured.
cenno, _dshěn'nŏ_, m. sign, nod, signal,
command; hint.
cenobio, _nŏ'bĭŏ_, m. monastery, convent.
cenobita, _nŏbē'tă_, m. monk.
censo, _dshěn'sŏ_, m. rent, tribute; census.
censore, _sŏ'rĕ_, m. censor, critic.

censorio, –sŏ́ rĭŏ, a. censorious.
censura, –sŏ́ rä, f. censure; censorship.
censurare, –sū̆rä́ rĕ, v. a. to censure, to
centauro, –tä́u̇ rŏ, m. centaur.　　[blame.
centellino, –tĕl̄lē̆ nŏ, m. sip, small draught.
centenario, –tĕnä́ rĭŏ, a. centenary, centennial.
centesimo, –tĕ́ sĭmŏ, a. hundredth; hundredfold; –, m. cent (American coin).
centina, –tĕ́ nä, f. hundred; wooden frame.
cento, dshĕn̄' tŏ, a. & m. hundred.
centomila, –mē̆ lä, a. hundred-thousand.
centrico, dshĕn̄' trĭkŏ, a. centrical.
centrifugo, –trē̆ fū̆gŏ, a. centrifugal.
centripeto, –trē̆ pĕtŏ, a. centripetal.
centro, dshĕn̄' trŏ, m. centre; heart.
centupede, –tä́pä dĕ̆, m. wood-louse.
centuplicare, –plĭkä́ rĕ, v. a. to cen-
centuplo, –tä́plŏ, a. centuple.　　[tuplicate.
centuria, –tŏ́ rä̆, f. roman century;
century, anything consisting of a hundred
parts.
centurione, –tū̆rĭŏ' nĕ, m. centurion.
ceppo, dshĕ́p pŏ, m. stump, block; stock.
cera, dshä́ rä, f. wax; wax-candle.
ceralacca, dshĕrälä̆k' kä, f. sealing-wax.
cerasa, dshĕrä́ sä, f. cherry.
cerbiatto, dshĕrbĭä̆t' tŏ, m. fawn.
cerbottana, –bŏt̄tä́ nä, f. pea-shooter;
speaking-tube.
cerca, dshĕr̄' kä, f. search, inquiry.
cercare, –kä́ rĕ, v. a. to seek; to search;
to endeavour; to shift (for bread).
cerchia, dshĕr̄' kĭä, f. hoop.
cerchiaio, –kĭä́ ŏ, m. hoop-maker; cooper.
cerchiare, –kĭä́ rĕ, v. a. to hoop; to surround.　　　[land; enclosure; assembly.
cerchio, dshĕr̄' kĭŏ, m. circle; hoop; gur-
cercine, dshĕr̄' dshĭnĕ̆, m. porter's knot,
circular pad for the head of a porter.
cereale, dshĕrĕä́ lĕ, a. of Ceres; cereal.
cerebrale, –brä́ lĕ, a. cerebral.
cerebro, dshä́ rĕbrŏ, m. brain.
cereo, dshä́ rĕŏ, a. waxen, of wax.
cereria, dshĕrĕrē̆ ä, f. wax-chandry.
cerimonia, dshĕrĭmŏ́ nĭä, f. ceremony.
cerimoniale, –mŏnĭä́ lĕ, a. & m. ceremonial.　　　　　　　　　[ceremonies.
cerimoniere, –nĭä́ rĕ, m. master of the
cerimonioso, –nĭŏ́ sŏ, a. ceremonious,
formal.　　　　　　　　　　[choose.
cerna, dshĕr̄' nä, f. refuse, scum; far –, to
cernere, dshĕr̄' nĕrĕ̆, cernire, dshĕrnē̆ rĕ,
v. a. to choose, to pick; to sift; to discuss.
cerniera, –nĭä́ rä, f. hinge, joint.
cero, dshä́ rŏ, m. wax-candle, wax-taper;
ceroso, dshĕrŏ́ sŏ, a. waxen.　　[simpleton.
cerotto, –rŏt̄' tŏ, m. vesicatory.
cerretano, dshĕrrĕtä́ nŏ, m. charlatan,
cerreto, –rē̆ tŏ, m. forest of green oak- or
beech-trees.　　　　　　　　[of hair.
cerro, dshĕr̄' rŏ, m. green oak; fringe; lock
certame, –tä́ mĕ, m. (poet.) combat, fight;
duel, single combat.
certamente, –mĕn̄' tĕ, ad. certainly, surely.
certezza, –tĕt̄' zä, f. certitude, evidence.

certificare, –tĭfĭkä́ rĕ, v. a. to certify, to
confirm.
certo, dshĕr̄' tŏ, a. certain, positive; al –,
di –, per –, certainly; un –, some one,
a certain person; –, ad. certainly, indeed.
certosa, –tŏ́ sä, f. Carthusian monastery.
certosino, –tŏ́ sē̆ nŏ, m. Carthusian monk.
ceruleo, dshĕrŏ́ lĕŏ, a. cerulean, sky-blue.
cerume, dshĕrŏ́ mĕ̆, m. cerumen.
cerusico, –rŏ́ sĭkŏ, m. surgeon.
cerussa, –rŭs̄' sä, f. white-lead.
cerva, dshĕr̄' vä, f. hind (female stag).
cervellata, –vĕl̄lä́ tä, f. thick short sausage.　　　　　　　　　　　[head-cloth.
cervellino, –lē̆ nŏ, m. queer or odd man;
cervello, –vĕ̄l' lŏ, m. brain, brains, pl.;
judgment, sense; genius.
cervice, dshĕrvē̆ dshĕ̆, f. neck, back of the
cerviere, –vĭä́ rĕ, m. lynx.　　　　[neck.
cervio, dshĕr̄' vĭŏ, m. stag, hart.
cervo, dshĕr̄' vŏ, m. stag, hart; – volante,
cervogia, –vŏ́ jä, f. beer.　　　　[paper-kite.
cerziorare, –tzĭŏrä́ rĕ, v. a. to certify, to
inform, to instruct; cerziorarsi, –rär'-
sĭ, to inform oneself.
Cesare, dshä́ zärĕ̆, m. emperor.
cesellare, dshĕsĕl̄lä́ rĕ, v. a. to chisel.
cesellatore, –tŏ́ rĕ̆, m. carver, engraver.
cesello, –sĕ̄l' lŏ, m. chisel, graver.
cesoie, –sŏ́ ĕ, f. pl. pair of scissors, pl.
cespite, dshĕ́s pĭtĕ̆, cespo, dshĕ́s pŏ, m.
turf; bush; furze.
cespuglio, –pŭl' yŏ, m. turf, bush.
cessare, –sä́ rĕ, v. a. & n. to avoid; to
cease, to stop.　　　　　　　[ruption.
cessazione, –tzĭŏ' nĕ̆, f. cessation, inter-
cessionario, –sĭŏnä́ rĭŏ, m. cessionary.
cessione, –sĭŏ' nĕ̆, f. cession.
cesso, dshĕ́s sŏ, m. ceasing, giving up;
water-closet; small debt.
cesta, dshĕ́s tä, f. basket, fishing-basket.
cesto, dshĕ́s tŏ, m. bush, tuft; bushy plant;
basket.
cestone, –tŏ́ nĕ̆, m. large basket, hamper.
cesura, dshĕsŏ́ rä, f. cesura.
ceterare, –tĕrä́ rĕ, v.n. to play on the harp.
cetine, –tē̆ nĕ̆, f. pl. burning pits, pl.
ceto, dshä́ tŏ, m. (poet.) whale.
cetra, dshä́ trä, f. cithern, harp, lyre.
cetriuolo, see cedriuolo.
che, kĕ̆, pn. that, which, what, who, whom;
–, ad. when, as soon as; till; after; otherwise; –, c. because; until; for; that, than;
whether.
cheppia, kĕp̄' pĭä, f. shad-fish.
cherca, see cherica.
cherco, see cherico.
cherica, kä́ rĭkä, f. tonsure, shaven crown.
chericale, –kä́ lĕ, a. clerical.
chericato, –kä́ tŏ, m. clerkship.
cherico, kä́ rĭkŏ, m. clerk, priest.
chermisi, kĕr̄' mĭsĭ̆, m. crimson.
cherubino, kĕrŭbē̆ nŏ, m. cherub.
chetare, kĕtä́ rĕ, v. a. to appease, to
silence; chetarsi, –tär̄' sĭ, to grow calm,
to be silent.
cheto, kä́ tŏ, a. quiet, noiseless; gentle.

chi, *kï*, pn. who, whom, whoever, any one, some.

chiacchiera, *kïăk' kïĕră*, f. idle talk.

chiacchierare, *-kïĕră' rĕ*, v. n. to prate, to tattle, to chat, to chatter.

chiacchierata, *-ră' tă*, f. tittle-tattle.

chiacchierone, *-rŏ' nĕ*, m. great babbler.

chiama, *kïă' mă*, f. call; election.

chiamare, *-mă' rĕ*, v. a. to call, to name; to send for; to ask; chiamarsi, *-măr' sï*, to be named, to be called, [tion.

chiamata, *-mă' tă*, f. appeal, calling; elec-

chiappare, *kïăppă' rĕ*, v. a. to snatch, to catch.

chiara, *kïă' ră*, f. white of an egg.

chiaramente, *-mĕn' tĕ*, ad. clearly, honestly. [clearness, evidence.

chiarezza, *-rĕt' ză*, f. light, brightness,

chiarificare, *-rïfïkă' rĕ*, v. a. to clear, to explain.

chiarificazione, *-tzïŏ' nĕ*, f., chiarimento, *-rïmĕn' tŏ*, m. clarification; explication.

chiarire, *-rï rĕ*, v. a. to clear up, to reveal, to determine.

chiaro, *kïă' rŏ*, a. clear, bright; evident; illustrious, honest; true, loyal; —, ad. clearly; evidently; —, m. brightness, clearness; — di luna, moonshine, moonlight.

chiarore, *-rŏ' rĕ*, m. brightness, lustre.

chiaroscuro, *kïărŏskŏ' rŏ*, m. clare-obscure.

chiassata, *kïăssă' tă*, f. uproar, riot.

chiasso, *kïăs' sŏ*, m. uproar, clatter; brothel.

chiatta, *kïăt' tă*, f. ferry-boat.

chiavaccio, *-vă' shŏ*, m. padlock, iron-bolt.

chiavaio, *-vă' ŏ*, chiavaiuolo, *-văïŭŏ' lŏ*, m. locksmith.

chiavarda, *-văr' dă*, f. bolt, iron pin.

chiave, *kïă' vĕ*, f. key; tuning-key; stopcock; (mus.) clef; — maestra, master-key.

chiavetta, *-vĕt' tă*, f. small key; (mar.) forelock.

chiavica, *kïă' vïkă*, f. common sewer, drain.

chiavistello, *-stĕl' lŏ*, m. padlock; screw-vice, screw-wrench, spanner.

chiazza, *kïăt' ză*, f. scab, scar, freckle.

chiazzare, *-tză' rĕ*, v. a. to speckle.

chiazzato, *-tză' tŏ*, a. speckled.

chicca, *kïk' kă*, f. sweet-meats.

chicchera, *kïk' kĕră*, f. cup.

chicchessia, (chi che sia) *-kĕssĕ' ă*, pn. whoever.

chicco, *kïk' kŏ*, m. grain, seed.

chiedere, *kïĕ' dĕrĕ*, v. a. ir. to demand, to ask; to beg; to inquire.

chiesa, *kïĕ' să*, f. church.

chiesta, *kïĕs' tă*, f. demand, request.

chiesto, *-tŏ*, a. demanded, requested; sought.

chietino, *kïĕtï' nŏ*, m. church-goer; bigot.

chiglia, *kïl' ÿă*, f. keel, careen.

chilifero, *-lï' fĕrŏ*, a. chylous.

chilificare, *-lïfïkă' rĕ*, v. a. to form into chyle; to digest.

chilo, *kĕ' lŏ*, m. (med.) chyle.

chimera, *kïmĕ' ră*, f. chimera, illusion.

chimerico, *-mĕ' rïkŏ*, a. chimerical, imaginary. [castles in the air.

chimerizzare, *-mĕrïtză' rĕ*, v. a. to build

chimica, *kĕ' mïkă*, f. chemistry.

chimicamente, *-mĕn' tĕ*, ad. chemically.

chimico, *kĕ' mïkŏ* m. chemist; —, a. chemical.

china, *kĕ' nă*, f. declivity, slope. [ical.

chinachina, *-năkĕ' nă*, f. quinquina, Peruvian bark.

chinare, *-nă' rĕ*, v. a. to bend, to bow; to stoop down; — gli occhi, to look down; chinarsi, *-năr' sï*, to be inclined; to begin to fall.

chincagliere, *kïnkălÿĕ' rĕ*, m. hardware-man.

chincaglieria, *-kălÿĕrï' ă*, f. hardware.

chinea, *-nĕ' ă*, f. ambling pad.

chino, *kĕ' nŏ*, a. bent; cast down; deep; —, m. declivity, slope.

chioccare, *kïŏkkă' rĕ*,v.a.to cuff,to thwack.

chioccia, *kïŏt' shă*, f. brood-hen.

chiocciare, *-tshă' rĕ*, v. n. to cluck.

chioccio, *kïŏt' shŏ*, a. hoarse; clucking.

chiocciola, *kïŏt' shŏlă*, f. snail; female-screw; scala a —, winding or screw staircase. [biscuit.

chiocciolino, *-shŏlï' nŏ*, m. small screw;

chiodagione, *-dăÿŏ' nĕ*, f. heap of nails; nail-work. [maker.

chiodaiuolo, *-dăïŭŏ' lŏ*, m. nailer, nail-chiodare, *-dă' rĕ*, v. a. to nail up, to fasten with nails. [nail-work; nail-trade.

chioderia, *-dĕrï' ă*, f. nail-manufactory; chiodetto, *-dĕt' tŏ*, chiodino, *-dï' nŏ*, m. small nail, peg, pin.

chiodo, *kïŏ' dŏ*, m. nail; hob-nail.

chioma, *kïŏ' mă*, f. man's hair, ringlet, curl.

chiomato, *-mă' tŏ*, a. hairy, covered with hair. [tration; freckle.

chiosa, *kïŏ' să*, f. glossary, comment; illus-

chiosare, *kïŏsă' rĕ*,v.a.to gloss,to comment.

chiosatore, *-tŏ' rĕ*, m. glosser. [walls.

chiostra, *kïŏs' tră*, f. place surrounded by

chiostro, *kïŏs' trŏ*, m. cloister, convent-porch; back-court (of a house).

chiotto, *kïŏt' tŏ*, a. still as a mouse.

chiragra, *kïră' gră*, f. chiragra.

chirografo, *-rŏ' grăfŏ*, m. bond under one's own hand.

chiromante, *-rŏmăn' tĕ*, m. chiromancer.

chiromanzia, *-măntză' ă*, f. chiromancy.

chirurgia, *-rŭrÿï' ă*, f. surgery.

chirurgico, *-rŭr' ÿïkŏ*, a. surgical.

chirurgo, *-rŭr' gŏ*, m. surgeon.

chitarra, *-tăr' ră*, f. guitar. [sical talk.

chiucchiurlaia, *kïŭkkïŭrlă' ă*, f. nonsen-

chiudenda, *-dĕn' dă*, f. enclosure, hedge.

chiudere, *kïŭ' dĕrĕ*, v. a. ir. to enclose, to shut, to fence. [owls).

chiurlare, *kïŭrlă' rĕ*, v. n. to hoot (of chiurlo, *kïŭr' lŏ*, m. bird-catching with bird-lime; dolt, dunce.

chiusa, *kïŭ' să*, f. enclosure; prison.

chiusino, *kïŭsï' nŏ*, m. cover, lid; stopper.

chiuso, *kïŭ' sŏ*, a. enclosed, shut up; —, m. enclosure, fence. [a door.

chiusura, *kïŭsŏ' ră*, f. enclosure; lock oi

ci, *dshï*, pn. us, to us; —, c. here, there.

ciaba, *dshă′bă*, **ciabattiere**, *-tǐǐ′rĕ*, m. cobbler, bungler.

ciaccherino, *-kĕrĕ′nŏ*, m. young pig.

ciacco, *dshăk′kŏ*, m. hog; spunger.

cialda, *dshăl′dă*, f. wafer, crackling cake.

cialtrone, *-trŏ′nĕ*, m. rogue, cheat.

ciambella, *dshămbĕl′lă*, f. cracknel, twisted bun.

ciambellotto, *-bĕllŏt′tŏ*, m. camlet.

ciamberlano, *-bĕrlă′nŏ*, m. chamberlain.

ciampicare, *-pĭkă′rĕ*, v. n. to stumble.

ciancia, *dshăn′dshă*, f. jest, banter; chit-chat; sport.   [prate, to trifle.

cianciare, *-dshă′rĕ*, v. n. to joke; to

ciancicare, *-dshĭkă′rĕ*, v. n. to stutter.

ciangolare, *-gŏlă′rĕ*, v. n. to prattle, to

ciano,*dshă′nŏ*, m. corn-flower. [chatter.

ciapperone, *dshăppĕrŏ′nĕ*, m. chaperon; hood.

ciaramella, *dshărămĕl′lă*, f. babbler.

ciaramellare, *-mĕllă′rĕ*, v. n. to tattle, to chat.

ciarla, *dshăr′lă*, **ciarlata**, *-lă′tă*, f. prattling, talkativeness; nonsense.

ciarlare, *-lă′rĕ*, v. n. to prattle.

ciarlataneria, *-tănĕrĕ′ă*, f. talkativeness; quackery.

ciarlatano, *-tă′nŏ*, m. quack, cheat.

ciarlatore, *-tŏ′rĕ*, m. babbler, tattler.

ciarleria, *-ĕrĕ′ă*, f. chit-chat, prattle.

ciarliere, *-lĭĕ′rĕ*, **ciarliero**, *-lĭĕ′rŏ*, m. babbler, idle talker.

ciarlone, *-lŏ′nĕ*, m. everlasting talker.

ciarpa, *dshăr′pă*, f. rags, tatters, pl.; frippery.

ciarpame, *-pă′mĕ*, m. heap of rags.

ciarpare, *-pă′rĕ*, v. a. & n. to botch; to cobble, to bungle.

ciascheduno, *dshăskĕdŏ′nŏ*, **ciascuno**, *-kŏ′nŏ*, pn. each, every one.

cibare, *dshĭbă′rĕ*, v. a. to feed; to nourish.

cibo, *dshĭ′bŏ*, m. food, aliment.

cibreo, *dshĭbrĕ′ŏ*, m. fricassee of chicken.

cica, *dshĭ′kă*, f. nothing; —, ad. not a bit.

cicala, *-kă′lă*, f. grasshopper; chatterer.

cicalare, *-lă′rĕ*, v. n. to prate.

cicalata, *-lă′tă*, f. chit-chat, prattle.

cicatrice, *-trĕ′dshĕ*, f. cicatrice, scar; fraud, cheat, deceit.

ciccantona, *-kăntŏ′nă*, f. strumpet.

ciccia, *dshĭt′shă*, f. flesh (nursery-word).

cicciolo, *-shŏlŏ*, m. flesh (nursery-word).

cicerbita, *dshĭdshĕr′bĭtă*, f. sow-thistle.

cicerchia, *-dshĕr′kĭă*, f. vetch, chick-peas.

cicisbeo, *-dshĭsbĕ′ŏ*, m. gallant, spark.

ciclo, *dshĭ′klŏ*, m. cycle, period of time.

cicogna, *-kŏn′yă*, f. stork; beam (of a bell).

cicognino, *-ȳĭ′nŏ*, m. young stork.

cicoria, *-kŏ′rĭă*, f. chicory, endive.

cicuta, *-kŏ′tă*, f. hemlock.

cieco, *dshĭĕ′kŏ*, a. blind; dark, gloomy; hidden; —, m. blind-man.

ciecolina, *-lĕ′nă*, f. grig (fish). [climate.

cielo, *dshĭĕl′ŏ*, m. heaven; sky; daylight;

cifra, *dshĭ′ră*, f. cipher; device.

cifrare, *-ră′rĕ*, v. a. to write in cipher.

ciglio, *dshĭl′yŏ*, m. eyebrow.

cigna, *dshĭn′yă*, f. girth, girdle.

cignare, *-yă′rĕ*, **cignere**, *dshĭn′yĕrĕ*, v. a. ir. to gird; to embrace.

cigno, *dshĭn′yŏ*, m. swan.   [band.

cignone, *-nŏ′nĕ*, m. under-girth, belly-band.

cigolare, *dshĭgŏlă′rĕ*, v. n. to rattle, to creak.   [vain promise.

cilecca, *-lĕk′kă*, f. balk; disappointment.

cilestro, *-lĕs′trŏ*, m. blue colour.

cilindro, *-lĭn′drŏ*, m. cylinder, roller.

cilizio, *-lĭ′dzĭŏ*, m. hair-cloth.

cima, *dshĕ′mă*, f. summit, top; (fig.) eminence.   [to lop.

cimare, *dshĭmă′rĕ*, v. a. to shear (cloth);

cimbotto(lo), *dshĕmbŏt′tŏ(lŏ)*, m. tumble.

cimelio, *-mă′lĭŏ*, m. antique remains or relics.   [try.

cimentare, *-mĕntă′rĕ*, v. a. to attempt, to

cimento, *-mĕn′tŏ*, m. trial, essay, proof.

cimice, *dshă′mĭdshĕ*, f. bug; poltroon.

cimiero, *dshĭmĭĕ′rŏ*, m. crest (of a helmet).

cimitero, *-tă′rŏ*, m. churchyard.

cimurro, *-mŭr′rŏ*, m. glanders, pl.

cina, *dshĕ′nă*, f. Jesuit's bark.

cinabro, *dshĭnă′brŏ*, m. cinnabar.

cincia, *-dshĭn′dshă*, **cingallegra**, *-găl-lă′gră*, f. tit-mouse, tom-tit.   [stammer.

cincischiare, *-dshĭskĭă′rĕ*, v.a. to hack; to

cincischio, *-dshĭs′kĭŏ*, **cincistio**, *-dshĭs′tĭŏ*, m. hacking; cut made with a tool.

cinerizio, *-nĕrĕ′dzĭŏ*, a. ash-coloured.

cingere, *see* **cignare**.   [lashen.

cinghia, *dshĭn′ghĭă*, f. girth for a horse.

cinghiale, *-ghĭă′lĕ*, m. wild boar.

cinghiare, *-ghĭă′rĕ*, v. a. to gird; to surround.

cinghio, *dshĭn′ghĭŏ*, m. circle, circuit.

cinguettare, *-gŭĕttă′rĕ*, v. n. to lisp, to chatter; to prate.

cinguettio, *-gŭĕttĕ′ŏ*, m. prattle.

ciniglia, *-nĭl′yă*, f. caterpillar; chenille.

cinnamo, *dshĭn′nămŏ*, **cinnamomo**, *-mŏ′mŏ*, m. cinnamon.

cinquanta, *-kŭăn′tă*, a. fifty.

cinquantesimo, *-tă′sĭmŏ*, a. fiftieth.

cinque, *dshĭn′kŭĕ*, a. five.   [years.

cinquennio, *-kŭĕn′nĭŏ*, m. space of five

cinta, *dshĭn′tă*, f. enclosure; girdle.

cinto, *dshĭn′tŏ*, m. cincture, girdle; halo.

cintura, *-tŏ′ră*, f. cincture, string.

ciò, *dshŏ′*, pn. this, that, what, which.

ciocca, *dshŏk′kă*, f. cluster (of flowers &c.), bunch, tuft.

ciocchè, *-kĕ′*, pn. what, that which.

ciocchetta, *-kĕt′tă*, f. small tuft.

ciocco, *dshŏk′kŏ*, m. log, billet (of wood); block-head.

cioccolatte, *-lăt′tĕ*, f. chocolate.

cioè, *dshŏĕ′*, ad. that is, that is to say, namely.

ciompo, *dshŏm′pŏ*, m. carder; clown.

cioncare, *dshŏnkă′rĕ*, v. n. to tipple; to mangle; to cut, to fell.

ciondolare, *-dŏlă′rĕ*, v. n. to hang dangling, to shake about.

ciondolo, *dshŏn′dŏlŏ*, m. thing that hangs dangling.

ciondolone, *-lŏ′nĕ*, m. lounger, sluggard.

ciotola, _dshŏ′ tŏlä_, f. cup, board.
ciottolo, _dshŏt′ tŏlŏ_, m. flint-stone, pebble.
cipiglio, _dshipil′ yŏ_, m. rancorous look, frowning. [onion, bulb.
cipolla, _–pŏl′lä_, cipollina, _–lĕ′nä_, f.
cipresso, _–prĕs′sŏ_, m. cypress; occiput.
circa, _dshir′kä_, pr. & ad. about; almost.
circo, _dshir′kŏ_, m. circus.
circolare, _–kōlä′rĕ_, v. n. to circulate, to go round; –, a. circular.
circolo, _dshir′kŏlŏ_, m. circle, circuit.
circoncidere, _–kŏndshĕ′dĕrĕ_, circon-cire, _–dshĕ′rĕ_, v. a. to circumcise.
circoncisione, _–dshĭsiŏ′nĕ_, f. circum-cision. [environ, to surround.
circondare, _–dä′rĕ_, v. a. to enclose, to
circondario, _–dä′riŏ_, m. boundaries, pl.; district, territory. [ference.
circonferenza, _–fĕrĕn′tzä_, f. circum-
circonflesso, _–flĕs′sŏ_, a., accento –, m. circumflex. [flex.
circonflettere, _–flĕt′tĕrĕ_, v. a. to circum-
circonlocuzione, _–lŏkŭtziŏ′nĕ_, f. circum-locution. [vent, to overreach.
circonvenire, _–vĕnĕ′rĕ_, v. a. to circum-
circoscritto, _–skrit′tŏ_, a. circumscribed, limited. [scribe, to limit.
circoscrivere, _–skrĕ′vĕrĕ_, v. a. to circum-
circostanza, _–stän′tzä_, f. circumstance; particularity.
circuire, _dshirkŭĕ′rĕ_, v. a. to surround, to enclose; –, v. n. to go round.
circuito, _–kŏ′ĭtŏ_, m. circuit, compass.
ciriegia, _dshiriĕ′dshä_, f. cherry.
cirro, _dshir′rŏ_, m. man's hair, curl, ringlet.
ciscranna, _dshiskrän′nä_, f. folding-chair.
cispa, _dshis′pä_, f. blearedness.
cisposo, _–pŏ′sŏ_, a. blear-eyed; rheumy.
cisterna, _–tĕr′nä_, f. cistern, tank.
citare, _dshitä′rĕ_, v. a. to cite, to summon; to quote.
citazione, _–tziŏ′nĕ_, f. citation, summons.
citeriore, _–tĕriŏ′rĕ_, a. nearer; hither-most.
citiso, _dshĕ′tisŏ_, m. heath, fern.
citrullo, _dshitrŭl′lŏ_, m. block-head.
città, _dshittä′_, f. city, town; burghership.
cittadella, _–dĕl′lä_,f.borough; (mil.) citadel.
cittadina, _–dĕ′nä_, f. citizen's wife.
cittadinanza, _–dĕnän′tzä_, f. burghership, citizenship; citizens,pl.; humanity, home.
cittadino, _–dĕ′nŏ_, m. citizen, burgess.
civaia, _dshä′ä_, f. all kinds of pulse; vege-tables, pl.
ciuco, _dshŭ′kŏ_, m. ass; block-head.
ciuffare, _dshŭffä′rĕ_, v. a. to catch, to snatch.
ciuffo, _dshŭf′fŏ_, m. lock of hair, toupet.
ciurma, _dshŭr′mä_, f. ship's crew; galley-slaves; rabble; deceit.
ciurmaglia, _–mäl′yä_, f. mob, rabble.
ciurmare, _–mä′rĕ_, v. a. to charm; to cheat.
civetta, _dshivĕt′tä_, f. screech-owl; coquette.
civettare, _–tä′rĕ_, v. n. to coquet; to trifle.
civile, _–vĕ′lĕ_, a. civil, polite; gracious.

civiltà, _–vĭltä′_, f. civility, politeness.
clandestino, _kländĕstĕ′nŏ_, a. clandestine, secret. [(of trumpets).
clangore, _–gŏ′rĕ_, m. clankour, flourish
claretto, _klärĕt′tŏ_, m. claret (wine).
classe, _kläs′sĕ_, f. class; rank, order.
classico, _kläs′sikŏ_, a. classical.
classificare, _–fikä′rĕ_, v. a. to classify.
clausola, _kläŭ′sŏlä_, f. clause.
claustrale, _–strä′lĕ_, a. claustral; solitary.
claustro, _kläŭs′trŏ_, m. (poet.) cloister.
clausura, _–sŏ′rä_, f. enclosure; monastery.
clava, _klä′vä_, f. club.
clavicembalo, _–vidshĕm′bälŏ_, m. harp-sichord, pianoforte.
clavicola, _–vĕ′kŏlä_, f. (an.) clavicule.
clavicordio, _–vikŏr′diŏ_, m. clavichord.
clavo, _klä′vŏ_, m. nail; helm.
clemente, _klĕmĕn′tĕ_, a. clement, gentle.
clemenza, _–mĕn′tzä_, f. clemency.
clericale, _klĕrikä′lĕ_, a. clerical.
clero, _klä′rŏ_, m. clergy.
cliente, _kliĕn′tĕ_, m. client.
clientela, _–tä′lä_, f. patronage; protection; clients.
clima, _klĕ′mä_, f. climate; country.
clinico, _klĕ′nikŏ_, a. clinical.
clipeo, _klĕ′pĕŏ_, m. shield, target.
clistere, _klistä′rĕ_, m. clyster.
clivo, _klĕ′vŏ_, a. & m. declivous, declivity, hill.
clizia, _klĕ′dziä_, f. sun-flower.
cloaca, _klŏä′kä_, f. sewer, sink.
co′, _kŏ_, abbrev. of coi, with them.
coabitare, _–äbitä′rĕ_, v. n. to cohabit.
coacervare, _–ädshĕrvä′rĕ_, v. a. to heap up.
coadiutore, _–tŏ′rĕ_, m. coadjutor.
coadiuvare, _–ŭvä′rĕ_, v. a. to help, to assist. [assemble.
coadunare, _–dŭnä′rĕ_, v. a. to collect, to
coagulare, _–gŭlä′rĕ_, v. a. & n. to co-agulate.
coagulo, _–ä′gŭlŏ_, m. rennet, runnet.
coartare, _–ärtä′rĕ_, v. a. to restrict, to con-tract. [sion.
coazione, _–ätziŏ′nĕ_, f. coaction, compul-
cocca, _kŏk′kä_, f. notch of an arrow.
coccarda, _–kär′dä_, f. cockade.
cocchiere, _–kiĕ′rĕ_, m. coachman.
cocchio, _kŏk′kiŏ_, m. coach, carriage.
cocchiume, _–kiŏ′mĕ_, m. bung-hole.
cocciniglia, _–tshinĕl′yä_, f. cochineal.
coccio, _kŏt′shŏ_, m. pot-sherd. [ness.
cocciutaggine, _–tshiŭtäd′jinĕ_, f. stubborn-
cocciuto, _–tshiŏ′tŏ_, a. stubborn, obstinate.
cocco, _kŏk′kŏ_, m. cocoa.
coccodrillo, _–kŏdril′lŏ_, m. crocodile.
coccola, _kŏk′kŏlä_, f. berry.
cocere, see cuocere.
cocolla, _–kŏl′lä_, f. cowl, frock (of a monk).
cocomeraio, _–kŏmĕrä′ŏ_, m. water-melon bed; seller of water-melons.
cocomero, _–kŏ′mĕrŏ_, m. water-melon.
cocuzzo, _–kŭt′zŏ_, cocuzzolo, _–zŏlŏ_, m. crown of the head, top, summit.
coda, _kŏ′dä_, f. tail; train, end, hinder-part.
codardia, _–därdĕ′ä_, f. cowardice.

codardo, –dăr' dŏ, a. coward, vile.
codazzo, –dăt' zŏ, m. attendants, train.
codiare, –dĭă' rĕ, v. n. to be at one's heels, to dog; to observe, to spy.
codice, kŏ' dĭdzhĕ, m. code.
codicillo, kŏdĭdshīl' lŏ, m. codicil.
cod(r)ione, –d(r)ĭŏ' nĕ, m. rump.
coerede, kŏĕră' dĕ, m. joint-heir.
coerente, –ĕrĕn' tĕ, a. coherent.
coerenza, –ĕrĕn' tză, f. coherence.
coesione, –ĕsĭŏ' nĕ, f. cohesion, connexion.
coesistere, –ĕsĭs' tĕrĕ, v. n. to coexist.
coetaneo, –ĕtă' nĕŏ, a. contemporary.
coevo, –ĕ' vŏ, a. coeval, contemporary.
cofaccia, –făt' shă, f. bun, cake.
cofano, kŏ' fănŏ, m. basket; trunk, coffer.
coffa, kŏf' fă, f. (mar.) scuttle.
cogliere, kŏl' yĕrĕ, v. a. ir. to gather; to pick up.   [allied, related, kindred.
cognato, kŏnyă' tŏ, m. brother-in-law; –, a.
cognito, kŏn' yĭtŏ, a. known.
cognazione, –yătzĭŏ' nĕ, f. cognation.
cognizione, –yĭtzĭŏ' nĕ, f. knowledge.
cognome, –yŏ' mĕ, m. surname.
coiame, kŏiă' mĕ, m. quantity of hides.
coincidere, kŏindshē' dĕrĕ, v. n. ir. to coincide.
coito, kŏ' ĭtŏ, m. coition, lying with.   [cide.
coiaio, kŏiă' ŏ, m. tanner, currier.
col, kŏl, for collo, con lo.
cola, kŏ' lă, f. strainer, filter.
colà, kŏlă', ad. there, yonder.
colaggiù, –lădjū', ad. down there.
colare, –lă' rĕ, v. a. to strain through, to
colassù, –lăssū', ad. there above.   [filter.
colazione, –tzĭŏ' nĕ, f. breakfast.
colcare, kŏlkă' rĕ, v. a. to lay down, to
colei, kŏlă' ĭ, pn. she.   [stretch.
colere, kŏ' lĕrĕ, v. a. (poet.) to worship.
colibrì, kŏlĭbrī', m. humming-bird.
colica, kŏ' lĭkă, f. colic.
colico, kŏ' lĭkŏ, a. colic, gripping.
colla, kŏl' lă, m. glue; cord.
colla, kŏl' lă, for con la.
collana, kŏllă' nă, f. necklace, necklet.
collare, –lă' rĕ, v. a. to scourge; to lower with a rope; –, m. collar.
collaterale, –lătĕră' lĕ, a. & m. collateral.
collazionare, –tzĭŏnă' rĕ, v. a. to collate, to confront.   [fronting.
collazione, –tzĭŏ' nĕ, f. collation; con-
colle, kŏl' lĕ, m. (poet.) hillock.
collega, –lă' gă, m. colleague, adjutor; –, f. league, alliance.   [to join.
collegare, –lĕgă' rĕ, v. a. to bind, to unite,
collegiale, –lĕjiă' lĕ, a. collegial.
collegio, –lă' jĭŏ, m. college; community.
collera, kŏl' lĕră, f. anger, wrath.
collerico, –lă' rĭkŏ, a. choleric, irascible.
colletta, –lĕt' tă, f. collection; harvest.
collettivo, –tĕ' vŏ, a. collective.
colletto, –lĕt' tŏ, m. hillock; tippet.
collezione, –lĕtzĭŏ' nĕ, f. collection; impost.
collimare, –lĭmă' rĕ, v. n. to aim at; to
collina, –lĕ' nă, f. hill, hillock.   [strive.
colliquare, –lĭkŭă' rĕ, v. a. to liquefy.
collisione, –sĭŏ' nĕ, f. collision; clash.

collo, kŏl' lŏ, for con lo.
collo, kŏl' lŏ, m. neck; summit, top.
collocare, –kă' rĕ, v. a. to place, to arrange.   [sation.
colloquio, –lŏ' kŭĭŏ, m. discourse, conver-
collotorto, –lŏtŏr' tŏ, m. wry-neck; hypocrite.
collottola, –lŏt' tŏlă, f. nape of the neck.
colluvie, –lŏ' vĭĕ, f. crowd, mob.
colmare, –mă' rĕ, v. a. to pile up, to heap; to overcharge.
colmata, –mă' tă, f. filling up; embankment, causeway.   [with.
colmo, kŏl' mŏ, a. full, overfull; loaded
colo, kŏ' lŏ, m. sieve, strainer; fan.
colomba, kŏlŏm' bă, f. dove; keel.
colombaia, –bă' ă, f., colombaio, –bă' ŏ, m. pigeon-house.
colombina, –bē' nă, f. pigeon's dung.
colombo, –lŏm' bŏ, m. pigeon, dove.
colonia, –lŏ' nĭă, f. colony, plantation.
colonna, –lŏn' nă, f. column; bed-post; file.
colonnata, –nă' tă, f. colonnade.
colonnello, –nĕl' lŏ, m. (mil.) colonel; little column.
colonnino, –nē' nŏ, m. little column.
colono, –lŏ' nŏ, m. colonist.
colorare, –lŏră' rĕ, colorire, –rē' rĕ, v. a. to dye, to paint; to adorn; to disguise.
colore, –lŏ' rĕ, m. colour; pretence; appearance.
coloro, –lŏ' rŏ, pn. they, those.
colossale, –lŏssă' lĕ, a. colossal, gigantic.
colosseo, –lŏssĕ' ŏ, m. coliseum (at Rome).
colosso, –lŏs' sŏ, m. colossus.
colpa, kŏl' pă, f. fault, error; offence, sin.
colpevole, –pă' vŏlĕ, a. culpable, faulty.
colpire, –pē' rĕ, v. a. to strike; to hit the mark; to wound.
colpo, kŏl' pŏ, m. blow, stroke; hit; wound; ad un –, di –, all at once; – di fucile, gun-shot; – di (da) maestro, masterly stroke.   [ing.
colta, kŏl' tă, f. collecting (of taxes); gather-
coltella, –tĕl' lă, f. cutlass, hanger; coulter; polishing-iron.
coltellata, –lă' tă, f. cut, stab (with a knife).
coltelliera, –tĕllĭĕ' ră, f. sheath, case.
coltello, –tĕl' lŏ, m. knife, dagger.
coltivare, –tĭvă' rĕ, v. a. to cultivate; to improve; to exercise.
coltivatore, –tŏ' rĕ, m. cultivator, ploughman, tiller.   [worship.
coltivazione, –tzĭŏ' nĕ, f. cultivation;
colto, kŏl' tŏ, a. cultivated; improved, refined; –, m. ploughed land; worship.
coltre, kŏl' trĕ, f. coverlet, counterpane; shroud, pall; perch, mete-wand.
coltrone, –trŏ' nĕ, m. coverlet, quilt.
coltura, –tŏ' ră, f. culture; worship.
colubrina, –lŭbrē' nă, f. culverin.
colubro, kŏlŭ' brŏ, m. (poet.) snake.
colui, kŏlŭ' ĭ, pn. he, that.   [chief.
comandante, –măndăn' tĕ, m. commander,
comandare, –măndă' rĕ, v. a. to command.
comando, –măn' dŏ, m. command, order.
comare, –mă' rĕ, f. midwife; gossip; godmother.

combaciare, *kŏmbādshā'rĕ,* v. a. & n. to join, together; to be contiguous.

combattere, *–bā'tĕrĕ,* v. a. & n. to fight; to harass; to oppose; to besiege.

combattimento, *–tĭmĕn'tŏ,* m. fight, battle.

combinare, *–bĭnā'rĕ,* v. a. to combine, to assemble. [union.

combinazione, *–tzĭŏ'nĕ,* f. combination,

combriccola, *–brēk'kŏlă,* f. conventicle.

combustibile, *–bŭstĕ'bĭlĕ,* a. combustible.

combustione, *–bŭstĭŏ'nĕ,* f. combustion, burning; conflagration.

come, *kŏ'mĕ,* ad. & c. so; as, like; when; as soon as; how? why? what? –, c. although.

comecchè, *kŏmĕkkĕ',* c. however, though.

cometa, *–mā'tă,* f. comet.

comico, *kŏ'mĭkŏ,* a. & m. comical; comic actor *or* writer.

comignolo, *kŏmĭn'yŏlŏ,* m. ridge of a roof.

cominciare, *–dshā'rĕ,* v. a. to begin, to commence.

comino, *–mĕ'nŏ,* m. cumin.

comitiva, *–mātĕ'vă,* f. attendants, pl.

comizio, *–mĕ'tzĭŏ,* m. assembly, diet.

commedia, *kŏmmā'dĭă,* f. comedy; play-house. [memorable.

commemorabile, *–mĕmŏrā'bĭlĕ,* a. com-

commemorare, *–rā'rĕ,* v. a. to commemorate. [mendam.

commenda, *–mĕn'dă,* f. commandery, com-

commendare, *–dā'rĕ,* v. a. to commend, to recommend.

commensale, *–sā'lĕ,* m. table-companion.

commensurabile, *–sŭrā'bĭlĕ,* a. commensurable.

commentare, *–tā'rĕ,* v. n. to comment.

commentario, *–tā'rĭŏ,* m. commentary.

commentatore, *–tŏ'rĕ,* m. commentator.

commento, *–mĕn'tŏ,* m. comment.

commerciante, *–mĕrdshăn'tĕ,* m. merchant, tradesman.

commercio, *–mĕr'dshŏ,* m. commerce, trade, traffic; affair; correspondence.

commestibile, *–mĕstĕ'bĭlĕ,* a. eatable.

commettere, *–mĕt'tĕrĕ,* v. a. ir. to commit; to sin; to lay in; to order.

commettitura, *–tītŏ'ră,* f. joining.

commiato, *–mĭā'tŏ,* m. leave, dismissal.

commilitone, *–mĭlĭtŏ'nĕ,*m.fellow-soldier; companion, school-fellow.

commischiare, *–mĭskĭā'rĕ,* v. a. to mix together.

commiserare, *–mĭsĕrā'rĕ,* v. a. to commiserate, to take pity. [truster.

commissario, *–mĭssā'rĭŏ,* m. commissary;

commissione, *–mĭssĭŏ'nĕ,* f. commission, order, charge.

commisto, *–mĭs'tŏ,* a. mixed, confounded.

commovimento, *–mŏvĭmĕn'tŏ,* m. commotion, tumult, uproar.

commozione, *–mŏtzĭŏ'nĕ,* f. commotion, emotion, trouble. [to strengthen.

communire, *–mănĕ'rĕ,* v. a. to fortify,

commuovere, *–mŭŏ'vĕrĕ,* v. a. ir. to move; to touch; to disturb, to vex.

comodare, *–mŏdā'rĕ,* v. a. to fit; to dress, to trim; to lend.

comodità, *–mŏdĭtă',* f. conveniency, opportunity, occasion; riches.

comodo, *kŏ'mŏdŏ,* a. convenient, useful; fit; opportune; –, m. conveniency, ease; advantage, profit; a vostro –, at your leisure. [panion.

compagna, *kŏmpan'yă,* f. female com-

compagnevole, *–yā'vŏlĕ,* a. sociable.

compagnia, *–yĕ'ă,* f. company, society.

compagno, *–pan'yŏ,* m. companion, comrade, school-fellow; mate, partner.

companatico, *–nā'tĭkŏ,* m. victuals eaten with bread, pl.

comparare, *–pārā'rĕ,* v. a. to compare.

compare, *–pā'rĕ,* m. godfather; compeer.

comparire, *–rĕ'rĕ,* v. n. to appear.

comparsa, *–păr'să,* f. appearance.

compartimento, *–tĭmĕn'tŏ,* m. compartment, partition. [share.

compartire, *–tĕ'rĕ,* v. a. to divide, to

compassare, *–păssā'rĕ,* v. a. to measure with compasses; to consider.

compassionare, *–sĭŏnā'rĕ,* v. a. to pity, to commiserate. [mercy.

compassione, *–sĭŏ'nĕ,* f. compassion,

compassionevole, *–sĭŏnā'vŏlĕ,* a. exciting pity, pitiful.

compasso, *–păs'sŏ,* m. compass, compartment; compasses, pl.

compatibile, *–pātĕ'bĭlĕ* a. compatible, pardonable.

compatire, *–tĕ'rĕ,* v. a. to pity; to excuse.

compatto, *–păt'tŏ,* a. compact, solid.

compendiare, *–pĕndĭā'rĕ,* v. a. to abridge.

compendio, *–pĕn'dĭŏ,* m. abridgment, compendium. [to permeate.

compenetrare, *–pĕnĕtrā'rĕ,* v. a. to

compensare, *–pĕnsā'rĕ,* v. a. to compensate, to indemnify.

competente, *kŏmpĕtĕn'tĕ,* a. competent, qualified. [competition.

competenza, *–tĕn'tză,* f. competency;

competere, *–pĕ'tĕrĕ,* v. a. to compete.

competitore, *–tĭtŏ'rĕ,* m. competitor.

compiacente, *–pĭādshĕn'tĕ,* a. complaisant, polite, obliging, kind.

compiacenza, *–dshĕn'tză,* f. complacency.

compiacere, *–dshā'rĕ,* v. a. ir. to please, to comply with. [wail.

compiangere, *–pĭăn'jĕrĕ,* v. n. ir. to bemoan.

compianto, *–pĭăn'tŏ,* m. condolence; lamentation.

compiere, *kŏm'pĭĕrĕ,* v.a.ir.to accomplish.

compieta, *–pĭā'tă,* f. evening prayers.

compilare, *–pĭlā'rĕ,* v. a. to compile.

compilatore, *–tŏ'rĕ,* m. compiler.

compilazione, *–tzĭŏ'nĕ,* f. compilation.

compire, *–pĕ'rĕ,* v. a. to finish; to perfect.

compitare, *–pĭtā'rĕ,* v. a. to compute; to spell. [–pĕ'tŏ, a. complete; polite.

compito, *kŏm'pĭtŏ,* m. task; account; –,

compiuto, *–pĭŭ'tŏ,* a. complete, perfect; formed.

complemento, *–plĕmĕn'tŏ,* m.complement.

complessione, *–plĕssĭŏ'nĕ,* f. complexion, constitution.

complesso, *–plĕs'sŏ,* a. fleshy; strong, powerful; **–,** m. complication; mass; **nel –,** in the lump.

completo, *–plḗ'tŏ,* a. complete, whole.

complicare, *–plĭkä'rĕ,* v. a. to complicate.

complicazione, *–tzĭŏ'nĕ,* f. complication.

complice, *kŏm'plḗdshĕ,* m. accomplice.

complicità, *–dshĭtä',* f. participation.

complimentare, *–plĭmĕntä'rĕ,* v. a. to compliment.

complimento, *–mĕn'tŏ,* m. compliment.

complire, *–plḗ'rĕ,* v. a. to suit; to fulfil.

comporre, *–pŏr'rĕ,* v. a. ir. to compose; to adjust; to arrange; to contrive.

comportabile, *–tä'bĭlĕ,* a. tolerable, supportable, sufferable.

comportare, *–tä'rĕ,* v. a. to tolerate, to bear; **comportarsi,** *–tär'sĭ,* to conduct oneself. [delay.

comporto, *–pŏr'tŏ,* m. indulgence; respite.

compositore, *–pŏsĭtŏ'rĕ,* m. (mus.) composer; compositor (printing).

composizione, *–tzĭŏ'nĕ,* f. composition.

composta, *see* **composto.**

compostezza, *–pŏstĕt'zä,* f. sedateness, self-possession; modesty, decency.

composto, *–pŏs'tŏ,* m. mixture, conserve.

compra, *kŏm'prä,* f. purchase. [chase.

comprare, *–prä'rĕ,* v. a. to buy, to purchase.

comprendere, *–prĕn'dĕrĕ,* v. a. ir. to comprehend; to contain.

comprensione, *–sĭŏ'nĕ,* f. comprehension.

compreso, *–prḗ'sŏ,* m. circumference, compass; **–,** a. compressed; strong.

comprimere, *–prḗ'mĕrĕ,* v. a. ir. to compress; to restrain. [mise.

compromesso, *–prŏmĕs'sŏ,* m. compromise.

compromettere, *–mĕt'tĕrĕ,* v.a.ir. to compromise, to expose.

comprovare, *–prŏvä'rĕ,* v. a. to approve; to admit, to allow. [to force.

compulsare, *–pŭlsä'rĕ,* v. a. to compel.

compunto, *–pŭn'tŏ,* a. contrite.

compunzione, *–tzĭŏ'nĕ,* f. compunction, contrition. [reckon amongst.

computare, *–pŭtä'rĕ,* v. a. to compute, to

computista, *–tĭs'tä,* m. computor, calculator, reckoner. [office.

computisteria, *–tĭstĕrḗ'ä,* f. accountant's

computo, *kŏm'pŭtŏ,* m. reckoning; account.

comune, *kŏmḗ'nĕ,* a. common, usual, ordinary; trivial; **–,** m. common people, public, commons, [p.] [generally.

comunemente, *–mḗnĕmĕn'tĕ,* ad. usually,

comunicare, *–mŭnĭkä'rĕ,* v. a. to communicate, to participate, to administer the sacrament. [cation; communion.

comunicazione, *–kätzĭŏ'nĕ,* f. communication.

comunione, *–nĭŏ'nĕ,* f. communion.

comunità, *–nĭtä',* f. community; **in –,** in common.

comunque, *–mḗn'kŭĕ,* ad. however.

con, *kŏn,* pr. with.

conato, *kŏnä'tŏ,* m. (poet.) attempt, effort.

conca, *kŏn'kä,* f. washing-tub; shell.

concatenare, *–kätĕnä'rĕ,* v. a. to chain; to join.

concatenazione, *–tzĭŏ'nĕ,* f. concatenation, connection.

concavo, *kŏn'kävŏ,* a. concave, hollow.

concedere, *–dshĕ'dĕrĕ,* v. a. r. & ir. to grant, to permit.

concento, *–dshĕn'tŏ,* m. harmony, concert.

concentrare, *–trä'rĕ,* v. a. to concentrate.

concentrazione, *–trätzĭŏ'nĕ,* f. concentration. [to imagine, to understand.

concepire, *–dshĕpḗ'rĕ,* v. a. to conceive,

concernere, *–dshĕr'nĕrĕ,* v. a. to concern.

concertare, *–tä'rĕ,* v. a. to concert; to adjust, to adapt, to fit to.

concerto, *–dshĕr'tŏ,* m. concert; agreement.

concessione, *–dshĕssĭŏ'nĕ,* f. concession, permission. [wit; idea.

concetto, *–dshĕt'tŏ,* m. conceit; flash of

concettoso, *–tŏ'sŏ,* a. full of pleasant fancies. [thought.

concezione; *–tzĭŏ'nĕ,* f. conception;

conchiglia, *–kḗl'yä,* f. sea-shell, conch.

conchiudere, *–kĭŭ'dĕrĕ,* v. a. ir. to conclude, to infer; to resolve.

concia, *kŏn'dshä,* f. tan-house; tanning.

conciare, *–dshä'rĕ,* v. a. to mend; to dress, to trim; to adjust; to tan. [dressing; seasoning.

conciatura, *–tŏ'rä,* f. mending, adjusting, dressing; seasoning.

conciliare, *–dshĭlĭä'rĕ,* v. a. to reconcile.

concilio, *–dshĭ'lĭŏ,* m. council, consistory.

concimare, *–dshĭmä'rĕ,* v. a. to manure, to dung. [compost.

concime, *–dshĭ'mĕ,* m. manure, dung;

concinnità, *–dshĭnnĭtä',* f. concinnity; elegance.

concio, *kŏn'dshŏ,* a. dressed, elegant; **–,** m. conciliation, agreement; attire, muck.

concionare, *–dshŏnä'rĕ,* v. n. to harangue, to address; to preach.

concione, *–dshŏ'nĕ,* f. harangue, sermon.

conciosiachè, *–dshŏsĭä'kĕ',* **conciossiacosachè,** *–sĭäkŏsä'kĕ',* c. because.

conciso, *–dshḗ'sŏ,* a. concise, short.

concistoriale, *–dshĭstŏrĭä'lĕ,* a. consistorial.

concistorio, *–tŏ'rĭŏ,* m. consistory.

concitare, *–dshĭtä'rĕ,* v. a. to stir up; to excite.

concittadino, *–tädd'nŏ,* m. fellow-citizen.

concludere, *–klŭ'dĕrĕ,* v. a. ir. to conclude; to end; to confine.

conclusione, *–klŭsĭŏ'nĕ,* f. conclusion; **in –,** finally. [agreement, conforming.

concordanza, *–kŏrdän'tzä,* f. concordance,

concordare, *–dä'rĕ,* v. n. to concord.

concordato, *–dä'tŏ,* m. concordate.

concordia, *–kŏr'dĭä,* f. unanimity, harmony, concord. [rival.

concorrente, *–kŏrrĕn'tĕ,* m. competitor.

concorrenza, *–rĕn'tzä,* f. competition, rivalship. [to concur, to co-operate.

concorrere, *–kŏr'rĕrĕ,* v. n. ir. to run to;

concorso, *–kŏr'sŏ,* m. concourse, crowd.

concozione, *–kŏtzĭŏ'nĕ,* f. concoction, digestion.

concreto, *–krä'tŏ,* a. concrete. [gestion.

concrezione, *–krĕtzĭŏ'nĕ,* f. concretion.

concubina, *–kŭbĕ'nä,* f. concubine.

concubinato, _bīnä'tŏ_, m. concubinage.
concubito, _kŏ'bĭtŏ_, m. lying together.
conculcare, _kŭlkä'rĕ_, v. a. to trample upon; to oppress. [coct, to digest.
concuocere, _kŭŏ'dshĕrĕ_, v. a. ir. to con-
concupiscenza, _kŭpĭsshĕn'tzä_, f. con-cupiscence. [tioner.
concussionario, _kŭsssīŏnä'rĭŏ_, m. extor-
concussione, _stŏ'nĕ_, f. concussion, ex-tortion. [tence.
condanna, _dän'nä_, f. condemnation, sen-
condannare, _dännä'rĕ_, v. a. to condemn.
condecente, _dĕdshĕn'tĕ_, a. decent; proper.
condegno, _dĕn'yŏ_, a. condign, worthy.
condensare, _dĕnsä'rĕ_, v. a. to condense.
condescendere, _dĕsshĕn'dĕrĕ_, v. n. ir. to condescend; to yield.
condimento, _dīmĕn'tŏ_, m. seasoning.
condire, _dē'rĕ_, v. a. to season, to preserve.
condizionale, _dītzĭŏnä'lĕ_, a. conditional.
condizionato, _nä'tŏ_, a. fit, qualified, proper. [upon condition.
condizione, _tzĭŏ'nĕ_, f. condition; a —,
condoglianza, _dŏlyän'tzä_, f. condolence.
condolersi, _dŏlĕr'sĭ_, v. r. ir. to complain.
condonare, _dŏnä'rĕ_, v. a. to pardon, to excuse. [escort.
condotta, _dŏt'tä_, f. conduct; behaviour;
condottiere, _tĭä'rĕ_, m. conductor; leader
condotto, _dŏt'tŏ_, m. conduct; road; con-duit. [conducive.
conducibile, _dŭdshĭ'bĭlĕ_, a. conducent,
conduplicazione, _dŭplĭkätzĭŏ'nĕ_, f. du-plicate. [to lead.
condurre, _dŭr'rĕ_, v. a. ir. to conduct,
conduttore, _dŭttŏ'rĕ_, m. conductor, guide; guard; lodger; — di locomotiva, engine-driver. [stable; police-officer.
conestabile, _kŏnĕstä'bĭlĕ_, m. high con-
confabulare, _fäbŭlä'rĕ_, v. n. to converse.
confarsi, _fär'sĭ_, v. r. ir. to suit, to fit; to agree. [federate.
confederarsi, _fĕdĕrär'sĭ_, v. r. to con-
confederato, _rä'tŏ_, a. & m. confederate.
confederazione, _tzĭŏ'nĕ_, f. confederacy.
conferenza, _fĕrĕn'tzä_, f. conference.
conferire, _fĕrē'rĕ_, v. a. to collate, to compare; —, v. n. to consult; to be of use.
confermare, _fĕrmä'rĕ_, v. a. to confirm, to approve; to ratify.
confermativo, _tē'vŏ_, a. confirmatory.
confermazione, _tzĭŏ'nĕ_, f. confirmation.
confessare, _fĕssä'rĕ_, v. a. to confess.
confessionale, _sĭŏnä'lĕ_, m. confessional (seat). [fession of faith; avowal.
confessione, _stŏ'nĕ_, f. confession; con-
confessore, _sŏ'rĕ_, m. confessor.
confettare, _fĕttä'rĕ_, v. a. to preserve, to candy. [f. sweet-meats, comfits.
confetto, _fĕt'tŏ_, m., confettura, _tō'rä_,
confezionare, _fĕtzĭŏnä'rĕ_, v. a. to confect.
confezione, _see_ confetto.
conficcare, _fīkkä'rĕ_, v. a. to nail, to fix; to commit to memory; to convince.
confidare, _fīdä'rĕ_, v. n. to trust, to con-fide; confidarsi, _där'sĭ_, to place one-self in someone's hands.

confidenza, _dĕn'tzä_, f. confidence, as-surance. [to configurate.
configurare, _fīgŭrä'rĕ_, v. a. to fashion,
configurato, _rä'tŏ_, a. like, resembling.
confinare, _fīnä'rĕ_, v. a. to confine; to banish; —, v. n. to border upon.
confine, _fē'nĕ_, confino, _fē'nŏ_, m. limits, pl. [to forfeit.
confiscare, _fĭskä'rĕ_, v. n. to confiscate,
confiscazione, _tzĭŏ'nĕ_, confisca, _fĭs'kä_, f. confiscation, forfeiture.
conflato, _flä'tŏ_, a. joined together.
conflitto, _flĭt'tŏ_, m. conflict, combat.
confluente, _flŭĕn'tĕ_, m. conflux.
confondere, _fŏn'dĕrĕ_, v. a. ir. to con-found, to mix; to puzzle, to abash; to destroy, to waste.
confondimento, _dīmĕn'tŏ_, m. confusion.
conformare, _fŏrmä'rĕ_, v. a. to conform; conformarsi, _fŏrmär'sĭ_, v. r. to con-form oneself to.
conforme, _fŏr'mĕ_, a. & ad. conformable, agreeing; conformably to. [ness.
conformità, _fŏrmĭtä'_, f. conformity; like-
confortare, _fŏrtä'rĕ_, v. a. to comfort, to fortify, to strengthen; to encourage.
confortino, _tē'nŏ_, m. ginger-bread.
confraternita, _frätĕr'nĭtä_, f. brotherhood.
confrontare, _frŏntä'rĕ_, v. n. to confront.
confronto, _frŏn'tŏ_, m. confronting.
confusione, _fŭsĭŏ'nĕ_, f. confusion.
confuso, _fō'sŏ_, a. confused.
confutare, _fŭtä'rĕ_, v. a. to refute.
confutazione, _tzĭŏ'nĕ_, f. refutation.
congedare, _jĕdä'rĕ_, v. a. to dismiss, to discharge, to give leave to.
congedo, _jä'dŏ_, m. dismissal; leave; farewell. [join, to unite.
congegnare, _jĕnyä'rĕ_, v. a. to connect, to
congegno, _jĕn'yŏ_, m. connexion, union.
congelare, _jĕlä'rĕ_, v. n. to. congeal, to freeze.
congenere, _jĕ'nĕrĕ_, a. congencrous.
congenito, _jä'nĭtŏ_, a. congenial.
congerie, _jä'rĭĕ_, f. heap, mass.
congestione, _jĕstĭŏ'nĕ_, f. congestion.
congettura, _jĕttŏ'rä_, f. conjecture, guess.
congetturare, _tŭrä'rĕ_, v. a. to conjecture, to guess. [to unite, to annex; to match.
congiungere, _jŭn'jĕrĕ_, v. a. ir. to join,
congiuntamente, _tämĕn'tĕ_, ad. jointly, together. [eye.
congiuntiva, _tē'vä_, f. conjunctive of the
congiuntivo, _tē'vŏ_, m. (gr.) conjunctive.
congiunto, _jŭn'tŏ_, a. joined, allied; re-lated; —, m. kinsman. [opportunity.
congiuntura, _tŏ'rä_, f. joint, juncture;
congiunzione, _tzĭŏ'nĕ_, f. conjunction.
congiura, _jō'rä_, f. conspiracy.
congiurare, _jŭrä'rĕ_, v.a. & n. to conspire.
congiurato, _rä'tŏ_, congiuratore, _tō'rĕ_, m. conspirator.
congiurazione, _tzĭŏ'nĕ_, f. conspiracy.
conglobare, _glŏbä'rĕ_, v. a. to conglobate.
conglutinare, _glŭtĭnä'rĕ_, v. a. to con-glutinate.
congratulare, _grätŭlä'rĕ_, v. a. & n. to

congratulate; **congratularsi**, –lăr' sĭ, to congratulate oneself. [tion.
congratulazione. –tzĭō' ne, f. congratula-
congrega, kŏn' grĕgă f. congregation.
congregamento, –men' tŏ, m. assembly.
congregare, –gā' rĕ, v. a. to assemble.
congregazione, –tzĭō' ne, f. congregation, assembly, meeting.
congresso, –grĕs' sŏ, m. congress, meeting.
congruente, –grŭen' tĕ, a. congruent, cor-respondent. [–grŭtă', f. congruity.
congruenza, –grŭen' tză, **congruità**,
congruo, kŏn' grŭŏ, a. congruous.
conguagliare, –gŭălyă' rĕ, v.a. to equalize.
conguaglio, –gŭă' yŏ, m. levelling, equa-lization. [money.
coniare, kŏnĭă' rĕ, v. a. to coin; to stamp
conico, kŏ' nĭkŏ, a. conical.
conifero, kŏnĭ' fĕrŏ, a. coniferous.
conigliera, kŏnĭlyă' ră, f. rabbit-warren.
coniglio, kŏnĭ' lyŏ, m. rabbit.
conio, kŏ' nĭŏ, m. wedge, coin.
coniugale, kŏnĭŭgă' lĕ, a. conjugal.
coniugare, –gā' rĕ, v. a. to conjugate, to inflect verbs. [tion.
coniugazione, –gătzĭō' ne, f. conjuga-
coniuge, kŏn' ĭŭjĕ, m. & f. consort; hus-band; spouse.
coniugio, –ĭō' jŏ, m. marriage.
connaturale, –nătŭră' lĕ, a. natural; suit-able. [nation.
connazionale, –nătzĭōnă' lĕ, a. of the same
connessione, –nĕssĭō' ne, **connessità**, –nĕssĭtă', f. connexion, union. [to join.
connettere, –nĕt' tĕrĕ, v. a. ir. to connect,
connivenza, –nĭven' tză, f. connivance.
connubio, –nŏ' bĭŏ, m. marriage.
connumerare, –nŭmĕră' rĕ,v.a. to number.
cono, kŏ' nŏ, m. cone.
conocchia, kŏnŏk' kĭă, f. distaff.
conoscenza, –nŏsshen' tză, f. acquaint-ance; knowledge.
conoscere, –nŏssh' ĕrĕ, v. a. ir. to know, to understand; to discern; to taste.
conoscitore, –nŏsshĭtō' rĕ, m. connoisseur; discerner. [rious.
conosciuto, –nŏsshŭ' tŏ, a. known, noto-
conquassare, kŏnkŭăssă' rĕ, v.a. to bruise, to crush; to ruin; to shake.
conquidere, –kŭĭ' dĕrĕ, v. a. ir. to afflict, to grieve; to cast down. [tion.
conquista, –kŭĭs' tă, f. conquest; acquisi-
conquistare, –tă' rĕ, v. a. to conquer, to subdue.
conquistatore, –tō' rĕ, m. conqueror.
consacrare, –săkră' rĕ, v. a. to consecrate.
consacrazione, –tzĭō' ne, f. consecration.
consanguineo, –sangŭĭ' nĕŏ, a. akin, con-sanguineous. [guinity.
consanguinità, –gŭĭnĭtă', f. consan-
consapevole, –săpă' vŏlĕ, a. conscious.
conscio, kŏn' sshĭŏ, a. conscious.
consecutivo, –sĕkŭtĭ' vŏ, a. consecutive, successive. [acquisition.
consecuzione, –tzĭō' ne, f. consecution;
consegnare, –sĕnyă' rĕ, v. a. to consign.

conseguente, –sĕgŭen' tĕ, a. following, ensuing; **per –**, in consequence.
conseguenza, –gŭen' tză, f. consequence, importance. [to happen.
conseguire, –gŭĭ' rĕ, v. a. & n. to obtain;
conseguitare, –gŭĭtă' rĕ, v. n. to get; to follow, to ensue. [tion.
consenso, –sen' sŏ, m. consent, approba-
consentaneo, –tă' nĕŏ, a. consentaneous, fit, adequate to.
consentimento, –tĭmen' tŏ, m. consent.
consentire, –tĭ' rĕ, v. n. to consent.
consequente, see **conseguente**.
conserto, –ser' tŏ, m. accord, intelligence.
conserva, –ser' vă, f. store-house; con-serve; **– di piante**, f. green-house.
conservare, –vă' rĕ, v. a. to conserve, to preserve.
conservativo, –tĭ' vŏ, a. conservative.
conservatorio, –tō' rĭŏ, m. infirmary; conservatory. [maintenance; health.
conservazione, –tzĭō' ne, f. preservation.
consesso, –ses' sŏ, m. assembly, meeting.
considerabile, –sĭdĕră' bĭlĕ, a. consider-able, important. [to reflect upon.
considerare, –dĕră' rĕ, v. n. to consider,
considerazione, –sĭdĕra-tzĭō' ne, f. considera-tion; regard. [consult.
consigliare, –sĭlyă' rĕ, v. a. to advise, to
consigliato, –yă' tŏ, a. advised; cautious.
consigliatore, –tō' rĕ, m. adviser, coun-seller. [under-pilot.
consigliere, –yĕ' rĕ, m. counsellor
consiglio, –sĭ' lyŏ, m. counsel, advice; council; resource; **– di guerra**, court-martial.
consistente, –sĭsten' tĕ, a. consistent, firm, solidity.
consistenza, –ten' tză, f. consistence, solidity.
consistere, –sĭs' tĕrĕ, v. n. ir. to consist.
consociare, –sŏdshă' rĕ, v. a. to consociate to ally. [a. consular.
consolare, –sŏlă' rĕ, v. a. to console; –,
consolato, –lă' tŏ, m. consulate.
consolazione, –tzĭō' ne, f. consolation, console, kŏn' sŏlĕ, m. consul. [comfort.
consolidare, –sŏlĭdă' rĕ, v. a. to consoli-date; to confirm. [nionious.
consonante, –sŏnăn' tĕ, a. consonant, har-
consonanza, –nān' tză, f. harmony, accord.
consonare, –nă' rĕ, v. n. to accord; to suit; to answer.
consono, kŏn' sŏnŏ, a. consonant, agreeing.
consorte, –sŏr' tĕ, **consorto**, –sŏr' tŏ, m. companion, associate. [society.
consorzio, –sŏr' tzĭŏ, m. partnership.
consueto, –sŭĕ' tŏ, a. accustomed, or-dinary, usual. [habit.
consuetudine, –sŭĕtŭ' dĭnĕ, f. custom,
consulta, –sŭl' tă, f. consultation, council
consultare, –tă' rĕ, v. a. to consult.
consultazione, –tzĭō' ne, f. consultation.
consulto, –sŭl' tŏ, m. counsel, advice.
consultore, –tō' rĕ, m. consulter, adviser.
consumare, –sŭmă' rĕ, v. a. to consume, to waste; to accomplish.
consumato, –mă' tŏ, m. jelly-broth; – a. consumed; perfect, accomplished.

consumo, *–sō'mō,* m. consumption; waste, decay. [out; phthisical.

consunto, *–sŭn'tō,* a. consumed, worn

consunzione, *–sŭntzō'ne,* f. consumption.

contadina, *–tădē'nă,* f. country-woman.

contadinesco, *–dēnēs'kō,* a. rustic; clownish, clumsy, unwieldy.

contadino, *–dē'nō,* m. country-man.

contado, *–tă'dō,* m. country; shire; territory of a town. [f. contagion, plague.

contagio, *–tă'jō,* m., **contagione,** *–jō'ne,*

contagioso, *–jō'sō,* a. contagious.

contaminare, *–tămină're,* v. a. to contaminate, to pollute. [tion.

contaminazione, *–tziō'ne,* f. contamination.

contante, *–tăn'te,* a. counting; reckoned; danaro –, ready money. [to prize.

contare, *–tă're,* v. a. to count; to value,

contatore, *–tō're,* m. accountant; teller.

contatto, *–tăt'tō,* m. contact, touch.

conte, *kōn'te,* m. count, earl.

contea, *–tă'ă,* f. county. [compute.

conteggiare, *–tēdjă're,* v. a. to count, to

contegno, *–tēn'yō,* m. circuit; appearance. behaviour; gravity; pride, pomp.

contegnoso, *–yō'sō,* a. grave, proud.

contemperare, *–tēmpēră're,* v. a. to proportion; to temper.

contemplare, *–plă're,* v. a. to contemplate, to meditate.

contemplativo, *–tē'vō,* a. contemplative.

contemplazione, *–tziō'ne,* f. contemplation. [porary.

contemporaneo, *–pōră'nēō,* a. contem-

contendere, *–tēn'dēre,* v. n. to contend, to contest.

contenente, *–tēnēn'te,* a. containing; sober; –, ad. directly, immediately.

contenenza, *–nēn'tză,* f. abstinence.

contenere, *–tēnē're,* v. a. ir. to contain.

contentare, *–tēntă're,* v. a. to content.

contento, *–tēn'tō,* a. content, pleased; –, m. contentment; contents, pl.

contenuto, *–tēnŭ'tō,* a. contained, comprised; –, m. contents, pl. [bate.

contenzione, *–tziō'ne,* a. contention, de-

contenzioso, *–tziō'sō,* a. contentious.

conterminare, *–tērmină're,* v. n. to border

contesa, *–tă'ză,* f. contest, dispute. [upon.

conteso, *–tă'sō,* a. prohibited, forbid.

contessa, *–tēs'să,* f. countess.

contessere, *–tēs'sēre,* v. a. to interweave.

contestabile, *–tēstă'bilē,* m. constable.

contestare, *–tēstă're,* v. a. to notify, to refer a cause. [fication.

contestazione, *–tziō'ne,* f. contest; noti-

contesto, *–tēs'tō,* m. context.

contezza, *–tēt'tză,* f. knowledge, advice.

contiguità, *–tigŭită',* f. contiguity, near-

contiguo, *–tē'gŭō,* a. contiguous. [ness.

continente, *–tinēn'te,* a. & m. containing; continent.

continenza, *–nēn'tză,* f. continence.

contingente, *–tinjēn'te,* a. contingent; casual; –, m. contingent, quota.

contingenza, *–jēn'tză,* f. contingence; casualty.

continuamente, *–tēnŭămēn'te,* ad. continually. [tion.

continuamento, *–mēn'tō,* m. continua-

continuare, *–nŭă're,* v. a. to continue; to pursue; –, v. n. to last, to persevere.

continuato, *–nŭă'tō,* a. continued, uninterrupted.

continuazione, *–tziō'ne,* **continuità,** *–nŭită',* f. continuation; continuity.

continuo, *–tē'nŭō,* a. continuous; lasting; –, m. close body.

conto, *kōn'tō,* m. account; computation; relation, story; – **corrente,** account current. [to writhe.

contorcere, *–tōr'dshēre,* v. a. ir. to twist,

contorno, *–tōr'nō,* m. circuit; outline; contorni, pl. environs, pl.

contorsione, *–sō'ne,* f. contortion.

contra, *kōn'tră,* pr. against, opposite to.

contrabbando, *–băn'dō,* m. contraband goods, contrabanded goods, pl. [bass.

contrabbasso, *–băs'sō,* m. (mus.) counter-

contrabbilanciare, *–bilăndshă're,* v. a. to counterbalance.

contraccambiare, *–kămbiă're,* v. a. to exchange, to truck; to reward. [street.

contrada, *–tră'dă,* f. country, region;

contraddanza, *–dăn'tză,* f. country-dance.

contraddetto, *–dēt'tō,* m. contradiction.

contraddire, *–dē're,* v. a. ir. to contradict.

contraffare, *–fă're,* v. a. ir. to counterfeit.

contraffatore, *–tō're,* m. counterfeiter.

contraffazione, *–tziō'ne,* f. counterfeiting.

contraffodera, *–fō'dēră,* f. double lining.

contrafforte, *–fōr'te,* m. counterfort, ironbar. [aversion.

contraggenio, *–djē'niō,* m. antipathy,

contralto, *kōntrăl'tō,* m. (mus.) countertenor. [countermand.

contrammandare, *–măndă're,* v. a. to

contrammandato, *–măndă'tō,* m. countermand. [march.

contrammarcia, *–măr'dshă,* f. counter-

contrammina, *–mē'nă,* f. countermine; stratagem. [termine.

contramminare, *–mină're,* v. a. to coun-

contrammiraglio, *–ămmiră'lyō,* m. rearadmiral. [grain.

contrappelo, *–pē'lō,* ad. (a–) against the

contrappeso, *–pē'sō,* m. counterpoise.

contrappunto, *–păn'tō,* m. (mus.) counterpoint. [rarily, the wrong way,

contrariamente, *–riămēn'te,* ad. con-

contrariare, *–riă're,* v. a. to contradict.

contrarietà, *–riētă',* f. contrariety, opposition; adversity. [on the contrary,

contrario, *kōntră'riō,* a. contrary; al –,

contrarre, *–trăr're,* v. a. ir. to contract.

contrassegnare, *–sēnyă're,* v. a. to countersign. [contest.

contrastare, *–trăstă're,* v. a. to resist, to

contrasto, *–trăs'tō,* m. contrast; opposition, contest.

contrattare, *–trăttă're,* v. a. to bargain; to contract; to handle, to touch.

contrattempo, *–tēm'pō,* m. wrong time; misfortune. [ment.

contratto, *–trăt'tō,* m. contract; agree-

contravvenire, –věnē′rě, v. n. ir. to contravene, to infringe.

contravvenzione, –věntzĭŏ′ně, f. contravention, infraction.

contrazione, –tzĭŏ′ně, f. contraction.

contribuire, –trĭbŭē′rě, v. a. to contribute, to concur. [levy, tax.

contribuzione, –bŭtzĭŏ′ně, f. contribution;

contristare, –trĭstā′rě, v. a. to sadden, to grieve, to afflict.

contrito, –trē′tŏ, a. contrite; crushed.

contro, kŏn′trŏ, pr. against, opposite to.

contromarca, –mär′kā, f. counter-mark, check.

controstomaco, see **controvolontà.**

controversia, –věr′sĭā, f. controversy.

controverso, –věr′sŏ, a. debated, doubtful. [trovert, to debate.

controvertere, –věr′těrě, v. a. ir. to con-

controvolontà, –vŏlŏntā′, ad. against one's will.

contumace, –tŭmā′dshě, a. contumacious.

contumacia, –tŭmā′dshĭā, f. contumacy.

contumelia, –mā′lĭā, f. contumely, outrage. [outrageous.

contumelioso, –mělĭŏ′sŏ, a. contumelious,

conturbare, –tŭrbā′rě, v. a. to disturb.

contuttoché, –tŭttŏkě′, c. although, though.

contuttociò, –dshŏ′, c. however, nevertheless. [lescent.

convalescente, –vălěsshěn′tě, a. conva-

convalescenza, –sshěn′tzā, f. convalescence, recovery.

convalidare, –vălĭdā′rě, v. a. to corroborate, to strengthen; to verify.

convalle, –văl′lě, f. valley, dale.

convenevole, –věně′vŏlě, a. suitable, convenient. [propriety.

convenevolezza, –něvŏlět′zā, f. decency;

conveniente, –věnĭěn′tě, a. & m. decent; agreement. [decency; fitness.

convenienza, –měn′tzā, f. conveniency;

convenire, –věnē′rě, v. n. ir. to agree; to assemble; to suit; to be convenient.

conventicola, –věntĭ′kŏlā, f. conventicle.

convento, –věn′tŏ, m. meeting, convent.

convenzione, –tzĭŏ′ně, f. covenant, agreement.

convergere, –věr′jěrě, v. n. to converge.

conversare, –sā′rě, v. a. to converse, to discourse.

conversazione, –tzĭŏ′ně, f. conversation.

conversione, –sĭŏ′ně, f. conversion.

converso, –věr′sŏ, a. converted; changed; **per –,** on the contrary.

convertere, –věr′těrě, v. a. to convert.

convesso, –věs′sŏ, a. convex. [vince.

convincere, –vēn′dshěrě, v. n. ir. to con-

convitare, –vĭtā′rě, v. a. to invite.

convito, –vē′tŏ, m. banquet, feast.

convitto, –vēt′tŏ, m. company at table.

convittore, –tŏ′rě, m. fellow-commoner.

convocare, –vŏkā′rě, v. a. to convoke; to summon. [to escort.

convogliare, –vŏlyā′rě, v. a. to convoy,

convoglio, –vŏl′yŏ, m. convoy; (rail.) train; **– delle mercanzie,** luggage-train.

convolare, –vŏlā′rě, v. n. to marry again.

convolgere, –vŏl′jěrě, v. a. ir. to swallow; to roll; to tumble.

cooperare, kŏŏpěrā′rě, v. n. to co-operate.

coordinare, –ŏrdĭnā′rě, v. a. to co-ordinate. [monish, to remind.

coortare, –ŏrtā′rě, v. a. to exhort, to ad-

coorte, –ŏr′tě, f. cohort, troop.

coperchio, –pěr′kĭŏ, m. cover; lid.

coperta, –pěr′tā, f. cover; curtain; pretext. [abundance.

copia, kŏ′pĭā, f. copy, transcript; plenty,

copiare, kŏpĭā′rě, v. a. to copy.

copiosità, –prŏsĭtā′, f. abundance, plenty.

copioso, –pĭŏ′sŏ, a. copious; rich.

coppa, kŏp′pā, f. back of the head.

coppella, –pěl′lā, f. coppel, crucible.

coppia, kŏp′pĭā, f. couple.

coppo, kŏp′pŏ, m. pitcher; socket of the eye.

coprire, –prē′rě, v. a. ir. to cover.

copula, kŏ′pŭlā, f. conjunction, coupling.

copulare, –lā′rě, v. a. to copulate; **copularsi,** –lär′sĭ, to match, to couple.

coraggio, kŏrād′jŏ, m. courage, valour.

coraggioso, –djŏ′sŏ, a. courageous, bold.

corale, –rā′lě, a. hearty; choral.

corallo, –răl′lŏ, m. coral.

corame, –rā′mě, m. dressed leather.

coratella, –těl′lā, f. liver.

corazza, kŏrāt′zā, f. cuirass.

corazziere, –tzĭě′rě, m. (mil.) cuirassier.

corba, kŏr′bā, f. basket.

corbellare, –běllā′rě, v. a. to quiz, to rally.

corbelleria, –lěrē′ā, f. trifle, fudge.

corbello, –běl′lŏ, m. basket.

corbezzola, –běz′zŏlā, f. arbute-berry.

corcare, see **coricare.**

corda, kŏr′dā, f. cord, rope.

cordame, –dā′mě, m. cordage, rigging.

cordella, –děl′lā, f. small cord, riband.

cordiale, –dĭā′lě, a. hearty.

cordiale, –dĭā′lě, m. cordial, restorative.

cordialità, –ātĭtā′, f. cordiality.

cordino, –dē′nŏ, m. cord, line, rope.

cordoglio, –dŏ′lyŏ, m. heart-grief, sorrow.

cordonata, –dŏnā′tā, f. sloping terrace leading to the front entrance of a building. [loop.

cordone, –dŏ′ně, m. string; hat-band;

cordovano, –vā′nŏ, m. cordwain.

core, see **cuore.**

coreggiato, –rědjā′tŏ, m. flail.

coreografia, –rěŏgrăfē′ā, f. chorography.

coreografo, –rěŏ′grāfŏ, m. chorographer.

coricare, –rĭkā′rě, v. a. to lay down; to prostrate.

corifeo, –fě′ŏ, m. chief, leader.

corista, –rĭs′tā, m. chorister.

cornacchia, kŏrnäk′kĭā, f. rook, crow; (fig.) chatterer. [to chatter.

cornacchiare, –kĭā′rě, v. n. to chatter,

cornamusa, –nāmŏ′sā, f. bag-pipe.

cornea, kŏr′něā, f. cornea, horny tunicle of the eye.

corneo, kŏr′něŏ, a. horny, callous.

cornetta, –nět′tā, f. postillion's horn; cornet; troop of horse.

cornetto, –nĕt'tŏ, m. little horn; gherkin; cupping-glass; bruise.
cornice, –nĕ'dshĕ, f. cornice; frame.
corniola, kŏr'nĭŏlā, f. cornelian cherry.
corniola, –nĭŏ'lā, f. cornelian (stone).
corniolo, kŏr'nĭŏlŏ, m. cornelian-tree.
corno, kŏr'nŏ, m. horn; pride.
cornuto, –nŭ'tŏ, a. horned. [wind.
coro, kŏ'rŏ, m. chorus; choir; north-west
corollario, kŏrŏllā'rĭŏ, m. corollary.
corona, –rŏ'nā, f. crown; glory; garland.
coronare, –rŏnā'rĕ, v. a. to crown.
corpacciuto, –pātshŭt'tŏ, a. big-bellied, corpulent. [corps.
corpo, kŏr'pŏ, m. body; mass; society;
corporale, –pŏrā'lĕ, a. corporeal, bodily.
corporalmente, –mĕn'tĕ, ad. bodily; actually.
corporatura, –tŏ'rā, f. corpulence, size.
corporeo, –pŏ'rĕŏ, a. corporeal.
corpulento, –pŭlĕn'tŏ, a. corpulent, fleshy. [atom.
corpuscolo, –pŭs'kŏlŏ, m. corpuscle,
corputo, –pŭ'tŏ, a. big-bellied.
corre, see **cogliere.** [adorn.
corredare, –rĕdā'rĕ, v. a. to equip; to
corredo, –rĕd'dŏ, m. furniture, equipment; bridal dress; (mar.) rigging and tackling; (poet.) feast, banquet.
correggere, –rĕd'jĕrĕ, v. a. ir. to correct; to revise; to chastise.
correlativo, –rĕlātĕ'vŏ, a. corelative.
correlazione, –tzĭŏ'nĕ, f. mutual relation.
correligionario, –rĕlĭjĭŏnā'rĭŏ, m. core-ligionist.
corrente, –rĕn'tĕ, a. current; general, usual; hasty; prone; –, m. current, stream.
correo, –rĕ'ŏ, m. accomplice.
correre, kŏr'rĕrĕ, v. n. ir. to turn, to flow; to pass on; to last; to extend.
correspettività, –rĕspĕttĭvĭtā', f. rela-tion; reciprocal correspondence.
correspettivo, –tĕ'vŏ, a. corresponding, equivalent.
correttivo, –rĕttĕ'vŏ, a corrective.
corretto, –rĕt'tŏ, a. corrected; exact.
correttore, –tŏ'rĕ, m. corrector.
correzione, –tzĭŏ'nĕ, f. correction, reform; censure.
corridoio, –rĭdŏ'ŏ, **corridore,** –dŏ'rĕ, m. corridor. [courier, messenger.
corriere, –rĭĕ'rĕ, **corriero,** –rŏ, m.
corrispondente, –rĭspŏndĕn'tĕ, m. cor-respondent; trustee; –, a. corresponding.
corrispondenza, –rĭspŏndĕn'tzā, f. cor-respondence. [correspond.
corrispondere, –pŏn'dĕrĕ, v. a. ir. to
corrivo, –rĕ'vŏ, m. simpleton, ninny.
corroborare, –rŏbŏrā'rĕ, v. a. to corro-borate, to strengthen. [to waste.
corrodere, –rŏ'dĕrĕ, v. a. ir. to corrode;
corrompere, –rŏm'pĕrĕ, v. a. ir. to cor-rupt, to seduce, to bribe.
corrosivo, –rŏsĕ'vŏ, a. corrosive.
corrotto, –rŏt'tŏ, a. corrupted; bribed; –, m. weeping, mourning.
corruccio, –rŭt'shŏ, m. wrath, passion.

corrugare, –rŭgā'rĕ, v. a. to corrugate, to frown. [lighten.
corruscare, –rŭskā'rĕ, v. n. to flash, to
corrusco, –rŭs'kŏ, a. flashing, shining.
corruzione, –rŭtzĭŏ'nĕ, f. corruption.
corsa, kŏr'sā, f. course, race; career; heat.
corsale, –sā'lĕ, m. pirate, corsair.
corsaletto, –lĕt'tŏ, m. corslet, cuirass.
corsaro, see **corsale.**
corseggiare, –sĕdjā'rĕ, v. a. & n. to pirate; to plunder. [scene.
corsia, –sĕ'ā, f. current, stream; side-
corsiere, –sĭĕ'rĕ, m. courser; war-horse.
corsivo, –sĕ'vŏ, a. running, flowing.
corso, kŏr'sŏ, m. course; career; tide; pro-grees; course of lectures; public walk; Corsican wine. [yard.
corte, kŏr'tĕ, f. court; banquet; hall, court-
corteccia, –tĕt'shā, f. bark, crust; out-side; rough-cast. [to attend.
corteggiare, –tĕdjā'rĕ, v. a. to court;
corteggio, –tĕd'jŏ, m. train, retinue.
cortese, –tĕ'sĕ, a. courteous, kind, affable.
cortesemente, –mĕn'tĕ, ad. courteously.
cortesia, –tĕsĕ'ā, f. courtesy, politeness.
cortezza, –tĕt'zā, f. brevity, conciseness.
corticale, –tĭkā'lĕ, a. cortical.
cortina, –tĕ'nā, f. (bed-)curtain.
cortinaggio, –tĭnād'jŏ, m. bed-curtain.
corto, kŏr'tŏ, a. short; brief; small; – di vista, short-sighted.
corvetta, –vĕt'tā, f. curvet; (mar.) sloop.
corvettare, –tā'rĕ, v. n. to curvet; to prance. [prance.
corvo, kŏr'vŏ, m. raven.
cosa, kŏ'sā, f. thing; matter; business.
coscia, kŏssh'ā, f. thigh. [scruple.
coscienza, –sshĕn'tzā, f. conscience;
coscritto, –skrĭt'tŏ, a. conscript; registered;
coscrivere, –skrĕ'vĕrĕ, v. a. to enroll; to register.
cosellina, –sĕllĕ'nā, **coserella,** –rĕl'lā, **cosetta,** –sĕt'tā, f. trifle; play-thing.
così, kŏsĕ', ad. so, thus; **così così,** so so, indifferently. [in this way.
cosifattamente, –fāttāmĕn'tĕ, ad. thus,
cosifatto, –fāt'tŏ, a. such like.
cosmetico, kŏsmā'tĭkŏ, a. cosmetic.
cosmogonia, –mŏgŏnĕ'ā, f. cosmogony.
cosmografia, –grāfĕ'ā, f. cosmography.
cosmopolita, –pŏlĕ'tā, m. cosmopolite.
coso, kŏ'sŏ, m. simpleton, ninny; penis.
cospargere, kŏspār'jĕrĕ, v. a. ir. to sprinkle, to strew, to scatter, to water.
cospergere, –spĕr'jĕrĕ, v.a.ir. to sprinkle, to water. [presence; –, i. zooks! zounds!
cospetto, –spĕt'tŏ, m. aspect, view;
cospicuo, –spĕ'kŭŏ, a. conspicuous, mani-fest; noble.
cospirare, –rā'rĕ, v. n. to conspire.
cospiratore, –tŏ'rĕ, m.conspirator, plotter.
cospirazione, –tzĭŏ'nĕ, f.conspiracy, plot.
cosso, kŏs'sŏ, m. pimple, wart; knob.
costa, kŏs'tā, f. rib; coast; hillock.
costà, kŏstā', ad. there, in that place; thither. [below.
costaggiù, –djā', ad. yonder, there

costante, –stăn'tĕ, a. constant; certain.
costanza, –stăn'tză, f. constancy, steadiness, steadfastness.
costare, –stă'rĕ, v. n. to cost; to be evident.
costassù, kŏstăssŭ', ad. there above.
costei, kŏstă'ĭ, pn. she. [tion.
costellazione, –stĕllătzĭŏ'nĕ, f. constellation.
costernare, –stĕrnă'rĕ, v. a. to confound; **costernarsi,** –stĕrnăr'sĭ, to be confounded. [tion.
costernazione, –tzĭŏ'nĕ, f. constellaconstì, kŏstĭ', ad. there.
costiera, kŏstĭĕ'ră, f. shore, coast.
costipare, –pă'rĕ, v. a. to constipate.
costituire, –stătŭĭ'rĕ, v. a. to constitute.
costituzione, –tzĭŏ'nĕ, f. constitution.
costituto, –tŭ'tŏ, m. judiciary examination.
costo, kŏs'tŏ, m. cost, expense. [tion.
costoro, –tŏ'rŏ, pn. these, those.
costringere, –strĭn'jĕrĕ, v. a. ir. to constrain, to force.
costruire, –strŭĭ'rĕ, v. a. to construct; to construe (words). [profit, gain.
costrutto, –strŭt'tŏ, m. construction; profit, gain.
costruttore, –strŭttŏ'rĕ, m. constructor.
costruzione, –tzĭŏ'nĕ, f. construction.
costui, kŏstŭ'ĭ, pn. this man, this fellow.
costumanza, –tŭmăn'tză, f., **costume,** –tŏ'mĕ, m. custom, use; way.
costumare, –tŭmă'rĕ, v. a. to frequent; to practise; to civilize; to instruct; –, v. n. to be customary; to be wont.
costumatezza, –tĕt'tză, f. politeness.
costumato, –mă'tŏ, a. accustomed; polite, civil, courteous, courtly.
costume, –tŏ'mĕ, m. custom, habit.
costura, –tŏ'ră, f. seam.
cotale, kŏtă'lĕ, pn. such a one.
cotanto, –tăn'tŏ, a. as much, as many; –, ad. so much, so long, very.
cote, kŏ'tĕ, f. whetstone.
cotesta, –tĕs'tă, pn. this (woman).
cotesti, –tĕs'tĭ, pn. this one, this man
cotesto, –tĕs'tŏ, pn. that, this.
cotestoro, –tŏ'rŏ, pn. these, those.
cotestui, see cotesti. [every day.
cotidianamente, –tĭdĭănămĕn'tĕ, ad.
cotidiano, –dĭă'nŏ, a. quotidian, daily.
cotogna, kŏtŏn'ya, f. quince.
cotognato, –yă'tŏ, m. quince-marmalade.
cotogno, –tŏn'yŏ, m. quince-tree.
cotone, –tŏ'nĕ, m. cotton; – esplosivo, gun-cotton. [ebriation.
cotta, kŏt'tă, f. gown, surplice; batch; in**cottimante,** –tĭmăn'tĕ, m. jobber, piece-worker, contract-worker.
cottimo, kŏt'tĭmŏ, m. piece-work, contract-work, job-work.
cottura, –tŏ'ră, f. cooking.
cova, kŏ'vă, f. den, lair. [cave.
covaccio(lo), kŏvăt'shŏ(lŏ), m. burrow, **covare,** –vă'rĕ, v. a. to sit brooding, to hatch; to foment; to devise.
covile, –vĕ'lĕ, m. den, haunt.
covo, kŏ'vŏ, m. den, lair, kennel.
covone, –vŏ'nĕ, m. sheaf.

cozzo, kŏt'zŏ, m. shock, knock, blow with **cranio,** kră'nĭŏ, m. skull. [the horn.
crapulare, –pŭlă'rĕ, v. n. to lead a debauched life.
crapulone, –lŏ'nĕ, m. debauchee.
crasso, krăs'sŏ, a. fat, thick, gross.
cratere, krătĕ'rĕ, f. crater; cup, goblet.
cravatta, –văt'tă, f. cravat; stock.
creanza, krĕăn'tză, f. breeding; education; politeness. [to breed.
creare, krĕă'rĕ, v. a. to create; to choose; **creatore,** –tŏ'rĕ, m. creator.
creatura, –tŏ'ră, f. creature; hireling.
creazione, –tzĭŏ'nĕ, f. creation; election.
credenza, krĕdĕn'tză, f. belief, faith; credit; buffet, cupboard.
credere, krĕ'dĕrĕ, v. a. & n. to believe; to suppose; to confide. [dulous.
credibile, krĕdĭ'bĭlĕ, a. credible; cre**credibilità,** –dĭbĭlĭtă', f. credibility.
credito, krĕ'dĭtŏ, m. credit, reputation.
creditore, krĕdĭtŏ'rĕ, m. creditor.
credo, krĕ'dŏ, m. creed, belief.
credulità, krĕdŭlĭtă', f. credulity.
credulo, krĕ'dŭlŏ, a. credulous.
crema, krĕ'mă, f. cream.
cremisi, krĕ'mĭsĭ, m. crimson. [to burst.
crepare, krĕpă'rĕ, v. a. to crack; –, v. n. **crepitare,** –pĭtă'rĕ, v. n. to crackle.
crepolare, –pŏlă'rĕ, v. n. to burst.
crepuscolo, –pŭs'kŏlŏ, m. twilight.
crescente, krĕsshĕn'tĕ, a. increasing.
crescenza, –sshĕn'tză, f. growth; excrescence. [to increase, to augment.
crescere, krĕssh'ĕrĕ, v. a. & n. ir. to grow, **crescione,** –sshŏ'nĕ, m. water-cresses.
cresima, krĕ'sĭmă, f. chrism. [baptise.
cresimare, –mă'rĕ, v. a. to confirm; to **crespa,** krĕs'pă, f. wrinkle, plait.
crespare, –pă'rĕ, v. a. to twist, to curl.
cresta, krĕs'tă, f. crest, tuft; summit.
crestaia, –tă'ă, f. milliner.
creta, krĕ'tă, f. chalk.
cretaceo, krĕtă'dshĕŏ, a. chalky.
cribrare, krĭbră'rĕ, v. a. to sift, to bolt.
cribro, krĕ'brŏ, m. sieve, searce. [pable.
criminale, krĭmĭnă'lĕ, a. criminal, cul**criminalista,** –lĭs'tă, m. one versed in penal law.
crimine, krĕ'mĭnĕ, m. crime, offence.
criminoso, –nŏ'sŏ, a. criminal, culpable.
crinale, –nă'lĕ, m. ornament for the hair.
crine, krĕ'nĕ, m. horse-hair. [mane.
criniera, krĭnĭĕ'ră, f. horse-hair; lion's **crino,** see crine.
crise, krĕ'sĕ, crisi, –sĭ, f. crisis.
crisma, see cresima.
cristallizare, krĭstăllĭtză'rĕ, v. a. to crystallize; **cristallizarsi,** –tzăr'sĭ, to crystalize. [gulate.
cristallo, –tăl'lŏ, m. crystal.
cristeo, –tĕ'ŏ, cristere, –tĕ'rĕ, m. clyster, injection.
cristanello, –tăn'ĕl'lŏ, m. silly fellow
cristanesimo, –nĕ'sĭmŏ, m., **cristianità,** –nĭtă', f. christianity.
cristiano, –tĭă'nŏ, a. & m. christian.

criterio, *krŭd'rĭŏ*, m. criterion, judgment.
critica, *krē'tĭkă*, f. critique, censure.
criticare, *–kā'rĕ*, v. a. to criticise.
critico, *krē'tĭkŏ*, a. critical.
crivellare, *–vĕllā'rĕ*, v. a. to sift, to riddle; to examine.
crivello, *–vĕl'lŏ*, m. sieve, riddle.
crocchiare, *krŏkkĭā'rĕ*, v. a. to strike, to clack. [ment.
croce, *krŏ'dshĕ*, f. cross; affliction, torment; to irritate.
crociare, *–dshā'rĕ*, v. a. to crucify; to torment; to irritate.
crociata, *–dshā'tă*, f. crusade; cross-way.
crocidare, *–dshĭdā'rĕ*, v. n. to croak, to caw.
crociera, *–dshā'ră*, f. (mar.) cruising.
crocifiggere, *–fĭd'jĕrĕ*, v. a. ir. to crucify.
crocifissione, *–fĭssĭŏ'nĕ*, f. crucifixion.
crocifisso, *–fĭs'sŏ*, m. crucifix.
croco, *krŏ'kŏ*, m. crocus, saffron.
crogiuolo, *krŏjŭŏ'lŏ*, m. crucible.
crollare, *krŏllā'rĕ*, v. a. to shake, to toss.
croma, *krŏ'mă*, f. (mus.) quaver; crotchet.
cromatico, *–māt'kŏ*, a. (mus.) chromatic.
cronaca, *krŏ'năkă*, cronica, *–nĭkă*, f. chronicle.
cronachista, *krŏnăkĭs'tă*, m. chronicler.
cronico, *krŏ'nĭkŏ*, a. (med.) chronic.
cronista, *–nĭs'tă*, m. chronicler.
cronologia, *–nŏlŏjē'ă*, f. chronology.
cronologico, *–lŏ'jĭkŏ*, a. chronological.
cronometro, *–nŏ'mĕtrŏ*, m. chronometer.
crosta, *krŏs'tă*, f. crust, scurf.
cruccia, *krŭt'shă*, f. pick-axe, mattock.
crucciare, *–tshā'rĕ*, v. a. to irritate, to exasperate.
cruccio, *krŭt'shŏ*, m. anger; grief, pain.
cruciare, *–dshā'rĕ*, v. a. to cruciate; to crucify.
crudele, *krŭdā'lĕ*, a. cruel. [torment.
crudelmente, *–mĕn'tĕ*, ad. cruelly.
crudeltà, *–dĕltā'*, f. cruelty.
crudezza, *–dĕt'ză*, crudità, *–dĭtā'* f. crudity, rawness; indigestion.
crudo, *krŏ'dŏ*, a. raw, unripe.
cruento, *krŭĕn'tŏ*, a. bloody; dreadful.
cruna, *krŏ'nă*, f. eye of a needle.
crusca, *krŭs'kă*, f. bran.
cubatura, *kŭbătŏ'ră*, f. cubature.
cubico, *kŏ'bĭkŏ*, a. cubic.
cubito, *kŏ'bĭtŏ*, m. elbow; angle.
cubo, *kŏ'bŏ*, m. cube, die.
cucchiaio, *kŭkkĭā'ĭŏ*, m. spoon; spoonful.
cuccia, *kŭt'shă*, f. couch; seat. [stretch.
cucciare, *–tshā'rĕ*, v. a. to lay down; to
cucciolo, *kŭt'shŏlŏ*, m. little dog; simple-
cucco, *kŭk'kŏ*, m. egg; darling. [ton.
cuccuma, *kŭ'kŭmă*, f. hatred, rancour.
cucina, *–dshē'nă*, f. kitchen.
cucinare, *–dshĭnā'rĕ*, v. a. to cook.
cuciniera, *–nĭĕ'ră*, f. cook-maid.
cuciniere, *–nĭĕ'rĕ*, m. man-cook.
cucino, *–dshē'nŏ*, m. cushion, pillow.
cucire, *–dshē'rĕ*, v. a. to sew, to stitch.
cucitrice, *–dshĭtrē'dshĕ*, f. seamstress.
cucitura, *–tŏ'ră*, f. suture. [mender.
cuculiare, *–kŭlĭā'rĕ*, v. a. to mock, to quiz.
cuculo, *kŏ'kŭlŏ*, m. cuckoo.

cucurbita, *kŭkŭr'bĭtă*, f. cucurbite, gourd.
cucuzza, *–kŭt'ză*, f. gourd; noddle, pate.
cuffia, *kŭf'fĭă*, f. coif, cap, bonnet.
cugina, *–jē'nă*, cugino, *–nŏ*, m. cousin.
cui, *kŭ'ĭ*, pn. which, whom.
culatta, *–lāt'tă*, f. breech (of firearms).
culla, *kŭl'lă*, f. cradle. [glass &c.).
culo, *kŏ'lŏ*, m. backside; bottom (of a
cumulare, *kŭmŭlā'rĕ*, v. a. to accumulate.
cumulativo, *–tĕ'vŏ*, a. cumulative.
cumulo, *kŏ'mŭlŏ*, m. heap; store.
cuna, *kŏ'nă*, f. cradle.
cuneo, *kŏ'nĕŏ*, m. wedge.
cunetta, *kŭnĕt'tă*, f. (mil.) cunette.
cunicolo, *–nē'kŏlŏ*, cuniculo. *–kŭlŏ*, m. mine; rabbit, cony.
cuoca, *kŭŏ'kă*, f. cook-maid.
cuocere, *kŭŏ'dshĕrĕ*, v. a. ir. to cook.
cuoco, *kŭŏ'kŏ*, m. cook, man-cook.
cuoio, *kŭŏ'ŏ*, m. leather, skin.
cuore, *kŭŏ'rĕ*, m. heart; (fig.) courage.
cupidigia, *kŭpĭdē'jă*, cupidità, *–dĭtā'*, f. cupidity.
cupido, *kŏ'pĭdŏ*, a. desirous, covetous..
cupo, *kŏ'pŏ*, a. deep; dark; reserved, pensive; —, m. depth.
cupola, *kŏ'pŏlă*, f. cupola, dome.
cura, *kŏ'ră*, f. care; cure; parish.
curabile, *kŭră'bĭlĕ*, a. curable.
curante, *–răn'tĕ*, a. careful.
curare, *–rā'rĕ*, v. a. to take care; to protect; to value; to cure.
curato, *–rā'tŏ*, m. parson.
curatore, *–tŏ'rĕ*, m. guardian, trustee.
curia, *kŏ'rĭă*, f. court of justice.
curiosità, *kŭrĭŏsĭtā'*, f. curiosity; rarity.
curioso, *kŭrĭŏ'sŏ*, a. curious; comical.
cursore, *kŭrsŏ'rĕ*, m. runner; messenger.
curva, *kŭr'vă*, f. curve.
curvare, *–vā'rĕ*, v. a. to curve, to crook.
curvezza, *–vĕt'ză*, curvità, *–vĭtā'*, f. curvity.
cuscino, *kŭsshĕ'nŏ*, m. cushion, pillow.
cuscuta, *kŭskŭ'tă*, f. monk's rhubarb.
cuspide, *kŭs'pĭdĕ*, f. (poet.) spear, javelin.
custode, *–tŏ'dĕ*, m. keeper, guardian.
custodia, *–tŏ'dĭă*, f. custody; care.
custodire, *–tŏdē'rĕ*, v. n. to keep, to guard; to watch.
cutaneo, *kŭtā'nĕŏ*, a. cutaneous.
cute, *kŏ'tĕ*, f. human skin.
cuticagna, *kŭtĭkăn'yă*, f. hair of the neck.
cuticola, *–tĕ'kŏlă*, f. cuticle.
czar, *tzăr*, m. czar.
czarina, *–rē'nă*, f. czarina.

D.

da, *dā*, pr. from, by; about; of; – che, since; – indi innanzi, thence-forward; – indi in poi, since that time; – prima, at first; – vero, indeed. [city.
dabbenaggine, *dăbbĕnăd'jĕnĕ*, f. simplicity.
dabbene, *–bĕ'nĕ*, a. good, upright.
dachè, *–kĕ'*, c. since, as.

daddovero, –dŏvă'rŏ, ad. in earnest, really.
dado, dă'dŏ, m. die; cube.
daga, dă'gă, f. dagger, stiletto.
daino, dă'inŏ, m. deer, buck.
dama, dă'mă, f. lady, mistress; **giuocar a –,** to play at draughts.
damascare, –măskă'rě, v. a. to damask.
damasco, –mă'kŏ, m. damask; raised work; inlaid work.
damaschinare, –kĭnă'rě, v.a. to damask.
damerino, –měrē'nŏ, m. dandy, coxcomb.
damigella, –mĭjěl'lă, f. young lady.
damigello, –mĭjěl'lŏ, m. young man, page.
damma, dăm'mă, f. (poet.) doe, deer.
damo, dă'mŏ, m. wooer, gallant.
danaro, see **denaro.**
dannare, dănnă'rě, v. n. to condemn, to blame; to erase.   [demned
dannato, –nnă'tŏ, m. reproved; –, a. condemned
dannazione, –tzĭŏ'ně, f. condemnation.
danneggiare, –nědjă'rě, v. a. to damage, to injure, to hurt.
danno, dăn'nŏ, m. damage; prejudice.
dannoso, –nŏ'sŏ, a. hurtful, noxious.
dante, dăn'tě, m. deer-skin.
danza, dăn'tză, f. dance.
danzare, –tză'rě, v. n. to dance.
danzatore, –dănnă'tŏ'rě, m., **danzatrice,** –trě'dshě, f. dancer.
dappiè, dăppiě', **dappiede,** –pĭd'dě, ad. from the foot or bottom.   [carelessness.
dappocaggine, –pŏkăd'jĭně, f. indolence.
dappoco, –pŏ'kŏ, a. lazy, cowardly, spiritless.
dappoi, –pŏ'i, ad. & pr. since, after.   [less.
dappoichè, –pŏ'kě, c. since, in as much as.
dappresso, –prěs'sŏ, pr. near, hard by.
dardeggiare, dărdědjă'rě, v. a. to dart,
dardo, dăr'dŏ, m. dart, spear.   [to shoot.
dare, dă'rě, v. a. ir. to give; to grant, to permit; to commit; to appoint; to announce; to produce, to yield; to show, to tell; to strike; to dart; to incline to.
darsena, dărsě'nă, f. wet-dock.
data, dă'tă, f. date.
dattero, dăt'těrŏ, m. date (fruit).
dattilo, dăt'tĭlŏ, m. dactyl; –, a. dactylic.
davante, dăvăn'tě, **davanti,** –tĭ, ad. & pr. before.
davvero, dăvvă'rŏ, ad. in truth.
dazio, dă'tzĭŏ, m. toll, duty, excise.
dea, dě'ă, f. goddess.   [subdue.
debellare, děběllă'rě, v. a. to conquer, to
debilità, see **debolezza.**
debilitare, –bĭlĭtă'rě, v. a. to enfeeble.
debito, dě'bĭtŏ, a. due; fit, suitable; –, m. debt, duty.
debitore, děbĭtŏ'rě, m. debtor.
debole, dě'bŏlě, a. feeble, weak.
debolezza, děbŏlět'ză, f. weakness.
decadenza, –kăděn'tză, f. decay, decline.
decadere, –kădă'rě, v. n. ir. to fall off, to decline.
decagono, –kă'gŏnŏ, m. decagon.
decalogo, –kă'lŏgŏ, m. Decalogue.
decampare, –kămpă'rě, v. n. to decamp.
decanato, –kănă'tŏ, m. deanery, deanship.
decano, –kă'nŏ, m. dean; senior.

decantare, –kăntă'rě, v. a. to decant.
decapitare, –kăpĭtă'rě, v. a. to behead.
decapitazione, –tzĭŏ'ně, f. beheading.
decembre, –dshěm'brě, m. December.
decennale, –dshěnnă'lě, a. decennial.
decennio, –dshěn'nĭŏ, m. space of ten years.
decente, –dshěn'tě, a. decent.   [years.
decenza, –dshěn'tză, f. decency.
decesso, –dshě'sŏ, m. decease, death.
decezione, –dshětzĭŏ'ně, f. deception, cheat, deceit, imposture.
decidere, –dshě'děrě, v. a. ir. to decide.
deciferare, –dshĭfěră'rě, v. a. to decipher.
decima, dě'dshĭmă, f. tithe.
decimale, –dědshĭmă'lě, a. decimal.
decimare, –mă'rě, v. a. to tithe, to decimate.   [part.
decimo, dě'dshĭmŏ, a. & m. tenth; tenth
decimottavo, dědshĭmŏttă'vŏ, a. eighteenth.
decisione, –dshĭzĭŏ'ně, f. decision, decree.
decisivo, –sě'vŏ, a. decisive, peremptory.
deciso, –dshě'sŏ, a. decided.
declamare, –klămă'rě, v. n. to declaim.
declamatore, –tŏ'rě, m. declaimer.
declamatorio, –tŏ'rĭŏ, a. declamatory.
declamazione, –tzĭŏ'ně, f. declamation, harangue.
declinare, –klĭnă'rě, v. n. to lower; to decay; (gr.) to decline.
declinazione, –tzĭŏ'ně, f. declination; (gr.) declension.
declive, –klě'vě, a. sloping.
declivio, –klě'vĭŏ, m. slope, declivity.
declività, –klĭvĭtă', f. declivity, descent.
declivo, see **declive.**
decollare, –kŏllă'rě, v. a. to decapitate.
decomporre, –kŏmpŏr'rě, v. a. to decompose, to analyse.   [adorn.
decorare, –kŏră'rě, v. a. to decorate, to
decorazione, –tzĭŏ'ně, f. decoration, ornament.
decoro, –kŏ'rŏ, m. decorum, decency.
decoroso, –kŏ'sŏ, a. decorous, decent.
decorso, –kŏr'sŏ, m. course, stream.
decozione, –kŏtzĭŏ'ně, f. decoction.
decremento, –krěměn'tŏ, m. decrease, de-
decrepito, –krě'pĭtŏ, a. decrepit.   [cay.
decrescere, –krěsh'ěrě, v. n. ir. to decrease.
decretare, –krětă'rě, v. a. to decree.
decreto, –krě'tŏ, m. decree.
decuplo, dě'kŭplŏ, a. tenfold.
dedalo, dě'dălŏ, a. dedalian, dedalious.
dedica, dě'dĭkă, f. dedication.
dedicare, –kă'rě, v. a. to dedicate; to consecrate.
dedito, dě'dĭtŏ, a. given, addicted.
dedizione, –dědĭzĭŏ'ně, f. surrender.
dedurre, –dŭr'rě, v. a. ir. to deduce.
dedutto, –dăt'tŏ, a. deducted; drawn.
defalcare, –fălkă'rě, v. a. to deduct, to retrench.   [spect.
deferenza, –fěrěn'tză, f. deference, re-
deferire, –rě'rě, v. n. to submit; to defer.
definire, see **diffinire &c.**
deflorare, –flŏră'rě, v. a. to deflower.

deflusso, –flús'sŏ, m. defluxion.
deformare, –fōrmä'rĕ, v. a. to disfigure.
deforme, –fōr'mĕ, a. deformed, ugly.
defraudare, –fräüdä'rĕ, v. a. to defraud.
defunto, –fün'tŏ, a. deceased, defunct.
degenerare, –jĕnĕrä'rĕ, v. n. to degenerate.
degnare, dĕnyä'rĕ, v. n. to value, to vouchsafe; to condescend, to be pleased.
degno, dĕn'yŏ, a. worthy.
degradare, dĕgrädä'rĕ, v. a. to degrade.
degradazione, –tzĭŏ'nĕ, f. degradation.
deificare, dĕĭfĭkä'rĕ, v. a. to deify.
deificazione, –tzĭŏ'nĕ, f. apotheosis.
deismo, dĕĭs'mŏ, m. deism.
deista, dĕĭs'tä, m. deist.
deità, dĕĭtä', f. deity; divinity.
del, dĕl, art. (for de il) of the.
delatore, dĕlätŏ'rĕ, m. accuser; spy.
delazione, –tzĭŏ'nĕ, f. delation.
delegare, –lĕgä'rĕ, v. a. to delegate.
delegato, –lĕgä'tŏ, m. delegate, deputy.
delegazione, –tzĭŏ'nĕ, f. deputation.
delfino, dĕlfĭ'nŏ, m. dolphin; dauphin.
delibare, dĕlĭbä'rĕ, v. a. (poet.) to taste.
deliberare, –lĭbĕrä'rĕ, v. n. to deliberate.
deliberazione, –tzĭŏ'nĕ, f. deliberation, consultation.
delicatezza, –lĭkätĕt'zä, f. delicacy.
delicato, –lĭkä'tŏ, a. delicate; gentle.
delineare, –lĭnĕä'rĕ, v. a. to draw, to sketch. [offender.
delinquente, –lĭnkwĕn'tĕ, m. delinquent.
delinquere, –lĭn'kwĕrĕ, v. n. to commit a crime.
deliquio, –lĕ'kwĭŏ, m. fainting fit.
delirante, –lĭrän'tĕ, a. delirious.
delirare, –lĭrä'rĕ, v. n. to rave; to dote.
delirio, –lĕ'rĭŏ, m. delirium, madness.
delitto, –lĭt'tŏ, m. crime, misdeed.
delizia, –lĕ'tzĭä, f. delight, pleasure.
delizioso, –lĭtzĭŏ'sŏ, a. delicious.
deludere, –lŏ'dĕrĕ, v. a. ir. to delude.
delusione, –lüsĭŏ'nĕ, f. delusion, cheat.
demagogo, –mägŏ'gŏ, m. demagogue.
demarcazione, –märkätzĭŏ'nĕ, f. demarcation.
demente, –mĕn'tĕ, a. mad, frantic.
demenza, –mĕn'tzä, f. madness.
demeritare, –mĕrĭtä'rĕ, v. a. to do amiss.
demerito, –mä'rĭtŏ, m. demerit; punishment. [cal.
democratico, –mŏkrä'tĭkŏ, a. democratical.
democrazia, –tzĕ'ä, f. democracy.
demolire, –mŏlĭ'rĕ, v. a. to demolish.
demolizione, –lĭtzĭŏ'nĕ, f. demolition, destruction.
demone, dä'mŏnĕ, m. demon. [furious.
demoniaco, dĕmŏnĕ'äkŏ, a. demoniacal.
demonio, –mä'nĭŏ, m. demon, devil.
denaro, –nä'rŏ, m. penny; money.
denaroso, –rŏ'sŏ, a. rich in money, monied.
denegare, –nĕgä'rĕ, v. a. to deny.
denigrare, –nĭgrä'rĕ, v. a. to blacken; to slander. [nominate, to name.
denominare, –nŏmĭnä'rĕ, v. a. to de-

denominatore, –tŏ'rĕ, m. (ar.) denominator. [tion.
denominazione, –tzĭŏ'nĕ, f. denomination.
denotare, –nŏtä'rĕ, v. a. to denote.
densità, dĕnsĭtä', f. density, thickness.
denso, dĕn'sŏ, a. dense, thick; solid.
dentale, –tä'lĕ, a. & s. dental.
dentatura, –tŏ'rä, f. set of teeth.
dente, dĕn'tĕ, m. tooth; notch. [notch.
dentellare, –tĕllä'rĕ, v. a. to dent, to
dentello, –tĕl'lŏ, m. lace; notching.
dentista, –tĭs'tä, m. dentist.
dentro, dĕn'trŏ, ad. within, inwardly.
denudare, dĕnüdä'rĕ, v. a. to denude; to divest; to expose. [ciate.
denunziare, –nüntzĭä'rĕ, v. a. to denunciate.
deplorare, –plŏrä'rĕ, v. a. & n. to deplore, to bewail. [(gr.) verb deponent.
deponente, –pŏnĕn'tĕ, a. & m. deposing;
deporre, –pŏr'rĕ, v. a. ir. to depose; to degrade; to resign; to bear witness.
deportazione, –lätzĭŏ'nĕ, f. transportation, banishment, exile.
depositare, –pŏsĭtä'rĕ, v. a. to deposit.
deposito, –pŏ'sĭtŏ, m. deposit.
deposto, –pŏs'tŏ, m. attestation.
depravare, –prävä'rĕ, v. a. to deprave.
depravato, –vä'tŏ, a. depraved.
depravazione, –tzĭŏ'nĕ, f. depravation.
depredare, –prĕdä'rĕ, v. a. to ravage, to pillage, to prey upon.
deprimere, –prĕ'mĕrĕ, v. a. to depress.
depurare, –pürä'rĕ, v. a. to depurate, to depure, to purify, to refine.
deputare, –pütä'rĕ, v. a. to depute.
deputato, –tä'tŏ, m. deputy; delegate.
deputazione, –tzĭŏ'nĕ, f. deputation.
derelitto, –rĕlĭt'tŏ, a. abandoned.
derisione, –rĭsĭŏ'nĕ, f. derision.
derivare, –vä'rĕ, v. n. to derive; to derivate.
derivativo, –tĕ'vŏ, a. derivative.
derivazione, –tzĭŏ'nĕ, f. derivation, origin.
deroga, dä'rŏgä, f. derogation.
derogare, –rŏgä'rĕ, v. a. to derogate, to disparage.
derogatorio, dĕrŏgätŏ'rĭŏ, a. derogatory.
derogazione, –tzĭŏ'nĕ, f. derogation.
derrata, –rä'tä, f. merchandise; ware;
desco, dĕs'kŏ, m. table, board. [portion.
descrittivo, dĕskrĭt'tĭvŏ, a. descriptive.
descrivere, –skrĕ'vĕrĕ, v. a. ir. to describe.
descrizione, –skrĭtzĭŏ'nĕ, f. description; inventory. [ness.
deserto, dĕsĕr'tŏ, a. & m. desert; wilderdesiare, –sĭä'rĕ, desiderare, –dĕrä'rĕ, v. a. to desire, to long for.
desiderio, –dĕ'rĭŏ, m. desire, longing.
desideroso, –dĕrŏ'sŏ, a. desirous.
desidia, –sĕ'dĭä, f. (poet.) sloth, indolence.
designare, –sĭnyä'rĕ, v. a. to design; to assign.
desinare, –sĭnä'rĕ, v. n. to dine.
desinenza, –nĕn'tzä, f. termination.
desio, –sĕ'ŏ, m. desire.
desistere, –sĕs'tĕrĕ, v. n. ir. to desist
desolare, –sŏlä'rĕ, v. a. to desolate, to deprive of.

despota, *dĕs'pŭtä*, m. despot.
dessa, *dĕs'sä*, pn. she, she herself.
desso, *dĕs'sŏ*, pn. he, he himself.
destare, *dĕstä'rĕ*, v. a. to awake.
destinare, *–tĭnä'rĕ*, v. a. to destine; to destinate.
destinazione, *–tzĭŏ'nĕ*, f. destination.
destino, *–tĕ'nŏ*, m. destiny, fate.
desto, *dĕs'tŏ*, a. awaked, sprightly.
destra, *dĕs'trä*, f. right hand or side.
destrezza, *–trĕt'zä*, f. dexterity, skill.
destriero, *–trĭä'rĕ*, **destriero**, *–rŏ*, m. courser, war-horse; fine horse.
destro, *dĕs'trŏ*, a. dexterous, right, skilful; cunning; propitious; –, m. opportunity; water-closet.
desumere, *–sū'mĕrĕ*, v. a. to deduce.
detenere, *dĕtĕnä'rĕ*, v. a. to detain.
detenzione, *–tĕntzĭŏ'nĕ*, f. detention; confinement, imprisonment.
detergere, *–tĕr'jĕrĕ*, v. a. ir. to deterge.
deteriorare, *–rĭŏrä'rĕ*, v. a. to deteriorate.
determinare, *–mĭnä'rĕ*, v. a. to determine.
determinativo, *–tĕ'vŏ*, a. decisive.
determinazione, *–tzĭŏ'nĕ*, f. determination, resolution.
detestare, *–tĕstä'rĕ*, v. a. to detest.
detrarre, *–trä'rĕ*, v. a. ir. to lessen; to slander; to deprive.
detrazione, *–trätzĭŏ'nĕ*, f. detraction.
detrimento, *–trĭmĕn'tŏ*, m. detriment, injury.   [throne.
detronizzare, *–trŏnĭdzä'rĕ*, v. a. to dethrone.
detta, *dĕt'tä*, f. debt; credit.
dettare, *dĕttä'rĕ*, v. a. to dictate; to teach.
dettato, *–tä'tŏ*, m. style, elocution; proverb.
dettatore, *–tŏ'rĕ*, m. author, writer; dictator.   [ship.
dettatura, *–tŏ'rä*, f. dictation; dictatorship.
detto, *dĕt'tŏ*, a. said; named; – fatto, no sooner said than done; –, m. word; maxim.
deturpare, *dĕtŭrpä'rĕ*, v. a. to disfigure.
devastare, *–västä'rĕ*, v. a. to devastate.
devastazione, *–tzĭŏ'nĕ*, f. devastation, havoc.
deviare, *–vĭä'rĕ*, v. n. to deviate.
devoto, *–vŏ'tŏ*, a. devout, devoted, attached.
devozione, *–vŏtzĭŏ'nĕ*, f. devotion, piety.
di, *dĭ*, pr. of, from, to; – certo, for certain.
dì, *dĭ*, m. day; day-time.
diabete, *dĭäbĕ'tĕ*, m. siphon.
diabolico, *–bŏ'lĭkŏ*, a. diabolical. devilish.
diacono, *dĭä'kŏnŏ*, m. deacon.
diadema, *–dĕ'mä*, m. diadem.
diafano, *dĭä'fänŏ*, a. transparent.
diagnosi, *dĭän'ȳ ŏsĕ*, f. diagnosis.
diagonale, *–gŏnä'lĕ*, a. diagonal.
diagramma, *–grăm'mä*, m. diagram.
dialettica, *–lĕt'tĭkä*, f. dialectic art, logic.
dialetto, *–lĕt'tŏ*, m. dialect, idiom.
dialogo, *dĭä'lŏgŏ*, m. dialogue.
diamante, *–män'tĕ*, m. diamond.
diametro, *dĭä'mĕtrŏ*, m. diameter.
dianzi, *dĭän'tzĕ*, ad. before, not long since.
diario, *dĭä'rĭŏ*, m. diary, journal.

diarrea, *–rȳ'ä*, f. diarrhœa.
diaspro, *dĭäs'prŏ*, m. jasper.
diatriba, *–trĕ'bä* (*dĭä'trĭbä*), f. dissertation.
dibassare, *dĭbässä'rĕ*, v. a. to debase.
dibattere, *–bät'tĕrĕ*, v. a. to shake, to beat, to debate.   [of trees.
diboscamento, *–bŏskämĕn'tŏ*, m. felling trees.   [peel; to husk.
diboscare, *–bŏskä'rĕ*, v. a. to cut down trees.
dibucciare, *–bŭtshä'rĕ*, v. a. to bark, to peel; to husk.
dicembre, *–dshĕm'brĕ*, m. December.
diceria, *–dshĕrĕ'ä*, f. saying; verbiage.
dicevole, *–dshĕ'vŏlĕ*, a. suitable, becoming.
dichiarare, *–kĭärä'rĕ*, v. a. to declare, to explain.   [explanation.
dichiarazione, *–tzĭŏ'nĕ*, f. declaration.
dichinare, *–kĭnä'rĕ*, v. n. to decline, to go down.
diciannove, *–dshĭänŏ'vĕ*, a. nineteen.
diciannovesimo, *–nŏvĕ'sĭmŏ*, a. nineteenth.
diciassette, *–sĕt'tĕ*, a. seventeen.
diciassettesimo, *–tĕ'sĭmŏ*, a. seventeenth.   [sible.
dicibile, *–dshĕ'bĭlĕ*, a. utterable, expressible.
diciferare, *–dshĭfĕrä'rĕ*, v. a. to decipher.
diciotto, *–ŏt'tŏ*, a. eighteen.
didascalico, *–däskä'lĭkŏ*, a. instructive.
didacciare, *–dätshä'rĕ*, v. a. to thaw.
dieci, *dĭĕ'dshĕ*, a. ten.
dieta, *dĭĕ'tä*, f. diet; assembly.
dietro, *dĭĕ'trŏ*, pr. & ad. behind, afterwards.   [to forbid, to prohibit.
difendere, *dĭfĕn'dĕrĕ*, v. a. ir. to defend;
difensivo, *–sĭ'vŏ*, a. defensive.
difensore, *–sŏ'rĕ*, m. defender, protector.
difesa, *–fĕ'sä*, f. defence.   [of, to want.
difettare, *–fĕttä'rĕ*, v. n. to stand in need
difettivo, *–tĕ'vŏ*, a. defective, imperfect.
difetto, *–fĕt'tŏ*, m. defect, blemish; want.
difettosamente, *–tŏsämĕn'tĕ*, ad. imperfectly.
difettoso, *–tŏ'sŏ*, a. defective, imperfect.
diffalcare, *–fälkä'rĕ*, v. a. to abate, to deduct; to abridge.
diffalta, *–fäl'tä*, f. fault; breach; dearth.
diffamare, *–fämä'rĕ*, v. a. to defame, to slander.
diffamatore, *–tŏ'rĕ*, m. defamer, slanderer.
diffamatorio, *–tŏ'rĭŏ*, a. defamatory.
diffamazione, *–tzĭŏ'nĕ*, f. defamation, calumny, slander.
differente, *–fĕrĕn'tĕ*, a. different, various.
differenza, *–rĕn'tzä*, f. difference.
differire, *–rĕ'rĕ*, v. a. & n. to defer; to differ.
difficile, *–fĕ'dshĭlĕ*, a. difficult.   [differ.
difficilmente, *–fĕdshĭlmĕn'tĕ*, ad. with difficulty.
difficoltà, *–kŏltä'*, f. difficulty.   [suspect.
diffidare, *–dä'rĕ*, v. a. to distrust, to
diffidenza, *–dĕn'tzä*, f. distrust, suspicion.
diffinire, *–fĕnĕ'rĕ*, v. a. to define.
diffondere, *–fŏn'dĕrĕ*, v. a. ir. to diffuse.
difformare, *–förmä'rĕ*, v. a. to deform, to disfigure.
difforme, *–för'mĕ*, a. deformed, ugly.
difformità, *–mĭtä'*, f. deformity.

diffusione, *—füsió'nĕ*, f. diffusion.
diffuso, *—fŏ'sŏ*, a. diffuse; copious.
diformare, *see* difformare.
diga, *dĕ'gä*, f. dike, bank, mole. [digest.
digerire, *dijĕrĕ'rĕ*, v. a. to concoct, to
digestione, *—jĕstiŏ'nĕ*, f. digestion.
dighiacciare, *—ghätshä'rĕ*, v. n. to thaw;
  to liquefy.
digiunare, *—jŭnä'rĕ*, v. n. to fast.
digiuno, *—jŏ'nŏ*, a. & m. fasting.
dignità, *dinyitä'*, f. dignity, rank.
digradare, *—grädä'rĕ*, v. a. & n. to degrade; to descend gradually.
digradazione, *—tziŏ'nĕ*, f. gradual descent.
digredire, *—grĕdĕ'rĕ*, v. n. to digress.
digressione, *—grĕssiŏ'nĕ*, f. digression.
digressivo, *—sĕ'vŏ*, a. digressive.
digrossare, *—grŏssä'rĕ*, v. a. to chip; to
  form; to teach. [ruminate, to consider.
digrumare, *—grŭmä'rĕ*, v. n. to chew, to
diguazzare, *—gŭätzä'rĕ*, v. a. to shake up.
dilacciare, *—lätshä'rĕ*, v. a. to unlace.
dilacerare, *—dshĕrä'rĕ*, v.a.to tear, to rend.
dilagare, *—lägä'rĕ*, v. a. to overflow.
dilapidare, *—pĭdä'rĕ*, v. a. to squander
  away, to waste. [to defer, to prolong.
dilatare, *—tä'rĕ*, v. a. to dilate, to extend;
dilatorio, *—tŏ'riŏ*, a. dilatory, tardy.
dilavare, *—vä'rĕ*, v. a. to wash away.
dilazione, *—tziŏ'nĕ*, f. delay, respite.
dileggiare, *—lĕdjä'rĕ*, v. a. to laugh at, to
  scoff at, to deride, to banter.
dileggiato, *—djä'tŏ*, a. impudent, insolent.
dileggio, *—lĕd'jŏ*, m. impudence.
dilegine, *—lĕ'jinĕ*, a. soft; thin (of texture);
  feeble.
dileguare, *—lĕgŭä'rĕ*, v. n. to vanish.
dileguo, *—lĕ'gŭŏ*, m. disappearance; distance.
dilemma, *—lĕm'mä*, m. dilemma, difficulty.
dileticare, *—lĕtĭkä'rĕ*, v. n. to tickle; to
diletico, *—lä'tĭkŏ*, m. tickling. [flatter.
dilettante, *—lĕttän'tĕ*, m. dilettante, amateur. [joice.
dilettare, *—tä'rĕ*, v. a. to delight, to re-
diletto, *—lĕt'tŏ*, m. delight, pleasure.
dilettoso, *—tŏ'sŏ*, a. delightful.
dilezione, *—tziŏ'nĕ*, f. love, affection.
diligente, *—lĭjĕn'tĕ*, a. diligent, careful.
diligenza, *—jĕn'tzä*, f. diligence, care.
dilucidare, *—lŭdshidä'rĕ*, v. a. to elucidate, to explain, to expound.
diluire, *—lŭĕ'rĕ*, v. a. to dilute.
dilungare, *—lŭngä'rĕ*, v. a. to stretch; to
  lengthen; to extend; dilungarsi, *—gär'-
  sĕ*, to ramble.
diluviare, *—lŭvĭä'rĕ*, v. a. & n. to devour;
  to rain hard, to overflow.
diluviatore, *—tŏ'rĕ*, m. glutton.
diluvio, *—lŏ'vĭŏ*, m. deluge.
diluvione, *—lŭvĭŏ'nĕ*, m. glutton.
dimagrare, *—mägrä'rĕ*, v. n. to get lean.
dimanda, *—män'dä*, f. question, request.
dimandare, *—dä'rĕ*, v. a. to ask, to request.
dimani, *—mä'nĕ*, ad. to-morrow.
dimembrare, *—mĕmbrä'rĕ*, v. a. to dismember, to tear asunder.

dimenare, *—mĕnä'rĕ*, v. a. to shake, to
  agitate, to loss.
dimensione, *—siŏ'nĕ*, f. dimension.
dimenticanza, *—tĭkän'tzä*, f.forgetfulness.
dimenticare, *—kä'rĕ*, v. a. & n. to forget.
dimentichevole, *—kä'vŏlĕ*, dimentico,
  —tĭkŏ, a. forgetful. [dispirited.
dimesso, *—mĕs'sŏ*, a. omitted, neglected;
dimesticare, *—tĭkä'rĕ*, v. a. to domesticate, to tame; dimesticarsi, *—kär'sĕ*,
  to grow familiar. [familiar.
dimestico, *—mĕs'tĭkŏ*, a. tame; intimate,
dimettere, *—mĕt'tĕrĕ*, v. a. n. to dismiss;
  to forgive.
dimezzare, *—mĕtzä'rĕ*, dimidiare, *—mĭ-
  dĭä'rĕ*, v. a. to halve, to divide in two.
diminuire, *—mĭnŭĕ'rĕ*, v. a. to diminish.
diminutivo, *—nŭtĕ'vŏ*, a. diminutive.
diminuzione, *—tziŏ'nĕ*, f. diminution.
dimissione, *—mĭssiŏ'nĕ*, f. dimission.
dimodochè, *—mŏdŏkĕ'*, c. so that.
dimora, *—mŏ'rä*, f. delay; abode.
dimorare, *—mŏrä'rĕ*, v. n. to dwell, to reside; dimorarsi, *—rär'sĕ*, to dwell, to
  reside, to live. [strate, to show.
dimostrare, *—mŏsträ'rĕ*, v. a. to demon-
dimostrativo, *—tĕ'vŏ*, a. demonstrative.
dimostrazione, *—tziŏ'nĕ*, f. demonstration.
dinanzi, *—nän'tzĭ*, pr. & ad. before one's
  face, in presence of; preceding.
dinegare, *—nĕgä'rĕ*, v. a. to deny.
dinegazione, *—tziŏ'nĕ*, f. denial.
dinervare, *—nĕrvä'rĕ*, v. a. to enervate, to
  weaken.
dinotare, *—nŏtä'rĕ*, v. a. to denote.
dintornare, *dĭntŏrnä'rĕ*, v. a. to trace the
  outline of.
dintorno, *—tŏr'nŏ*, m. environs, pl.
dinudare, *dĭnŭdä'rĕ*, v. a. to strip naked.
dinumerare, *—mĕrä'rĕ*, v. a. to number;
Dio, *dĕ'ŏ*, m. God. [to reckon.
diocesano, *dĭŏdshĕsä'nŏ*, a. & m. diocesan.
diocesi, *dĭŏ'dshĕsĕ*, f. diocese, [reel.
dipanare, *dĭpänä'rĕ*, v. a. to wind up, to
dipartenza, *—pärtĕn'tzä*, f. departure.
dipartimento, *—tĭmĕn'tŏ*, m. departure;
  division. [depart.
dipartire, *—tĕ'rĕ*, v. a. & n. to divide; to
dipartita, *—tĕ'tä*, f. going away.
dipendenza, *—pĕndĕn'tzä*, f. dependence.
dipendere, *—pĕn'dĕrĕ*, v. n. to depend on.
dipingere, *—pĭn'jĕrĕ*, v. a. ir. to paint; to
dipinto, *—pĭn'tŏ*, m. picture. [describe.
dipintore, *—tŏ'rĕ*, m. painter.
dipintura, *—tŏ'rä*, f. painting, picture.
diploma, *—plŏ'mä*, m. diploma.
diplomatico, *—plŏmä'tĭkŏ*, a. diplomatic.
diportarsi, *—pŏrtär'sĕ*, v. r. to divert oneself; to conduct oneself.
diporto, *—pŏr'tŏ*, m. diversion, amusement.
diradare, *—rädä'rĕ*, v. a. to make thin; to
  rarefy. [exterminate.
diradicare, *—dĭkä'rĕ*, v. a. to root up, to
diramare, *—mä'rĕ*, v. a. to prune, to lop.
dire, *dĕ'rĕ*, v. a. ir. to say, to tell.
diredare, *dĭrĕdä'rĕ*, v. a. to disinherit.

diretto, —*rět'tŏ*, a. direct, straight; ad-
direttore, —*tŏ'rě*, m. director. [dressed.
direzione, —*tzĭŏ'ně*, f. direction.
dirigere, —*rě'jěrě*, v. a. ir. to direct; to
    guide, to lead, to conduct. [vorce.
dirimere, —*rě'měrě*, v. a. to disjoin, to di-
dirimpetto, —*rĭmpět'tŏ*, pr. over against,
    opposite to.
dirittezza, —*rĭttět'zā*, f. level; rectitude;
    honesty; justice.
diritto, —*rĭt'tŏ*, a. straight; upright;
    crafty; —, ad. straight, directly. precisely;
    —, m. right, reason; duty, custom.
dirittura, —*tŏ'rā*, f. straightness; upright-
    ness. [rectify, to correct.
dirizzare, —*rĭtzā'rě*, v. a. to direct; to
dirizzatore, —*tŏ'rě*, m. director; manager.
diroccare, —*rŏkkā'rě*, v. a. to demolish.
dirompere, —*rŏm'pěrě*, v. n. to break, to
    interrupt. [cessive.
dirotto, —*rŏt'tŏ*, a. steep; broken; ex-
dirozzare, —*rŏtzā'rě*, v. a. to rough-hew;
    to dress.
dirupare, —*rūpā'rě*, v. a. to precipitate.
dirupo, —*rū'pŏ*, m. steepness, precipice.
disabitare, —*ăsăbĭtā'rě*, v. a. to depopulate.
disacconcio, —*ăkkŏn'dshŏ*, a. indecent.
disacerbare, —*ădshěrbā'rě*, v. a. to ap-
    pease; to calm. [to waste.
disacquistare, —*ăkkŭĭstā'rě*, v. a. to lose;
disadatto, —*ădāt'tŏ*, a. unfit, unseemly;
    awkward, clumsy.
disagevole, —*ăjě'vŏlě*, a. difficult, hard.
disaggradare, —*ăggrădā'rě*, v. n. to dis-
    please. [able.
disaggradevole, —*dě'vŏlě*, a. disagree-
disagguagliarsi, —*gŭālyār'sĭ*, v. r. to
    differ, to be unlike. [to trouble.
disagiare, —*ăjā'rě*, v. a. to incommode,
disagio, —*ā'jĭŏ*, m. hardship, want.
disameno, —*āmě'nŏ*, a. disagreeable, un-
    pleasant.
disaminare, —*mĭnā'rě*, v. a. to examine.
disamore, —*āmŏ'rě*, m. spite, indifference.
disanimare, —*ănĭmā'rě*, v. a. to kill; to
    dispirit.
disapparare, —*ăppārā'rě*, v. a., **disap-**
    prendere, —*prěn'děrě*, v. a. ir. to un-
    learn, to forget. [prove.
disapprovare, —*prŏvā'rě*, v. a. to disap-
disapprovazione, —*tzĭŏ'ně*, f. disappro-
    bation, disapproval.
disarmare, —*ărmā'rě*, v. a. to disarm.
disarmonia, —*mŏně'ă*, f. discord.
disarmonico, —*mŏ'nĭkŏ*, a. discordant.
disastro, —*ăs'trŏ*, m. disaster, misfortune.
disavanzare, —*ăvāntzā'rě*, v. n. to go
    back; to suffer loss. [age.
disavanzo, —*ăvăn'tzŏ*, m. detriment, dam-
disavvantaggio, —*tăd'jŏ*, m. disadvan-
    tage, injury. [careless.
disavveduto, —*vědŭ'tŏ*, a. inconsiderate,
disavvenente, —*něn'tě*, a. ill-looking,
    ugly. [ugly.
disavvenevole, —*ně'vŏlě*, a. ill-mannered;
disavventura, —*tŏ'rā*, f. mishap, mis-
    chance. [custom.
disavvezzare, —*větzā'rě*, v. a. to disac-

disbarbare, *see* **sbarbare.**
disbarcare, *see* **sbarcare.**
disbramare, *see* **sbramare.**
disbranare, *see* **sbranare.**
disbrancare, —*brănkā'rě*, v. a. to sever,
    to part. [to despatch.
disbrigare, —*brĭgā'rě*, v. a. to disentangle;
discacciare, —*kātshā'rě*, v. a. to expel.
discapito, —*kā'pĭtŏ*, m. loss, damage.
discaricare, —*rĭkā'rě*, v. a. to unload; to
discaro, —*kā'rŏ*, a. disagreeable. [ease.
discendere, —*dĭshěn'děrě*, v. n. ir. to de-
    scend from.
discepolo, —*sshě'pŏlŏ*, m. scholar, pupil.
discernere, —*sshěr'něrě*, v. a. to discern.
discesa, —*sshā'sā*, f. descent.
dischiudere, *dĭskŏ'děrě*, v. a. ir. to dis-
    close. [cut.
discindere, —*sshĭn'děrě*, v. a. to dissect, to
disciogliere, —*sshŏl'yěrě*, v. a. ir. to un-
    tie; to dissolve; to melt.
disciorre, *see* **disciogliere.**
disciplina, —*sshĭplě'nā*, f. discipline; in-
    struction. [to instruct.
disciplinare, —*plĭnā'rě*, v. a. to discipline;
discipolo, —*sshĭ'pŏlŏ*, m. disciple, pupil.
discolo, *dĭs'kŏlŏ*, a. quarrelsome, riotous,
    wild. [rě, v. a. to discolour.
discolorare, —*rā'rě*, v. a. **discolorire,** —*rě'*-
discolpa, —*kŏl'pā*, f. excuse, justification.
discolpare, —*pā'rě*, v. a. to excuse, to
    justify.
disconoscere, —*kŏnŏssh'ěrě*, v. a. ir. to
    mistake for another. [become.
disconvenire, —*kŏnvěně'rě*, v. a. ir. to mis-
discoprire, —*kŏprě'rě*, v. a. ir. to discover.
discordanza, —*kŏrdăn'tzā*, f. discordance.
discordare, —*kŏrdā'rě*, v. n. to disagree;
    to jar; (mus.) to be out of tune.
discorde, —*kŏr'dě*, a. dissonant; incom-
    patible, disagreeing; contrary.
discordia, —*kŏr'dĭā*, f. discord, dissension.
discorrere, —*kŏr'rěrě*, v. n. ir. to ramble
    about; to discourse.
discorsivo, —*sě'vŏ*, a. discursive.
discorso, —*kŏr'sŏ*, m. discourse; treatise.
discortese, —*tā'sě*, a. uncivil, rude.
discosceso, —*kŏsshā'sŏ*, a. steep, pre-
    cipitous, sloping, declivous.
discostare, —*kŏstā'rě*, v. a. to remove.
discosto, —*kŏs'tŏ*, a. far, remote.
discredito, —*krā'dĭtŏ*, m. discredit.
discrepante, —*krěpăn'tě*, a. differing.
discrepanza, —*păn'tzā*, f. difference.
discrepare, —*pā'rě*, v. n. to disagree.
discreto, —*krā'tŏ*, a. discreet.
discrezione, —*krětzĭŏ'ně*, f. discretion.
discussione, —*kŭssĭŏ'ně*, f. discussion.
discutere, —*kŏ'těrě*, v. a. ir. to discuss.
disdegnare, —*děnyā'rě*, v. a. to disdain;
    disdegnarsi, —*yār'sĭ*, to be angry.
disdegno, —*děn'yŏ*, m. disdain, scorn;
    indignation. [ful.
disdegnoso, —*yŏ'sŏ*, a. indignant, scorn-
disdetta, —*dět'tā*, f. denial, refusal.
disdire, —*dě'rě*, v. a. ir. to deny, to refuse.
disdoro, —*dŏ'rŏ*, m. dishonour.
disegnare, —*sěnyā'rě*, v. a. to design.

disegnatore, –tō'rĕ, m. designer.
disegnatura, –tū'rā, f. sketch, design.
disegno, –sĕn'yŏ, m. design, drawing; intention, purpose.
diseredare, diśĕrĕdā'rĕ, v. a. to disinherit.
diseredazione, –tziō'nĕ, f. disinheriting.
disertare, –sĕrtā'rĕ, v. a. to ravage, to lay waste; –, v. n. to desert.
disertore, –tō'rĕ, m. deserter, runaway.
disfamare, disfamā'rĕ, v. a. to satiate; to defame. [stroy.
disfare, –fā'rĕ, v. a. ir. to undo, to de-
disfatta, –fāt'tā, f. defeat [to shine.
disfavillare, –villā'rĕ, v. n. to sparkle,
disfavore, –vō'rĕ, m. disfavour.
disfida, –fē'dā, f. defiance, challenge.
disfidare, –fēdā'rĕ, v. a. & n. to challenge; to mistrust.
disfigurare, –gūrā'rĕ, v. a. to disfigure.
disfiorare, –fiōrā'rĕ, v. a. to deflower.
disgiungere, –jūn'jĕrĕ, v. a. ir. to disjoin, to separate. [to discharge.
disgombrare, –gōmbrā'rĕ, v. a. to remove,
disgradevole, –grādĕ'vŏlĕ, a. disagreeable.
disgradire, –dē'rĕ, v. a. to dislike.
disgrazia, –grā'tziā, f. disgrace.
disgraziare, –tziā'rĕ, v. a. to disgrace.
disgraziatamente, –tāmĕn'tĕ, ad. unhappily, by chance.
disgraziato, –tziā'tŏ, a. unlucky; disagreeable. [to scatter.
disgregare, –grĕgā'rĕ, v. a. to disperse,
disguaglio, –gūāl'yŏ, m. disparity.
disgustare, –gūstā'rĕ, v. a. to disgust, to displease; to vex. [disagreeable.
disgustevole, –tĕ'vŏlĕ, a. disgusting,
disgusto, –gūs'tŏ, m. disgust.
disgustoso, –tō'sŏ, a. disgusting.
disiare, disiā'rĕ, a. to desire.
disimparare, disimpārā'rĕ, v. a. to unlearn, to forget. [engage.
disimpegnare, –pĕnyā'rĕ, v. a. to dis-
disingannare, –ingānnā'rĕ, v. a. to undeceive.
disinganno, –gān'nŏ, m. undeceiving.
disinteressato, –tĕressā'tŏ, a. disinterested. [ness.
disinteresse, –rĕs'sĕ, m. disinterested-
disinvolto, –vōl'tŏ, a. free, easy; clever.
disio, see desio.
disistima, disistē'mā, f. disesteem, contempt. [tempt.
dislacciare, dislātshā'rĕ, v. a. to unlace.
disleale, –lĕā'lĕ, a. disloyal, false.
dislealtà, –lĕāltā', f. disloyalty; perfidy.
dislegare, –lĕgā'rĕ, v. a. to untie.
dislogare, –lōgā'rĕ, v. a. to dislocate.
dismettere, –mĕt'tĕrĕ, v. a. ir. to abandon, to give up; to omit.
dismisura, –misū'rā, f. excess, superfluity.
dismontare, –mōntā'rĕ, v. n. to dismount, to descend. [move.
dismuovere, –mūŏ'vĕrĕ, v. a. ir. to re-
disnervare, –nĕrvā'rĕ, v. a. to enervate.
disnodare, –nōdā'rĕ, v. a. to untie a knot.
disobbediente, disŏbbĕdiĕn'tĕ, a. disobedient. [dience.
disobbedienza, –diĕn'tzā, f. disobe-

disobbedire, –dē'rĕ, v. a. to disobey.
disobbligare, –bligā'rĕ, v. a. to disoblige.
disoccupato, –ŏkkūpā'tŏ, a. unoccupied, at leisure. [scenity.
disonestà, –ŏnĕstā', f. dishonesty; ob-
disonestare, –tā'rĕ, v. a. to dishonour;
disonestarsi, –tār'sĕ, v. r. to disgrace oneself.
disonesto, –ŏnĕs'tŏ, a. dishonest, indecent.
disonnarsi, –nār'sĕ, v. r. to awake.
disonorare, –ŏnōrā'rĕ, v. a. to dishonour, to disgrace.
disonore, –ŏnō'rĕ, m. dishonour, infamy.
disonorevole, –rĕ'vŏlĕ, a. dishonourable, shameful.
disorbitante, –ŏrbitān'tĕ, a. exorbitant.
disordinare, –dinā'rĕ, v. a. to disorder; to disturb. [bauchery.
disordine, –ŏr'dinĕ, m. disorder; de-
dispaccio, –dispāt'shŏ, m. despatch, speed.
disparato, –pārā'tŏ, a. disparate, unequal.
disparere, –pārĕ'rĕ, m. discrepancy.
dispari, dis'pārĕ, a. unequal, uneven, different, diverse.
disparire, –rē'rĕ, v. n. to disappear.
disparità, –ritā', f. disparity, inequality.
disparito, –rē'tŏ, a. altered; pale.
dispartire, –pārtē'rĕ, v. a. to distribute; to separate.
dispendio, –pĕn'diŏ, m. expense, cost.
dispendioso, –diŏ'sŏ, a. expensive, costly.
dispensa, –pĕn'sā, f. distribution; pantry; dispensation. [with; to distribute.
dispensare, –sā'rā, v. a. to dispense
dispensiere, –siĕrĕ, m. butler, steward.
disperare, –spĕrā'rĕ, v. a. to deprive of hope; disperarsi, –rār'sĕ, to despair (of).
disperazione, –tziō'nĕ, f. despair, desperation, rage. [to scatter.
dispergere, –spĕr'jĕrĕ, v. a. ir. to disperse,
dispetto, –spĕt'tŏ, a. despised; mean, vile; –, m. affront, contempt.
dispiacere, –piāshĕ'rĕ, v. a. ir. to displease; –, m. displeasure.
dispiacevole, –shĕ'vŏlĕ, a. unpleasant.
dispiegare, –piĕgā'rĕ, v. a. to display.
dispietato, –tā'tŏ, a. pitiless.
disponibile, –pŏnē'bilĕ, a. ready at hand.
disporre, –pŏr'rĕ, v. a. ir. to dispose, to set in order; to prepare.
disposare, –pŏsā'rĕ, v. a. to affiance, to espouse.
disposizione, –sitziō'nĕ, f. disposition.
dispostezza, –pŏstĕt'zā, f. neatness, nicety. [disdain.
dispregiare, –prĕjā'rĕ, v. a. to despise, to
dispregio, –prĕ'jŏ, m. contempt.
disprezzare, –prĕtzā'rĕ, v. a. to despise.
disprezzo, –prĕt'zŏ, m. contempt, disdain.
disproporzione, –prŏpŏrtziō'nĕ, f. disproportion.
disputa, dis'pūtā, f. dispute, strife.
disputare, –tā'rĕ, v. a. to dispute.
disquisizione, –kūisitziō'nĕ, f. disquisition, inquiry.
dissagrare, –sāgrā'rĕ, v. a. to profane.

dissapore, *–săpŏ'rĕ,* m. discord, disagreement.

dissecare, *–sĕkkă'rĕ,* v. a. to dry up.

disseminare, *–sĕmĭnă'rĕ,* v. a. to disseminate.

dissennato, *–sĕnnă'tŏ,* a. senseless, mad.

dissensione, *–sĕn'nĕ,* f. dissension, strife.

dissenteria, *–tĕrĕ'ă,* f. dysentery.

dissentire, *–tĕ'rĕ,* v. n. to dissent. [lock.

disserrare, *–sĕrră'rĕ,* v. a. to open, to un-

dissertare, *–sĕrtă'rĕ,* v. n. to dissert.

dissertazione, *–tzĭŏ'nĕ,* f. dissertation.

disservire, *–vĕ'rĕ,* v. a. to disserve, to injure. [disorder.

dissestare, *–sĕstă'rĕ,* v. a. to derange, to

dissetare, *–sĕtă'rĕ,* v. n. to quench thirst.

dissezione, *–tzĭŏ'nĕ,* f. dissection, incision, cut. [ference.

dissidio, *–sĕ'dĭŏ,* m. dissension, dif-

dissigillare, *–sĭjĭllă'rĕ,* v. a. to unseal.

dissimigliare, *–sĭmĭlyă'rĕ,* v. n. to be

dissimile, *–sĕ'mĭlĕ,* a. unlike. [unlike.

dissimulare, *–sĭmŭlă'rĕ,* v. a. to dissemble. [tion, disguise.

dissimulazione, *–tzĭŏ'nĕ,* f. dissimula-

dissipare, *–sĭpă'rĕ,* v. a. to dissipate, to spend, to squander, to waste.

dissipatore, *–tŏ'rĕ,* m. squanderer.

dissipazione, *–tzĭŏ'nĕ,* f. dissipation, prodigality. [solve.

dissolvere, *–sŏl'vĕrĕ,* v. a. ir. to dis-

dissoluto, *–lŭ'tŏ,* a. dissolute, debauched.

dissoluzione, *–tzĭŏ'nĕ,* f. dissolution.

dissomigliare, *–sŏmĭlyă'rĕ,* v. n. to be un-

dissonante, *–năn'tĕ,* a. dissonant. [like.

dissonanza, *–năn'tză,* f. dissonance.

dissotterrare, *–sŏtterră'rĕ,* v. a. to disinter.

dissuadere, *–sŭădă'rĕ,* v. a. ir. to dissuade.

dissuasione, *–sĭŏ'nĕ,* f. dissuasion.

dissuetudine, *–sŭĕtŭ'dĭnĕ,* f. want of practice. [to disjoin.

distaccare, *–tăkkă'rĕ,* v. a. to separate, to

distacco, *dĭs'tăkŏ,* m. disengagement, alienation.

distante, *–stăn'tĕ,* a. distant, far off.

distanza, *–stăn'tză,* f. distance.

distare, *–stă'rĕ,* v. n. ir. to be distant.

distemperare, *–tĕmpĕră'rĕ,* v. a. to melt, to weaken. [to stretch.

distendere, *–tĕn'dĕrĕ,* v. a. ir. to extend,

distensione, *–sĭŏ'nĕ,* f. extension, expansion.

distesa, *dĭstă'să,* f. extent, stretching.

disteso, *–tă'sŏ,* a. spread, spacious.

distico, *dĭs'tĭkŏ,* m. distich.

distillare, *–tĭllă'rĕ,* v. a. & n. to distil.

distillatoio, *–lătŏ'ŏ,* m. still, alembic.

distillazione, *–tzĭŏ'nĕ,* f. distillation.

distinguere, *–tĭn'gŭĕrĕ,* v. a. ir. to distinguish.

distintivo, *–tĭntĕ'vŏ,* m. mark, token; characteristic.

distinto, *–tĭn'tŏ,* a. distinguished; clear.

distinzione, *–tzĭŏ'nĕ,* f. distinction.

distogliere, *–tŏl'yĕrĕ,* v. a. ir. to divert from, to draw off. [wreath.

distorcere, *–tŏr'dĕhĕrĕ,* v. a. to twist; to

distornare, *–nă'rĕ,* v. a. to divert.

distorre, *–tŏr'rĕ,* v. a. ir. to divert, to dissuade.

distrarre, *–tră'rĕ,* v. a. ir. to distract.

distratto, *–tră'tŏ,* a. distracted, absent.

distrazione, *–tzĭŏ'nĕ,* f. distraction, absence of mind.

distretta, *–trĕ'tă,* f. distress, need.

distretto, *–trĕ'tŏ,* a. pressed, pinched; rigorous; needy; –, m. district, territory.

distribuire, *–trĭbŭĕ'rĕ,* v. a. to distribute.

distributivo, *–tĕ'vŏ,* a. distributive.

distribuzione, *–tzĭŏ'nĕ,* f. distribution, portion.

distrigare, *–trĭgă'rĕ,* v. a. to disentangle.

distrignere, *–strĭn'yĕrĕ,* **distringere,** *–jĕrĕ,* v. a. ir. to bind close; to pinch.

distruggere, *–strŭd'jĕrĕ,* v. a. ir. to destroy, to ruin; **distruggersi,** *–strŭd'-jĕrsĭ,* to melt.

distruttore, *–tŏ'rĕ,* m. destroyer.

distruzione, *–tzĭŏ'nĕ,* f. destruction, ruin. [vex.

disturbare, *–tŭrbă'rĕ,* v. a. to disturb; to

disturbo, *–tŭr'bŏ,* m. disturbance, trouble.

disubbidiente, *see* **disobbediente.**

disubbidienza, *see* **disobbedienza.**

disubbidire, *see* **disobbedire.**

disuguale, *–ăgŭă'lĕ,* a. unequal, uneven.

disugualità, *–lĭtă',* f. inequality.

disumidire, *–ămĭdă'rĕ,* v. a. to dry up.

disunire, *–ănĕ'rĕ,* v. a. to disunite.

disunto, *–ăn'tŏ,* a. lean, thin.

disusare, *–ŭsă'rĕ,* v. a. to disuse.

disutile, *–ŏ'tĭlĕ,* a. useless, unserviceable.

disvalere, *–vălă'rĕ,* v. a. to hurt, to harm.

disvantaggio, *–văntăd'jŏ,* m. disadvantage. [cover.

disvelare, *–vĕlă'rĕ,* v. a. to unveil, to dis-

disvezzare, *–vĕtză'rĕ,* v. a. to disaccustom; to wean (a child).

disviare, *–vĭă'rĕ,* v. a. to lead astray; **disviarsi,** *–vĭăr'sĭ,* to stray.

ditale, *dĭtă'lĕ,* m. thimble; finger-stall.

ditata, *–tă'tă,* f. tap with the finger.

ditello, *–tĕl'lŏ,* m. arm-pit.

ditirambico, *–trăm'bĭkŏ,* a. dithyrambic.

ditirambo, *–răm'bŏ,* m. dithyramb.

dito, *dĭ'tŏ,* (**dita,** f. pl.) finger, inch.

ditta, *dĭt'tă,* f. firm.

dittatore, *–tŏ'rĕ,* m. dictator.

dittatorio, *–tŏ'rĭŏ,* a. dictatorial.

dittatura, *–tŏ'ră,* f. dictation; dictatorship.

dittongo, *–tŏn'gŏ,* m. diphthong.

diurno, *dĭŭr'nŏ,* a. diurnal, quotidian.

diuturnità, *–tŭrnĭtă',* f. long duration.

diuturno, *–tŭr'nŏ,* a. long, of long duration.

diva, *dĕ'vă,* f. goddess; mistress.

divagare, *dĭvăgă'rĕ,* v. n. to rove, to ramble. [come down.

divallare, *–văllă'rĕ,* v. n. to descend, to

divampare, *–vămpă'rĕ,* v. n. to flash, to

divano, *–vă'nŏ,* m. divan. [blaze.

divario, *–vă'rĭŏ,* m. variety, inequality.

divecchiare, *–vĕkkĭă'rĕ,* v. n. to grow young.

divellere, *–vĕl'lĕrĕ,* v. a. to pluck or to root up.

diveltare, –vĕltä´rĕ, v. n. to plough.
divelto, –vĕl´tŏ, m. ploughed ground.
divenire, –vĕnē´rĕ, v. n. ir. to become, to get; to happen.
diventare, –tä´rĕ, v. n. to become.
diverbio, –vĕr´bŏ, m. talk, conversation.
divergere, –vĕr´jĕrĕ, v. n. ir. to diverge.
diversificare, –sĭfĭkä´rĕ, v.a. to diversify.
diversione, –sĭō´nĕ, f. diversion, amusement; (mil.) diversion.
diversità, –sĭtä´, f. diversity.
diverso, –vĕr´sŏ, a. different, unlike.
diverticolo, –tĕ´kŏlŏ, m. digression.
divertimento, –tĭmĕn´tŏ, m. diversion, interruption; amusement.
divertire, –tĭr´ĕ, v.a. to divert, to amuse;
divertirsi, –tĭr´sĭ, to take one's pleasure.
divezzare, –vĕtzä´rĕ, v. a. to wean.
diviato, –vĭä´tŏ, a. quick, nimble.
dividere, –vē´dĕrĕ, v. a. to divide, to part.
divietare, –vĭĕtä´rĕ, v. a. to prohibit, to interdict, to forbid.
divieto, –vĭĕ´tŏ, m. prohibition, veto.
divinare, –vĭnä´rĕ, v.a. to divine, to foredivinatore, –tō´rĕ, m. diviner. [tell.
divinazione, –tzĭō´nĕ, f. divination.
divincolare, –kŏlä´rĕ, v. a. to twist, to wrest, to wring, to writhe; **divincolarsi,** –lär´sĭ, to turn, to writhe.
divinità, –nĭtä´, f. divinity; goddess.
divino, –vē´nŏ, a. divine; excellent.
divisa, –vē´sä, f. share; way, manner; uniform, livery. [thought, design; device.
divisamento, –vĭsämĕn´tŏ, m. division;
divisare, –sä´rĕ, v.a. to think, to imagine, to devise; to diversify.
divisato, –sä´tŏ, a. disfigured; unlike.
divisione, –sĭō´nĕ, f. division; discord.
divisore, –sō´rĕ, m. (ar.) divider.
divo, dē´vŏ, (poet.) divine, heavenly.
divorare, dĭvōrä´rĕ, v.a. to devour, to swallow up, to consume.
divorzio, –vŏr´tzĭŏ, m. divorce.
divoto, –vŏ´tŏ, a. devout; attached.
divozione, –vōtzĭō´nĕ, f. devotion; attachment, adherence.
divulgare, –vŭlgä´rĕ, v. a. to divulge.
dizionario, dĭtzĭōnä´rĭŏ, m. dictionary.
dizione, –tzĭō´nĕ, f. diction, district, circuit.
do, dŏ, m. (mus.) do, ut.
doblone, dŏblō´nĕ, m. doubloon.
doccia, dŏt´shä, f. conduit, tube, pipe; canal, rivulet.
docciare, –tshä´rĕ, v. n. to drop.
doccio, dŏt´shŏ, **doccione,** –shō´nĕ, m. earthen conduit-pipe.
docile, dō´dshĭlĕ, a. docible, docile.
docilità, dōdshĭlĭtä´, f. docility, tractableness. [precept.
documento, dōkŭmĕn´tŏ, m. document;
dodicesimo, dōdĭtshä´sĭmŏ, a. twelfth.
dodici, dŏ´dĭtshĭ, a. twelve.
doga, dŏ´gä, f. staff (of a barrel, &c.).
dogana, dōgä´nä, f. custom-house; custom.
doganiere, –nĭä´rĕ, m. custom-house officer.
doge, dŏ´jĕ, m. Doge (of Venice). [ficer.
doglia, dŏl´yä, f. grief, pain.
doglianza, –yän´tzä, f. lamentation, grief.

doglio, dŏl´yŏ, m. cask, tun, barrel.
doglioso, –yŏ´sŏ, a. grievous.
dogma, dŏg´mä, m. dogma, principle.
dogmatico, –mä´tĭkŏ, a. dogmatical.
dogmatizzare, –tĭtzä´rĕ, v. n. to dogmatize. [–, ad. agreeably.
dolce, dŏl´dshĕ, a. sweet, pleasant, soft;
dolcezza, –dshĕt´zä, f. sweetness, pleasure.
dolcificare, –dshĭfĭkä´rĕ, v. a. to sweeten.
dolcigno, –dshĭn´yŏ, a. sweetish.
dolco, dŏl´kŏ, a. mild; pleasant.
dolente, dōlĕn´tĕ, a. doleful, afflicted.
dolere, –lĕ´rĕ, v. n. ir. to suffer, to feel pain; to take pity; **dolersi,** –lĕr´sĭ, to complain.
dollaro, dŏl´lärŏ, m. dollar. [complain.
dolo, dŏ´lŏ, m. fraud, artifice.
dolore, dōlō´rĕ, m. pain, grief.
doloroso, –lŏrō´sŏ, a. dolorous.
doloso, –lŏ´sŏ, a. fraudulent, deceitful.
domanda, –män´dä, f. demand.
domandare, –dä´rĕ, v. a. to demand, to request, to claim, to ask, to require.
domani, –mä´nĭ, ad. to-morrow.
domare, –mä´rĕ, v. a. to tame, to humble.
domattina, –mättē´nä, f. to-morrow morning.
domenica, –mä´nĭkä, f. Sunday. [ing.
domenicale, –mĕnĭkä´lĕ, m. Sunday-clothes, pl.; –, a. dominical.
domesticare, –mĕstĭkä´rĕ, v. a. to domesticate. [miliar; –, m. servant.
domestico, –mĕs´tĭkŏ, a. domestic, fa-
domiciliato, –mĭdshĭlĭä´tŏ, a. domiciled.
domicilio, –dshĕ´lĭŏ, m. residence, abode.
dominare, –nä´rĕ, v. a. to rule over, to reign over, to command.
dominatore, –tō´rĕ, m. ruler, sovereign.
dominazione, –tzĭō´nĕ, f. power, empire.
dominio, –mĕ´nĭŏ, domino, dŏ´mĭnŏ, m. dominion, empire.
dommasco, –mä´skŏ, m. damask.
donare, –nä´rĕ, v. a. to give, to bestow upon, to present with.
donatario, –tä´rĭŏ, m. (jur.) donee.
donativo, –tē´vŏ, m. donative, present.
donatore, –tō´rĕ, m. giver, donor.
donazione, –tzĭō´nĕ, f. donation, gift.
donde, dŏn´dĕ, pn. & ad. whence, from whence; why. [dally.
dondolare, –dŏlä´rĕ, v. a. to swing; to
donna, dŏn´nä, f. wife, lady, mistress.
donnesco, –nĕs´kŏ, a. womanlike; courteous, courtly. [master, lord.
donno, dŏn´nŏ, a. kind, benevolent; –, m.
donnola, dŏn´nŏlä, f. weasel.
donnuccia, –nät´shä, f. silly little woman.
dono, dŏ´nŏ, m. gift, present.
donzella, dŏntzĕl´lä, f. virgin; damsel; lady's maid. [spark; sergeant, bailiff.
donzello, –tzĕl´lŏ, m. knight's esquire;
dopo, dŏp´ŏ, ad. & pr. after, behind, since.
dopoché, –kĕ´, ad. & c. after that, since.
doppia, dŏp´pĭä, f. pistole (coin); flounce.
doppiare, –pĭä´rĕ, v. a. & n. to double, to multiply; to increase. [torch, tapper.
doppiere, –pĭä´rĕ, doppiero, –rŏ, m.
doppiezza, –pĭĕt´zä, f. duplicity; dissimulation, deceitfulness.

doppio, *dŏp'pĭŏ*, a. double; deceitful.
doppione, *–pĭŏ'nĕ*, m. doubloon.
dorare, *dōrā'rĕ*, v. a. to gild.
doratore, *–tŏ'rĕ*, m. gilder.
doratura, *–tŭ'rä*, f. gilding.
dormentorio, *–mĕntŏ'rĭŏ*, m. dormitory.
dormicchiare, *–mĭkkĭä'rĕ*, **dormigliare**, *–mĭlyä'rĕ*, v. n. to slumber.
dormiglione, *–yŏ'nĕ*, m. lazy drone, dullard. [somnolent, sluggish.
dormiglioso, *–mĭlyŏ'sŏ*, a. sleepy, drowsy,
dormire, *–mē'rĕ*, v. n. to sleep.
dormita, *–mī'tä*, f. slumber, nap, doze.
dormitorio, *see* **dormentorio**.
dorsale, *–sä'lĕ*, a. dorsal.
dorso, *dŏr'sŏ*, m. back; ridge of a mountain.
dosare, *dŏsä'rĕ*, v. a. to dose; to mix.
dose, *dŏ'sĕ*, f. dose, portion.
dossiere, *dŏssĭä'rĕ*, m. blanket; coverlet.
dosso, *dŏs'sŏ*, m. back; **non ho moneta in –**, I have no money about me.
dotare, *dŏtä'rĕ*, v. a. to endow, to bestow.
dotazione, *–tzĭŏ'nĕ*, f. dotation, portion.
dote, *dŏ'tĕ*, f. dowry, portion; endowment, gift; talent.
dottare, *–tä'rĕ*, v. n. to fear, to doubt.
dotto, *dŏt'tŏ*, a. learned, erudite.
dottorale, *–rä'lĕ*, a. doctoral.
dottorato, *–rä'tŏ*, m. doctorship.
dottore, *–tŏ'rĕ*, m. doctor, master.
dottrina, *–trē'nä*, f. doctrine; knowledge.
dottrinale, *–trinä'lĕ*, a. doctrinal, instructive. [struct.
dottrinare, *–nä'rĕ*, v. a. to teach, to instruct.
dove, *dŏ'vĕ*, ad. where, whither, whence; **–, c.** when, whereas; **dove che, dove che sia**, wherever.
dovere, *dŏvā'rĕ*, v. a. & n. ir. to owe, to be obliged; **–,** m. duty, task; part.
doveroso, *–vĕrŏ'sŏ*, a. dutiful, rightful.
dovizia, *–vē'tzĭä*, f. riches, wealth; store.
dovizioso, *–vĭtzĭŏ'sŏ*, a. rich; copious.
dovunque, *–vŭn'kŏĕ*, ad. wheresoever.
dovuto, *–vŭ'tŏ*, a. due, obliged; fit; **–,** m. debt; duty; obligation.
dozzina, *dŏdzē'nä*, f. dozen; **tenere a –**, to board a person. [mean.
dozzinale, *–dzĭnä'lĕ*, a. common, vulgar.
dozzinante, *–nän'tĕ*, m. boarder.
dragante, *drägän'tĕ*, m. dragacanth.
drago(ne), *drä'gŏ('nĕ)*, m. dragon, dragoon.
dramma, *dräm'mä*, f. dram; **–,** m. drama.
drammatico, *–mä'tĭkŏ*, a. dramatic.
drappello, *dräppĕl'lŏ*, m. colours, pl.; flag, banner; troop of soldiers, band.
drapperia, *–pĕrē'ä*, f. drapery; silk stuffs, pl.
drappo, *dräp'pŏ*, m. stuffs; cloth; silks.
dritto, *see* **diritto**.
drizzare, *drĭtzä'rĕ*, v. a. to raise, to erect.
droga, *drŏ'gä*, f. drug; **droghe**, pl. groceries, pl. [pl.
drogheria, *drŏghĕrē'ä*, f. drugs, groceries,
droghiere, *–ghĭĕ'rĕ*, m. druggist.
dromedario, *drŏmĕdä'rĭŏ*, m. dromedary.
drudo, *drŏ'dŏ*, a. clever, bold; amorous; **–,** m. lover, gallant.

dubbiezza, *dŭbbĭĕt'zä*, **dubbio**, *dŭb'bĭŏ*, m. doubt, scruple. [doubtful.
dubbio, *dŭb'bĭŏ*, **dubbioso**, *–bĭŏ'sŏ*, a. doubtful.
dubitare, *–bĭtä'rĕ*, v. n. to doubt.
dubitativo, dubitoso, *see* **dubbio**.
duca, *dŏ'kä*, m. general, chief; duke.
ducato, *dŭkä'tŏ*,m. dukedom; ducat (coin).
duce, *dŏ'dshĕ*, m. commander; duke.
ducea, *see* **duchea**.
duchea, *dŭkä'ä*, f. duchy, dukedom.
duchessa, *dŭkĕs'sä*, f. duchess.
due, *dŏ'ĕ*, a. two.
duecento, *dŭĕdshĕn'tŏ*, a. two hundred.
duellante, *dŭĕllän'tĕ*, m. duellist, dueller.
duellare, *–lä'rĕ*, v. a. to fight a duel.
duellatore, *–tŏ'rĕ*, **duellista**, *–lĭs'tä*, m. duellist, dueller.
duello, *dŭĕl'lŏ*, m. duel, single combat.
du(e)mila, *dŭ(ĕ)mē'lä*, a. two thousand.
duetto, *dŭĕt'tŏ*, m. duet.
dugento, *dŭjĕn'tŏ*, a. two hundred.
dumila, *–mē'lä*, a. two thousand.
duna, *dŏ'nä*, f. downs, dunes, pl.
dunque, *dŭn'kŏĕ*, c. then, what.
duo, *dŏ'ŏ*, a. duet.
duodecimo, *dŭŏdä'dshĭmŏ*, a. twelfth.
duolo, *dŭŏ'lŏ*, m. grief, pain.
duomo, *dŭŏ'mŏ*, m. dome, cathedral.
duplicare, *dŭplĭkä'rĕ*, v. a. to double.
duplice, *dŭ'plĭdshĕ*, a. double.
duplicità, *–dshĭtä'*, f. duplicity; dissimulation. [lation.
duplo, *dŭp'lŏ*, m. double.
durabile, *dŭrä'bĭlĕ*, a. durable, lasting.
durabilità, *–bĭlĭtä'*, f. durability.
durante, *–rän'tĕ*, a. during, lasting.
durare, *–rä'rĕ*, v. n. to last, to hold out, to endure; to abide.
durata, *–rä'tä*, f. durability, continuance.
duro, *dŏ'rŏ*, a. hard, strong; stubborn, inexorable, cruel.
duttile, *dŭt'tĭlĕ*, a. ductile; malleable.
dutto, *dŭt'tŏ*, m. duct, canal.

E.

e, *ĕ̃*, c. and.
e', *ĕ̃*, for: **egli**.
ebano, *ĕ̃'bänŏ*, m. ebony; ebony-tree.
ebbro, *ĕb'brŏ*, a. drunk; foolish.
ebete, *ĕ̃'bĕtĕ*, a. weak; dull, blunted.
ebraismo, *ĕbrä̃ĭs'mŏ*, m. hebraism.
ebrietà, *ĕbrĭĕtä'*, **ebbrezza**, *ĕbbrĕt'zä*, f. drunkenness; (fig.) intoxication.
ebullizione, *ĕbŭllĭtzĭŏ'nĕ*, f. ebullition.
eburneo, *ĕbŭr'nĕŏ*, **eburno**, *–nŏ*, a. of ivory, white as ivory.
ecatombe, *ĕkätŏm'bĕ*, f. hecatomb.
eccedente, *ĕtshĕdĕn'tĕ*, a. exceeding; immoderate. [fluity.
eccedenza, *–dĕn'tzä*, f. excess; super-
eccedere, *ĕtshĕd'dĕrĕ*, v. a. & n. ir. to exceed, to surpass.
eccellente, *ĕtshĕllĕn'tĕ*, a. excellent.
eccellenza, *ĕtshĕllĕn'tzä*, f. excellency.
eccellere, *ĕtshĕl'lĕrĕ*, v. a. to excel.

eccelso, ĕtshĕl'sŏ, a. high, lofty; eminent, sublime.

eccentrico, ĕtshĕn'trĭkŏ, a. eccentric; odd.

eccessivo, ĕtshĕssē'vŏ, a. excessive, immoderate, exorbitant.

eccesso, ĕtshĕs'sŏ, m. excess, superfluity.

eccetera, ĕtshĕt'ĕrä, m. and so on.

eccetto, ĕtshĕt'tŏ, pr. & c. except, unless; but, save. [restrict.

eccettuare, −tŭä'rē, v. a. to except; to

eccezione, −tzĭō'nē, f. exception.

eccidio, ĕtshē'dĭŏ, m. slaughter, ruin.

eccitare, ĕtshētä'rē, v. a. to excite.

ecclesiastico, ĕkklēsäs'tĭkŏ, m. priest; —, a. ecclesiastical.

ecclissare, see eclissare.

ecco, ĕk'kŏ, ad. here is, there is, here are, there are; —, i. behold! [obscure.

eclissare, ĕklēssä'rē, v. a. to eclipse, to

eclisse, ĕklēs'sē, eclissi, −sē, f. eclipse.

economia, ĕkŏnŏmē'ä, f. economy.

economico, −nŏ'mĭkŏ, a. economic; frugal.

economo, ĕkŏ'nŏmŏ, m. steward, manager. ed, ĕd, c. and.

edace, ĕdä'dshē, a. voracious.

edera, d'dĕrä, f. ivy.

edicola, ĕdē'kŏlä, f. little chapel. [edify.

edificare, ĕdĭfĭkä'rē, v. a. to build; to

edificio, −fē'dshŏ, edifizio, −dzĭŏ, m. edifice; fabric.

editore, −tŏ'rē, m. editor, publisher.

editto, ĕdĭt'tŏ, m. edict, decree.

edizione, −tzĭō'nē, f. edition; publication.

edra, see edera. [struct.

educare, ĕdŭkä'rē, v. a. to educate, to instruct.

educato, −kä'tŏ, a. educated. [struction.

educazione, −tzĭō'nē, f. education, instruction.

effeminare, ĕffĕmĭnä'rē, v.a. to effeminate.

effeminatezza, −tĕt'zä, f. effeminacy.

efferato, −rä'tŏ, a. cruel, inhuman.

effervescenza, −fĕrvĕsshĕn'tzä, f. effervescence; fervour.

effettivamente, −tĭvämĕn'tē, ad. in fact,

effettivo, −tē'vŏ, a. effective, real.

effetto, −fĕt'tŏ, m. effect; result; in −, in fact, indeed.

effettuare, −tŭä'rē, v. a. to effectuate.

efficace, −fēkä'dshē, a. efficacious.

efficacia, −kä'dshä, f. efficacy.

effigiare, −fē'rē, v. a. to image, to paint.

effigie, −fē'jē, f. effigy. [day.

effimero, −fē'mĕrŏ, a. ephemeral, of one

efflorescenza, −flŏrĕsshĕn'tzä, f. efflorescence; mould.

efflusso, −flŭs'sŏ, m. efflux, effusion.

effluvio, −flŏ'vĭŏ, m. evaporation.

effondere, −fŏn'dĕrē, v. a. ir. to pour out, to shed, to spill.

effusione, −fŭsĭō'nē, f. effusion.

egestione, −jĕstĭō'nē, f. evacuation.

egida, d'jĭdä, f. shield, protection.

egli, ĕl'yĭ, pn. he, it; −stesso, he himself.

eglino, ĕl'yēnŏ, pn. pl. they.

egloga, ĕ'glŏgä, f. eclogue.

egregio, ĕgrä'jŏ, a. egregious, famous.

egro, d'grŏ, a. (poet.) ill, infirm, sick.

eguale, ĕgŭä'lē, a. equal.

eguaglianza.−lᵘᵃⁿ't·ä.f. equality, parity.

eguagliare, −lyä'rē, v. a. to make equal.

egualità, −tä', f. equality, evenness.

ehi! ĕh'ē, i. ha! hem!

ei, d'ē, for: egli.

elasticità, ĕlästĭdshĭä', f. elasticity.

elastico, −läs'tĭkŏ, a. elastic.

elce, ĕl'dshē, f. holm-oak.

elefante, ĕlēfän'tē, m. elephant.

elegante, −gän'tē, a. elegant.

eleganza, −gän'tzä, f. elegance.

eleggere, ĕlĕd'jĕrē, v. a. ir. to elect, to

elegia, −jē'ä, f. elegy. [choose.

elegiaco, −jē'äkŏ, a. & m. elegiac; writer of elegies.

elementare, −mĕntä'rē, a. elementary.

elemento, −mĕn'tŏ, m. element, principle.

elemosina, −mŏ'sēnä, f. alms, pl., charity.

elemosinare, −mŏsēnä'rē, v. n. to give alms.

elemosiniero, −nä'rĭŏ, m. almoner.

elenco, ĕlĕn'kŏ, m. catalogue, index.

eletto, ĕlĕt'tŏ, a. elected, chosen; rare.

elettore, −tŏ'rē, m. elector. [force.

elettricismo, −trĭshĭs'mŏ, m. electric

elettricità, −dshĭtä', f. electricity.

elettrico, ĕlĕt'trĭkŏ, a. electric.

elettrizzare, −trĭzä'rē, v. a. to electrify.

elettro, ĕlĕt'trŏ, m. amber.

elettuario, −tŭä'rĭŏ, m. electuary.

elevare, −vä'rē, v. a. to elevate.

elezione, −tzĭō'nē, f. election; deliberation.

elidere, ĕlē'dĕrē, v. a. ir. to elide.

eligibile, ĕlĭjē'bĭlē, a. eligible.

elisione, −sĭō'nē, f. (gr.) elision.

ella, ĕl'lä, f. elecampane, starwort.

ella, ĕl'lä, pn. she, it; elle, elleno, pl.

elleboro, ĕllĕ'bŏrŏ, m. hellebore. [they.

ellenismo, ĕllĕnĭs'mŏ, m. hellenism.

ellera, ĕl'lĕrä, f. ivy.

ellisse, −lĭs'sē, f. ellipsis.

ellittico, −lĭt'tĭkŏ, a. elliptical.

elmetto, ĕlmĕt'tŏ, elmo, ĕl'mŏ, m. helmet.

elocuzione, ĕlŏkŭtzĭō'nē, f. elocution, eloquence.

elogio, ĕlŏ'jĭŏ, m. eulogy. [quence.

eloquente, ĕlŏkŭĕn'tē, a. eloquent.

eloquenza, −kŭĕn'tzä, f. eloquence.

eloquio, ĕlŏ'kŭĭŏ, m. reasoning.

elsa, ĕl'sä, f., elso, ĕl'sŏ, m. sword-hilt.

elucubrato, ĕlŭkŭbrä'tŏ, a. elaborate.

elucubrazione, −tzĭō'nē, f. lucubration, careful study.

eludere, ĕlŭ'dĕrē, v. a. ir. to elude.

elusione, ĕlŭsĭō'nē, f. elusion, evasion.

elusorio, −sŏ'rĭŏ, a. illusory, fraudulent.

emaciato, ĕmädshä'tŏ, a. emaciated.

emaciazione, −tzĭō'nē, f. emaciation, leanness. [issue.

emanare, −nä'rē, v. n. to emanate, to

emanazione, −tzĭō'nē, f. emanation, origin.

emancipare, ĕmändshĭpä'rē, v.a. to emancipate. [tion, freedom.

emancipazione, −tzĭō'nē, f. emancipation.

emblema, ĕmblĕ'mä, m. emblem.

embrione, −brĭō'nē, m. embryo.

emenda, ĕmĕn'dä, f. emendation, correction; amendment.

emendare, –dā′rĕ, v. a. to amend, to mend ; to correct. [revisal.
emendazione, –tzĭō′nĕ, f. emendation ;
emergere, ĕmĕr′jĕrĕ, v. n. to emerge.
emerito, ĕmā′rĭtŏ, a. emerited.
emersione, ĕmĕrsĭō′nĕ, f. emersion.
emetico, ĕmā′tĭkŏ, a. emetic, vomitive.
emigrare, ĕmĭgrā′rĕ, v. n. to emigrate.
emigrato, –grā′tŏ, m. emigrant.
emigrazione, –tzĭō′nĕ, f. emigration.
eminente, –nĕn′tĕ, a. eminent, lofty ; re- markable, conspicuous.
eminenza, –nĕn′tzā, f. eminence.
emisfero, ĕmĭsfā′rŏ, m. hemisphere.
emissario, –sā′rĭŏ, m. emissary ; stone-
emissione, –sĭō′nĕ, f. emission. [horse.
emolliente, ĕmŏllĭĕn′tĕ, a. emollient.
emolumento, –lŭmĕn′tŏ, m. emolument.
emozione, –tzĭō′nĕ, f. emotion, alteration.
empiastro, –pĭās′trŏ, m. plaster.
empiere, ĕm′pĭĕrĕ, v. a. ir. to fill up, to complete. [impiety.
empietà, –pĭĕtā′, empiezza, –pĭĕt′zā, f.
empio, ĕm′pĭŏ, a. impious.
empire, see empiere.
empirico, –pē′rĭkŏ, m. empiric, charlatan.
empirismo, –pĭrĭs′mŏ, m. empirism.
empito, ĕm′pĭtŏ, m. impetuosity.
emporio, –pō′rĭŏ, m. fair, market.
emulare, ĕmŭlā′rĕ, v. a. to emulate.
emulazione, –tzĭō′nĕ, f. emulation.
emulo, ĕ′mŭlŏ, m. competitor, rival.
emulsione, ĕmŭlsĭō′nĕ, f. emulsion.
enciclopedia, ĕnchĭklŏpĕdē′ā, f. ency- clopædia.
enciclopedico, –pā′dĭkŏ, a. encyclopædic.
encomiare, –kŏmĭā′rĕ, v. a. to praise.
encomio, –kō′mĭŏ, m. praise, eulogy.
energia, ĕnĕrjē′ā, f. energy.
energico, ĕnĕr′jĭkŏ, a. energetic.
enervare, –vā′rĕ, v. a. to enervate.
enfasi, ĕn′fāsĭ, f. emphasis.
enfatico, –fā′tĭkŏ, a. emphatical.
enfiagione, –fĭājō′nĕ, f. & m. swelling ; pride, inflation, conceit.
enfiarsi, –fĭār′sĭ, v. r. to swell, to puff up.
enfiato, –fĭā′tŏ, enfiore, –fĭō′rĕ, m. swelling ; conceit. [enigma, riddle.
enigma, ĕnĭg′mā, enimma, ĕnĭm′mā, m.
enorme, ĕnŏr′mĕ, a. enormous.
enormezza, –mĕt′zā, enormità, –mĭtā′, f. enormity.
ente, ĕn′tĕ, m. being ; existence.
entità, –tĭtā′, f. entity, existence.
entrambi, –trăm′bĭ, entrambo, –trăm′bŏ, a. both.
entrare, –trā′rĕ, v. a. & n. to enter.
entrata, –trā′tā, f. entrance ; income ; pre-
entro, ĕn′trŏ, ad. & pr. within. [lude.
entusiasmo, –tŭsĭās′mŏ, m. enthusiasm.
entusiasta, –stās′tā, m. enthusiast.
entusiastico, –stās′tĭkŏ, a. enthusiastic.
enumerare, ĕnŭmĕrā′rĕ, v. a. to enu- merate. [to express.
enunciare, ĕnŭndshā′rĕ, v. a. to declare,
enunciazione, –tzĭō′nĕ, f. enunciation, declaration, expression.
epa, ā′pā, 1. belly, paunch.

epicarpo, ĕpĭkār′pŏ, m. epicarpium.
epidemia, –dĕmē′ā, f. epidemy.
epidemico, –dā′mĭkŏ, a. epidemic.
epigramma, –grām′mā, m. epigram.
epigrammatico, –mā′tĭkŏ, a. epigram- matic. [sickness.
epilessia, –lĕssā′ā, f. epilepsy, falling
epilettico, –lĕt′tĭkŏ, a. epileptic.
epilogo, ĕpē′lŏgŏ, m. epilogue.
episcopale, ĕpĭskŏpā′lĕ, a. episcopal.
episcopato, –pā′tŏ, m. bishopric.
episodio, ĕpĭsō′dĭŏ, m. episode, digression.
epistola, ĕpĭs′tŏlā, f. epistle, letter.
epitaffio, ĕpĭtāf′fĭŏ, m. epitaph.
epulone, ĕpŭlō′nĕ, m. glutton, gormand.
equabile, ĕkŭā′bĭlĕ, a. equable, equal.
equanime, ĕkŭā′nĭmĕ, a. equanimous ; smooth. [possession.
equanimità, –nĭmĭtā′, f. equanimity, self-
equatore, –tō′rĕ, m. equator.
equazione, –tzĭō′nĕ, f. equation.
equestre, ĕkŭĕs′trĕ, a. equestrian.
equidistante, ĕkŭĭdĭstăn′tĕ, a. equidistant.
equidistanza, –tăn′tzā, f. equal distance.
equilatero, –lā′tĕrŏ, a. equilateral.
equilibrare, –lĭbrā′rĕ, v. a. to equipoise, to balance equally.
equilibrio, –lē′brĭŏ, m. equilibrium.
equinoziale, –nŏtzĭā′lĕ, a. equinoctial.
equinozio, –nō′tzĭŏ, m. equinox.
equipaggiare, –pādjā′rĕ, v. a. to equip, to fit out ; (mar.) to man.
equipaggio, –pād′jŏ, m. equipage, equip- ment, baggage. [compare.
equiparare, –pārā′rĕ, v. a. to equal, to
equità, ĕkŭĭtā′, f. equity, right.
equivalente, –vālĕn′tĕ, m. equivalent.
equivalere, –vālā′rĕ, v. n. ir. to be of the same value, to equal. [to mistake.
equivocare, –vŏkā′rĕ, v. a. to equivocate ;
equivoco, –ĕkŭā′vŏkŏ, a. equivocal.
equo, ā′kŭŏ, a. just, equitable.
era, ā′rā, f. era, epoch, period.
erario, ĕrā′rĭŏ, m. treasury, exchequer.
erba, ĕr′bā, f. herb, grass.
erbaggio, –bād′jŏ, m. pot-herbs, pl.
erbaio, –bā′ĭŏ, m. pasture-ground.
erbaiuolo, –bāĭŭō′lŏ, m. herbalist.
erborare, –bŏrā′rĕ, v. n. to herbalize.
eredare, ĕrĕdā′rĕ, v. a. to inherit.
erede, ĕrā′dĕ, m. & f. heir ; heiress.
eredità, ĕrĕdĭtā′, f. inheritance, heritage.
ereditare, –tā′rĕ, v. a. to inherit.
ereditario, –tā′rĭŏ, a. hereditary.
eremita, –mē′tā, m. hermit.
eremitaggio, –tād′jŏ, m. hermitage.
eremo, ā′rĕmŏ, m. hermitage.
eresia, ĕrĕsē′ā, f. heresy.
ereticale, –tĭkā′lĕ, a. heretical.
eretico, ĕrā′tĭkŏ, m. heretic.
eretto, ĕrĕt′tŏ, a. erect, upright.
ergastolo, ĕrgās′tŏlŏ, m. prison, dungeon.
ergere, ĕr′jĕrĕ, v. a. ir. to erect, to raise.
erica, ā′rĭkā, f. heath, sweet broom.
ermellino, ĕrmĕllē′nŏ, m. ermine.

ormo, ĕr'mŏ, a. solitary, desert.
ernia, ĕr'nĭă, f. hernia, rupture.
eroe, ĕrŏ'ĕ, m. hero.
eroico, ĕrŏ'ĭkŏ, a. heroic.
eroina, ĕrŏĕ'nă, f. heroine.
eroismo, –ĭs'mŏ, m. heroism.　[forth.
erompere, ĕrŏm'pĕrĕ, v. n. ir. to burst
erosione, –sĭŏ'nĕ, f. corrosion.
erotico, ĕrŏ'tĭkŏ, a. erotic.
erpicare, ĕrpĭkā'rĕ, v. a. to harrow.
erpice, ĕr'pĭdshĕ, m. harrow.
errabondo, –răbŏn'dŏ, a. errant, vagrant.
errare, –rā'rĕ, v. n. to err; to wander, to
　roam ; to mistake.
errata, –rā'tă, f. erratum, misprint.
erroneo, –rŏ'nĕŏ, a. erroneous.
errore, –rŏ'rĕ, m. error, mistake, fault.
erta, ĕr'tă, f. steep, declivity, slope.
erto, ĕr'tŏ, a. steep; arduous.
erudire, ĕrŭdē'rĕ, v. a. to instruct, to teach.
erudito, –dē'tŏ, a. erudite, learned. [ing.
erudizione, –dĭzĭŏ'nĕ, f. erudition, learn-
eruttare, ĕrŭttā'rĕ, v. n. to eruct, to belch.
eruzione, –tzĭŏ'nĕ, f. eruption.
esacerbare, ĕsădshĕrbā'rĕ, v. a. to ex-
　asperate, to provoke.
esagerare, –jĕrā'rĕ, v. a. to exaggerate.
esagerazione, –ăjĕrătzĭŏ'nĕ, f. exaggera-
　tion.　　　　　　　　　　　　　[harass.
esagitare, –ăjĭtā'rĕ, v. a. to vex, to
esalare, –ālā'rĕ, v. a. to exhale; to ex-
　pire.　　　　　　　　　　　　　[poration.
esalazione, –tzĭŏ'nĕ, f. exhalation, eva-
esaltare, –āltā'rĕ, v. a. to exalt, to extol.
esame, ĕsā'mĕ, m. examination, exam.
esametro, ĕsā'mĕtrŏ, m. hexameter.
esaminare, –mĭnā'rĕ, v. a. to exa'ine;
　to discuss ; to search.
esaminatore, –tŏ'rĕ, m. examiner.
esangue, ĕsăn'gŭĕ, a. bloodless ; half dead.
esanimare, –ănĭmā'rĕ, v. a. to terrify, to
　dishearten.　　　　　　　　　　[couraged.
esanime, ĕsă'nĭmĕ, a. terrified, dis-
esarcato, –ārkā'tŏ, m. exarchate.
esasperare, ĕsăspĕrā'rĕ, v. a. to exasperate,
　to provoke.
esattezza, ĕsăttĕt'ză, f. exactness, punc-
　tuality.
esatto, ĕsăt'tŏ, a. exact, accurate, careful.
esattore, –tŏ'rĕ, m. tax-gatherer.
esaudire, –ădē'rĕ, v. a. to grant, to hear.
esaurire, –rē'rĕ, v. a. to exhaust, to dry up.
esazione, –zĭŏ'nĕ, f. exaction.
esca, ĕs'kă, f. bait; allurement.　[anger.
escandescenza, ĕskăndĕsshĕn'tză, f. wrath,
escavare, –kāvā'rĕ, v. a. to excavate.
escire, see uscire.
esclamare, –klāmā'rĕ, v. n. to exclaim.
escludere, –klŏ'dĕrĕ, v. a. ir. to exclude.
esclusione, –klŭsĭŏ'nĕ, f. exclusion.
escogitare, –kŏjĭtā'rĕ, v. a. to meditate,
　to invent.
escoriato, –rĭā'tŏ, a. excoriated.
escoriazione, –tzĭŏ'ne, f. excoriation.
escremento, –krĕmĕn'tŏ, m. excrement.
escrescenza, –krĕsshĕn'tză, f. excrescence.

escursione, –kŭrsĭŏ'nĕ, f. excursion, in-
　vasion.　　　　　　　　　　　　[detest, to hate.
esecrare, ĕsĕkrā'rĕ, v. a. to execrate, to
esecrazione, –tzĭŏ'nĕ, f. execration.
esecutore, –kŭtŏ'rĕ, m. hangman.
esecuzione, –tzĭŏ'nĕ, f. execution, per-
　formance.　　　　　　　　　　　[perform.
eseguire, –gŭē'rĕ, v. a. to execute, to
esempio, ĕsĕm'pĭŏ, m. example, copy;
　per –, for instance.
esemplare, –plā'rĕ, a. exemplary, –, m.
　copy, model ; –, v. a. to copy, to imitate.
esemplificare, –plĭfĭkā'rĕ, v. a. to ex-
　emplify.　　　　　　　　　　　[fication.
esemplificazione, –tzĭŏ'nĕ, f. exempli-
esentare, ĕsĕntā'rĕ, v. a. to exempt, to
　privilege.
esente, ĕsĕn'tĕ, a. exempt.　　　[burial.
esequie, ĕsā'kŭĕ, f. pl. obsequies, pl.,
esercitare, ĕsĕrdshĭtā'rĕ, v. a. to exercise.
esercito, ĕsĕr'dshĭtŏ, m. army.
esercizio, –dshē'tzĭŏ, m. exercise, prac-
　tice; theme.
esergo, ĕsĕr'gŏ, m. exergue (of a coin).
esibire, ĕsĭbē'rĕ, v. a. to exhibit, to show.
esibizione, –bĭzĭŏ'nĕ, f. exhibition.
esigente, ĕsĭjĕn'tĕ, a. exigent.
esigenza, –jĕn'ză, f. exigency, want.
esigere, ĕsĭ'jĕrĕ, v. a. ir. to exact; to re-
　quire.
esiguo, ĕsĭ'gŭŏ, a. exiguous, small.
esilarare, –lārā'rĕ, v. a. to exhilarate,
　to cheer up.
esile, ĕsĭ'lĕ, a. slender, lean.
esiliare, –lĭā'rĕ, v. a. to exile
esilio, ĕsĭ'lĭŏ, esiglio, ĕsĭ'lyŏ, m. exile,
　banishment.
esimere, ĕsĭ'mĕrĕ, v. a. to exempt, to free.
esimio, ĕsĭ'mĭŏ, a. exquisite, extraordinary.
esinanire, ĕsĭnănē'rĕ, v. a. to annihilate,
　to destroy ; to annul ; to void.
esistente, ĕsĭstĕn'tĕ, a. existent, living.
esistenza, –tĕn'tză, f. existence, life.
esistere, ĕsĭs'tĕrĕ, v. n. ir. to exist.
esitare, ĕsĭtā'rĕ, v. a. to sell, to retail ; –,
　v. n. to hesitate.
esito, ĕ'sĭtŏ, m. issue, event; success ; sale.
esiziale, ĕsĭtzĭā'lĕ, a. destructive; fatal.
esizio, ĕsĭ'tzĭŏ, m. destruction, ruin.
Esodo, ĕ'sŏdŏ, m. Exodus.
esofago, ĕsŏ'făgŏ, m. (an.) æsophagus.
esorbitante, ĕsŏrbĭtăn'tĕ, a. exorbitant.
esorcismo, –dshĭs'mŏ, m. exorcism.
esorcista, –dshĭs'tă, m. exorcist.
esorcizzare, –dshĭtzā'rĕ, v. a. to exorcise.
esordio, ĕsŏr'dĭŏ, m. exordium, preamble.
esortare, –tā'rĕ, v. a. to exhort, to advise.
esortazione, –tzĭŏ'nĕ, f. exhortation.
esoso, ĕsŏ'sŏ, a. hateful, detestable.
esotico, ĕsŏ'tĭkŏ, a. exotic, foreign.
espansione, ĕspănsĭŏ'nĕ, f. expansion,
　display.　　　　　　　　　　　[means, pl.
espediente, –pĕdĭĕn'tĕ, m. expedient,
espellere, –pĕl'lĕrĕ, v. a. ir. to expel, to
　banish.　　　　　　　　　[experiment, trial.
esperienza, –pĕrĭĕn'tză, f. experience,

esperimentare, –mĕntă'rĕ, v. a. to experience, to try. [experience.
esperimento, –mĕn'tŏ, m. experiment.
Espero, ĕs'pĕrŏ, m. evening-star.
esperto, –pĕr'tŏ, a. expert, skilful.
espettativa, ĕspĕttătĕ'vă, **espettazione,** –tzĭŏ'nĕ, f. expectation.
espettorare, –tŏră'rĕ, v.a. to expectorate.
espiare, ĕspĭă'rĕ, v. a. to expiate; to spy.
espilare, –pĕlă'rĕ, v. a. to swindle, to rob slyly, to purloin, to filch.
esplicare, –plĕkă'rĕ, v. a. to explain.
esplicito, –plĕ'dshĭtŏ, a. explicit, plain, clear; formal. [sound.
esplorare, –plŏră'rĕ, v. a. to explore, to
esplosione, –sĭŏ'nĕ, f. explosion.
esponente, –pŏnĕn'tĕ, m. exponent, explainer, expounder. [explain.
esporre, –pŏr'rĕ, v. a. ir. to expose; to
esportare, –pŏrtă'rĕ, v. a. to export.
espositore, –pŏsĭtŏ'rĕ, m. expositor, interpreter. [planation.
esposizione, –tzĭŏ'nĕ, f. exposition, explanation.
espressione, –prĕssĭŏ'nĕ, f. expression.
espressivo, –sĕ'vŏ, a. expressive, significant. [firm; –, ad. expressly.
espresso, –prĕs'sŏ, a. express, precise,
esprimere, –prĕ'mĕrĕ, v. a. ir. to express; to utter. [propriate.
espropriare, –prŏprĭă'rĕ, v. a. to expropriation. [conquer.
espropriazione, –tzĭŏ'nĕ, f. expropriation.
espugnare, –pŭnyă'rĕ, v.a. to subdue, to
espugnatore, –tŏ'rĕ, m. conqueror.
espugnazione, –tzĭŏ'nĕ, f. conquest; taking by assault.
espulsione, –pŭlsĭŏ'nĕ, f. expulsion.
espurgare, –pŭrgă'rĕ, v. a. to purge, to scour. [they.
essa, ĕs'să, pn. she, it, the same; **esse,** pl.
essenza, –sĕn'tză, f. essence.
essenziale, –tzĭă'lĕ, a. essential.
essere, ĕs'sĕrĕ, v. ir. to be, to become; to belong; to be about.
essi, ĕs'sĭ, pn. pl. they.
essiccare, –kă'rĕ, v. a. to dry up.
esso, ĕs'sŏ pn. he, it.
estasi, ĕs'tăsĭ, f. ecstasy, trance, rapture.
estate, –tă'tĕ, f. summer.
estatico, –tă'tĭkŏ, a. ecstatic, ravishing.
estendere, –tĕn'dĕrĕ, v. a. ir. to extend, to stretch. [in a wider sense.
estensione, –sĭŏ'nĕ, f. extension; **per –,**
estenuare, –nŭă'rĕ, v. a. to extenuate.
esteriore, –tĕrĭŏ'rĕ, a. exterior, external.
esterminare, –mĭnă'rĕ, v. a. to exterminate. [havoc.
esterminio, –mĕ'nĭŏ, m. destruction,
esternare, –nă'rĕ, v. a. to reveal; to avow. [day.
esterno, –tĕr'nŏ, a. external; of yesterday.
esteso, –tă'sŏ, a. extended, ample.
estimazione, ĕstĭmătzĭŏ'nĕ, f. estimation; value. [to destroy.
estinguere, –tĭn'gŭĕrĕ, v.a. to extinguish;
estinto, –tĭn'tŏ, a. extinguished; dead.

estinzione, –tzĭŏ'nĕ, f. extinction, destruction. [destroy.
estirpare, ĕstĭrpă'rĕ, v. a. to extirpate, to
estorcere, –tŏr'dshĕrĕ, **estorquere,** –kŭĕrĕ, v. a. ir. to extort; to wring.
estraneo, –tră'nĕŏ, a. strange; odd.
estrarre, –trăr'rĕ, v. a. ir. to extract.
estratto, –trăt'tŏ, m. extract; essence; abridgment. [descent.
estrazione, –tzĭŏ'nĕ, f. extraction;
estremità, –trĕmĭtă', f. extremity; misery.
estremo, –trĕ'mŏ, a. extreme, last, utmost; excessive.
estrinseco, –trĭn'sĕkŏ, a. extrinsic.
estro, ĕs'trŏ, m. poetic rage.
estrudere, –trŏ'dĕrĕ, v. a. ir. to extrude, to thrust out. [dundant.
esuberante, ĕsŭbĕrăn'tĕ, a. exuberant, redundant.
esuberanza, –răn'tză, f. exuberance. superabundance.
esulare, ĕsŭlă'rĕ, v. a. to exile.
esulcerare, –ŭldshĕră'rĕ, v.a.to exulcerate.
esulcerazione, –tzĭŏ'nĕ, f. exulceration.
esule, ĕ'sŭlĕ, a. exiled. [light.
esultanza, ĕsŭltăn'tză, f. exultation, delight.
esultare, –tă'rĕ, v. n. to exult. [age.
età, ĕtă', f. age, century; **– minore,** under age.
etere, ĕ'tĕrĕ, m. ether, air; firmament, sky.
etereo, ĕtĕ'rĕŏ, a. ethereal, celestial.
eternale, ĕtĕrnă'lĕ, a. eternal.
eternamente, –mĕn'tĕ, ad. eternally.
eternare, –mĕ'rĕ, v. a. to eternize.
eternità, –nĭtă', f. eternity.
eterno, ĕtĕr'nŏ, a. eternal.
eterodosso, –rŏdŏs'sŏ, a. heterodox.
eterogeneo, –rŏjă'nĕŏ, a. heterogeneous.
etica, ĕ'tĭkă, f. ethics; consumption.
etichetta, ĕtĭkĕt'tă, f. etiquette, ceremony; ticket, label.
etico, ĕ'tĭkŏ, a. hectic, consumptive.
etimologia, ĕtĭmŏlŏjĕ'ă, f. etymology.
etnico, ĕt'nĭkŏ, m. pagan, heathen.
etra, ĕ'tră, f. (poet.) ether, sky.
eucaristia, ĕŭkărĕstĕ'ă, f. eucharist, communion.
eunuco, ĕŭnŭ'kŏ, m. eunuch.
evacuare, ĕvăkŭă'rĕ, v. n. to evacuate.
evacuazione, –tzĭŏ'nĕ, f. evacuation.
evadere, ĕvă'dĕrĕ, v. n. ir. to escape.
evangelico, ĕvănjĕ'lĭkŏ, a. evangelical.
evangelista, –jĕlĭs'tă, m. evangelist.
evangelizzare, –lĭtză'rĕ, v. n. to preach the Gospel.
evangelo, –jă'lŏ, m. Gospel.
evaporare, –pŏră'rĕ, v. n. to evaporate; to fly off.
evaporazione, –tzĭŏ'nĕ, f. evaporation.
evento, ĕvĕn'tŏ, m. event.
eventuale, ĕvĕntŭă'lĕ, a. eventual, casual.
evidente, ĕvĭdĕn'tĕ, a. evident.
evidenza, –dĕn'tză, f. evidence; proof.
evitare, –tă'rĕ, v. a. to avoid, to escape.
evo, ĕ'vŏ, m. age, century. [jure.
evocare, ĕvŏkă'rĕ, v. a. to evocate; to conjure.
evoluzione, –lŭtzĭŏ'nĕ, f. (mil.) evolution.
eziandio, ĕtzĭănde'ŏ, ad. even, also, yet.

F.

fa, *fã*, m. (mus.) fa.
fabbrica, *fãb'brĭkă*, f. building; fabric, manufactory.
fabbricare, *–kā'rĕ*, v. a. to build; to forge.
fabbricatore, *–tō'rĕ*, m. builder, mason; forger; intriguer, liar.
fabro, *fã'brŏ*, fabbro, *fãb'brŏ*, m. smith, blacksmith; forger; inventor.
faccenda, *fātshĕn'dă*, f. business.
faccendiere, *–dĭd'rĕ*, m. intriguer acto-tum; manager.
faccetta, *–tshĕt'tă*, f. angular cut, facet.
facchino, *fākkē'nŏ*, m. porter; scoundrel.
faccia, *fãt'shă*, f. face; appearance.
facciata, *–tshă'tă*, f. façade, front.
faceto, *fădshē'tŏ*, a. facetious, gay.
facezia, *–dshē'tzĭă*, f. merry conceit.
facidanno, *fădshĭdăn'nŏ*, a. prejudicial.
facile, *fã'dshĭlĕ*, a. easy, pliant; (of per-sons) affable.
facilità, *–dshĭlĭtă'*, f. facility.
facilitare, *–tā'rĕ*, v. a. to make easy.
facilmente, *–mĕn'tĕ*, ad. easily.
facimale, *–mă'lĕ*, m. mischievous boy.
facinoroso, *–nŏrŏ'sŏ*, a. atrocious.
facoltà, *făkŏltă'*, f. faculty, power.
facoltoso, *–tŏ'sŏ*, a. wealthy.
facondia, *–kŏn'dĭă*, f. eloquence.
facondo, *–kŏn'dŏ*, a. eloquent.
faggio, *fãd'jŏ*, m. beech-tree.
fagiana, *făjă'nă*, f. hen-pheasant.
fagiano, *–jă'nŏ*, m. pheasant.
fagiolata, *–jŏlă'tă*, f. awkwardness, sil-liness.
fagiuolo, *–jăŏ'lŏ*, m. kidney-bean; ninny, blockhead.
fagotto, *–gŏt'tŏ*, m. bundle, packet; (mus.) bassoon.
faina, *fă'ĭnă*, f. pole-cat.
falange, *fălăn'jĕ*, f. phalanx.
falbo, *fãl'bŏ*, a. light brown.
falcare, *–kā'rĕ*, v. a. to hook, to bend.
falce, *fãl'dshĕ*, f. sickle.
falciare, *–dshă'rĕ*, v. a. to mow.
falciata, *–dshă'tă*, f. cut of the scythe.
falcione, *–dshŏ'nĕ*, m. falchion.
falco, *fãl'kŏ*, m. falcon.
falcone, *–kŏ'nĕ*, m. falcon, hawk; (mil.) falconet.
falconeria, *–nĕră'ă*, f. hawking, falconry.
falconiere, *–nĭd'rĕ*, m. falconer.
falda, *fãl'dă*, f. fold, plait; skirt; side of a hill.
faldato, *–dā'tŏ*, a. folded.
faldella, *–dĕl'lă*, f. lint.
faldiglia, *–dēl'yă*, f. hoop-petticoat.
faldistorio, *–dĭstŏ'rĭŏ*, m. bishop's arm-chair.
falegname, *fălĕnyă'mĕ*, m. carpenter; [joiner.
fallace, *făllă'dshĕ*, a. fallacious.
fallacia, *–lă'dshă*, f. fallacy, deceit.
fallare, *–lă'rĕ*, v. n. to fail, to err, to mis-take; to offend; to omit.
fallibile, *–lē'bĭlĕ*, a. fallible; frail.
fallimento, *–lĭmĕn'tŏ*, m. failure; bank-ruptcy. [cheat.
fallire, *–lē'rĕ*, v. n. to fail; to sin; to

fallito, *–lē'tŏ*, m. bankrupt.
fallo, *fãl'lŏ*, m. error, failure.
falotico, *–lŏ'tĭkŏ*, a. whimsical.
falsare, *–sā'rĕ*, v. n. to falsify.
falsariga, *–sărē'gă*, f. ruled black lines for straight writing. [falsifier, forger.
falsario, *–să'rĭŏ*, falsatore, *–tŏ'rĕ*, m.
falsetto, *–sĕt'tŏ*, m. (mus.) falsetto, treble.
falsificare, *–sĭfĭkă'rĕ*, v. a. to falsify.
falsificazione, *–tzĭŏ'nĕ*, f. falsification, adulteration.
falsità, *–stă'*, f. falsity, falseness.
falso, *fãl'sŏ*, a. (& ad.) false(ly).
fama, *fă'mă*, f. fame, renown.
fame, *fă'mĕ*, f. hunger; eagerness.
famelico, *–mă'lĭkŏ*, a. dying with hunger.
famigerato, *–mĭjĕră'tŏ*, a. famed, famous.
famiglia, *–mīl'yă*, f. family; servants.
familiare, *–mīlĭă'rĕ*, a. familiar, intimate.
familiarità, *–lĭărĭtă'*, f. familiarity.
famoso, *–mŏ'sŏ*, a. famous, public.
fanale, *–nă'lĕ*, m. beacon, light-house.
fanatico, *–nă'tĭkŏ*, a. fanatic.
fanatismo, *–tĭs'mŏ*, m. fanaticism.
fanciulla, *făndshŭl'lă*, f. young girl, lass.
fanciullaggine, *–lăd'jĭnĕ*, f. childishness, puerility, childish trick.
fanciullesco, *–lĕs'kŏ*, a. childish, puerile.
fanciullezza, *–lĕt'ză*, f. childhood.
fanciullo, *–dshŭl'lŏ*, a. childish, young; –, m. young child, boy.
fandonia, *–dŏ'nĭă*, f. idle story, fable.
fanello, *fănĕl'lŏ*, m. linnet. [gaw.
fanfaluca, *–fălă'kă*, f. spark; trifle, gew-
fanfano, *făn'fănŏ*, m. boaster, romancer.
fango, *făn'gŏ*, m. mud, mire; clay; trouble.
fangoso, *–gŏ'sŏ*, a. muddy, miry.
fantaccino, *–tătshē'nŏ*, m. foot-soldier.
fantasia, *–tăsē'ă*, f. fancy.
fantasima, *–tă'sĭmă*, f., fantasma, *–tăs'mă*, m. phantom.
fantasticaggine, *–tăstĭkăd'jĭnĕ*, f. whim.
fantasticare, *–tăstĭkă'rĕ*, v. n. to fancy, to muse, to meditate.
fantasticheria, *see* fantasticaggine.
fantastico, *–tăs'tĭkŏ*, a. fantastic.
fante, *făn'tĕ*, m. man-servant; foot-soldier; knave (at cards).
fanteggiare, *–tĕdjă'rĕ*, v. a. to serve.
fanteria, *–tĕrē'ă*, f. infantry.
fantesca, *–tĕs'kă*, f. maid-servant.
fanticino, *–tĭdshē'nŏ*, m. boy, child.
fantino, *–tē'nŏ*, m. child, little boy; groom.
fantoccio, *–tŏt'shŏ*, m. puppet; baboon.
fardello, *fărdĕl'lŏ*, m. bundle, pack.
fare, *fă'rĕ*, v. a. ir. to do, to make; to com-pose; to finish; to act, to play; to bid, to cause; to be of consequence, to matter; – freddo, to be cold weather; farsi, to make oneself; to become; to come to.
faretra, *fă'tră*, f. quiver.
farfalla, *fărfăl'lă*, f. butterfly.
farfallone, *–lŏ'nĕ*, m. large butterfly; fib.
farfaro, *făr'fărŏ*, m. (bot.) colt's foot.
farina, *–rē'nă*, f. flour, meal.
farinaceo, *–rĭnă'dshĕŏ*, a. farinaceous,

farinata, –nä′ tä, f. porridge made of meal and water.

farinello, –nĕl′ lŏ, m. rogue, wretch.

faringe, –rin′jĕ, f. (an.) pharynx.

farmacia, –mädshĕ′ ä, f. pharmacy.

farmacista, –dshis′ tä, m. apothecary.

farmaco, fär′ mäkŏ, m. drug; medicament.

farneticare, –nĕtikä′ rĕ, v. n. to dote, to rave.

farnetico, –nä′ tikŏ, a. frenetic. [drivel.

faro, fä′ rŏ, m. watch-tower; strait.

farragine, färrä′jinĕ, f. medley; hotch-potch.

farro, fär′ rŏ, m. corn, rye. [potch.

farsa, fär′ sä, f. farce.

farsetto, –sĕt′ tŏ, m. doublet.

fascetta, fässhĕt′ tä, f. little bundle.

fascia, fäs′shä, f. band, fillet; fasce, pl. swaddling-clothes; sotto –, by bookpost, under open cover.

fasciare, –sshä′ rĕ, v. a. to bind, to bondage.

fasciatura, –tö′ rä, f. bandage, ligature.

fascina, –sshĕ′ nä, f. fascine, fagot.

fascinare, –sshinä′ rĕ, v. a. to make fagots.

fascino, –sshĕ′ nŏ, m. fascination.

fascio, fäs′ shŏ, m. bundle.

fasciume, –sshŏ′ mĕ, m. heap of rubbish.

fastello, fästĕl′ lŏ, m. fagot, bundle.

fasti, fäs′ tĭ, m. pl. annals, pl.

fastidio, –tĕ′ diŏ, m. weariness.

fastidiosaggine, –tidiŏsäd′jinĕ, f. troublesomeness. [some.

fastidioso, –diŏ′ sŏ, a. tiresome, troublesome.

fastidire, –dĕ′ rĕ, v. a. to weary, to vex.

fastigio, –tĕ′ jiŏ, m. top, summit.

fasto, fäs′ tŏ, m. pomp, ostentation.

fastoso, –tŏ′ sŏ, a. haughty.

fata, fä′ tä, f. fairy, witch.

fatale, –tä′ lĕ, a. fatal, predestined.

fatalità, –tälitä′, f. fatality.

fatare, –tä′ rĕ, v. a. to charm; to render invulnerable.

fatica, –tĕ′ kä, f. fatigue, toil.

faticare, –tikä′ rĕ, v. a. to fatigue, to toil.

faticatore, –tŏ′ rĕ, m. hard-worker, painstaker.

fatichevole, –kä′ vŏlĕ, a. laborious.

faticoso, –kŏ′ sŏ, a. fatiguing, laborious.

fatidico, –tĕ′ dikŏ, m. foreteller.

fato, fä′ tŏ, m. fate.

fatta, fät′ tä, f. sort, kind.

fattamente, –mĕn′ tĕ, ad. in fact, really.

fattezza, –tĕt′ zä, f. feature, fashion.

fattibile, –tĕ′ pĭlĕ, a. feasible.

fatticcio, –tĭt′ shŏ, a. robust; stout.

fattizio, –tĕ′ tziŏ, a. artificial, artful.

fatto, fät′ tŏ, a. made, done.

fattoiano, –tŏiä′ nŏ, m. oil-presser.

fattoio, –tŏ′ ŏ, m. oil-press.

fattore, –tŏ′ rĕ, m. maker; artisan; factor.

fattoressa, –tŏrĕs′ sä, f. steward's wife.

fattoria, –tŏrĕ′ ä, f. factory; stewardship;

fattorino, –tŏrĕ′ nŏ, m. shopman. [farm.

fattucchiera, –tükkĭä′ rä, f. witch, hag, sorceress.

fattucchieria, –kĕrĕ′ ä, f. witchcraft.

fattucchiero, –kĭä′ rŏ, m. wizard, sorcerer.

fattura, –tŏ′ rä, f. work, making; fashion; invoice; bill of lading; witchcraft.

fatturare, –tŏrä′ rĕ, v. a. to adulterate (wine).

fatuità, fätäitä′, f. fatuity.

fatuo, fä′ täŏ, a. infatuated, foolish, giddy.

fauci, fäŭ′ dshĭ, f. pl. throat; strait; river's mouth.

fauno, fäŭ′ nŏ, m. faun, satyr.

fautore, –tŏ′ rĕ, m. favourer, protector.

fava, fä′ vä, f. bean; vote; foolish pride.

favata, –vä′ tä, f. ragout made with beans; foolish pride, inflation, conceit.

favella, fävĕl′ lä, f. speech, dialect; language.

favellare, –vĕllä′ rĕ, v. a. & n. to speak.

favellio, –vĕllĕ′ ŏ, m. prate, prattle.

favilla, –vĭl′ lä, f. spark, sparkle.

favillare, –lä′ rĕ, v. n. to sparkle, to twinkle.

favo, fä′ vŏ, m. honey-comb.

favola, fä′ vŏlä, f. fable, story tale.

favoleggiare, –vŏlĕdjä′ rĕ, v. n. to tell tales; to banter.

favoloso, –lŏ′ sŏ, a. fabulous. [zephyr.

favonio, –vŏ′ niŏ, m. (poet.) west-wind,

favore, –vŏ′ rĕ, m. favour, protection.

favoreggiare, –rĕdjä′ rĕ, v. a. to favour.

favorevole, –rä′ vŏlĕ, a. favourable, propitious, friendly.

favorire, –rĕ′ rĕ, v. a. to be so kind as.

favorito, –rĕ′ tŏ, m. favourite.

fazione, fätziŏ′ nĕ, f. fashion; faction.

fazioso, –tziŏ′ sŏ, a. factious.

fazzoletto, –tzŏlĕt′ tŏ, m. handkerchief.

fè, see fede.

febbraio, fĕbbrä′ ŏ, m. February.

febbre, fĕb′ brĕ, f. fever. [feverish.

febbricitare, –brădshitä′ rĕ, v. a. to be feverish.

febbricone, –kŏ′ nĕ, m. violent fever.

febbrifugo, –brĕ′ fŭgŏ, m. febrifuge.

febbrile, –brĕ′ lĕ, a. febrile.

febeo, fĕbĕ′ ŏ, a. poetical. [dross.

feccia, fĕtsh′ ä, f. dregs, pl.; sediment;

feccioso, –thŏ′ sŏ, a. full of dregs; tiresome. [ful, to fertilize.

fecondare, fĕkŏndä′ rĕ, v. a. to make fruitful, to fertilize.

fecondità, –ditä′, f. fecundity.

fecondo, –kŏn′ dŏ, a. fruitful.

fede, fä′ dĕ, f. faith; fidelity, loyalty, sincerity; trust, credit, confidence.

fedecommessario, fĕdĕkŏmmĕssä′ rĭŏ, m. trustee, feoffee.

fedecommesso, –mĕs′ sŏ, m. deed of trust.

fedecommettere, –mĕt′ tĕrĕ, v. a. ir. to make a deed of trust.

fededegno, –dĕn′ yŏ, a. worthy of trust.

fedele, fĕdä′ lĕ, m. christian, believer; –, a. faithful, loyal, true.

fedelmente, –dĕlmĕn′ tĕ, ad. faithfully, loyally.

fedeltà, –dĕltä′, f. fidelity, loyalty.

federa, fĕ′ dĕrä, f. ticking; pillow-case.

fedifrago, fĕdĕ′ frägŏ, a. faithless.

fegatello, –gätĕl′ lŏ, m. bit of roasted liver.

fegato, fĕgä′ tŏ, m. liver.

fegatoso, –tŏ′ sŏ, a. diseased in the liver.

felce, fĕl′ dshĕ, f. (bot.) fern.

felice, fĕlĕ′ dshĕ, a. happy, lucky.

felicità, –lĭshĭtä′, f. felicity.

felicitare, –dshitä′ rĕ, v. a. to make happy.

fello, fĕl′ lŏ, a. wicked; perfidious.

fellone, –lŏ′ nĕ, m. (poet.) thief.

fellonesco, –lŏnĕs'kŏ, a. perfidious, cruel.
fellonia, –lŏnē'ä, f. felony. [to refine.
feltrare, –trä'rĕ, v. a. to filter, to strain;
feltro, fĕl'trŏ, m. felt.
femmina, fĕm'minä, f. female, woman.
femminella, –nĕl'lä, f. poor, common
woman.
femmineo, –mĕ'nĕŏ, a. feminine, womanish.
femminile, –minē'lĕ, a. feminine.
femminilità, –nĭlĭtä', f. feminality;
womanhood, womanliness.
femminino, –nĕ'nŏ, a. feminine, female.
femore, fĕ'mŏrĕ, m. thigh-bone.
fendente, fĕndĕn'tĕ, m. cut, gash, stroke.
fendere, fĕn'dĕrĕ, v. a. ir. to cleave, to
split; to plough.
fenditura, –dĭtŏ'rä, f. chink, cleft.
fenice, fĕnē'dshĕ, f. phœnix; rarity.
fenile, –nē'lĕ, m. hay-loft.
fenomenale, –nŏmĕnä'lĕ, a. phenomenal.
fenomeno, –nŏ'mĕnŏ, m. phenomenon.
fera, fĕ'rä, f. wild beast.
ferace, fĕrä'dshĕ, a. fruitful, fertile.
feracità, –rädshĭtä', f. fertility.
ferale, –rä'lĕ, a. fatal, funeral.
feretro, fĕ'rĕtrŏ, m. bier, litter.
feria, fĕ'rĭä, f. holiday.
feriale, fĕrĭä'lĕ, a. daily, trivial.
feriare, –rĭä'rĕ, v. n. to keep holiday; to
have vacations.
ferimento, –rĭmĕn'tŏ, m. wounding.
ferino, –rē'nŏ, a. savage, cruel.
ferire, –rē'rĕ, v. a. to strike, to wound.
ferita, –rē'tä, f. wound, co tusion.
ferità, –rĭtä', f. ferocity, fierceness.
feritoia, –rĭtŏ'ä, f. loop-hole.
ferma, fĕr'mä, f. farming, leasing; arrest.
fermaglio, –mäl'yŏ, m. clasp, buckle.
fermare, –mä'rĕ, v. a. to stop, to stay; to
fix; to confirm; fermarsi, –mär'sĭ, to
fermata, –mä'tä, f. pause, stop. [pause.
fermentare, –mĕntä'rĕ, v. n. to ferment;
to effervesce; to work.
fermentativo, –tĕ'vŏ, a. fermentative.
fermentazione, –tzĭŏ'nĕ, f. fermentation.
fermento, –mĕn'tŏ, m. ferment, yeast.
fermezza, –mĕt'zä, f. firmness.
fermo, fĕr'mŏ, a. firm, steady, fast; stable;
solid; constant; determined, intrepid;
canto –, m. plain song; –, m. agreement.
fero, fĕ'rŏ, a. (poet.) fierce.
feroce, fĕrŏ'dshĕ, a. ferocious, fierce.
ferocemente, –mĕn'tĕ, ad. fiercely.
ferocia, –rŏ'dshä, ferocità, –rŏdshĭtä', f.
ferocity, cruelty.
ferraccio, fĕrrät'shŏ, m. old iron.
ferragosto, –rägŏs'tŏ, m. first day of
August.
ferraio, –rä'ŏ, m. iron-monger; cutler.
ferraiuolo, –rä-iŏŏ'lŏ, m. cloak; smith,
cutler. [to shoe (a horse).
ferrare, fĕrrä'rĕ, v. a. to bind with iron;
ferrareccia, –rä'tshä, f. all sorts of iron
tools, pl. [cavalli, tramway.
ferrata, –rä'tä, f. iron-grate; railway; – a
ferratore, –rä-tŏ'rĕ, m. farrier, smith.
ferratura, –tŏ'rä, f. horse-shoeing; iron-
ferreo, fĕr'rĕŏ, a. ferrous. [work.

ferriera, –rĭä'rä, f. farrier's leathern bag;
forge; iron-mine. [coloured.
ferrigno, –rēn'yŏ, a. ferruginous; iron-
ferro, fĕr'rŏ, m. iron; sword.
ferrovia, –rŏvē'ä, f. railway.
ferruginoso, –rŭjĭnŏ'sŏ, a. ferruginous.
fertile, fĕr'tĭlĕ, a. fertile, fruitful.
fertilità, –tĭlĭtä', f. fertility.
fertilizzare, –lĭdzä'rĕ, v. a. to fertilize.
fervente, –vĕn'tĕ, a. fervent; vehement;
eager; passionate.
fervere, fĕr'vĕrĕ, v. n. to boil, to be hot.
fervido, fĕr'vĭdŏ, a. fervent.
fervore, –vŏ'rĕ, m. fervour; zeal.
fervoroso, –rŏrŏ'sŏ, a. ardent, zealous.
ferza, fĕr'tzä, f. whip, lash.
fesso, fĕs'sŏ, m. fissure, cleft; crack.
fessura, –sŏ'rä, f. fissure; opening.
festa, fĕs'tä, f. holiday; feast.
festante, –tän'tĕ, a. joyful.
festare, –tä'rĕ, v. a. to feast.
festeggiamento, –tĕdjämĕn'tŏ, m. re-
joicings, pl. [feast.
festeggiare, –tĕdjä'rĕ, v. a. to give a
festereccio, –tĕrĕ'shŏ, a. festive, joyous.
festevole, –tĕ'vŏlĕ, a. merry.
festino, –tē'nŏ, m. ball, feast, entertain-
festività, –tĭvĭtä', f. festivity. [ment.
festivo, –tē'vŏ, a. festive.
festone, –tŏ'nĕ, m. festoon.
festuca, –tŏ'kä, f. bit of straw, mote.
fetente, fĕtĕn'tĕ, a. stinking.
fetido, fĕ'tĭdŏ, a. fetid.
feto, fĕ'tŏ, m. fœtus, embryo.
fetore, fĕtŏ'rĕ, m. fetidness.
fetta, fĕt'tä, f. slice, cut, steak.
feudale, fĕŭdä'lĕ, a. feudal.
feudatario, –dä-tä'rĭŏ, m. feudatory.
feudo, fĕ'ŭdŏ, m. fief, fee; tenure.
fiaba, fĭä'bä, f. fib, story.
fiacca, fĭäk'kä, f. noise, clatter.
fiaccare, –kä'rĕ, v. a. to break.
fiacchezza, –kĕt'zä, f. weakness.
fiacco, fĭäk'kŏ, m. ruin, destruction.
fiaccola, fĭäk'kŏlä, f. torch, flambeau.
fiala, fĭä'lä, f. phial, flask.
fiamma, fĭäm'mä, f. flame; (fig.) passion.
fiammata, –mä'tä, f. great flame.
fiammeggiare, –mĕdjä'rĕ, v. n. to sparkle,
to glitter, to blaze.
fiammiferaio, –fĕrä'ŏ, m. seller of luci-
fers or safety-matches.
fiammifero, –mĕ'fĕrŏ, m. lucifer, match,
safety-match. [flames.
fiammifero, –mĕ'fĕrŏ, a. flaming, darting
fiancata, fĭänkä'tä, f. thrust in the flank.
fiancheggiare, –kĕdjä'rĕ, v. a. to support; to wound in the side.
fianco, fĭän'kŏ, m. flank, side.
fiancuto, –kŭ'tŏ, a. broad-sided.
fiasca, fĭäs'kä, f. flat bottle.
fiascaio, –kä'ŏ, m. bottle-maker.
fiascheggiare, –kĕdjä'rĕ, v. a. to buy
(wine) by the bottle.
fiasco, fĭäs'kŏ, m. bottle, flask.
fiata, fĭä'tä, f. time; una –, once.
fiatare, –ä'rĕ, v. n. to breathe.

fiato, *fĭä′tŏ,* m. breath.
fibbia, *fēb′bĭä,* f. buckle, clasp.
fibbiaio, *fēb′bĭä′ŏ,* m. spangle-maker.
fibra, *fē′brä,* f. fibre, filament.
fibrilla, *fĭbrēl′lä,* f. small fibre.
fibrina, *–brē′nä,* f. fibrine.
fibroso, *–brŏ′sŏ,* a. fibrous.
ficaia, *–kä′ä,* f. fig-tree.
ficcare, *fēkkä′rē,* v. a. to drive in.
fico, *fē′kŏ,* m. fig; fig-tree.
ficosecco, *fēkŏsĕk′kŏ,* m. dried fig.
fida, *fē′dä,* f. security, pledge.
fidanza, *fĭdän′tzä,* f. confidence, faith.
fidanzare, *–tzä′rē,* v. a. to warrant; to betroth, to affiance.
fidanzato, *–tzä′tŏ,* a. warranted.
fidare, *–dä′rē,* v. a. to trust.
fidato, *–dä′tŏ,* a. faithful, loyal.
fidecommesso, *see* **fedecommesso &c.**
fido, *fē′dŏ,* a. faithful, trusty, honest.
fiducia, *fĭdŏ′dsˏä,* f. confidence.
fiduciario, *–dŭdshä′rĭŏ,* a. fiduciary.
fiedere, *fĭĕ′dĕrē,* v. a. to strike.
fiele, *fĭĕ′lē,* m. gall; bitterness; rancour.
fienaia, *fĭĕnä′ä,* f. scythe.
fienile, *–nē′lē,* m. hay-loft.
fieno, *fĭĕ′nŏ,* m. hay.
fiera, *fĭĕ′rä,* f. wild beast; public fair.
fierezza, *fĭĕrĕt′zä,* f. fierceness; alacrity.
fiero, *fĭĕ′rŏ,* a. fierce, cruel; proud, haughty; lively.
fievole, *fĭĕ′vŏlē,* a. feeble.
fievolezza, *fĭĕvŏlĕt′zä,* f. weakness.
figgere, *fēd′jĕrē,* v. a. ir. to fix, to drive [in.
figlia, *fēl′yä,* f. daughter; child.
figliare, *–yä′rē,* v. a. to bring forth.
figliastra, *–yäs′trä,* f. step-daughter.
figliastro, *–yäs′trŏ,* m. step-son.
figliatura, *–yätŏ′rä,* f. gestation; child-birth, delivery.
figlio, *fēl′yŏ,* m. son; child.
figlioccia, *–yŏt′shä,* f. goddaughter.
figlioccio, *–yŏt′shŏ,* m. godson.
figliuola, *–yŏŏ′lä,* f. daughter.
figliuolanza, *–yŏŏlän′tzä,* f. off-spring;
figliuolo, *–yŏŏ′lŏ,* m. son. [children.
fignolo, *fēn′yŏlŏ,* m. bile.
figura, *fĭgŏ′rä,* f. figure; statue.
figurabile, *–gŭrä′bĭlē,* a. figurable.
figurante, *–rän′tē,* m. super, walking gentleman *or* lady.
figurare, *–rä′rē,* v. a. to figure, to represent.
figuratamente, *–rätämĕn′tē,* **figurativamente,** *–tĭvämĕn′tē,* ad. figuratively.
figurativo, *–tē′rŏ,* a. figurative.
figurazione, *–tzĭŏ′nē,* f. imagination.
fila, *fē′lä,* f. file, row. [idea, fancy.
filaloro, *fĭlälŏ′rŏ,* m. gold-wire-drawer.
filamento, *–mēn′tŏ,* m. filament; thread.
filamentoso, *–tŏ′sŏ,* a. fibrous.
filanda, *fĭlän′dä,* f. spinning-mill.
filantropia, *–trŏpē′ä,* f. philanthropy.
filantropo, *–län′trŏpŏ,* m. philanthropist.
filare, *–lä′rē,* v. a. to spin, to wiredraw.
filastrocca, *–lästrŏk′kä,* f. cock-and-bull story, rigmarole.

filatessa, *–lätĕs′sä,* f. entangled thread.
filaticcio, *–tĭt′shŏ,* m. coarse silk thread.
filato, *–lä′tŏ,* m. spun yarn.
filatoio, *–tŏ′ŏ,* m. spinning-wheel.
filatura, *–tŏ′rä,* f. spinning-fabric.
filettare, *–lĕttä′rē,* v. a. to stitch with gold thread, to embroider in gold.
filetto, *–lĕt′tŏ,* m. small thread.
filiale, *–lĭä′lē,* a. filial.
filiazione, *–tzĭŏ′nē,* f. filiation.
filiera, *–lĭĕ′rä,* f. wire-drawing-plate;
filiggine, *–lĭd′jĭnē,* f. soot.
filigrana, *–lĭgrä′nä,* f. filigree. [wire.
filo, *fē′lŏ,* m. (fila, pl.) thread; string;
filologia, *fĭlŏlŏjē′ä,* f. philology.
filologo, *–lŏ′lŏgŏ,* m. philologer.
filone, *–lŏ′nē,* m. vein (of ore, water, &c.).
filosofale, *–lŏsŏfä′lē,* a. philosophical.
filosofare, *–fä′rē,* **filosofeggiare,** *—fĕdjä′rē,* v. n. to philosophize.
filosofessa, *–fĕs′sä,* f. female philosopher.
filosofia, *–fē′ä,* f. philosophy.
filosofico, *–sŏ′fĭkŏ,* a. philosophical.
filosofo, *–lŏ′sŏfŏ,* m. philosopher.
filtro, *fēl′trŏ,* m. love-potion.
filugello, *fĭlŭjĕl′lŏ,* m. silk-worm.
filuzzo, *–lŭt′zŏ,* m. fine thread.
filza, *fēl′tzä,* f. row, string.
fimbria, *fēm′brĭä,* f. edge, border.
fimbriato, *–brĭä′tŏ,* a. bordered, fringed.
fime, *fē′mē,* **fimo,** *–mŏ,* m. soil, dung.
finale, *fēnä′lē,* a. final, definitive.
finanze, *–nän′tzē,* f. pl. finances; revenue.
finanziere, *–tzĭä′rē,* m. financier.
finattantoché, *–nättäntŏkē′,* **finché,** *fĭnkē′,* ad. until, whilst. [clever.
fine, *fē′nē,* m. & f. end; –, a. fine; elegant,
finestra, *fĭnĕs′trä,* f. window.
finestrato, *–trä′tŏ,* m. row of windows.
finestrino, *–trē′nŏ,* m. little window.
finezza, *–nĕt′zä,* f. fineness; civility.
fingente, *fĭnjĕn′tē,* a. feigning.
fingere, *fĭn′jĕrē,* v. a. ir. to feign.
fingimento, *–jĭmĕn′tŏ,* m. fiction.
finimento, *fĭnĭmĕn′tŏ,* m. end, conclusion.
finimondo, *–mŏn′dŏ,* m. end of the world.
finire, *fĭnē′rē,* v. a. to finish.
finita, *–nē′tä,* f. end, determinate quantity.
finitimo, *–nē′tĭmŏ,* a. neighbouring.
fino, *fē′nŏ,* a. fine, nice; thin, subtile; crafty, skilful; –, ad. & pr. as far as, till,
finocchio, *–nŏk′kĭŏ,* m. fennel. [until.
finora, *–ŏ′rä,* ad. till now.
finta, *fēn′tä,* f. feint, dissimulation.
finto, *fēn′tŏ,* a. feigned; hidden.
finzione, *–tzĭŏ′nē,* f. fiction.
fio, *fē′ŏ,* m. fief.
fiocaggine, *fĭŏkäd′jĭnē,* f. hoarseness.
fiocca, *fĭŏk′kä,* f. flake, tassel. [flakes.
fioccare, *–kä′rē,* v. n. to snow in large
fiocco, *fĭŏk′kŏ,* m. lock of wool; flake; tassel; (mar.) jib.
fiocchezza, *–kĕt′zä,* f. hoarseness.
fiocina, *–dshē′nä,* f. harpoon.
fioco, *fĭ′kŏ,* a. hoarse; faint.
fionda, *fĭŏn′dä,* f. sling.
fioraia, *fĭŏrä′ä,* f. flower-girl.

fioraliso, *–rälö'sö*, m. corn-flower, blue-bottle. [pl.

fiorame, *–rä'mĕ* m. all sorts of flowers.

fiordaliso, *–dälĕ'sö*, m. fleur-de-lis, iris.

fiore, *fĕö'rĕ*, m. flower; blossom.

fiorente, *–rĕn'tĕ*, a. flourishing, in flower.

fioretto, *–rĕt'tö*, m. little flower; fencing-foil; blotting-paper; the best part.

fiorino, *–rĕ'nö*, m. florin.

fiorire, *–rĕ'rĕ*, v. n. to bloom; to prosper.

fiorista, *–rĕs'tä*, m. florist.

fioritura, *–rĕtöö'rä*, f. flowering.

fiorrancio, *–rän'dshö*, m. marigold; crested wren.

fiottare, *fĕöttä'rĕ*, v. n. to float.

fiotto, *fĕöt'tö*, m. surge, wave; tide, flood.

fiottoso, *–tö'sö*, a. billowy, tempestuous.

firma, *fĕr'mä*, f. signature, subscription.

firmamento, *–mämĕn'tö*, m. firmament.

firmare, *–mä'rĕ*, v. a. to sign, to subscribe.

fiscale, *fĕskä'lĕ*, m. attorney-general.

fiscalità, *–kälitä'*, f. fisc, exchequer.

fiscella, *fĕsshĕl'lä*, f. wicker-basket.

fischiare, *fĕskĕä'rĕ*, v. n. to whistle, to whistle. [hiss.

fischiata, *–kĕä'tä*, f. whistling.

fischietto, *–kĕĕt'tö*, m. little whistle.

fischio, *fĕs'kĕö*, m. hiss, whistle.

fisciù, *fĕsshö'*, m. neckerchief, wrapper.

fisco, *fĕs'kö*, m. exchequer.

fisica, *fĕ'sikä*, f. physics.

fisicaggine, *fĕsikäd'jĕnĕ*, f. caprice, whim.

fisicare, *–kä'rĕ*, v. a. to fancy.

fisico, *fĕ'sikö*, m. physician.

fisicoso, *fĕsikö'sö*, a. scrupulous; fantastic.

fisima, *fĕ'simä*, f. whim.

fisiologia, *fĕsiölöjĕ'ä*, f. physiology.

fisiologico, *–lö'jikö*, a. physiological.

fisiologo, *–sĕö'lögö*, m. physiologist.

fisiomante, *fĕsiömän'tĕ*, m. physiognomist.

fisionomia, *–nömĕ'ä*, f. physiognomy.

fisionomo, *–sĕö'nömö*, m. physiognomist.

fiso, *fĕ'sö*, a. (& ad.) fixed(ly); intently.

fisonomia, *see* fisonomia.

fissare, *fĕssä'rĕ*, v. a. to fix the eyes on.

fissazione, *–tzĕö'nĕ*, fissezza, *–sĕt'zä*, f. fixation; stability.

fisso, *fĕs'sö*, a. fixed; firm, permanent.

fistola, *fĕs'tölä*, f. fistula; flageolet, pipe.

fistolare, *–tölä'rĕ*, a. fistular.

fistolo, *fĕs'tölö*, m. demon.

fitta, *fĕt'tä*, f. quagmire; stitch, acute pain.

fittaiuolo, *–tä'iöö'lö*, m. farmer.

fittile, *–tĕ'lĕ*, a. earthen.

fittivo, *–tĕ'vö*, a. fictitious.

fittizio, *–tĕ'tzĕö*, a. fictitious, false.

fitto, *fĕt'tö*, m. rent, hire.

fittone, *–tö'nĕ*, m. main root.

fittuario, *–tŭä'rĕö*, m. farmer.

fiumana, *fĕŭmä'nä*, f. flood, inundation.

fiumatico, *–mä'tikö*, a. fluviatic.

fiume, *fĕö'mĕ*, m. river, stream.

fiumicello, *–mĕshĕl'lö*, fiumicino, *–dshĕ'nö*, m. rivulet.

fiutare, *fĕŭtä'rĕ*, v. a. to smell.

fiuto, *fĕö'tö*, m. smell.

flaccido, *flät'shidö*, a. flaccid, languid.

flagellare, *–jĕllä'rĕ*, v. a. to flagellate, to whip. [ruin.

flagello, *–jĕl'lö*, m. whip; punishment;

flanella, *–nĕl'lä*, f. flannel. [flatulency.

flato, *flä'tö*, m., flatuosità, *–tŭösitä'*, f.

flatuoso, *–tŭö'sö*, a. flatulent.

flautista, *flaŭtĕs'tä*, m. flute-player.

flauto, *flaŭ'tö*, m. flute.

flebile, *flĕ'bĭlĕ*, a. mournful.

flebilmente, *flĕbĭlmĕn'tĕ*, ad. mournfully.

flebotomia, *–bötömĕ'ä*, f. blood-letting.

flebotomo, *–bö'tömö*, m. blood-letter, [bleeder.

flemma, *flĕm'mä*, f. phlegm.

flemmatico, *–mä'tikö*, a. phlegmatic.

flessibile, *flĕssĕ'bĭlĕ*, a. flexible, pliable.

flessione, *–sĕö'nĕ*, f. flexion.

flessuoso, *–sŭö'sö*, a. bent, curved

flibustiero, *flĭbŭstĕĕ'rö*, m. buccaneer.

floridezza, *flörĭdĕt'zä*, f. floridness.

florido, *flö'rĭdö*, a. florid, flowery.

florifero, *flörĭfĕ'rö*, a. full of flowers.

floscezza, *flösshĕt'zä*, f. flaccidity, laxness.

floscio, *flössh'ö*, a. flabby; weak.

flotta, *flöt'tä*, f. fleet, navy.

flottiglia, *–tĕl'yä*, f. flotilla.

fluente, *flŭĕn'tĕ*, a. flowing. [fluidity.

fluidezza, *flŭĭdĕt'zä*, fluidità, *–ditä'*, f.

fluido, *flŭ'ĭdö*, a. & m. fluid.

fluire, *flŭĕ'rĕ*, v. n. to flow.

flussione, *flŭssĕö'nĕ*, f. fluxion, catarrh.

flusso, *flŭs'sö*, m. looseness of body.

flutto, *flŭt'tö*, m. surge, billow.

fluttuamento, *–tŭämĕn'tö*, m. fluctuation.

fluttuare, *–tŭä'rĕ*, v. n. to fluctuate.

fluttuoso, *–tŭö'sö*, a. billowy; stormy.

fluviale, *flŭvĕä'lĕ*, a. fluviatic.

foca, *fö'kä*, f. seal, sea-calf.

focaccia, *fökät'shä*, f. cake; bun; **render pane per –**, to render like for like.

focaia, *–kä'yä*, f. flint-stone.

foce, *fö'dshĕ*, f. gullet; mouth (of a river).

focherello, *fökĕrĕl'lö*, m. small fire.

focile, *see* fucile.

foco, *fö'kö*, m. fire; ardour; passion; focus.

focolare, *fökölä'rĕ*, m. hearth, fire-place.

focone, *–kö'nĕ*, m. great fire; powder-pan.

focoso, *–kö'sö*, a. fiery; furious.

fodera, *fö'dĕrä*, f. lining; scabbard.

foderaio, *födĕrä'ö*, m. furrier.

foderare, *–dĕrä'rĕ*, v. a. to line.

fodero, *fö'dĕrö*, m. lining.

foga, *fö'gä*, f. fury. [manner.

foggia, *föd'jä*, f. fashion, form, shape;

foggiare, *–djä'rĕ*, v. a. to form, to fashion.

foglia, *föl'yä*, f. leaf.

fogliame, *–yä'mĕ*, f. leaves, pl.

fogliare, *–yä'rĕ*, v. n. to produce leaves.

foglietta, *–yĕt'tä*, f. small leaf; pint.

foglietto, *–yĕt'tö*, m. leaf of a book; small sheet of paper.

foglio, *föl'yö*, m. sheet of paper; page.

foglioso, *–yö'sö*, a., fogliuto, *–yŭ'tö*, a. leafy.

fogna, *fön'yä*, f. common sewer.

fognare, *–yä'rĕ*, v. a. to make a sewer.

foia, *fö'yä*, f. rut, lust.

fola, *fö'lä*, f. story; crowd.

folaga, folä'gä, f. moor-hen.
folata, -lä'tä, f. gust of wind; flight of birds. [shine.
folgorare, folgōrä're, v. n. to lighten; to **folgore,** fol'gore, m. lightning.
folgoreggiare, -rēdjä're, v. n. to lighten.
folla, fol'lä, f. crowd, press.
folleggiamento, -lēdjämēn'tő, m. folly.
folleggiare, -lēdjä're, v. a. to play the fool.
follemente, -lēmēn'tē, ad. foolishly.
folletto, -lēt'tő, m. hobgoblin.
follia, follī'ä, f. folly. [m. husk, shell.
follicola, -lē'kőlä, f.; **follicolo,** -kőlő,
follone, -lő'nē, m. fuller.
folta, fol'tä, f. crowd; heap.
foltezza, -tēt'zä, f. thickness.
folto, fol'tő, a. thick; dense. [excite.
fomentare, főmēntä're, v. a. to foment; to **fomento,** -mēn'tő, m. fomentation.
fomite, fő'mītē, m. tinder.
fonda, fon'dä, f. purse; sling. [ment.
fondaccio, -dät'shő, m. dregs, pl., sedi-
fondamentale, -dämēntä'tē, a. funda-mental.
fondamento, -mēn'tő, m. foundation.
fondare, -dä're, v. a. to found, to etablish.
fondata, -dä'tä, f. wine-lees, pl. [reason.
fondatamente, -dätämēn'tē, ad. with
fondatore, -tő're, m. founder.
fondatrice, -trē'dshē, f. foundress.
fondazione, -tzið'nē, f. foundation.
fondello, -dēl'lő, m. button-hole.
fondere, fon'dērē, v. a. ir. to melt.
fonderia, -dērī'ä, f. foundry.
fondigliuolo, see **fondaccio.**
fonditore, -dītő're, m. iron-founder; spendthrift. [depth.
fondo, fon'dő, a. deep; thick; —, m. bottom,
fonduto, -dä'tő, a. melted.
fontale, -tä'lē, a. original.
fontana, -tä'nä, f. fountain.
fontanella, -nēl'lä, f. small fountain.
fontaniere, -nä're, m. water-bailiff.
fontano, -tä'nő, a. of a fountain.
fonte, fon'tē, m. & f. fountain, source.
foracchiare, főrákkä're, v. a. to bore.
foraggiare, -djä're, v. a. to forage.
foraggiere, -djä're, m. forager.
foraggio, főräd'jő, m. forage, provisions.
forame, -rä'mē, m. hole.
foraneo, -rä'nēő, a. forensic, of the bar.
forare, -rä're, v. a. to pierce, to bore.
forasiepe, -stä'pē, m. hedge-sparrow; poor little man.
foraterra, -tēr'rä, f. dibble.
foratoio, -tő'ő, m. wimble; gimlet.
forbici, for'bidshī, f.pl. scissors, pl.; claws (of a crab), pl.
forbire, -bē're, v. a. to furbish, to rub up.
forbitezza, -bītēt'zä, f. polish, lustre.
forbito, -bē'tő, a. polished; elegant.
forbitoio, -tő'ő, m. burnishing-tool.
forca, for'kä, f. pitchfork.
forcata, -kä'tä, f. fork of the legs; pitch-
forcato, -kä'tő, a. forked. [fork-full].

forcatura, see **forcata.**
forcella, -dshēl'lä, f. little fork; vine-prop.
forchetta, -kēt'tä, f. fork; **favellare in punta di —,** to speak with affectation.
forcina, see **forchetta.**
forcone, -kő'nē, m. spear with three iron-
forcuto, -kü'tő, a. forked. [prongs.
forese, főrä'sē, m. rustic.
foresozzo, -rēsőt'ző, m. young peasant.
foresta, -rēs'tä, f. forest.
foresteria, -tērī'ä, f. crowd of strangers.
forestiere, -tiä'rē, m. stranger, guest.
foresto, -rēs'tő, a. wild, savage; desert.
forfecchia, -fēk'kiä, f. ear-wig.
forfice, for'fidshē, f. scissors.
forfora, for'fōrä, f. scruff; scald-head.
foriera, -riä'rä, f. fore-runner.
foriere, -riä're, m. fore-runner; quarter-master. [model; way.
forma, for'mä, f. form, figure; fashion;
formaggio, -mäd'jő, m. cheese.
formaio, -mä'ő, m. maker of shoe-lasts.
formale, -mä'lē, a. formal, external.
formalità, -mälitä', f. formality.
formalmente, -mälmēn'tē, ad. formally, precisely.
formare, -mä're, v. a. to form, to fashion.
formatamente, -tämēn'tē, ad. positively, perfectly.
formativo, -tē'vő, a. giving form.
formazione, -tzið'nē, f. formation.
formella, -mēl'lä, f. hole (for planting trees); furrow.
formentone, -mēntő'nē, m. Indian corn.
formica, -mē'kä, f. ant, emmet.
formicaio, -mikä'ő, m. ant-hill.
formicola, -mē'kőlä, f. small ant.
formicolaio, -mikőlä'ő, m. ant-hill; crowd.
formicolamento, -lämēn'tő, **formi-colio,** -kőlő'ő, m. prickling like the sting-ing of ants. [crowd; to tickle.
formicolare, -kőlä're, v. n. to swarm; to
formicone, -kő'nē, m. large ant.
formidabile, -dä'bilē, a. dreadful.
formisura, -miső'rä, ad. beyond measure.
formola, see **formula.**
formosità, -mősitä', f. beauty.
formoso, -mő'ső, a. beautiful.
formula, for'mälä, f. form; rule.
formulario, -mälä'riő, m. formulary.
fornace, for'nä'dshē, f. furnace.
fornaio, -nä'ő, m. baker.
fornata, -nä'tä, f. batch; an oven full.
fornello, -nēl'lő, m. small furnace.
fornicare, -nikä're, v. a. to fornicate.
fornicatore, -tő're, m. fornicator.
fornicazione, -tzið'nē, f. fornication.
fornimento, -mēn'tő, m. furniture.
fornire, -nē're, v. a. to finish; to furnish, to provide. [f. furniture, ornament.
fornito, -nē'tő, m. **fornitura,** -tő'rä,
forno, for'nő, m. oven.
foro, fő'rő, m. hole; court of justice.
forosetta, főrősēt'tä, f. young peasant
forra, for'rä, f. glen, defile. [woman.

forse, fōr'sĕ, ad. perhaps; about.
forsennatezza, –sĕnnātĕt'zā, f.folly, rage.
forsenato, –nā'tŏ, a. mad, extravagant.
forte, fōr'tĕ, a. strong, brave, bold, firm; –, ad. strongly, valiantly; extremely; hard; loud; –, m. fort, fortress; strength; flower. [ly, forcibly.
fortemente, –mĕn'tĕ, ad. stoutly, valiant-
fortezza, –tĕt'zā, f. constancy; force, energy; fortress. [to strengthen.
fortificare, –tĭfĭkā'rĕ, v. a. to fortify.
fortificazione, –tzĭŏ'nĕ, f. fortification.
fortino, –tē'nŏ, m. small fortress, redoubt.
fortore, –tŏ'rĕ, m. force; sourness.
fortuito, –tŏ'ĭtŏ, a. fortuitous, acci-dental, casual. [tasted.
fortume, –tŏ'mĕ, m. things strongly,
fortuna, –tŏ'nā, f. fortune, chance, hap-piness, good luck.
fortunato, –tūnā'tŏ, a. fortunate, lucky.
fortunoso, –nŏ'sŏ, a.fortuitous,hazardous.
forviare, –vĭā'rĕ, v. n. to miss the road;
forza, fōr'tzā, f. force, power. [to err.
forzare, –tzā'rĕ, v. a. to force.
forzatamente, –tāmĕn'tĕ, ad. by force.
forzato, –tzā'tŏ, m. galley-slave.
forziere, –tzĭĕ'rĕ, m. iron chest, trunk.
forzoso, –tzŏ'sŏ, forzuto, –tzū'tŏ, a. strong, sturdy.
fosco, fŏs'kŏ, a. blackish; dark. [phorus.
fosforo, fŏs'fŏrŏ, m. morning-star; phos-
fossa, fŏs'sā, f. ditch; grave.
fossato, –sā'tŏ, m. trench, moat, ditch.
fossetta, –sĕt'tā, f. small ditch; dimple.
fossile, fŏs'sĭlĕ, a. fossil.
fosso, fŏs'sŏ, m. large ditch, trench.
fotografia, fŏtŏgrāfē'ā, f. photography.
fotografico, –grā'fĭkŏ, a. photographic.
fotografo, –tŏ'grāfŏ, m. photograph; pho-fra, frā, pr. amongst, between. [tographer.
fracassare, –kāssā'rĕ, v. a. to splinter, to smash, to destroy.
fracassio, –kāssē'ŏ, fracasso, –kās'sŏ, m. noise, tumult; destruction. [legs.
fraccurrado, –kūrrā'dŏ, m. doll without
fracidezza, –dshĭdĕt'zā, f. rottenness.
fracidiccio, –dĭt'dshŏ, a. mouldy, musty; –, m. mustiness.
fracido, frā'dshĭdŏ, a. rotten.
fracidume, –dshĭdŏ'mĕ, m. dung-hill; an-noyance. [very damp.
fradicio, –dĭ'dshĭŏ, a. extremely wet,
fraga (poet.), see fragola.
fragile, frā'jĭlĕ, a. frail, weak.
fragilità, –jĭlĭtā', f. fragility, weakness.
fragola,frā'gŏlā, f. straw-berry. [smell.
fragore, –gŏ'rĕ, m. great noise; sweet
fragrante, –grān'tĕ, a. odorous.
fragranza, –grān'tzā, f. fragrance.
frale, frā'lĕ, a. frail, weak.
fralezza, –lĕt'zā, f. frailness. [tween.
framezzare, –mĕdzā'rĕ, v. a. to put be-
frammassone, frāmmāssō'nĕ, m. free-mason. [masonry.
frammassoneria, –sŏnĕrē'ā, f. free-
frammento, –mĕn'tŏ, m. fragment.

frammescolare, –mĕskōlā'rĕ, v. a. to intermix.
frammesso, –mĕs'sŏ, m. insertion.
frammettere, –mĕt'tĕrĕ, v. a. ir. to inter-pose; to insert. [tion.
frammettimento, –tĭmĕn'tŏ, m. interposi-
frammezzare, –mĕtzā'rĕ, v.a. to intermix.
frammischiare, –mĭskĭā'rĕ, v. a. to inter-mix.
frana, frā'nā, f. precipice. [mix.
franare, –nā'rĕ, v. n. to roll down.
francamento, frānkāmĕn'tŏ, m. delivery.
francescano, –dshĕskā'nŏ, m. Franciscan friar. [frenchify.
franceseggiare, –dshĕsĕdjā'rĕ, v. a. to
francheggiare, –kĕdjā'rĕ, v. a. to free to exempt; to encourage.
franchezza, –kĕt'zā, f. frankness.
franchigia,–kē'jĭā, f. exemption; privilege.
franco, frān'kŏ, a. free; bold; privileged; –, m. frank (coin).
francolino, –kŏlē'nŏ, m. heath-cock.
frangente, –jĕn'tĕ, m. breaker; (fig.) cri-sis, extremity.
frangere, frān'jĕrĕ, v. a. &n. ir. to break.
frangia, frān'jā, f. fringe.
frangiare, –jā'rĕ, v. a. to fringe.
frangibile, –jē'bĭlĕ, a. fragile, brittle.
frangibilità, –jbĭlĭtā', f. fragility.
frangimento, –mĕn'tŏ, m. breaking, frac-ture; fragment.
frannonnolo, –nŏn'nŏlŏ, m. dotard.
frantendere, frāntĕn'dĕrĕ, v. a. ir. to misunderstand.
frantoio, –tŏ'ĭŏ, m. oil-mill, oil-press.
frantume, –tŏ'mĕ, m. heap of splinters.
frappa, frāp'pā, f. shred, jag.
frappare, –pā'rĕ, v. a. to snip, to cheat.
frappeggiare, –pĕdjā'rĕ, v. a. to paint foliage. [position.
frapponimento, –pŏnĭmĕn'tŏ, m. inter-
frapporre, –pŏr'rĕ, v. a. ir. to interpose.
frasario, frāsā'rĭŏ, m. phrase-book.
frasca, frās'kā, f. branches, pl., foliage; foolish man; idle story.
frascato, –kā'tŏ, m. bower.
frascheggiare, –kĕdjā'rĕ, v. n. to rustle, to flirt; to trifle.
frascheria, –kĕrē'ā, f. wantonness.
fraschetta, –kĕt'tā, f. small bough; wan-ton person.
frasconaia, –kŏnā'ā, f. bird-catching.
frascone, –kŏ'nĕ, m. great bough; dead
frase, frā'sĕ, f. phrase. [branches, pl.
fraseggiamento, –sĕdjāmĕn'tŏ, m. use of phrases.
fraseggiare, –sĕdjā'rĕ, v.a. to use phrases.
fraseggiatore, –tŏ'rĕ, m. phrase-maker.
frassineto, frāssĭnĕ'tŏ, m. grove of ash-
frassino, –sē'nŏ, m. ash-tree. [trees.
frastagliamento, –tālyāmĕn'tŏ, m. cut-ting, notch. [to notch.
frastagliare, –tālyā'rĕ, v. a. to cut out,
frastagliatura, –tŏ'rā, f. cut, notch; eyelet. [work.
frastaglio, –tāl'yŏ, m. cut, slit; open
frastornare, –tŏrnā'rĕ, v. a. to divert from; to hinder.

frastornio, –tŏr'nĭŏ, **frastuono,** –tŭŏ'nŏ, m. confused noise.

frataccio, frătăt'shŏ, m. wicked monk.

frataio, –tăī'ŏ, m. monkish man.

frate, frā'tĕ, m. brother; monk, friar.

fratellanza, –tĕllăn'tză, f. brotherhood.

fratellevole, –tĕllĕ'vŏlĕ, a. brotherly.

fratello, –tĕl'lŏ, m. brother; intimate friend. [tery.

frateria, –tĕrĕ'ă, f. brotherhood; monas-

fraternità, –tĕrnĭtă', f. fraternity.

fraterno, –tĕr'nŏ, a. brotherly.

fratesco, –tĕs'kŏ, a. monkish.

fraticida, –tĭdshĕ'dă, m. fratricide.

fraticidio, –tĭdshĕ'dĭŏ, m. fratricide, murder of a brother.

fratismo, –tĭs'mŏ, m. monkery.

fratta, frăt'tă, f. hedge, bush, jungle.

frattaglie, –tăl'yĕ, f. pl. heart, liver and lights.

frattanto, –tăn'tŏ, ad. in the mean time.

fratto, frăt'tŏ, a. broken, split.

frattura, –tŏo'ră, f. fracture. [frustrate.

fraudare, frăŭdă'rĕ, v. a. to defraud, to

fraude, frā'ŭdĕ, f. fraud.

fraudolento, –dŏlĕn'tŏ, a. fraudulent.

fraudolenza, –dŏlĕn'tză, f. fraud, deceit.

fravola, see **fragola.** [fraction.

frazione, frătzĭŏ'nĕ, f. breaking, fracture;

freccia, frĕt'shă, f. arrow.

frecciare, –tshā'rĕ, v. a. to shoot, to dart.

frecciata, –tshă'tă, f. arrow-shot.

freddare, frĕddă'rĕ, v. a. to cool; –, v. n. to grow cold; to shiver. [ence.

freddezza, –dĕt'ză, f. coldness, indiffer-

freddo, frĕd'dŏ, a. cold; slow; indifferent; –, m. cold, coldness, chilliness.

freddura, –dŏ'ră, f. coldness; slowness.

frega, frĕ'gă, f. ardent desire, lust; friction.

fregagione, –găjŏ'nĕ, **fregamento,** –mĕn'tŏ, m. rubbing, friction.

fregare, –gā'rĕ, v. a. to rub; to play a

fregata, –gā'tă, f. frigate. [trick on.

fregatura, see **fregagione.**

fregiare, frĕjā'rĕ, v. a. to trim, to adorn.

fregio, frĕ'jŏ, m. trimming; lace.

frego, frĕ'gŏ, m. stroke, dash, scar.

fregola, frĕ'gŏlă, f. spawning.

fregolo, frĕ'gŏlŏ, m. spawning-time; spawn. [neighing.

fremente, frĕmĕn'tĕ, a. raging, fuming;

fremere, frĕ'mĕrĕ, v. n. to roar, to rage.

fremito, frĕ'mĭtŏ, m. noise; neighing.

frenaio, frĕnăī'ŏ, m. bridle-maker; (rail.) breaksman.

frenare, –nā'rĕ, v. a. to bridle, to restrain; to apply the brake.

frenella, –nĕl'lă, f. bridle-bit; flannel.

frenello, –nĕl'lŏ, m. muzzle: filament under the tongue.

frenesia, –nĕsĕ'ă, f. frenzy.

freneticare, –nĕtĭkā'rĕ, v. n. to rave

frenetico, –nĕ'tĭkŏ, a. frantic.

frenitide, –nĕ'tĭdĕ, f. phrenitis.

freno, frĕ'nŏ, m. bit, bridle; (rail.) brake.

frenologia, frĕnŏlŏjĕ'ă, f. phrenology.

frequentare, frĕkŭĕntă'rĕ, v. a. to frequent.

frequentazione, –tzĭŏ'nĕ, f. frequenting, frequentation.

frequente, –kŭĕn'tĕ, a. frequent, ordinary.

frequenza, –kŭĕn'tză, f. frequency.

frescante, frĕskăn'tĕ, m. painter in fresco.

freschezza, –kĕt'ză, f. freshness; bloom, prime. [di –, lately, just now.

fresco, frĕs'kŏ, a. fresh, cool; green; new;

frescura, –kŏ'ră, f. coolness.

fretta, frĕt'tă, f. haste, hurry.

frettoloso, –tŏlŏ'sŏ, a. quick, hasty.

friabile, frĭ'ăbĭlĕ, a. friable.

friabilità, –bĭlĭtă', f. friability.

fricassea, frĭkăssĕ'ă, f. fricassee.

friggere, frĭd'jĕrĕ, v. a. ir. to fry.

frigidezza, –djĭdĕt'ză, **frigidità,** –dĭtă', f. frigidity; impotence.

frigido, frĕ'djĭdŏ, a. frigid, cold; impotent.

frignare, frĭnyā'rĕ, v. n. to whine, to whimper.

fringuello, frĭngŭĕl'lŏ, m. chaffinch.

frinzello, –tzĕl'lŏ, m. patch-work; cicatrice.

friscello, frĭsshĕl'lŏ, m. mill-dust: flour.

fritta, frĭt'tă, f. frit.

frittata, –tă'tă, f. omelet.

frittella, –tĕl'lă, f. fritter; pancake.

fritto, frĭt'tŏ, a. fried; undone; ruined.

frittura, –tŏ'ră, f. fried dishes.

frivolezza, frĭvŏlĕt'ză, f. frivolity.

frivolo, frĕ'vŏlŏ, a. frivolous.

frizzamento, frĭtzămĕn'tŏ, m. itching.

frizzante, –tsăn'tĕ, a. smart, sharp, biting, pungent. [be piquant.

frizzare, –tză'rĕ, v. a. & n. to smart; to

frizzo, see **frizzamento.**

frodare, see **fraudare.**

frode, frŏ'dĕ, f. fraud. [tender.

frollamento, frŏllămĕn'tŏ, m. making

frollare, –lā'rĕ, v. a. to make tender.

frollatura, see **frollamento.**

frollo, frŏl'lŏ, a. made tender.

fromba, see **frombola.**

frombatore, –bātŏ'rĕ, m. slinger.

frombo, see **frombatore.**

frombola, frŏm'bŏlă, f. sling, sling-stone.

frombolare, –bŏlā'rĕ, v. a. to sling stones.

frombolatore, –tŏ'rĕ, **fromboliere,** –bŏlĭĕ'rĕ, m. slinger. [pl., foliage.

fronda, frŏn'dă, **fronde,** –dĕ, f. leaves.

frondeggiante, –dĕdjăn'tĕ, a. covered with leaves. [leaves.

frondeggiare, –djĕ'rĕ, v. n. to bear

frondifero, –dĕ'fĕrŏ, a. bearing leaves.

frondire, frŏndĕ'rĕ, v. n. to bear leaves.

frondoso, –dŏ'sŏ, a. leafy.

fronduto, see **fronzuto.**

frontale, –tă'lĕ, m. frontlet.

fronte, frŏn'tĕ, f. front; forehead, face.

fronteggiare, –tĕdjā'rĕ, v. a. to face, to oppose. [border.

frontiera, –tĭĕ'ră, f. frontier, confine.

frontispizio, –tĭspĕ'tzĭŏ, m. frontispiece; title of a book.

frontoso, –tŏ'sŏ, a. bold, audacious.

fronzuto, –tzŏ'tŏ, a. leafy, green.

frosone, frŏsŏ'nĕ, m. ospray.

frotta, *frŏt'tä,* f. crowd, troop.
frottola, *frŏt'tŏlä,* f. ballad; old wives' tale. [to jeer.
frottolare, *-tŏlä're,* v. a. to write ballads;
frucone, *fräkō'nĕ,* m. bludgeon; fisticuff.
frugacchiare, *-gäkkiä're,* v. a. to sound with a stick; to grope.
frugale, *-gä'lĕ,* a. frugal; thrifty.
frugalità, *-gälitä',* f. frugality.
frugalmente, *-mĕn'tĕ,* ad. frugally.
frugare, *-gä're,* v. a. to grope, to sound with a stick.
frugifero, *-jĕ'fĕrŏ,* a. fruit-bearing.
frugivoro, *-jĕ'vŏrŏ,* a. frugiverous.
frugnolare, *fränyŏlä're,* v. a. to go a-fishing or fowling with a lantern.
frugnolo, *frän'yŏlŏ,* m. fowling-lantern.
frugolo, *frü'gŏlŏ,* m. waggish child.
frugone, *frägō'nĕ,* m. sounding-pole; blow with the fist.
fruire, *frü'ē're,* v. a. (poet.) to enjoy.
fruizione, *früītzĭō'nĕ,* f. fruition, enjoyment. [roar.
frullare, *früllä're,* v. a. & n. to twirl; to
frullo, *frül'lŏ,* m. whirring, whizzing; twirling-stick, nothing, fig.
frullone, *-lō'nĕ,* m. bolter to sift meal.
frumentario, *frümĕntä'riŏ,* a. frumentarious.
frumento, *-mĕn'tŏ,* m. wheat, corn.
fruscio, *früsshē'ŏ,* m. noise, rustling.
frusta, *früs'tä,* f. whip, switch.
frustagno, *-tän'yŏ,* m. fustian.
frustare, *-tä're,* v. a. to whip; to wear out.
frustatura, *-tätō'rä,* f. whipping.
frustino, *-tē'nŏ,* m. small whip. [out.
frusto, *früs'tŏ,* m. bit, morsel; —, a. worn
frustrare, *-trä're,* v. a. to frustrate.
frutice, *frū'tĭdshĕ,* m. shrub.
frutta, *frŭt'tä,* f. pl. fruit; dessert.
fruttaiuolo, *-täiuō'lŏ,* m. fruiterer.
fruttare, *früttä're,* v. a. & n. to produce or to yield fruit.
fruttato, *-tä'tŏ,* a. planted with fruit-trees.
fruttiera, *-tiĕ'rä,* f. fruit-dish. [ful.
fruttifero, *-tē'fĕrŏ,* a. bearing fruit, fruitful.
fruttificare, see **fruttare.** [profit.
fruttificazione, *-tĭfĭkätzĭō'nĕ,* f. fruit;
frutto, *frŭt'tŏ,* m. fruit; produce.
fruttuoso, *-tuō'sŏ,* a. a fruitful, profitable.
fucato, *fŭkä'tŏ,* a. painted; disguised.
fucilare, *-dshīlä're,* v. a. to shoot.
fucilata, *-lä'tä,* f. shooting.
fucile, *-dshē'lĕ,* m. steel to strike fire with; fire-lock.
fuciliere, *-dshīliĕ're,* m. fusileer.
fucina, *-dshē'nä,* f. forge.
fuco, *fū'kŏ,* m. drone. [(mus.) fugue.
fuga, *fū'gä,* f. flight; suit (of rooms);
fugace, *fügä'dshĕ,* a. fugitive, transient.
fugacità, *-gädshĭtä',* f. fugacity.
fugamento, *-mĕn'tŏ,* m. rout, disorder.
fugare, *-gä're,* v. a. to put to flight, to [chase.
fuggevole, see **fugace.**
fuggiasco, *-djäs'kŏ,* a. fugitive.
fuggifatica, *-djĭfä'tĭkä,* m. & f. sluggard.
fuggire, *-djē're,* v. n. to fly away.

fuggita, *-djē'tä,* f. hasty flight.
fuggitivo, *-tē'vŏ,* a. fugitive.
fuggito, *-djē'tŏ,* a. run away, escaped.
fulcire, *füldshē're,* v. a. to underprop.
fulgere, *fül'jĕrĕ,* v. n. to shine.
fulgidezza, *-jĭdĕt'zä,* **fulgidità,** *-dĭtä',* f. fulgency.
fulgido, *fül'jĕdŏ,* a. fulgid, brilliant.
fulgore, *-gō'rĕ,* m. splendour, brightness.
fuliggine, *-lĭd'jĕnĕ,* f. soot.
fuligginoso, *-djĭnō'sŏ,* a. sooty.
fulminante, *-mĭnän'tĕ,* a. fulminant, thundering, [thunder; to rage.
fulminare, *-nä'rĕ,* v. a. to fulminate, to
fulmine, *fül'mĭnĕ,* m. lightning.
fulmineo, *-mē'nĕŏ,* a. fulminatory.
fulvo, *fül'vŏ,* a. tawny, of a deep yellow.
fumacchio, *fümäk'kiŏ,* m. fumigation, smoking coal.
fumido, *fō'mĭdŏ,* a. smoky.
fumaiuolo, *fämäiuō'lŏ,* m. smoky coal; funnel of a chimney.
fumare, *-mä're,* v. a. to smoke tobacco; —, v. n. to emit smoke, to fume.
fumata, *-mä'tä,* f. smoke signal.
fumatore, *-tō'rĕ,* m. smoker.
fumicare, *-mĭkä're,* v. n. to smoke; to perfume.
fumigazione, *-mĭgätzĭō'nĕ,* f. fumigation.
fumista, *-mĭs'tä,* m. chimney-doctor.
fumo, *fō'mŏ,* m. smoke, fume; vanity.
fumosità, *fämōsĭtä',* f. smokiness.
fumoso, *-mō'sŏ,* a. smoking; proud, haughty, conceited.
fumosterno, *-stĕr'nŏ,* m. (bot.) fumitory.
funaio, *fünä'ŏ,* **funaiolo,** *-ŏ'lŏ,* m. rope-maker.
funambolo, *-näm'bŏlŏ,* m. rope-dancer.
funata, *-nä'tä,* f. chain of prisoners.
fune, *fō'nĕ,* f. rope.
funebre, *fō'nĕbrĕ,* **funerale,** *fänĕrä'lĕ,* a. funereal.
funereo, *-nä'rĕŏ,* a. funereal.
funestare, *-nĕstä're,* v. a. to sadden, to [afflict.
funesto, *-nĕs'tŏ,* a. fatal.
fungaia, *fängä'ä,* f. mushroom-bed.
fungo, *fän'gŏ,* m. mushroom.
fungoso, *-gō'sŏ,* a. fungeous, spungy.
funicella, *fänĭdshĕl'lä,* **funicolo,** *fänĕ'kŏlŏ,* m. little rope, small cord.
funzione, *fäntzĭō'nĕ,* f. function, office.
fuochista, *füŏkĭs'tä,* m. (rail.) fireman, stoker. [anger; hearth; focus.
fuoco, *fäŏ'kŏ,* m. fire; (fig.) passion, love;
fuocoso, *-kō'sŏ,* a. fiery, ardent.
fuora, *fäŏ'rä,* ad. & pr. out of, without, except. [that.
fuorchè, *fäŏrkĕ',* c. save, except, except
fuori, *fäŏ'rĕ,* ad. & pr. out of, without, except.
fuormisura, *fäŏrmĭsä'rä,* ad. excessively.
fuoruscito, *-dsshĕ'tŏ,* m. outlaw.
furace, *färä'dshĕ,* a. thievish.
furare, *-rä're,* v. a. to steal.
furbamente, *-mĕn'tĕ,* ad. cunningly.
furberia, *-bĕrē'ä,* f. knavery; cheat.
furbesco, *-bĕs'kŏ,* a. knavish; crafty.

furbo, *fŭr'bŏ,* m. knave.

furente, *fūrĕn'tĕ,* a. furious, enraged.

furfantare, *–fäntă'rĕ,* v. n. to lead a rogue's life.

furfante, *–fän'tĕ,* m. rascal.

furfantello, *–tĕl'lŏ,* m. little rogue.

furfanteria, *–tĕrĕ'ä,* f. roguery.

furfantone, *–tō'nĕ,* m. great rogue.

furia, *fō'rĭä,* f. fury, frenzy.

furiare, *fūrĭä'rĕ,* v. n. to rage.

furibondo, *–rĭbŏn'dŏ,* a. furious.

furiere, *–rĭĕ'rĕ,* m. quarter-master.

furiosamente, *–rĭŏsämĕn'tĕ,* ad. furiously.

furioso, *–rĭŏ'sŏ,* a. furious, mad.

furo, *fō'rŏ,* m. thief.

furore, *fūrō'rĕ,* m. fury.

furtivo, *–tĕ'vŏ,* a. stealthy; hidden.

furto, *fŭr'tŏ,* m. theft, stealth; **di —,** by stealth, privately.

furuncolo, *–rŭn'kŏlŏ,* m. furuncle, boil.

fusaio, *fūsä'ŏ,* m. turner.   [spindle.

fusaiuolo, *–säiŏ'lŏ,* m. whirl put to a

fuscello, *fūsshĕl'lŏ,* m. straw; skewer.

fusciacca, *–sshäk'kä,* f. bow of ribbon,

fusibile, *fūsĕ'bĭlĕ,* a. fusible.   [favour.

fusibilità, *–sĭbĭlĭtä',* f. fusibility.

fusione, *–sĭō'nĕ,* f. fusion.

fuso, *fō'sŏ,* m. spindle; shaft of a column.

fusolo, *fō'sŏlŏ,* m. shin-bone.

fusta, *fūs'tä,* f. light galley.

fustagno, *–tän'yŏ,* m. fustian.

fusto, *fūs'tŏ,* m. stalk; trunk.

futile, *fō'tĭlĕ,* a. trifling, frivolous.

futilità, *fūtĭlĭtä',* f. futility.

futuro, *–tō'rŏ,* a. future; **—,** m. time to come; (gr.) future tense.

G.

gabbadeo, *gäbbädĕ'ŏ,* m. hypocrite.

gabbamento, *–mĕn'tŏ,* m. cheat.

gabbanella, *–nĕl'lä,* f. riding-hood.

gabbano, *–bä'nŏ,* m. gabardine.

gabbare, *–bä'rĕ,* v. a. to deceive.

gabbatore, *–tō'rĕ,* m. deceiver.

gabbia, *gäb'bĭä,* f. cage.

gabbiaio, *–bĭä'ŏ,* m. cage-maker.

gabbiano, *–bĭä'nŏ,* a. clownish; **—,** m.

gabbiata, *–bĭä'tä,* f. cage-full.   [sea-gull.

gabbiere, *–bĭĕ'rĕ,* m. (mar.) top-man, look-out-man.   [gabion.

gabbione, *–bĭō'nĕ,* m. large cage; (bot.)

gabbionnata, *–nä'tä,* f. (fort.) gabionade.

gabbo, *gäb'bŏ,* m. jeering.

gabella, *gäbĕl'lä,* f. tax, custom, duty.

gabellabile, *–lä'bĭlĕ,* a. subject to excise.

gabellare, *–lä'rĕ,* v. a. to pay the duty.

gabelliere, *–lĭĕ'rĕ,* m. custom-house officer.

gabinetto, *–bĭnĕt'tŏ,* m. cabinet, closet.

gaggia, *gäd'jä,* f. (mar.) scuttle of a mast; acacia.

gaggio, *gäd'jŏ,* m. pledge; wages.

gagliardamente, *gälyärdämĕn'tĕ,* ad. valiantly, stoutly.

gagliardezza, *–dĕt'zä,* **gagliardia,** *–dĕ'ä,* f. strength, prowess.

gagliardo, *–yär'dŏ,* a. strong, stubborn.

gaglioffaria, *–yŏffĕrĕ'ä,* f. scurrility, cheat.

gaglioffo, *–yŏf'fŏ,* m. blackguard.   [ing.

gagnolamento, *gänyŏlämĕn'tŏ,* m. howl-

gagnolare, *–lä'rĕ,* v. n. to howl.

gaiezza, *gäĕt'zä,* f. gaiety.

gaio, *gä'ŏ,* a. gay, merry.

gala, *gä'lä,* f. tucker; finery, dress.

galante, *–län'tĕ,* a. gallant, gay; gracious.

galanteggiare, *–tĕdjä'rĕ,* v. a. to play the gallant.   [knacks, pl.

galanteria, *–tĕrĕ'ä,* f. gentility; knick-

galantuomo, *–tŭŏ'mŏ,* m. honest man; gentleman.

galappio, *–läp'pĭŏ,* m. trap, snare.

galassia, *–läs'sĭä,* f. Milky Way.

galbano, *gälbä'nŏ,* m. gum albanum.

galea, *gälĕ'ä,* f. galley.

galeazza, *–lĕät'zä,* f. galeas.

galeone, *–lĕō'nĕ,* m. galleon.

galeotto, *–lĕŏt'tŏ,* m. galley-slave.

galera, *–lĕ'rä,* f. galley.

galetta, *–lĕt'tä,* f. sea-biscuit.

gallare, *gällä'rĕ,* v. n. to float; to exult; to tread (as a cock).   [swim.

galleggiare, *–lĕdjä'rĕ,* v. n. to float, to

galleria, *–lĕrĕ'ä,* f. gallery.

galletto, *–lĕt'tŏ,* m. young cock.

gallicinio, *–lĭsshĕ'nĭŏ,* m. cock-crowing.

gallina, *–lĕ'nä,* f. hen.

gallinaccio, *–lĭnät'shŏ,* m. turkey-cock; mushroom; **—,** a. gallinaceous.

gallinaio, *–nä'ŏ,* m. hen-roost.

gallinella, *–nĕl'lä,* f. water-hen; **galli-nelle,** pl. Pleiads.

gallo, *gäl'lŏ,* m. cock.

gallonare, *–lŏnä'rĕ,* v. a. to lace.

gallone, *–lŏ'nĕ,* m. side; galoon.

galloria, *–lŏ'rĭä,* f. exultation, transport.

gallozza, *–lŏt'zä,* **gallozzola,** *–zŏlä,* f. gall-nut; bubble in water.

galoppare, *gälŏppä'rĕ,* v. n. to gallop.

galoppata, *–pä'tä,* f. galloping.

galoppo, *–lŏp'pŏ,* m. gallop.

galoscia, *–lŏssh'ä,* f. pl. galoshes, pl.

galuppo, *–lŭp'pŏ,* m. soldier's scrub.

gamba, *gäm'bä,* f. leg, shank.

gambale, *–bä'lĕ,* m. stem, stalk.

gambata, *–bä'tä,* f. kick.

gambero, *gäm'bĕrŏ,* m. cray-fish.

gamberuola, *–bĕrŭŏ'lä,* f. greave, leg armour.   [legs about.

gambettare, *–bĕttä'rĕ,* v. n. to kick one's

gambetto, *–bĕt'tŏ,* m., **dare il —,** to sup-

gambiera, *see* **gamberuola.**   [plant.

gambo, *gäm'bŏ,* m. stem, stalk; stroke.

gambone, *–bō'nĕ,* m. big leg.

gambuto, *–bü'tŏ,* a. high-stalked.

gammura, *–mō'rä,* f., **gamurrino,** *–mü-rrĕ'nŏ,* m. long petticoat.

gana, *gä'nä,* f. eagerness.

ganascia, *–nässh'ä,* f. jaw-bone.

gancio, *gän'dshŏ,* m. hook.

gangherare, *–ghĕrä'rĕ,* v. a. to set on hinges.

ganghero, *găn′ ghĕrŏ*, m. hinge, hook, pivot, clasp. [evil.
gangola, *găn′ gŏlă*, f. tonsil, gland; king's
gangoloso, *–gŏlŏ′ sŏ*, a. scrofulous.
gangrena, *–grā′ nă*, f. gangrene.
ganimede, *gănĭmā′ dĕ*, m. dandy, fop.
ganza, *găn′ tză*, f. (mar.) knot at a rope's
ganzo, *găn′ tzŏ*, m. lover. [end.
gara, *gā′ ră*, f. strife; rivalry.
garabullare, *–būllā′ rĕ*, v. a. to deceive.
garantire, *gărăntē′ rĕ*, v. a. to warrant.
garante, *–răn′ tĕ*, m. guarantee; (mar.) rope's end.
garanzia, *–răntzē′ ă*, f. guarenty.
garbare, *gărbā′ rĕ*, v. n. to please, to have a genteel air, to be agreeable.
garbatezza, *–tĕt′ ză*, f. gracefulness.
garbato, *–bā′ tŏ*, a. graceful.
garbino, *–bē′ nŏ*, m. southwest-wind.
garbo, *găr′ bŏ*, m. gracefulness.
garbuglio, *–būl′ yŏ*, m. disorder, tumult.
gareggiamento, *–rēdjămĕn′ tŏ*, m. strife.
gareggiare, *–rēdjā′ rĕ*, v. n. to rival, to
garetto, *–rĕt′ tŏ*, m. ham, thigh. [dispute.
gargarismo, *gărgărĭs′ mŏ*, m. gargarism, gargling. [to gargle.
gargarizzare, *–rătzā′ rĕ*, v. a. to gargarize,
gargozza, *–gŏt′ ză*, f. throat.
garofanare, *gărŏfănā′ rĕ*, v. a. to season with cloves.
garofano, *–rŏ′ fănŏ*, m. clove, gilliflower.
garontolare, *–rŏntŏlā′ rĕ*, v. a. to strike with one's fist.
garontolo, *–rŏn′ tŏlŏ*, m. fisticuff.
garoso, *–rŏ′ sŏ*, a. quarrelsome.
garretta, *–rĕt′ tă*, f. knee-hollow, hough.
garrire, *–rē′ rĕ*, v. a. to chirp, to warble; to chide; to chatter.
garrito, *–rē′ tŏ*, m. chirping; reproof.
garritore, *–tŏ′ rĕ*, m., **garritrice**, *–trē′ - dshĕ*, f. grumbler; scolding woman.
garrulità, *–rūlĭtă′*, f. garrulity.
garrulo, *găr′ rūlŏ*, a. garrulous.
garza, *găr′ dză*, f. white heron.
garzoncello, *–dzŏndshĕl′ lŏ*, m. young lad.
garzone, *–dzŏ′ nĕ*, m. boy; shop-boy.
garzonile, *–nē′ lĕ*, a. boyish.
garzuolo, *–dzūŏ′ lŏ*, m. heart (of cabbage, lettuce, &c.); fine hemp.
gastigamatti, *–găstĭgămăt′ tĭ*, m. whip.
gastigare, *–gā′ rĕ*, v. a. to chastise.
gastigo, *găst′ gŏ*, m. chastisement.
gastrico, *găs′ trĭkŏ*, a. stomachic.
gatta, *găt′ tă*, f. (she) cat.
gattaiuola, *–tāĭŭŏ′ lă*, f. cat's hole.
gattice, *–găt′ tŭtshĕ*, m. abel-tree, white poplar.
gatto, *găt′ tŏ*, m. cat. [moset.
gattomammone, *–mămmŏ′ nĕ*, m. mar-
gattone, *–tŏ′ nĕ*, m. large cat.
gavazzare, *găvătzā′ rĕ*, v. n. to jump for
gaudio, *gă′ ŭdĭŏ*, m. joy. [joy.
gaudioso, *găŭdĭŏ′ sŏ*, a. joyful.
gavetta, *găvĕt′ tă*, f. bundle of musical strings; seamen's wooden bowl.
gavigne, *–vīn′ yĕ*, f. pl. tonsils, almonds of the throat.
gavocciolo, *–vŏt′ shŏlŏ*, m. tumour

gaz, **gas**, *găs*, m. gas.
gazza, *găd′ ză*, f. magpie.
gazzarra, *–dză′ ră*, f. feast in a camp with shooting and music.
gazzella, *–dzĕl′ lă*, f. antelope.
gazzera, *see* **gazza**.
gazzetta, *–dzĕt′ tă*, f. newspaper.
gazzettiere, *–tĭĕ′ rĕ*, m. gazetteer.
gelamento, *jĕlămĕn′ tŏ*, m. freezing, frost.
gelare, *–lā′ rĕ*, v. a. & n. to freeze.
gelata, *–lā′ tă*, f. frost.
gelatina, *–lătē′ nă*, f. jelly.
gelatinoso, *–tĭnŏ′ sŏ*, a. gelatinous.
gelato, *–lā′ tŏ*, a. frozen, chilly.
geldra, *jĕl′ dră*, f. rabble, mob. [frost.
gelicidio, *–lĭdshē′ dĭŏ*, m. frosty weather;
gelido, *jĕ′ lĭdŏ*, a. frozen, cold; terrified.
gelo, *jā′ lŏ*, m. ice, cold.
gelone, *jĕlŏ′ nĕ*, m. hard frost; chilblain.
gelosia, *–lŏsē′ ă*, f. jealousy; lattice, per-
geloso, *–lŏ′ sŏ*, a. jealous. [sian.
gelso, *jĕl′ sŏ*, m. mulberry-tree.
gelsomino, *–sŏmē′ nŏ*, m. jessamine.
gemebondo, *jĕmĕbŏn′ dŏ*, a. groaning.
gemello, *–mĕl′ lŏ*, m. twin. [down, to ooze.
gemere, *jā′ mĕrĕ*, v. n. to groan; to trickle
gemicare, *jĕmĭkā′ rĕ*, v. n. to groan.
geminare, *–nā′ rĕ*, v. a. to double; to repeat. [tion).
gemini, *jā′ mĭnĭ*, m. pl. Twins (constella-
gemino, *jā′ mĭnŏ*, a. double.
gemitio, *–mĭtĭŏ′ ŏ*, m. sweating of a cave.
gemito, *jā′ mĭtŏ*, m. groan, complaint.
gemma, *jĕm′ mă*, f. gem; bud.
gemmante, *–măn′ tĕ*, a. brilliant.
gemmare, *–mā′ rĕ*, v. n. to bud.
genealogia, *jĕnĕălŏjē′ ă*, f. genealogy.
genealogico, *–lŏ′ jĭkŏ*, a. genealogical.
generabile, *–rā′ bĭlĕ*, a. generable.
generabilità, *–bĭlĭtă′*, f. power of en-gendering.
generalato, *–lā′ tŏ*, m. generalship.
generale, *–rā′ lĕ*, m. general; –, a. general, universal.
generalità, *–rălĭtă′*, f. generality.
generalizzare, *–răltĭzā′ rĕ*, v. a. to generalize.
generalmente, *–rălmĕn′ tĕ*, ad. generally.
generare, *–rā′ rĕ*, v. a. to produce, to en-gender, to generate, to beget.
generativo, *–rătē′ vŏ*, a. generative.
generatore, *–tŏ′ rĕ*, m., **generatrice**, *–trē′ dshĕ*, f. begetter, progenitor.
generazione, *–rătzĭŏ′ nĕ*, f. generation; progeny, race.
genere, *jā′ nĕrĕ*, m. kind, sort; gender.
genericamente, *jĕnĕrĭkămĕn′ tĕ*, ad. generically.
generico, *–nā′ rĭkŏ*, a. generical.
genero, *jā′ nĕrŏ*, m. son-in-law.
generosità, *jĕnĕrŏsĭtă′*, f. generosity.
generoso, *–rŏ′ sŏ*, a. generous, noble.
genesi, *jā′ nĕsĭ*, m. & f. genesis.
genetliaco, *jĕnĕtlē′ ăkŏ*, m. horoscopist.
gengia, *see* **gengiva**.
gengiovo, *jĕnjŏ′ vŏ*, m. ginger.
gengiva, *–jē′ vă*, f. gum

genia, *jĕnĕ'ä*, f. low race, mob.
geniale, *–nēä'lĕ*, a. genial; pleasing.
genialità, *–nēälĭtä'*, f. natural disposition.
genialmente, *–mĕn'tĕ*, ad. genially; by natural disposition.
genio, *jä'nĭŏ*, m. genius, guardian angel; talent; **andare a –**, to please.
genitale, *jĕnĭtä'lĕ*, a. genital, inborn.
genitivo, *–tē'vŏ*, m. (gr.) genitive case.
genito, *jä'nĭtŏ*, m. son.
genitore, *jĕnĭtō'rĕ*, m. father.
genitrice, *–trē'dshĕ*, f. mother.
genitura, *–tŏŏ'rä*, f. birth.   [January.
gennaio, *jĕnnä'ŏ*, **gennaro**, *–nä'rŏ*, m.
gentaglia, *–tä'lyä*, f., **gentame**, *–tä'mĕ*, m. rabble, mob.   [troops.
gente, *jĕn'tĕ*, f. people, nation; kindred;
genterella, *–tĕrĕl'lä*, f. common people.
gentildonna, *–tĭldŏn'nä*, f. lady.
gentile, *–tē'lĕ*, a. genteel, noble; **–**, m.pagan.
gentilesco, *–tĭlĕs'kŏ*, a. genteel; heathenish.
gentilesimo, *–lä'sĭmŏ*, m. paganism.
gentilezza, *–lĕt'zä*, f. gentility, politeness.
gentilità, *–tĭlĭtä'*, f. heathenism; nobility.
gentilizio, *–lē'tzĭŏ*, a. gentilitious.
gentiluomo, *–tĭlŏŏ'mŏ*, m. gentleman.
gentuccia, *–tĭt'shä*, f. common people.
genuflessione, *jĕnŭflĕssĭō'nĕ*, f. kneeling.
genuflesso, *–flĕs'sŏ*, a. kneeling.
genuino, *jĕnŭĭ'nŏ*, a. genuine; true.
genziana, *jĕntzĭä'nä*, f. (bot.) gentian.
geodesia, *jĕŏdĕsē'ä*, f. land-surveying.
geodetico, *–dä'tĭkŏ*, a. geodetical.
geografia, *–gräfē'ä*, geography.
geografico, *–grä'fĭkŏ*, a. geographical.
geografo, *jĕŏ'gräfŏ*, m. geographer.
geologia, *jĕŏlŏjē'ä*, f. geology.
geologico, *–lŏ'jĭkŏ*, a. geological.
geologo, *jĕŏ'lŏgŏ*, m. geologist.
geometra, *jĕŏ'mĕträ*, m. geometrician.
geometria, *jĕŏmĕtrē'ä*, f. geometry.
geometrico, *–mä'trĭkŏ*, a. geometrical.
gerarca, *jĕrär'kä*, m. high-priest.
gerarchia, *–rär'kē'ä*, f. hierarchy.
gerarchico, *–rär'kĭkŏ*, a. hierarchical.
gergo, *jĕr'gŏ*, **gergone**, *–gŏ'nĕ*, m. gibberish.
gerla, *jĕr'lä*, f. back-basket.   [berish.
germana, *–mä'nä*, f. sister, full sister.
germano, *–mä'nŏ*, m. brother; **–**, a. true, real, genuine.
germe, *jĕr'mĕ*, m. germ, bud.
germinare, *–mĭnä'rĕ*, v. n. to bud.
germinativo, *–nätē'vŏ*, a. fit to germinate.
germogliare, *–mŏlyä'rĕ*, v. n. to bud, to sprout, to shoot.
germoglio, *–mŏl'yŏ*, m. bud, sprout, shoot.
geroglifico, *jĕrŏglē'fĭkŏ*, m. & a. hieroglyphic.
gersa, *jĕr'sä*, f. red paint.   [glyphic.
gerundio, *jĕrŭn'dĭŏ*, m. (gr.) gerund.
gessare, *jĕssä'rĕ*, v. a. to plaster.
gesso, *jĕs'sŏ*, m. plaster; chalk.
gesta, *jĕs'tä*, f. pl. exploits, deed.
gesticolazione, *–tĭkŏlätzĭō'nĕ*, f. gesticulation.
gestire, *–tē'rĕ*, v. n. to gesticulate.   [tion.
gesto, *jĕs'tŏ*, m. gesture; deed.
gettare, *jĕttä'rĕ*, v. a. to throw, to cast.

getto, *jĕt'tŏ*, m.throw, jet; plaster; foundry; copy; **d'un –**, at one cast.
gettone, *–tŏ'nĕ*, m. counter (at cards).
gheppio, *ghĕp'pĭŏ*, m. kestrel.
gheriglio, *ghĕrĭl'yŏ*, m. kernel of a nut.
gherminella, *ghĕrmĭnĕl'lä*, f. juggling trick.
ghermire, *–mĕ'rĕ*, v. a. to snatch, to catch;
ghermirsi, *–mĭr'sĕ*, to get hold of one another.
gherone, *–rŏ'nĕ*, m. piece; gusset; cutting.
ghetto, *ghĕt'tŏ*, m. Jews' quarter.
ghezzo, *ghĕd'zŏ*, a. black as a Moor.
ghiabaldana, *ghĭäbäldä'nä*, f. trifle, toy.
ghiacciaia, *–tshä'ä*, f. ice-house.
ghiacciare, *–tshä'rĕ*, v. a. & n. to freeze.
ghiaccio, *ghĭät'shŏ*, m. ice.
ghiado, *ghĭä'dŏ*, m. extreme cold; dagger.
ghiaia, *ghĭä'ä*, f. gravel.
ghiaiata, *–ä'tä*, f. highway.
ghiaioso, *–ŏ'sŏ*, a. gravelly.
ghianda, *ghĭän'dä*, f. acorn.
ghiandaia, *–dä'ä*, f. jackdaw.   [river.
ghiareto, *ghĭärĕ'tŏ*, m. gravelly bed of a
ghignare, *ghĭnyä'rĕ*, v. n. to smile.
ghignata, *–yä'tä*, f. derisive laughter.
ghignazzare, *–yätzä'rĕ*, v. n. to burst with laughter.
ghigno, *ghĭn'yŏ*, m. smile, sneer.
ghinea, *ghĭnĕ'ä*, f. guinea.
ghiotta, *ghĭŏt'tä*, f. dripping-pan.
ghiotto, *ghĭŏt'tŏ*, a. gluttonous.
ghiottone, *–tŏ'nĕ*, m. glutton; great cheat.
ghiottoneria, *–tŏnĕrē'ä*, f. roguery.   [pl.
ghiottornia, *–tŏrnē'ä*, f. gluttony; dainties,
ghiozzo, *ghĭŏd'zŏ*, m. gudgeon; block-head; little bit.
ghiribizzare, *ghĭrĭbĭdzä'rĕ*, v. n. to fancy.
ghiribizzo, *–bĭd'zŏ*, m. whim, fancy.
ghirigoro, *–gŏ'rŏ*, m. flourish (in writing); round-about way.
ghirlanda, *ghĭrlän'dä*, f. garland.
ghirlandare, *–dä'rĕ*, v. a. to crown with a garland, to wreathe.
ghiro, *ghĕ'rŏ*, m. dormouse.
ghironda, *ghĭrŏn'dä*, f. hurdy-gurdy.
già, *jä'*, ad. formerly; already.
giacchè, *jäkkĕ'*, c. since.
giacchiata, *–kĭä'tä*, f. draught.
giacchio, *jäk'kĭŏ*, m. sweep-net.
giacere, *jädshä'rĕ*, v. n. ir. to lie down; to be situated.
giacimento, *–dshĭmĕn'tŏ*, m. lying down.
giacinto, *–dshĭn'tŏ*, m. hyacinth.
giacitura, *–dshĭtŏŏ'rä*, f. act of lying down; posture; arrangement of words.
giaco, *jä'kŏ*, m. coat of mail.
giallamina, *jällämĕ'nä*, f. calamine.
gialleggiare, *–lĕdjä'rĕ*, v. n. to turn to yellow.
giallezza, *–lĕt'zä*, f. yellowness.
gialliccio, *–lĭt'shŏ*, a. yellowish.
giallo, *jäl'lŏ*, a. & m. yellow.
giallognolo, *–lŏ'nyŏlŏ*, a. yellowish.
giallume, *–lŏŏ'mĕ*, m. yellowness; paleness.
giambare, *jämbä'rĕ*, v. n. to jest.
giambo, *jäm'bŏ*, m. iambic; jest.
giammai, *jämmä'ĕ*, ad. never; ever.

giammengola, —měn' gŏlă, f. trifle.
giannetta, jănnět' tă, f. spear; cane.
giannettata, —tă' tă, f. thrust with a pike.
giannizzero, —nĭt' zěrŏ, m. janissary.
giara, jă' ră, f. jar, mug, pitcher.
giarda, jăr' dă, f. spavin; trick.
giardinaggio, —dĭnăd' jŏ, m. gardening.
giardinetto, —nět' tŏ, m. small garden.
giardiniera, —nĭd' ră, f. gardener's wife.
giardiniere, —nĭd' rě, m. gardener.
giardino, —dě' nŏ, m. garden.
giarrettiera, —rĕttĭd' ră, f. order of the Garter.
giava, jă' vă, f. store-room.
giavellotto, —vĕllŏt' tă, m. javelin.
gibbo, jĭb' bŏ, m. protuberance; hump.
gibboso, —bŏ' sŏ, gibbuto, —bŭ' tŏ, a. gibbous, hunch-backed.
giberna, —běr' nă, f. cartridge-box.
gigante, —găn' tě, m. giant. [a. gigantic.
giganteo, —găntě' ŏ, gigantesco, —těs' kŏ,
gigantessa, —těs' să, f. giantess.
gigliato, jĭlyă' tŏ, a. lilied.
giglieto, —yă' tŏ, m. bed of lilies.
giglio, jěl' yŏ, m. lily.
ginepra, jĭnă' pră, f. juniper-berry.
ginepraio, —něpră' ŏ, ginepreto, —prě'-tŏ, m. place where juniper grows.
ginepro, —ně' prŏ, m. juniper.
ginestra, —něs' tră, f. broom, genet.
gingillarsi, —jĭllăr' sĭ, v. r. to build castles in the air. [invention.
gingillo, —jĭl' tŏ, m. subtle but fantastic
ginnasiale, —năsĭă' lě, a. belonging to a gymnasium.
ginnasio, —nă' sĭŏ, m. gymnasium.
ginnastica, —năs' tĭkă, f. gymnastics, pl.
ginnastico, —năs' tĭkŏ, a. gymnastic.
ginnetto, —nět' tŏ, m. Spanish horse.
ginnico, jĭn' nĭkŏ, a. gymnastic.
ginocchiello, jĭnŏkkĭěl' lŏ, m. hog's foot; knee-piece.
ginocchio, —ŏk' kĭŏ, m. knee.
giocare, see giuocare.
giocoforza, jŏkŏfŏr' tză, f. necessity.
giocolare, —lă' rě, m. juggler; —, v. n. to
giocolatore, —tŏ' rě, m. juggler. [juggle.
giocondare, —kŏndă' rě, v. n. to rejoice; to cheer oneself.
giocondevole, —dă' vŏlě, a. pleasing, rejoicing.
giocondezza, —dět' ză, giocondità, —dĭ-tă', f. joy, mirth.
giocondo, —kŏn' dŏ, a. joyful.
giocoso, —kŏ' sŏ, a. jocose, mirthful.
giogaia, —gă' ĭă, f. dew-lap; ridge (of mountains).
giogliato, jŏlyă' tŏ, a. mixed with tares.
gioglio, jŏl' yŏ, m. (bot.) tare; darnel.
giogo, jŏ' gŏ, m. yoke; slavery; summit.
gioia, jŏ' ă, f. jewel; joy.
gioielliere, jŏĭĕllĭě' rě, m. jeweller.
gioiello, —ěl' lŏ, m. jewel.
gioioso, jŏĭ' sŏ, a. joyful.
gioire, jŏě' rě, v. a. & n. to rejoice.
giomella, jŏměl' lă, f. two handfuls.

giornale, jŏrnă' lě, m. journal; —, a. daily.
giornaliere, —lĭě' rě, m. day-labourer.
giornaliero, —lĭě' rŏ, a. daily, variable.
giornalista, —lĭs' tă, m. journalist.
giornalmente, —nălměn' tě, ad. every day.
giornata, —nă' tă, f. day, day's work; journey.
giornea, —nă' ă, f. coat; soldier's cloak.
giorno, jŏr' nŏ, m. day; day-light.
giostra, jŏs' tră, f. joust, tilt; trick.
giostrare, —tră' rě, v. n. to joust, to tilt.
giostratore, —tŏ' rě, m. tilter.
giovamento, jŏvăměn' tŏ, m. help, benefit.
giovanaglia, —vănă' lyă, f. young people.
giovane, jŏ' văně, m. & f. young man; young woman. [the youth.
giovaneggiare, —vănědjă' rě, v. n. to act
giovanesco, —něs' kŏ, a. very young.
giovanezza, —nět' ză, f. youth.
giovanile, —nĭ' lě, a. juvenile, young.
giovanilmente, —nĭlměn' tě, ad. in a youthful manner.
giovanotto, —nŏt' tŏ, m. vigorous young man.
giovare, —vă' rě, v. a. to help; to please.
giovatore, —tŏ' rě, m.
giovedì, jŏvědĭ', m. Thursday.
giovenca, —věn' kă, f. heifer.
giovenco, —věn' kŏ, m. bullock.
giovenile, see giovanile.
gioventù, —věntŭ', f. youth, young people.
giovevole, —vě' vŏlě, a. profitable.
giovevolezza, —vĕvŏlět' ză, f. utility.
gioviale, —vĭă' lě, a. jovial.
giovine, see giovane.
giracapo, jĭrăkă' pŏ, m. dizziness, vertigo.
giraffa, —răf' fă, f. giraffe, camelopard.
giramento, —răměn' tŏ, m. turning round.
giramondo, —mŏn' dŏ, m. vagrant.
girandola, —răn' dŏlă, f. chandelier; fire-wheel; wheeling. [to muse.
girandolare, —dŏlă' rě, v. n. to revolve,
girare, jĭră' rě, v. a. & n. to turn, to wheel; (merch.) to endorse.
girarrosto, —ărrŏs' tŏ, m. turn-spit.
girata, —ră' tă, f. turn; (com.) circulation; endorsement; dar la —, to endorse.
girasole, —sŏ' lě, m. sun-flower; opal.
giratario, —tă' rĭŏ, m. endorsee.
giravolta, —vŏl' tă, f. going to and fro.
giravoltare, —vŏltă' rě, v. n. to go mad.
gire, jě' rě, v. n. (poet.) to go; to die.
girella, jĭrěl' lă, f. pulley; weather-cock.
girevole, —rě' vŏlě, a. moveable, changeable.
giro, —jě' rŏ, m. turn, circumference. [able.
girone, jĭrŏ' ně, m. great circuit; whirl-wind. [about.
gironzolare, —rŏnzŏlă' rě, v. n. to ramble
girovago, —rŏ' văgŏ, a. roving, rambling.
gita, jě' tă, f. journey, excursion.
gittaione, jĭttă' ŏ' ně, m. corn-cockle.
gittare, see gettare.
gitto, jĭt' tŏ, ad. exactly.
giù, jŏ', ad. down, below.
giubba, jŏŭ' bă, m. under-waistcoat; mane.
giubbetto, —bět' tŏ, m. gallows, pl.

giubbilare,—_bĭlă′rĕ_, v. n. to rejoice.
giubbileo,—_bĭlĕ′ō_, m. jubilee.
giubbilo,—_jŭb′bĭlō_, **giubbilio,**—_jŭbĕ′lĭō_, m. rejoicing, feasting.
giubbiloso,—_jŭbbĭlō′sō_, a. overjoyed.
giubbone,—_bō′nĕ_, m. doublet.
giudaico,—_jŭdā′ĭkō_, a. jewish.
giudaismo,—_dăĭs′mō_, m. judaism.
giudaizzare,—_dăĭdză′rĕ_, v. n. to judaize.
giudicare,—_dĭkă′rĕ_, v. a. to judge; to think.
giudicativo,—_kătĭ′vō_, a. judicial.
giudicato,—_kă′tō_, m. judgment; jurisdiction.
giudicatore,—_tō′rĕ_, m. judge.
giudicatorio,—_tō′rĭō_, a. judicial.
giudicazione,—_tzĭō′nĕ_, f. judgment.
giudice,_jō′dĭdshĕ_, m. judge.
giudiciale,_jŭdĭdshĭă′lĕ_, a. judicial.
giudiciario,—_ăĭdshĭă′rĭō_, a. judicial.
giudicio,—_dĕ′dshō_, m., **guidizio,**—_dĕ′tzĭō_, m. judgment; court of justice.
giudiziosamente,—_dĭtzĭōsămĕn′tĕ_, ad. judiciously, prudently.
giudizioso,—_tzĭō′sō_, a. judicious, prudent.
giuggiola,_jŭd′jōlă_, f. jujube. [loured.
giuggiolino,—_djŏlĭ′nō_, a. yellow-red co-
giuggiolo,_jŭd′jōlō_, m. jubebe-tree.
giugno,_jō′nyō_, m. June.
giulebbare,_jŭlĕbbă′rĕ_, v. a. to boil into
giulebbe,—_lĕb′bĕ_, m. julep. [a jelly.
giulività,—_lĭvĭtă′_, f. gaiety.
giulivo,—_lĕ′vō_, a. joyous.
giumella, see **giomella.**
giumenta,—_mĕn′tă_, f. mare; whore.
giumento,—_mĕn′tō_, m. cart- or pack-horse.
giuncaia,_jănkă′ĭă_, f. place full of rushes.
giuncare,—_kă′rĕ_, v.a. to strew with rushes.
giuncata,—_kă′tă_, f. cream-cheese.
giunco,_jŭn′kō_, m. rush.
giungere,_jŭn′jĕrĕ_, v. a. ir. to arrive at; to overreach; to join. [ing; cheat.
giunta,_jŭn′tă_, f. arrival; overplus; meet-
giuntare,—_tă′rĕ_, v. a. to deceive.
giuntatore,—_tă′rĕ_, m. cheat, swindler.
giunteria,—_tĕrĕ′ă_, f. fraud.
giunto,_jŭn′tō_, a. joined; arrived.
giuntura,—_tō′ră_, f. juncture, joint.
giuocare,_jŭŏkă′rĕ_, v. a. to play; to jest.
giuoco,_jŭŏ′kō_, m. game, play.
giuocoforza,_jŭŏkŏfŏr′tză_, f. unavoidable necessity.
giuocolare,—_lă′rĕ_, v. n. to juggle.
giuocolatore,—_tō′rĕ_, m. juggler.
giuramento,_jūrămĕn′tō_, m. oath.
giurare,—_ră′rĕ_, v. a. to swear.
giurato,—_ră′tō_, m. juryman, juror.
giuratorio,—_tō′rĭō_, a. juratory, sworn.
giure,_jō′rĕ_, m. law, jurisprudence.
giureconsulto,—_jūrĕkŏnsŭl′tō_, m. jurisconsult.
giuria,—_rĕ′ă_, f. jury. [consult.
giuridico,—_rĕ′dĭkō_, a. legal.
giurisdizionale,—_rĭsdĭtzĭōnă′lĕ_, a. judicial. [tion.
giurisdizione,—_rĭsdĭtzĭō′nĕ_, f. jurisdic-
giurisperito,—_rĭspĕrĭ′tō_, m. lawyer.

giurista,—_rĭs′tă_, m. jurist.
gius,_jŭs_, m. right, justice.
giusdicente,—_dĭdshĕn′tĕ_, m.(poet.) judge.
giuso,_jō′sō_, ad. (poet.) down.
giusquiamo,_jŭskŭĭă′mō_, m. hen-bane.
giusta,_jŭs′tă_, pr. according to.
giustacore,—_kō′rĕ_, m. bodice.
giustamente,—_mĕn′tĕ_, ad. justly, rightly.
giustezza,—_tĕt′ză_, f. justness.
giustificare,—_tĭfĭkă′rĕ_, v. a. to justify.
giustificativo,—_tĕ′vō_, a. justificative.
giustificazione,—_tzĭō′nĕ_, f. justification.
giustizia,—_tĕ′tzĭă_, f. justice, equity; court of law; execution; gallows. [to ruin.
giustiziare,—_tĭtzĭă′rĕ_, v. a. to execute;
giustiziere,—_tzĭă′rĕ_, m. justiciary; executioner.
giusto,_jŭs′tō_, a. just; equal; —, ad. justly.
glaciale,_glădshĭă′lĕ_, a. icy.
glandula,_glăn′dŭlă_, f. (an.) gland; kernel.
glanduloso,—_dŭlō′sō_, a. glandulous.
glastro,_glăs′trō_, m. woad.
gleba,_glĕ′bă_, f. glebe.
gli,_lyĭ_, art. pl. the; —, pn. to him; to them; they, them; —, ad. there.
globo,_glŏ′bō_, m. globe, sphere; ball.
globosità,—_glŏbŏsĭtă′_, f. rotundity.
globoso,—_bŏ′sō_, a. globular.
gloria,_glŏ′rĭă_, f. glory; fame.
gloriare,_glŏrĭă′rĕ_, v. a. to praise; **gloriarsi,**—_rĭar′sĕ_, to boast. [fication.
glorificamento,—_rĭfĭkămĕn′tō_, m. glori-
glorificare,—_fĭkă′rĕ_, v. a. to glorify; **glorificarsi,**—_fĭkăr′sĕ_, to boast.
glorificazione,—_tzĭō′nĕ_, f. glorification.
glorioso,—_rĭō′sō_, a. glorious.
glossa,_glŏs′să_, f. gloss.
glossare,—_să′rĕ_, v. a. to gloss.
glossario,—_să′rĭō_, m. glossary.
glossatore,—_tō′rĕ_, m. glosser.
glottide,_glŏt′tĭdĕ_, f. (an.) glottis.
glutine,_glō′tĭnĕ_, f. glue.
glutinoso,—_dălō′sō_, a. glutinous.
gnaffè,_nyăfĕ′_, i. by my troth!
gnao,_nyă′ō_, m. mewing (of a cat).
gnaulare,_nyăŭlă′rĕ_, v. n. to mew.
gnocco,_nyŏk′kō_, m. dumpling; blockhead.
gnorri,_nyŏr′rĭ_, **far lo —,** to feign ignorance.
gobba,_gŏb′bă_, f. hump. [ance.
gobbo,_gŏb′bō_, m. hunch-back, hump-back.
goccia,_gŏt′shă_, f. drop.
gocciare,—_tshă′rĕ_, v. n. to fall in drops.
gocciola,_gŏt′shŏlă_, f. droplet; gutter; crack in a wall.
gocciolamento,—_lămĕn′tō_, m. dropping.
gocciolare,—_lă′rĕ_, v. n. to drop.
goccialatoio,—_lătŏ′jŏ_, m. gutter.
gocciolatura,—_tō′ră_, f. spot or indentation caused by dropping. [quantity.
gocciolo,_gŏt′shŏlō_, m. drop; small
gocciolone,—_lō′nĕ_, m. dunce.
godere,_gŏdĕ′rĕ_, v. n. to rejoice, to enjoy.
godereccio,—_dĕrĕt′shō_, a. giving pleasure.
godimento,—_dĭmĕn′tō_, m. enjoyment; pleasure.

goditore, –tŏ'rĕ, m. jovial fellow.
goffaggine, gŏffăd'jĭnĕ, **goffezza,**–fĕt'ză, m. awkwardness.
goffo, gŏf'fŏ, a. awkward.
gogna, gŏn'yă, f. iron-collar; trouble.
gola, gŏ'lă, f. throat; gluttony; lust.
goletta, gŏlĕt'tă, f. gorget.
golfo, gŏl'fŏ, m. gulf, bay.
golosità, gŏlŏsĭtă', f. gluttony.
goloso, –lŏ'sŏ, a. gluttonous; covetous.
golpato, gŏlpă'tŏ, a. mildewed.
golpe, gŏl'pĕ, f. mildew; fox.
gombina, gŏmbĕ'nă, f. thong of a flail.
gomena, gŏ'mĕnă, f. (mar.) cable.
gomitata, gŏmĭtă'tă, f. blow with the elbow.
gomito, gŏ'mĭtŏ, m. elbow, corner; gulf; commander of galley-slaves.
gomitolo, gŏmĭ'tŏlŏ, m. clew of thread.
gomma, gŏm'mă, f. gum.
gommarabica, –ără'bĭkă, f. gum arabic.
gommato, –mă'tŏ, a. gummed.
gommifero, –mĕ'fĕrŏ, a. gum-producing.
gommoso, –mŏ'sŏ, a. gummy.
gondola, gŏn'dŏlă, f. gondola.
gondoliere, –dŏlĭă'rĕ, m. gondolier.
gonfalone, –fălŏ'nĕ, m. standard, flag.
gonfaloniere, –lŏnĭă'rĕ, m. standard-bearer; lord-mayor.
gonfia, gŏn'fĭă, m. glass-blower.
gonfiagione, –fĭăjŏ'nĕ, f., **gonfiamento,**–fĭămĕn'tŏ, m. swelling; pride.
gonfianuvoli, –fĭă nŭ'vŏlĭ, m. boaster.
gonfiare, –fĭă'rĕ, v. a. & n. to swell; to grow proud. [lows.
gonfiatoio, –fĭătŏ'ŏ, m. syringe; bellows.
gonfiatura, –fĭă'ră, f. swelling; flattery.
gonfietto, –fĭĕt'tŏ, m. small swelling; little conceit. [m. swelling; pride.
gonfiezza, –fĭĕt'ză, f., **gonfio,** gŏn'fĭŏ,
gonfio, gŏn'fĭŏ, a. swelled; vain, proud.
gonfiotto, –fĭŏt'tŏ, m. swimming-bladder.
gonga, gŏn'gă, f. sore throat.
gongolare, –lă'rĕ, v. n. to leap for joy.
gonna, gŏn'nă, f. (poet.) petticoat.
gonzo, gŏn'tzŏ, a. clownish; –, m. stupid fellow.
gora, gŏ'ră, f. conduit; mill-dam.
gorbia, gŏr'bĭă, f. ferrule; arrow-head.
gorello, gŏrĕl'lŏ, m. small water-pipe.
gorga, gŏr'gă, f. gullet, throat.
gorgheggiare, gŏrghĕdjă'rĕ, v. n. to trill, to quaver.
gorgia, gŏr'jă, f. throat; canal; rivulet.
gorgiera, –jĕ'ră, f. ruff, gorget.
gorgo, gŏr'gŏ, m. whirl-pool, gulf.
gorgogliare, –gŏlyă'rĕ, v. n. to gargle, to bubble up, to purl.
gorgoglio, –gŏl'yŏ, m. gargling, purling.
gorgoglione, –yŏ'nĕ, m. weevil, mite.
gota, gŏ'tă, f. cheek; side.
gotata, gŏtă'tă, f. slap, cuff.
gotta, gŏt'tă, f. gout.
gotto, gŏt'tŏ, m. goblet, cup, bowl.
gotteso, –tŏ'sŏ, a. gouty.
governale, gŏvĕrnă'lĕ, m. helm, rudder.

governare, –nă'rĕ, v. a. to govern, to manage, to steer.
governatore, –tŏ'rĕ, m. governor.
governo, –vĕr'nŏ, m. government.
gozzaia, gŏtzăĭ'ă, f. wen; inveterate hate.
gozzo, gŏt'zŏ, m. bird's crop.
gozzoviglia, –vĭ'lyă, f. merrimaking.
gozzovigliare, –vĭlyă'rĕ, v. n. to make merry, to revel. [prate.
gracchiare, grăkkĭă'rĕ, v. n. to croak; to
gracidare, grădshĭdă'rĕ, v. a. to croak.
gracile, gră'dshĭlĕ, a. slender, slight, thin.
gradare, –dă'rĕ, v. n. to descend by degrees.
gradazione, –tzĭŏ'nĕ, f. gradation.
gradevole, –dă'vŏlĕ, a. agreeable.
gradimento, –dĭmĕn'tŏ, m. kindness, favour, approbation; acceptance.
gradina, –dĕ'nă, f. dented chisel.
gradino, –dĕ'nŏ, m. step (of a staircase).
gradire, –dĕ'rĕ, v. a. to accept, to approve of. [dignity; will, pleasure.
grado, gră'dŏ, m. degree, step; rank,
graduale, –dăŭ'ălĕ, a. gradual.
graduare, –dŭă'rĕ, v. a. to graduate.
graduazione, –tzĭŏ'nĕ, f. graduation.
graduire, –dŭĭ'rĕ, v. a. to refine. [claw.
graffiare, grăffĭă'rĕ, v. a. to scratch, to
graffiatura, –fĭătŏ'ră, f. scratch; book.
graffio, grăf'fĭŏ, m. scratch; hook.
gragnuola, grănyŭŏ'lă, f. hail. [clothes.
gramaglia, grămă'lyă, f. mourning.
gramezza, –mĕt'ză, f. affliction, pain.
gramigna, –mĭn'yă, f. dog's grass.
grammatica, –mă'tĭkă, f. grammar.
grammaticale, –tĭkă'lĕ, a. grammatical.
grammaticalmente, –kălmĕn'tĕ, ad. grammatically.
grammatico, –mă'tĭkŏ, m. grammarian.
grammo, grăm'mŏ, m. gram.
gramo, gră'mŏ, a. wretched, sad.
gramolare, –mŏlă'rĕ, v. a. to bruise flax.
grampa, grăm'pă, f. claw, talon.
gran, grăn, for: **grande.**
grana, gră'nă, f. cochineal; grain.
granaio, –nă'ŏ, m. granary.
granare, –nă'rĕ, v. n. to grain.
granata, –nă'tă, f. broom; grenade.
granatiere, –tĭă'rĕ, m. grenadier.
granato, –nă'tŏ, m. garnet; pomegranate; –, a. grained, hard.
granbestia, grănbĕs'tĭă, f. elk.
granchio, grăn'kĭŏ, m. cray-fish; cramp, blunder; Cancer.
grancire, –dshĕ'rĕ, v. a. to snatch, to seize.
grande, grăn'dĕ, m. nobleman; –, a. great; high, sublime; –, ad. greatly, extremely.
grandeggiare, –dĕdjă'rĕ, v. n. to lord it.
grandemente, –dĕmĕn'tĕ, ad. greatly, extremely.
grandetto, –dĕt'tŏ, a. pretty tall. [tremely.
grandezza, –dĕt'ză, f. limity; lordship.
grandicello, see **grandetto.**
grandigia, –dĕ'jă, f. pride, haughtiness.
grandinare, –dĭnă'rĕ v. imp. to hail.
grandine, grăn'dĭnĕ, f. hail.
grandiosità, –ŏsĭtă', f. sumptuousness; magnificence.

grandioso, –dĭŏ'sŏ, a. sumptuous, magnificent, pompous.

granduca, –dŏ'kä, m. grand-duke.

granducato, –dŭkä'tŏ, m. grand-duchy.

granduchessa, –kĕs'sä, f. grand-duchess.

granello, grănĕl'lŏ, m. grain, kernel; stone.

granigione, –nĭjŏ'nĕ, f. running to seed.

granire, –nĕ'rĕ, v. n. to granulate.

grano, grä'nŏ, m. grain; corn; trifle.

grappare, grăppä'rĕ, v. a. to grapple, to catch. [ninny.

grappolo, grăp'pŏlŏ, m. bunch of grapes.

grascia, grăssä'ä, f. provisions, victuals, pl.; winnings, pl., gain.

grassatore, grăssätŏ'rĕ, m. highwayman.

grassazione, grăssätzĭŏ'nĕ, f. highway-robbery.

grassetto, –sĕt'tŏ, a. pretty fat.

grassezza, –sĕt'zä, f. fatness, plumpness.

grasso, grăs'sŏ, a. fat, greasy; plump; rich; stupid; –, m. fat; abundance.

grassoccio, –sŏt'shŏ, a. pretty fat.

grassume, –sŏ'mĕ, m. tallow.

grata, see **graticola.**

gratella, –tĕl'lä, f. small grate; fish-basket.

graticcio, –tĭt'shŏ, m. hurdle; lattice.

graticola, –tĭ'kŏlä, f. gridiron, grate.

gratificare, –tĭfĭkä'rĕ, v. a. to gratify, to indulge; to please. [gratitude.

gratitudine, –tŏ'dĭnĕ, f. thankfulness.

grato, grä'tŏ, a. grateful; pleasing, welcome; –, m. will, desire; pleasure.

grattacapo, grăttäkä'pŏ, m. itching of the head. [flatter.

grattare, grăttä'rĕ, v. a. to scratch; to

grattugia, –tŏ'jä, f. grater, rasp. [rasp.

grattugiare, –tŭjä'rĕ, v. a. to grate, to

gratuire, grătŭĕ'rĕ, v. a. to gratify.

gratuito, –tŏ'ĭtŏ, a. gratuitous, voluntary.

gratulare, –tŭlä'rĕ, v. a. to congratulate, to wish joy. [complaint.

gravame, –vä'mĕ, m. weight, burden;

gravare, –vä'rĕ, v. a. to charge, to burden; to vex. [m. gravity, weight.

grave, grä'vĕ, a. grave, heavy, strong; –,

gravemente, –mĕn'tĕ, ad. heavily; grievously. [trouble, vexation.

gravezza, –vĕt'zä, f. heaviness; weight;

gravicembalo, –vĭdshĕm'bälŏ, m. piano-forte. [gravidity.

gravidanza, –dän'tzä, f. pregnancy;

gravido, grä'vĭdŏ, a. laden; full; pregnant.

gravità, grăvĭtä', f. gravity; seriousness.

gravitare, –tä'rĕ, v. n. to gravitate; to weigh.

gravitazione, –tätzĭŏ'nĕ, f. gravitation.

gravoso, –vŏ'sŏ, a. heavy; hard, rigid; hurtful.

grazia, grä'tzĭä, f. grace, beauty; favour; kindness; thanks, pl.; privilege.

graziare, –tzĭä'rĕ, v. a. to grant a favour; to absolve. [ciously.

graziosamente, –tzĭŏsämĕn'tĕ, ad. gra-

graziosità, –sĭtä', f. gracefulness, comeliness; elegance.

grazioso, –tzĭŏ'sŏ, a. graceful; polite.

gregario, grĕgä'rĭŏ, a. gregarious; vulgar.

gregge, grĕd'jĕ, m., **greggia,** –jä, f. flock; herd; crowd; sheep-fold.

greggio, grĕd'jŏ, a. rough, raw; clownish.

grembiale, grĕmbĭä'lĕ, m. apron.

grembo, grĕm'bŏ, m. lap; bosom; apron.

gremire, grĕmĭ'rĕ, v. a. to gripe, to snatch.

gremito, –mĭ'tŏ, a. full, thick; crowded.

greppo, grĕp'pŏ, m. mound of earth, bank; precipice.

greppia, grĕp'pĭä, f. rack, manger.

greto, grĕ'tŏ, m. sandy or marshy ground.

gretola, grĕ'tŏlä, f. bar of a cage; opportunity; subterfuge.

gretto, grĕt'tŏ, a. niggardly, stingy.

grezzo, grĕt'zŏ, a. rough, coarse.

gricciolo, –grĭt'shŏlŏ, m. fancy, caprice.

grida, grĕ'dä, f. proclamation; report.

gridare, grĭdä'rĕ, v. a. & n. to cry; to bawl; to divulge; to scold.

gridio, –dĕ'ŏ, m. bawling, brawling.

grido, –grĕ'dŏ, m. cry, shriek; report, fame.

grieve, grĭä'vĕ, a. (poet.) heavy; grievous.

grifagno, grĭfän'yŏ, a. rapacious.

grifo, grĕ'fŏ, m. snout, muzzle; net; riddle.

grifone, grĭfŏ'nĕ, m. griffin; slap on the face.

grigio, grĕ'jŏ, a. grizzly.

grillanda, grĭllän'dä, f. garland.

grillare, –grĭllä'rĕ, v. n. to simmer.

grillo, grĭl'lŏ, m. cricket; whim, freak.

grimaldello, grĭmäldĕl'lŏ, m. pick-lock.

grinta, grĭn'tä, f. grim face.

grinza, grĭn'tzä, f. wrinkle. [wrinkled.

grinzo, grĭn'tzŏ, **grinzoso,** –tzŏ'sŏ, a.

gromma, grŏm'mä, f. tartar; crust. [tile.

gronda, grŏn'dä, f. eaves; gutter; hollow

grondaia, –dä'ä, f. dropping from a roof or gutter. [from a gutter.

grondare, –dä'rĕ, v. n. to fall in drops

grongo, grŏn'gŏ, m. conger.

groppa, grŏp'pä, f. rump, croup, crupper.

groppo, grŏp'pŏ, m. knot, knob; group; difficulty. [gross; alla –, in the lump.

grossa, grŏs'sä, f. mass, quantity, whole;

grosseria, –sĕrĕ'ä, f. coarse ironware, wholesale dealing. [clownishness.

grossezza, –sĕt'zä, f. bigness; coarseness.

grossiere, –sĭĕ'rĕ, a. coarse, heavy; stupid; –, m. wholesale-merchant.

grosso, grŏs'sŏ, a. big, thick, large, heavy; coarse, fat; stupid; –, ad. in great quantities; heavily, rudely; –, m. main body; bulk; mass; whole.

grossolano, –sŏlä'nŏ, a. coarse; dull.

grotta, grŏt'tä, f. grotto, cave.

grottesco, –tĕs'kŏ, a. grotesque, odd.

gru, grŏ, f. crane (bird). [nozzle.

grufolare, grŭfŏlä'rĕ, v. a. to grub up, to

grugnire, grŭnyĕ'rĕ, v. n. to grunt.

grugnito, –yĕ'tŏ, m. grunting. [ing.

grugno, grŭn'yŏ, m. snout, muzzle; frown-

grullo, grŭl'lŏ, a. drowsy; benumbed.

gruma, grŏ'mä, f. tartar; crust. [tion.

grumo, grŏ'mŏ, m. clot of blood; concre-

grumoso, grŭmŏ'sŏ, a. clotted, thickened.

gruppito, grŭppĭ'tŏ, a. naturally polished

gruppo, see **groppo.** [(of diamonds).

gruzzolo, grŭt'zŏlŏ, m. hoard, heap.

guadagnare, *gŭădăny⁸' r̄ĕ*, v. a. to gain, to win, to profit. [come.
guadagno, *–dăn' yŏ*, m. gain, lucre; in-
guadare, *–dā' rĕ*, v. a. to ford.
guado, *gŭă' dŏ*, m. ford, shallow passage.
guai, *see* guaio.
guai, *gŭă' ĭ*, i. woe! alas!
guaime, *gŭă' mĕ*, m. after-grass.
guaina, *gŭă' nă*, f. sheath.
guaio, *gŭă' ŏ*, m. howling; woe, calamity.
guaiolare, *gŭăiŏlă' rĕ*, guaire, *gŭă' rĕ*,
  v. n. to wail, to howl, to lament.
gualca, *gŭăl' kă*, f. fuller's mill.
gualcare, *–kă' rĕ*, v. a. to full, to mill
  (cloth). [crush.
gualcire, *–dshĕ' rĕ*, v. a. to rumple, to
gualdrappa, *–drăp' pă*, f. horse-cloth.
guancia, *gŭăn' dshă*, f. cheek.
guanciale, *–dshĕ' lĕ*, m. pillow.
guancialetto, *–lĕt' tŏ*, m. small pillow.
guanciata, *–dshă' tă*, f. slap on the face.
guantiera, *–tĭă' ră*, f. glove-box.
guanto, *gŭăn' tŏ*, m. glove. [ranger.
guardaboschi, *gŭărdăbŏs' kĭ*, m. wood-
guardacoste, *–kŏs' tĕ*, m. coast-guard.
guardaportone, *–pŏrtŏ' nĕ*, m. door-
  keeper, porter.
guardare, *–dă' rĕ*, v. a. to look, to behold,
  to consider; to guard, to take care of;
  guardarsi, *–dăr' sĭ*, to look at oneself;
  to abstain from. [wardrobe-keeper.
guardaroba, *–rŏ' bă*, f. & m. wardrobe;
guardia, *gŭăr' dĭă*, f. guard, watch.
guardiano, *–dĭă' nŏ*, m. guardian, keeper.
guardigno, *–dĭn' yŏ*, a. guarded.
guardinfante, *gŭărdĭnfăn' tĕ*, m. hoop-
  petticoat, farthingale.
guardo, *gŭăr' dŏ*, m. view, look, aspect.
guarentigia, *gŭărĕntĭ' jă*, f. guarantee,
  warranty. [warrant.
guarentire, *–tĭ' rĕ*, v. a. to guarantee, to
guari, *gŭă' rĭ*, ad. much, many.
guarigione, *gŭărĭjŏ' nĕ*, f. cure, recovery.
guarire, *–rĕ' rĕ*, v. a. to cure, to heal.
guarnacca, *gŭărnăk' kă*, f. night-gown.
guarnelletto, *–nĕllĕt' tŏ*, m. small fustian
  petticoat.
guarnello, *–nĕl' lŏ*, m. fustian.
guarnire, *–nĕ' rĕ*, v. a. to furnish, to store;
  to adorn, to fortify.
guarnizione, *–nĭtsĭŏ' nĕ*, f. trimming.
guastada, *gŭăstă' dă*, f. decanter.
guastare, *–tă' rĕ*, v. a. to spoil, to deprave, to waste, to destroy.
guasto, *gŭăs' tŏ*, m. ruin, waste.
guatare, *gŭătă' rĕ*, v. a. & n. to look at,
  to spy; to aim at. [lion.
guattero, *gŭăt' tĕrŏ*, m. kitchen-boy, scul-
guazza, *gŭăt' ză*, f. dew.
guazzabuglio, *–tzăbŭl' yŏ*, m. hotch-potch.
guazzare, *gŭăzză' rĕ*, v. a. & n. to shake;
  to rejoice; to fluctuate.
guazzatoio, *–tŏ' ŏ*, m. watering-place.
guazzetto, *–dzĕt' tŏ*, m. minced meat.
guazzo, *gŭăz' zŏ*, m. ford, puddle, splash;
  water-colour.

guazzoso, *–dzŏ' sŏ*, a. splashy, muddy.
guercio, *gŭĕr' dshŏ*, a. squint-eyed.
guernire, *–nĕ' rĕ*, v. a. to furnish, to equip;
  to trim. [enmity; vexation.
guerra, *gŭĕr' ră*, f. war, fight; obstacle;
guerreggiare, *–rĕdjă' rĕ*, v. a. to wage
  war, to fight, to make war.
guerresco, *–rĕs' kŏ*, a. warlike.
guerriere, *–rĭĕ' rĕ*, m. warrior, soldier.
guerriero, *–rĭĕ' rŏ*, a. warlike.
gufare, *gŭfă' rĕ*, v. a. to mock.
gufo, *gŏ' fŏ*, m. (screech-)owl.
guglia, *gŭl' yă*, f. obelisk; needle.
gugliata, *gŭlyă' tă*, f. needleful.
guida, *gŭĕ' dă*, f. guide, conductor.
guidare, *gŭĭdă' rĕ*, v. a. to guide, to lead,
  to rule. [ward.
guiderdonare, *–dĕrdŏnă' rĕ*, v. a. to re-
guiderdone, *–dŏ' nĕ*, m. recompense.
guiggia, *gŭĭd' jă*, f. vamp.
guindolo, *gŭĭn' dŏlŏ*, m. reel, spindle.
guinzaglio, *–tză' lyŏ*, m. leash, string.
guisa, *gŭĕ' să*, f. way, manner; fashion.
guitto, *gŭĭt' tŏ*, a. filthy, nasty.
guizzare, *gŭĭtză' rĕ*, v. a. & n. to brandish; to glide, to slide along.
guizzo, *gŭĭt' zŏ*, a. withered, wrinkled.
guscio, *gŭsshˈ ŏ*, m. shell; bark; body (of
  a coach); case; scales, pl., balance.
gustare, *gŭstă' rĕ*, v. a. to taste, to relish.
gusto, *gŭs' tŏ*, m. taste, savour; relish;
  pleasure, enjoyment.
gustoso, *–tŏ' sŏ*, a. agreeable, pleasant.
gutturale, *gŭttŭră' lĕ*, a. guttural.

I.

ialino, *ĭălĕ' nŏ*, a. hyaline, glassy, trans-
iaspide, *ĭăs' pĭdĕ*, m. jasper. [parent.
iato, *ĭă' tŏ*, m. hiatus; abyss.
iattanza, *ĭăttăn' tză*, f. brag, boasting.
iattura, *–tŏ' ră*, f. loss, damage.
iberno, *ĭbĕr' nŏ*, a. (poet.) hibernal, wintry.
ibi, *ĕ' bĭ*, m. ibis.
iconoclasta, *ĭkŏnŏklăs' tă*, m. iconoclast.
iconografia, *–grăfĕ' ă*, f. iconography.
Iddio, *ĭddĕ' ŏ*, m. (poet.) God.
idea, *ĭdă' ă*, f. idea, fancy.
ideale, *ĭdĕă' lĕ*, a. ideal; intellectual.
idealismo, *–lĭs' mŏ*, m. idealism.
idealista, *–lĭs' tă*, m. idealist.
idealità, *–lĭtă'*, f. ideality.
idealizare, *–lĭdză' rĕ*, v. a. to idealize.
idealmente, *–mĕn' tĕ*, a. ideally.
identico, *ĭdĕn' tĭkŏ*, a. identical.
identità, *–tĭtă'*, f. identity.
idioma, *ĭdĭŏ' mă*, m. idiom, dialect.
idiota, *ĭdĭŏ' tă*, m. idiot. [pacity.
idoneità, *ĭdŏnĕĭtă'*, f. fitness, ability, ca-
idoneo, *ĭdŏ' nĕŏ*, a. fit, able; suitable.
idra, *ĕ' dră*, f. hydra.
idromele, *ĭdrŏmĕ' lĕ*, m. hydromel, mead.
idropico, *ĭdrŏ' pĭkŏ*, a. dropsical.
idrope, *see* idropisia.

idropisia, *idròpìsè'â*, f. dropsy.
iena, *ìè'nà*, iene, *ìè'nè*, f. hyena.
ieri, *ìè'rè*, m. yesterday. [morning.
iermattina, *ìermàttè'nà*, f. yesterday
iernotte, *-nòt'tè*, f. last night.
iersera, *-sè'rà*, f. yesterday evening.
ignaro, *ìnyà'rò*, a. ignorant.
ignavia, *ìnyà'vìà*, f. idleness; cowardice.
ignavo, *-yà'vò*, a. lazy; cowardly.
igneo, *ìn'yèò*, a. igneous, fiery.
ignito, *ìnyì'tò*, a. inflamed, burning.
ignivomo, *-yè'vòmò*, a.ignivomous,flame-vomiting.
ignobile, *-yò'bìlè*, a. ignoble, base.
ignobilmente, *-mèn'tè*, ad. ignobly; meanly. [traction.
ignobiltà, *-bìltà'*, f. ignobility; mean ex-
ignominia, *-yòmìnè'â*, f. ignominy.
ignominioso, *-mìò'sò*, a. ignominious.
ignorante, *-yòràn'tè*,a.ignorant,illiterate.
ignoranza, *-ràn'tzà*, f. ignorance.
ignorare, *-rà'rè*, v. a. not to know, to be ignorant of.
ignoto, *-yò'tò*, a. unknown; hidden.
ignudare, *-yüdà'rè*, v. a. to strip naked.
ignudo, *-yò'dò*, a. naked. [to undress.
il, *ìl*, art. & pn. the; him, it. [to soil.
illaidire, *ìllàìdè'rè*, v. a. to make ugly;
illanguidire, *-làngüìdè'rè*, v. n. to languish. [enslave.
illaqueare, *-làküèà'rè*, v. a. to ensnare; to
illativo, *-làtì'vò*, a. illative, consequential.
illecitamente, *-lèdshìtàmèn'tè*,ad.illicity, unlawfully.
illecito, *-lè'dshìtò*, a. illicit, unlawful.
illegale, *-lègà'lè*, a. illegal.
illegittimo, *-lèjìt'tìmò*, a. illegitimate.
illeso, *-lè'sò*, a. unhurt, safe. [rant.
illetterato, *-lèttèrà'tò*, a. illiterate, igno-
illibatezza, *-lìbàtèt'zà*, f. integrity, stain-less purity.
illibato, *-lìbà'tò*, a. spotless, stainless.
illiquidire, *-lìküìdè'rè*, v. n. to become liquid, to melt.
illuminare, *-lümìnà'rè*, v.a. to illumine,
illuminazione, *-tzìò'nè*, f. illumination.
illusione, *-lüsì'ò'nè*, f. illusion; error.
illusorio, *-sò'rìò*, a. illusory, vain.
illustrare, *-lüstrà'rè*, v. a. to illustrate; to explain, to adorn. [explanation.
illustrazione, *-tzìò'nè*, f. illustration;
imbalconato, *ìmbàlkònà'tò*, a. flesh-coloured. [bold.
imbaldanzire, *-dàntzà'rè*, v. n. to grow
imballare, *-là'rè*, v. a. to embale, to pack up, to bundle up.
imbalsamare, *-sàmà'rè*, v.a. to embalm.
imbandire, *-bàndè'rè*, v. a. to dress, to serve up; to cook.
imbarazzare, *-bàràtzà'rè*, v. n. to embarrass, to trouble; to entangle.
imbarazzo, *-bàràt'zò*, m. embarrassment: confusion.
imbarcare, *-bàrkà'rè*, v. a. to embark; imbarcarsi, *-kàr'sì*, to embark in.
imbarcazione, *-tzìò'nè*, f. embarkation.

imbarco, *-bàr'kò*, m. embarkation; enter-prize; (jur.) embargo. [foundation.
imbasamento, *-bàsàmèn'tò*, m. basis,
imbastardire, *-bàstàrdè'rè*, v. n. to de-generate.
imbastire, *-bàstè'rè*, v. a. to baste.
imbastitura, *-tö'rà*, f. basting.
imbasto, *-bàs'tò*, m. pack-saddle.
imbattersi, *-bàt'tèrsì*, v. r. to meet with.
imbavagliare, *-bàvàlyà'rè*, v. a. to blind-fold, to hood-wink.
imbavare, *-bàvà'rè*, v. a. to slabber.
imbeccare, *-bèkkà'rè*, v. a. to feed a young bird.
imbeccata, *-kà'tà*, f. bill-full; bribe.
imbecille, *-bèdshìl'lè*, a. imbecile, weak.
imbecillità, *-dshìlìtà'*, f. imbecility.
imbellettare, *-bèllèttà'rè*, v. a., imbel-lettarsi, *-tàr'sì*, to paint one's face,to fard.
imbellire, *-bèllè'rè*, v. a. to embellish.
imberbe, *-bèr'bè*, a. beardless.
imberciare, *-dshà'rè*, v. a. to hit the mark.
imbertescare, *-tèskà'rè*, v. a. to fortify with battlements. [white.
imbiaccare, *-bìàkkà'rè*, v. a. to paint
imbiutare, *-bìütà'rè*, v. a. to plaster, to daub. [a violent passion.
imbizzarrire, *-bìdzàrrè'rè*,v. n. to fly into
imboccare, *-bòkkà'rè*, v. a. & n. to feed; to disembogue.
imboccatura, *-kàtö'rà*, f. mouth (of a river); bridle-pit; entrance (of a street).
imborsare, *-bòrsà'rè*, v. a. to purse, to pocket.
imbottatoio, *-bòttàtò'ò*, m. funnel.
imbozzimare, *-bòdzìmà'rè*, v. a. to starch.
imbracciare, *-bràtshà'rè*, v.a. to embrace.
imbrattare, *-bràttà'rè*, v. a. to soil, to daub, to foul, to dirty.
imbratto, *-bràt'tò*, m. dirt; hog's wash.
imbrodolare, *-bròdòà'rè*, v. a. to grease, to daub. [to embroil.
imbrogliare, *-bròlyà'rè*, v. a. to perplex,
imbroglio, *-bròl'lyò*, m.perplexity,trouble.
imbroncire, *-bròndshè'rè*, v. n. to get or to grow angry.
imbrunare, *-brünà'rè*, imbrunire, *-nè'rè*, v. a. to make brown; to burnish.
imbucatare, *-bükàtà'rè*, v. a. to buck.
imbullettare, *-büllèttà'rè*, v. a. to fasten with tacks. [to instruct.
imburiassare, *-bürìàssà'rè*, v. a. to teach,
imbusto, *-büs'tò*, m. bust, trunk; body; [corset.
imbuto, *-bö'tò*, m. funnel.
imitare, *ìmìtà'rè*, v. a. to imitate, to counterfeit.
imitazione, *-tzìò'nè*, f. imitation.
immaginare, *ìmmàjìnà'rè*, v. a. & n. to imagine, to fancy.
immaginario, *-nà'rìò*, a. imaginary.
immaginativa, *-tè'và*, f. imaginative faculty. [fancy.
immaginazione, *-tzìò'nè*, f. imagination,
immagine, *-mà'jìnè*, f. image, figure; likeness.
immagrire, *-màgrè'rè*, v. a. to grow lean.
immalinconire, *-lìnkònè'rè*, v. a. & n. to afflict; to be afflicted.

immane, —mä'nĕ, a. (poet.) cruel, savage.
immanente, —nĕn'tĕ, a. immanent, in- [herent.
immanità, —mänită', f. cruelty.
immantinente, —mäntinĕn'tĕ, ad. im- mediately, instantly. [maturely.
immaturamente, —mäturämĕn'tĕ, ad. pre-
immaturità, —türită', f. immaturity, un- ripeness.
immaturo, —mätü'rŏ, a. immature, unripe.
immedesimare, —mĕdĕsimä'rĕ, v. a. to identify. [sent.
immediato, —mĕdiä'tŏ, a. immediate; pre-
immemore, —mä'mŏrĕ, a. unmindful, un- grateful.
immensità, —mĕnsită', f. immensity.
immenso, —mĕn'sŏ, a. immense, huge.
immensurabile, —sürä'bĭlĕ, a. immen- surable. [to plunge.
immergere, —mĕr'jĕrĕ, v.a. ir. to immerse,
immettere, —mĕt'tĕrĕ, v. a. ir. to put in; to insert, to embody. [threatening.
imminente, —minĕn'tĕ, a. impending,
immobile, —mŏ'bĭlĕ, a. immoveable.
immoderato, —mŏdĕrä'tŏ, a. immoderate; excessive.
immodestia, —mŏdĕs'tiä, f. immodesty.
immodesto, —mŏdĕs'tŏ, a. immodest.
immolare, —mŏlä'rĕ, v. a. to immolate, to sacrifice. [soak; to mollify.
immollare, —mŏllä'rĕ, v. a. to moisten, to
immondezza, —mŏndĕt'zä, f. filth, dirt.
immondo, —mŏn'dŏ, a. filthy, impure.
immorale, —mŏrä'lĕ, a. immoral.
immortalare, —mŏrtälä'rĕ, v. a. to im- mortalize.
immortale, —mŏrtä'lĕ, a. immortal, eternal.
immortalità, —tälită', f. immortality.
immoto, —mŏ'tŏ, a. unmoved, steadfast.
immune, —mŏ'nĕ, a. exempt, privileged.
immunità, —münită', f. immunity.
immutare, —mütä'rĕ, v.a. to change, to
imo, è'mŏ, a. low, deep; vile. [alter.
impacciare, ĭmpätshä'rĕ, v. a. to en- cumber, to embroil, to embarrass; to bar.
impaccio, —pät'shŏ, m. trouble, perplexity; pain. [oneself master of.
impadronirsi, —pädrŏnĭr'sĭ, v. r. to make
impalare, —pälä'rĕ, v. a. to impale.
impalcare, —pälkä'rĕ, v.a. to ceil, to plank.
impallidire, —pällĭdĭ'rĕ, v. n. to get pale.
impalmare, —pälmä'rĕ, v. a. to give the hand; to betroth, to affiance.
impalpabile, —pä'bĭlĕ, a. impalpable.
impaludare, —pälüdä'rĕ, v. a. to grow marshy. [to learn.
imparare, —pärä'rĕ, v. a. & n. to teach;
impareggiabile, —pärĕd'jä'bĭlĕ, a. incom- parable. [kindred.
imparentato, —pärĕntä'tŏ, a. related,
impari, ĭm'pärĭ, a. uneven, unequal.
impartibile, —pärtĭ'bĭlĕ, a. indivisible.
imparziale, —pärzĭä'lĕ, a. impartial; just.
imparzialità, —tzĭälĭtă', f. impartiality.
imparzialmente, —mĕn'tĕ, ad. impartially.
impassibile, —päsĕ'bĭlĕ, a. impassible.
impassibilità, —sĭbĭlĭtă', f. impassibility.
impastare, —pästä'rĕ, v. a. to knead.

impasto, —päs'tŏ, a. fasting.
impaurire, —päürĭ'rĕ, v. a. to frighten, to terrify.
impavido, —pä'vĭdŏ, a. fearless. [eager.
impaziente, —pätzĭĕn'tĕ, a. impatient;
impazienza, —tzĭĕn'tzä, f. impatience.
impazzare, —pätzä'rĕ, impazzire, —tzĕ'rĕ, v. n. to go mad. [ment, hindrance.
impedimento, —pĕdĭmĕn'tŏ, m. impedi-
impedire, —pĕdĭ'rĕ, v. a. to hinder, to prevent.
impegnare, —pĕnyä'rĕ, v. a. to pledge; to engage; impegnarsi, —pĕnyär'sĭ, to oblige oneself. [tion.
impegno, —pĕn'yŏ, m. engagement, obliga-
impegolare, —pĕgŏlä'rĕ, v. a. to pitch.
impelagare, —lägä'rĕ, v. a. to embarrass, to hinder.
impelare, —pĕlä'rĕ, v. n. to grow hairy.
impellere, —pĕl'lĕrĕ, v. a. ir. to impel.
impennare, —pĕnnä'rĕ, v. a. to fledge; to describe; to book.
impensato, —pĕnsä'tŏ, a. unthought of.
imperante, —pĕrän'tĕ, m. commander.
imperativo, —pĕrätĭ'vŏ, a. imperative, im- perious.
imperatore, —tŏ'rĕ, m. emperor.
imperatorio, —tŏ'rĭŏ, a. imperial.
imperatrice, —trĕ'dshĕ, f. empress.
impercettibile, —dshĕttĕ'bĭlĕ, a. impei- ceptible. [whereas.
imperciocchè, —dshŏkĕ', ad. for, because,
imperfetto, —fĕt'tŏ, a. & m. (gr.) imperfect.
imperiale, —pĕriä'lĕ, a. imperial; excellent.
imperio, see impero. [haughty.
imperioso, —pĕrĭŏ'sŏ, a. imperious,
imperito, —pĕrĭ'tŏ, a. unskilled; awkward.
imperlaqualcosa, —läkŭälkŏ'sä, ad. there- fore. [mand.
impero, —pä'rŏ, m. empire; reign; com-
imperò, —pĕrŏ', ad. therefore.
imperocchè, —kĕ', ad. because; since.
impertinente, —pĕrtĭnĕn'tĕ, a. insolent; absurd.
impertinenza, —nĕn'tzä, f. impertinence.
imperturbabile, —türbä'bĭlĕ, a. imper- turbable; calm. [turbability.
imperturbabilità, —bäbĭlĭtă', f. imper-
imperturbato, —türbä'tŏ, a. undisturbed, tranquil. [to rave; to disturb.
imperversare, —vĕrsä'rĕ, v. n. to rage,
impetigine, —pĕtĭ'jĭnĕ, f. tetter, ring-worm.
impetrare, —pĕträ'rĕ, v. a. to obtain by entreaty.
impettito, —pĕttĭ'tŏ, a. upright, straight.
impetuoso, —tŭŏ'sŏ, a. impetuous, violent.
impiagare, —piägä'rĕ, v. a. to wound, to hurt.
impiastrare, —piästrä'rĕ, v. a. to apply a plaster; to ingraft; (fig.) to reconcile.
impiastro, —piäs'trŏ, m. plaster.
impiattare, —piättä'rĕ, v. a. to conceal.
impiccare, —piĕkä'rĕ, v. a. to hang; im- piccarsi, —kär'sĭ, to hang oneself.
impicciare, —pĭtshä'rĕ, v. a. to embroil, to perplex. [hindrance.
impiccio, —pĭt'shŏ, m. perplexity, trouble;

impiegare, –*piēgā'rĕ,* v. a. to employ, to make use of. [ployé.

impiegato, –*gā'tŏ,* m. place-man; em-

impiego, –*pĭā'gŏ,* m. employ, employment, office. [to pity; to feel compassion.

impietosire, –*piĕtŏsē'rĕ,* v. a. & n. to move

impietrare, –*piĕtrā'rĕ,* **impietrire,** –*trē'rĕ,* v. a. & n. to petrify.

impigliare, –*pĭlyā'rĕ,* v. n. to entangle, to embroil, to stop. [to manure.

impinguare, –*pĭngŭā'rĕ,* v. a. to fatten,

impinzare, –*tzā'rĕ,* v. a. to overfill.

implacabile, –*plākā'bĭlĕ,* a. implacable.

implicare, –*plĭkā'rĕ,* v. a. to implicate; to embarrass, to embroil.

implicito, –*plĭ'dshĭtŏ,* a. implicit.

implorare, –*plŏrā'rĕ,* v. a. to implore.

impoltronire, –*pŏltrŏnē'rĕ,* v. a. to make lazy; –, v. n. to grow lazy.

impolverare, –*pŏlvĕrā'rĕ,* v. a. & n. to powder; to dust oneself. [derable.

imponderabile, –*pŏndĕrā'bĭlĕ,* a. impon-

imporre, –*pŏr'rĕ,* v. a. ir. to impose, to lay upon; to order; to deceive.

importante, –*tän'tĕ,* a. important, weighty.

importanza, –*tän'tzā,* f. importance.

importare, –*tā'rĕ,* v. a. & n. to import; to be of consequence; **non importa,** no matter! [to tease.

importunare, –*tŭnā'rĕ,* v.a. to importune,

importuno, –*tŏ'nŏ,* a. importunate, trouble-some. [import, duty, toll.

imposizione, –*pŏsĭtzĭŏ'nĕ,* f. imposition;

impossibile, –*pŏssē'bĭlĕ,* a. impossible.

impossibilità, –*stbĭlĭtā',* f. impossibility.

impossibilitare, –*bĭlĭtā'rĕ,* v. a. to render impossible. [door-post; window-frame.

imposta, –*pŏs'tā,* f. impost, tax, custom;

impostore, –*tŏ'rĕ,* m. impostor, cheat.

impostura, –*tŏ'rā,* f. imposture, deceit.

impotente, –*pŏtĕn'tĕ,* a. impotent.

impotenza, –*tĕn'tzā,* **impotenzia,** –*tĕn'-tzĭā,* f. impotence, weakness.

impoverire, –*pŏvĕrē'rĕ,* v. a. & n. to im-poverish; to grow poor.

impraticabile, –*prātĭkā'bĭlĕ,* a. imprac-ticable; unsociable.

imprecare, –*prĕkā'rĕ,* v. a. to imprecate.

impregnare, –*prĕnyā'rĕ,* v. a. to impreg-nate. [take; to learn.

imprendere, –*prĕn'dĕrĕ,* v. a. ir. to under-

impresa, –*prā'sā,* f. enterprise; emblem.

impresario, –*prĕsā'rĭŏ,* m. undertaker; stage-manager.

impressione, –*prĕssĭŏ'nĕ,* f. impression, print; mark; idea; image.

impressivo, –*sē'vŏ,* a. impressive.

imprestare, –*prĕstā'rĕ,* v. a. to lend; to grant. [unavoidable.

impreteribile, –*prĕtĕrē'bĭlĕ,* a. unfailing,

imprigionare, –*prĭjŏnā'rĕ,* v. a. to im-prison. [to imprint; to stamp.

imprimere, –*prē'mĕrĕ,* v. a. ir. to impress;

improbabile, –*prŏbā'bĭlĕ,* a. improbable; unlikely. [ness.

improbità, –*prŏbĭtā',* f. improbity, wicked-

improbo, *ĭm'prŏbŏ,* a. wicked, ungodly.

impromettere, *see* **promettere.**

impronta, –*prŏn'tā,* f. print, stamp.

improntare, –*tā'rĕ,* v.a. to print, to stamp; to borrow; to importune.

impronto, –*prŏn'tŏ,* a. importunate, troublesome; –, m. impression, mark; print. [jury.

improperio, –*prŏpā'rĭŏ,* m. reproach; in-

improprietà, –*prŏprĭĕtā',* f. impropriety; unfitness.

improprio, –*prŏp'rĭŏ,* a. improper.

improsperire, –*prŏspĕrē'rĕ,* v. n. to prosper.

improvvido, –*prŏv'vĭdŏ,* a. improdent.

improvvisamente, –*prŏvvĭsāmĕn'tĕ,* ad. unexpectedly, suddenly.

improvvisare, –*vĭsā'rĕ,* v. n. to make verses extempore.

improvvisata, –*vĭsā'tā,* f. impromptu.

improvviso, –*vē'sŏ,* a. unprovided, un-expected, unthought of; sudden; –, ad. upon a sudden, unexpectedly.

imprudente, –*prūdĕn'tĕ,* a. imprudent.

imprudenza, –*dĕn'tzā,* f. imprudence.

impubere, –*pŏ'bĕrĕ,* a. beardless, under age.

impudente, –*pŭdĕn'tĕ,* a. impudent.

impudenza, –*dĕn'tzā,* f. impudence.

impudico, –*pŏ'dĭkŏ,* a. unchaste.

impugnare, –*pŭnyā'rĕ,* v. a. to gripe, to grasp, to lay hold of; to oppose; to impugn.

impugnatura, –*tŏ'rā,* f. grasping; handle; hilt (of a sword).

impulito, –*pŭlē'tŏ,* a. unpolished.

impulsione, –*pŭlsĭŏ'nĕ,* f. impulsion; action.

impulso, –*pŭl'sŏ,* m. impulse, motive.

impunemente, –*pănĕmĕn'tĕ,* ad. with im-punity.

impunità, –*pănĭtā',* f. impunity.

impunito, –*pănē'tŏ,* a. unpunished.

impuntare, –*păntā'rĕ,* v. a. to point, to pierce; –, v. n. to stop, to halt.

impuntire, –*tē'rĕ,* v. a. to sew closely.

impuntura, –*tŏ'rā,* f. knotted needle-work.

impurità, –*pŭrĭtā',* f. impurity. [work.

impuro, –*pŏ'rŏ,* a. impure, obscene.

imputare, –*pŭtā'rĕ,* v. a. to impute, to accuse. [charge.

imputazione, –*tzĭŏ'nĕ,* f. imputation,

imputridire, –*trĭdē'rĕ,* v. n. to putrefy.

impuzzare, –*pŭtzā'rĕ,* **impuzzolire,** –*tzŏlē'rĕ,* v. n. to stink; to rot.

in, pr. in, into, at, on, upon.

inabile, *ĭnā'bĭlĕ,* a. incapable.

inabilità, –*bĭlĭtā',* f. inability.

inabilitare, –*pŭrĭtā',* v. a. to disable.

inabitabile, –*tā'bĭlĕ,* a. uninhabitable.

inacerbire, –*dshĕrbē'rĕ,* v. a. & n. to ex-asperate; to grow angry.

inacetire, –*dshĕtē'rĕ,* v. n. to grow sour.

inacutire, –*ākŭtē'rĕ,* v. a. to whet, to sharpen.

inalberare, –*ālbĕrā'rĕ,* v. a. to climb upon a tree; to plant; to hoist a flag.

inalienabile, –*ălĭĕnā'bĭlĕ,* a. unalienable.

inalterato, –*tĕrā'tŏ,* a. unaltered.

inalzare, –*āltzā'rĕ,* v. a. to raise; to ad-vance.

inamabile, *—ämä′bĕlĕ,* a. disagreeable.

inamidare, *—ämĭdä′rĕ,* v. a. to starch.

inane, *ĭnä′nĕ,* a. inane. [rings, to curl.

inanellare, *—änĕllä′rĕ,* v. a. to put in

inanimato, *—änĭmä′tŏ,* a. lifeless.

inanimire, *—mĕ′rĕ,* v. n. to stimulate, to encourage.

inanità, *—nĭtä′,* f. inanity, futility.

inarcare, *—ärkä′rĕ,* v. a. to arch, to bend.

inargentare, *—ärjĕntä′rĕ,* v. a. to silver over. [dry; to become dry.

inaridire, *—ärĭdĭ′rĕ,* v. a. & n. to make

inaridito, *—ärĭdĭ′tŏ,* a. dried up, withered.

inaspettato, *—äspĕttä′tŏ,* a. unexpected.

inasprire, *—äsprĭ′rĕ,* v. a. to exasperate.

inaugurare, *—äŭgŭrä′rĕ,* v. n. to inaugurate. [to run aground, to stand.

incagliare, *—kälyä′rĕ,* v. a. & n. to stick;

incalciare, *see* **incalzare.**

incallire, *—källĕ′rĕ,* v. n. to grow callous, to indurate.

incalzare, *—kältzä′rĕ,* v. a. to chase, to pursue hotly. [prison.

incamerare, *—kämĕrä′rĕ,* v. a. to im-

incamiciata, *—kämĭdshä′tä,* f. attack by night.

incamminare, *—mĭnä′rĕ,* v. a. to set on foot; to begin; **incamminarsi,** *—när′sĭ,* to set out. [candescent.

incandescente, *—kändĕsshĕn′tĕ,* a. in-

incandescenza, *—sshĕn′tzä,* f. incandescence. [bins; to swallow up.

incannare, *—kännä′rĕ,* v. a. to wind bo-

incantare, *—tä′rĕ,* v. a. to enchant, to bewitch.

incantevole, *—tĕ′vŏlĕ,* a. enchanting.

incanto, *—kän′tŏ,* m. enchantment, charm; public sale. [oneself in a corner.

incantucciarsi, *—tŭtshär′sĭ,* v. r. to hide

incanutire, *—känŭtĕ′rĕ,* v. n. to grow grey.

incapace, *—käpä′dshĕ,* a. incapable, unable.

incapamento, *—mĕn′tŏ,* m. obstinacy.

incaponirsi, *—pŏnĭr′sĭ,* v. r. to grow stubborn.

incappare, *—käppä′rĕ,* v. a. to tie; to wrap up in a cloak; —, v. n. to be caught; to stumble. [love, to be smitten.

incapricciarsi, *—prĭtshär′sĭ,* v. r. to fall in

incarcerare, *—kärdshĕrä′rĕ,* v. a. to im-prison. [charge.

incaricare, *—kärĭkä′rĕ,* v. a. to load, to

incarico, *—kä′rĭkŏ,* m. charge, burden; tax, custom; care; injury, wrong.

incarnare, *—kärnä′rĕ,* v. a. to paint to the life; to stick in the flesh; —, v. n. to in-carnate.

incarnatino, *—tĕ′nŏ,* a. flesh-coloured.

incarnato, *—nä′tŏ,* a. flesh-coloured.

incarnazione, *—tzĭŏ′nĕ,* f. flesh-colour.

incartare, *—tä′rĕ,* v. a. to put in paper.

incartocciare, *—tŏtshä′rĕ,* v. a. to roll up in paper. [up; to cash.

incassare, *—kässä′rĕ,* v. a. to case, to pack

incastonare, *—kästŏnä′rĕ,* v. a. to enchase; to set in. [enchase.

incastrare, *—kästrä′rĕ,* v. a. to mortise, to

incattivire, *—kättĭvĕ′rĕ,* v. n. to grow wicked.

incauto, *—kä′ŭtŏ,* a. incautious, incon-siderate. [hollow.

incavare, *—kävä′rĕ,* v. a. to scoop, to

incavo, *—kä′vŏ,* m. cavity, hollow, hole.

incedere, *—dshĕ′dĕrĕ,* v. n. to walk on, to proceed, to march.

incendio, *—dshĕn′dĭŏ,* m. conflagration.

incenerire, *—dshĕnĕrĕ′rĕ,* v. a. to burn to ashes. [with incense; to extol, to praise.

incensare, *—dshĕnsä′rĕ,* v. a. to perfume

incenso, *—dshĕn′sŏ,* m. incense; (fig.) adulation. [to fetter.

inceppare, *—dshĕppä′rĕ,* v. a. to shackle,

incertezza, *—dshĕrtĕt′zä,* f. uncertainty.

incerto, *—dshĕr′tŏ,* a. uncertain.

incespicare, *—dshĕspĭkä′rĕ,* v. n. to grow, to increase; to cover with turf.

incesto, *—dshĕs′tŏ,* m. incest. [engros-

incettare, *—dshĕttä′rĕ,* v. a. to buy up, to

inchiedere, *—kĭĕ′dĕrĕ,* v. a. ir. to inquire, to search into.

inchiesta, *—kĭĕs′tä,* f. inquest, search.

inchinare, *—kĭnä′rĕ,* v. a. to bend, to bow, to incline; to nod, to assent; —, v. n. to decline.

inchinevole, *—nä′vŏlĕ,* a. inclined, prone.

inchino, *—kĕ′nŏ,* m. bow, salutation.

inchiodare, *—kĭŏdä′rĕ,* v. a. to nail (up); to spike. [nail.

inchiodatura, *—tŏ′rä,* f. prick (of a

inchiostro, *—kĭŏs′trŏ,* m. ink.

inchiudere, *—kĭŏ′dĕrĕ,* v. a. ir. to include, to enclose, to contain. [to trip.

inciampare, *—dshämpä′rĕ,* v.n. to stumble.

inciampo, *—dshäm′pŏ,* m. stumbling; dif-ficulty; risk. [casual event.

incidente, *—dshĭdĕn′tĕ,* a. & m. incidental;

incidenza, *—dĕn′tzä,* f. incidence; hap, chance; digression.

incidere, *—dshĕ′dĕrĕ,* v. a. ir. to cut into, to engrave; to interrupt. [nant.

incingere, *—dshĭn′jĕrĕ,* v. n. ir. to be preg-

incinta, *—dshĕn′tä,* a. pregnant.

incipiente, *—dshĭpĭĕn′tĕ,* a. & m. begin-ning; novice. [virulent.

inciprignire, *—prĭnyĕ′rĕ,* v. n. to grow

incirca, *—dshĕr′kä,* pr. about, concerning.

incisione, *—dshĭsĭŏ′nĕ,* f. incision, slash.

incisore, *—sŏ′rĕ,* m. engraver.

incitamento, *—tämĕn′tŏ,* m. incitement.

incitare, *—tä′rĕ,* v. a. to incite.

incivile, *—vĕ′lĕ,* a. uncivil, ill-bred.

inclemente, *—klĕmĕn′tĕ,* a. inclement.

inclemenza, *—mĕn′tzä,* f. inclemency.

inclinare, *—klĭnä′rĕ,* v. a. & n. to incline, to be prone. [propensity, disposition.

inclinazione, *—tzĭŏ′nĕ,* f. inclination,

inclinevole, *—nä′vŏlĕ,* a. disposed; prone.

inclito, *ĕn′klĭtŏ,* a. illustrious, famous.

includere, *see* **inchiudere.**

inclusa, *—klŏ′sä,* f. enclosed letter.

inclusivo, *—klŭsĕ′vŏ,* a. inclusive.

incogliere, *—kŏl′yĕrĕ,* v. a. ir. to catch; to surprise; —, v. n. to happen.

incognito, *—kŏn′yĭtŏ,* a. unknown; in-cognito.

incollare, *—kŏllä′rĕ,* v. a. to glue.

incollerirsi, *–lĕrŭr'sĭ,* v. r. to fly into a passion.

incolpare, *–pā'rĕ,* v. a. to accuse.

incolto, *–kŏl'tŏ,* a. & p. uncultivated, rude; waste; befallen, happened.

incombenza, *–kŏmbĕn'tzā,* f. incumbency; charge. [mencement, beginning.

incominciamento, *–dshāmĕn'tŏ,* m. commence.

incominciare, *–kŏmĭndshā'rĕ,*v.a.to commence, to begin.

incomodare, *–kŏmŏdā'rĕ,* v. a. to incommode, to disturb, to trouble.

incomodità, *–dĭtā',* f. inconvenience.

incomodo, *–kŏ'mŏdŏ,* a. inconvenient, troublesome; —, m. disadvantage, trouble.

incompetente, *–kŏmpĕtĕn'tĕ,* a. incompetent, unqualified.

incompetenza, *–tĕn'tzā,* f. incompetency.

inconsolabile, *–kŏnsŏlā'bĭlĕ,* a. inconsolable.

incontaminato, *–kŏntāmĭnā'tŏ,* a. incorrupt. [tely, at once.

incontanente, *–tānĕn'tĕ,* ad. immediately.

incontinente, *–tĭnĕn'tĕ,* a. incontinent, unchaste.

incontinenza, *–nĕn'tzā,* f. incontinence.

incontra, *–kŏn'trā,* pr. against; **all –,** on the contrary.

incontrare, *–trā'rĕ,* v. a. to meet (with); —, v. n. to happen, to befall; **incontrarsi,** *–trăr'sĭ,* to fall in with.

incontro, *–kŏn'trŏ,* pr. against, opposite, towards; **andare all' – di uno,** to go to meet; —, ad. contrarily; —, m. meeting, encounter; chance.

inconveniente, *–vĕnĭĕn'tĕ,* m. inconveniency. [–dji'rĕ, v. a. to encourage.

incoraggiare, *–kŏrădjā'rĕ,* **incoraggire,** *–kŏrā'rĕ,* v. a.& n. to persuade; to animate; to take into one's head.

incordare, *–kŏrdā'rĕ,* v. a. & n. to string an instrument; to grow stiff. [to border.

incorniciare, *–nĭdshā'rĕ,* v. a. to frame;

incoronare, *–kŏrŏnā'rĕ,* v. a. to crown.

incoronazione, *–tzĭŏ'nĕ,* f. coronation.

incorporare, *–kŏrpŏrā'rĕ,* v. a. to incorporate, to embody. [tion.

incorporazione, *–tzĭŏ'nĕ,* f. incorporation.

incorporeo, *–pŏ'rĕŏ,* a. incorporeal, immaterial. [material.

incorre, *see* **incogliere,**

incorreggibile, *–rĕdjĕ'bĭlĕ,*a. incorrigible.

incorrere, *–kŏr'rĕrĕ,* v. a. & n. ir. to incur, to fall into, to become liable to.

incorrotto, *–rŏt'tŏ,* a. incorrupt, pure.

incorso, *–kŏr'sŏ,* m. meeting, encounter,

incoscienza, *–kŏsshĕn'tzā,*f. unconsciousness. [stable.

incostante, *–kŏstān'tĕ,* a. inconstant, unstable.

incostanza, *–tān'tzā,* f. inconstancy, variableness; fickleness.

incotto, *–kŏt'tŏ,* a. scorched, sun-burnt.

increato, *–krĕā'tŏ,* a. increate.

incredibile, *–krĕdĭ'bĭlĕ,* a. incredible.

incredulità, *–dŭlĭtā',* f. incredulity.

incredulo, *–krĕ'dŭlŏ,* a. incredulous.

incremento, *–krĕmĕn'tŏ,* m. increase.

increscere, *–krĕssh'ĕrĕ,* v. n. ir. to be sorry; to be tired; to commiserate.

increscioso, *–sshŏ'sŏ,* a. tiresome, tedious.

increspare, *–krĕspā'rĕ,* v. a. to curl, to crisp. [(mar.) to cruise,

incrociare, *–krŏdshā'rĕ,* v. a. to cross;

incrociatura, *–tŏ'rā,* (mar.) stack *or* crown of the anchor.

incrostare, *–krŏstā'rĕ,* v. a. to incrust, to plaster. [cruel.

incrudelire, *–krŭdĕlĭ'rĕ,* v. n. to grow

incruento, *–krŭĕn'tŏ,* a. bloodless, unstained with blood.

incubo, *ĭn'kŭbŏ,* m. incubus, night-mare.

incudine, *–kŏ'dĭnĕ,* f. anvil.

inculcare, *–kĭlkā'rĕ,* v. a. to inculcate,

inculto, *–kŭl'tŏ,* a. uncultivated.

incumbenza, *–kŭmbĕn'tzā,* f.incumbency, charge. [one's head.

incuorare, *–kŏŏrā'rĕ,* v. a. & n. to put into

incuria, *–kŏ'rĭā,* f. negligence, carelessness.

incursione, *–kŭrsĭŏ'nĕ,* f. invasion.

incurvare, *–vā'rĕ,* v. a. to curve, to bend.

incutere, *–kŏ'tĕrĕ,* v. a. ir. to strike into; [to instil.

indaco, *ĭn'dākŏ,* m. indigo. [to instil.

indagare, *–dāgā'rĕ,* v. a. to search into, to inquire.

indagine, *–dā'jĭnĕ,* f. investigation.

indanaiare, *–dānāĭā'rĕ,* v. a. to speckle, to stain.

indarno, *–dăr'nŏ,* ad. in vain.

indebitamente, *–dĕbĭtāmĕn'tĕ,*ad.unduly, wrongfully.

indebitirsi, *–tĭr'sĭ,* v. r. to run into debt.

indebolire, *–dĕbŏlĭ'rĕ,* v. a. & n. to weaken; to grow weak.

indefesso, *–fĕs'sŏ,* a. unwearied.

indefinito, *–fĭnĭ'tŏ,* a. indefinite.

indegnamente, *–dĕnyāmĕn'tĕ,* ad. unworthily.

indegnità, *–nyĭtā',* f. indignity, affront.

indegno, *–dĕn'yŏ,* a. unworthy, bad, dishonourable.

indelebile, *–dĕlĕ'bĭlĕ,* a. indelible.

indemoniato, *–mŏnĭā'tŏ,* a. possessed with a devil.

indenne, *–dĕn'nĕ,* a. indemnified, unhurt.

indennità, *–nĭtā',* f. indemnity; compensation. [demnify.

indennizzare, *–nĭdzā'rĕ,* v. a. to indemnify.

indennizzazione, *–tzĭŏ'nĕ,* f. indemnification. [termine.

indettare, *–dĕttā'rĕ,* v. a. to agree, to determine.

indi, *ĭn'dĭ,* ad. thence, afterwards; **– a poco,** soon after.

indiana, *–dĭā'nā,* f. printed calico.

indiavolato, *see* **indemoniato.**

indicare, *–dĭkā'rĕ,* v. a. to indicate.

indicativo, *–tĭ'vŏ,* m. (gr.) indicative mood.

indice, *ĭn'dĭdshĕ,* m. index; forefinger.

indicibile, *–dshĕ'bĭlĕ,* a. unspeakable, ineffable. [back; to recoil.

indietreggiare, *–dĭĕtrĕdjā'rĕ,* v. n. to go

indietro, *–dĭĕ'trŏ,* ad. backwards, after, behind. [careless.

indifferente, *–dĭffĕrĕn'tĕ,* a. indifferent,

indifferenza, *–rĕn'tzā,* f. indifference.

indigeno, *–dĕ'jĕnŏ,* a. indigenous.

indigente, *–dĭjĕn'tĕ,* a. indigent, in want.

indigenza, –jĕn′tzā, f. indigence, want.
indigestione, –jĕstĭŏ′nĕ, f. indigestion.
indigesto, –jĕs′tŏ, a. undigested; crude.
indignarsi, –dīnyär′sĭ, v. r. to be indignant, to grow angry.
indignato, –yā′tŏ, a. angry, provoked.
indignazione, –yätzĭŏ′nĕ, f. indignation.
indigrosso, –ātgrŏs′sŏ, a. one with another, in the gross, in a lump.
indipendente, –pĕndĕn′tĕ, a. independent.
indipendenza, –dĕn′tzā, f. independence;
freedom.
indire, –dĕ′rĕ, v. a. to intimate.
indirettamente, –dīrĕttämĕn′tĕ, ad. in-
indiretto, –rĕt′tŏ, a. indirect. [directly.
indirizzare, –rĭtzär′rĕ, v. a. to show the
way; to address (a letter).
indirizzo, –rĭt′zŏ, m. direction; address.
indiscreto, –dĭskrĕ′tŏ, a. indiscreet.
indiscrezione, –krĕtzĭŏ′nĕ, f. indiscretion.
indispensabile, –pĕnsā′bĭlĕ, a. indispensable. [sition; disinclination.
indisposizione, –pŏsĭtzĭŏ′nĕ, f. indispo-
indisposto, –pŏs′tŏ, a. out of order, confused; indisposed, ill; disinclined.
indissolubile, –sŏlŏ′bĭlĕ, a. indissoluble.
indissolubilità, –lĭbĭlĭtā′ f. indissolu-
bility. [distinctly.
indistintamente, –tĭntämĕn′tĕ, ad. in-
indistinto, –tĭn′tŏ, a. indistinct.
indivia, –dĕ′vĭā, f. (bot.) endive, succory.
individuale, –dĭvĭdŏā′lĕ, a. individual,
personal.
individualità, –dāhĭtā′, f. individuality.
individuare, –dŏā′rĕ, v. a. to individuate,
to specify. [tion, specification.
individuazione, –tzĭŏ′nĕ, f. individua-
individuo, –vĕ′dŏŏ, a. individual; inseparable; –, m. individual.
indivisibile, –vĭsĭ′bĭlĕ, a. indivisible, inseparable.
indiviso, –vĕ′sŏ, a. undivided, whole.
indiziare, –dĭtzĭā′rĕ, v. a. to indicate; to
cause suspicion.
indizio, –dĕ′tzĭŏ, m. sign, token.
indocile, –dŏ′dshĭlĕ, a. indocile.
indole, ĕn′dŏlĕ, f. natural disposition; nature, inclination.
indolente, –dŏlĕn′tĕ, a. indolent, inert.
indolenza, –lĕn′tzā, f. indolence.
indolenzire, –lĕntzĕ′rĕ, v. n. to become
benumbed. [ache.
indolorimento, –dŏlŏrēmĕn′tŏ, m. pain,
indomito, –dŏ′mĭtŏ, a. untamed, unruly;
fierce.
indorare, –dŏrä′rĕ, v. a. to gild; to adorn.
indossare, –dŏssä′rĕ, v. a. to wear (clothes);
(com.) to indorse. [about.
indosso, –dŏs′sŏ, ad. upon one's back, on;
indotto, –dŏt′tŏ, a. induced, persuaded.
indovinare, –dŏvēnä′rĕ, v. a. to divine.
indovinello, –nĕl′lŏ, m. riddle, enigma.
indovino, –vĕ′nŏ, m. diviner. [to rage.
indracare, –drākä′rĕ, v. n. to get furious,
indubitabile, –dŭbĭtā′bĭlĕ, a. indubitable.
indubitabilmente, –bĭlmĕn′tĕ, ad. un-
doubtedly. [long.
indugiare, –dŭĭä′rĕ, v. a. to delay, to pro-

indugio, –dŏ′jŏ, m. delay, prolonging.
indulgente, –dŭljĕn′tĕ, a. indulgent, kind.
indulgenza, –jĕn′tzā, f. indulgence. [pl.
indumento, –dŭmĕn′tŏ, m. dress, clothes,
indurare, –dŭrä′rĕ, indurire, –rĕ′rĕ,
v. a. & n. to harden; to grow hard; to
grow hard-hearted; indurarsi, –rär′sĭ,
to grow stubborn.
indurre, –dŭr′rĕ, v. a. ir. to induce, to
draw on; to occasion; indursi. –dŭr′sĭ,
to decide, to determine.
industre, see industrioso.
industria, –dŭs′trĭā, f. industry; diligence; skill. [hard, to do one's best.
industriarsi, –trĭär′sĭ, v. r. to strive
industrioso, –trĭŏ′sŏ, a. industrious.
induzione, –dŭtzĭŏ′nĕ, f. inducement.
inebriare, –ĕbrĭä′rĕ, v. a. to make drunk.
inedia, –ĕ′dĭā, f. abstinence, diet; utmost
necessity or exigency.
inedito, –ĕ′dĭtŏ, a. unedited, unpublished.
ineffabile, –ĕffā′bĭlĕ, a. unspeakable.
ineguale, –ĕgŭā′lĕ, a. unequal; rough,
rugged. [ness, disparity.
ineguralità, –lĭtā′, f. inequality, uneven-
inerente, –ĕrĕn′tĕ, a. inherent; inborn.
inerme, –ĕr′mĕ, a. unarmed; defenceless.
inerpicare, –pĭkä′rĕ, v. r. to climb.
inerte, –ĕr′tĕ, a. inert, lazy, dull.
inescare, –ĕskä′rĕ, v. a. to bait, to allure.
inesorabile, –ĕsŏrā′bĭlĕ, a. inexorable.
inesorabilmente, –bĭlmĕn′tĕ, ad. in-
exorably. [ence.
inesperienza, –ĕspĕrĭĕn′tzā, f, inexperi-
inesperto, –pĕr′tŏ, a. inexpert, unskilful.
inestimabile, –ĕstĭmā′bĭlĕ, a. inestimable
inetto, –ĕt′tŏ, a. inept, unfit.
inevitabile, –ĕvĭtā′bĭlĕ, a. inevitable.
inezia, –ĕ′tzĭā, f. folly, nonsense.
infallibile, –fällĭ′bĭlĕ, a. infallible.
infamare, –fämä′rĕ, v. a. to defame.
infamatorio, –tŏ′rĭŏ, a. defamatory.
infame, –fä′mĕ, a. infamous; base, mean.
infamia, –fä′mĭā, f. infamy.
infanciullire, –fändshĭllĕ′rĕ, v. n. to become childish.
infante, –fän′tĕ, m. child; Infant (title).
infanteria, –tĕrĕ′ā, f. infantry. [child.
infanticida, –tĭdshĕ′dā, m. murderer of a
infanticidio, –dshĕ′dĭŏ, m. infanticide.
infarcire, –färdshĕ′rĕ, v. a. to stuff.
infardare, –dä′rĕ, v. a. to besmear with
spittle, to foul. [flour.
infarinare, –färĭnä′rĕ, v. a. to cover with
infastidire, –fästĭdĕ′rĕ, v. a. to make
fastidious; to disturb.
infatuare, –fätŭä′rĕ, v. a. to infatuate.
infecondo, –fĕkŏn′dŏ, a. unfruitful, sterile.
infecondità, –dĭtā′, f. infecundity, sterility.
infedele, –fĕdĕ′lĕ, a. unfaithful; disloyal.
infedeltà, –dĕltā′, f. infidelity, perfidy.
infelice, –fĕlĕ′dshĕ, a. unhappy.
inferiore, –rĭŏ′rĕ, a. inferior; subordinate.
inferire, –rĕ′rĕ, v. a. to infer, to conclude.
infermare, –fĕrmä′rĕ, v. a. to make sick;
infermarsi, –mär′sĭ, to get infirm; to
fall sick. [tagion.
infermeria, ĭĕrĕ′ā, f. infirmary; con-

infermiccio, *—mĕt′shŏ,* a. rather infirm; sickly, poorly.

infermità, *—mĭtä′,* f. infirmity; sickness.

infermo, *—fĕr′mŏ,* a. infirm; sick.

infernale, *—nä′lĕ,* a. hellish. [—, m. hell.

inferno, *—fĕr′nŏ,* a. infernal; very wicked;

infervorare, *—vŏrä′rĕ,* v. a. to animate, to make fervid, to render zealous.

infestare, *—fĕstä′rĕ,* v. a. to importune, to tease.

infesto, *—fĕs′tŏ,* a. importunate, tiresome.

infettare, *—fĕttä′rĕ,* v. a. to infect.

infettivo, *—tĕ′vŏ,* a. infective, tainting.

infeudare, *—fĕŭdä′rĕ,* v. a. to enfeoff.

infezione, *—fĕtzĭŏ′nĕ,* f. infection.

infiacchire, *—fĭäkkĕ′rĕ,* v. a. to weaken, to slacken, to flag.

infiammare, *—fĭämmä′rĕ,* v. a. to inflame, to kindle; to illuminate; to excite.

infiammatorio, *—mätŏ′rĭŏ,* a. inflammatory.

infiammazione, *—tzĭŏ′nĕ,* f. inflammation.

infiascare, *—fĭäskä′rĕ,* v. a. to bottle.

infievolire, *—fĭĕvŏlĕ′rĕ,* v. a. to enfeeble.

infiggere, *—fĭd′jĕrĕ,* v. a. ir. to nail, to drive in.

inficcappi, *—fĭäkäp′pĭ,* m. hair-pin.

infilare, *—fĭlä′rĕ,* v. a. to thread; to file.

infilzare, *—fĭltzä′rĕ,* v. a. to string, to thread.

infimo, *ĭn′fĭmŏ,* a. lowest; vilest; utmost.

infinattanto(chè), *—fĭnättän′tŏ(kĕ′),* ad.

infin, *ĭnfĭn′,* for: infino. [until (that).

infine, *—fĕ′nĕ,* ad. at last.

infingardaggine, *—ĭngärdäd′jĭnĕ,* f. laziness, idleness.

infingardo, *—gär′dŏ,* a. lazy, slothful.

infingere, *—fĭn′jĕrĕ,* v. n. ir. to feign, to dissemble.

infinità, *—fĭnĭtä′,* f. infinity.

infinitamente, *—mĕn′tĕ,* ad. infinitely.

infinitivo, *—tĕ′vŏ,* m. (gr.) infinitive mood.

infinito, *—fĭnĭ′tŏ,* a. endless.

infino, *—fĕ′nŏ,* pr. till, until, from, as far as; — ad ora, till now; — allora, till then; — a qui, hitherto; — a quando? till when? how long?

infinocchiare, *—fĭnŏkkĭä′rĕ,* v. a. to make one believe; to deceive.

infinta, *—fĕn′tä,* f. feint, dissimulation.

infiorare, *—fĭŏrä′rĕ,* v. a. to adorn with flowers.

inflessibile, *—flĕss′ĭbĭlĕ,* a. inflexible.

inflettere, *—flĕt′tĕrĕ,* v. a. ir. to bow, to bend.

infliggere, *—flĭd′jĕrĕ,* v. a. to inflict.

influenza, *—flŭĕn′tzä,* f. influence.

influire, *—flŭĕ′rĕ,* v. a. to influence, to sway.

influsso, *—flŭs′sŏ,* m. influx; influence.

infocare, *—fŏkä′rĕ,* v. a. to inflame; to make red-hot. [mud.

infognare, *—fŏnyä′rĕ,* v. a. to stick in the

infondere, *—fŏn′dĕrĕ,* v. a. ir. to infuse; to soak. [fork; to mount; to hang.

inforcare, *—fŏrkä′rĕ,* v. a. to catch with a

informare, *—mä′rĕ,* v. a. to inform, to instruct; to prepare, to qualify.

informazione, *—tzĭŏ′nĕ,* f. information, instruction.

informe, *—fŏr′mĕ,* a. formless, shapeless.

infornare, *—nä′rĕ,* v. a. to put into the oven.

infortire, *—tĕ′rĕ,* v. a. & n. to strengthen, to grow sour. [unhappy.

infortunato, *—tŭnä′tŏ,* a. unfortunate,

infortunio, *—tŏ′nĭŏ,* m. ill-fortune, disaster.

inforzare, *see* infortire.

infossare, *—fŏssä′rĕ,* v. a. to lay in the grave.

infossato, *—sä′tŏ,* a. deepened, hollow.

infra, *ĭn′frä,* pr. among, between; about.

infracidamento, *—frädshĭdämĕn′tŏ,* m. putrefaction.

infracidare, *—dshĭdä′rĕ,* v. a. & n. to importune, to weary; to putrefy.

infralire, *—frälĕ′rĕ,* v. a. & n. to weaken; to grow frail or weak.

inframmessa, *—mĕs′sä,* f. interposition, mediation.

inframmettere, *—mĕt′tĕrĕ,* v. a. ir. to interpose, to mediate. [to crush.

infrangere, *—frän′jĕrĕ,* v. a. ir. to break,

infrangibile, *—jĕ′bĭlĕ,* a. infrangible, inviolable. [branches.

infrascare, *—fräskä′rĕ,* v. a. to cover with

infreddare, *—frĕddä′rĕ,* v. a. to make cold, to cool; —, v. n. to catch cold.

infreddatura, *—tŏŏrä,* f. cold, rheum.

infrenare, *—frĕnä′rĕ,* v. a. to bridle; to restrain, to keep in check.

infruscare, *—früskä′rĕ,* v. a. to confuse.

infruttifero, *—früttĭ′fĕrŏ,* a. fruitless, useless.

infundibolo, *—fŭndĕ′bŏlŏ,* m. funnel.

infuocare, *see* infocare.

infuriare, *—fŭrĭä′rĕ,* v. n., **infuriarsi,** *—rär′sĭ,* to be furious, to rage. [tion.

infusione, *—fŭsĭŏ′nĕ,* f. infusion; inspira-

infuturarsi, *—fŭtŭrär′sĭ,* v. r. to stretch into the future; to grow old.

ingabbiare, *—gäbbĭä′rĕ,* v. a. to cage; to shut up.

ingaggiare, *—gädjä′rĕ,* v. a. to engage, to pledge; to oppose, to fight.

ingagliardire, *—gälyärdĕ′rĕ,* v. a. & n. to make strong; to reinforce; to grow strong.

ingalluzzarsi, *—gälltĭtzär′sĭ,* v. r. to carry one's head high; to be proud.

ingannare, *—gännä′rĕ,* v. a. to deceive, to cheat; **ingannarsi,** *—när′sĭ,* to be mistaken.

ingannatore, *—tŏ′rĕ,* m. deceiver.

ingannevole, *—nä′vŏlĕ,* a. deceitful.

inganno, *—gän′nŏ,* m. deceit, trick; mistake.

ingegnarsi, *—jĕnyär′sĭ,* v. r. to endeavour, to exert oneself.

ingegnere, *—yĕ′rĕ,* m. engineer.

ingegneria, *—yĕrĕ′ä,* f. art of engineering.

ingegno, *—jĕn′yŏ,* m. natural talent; wit, genius; cunning.

ingegnoso, *—yŏ′sŏ,* a. ingenious, witty.

ingenerare, *—jĕnĕrä′rĕ,* v. a. to engender.

ingenito, *—jĕ′nĭtŏ,* a. innate, inborn.

ingentilire, *—jĕntĭlĕ′rĕ,* v. a. to make noble; to tame.

ingenuo, *—jĕ′nŭŏ,* a. ingenuous, sincere.

ingerire, *—jĕrĕ′rĕ,* v. a. to adduce; **ingerirsi,** *—rĕr′sĭ,* to meddle with.

inghiottire, *-ghêŏttê'rê,* v. a. to swallow, to absorb. [crown with a garland.
inghirlandare, *-ghîrlândä'rê,* v. a. to
ingiallire, *-jâllê'rê,* v. a. & n. to make yellow; to grow yellow.
inginocchiarsi, *-jînŏkkêâr'sî,* v. r. to kneel down. [stool.
inginocchiatoio, *-kêâtō'ŏ,* m. kneeling-
ingiovanire, *-jŏvânê'rê,* v. n. to grow young again.
ingiù, *-jû',* ad. down. [to command.
ingiungere, *-jûn'jerê,* v. a. ir. to enjoin;
ingiuria, *-jô'rîä,* f. injury, wrong, offence.
ingiuriare, *-jûrä'rê,* v. a. to injure, to offend.
ingiurioso, *-rî'ŏ'sŏ,* a. injurious.
ingiustamente, *-jûstämên'tê,* ad. unjustly, wrongfully.
ingiustizia, *-jûsî'tzîä,* f. injustice; injury.
ingiusto, *-jûs'tŏ,* a. unjust, wrongful.
ingoiare, *-gŏä'rê,* v. a. to swallow down, to swallow up, to ingulf.
ingolfare, *-gŏlfä'rê,* v. a. to enter a gulf.
ingollare, *-gŏllä'rê,* v. a. to swallow.
ingombrare, *-gŏmbrä'rê,* v. a. to encumber, to embarrass.
ingombro, *-gŏm'brŏ,* m. incumbrance, clog; nuisance.
ingordigia, *-gŏrdâ'jä,* f. greediness.
ingordo, *-gŏr'dŏ,* a. greedy, eager; exorbitant. [to fill up.
ingorgare, *-gä'rê,* v. a. to gorge, to stuff,
ingozzare, *-gŏtzä'rê,* v. a. to swallow, to gorge.
ingrandire, *-grândê'rê,* v. a. & n. to aggrandize; to rise; to increase.
ingrassare, *-grässä'rê,* v. a. to fatten.
ingraticolare, *-grätîkŏlä'rê,* v. a. to enclose with rails, to rail in.
ingratitudine, *-ttû'dînê,* f. ingratitude.
ingrato, *-grä'tŏ,* a. ungrateful; disagreeable. [impregnate; to be pregnant.
ingravidare, *-grävîdä'rê,* v. a. & n. to
ingrediente, *-grêdiên'tê,* m. ingredient.
ingresso, *-grês'sŏ,* m. ingress, entrance.
ingrognare, *-grŏnyä'rê,* v. n. to be angry, to grow surly.
ingrossare, *-grŏssä'rê,* v. a. & n. to make big; **ingrossarsi,** *-sär'sî,* to grow big or thick; to grow angry; to swell up; to get with child; to conceive. [lump.
ingrosso, *-grŏs'sŏ,* ad. wholesale, in the
inguine, *în'gûînê,* m. groin.
inibire, *-îbê'rê,* v. a. to inhibit, to forbid.
inibizione, *-îbîtziŏ'nê,* f. inhibition, prohibition, interdiction.
inimicare, *-îmîkä'rê,* v. a. to treat like an enemy. [trary.
inimichevole, *-kâ'vŏlê,* a. hostile; con-
inimicizia, *-îshî'tzîä,* f. enmity.
inimico, *-îmê'kŏ,* m. enemy. [tously.
iniquamente, *-îkûämên'tê,* ad. iniqui-
iniquità, *-îkûîtä',* f. iniquity.
iniquo, *-ê'kûŏ,* a. iniquitous.
iniziale, *-îtziä'lê,* a. initial, first.
iniziare, *-îtziä'rê,* v. a. to initiate.
inizio, *-ê'tziŏ,* m. beginning.
iniettare, *-îêttä'rê,* v. a. to inject.

innacquare, *-äkkûä'rê,* v. a. to water; to dilute. [moisten, to sprinkle.
innaffiare, *-äfiä'rê,* v. a. to water, to
innaffiatoio, *-tô'ŏ,* m. watering-pot.
innamorare, *-ïnnämŏrä'rê,* v. a. to inspire with love; **innamorarsi,** *-rär'sî,* to become enamoured, to fall in love. [heart.
innamorata, *-rä'tä,* f. mistress, sweet-
innamorato, *-rä'tŏ,* m. lover, [before.
innante, *-än'tê,* **innanti,** *-tê,* pr. (poet.)
innanzi, *-än'tzî,* pr. before; above; in presence; of in preference to; —, ad. sooner, forward, before; rather, better; afterwards; —, m. model, pattern, original.
innaspare, *-äspä'rê,* v. a. & n. to wind up; to be delirious.
innato, *-nä'tŏ,* a. inborn.
innaturale, *-nätûrä'lê,* a. unnatural.
innestare, *-nêstä'rê,* v. a. to graft, to inoculate.
innesto, *-nês'tŏ,* m. graft, shoot.
inno, *ên'nŏ,* m. hymn. [less.
innocente, *-nŏdshên'tê,* a. innocent, harm-
innocenza, *-dshên'tzä,* f. innocence; simplicity.
innocuo, *-nŏ'kûŏ,* a. innocuous, harmless.
innovare, *-nŏvä'rê,* v. a. to renew.
innovazione, *-tziŏ'nê,* f. innovation.
innumerabile, *-nûmêrä'bîlê,* a. innumerable. [desire.
innuzzolire, *-nätzŏlê'rê,* v. a. to excite ?
inobbedienza, *see* disubbidienza.
inoculare, *-ŏkûlä'rê,* v. n. to inoculate.
inoculazione, *-tziŏ'nê,* f. inoculation.
inoliare, *-ŏliä'rê,* v. a. to anoint, to oil.
inoltrarsi, *-ŏlträr'sî,* v. r. to advance to exceed.
inoltre, *-ŏl'trê,* ad. besides, moreover.
inondare, *-ŏndä'rê,* v. a. to inundate, to submerge, to flood.
inondazione, *-tziŏ'nê,* f. inundation.
inonestà, *-ŏnêstä',* f. dishonesty.
inonesto, *-ŏnês'tŏ,* a. dishonest.
inopia, *-ŏ'pîä,* f. want, penury, need.
inopinato, *-ŏpînä'tŏ,* a. unexpected.
inopportuno, *-ŏppŏrtû'nŏ,* a. unseasonable. [to honour.
inorare, *-ŏrä'rê,* v. a. to gild; to respect,
inorgoglire, *-ŏrgŏlyê'rê,* v. a. to make proud; **inorgogliarsi,** *-lyär'sî,* **inorgoglirsi,** *-lyîr'sî,* to grow proud.
inottusire, *-ŏttûsê'rê,* v. n. to grow blunt or blunt.
inquietare, *-kûêtä'rê,* v. a. to disquiet, to disturb; to vex; **inquietarsi,** *-tär'-sî,* to be uneasy.
inquieto, *-kûîê'tŏ,* a. uneasy, restless.
inquilino, *-kûîlê'nŏ,* m. tenant, inmate.
inquinare, *-kûînä'rê,* v. a. to soil, to stain.
inquisire, *-kûîsê'rê,* v. a. to impeach, to charge, to accuse. [sitor.
inquisitore, *-sîtô'rê,* m. inquirer; inqui-
inquisizione, *-sîtziô'nê,* f. inquisition, search, examination.
insaccare, *-säkkä'rê,* v. a. to put into a sack or bag; to pocket.
insalata, *-sälä'tä,* f. salad.

insalatiera, –tĭă´ră, f. salad-dish.
insaldare, –săldă´rĕ, v. a. to solder; to starch; to fortify; to heal up.
insania, –să´nĭĭ, f. insanity, madness.
insanire, –săné rĕ, v. n. to grow insane or mad.
insano, –să´nŏ, a. insane, mad.
insaponare, –săpŏnă´rĕ, v. a. to wash with soap; (fig.) to flatter.
insaziabile, –sătsĭă´bĭlĕ, a. insatiable; insatiate.
insaziabilità, –bĭlĭtă´, f. insatiableness.
insciente, –sshĭĕn´tĕ, a. ignorant.
inscrivere, –skré vĕrĕ, v. a. ir. to inscribe; to address (a letter). [title, address.
inscrizione, –skrĭtzĭŏ´nĕ, f. inscription;
insecutore, –sĕkŭtŏ´rĕ, m. prosecutor, pursuer. [session.
insediare, –sădĭă´rĕ, v. a. to put in possession.
insegna, –sĕn´yă, f. banner, standard; ensign; flag; sign, mark; arms; ensign-bearer. [inform.
insegnare, –yă´rĕ, v. a. to instruct, to
inseguimento, –sĕgŭĭmĕn´tŏ, m. pursuit.
inseguire, –sĕgŭé rĕ, v. . to pursue.
inselvarsi, –sĕlvăr´sĭ, v. r. to get woody; to grow savage. [wild.
inselvaticare, –tĭkă´rĕ, v. n. to grow
insenatura, –sĕnătŏ´ră, f. creek, bay.
insensato, –sĕnsă´tŏ, a. insensate, foolish.
insensibile, –sĕ´bĭlĕ, a. insensible.
insensibilmente, –mĕn´tĕ, ad. insensibly; gradually.
inseparabile, –săpără´bĭlĕ, a. inseparable.
inserire, –sĕré rĕ, v. a. to insert.
inserviente, –vĭĕn´tĕ, a. serviceable, useful.
inserzione, –tzĭŏ´nĕ, f. insertion. [ful.
insetto, –sĕt´tŏ, m. insect.
insidia, –sĕ´dĭă, f. ambush, snare, deceit.
insidiare, –sĭdĭă´rĕ, v. a. to lie in wait.
insidioso, –dĭŏ´sŏ, a. insidious, treacherous, sly. [whole, mass.
insieme, –sĭă´mĕ, ad. together; –, m.
insigne, –sĭn´yĕ, a. notable, famous.
insignificante, –yĭfĭkăn´tĕ, a. insignificant. [adorn; to signalize.
insignire, –yĕ´rĕ, v. a. to decorate; to
insignorire, –yŏré´rĕ, v. a. to make master of; **insignorirsi,** –rĭr´sĭ, to make oneself master of.
insino, –sé nŏ, c. till, until.
insinuare, –sĭnŭă´rĕ, v. a. to insinuate.
insinuazione, –tzĭŏ´nĕ, f. insinuation.
insipido, –sé pĭdŏ, a. insipid.
insipiente, –sĭpĭĕn´tĕ, a. silly.
insipienza, –pĭĕn´tză, f. want of understanding. [persist.
insistere, –sĭs´tĕrĕ, v. n. ir. to insist, to
insito, ĭn´sĭtŏ, a. innate, natural.
insolcare, –sŏlkă´rĕ, v. a. to trace the plan of an edifice; to furrow.
insolente, –sŏlĕn´tĕ, a. insolent, arrogant.
insolenza, –lĕn´tză, f. insolence, sauciness.
insolito, –sŏ´lĭtŏ, a. unusual, rare.
insollare, –sŏllă´rĕ, v. a. to soften; to weaken; to frustrate; –, v. n. to soften.
insollire, –lĭ´rĕ, v. n. to rise up in arms.
insonne, –sŏn´nĕ, a. unsleeping.

insorgere, –sŏr´jĕrĕ, v. n. ir. to rise up; to rebel.
insozzare, –sŏtză´rĕ, **insozzire,** –sŏtzĕ´rĕ, v. a. & n. to soil.
instigare, ĭnstĭgă´rĕ, v. n. to instigate.
instillare, ĭnstĭllă´rĕ, v a. to instil; to insinuate. [to foul.
insudiciare, –sădĭdshă´rĕ, v. a. to soil,
insueto, –sŭĕ´tĭ, a. unused.
insulso, –sŭl´sŏ, a. foolish, silly, stupid.
insultare, –sŭltă´rĕ, v. a. to insult.
insulto, –sŭl´tŏ, m. insult.
insuperbire, –săpĕrbé rĕ, v.n., **insuperbirsi,** –bĭr´sĭ, to grow proud.
insuso, –să´sŏ, ad. on high, above.
insussistente, –sŭssĭstĕn´tĕ, a. non-existent; unreal.
insussistenza, –tĕn´tză, f. unreality.
intaccare, –tăkkă´rĕ, v. a. to notch; to hurt.
intagliare, –tălyă´rĕ, v. a. to engrave, to carve; – **ad acqua forte,** to etch.
intagliatore, –tŏ´rĕ, m. carver, engraver.
intaglio, –tăl´yŏ, m. engraving, cut, sculpture; (rail.) open cutting. [in a den.
intanarsi, –tănăr´sĭ, v. n. to hide oneself
intangibile, –tănjé´bĭlĕ, a. intangible.
intanto, –tăn´tŏ, ad. in so far, inasmuch; whilst.
intantochè, –tŏkĕ´, ad. & c. whilst, till.
intarlare, –tărlă´rĕ, v. n. to grow worm-eaten. [up.
intasare, –tăsă´rĕ, v. a. to stop or bung
intascare, –tăskă´rĕ, v. a. to pocket; to seize. [pure; whole.
intatto, –tăt´tŏ, a. untouched; untainted,
intavolare, –tăvŏlă´rĕ, v. a. to wainscot, to rail in; to set to music.
intavolato, –lă´tŏ, m. ceiling, wainscot.
integerrimo, –tĕjĕr´rĭmŏ, a. very integral; incorruptible.
integrale, –tĕgră´lĕ, a. integral, principal.
integrare, –gră´rĕ, v. a. to make entire, to complete.
integrità, –grĭtă´, f. integrity.
integro, ĭntĕ´grŏ, a. entire, complete; upright. [cover.
integumento, –tĕgŭmĕn´tŏ, m. integument,
intelaiare, –lăă´rĕ, v. a. to put in the loom. [cass.
intelaiatura, –tŏ´ră, f. frame-work; car-
intellettivo, –tĕllĕtĭ´vŏ, a. intellectual.
intelletto, –lĕt´tŏ, m. intellect, understanding; sense.
intellettuale, –lĕttŭă´lĕ, a. intellectual.
intellezione, –tzĭŏ´nĕ, f. intelligence; judgment. [learned.
intelligente, –lĭjĕn´tĕ, a. intelligent,
intelligenza, –jĕn´tză, f. intelligence, cleverness.
intelligibile, –jé´bĭlĕ, a. intelligible.
intemerato, –tĕmĕră´tŏ, a. inviolate.
intempestivo, –pĕstĭ´vŏ, a. unseasonable.
intendente, –tĕndĕn´tĕ, m. intendant; –, a. intelligent, attentive.
intendenza, –dĕn´tză, f. understanding, knowledge; intendant. [stand; to intend.
intendere, –tĕn´dĕrĕ, v. a. ir. to under-

intendimento, –dĭmĕn'tŏ, m. judgment; intention.

intenebrare, –tĕnĕbrä'rĕ, v. a. to darken.

intenerire, –tĕnĕrē'rĕ, v. a. to make tender, to soften; **intenerirsi,** –rīr'sī, to be moved. [intense, piercing.

intensivo, –sē'vŏ, **intenso,** –tĕn'sŏ, a.

intentare, –tĕntä'rĕ, v. a. to attempt.

intento, –tĕn'tŏ, a. attentive, diligent; –, m. intention, purpose. [meaning.

intenzione, –tzĭŏ'nĕ, f. intention, purpose;

intepidire, see **intiepidire.**

interamente, –tĕrämĕn'tĕ, ad. entirely, quite. [calate.

intercalare, ĭntĕrkälä'rĕ, v. a. to inter-

intercedere, –dshä'dĕrĕ, v. n. r. & ir. to intercede. [cession.

intercessione, –dshĕssĭŏ'nĕ, f. inter-

intercettare, –dshĕttä'rĕ, v. a. to inter-cept. [close.

interchiudere, –kĭŏ'dĕrĕ, v. a. ir. to en-

intercidere, –dshĭ'dĕrĕ, v. a. to divide in two; to hinder.

interdetto, –dĕt'tŏ, m. interdict.

interdire, –dē'rĕ, v. a. ir. to interdict.

interdizione, –dĭtzĭŏ'nĕ, f. interdiction.

interessante, –rĕssän'tĕ, a. interesting.

interessare, –sä'rĕ, v. a. to interest; to concern. [gain; affair, concern.

interesse, –rĕs'sĕ, m. interest, advantage,

interezza, –rĕt'zä, f. integrity; vigour.

interiezione, –rĭĕtzĭŏ'nĕ, f. interjection.

interiora, –rĭŏ'rä, f. pl. entrails, pl.

interiore, –rĭŏ'rĕ, a. interior; –, m. heart, thought.

interlineare, –lĭnĕä'rĕ, v. a. to interline.

intermedio, –mĕ'dĭŏ, a. intermediate; –, m. interlude; interval. [mit.

intermettere, –mĕt'tĕrĕ, v. a. ir. to inter-

intermezzo, –mĕt'zŏ, m. interlude; –, a. intermediate. [discontinuing.

intermittente, –mĭttĕn'tĕ, a. intermitting,

intermittenza, –tĕn'tzä, f. intermission, interval. [nally.

internamente, –tĕrnämĕn'tĕ, ad. inter-

internarsi, –när'sī, v. r. to penetrate deeply. [inward.

interno, –tĕr'nŏ, m. interior; –, a. internal,

intero, –tĕ'rŏ, a. entire, whole; hones.

interpellare, –pĕllä'rĕ, v. a. to summon.

interpellazione, –lätzĭŏ'nĕ, **interpel-lanza,** –län'tzä, f. interpellation, summons, pl.

interpolare, –pŏlä'rĕ, v. a. to interpolate.

interpolazione, –tzĭŏ'nĕ, f. interpolation.

interporre, –pŏr'rĕ, v. a. ir. to interpose, to interfere; to insert; **interporsi,** –pŏr'-sī, to intermeddle.

interpretare, –prĕtä'rĕ, v. a. to interpret.

interpretazione, –tzĭŏ'nĕ, f. interpretation.

interprete, –tĕr'prĕtĕ, m. interpreter.

interpunzione, –pŭntzĭŏ'nĕ, f. punctua-

interrare, –tĕrrä'rĕ, v. a. to bury. [tion.

interrogare, –rŏgä'rĕ, v. a. to interrogate.

interrogatorio, –tŏ'rĭŏ, m. interrogatory.

interrogazione, –tzĭŏ'nĕ, f. interrogation, inquiry. [terrupt.

interrompere, –rŏm'pĕrĕ, v. a. ir. to in-

interruzione, –rŭtzĭŏ'nĕ, f. interruption

intersecare, –sĕkä'rĕ, v. a. to intersect.

intersezione, –sĕtzĭŏ'nĕ, f. intersection.

interstizio, –stĭ'tzĭŏ, m. interval.

intertenere, –tĕnĕ'rĕ, v. a. ir. to entertain.

intervallo, –väl'lŏ, m. interval; space.

intervenire, –vĕnē'rĕ, v. n. ir. to happen; to come to pass. [sistance.

intervento, –vĕn'tŏ, m. intervention; as-

intesa, –tä'sä, f. intention, meaning; pur-pose, aim, design, object.

inteso, –tä'sŏ, a. intent, understood; at-tentive; **star sull'** –, to be on one's guard.

intessere, –tĕs'sĕrĕ, v. a. to interweave.

intestino, –tĕstē'nŏ, m. bowel, intestine; –, a. intestine, inward.

intiepidire, –tĭĕpĭdē'rĕ, v. a. & n. to make tepid; to become tepid; to grow indifferent.

intimare, –tĭmä'rĕ, v. a. to intimate.

intimazione, –tzĭŏ'nĕ, f. intimation, de-claration. [ful.

intimidire, –tĭmĭdē'rĕ, v. n. to grow fear-

intimo, ĭn'tĭmŏ a. intimate; inmost.

intimorire, –tĭmŏrē'rĕ, v. a. to make afraid, to terrify.

intingere, –tĭn'gĕrĕ, v. a. ir. to dip, to steep; to soak.

intingolo, –tĭn'gŏlŏ, m. ragout.

intinto, –tĭn'tŏ, m. sauce, gravy.

intirizzire, –tĕrĭtzē'rĕ, v. n. to be or to grow benumbed.

intitolare, –tĭtŏlä'rĕ, v. a. to entitle.

intitolazione, –tzĭŏ'nĕ, f. title; dedication.

intollerabile, –tŏllĕrä'bĭlĕ, a. intolerable.

intonacare, –tŏnäkä'rĕ, **intonicare,** –nĭkä'rĕ, v. a. to plaster.

intonaco, –tŏ'näkŏ, **intonico,** –nĭkŏ, m. rough-cast; plaster, paint.

intonare, –tŏnä'rĕ, v. a. to tune; to sing.

intonazione, –tzĭŏ'nĕ, f. intonation, tuning.

intoppare, –tŏppä'rĕ, v. n. to meet with; to stumble upon. [obstacle.

intoppo, –tŏp'pŏ, m. meeting, encounter;

intorbare, –tŏrbä'rĕ, **intorbidare,** –bĭ-dä'rĕ, v. a. to make turbid, to trouble; to vex, to plague.

intorbidire, –bĭdē'rĕ, v. n. to get turbid, to become muddy; to grow dim.

intormentire, –mĕntē'rĕ, v.n.to grow stiff.

intorniare, –nĭä'rĕ, v. a. to surround, to encompass. [concerning.

intorno, –tŏr'nŏ, ad. & pr. about, around;

intra, ĭn'trä, pr. between, amongst.

intraducibile, –trädǔdshē'bĭlĕ, a. un-translatable. [rupt; to omit.

intralasciare, –läshä'rĕ, v. a. to inter-

intralciare, –träldshä'rĕ, v. a. to inter-weave; to embarrass.

intramettere, –mĕt'tĕrĕ, v. a. ir. to put between; to insert.

intramezzare, –mĕdzä'rĕ, v. a. to inter-pose; to intermeddle; to intermix.

intraprendere, –prĕn'dĕrĕ, v. a. ir. to undertake; to catch.

intraprenditore, –dĭtŏ'rĕ, m. undertaker.

intrapresa, –prĕ'sä, f. enterprise.

intrattabile, –trättä'bĭlĕ, a. intractable.

intrattenere, –těnd' rě, v. a. ir. to entertain.
intravvenire, see intervenire.
intrecciare, –trětshä' rě, v. a. to inter-
weave. [twist; plot.
intreccio, –trět' shǒ, m. wreath, garland;
intrepidezza, –trěpĭdět' zä, f. intrepidity.
intrepido, –trě' pĭdǒ, a. intrepid, courageous. [v. a. to intrigue; to confuse.
intricare, –trĭkä' rě, intrigare, –gä' rě,
intridere, –trě' děrě, v. a. to dilute; to
knead; to splash.
intrigo, –trě' gǒ, m. intrigue.
intrinseco, –trĭn' sěkǒ, a. intrinsic, inward; intimate. [to thrive ill.
intristire, –trĭstě' rě, v. n. to grow wicked;
introdotto, ĭntrǒdǒt' tǒ, m. introduction.
introdurre, –důr' rě, v. a. ir. to introduce,
to bring in.
introduzione, –dǎtzĭǒ' ně, f. introduction; preface. [duce; to insert.
intromettere, –mět' těrě, v. a. ir. to intro-
intronare, –trǒnä' rě, v. a. to stun.
intronizzare, –nĭdzä' rě, v. a. to enthrone.
intrudere, –trǒ' děrě, v. a. ir. to thrust
in; to drive in.
intrusione, –trǔsĭǒ' ně, f. intrusion.
intruso, –trǔ' sǒ, a. intruded, thrust in.
intuito, –ĭǒ' ĭtǒ, m. looking into, glance;
perception. [tion.
intuizione, –tǎĭtzĭǒ' ně, f. mental percep-
intonare, see intonare.
inuguale, see ineguale.
inulto, –ǔl' tǒ, a. unrevenged.
inumanità, –ǔmänĭtà', f. inhumanity.
inumano, –ǔmä' nǒ, a. inhuman.
inumidire, –ǔmĭdě' rě, v. a. to moisten.
inusto, –ǔs' tǒ, a. burnt.
inutile, –ǒ' tĭlě, a. useless.
inutilità, –ǔtĭlĭtà', f. inutility.
inutilmente, –měn' tě, ad. uselessly.
invadere, –vä' děrě, v. a. ir. to invade;
to assail. [with desire.
invaghire, –väghě' rě, v. a. to inflame
invaghito, –väghě' tǒ, a. enamoured, fond.
invalidare, –välĭdä' rě, v. a. to invalidate.
invalido, –vä' lĭdǒ, a. invalid, infirm; null.
invanire, –väně' rě, v. a. to render fruitless, to baffle; –, v. n. to grow proud.
invano, –vä' nǒ, ad. in vain.
invasare, –väsä' rě, v. a. to put into a
vase; to rush in; to assault.
invasione, –säǒ' ně, f. invasion; irruption.
invecchiare, –věkkĭä' rě, v. a. & n. to make
old; to grow old.
inveire, –věě' rě, v. n. to inveigh.
invenia, –vě' nĭä, f. humiliation; respects,
pl.; pardon.
inventare, –věntä' rě, v. a. to invent.
inventore, –tǒ' rě, m. inventor.
invenzione, –tzĭǒ' ně, f. invention; fiction.
inverdire, –věrdě' rě, v. n. to grow green.
invernale, –nä' lě, a. winterly, wintry.
invernare, –nä' rě, v. n. to pass the winter.
inverniciare, –nĭdshä' rě, v. a. to varnish.
inverno, –věr' nǒ, m. winter.
invero, –vě' rǒ, ad. truly, indeed.
inversione, –věrsĭǒ' ně, f. inversion.

inverso, –věr' sǒ, pr. towards, in comparison. [turn upside down, to overturn.
invertere, –věr' těrě, v. a. ir. to invert, to
investigare, –věstĭgä' rě, v. a. to investigate, to search out.
investigazione, –gätzĭǒ' ně, f. investigation, search.
investimento, –měn' tǒ, m. investment.
investire, –věstě' rě, v. a. to invest; to
spend; to employ; to suit; to strike, to
attack, to assault; to blockade.
investitura, –tĭǒ' rä, f. investiture.
invetrare, –věträ' rě, v. a. to vitrify, to
glaze.
invettiva, –věttě' vä, f. invective, abuse.
inviare, –vĭǒ' rě, v. a. to put in the way,
invidia, –vě' dĭä, f. envy. [to despatch.
invidiare, –vĭdĭä' rě, v. a. to envy, to
grudge. [invidious, envious.
invidioso, –dĭǒ' sǒ, invido, ĭn' vĭdǒ, a.
invietire, –vĭětě' rě, v. n. to grow obsolete.
invigilare, –vĭjĭlä' rě, v. a. & n. to watch
carefully.
invigorire, –gǒrě' rě, v. a. to invigorate,
to encourage; –, v. n. to grow strong.
invilire, –lě' rě, v. a. & n. discourage;
to get disheartened. [up; to perplex.
inviluppare, –lǔppä' rě, v. a. to wrap
inviluppo, –lǔp' pǒ, m. enveloppe, packet;
confusion, complication.
invincibile, –vĭndshě' bĭlě, a. invincible.
invincidire, –dshĭdě' rě, v. a. & n. to
make soft; to get flabby.
invio, –vě' ǒ, a, envoy, address, sending.
invitare, –vĭtä' rě, v. a. to invite, to allure.
invitazione, –tzĭǒ' ně, f. invitation.
invito, –vě' tǒ, a. against one's will.
invitto, –vĭt' tǒ, a. unconquered. [spoil.
inviziare, –vĭtzĭä' rě, v. a. to vitiate, to
invizzire, –tzě' rě, v. n. to fade.
invocare, –vǒkä' rě, v. a. to invoke, to
implore, to beseech, to entreat.
invocazione, –tzĭǒ' ně, f. invocation.
invoglia, –vǒ' yä, f. pack-cloth, wrapper.
invogliare, –yä' rě, v. a. to wrap up, to
pack up. [parcel.
invoglio, –vǒ' yǒ, m. packing-cloth;
involare, –vǒlä' rě, v. a. to steal, to rob.
involgere, –vǒl' jěrě, v. a. ir. to involve;
to wrap up. [tary.
involontario, –vǒlǒntä' rĭǒ, a. involun-
involtare, –vǒltä' rě, v. a. to wrap up, to
envelop.
involto, –vǒl' tǒ, m. packet, parcel.
involvere, –vǒl' věrě, v. a. to involve; to
wrap up.
inzavardare, –dzävärdä' rě, v. a. to soil.
inzeppare, –dzěppä' rě, v. a. to pile up;
to press down, to thrust in.
inzotichire, –dzǒtĭkě' rě, v. n. to grow
awkward.
insuppare, –dzǔppä' rě, v. a. to suck in,
io, ě' ǒ, pn. I. [to soak in.
iperbole, ĭpěr' bǒlě, f. hyperbole.
iperboleggiare, –lědjä' rě, v. a. to exaggerate.
ipocondria, ĭpǒkǒndrě' ä, f. spleen, vapours.

ipocondriaco, *–drĕ'ākŏ,* a. hypochondriacal. [hypocrite.
ipocrita, *ĭpŏ'krĭtă,* **ipocrito,** *–krĭtŏ,* m.
ipoteca, *ĭpŏtĕ'kă,* f. mortgage.
ipotecare, *–tĕkā'rĕ,* v. a. to mortgage.
ipotesi, *ĭpŏ'tĕsĭ,* f. hypothesis.
ipotetico, *ĭpŏtĕ'tĭkŏ,* a. conditional.
ippodromo, *ĭppŏ'drŏmŏ* m. race-ground.
ippogrifo, *–grĕ'fŏ,* m. hippogriff, winged horse.
ippopotamo, *–pŏ'tămŏ,* m. hippopotamus, sea-horse.
ira, *ē'rā,* f. anger, wrath, rage, passion.
iracondia, *ĭrākŏn'dĭā,* f. anger, wrath.
iracondo, *–kŏn'dŏ,* a. irascible.
irascibile, *ĭrāsshĕ'bĭlĕ,* a. irascible.
irato, *ĭrā'tŏ,* a. angry.
irco, *ĭr'kŏ,* m. he-goat.
iride, *ē'rĭdĕ,* f. rainbow; iris.
ironia, *ĭrŏnē'ā,* f. irony.
ironico, *ĭrŏ'nĭkŏ,* a. ironical.
irradiare, *ĭrrādĭā'rĕ,* **irraggiare,** *–rād-djā'rĕ,* v. a. & n. to irradiate.
irragionevole, *–rādjŏnĕ'vŏlĕ,* a. unreasonable. [unreasonably.
irragionevolmente, *–nĕvŏlmĕn'tĕ,* ad.
irrazionale, *–rātzĭŏnā'lĕ,* a. irrational.
irrazionalità, *–nālĭtā',* f. irrationality.
irregolare, *–rĕgŏlā'rĕ,* a. irregular.
irregolarità, *–ārĭtā',* f. irregularity.
irregolarmente, *–mĕn'tĕ,* ad. irregularly.
irreparabile, *–rĕpārā'bĭlĕ,* a. irreparable, irrecoverable.
irretire, *–rĕtē'rĕ,* v. a. to catch in nets.
irrigare, *–rĭgā'rĕ,* v. a. to irrigate, to wet.
irrigazione, *–tzĭŏ'nĕ,* f. irrigation, watering. [or stiff.
irrigidire, *–rĭjĭdē'rĕ,* v. n. to grow rigid
irriguo, *–rē'gŭŏ,* a. watered, moist.
irrisione, *–rĭsĭŏ'nĕ,* f. derision, scorn.
irritare, *–rĭtā'rĕ,* v. a. & n. to irritate, to provoke. [tion.
irritazione, *–tzĭŏ'nĕ,* f. irritation, provoca-
irriverente, *–rĕvĕrĕn'tĕ,* a. irreverent.
irriverenza, *–rĕn'tzā,* f. irreverence.
irrorare, *–rŏrā'rĕ,* v. a. to besprinkle, to water. [rusty.
irrugginire, *–rŭdjĭnē'rĕ,* v. n. to grow
irruzione, *–rŭtzĭŏ'nĕ,* f. irruption, inroad.
irsuto, *ĭrsŭ'tŏ,* a. hirsute; hideous.
isabella, *ĭsăbĕl'lă,* m. light bay.
ischio, *ĭs'kĭŏ,* m. holm-oak.
iscrizione, *ĭskrĭtzĭŏ'nĕ,* f. inscription; title; label.
isola, *ē'sŏlă,* f. island, isle.
isolano, *ĭsŏlā'nŏ,* m. islander.
isolare, *–lā'rĕ,* v. a. to isolate.
isonne, *ĭsŏn'nĕ,* ad. in great quatities, in plenty.
isopo, *ĭsŏ'pŏ,* m. (bot.) hyssop.
ispettore, *ĭspĕt'tŏrĕ,* m. surveyor, overseer; (rail.) – dell'atrio, station-master, inspector.
ispettrice, *–trē'dshĕ,* f. female surveyor.
ispezione, *–tzĭŏ'nĕ,* f. inspection.
ispido, *ĭs'pĭdŏ,* a. rough; shaggy; bristly.

ispirare, *–ĭspĭrā'rĕ,* v. a. & n. to inspire.
ispirazione, *–tzĭŏ'nĕ,* f. inspiration.
issofatto, *–sŏfā'tŏ,* ad. immediately.
istallare, *ĭstāllā'rĕ,* v. a. to install.
istantaneamente, *ĭstāntānĕāmĕn'tĕ,* ad. instantaneously.
istantaneo, *–tā'nĕŏ,* a. instantaneous.
istante, *ĭstān'tĕ,* a. instant, moment.
istanza, *–tān'tzā,* f. instance. [urge.
istare, *ĭstā'rĕ,* v. a. to press, to insist, to
isterico, *ĭstĕ'rĭkŏ,* a. hysterical.
istesso, *ĭstĕs'sŏ,* a. self, same.
istinto, *ĭstĭn'tŏ,* m. instinct.
istituire, *–tĭtŭĭ'rĕ,* v. a. to institute; to instruct.
istituto, *–tĭ'tŏ,* m. precept, maxim.
istitutore, *–tŏ'rĕ,* m. instiutor, preceptor.
istituzione, *–tzĭŏ'nĕ,* f. institution.
istmo, *ĭst'mŏ,* m. isthmus.
istoria, *ĭstŏ'rĭă,* f. history, story.
istorico, *ĭstŏ'rĭkŏ,* m. historian; –, a. historical.
istrice, *ĭs'trĭdshĕ,* m. porcupine.
istrione, *ĭstrĭŏ'nĕ,* m. player, comedian.
istruire, *ĭstrŭĭ'rĕ,* v. a. to instruct, to teach; to inform of, to give notice of.
istrumentale, *–mĕntā'lĕ,* a. instrumental.
istrumento, *–mĕn'tŏ,* m. instrument, tool : deed, bond ; contract.
istruttivo, *–tĭ'vŏ,* a. instructive; tutor.
istruttore, *–tŏ'rĕ,* m. instructor; tutor.
istruzione, *–tzĭŏ'nĕ,* f. instruction.
istupidire, *ĭstŭpĭdē'rĕ,* v. n. to be stupefied.
iterare, *ĭtĕrā'rĕ,* v. a. to repeat.
itinerario, *ĭtĭnĕrā'rĭŏ,* m. itinerary.
itterico, *ĭttĕ'rĭkŏ,* a. iterical, jaundiced.
itterizia, *ĭttĕrē'tzĭă,* f. jaundice.
ivi, *ē'vĭ,* ad. there.
izza, *ē'tză,* f. wrath, anger.

L.

la, *lā,* art. & pn. the; her, it.
là, *lā',* ad. there; **quà e –,** here and there.
labbro, *lăb'brŏ,* m. (**labbra,** f. pl.) lip.
laberinto, *lābĕrĭn'tŏ,* m. labyrinth.
labiale, *–bĭā'lĕ,* a. labial.
labile, *lā'bĭlĕ,* a. slippery; frail.
labirinto, see **laberinto.**
laboratorio, *–bŏrā'tŏrĭŏ,* m. laboratory.
laborioso, *–rĭŏ'sŏ,* a. laborious, toilsome.
lacca, *lăk'kă,* f. bank, shore; leg, haunch; lake-colour.
lacchè, *lăkkĕ',* m. lackey, foot-boy.
lacchezzo, *–kĕt'zŏ,* m. tit-bit; merry jest.
laccio, *lăt'shŏ,* m. snare, gin; lasso; ambush. [to slander;
lacerare, *–dshĕrā'rĕ,* v. a. to tear; to rend;
lacerazione, *–tzĭŏnĕ,* f. laceration, tearing; slander. [famed.
lacero, *lā'dshĕrŏ,* lacerated, in rags; de-
lacerto, *–dshĕr'tŏ,* m. fore-arm.
laco, see **lago.**
lacrima, see **lagrima.**
lacrimare, see **lagrimare.**

lacuna, _–kō′nă,_ f. lagoon; marsh; gap; defect.   [because; whereas.
laddove, _lăddō′vĕ,_ ad. there where; —, c.
ladramente, _lădrămĕn′tĕ,_ ad. thievishly; wretchedly.
ladreria, _–drĕr′ă,_ f. roguery, pilfering, thieving, theft.
ladro, _lă′drŏ,_ m. thief, robber.
ladrone, _–drŏ′nĕ,_ m. highwayman, bandit.
ladroneccio, _–nĕt′shŏ,_ m. robbery, theft.
laggiù, _lădjū′,_ ad. there below.
lagnarsi, _lănyăr′sĭ,_ v. r. to complain, to moan.
lago, _lă′gŏ,_ m. lake; stream; depth.
lagone, _–gŏ′nĕ,_ m. pool, marsh, gap.
lagrima, _lă′grĭmă,_ f. tear, drop.
lagrimare, _–mă′rĕ,_ v. a. & n. to bewail, to shed tears, to weep; to trickle.
lagrimevole, _–mă′vŏlĕ,_ a. deplorable.
lagrimoso, _–mŏ′sŏ,_ a. weeping, dripping
laguna, see **lacuna.**   [wet; tearful.
lai, _lă′ĭ,_ m. pl. (poet.) lamentations.
laicale, _–kă′lĕ,_ a.laical, profane; temporal.
laico, _lă′ĭkŏ,_ m. lay-brother; —, a. lay,
laido, _lă′ĭdŏ,_ a. ugly, foul.   [secular.
lama, _lă′mă,_ f. plain, open field; thin plate of metal; blade.
lambiccare, _lămbĭkkă′rĕ,_ v. a. to distil.
lambicco, _–bĭk′kŏ,_ m. alembic.   [graze.
lambire, _–bē′rĕ,_ v. a. to lick, to lap; to
lamentare, _lămĕntă′rĕ,_ v.a.& n. to lament, to complain.
lamentazione, _–tzĭō′nĕ,_ f. lamentation.
lamento, _–mĕn′tŏ,_ m. lament, wailing.
lamina, _lă′mĭnă,_ f. plate of metal; blade.
laminare, _–nă′rĕ,_ v. a. to cover with plates.
lammia, _lăm′mĭă,_ f. sorceress.
lampada, _lăm′pădă,_ lamp; (rail.) – **di signale,** signal-lamp.
lampadario, _–dă′rĭŏ,_ m.chandelier, lustre.
lampeggiare, _–pĕdjă′rĕ,_ v. n. to shine, to glitter.   [berry.
lampone, _–pŏ′nĕ,_ m. small lamp; rasp-
lampone, _–pŏ′nĕ,_ m. raspberry.
lampreda, _–prĕ′dă,_ f. lamprey.
lana, _lă′nă,_ f. wool; fleece.
lance, _lăn′dshĕ,_ f. balance, scales, pl.
lancetta, _–dshĕt′tă,_ f. lancet; small lance; gnomon (of a dial); hand (of a watch).
lancia, _lăn′dshă,_ f. lance, spear.
lanciare, _–dshă′rĕ,_ v. a. to dart, to fling.
lanciatore, _–tŏ′rĕ,_ m. lancer, spearman.
lancio, _lăn′dshŏ,_ m. great leap.
lanciotto, _–dshŏt′tŏ,_ m, javelin, short lance.
landa, _lăn′dă,_ f. flat open country; heath.
landra, _lăn′dră,_ f. prostitute.
languente, _–gŏĕn′tĕ,_ a. languid, dull.
languidezza, _–gŏĭdĕt′ză,_ f. languidness.
languido, _lăn′gŏĭdŏ,_ a. languid, faint.
languire, _–gŏē′rĕ,_ v.n. to languish, to fade.
languore, _–gŏŏ′rĕ,_ m. languor, faintness.
lanificio, _lănĭf′dshŏ,_ m. woollen manu- factory.
lanigero, _–nĕ′jĕrŏ,_ a. wool-bearing.
lanino, _–nĕ′nŏ,_ m. wool-worker.
lano, _lă′nŏ,_ a. woollen.
lanterna, _lăntĕr′nă,_ f. lantern.

lanternone, _–nŏ′nĕ,_ m. large lantern.
lanugine, _lănō′jĭnĕ,_ f. down, soft hair.
lanuginoso, _–nājĭnŏ′să,_ a. downy.
lanzo, _lăn′tzŏ,_ m. German foot-soldier.
laonde, _lăŏn′dĕ,_ ad. therefore, whence.
lapidare, _lăpĭdă′rĕ,_ v. a. to stone.
lapidario, _–dă′rĭŏ,_ m. lapidary, diamond- cutter.   [ing.
lapidazione, _–tzĭō′nĕ,_ f. lapidation, ston-
lapide, _lă′pĭdĕ,_ f. grave-stone; precious stone.
lapideo, _–pĕ′dĕŏ,_ a. stony, of stone.
lapillo, _–pĕl′lŏ,_ m. precious stone; pebble.
lapis, _lă′pĭs,_ m. red chalk, hematite.
lappola, _lăp′pŏlă,_ f. bur-dock; trifle.
lardare, _lărdă′rĕ,_ v. a. to lard.
lardo, _lăr′dŏ,_ m. lard, bacon.   [amply.
largamente, _–gămĕn′tĕ,_ ad. largely,
largheggiare, _–ghĕdjă′rĕ,_ v. a. to give full liberty; to give presents.
larghezza, _–ghĕt′za,_ f. largeness,liberality, bounty; abundance.   [grant.
largire, _lărjē′rĕ,_ v. a. to give liberally; to
largizione, _–gĭtzĭō′nĕ,_ f. gift.
largo, _lăr′gŏ,_ a. broad, large; liberal bountiful; —, ad. largely, abundantly.
largura, _–gŏ′ră,_ f. wide extent.
lari, _lă′rĭ,_ m. pl, lares, household gods, pl.
larice, _lă′rĭdshĕ,_ f. larch-tree.
laringe, _–rĕn′jĕ,_ f. larynx, throat.
larva, _lăr′vă,_ f. ghost, phantom; mask; chrysalis.
larvato, _–vă′tŏ,_ a. masked; hidden.
lasca, _lăs′kă,_ f. mullet.   [don.
lasciare, _lăsshă′rĕ,_ v. a. to leave, to aban-
lascito, _lăssh′ĭtŏ,_ m. legacy.
lascivia, _–sshĭ′vĭă,_ f. lasciviousness.
lascivo, _–sshĭ′vŏ,_ a. lascivious, wanton.
lassezza, _–sĕt′ză,_ f. lassitude, relaxation.
lasso, _lăs′sŏ,_ a. tired, relaxed; miserable.
lassù, _lăssū′,_ ad. there above.
lastra, _lăs′tră,_ f. flat broad stone, slate; – **stereotipata,** stereotype-plate.
lastricare, _–trĭkă′rĕ,_ v. a. to pave with broad stones.
lastrico, _lăs′trĭkŏ,_ m. pavement.
latente, _lătĕn′tĕ,_ a. latent, concealed.
laterale, _lătĕră′lĕ,_ a. lateral.
laterizio, _–rē′tzĭŏ,_ a. of brick.
latino, _lătē′nŏ,_ m. Latin language; —, a. Latin; easy, plain, intelligible.
latitudine, _–tĭtō′dĭnĕ,_ f. breadth, extent.
lato, _lă′tŏ,_ m. side; place; part; —, a. wide, large, spacious.
latomia, _–tŏ′mĭă,_ f. marble-quarry.
latore, _–tŏ′rĕ,_ m. bearer, porter; – **di leggi,** legislator.
latrare, _–tră′rĕ,_ v. n. to bark; to cry.
latrato, _–tră′tŏ,_ m. barking.   [privy.
latrina, _–trē′nă,_ f. place of retirement,
latrocinio, _–trŏdshĕ′nĭŏ,_ m. larceny, theft.
latta, _lăt′tă,_ f. sheet of iron tinned over.
latte, _lăt′tĕ,_ m. milk; soft roe.
latteo, _lăt′tĕŏ,_ a. lacteous, milky.
latticinio, _–tdshĕ′nĭŏ,_ m. milk-food.
lattime, _lăttĕ′mĕ,_ m. scurf (on children's heads).

lattovaro, _–tõvä'rõ,_ m. electuary.
lattuga, _–tõ'gä,_ f. lettuce.
laudare, see lodare.
laude, _lä'ŭdĕ,_ f. hymn, praise.
laurea, _lä'rĕä,_ f. crown of laurel.
lauro, _lä'rõ,_ m. laurel; glory. [stately.
lauto, _lä'ŭtõ,_ a. magnificent, sumptuous,
lava, _lä'vä,_ f. lava.
lavacro, _–vä'krõ,_ m. washing-place, bath.
lavagna, _–vän'yä,_ f. slate (to write upon).
lavanda, _–vän'dä,_ f. lavender.
lavandaia, _–dä'ä,_ f. washer-woman.
lavare, _–vä'rĕ,_ v. a. to wash.
lavativo, _–tē'võ,_ m. clyster. [trough.
lavatoio, _–tõ'õ,_ m. wash-house; washing-
laveggio, _–vĕd'jõ,_ m. broth-pot; small
  brazier.   [labour; to plough.
lavorare, _–võrä'rĕ,_ v. a. & n. to work, to
lavoro, _lävõ'rõ,_ m. work, piece of work;
  brick-work.
lazzarone, _lädzär'õ'nĕ,_ m. lazzarone, laz-
  zaroni, pl. (fig.) lounger.   [house.
lazzaretto, _–rĕt'tõ,_ m. lazaretto; pest-
lazzo, _lät'zõ,_ m. buffoonery; –, a. tart,
  sharp; droll, jocose.
le, _lĕ,_ pn. pl. the; them.
leale, _lĕä'lĕ,_ a. loyal, faithful, honest.
lebbra, _lĕb'brä,_ f. leprosy.
leccarda, _lĕkkär'dä,_ f. dripping-pan.
leccare, _–kä'rĕ,_ v. a. to lick; to skim, to
  graze.
leccato, _–kä'tõ,_ a. licked; affected, neat.
leccio, _lĕt'shõ,_ m. holm-oak.
leccume, _lĕkkõ'mĕ,_ m. tit-bit; allurement.
lecito, _lĕ'dshītõ,_ a. lawful, permitted.
ledere, _lĕ'dĕrĕ,_ v. a. ir. to hurt, to injure.
lega, _lä'gä,_ f. league.
legaccia, _lĕgät'shä,_ f. tie, garter, string.
legale, _–gä'lĕ,_ a. legal, lawful.
legalità, _–litä',_ f. legality, authenticity.
legalizzare, _–dzä'rĕ,_ v. a. to legalize.
legalizzazione, _–dzatzõ'nĕ,_ f. legaliza-
  tion.
legalmente, _–gälmĕn'tĕ,_ ad. legally.
legame, _–gä'mĕ,_ m. ligature; chain.
legare, _–gä'rĕ,_ v. a. to tie, to bind; to
  leave by will, to bequeath.
legato, _–gä'tõ,_ m. legate; legacy.
legazione, _–tzõ'nĕ,_ f. legation, embassy.
legge, _lĕd'jĕ,_ f. law, rule.
leggenda, _lĕdjĕn'dä,_ f. legend.
leggendario, _–dä'rõ,_ m. legendary.
leggere, _lĕd'jĕrĕ,_ v. a. ir. to read; to teach,
  to instruct.   [charming.
leggiadro, _–jä'drõ,_ a. nice, pretty, elegant,
leggibile, _–jē'bīlĕ,_ a. legible. [frivolous.
leggiero, _–jĕ'rõ,_ a. light, swift, nimble;
leggio, _lĕd'jõ,_ m. reading desk; easel;
  hump-back.
legione, _lĕjõ'nĕ,_ f. legion; great number.
legislativo, _–jislätē'võ,_ a. legislative.
legislatore, _–tõ'rĕ,_ m. lawgiver.
legislatura, _–tõ'rä,_ f. legislature.
legislazione, _–tzõ'nĕ,_ f. legislation.
legista, _–jē'stä,_ m. lawyer, jurisconsult.
legittimare, _–jīttimä'rĕ,_ v. a. to legitimize.
legittimazione, _–tzõ'nĕ,_ f. legitimation.
legittimità, _–timītä',_ f. legitimacy.

legittimo, _–jēt'tīmõ,_ a. legitimate.
legna, _lĕn'yä,_ f. pl. fire-wood.
legnaggio, _–yäd'jõ,_ m. lineage, family.
legnaia, _–yä'ä,_ f. pile of wood; wood-
  house.
legnaiuolo, _–yäiõ'lõ,_ m. carpenter.
legname, _–yä'mĕ,_ m. timber.
legnare, _–yä'rĕ,_ v. n. to cut wood (for fuel).
legno, _lĕn'yõ,_ m. wood; coach.
leguleco, _lĕgŭlä'kõ,_ m. lawyer.
legume, _–gõ'mĕ,_ m. pulse(pease, beans,&c.).
lei, _lä'ī,_ pn. her; **da –,** from her; **di –,**
  of her.
lellare, _lĕllä'rĕ,_ v. n. to dally, to hesitate.
lembo, _lĕm'bõ,_ m. hem, edge.
lena, _lĕ'nä,_ f. breath; vigour.
lene, _lĕ'nĕ,_ a. (poet.) humane, gentle.
lenire, _lĕnē'rĕ,_ v. a. to soften, to mitigate.
lenità, _–nītä',_ f. lenity, mildness.
lenocinio, _–nõdshē'nīõ,_ m. pimping.
lenone, _–nõ'nĕ,_ m. pimp.
lentare, _lĕntä'rĕ,_ v. a. to loose, to relax.
lente, _lĕn'tĕ,_ f. lentil; convex glass.
lenticolare, _–tīkõlä'rĕ,_ a. lenticular.
lentiggine, _–tīd'jinĕ,_ f. freckle.
lento, _lĕn'tõ,_ a. slow, tardy, sluggish; loose.
lentore, _–tõ'rĕ,_ m. slowness.
lenza, _lĕn'tzä,_ f. angling-line.
lenzuolo, _–tzüõ'lõ,_ m. sheet (for a bed).
leone, _lĕõ'nĕ,_ m. lion; dandy, fashionable;
  Leo (sign of the zodiac).
leonessa, _lĕõnĕs'sä,_ f. lioness.
leonino, _–nõ'nõ,_ a. a leonine.
leopardo, _–pär'dõ,_ m. leopard.
lepidezza, _lĕpīdĕt'zä,_ f. cheerfulness, face-
  tiousness, sportiveness.
lepido, _lä'pīdõ,_ a. pleasant, droll, sportive,
  waggish.
lepre, _lä'prĕ,_ f. hare.
leprotto, _lĕprõt'tõ,_ m. young hare.
lesina, _lä'sīnä,_ f. awl; (fig.) sordidness.
lesione, _lĕsī'õnĕ,_ f. damage, injury.
leso, _lä'sõ,_ a. wronged, hurt.
lessare, _lĕssä'rĕ,_ v. a. to boil.
lesso, _lĕs'sõ,_ m. boiling; boiled meat.
lestezza, _–lĕt'zä,_ f. nimbleness; cunning.
lesto, _lĕs'tõ,_ a. nimble, quick; sly.
letale, _lĕtä'lĕ,_ a. (poet.) deadly.
letame, _–tä'mĕ,_ m. dung; manure; mari.
letaminare, _–mīnä'rĕ,_ v. a. to dung, to
letanie, _–tänē'ĕ,_ f. pl. litany.   [manure.
letargia, _–tärjī'ä,_ f. lethargy.
letargico, _–tär'jīkõ,_ a. lethargic.
letificare, _–tīfīkä'rĕ,_ v. a. to make glad.
letizia, _–lĕ'tzīä,_ f. (poet.) gladness.
lettera, _lĕt'tĕrä,_ f. letter; learning, letters;
  –, di cambio, bill of exchange.
letterale, _–tĕrä'lĕ,_ a. literal.
letterario, _–rä'rīõ,_ a. literary; learned.
letterato, _–rä'tõ,_ m. learned man.
letteratura, _–tõ'rä,_ f. literature; learning,
lettiera, _lĕttiĕ'rä,_ f. bedstead.   [science.
lettiga, _lĕttē'gä,_ f. litter.
letto, _lĕt'tõ,_ m. bed; layer.
letto, _lĕt'tõ,_ a. read, perused.
lettore, _–tõ'rĕ,_ m. reader; lecturer.
lettura, _–tõ'rä,_ f. lecture.

leva, lĕ'vä, f. levy, raising; lever; —, di **baratto,** (rail.) switch, siding; — di **acqua,** siphon; — di **milizia,** levy of troops.

levante, lĕvän'tĕ, m. East, Levant, Orient.

levare, —vä'rĕ, v. a. to raise up, to lift up; to take away, to carry; to prohibit; to levy; **levarsi,** —vär'sĭ, to rise, to stand up; to go away; to get proud.

levata, —vä'tä, f. rising, lifting up; departure; sunrise.

levato, —vä'tŏ, a. raised up, lifted up; drawn from; haughty. [bridge.

levatoio, —ĭtŏ'ŏ, a., **ponte** —, m. draw-

levatrice, —trĕ'dshĕ, f. midwife.

levigare, —vĭgä'rĕ, v. a. to polish, to smooth. [hound.

levriere, —vrĭĕ'rĕ, m. gray-hound, grey-

lezio, lä'tzĭŏ, m. affection, caresses, pl. coaxing, pampering; **lezi dello stile,** pl. quaintness of style.

lezioncina, lĕtzĭŏndshĕ'nä, f. short lesson.

lezione, —tzĭŏ'nĕ, f. lesson, lecture; election.

lezioso, —tzĭŏ'sŏ, a. delicate; affected.

lezzare, —dsä'rĕ, v. a. & n. to emit an offensive smell, to stink.

lezzo, lĕd'zŏ, m. stink.

li, lĭ', ad. there, yonder.

libare, lĭbä'rĕ, v. a. to taste, to sip.

libbra, lĭb'brä, f. pound (weight); livre, franc (coin).

libeccio, lĭbĕt'shŏ, m. south-west-wind.

libello, —bĕl'lŏ, m. libel, pamphlet.

liberale, —bĕrä'lĕ, a. liberal; affable, generous.

liberalità, —rälĭtä', f. liberality, bounty, generosity. [all means.

liberamente, —rämĕn'tĕ, ad. freely; by

liberare, —rä'rĕ, v. a. to deliver, to free.

libero, lĕ'bĕrŏ, a. free; open, frank.

libertà, lĭbĕrtä', f. liberty, freedom; privilege. [tious.

libertino, —tĭ'nŏ, a. emancipated; licen-

liberto, —bĕr'tŏ, m. freed-man.

libidine, —bĕ dĭnĕ, f. lust, sensuality.

libidinoso, —bĭdĭnŏ'sŏ, a. libidinous, wanton. [a —, at pleasure.

libito, lĕ'bĭtŏ, m. will, pleasure, mind;

libra, lĕ'brä, f. balance; Libra (sign of the zodiac).

libraio, lĭbrä'ĕŏ, m. bookseller.

librare, —brä'rĕ, v. a. to balance, to weigh; to consider; **librarsi,** —brär'sĭ, to be balanced. [shop.

libreria, —brĕrĕ'ä, f. library, bookseller's

libretto, —brĕt'tŏ, m. little book.

libro, lĕ'brŏ, m. book. [mission.

licenza, lĭtshĕn'tzä, f. licence, license, per-

licenziare, —tzĭä'rĕ, v. a. disband, to give permission to. [solute.

licenzioso, —tzĭŏ'sŏ, a. licentious, dis-

lido, lĕ'dŏ, m. shore, bank; country.

lieto, lĭĕ'tŏ, a. joyous, merry, gay.

lieve, lĭĕ'vĕ, a. light, easy; trifling.

lievemente, lĭĕvĕmĕn'tĕ, ad. lightly, easily; kindly.

lievitare, —vĭtä'rĕ, v. n. to ferment.

lievito, lĭĕ'vĭtŏ, m. leaven, ferment; poultice.

ligio, lĕ'jŏ, a. liege, subject. [family.

lignaggio, lĭnyää'jŏ, m. lineage, race;

ligneo, lĭn'yĕŏ, a. ligneous, wooden.

liliaceo, lĭlĭä'dshĕŏ, a. of lilies. [der.

lima, lĕ'mä, f. file; muddy ground; floun-

limaccio, lĭmät'shŏ, m. mud, mire.

limaccioso, —tshŏ'sŏ, a. muddy, miry.

limare, —mä'rĕ, v. a. to file, to polish; to consume.

limatura, —tä'rä, f. file-dust.

limitare, —mĭtä'rĕ, v. a. to limit, to circumscribe; —, m. threshold.

limite, lĕ'mĭtĕ, m. limit, boundary.

limitrofo, lĭmĕ'trŏfŏ, a. bordering upon.

limo, lĕ'mŏ, m. mud, mire.

limonaio, lĭmŏnä'ŏ, m. lemon-seller.

limone, lĭmŏ'nĕ, m. lemon, citron; lemon-

limosina, —mŏ'sĭnä, f. alms, pl. [tree.

limosinare, —mŏsĭnä'rĕ, v. a. & n. to give alms; to beg alms.

limpidità, lĭmpĭdĭtä', **limpidezza,** —pĭdĕt'zä, f. limpidness; brightness; transparency. [lucid.

limpido, lĭm'pĭdŏ, a. limpid, clear; pel-

lince, lĭn'dshĕ, m. lynx.

lindo, lĭn'dŏ, a. spruce, neat, elegant.

linea, lĕ'nĕä, f. line; lineage. [feature.

lineamento, lĭnĕämĕn'tŏ, m. lineament;

lineare, —nĕä'rĕ, v. a. to draw lines, to sketch.

lineatura, —tĕ'rä, f. lineament; sketch.

lingua, lĭn'gää, f. tongue; language.

linguaccia, —gät'shä, f. slanderous tongue. [idiom.

linguaggio, —gää'jŏ, m. language;

linguaio, —gää'ŏ, m. affected speaker.

lingueggiare, —gĕdjä'rĕ, v. n. to chatter.

linguettare, —gĕtä'rĕ, v. a. to stutter, to stammer.

lino, lĕ'nŏ, m. flax; lint.

linseme, lĭnsä'mĕ, m. linseed.

liocorno, lĭŏkŏr'nŏ, m. unicorn.

liofante, —fän'tĕ, m. elephant.

lionato, —nä'tŏ, a. light-brown.

lione, see **leone.**

lippo, lĭp'pŏ, a. blear-eyed.

liquefare, lĭkĕfä'rĕ, v. a. ir., **liquidare,** —kĭdä'rĕ, v. a. to liquefy, to melt; to liquidate, to pay off, to settle.

liquidazione, —kĭdätzĭŏ'nĕ, f. liquefaction; liquidation.

liquidità, —dĭtä', f. liquidness, fluency.

liquido, lĕ'kĭdŏ, m. liquid substance; —, a. liquid, fluid; clear.

liquirizia, lĭkĭrĕ'tzä, f. licorice.

liquore, lĭkĭŏ'rĕ, m. liquor; — **amaro stomatico,** bitters, pl.

lira, lĕ'rä, f. livre (money); lyre.

lirico, lĕ'rĭkŏ, a. lyric.

lisca, lĭs'kä, f. fish-bone; trifle.

lisciare, lĭsshä'rĕ, v. a. to smoothe, to polish; to flatter, pl.

liscio, lĭssh'ŏ, a. smooth, glossy; —, m. paint for the face.

lisciva, lĭsshĕ'vä, f. lye, lessive.

lista, lĭs'tă, f. list, stripe; roll, catalogue.
listare, lĭstä'rĕ, v. a. to lace, to stripe.
litanie, lĭtä'nĕ, f. pl. litany.
litargirio, -tärjē'rĭŏ, m. litharge.
lite, lē'tĕ, f. quarrel: lawsuit.
liticare, lĭtĭkä'rĕ, litigare, -gä'rĕ, v. a. & n. to litigate, to plead.
litigio, -tē'jŏ, m. quarrel; law-suit.
litigioso, -tĭjŏ'sŏ, a. litigious, quarrel-
lito, see lido. [some.
litografia, -tŏgräfē'ă, f. lithography.
litografico, -grä'fĭkŏ, a. lithographic.
litterale, see letterale.
littorale, lĭttŏrä'lĕ, a. littoral.
littore, -tŏ'rĕ, m. lictor.
liturgia, -tŭrjē'ă, f. liturgy.
livella, lĭvĕl'lă, f. plummet, level.
livello, -vĕl'lŏ, m. level; tribute-money.
lividezza, -vĭdĕz'ză, f. (fig.) grudge, ran-
livido, lĭ'vĭdŏ, a. black and blue. [cour.
lividura, lĭvĭdŏ'ră, f. lividness; bruise.
livore, -vŏ'rĕ, m. envy, rancour.
livrea, lĭvrĕ'ă, f. livery; servants, pl.
lizza, lĭt'ză, f. list; palisades, barriers, pl.;
lo, lŏ, art. the; –, pn. him, it. [course.
locale, lŏkä'lĕ, a. local. [chamber.
locanda, -kän'dă, f. lodging-house; hired
locare, -kä'rĕ, v. a. to place, to settle; to form; to hire; to apply.
loco, lŏ'kŏ, m. (poet.) place; opportunity.
locomotiva, lŏkŏmŏtē'vă, f. (rail.) loco-motive-engine.
locomozione, -mŏtzĭŏ'nĕ, f. locomotion.
locusta, -kŭs'tă, f. locust; lobster.
locuzione, -kŭtzĭŏ'nĕ, f. expression, phrase.
lodabile, -dä'bĭlĕ, a. laudable.
lodare, -dä'rĕ, v. a. to praise, to commend.
lode, lŏ'dĕ, f. praise, commendation.
lodevole, lŏdä'vŏlĕ, a. praiseworthy.
lodevolmente, -dĕvŏlmĕn'tĕ, ad. com-
lodola, lŏ'dŏlă, f. lark. [mendably.
logaritmo, lŏgärĭt'mŏ, m. logarithm.
loggia, lŏd'jă, f. lodge, open gallery; high terrace.
loggiato, -jä'tŏ, m. covered gallery.
logica, lŏ'jĭkă, f. logic.
logico, lŏ'jĭkŏ, a. logical.
loglio, lŏl'yŏ, m. darnel, cockle-weed.
logorare, lŏgŏrä'rĕ, v. a. to wear out, to waste.
logoro, lŏ'gŏrŏ, a. worn out, wasted.
lombaggine, lŏmbäd'jĭnĕ, f. lumbago.
lombo, lŏm'bŏ, m. loin, hip.
lombrico, lŏm'brĭkŏ, m. earth-worm.
longanime, lŏngä'nĭmĕ, a. forbearing.
longanimità, -änĭmĭtä', f. longanimity; forbearance, patience.
longevità, -jĕvĭtä', f. longevity.
longevo, -jä'vŏ, a. (poet.) long-lived.
longitudine, -jĭtŏ'dĭnĕ, f. longitude; length. [distance.
lontananza, -tänän'tză, f. remoteness,
lontano, -tä'nŏ, a. distant, remote; –, ad. afar off.
lontra, lŏn'tră, f. common otter.
lonza, lŏn'tză, f. ounce (small panther).
loppa, lŏp'pă, f. chaff.
loquace, lŏkä'dshĕ, a. loquacious.

loquacità, -dshĭtä', f. loquacity, talkative-ness.
loquela, -kä'lă, f. speech; tongue.
lordo, lŏr'dŏ, a. filthy, foul; lewd.
lordume, -dŏ'mĕ, m., lordura, -dŏ'ră,
lorica, lŏrē'kă, f. cuirass. [f. nastiness.
loro, lŏ'rŏ, pn. them, to them, their.
losco, lŏs'kŏ, a. purblind, short-sighted;
loto, lŏ'tŏ, m. mud, dirt. [stupid.
lotoso, lŏtŏ'sŏ, a. dirty.
lotta, lŏt'tă, f. wrestling; combat.
lottare, -tä'rĕ, v. a. to wrestle; to combat.
lottatore, -tŏ'rĕ, m. wrestler, struggler.
lozione, lŏtzĭŏ'nĕ, f. lotion. [ness.
lubricità, lŭbrĭdshĭtä', f. lubricity, lewd-
lubrico, lŏ'brĭkŏ, a. slippery, fallacious.
lucchetto, lŭkkĕt'tŏ, m. padlock.
lucciare, -tshĭkä'rĕ, v. n. to glitter, to
luccio, lŭt'shŏ, m. pike (fish). [twinkle.
lucciola, lŭt'shŏlă, f. fire-fly.
lucciolato, -lä'tŏ, m. glow-worm.
luce, lŏ'dshĕ, f. light, splendour; (fig.) eye; opening.
lucere, lŏ'dshĕrĕ, v. n. ir. to shine.
lucerna, lŭdshĕr'nă, f. lamp, light, shine; Spanish trefoil; (fig.) guide. [skylight.
lucernario, -nä'rĭŏ, m. dormer-window;
lucert(ol)a, -dshĕr't(ŏl)ă, a. lizard.
lucidare, -dshĭdä'rĕ, v. a. to elucidate, to explain.
lucidità, -dshĭdĭtä', f. light, splendour.
lucido, lŏ'dshĭdŏ, a. lucid, bright.
lucifero, lŭdshĕ'fĕrŏ, m. morning-star.
lucignolo, -dshĭn'yŏlŏ, m. wick.
lucrare, lŭkrä'rĕ, v. a. to gain, to win.
lucrativo, -tĭ'vŏ, a. lucrative.
lucro, lŏ'krŏ, m. gain, lucre, profit.
lucroso, lŭkrŏ'sŏ, a. lucrative. [borate.
lucubrato, lŭkŭbrä'tŏ, a. lucubrated; ela-
lucubrazione, -tzĭŏ'nĕ, f. lucubration.
ludibrio, -dĕ'brĭŏ, m. mockery, laughing-stock.
ludo, lŏ'dŏ, m. (poet.) play; game; diversion.
lue, lŏ'ĕ, f. plague, pestilence; – venerea, venereal disease.
luglio, lŭl'yŏ, m. July.
lugubre, lŏgŏ'brĕ, a. mournful.
lui, lŏ'ĭ, m. wren.
lui, lŏ'ĭ, pn. him, it. [snail.
lumaca, lämä'kă, lumaccia, -mät'shă, f.
lumaio, -mä'ĭŏ, m. lamp-lighter.
lume, lŏ'mĕ, m. light; knowledge; genius.
lumiera, lämĭ'dră, f. light, torch, chan-delier. [stick.
luminello, -nĕl'lŏ, m. socket of a candle-
luminoso, -nŏ'sŏ, a. luminous, shining.
luna, lŏ'nă, f. moon; month.
lunare, länä'rĕ, a. lunar course.
lunario, -nä'rĭŏ, m. almanac, calendar.
lunatico, -nä'tĭkŏ, a. lunatic; whimsical.
lunazione, -tzĭŏ'nĕ, f. lunation.
lunedì, länĕdē', m. Monday.
lunetta, -nĕt'tă, f. (mil.) lunette, small half-moon. [of time.
lunga, län'gă, f. leather thong, strap; length
lungheria, -ghĕrē'ă, f. length, extent.
lunghesso, -ghĕs'sŏ, ad. by, along, near.
lunghezza, -ghĕt'ză, f. length; duration.

lungi, *lŭn'jĕ,* ad. & pr. far, far off.
lungo, *lŭn'gō,* a. long; slow, lazy; irresolute; —, ad. a long while; at length; —, pr. along; by, near.   [employ; need.
luogo, *lŭō'gō,* m. place; family, lineage;
luogotenente, *–tĕnĕn'tĕ,* m. lieutenant.
lupa, *lō'pä,* f. she-wolf; whore.
lupino, *lŭpē'nō,* m. (bot.) lupine.
lupo, *lō'pō,* m. wolf; **– cerviere,** lynx.
luppolo, *lŭp'pōlō,* m. hops, pl.
lurco, *lŭr'kō,* a. gluttonous, voracious.
lurido, *lō'rĭdō,* a. fawn-coloured.
lusco, *lŭs'kō,* a. purblind; stupid.
lusinga, *lŭsēn'gä,* f. flattery.   [coax.
lusingare, *–sĭngä'rĕ,* v. a. to flatter, to
lusinghevole, *–sĭnghā'vōlĕ,* a. flattering.
lusinghiero, *–sĭnghiä'rō,* a. flattering.
lussare, *lŭssä'rĕ,* v. a. to luxate.
lussazione, *–tzĭō'nĕ,* f. luxation.
lusso, *lŭs'sō,* m. luxury.
lussuria, *–sō'rĭä,* f. luxury wantonness.
lussuriare, *–sŭriä'rĕ,* v. n. to live luxuriously.
lussurioso, *–rĭō'sō,* a. luxurious; wanton.
lustra, *lŭs'trä,* f. den, cave.
lustrale, *–trä'lĕ,* a. of five years; lustral.
lustrare, *–trä'rĕ,* v. a. to illustrate, to lighten; to burnish; to gloss; —, v. n. to shine, to sparkle.
lustrino, *–trē'nō,* m. lute-string; tinsel.
lustro, *lŭs'trō,* a. polished, bright; — ,m. lustre, splendour; space of five years.
Luteranismo, *lūtĕränĭs'mō,* m. Lutheranism.
luterano, *–rä'nō,* m. Lutheran.   [ism.
lutto, *lŭt'tō,* m. mourning, wailing; mourning-clothes.
luttuoso, *–tŭō'sō,* a. mournful.
lutulento, *lŭtŭlĕn'tō,* a. muddy.

M.

ma, *mä,* c. but.
macca, *mäk'kä,* f. abundance, store.
maccatella, *–tĕl'lä,* f. defect.
maccherone, *mäkkĕrō'nĕ,* m. macaroon; blockhead.
macchia, *mäk'kĭä,* f. spot, stain; blemish.
macchiare, *–kĭä'rĕ,* v. a. to stain.
macchina, *mäk'kĭnä,* f. machine; engine; frame; plot.   [to plot.
macchinare, *–kĭnä'rĕ,* v. a. to machinate;
macchinatore, *–tō'rĕ,* m. plotter.
macchinazione, *–tzĭō'nĕ,* f. machination; plot.   [(rail.) engine-driver.
macchinista, *–nĭs'tä,* m. engine-maker;
macchione, *–kĭō'nĕ,* m. bushy place.
macco, *mäk'kō,* m. beans boiled to a mash; massacre; defeat.
macellaio, *mädshĕllä'ō,* **macellaro,** *–lä'rō,* m. butcher.   [to destroy.
macellare, *–dshĕllä'rĕ,* v. a. to butcher;
macello, *–dshĕl'lō,* m. slaughter-house; massacre.   [to soak.
macerare, *–dshĕrä'rĕ,* v. a. to macerate;
macigno, *–dshĭn'yō,* m. hard greystone; rock.   [meager.
macilente, *–dshĭlĕn'tĕ,* a. lean, lank,

macina, *mä'dshĭnä,* f. mill-stone.
macinare, *–dshĭnä'rĕ,* v. a. to grind; to pulverize, to powder.
maciulla, *–dshŭl'lä,* f. hemp-brake. [sin.
macula, *mä'kŭlä,* f. stain, spot; blemish;
maculare, *–kŭlä'rĕ,* v. a. to stain, to spot.
madama, *–dä'mä,* f. madam.   [lady.
madamigella, *–mĭjĕl'lä,* f. Miss; young
madia, *mä'dĭä,* f. kneading-trough, hutch.
madido, *mä'dĭdō,* a. humid, wet.
madonna, *–dōn'nä,* f. mistress, lady; Virgin Mary.
madore, *–dō'rĕ,* m. moisture.   [mould.
madre, *mä'drĕ,* f. mother; (fig.) origin;
madreperla, *–pĕr'lä,* f. mother of pearl.
madreselva, *–sĕl'vä,* f. honey-suckle.
madrevite, *–vē'tĕ,* m. female screw.
madrina, *–drē'nä,* f. godmother, midwife.
maestà, *mäĕstä',* f. majesty; **delitto di lesa –,** m. high-treason.   [a. majestic.
maestevole, *–tä'vōlĕ,* **maestoso,** *–tō'sō,*
maestra, *mäĕs'trä,* f. (school-)mistress.
maestrevole, *–trä'vōlĕ,* a. masterly.
maestria, *–trē'ä,* f. skill; authority.
maestro, *mäĕs'trō,* m. master; teacher, professor; director; artist; —, a. skilful; chief, main.
maga, *mä'gä,* f. (poet.) sorceress.
magagna, *–gän'yä,* f. defect; flaw.
magagnare, *–gänyä'rĕ,* v. a. to spoil; to corrupt.   [house-keeper.
magazziniere, *–gädzĭnĭä'rĕ,* m. warehouse
magazzino, *–dzē'nō,* m. magazine.
maggese, *mädjā'sĕ,* **maggiatica,** *–djä'tĭkä,* f. fallow ground.
maggio, *mäd'jō,* m. May.
maggiorana, *mädjōrä'nä,* f. sweet marjoram.   [superiority.
maggioranza, *–rän'tzä,* f. mastership,
maggiordomo, *–djōrdō'mō,* m. steward.
maggiore, *–djō'rĕ,* a. greater, elder; of age.
maggiorente, *–rĕn'tĕ,* m. chief man.
maggiori, *–jō'rĭ,* m. pl. ancestors, pl.
maggiorità, *–jōrĭtä',* f. majority; majority (in age).   [ter; particularly.
maggiormente, *–mĕn'tĕ,* ad. more; better.
magia, *mädjē'ä,* f. magic, witchcraft.
magico, *mä'jĭkō,* a. magical, magic.
magione, *–jō'nĕ,* f. mansion.
magistero, *–jĭstä'rō,* m. skilfulness; instruction; doctorship; engine.
magistrato, *–jĭsträ'tō,* m. magistrate.
magistratura, *–tō'rä,* f. magistracy.
maglia, *mä'lyä,* f. mail; coat of mail; link; net-work, stitch.
maglio, *mä'lyō,* m. mallet, beetle.
magnanimità, *mänyänĭmĭtä',* f. magnanimity.
magnanimo, *–yä'nĭmō,* a. magnanimous.
magnano, *–yä'nō,* m. locksmith.
magnete, *–yä'tĕ,* f. loadstone.   [netize.
magnetizzare, *–yĕtĭdzä'rĕ,* v. a. to magnify
magnificare, *–yĭfĭkä'rĕ,* v. a. to magnify;
magnificente, *–dshĕn'tĕ,* a. magnificent.
magnificenza, *–dshĕn'tzä,* f. magnificence, pomp.

magnifico, –yĭ'fĭkô, a. magnificent.
magno, măn'yŏ, a. great, mighty.
mago, mă'gŏ, a. & m. magical, magician.
magona, –gŏ'nă, f. refining-smithy, large forge; great store.   [dry; bad.
magro, mă'grŏ, a. meagre; thin; weak;
mai, mă'ĭ, ad. ever, always; never, yet; – più, at last; never more.
maio, mă'ŏ, m. green bough, bunch.
maiolica, măiŏ'lĭkă, f. delf-ware.
malaccorto, mălăkkŏr'tŏ, a. inconsiderate.
malacreanza, –krĕăn'tză, f. impoliteness.
malagevole, –ăjĕ'vŏlĕ, a. hard, difficult, dangerous.   [vided.
malagiato, –ăjă'tŏ, a. ill at ease; unpro-
malamente, –mĕn'tĕ, ad. badly; barbarously.
malandare,|–ăndă'rĕ, v. n. ir. to go to ruin.
malandato, –dă'tŏ, a. ruined, lost.
malandrino, –drĕ'nŏ, m. highwayman.
malanno, –ăn'nŏ, m. disaster, misery.
malaticcio, –tĭt'shŏ, a. sickly.
malato, –lă'tŏ, a. sick.
malattia, –lăttĕ'ă, f. sickness, disease.
malavoglia, –vŏĭ'yă, f. malevolence.
malavvezzo, –ăvĕt'zŏ, a. ill-bred; depraved.
malazzato, –ădză'tŏ, a. sickly.
malcontento, –kŏntĕn'tŏ, a. discontented.
malcreato, –krĕă'tŏ, a. ill-bred, impolite.
maldicente, –dĭdshĕn'tĕ, a. slanderous.
maldicenza, –dshĕn'tză, f. slander.
maldisposto, –dĭspŏs'tŏ, a. evil-minded.
male, mă'lĕ, m. evil, mischief; harm, pain; grief; hurt, damage; sickness; –, ad. ill, badly; hardly; – detto, a. cursed.
maledico, mălĕ'dĭkŏ, a. calumnious.
maledire, mălĕdă'rĕ, v. a. ir. to curse, to execrate.
maledizione, –dĭtzĭŏ'nĕ, f. malediction.
maleficio, –fĭ'dshĭŏ, m. crime; witchcraft.
malefico, mălĕ'fĭkŏ, a. maleficent, hurtful.
malevolo, mălĕ'vŏlŏ, a. malevolent.
malfatto, –făt'tŏ, m. misdeed, crime.
malfattore, –tŏ'rĕ, m. malefactor.
malgoverno, –gŏvĕr'nŏ, m. slaughter; destruction.
malgrado, –gră'dŏ, ad. in spite of.
malia, mălĕ'ă, f. witchcraft.
maliardo, –lĭăr'dŏ, m. sorcerer.
malignità, –lĭnyĭtă', f. malignity.
maligno, –lĭn'yŏ, a. malignant.
malinconia, –kŏnĕ'ă, f. melancholy.
malinconico, –kŏ'nĭkŏ, m. melancholy.
malincorpo (a –), –kŏr'pŏ, melincuore (a –), –kŭŏ'rĕ, ad. unwillingly.
malinteso, –ĭntĕ'zŏ, a. ill informed.
malizia, mălĭt'zĭă, f. malice, craftiness; grudge; sickness; contagion.
maliziosamente, –tzĭŏsămĕn'tĕ, ad. maliciously, craftily.   [chievous.
malizioso, –tzĭŏ'sŏ, a. malicious, mis-
malleabile, mălĕ'ăbĭlĕ, a. malleable.
malleolo, –lĕ'ŏlŏ, m. ankle-bone.
mallevare, –lĕvă'rĕ, v. a. to go bail for.

malmenare, –mĕnă'rĕ, v. a. to ill-use, to
malo, mă'lŏ, a. bad, ill.   [torment.
malora, mălŏ'ră, f. ruin, perdition.
malore, –ŏ'rĕ, m. disease, trouble.
malsano, –să'nŏ, a. unhealthy; insane.
malta, măl'tă, f. mire, dirt; mortar.
maltalento, –tălĕn'tŏ, m. grudge, rancour.
maltrattamento, –trăttămĕn'tŏ, m. ill-treatment, ill-usage.
maltrattare, –trăttă'rĕ, v. a. to ill-treat.
malva, măl'vă, f. mallow.
malvagia, –văjĕ'ă, f. Malmsey wine.
malvagio, –vă'jŏ, a. wicked, malicious.
malvisto, –vĭs'tŏ, a. ill-looked-on, disliked; unpopular.
malvivente, –vĭvĕn'tĕ, a. lewd, dissolute.
malvogliente, –vŏlyĕn'tĕ, a. malevolent.
malvoluto, –vŏlŭ'tŏ, a. hated, detested.
mamma, măm'mă, f. Mamma; breast.
mammana, –mă'nă, f. midwife; governess.
mammella, –mĕl'lă, f. woman's breast.
mammola, măm'mŏlă, f. nurse-child.
manata, mănă'tă, f. handful; bundle.
mancamento, mănkămĕn'tŏ, m. deficiency, want; defect; slip.   [crime.
mancanza, –kăn'tză, f. want; defect;
mancare, –kă'rĕ, v. n. to want; to fail, to miss; to cease.   [fective.
manchevole, –kĕ'vŏlĕ, a. imperfect, de-
manchevolezza, –kĕvŏlĕt'ză, f. want; defect; error.
mancia, măn'dshă, f. drinking-money
mancino, –dshĕ'nŏ, a. left-handed.
mancipio, –dshĕ'pĭŏ, m. slave.
manco, măn'kŏ, a. defective, faulty, imperfect; –, m. want, defect; v. fault, failure.
mandare, –dă'rĕ, v. a. to send; to order; to inform; to waste.   [trustee.
mandatario, –dătă'rĭŏ, m. commissioner,
mandato, –dă'tŏ, m. mandate, order.
mandibula, –dĕ'bĭlă, f. upper jaw.
mandorla, –dŏr'lă, f. almond.
mandorlo, –dŏr'lŏ, m. almond-tree.
mandra, măn'dră, f. flock; sheep-fold.
mandriano, –drĕă'nŏ, m. herdsman.
manducare, –dŭkă'rĕ, v. a. (poet.) to eat;
mane, mă'nĕ, f. (poet.) morning. [to chew.
maneggiare, –nĕdjă'rĕ, v. a. to handle, to touch; to manage; to govern, to direct.
maneggio, –nĕd'jŏ, m. management, treatment; riding-school.   [rier.
manescalco, –nĕskăl'kŏ, m. marshal; far-
manesco, –nĕs'kŏ, a. of the hands; handy; passionate.
manette, –nĕt'tĕ, f. pl. hand-cuffs, pl.
manevole, –nă'vŏlĕ, a. manageable, pliable.
manfanile, –fănĕ'lĕ, m. handle of a flail.
manganare, –gănă'rĕ, v. a. to cast stones; to mangle (linen).
manganella, –nĕl'lă, f. crossbow.
mangano, măn'gănŏ, m. sling; calender.
mangiapane, mănjăpă'nĕ, m. idler.
mangiare, –jă'rĕ, v. a. to eat.
mangiata, –jă'tă, f. belly-full.
mangiatoia, –tŏĭ'ă, f. manger.

Italian and English.

mangione, –jõ' nẽ, m. great eater.
mania, mănĭ' ă, f. frenzy, madness.
maniaco, –mẽ' ăkŏ, a. maniacal, furious.
manica, mă' nĭkă, f. sleeve; handle.
manicare, –nĭkă' rẽ, v. a. (poet.) to eat.
manichino, –nĭkẽ' nŏ, m. small sleeve, ruffle. [fiddle.
manico, mă' nĭkŏ, m. handle; neck of a
manicotto, –nĭkŏt' tŏ, m. muff.
maniera, mănĭă' ră, f. manner; fashion;
di – che, so that. [give grace to.
manierare, –nĭĕră' rẽ, v. a. to adorn; to
manieroso, –rõ' sŏ, a. well-mannered.
manifattore, –făttõ' rẽ, m. workman.
manifattura, –tõ' ră, f. manufacture;
workmanship. [to publish.
manifestare, –fĕstă' rẽ, v. a. to manifest,
manifesto, –fĕs' tŏ, m. manifesto, edict;
–, a. manifest.
maniglia, mănĭl' yă, f. bracelet.
maniglio, –nĭl' yŏ, m. handle.
manigoldo, –nĭgŏl' dŏ, m. executioner.
maninconia, mănĭkŏnĭ' ă, f. melancholy.
manipolare, –nĭpŏlă' rẽ, m. common soldier; –, v. a. to manipulate; to handle,
to manage; to mingle.
manipolazione, –tzĭõ' nẽ, f. manipulation,
manual work; composition.
manipolo, –nẽ' pŏlŏ, m. maniple; handful.
maniscalco, –nĭskăl' kŏ, m. farrier.
manna, –măn' nă, f. manna; sheaf of corn.
mannaia, –nă' ă, f. hatchet.
mannerino, –nĕrĭ' nŏ, m. young wether.
mano, mă' nŏ, f. hand; help; side; writing;
a –, at hand; – –, by degrees.
manomettere, –mĕt' tĕrẽ, v. n. ir. to lay
hands upon; to make the first cut; to
begin; to ill-use, to ruin; to emancipate.
manopola, mănŏ' pŏlă, f. gauntlet; half-
sleeve. [–, a. written.
manoscritto, –skrĭt' tŏ, m. manuscript;
manoso, mănõ' sŏ, a. soft, gentle; tractable.
manovella, –vĕl' lă, f. lever.
manovra, –õ' vră, f. (mar.) tackling;
military manœuvre.
manovrare, –õvră' rẽ, v. a. to work a
ship; to manœuvre.
mansione, –sĭõ' nẽ, f. abode.
mansueto, –sŭĕ' tŏ, a. mild, gentle, affable.
mansuetudine, –sŭĕtŏ' dĭnẽ, f. mildness,
gentleness.
manteca, –tẽ' kă, f. pomatum.
mantello, –tĕl' lŏ, m. cloak, mantle; (fig.)
pretence. [to support.
mantenere, –tĕnĕ' rẽ, v. a. ir. to maintain;
mantice, măn' tĭdshẽ, m. bellows, pl.;
mantiglia, –tĭl' yă, f. mantilla. [lungs, pl.
manto, măn' tŏ, m. mantle, veil; (fig.)
pretence.
manuale, mănŭă' lẽ, a. of the hand.
manubrio, –nõ' brĭŏ, m. handle, hilt.
manzo, măn' tzŏ, m. ox; beef.
mappamondo, măppămŏn' dŏ, m. map of
the world.
marachella, mărăkĕl' lă, f. spy; deceit.
marame, –ră' mẽ, m. refuse; sweepings,
parings, pl.

marangone, –răngõ' nẽ, m. diver (man);
diver (bird); joiner's journeyman.
marasmo, –răs' mŏ, m. marasmus.
maraviglia, –răvĭl' yă, f. wonder, miracle;
balsamine; a –, admirably.
maravigliarsi, –yăr' sĭ, v. r. to wonder.
maraviglioso, –yõ' sŏ, a. wonderful, marvellous. [token.
marca, măr' kă, f. border; region; mark,
marcare, mărkă' rẽ, v. a. & n. to mark;
to border upon. [nă, f. marchioness.
marchesa, –kẽ' să, marchesana, –kẽsă'-
marchesato, –kẽsă' tŏ, m. marquisate.
marchese, –kẽ' sẽ, m. marquis.
marchiare, –kĭă' rẽ, v.a. to mark, to stamp.
marcia, măr' tshă, f. pus; march.
marcio, măr' tshŏ, a. rotten; despicable.
marcire, –tshĭ' rẽ, v. n. to rot; to fester.
marco, măr' kŏ, m. mark; sign.
mare, mă' rẽ, m. sea.
marea, –rẽ' ă, f. tide, ebb and flow; –
massima, spring-tide.
mareggiare, –rĕdjă' rẽ, v. n. to float upon
the sea.
maremma, –rẽm' mă, f. country contiguous
to the sea.
maremmano, –mă' nŏ, a. maritime; marshy.
maresciallo, –rĕsshăl' lŏ, m. marshal.
margarita, –gărĭ' tă, margherita,
–ghĕrĭ' tă, f. pearl. [brim.
margine, măr' jĭnẽ, m. margin, border,
margutto, –gŭt' tŏ, a. silly. [marine.
marina, –rĭ' nă, f. sea-coast, shore; navy,
marinaio, –rĭnă' ŏ, m. mariner, sailor.
marinare, –nă' rẽ, v. a. to pickle.
marinaro, see marinaio. [wind.
marino, –rẽ' nŏ, a. & m. maritime; west-
maritaggio, –tăd' jŏ, m. marriage.
maritale, –tă' lẽ, a. conjugal.
maritare, –tă' rẽ, v. a. to marry; to unite.
marito, mărĭ' tŏ, m. husband.
marittimo, –rĭt' tĭmŏ, a. maritime; marine.
marmaglia, –mă' yă, f. rabble, mob.
marmo, măr' mŏ, m. marble.
marmoreo, –mõ' rĕŏ, a. of marble.
marmorizzato, –rĭtză' tŏ, a. marbled.
marmotta, –mŏt' tă, f. marmot.
maroso, mărõ' sŏ, m. wave, surge; marsh;
trouble of mind.
marra, măr' ră, f. mattock, pick-axe.
marrano, –ră' nŏ, m. traitor. [leather.
marrocchino, –rŏkkĭ' nŏ, m. morocco-
marrone, –rõ' nẽ, m. large mattock; large
French chestnut; blunder.
marruca, –rŏ' kă, f. bramble.
martedì, –tĕdĭ', m. Tuesday; – grasso,
Shrove-Tuesday. [torture.
martellare, –tĕllă' rẽ, v. a. to hammer; to
martellata, –lă' tă, f. blow with a hammer.
martello, –tĕl' lŏ, m. hammer; torment;
anxiety, care; jealousy.
martire, măr' tĭrẽ, m. martyr.
martirio, –tĭ' rĭŏ, m. martyrdom.
martirizzare, –tĭrĭdză' rẽ, v. a. to torture
to death.
martirologio, –tĭrŏlŏ' jĭŏ, m. martyrology.
martora, măr' tŏră, f. marten. [torture.
martoriare, –tŏrĭă' rẽ, v. a. to rack, to

martorio, _–tŏ′ rĭŏ_, m. rack, torture; pain.
marza, _măr′ tză_, f. graft.
marzapane. _–pä′ nĕ_, m. marchpane.
marziale, _–tzĭä′ lĕ_, a. martial, warlike.
marzo, _măr′ tzŏ_, m. March (month).
marzolino, _–tzŏlē′ nŏ_, a. of March, made in March.
mascagno, _măskăn′ yŏ_, a. cunning.
mascella, _măsshĕl′ lă_, f. jaw, cheek.
mascellare, _–sshĕllä′ rĕ_, m. grinder, cheek-tooth.
maschera, _măs′ kĕră_, f. mask; (fig.) pretext.
mascherare, _–kĕrä′ rĕ_, v. a. to mask; to disguise.
mascherata, _–kĕrä′ tă_, f. masquerade.
maschile, _–kē′ lĕ_, a. manly, of man.
maschio, _măs′ kĭŏ_, a male, manly; noble.
mascolino, _–kŏlē′ nŏ_, a. masculine.
masnada, _–nä′ dă_, f. troop of soldiers; family.   [man.
masnadiere, _–dĭĕ′ rĕ_, m. soldier; highwayman.
massa, _măs′ să_, f. mass, hoard.
massaia, _–sä′ ă_, f. house-wife; maid-servant.   [husband; farmer.
massaio, _–sä′ ŏ_, m. house-steward; good
massaro, _–sä′ rŏ_, a. old, aged.
masseria, _–sĕrē′ ă_, f. farm-house; quantity of goods.   [furniture; sparingness.
masserizia, _–sĕrē′ tzĭă_, f. household goods,
massiccio, _–sĭt′ shŏ_, a. massy; strong.
massima, _măs′ sĭmă_, f. maxim, rule.
massimo, _măs′ sĭmŏ_, a. supreme, very great.
masso, _măs′ sŏ_, m. rock, boulder.
mastello, _–tĕl′ lŏ_, m. bathing-tub, bucket.
masticare, _–tĭkä′ rĕ_, v. a. to chew; to deliberate upon.   [ment.
mastice, _măs′ tĭdshĕ_, m. mastic, glue, cement.
mastino, _–tē′ nŏ_, m. mastiff.
mastro, _mä′ strŏ_, m. master.   [set.
matassa, _–tăs′ să_, f. skein; heap; parcel,
matematica, _–tēmä′ tĭkă_, f. mathematics, pl.   [tical; mathematician.
matematico, _–mä′ tĭkŏ_, a. & m. mathematical.
materasso, _–tĕräs′ sŏ_, m. mattress.
materia, _–tä′ rĭă_, f. matter; cause.
materiale, _–tĕrĭä′ lĕ_, a. material; heavy.
materialità, _–rĭälĭtä′_, f. materiality.
maternale, _–tĕrnä′ lĕ_, a. motherly.
maternità, _–tĕrnĭtä′_, f. motherhood.
materno, _–tĕr′ nŏ_, a. motherly.
matita, _–tē′ tă_, f. pencil, crayon.
matrice, _–trē′ dshĕ_, f. womb; mould, matrix.
matricola, _–trē′ kŏlă_, f. matricular book.
matricolare, _–trĭkŏlä′ rĕ_, v. a. to matriculate.   [cruel mother.
matrigna, _–trēn′ yă_, f. mother-in-law;
matrimoniale, _–trĭmŏnĭä′ lĕ_, a. matrimonial.
matrimonio, _–mŏ′ nĭŏ_, m. matrimony.
matrina, _–trē′ nă_, f. midwife, godmother.
matrona, _–trŏ′ nă_, f. matron.
mattana, _măttä′ nă_, f. ill-humour, disgust.
mattezza, _–tĕt′ ză_, materia, _–tĕr′ ă_,
matta, _–ĭt′ ă_, f. folly, madness.
mattina, _–tē′ nă_, f. morning.
mattinata, _–tĭnä′ tă_, f. morning-serenade; whole morning.

mattino, _–tē′ nŏ_. m. morning.
matto, _măt′ tŏ_, a. mad; terrible.
mattone, _–tŏ′ nĕ_, m. brick; arrant fool.
mattutino, _–tătē′ nŏ_, m. morning; morning prayer.
maturare, _mătŭrä′ rĕ_, v. a. to make ripe; to suppurate; to finish, to perfect; to consider well; –, v. n. to ripen, to grow ripe.
maturazione, _–tzĭŏ′ nĕ_, f. maturation, ripeness; suppuration.
maturità, _–tŭrĭtä′_, f. maturity, ripeness.
maturo, _–tŏ′ rŏ_, a. mature, ripe.   [mallet.
mazza, _măt′ ză_, f. stick, staff; club, mace;
mazzafrusto, _–frŭs′ tŏ_, m. balista.
mazzeranga, _–zĕrän′ gă_, f. beetle.
mazzetta, _–zĕt′ tă_, f. mallet, rammer.
mazzo, _măt′ zŏ_, m. bunch, bundle; packet; mallet; –, di fiori, nosegay.   [nosegay.
mazzuolo, _–zŭŏ′ lŏ_, m. small bunch; little
me′, _mĕ_, for meglio.
meato, _mĕä′ tŏ_, m. pore.
meccanica, _mĕkkä′ nĭkă_, f. mechanics, pl.
meccanico, _kä′ nĭkŏ_, m. mechanician, mechanic; –, a. mechanical.
meccanismo, _–nĭs′ mŏ_, m. mechanism.
meco, _mä′ kŏ_, pn. with me.
medaglia, _mĕdä′ yă_, f. medal; coin.
medaglione, _–yŏ′ nĕ_, m. medallion.
medesimamente, _–dĕsĭmämĕn′ tĕ_, ad. likewise, also.
medesimo, _–dĕ′ sĭmŏ_, pn. same, self.
mediano, _–dĭä′ nŏ_, a. middle, middling.
mediante, _–dĭän′ tĕ_, pr. by means of, through; amidst; between.   [dious.
mediato, _–dĭä′ tŏ_, a. middle; fit, commodious.
medicamento, _–dĭkämĕn′ tŏ_, m. medicament.   [cure.
medicare, _–dĭkä′ rĕ_, v. n. to medicate, to
medicina, _–dĭdshē′ nă_, f. medicine.
medico, _mä′ dĭkŏ_, m. physician, doctor.
medio, _mä′ dĭŏ_, a. middle.
mediocre, _mĕdĭŏ′ krĕ_, a. middling, moderate; indifferent.
mediocremente, _–mĕn′ tĕ_, ad. indifferently, so so.   [middle way.
mediocrità, _–dĭŏkrĭtä′_, f. mediocrity;
meditare, _–dĭtä′ rĕ_, v. n. to meditate, to muse, to ponder, to ruminate.
meditazione, _–tzĭŏ′ nĕ_, f. meditation.
meglio, _mĕl′ yŏ_, ad. better; more, rather.
mela, _mä′ lă_, f. apple.
melacotogna, _mĕlăkŏtŏn′ yă_, f. quince.
melarancia, _–ărän′ dshă_, f. orange.
melata, _–lä′ tă_, f. August-dew; apple-mildew.   [marmalade.
melato, _–lä′ tŏ_, a. honied.
mele, _mä′ lĕ_, m. honey.
melenso, _mĕlĕn′ sŏ_, a. foolish, dull.
meleto, _–lä′ tŏ_, m. apple-orchard.
meliaca, _–lĭä′ kă_, f. apricot.
meliaco, _–lĭä′ kŏ_, m. apricot-tree.
melico, _mä′ lĭkŏ_, a. melodious.
meliga, _mä′ lĭgă_, f. buckwheat.
melissa, _mĕlĭs′ să_, f. balm-mint.   [honey.
mellificare, _mĕllĭfĭkä′ rĕ_, v. a. to make
mellifluo, _–lē′ flŭŏ_, a. sweet as honey.
mellone, _–lŏ′ nĕ_, m. water-melon.
melma, _mĕl′ mă_, f. mud, puddle.

melo, *mā'lŏ*, m. apple-tree. [tree.
melocotogno, *mĕlŏkŏtōn'yŏ*, m. quince-
melodia, *–lŏdē'ä*, f. melody.
melodico, *–lŏ'dĭkŏ*, melodioso, *–lŏdĭŏ'-
sŏ*, a. melodious. [drama.
melodramma, *–lŏdräm'mä*, m. melo-
melodrammatico, *–mä'tĭkŏ*, a. melo-
dramatical. [tree.
melogranato, *–grän̄ä'tŏ*, m. pomegranate-
membrana, *mĕmbrä'nä*, f. membrane.
membranaceo, *–nä'dshĕŏ*, a. membra-
neous, filmy. [remember.
membrare, *–brä'rĕ*, v. a. & n. (poet.) to
membro, *mĕm'brŏ*, m. member; limb.
membruto, *–brŏ'tŏ*, a. strong-limbed.
memorabile, *–mŏrä'bĭlĕ*, a. memorable,
remarkable. [to recollect.
memorare, *–mŏrä'rĕ*, v. a. to remember;
memoria, *–mŏ'rĭä*, f. memory, remembrance; memorandum.
memoriale, *–mŏrĭä'lĕ*, m. memorial, memorandum; monument; petition.
mena, *mā'rĕ*, f. work, business; underhand dealing; condition; kind.
menare, *–nä'rĕ*, v. a. to lead, to guide, to
agitate; to produce; to manage, to handle;
to plot.
mencio, *mĕn'dshŏ*, a. flappy, loose.
menda, *mĕn'dä*, f. fault; forfeit; reparation.
mendace, *–dä'dshĕ*, a. mendacious, lying.
mendacio, *–dä'dshŏ*, m. (poet.) falsehood.
mendare, *–dä'rĕ*, v. a. to make amends,
to repair.
mendicare, *–dĭkä'rĕ*, v. a. to beg.
mendico, *–dē'kŏ*, a. beggarly.
menno, *mĕn'nŏ*, a. castrated; vain; beardless; defective.
meno, *mā'nŏ*, ad. less; al –, at least.
menomare, *mĕnŏmä'rĕ*, v. a. to diminish.
menomo, *mĕ'nŏmŏ*, a. least, less; smallest.
mensa, *mĕn'sä*, f. table.
menstruo, *mĕn'strŏŏ*, m. menstrual flux.
mensuale, *–sŏä'lĕ*, a. monthly.
menta, *mĕn'tä*, f. (bot.) mint.
mentale, *–tä'lĕ*, a. mental, intellectual.
mente, *mĕn'tĕ*, f. mind, understanding, intellect, judgment; memory.
mentecatto, *–kät'tŏ*, a. mad, imbecile.
mentire, *–tē'rĕ*, v. a. & n. to pretend; to
adulterate; to lie.
mento, *mĕn'tŏ*, m. chin.
mentovare, *–tŏvä'rĕ*, v. a. to mention.
mentre, *mĕn'trĕ*, ad. while, whilst.
menzionare, *–tzĭŏnä'rĕ*, v. a. to make
mention.
menzione, *–tzĭŏ'nĕ*, f. mention.
menzogna, *–tzŏn'yä*, f. falsehood, fib.
menzognere, *–tzŏnyä'rĕ*, a. lying, false.
meramente, *mĕrämĕn'tĕ*, ad. merely.
meraviglia, see maraviglia.
mercantare, *mĕrkäntä'rĕ*, v. n. to traf-
fick, to trade, to do business.
mercante, *–kän'tĕ*, mercatante, *–kä-
tän'tĕ*, m. merchant, shop-keeper.
mercantile, *–käntē'lĕ*, a. commercial.
mercanzia, *–käntzē'ä*, f. merchandise.
goods, wares, pl.
mercare, *–kä'rĕ*, v. a. to deal in.

mercatare, *–kätä'rĕ*, v. a. & n. to trade;
to cheapen.
mercato, *–kä'tŏ*, m. market, market-place;
bargain; price; provision; a buon –,
cheap. [goods, pl.
merce, *mĕr'dshĕ*, f. merchandise, wares,
mercè, *mĕrdshĕ'*, mercede, *–dshĕ'dĕ*, f.
recompense, reward; salary; merit; help,
aid; compassion; kindness, favour.
mercenario, *–dshĕnä'rĭŏ*, a. & m. venal,
mercenary.
merceria, *–dshĕrē'ä*, f. mercer's wares.
merciaio, *–dshä'yŏ*, m. mercer.
mercoledì, *–kŏlĕdē'*, m. Wednesday.
mercurio, *–kŏ'rĭŏ*, m. mercury, quick-
merenda, *mĕrĕn'dä*, f. luncheon. [silver.
meretrice, *–rĕtrē'dshĕ*, f. prostitute.
mergo, *mĕr'gŏ*, m. diver; arsefoot (ave);
vine-shoot.
meridiano, *mĕrĭdĭä'nŏ*, a. & m. meridian.
meriggio, *–rĭd'jŏ*, m. south; mid-day.
meritamente, *–rĭtämĕn'tĕ*, ad. deservedly.
meritare, *–tä'rĕ*, v. a. to merit, to deserve.
meritevole, *mĕrĭtĕ'vŏlĕ*, a. deserving,
worthy.
merito, *mā'rĭtŏ*, m. merit, reward.
merla, *mĕr'lä*, f. blackbird.
merlare, *–lä'rĕ*, v. a. to raise battlements;
to indent.
merletto, *–lĕt'tŏ*, m. lace, bone-lace.
merlo, *mĕr'lŏ*, m. battlement; lace; black-
bird. [silk-lace; stockfish.
merluzzo, *–lŭt'zŏ*, m. young blackbird;
mero, *mā'rŏ*, a. pure, clear.
merolla, *mĕrŏl'lä*, f. marrow, pith; best.
mesata, *mĕsä'tä*, f. whole month; month's
pay. [pour out.
mescere, *mĕssh'ĕrĕ*, v. a. ir. to mix; to
meschinità, *–kĭnĭtä'*, f. misery, extreme
poverty.
meschino, *–kē'nŏ*, a. poor, miserable.
meschita, *–kē'tä*, f. mosque.
mescolanza, *–kŏlän'tzä*, f. mixture,
medley; salad.
mescolare, *–kŏlä'rĕ*, v. a. to mix, to mingle.
mese, *mā'sĕ*, m. month.
mesenterio, *mĕsĕntä'rĭŏ*, m. mesentery.
messa, *mĕs'sä*, f. mass; set of dishes;
shoot; stock; fund; stake.
messaggeria, *–sädjĕrē'ä*, f. embassy.
messaggiere, *–sädjĕ'rĕ*, m. messenger.
messaggio, *–sĕd'jŏ*, m. message.
messe, *–mĕs'sĕ*, f. (poet.) harvest, crop.
messere, *mĕssä'rĕ*, m. master, sir.
messo, *mĕs'sŏ*, m. messenger; serjeant;
course at table. [sadly.
mestamente, *–tämĕn'tĕ*, ad. gloomily
mestare, *–tä'rĕ*, v. a. to stir with a pot-
stick; to mingle.
mestatoio, *–tätŏ'ŏ*, m. pot-ladle; spattle.
mestiere, *–tĭä'rĕ*, mestiero, *–rŏ*, m.
trade, business; need, necessity; far –,
to be wanted.
mestizia, *–tē'tzĭä*, f. sadness, grief, gloom.
mesto, *mĕs'tŏ*, a. sad, gloomy.
mestola, *mĕs'tŏlä*, f., mestolo, *–tŏlŏ*, m.
ladle, trowel.

mestura, –tŏ'rä, f. mixture.
metà, mĕtä', f. half, moiety.
meta, mä'tä, f. turd, cow-dung; limit,
boundary; aim. [pl.
metafisica, mĕtäf'sikä, f. metaphysics,
metafisico, –f' sikŏ, a. metaphysical.
metafora, –tä'fŏrä, f. metaphor.
metallico, –täl'likŏ, metallino, –lĕ'nŏ, a.
metallo, –täl'lŏ, m. metal. [metallic.
metallurgia, –lärjĕ'ä, f. metallurgy.
meteora, –tĕŏ'rä, f. meteor.
meteorologia, –tĕŏrŏlŏjē'ä, f. meteorology.
metodico, –tŏ'dikŏ, a. methodical.
metodo, mä'tŏdŏ, m. method; rule.
metrica, mä'trikä, f. metrics.
metrico, mä'trikŏ, a. metrical.
metro, mä'trŏ, m. metre; poetical measure.
metropoli, mĕtrŏ'pŏlĭ, f. metropolis.
metropolita, –trŏpŏlĭ'tä, m. metropolitan
bishop. [politan.
metropolitano, –pŏlitä'nŏ, a. metro-
mettere, mĕt'tĕrĕ, v. a. to put, to place,
to set; to dispose; to admit; to bud, to
sprout. [curess; (mar.) mizzen.
mezzana, mĕdzä'nä, f. square brick; pro-
mezzanino, –dzäně'nŏ, m. small low storey
between two higher ones, entresol.
mezzano, –dzä'nŏ, m. mediator, go-between; –, a. middle, mediocre.
mezzina, –dzē'nä, f. pitcher.
mezzo, mĕ'dzŏ, m. middle, half; centre;
means, pl.; –, a. middle, half; moderate;
–, ad. half, almost, nearly.
mezzo, mĕz'zŏ, a. over-ripe, withered.
mezzodì, mĕdzŏdē', mezzogiorno, –jŏr'-
nŏ, m. south; south-wind; noon, noon-
day.
mezzorilievo, –rĭliĕ'vŏ, m. half-relief.
mi, mĭ, pn. me, to me.
miagolare, mĭägŏlä'rĕ, v. n. to mew.
mica, mĕ'kä, ad. not at all.
miccia, mĭt'shä, f. match.
miccino, mĭtshĕ'nŏ, a. little; many, some.
miccio, mĭt'shŏ, m. jack-ass.
micio, mĕ'dshŏ, m, cat, puss.
microscopio, mĭkrŏskŏ'pĭŏ, m. microscope.
midolla, mĭdŏl'lä, f., midollo, –lŏ, m.
marrow; crum of bread.
miele, mĭĕ'lĕ, m. honey.
mietere, mĭĕ'tĕrĕ, v. a. to reap, to gather in.
migliarola, mĭlyärŏ'lä, f. sparrow-shot,
hail-shot. [millet.
miglio, mĭl'yŏ, m. (miglia, f. pl.) mile;
migliorare, –yŏrä'rĕ, v. a. to better; to
migliore, –yŏ'rĕ, a. better. [improve.
mignatta, mĭnyät'tä, f. leech; usurer.
mignolo, mĭn'yŏlŏ, m. little finger; olive-
blossom.
migrare, mĭgrä'rĕ, v. n. to migrate.
mila, mĕ'lä, pl. of mille.
miliardo, mĭlĭär'dŏ, m. milliard.
milione, –lĕ'ŏnĕ, m. million. [militate.
militare, –lĭtä'rĕ, a. military; –, v. n. to
milite, mĕ'lĭtĕ, m. soldier.
milizia, mĭlē'tzĭä, f. art of war; militia.
millantare, mĭlläntä'rĕ, v.a. to exaggerate,
to boast; millantarsi, –tär'si, to boast.

mille, mĭl'lĕ, a. & m, thousand.
millefoglie, –fŏl'yĕ, f. milfoil.
millesimo, –lä'simŏ, a. thousandth; –, m.
(poet.) millenium.
milza, mĭl'tzä, f. spleen.
mimico, mĕ'mĭkŏ, a. mimic.
mina, mĕ'nä, f. half a bushel; mine.
minaccia, mĭnät'shä, f. menace, threat.
minacciare, –tshä'rĕ, v. a. to menace, to
threaten.
minaccioso, –tshŏ'sŏ, a. threatening.
minare, mĭnä'rĕ, v. a. to mine, to sap; to
minatore, –tŏ'rĕ, m. miner. [ruin.
minatorio, –tŏ'rĭŏ, a. minatory, threatening. [to banter, to jest.
minchionare, mĭnkĭŏnä'rĕ, v. a. to quiz,
minchione, –kĭŏ'nĕ, m. blockhead.
minerale, mĭnĕrä'lĕ, a. & m. mineral.
mineralogia, –lŏjē'ä, f. mineralogy.
minestra, –nĕs'trä, f. pottage, soup, broth.
mingherlino, mĭnghĕrlē'nŏ, a.lean,slender.
miniatore, –nĭätŏ'rĕ,m. miniature-painter.
miniatura, –tŏ'rä, f. miniature-painting.
miniera, –nĭĕ'rä, f. metallic mine.
minimo, mĕ'nĭmŏ, a. least, meanest,
smallest.
minio, mĕ'nĭŏ, m. vermilion; miniature.
ministero, mĭnĭstä'rŏ, m. ministry, administration, office.
ministrare, –trä'rĕ, v. a. & n. to afford;
to minister, to officiate.
ministro, –nĭs'trŏ, m. minister.
minoranza,–nŏrän'tzä,f. minority; smallness; diminution.
minorare, –nŏrä'rĕ, v. a. to diminish.
minore, –nŏ'rĕ, a. less, smaller; younger,
under age. [(in age).
minorità, –nŏrĭtä', f. minority; minority
minugia, –nŏ'jä, f. pl. gut, intestines, pl.
minuto, –nŏ'tŏ, a. slender, thin, small;
vulgar; circumstantial.
minuzia, –nŏ'tzĭä, f. trifle.
mio, mĕ'ŏ, pn. my, mine.
miope, mĕ'ŏpĕ, m. short-sighted person.
miopia, mĕŏpĕ'ä, f. myopy, shortness of
sight.
mira, mĕ'rä, f. aim, sight; purpose.
mirabile, mĭrä'bĭlĕ, a. wonderful.
miracolo, –rä'kŏlŏ, m. miracle.
miracoloso, –kŏlŏ'sŏ, a. miraculous, marvellous. [template; to aim at.
mirare, –rä'rĕ, v. a. & n. to view, to con-
miriade, –rĕ'ädĕ, f. myriad.
mirra, mĕr'rä, f. myrrh.
mirto, mĭr'tŏ, m. myrtle-tree. [thropy.
misantropia, mĭsäntrŏpĕ'ä, f. misan-
misantropo, –än'trŏpŏ, m. misanthrope.
miscea, mĭsshä'ä, f. old stuffs, trifles, pl.
miscellaneo, –sshĕllä'nĕŏ, a. miscellaneous.
mischia, mĭs'kĭä, f. scuffle, fray.
mischiare, –kĭä'rĕ,v. a. to mix, to mingle.
mischio, mĭs'kĭŏ, m. mixture, medley;
–, a. chequered. [infidel.
miscredente, –krĕdĕn'tĕ, m. unbeliever,
miscredenza, –krĕn'tzä, f. incredulity.
miserabile, mĭsĕrä'bĭlĕ, a. miserable.

miserazione, −tzĭŏ′ nĕ, f. pity, commiseration.
miseria, mĭsĕ′rĭă, f. misery. [tion.
misericordia, −sĕrĭkŏr′ dĭă, f. mercy, compassion.
misericordioso, −kŏrdĭŏ′ sŏ, a. merciful.
misero, mĕ′sĕrŏ, a. miserable, wretched; stingy, niggardly, avaricious.
misfatto, mĭsfät′ tŏ, m. misdeed, crime.
missionario, mĭssĭŏnä′rĭŏ, m. missionary.
missione, −sĭŏ′nĕ, f. mission, discharge.
missiva, −sĕ′vă, f. missive, epistle.
mistero, mĭstä′rŏ, m. mystery, secret.
misterioso, −tĕrĭŏ′sŏ, a. mysterious.
mistico, mĭs′tĭkŏ, a. mystical.
mistione, −tĭŏ′nĕ, f. mixture; complex.
misto, mĭs′tŏ, a. mixed.
mistura, −tŏ′ră, f. mixture.
misura, mĭsŏ′ră, f. measure.
misurare, −sŏră′rĕ, v. a. to measure.
misurazione, −tzĭŏ′nĕ, f. measuring.
mite, mĕ′tĕ, a. mild, meek.
mitezza, mĭtĕ′ză, f. mildness. [standing.
mitidio, −tĭ′dĭŏ, m. order, rule; under-
mitigare, −tĭgä′rĕ, v. a. to mitigate.
mitologia, −tŏlŏjĕ′ă, f. mythology.
mitologico, −lŏ′jĭkŏ, a. mythological.
mitra, mĕ′tră, f. mitre, episcopal crown.
mo', mŏ, ad. now; mo' mo', in just now.
mobile, mŏ′bĭlĕ, a. moveable; variable, fickle. [furniture.
mobilia, mŏbĕ′lĭă, f. household-goods, pl.,
mobilità, −bĭlĭtä′, f. mobility, fickleness.
mobilitare, −tä′rĕ, v. a. to put into movement. [kerchief.
moccichino, mŏtschĭkĕ′nŏ, m. pocket-hand-
moccio, mŏt′shŏ, m. snot; mucus.
moccolaia, mŏkkŏlä′ĭă, f. candle-snuffer.
moccolo, mŏk′kŏlŏ, m. bit of candle; tip of the nose. [fashionably.
moda, mŏ′dă, f. mode, fashion; alla −,
modano, mŏ′dänŏ, m. mould, frame; netting-mesh.
modellare, mŏdĕllä′rĕ, v. a. to model.
modello, −dĕl′lŏ, m. model, pattern, type; example.
moderare, −dĕrä′rĕ, v. a. to moderate.
moderato, −rä′tŏ, a. moderate; sober.
moderatore, −tŏ′rĕ, m. director.
moderazione, −tzĭŏ′nĕ, f. moderation.
modernità, −dĕrnĭtä′, f. novelty, newness.
moderno, −dĕr′nŏ, a. modern.
modestia, −dĕs′tĭă, f. modesty; chastity.
modesto, −dĕs′tŏ, a. modest; shy; chaste; sober.
modificare, −dĭfĭkä′rĕ, v. a. to modify.
modificazione, −tzĭŏ′nĕ, f. modification.
modista, mŏdĭs′tă, f. milliner.
modo, mŏ′dŏ, m. manner, means; custom, use; measure; (gr.) mood; in − che, so that; in che −? in what way?
modulo, mŏ′dŭlŏ, m. model, form, module.
moggio, mŏd′jŏ, m. 12 bushels.
mogio, mŏ′jŏ, a. sleepy, lazy.
moglie, mŏl′yĕ, f. wife, spouse.
mola, mŏ′lă, f. mill-stone.
molcere, mŏl′dshĕrĕ, v. a. to ally, to soften.

mole, mŏ′lĕ, f. pile, heap; mass of buildings; vaste structure, size; bulk.
molecola, mŏlä′kŏlă, f. molecule.
molestare, −lĕstä′rĕ, v. a. to molest, to importune.
molestia, −lĕs′tĭă, f. molestation, vexation.
molesto, −lĕs′tŏ, a. troublesome, irksome.
molla, mŏl′lă, f. spring.
mollare, −lä′rĕ, v. a. to slacken, to loosen.
molle, mŏl′lĕ, a. humid, moist; gentle, tender; soft, delicate; weak.
mollezza, −lĕt′ză, f. softness; effeminacy.
molli, mŏl′lĭ, f. pl. fire-tongs, pl.
mollica, −lĭ′kă, f. crumb.
molo, mŏ′lŏ, m. mole, quay.
moltiplicare, −tĭplĭkä′rĕ, v. a. to multiply.
moltiplicazione, −tzĭŏ′nĕ, f. multiplication.
moltitudine, −tŏ′dĭnĕ, f. multitude.
molto, mŏl′tŏ, a. much, many, great; −, ad. much, greatly, very.
momentaneo, mŏmĕntä′nĕŏ, a. momentaneous; perishable.
momento, −mĕn′tŏ, m. moment, instant; importance, weight.
monaca, mŏ′näkă, f. nun.
monacale, mŏnäkä′lĕ, a. monastic, monkish.
monachino, −kĕ′nŏ, m. gnat-snapper; −, a. tan-coloured.
monaco, mŏ′näkŏ, m. monk; bullfinch.
monarca, mŏnär′kă, m. monarch.
monarchia, −närkĕ′ă, f. monarchy.
monarchico, −när′kĭkŏ, a. monarchical.
monastero, −nästä′rŏ, m. monastery.
monastico, −näs′tĭkŏ, a. monastical.
monco, mŏn′kŏ, a. maimed, one-handed.
mondano, −dä′nŏ, m. worldling; −, a. worldly. [to cleanse.
mondare, −dä′rĕ, v. a. to peel; to pare;
mondezza, −dĕt′ză, f. neatness.
mondezzaio, −dĕtzä′ĭ ŏ, m. dunghill.
mondiale, −dĭä′lĕ, a. worldly.
mondiglia, −dĭl′yă, f. parings, pl.; chaff.
mondizia, −dĕ′tzĭă, f. cleanliness.
mondo, mŏn′dŏ, m. world, universe; −, a. pure, clean, neat. [pocket, rogue.
monello, −nĕl′lŏ, m. swindler, pick-
moneta, −nä′tă, f. coin, money.
monetare, −nĕtä′rĕ, v. a. to coin, to mint.
monetiere, −tĭä′rĕ, m. coiner.
mongana, −gä′nă, f. milk-calf.
mongibello, −jĭbĕl′lŏ, m. volcano.
monile, mŏnĕ′lĕ, m. necklace.
monna, mŏn′nă, f. mistress; she-ape.
monocolo, mŏnŏ′kŏlŏ, a. one-eyed.
monotonia, −nŏtŏnĕ′ă, f. monotony.
monotono, −nŏ′tŏnŏ, a. monotonous.
Monsignore, mŏnsĭnyŏ′rĕ, m. my Lord, your Lordship.
montagna, −tän′yă, f. mountain.
montagnuolo, −yŭŏ′lŏ, montanino, −nĕ′nŏ, m. small mountain.
montanaro, −tänä′rŏ, m. mountaineer.
montanello, −nĕl′lŏ, m. linnet.
montano, −tä′nŏ, a. mountainous.
montare, −tä′rĕ, v. a. & n. to mount, to ascend; to rise; to amount to; to increase.

montata, _-tä' tä_, f. mounting; ascent, height.
montatoio, _-tô̆'ŏ_, m. mounting-block.
montatore, _-tŏ̆' rĕ_, m. stallion.
monte, _mŏn' tĕ_, m. mountain, hill; heap; - di pieta, lombard. [heap.
monticello, _-tätshĕl' lŏ_, m. hill, hillock; montone, _-tŏ̆' nĕ_, m. ram, wether; dunce.
montuoso, _-tŭŏ'sŏ_, a. mountainous.
monumento, _mŏnŭmĕn' tŏ_, m. monument, tomb. [of stones; delay,
mora, _mŏ' rä_, f. mulberry, blackberry; heap
moraiuola, _mŏräĕŭ̈' lä_, f. mulberry.
moraiuolo, _-räŭ̈ŏ' lŏ_, m. mulberry-tree.
morale, _-rä' lĕ_, f. morals, pl. ; -, a. moral.
moralità, _-rälĕtä'_, f. morality.
morato, _mŏrä' tŏ_, a. of blackberry colour.
morbido, _mŏr' bĭdŏ_, a. soft, delicate; downy; tender; effeminate.
morbo, _mŏr' bŏ_, m. disease; contagion.
morboso, _-bŏ' sŏ_, a. morbid.
mordace, _-dä' dshĕ_, a. biting; pungent, sharp, satirical.
mordacità, _-däsh̆ĭtä'_, f. mordacity.
mordere, _mŏr' dĕrĕ_, v. a. ir. to bite; to backbite, to satirise, to censure. [ing.
mordicamento, _-dĭkämĕn' tŏ_, m. bite, bit-
mordicante, _-dĭkän' tĕ_, a. biting; sharp, tart. [smart, to fret, to burn.
mordicare, _-kä' rĕ_, v. a. to nibble; to
morditore, _-tŏ̆' rĕ_, m. slanderer.
morello, _mŏrĕl' lŏ_, a. blackish.
moresco, _mŏrĕs' kŏ_, a. Moorish.
moria, _mŏrĕ' ä_, f. plague; contagion.
moribondo, _-rĭbŏn' dŏ_, a. dying.
moriccia, _-rĭt' shä_, f. rubbish, ruins, pl.
morigerare, _-rĭ̆̆gĕrä' rĕ_, v. a. to teach good manners.
morigeratezza, _-tĕt' zä_, f. good manners.
morigerato, _-rä' tŏ_, a. well brought up.
morione, _-rĭ̆ŏ' nĕ_, m. helmet, head-piece.
morire, _-rĕ' rĕ_, v. n. ir. to die, to expire.
mormorare, _mŏrmŏrä' rĕ_, v. n. to warble, to purl; to murmur.
mormorio, _-mŏrĕ' ŏ_, m. murmur, war-bling; calumny.
moro, _mŏ' rŏ_, m. mulberry-tree; negro.
moroso, _mŏrŏ' sŏ_, a. tardy, slow.
morsa, _mŏr' sä_, f. screw-vice, pincers, pl.
morsecchiare, _-sĕkkĭä' rĕ_, morseg-giare, _-sĕdjä' rĕ_, v. a. to nibble.
morsello, _-sĕl' lŏ_, m. morsel, mouthful.
morsicare, see morsecchiare.
morso, _mŏr' sŏ_, m. bite; bit of a horse; mortaio, _-tä̆' ŏ_, m. mortar. [mouthful.
mortale, _-tä' lĕ_, a. deadly; capital.
mortalità, _-tälĭtä'_, f. mortality. [deadly.
mortalmente, _-mĕn' tĕ_, ad. mortally, morte, _mŏr' tĕ_, f. death; a -, mortally, to the death.
mortella, _-tĕl' lä_, f. myrtle. [ous.
mortifero, _-tĕ' fĕrŏ_, a. deadly, mortifer-
mortificare, _-tĭfĭkä' rĕ_, v. a. to mortify.
mortificazione, _-tzĭŏ' nĕ_, f. mortification; abstinence. [corpse.
morto, _mŏr' tŏ_, a. dead; -, m. dead body;
mortorio, _-tŏ̆' rĭŏ_, m. funeral.

morvido, see morbido. [buff.
mosca, _mŏs' kä_, f. fly; - cieca, blindman's
moscadello, _-kädĕl' lŏ_, m. muscat-wine.
moscado, _-kä' dŏ_, m. musk.
moschea, _-kä' ä_, f. mosque.
moscherino, _-kĕrĕ' nŏ_, m. gnat, midge.
moschettare, _-kĕttä' rĕ_, v. a. to kill with a musket-ball.
moschetto, _-kĕt' tŏ_, m. musket.
moscino, _mŏsshĕ' nŏ_, m. small fly.
moscio, _mŏssh' ŏ_, a. flabby, flaccid; soft.
moscione, _mŏsshŏ' nĕ_, m. gnat; tippler.
mossa, _mŏs' sä_, f. movement, motion.
mosso, _mŏs' sŏ_, a. moved.
mossolina, _-sŏlĕ' nä_, f. muslin.
mostacciata, _-tätshä' tä_, f. slap on the mostaccio, _-tät' shŏ_, m. face. [face.
mostarda, _-tär' dä_, f. mustard.
mosto, _mŏs' tŏ_, m. must, new wine.
mostra, _mŏs' trä_, f. show, display; review; appearance, semblance; sample, pattern; show-window, glass-case; dial-plate.
mostrare, _-trä' rĕ_, v. a. & n. to show; to demonstrate, to appear.
mostro, _mŏs' trŏ_, m. monster.
mostruoso, _-trŭŏ' sŏ_, a. monstrous.
mota, _mŏ' tä_, f. mud, mire, dirt. [propose.
motivare, _mŏtĭvä' rĕ_, v. a. to mention; to
motivo, _-tĕ' vŏ_, m. motive. [pulse.
moto, _mŏ' tŏ_, m. movement, motion; im-
motore, _mŏtŏ' rĕ_, m. mover, contriver.
motoso, _-tŏ' sŏ_, a. muddy, miry.
motta, _mŏt' tä_, f. clod, lump of earth.
motteggevole, _-tĕdjĕ' vŏlĕ_, a. facetious, merry, sportive. [quiz.
motteggiare, _-tĕdjä' rĕ_, v. a. to jeer, to
motteggio, _-tĕd' jŏ_, m. jest, banter.
motto, _mŏt' tŏ_, m. motto, device; word; movere, see muovere. [joke.
movimento, _mŏvĭmĕn' tŏ_, m. movement, motion. [tion.
mozione, _-tzĭŏ' nĕ_, f. movement; commo-
mozzare, _-tzä' rĕ_, v. n. to mutilate, to cut off. [remainder.
mozzicone, _-tzĭkŏ' nĕ_, m. trunk, stump;
mozzino, _-tzĕ' nŏ_, a. cunning.
mozzo, _mŏt' zŏ_, m. stump, fragment; stable-boy; -, a. cut off; mutilated.
mucchio, _mŭk' kĭŏ_, m. heap, pile; mass.
mucido, _mŏ' dshĭdŏ_, a. musty, moist; ef-feminate. [gum.
mucilaggine, _mŭdshĭlädʹjĭnĕ_, f. mucilage,
mucoso, _mŭkŏ' sŏ_, a. mucous.
muffa, _mŭf' fä_, f. mouldiness. [mouldy.
muffare, _-fä' rĕ_, v. n. to grow musty or
mugghiare, _mŭgghĭä' rĕ_, muggire, _mŭdjĕ' rĕ_, v. n. to low, to bellow.
muggito, _-djĕ' tŏ_, m. lowing, roar.
mughetto, _-ghĕt' tŏ_, m. lily of the valley.
mugnaio, _mŭnyä̆' ŏ_, m. miller; sea-gull.
mugnere, _mŭn' yĕrĕ_, v. a. ir. to milk; to extract. [groan.
mugolare, _mŭgŏlä' rĕ_, v. n. to yelp; to
mula, _mŏ' lä_, f. mule; slipper.
mulacchia, _mŭläk' kĭä_, f. jack-daw, crow.
mulatto, _-lät' tŏ_, m. mulatto.
muliebre, _-lĭä' brĕ_, a. womanish.

mulinare, _-lĭnă'rĕ_, v. n. to revolve in one's mind; to refine.
mulinello, _-nĕl'lŏ_, m. hand-mill.
mulino, _-lĭ'nŏ_, m. mill.
mulo, _mŏ'lŏ_, m. mule; (fig.) bastard.
multa, _mŭl'tă_, f. fine, penalty.
mungere, see **mugnere**.
municipale, _mănĭdshĭpă'lĕ_, a. municipal.
municipio, _-dshĕ'pĭŏ_, m. free-town.
munificenza, _-fĭdshĕn'tză_, f. munificence, bounty.
munifico, _-nĕ'fĭkŏ_, a. munificent, liberal.
munimento, _-nĭmĕn'tŏ_, m. monument; admonition.
munire, _-nĕ'rĕ_, v. a. to provide; to fortify.
munizione, _-nĭtzĭŏ'nĕ_, f. ammunition; fortification.   [meagre.
munto, _-mŭn'tŏ_, a. milked, drained; lean.
muovere, _mŭŏ'vĕrĕ_, v. a. ir. to move; to touch; to excite, to instigate; to persuade.
muraglia, _mŭră'lyă_, f. wall.
murare, _-ră'rĕ_, v. a. to wall; to build.
muratore, _-tŏ'rĕ_, m. mason.
muratura, _-tŏ'ră_, f. masonry.
murena, _-rĕ'nă_, f. lamprey.
muricciuolo, _-rĭtshŏ'lŏ_, m. little wall.
muro, _mŏ'rŏ_, m. (muri and mura, pl.) wall; rampart; home.
musa, _mŏ'să_, f. muse; pipe.   [lazy.
musardo, _mŏsăr'dŏ_, a. musing, loitering.
musare, _-să'rĕ_, v. n. to muse, to stare, to loiter.
muschio, _mŭs'kĭŏ_, m. moss; musk.
muschioso, _-kĭŏ'sŏ_, a. mossy.
muscolatura, _mŭskŏlătŏ'ră_, f. muscling.
muscolo, _mŭs'kŏlŏ_, m. _-kŭlŏ_, m. [muscle.
museo, _mŭsĕ'ŏ_, m. museum.
musica, _mŏ'sĭkă_, f. music.
musicale, _mŭsĭkă'lĕ_, a. musical.
musicista, _-dshĕs'tă_, m. musician.
musico, _mŏ'sĭkŏ_, m. musician; —, a. musical.   [—, a. moping, pouting.
muso, _mŏ'sŏ_, m. muzzle, snout; grimace;
musoliera, _mŭsŏlĭĕ'ră_, f. muzzle.
mussolina, _mŭssŏlĭ'nă_, m. muslin.
mustacchi, _-tăk'kĭ_, m. pl. whiskers.
mustio, _mŭs'tĭŏ_, m. moss.
muta, _mŏ'tă_, f. change, exchange; mutation; a – a – by turns.   [stant.
mutabile, _mŭtă'bĭlĕ_, a. mutable; incon-
mutande, _-tăn'dĕ_, f. pl. drawers, pl.
mutare, _-tă'rĕ_, v. a. to change, to alter.
mutazione, _-tzĭŏ'nĕ_, f. mutation.
mutilare, _-tĭlă'rĕ_, v. a. to mutilate.
mutilo, _mŏ'tĭlŏ_, a. mutilated, truncated.
muto, _mŏ'tŏ_, mutolo, _-tŏlŏ_, a. dumb, mute; —, m. dumb person.
mutuo, _mŏ'tŭŏ_, a. mutual, reciprocal.

N.

nacchera, _năk'kĕră_, f. kettle-drum.
nano, _nă'nŏ_, m. dwarf.
napo, _nă'pŏ_, m. turnip.
nappa, _năp'pă_, f. tuft, tassel.
nappo, _năp'pŏ_, m. cup, goblet; basin.

narciso, _nărdshĕ'sŏ_, m. daffodil, narcissus.
narcotico, _-kŏ'tĭkŏ_, m. narcotic.
nare, _nă'rĕ_, **narice**, _-rĕ'dshĕ_, f. nostril.
narrare, _nărră'rĕ_, v. a. to relate, to tell
narrativo, _-tĕ'vŏ_, a. narrative.
narratore, _-tŏ'rĕ_, m. relater, teller.
narrazione, _-tzĭŏ'nĕ_, f. narration; account.
nasata, _năsă'tă_, f. rebuff, reprimand.
nascenza, _năsshĕn'tză_, f. birth, nativity.
nascere, _năssh'ĕrĕ_, v. n. ir. to be born; to arise, to proceed.
nascita, _năssh'ĭtă_, f. extraction; descent.
nascondere, _năskŏn'dĕrĕ_, v. a. ir. to conceal, to hide.   [lurking-place.
nascondiglio, _-dĕl'yŏ_, m. hiding-place,
nascoso, _-kŏ'sŏ_, **nascosto**, _-kŏs'tŏ_, a. hidden; secret.   [bolt, catch.
nasello, _-sĕl'lŏ_, m. small _or_ snub-nose.
naso, _nă'sŏ_, m. nose.
naspo, _năs'pŏ_, m. reel; winder.
nassa, _năs'să_, f. bow-net.
nastraio, _năstră'ŏ_, m. riband-weaver.
nastro, _năs'trŏ_, m. ribbon.
nasturzio, _-tŭr'tzĭŏ_, m. water-cress.
nasuto, _năsŭ'tŏ_, a. big- _or_ long-nosed.
natale, _nătă'lĕ_, m. nativity; —, a. natal; native.
natatoria, _-tătŏ'rĭă_, f. fish-pond.
natica, _nă'tĭkă_, f. buttock.
natio, _nătĕ'ŏ_, a. natal, native.
natività, _-tĭvĭtă'_, f. nativity, birth.
nativo, _-tĕ'vŏ_, a. native, natal.
nato, _nă'tŏ_, m. (poet.) son, child.
natta, _năt'tă_, f. trick; tumour in the mouth; mat; twist.
natura, _nătŏ'ră_, f. nature.
naturale, _-tŭră'lĕ_, a. natural.
naturalezza, _-lĕt'ză_, f. naturalness; natural property; nature.   [ralize.
naturalizzare, _-lĭdză'rĕ_, v. a. to natu-
naturalmente, _-mĕn'tĕ_, ad. naturally.
naturare, _-tŭră'rĕ_, v. a. to render natural, to accustom.   [wreck.
naufragare, _năŭfrăgă'rĕ_, v. n. to ship-
naufragio, _-fră'gĭŏ_, m. ship-wreck.
naufrago, _năŭ'frăgŏ_, a. wrecked, ruined.
nausea, _năŭ'sĕă_, f. nausea, loathing.
nauseabondo, _-sĕăbŏn'dŏ_, **nauseante**, _-sĕăn'tĕ_, a. nauseous.
nauseare, _-sĕă'rĕ_, v. n. to nauseate.
nauseoso, _-sĕŏ'sŏ_, a. nauseous.
nauta, _năŭ'tă_, m. (poet.) sailor, boatman.
nautica, _nă'ŭtĭkă_, f. art of sailing.
nautico, _nă'ŭtĭkŏ_, a. nautical.
navale, _năvă'lĕ_, m. dockyard; —, a. naval, maritime.
navata, _nă'tă_, f. ship's freight, boat-ful.
nave, _nă'vĕ_, f. ship, vessel; nave (of a church).
navicella, _-vĭdshĕl'lă_, f. bark, boat, barge.
navigare, _vĭgă'rĕ_, v. n. to navigate, to sail.
navigatore, _-tŏ'rĕ_, m. seaman.   [sail.
navigazione, _-tzĭŏ'nĕ_, f. navigation.
naviglio, _-vĭl'yŏ_, m. fleet; ship.
nazionale, _nătzĭŏnă'lĕ_, a. national.
nazionalità, _-nălĭtă'_, f. nationality.
nazione, _-tzĭŏ'nĕ_, f. nation.

ne, nĕ, pn. (some) of it, (some) of them.
nè, nĕ, c. neither, nor.
nebbia, nĕb'bĕa, f. fog, mist; (fig.) ignorance.
nebbioso,—bĕ' sŏ, a. foggy, misty.
nebuloso, nĕbŭlŏ' sŏ, a. nebulous, misty.
necessariamente,—dshĕssăriāmĕn'tĕ, ad. necessarily.   [—, a. necessary.
necessario,—dshĕssă' rĕŏ, m. water-closet;
necessità,—dshĕssĭtä' f. necessity.
necessitare,—tä' rĕ, v. a. to necessitate.
necrologia,—krŏlŏjä' ä, f. necrology.
ned, nĕd, for : nè.
nefandezza,—fāndĕt'zä, f. wickedness.
nefando,—făn' dŏ, a. most execrable.
nefario,—fä' rĕŏ, a. nefarious.
nefasto,—fäs'tŏ, a. unlucky, inauspicious.
negare, nĕgä' rĕ, v. a. to deny, to disown.
negativa,—gätĭ' vä, f. negation, denial.
negativo,—tĕ' vŏ, a. negative.
negazione,—tzĭŏ' nĕ, f. negation, refusal.
neghittoso,—ghĭttŏ' sŏ, a. idle, lazy.
negligente,—glĭjĕn' tĕ, a. negligent.
negligenza,—glĭjĕn' tzä, f. negligence.
negligere,—glĕ' jĕrĕ, v. a. ir. to neglect.
negoziante,—gŏdzĭän' tĕ, m. merchant, trader.
negoziare,—gŏdzĭä' rĕ, v. n. to negotiate.
negozio,—gŏ' dzĭŏ, m. business; trade, traffic.   [gloomy, sad.
negro, nĕ' grŏ, m. negro; —, a. black,
negromante, nĕgrŏmän' tĕ, m. necromancer.
negromanzia,—mäntzĭ' ä, f. necromancy.
nembo, nĕm' bŏ, m. sudden rain, shower.
nemicare, nĕmĭkä' rĕ, v. a. to hate, to pursue, to persecute.
nemichevole,—kĕ' vŏlĕ, a. inimical, cruel.
nemico, nĕmĕ' kŏ, m. enemy, fiend, foe; —, a. hostile; contrary.
neo, nĕ' ŏ, m. mole; patch, spot.
neologismo, nĕŏlŏjĭs' mŏ, m. neologism.
nepitella, nĕpĭtĕl' lä, f. (bot.) cap-mint.
nepote, nĕpŏ' tĕ, m. & f. nephew; niece.
neppure, nĕppŏ' rĕ, ad. not even, not so much as.
nerbo, nĕr' bŏ, m. nerve; sinew.
nerboruto,—bŏrŏ' tŏ, a. nervous, vigorous.
nereggiare, nĕrĕdjä' rĕ, v. n. to incline to black.
nerezza,—rĕt' zä, f. blackness, swarthiness.
nero, nĕ' rŏ, a. black; wicked.
nerveo, nĕr' vĕŏ, a. nervous; vigorous.
nervo, nĕr' vŏ, m. nerve, sinew; strength.
nervoso, nĕrvŏ' sŏ, a. nervous.   [ignorant.
nesciente, nĕsshĕn' tĕ, nescio, nĕssh' ĭŏ, a.
nespola, nĕs' pŏlä, f. medlar.
nespolo, nĕs' pŏlŏ, m. medlar-tree.
nesso, nĕs' sŏ, m. connection.
nessuno,—sŏ' nŏ, a. none, nobody, not one.
nesto, nĕs' tŏ, m. graft, scion.
nettare, nĕttä' rĕ, v. a. & n. to clean; to make a sudden flight.
nettare, nĕt' tärĕ, m. nectar.   [ness.
nettezza,—tĕt' zä, f. cleanliness; uprightaetto, nĕt' tŏ, a. clean, neat, pure; clear, net; faithful; —, ad. cleanly; honestly; frankly.

neutrale, nĕŭträ' lĕ, a. neutral, indifferent.
neutralità,—trälĭtä' f. neutrality.
neutro, nĕ' ŭtrŏ, a. neuter; indifferent.
neve, nä' vĕ, f. snow.
nevicare, nĕvĭkä' rĕ, v. imp. to snow.
nevicata,—kä' tä, f. snow-drift.
nevoso,—vŏ' sŏ, a. snowy.
nibbio, nĭb' bĭŏ, m. kite; simpleton.
nicchia, nĭk' kĕä, f. niche.
nicchiare,—kĕä' rĕ, v. n. to whine, to complain; to be irresolute.
nicchio, nĭk' kĭŏ, m. cockle-fish.
nidificare, nĭdĭfĭkä' rĕ, v. n. to nest, to make a nest; to settle.
nido, nĕ' dŏ, m. nest; home.
niego, nĭĕ' gŏ, m. denial, refusal.
niente, nĭĕn' tĕ, m. nothing; — affatto, nothing at all.
nientedimanco,—dĭmän' kŏ, nientedimeno,—mä' nŏ, nientemeno,—tĕmä' nŏ ad. nevertheless, however.
nimicare, see nemicare.
nimicizia,—dshĕ tzĭä, f. enmity.
ninfa, nĭn' fä, f. nymph.
ninfea,—fĕ' ä, f. water-lily.
ninnare,—nä' rĕ, v. a. to lull to sleep.
nipote, see nepote.
nissuno, see nessuno.
nitidezza, nĭtĭdĕt' zä, f. brightness.
nitido, nĕ' tĭdŏ, a. neat, clean, bright; shining.
nitrire, nĭtrĕ' rĕ, v. n. to neigh.
nitrito,—trĕ' tŏ, m. neighing.
nitro, nĕ' trŏ, m. nitre, saltpetre.
niuno, nĭŏ' nŏ, pn. no one, nobody, none.
niveo, nĕ' vĕŏ, a. niveous, snow-white.
no, nŏ, ad. no; not.
nobile, nŏ' bĭlĕ, m. nobleman; —, a. noble.
nobilitare, nŏbĭlĭtä' rĕ, v. a. to ennoble.
nobilmente,—bĭlmĕn' tĕ ad. nobly, generously.
nobiltà,—bĭltä' f. nobility; generosity.
nocca, nŏk' kä, f. knuckle, joint.
nocchiere,—kĕä' rĕ, m. pilot.
nocchio, nŏk' kĭŏ, m. knot, knob, hole (in trees &c.).   [fruit].
nocciolo, nŏtsh' ŏlŏ, m. kernel, stone (or
nocciuola,—tshŭŏ' lä, f. hazel-nut.
nocciuolo,—tshŭŏ' lŏ, m. hazel, filbert-tree.
noce, nŏ' dshĕ, f. nut; —, m. nut-tree.
nocella, see nocciuola.
nocente,—dshĕn' tĕ, a. noxious, hurtful.
nocevole,—dshĕ' vŏlĕ, a. hurtful.
nocivo,—dshĕ' vŏ, a. hurtful.
nocumento,—kŭmĕn' tŏ, m. damage, wrong.
noderoso,—dĕrŏ' sŏ, a. knotty, knobby.
nodo, nŏ' dŏ, m. knot; joint.
nodoso,—dŏ' sŏ, a. knotty.
noi, nŏ' ĭ, pn. pl. we, us.
noia, nŏ' ä, f. weariness, trouble, vexation.
noiare, nŏĭä' rĕ, v. a. to weary, to tease.
noioso, nŏĭŏ' sŏ, a. wearisome, tiresome, tedious.
noleggiare, nŏlĕdjä' rĕ, v. a. to freight.
noleggio,—lĕd' jŏ, nolo, nŏ' lŏ, m. freighting, hire.
nome, nŏ' mĕ, m. name; renown, noun.

nomignolo, *nōmēn'yōlō,* m. surname, nickname, by-name.

nomina, *nō'mīnä,* f. nomination.

nominale, *nōmīnä'lĕ,* a. nominal.

nominare, *—nä'rĕ,* v. a. to name, to call, to appoint.   [case.

nominativo, *—tĕ'vō,* m. (gr.) nominative

nompariglia, *nōmpärĕl'yä,* f. (print.) non pareil.

non, *nōn,* ad. not; no ; **– che,** not only.

noncurante, *nōnkūrän'tĕ,* a. careless.

noncuranza, *—rän'tzä,* f. carelessness.

nondimanco, *—dīmän'kō,* **nondimeno,** *—mä'nō,* ad. nevertheless, however.

nonna, *nōn'nä,* f. grandmother.

nonno, *nōn'nō,* m. grandfather.

nonnulla, *—nūl'lä,* f. thing of no moment.

nono, *nō'nō,* a. ninth.

nonostante(chè), *nōnōstän'tä(kĕ'),* c. notwithstanding that.

nonuplo, *nōnō'plō,* a. ninefold.

norcino, *nōrdshĕ'nō,* m. hog-butcher; bad surgeon.

norma, *nōr'mä,* f. rule, model. [surgeon.

normale, *nōrmä'lĕ,* a. normal.

norte, *nōr'tĕ,* m. North.

nostalgia, *nōstäljĕ'ä,* f. home-sickness.

nostrale, *—trä'lĕ,* a. of our own country.

nostro, *nō'strō,* pn. ours ; our.

nota, *nō'tä,* f. note ; mark, sign ; stain.

notabile, *nōtä'bīlĕ,* a. notable, remarkable.

notare, *—tä'rĕ,* v. a. to note, to mark; to remark; to sing by note ; **–,** v. n. to swim.

notarile, *—tärĕ'lĕ,* a. attested before a notary. *—tä'rō,* m. notary.   [tary.

notificare, *—tīfīkä'rĕ,* v. a. to notify.

notificazione, *—tzīō'nĕ,* f. notification.

notizia, *—tĕ'tzä,* f. notice, information.

notomia, *—tōmē'ä,* f. anatomy. [tomize.

notomizzare, *—mēdzä'rĕ,* v. a. to ana-

notorio, *—tō'rēō,* a. notorious.

nottambulo, *nōttäm'būlō,* m. night-walker.

nottata, *—tä'tä,* f. whole night.

notte, *nōt'tĕ,* f. night; **di –,** by night.

nottetempo, *—tĕm'pō,* ad. in the nighttime.

nottola, *nōt'tōlä,* f. wooden latch; bat.

nottolone, *—tōlō'nĕ,* m. night-walker.

notturno, *nōttūr'nō,* a. nocturnal, nightly.

novamente, *nōvämĕn'tĕ,* ad. newly.

novanta, *—vän'tä,* a. ninety.

novantesimo, *—tĕ'sīmō,* a. ninetieth.

nove, *nō'vĕ,* a. nine.

novecento, *nōvĕdshĕn'tō,* a. nine hundred.

novella, *—vĕl'lä,* f. story, tale ; news.

novellamente, *see* **novamente.**

novellare, *—lä'rĕ,* v. n. to tell stories; to prattle, to prate, to chat.

novellista, *—lis'tä,* m. writer of novels.

novello, *—vĕl'lō,* a. new, young; modern.

novembre, *—vĕm'brĕ,* m. November.

noverare, *—vĕrä'rĕ,* v. a. to number, to compute.   [mother-in-law.

noverca, *—vĕr'kä,* f. (poet.) step-mother;

novero, *nō'vĕrō,* m. number.

novilunio, *nōvīlō'nēō,* m. new moon.

novità, *nōvītä',* f. novelty, novity.

novizio, *—vĕ'tzīō,* m. novice ; beginner.

novo, *see* **nuovo.**

nozione, *nōtzīō'nĕ,* f. notion, idea.

nozze, *nōt'zĕ,* f. pl. wedding; marriage.

nube, *nō'bĕ,* f. (poet.) cloud.

nubile, *nō'bīlĕ,* a. marriageable.

nubiloso, *nūbīlō'sō,* a. cloudy.

nuca, *nō'kä,* f. nape of the neck.

nudare, *nūdä'rĕ,* v. a. to strip naked.

nudità, *—dītä',* f. nakedness.

nudo, *nō'dō,* a. naked, bare.

nulla, *nūl'lä,* m. nothing.

nulladimeno, *—dīmä'nō,* ad. nevertheless.

nullità, *nūllītä',* f. nullity, nothingness; non-existence.   [invalid.

nulle, *nūl'lĕ,* a. no, no one, none; void,

nume, *nō'mĕ,* m. (poet.) deity, divinity.

numerare, *nūmĕrä'rĕ,* v. a. to number, to count.

numeratore, *—tō'rĕ,* m. (ar.) numerator.

numerazione, *—tzīō'nĕ,* f. numeration, numbering.

numerico, *—mä'rīkō,* a. numerical.

numero, *nū'mĕrō,* m. number; cipher.

numeroso, *—mĕrō'sō,* a. numerous.

nunzio, *nūn'tzīō,* m. nuncio, ambassador.

nuocere, *nwō'dshĕrĕ,* v. a. ir. to hurt, to prejudice.

nuora, *nwō'rä,* f. daughter-in-law.

nuotare, *nūōtä'rĕ,* v. n. to swim.

nuova, *nwō'vä,* f. notice, news.

nuovamente, *—mĕn'tĕ,* ad. newly ; again.

nuovo, *nwō'vō,* a. new; fresh; **di –,** again.

nutricare, *nūtrīkä'rĕ,* v. a. to nourish, to feed.

nutrice, *—trē'dshĕ,* f. nurse, foster-mother.

nutrimento, *—trēmĕn'tō,* m. nourishment, aliment, food.   [tain.

nutrire, *—trē'rĕ,* v. a. to nourish ; to main-

nutritivo, *—trītē'vō,* a. nourishing, nutritious.

nuvola, *nō'vōlä,* f. cloud; flight. [tious.

nuvolo, *nō'vōlō,* m. cloud, clouds, pl.

nuvoloso, *—vōlō'sō,* a. cloudy.

nuziale, *nūtzīä'lĕ,* a. nuptial.

O.

o, *ō,* c. either, or.

obbediente, *ōbbĕdīĕn'tĕ,* a. obedient.

obbedienza, *—dīĕn'tzä,* f. obedience.

obbedire, *—dī'rĕ,* v. a. to obey. [compel.

obbligare, *ōbblīgä'rĕ,* v. a. to oblige; to

obbligazione, *—tzīō'nĕ,* f. obligation; bond.

obbligo, *ōb'līgō,* m. obligation, bond, duty.

obbrobrio, *ōbbrō'brīō,* m. dishonour, infamy, shame.

obbrobrioso, *—brīō'sō,* a. opprobrious.

obeso, *ōbĕ'sō,* a. corpulent, paunchy.

obiettare, *ōbīĕttä'rĕ,* v. a. to object to, to resist.

obiettivo, *—tē'vō,* a. objective. [resist.

obietto, *ōbīĕt'tō,* m. object, aim, intent; **–,** a. opposed.

obiezione, *—tzīō'nĕ,* f. objection.

oblazione, *—lätzīō'nĕ,* f. offering.

obliare, *—līä'rĕ,* v. a. to forget.

oblio, *—lī'ō,* m. oblivion, forgetfulness.

obliquare, *–lŭĕ-kŭă' rĕ*, v. n. to decline.
obliquità, *–kŭĕtŭ'*, f. obliquity.
obliquo, *–lĕ' kŭŏ*, a. oblique; indirect.
oblivione, *–lĭvĕŏ' nĕ*, f. oblivion, forgetfulness.
oblungo, *–lŭn' gŏ*, a. oblong. [ness.
oboe, *ŏ' bŏĕ*, m. (mus.) hautbois.
oca, *ŏk' ă*, f. goose. [sion.
occasionare, *ŏkḱā̆sĭŏnă' rĕ*, v. a. to occasion.
occasione, *–sĭŏ' nĕ*, f. occasion.
occaso, *–kă' sŏ*, m. sunset; West; (fig.) death.
occhiale, *–kḱĕ' ă lĕ*, m. spectacles; telescope.
occhiare, *–kŭ' rĕ*, v. a. to eye, to ogle.
occhiata, *–kŭă' tă*, f. look; ogle; rock.
occhieggare, *–kĕĕdjă' rĕ*, v. n. to ogle, to look amorously; to make eyes.
occhiello, *–kĕĕ' lŏ*, m. button-hole; eyelet.
occhio, *ŏk' kĭŏ*, m., occhi, pl. eye, look, sight; bud; skylight. [western.
occidentale, *ŏtshĭdĕntă' lĕ*, a. occidental.
occidente, *–dĕn' tĕ*, m. occident, West.
occipizio, *–pĕ' tzĭŏ*, m. occiput.
occorrente, *ŏkkŏrrĕn' tĕ*, a. occurring; happening.
occorrenza, *–rĕn' tză*, f. occurrence; want.
occorrere, *–kŏr' rĕrĕ*, v. n. ir. to occur, to happen; to meet; to want; to remember.
occultare, *–kŭltă' rĕ*, v. a. to conceal, to hide.
occulto, *–kŭl' tŏ*, a. hidden; latent. [hide.
occupare, *–kŭpă' rĕ*, v. a. to occupy; to employ.
occupazione, *–tzĭŏ' nĕ*, f. occupation.
oceano, *ŏdshĕ' ănŏ*, m. ocean.
oculare, *ŏkŭlă' rĕ*, a. ocular.
oculato, *–lŭ' tŏ*, a. cautious, circumspect.
oculista, *–lĭs' tă*, m. oculist.
od, *ŏd*, c. or, either.
odiare, *ŏdĭă' rĕ*, v. a. to hate.
odierno, *ŏdĭĕr' nŏ*, a. of to-day.
odio, *ŏ' dĭŏ*, m. hatred. [able.
odioso, *ŏdĭŏ' sŏ*, a. odious, hateful, detestodontalgia, *ŏdŏntăljĕ' ă*, f. odontalgia.
odontalgico, *–tăl' jĭkŏ*, a. odontalgic.
odorare, *ŏdŏră' rĕ*, v. a. & n. to smell, to scent; to have a smell. [ing.
odorato, *–ră' tŏ*, m. smell; sense of smelling.
odore, *ŏdŏ' rĕ*, m. odour, smell, scent; (fig.)
odorifero, *–rĕ' fĕrŏ*, a. odoriferous. [hint.
odoroso, *–rŏ' sŏ*, a. odorous.
offendere, *ŏffĕn' dĕrĕ*, v. a. & n. ir. to offend, to injure; to displease.
offensivo, *–sĕ' vŏ*, a. offensive.
offerire, *–fĕrĕ' rĕ*, offrire, *–frĕ' rĕ*, v. a. to offer, to present; to sacrifice.
offerta, *–fĕr' tă*, f. offer, proposal; offering.
offesa, *–fĕ' să*, f. offence.
officiale, *–fĭdshĭ' lĕ*, m. officer; official.
officiare, *–dshă' rĕ*, v. n. to officiate; to say mass. [tory.
officina, *–dshĕ' nă*, f. work-shop; laboraofficio, *–fĕ' dshĭŏ*, m. office, charge; duty.
officioso, *–fĭdshĭ' sŏ*, a. officious.
offuscare, *–fŭskă' rĕ*, v. a. to obfuscate, to darken.
oggettivo, *ŏdjĕttĕ' vŏ*, a. objective.
oggetto, *ŏdjĕt' tŏ*, m. object.
oggi, *ŏd' jĕ*, ad. to-day, now-a-days.

oggidì, *–dĕ'*, oggigiorno, *–jŏr' nŏ*, ad. now-a-days.
oggimai, *–mă' ĕ*, ad. now, henceforth; at last. [every time that.
ogni, *ŏn' yĕ*, a. every, all; – volta che, every time that.
ognora, *–yŏ' ră*, ad. always, continually.
ognorache, *–yŏrăkĕ'*, ad. every time that.
ognuno, *–yŏ' nŏ*, pn. every one.
oh! oi! *ŏĕ'*, i. alas! ah!
oibò! *ŏĭbŏ'*, i. fy! shame!
oimè, *ŏĭmĕ'*, i. alas!
olà! *ŏlă'*, i. ho there! stop!
oleastro, *ŏlĕăs' trŏ*, m. wild olive-tree.
oleoso, *ŏlĕŏ' sŏ*, a. oily.
olezzare, *ŏlĕdză' rĕ*, v. n. to smell sweet.
olezzo, *ŏlĕd' zŏ*, m. odour, fragrance. [ing.
olfatto, *ŏlfăt' tŏ*, m. smell, sense of smelloliandolo, *ŏlĭăn' dŏlŏ*, m. oil-merchant.
olibano, *ŏlĕ' bănŏ*, m. frankincense.
olio, *ŏ' lĭŏ*, m. oil.
olioso, *ŏlĭŏ' sŏ*, a. oily, greasy.
oliva, *ŏlĕ' vă*, f. olive; olive-tree.
olivastro, *–lĭvăs' trŏ*, a. olive-coloured.
oliveto, *–vĕ' tŏ*, m. olive-grove.
olivo, *ŏlĕ' vŏ*, m. olive-tree.
olla, *ŏl' lă*, f. pot; – podrida, hotch-potch.
olmo, *ŏl' mŏ*, m. elm-tree.
oltracciò, *ŏltrătshŏ'*, ad. moreover, besides.
oltracotante, *–kŏtăn' tĕ*, a. presumptuous.
oltracotanza, *–tăn' tză*, f. forwardness, superciliousness. [to insult.
oltraggiare, *–trădjă' rĕ*, v. a. to outrage.
oltraggio, *–trăd' jŏ*, m. outrage, insult; a –, excessively.
oltraggioso, *–djŏ' sŏ*, a. outrageous.
oltramontano, *–mŏntă' nŏ*, a. beyond the mountains.
oltranza, *ŏltrăn' tză*, f. outrage.
oltre, *ŏl' trĕ*, pr. besides, beyond, more than, above; –, ad. very far, very forward.
oltrechè, *–trĕkĕ'*, ad. & c. besides that, moreover. [yond; to exceed.
oltrepassare, *–păssă' rĕ*, v. a. to go beomaggio, *ŏmăd' jŏ*, m. homage, submission.
omai, *ŏmă' ĕ*, ad. now; at length.
ombè, *ŏmbĕ'*, ad. now then, well!
ombelico, *–bĕ' lĭkŏ*, ombilico, *–bĕ' lĭkŏ*, m. navel.
ombra, *ŏm' bră*, f. shade, shadow; spectre; appearance; pretext; suspicion.
ombracolo, *–bră' kŏlŏ*, m. bower, shady place; protection. [shadow.
ombrare, *–bră' rĕ*, v. a. to shade, to overombratile, *–tĕ' lĕ*, a. shady; feigned.
ombreggiare, *–brĕdjă' rĕ*, v. a. to shade to overshadow.
ombrello, *–brĕl' lŏ*, m. umbrella.
ombroso, *–brŏ' sŏ*, a. shady.
omero, *ŏ' mĕrŏ*, m. shoulder. [leave out.
omettere, *ŏmĕt' tĕrĕ*, v. a. ir. to omit, to
omicida, *ŏmĭdshĕ' dă*, m. murderer.
omicidio, *–dshĕ' dĭŏ*, m. murder, manslaughter.
omissione, *ŏmĭssĭŏ' nĕ*, f. omission; fault.
omnibus, *ŏm' nĭbŭs*, m. omnibus, 'bus.
omogeneo, *ŏmŏjă' nĕŏ*, a. homogeneous.

omologo, ŏmŏ'lŏgŏ, a. homologous.
omonimo, ŏmŏ'nĭmŏ, a. homonymous.
onagro, ŏ'năgrŏ, m. wild ass.
oncia, ŏn'dshă, f. ounce; inch.
onda, ŏn'dă, f. wave, billow.
ondare, -dă'rĕ, v. n. to float.
ondata, -dă'tă, f. surge, billow.
ondato, -dă'tŏ, a. watered. [this reason.
onde, ŏn'dĕ, ad. whence, wherefore, for
ondechè, -dĕkĕ', ad. from whatever place.
ondeggiare, -dĕdjă'rĕ, v. n. to waver, to be agitated.
onerario, ŏnĕră'rĭŏ, a. having the care of.
oneroso, -rŏ'sŏ, a. burdensome, heavy.
onestà, ŏnĕstă', f. honesty; decency.
onestamente, -mĕn'tĕ, ad. honestly; decently.
onestare, ŏnĕstă'rĕ, v. a. to embellish.
onesto, ŏnĕs'tŏ, a. honest; modest.
onninamente, ŏnnĭnămĕn'tĕ, ad. entirely.
onnipossente, -pŏssĕn'tĕ, **onnipotente,** -tĕn'tĕ, a. almighty.
onnipotenza, -pŏtĕn'tză, f. omnipotence.
onniscienza, -sshĕn'tză, f. omniscience.
onorare, ŏnŏră'rĕ, v. a. to honour.
onorario, -ră'rĭŏ, m. fee, reward, salary.
onore, ŏnŏ'rĕ, m. honour, respect; rank.
onorevole, -rĕ'vŏlĕ, a. honourable; splendid.
onta, ŏn'tă, f. shame, disgrace. [did.
ontano, -tă'nŏ, m. elder-tree.
ontoso, -tŏ'sŏ, a. shameful.
onusto, ŏnŭs'tŏ, a. loaded, laden.
opacità, ŏpădshĭtă', f. opacity. [pellucid.
opaco, ŏpă'kŏ, a. opaque, obscure; not
opera, ŏ'pĕră, f. work; action, deed; business; opera.
operaio, ŏpĕră'ŏ, m. workman. [work.
operare, -ră'rĕ, v. a. to operate, to do, to
operatore, -rătŏ'rĕ, m. operator, workman, artificer.
operazione, -tzĭŏ'nĕ, f. operation.
operoso, -rŏ'sŏ, a. laborious, busy.
opimo, ŏpĭ'mŏ, a. abundant, fertile; rich.
opinabile, ŏpĭnă'bĭlĕ, a. probable.
opinare, -nă'rĕ, v. a. to opine, to think.
opinione, -nĭŏ'nĕ, f. opinion; esteem.
oppilare, ŏppĭlă'rĕ, v. a. to oppilate, to obstruct.
oppilazione, -tzĭŏ'nĕ, f. obstruction.
oppio, ŏp'pĭŏ, m. white poplar; opium.
opporre, -pŏr'rĕ, v. a. ir. to oppose; to object; **opporsi,** -pŏr'sĭ, to set oneself against. [opportunely, seasonably.
opportunamente, -pŏrtŭnămĕn'tĕ, ad.
opportunità, -tănĭtă', f. opportunity.
opportuno, -tŏ'nŏ, a. seasonable.
opposito, see **opposto.**
opposizione, -pŏsĭtzĭŏ'nĕ, f. opposition.
opposto, -pŏs'tŏ, a. opposite, contrary.
oppressione, -prĕssĭŏ'nĕ, f. oppression.
opprimere, -prĭ'mĕrĕ, v. a. to oppress.
oppugnare, -pŭnyă'rĕ, v. a. to oppugn.
opra, see **opera.**
oprare, see **operare.**
opulento, ŏpŭlĕn'tŏ, a. opulent, wealthy.
ora, ŏ'ră, f. hour; time; -, ad. now, at
oracolo, ŏră'kŏlŏ, m. oracle. [present.

orafo, ŏ'răfŏ, m. goldsmith.
oramai, see **ormai.**
orare, ŏră'rĕ, v. a. to pray; to harangue.
orario, ŏră'rĭŏ, m. (rail.) time-table; -,
orata, ŏră'tă, f. gold-fish. [a. horary.
oratore, -tŏ'rĕ, m. haranguer; preacher.
oratoria, -tŏ'rĭă, f. eloquence.
oratorio, -tŏ'rĭŏ, m. oratory; (mus.) oratorio; -, a. rhetorical.
orazione, -tzĭŏ'nĕ, f. prayer; speech, rhetorical harangue.
orbare, ŏrbă'rĕ, v. a. to deprive of.
orbe, ŏr'bĕ, m. orb, globe.
orbè, ŏrbĕ', **orbene,** -bă'nĕ, ad. well and good; be it so; all in good time.
orbicolare, -bĭkŏlă'rĕ, a. spherical.
orbita, ŏr'bĭtă, f. orbit.
orbità, ŏrbĭtă', f. blindness; privation.
orbo, ŏr'bŏ, a. blind; bereft.
orca, ŏr'kă, f. sea-monster.
orcio, ŏr'dshŏ, m. oil-pot, cruet; jar, pitcher.
orciuolo, -dshŭŏ'lŏ, m. pitcher, jug.
orco, ŏr'kŏ, m. hobgoblin; hell.
orda, ŏr'dă, f. horde, tribe.
ordegno, -dĕn'yŏ, **ordigno,** -dĭn'yŏ, m. machine, engine; tool; structure.
ordinale, -dĭnă'lĕ, a. ordinary, usual.
ordinanza, -năntză, f. ordinance; decree; crew. [speak.
ordinare, -nă'rĕ, v. a. to order, to be
ordinario, -nă'rĭŏ, a. ordinary; usual; common, vulgar.
ordinazione, -tzĭŏ'nĕ, f. order, decree; medical prescription; ordination.
ordine, ŏr'dĭnĕ, m. order. [machinate.
ordire, -dĕ'rĕ, v. a. to warp; to frame, to
ordito, -dĕ'tŏ, m. warp; weaver's warp.
orditoio, -tŏ'ŏ, m. loom.
orecchiare, ŏrĕkkĭă'rĕ, v. a. & n. to listen.
orecchiata, -kă'tă, f. box on the ear.
orecchino, -kĕ'nŏ, m. ear-ring.
orecchio, ŏrĕk'kĭŏ, m. ear.
orefice, ŏră'fĭdshĕ, m. goldsmith.
oreria, ŏrĕră', f. gold-plate.
orfana, ŏr'fănă, f. orphan girl.
orfano, ŏr'fănŏ, m. orphan.
organico, ŏrgă'nĭkŏ, a. organic.
organizzare, -gănĭdză'rĕ, v. a. to organise.
organizzazione, -dzătzĭŏ'nĕ, f. organisation.
organo, ŏr'gănŏ, m. organ.
orgasmo, -găs'mŏ, m. orgasm.
orgoglio, -gŏl'yŏ, m. pride, haughtiness.
orgoglioso, -glĭŏ'sŏ, a. proud, haughty.
oricalco, ŏrĭkăl'kŏ, m. yellow brass.
orientale, ŏrĭĕntă'lĕ, a. oriental.
oriente, ŏrĭĕn'tĕ, m. Orient, East.
orifizio, ŏrĭfĭ'tzĭŏ, m. opening, mouth.
originale, ŏrĭjĭnă'lĕ, m. original; -, a. original. [to take its rise.
originare, -nă'rĕ, v. a. & n. to originate;
originario, -nă'rĭŏ, a. original.
origine, ŏrĭ'jĭnĕ, f. origin. [quire.
origliare, ŏrĭlyă'rĕ, v. n. to listen; to in-
origliere, -yĕ'rĕ, m. cushion.
orina, ŏrĕ'nă, f. urine.

orinale, *orinā′ lĕ*, m. chamber-pot.
orinare, *–nā′ rĕ*, v. n. to urine, to pass water.
oriolaio, *orĭōlā′ ŏ*, m. watch-maker.
oriolo, *orĭō′ lŏ*, m. watch, clock.
orizzontale, *orĭdzōntā′ lĕ*, a. horizontal.
orizzontalmente, *–mēn′ tĕ*, a. horizont-
orizzonte, *–tzŏn′ tĕ*, m. horizon. [ally.
orlare, *orlā′ rĕ*, v. a. to hem; to border.
orliccio, *–lĭt′ shŏ*, m. kissing-crust; hem.
orlo, *or′ lŏ*, m. hem.
orma, *or′ mă*, f. trace, footstep.
ormai, *ormā′ ĭ*, ad. now; at length.
ormare, *–mā′ rĕ*, v. a. to trace, to pursue.
ormeggiarsi, *–mēdjār′ sĭ*, v. r. to cast
anchor.
ormeggio, *–mēd′ jŏ*, m. (mar.) stern-fast.
ornamento, *ornămēn′ tŏ*, m. ornament.
ornare, *–nā′ rĕ*, v. a. to adorn, to trim.
orno, *or′ nŏ*, m. wild ash.
oro, *ŏ′ rŏ*, m. gold.
orologio, *orŏlŏ′ jŏ*, m. clock, watch.
oroscopo, *orŏs′ kŏpŏ*, m. horoscope.
orpello, *orpĕl′ lŏ*, m. tinsel; (fig.) disguise.
orrendo, *orrĕn′ dŏ*, a. horrible, dreadful.
orrettizio, *–rĕttĭ′ tzĭŏ*, a. obreptitious.
orribile, *–rĭ′ bĭlĕ*, orrido, *ŏr′ rĭdŏ*, a. hor-
orrore, *ŏrrŏ′ rĕ*, m, horror, fright. [rible.
orso, *ŏr′ sŏ*, m. bear; paring-shovel.
orsù, *orsŭ′*, i. come on !
ortaggio, *–tăd′ jŏ*, m. greens, pot-herbs.
ortense, *–tĕn′ sĕ*, a. garden-, of a garden.
ortica, *–tĭ′ kă*, f. nettle; (fig.) remorse.
orto, *ŏr′ tŏ*, m. kitchen-garden; sun-rise;
East; birth.
ortodossia, *–dŏssĭ′ ă*, f. orthodoxy.
ortodosso, *–dŏs′ sŏ*, a. orthodox.
ortografia, *–grăfĭ′ ă*, f. orthography.
ortografico, *–grā′ fĭkŏ*, a. orthographical.
ortolano, *–lā′ nŏ*, m. gardener; ortolan.
orzata, *–dzā′ tă*, f. barley-water.
orzo, *ŏr′ dzŏ*, m. barley.
osare, *ŏsā′ rĕ*, v. a. to dare.
oscenità, *ŏsshĕnĭtă′*, f. obscenity.
osceno, *ŏsshā′ nŏ*, a. obscene, unchaste.
oscillare, *ŏsshĭllā′ rĕ*, v. n. to oscillate.
oscurare, *ŏskŭrā′ rĕ*, v. a. to darken.
oscurazione, *–kŭrătzĭŏ′ nĕ*, f. darkening.
oscurità, *–kŭrĭtă′*, f. obscurity.
oscuro, *–kŏ′ rŏ*, a. obscure, dark, abstruse.
oso, *ŏ′ sŏ*, a. (poet.) daring, bold.
ospedale, *ŏspĕdā′ lĕ*, m. hospital.
ospitare, *ŏspĭtā′ rĕ*, v.a. to lodge; to attend.
ospite, *ŏs′ pĭtĕ*, m. guest, host, landlord.
ospizio, *–pĭ′ tzĭŏ*, m. hospice, asylum.
ossame, *ŏssā′ mĕ*, m. heap of bones.
ossecrazione, *–sĕkrătzĭŏ′ nĕ*, f. supplication, entreaty, request.
osseo, *ŏs′ sĕŏ*, a. bony, made of bone.
ossequente, *–sĕkŭĕn′ tĕ*, a. obsequious.
ossequiare, *–sĕkŭĭā′ rĕ*, v. a. to revere, to
honour.
ossequio, *–sā′ kŭĭŏ*, m. obsequiousness,
respect.

osservanza, *–sērvān′ tză*, f. observation;
respect; custom; rule.
osservare, *–vā′ rĕ*, v. a. to observe, to
keep; to watch; to regard. [tator.
osservatore, *–tŏ′ rĕ*, m. observer, spec-
osservatorio, *–tŏ′ rĭŏ*, m. observatory.
osservazione, *–tzĭŏ′ nĕ*, f. observation,
note. [spirits; oppressed.
ossesso, *ŏssĕs′ sŏ*, a. possessed by evil
osso, *ŏs′ sŏ*, m. (ossa, f. pl.) bone; stone of a
ossuto, *–sū′ tŏ*, a. bony; scraggy. [fruit.
ostacolo, *ŏstā′ kŏlŏ*, m. obstacle, hinderance.
ostaggio, *–tăd′ jŏ*, m. hostage.
ostare, *–tā′ rĕ*, v. a. to oppose, to resist.
oste, *ŏs′ tĕ*, m. host, innkeeper; guest.
osteggiamento, *–tēdjāmēn′ tŏ*, m. encampment. [to encamp.
osteggiare, *–djā′ rĕ*, v. a. & n. to attack;
ostello, *–tĕl′ lŏ*, m. (poet.) inn; lodging.
ostensibile, *–tĕnsĭ′ bĭlĕ*, a. ostensible.
ostentare, *–tĕntā′ rĕ*, v. a. to boast, to
parade; to vaunt. [boast.
ostentazione, *–tzĭŏ′ nĕ*, f. ostentation,
osteria, *–tĕrĭ′ ă*, f. inn, tavern.
ostessa, *–tĕs′ să*, f. hostess.
ostetrico, *–tĕ′ trĭkŏ*, m. man-midwife, ob-
stetrician.
ostia, *ŏs′ tĭă*, f. host, consecrated wafer.
ostiario, *–tĭā′ rĭŏ*, m. door-keeper; ostiary.
ostiere, *–tĭā′ rĕ*, m. innkeeper; lodging.
ostile, *ŏstĭ′ lĕ*, a. hostile, inimical.
ostilità, *ŏstĭlĭtă′*, f. hostility.
ostinato, *–nā′ tŏ*, a. obstinate, stubborn.
ostinazione, *–tzĭŏ′ nĕ*, f. obstinacy, stub-
ostrica, *ŏs′ trĭkă*, f. oyster. [bornness.
ostro, *ŏs′ trŏ*, m. purple; (poet.) south-wind.
ostruire, *ŏstrŭĭ′ rĕ*, v. a. to obstruct.
ostruzione, *–trătzĭŏ′ nĕ*, f. obstruction.
otre, *ŏ′ trĕ*, m. leather bottle or bag.
ottanta, *ŏttān′ tă*, a. eighty.
ottantesimo, *–tā′ sĭmŏ*, a. eightieth.
ottarda, *ŏttār′ dă*, f. bustard.
ottava, *–tā′ vă*, f. stanza of eight lines;
ottavo, *–tā′ vŏ*, a. eighth. [eight-days.
ottemperare, *–tĕmpĕrā′ rĕ*, v. a. to obey.
ottenebrare, *–tĕnēbrā′ rĕ*, v. a. to darken.
ottenere, *–tĕnā′ rĕ*, v. a. ir. to obtain, to
ottica, *ŏt′ tĭkă*, f. optics, pl. [acquire.
ottimamente, *–tĭmāmēn′ tĕ*, ad. perfectly
well.
ottimo, *ŏt′ tĭmŏ*, a. perfectly good, best.
otto, *ŏt′ tŏ*, a. eight.
ottobre, *ŏttŏ′ brĕ*, m. October.
ottocento, *–dshĕn′ tŏ*, a. eight hundred.
ottone, *ŏttŏ′ nĕ*, m. brass.
ottuagesimo, *ŏttŭājā′ sĭmŏ*, a. eightieth.
ottuplo, *ŏt′ tŭplŏ*, m. eightfold. [dam.
otturare, *ŏttŭrā′ rĕ*, v. a. to stop up, to
ottusità, *–tŭsĭtă′*, f. obtuseness, bluntness.
ottuso, *–tŏ′ sŏ*, a. blunt; stupid.
ovaia, *ŏvā′ ă*, f. ovary.
ovale, *ŏvā′ lĕ*, a. oval, elliptical.
ovazione, *–tzĭŏ′ nĕ*, f. ovation. [wherever.
ove, *ŏ′ vĕ*, ad. where; – che, – che sia,
ovile, *ŏvĭ′ lĕ*, m. sheepfold; dwelling-
oviparo, *ŏvĭ′ părŏ*, a. oviparous. [place,

ovo, ŏ'vŏ, m. egg.
ovvero, ŏvvĕ'rŏ, c. or else, or, either, alias.
ovviare, –vĭä'rĕ, v.a. to obviate, to prevent.
ovvio, ŏv'vĭŏ, a. obvious; trivial, common.
oziare, ŏtzĭä'rĕ, v. n. to idle, to lounge.
ozio, ŏ'tzĭŏ, m. leisure; ease; idleness.
oziosità, ŏtzĭŏsĭtä', f. laziness, indolence.
ozioso, ŏtzĭŏ'sŏ, a. idle, lazy; vain.

P.

pacatamente, –päkätämĕn'tĕ, ad. placidly.
pacatezza, –tĕt'zä, f. tranquillity.
pacato, –kä'tŏ, a. placid, tranquil; serene.
pacchetto, –kĕt'tŏ, m. packet.
pacchia, päk'kĭä, f. pasture; food, proven-
    der; good cheer.
pacciame, pätshä'mĕ, m. sweepings, pl.
pace, pä'dshĕ, f. peace; tranquillity; truce.
paciero, –dshĕ'rŏ, m. peace-maker.
pacificare, –dshĭfĭkä'rĕ, v. a. to pacify.
pacifico, –dshĕ'fĭkŏ, a. pacific, peaceable.
padella, –dĕl'lä, f. frying-pan; knee-pan.
padiglione, –dĭlyŏ'nĕ, m. pavilion.
padre, pä'drĕ, m. father; (fig.) author.
padrona, –drŏ'nä, f. patroness; mistress.
padronanza, –drŏnän'tzä, f. superiority.
padrone, –drŏ'nĕ, m. master; patron;
    protector.
paesano, päĕsä'nŏ, a. of the same country.
paese, pä'ĕ'sĕ, m. country, land.
paesello, päĕsĕl'lŏ, m. small village,
    hamlet.
paesetto, päĕsĕt'tŏ, m. landscape.
paesista, –sĭs'tä, m. landscape-painter.
paffuto, pĕffä'tŏ, a. plump, fat.
paga, pä'gä, f. pay, salary.
pagamento, –mĕn'tŏ, m. payment.
pagano, –gä'nŏ, a. pagan.
pagare, –gä'rĕ, v. a. to pay.
paggio, päd'jŏ, m. page.
pagherò, –päghĕrŏ', m. bill payable at
    sight, promissory note.
pagina, pä'jĭnä, f. page of a book.
paglia, pä'lyä, f. straw, chaff.
pagliaccio, –yät'shŏ, m. chopped straw.
pagliaio, –yä'ŏ, m. stack of straw.
pagliuola, –yŏŏ'lä, f. spangle.
pagnotta, –pänyŏt'tä, f. small loaf.
pago, pä'gŏ, m. payment; –, a. content,
    satisfied.
paio, pä'ŏ, m. (paia, f. pl.) pair, couple.
paiuolo, päŏŏ'lŏ, m. boiler, kettle.
pala, pä'lä, f. shovel; spade.
paladino, pälädĕ'nŏ, m. paladin.
palafitta, –fĭt'tä, f. fence of piles.
palafittare, –fĭttä'rĕ, v. a. to drive in
    piles; to fence with palings.   [man.
palafreniere, –frĕnĕä'rĕ, m. groom, stable-
palafreno, –frä'nŏ, m. palfrey.
palagio, pälä'jŏ, m. palace.
palanca, –län'kä, f. stake, palisade.
palancato, –kä'tŏ, m. stockade, enclosure.

palandrana, –ländrä'nä, f., palandrano,
    –nŏ, m. old-fashioned great coat.
palare, pälä'rĕ, v. a. to pale; to fence.
palata, –lä'tä, f. palisade; shovel-full.
palato, –lä'tŏ, m. palisade; palate.
palazzo, –lät'zŏ, m. palace.
palchetto, pälkĕt'tŏ, m. balcony; gallery;
    – di teatro, box in a theatre.
palco, päl'kŏ, m. floor; scaffold; box in a
paleo, päld'ŏ, m. whipping-top.   [theatre.
palesare, –lĕsä'rĕ, v. a. to reveal, to make
    known, to proclaim.
palese, –lä'sĕ, a. evident, known. [festly.
palesemente, –mĕn'tĕ, ad. openly, mani-
paletta, –lĕt'tä, f. fire-shovel; spattle.
paletto, –lĕt'tŏ, m. hasp (of windows).
palinodia, –lĭnŏdĭ'ä, f. palinode.
palio, pä'lĭŏ, m. canopy; mantle. [piece.
paliotto, –lĭŏt'tŏ, m. small mantle; altar-
palizzata, –lĭdzä'tä, f. palisade.
palla, päl'lä, f. ball; bullet; bowl.
palladio, –lä'dĭŏ, m. palladium; (fig.)
    protection.   [tennis; to banter, to quiz.
palleggiare, –lĕdshä'rĕ, v. n. to play at
palleggio, –lĕä'jŏ, m. tennis-court; lawn-
    tennis.   [cuse.
palliare, –lĭä'rĕ, v. a. to palliate; to ex-
palliativo, –tĭ'vŏ, a. palliative.
pallido, päl'lĭdŏ, a. pallid, pale.
pallino, –lĕ'nŏ, m. small shot.
pallio, päl'lĭŏ, m. pallium, mantle.
pallone, –lŏ'nĕ, m. air-balloon; large
    foot-ball,   [hand]; (fig.) victory.
palma, päl'mä, f. palm-tree, palm (of the
palmento, –mĕn'tŏ, m. wine-press; mill-
    stone frame.   [trees.
palmeto, –mä'tŏ, m. plantation of palm-
palmite, päl'mĭtĕ, m. vine-branch.
palmo, päl'mŏ, m. span (measure).
palo, pä'lŏ, m. pale; lever.   [fish.
palombo, pälŏm'bŏ, m. wood-pigeon; dog-
palpare, pälpä'rĕ, v. a. to touch, to grope;
palpebra, –pä'brä, f. eye-lid. [to cajole.
palpeggiare, –pĕdjä'rĕ, v. a. to touch,
    to grope.
palpitare, –pĭtä'rĕ, v. n. to palpitate.
palpitazione, –tzĭŏ'nĕ, f. palpitation,
palpito, päl'pĭtŏ, m. throb.   [throbbing.
paludamento, pälüdämĕn'tŏ, m. roman
    coat of mail.   [fen.
palude, pä'lüdĕ, f. marsh, morass,
paludoso, –lüdŏ'sŏ, palustre, –lüs'trĕ, a.
    marshy, fenny, swampy.
palvese, pälvĕ'sĕ, m. large shield.
panata, pänä'tä, f. panada.
panattiera, –nättĭä'rä, f. bread-basket;
    shepherd's scrip; pantry.
panattiere, –tĭä'rĕ, m. pantler, bread-
panca, pän'kä, f. bench.   [baker.
pancia, pän'dshä, f. paunch; belly.
panciera, –dshĭä'rä, f. cuirass.
panciolle, –dshŏl'lĕ, ad. comfortably.
panconcello, –kŏndshĕl'lŏ, m. lath.
pancone, –kŏ'nĕ, m. plank, thick board;
    joiner's bench.   [nance.
pane, pä'nĕ, m. bread; loaf; (fig.) suste-

pania, *pă'nĭă*, f. bird-lime; snare.
paniccia, *–nĭt'shă*, f. paste.
panico, *–nĕ'kŏ*, m. millet; –, *pă'nĭkŏ*, a. panic.
paniera, *–nĭĕ'ră*, f. (bread-)basket.
panificio, *–nĭfĭ'dshŏ*, m. bread-making.
paniuzza, *–nĭut'ză*, f. lime-twig.
panna, *păn'nă*, f. bloom; cream; dew.
pannaiuolo, *–naiŭŏ'lŏ*, m. woollen-draper.
pannicolo, *–nĕ'kŏlŏ*, m. bit of cloth; midriff.
panno, *păn'nŏ*, m. (woollen) cloth, stuff; sail-cloth; – **lino,** linen-cloth; **panni,** pl. clothes, dress; **panni da gamba,** breeches, pantaloons, pl.
pantano, *păntă'nŏ*, m. slough, puddle.
pantera, *–tĕ'ră*, f. panther; draw-net.
pantofola, *–tŏ'fŏlă*, f. pantofle, slipper.
pantomima, *–tŏmĕ'mă*, f. pantomime.
pantomimo, *–mĕ'mŏ*, m. pantomime player.
papa, *pă'pă*, m. pope.
papale, *–pă'lĕ*, a. papal.
papato, *–pă'tŏ*, m. papacy.
papavero, *–pă'vĕrŏ*, m. poppy.
papero, *pă'pĕrŏ*, m. young goose.
papilione, *–pĭlĭŏ'nĕ*, m. butterfly.
papilla, *–pĭl'lă*, f. nipple, teat.
papiro, *–pĕ'rŏ*, m. paper.
pappa, *păp'pă*, f. pap (infants' food).
pappafico, *–fĕ'kŏ*, m. rain-hood.
pappagallo, *–găl'lŏ*, m. parrot.
pappalardo, *–lăr'dŏ*, m. hypocrite; glutton.
pappare, *–pă'rĕ*, v. n. to eat to excess, to gorge.
pappino, *–pĕ'nŏ*, m. servant in an hospital.
pappolata, *–pŏlă'tă*, f. tasteless dish; insipid story.
pappone, *–pŏ'nĕ*, m. glutton, devourer.
parabola, *pără'bŏlă*, f. parable; parabola.
parabolano, *–bŏlă'nŏ*, m. great prattler; –, a. false, vain.
paracuore, *–kŭŏ'rĕ*, m. lungs, pl.
paradiso, *–dē'zŏ*, m. paradise; upper-gallery (in a theatre). |paradoxical.
paradosso, *–dŏs'sŏ*, m. paradox; –, a.
paraggio, *părăd'jŏ*, m. comparison; descent, lineage, extraction; naval station.
paragonare, *–gŏnă'rĕ*, v. a. to compare, to equal. |parison.
paragone, *–gŏ'nĕ*, m. touch-stone; com-
paragrafo, *pără'grăfŏ*, m. paragraph.
paralello, *–lĕl'lŏ*, a. parallel.
paralisi, *pără'lĭsĭ*, f. palsy.
paralitico, *–lĕ'tĭkŏ*, a. palsied.
paralume, *–lŏ'mĕ*, m. screen.
paramento, *–mĕn'tŏ*, m. sacerdotal ornaments, pl.; drapery. |man.
paraninfo, *–nĭn'fŏ*, m. paranymph; bride's
parapiglia, *–pĭl'yă*, f. crowd; throng.
parare, *pără'rĕ*, v. a. to deck, to dress; to parry, to keep off; to offer.
parasole, *–sŏ'lĕ*, m. parasol.
parasito, *părăsĭ'tŏ*, m. parasite, sponger.
parata, *pără'tă*, f. parade.
paratio, *–ră'tĭŏ*, m. partition-wall.
parato, *–ră'tŏ*, m. finery; drapery.
paratura, *–tŏ'ră*, f. attire, ornament.

paravento, *–vĕn'tŏ*, m. folding-screen.
parca, *păr'kă*, f., le **parche,** pl. the Fates.
parcamente, *–mĕn'tĕ*, ad. sparingly.
parco, *păr'kŏ*, m. (deer-)park; –, a. sparing, thrifty.
pardo, *păr'dŏ*, m. leopard.
parecchi, *părĕk'kĭ*, a. pl. several, divers.
parecchio, *–rĕk'kĭŏ*, a. equal, similar.
pareggiare, *–rĕdjă'rĕ*, v. a. to equal, to compare; to settle an account.
parenesi, *–rĕnĕ'sĭ*, f. exhortation.
parenetico, *–nĕ'tĭkŏ*, a. exhorting.
parentado, *părĕntă'dŏ*, m. parentage, kindred, extraction.
parente, *–rĕn'tĕ*, m. kinsman.
parentela, *–rĕntĕ'lă*, f. relationship.
parentesi, *–rĕn'tĕsĭ*, f. parenthesis.
parere, *–ră'rĕ*, v. n. to appear; to think, to judge; –, m. opinion, mind, advice.
parete, *–rĕ'tĕ*, f. wall; rampart.
pargoletto, *părgŏlĕt'tŏ*, a. childish; young.
pargolo, *păr'gŏlŏ*, m. (poet.) infant.
pari, *pă'rĭ*, a. alike, equal; like, similar; **al** –, equally; –, ad. equally, evenly.
pariglia, *–rĭl'yă*, f. double point at dice.
parimente, *–rĭmĕn'tĕ*, ad. also, likewise.
parità, *–rĭtă'*, f. parity, equality.
parlamentare, *părlămĕntă'rĕ*, v. n. to (hold a) parley.
parlamento, *–mĕn'tŏ*, m. parley; Parliament.
parlare, *părlă'rĕ*, v. a. & n. to speak, to talk, to converse.
parlata, *–lă'tă*, f. talk, conversation.
parlatore, *–tŏ'rĕ*, m. speaker, orator.
parlatorio, *–tŏ'rĭŏ*, m. parlour.
parletico, *–lĕ'tĭkŏ*, a. palsied.
parlottare, *–lŏttă'rĕ*, v. n. to speak low,
paro, *pă'rŏ*, m. pair, couple. |to mutter.
paroco, see **parroco.**
parodia, *părŏdĭ'ă*, f. parody; travesty.
parodiare, *–dĭă'rĕ*, v. a. to parody; to travesty.
parola, *părŏ'lă*, f. word; term; maxim; proverb; **avere la** –, to be allowed to speak.
parolaccia, *–rŏlăt'shă*, f. coarse or lewd language.
parolaio, *–lăĭ'ŏ*, m. great talker, prater; prosy fellow. |word.
parolina, *–lĭ'nă*, f. honied or flattering
parolona, *–lŏ'nă*, f., **parolone,** *–nĕ*, m. high-flown word,
parossismo, *–rŏssĭs'mŏ*, m. paroxysm.
parpaglione, *părpăl'yŏne*, m. butterfly.
parricida, *părrĭdshĭ'dă*, m. parricide.
parricidio, *–dshĭ'dĭŏ*, m. parricide.
parrocchia, *părrŏk'kĭă*, f. parish, parish-church.
parrocchiano, *–kĭă'nŏ*, m. parishioner, parish-priest.
parroco, *păr'rŏkŏ*, m. parish-priest, parson.
parrucca, *părrŭk'kă*, f. wig, periwig.
parsimonia, *părsĭmŏ'nĭă*, f. parsimony.
parte, *păr'tĕ*, f. part, share; side, place; party; country; **a** –, **da** –, aside; **da** – **a** –, through and through; – **per** –, one by one, piece by piece.

partecipare, –tĕdshĭpä´re, v. a. to participate in, to partake of.

partecipazione, –pätzĭ´nē, f. participation.

partecipe, –tĕ´dshĭpē, a. & m. participant; sharer.

parteggiare, –tĕdjä´rē, v. n. to follow one's party; to take one's part, to side with.

partenza, –tĕn´tzā, f. departure.

particella, –tĭdshĕl´lā, f. particle, parcel.

participio, –tĭdshĕ´pĭō, m. (gr.) participle.

particola, –tĭ´kŏlā, f. particle, parcel.

particolare, –kŏlä´rē, a. particular; singular.

particolarità, –lărĭtä´, f. particularity.

particolarizzare, –lărĭdzä´rē, v. a. to particularize.

particolarmente, –lărmĕn´tē, ad. particularly.

partigiana, –tĭjä´nā, f. partisan, halberd.

partigiano, –jä´nŏ, m. partisan, factionary.

partimento, –tĭmĕn´tō, m. partition, division; sharing.

partire, –tē´rē, v. a. to share, to divide; –, v. n., **partirsi,** –tĭr´sĭ, to depart; to retire.

partita, –tē´tā, f. departure; share, portion; party, faction; entry in a ledger.

partito, –tē´tō, m. way, means; manner; condition; bargain; resolution.

partizione, –tzĭō´nē, f. partition, division.

parto, –pär´tō, m. child-bed, birth.

partoriente, –tŏrĭĕn´tē, f. woman in labour.

partorire, –tŏrē´rē, v. a. & n. to bring forth; to be delivered.

parvente, –vĕn´tē, a. visible, manifest.

parvenza, –vĕn´zā, f. appearance; smallness.

parvità, –vĭtä´, f. smallness, minuteness.

paruta, –pärō´tā, f. appearance; outside.

parziale, –pärtzĭä´lē, a. partial, unjust.

parzialità, –tzĭälĭtä´, f. partiality.

parzialmente, –mĕn´tē, ad. partially.

pascere, –päsh´ĕrē, v. a. ir. to feed, to nourish; –, v. n. to graze; **pascersi,** –päsh´ersĭ, to feed upon. [ance.

pasciona, –päshō´nā, f. fat pasture; abund

pascolo, –päs´kŏlō, m. (poet.) pasture, pas

pasqua, –päs´kŭā, f. Easter. [turage.

pasquale, –kŭä´lē, a. of Easter.

pasquinata, –kŭĭnä´tā, f. pasquinade, lampoon.

passabile, –pässä´bĭlē, a. passable, tolerable.

passaggiere, –sädjä´rē, **passaggiero,** –rŏ, m. passenger.

passaggio, –säd´jŏ, m. passage, way; transition; toll; passage-money; (rail.) cross

passaporto, –pŏr´tō, m. passport. [ing.

passare, –pässä´rē, v. a. & n. to pass, to go through, to cross; to transgress.

passata, –sä´tā, f. passage; omission.

passatempo, –tĕm´pō, m. pastime.

passato, –sä´tō, m. past time; **passati,** pl. ancestors, forefathers; –, a. passed, past.

passeggiare, –sĕdjä´rē, v. n. to walk, to take a walk; to pace a horse.

passeggiata, –djä´tā, f. walk, turn.

passeggiere, –djä´rē, m. passenger; toll-gatherer. [menade.

passeggio, –sĕd´jŏ, m. public walk, pro-

passera, päs´sĕrā, f., **passero,** –sĕrŏ, m. sparrow; – di canaria, canary-bird.

passerotto, –rŏt´tŏ, m. young or little sparrow.

passetto, –sĕt´tō, a. somewhat withered.

passionare, –sĭŏnä´rē, v. a. to torment, to torture; –, v. n. to suffer.

passione, –sĭ´nē, f. passion. [bility.

passività, –sĭvĭtä´, f. passiveness, passi-

passivo, –sĭ´vŏ, a. passive.

passo, päs´sŏ, m. step, pace; passage; course; walk; ford; –, a. withered.

pasta, päs´tā, f. paste, dough.

pasteggiare, –tĕdjä´rē, v. a. & n. to feast, to dine or sup together.

pastello, –tĕl´lō, m. bit of paste; pastil.

pasticca, –tĭk´kā, f. pastil.

pasticciere, –tĭtshä´rē, m. pastry-cook.

pasticcio, –tĭt´shŏ, m. pie, pasty.

pastinaca, –tĭnä´kā, f. (bot.) parsnip.

pastinare, –nä´rē, v. a. to hoe. [repast.

pasto, päs´tō, m. food, aliment; meal,

pastocchia, –tŏk´kĭā, f. fib; nonsense.

pastoia, –tŏ´ĭā, f. pastern; impediment.

pastora, –tŏ´rā, f. shepherdess.

pastorale, –tŏrä´lē, m. crosier; –, f. pastoral poem.

pastore, –tŏ´rē, m. pastor; shepherd.

pastorella, –tŏrĕl´lā, f. shepherdess.

pastorizia, –tŏrĭtzĭä´, f. shepherd's profession; pastoral condition.

pastoso, –tŏ´sŏ, a. doughy, pulpy; mellow.

pastume, –tŏ´mē, m. all sorts of pastry.

pastura, –tŏ´rä, f. pasture, pasturage; food. [feed.

pasturare, –tŭrä´rē, v. a. to pasture; to

patata, pätä´tā, f. potato.

patena, –tä´nā, f. cover of the chalice.

patente, –tĕn´tē, a. evident, manifest; –, m. letter-patent, brevet.

patera, pä´tĕrā, f. offering-cup.

paternale, –tĕrnä´lē, a. fatherly.

paternità, –tĕrnĭtä´, f. fatherhood.

paterno, –tĕr´nŏ, a. paternal.

paternostro, –nŏs´trŏ, m. Lord's prayer.

patetico, –tĕ´tĭkŏ, a. pathetic.

patibolo, –tĕ´bŏlō, m. gibbet, gallows, pl.

patimento, –tĭmĕn´tō, m. suffering, pain, grief, affliction, misfortune.

patire, –tē´rē, v. a. & n. to suffer, to endure.

patologia, –tŏlŏjĭ´ā, f. pathology.

patologico, –lŏ´jĭkŏ, a. pathologic.

patria, pä´trĭā, f. fatherland.

patriarca, –trĭär´kā, m. patriarch.

patriarcale, –kä´lē, a. patriarchal.

patriarcato, –kä´tō, m. patriarchate.

patricida, –trĭdshĕ´dā, m. parricide (murderer).

patricidio, –dshĕ´dĭō, m. parricide (murder).

patrigno, –trĭn´yŏ, step-father; father-in-law.

patrimoniale, –trĭmŏnĭä´lē, a. patrimonial.

patrimonio, –trĭmŏ´nĭō, m. patrimony.

patrino, *–trĕ' nŏ*, m. godfather; second in a duel.
patrio, *pă' trĭŏ*, a. paternal; native.
patriottismo, *–trĭŏttĭs' mŏ*, m. patriotism.
patriottico, *–trĭŏt' tĭkŏ*, a. patriotic.
patriotto, *–trĭŏt' tŏ*, m. patriot.
patrizio, *–trĕ' tzĭŏ*, m. patrician; –, a. patrician. [tronize.
patrocinare, *–trŏdshĭnă' rĕ*, v. a. to pa-
patrocinio, *–dshĕ' nĭŏ*, m. patronage, protection. [to bargain.
patteggiare, *păttĕdjă' rĕ*, v. n. to contract,
pattino, *–tĕ' nŏ*, m. skate.
patto, *păt' tŏ*, m. pact, convention; bargain.
pattuglia, *–tŭl' yă*, f. (mil.) patrol.
pattugliare, *–yă' rĕ*, v. n. (mil.) to patrol.
pattume, *–tŭ' mĕ*, m. sweepings, pl., dirt.
paura, *pă' ŭră*, f. fear, fright.
pauroso, *–rŏ' sŏ*, a. timorous, fearful.
pausa, *pă' ŭsă*, f. pause, stop. [stop.
pausare, *–să' rĕ*, v. n. to pause, to make a
paventare, *păvĕntă' rĕ*, v. n. to fear, to be afraid.
pavido, *pă' vĭdŏ*, a. timid, timorous.
pavimentare, *–vĭmĕntă' rĕ*, v. a. to pave, to floor. [way,
pavimento, *–mĕn' tŏ*, m. pavement; cause-
pavonazzo, *–vŏnăt' zŏ*, m. violet.
pavoncella, *–vŏndshĕl' lă*, f. lapwing.
pavone, *–vŏ' nĕ*, m. peacock.
pavoneggiarsi, *–nĕdjăr' sĭ*, v. r. to walk proudly, to strut.
pavonessa, *–nĕs' să*, f. peahen. [patient.
paziente, *pătzĭĕn' tĕ*, m. patient; –, a.
pazienza, *–tzĭĕn' tză*, f. patience.
pazzeggiare, *–tzĕdjă' rĕ*, v. n. to dote, to rave.
pazzerello, *–tzĕrĕl' lŏ*, m. little fool.
pazzeria, *–tzĕrĕ' ă*, f. folly, madness.
pazzesco, *–tzĕs' kŏ*, a. mad, foolish.
pazzia, *–tzĕ' ă*, f. madness; extravagance.
pazzo, *păt' zŏ*, m. madman; –, a. mad; whimsical. [foible.
pecca, *pĕk' kă*, f. slight defect, blemish.
peccabile, *–kă' bĭlĕ*, a. peccable.
peccare, *–kă' rĕ*, v. n. to sin, to transgress.
peccato, *–kă' tŏ*, m. sin, transgression; crime. [dshĕ, f. sinner.
peccatore, *–tŏ' rĕ*, m., **peccatrice**, *–trĕ'-*
pecchia, *pĕk' kĭă*, f. bee.
peccia, *pĕt' shă*, f. paunch.
pece, *pă' dshĕ*, f. pitch; – **greca**, resin.
pecora, *pă' kŏră*, f. sheep, ewe.
pecoraio, *pĕkŏră' ŏ*, m. shepherd.
pecorella, *–rĕl' lă*, f. young sheep.
pecorile, *–rĕ' lĕ*, m. sheep-fold.
pecorino, *–rĕ' nŏ*, m. lamb; –, a. of a sheep; stupid.
peculato, *pĕkŭlă' tŏ*, m. peculation.
peculiare, *–kŭlĭă' rĕ*, a. peculiar, particular. [exclusive property.
peculio, *–kŏ' lĭŏ*, m. herd; stock; hoard;
pecunia, *–kŏ' nĭă*, f. money, cash.
pecuniario, *–kŭnĭă' rĭŏ*, a. pecuniary, of money.
pecunioso, *–nĭŏ' sŏ*, a. monied, rich.
pedaggio, *pĕdăd' jŏ*, m. turnpike-money.

Italian and English.

pedagogia, *pĕdăgŏjĕ' ă*, f. pedagogy, teaching of children.
pedagogo, *–gŏ' gŏ*, m. pedagogue.
pedale, *pĕdă' lĕ*, m. stock, trunk of a tree;
pedante, *–dăn' tĕ*, m. pedant. [pedal.
pedanteria, *–tĕrĕ' ă*, f. pedantry.
pedantesco, *–tĕs' kŏ*, a. pedantic. [kick.
pedata, *pĕdă' tă*, f. track, trace, footstep;
pedestre, *–dĕs' trĕ*, a. on foot; low, mean.
pediculare, *pĕdĭkŭlă' rĕ*, a. lousy.
pedignone, *–dĭnyŏ' nĕ*, m. chilblain.
pediluvio, *–dĭlŭ' vĭŏ*, m. foot-bath.
pedone, *–dŏ' nĕ*, m. foot-soldier; stem.
peggio, *pĕd' jŏ*, a. worse; **di male in –**, worse and worse.
peggiorare, *–djŏră' rĕ*, v. a. & n. to make worse; to grow worse. [worst.
peggiore, *–djŏ' rĕ*, a. worse; **il –**, the
pegno, *pĕn' yŏ*, pledge, pawn; token.
pegnorare, *–yŏră' rĕ*, v. a. to seize property by law.
pegola, *pă' gŏlă*, f. bee's wax; tar.
pel, *pĕl*, for: **per lo**.
pelacani, *pĕlăkă' nĭ*, m. tanner. [fusion.
pelago, *pă' lăgŏ*, m. ocean; abyss; con-
pelame, *pĕlă' mĕ*, m. hair.
pelare, *–lă' rĕ*, v. a. to pluck out the feathers; to pull out the hair; to pick.
pelatina, *–tĕ' nă*, f. scald, loss of hair.
pelle, *pĕl' lĕ*, f. skin, hide; (fig.) pretence.
pellegrinaggio, *–lĕgrĭnăd' jŏ*, m. pilgrimage. [a pilgrim.
pellegrinare, *–grĭnă' rĕ*, v. n. to travel as
pellegrino, *–grĕ' nŏ*, m. pilgrim; –, a. foreign; singular; exquisite.
pellicano, *–lĭkă' nŏ*, m. pelican.
pelliccia, *–lĭt' shă*, f. fur-coat.
pellicciaio, *–lĭtshă' ŏ*, m. furrier.
pellicella, *–lĭdshĕl' lă*, **pellicina**, *–dshĕ'-nă*, **pellicola**, *–lĕ' kŏlă*, **pellolina**, *–lŏ-lĕ' nă*, f. pellicle, cuticle.
pellucido, *–lŏ' dshĭdŏ*, a. pellucid, clear.
pelo, *pă' lŏ*, m. hair; nap; surface; (fig.) rank, condition.
peloso, *pĕlŏ' sŏ*, a. hairy, shaggy.
peltro, *pĕl' trŏ*, m. pewter.
peluria, *pĕlŭ' rĭă*, f. soft down; fine hair.
peluzzo, *–lŭt' zŏ*, m. slight hair.
pena, *pă' nă*, f. pain, punishment; grief; labour; **a –**, **a mala –**, scarcely.
penalità, *pĕnălĭtă'*, f. penalty.
penare, *–nă' rĕ*, v. n. to loiter, to delay; to suffer, to endure.
pendaglio, *pĕndăl' yŏ*, m. belt, girdle.
pendente, *–dĕn' tĕ*, m. ear-ring, drop; declivity; –, a. hanging, dangling; depending. [tion.
pendenza, *–dĕn' tză*, f. declivity; inclina-
pendere, *pĕn' dĕrĕ*, v. n. to hang, to be suspended; to incline; to depend.
pendice, *–dĕ' tshĕ*, m. declivity.
pendio, *–dĕ' ŏ*, m. declivity, steepness.
pendolo, *pĕn' dŏlŏ*, m. plummet, pendulum; –, a. hanging, suspended.
penetrare, *–nĕtră' rĕ*, v. a. to penetrate, to pierce; to understand.
penisola, *pĕnĕ' sŏlă*, f. peninsula.
penitente, *pĕnĭtĕn' tĕ*, a. penitent, contrite

penitenza, –těn'tzå, f. penitence, repentance.   [top; (fig.) style, writer.

penna, pěn'nå, f. feather; quill, pen; summit,

pennacchio, –nåk'kiå, m. tuft of feathers.

pennaiuolo, –nåiŭŏ'lŏ, m. pen-case; seller of pens.

pennato, –nå'tå, m, pruning-knife.

pennelleggiare, –něllěĕdjå'rě, v. a. to paint; to draw.

pennello, –něl'lŏ, m. hair-pencil.

pennone, –nŏ'ně, m. banner, ensign.

pennuto, –nŭ'tŏ, a. feathered, feathery.

penombra, pěnŏm'brå, f. penumbra.

penoso, –nŏ'sŏ, a. painful, hard.

pensare, pěnså'rě, v. a. & n. to think; to intend; to believe.

pensata, –så'tå, f. thought, sentiment.

pensiere, –sĕ'rě, **pensiero,** –rŏ, m. thought, meaning; mind.

pensieroso, –sĕrŏ'sŏ, a. thoughtful.

pensile, pěn'silě, a. hanging, suspended.

pensionario, –siŏnå'riŏ, m. pensioner; boarder.   [house; annuity.

pensione, –siŏ'ně, f. pension, boarding-

pensoso, –sŏ'sŏ, a. thoughtful.

Pentecoste, pěntěkŏs'tě, f. Pentecost.

pentimento, pěntiměn'tŏ, m. repentance.

pentirsi, pěntir'si, v. r. to repent.

pentola, pěn'tŏlå, f., **pentolo,** –tŏlŏ, m. earthen pot, broth-pot.

pentolino, –tŏli'nŏ, m. poor fare.

penuria, pěnŭ'riå, f. penury, indigence.

penuriare, –nŭriå'rě, v. n. to be in need.

penzolo, pěn'tzŏlŏ, a. hanging, dangling.

penzolone, –tzŏlŏ'ně, ad. in a dangling manner.

peonia, pěŏ'niå, f. peony.

pepato, pěpå'tŏ, a. spiced; **pane –,** m. ginger-bread.

pepe, pě'pě, m. pepper.

per, pěr, pr. for, by, from, in, through.

pera, pě'rå, f. pear.

percepire, pěrchěpě'rě, v. a. to perceive.

percettibile, –dshěttě'bilě, a. perceptible, perceivable, observable.

percezione, –tziŏ'ně, f. perception.

perchè, pěrkě', ad. why? because.

perciò, pěrshŏ', ad. therefore, however.

perciocchè, –dshŏkkě', ad. & c. since, for; that.

percipere, –dshi'pěrě, v. a. to perceive.

percorrere, –kŏr'rěrě, v. a. ir. to run rapidly through; to peruse hastily.

percossa, –kŏs'så, f. striking, hit, blow; percussion.

percuotere, –kŭŏ'těrě, v. a. ir. to strike, to beat.   [stroke.

percussione, –kŭssŏ'ně, f. percussion.

perdere, pěr'děrě, v. a. ir. to lose, to let slip, to waste, to destroy; **–,** v. n. to decay, to wither.

perdigiorno, –djŏr'nŏ, m. idle fellow.

perdita, pěr'ditå, f. detriment; waste.

perdizione, –ditziŏ'ně, f. perdition; destruction.   [forgive.

perdonare, –dŏnå'rě, v. a. to pardon, to

perdono, –dŏ'nŏ. m. pardon, remission.

perdurare, –dŭrå'rě, v. n. to last, to hold

perduto, –dŭ'tŏ, a. lost, ruined.   [out.

peregrinare, pěrěgrinå'rě, v. n. to go on a pilgrimage.

peregrinazione, –tziŏ'ně, f. peregrination.

peregrino, –grě'nŏ, a. foreign; **–,** m. pilgrim.

perentorio, pěrěntŏ'riŏ, a. peremptory.

perfettamente, pěrfěttåměn'tě, ad. perfectly, wholly, entirely.   [perfected.

perfettibile, –ěttě'bilě, a. that can be

perfetto, –fět'tŏ, m. perfection; **–,** a. perfect, complete, finished.   [to perfection.

perfezionare, –fětziŏnå'rě, v. a. to bring

perfezione, –tziŏ'ně, f. perfection.

perfidamente, –fidåměn'tě, ad. perfidiously.

perfidia, –fĭ'diå, f. perfidy.

perfido, pěr'fidŏ, a. perfidious.

perforare, –fŏrå'rě, v. a. to pierce through.

pergamena, –gåmě'nå, f. parchment.

pergamo, pěr'gåmŏ, m. pulpit; scaffold, hustings, pl.

pergola, pěr'gŏlå, f. bower, arbour.

pericolare, pěrikŏlå'rě, v. a. to ruin, to destroy; to neglect; **–,** v. n. to be in danger, to run the risk.

pericolo, –rě'kŏlŏ, m. danger, peril.

pericoloso, –kŏlŏ'sŏ, a. perilous, dangerous.

perifrasi, –rě'fråsi, f. paraphrase.

periglio, see **pericolo.**

perimetro, –rě'mětrŏ, m. circumference, compass.   [periodical.

periodico, –rĭ'ŏ dikŏ, m. journal; **–,** a.

periodo, –rĭ'ŏdŏ, m. period, circuit.

perire, pěrě'rě, v. n. to perish.

peritanza, –rĭtån'tzå, f. bashfulness, modesty.   [be timid.

peritarsi, –tår'si, v. r. to be bashful; to

perito, pěrĭ'tŏ, a. expert, skilful; **–,** p. perished, dead.

peritoso, –tŏ'sŏ, a. bashful, shy.

perituro, –tŏ'rŏ, a. transitory, unstable.

perizia, –rě'tziå, f. skill, expertness.

perizoma, –rĭtzŏ'må, f. cincture of modesty.   [desty.

perla, pěr'lå, f. pearl.

permaloso, pěrmålŏ'sŏ, a. peevish, sullen.

permanente, –måněn'tě, a. permanent, lasting, continual.

permanenza, –něn'tzå, f. permanence.

permanere, –måně'rě, v. n. ir. to be continuous; to last.

permeabile, –měå'bilě, a. permeable.

permesso, –měs'sŏ, m. permission, leave.

permettere, –mět'těrě, v. a. ir. to permit, to allow.   [leave.

permissione, –missiŏ'ně, f. permission.

permuta, –mŏ'tå, f. permutation, change.

permutare, –mŭtå'rě, v. a. to permute; to exchange.

pernice, pěrnĭ'dshě, f. partridge.

pernicioso, –nidshŏ'sŏ, a. hurtful, pernicious.   [tridge.

perniciotto, –dshŏt'tŏ, m. young par-

perno, pěr'nŏ, m. pivot, hinge; ornament, support, basis.   [whole night.

pernottare, –nŏttå'rě, v. n. to pass the

pero, pě'rŏ, m. pear-tree.

però, *pĕrŏ',* ad. for that; therefore; **però,** in short.

perocchè, *pĕrŏkkĕ',* c. for, because.

perorare, *pĕrŏrā',rĕ,* y. a. to harangue.

perorazione, *–tzĭŏ'nĕ,* f. peroration.

perpendicolare, *–pĕndĭkŏlā'rĕ,* a. perpendicular.

perpendicolarmente, *–lărmĕn'tĕ,* ad. perpendicularly.   [perpendicle.

perpendicolo, *–dĕ'kŏlŏ,* m. plumb-line;

perpetrare, *–pĕtrā'rĕ,* v. a. to perpetrate; to commit.   [tually.

perpetuamente, *–pĕtŭămĕn'tĕ,* ad. perpetuate,—*tŭā'rĕ,* v. a. to perpetuate; to eternize, to eternalize.

perpetuazione, *–tzĭŏ'nĕ,* f. perpetuation.

perpetuità, *–pĕtŭĭtā',* f. perpetuity.

perpetuo, *–pĕ'tŭŏ,* a. perpetual, endless.

perplessità, *–plĕssĭtā',* f. perplexity.

perplesso, *–plĕs'sŏ,* a. perplexed.

perquisizione, *–kŭĭsĭtzĭŏ'nĕ,* f. perquisition, search.   [tion.

persecuzione, *–sĕkŭtzĭŏ'nĕ,* f. persecution.

perseguire, *–gŭĕ'rĕ,* v. a. to persecute; to continue, to pursue.   [to molest.

perseguitare, *–gŭĭtā'rĕ,* v. a. to persecute,

perseverante, *–sĕvĕrăn'tĕ,* a. persevering.

perseveranza, *–sĕvĕrăn'tzā,* f. perseverance.   [to persist.

perseverare, *–rā'rĕ,* v. n. to persevere,

persia, *pĕr'sĭā,* f. majoram.

persica, *pĕr'sĭkā,* f. peach.

persico, *pĕr'sĭkŏ,* m. peach-tree.

persistere, *–sĭs'tĕrĕ,* v. n. ir. to persist.

perso, *pĕr'sŏ,* a. lost; ruined.

persona, *pĕrsŏ'nā,* f. person; **in —,** personally, in person; **in — de,** instead of.

personaggio, *–sŏnăd'jŏ,* m. personage.

personale, *–nā'lĕ,* a. personal.

personalità, *–nālĭtā',* f. personality.

personalmente, *–nālmĕn'tĕ,* ad. personally, in person.   [cious.

perspicace, *pĕrspĭkā'dshĕ,* a. perspicacious.

perspicacia, *–kā'dshā,* f. perspicacity.

persuadere, *–sŭādĕ'rĕ,* v. a. ir. to persuade.

persuasione, *–sŭŏ'nĕ,* f. persuasion.

pertica, *pĕr'tĭkā,* f. perch, pole.

pertinace, *–tĭnā'dshĕ,* a. pertinacious, stubborn, headstrong.

pertinacia, *–nā'dshā,* f. stubbornness.

pertinente, *–nĕn'tĕ,* a. belonging to.

pertinenza, *–nĕn'tzā,* f. appurtenance; dependency.   [make a hole.

pertugiare, *–tŭjā'rĕ,* v. a. to pierce, to

pertugio, *–tŭ'jŏ,* m. hole.   [trouble.

perturbare, *–tŭrbā'rĕ,* v. a. to disturb, to

pervenire, *–vĕnĕ'rĕ,* v. n. ir. to attain to, to reach, to arrive at.

perversità, *–vĕrsĭtā',* f. perversity.

perverso, *–vĕr'sŏ,* a. perverse, depraved.

pervertire, *–vĕrtĕ'rĕ,* v. a. to pervert, to deprave, to corrupt.   [headstrong.

pervicace, *–vĭkā'dshĕ,* a. pervicacious.

pervicacia, *–kā'dshā,* f. obstinacy.

pervinca, *–vĭn'kā,* f. periwinkle.

pervio, *pĕr'vĭŏ,* a. pervious, open.   [grave.

pesante, *pĕsăn'tĕ,* a. heavy; important,

---

pesantezza, *–tĕt'zā,* f. weight, heaviness; sorrow.

pesare, *pĕsā'rĕ,* v. a. to weigh, to poise; to examine, to ponder, –. v. n. to be heavy.

pesca, *pĕs'kā,* f. peach.   [f. fishing.

pesca, *pĕs'kā,* **pescagione,** *–kājŏ'nĕ,*

pescaia, *–kā'ā,* f. sluice.

pescare, *–kā'rĕ,* y. a. to fish.

pescatore, *–tŏ'rĕ,* m. fisherman, angler.

pesce, *pĕssh'ĕ,* m. fish; Pisces (sign of the zodiac).   [market.

pescheria, *pĕskĕrĭ'ā,* f. fishery; fish-

peschiera, *–kĭā'rā,* f. fish-pond.

pesciaiulo, *pĕsshāĭŭŏ'lŏ,* m. fish-monger.

pesciatello, *–sshătĕl'lŏ,* m. little fish; fry.

pescivendolo, *–sshĭvĕn'dŏlŏ,* m. fish-monger.

pesco, *pĕs'kŏ,* m. peach-tree.   [monger.

peso, *pā'sŏ,* m. weight, load, charge; importance.   [wickedly.

pessimamente, *pĕssĭmāmĕn'tĕ,* ad. most

pessimo, *pĕs'sĭmŏ,* a. most wicked, infamous.   [crowd.

pesta, *pĕs'tā,* f. footstep, track, trace;

pestare, *pĕstā'rĕ,* v. a. to pound, to bruise; to trample upon.

peste, *pĕs'tĕ,* f. plague, pestilence.

pestello, *–tĕl'lŏ,* m. pestle.

pestilente, *–tĭlĕn'tĕ,* a. pestilent, pestiferous.

pestilenza, *–lĕn'tzā,* f. pestilence, plague.

pestilenziale, *–tzā'lĕ,* a. pestilential.

pestio, *pĕstī'ŏ,* m. trampling upon.

petecchiale, *pĕtĕkkĭā'lĕ,* a. spotted.

petecchie, *–tĕk'kĭĕ,* f. pl. purple-fever.

petizione, *–tĭtzĭŏ'nĕ,* f. petition; entreaty.

peto, *pā'tŏ,* m. fart.

petraia, *pĕtrā'ā,* f. stone-quarry.

petrella, *–trĕl'lā,* f. small stone.

petrificare, *–trĭfĭkā'rĕ,* v. a. to petrify.

petrolio, *–trŏ'lĭŏ,* m. petrolium, rock-oil.

petrosello, *–trŏsĕl'lŏ,* m. parsley.

petroso, *–trŏ'sŏ,* a. stony; hard.

petruzza, *see* petrella.

pettabbotta, *pĕttăbbŏt'tā,* f. breast-plate.

pettegola, *–tā'gŏlā,* f. strumpet, wench.

pettegolezzo, *–tĕgŏlĕt'zŏ,* m. gossip, prattle.   [(fig.) to scratch.

pettinare, *–tĭnā'rĕ,* v. a. to comb, to card;

pettine, *pĕt'tĭnĕ,* m. comb; hatchel.

pettinella, *–tĭnĕl'lā,* f. hairpoon.

pettirosso, *–rŏs'sŏ,* m. robin red-breast.

petto, *pĕt'tŏ,* m. breast, bosom; mind.

pettorale, *–tŏrā'lĕ,* m. breast-strap; –, a. pectoral.   [marily.

pettoralmente, *–rālmĕn'tĕ,* ad. sum-

petulante, *pĕtŭlăn'tĕ,* a. petulant, arrogant.

petulanza, *–lăn'tzā,* f. petulancy.

peverada, *pĕvĕrā'dā,* f. meat-broth.

pezza, *pĕt'zā,* f. piece; strip; remnant, bit; **a questa —,** at present, now; **una gran —,** a long while.

pezzato, *–tzā'tŏ,* a. speckled.

pezzente, *–tzĕn'tĕ,* m. beggar.

pezzo, *pĕt'zŏ,* m. bit, piece, morsel; **— d'artiglieria,** piece of ordnance.

pezzuola, –tzŭd'lǎ, f. handkerchief.
pezzuolo, –tzŭd'lŏ, m. little piece, small rag. [able.
piacente, pĭădshĕn'tĕ, a. pleasing, agree-
piacentemente, –tĕmĕn'tĕ, ad. pleasantly; calmly, peaceably.
piacenteria, –dshĕntĕrĕ'ă, f. flattery.
piacere, –dshá'rĕ, v. a. ir. to please, to charm ; –, m. pleasure, delight, favour.
piacevole, –dshá'vŏlĕ, a. pleasing, affable, agreeable ; droll, merry.
piacevolezza, –dshĕvŏlĕt'ză, f. affability, gentleness, playfulness, sportiveness.
piacimento, –dshĭmĕn'tŏ, m. pleasure, delight ; will.
piaga, pĭă'gă, f. sore, wound, calamity.
piagare, –gá'rĕ, v. a. to wound.
piaggia, pĭăd'jă, f. side of a hill ; seashore; country-side.
piaggiare, –djá'rĕ, v. a. to walk or stand on the sea-shore; to blandish, to wheedle.
piagnucolare, pĭănyŭkŏlá'rĕ, v. n. to weep a little, to whine, to wail.
pialla, pĭăl'lă, f. carpenter's plane.
piallare, –lá'rĕ, v. a. to plane.
piana, pĭă'nă, f. plank, rafter, joist ; stave.
pianamente, –mĕn'tĕ, ad. softly, gently.
pianare, –ná'rĕ, v. a. to plane, to make plain, to smooth.
pianella, –nĕl'lă, f. slipper; flat tile.
pianeta, –ná'tă, m. planet ; –, f. priest's cope. [to lament.
piangere, pĭăn'jĕrĕ, v. a. ir. to weep ;
piangolare, see **piagnucolare**.
piano, pĭă'nŏ, m. plain; floor, storey; sounding-board ; –, a. level, flat; plain ; smooth ; even ; clear, intelligible; meek ; –, ad. softly, gently; slowly, low; **pian** –, very softly.
pianoforte,–fŏr'tĕ, m. pianoforte, piano.
pianta, pĭăn'tă, f. plant; scion; sole of the foot; plan of a house.
piantaggine, –tăd'jĭnĕ, f. plantain.
piantagione, –tăjŏ'nĕ, f. planting, plantation. [to place; to point.
piantare, pĭăntá'rĕ, v. a. to plant, to set,
piantazione, –tă̆tzĭŏ'nĕ, f. plantation.
pianterreno, –tĕrrá'nŏ, m. ground-floor.
pianto, pĭăn'tŏ, m. weeping, lamentation.
piantone, –tŏ'nĕ, m. sucker; sapling.
pianura, pĭănŏ'ră, f. plain, open plain.
piare, pĭă'rĕ, v. n. to chirp.
piastra, pĭăs'tră, f. thin plate of metal; piaster ; dry scab. [plastron.
piastrone, –trŏ'nĕ, m. coat of mail.
piatire, pĭătĕ'rĕ, v. n. to plead, to dispute.
piato, pĭă'tŏ, m. plea, law-suit, dispute, debate ; affair. [(rail.) turn-plate.
piattaforma, pĭăttăfŏr'mă, f. platform ;
piatteria, –tĕrĕ'ă, f. table-service, dishes.
piatto, pĭăt'tŏ, m. dish, meat, mess, course; –, a. flattened, flat; hidden.
piattola, pĭăt'tŏlă, f. crab-louse.
piazza, pĭăt'ză, f. place, room; square; market-place. [boy.
piazzaiuolo, –tzăiŭd'lŏ, m. blackguard-

piazzetta, –tzĕt'tă, f. small place, spot.
pica, pĕ'kă, f. magpie; spear, pike; pique; dispute; chatterer. [dispute.
picca, pĭk'kă, f. spear, pike; grudge;
piccare, –kă'rĕ, v. a. to prick, to sting, to injure; **piccarsi**, –kăr'sĕ, to pretend to.
picchetto, –kĕt'tŏ, m. piquet (game); (mil.) picket.
picchiare, –kĭă'rĕ, v. a. to knock (at a door); to strike, to beat.
picchiettare, –kĭĕttá'rĕ, v. a. to mark with spots.
picchio, pĭk'kĭŏ, m. wood-pecker, blow, rap.
piccino, pĭtshĕ'nĕ, a. small, little; short.
piccione, –tshŏ'nĕ, m. pigeon; ninny.
picciuolo, –tshăd'lŏ, m. stem, stalk; penis.
picco, pĭk'kŏ, a. stung; nettled.
piccoletto, –lĕt'tŏ, **piccolino**, –lĕ'nŏ, a. very little.
piccolo, pĭk'kŏlŏ, a. small, little; short.
piccone, –kŏ'nĕ, m. pick-axe, mattock; (cant) alderman.
picconiere, –kŏnĭă'rĕ, m. pioneer; digger.
piccoso, –kŏ'sŏ, a. captious, touchy.
piceo, pĕ'dshĕŏ, a. pitch-coloured.
pidocchio, pĭdŏk'kĭŏ, m. louse.
pidocchioso, –kĭŏ'sŏ, a. lousy.
pie, pĭĕ', **piede**, pĭĕ'dĕ, m. foot; stem, plant, base, ground; support; **a** –, on foot.
piega, pĭĕ'gă, f. plait, fold.
piegare, pĭĕgá'rĕ, v. a. to fold, to bend; to incline, **piegarsi**, –gár'sĕ, to yield, to resign. [easy.
pieghevole, –ghĕ'vŏlĕ, a. pliant, flexible;
piena, pĭĕ'nă, f. flood; throng.
pienamente, –mĕn'tĕ, ad. fully, quite.
pienezza, –nĕt'ză, f. fulness.
pieno, pĭĕ'nŏ, a. full, filled.
pietà, pĭĕ'tă, f. (poet.) sorrow, affliction.
pietà, pĭĕtá', f. piety; pity, compassion.
pietanza, –tăn'tză, f. plate of meat, portion.
pietoso, –tŏ'sŏ, a. pitiful, exciting pity.
pietra, pĭĕ'tră, f. stone; gem ; – **da fuoco**, flint; – **di paragone**, touch-stone ; – **di scandalo**, stumbling-block.
pietrame, pĭĕtră'mĕ, m. heap of stones.
pietrificare, –trĭfĭká'rĕ, v. a. to petrify.
pietrificazione, –tzĭŏ'nĕ, f. petrifaction.
pietroso, –trŏsŏ, a. stony.
piffero, pĭf'fĕrŏ, m. fife; fifer. [crush.
pigiare, pĭjá'rĕ, v. a. to trample upon; to
pigiatura, –tŏ'ră, f. grape-pressing.
pigio, pĕ'jŏ, m. press, crowd, throng.
pigionale, pĭjŏná'lĕ, m. lodger, tenant.
pigione, –jŏ'nĕ, m. house-rent.
pigliare, pĭlyá'rĕ, v. a. to take, to seize; to receive ; – **terra**, to land ; – **di mira**, to aim at ; – **partito**, to determine.
piglio, pĭl'yŏ, m. taking, hold, look, glance.
pigmeo, pĭgmă'ŏ, m. pigmy, dwarf.
pignatta, pĭnyăt'tă, f., **pignatto**, –tŏ, m. broth-pot, kettle.
pignere, see **pingere**.
pignone, –yŏ'nĕ, m. dike, wharf.
pignorare, –yŏrá'rĕ, v. a. to give as a pledge, to mortgage.

pigolare, *pĭgōlä´rĕ,* v. a. to pip, to chirp.
pigrezza, *pĭgrĕt´zä,* **pigrizia,** *–grĭt´zĭä,*
pigro, *pĕ´grō,* a. lazy, idle. [f. idleness.
pila, *pĕ´lä,* f. pillar ; stone cistern ; mortar.
piliere, *pĭlĭä´rĕ,* m. pillar, column.
pillare, *pĭllä´rĕ,* v. a. to pound, to grind,
pillo, *pĭl´lō,* m. pestle. [to bruise.
pillola, *pĭl´lōlä,* f. pill. [to singe.
pillottare, *–lōttä´rĕ,* v. a. to baste meat;
pilo, *pĕ´lō,* m. javelin.
pilone, *pĭlō´nĕ,* m. pilaster.
pilota, *pĭlō´tä,* **piloto,** *–tō,* m. pilot.
pimmeo, *see* **pigmeo.**
pina, *pĕ´nä,* f. pine-apple. [paintings.
pinacoteca, *pĭnäkōtä´kä,* f. gallery of
pincione, *pĭnchōˈnĕ,* m. chaffinch.
pineta, *pĭnä´tä,* f., **pineto,** *–tō,* m. pine-
grove. [to thrust.
pingere, *pĭn´jĕrĕ,* v.a. ir. to paint ; to push,
pingue, *pĭn´gŭĕ,* a. fat, plump.
pinguedine, *–gŭĕ´dĭnĕ,* f. fatness.
pinna, *pĭn´nä,* f. fin.
pinnacolo, *–nä´kōlō,* m. pinnacle.
pino, *pĕ´nō,* m. pine, pine-tree; (poet.) ship.
pinocchio, *pĭnōk´kĭō,* m. pine-seed.
pinta, *pĭn´tä,* f. push, thrust ; impulse.
pinzacchio, *–zäk´kĭō,* m. mite, weevil.
pinzo, *pĭn´tzō,* a. very full.
pinzochero, *–tzō´kĕrō,* m. bigot, hypocrite, dissembler. [sionate.
pio, *pĕ´ō,* a. pious, religious ; compas-
pioggia, *pĭōd´jä,* f. rain.
piombare, *pĭōmbä´rĕ,* v. a. to plumb ; –,
v.n. to be perpendicular ; to sink like lead ;
piombarsi, *–bär´sĭ,* to lay heavy upon.
piombatura, *–bätō´rä,* f. leaden ball or
bullet. [line.
piombino, *–bĕ´nō,* m. plummet ; plumb-
piombo, *pĭōm´bō,* m. lead ; plummet, level ;
a –, perpendicular.
pioppo, *pĭōp´pō,* m. poplar-tree.
piota, *pĭō´tä,* f. sole of the foot ; grassy sod,
piova, *pĭō´vä,* f. (poet.) rain. [turf.
piovano, *pĭōvä´nō,* m. country-parson.
piovigginare, *pĭōvĭdjĭnä´rĕ,* v. n. to
drizzle.
piovere, *pĭō´vĕrĕ,* v. n. ir. to rain.
pipa, *pĕ´pä,* f. tobacco-pipe.
pipare, *pĭpä´rĕ,* v. a. to smoke (a pipe).
pipistrello, *–pĭstrĕl´lō,* m. bat.
pipita, *–pĭ´tä,* f. pip (disease of fowls);
sprout.
pippione, *pĭppĭō´nĕ,* f. young pigeon.
pira, *pĕ´rä,* f. funeral pile ; perfuming-pot.
piramide, *pĭrä´mĭdĕ,* f. pyramid.
pirata, *–rä´tä,* m. pirate ; plagiarist.
piroetta, *–rōĕt´tä,* f. whirligig.
pirone, *–rō´nĕ,* m. lever. [fire-works, pl.
pirotecnia, *–rōtĕknĕ´ä,* f. pyrotechnics,
pirotecnico, *–tĕk´nĭkō,* a. pyrotechnic.
piscia, *pĭssh´ä,* f. piscio, *pĭssh´ō,* m.
urine. [water.
pisciare, *pĭsshä´rĕ,* v. n. to piss, to make
pisciatoio, *–tō´ō,* m. chamber-pot.
piscina, *pĭsshĕ´nä,* f. fish-pond.
pisello, *pĭsĕl´lō,* m. pease.

pispigliare, *pĭspĭlyä´rĕ,* v. n. to whisper,
to speak low.
pisside, *pĭs´sĭdĕ,* f. pyx ; cavity.
pistagna, *–tän´yä,* f. flounce, furbelow.
pistola, *pĭs´tōlä,* f. letter, epistle ; –, *pĭs-
tō´lä,* f. pistol.
pitaffio, *pĭtäf´fĭō,* m. epitaph.
pitocco, *–tōk´kō,* m. beggar.
pittore, *pĭttō´rĕ,* m. painter.
pittoresco, *–tōrĕs´kō,* a. picturesque.
pittura, *–tō´rä,* f. painting, picture.
pitturare, *–tūrä´rĕ,* v. a. to paint ; to de-
pituita, *pĭtō´ĭtä,* f. phlegm. [pict.
più, *pĭŭ´,* ad. more ; **al –,** at (the) most;
di –, moreover ; **– che –,** much more ;
– fa, a long while ago ; **i –,** most of them.
piva, *pĕ´vä,* f. bag-pipe. [plover (bird).
piviere, *pĭvĭä´rĕ,* m. precinct of a parish ;
piuma, *pĭō´mä,* f. plume, down.
piumaccio, *pĭōmät´shō,* m. bolster, cushion.
piumino, *–mē´nō,* m. tuft of feathers.
piuolo, *pĭō´lō,* m. peg.
piuttosto, *pĭōttōs´tō,* ad. rather, sooner.
pizzicagnolo, *pĭtzĭkän´yōlō,* m. pork-
butcher. [to bite ; to itch.
pizzicare, *–kä´rĕ,* v. a. to pinch, to peck,
pizzicheria, *–kĕrĕ´ä,* f. trade in victuals.
pizzico, *pĭt´zĭkō,* m. pinch.
pizzo, *pĭt´zō,* m. pointed beard, imperial.
placabile, *pläkä´bĭlĕ,* a. placable.
placare, *–kä´rĕ,* v. a. to appease, to pacify.
placidamente, *plädshĭdämĕn´tĕ,* ad.
placidly.
placidità, *–dshĭdĭtä´,* f. placidity.
placido, *plä´dshĭdō,* a. placid, mild, calm.
placito, *plä´dshĭtō,* m. good-will, pleasure.
plaga, *plä´gä,* f. shore ; region ; coast.
plagiario, *pläjä´rĭō,* m. plagiarism ; pla-
plagio, *plä´jō,* m. plagiarism. [giarist.
planetario, *–nĕtä´rĭō,* a. planetary.
plastica, *pläs´tĭkä,* f. plastic art.
plastico, *pläs´tĭkō,* a. plastic.
platea, *plätä´ä,* f. area (of a building) ; pit
(of a theatre).
plaudire, *plädä´rĕ,* v. n. to applaud.
plausibile, *–sĕ´bĭlĕ,* a. plausible.
plauso, *plä´ūsō,* m. applause.
plaustro, *plä´ūstrō,* m. chariot.
plebaglia, *plĕbä´lyä,* f. mob, rabble.
plebe, *plä´bĕ,* f. common people.
plebeo, *plĕbä´ō,* a. plebeian, low.
plenario, *–nä´rĭō,* a. plenary, full.
plenilunio, *plĕnĭlō´nĭō,* m. full moon.
plenipotenza, *–pōtĕn´tzä,* f. absolute
power. [potentiary.
plenipotenziario, *–tzĭä´rĭō,* m. pleni-
plenitudine, *–tō´dĭnĕ,* f. fulness.
plico, *plĕ´kō,* m. packet of letters.
plorare, *plōrä´rĕ,* v. n. to weep.
plurale, *plōrä´lĕ,* m. (gr.) plural number.
pluralità, *–rälĭtä´,* f. plurality.
pluviale, *–vĭä´lĕ,* **pluvio,** *plŭ´vĭō,* a. rainy.
po', *pō,* for **poco.**
pocciare, *pōtshä´rĕ,* v. a. to suck.
pochetto, *–kĕt´tō,* ad. very little.
pochezza, *–kĕt´zä,* f. littleness ; scarcity.
poco, *pō´kō,* a. little, small ; few ; slender,

thin; –, ad. little, not much; **a – a –**, little by little; **– anzi**, not long ago; **fra –, shortly; – stante**, soon after.

pocolino, *pŏkŏlē′nŏ*, ad. very little.

podere, *pŏdā′rĕ*, m. power; manor.

poderoso, *–dĕrō′sŏ*, a. powerful; vigorous, sturdy, stout.

podestà, *–dĕstā′*, f. power; dominion; authority.

podice, *pŏ′dădshĕ*, m. buttock.

poema, *pŏā′mă*, m. poem.

poesia, *pŏĕsē′ă*, f. poetry, poesy.

poeta, *pŏā′tă*, m. poet.

poetare, *pŏĕtā′rĕ*, v. n. to compose poems.

poetastro, *–tās′trŏ*, m. poetaster.

poeteggiare, *–tĕdjā′rĕ*, v. n. to poetize.

poetesco, *–tĕs′kŏ*, a. poetical.

poetessa, *–tĕs′să*, f. poetess.

poetica, *pŏĕ′tĭkă*, f. poetry.

poetico, *pŏĕ′tĭkŏ*, a. poetical.

poggia, *pŏd′jă*, f. (mar.) starboard-side.

poggiare, *–djā′rĕ*, v. n. to mount, to ascend.

poggio, *pŏd′jŏ*, m. hill, cliff.

pogginolo, *–djŏ′lŏ*, m. verandah.

poi, *pŏ′ĭ*, ad. then, after; **in –**, except, unless; **po' –**, in short.

poichè, *pŏĭkĕ′*, ad. & c. since; considering that.

poledro, *pŏlĕ′drŏ*, m. colt, foal.

polenda, *–lĕn′dă*, f. pudding (of chestnut flour).

poligamia, *pŏlĭgămē′ă*, f. polygamy.

poligamo, *pŏlĭ′gămŏ*, m. polygamist.

poliglotta, *–lĭglŏt′tă*, m. polyglot.

poligono, *–lĕ′gŏnŏ*, m. polygon; –, a. polygonal.

polipo, *pŏ′lĭpŏ*, m. polypus.

polire, *–lĕ′rĕ*, v. a. to polish.

politica, *–lĕ′tĭkă*, f. politics, pl., policy.

politico, *–lĕ′tĭkŏ*, m. politician; –, a. political.

politto, *–lĕ′tŏ*, a. polished.

polizza, *–lĕ′tză*, f. note, bill; lottery-ticket.

polla, *pŏl′lă*, f. spring of water.

pollaio, *–lā′ŏ*, m. hen-roost; poultry-yard.

pollaiuolo, *–lăŏŏlŏ*, m. poulterer.

pollame, *–lā′mĕ*, m. poultry.

pollastra, *–lās′tră*, f. fat pullet.

pollastro, *–lās′trŏ*, m. fowl, chicken.

pollezzola, *–lĕt′zŏlă*, f. sprout, shoot.

pollice, *pŏl′lădshĕ*, m. thumb; big toe.

pollo, *pŏl′lŏ*, m. chicken.

pollone, *–lŏ′nĕ*, m. sprout, sucker.

polluto, *–lŭ′tŏ*, a. polluted.

polluzione, *–tzŏ′nĕ*, f. pollution.

polmonare, *–mŏnā′rĕ*, a. pulmonary.

polmone, *–mŏ′nĕ*, m. lungs, pl.

polo, *pŏ′lŏ*, m. pole.

polpa, *pŏl′pă*, f. pulp, fleshy part.

polpaccio, *–pāt′shŏ*, m. calf of the leg.

polpastrello, *–pāstrĕl′lŏ*, m. fleshy end of the finger.

polpetta, *–pĕt′tă*, f. sausage.

polputo, *–pŭ′tŏ*, a. pulpous.

polsetto, *–sĕt′tŏ*, m. bracelet.

polso, *pŏl′sŏ*, m. pulse; vigour.

polta, *pŏl′tă*, f. pap; hasty-pudding.

poltiglia, *–tĭl′yă*, f. mud, mire.

poltrire, *–trē′rĕ*, v. a. to lie abed lazily; to loiter, to be idle.

poltrona, *–trŏ′nă*, f. easy-chair.

poltrone, *–trŏ′nĕ*, m. sluggard, poltroon.

poltroneria, *–trŏnĕrē′ă*, f. cowardice; idleness.

poltronesco, *–nĕs′kŏ*, a. lazy, cowardly.

polve, *pŏl′vĕ*, (poet.) **polvere**, *–vĕrĕ*, f. dust, powder; gun-powder.

polveriera, *–vĕrĭĕ′ră*, f. gun-powder mill.

polverino, *–rē′nŏ*, m. sand-box; powder-box; priming-powder.

polverio, *–rē′ŏ*, m. whirlwind of dust.

polverizzare, *–rĭdzā′rĕ*, v. a. to pulverise.

polverone, *–rŏ′nĕ*, m. dust-cloud.

polveroso, *–rŏ′sŏ*, a. dusty.

pomario, *pŏmā′rĭŏ*, m. apple-orchard.

pomata, *–mā′tă*, f. pomatum.

pomice, *pŏ′mĭdshĕ*, f. pumice-stone.

pomidoro, *pŏmĭdŏ′rŏ*, m. tomato, love-apple.

pommelato, *pŏmmĕlā′tŏ*, a. dappled.

pomo, *pŏ′mŏ*, m. apple; pommel; hilt; **– di terra**, potato.

pompa, *pŏm′pă*, f. pomp.

pomposo, *–pŏ′sŏ*, a. pompous.

ponderabile, *pŏndĕrā′bĭlĕ*, a. ponderable.

ponderare, *–rā′rĕ*, v. a. & n. to ponder, to weigh; to consider.

ponderoso, *–rŏ′sŏ*, a. ponderous, weighty.

pondi, *pŏn′dĭ*, m. pl. bloody flux.

pondo, *pŏn′dŏ*, m. weight, load; pound; importance.

ponente, *pŏnĕn′tĕ*, m. west; westwind.

pontare, *pŏntā′rĕ*, v. a. to thrust; to shove; to support.

ponte, *pŏn′tĕ*, m. bridge, scaffold; (mar.) deck.

pontefice, *–tĕ′fĭdshĕ*, m. pontiff, high-priest.

pontico, *pŏn′tĭkŏ*, a. sharp, tart.

pontificare, *–tĭfĭkā′rĕ*, v. a. to hold the charge of a pontiff.

pontificato, *–kā′tŏ*, m. pontificate.

pontificio, *–fē′dshŏ*, a. pontifical.

ponto, *pŏn′tŏ*, m. (poet.) sea, ocean; –, a. pricked, stung.

pontonaio, *–tŏnā′ŏ*, m. bridge-guard.

pontone, *–tŏ′nĕ*, m. pontoon.

ponzare, *tzā′rĕ*, v. a. to make an effort, to strain.

popolaccio, *pŏpŏlāt′shŏ*, m. populace, mob.

popolano, *–lā′nŏ*, a. & m. popular; parishioner, inhabitant of a village.

popolare, *–lā′rĕ*, a. popular, vulgar; –, v. a. to people.

popolarità, *–lārĭtā′*, f. popularity.

popolazione, *–lātzĭŏ′nĕ*, f. population.

popolazzo, *–lāt′zŏ*, m. common people.

popolo, *pŏ′pŏlŏ*, m. people, nation; mass, quantity; poplar.

popoloso, *pŏpŏlŏ′sŏ*, a. populous.

poppa, *pŏp′pă*, f. woman's breast; poop (of a vessel).

poppare, *pŏp′pā′rĕ*, v. a. to suck (milk).

poppatoio, *–pātŏ′ŏ*, m. nipple-glass, sucker.

poppatola, *–pă′tŏlă*, f. doll, puppet.

popputo, *–pŭ′tŏ*, a. full breasted.

porca, *pŏr′kă*, f. sow.

porcaio, *–kā′ŏ*, m. swine-herd.

porcella, *–dshĕl′lă*, f. young sow.

porcellana, *–lā′nă*, f. porcelain.

porcello, *–dshĕl′lŏ*, m. sucking-pig.

porcheria, –kèr'ă, f. nastiness, filth.
porcile, –dshè'lĕ, m. pig-sty.
porco, pŏr'kŏ, m. hog, pig, swine; – spino, porcupine; –, a. dirty, nasty.
porgere, pŏr'jèrĕ, v. a. ir. to present, to offer; to afford.
poro, pŏ'rŏ, m. pore. [offer; to afford.
porosità, pŏrŏsĭtă', f. porosity.
poroso, –rŏ'sŏ, a. porous. [cloth.
porpora, pŏr'pŏră, f. purple colour; purple
porre, pŏr'rĕ, v. a. ir. to put, to pose, to place; to order.
porrina, –rē'nă, f. (bot.) small leek.
porro, pŏr'rŏ, m. (bot.) leek; wart.
porta, pŏr'tă, f. door, gate.
portabile, pŏrtă'bĭlĕ, a. portable.
portacappe, –kăp'pĕ, m. travelling-bag.
portafiaschi, –fĭăs'kĭ, m. hamper, basket.
portafogli, –fŏl'yĭ, m. letter-case.
portalettere, –lèt'tèrĕ, m. letter-carrier, postman.
portamantello, –măntèl'lŏ, m. carpet-bag.
portamento, –mèn'tŏ, m. carrying; bearing; look, mien, behaviour.
portantina, pŏrtăntē'nă, f. sedan-chair.
portare, –tă'rĕ, v. a. to carry, to bring, to bear, to wear; to bring forth, to yield, to produce; to allege; to induce; portarsi, –tăr'sĭ, to behave oneself.
portata, –tă'tă, f. calibre; load; condition; means, pl., import.
portatile, –tă'tĭlĕ, a. portable.
portato, –tă'tŏ, m. brood; litter; course of dishes. [brood.
portatura, –tŏ'ră, f. carriage; fashion;
portello, –tèl'lŏ, m. little door, postern.
portento, –tèn'tŏ, m. prodigy. [digious.
portentoso, –tŏ'sŏ, a. monstrous, proporticato, –ĭtkă'tŏ, m. portico.
porticciuola, –tĭtshŏŏ'lă, f. postern.
portico, pŏr'ĭtkŏ, m. porch, portico.
portiera, –tĭă'ră, f. door-curtain; coachdoor; portress. [door-keeper.
portiere, –tĭă'rĕ, portinaio, –nă'ŏ, m.
porto, pŏr'tŏ, m. port, haven, harbour; carriage.
portolano, –tŏlă'nŏ, m. pilot; door-keeper.
portulaca, –tŭlă'kă, f. (bot.) purslain.
porzione, –tzĭŏ'nĕ, f. portion, share; lot.
posa, pŏ'să, f. repose, quiet; pause.
posare, pŏsă'rĕ, v. a. & n. to set or to lay down; to sit down; to repose, to stand.
posato, –să'tŏ, a. laid down; sedate, staid.
posatoio, –tŏ'ŏ, m. bench; perch; place of repose.
posatura, –tŏ'ră, f. sediment, dregs, pl.
poscia, pŏssh'ă, ad. after, afterwards.
posciachè, pŏsshăkè', ad. & c. since, since that; although. [m. postscript.
poscritta, pŏskrĭt'tă, f., poscritto, –tŏ, posdomani, –dŏmă'nĭ, ad. after to-morrow.
positivo, –sĭtē'vŏ, a. positive. [row.
positura, –tŏ'ră, f. posture, situation.
posizione, –tzĭŏ'nĕ, f. position, situation;
poso, see posa. [proposition.
posporre, pŏspŏr'rĕ, v. a. ir. to postpone, to neglect. [delay.
posposizione, –pŏsĭtzĭŏ'nĕ, f. postponing;

possa, pŏs'să, possanza, –săn'tză, f. power, force; virtue.
possedere, –sèdd'rĕ, v. a. to possess.
possente, –sèn'tĕ, a. powerful, potent.
possessione, –sèssŏ'nĕ, f. possession; estate.
possessivo, –sèssĕ'vŏ, a. possessive.
possesso, –sès'sŏ, m. possession, holding.
possessore, –sèssŏ'rĕ, m. possessor.
possibile, –sē'bĭlĕ, a. possible.
possibilità, –sĭbĭlĭtă', f. possibility.
possibilmente, –mèn'tĕ, ad. possibly.
posta, pŏs'tă, f. post, station, place; stall, post-house; rendezvous, opportunity; ambush; footstep, trace; stake, bet; situation; posture; planting; – fatta, on purpose; – ferma, settled affair; a –, expressly; a – d'alcuno, as any one pleases; far la –, to lay in ambuscade.
postare, –tă'rĕ, v. n. to take station.
postema, –tĕ'mă, f. abscess. [posterity.
posteri, pŏs'tèrĭ, m. pl. descendants, pl., posteriore, –tèrĭŏ'rĕ, m. posterior; backside; –, a. posterior.
posterità, –tèrĭtă', f. posterity.
posticcio, –tĭt'shŏ, a. borrowed, false.
posticipare, –tĭdshĭpă'rĕ, v. a. to defer, to delay.
postiere, –tĭă'rĕ, m. post-master.
postierla, –tĭèr'lă, f. small gate, postern.
postiglione, –tĭlyŏ'nĕ, m. post-boy.
postilla, –tĭl'lă, f. postil.
postino, –tĕ'nŏ, m. letter-carrier, postman.
posto, pŏs'tŏ, m. place, post; stand; situation, station.
postochè, pŏstŏkè', c. in case that.
postremo, –trĕ'mŏ, a. last, hindmost.
postribolo, –trē'bŏlŏ, m. brothel.
postumo, pŏs'tŭmŏ, a. posthumous.
postura, –tŏ'ră, f. posture; situation.
potabile, pŏtă'bĭlĕ, a. drinkable.
potare, –tă'rĕ, v. a. to prune, to lop.
potatoio, –tŏ'ŏ, m. pruning-knife.
potatore, –tŏ'rĕ, m. vine-dresser.
potatura, –tŏ'ră, f. pruning, lopping of branches.
potentato, –tèntă'tŏ, m. potentate.
potente, –tèn'tĕ, a. potent, powerful. [pl.
potenza, –tèn'tză, f. potency, power; forces, potere, –tă'rĕ, v. a. ir. to be able; –, m. power.
potestà, –tèstă', f. power, government.
potissimo, –tĭs'sĭmŏ, a. principal, chief.
poveraglia, pŏvèră'lyă, f. poor people.
poverello, –rèl'lŏ, a. poor, unfortunate.
poveretto, –rèt'tŏ, m. poor creature.
poverino, –rē'nŏ, a. poor, miserable.
povero, pŏ'vèrŏ, a. poor, indigent.
povertà, pŏvèrtă', f. poverty.
pozione, pŏtzĭŏ'nĕ, f. portion; draught.
poziore, –tzĭŏ'rĕ, a. prior, preceding.
pozza, pŏt'ză, pozzanghera, –zăn'ghèră, f. puddle, dirty plash.
pozzetta, pŏtzèt'tă, f. small puddle, dimple.
pozzo, pŏt'zŏ, m. well; – nero, sink.
pranzare, prăntză'rĕ, v. a. to dine.
pranzo, prăn'tzŏ, m. dinner; –, a. saturated.
pratellina, prătèllē'nă, f. daisy.

prateria, –těr'ĭ ā̆, f. meadows, prairies, pl.
pratica, prä'tīkä, f. practice, usage; **di –,** freely; easily.
praticabile, –tĭkä'bĭlě, a. practicable.
praticare, –kä'rě, v. a. to practise; to negotiate. [practical.
pratico, prä'tĭkŏ, a. practised, versed,
prato, prä'tŏ, m. meadow, pasture-field.
pravità, prävĭtä', f. depravity.
pravo, prä'vŏ, a. depraved, wicked.
preaccennare, preätshěnnä'rě,v.a.to mention before. [tioned.
preallegato, –ällěgä'tŏ, a. above-mentioned.
preambolo, –äm'bŏlŏ, m. preamble, preface.
preavvisare, –avvĭsä'rě, v.a. to forewarn.
preavviso, –ävvē'sŏ, m. forewarning.
prebenda, –běn'dä, f. prebend; stipend; provision.
precario, –kä'rĭŏ, a. precarious; uncertain.
precauzione, –käŭtzĭŏ'ně, f. precaution, care, circumspection.
prece, prě'dshě, f. prayer, entreaty.
precedente, prědshěděn'tě, m. antecedent.
precedentemente, –měn'tě, ad. previously. [priority.
precedenza, –děn'tzä, f. precedence.
precedere, –dshě'děrě, v. a. to precede.
precettare, –dshěttä'rě, v. a. to summon, [to cite.
precetto, –dshět'tŏ, m. precept.
precettore, –tŏ'rě, m. preceptor, teacher.
precidere, –dshě'děrě, v. a. ir. to cut off, to shorten. [surround.
precingere, –dshĭn'jěrě, v. a. to gird, to
precinto, –dshĭn'tŏ, m. precinct, compass.
precipitare, –dshĭpĭtä'rě, v. a. & n. to precipitate; to fall down headlong.
precipite, –dshě'pĭtě, **precipitoso,** –dshĭpĭtŏ'sŏ, a. precipitous; overhasty.
precipizio, –dshĭpē'tzĭŏ, m. precipice.
precipuo, –dshě'pŭŏ, a. principal, chief.
precisamente, –dshĭsäměn'tě, ad. precisely. [ness.
precisione, –sĭŏ'ně, f. precision, exact-
preciso, –dshě'sŏ, a. precise, exact, strict; **–,** ad. precisely, exactly. [famous.
preclaro, –klä'rŏ, a. noble, illustrious,
precludere, –klŭ'děrě, v. a. ir. to preclude; to hinder.
precoce, –kŏ'dshě, a. precocious.
preconio, –kŏ'nĭŏ, m. (poet.) praise.
preconizzare, –kŏnĭzzä'rě, v. n. to preconize, to extol.
preda, prě'dä, f. prey, booty. [plunder.
predare, –dä'rě, v. a. to pillage, to
predecessore, –dědshěssŏ'rě, m. predecessor; ancestor.
predella, –děl'lä, f. stool, foot-stool; close-stool; confessional; reins of a bridle.
predestinare, –děstĭnä'rě, v. a. to predestine.
predica, prě'dĭkä, f. sermon; auditory.
predicamento, –prědĭkäměn'tŏ, m. predicament; preaching.
predicare, –kä'rě, v. a. & n. to preach; to sermonise, to lecture.
predicato, –kä'tŏ, m. predicate.

prediletto, –lět'tŏ, a. beloved, dearest.
predilezione, –lětzĭŏ'ně, f. predilection; partiality.
prediligere, –lě'jěrě, v. a. to be partial to.
predire, –dě'rě, v. a. ir. to foretell, to prophesy.
predizione, –dĭtzĭŏ'ně, f. prediction.
predominare, –dŏmĭnä'rě, v. n. to predominate; to prevail.
predominio, –dŏmě'nĭŏ, m. predominance.
predone, –dŏ'ně, m. plunderer, highwayman.
preesistente, –ěsĭstěn'tě, a. pre-existent.
preesistenza, –ěsĭs'tzä, f. pre-existence.
preesistere, –ěsĭs'těrě, v. n. ir. to pre-exist.
prefato, –fä'tŏ, a. aforesaid. [exist.
prefazione, –tzĭŏ'ně, f. preface.
preferenza, –fěrěn'tzä, f. preference, precedence.
preferire, –fěrě'rě, v. a. to prefer.
prefetto, –fět'tŏ, m. prefect, magistrate.
prefettura, –fěttŏ'rä, f. prefecture.
prefiggere, –fĭd'jěrě, v. a. ir. to prefix.
prefisso, –fĭs'sŏ, a. prefixed, determined.
pregare, prěgä'rě, v. a. to pray, to entreat.
pregevole, –jä'vŏlě, a. worthy, valuable.
preghevole, –ghě'vŏlě, a. suppliant.
preghiera, –ghĭě'rä, f. prayer, supplication, entreaty, request.
pregiare, –jä'rě, v. a. to prize, to value, to esteem; **pregiarsi,** –jär'sĭ, to pretend to. [tion.
pregio, prě'jŏ, m. value, worth, appreciation.
pregiudicare, prějŭdĭkä'rě, v. a. to prejudice, to hurt.
pregiudicevole, –dshě'vŏlě,a. prejudicial.
pregiudiziale, –tzĭä'lě, a. prejudicial.
pregiudizio, –dě'tzĭŏ, m. prejudice, damage, wrong. [a. pregnant, full.
pregnante, prěnyän'tě, **pregno,** prě'nyŏ,
prego, prě'gŏ, m. prayer, entreaty.
prelato, prělä'tŏ, m. prelate.
prelatura, –tŏ'rä, f. prelacy. [ferenco.
prelazione, –tzĭŏ'ně, f. prelation, preference.
prelibare, –lĭbä'rě, v. a. to have a slight foretaste of; to try before.
preliminare, –lĭnĭnä'rě, a. preliminary.
preludiare, –lŭdĭä'rě, v. a. to prelude.
preludio, –lŏ'dĭŏ, m. prelude.
prematuro, –mätŏ'rŏ, a. premature.
premere, prě'měrě, v. a. to press, to squeeze, to urge; to oppress.
premettere, prěmět'těrě, v. a. ir. to put or lay before; to premise.
premiare, –mĭä'rě, v. a. to reward.
premiazione, –tzĭŏ'ně, f. distribution of prizes.
preminente, –mĭněn'tě, a. pre-eminent.
preminenza, –něn'tzä, f. pre-eminence.
premio, prě'mĭŏ, m. recompense; prize.
premorire, –mŏrě'rě, v. n. to die before, to predecease.
premunire, –prěmŭně'rě, v. a. to forewarn, to provide; **premunirsi,** –nĭr'sĭ, to stand prepared.
premura, –mŏ'rä, f. eagerness; importance.
premuroso, –mŭrŏ'sŏ, a. pressing, urgent.

prence, *prĕn' dshĕ*, m. (poet.) prince.
prendere, *prĕn' dĕrĕ*, v. a. ir. to take, to seize; to receive; to surprise; **prendersi**, *prĕn' dĕrsĭ*, to be caught.
prenome, *prĕnō' mĕ*, m. Christian name.
preoccupare, *–ŏkkŭpā' rĕ*, v. a. to pre-occupy.   [tion.
preoccupazione, *–tzĭō' nĕ*, f. preoccupa-
preparare, *–pārā' rĕ*, v. a. to prepare.
preparazione, *–tzĭō' nĕ*, f. preparation.
preponderare, *–pŏndĕrā' rĕ*, v. a. to pre-ponderate.   [propose.
preporre, *–pōr' rĕ*, v. a. ir. to prefer; to
prepositura, *–pŏsĭtō' rā*, f. provostship.
preposizione, *–sĭtzĭō' nĕ*, f. (gr.) prepo-sition.
prepostero, *–pōs' tĕrō*, a. preposterous, perverted, absurd.
prepotente, *–pōtĕn' tĕ*, a. very powerful, all-powerful.
prepotenza, *–tĕn' tza*, f. supreme power.
prepuzio, *–pō' tzĭō*, m. prepuce.
prerogativa, *–rōgātĕ' vā*, f. prerogative.
presa, *prā' sā*, f. taking; capture; prize, prize-money; dose, pinch; handle; **di prima –**, at first sight.
presagio, *prāsā' jō*, m. presage.
presagire, *–sājē' rĕ*, v. a. to presage.
presago, *–sā' gō*, m. diviner.
presame, *–sā' mĕ*, m. rennet.
presbite, *prĕs' bĭtĕ*, m. long-sighted.
presbiterio, *–bĭtā' rĭō*, m. priesthood; presbytery.
prescia, *prĕssh' ā*, f. haste, hurry.
prescienza, *–sshĕn' tzā*, f. foreknowledge.
prescindere, *–sshĭn' dĕrĕ*, v. a. to prescind.
presciutto, *–sshĭt' tō*, m. bacon, ham.
prescritto, *–skrĭt' tō*, m. prescript.
prescrivere, *–skrē' vĕrĕ*, v. a. & n. ir. to prescribe; to limit.
prescrizione, *–skrĭtzĭō' nĕ*, f. prescrip-tion; (med.) recipe.
presedere, *–sĕdā' rĕ*, v. n. ir. to preside.
presentaneo, *–sĕntā' nĕō*, a. ready; quick.
presentare, *–tā' rĕ*, v. a. to present.
presentazione, *–tzĭō' nĕ*, f. presentation.
presente, *–sĕn' tĕ*, m. present, gift; (gr.) present tense; **–**, a. present, at hand; ready.   [ment.
presentimento, *–tĭmĕn' tō*, m. presenti-
presentire, *–tē' rĕ*, v. a. to have a pre-sentiment of, to forebode.
presenza, *–sĕn' tzā*, f. presence.
presenzialmente, *–tzĭālmĕn' tĕ*, ad. per-sonally, in one's presence.
presepio, *–sā' pĭō*, m. stable; manger.
preservare, *–sĕrvā' rĕ*, v. a. to preserve.
preservativo, *–tē' vō*, a. preservative.
preside, *prā' sĭdĕ*, **presidente**, *prĕsĭdĕn' tĕ*, m. president.
presidenza, *prĕsĭdĕn' tzā*, f. presidency.
presidiare, *–sĭdĭā' rĕ*, v. a. to garrison.
presidio, *–sĕ' dĭō*, m. garrison.
pressa, *prĕs' sā*, f. throng, crowd; haste.
pressante, *–sān' tĕ*, a. pressing, urgent.
pressappoco, *–sāppō' kō*, ad. nearly, there-about.

pressare, *–sā' rĕ*, v. a. to press, to urge; to hurry.
presso, *prĕs' sō*, a. near, neighbouring; **–**, ad. & pr. near, hard by; almost, about; **presso presso**, close by, quite near; **– a poco**, thereabout.
prestante, *prĕstān' tĕ*, a. excellent.
prestanza, *–tān' tzā*, f. lending, loan.
prestare, *–tā' rĕ*, v. a. to lend; to grant, to yield; **– giuramento**, to give oath; **– orecchi**, to give ear.
prestito, *prĕs' tĭtō*, m. loan, lending.
prestigio, *–tĕ' jō*, m. illusion; juggling.
presto, *prĕs' tō*, a. quick, prompt; ready; **–**, ad. quickly, nimbly.   [persuasion.
presuasione, *–prĕsŭāsĭō' nĕ*, f. previous
presumere, *–sō' mĕrĕ*, v. n. ir. to presume.
presuntuoso, *–sŭntŭō' sō*, a. presumptuous.
presunzione, *–tzĭō' nĕ*, f. presumption.
prete, *prā' tĕ*, m. priest.
pretendere, *prĕtĕn' dĕrĕ*, v. a. ir. to pre-tend.   [boldness.
pretensione, *–tĕnsĭō' nĕ*, f. pretension;
preterire, *–tĕrē' rĕ*, v. a. to pass over, to pass by; to neglect, to omit.   [a. past.
preterito, *–tā' rĭtō*, m. (gr.) past tense; **–**,
preterizione, *–tĕrĭtzĭō' nĕ*, f. preterition.
pretermettere, *prĕtĕrmĕt' tĕrĕ*, v. a. ir. to pretermit.   [natural.
preternaturale, *–nātŭrā' lĕ*, a. preter-
pretesto, *prĕtĕs' tō*, m. pretext, pretence.
pretto, *prĕt' tō*, a. pure, unmixed.
prevalenza, *prĕvālĕn' tzā*, f. prevalence.
prevalere, *–vālē' rĕ*, v. n. ir. to prevail.
prevaricare, *–rĭkā' rĕ*, v. a. & n. to pre-varicate, to transgress.
prevaricazione, *–tzĭō' nĕ*, f. prevarication, shuffling.   [to foreknow.
prevedere, *–vĕdē' rĕ*, v. a. ir. to foresee;
prevenire, *–vĕnē' rĕ*, v. a. ir. to come be-fore, to anticipate; to prepossess; to pre-vent; to hinder.   [anticipation.
prevenzione, *–vĕntzĭō' nĕ*, f. prevention;
previo, *prā' vĭō*, a. previous.
previsione, *prĕvĭsĭō' nĕ*, f. foresight.
prevosto, *–vōs' tō*, m. provost; overseer.
prezioso, *–tzĭō' sō*, a. precious, costly.
prezzare, *prĕtzā' rĕ*, v. a. to rate, to fix the price; to appreciate, to esteem.
prezzemolo, *–tzā' mōlō*, m. parsley.
prezzo, *prĕt' zō*, m. price, rate, value; reward.
prezzolare, *–tzōlā' rĕ*, v. a. to cheapen.
pria, *prē' ā*, ad. (poet.) before, sooner.
prigione, *prĭjō' nĕ*, f. prison; **–**, m. prisoner.
prigioniero, *–nĭā' rō*, m. prisoner.
prima, *prē' mā*, ad. before, sooner, first, formerly; **como –**, as soon as.
primamente, *prĭmāmĕn' tĕ*, ad. firstly.
primario, *–mā' rĭō*, a. primary.
primaticcio, *–tĭt' shō*, a. precocious, early.
primato, *–mā' tō*, m. highest place; primate.
primavera, *–vā' rā*, f. spring.
primaverile, *–vĕrē' lĕ*, a. vernal.
primeggiare, *–mĕdjā' rĕ*, v. n. to excel, to surpass, to outdo.
primiera, *–mĭā' rā*, f. lead at cards.

primiero, *—mìá'rŏ*, a. first, former.
primigenio, *—mĭjá'nĭŏ*, a. primitive, original.
primitivo, *—tĕ'vŏ*, a. primitive, original.
primizia, *—mĕ'tzĭă*, f. first-fruits.
primo, *prĕ'mŏ*, a. first, principal. [son.
primogenito, *primŏjĕ'nĭtŏ*, m. first-born
primogenitura, *—jĕnĭtŏ'ră*, f. birth-right; eldership. [original.
primordiale, *—mŏrdĭá'lĕ*, a. primordial.
principale, *prĭndshĭpá'lĕ*, a. principal, chief. [cipally, chiefly.
principalmente, *—pálmĕn'tĕ*, ad. principrincipato, *—pá'tŏ*, m. principality.
principe, *prìn'dshĭpĕ*, m. prince; chief.
principesco, *—dshĕpĕs'kŏ*, a. of a prince, princely, prince-like.
principessa, *—pĕs'să*, f. princess.
principiare, *—pĭá'rĕ*, v. a. to begin.
principio, *—dshĕ'pĭŏ*, m. principle; beginning.
priorità, *prĭŏrĭtá'*, f. priority. [ning.
prisco, *prĭs'kŏ*, a. ancient, of olden times.
pristino, *—tĕ'nŏ*, a. ancient, primitive, former, previous.
privare, *prĭvá'rĕ*, v. a. to deprive; **privarsi**, *—vár'sĭ*, to abstain from.
privativo, *—tĕ'vŏ*, a. privative, exclusive.
privato, *prĭvá'tŏ*, m. privy; —, a. private.
privazione, *—tzĭŏ'nĕ*, f. privation.
privilegiare, *—vĭlĕjá'rĕ*, v. a. to privilege.
privilegio, *— d'jŏ*, m. privilege.
privo, *prĕ'vŏ*, a. deprived of.
prizzato, *prĭtzá'tŏ*, a. spotted, speckled.
pro, *prŏ*, m. utility, profit, advantage; —, a. valiant, bold, courageous.
proavo, *prŏá'vŏ*, m. great-grandfather.
probabile, *—bá'bĭlĕ*, a. probable, likely.
probabilità, *—bĭlĭtá'*, f. probability, likelihood.
probabilmente, *—mĕn'tĕ*, ad. probably.
probità, *prŏbĭtá'*, f. probity.
probo, *prŏ'bŏ*, a. honest; upright.
proboscide, *prŏbŏs'shĭdĕ*, f. proboscis.
procacciare, *—kátshá'rĕ*, v. a. to procure.
procaccia, *—kát'shă*, m. letter-carrier, postman. [carrier.
procaccio, *—kát'shŏ*, m. provision; letter-**procace**, *—ká'dshĕ*, a. petulant, saucy.
procedere, *—dshĕ'dĕrĕ*, v. n. ir. to proceed, to continue; to result.
procella, *—dshĕl'lă*, f. storm, tempest.
procelloso, *—lŏ'sŏ*, a. stormy.
processare, *—dshĕssá'rĕ*, v. a. & n. to suc.
processione, *—sĭŏ'nĕ*, f. procession.
processo, *—dshĕs'sŏ*, m. progression; process, law-suit.
procinto, *—dshĭn'tŏ*, m. precinct.
proclama, *—klá'mă*, f. proclamation, ban.
proclamare, *—klámá'rĕ*, v. a. to proclaim.
proclamazione, *—tzĭŏ'nĕ*, f. proclamation.
proclive, *—klĕ'vĕ*, m. slope; —, a. inclined.
proco, *prŏ'kŏ*, m. suitor, gallant. [prone.
procrastinare, *prŏkrăstĭná'rĕ*, v. a. to procrastinate. [beget.
procreare, *—krĕá'rĕ*, v. a. to procreate; to
procreazione, *—tzĭŏ'nĕ*, f. generation.
procura, *—kŏ'ră*, f. procuration.

procurare, *—kŏrá'rĕ*, v. a. to procure; to strive. [torney.
procuratore, *—tŏ'rĕ*, m. solicitor; attorney.
procurazione, *—tzĭŏ'nĕ*, f. procuration; power of attorney.
proda, *prŏ'dă*, f. bank, shore; (mar.) prow.
prode, *prŏ'dĕ*, m. profit; —, a. brave, valiant.
prodigalità, *prŏdĭgălĭtá'*, f. prodigality.
prodigio, *—dĭ'jŏ*, m. prodigy, wonder.
prodigioso, *—dĭjŏ'sŏ*, a. prodigious, wonderful. [prodigal.
prodigo, *prŏ'dĭgŏ*, m. spendthrift; —, a.
prodizione, *prŏdĭtzĭŏ'nĕ*, f. treason, perfidy.
prodotto, *—dŏt'tŏ*, m. product. [fidy.
produrre, *—dŭr'rĕ*, v. a. ir. to produce.
produzione, *—dŭtzĭŏ'nĕ*, f. production, produce; fruit.
proemio, *prŏĕ'mĭŏ*, m. preface, introduction.
profanare, *—fáná'rĕ*, v. a. to profane; to abuse.
profanazione, *—tzĭŏ'nĕ*, f. profanation.
profanità, *—fănĭtá'*, f. profaneness.
profano, *—fá'nŏ*, a. profane, impious.
proferire, *—fĕrĕ'rĕ*, v. a. to utter, to pronounce.
proferta, *—fĕr'tă*, f. offer. [nounce.
professare, *—fĕssá'rĕ*, v. a. to profess; to teach publicly. [religious order.
professione, *—sĭŏ'nĕ*, f. profession; trade;
professore, *—sŏ'rĕ*, m. professor.
profeta, *—fĕ'tă*, m. prophet.
profetare, *—fĕtá'rĕ*, **profetizzare**, *—fĕtĭdzá'rĕ*, v. a. to prophesy.
profetessa, *—tĕs'să*, f. prophetess.
profetico, *—fĕ'tĭkŏ*, a. prophetical.
profezia, *—fĕtzĕ'ă*, f. prophecy.
proficuo, *—fĕ'kŭŏ*, a. profitable.
profilo, *—fĕ'lŏ*, m. profile, side-face.
profittare, *—fĭt'tá'rĕ*, v. n. to profit.
profittevole, *—tĕ'vŏlĕ*, a. profitable.
profitto, *—fĭt'tŏ*, m. profit, advantage.
profluvio, *—flŏ'vĭŏ*, m. overflowing; abundance; flow of words.
profondamente, *—fŏndámĕn'tĕ*, ad. profoundly.
profondare, *—dá'rĕ*, v. a. to deepen; to dive into; to dig; —, v. n. to sink into.
profondere, *—fŏn'dĕrĕ*, v. a. ir. to pour out.
profondità, *—fŏndĭtá'*, f. profundity, depth.
profondo, *—fŏn'dŏ*, m. depth; bottom; —, a. deep; profound.
profugo, *prŏ'fŭgŏ*, a. & m. fugitive.
profumare, *prŏfŭmá'rĕ*, v. a. to perfume, to scent.
profumiera, *—mĭĕ'ră*, f. perfuming-pan.
profumiere, *—mĭĕ'rĕ*, m. perfumer.
profumo, *—fŭ'mŏ*, m. perfume. [ness.
profusione, *—fŭsĭŏ'nĕ*, f. profusion, lavish-**profuso**, *—fŏ'sŏ*, a. profuse; copious.
progenie, *—jĕ'nĭĕ*, f. issue, offspring.
progenitore, *—jĕnĭtŏ'rĕ*, m. progenitor, ancestor.
progettare, *—jĕttá'rĕ*, v. a. to project.
progetto, *—jĕt'tŏ*, m. project.
programma, *—grám'mă*, m. programme, prospectus. [to proceed.
progredire, *—grĕdĕ'rĕ*, v. n. to advance, **progresso**, *—grĕs'sŏ*, m. progress.

proibire, _proïbi'rĕ_, v. a. to prohibit, to forbid.
proibizione, _-bïtziŏ'nĕ_, f. prohibition
proiezione, _-iĕtziŏ'nĕ_, f. projection.
prole, _prŏ'lĕ_, f. offspring.
prolifico, _prŏlï'fïkŏ_, a. prolific, fruitful.
prolissità, _-lïssïtä'_, f. prolixity.
prolisso, _-lïs'sŏ_, a. prolix, diffuse.
prologo, _-prŏ'lŏgŏ_, m. prologue, preface.
prolungamento, _-lŭngämĕn'tŏ_, m. prolongation, delay.
prolungare, _-gä'rĕ_, v. a. to prolong.
prolungazione, _-tzïŏ'nĕ_, f. prolongation.
prolusione, _-lïsïŏ'nĕ_, f. prelude.
promessa, _-mĕs'sä_, f. promise; warranty.
promettere, _-mĕt'tĕrĕ_, v. a. ir. to promise.
prominente, _-mïnĕn'tĕ_, a. prominent.
prominenza, _-nĕntzä_, f. prominence, protuberance. [ness.
promiscuità, _-skŭïtä'_, f. promiscuous-
promiscuo, _-mïs'kŭŏ_, a. promiscuous.
promissione, _-mïssïŏ'nĕ_, f. promise; permission.
promontorio, _-mŏntŏ'rïŏ_, m. promontory.
promotore, _-mŏtŏ'rĕ_, m. promoter, forwarder, furtherer. [mote.
promovere, _-mŏ'vĕrĕ_, v. a. ir. to pro-
promozione, _-mŏtziŏ'nĕ_, f. promotion.
promulgare, _-mŭlgä'rĕ_, v. a. to promulgate. [tion.
promulgazione, _-tzïŏ'nĕ_, f. promulga-
promuovere, _see_ promovere.
pronipote, _-nïpŏ'tĕ_, m. great grandnephew; **pronipoti,** _-pŏ'tï_, pl. descendants.
prono, _prŏ'nŏ_, a. prone, inclined. [dants.
pronome, _prŏnŏ'mĕ_, m. (gr.) pronoun.
prontezza, _prŏntĕt'zä_, f. promptitude.
pronto, _prŏn'tŏ_, a. ready, at hand; quick.
pronuba, _prŏ'nŭbä_, f. bridesmaid.
pronubo, _prŏ'nŭbŏ_, m. bride-man.
pronunciare, _prŏnŭndshä'rĕ_, **pronunziare,** _-tzïä'rĕ_, v. a. to pronounce.
pronunziazione, _-tzïätzïŏ'nĕ_, f. pronunciation.
propaganda, _-pägän'dä_, f. propaganda.
propagare, _-pägä'rĕ_, v. a. to propagate.
propagginare, _-pädjïnä'rĕ_, v. a. to provine, to plant layers; to propagate.
propaggine, _-päd'jïnĕ_, f. vine-layer.
propalare, _-pälä'rĕ_, v. a. to divulge.
propendere, _-pĕn'dĕrĕ_, v. n. to propend, to incline. [inclination.
propensione, _-sïŏ'nĕ_, f. propensity.
propinare, _-pïnä'rĕ_, v. a. to drink a toast to.
propinquità, _-pïnkŭïtä'_, f. propinquity.
propinquo, _-pïn'kŭŏ_, a. near; nigh.
propiziare, _-pïtzïä'rĕ_, v. a. to propitiate.
propizio, _-pĕ'tzïŏ_, a. propitious.
proponente, _-pŏnĕn'tĕ_, a. proposing.
proporre, _-pŏr'rĕ_, v. a. ir. to propose.
proporzionale, _-pŏrtzïŏnä'lĕ_, a. proportional. [tion.
proporzionare, _-nä'rĕ_, v. a. to propor-
proporzione, _-tzïŏ'nĕ_, f. proportion.
proposito, _-pŏ'sïtŏ_, m. intention, purpose; motive; **a –,** seasonably.

propositura, _-pŏsïtŏ'rä_, f. provostship.
proposizione, _-tzïŏ'nĕ_, f. proposition, proposal, offer.
proposta, _-pŏs'tä_, f. proposition.
proposto, _-pŏs'tŏ_, m. purpose; provost.
proprietà, _-prïĕtä'_, f. property, ownership; estate. [owner.
proprietario, _-tä'rïŏ_, m. proprietor.
proprio, _prŏ'prïŏ_, m. property, peculiar quality; **–,** a. proper, own, peculiar; fit; **–,** ad. properly, precisely.
propugnacolo, _prŏpŭnyä'kŏlŏ_, m. rampart, bulwark.
propugnare, _-yä'rĕ_, v. a. to defend.
propulsare, _-pŭlsä'rĕ_, v. a. to repulse, to prora,** _prŏ'rä_, f. (mar.) prow. [drive off.
proroga, _prŏ'rŏgä_, f. prorogation, putting off. [to put off.
prorogare, _prŏrŏgä'rĕ_, v. a. to prorogue,
prorompere, _-rŏm'pĕrĕ_, v. a. ir. to burst out, to break forth.
prosa, _prŏ'sä_, f. prose.
prosaico, _prŏsä'ïkŏ_, a. prosaic.
prosapia, _-sä'pïä_, f. progeny, lineage.
prosastico, _prŏsäs'tïkŏ_, a. prose, in prose.
prosatore, _-tŏ'rĕ_, m. prose-writer.
proscenio, _-sshä'nïŏ_, m. proscenium.
prosciogliere, _-sshŏl'yĕrĕ_, v. a. ir. to absolve, to deliver.
prosciugare, _-sshŭgä'rĕ_, v. a. to dry up.
prosciutto, _-sshŭt'tŏ_, m. gammon.
proscrivere, _-skrï'vĕrĕ_, v. a. ir. to proscribe, to banish. [tion.
proscrizione, _-skrïtzïŏ'nĕ_, f. proscrip-
proseguire, _-sĕgŭï'rĕ_, v. a. to prosecute.
proselito, _-sĕ'lïtŏ_, m. proselyte.
prosodia, _-sŏdï'ä_, f. prosody.
prosperare, _-spĕrä'rĕ_, v. a. & n. to prosper, to thrive.
prosperità, _-spĕrïtä'_, f. prosperity.
prospero, _prŏs'pĕrŏ_, a. prosperous, propitious, thriving.
prospettiva, _-spĕt'ïvä_, f. perspective.
prospettare, _-tä'rĕ_, v. a. to take a prospective view.
prospetto, _-spĕt'tŏ_, m. prospect, view.
prossimo, _prŏs'sïmŏ_, a. next, near; related.
prosternarsi, _-stĕrnär'sï_, v. r. to be terrified. [tion.
prosternazione, _-tzïŏ'nĕ_, f. prostra-
prosternere, _-stĕr'nĕrĕ_, v. a. ir. to prostrate, to overthrow.
prostituire, _-stïtŭï'rĕ_, v. a. to prostitute.
prostituta, _-tï'tä_, f. whore.
prostituzione, _-tzïŏ'nĕ_, f. prostitution.
prostrare, _-strä'rĕ_, v. a. to prostrate.
prostrazione, _-tzïŏ'nĕ_, f. prostration.
proteggere, _prŏtĕd'jĕrĕ_, v. a. ir. to protect, to defend. [out, to widen.
protendere, _-tĕn'dĕrĕ_, v. a. ir. to stretch
protervia, _-tĕr'vïä_, f. arrogance, insolence.
protervo, _-tĕr'vŏ_, a. arrogant, saucy.
protestante, _-tĕstän'tĕ_, m. Protestant.
protestare, _-tĕstä'rĕ_, v. a. to protest; to declare.
protestazione, _-tzïŏ'nĕ_, f. protestation.

protettorato,–tĕttŏrā′tŏ, m. protectorship.
protettore,–tĕttŏ′rĕ, m. protector.
protettrice,–trĕ′dshĕ, f. protectress.
protezione,–tziŏ′nĕ, f. protection.
proto, prŏ′tŏ, m. chief; factor in a printing-office.
protocollo, prŏtŏkŏl′lŏ, m. protocol.
protomartire, –mār′tirĕ, m. protomartyr.
protomedico, –mā′dikŏ,m. first physician.
protonotario, –nŏtā′riŏ, m. protonotary.
prototipo, prŏtŏ′tipŏ, m. prototype; –, a. original.
protrarre, prŏtrār′rĕ, v. a. ir. to protract, to lengthen.　　　　　[ance.
protuberanza, –tūbĕrān′tzā, f. protuber-
prova, prŏ′vā, f. proof, experiment, essay; proof-sheet; witness.
provare, prŏvā′rĕ, v. a. to try, to taste; to prove; –, v. n. to thrive.　　[origin.
provenienza, –vĕniĕn′tzā, f. derivation,
provenire, –vĕnī′rĕ, v. n. ir. to grow, to proceed, to arise; to thrive.
provento, –rĕn′tŏ, m. rent, revenue.
proverbialmente, –vĕrbiāl′mĕntĕ, ad. proverbially.
proverbiare, –biā′rĕ, v. a. to scold.
proverbio, –vĕr′biŏ, m. proverb.
proverbioso, –biŏ′sŏ, a. injurious.
provianda, –viān′dā, f. victuals, pl.
provincia, –vin′dshā, f. province, region.
provocare, –vŏkā′rĕ, v. a. to provoke, to rouse.
provocazione, –tziŏ′nĕ, f. provocation.
provveditore, prŏvvĕditŏ′rĕ, m. purveyor, furnisher.
provvidenza, –vidĕn′tzā, f. providence.
provvido, prŏv′vidŏ, a. careful, provident.
provvisione, –rtsiŏ′nĕ, f. provision; pension, commission.
provvisto, –vis′tŏ, a. provided, ready.
prua, prŏ′ā, f. prow of a ship.
prudente, prūdĕn′tĕ, a. prudent.
prudenza, –dĕn′tzā, f. prudence, wisdom.
prudere, prŏ′dĕrĕ, v. n. to itch.
prudore, prūdŏ′rĕ, m. itching, pruriency.
prugna, prŏn′yā, f. plum.
prugno, prŏn′yŏ, m. plum-tree.
prugnola, prŏn′yŏlā, f. sloe.
pruina, prŏĭ′nā, f. hoar-frost.
pruna, see **prugna**.
prunaio, –nā′ŏ, **pruneto,** –nĕ′tŏ, m. thorny bush.
pruno, prŏ′nŏ, m. black-thorn.
pruova, see **prova.**
prurigine, prūrĭ′jinĕ,f.pruriency, itching.
prurire, –rī′rĕ, v. n. to itch.
prurito, see **prurigine.**
pruzza, prŭt′zā, f. itching, pricking.
pseudonimo, psĕŭdŏ′nimŏ, a. pseudonymous
psicologia, psīkŏlŏjī′ā, f. psychology.
psicologico, –lŏ′jikŏ, a. psychological.
pubblicano, pŭbblikā′nŏ, m. publican.
pubblicare, –kā′rĕ, v. a. to publish.
pubblicatore, –tŏ′rĕ, m. publisher.
pubblicazione, –tziŏ′nĕ, f. publication.

pubblicità, –dshĭtā′, f. publicity.
pubblico, pŭb′blikŏ,m. public; –, a. public; known.　　　　　　　[ringeable.
pubere, pŏ′bĕrĕ, a. puberal, manly, mar-
pubertà, pŭbĕrtā′, f. puberty.
pudicizia, –dĭdshĕ′tzā, f. pudicity.
pudico, pŏ′dīkŏ, a. chaste.
pudore, pŭdŏ′rĕ, m. pudicity.
puerile, pŭĕrī′lĕ, a. puerile, childish.
puerizia, –rĕ′tzĭā, f. childishness.
puerpera, pŭĕr′pĕrā, f. woman in labour.
puerperio, –pĕ′riŏ, m. child-bed.
pugilato, pŭjīlā′tŏ, m. boxing.
pugna, pŭn′yā, f. fight, combat, battle.
pugnace, –yā′dshĕ, a. pugnacious; war-
pugnale, –yā′lĕ, m. dagger.　　　[like.
pugnare, –yā′rĕ, v. a. & n. to fight, to prove; –, v. n. to thrive.　　[combat.
pugnello, –yĕl′lŏ, m. handful.
pugnetto, –yĕt′tŏ, m. handful.
pugno, pŭn′yŏ, m. fist; fisticuff; handful.
pula, pŏ′lā, f. husk, hull.
pulce, pŭl′dshĕ, f. flea.
pulcella, –dshĕl′lā, f. mĭdd, virgin.
pulsesecca, –dshĕsĕk′kā, f. pinch.
pulcinella, –dshĭnĕl′lā, m. punchinello, punch.
pulcino, –dshĭ′nŏ, m. young chicken.
puledro, pŭlĕ′drŏ, m. colt, foal.
puleggia, –lĕd′jā, f. pulley.　　[smoothe.
pulire, –lĕ′rĕ, v. a. to clean, to polish; to
pulitamente, –lĭtāmĕn′tĕ, ad. neatly, cleanly; politely.　　　　　[politeness.
pulitezza, –tĕt′zā, f. neatness, cleanness.
pulito, –lĕ′tŏ, a. clean, smooth; polished; refined; polite.
pulitura, –tŭ′rā, f. polish; gloss.
pulizia, –lĕ′tziā, f. cleanliness, neatness.
pullulare, pŭllŭlā′rĕ, v. n. to bud forth; to swarm, to crawl, to crowd.
pulpito, pŭl′pitŏ, m. pulpit.
pulsazione, –sātziŏ′nĕ, f. pulsation, throb.
pulzella, see **pulcella.**
pungello, pŭnjĕl′lŏ, m. goad; spur.
pungere, pŭn′jĕrĕ, v. a. ir. to sting, to prick; to vex.
punire, pŭnī′rĕ, v. a. to punish.
punizione, –nĭtziŏ′nĕ, f. punishment.
punta, pŭn′tā, f. point; top; edge.
puntale, –tā′lĕ, m. tag, aglet.
puntare, –tā′rĕ, v. a. to point; to sting; to insist upon.　　　　　[instrument.
puntata, –tā′tā, f. thrust with a pointed
puntatura, –tŏ′rā, f. punctuation.
punteggiare, –tĕdjā′rĕ, v. a. to point in writing.
punteggiatura, –tŏ′rā, f. punctuation.
puntellare, –tĕl′lā′rĕ, v. n. to prop, to support; to stay.
puntello, –tĕl′lŏ, m. prop, support; stay.
punteruolo, –tĕrŭŏ′lŏ, m. bodkin; weevil.
puntiglio, –tĭl′yŏ, m. point of honour;
puntino, –tĕ′nŏ, m. little point.　　[cavil.
punto, pŭn′tŏ, m. point; stitch; moment; article; condition; wrangling; –, ad. by no means; a –, exactly; di – in –, per –, distinctly.

puntuale, *–tŭă' lĕ*, a. punctual, exact.
puntualità, *–tŭălĭtă'*, f. punctuality.
puntualmente, *–mĕn' tĕ*, ad. punctually.
puntura, *–tō' rä*, f. puncture; anguish; pang. [to incite.
punzecchiare, *–dzĕkkĭä' rĕ*, v. a. to spur;
punzone, *–tzō' nĕ*, m. puncheon.
pupilla, *pŭpĭl' lä*, f. pupil of the eye.
pupillo, *pŭpĭl' lō*, m. pupil.
pur, *pŏr*, for pure. [ever.
purchè, *pŭrkĕ'*, c. provided that, if, how-
pure, *pō' rĕ*, ad. yet, although, moreover, however.
puretto, *pŭrĕt' tō*, a. pure, genuine.
purezza, *–rĕt' zä*, f. pureness, purity.
purga, *pŭr' gä*, f. purge, purging.
purgare, *–gä' rĕ*, v. a. to purge, to cleanse, to purify.
purgatorio, *–tō' rĭō*, m. purgatory.
purgazione, *–tzĭō' nĕ*, f. purgation.
purgo, *pŭr' gō*, m. fulling-mill.
purificare, *pŭrĭfĭkä' rĕ*, v. a. to purify.
purificazione, *–tzĭō' nĕ*, f. purification.
puro, *pō' rō*, a. pure; clean; chaste; sincere.
purpureo, *pŭrpō' rĕō*, a. purple-coloured.
purulento, *–rŭlĕn' tō*, a. putrid; rotten.
pusigno, *–sĭn' yō*, m. refreshments after supper, pl.
pusillanime, *–sĭllä' nĭmĕ*, a. pusillani-mous, faint-hearted. [mity.
pusillanimità, *–länĭmĭtä'*, f. pusillani-
pusillo, *–sĭl' lō*, a. little, small; mean.
pustola, *pŭs' tōlä*, pustula, *–tŭlä*, f. pus-tule, pimple.
putativo, *–tä' tĭvō*, a. supposed.
putire, *–tĭ' rĕ*, v. n. to stink.
putre, *pō' trĕ*, a. putrid, rotten.
putredine, *pŭtrĕ' dĭnĕ*, f. putridness.
putredinoso, *–trĕdĭnō' sō*, a. putrescent.
putrefare, *–fä' rĕ*, v. n. ir. to putrefy.
putridire, *–rĭdĭ' rĕ*, v. n. to get rotten.
putrido, *pō' trĭdō*, a. putrid. [things.
putridume, *–trĭdō' mĕ*, m. mass of rotten
putta, *pŭt' tä*, f. magpie. [cenary.
putto, *pŭt' tō*, m. boy, lad; –, a. venal, mer-
puzza, *pŭt' zä*, f. pus; stink, stench.
puzzare, *–tzä' rĕ*, v. n. to stink.
puzzo, *pŭt' zō*, m. stench; corruption.
puzzola, *pŭt' zōlä*, f. pole-cat, pismire.
puzzolente, *–tzōlĕn' tĕ*, puzzoso, *–tzō' sō*, a. stinking; obscene

Q.

qua, *kŭä'*, ad. here, this side, hither, in this place; – e là, here and there; di –, this way, on this side.
quaderno, *kŭädĕr' nō*, m. writing-book; quire of paper; two fours (at dice); bed in a garden. [years old.
quadragenario, *kŭädrädjĕnä' rĭō*, a. forty
quadragesima, *see* quaresima.
quadragesimo, *–jä' sĭmō*, a. fortieth.
quadrangolo, *kŭädrän' gōlō*, m. quad-rangle, square.

quadrante, *–drän' tĕ*, m. quadrant.
quadrare, *–drä' rĕ*, v. a. & n. to square; to fit, to be fitting.
quadrato, *–drä' tō*, m. square; quadrate; –, a. square; well knit, well made; strong.
quadrellare, *–drĕllä' rĕ*, v. a. to dart ar-rows, to shoot.
quadrello, *–drĕl' lō*, m. arrow, bolt; pack-ing-needle; square brick.
quadreria, *–drĕrĭ' ä*, f. gallery of paintings.
quadretto, *–drĕt' tō*, m. small square; little picture; square stone.
quadriennio, *–drĭĕn' nĭō*, m. space of four years.
quadriga, *–drĭ' gä*, f. (poet.) quadriga, car drawn by four horses.
quadrivio, *–drĭ' vĭō*, m. crossway.
quadro, *kŭä' drō*, m. square; frame; pic-ture; garden-bed; –, a. square.
quadrupede, *–drō' pĕdĕ*, m. four-footed animal. [quadruplicate.
quadruplicare, *–drŭplĭkä' rĕ*, v. a. to
quadruplice, *–drō' plĭdshĕ*, quadruplo, *–kŭä' drŭplō*, a. fourfold.
quaggiù, *kŭädjä'*, ad. here below.
quaglia, *kŭäl' yä*, f. quail.
qual, *kŭäl*, i. what!
qualche, *kŭäl' kĕ*, a. some, any; what-ever, whoever; – cosa, something.
qualcheduno, *–kĕdō' nō*, a. somebody, anybody, some one, some.
qualcosa, *–kō' sä*, f. something.
qualcuno, *see* qualcheduno.
quale, *kŭä' lĕ*, pn. what, which; that; who; such as, like. [to distinguish.
qualificare, *–lĭfĭkä' rĕ*, v. a. to qualify;
qualificazione, *–tzĭō' nĕ*, f. qualification.
qualità, *kŭälĭtä'*, f. quality.
qualmente, *–mĕn' tĕ*, ad. like, how, as.
qualora, *–ō' rä*, ad. whenever; as often as.
qualsisia, *–sĭsĕ' ä*, qualsivoglia, *–vōl' yä*, pn. whoever, whatever.
qualunque, *kŭälōn' kŭĕ*, pn. whatever, whoever; – ora, – volta, whenever.
quando, *kŭän' dō*, quandochè, *–dōkĕ'*, ad. when, if; whenever; quandochesia, *–dōkĕsĕ' ä*, at one time, once.
quantità, *kŭäntĭtä'*, f. quantity.
quanto, *kŭän' tō*, a. how much, how many, as many as; –, ad. as far, as long; as for; how long; – a me, as for me; – prima, as soon as possible.
quantunque, *–tŭn' kŭĕ*, c. & a. although, though; how much, how many.
quaranta, *kŭärän' tä*, a. forty.
quarantesimo, *–tĕ' sĭmō*, a. fortieth.
quarantina, *–tĕ' nä*, f. forty; quarantine.
quare, *kŭä' rĕ*, ad. why? wherefore?
quaresima, *–rĕ' sĭmä*, f. forty days; Lent.
quarta, *kŭär' tä*, f. quarter; quart, quart-pot; quadrant. [well-set.
quartato, *–lä' tō*, a. square, quartered;
quarterone, *–tĕrō' nĕ*, m. quarter of the
quarteruola, *–tĕrŭō' lä*, f. peck. [moon.
quartiere, *–tĭĕ' rĕ*, m. quarter, fourth part.
quartiermastro, *–tĭĕrmä' strō*, m. quarter-master.

quarto, *kŭăr'tŏ,* m. quarter, fourth part; quarto; —, a. fourth.

quartodecimo, *–tŏdā'dshĭmŏ,* a. fourteenth. [almost.

quasi, *kŭă'sĕ,* ad. as if, like; **quasi** quasi.

quasimente, *–sĭmĕn'tĕ,* ad. almost, about;

quassù, *kŭăssŭ',* ad. here above. [as if.

quaternario, *kŭătĕrnă'rĭŏ,* a. quaternary.

quatto, *kŭăt'tŏ,* a. squat, quiet.

quattordici, *–tŏr'dĭdshĭ,* a. fourteen.

quattrino, *–trē'nŏ,* m. farthing.

quattro, *kŭăt'trŏ,* a. four.

quei, *kŭĕ'ĕ,* **quegli,** *kŭĕ'yĭ,* for **quelli.**

quel, *kŭĕl',* for **quello.**

quello, *kŭĕl'lŏ,* pn. he; that.

querce, *kŭĕr'dshĕ,* f. oak-tree.

querceto, *–dshā'tŏ,* m. oak-forest.

quercio, *see* **guercio.** [plaint.

querela, *kŭĕrā'lă,* f. lamentation, com-

querelare, *–rēlā'rĕ,* v. a. to accuse; **querelarsi,** *–lār'sĕ,* to complain.

querimonia, *–rĭmŏ'nĭă,* f. complaint, moan. [ing.

querulo, *kŭĕ'rŭlŏ,* a. querulous, complain-

quesito, *kŭĕsĕ'tŏ,* m. question; theme.

questi, *kŭĕs'tĭ,* pn. this one, this.

questionare, *–tĭŏnā'rĕ,* v. a. & n. to question; to dispute. [suit.

questione, *kŭĕstĭŏ'nĕ,* f. question; law-

questo, *kŭĕs'tŏ,* pn. this.

questore, *–tŏ'rĕ,* m. quastor; treasurer.

questua, *kŭĕs'tŭă,* f. begging.

questuare, *–tŭā'rĕ,* v. a. to go a-begging.

questura, *–tŏ'ră,* f. police-office.

quetamente, *kŭĕtămĕn'tĕ,* ad. quietly; stealthily. [charge.

quetanza, *–tăn'tză,* f. quittance, dis-

quetare, *–tā'rĕ,* v. a. to quiet, to calm; to acquit. [still.

queto, *kŭĕtā'tŏ,* m. quittance; —, a. quiet,

qui, *kŭī',* ad. here, hither.

quietare, *kŭĭĕtā'rĕ,* v. a. to quiet, to appease; to acquit.

quiete, *kŭĭĕ'tĕ,* **quietezza,** *kŭĭĕtĕt'ză,* f. quietness, quietude.

quieto, *kŭĭĕ'tŏ,* a. quiet, calm.

quinci, *kŭĭn'dshĭ,* ad. from here, from hence; hence; after, afterwards.

quindi, *kŭĭn'dĭ,* ad. hence, then, afterwards; therefore; **da — innanzi,** thenceforward; — **per —,** from the same place.

quindicesimo, *–dĭdshā'sĭmŏ,* a. fifteenth.

quindici, *kŭĭn'dĭdshĭ,* a. fifteen.

quinquagenario, *–kŭăjĕnā'rĭŏ,* a. fifty years old.

quinquagesimo, *–jā'gĭmŏ,* a. fiftieth.

quinquennio, *–kŭĕn'nĭŏ,* m. space of five years.

quintale, *–tā'lĕ,* m. hundred weight.

quintana, *–tā'nă,* f. tilting-post.

quintessenza, *kŭĭntĕssĕn'tză,* f. quint-

quinto, *kŭĭn'tŏ,* a. fifth. [essence.

quintodecimo, *–dā'dshĭmŏ,* a. fifteenth.

quintuplo, *kŭĭn'tŭplŏ,* a. fivefold.

quisquiglia, *kŭĭskŭĭl'yă,* **quisquilia,** *–kŭĕ'lĭă,* f. sweepings, pl., filth.

quivi, *kŭĕ'vĭ,* ad. there, in that place, then.

quota, *kŭŏ'tă,* f. quota, share, portion.

quotare, *kŭŏtā'rĕ,* v. a. to set in order.

quotidiano, *–tĭdĭā'nŏ,* a. daily.

quoto, *kŭŏ'tŏ,* m. order; rank.

quoziente, *kŭŏtzĭĕn'tĕ,* m. quotient.

R.

rabarbaro, *răbăr'bărŏ,* m. rhubarb.

rabbellire, *răbbĕllē'rĕ,* v. a. to embellish anew. [to bungle.

rabberciare, *–bĕrdshā'rĕ,* v. a. to patch,

rabbia, *răb'bĭă,* f. fury, violent passion.

rabbino, *–bē'nŏ,* m. rabbi.

rabbioso, *–bĭŏ'sŏ,* a. enraged, furious; excessive. [to fill up again.

rabboccare, *–bŏkkā'rĕ,* v a. to bite again;

rabbonacciare, *–bŏnătshā'rĕ,* v. a. & n. to make calm, to appease; to grow calm.

rabbonire, *–bŏnē'rĕ,* v. a. to appease, to pacify [to dishevel.

rabbuffare, *–bŭffā'rĕ,* v. a. to disorder,

rabbuffo, *–bŭf'fŏ,* m. rebuke, reprimand.

rabbuiare, *–bŭĭā'rĕ,* v. n., **rabbuiarsi,** *–bŭĭār'sĕ,* to grow cloudy or dark.

rabido, *ră'bĭdŏ,* a. rabid, furious.

raccapezzare, *–kăpĕtzā'rĕ,* v. a. to find out again.

raccapricciare, *–prĭtshā'rĕ,* **raccapriccire,** *–tshē'rĕ,* v. a. & n. to terrify; to be frightened.

raccapriccio, *–prĭt'shŏ,* m. horror, fright.

raccattare, *–kăttā'rĕ,* v. a. to redeem, to recover. [up.

raccenciare, *–tshĕndshā'rĕ,* v. a. to patch

raccertare, *–tshĕrtā'rĕ,* v. a. to reassure.

raccettare, *–tshĕttā'rĕ,* v. a. to take to one's home, to harbour.

raccetto, *–tshĕt'tŏ,* m. lodging, shelter, retreat, asylum. [up.

racchiudere, *–kĭŭ'dĕrĕ,* v. a. ir. to shut

racchiuso, *–kĭŭ'sŏ,* a. shut up, enclosed, included.

raccogliere, *–kŏl'yĕrĕ,* v. a. ir. to gather, to collect; to infer; to receive, to lodge; to understand.

raccolta, *–kŏl'tă,* f. collection; harvest.

raccomandare, *–kŏmăndā'rĕ,* v. a. to recommend; to suspend; to fasten.

raccomandazione, *–tzĭŏ'nĕ,* f. recommendation. [to mend.

raccomodare, *–kŏmŏdā'rĕ,* v. a. to repair,

raccompagnare, *–kŏmpănyā'rĕ,* v. a. to accompany again.

racconciare, *–kŏndshā'rĕ,* v. a. to repair, to mend; to reconcile. [fort, to console.

racconsolare, *–kŏnsŏlā'rĕ,* v. a. to com-

raccontare, *–kŏntā'rĕ,* v. a. to relate, to recite; **raccontarsi,** *–tār'sĕ,* to be reconciled.

racconto, *–kŏn'tŏ,* m. account, relation.

raccorciare, *–kŏrdshā'rĕ,* **raccorcire,** *–dshē'rĕ,* v. a. to shorten, to abridge.

raccordamento, *–dămĕn'tŏ,* m. remembrance. [to reconcile.

raccordare, *–dā'rĕ,* v. a. to remember;

raccorre, *see* raccogliere. [again.

raccostare, *–kŏstā' rĕ*, v. a. to approach

raccozzare, *–kŏtzā' rĕ*, v. a. to collect, to bring together. [to pluck.

racimolare, *–dshĭmŏlā' rĕ*, v. a. to glean,

racimolo, *–dshĕ' mŏlŏ*, m. cluster of grapes.

racquattarsi, *–kwăttăr' sĭ*, v. r. to sit cowering.

racquetare, *–kwĕtā' rĕ*, racquietare, *–kwĭĕtā' rĕ*, v. a. to calm, to pacify.

racquistare, *–kwĭstā' rĕ*, v. a. to recover.

rada, *rä' dă*, f. bay, road, roadstead.

radamentè, *–mĕn' tĕ*, ad. rarely, seldom.

raddolcare, *–dŏlkā' rĕ*, raddolcire, *–dshē' rĕ*, v. a. to sweeten; to calm, to pacify.

raddoppiare, *–dŏppĭā' rĕ*, v. a. to redouble.

raddotto, *–dŏt' tŏ*, m. place of meeting; assembly; rout.

raddrizzare, *–drĭtzā' rĕ*, v. a. to make straight; to redress; to set upright.

raddurre, *–dūr' rĕ*, v. a. to lead back.

radere, *rä' dĕrĕ*, v. a. ir. to shave, to shear;

radezza, *–dĕt' ză*, f. rarity. [to erase.

radiare, *–dĭā' rĕ*, v. n. to emit rays; to

radica, *rä' dĭkă*, f. root. [radiate.

radicale, *–kä' lĕ*, a. radical.

radicalmente, *–kälmĕn' tĕ*, ad. radically.

radicare, *–kä' rĕ*, v. n. to take root.

radice, *–dĕ' dshĕ*, f. root; (fig.) origin.

radificare, *see* rarefare.

radio, *see* raggio.

rado, *see* raro. [bring together.

radunare, *–dūnā' rĕ*, v. a. to assemble, to

rafano, *rä' fănŏ*, m. horse-radish.

raffacciare, *–räffätshā' rĕ*, v.a. to reproach.

raffardellare, *–färdĕllā' rĕ*, v.a. to pack up.

raffazzonare, *–fätzōnā' rĕ*, v. a. to trim, to embellish. [to ratify.

raffermare, *–fĕrmā' rĕ*, v. a. to confirm,

raffibbiare, *–fĭbbĭā' rĕ*, v. a. to buckle; to repeat. [mind; to compare.

raffigurare, *–fĭgūrā' rĕ*, v. a. to call to

raffilare, *–fĭlā' rĕ*, v. a. to pare, to clip.

raffinare, *–fĭnā' rĕ*, v. a. to refine.

raffinire, *–nē' rĕ*, v. n. to get refined.

raffio, *räf' fĭŏ*, m. iron hook. [deeper.

raffondare, *–fŏndā' rĕ*, v. a. to hollow out

rafforzare, *–fŏrdzā' rĕ*, v. a. to reinforce.

raffrancare, *–fränkā' rĕ*, v. a. to re-establish; to free again. [to cool.

raffreddare, *–frĕddā' rĕ*, v.a. to make cold,

raffreddore, *–dŏ' rĕ*, m. cold, rheum.

raffrenare, *–frēnā' rĕ*, v. a. to curb, to restrain. [ment; cooling; coolness.

raffrescamento, *–frĕskämĕn' tŏ*, n. refresh-

raffrontare, *–frŏntā' rĕ*, v. a. to encounter again; to attack.

ragazza, *răgät' ză*, f. young girl.

ragazzata, *–tzä' tă*, f. childish trick.

ragazzo, *răgät' zŏ*, m. boy; lad.

raggentilire, *–djĕntĭlē' rĕ*, v. a. to render genteel. [beam.

raggiare, *rädjā' rĕ*, v. a. to radiate, to

raggio, *räd' jŏ*, m. ray, beam; radius.

raggiornare, *–ljŏnā' rĕ*, v. n. to grow light.

raggirare, *–djrā' rĕ*, v. n. to turn round, to whirl; to deceive.

raggiro, *–djē' rŏ*, m. subterfuge, evasion.

raggiustare, *–djūstā' rĕ*, v. a. to mend, to refit. [gather, to glean.

raggranellare, *–grănĕllā' rĕ*, v. a. to

raggravare, *–grävā' rĕ*, v. a. to aggravate.

raggricchiare, *–grĭkkĭā' rĕ*, v. a. & n. to contract, to shrink, to shrivel; rag-grichiarsi, *–kĭār' sĭ*, to shrivel up; to cuddle up.

raggrinzare, *–grĭntzā' rĕ*, v. a. & n. to wrinkle; raggrinzarsi, *–tzär' sĭ*, to lose courage.

raggruppare, *–grŭppā' rĕ*, v. a. to tie up together; to make up in parcels. [up.

raggruzzolare, *–grŭtzŏlā' rĕ*, v.a. to hoard

ragguagliare, *–gŭälyā' rĕ*, v. a. to level, to make even, to equalise; to compare; to advise.

ragguaglio, *–gŭäl' yŏ*, m. balancing, equality, relation, account, advice.

ragguardare, *–gŭärdā' rĕ*, v. a. to regard, to consider; to examine; to concern.

ragguardevole, *–dă' vŏlĕ*, a. remarkable, considerable.

ragia, *rä' jă*, f. resin; snare, fraud.

ragionamento, *răjŏnämĕn' tŏ*, m. reasoning, discourse.

ragionare, *–jŏnā' rĕ*, v. a. & n. to reason. to discourse, to infer, to conclude.

ragionato, *–nä' tŏ*, a. reasonable; afore-said; known.

ragione, *–jŏ' nĕ*, f. reason, judgment; sense; cause, motive; right, justice; subject, theme; account; rate; a – di, at the rate of.

ragionevole, *–nĕ' vŏlĕ*, a. reasonable; just.

ragliare, *rälyā' rĕ*, v. a. to bray.

raglio, *räl' yŏ*, m. braying of an ass.

ragna, *răn' yă*, f. spider; cob-web; fowling-net; snare, ambush.

ragnaia, *–yä' ră*, f. fowling-floor.

ragnare, *–yä' rĕ*, v. a. to lay bird-nets, to net birds; –, v. n. to get threadbare.

ragnatelo, *–yätĕ' lŏ*, ragno, *rän' yŏ*, m. spider; cob-web.

rallargare, *rällärgā' rĕ*, v. a. to widen, to extend, to stretch, to enlarge.

rallegrare, *–lĕgrā' rĕ*, v. a. to rejoice, to delight, to cheer up; rallegrarsi, *–grär' sĭ*, to be delighted; to take one's pleasure.

rallentare, *–lĕntā' rĕ*, v. a. to slacken, to retard, to abate.

rallevare, *–lĕvā' rĕ*, v. a. to educate, to rear.

rallungare, *–lüngā' rĕ*, v. a. to lengthen.

rama, *rä' mă*, f. branch. [out.

ramaiolo, *–mäĭŏ' lŏ*, m. ladle.

ramarro, *–mär' rŏ*, m. lizard.

rame, *rä' mĕ*, m. copper, brass; copper-money; figura in –, engraving.

ramerino, *–mĕrē' nŏ*, m. rosemary.

rametto, *–mĕt' tŏ*, m. small branch.

ramificare, *–mĭfĭkā' rĕ*, v. n., ramifi-carsi, *–kär' sĭ*, to ramify.

ramingare, *–mĭngā' rĕ*, v. n. to rove up and down homeless.

ramingo, *–mĭn' gŏ*, a. roving up and down.

rammantarsi, *–mäntăr′sĭ,* v. r. to adorn oneself.   [to heal up; to cicatrise.

rammarginare, *–mărjĭnă′rĕ,* v. a. & n.

rammaricarsi, *–mărĭkăr′sĭ,* v. r. to complain, to lament.

rammarico, *–mă′rĭkŏ,* m. complaint, lamentation.   [together, to collect.

rammassare, *–măssă′rĕ,* v. a. to scrape

rammemorare, *–mĕmŏră′rĕ,* v. a. to remind, to remember, to mention; **rammemorarsi,** *–răr′sĭ,* to remember oneself.

rammendare, *–mĕndă′rĕ,* v. a. to mend.

rammendo, *–mĕn′dŏ,* m. mending, patching.   [to put in mind, to mention.

rammentare, *–mĕntă′rĕ,* v. a. to remind,

rammollare, *–mŏllă′rĕ,* **rammollire,** *–mŏllĭ′rĕ,* v. a. to mollify.

rammontare, *–mŏntă′rĕ,* v. a. to heap up.

rammorbidare, *–mŏrbĭdă′rĕ,* **rammorbidire,** *–dĭ′rĕ,* v. a. to soften, to mitigate.

rammucchiare, *–mŭkkĭă′rĕ,* **rammuricare,** *–mŭrĭkă′rĕ,* v. a. to heap up.

ramo, *ră′mŏ,* m. branch, bough.

ramolaccio, *–mŏlăt′shŏ,* m. horse-radish.

ramoso, *–mŏ′sŏ,* a. branchy.

rampa, *răm′pă,* f. paw, clutch.

rampare, *–pă′rĕ,* v. a. to paw (like a lion).

rampicare, *–pĭkă′rĕ,* v. n. to climb, to crawl.

rampicone, *–pĭkŏ′nĕ,* **rampino,** *–pĕ′nŏ,* **rampo,** *răm′pŏ,* m. hook, harping-iron.

rampogna, *–pŏn′yă,* f. rebuke, reproof.

rampognare, *–yă′rĕ,* v. a. to rebuke, to abuse.

rampollare, *–pŏllă′rĕ,* v. a. to produce; –, v. n. to spring forth, to gush out.

rampollo, *–pŏl′lŏ,* m. small spouting spring of water; young shoot.

ramuscello, *răm̆ŭsshĕl′lŏ,* m. small branch.

rana, *ră′nă,* f. frog.

rancare, *rănkă′rĕ,* v. n. to limp; to hobble.

ranciato, *–dshă′tŏ,* a. orange-coloured.

rancido, *răn′dshĭdŏ,* a. rancid.   [rancid.

rancio, *răn′dshŏ,* a. orange-coloured; stale,

ranco, *răn′kŏ,* lame, hobbling.

rancore, *–kŏ′rĕ,* m. rancour, grudge.

randello, *–dĕl′lŏ,* m. cudgel.

rango, *răn′gŏ,* m. rank, degree.

rannicchiare, *rănnĭkkĭă′rĕ,* v. a. to shrink in, to shrivel up; **rannicchiarsi,** *–kĭăr′sĭ,* to squat; to crouch.

ranno, *răn′nŏ,* m. lye.   [to dignify.

rannobilire, *–nŏbĭlĭ′rĕ,* v. a. to ennoble,

rannochia, *–nŏk′kĭă,* **rannochio,** *–kĭŏ,* m. frog.   [cloudy.

rannuvolare, *–nŭvŏlă′rĕ,* v. n. to grow

rantolo, *răn′tŏlŏ,* m. rattling in the throat; hoarseness.   [crowfoot.

ranuncolo, *rănŭn′kŏlŏ,* m. ranunculus.

rapa, *ră′pă,* f. turnip.

rapace, *–pă′dshĕ,* a. rapacious.

rapacità, *–pădshĭtă′,* a. rapacity.

rapatumarsi, *–pătŭmăr′sĭ,* v. r. to reconcile oneself.

rapè, *răpĕ′,* m. rappee (snuff).

raperella, *–pĕrĕl′lă,* f. ferule.

raperonzo, *–rŏn′tzŏ,* m. rampion.

rapidamente, *–pĭdămĕn′tĕ,* ad. rapidly.

rapidità, *–pĭdĭtă′,* f. rapidity.

rapido, *ră′pĭdŏ,* a. rapid; swift; greedy.

rapimento, *–pĭmĕn′tŏ,* m. rapture, ecstasy; kidnapping.

rapina, *–pĕ′nă,* f. rapine, prey; fury; spite.

rapire, *–pĕ′rĕ,* v. a. to carry off by force, to ravish, to rape; to charm.

rappaciare, *răppădshă′rĕ,* **rappacificare,** *–dshĭfĭkă′rĕ,* v. a. to pacify, to appease, **rappacciarsi,** *–dshăr′sĭ,* **rappacificarsi,** *–kăr′sĭ,* to make oneself easy, to calm oneself.   [gether, to patch up.

rappezzare, *–pĕtză′rĕ,* v. a. to piece to-

rappianare, *–pĭănă′rĕ,* v. a. to smoothe, to level.

rappiattarsi, *–pĭăttăr′sĭ,* v. r. to lie squat, to hide oneself.   [again.

rappiccare, *–pĭkkă′rĕ,* v. a. to hang up

rappiccinire, *–pĭtshĭnĕ′rĕ,* **rappiccolire,** *–pĭkkŏlĕ′rĕ,* v. a. to lessen.

rappigliare, *–pĭlyă′rĕ,* v. a. to curdle; to make reprisals; to detain, **rappigliarsi,** *–yăr′sĭ,* to become curdled, to begin afresh.

rapportare, *–pŏrtă′rĕ,* v. a. to report, to relate, to recount; to cause.

rapporto, *–pŏr′tŏ,* m. report, relation.

rapprendere, *–prĕn′dĕrĕ,* v. a. ir. to take back again; **rapprendersi,** *–prĕn′dĕrsĭ,* to coagulate.   [retaliation.

rappresaglia, *–prĕsăl′yă,* f. reprisals, pl.,

rappresentante, *–prĕsĕntăn′tĕ,* m. representative.   [ing of a play.

rappresentanza, *–tăn′tză,* f. image; act-

rappresentare, *–tă′rĕ,* v. a. to represent; to exhibit.   [sentation; acting.

rappresentazione, *–tzĭŏ′nĕ,* f. repre-

rappreso, *–prĕ′sŏ,* a. curdled; benumbed; foundered; asleep.

rapsodia, *răpsŏdĕ′ă,* f. rhapsody.

rapsodo, *–să′dŏ,* m. rhapsodist.

raramente, *rără̆mĕn′tĕ,* ad. rarely.

rarefare, *rărĕfă′rĕ,* v. a. ir. to rarefy; to dilate.

rarefazione, *–fătzĭŏ′nĕ,* f. rarefaction.

rarezza, *rărĕt′ză,* f. rarity; thinness.

rarificare, *see* **rarefare.**   [scarcity.

rarità, *–rĭtă′,* f. rarity; scarcity; curiosity.

raro, *ră′rŏ,* a. rare; thin; scarce; exquisite; –, ad. rarely, seldom.

raschia, *răs′kĭă,* f. rasp, slight itch.

raschiare, *–kĭă′rĕ,* v. a. to scrape, to grate.

rasciugare, *răsshŭgă′rĕ,* v. a. to dry up.

rasciutto, *–sshăt′tŏ,* a. dried up, wiped.

rasentare, *răsĕntă′rĕ,* v. a. to graze, to touch slightly.

rasente, *–sĕn′tĕ,* pr. grazing, close to.

rasiera, *–sĭă′ră,* f. scraper.

raso, *ră′sŏ,* m. satin; –, a. shaved, shorn.

rasoio, *–sŏ′ŏ,* m. razor.   [even, smooth.

raspa, *răs′pă,* f. rasp; dough-knife.

raspare, *–pă′rĕ,* v. a. to rasp, to scrape.

raspo, *răs′pŏ,* m. bunch of grapes; mange, itch.   [after vintage.

raspollare, *–pŏllă′rĕ,* v. a. to glean grapes

rassegare, _–sĕgä′rĕ_, v. n. to curdle again.
rassegna, _–sĕn′yä_, f. review of troops.
rassegnare, _–yä′rĕ_, v. a. to resign; to restore; to review (troops); **rassegnarsi**, _–när′sĭ_, to resign oneself.
rassembrare, _–sĕmbrä′rĕ_, v. n. to resemble; to assemble.
rasserenare, _–sĕrĕnä′rĕ_, v. a. to clear up; **rasserenarsi**, _–när′sĭ_, to clear up.
rassettare, _–sĕttä′rĕ_, v. a. to settle, to set in order; to mend.
rassicurare, _–sĭkŭrä′rĕ_, v. a. to re-assure; to encourage.
rassodare, _–sŏdä′rĕ_, v. a. to consolidate; to strengthen.
rassomiglianza, _–sŏmĭlyän′tzä_, f. resemblance; comparison.
rassomigliare, _–yä′rĕ_, v. a. & n. to resemble.
rastrellare, _rästrĕllä′rĕ_, v. a. to rake, to scrape, to scour; to rob, to steal.
rastrello, _rästrĕl′lŏ_, m. rake; stile; ward of a lock.
rastro, _räs′trŏ_, m. rake.
rata, _rä′tä_, f. rate, share, quota.
ratificare, _–tĭfĭkä′rĕ_, v. a. to ratify.
ratificazione, _–tzĭŏ′nĕ_, f. ratification.
rattaccare, _rättäkkä′rĕ_, v. n. to attach again, to reunite.
rattacconare, _–kŏnä′rĕ_, v. a. to patch.
rattenere, _–tĕnĕ′rĕ_, v. a. ir. to detain, to keep back; to hinder; **rattenersi**, _–tĕ-nĕr′sĭ_, to pause.
rattenitiva, _–nĭtĕ′vä_, f. retentive faculty; memory.
rattenitivo, _–tĕ′vŏ_, m. rails, pl.
rattestare, _–tĕstä′rĕ_, v. a. to reunite.
rattiepidire, _–tĭĕpĭdĕ′rĕ_, v. a. to make lukewarm.
rattizzare, _–tĭtzä′rĕ_, v. a. to stir the fire.
ratto, _rät′tŏ_, m. robbery, rape; rapture; ecstasy; rat; –, a rapid, swift; steep; ravished, snatched away.
rattoppare, _–tŏppä′rĕ_, v. a. to patch, to botch.
rattrappire, _–träppĕ′rĕ_, v. n. to become paralised; to shrink.
rattrarre, _–trär′rĕ_, v. n. ir. to shrink.
rattristare, _–trĭstä′rĕ_, v. a. to grieve.
raucedine, _räŭdshĕ′dĭnĕ_, f. hoarseness.
rauco, _räŭ′kŏ_, a. hoarse; rough.
raumiliare, _–ămĭlĭä′rĕ_, v. a. to humble, to pacify.
raunare, _see_ radunare.
ravanello, _rävänĕl′lŏ_, **ravano**, _rä′vänŏ_, m. radish.
ravvalorare, _rävvälŏrä′rĕ_, v. a. to encourage, to fortify.
ravvedersi, _–vĕdĕr′sĭ_, v. r. ir. to correct oneself.
ravviare, _–vĭä′rĕ_, v. a. to set again in the right way; to arrange.
ravviluppare, _–vĭlŭppä′rĕ_, v. a. to wrap up, to entangle; to embroil.
ravvisare, _–vĭsä′rĕ_, v. a. to advise; to recognise.
ravvivare, _–vĭvä′rĕ_, v. a. to revive.
ravvolgere, _–vŏl′jĕrĕ_, v. a. ir. to wrap up; to turn; **ravvolgersi**, _–vŏl′jĕrsĭ_, to ramble.
ravvoltare, _–vŏltä′rĕ_, v. a. to wrap up.
ravvolto, _–vŏl′tŏ_, m. bundle, packet.

Italian and English.

raziocinare, _rätzĭŏdshĭnä′rĕ_, v. n. to reason, to argue; to reasoning.
raziocinio, _–dshĕ′nĭŏ_, m. ratiocination.
razionabile, _see_ razionevole.
razionabilità, _–näbĭlĭtä′_, f. reasonableness, reason; able.
razionale, _–tzĭŏnä′lĕ_, a. rational, reasonable.
razione, _–tzĭŏ′nĕ_, f. ration, daily portion; proportion; breed; sort.
razza, _rät′zä_, f. race, family, lineage; thorn-back (fish); ray (fish); spoke of a wheel.
razza, —, f.
razzare, _rätzä′rĕ_, v. n. to radiate; to shine.
razzo, _rät′zŏ_, m. ray, beam; spoke; cracker.
razzolare, _–tzŏlä′rĕ_, v. a. to scratch the ground (of fowls); to investigate.
re, _rĕ_, m. king.
reale, _rĕä′lĕ_, a. royal, kingly; real, positive; true, loyal, sincere.
realizzare, _–lĭtzä′rĕ_, v. a. to realise.
realtà, _rĕältä′_, f. reality; existence.
reame, _rĕä′mĕ_, m. kingdom.
reato, _rĕä′tŏ_, m. crime, transgression.
reattivo, _–ättĕ′vŏ_, a. reactive.
rebbio, _rĕb′bĭŏ_, m. prong of a fork.
recare, _–kä′rĕ_, v. a. to bring, to carry; to impute; to inform; to cause; to induce.
recedere, _–dshĕ′dĕrĕ_, v. n. ir. to recede, to draw back; to desist.
recente, _–dshĕn′tĕ_, a. recent, new; late.
recentemente, _–mĕn′tĕ_, ad. recently.
recere, _rĕ′dshĕrĕ_, v. n. to retch, to vomit.
recesso, _rĕdshĕs′sŏ_, m. recess, retreat.
recettacolo, _–dshĕttä′kŏlŏ_, m. receptacle; shelter, asylum.
recettivo, _–dshĕttĕ′vŏ_, a. receiving.
recettore, _–tŏ′rĕ_, m. receiver.
recidere, _–dshĕ′dĕrĕ_, v. a. ir. to cut off; to shorten; –, v. n. to cross.
recidiva, _–dshĭdĕ′vä_, f. relapse.
recidivo, _–dĕ′vŏ_, a. relapsing.
recinto, _–dshĕn′tŏ_, m. enclosure, circuit.
recipe, _rĕ′dshĕpĕ_, m. (med.) recipe, prescription.
recipiente, _rĕdshĭpĭĕn′tĕ_, m. recipient; –, a. receiving, hospitable; polite.
reciprocare, _–dshĭprŏkä′rĕ_, v. n. to reciprocate; tual.
reciproco, _–dshĕ′prŏkŏ_, a. reciprocal, mutual.
reciso, _–dshĕ′sŏ_, a. cut off; concise.
recitare, _–dshĭtä′rĕ_, v. a. to recite.
recitativo, _–tĕ′vŏ_, m. (mus.) recitative.
recitazione, _–tzĭŏ′nĕ_, f. recitation, recital.
reclamare, _–klämä′rĕ_, v. n. to reclaim; to complain; to protest.
reclamo, _–klä′mŏ_, m. reclamation.
reclinare, _–klĭnä′rĕ_, v. a. to recline, to lean upon or against; to repose.
recluta, _–klŭ′tä_, f. recruit; recruits, pl.
reclutare, _–tä′rĕ_, v. a. to recruit.
recondito, _–kŏn′dĭtŏ_, a. secret, hidden.
reda, _rĕ′dä_, f. heiress.
redare, _rĕdä′rĕ_, v. a. to inherit.
redarguire, _–därgŭĕ′rĕ_, v. a. to disprove, to rebuke.
redattore, _–dättŏ′rĕ_, m. redactor.

redazione, —dātzĭŏ'nĕ, f. redaction.

reddire, rĕddŏ'rĕ, v. n. (poet.) to come back.

redentore', —dĕntŏ'rĕ, m. redeemer, saviour. [ransom.

redenzione, —tzĭŏ'nĕ, f. redemption;

redimere, —dĕ'mĕrĕ, v. a. ir. to redeem.

redimire, —dĭmŏ'rĕ, v. a. (poet.) to crown.

redine, rĕ'dĭnĕ, f, rein of a bridle.

redintegrare, rĕdĭntĕgrā'rĕ, f. renovation, re-establishment.

redivivo, —dĭvĕ'vŏ, a. returned to life.

reduplicare, —dūplĭkā'rĕ, v. a. to redouble; to repeat.

refe, rŏ'fĕ, m. thread.

referire, rĕfĕrĭ'rĕ, v. a. to refer.

referto, —fĕr'tŏ, m. report; relation.

refettorio, —fĕttŏ'rĭŏ, m. refectory.

refezione, —fĕtzĭŏ'nĕ, f. restoration; refreshment. [cussion.

reflesso, —flĕs'sŏ, m. reflection, repercussion.

refocillare, —fŏdshĭllā'rĕ, v. a. to restore, to give new life. [fracted.

refrangersi, —frān'jĕrsĭ, v. r. ir. to be refracted.

refrangibile, —jĕ'bĭlĕ, a. refrangible.

refrattario, —frāttā'rĭŏ, a. refractory; disobedient.

refrazione, —tzĭŏ'nĕ, f. refraction.

refrigerare, —frĭjĕrā'rĕ, v. a. to cool, to refresh, to freshen.

refrigerio, —jĕ'rĭŏ, m. relief, comfort.

refugio, see **rifugio.**

regalare, —gālā'rĕ, v. a. to make a present of, to regale.

regalato, —lā'tŏ, a. bestowed; regaled, treated; exquisite, delicious.

regale, —gā'lĕ, m. hand-organ; —, a. royal.

regalia, —gālĕ'ā, f. regalia, pl.

regalo, —gā'lŏ, m. present, donation.

regata, —gā'tā, f. regatta, boat's race.

rege, rŏ'jĕ, m. (poet.) king.

reggente, rĕdjĕn'tĕ, a. regent, governing.

reggenza, —djĕn'tzā, f. regency.

reggere, rĕdj'ĕrĕ, v. a. ir. to support; to rule, to govern; to withstand, to oppose; —, v. n. ir. to last, to hold out; to subsist, to live.

reggia, rĕd'jā, f. royal palace.

reggimento, rĕdjĭmĕn'tŏ, m. government; behaviour; support; foundation; (mil.) regiment.

regia, see **reggia.** [derer).

regicida, rĕjĭdshĕ'dā, m. regicide (murderer).

regicidio, —dshĕ'dĭŏ, m. regicide (murder).

regina, rĕjĕ'nā, **reina,** rĕĕ'nā, f. queen.

regio, rŏ'jŏ, a. royal; noble.

regionale, rĕjŏnā'lĕ, a. local, peculiar to any region.

regione, —jŏ'nĕ, f. region, country.

registrare, —jĭstrā'rĕ, v. a. to register, to record, to note. [registry.

registrazione, —tzĭŏ'nĕ, f. registering;

registro, —jĕs'trŏ, m. register.

regnare, rĕnyā'rĕ, v. a. to reign, to rule; to manage; to predominate.

regnicolo, —yĕ'kŏlŏ, a. native.

regno, rĕn'yŏ, m. kingdom, reign.

regola, rŏ'gŏlā, f. rule, law; religious order. [rule; —, a. regular.

regolare, rĕgŏlā'rĕ, v. a. to regulate, to

regolarità, —lārĭtā', f. regularity.

regolizia, —lĕ'tzĭā, f. licorice.

regolo, rŏ'gŏlŏ, m. petty king; basilisk; ruler for ruling lines; wren.

regresso, rĕgrĕs'sŏ, m. regress, return.

reietto, rĕĕt'tŏ, a. rejected. [grate.

reintegrare, —ĭntĕgrā'rĕ, v. a. to reintereità, rĕĕtā', f, fault, crime.

reiterare, —tĕrā'rĕ, v. a. to reiterate, to repeat again. [tively.

relativamente —lātĭvāmĕn'tĕ, ad. relative.

relativo, —tĕ'vŏ, a. relative.

relatore, —tŏ'rĕ, m. relater, reporter.

relazione, —tzĭŏ'nĕ, f. relation; account.

relegare, —lĕgā'rĕ, v. a. to relegate, to banish. [ment.

relegazione, —tzĭŏ'nĕ, f. relegation, banishment.

religione, —lĕjŏ'nĕ, f. religion; religious order.

religiosità, —jŏsĭtā', f. religiousness.

religioso, —jŏ'sŏ, m. monk; —, a. religious.

reliquia, —lĕ'kŏā, f. relic. [relics.

reliquiario, —lĭkŏā'rĭŏ, m. shrine for

reluttante, —lŭttān'tĕ, a. reluctant.

reluttanza, —tān'tzā, f. reluctance.

reluttare, —tā'rĕ, v. n. to resist.

remare, rĕmā'rĕ, v. a. **remigare,** —mĭgā'rĕ, v. a. & n. to row. [niscence.

reminiscenza, —mĭnĭsshĕn'tzā, f. reminiscence.

remissibile, —mĭssĕ'bĭlĕ, a. pardonable.

remissione, —sĭŏ'nĕ, f. pardon; abatement.

remo, rŏ'mŏ, m. oar; hard labour.

remoto, rĕmŏ'tŏ, a. remote, distant.

remunerare, —mŭnĕrā'rĕ, v. a. to remunerate, to reward. [tion.

remunerazione, —tzĭŏ'nĕ, f. remunerarena, rŏ'nā, f. sand, gravel.

renaccio, rĕnāt'shŏ, m. sandy ground.

rendere, rĕn'dĕrĕ, v. a. r. & ir. to render, to restore; to return, to compensate; to produce, to yield; **rendersi,** rĕn'dĕrsĭ, to surrender, to yield.

rendita, rĕn'dĭtā, f. rent, revenue. [pl.

rene, rŏ'nĕ, m. (rene, f., reni, f. pl.) loins,

renella, —nĕl'lā, f. small sand; gravel (disease). [sandy.

renischio, —nĭs'kĭŏ, **renistio,** —tĭŏ, a.

renitente, —nĭtĕn'tĕ, a. restive, stubborn.

renitenza, —tĕn'tzā, f. obstinacy.

renoso, —nŏ'sŏ, a. sandy.

renunzia, see **rinunzia.**

renunziare, see **rinunziare.**

reo, rŏ'ŏ, a. guilty, criminal. [pulse.

repellere, rĕpĕl'lĕrĕ, v. a. ir. to repel, to repentaglio, —pĕntā'lyŏ, m. peril; risk.

repente, —pĕn'tĕ, a. & ad. sudden(ly); unexpected(ly).

repentemente, —mĕn'tĕ, ad. suddenly.

repere, rŏ'pĕrĕ, v. n. to creep. [discover.

reperire, rĕpĕrĭ'rĕ, v. a. ir. to find out, to repertorio, —tŏ'rĭŏ, m. repertory.

replica, rŏ'plĭkā, f. reply, repartee.

replicare, rĕplĭkā'rĕ, v. a. to reply, to answer.

replicatamente, –kätämen'te, ad. repeatedly.

replicazione, –tzio'ne, f. reply, answer.

repositorio, –pŏsĭto'rĭŏ, m. repository; wardrobe.

reprimere, –pre'mere, v. a. ir. to repress, to restrain.

reprobo, rĕ'prŏbŏ, a. reprobate.

repubblica, rĕpŭb'blĭkä, f. republic.

repubblicano, –blĭkä'nŏ, a. & m. republican.

repudiare, see **ripudiare.**

repudio, see **ripudio.**

repugnare, –pŭnyä're, v. n. to be repugnant.

repulsa, –pŭl'sä, f. refusal. [pugnant.

reputare, –pŭtä're, v. a. & n. to repute; to esteem.

reputazione, –tzio'ne, f. reputation, esteem.

requie, rĕ'kŭĭe, f. repose, rest; quiet.

requisito, rĕkŭĭsĭ'tŏ, a. required.

requisizione, –sĭtzĭo'ne, f. requisition.

resa, rĕ'sä, f. surrender.

rescindere, rĕsshĭn'dĕrĕ, v. a. ir. to rescind; to annul.

rescritto, –skrĭt'tŏ, m. rescript, decree.

resecare, –sĕkä're, v. a. to cut off.

residente, –sĭdĕn'te, a. residing.

residenza, –sĭdĕn'tzä, f. residence, dwelling.

residuare, –dĭlä're, v. a. to form a residue.

residuo, –sĕ'dŭŏ, m. remainder, sediment.

resina, –rĕsĕ'nä, f. resin.

resinoso, –sĭnŏ'sŏ, a. resinous.

resistente, –sĭstĕn'te, a. resisting, opposing.

resistenza, –tĕn'tzä, f. resistance.

resistere, –sĭs'tĕrĕ, v. a. ir. to resist.

respettivamente, –spĕttĭvämĕn'te, ad. respectively.

respettivo, –tĕ'vŏ, a. relative.

respingere, –spĭn'jĕrĕ, v. a. ir. to push back.

respirare, –spĭrä're, v. n. to respire, to breathe. [breathing.

respirazione, –tzio'ne, f. respiration.

respiro, –spĕ'rŏ, m. breath, pause; rest; relief, ease.

ressa, rĕs'sä, f. importunity; dispute.

resta, rĕs'tä, f. beard of corn; pause, delay.

restante, –tän'te, m. remainder, residue.

restare, –tä're, v. n. to remain, to stay, to cease; **restarsi,** –tär'sĭ, to stand still.

restata, –tä'tä, f. stop, halt.

restaurare, rĕstäŭrä're, v. a. to restore; to indemnify. [recovery.

restaurazione, –tzio'ne, f. restoration.

restauro, rĕstä'ŭrŏ, m. recovery; comfort; reward.

restio, rĕstĭ'ŏ, m. pig-headedness; –, a. restive, stubborn.

restituire, –stĭtŭĭ're, v. a. to restore, to pay back. [payment.

restituzione, –tzio'ne, f. restoring; restoration.

resto, rĕs'tŏ, m. remainder, rest, surplus.

restringere, rĕstrĭn'jĕrĕ, v. a. ir. to restrain.

restrizione, –strĭtzio'ne, f. restriction, limitation.

resultare, –sŭltä're, v. n. to result.

resultato, –tä'tŏ, m. result.

resupino, –sŭpĭ'nŏ, a. lying on one's back.

retaggio, rĕtäd'jŏ, m. inheritance.

rete, rĕ'te, f. net, snare. [cealment.

reticenza, rĕtĭshĕn'tzä, f. reticence, concealment.

retore, rĕ'tŏrĕ, m. rhetorician.

retorica, rĕtŏ'rĭkä, f. rhetoric.

retorico, –tŏ'rĭkŏ, a. rhetorical.

retribuire, –trĭbŭĭ're, v. a. to recompense, to requite.

retribuzione, –tzio'ne, f. retribution.

retro, rĕ'trŏ, ad. behind, backward.

retroazione, rĕtrŏäzĭo'ne, f. retroaction.

retrocedere, –dshĕ'dĕrĕ, v. n. ir. to go back, to recede.

retrogrado, –grä'dŏ, a. retrograde.

retrorso, –trŏr'sŏ, ad. (poet.) backwards.

retta, rĕt'tä, f. resistance.

rettangolo, rĕttän'gŏlŏ, m. rectangle.

rettificare, –tĭfĭkä're, v. a. to rectify.

rettificazione, –tzio'ne, f. rectification.

rettile, rĕt'tĭlĕ, m. reptile. [rightness.

rettitudine, –tĭtŏ'dĭnĕ, f. rectitude, uprightness.

retto, rĕt'tŏ, a. ruled; right, upright; just.

rettore, rĕttŏ're, m. rector, ruler.

reverberare, rĕvĕrbĕrä're, v. a. & n. to reverberate; to rebound.

reverbero, –vĕr'bĕrŏ, m. reflector.

reverendo, –vĕrĕn'dŏ, a. reverend. [ful.

reverente, –vĕrĕn'te, a. reverent, respectful.

reverenza, –vĕrĕn'tzä, f. reverence, bow.

reverire, –vĕrĕ're, v. a. to revere.

revisione, –vĭsĭo'ne, f. revising, revisal.

revisore, –vĭsŏ're, m. reviser, censor.

reuma, rĕ'ŭmä, m. rheum, catarrh, cold.

reumatico, rĕŭmä'tĭkŏ, a. rheumatic.

reumatismo, –mätĭs'mŏ, m. rheumatism.

rialto, rĭäl'tŏ, m. eminence, height; –, a. elevated; high.

rialzare, –älzä're, v. a. to raise higher.

riapparire, –äppärĕ're, v. n. ir. to reappear.

ribadire, –bädĕ're, v. a. to rivet.

ribalderia, –bäldĕrĕ'ä, f. ribaldry; rascality. [beggarly.

ribaldo, –bäl'dŏ, a. rascally, roguish;

ribalta, –bäl'tä, f. trap, pitfall.

ribaltare, –bältä're, v. a. to overturn; (mar.) to capsize.

ribassare, –bässä're, v. a. to discount.

ribasso, –bäs'sŏ, m. abatement, discount.

ribellare, –bĕllä're, v. a. & n. to rebel; **ribellarsi,** –lär'sĭ, to revolt.

ribelle, rĭbĕl'lĕ, m. rebel, insurgent.

ribellione, –bĕllĭo'ne, f. rebellion.

ribes, rĕ'bĕs, m. gooseberry bush; gooseberry. [quibble.

ribobolo, rĭbŏ'bŏlŏ, m. silly saying; jest,

riboccare, –bŏkkä're, v. n. to overflow, to be brimful. [abundance.

ribocco, –bŏk'kŏ, m. overflow; super-

ribollire, –bŏllĕ're, v. n. to boil again, to boil up; to overheat oneself.

ribrezzare, –brĕtzä're, v. n. to shiver.

ribrezzo, –brĕt'zŏ, m. shivering, chilliness; fright. [reject; to vomit.

ributtare, –bŭttä're, v. a. to repulse, to

ricadere, –kädĕ're, v. n. ir. to fall again; to relapse; to lie down (of grain).

ricadia, –kåd̯ă, f. relapse; trouble, misfortune.

ricamare, –kåmă̄ rĕ, v. a. to embroider.

ricamatrice, –trē̍ dshĕ, f. embroiderer.

ricamatura, –tṓ rā, f. embroidery.

ricambiare, –kåmbiă̄ rĕ, v. a. to requite, to reward.

ricambio, –kăm'biŏ, m. re-exchange; recompense, reward, requital, return.

ricamo, rĭkă̄ mŏ, m. embroidery.

ricapitare, –kåpĭtă̄ rĕ, v. a. to direct; to remit.   [tion.

ricapito, –kă̍ pĭtŏ, m. address; satisfaction.

ricapitolare, –kåpĭtŏlā̄ rĕ, v. a. to recapitulate.   [tion.

ricapitolazione, –tziŏ'nĕ, f. recapitulation.

ricattare, –kåttă̄ rĕ, v. a. to redeem, to recover; **ricattarsi,** –tăr'sĭ, to be avenged.

ricatto, –kă̍t'tŏ, m. redemption; vengeance.

ricavare, –kåvă̄ rĕ, v. a. to gain, to profit; to recover; to copy out.

ricchezza, rĭkkĕ̍t'zā, f. riches, pl.

ricciaia, rĭtshă̄ĭ', f. curly head.

riccio, rĭt'shŏ, m. husk of chestnuts; curl; false jewel; hedge-hog; –, a. frizzled, curled; shaggy.

ricciuto, rĭtshū'tŏ, a. frizzled, in ringlets.

ricco, rĭk'kŏ, a. rich, wealthy.

ricerca, rĭdshĕr'kā, f. inquiry, search, research.

ricercare, –dshĕrkă̄ rĕ, v. a. to seek again, to search, to inquire into; to request.

ricetta, –dshĕt'tā, f. medical prescription, receipt.   [asylum.

ricettacolo, –tă̍ kŏlŏ, m. receptacle;

ricettare, –tă̄ rĕ, v. a. to receive, to accept; to lodge, to shelter; to entertain.

ricetto, –dshĕt'tŏ, m. shelter, asylum.

ricevere, –dshā vĕrĕ, v. a. to receive; to lodge.

ricezione, –dshĕtzĭŏ'nĕ, f. reception.

richiamare, –kĭămă̄ rĕ, v. a. to call back, to recall, to summon.

richiamo, –kĭă̄ mŏ, m. reclaiming; appeal; bird-call, decoy; complaint.

richiedere, –kĭă̍ dĕrĕ, v. a. ir. to request, to require, to demand.

richiesta, –kĭĕ̄s'tā, f. request, petition; summons, pl.

richiudere, –kĭŏ̄ dĕrĕ, v. a. ir. to shut up.

ricognizione, –kŏnyĭtzĭŏ'nĕ, f. acknowledgment; (mil.) reconnoitring.

ricolta, –kŏl'tā, f., **ricolto,** –tŏ, m. crop, harvest.   [begin again.

ricominciare, –kŏmĭndshă̄ rĕ, v. a. & n. to

ricompensa, –kŏmpĕn'sā, f. recompense, reward.

ricompensare, –pĕnsă̄ rĕ, v. a. to recompense, to reward.

ricompiere, –kŏm'pĭĕrĕ, v. a. ir. to fill again, to fulfil; to reward; to accomplish; to supply.

ricomprare, –pră̄ rĕ, v. a. to repurchase; to redeem, to ransom.

riconciliare, –kŏndshĭlĭă̄ rĕ, v. a. to reconcile.

riconciliazione, –tzĭŏ'nĕ, f. reconciliation.   [join again, to re-unite.

ricongiungere, –jăn'jĕrĕ, v. a. ir. to

riconoscente, –kŏnŏsshĕn'tĕ, a. thankful.

riconoscenza, –sshĕn'tzā, f. thankfulness; acknowledgment; reward.

riconoscere, –nŏssh'ĕrĕ, v. a. ir. to recognise, to acknowledge.

ricordare, –kŏrdă̄ rĕ, v. a. to remember, to mention.

ricordevole, –dā'vŏlĕ, a. memorable.

ricordo, –kŏr'dŏ, m. remembrance; keepsake; warning.   [to retrieve.

ricoverare, –kŏvĕră̄ rĕ, v. a. to recover, to retrieve.

ricreare, –krĕă̄ rĕ, v. a. to recreate, to amuse; to rejoice.

ricredere, –krĕ'dĕrĕ, v. a. to undeceive.

ricrescere, –krĕssh'ĕrĕ, v. a. & n. ir. to augment; to grow, to increase.

ricucire, –kŭdshĕ'rĕ, v. a. to sew again; to repair.

ricuocere, –kŭŏ'dshĕrĕ, v. a. ir. to cook again; to digest; to consider.

ricuperare, –kŭpĕră̄ rĕ, v. a. to recover, to retrieve.

ricurvo, –kŭr'vŏ, a. curved, crooked.

ricusa, –kŏ'sā, f. refusal, denial.

ricusare, –kŭsă̄ rĕ, v. a. to refuse, to reject.

ridere, rĕ'dĕrĕ, v. n. ir. to laugh; to smile; to jeer.   [able.

ridicolo, rĭdĭ'kŏlŏ, a. ridiculous, laughable.

ridire, –dĕ'rĕ, v. a. ir. to tell again, to repeat; to refer, to tell; **ridirsi,** –dĭr'sĭ, to unsay, to retract.

ridolere, –dŏlĕ'rĕ, v. n. ir. to smell sweet.

ridondare, –dŏndă̄ rĕ, v. n. to superabound; to result.

ridosso (a –), –dŏs'sŏ, ad. astraddle.

ridotto, –dŏt'tŏ, m. place, retreat, shelter.

ridurre, –dŭr'rĕ, v. a. ir. to reduce, to bring back; to force; **ridursi,** –dŭr'sĭ, to assemble; to arrive at.

riduzione, –dătzĭŏ'nĕ, f. reduction.

riesaminare, –ĕsămĭnă̄ rĕ, v. a. to re-examine.   [prosper.

riescire, –ĕsshĕ'rĕ, v. n. to succeed, to

rifabbricare, –făbbrĭkă̄ rĕ, v. a. to rebuild.

rifacimento, –fādshĭmĕn'tŏ, m. re-making; re-polishing; re-establishment.

rifacitore, –tŏ'rĕ, m. repairer.

rifare, –fă̄ rĕ, v. a. ir. to do or to make again; to re-polish, to re-cast, to repair; to mend; **rifarsi,** –făr'sĭ, to recover one's strength.   [to ascribe.

riferire, –fĕrĕ'rĕ, v. a. to relate, to refer,

rifermare, –fĕrmă̄ rĕ, v. a. to confirm.

rifinare, –fĭnă̄ rĕ, v. n., **rifinarsi,** –năr'sĭ, **rifinire,** –fĭnĕ'rĕ, v. n. to leave off, to stop.

rifiutare, –fĭŭtă̄ rĕ, v. a. to refuse; to renounce.

rifiuto, –fĭŭ'tŏ, m. refusal; divorce; outcast; sweepings, pl.

riflessione, –flĕssĭŏ'nĕ, f. reflection.

riflessivo, –vŏ, a. reflective.

riflesso, –flĕs'sŏ, m. reflex; reflection; lights (in painting) pl.

riflettere, —flĕt'tĕrĕ, v. a. ir. to reflect; to reverberate; to consider.

riflusso, —flŭs'sŏ, m. reflux, ebb-tide.

riforma, —fŏr'mă, f. reform, reformation.

riformare, —mā'rĕ, v. a. to reform.

riformatore, —tŏ'rĕ, m. reformer.

riformazione, —tziŏ'nĕ, f. reformation.

rifrancare, —frănkā'rĕ, v. a. to strengthen.

rifrustrare, —frŭstrā'rĕ, v. a. to rummage, to search; to cane.

rifuggire, —fŭdjĕ'rĕ, v. n., rifuggirsi, —djĕr'sĕ, to take refuge.

rifugio, —fŏ'jŏ, m. refuge, asylum.

rifulgere, —fŭl'jĕrĕ, v. n. to shine; to glitter.

rifutare, —fūtā'rĕ, v. a. to refute.

riga, rĕ'gă, f. line, ruled line.

rigaglie, rĭgāl'yĕ, f. pl. by-profit.   [let.

rigagnolo, —găn'yŏlŏ, m. streamlet, rivulet.

rigare, —gā'rĕ, v. a. to draw lines; to water.

rigattiere, —gāttiĕ'rĕ, m. broker, huckster.

rigenerare, —jĕnĕrā'rĕ, v. a. to regenerate.

rigidità, —jidĭtă', f. rigidity, stiffness; rigour, severity.

rigido, rĕ'jidŏ, a. rigid, stiff; severe.

rigirare, rijirā'rĕ, v. a. to surround; to deceive; v. n. to turn about, tŏ whirl.

rigiro, —jĕ'rŏ. m. turning round, evasion, subterfuge, poor excuse.

rigo, rĕ'gŏ, m. line; ruler.

rigoglio, rĭgŏl'yŏ, m. rankness (of plants); boldness; pride.

rigoletto, —gŏlĕt'tŏ, m. round dance.

rigonfiare, —gŏnfiā'rĕ, v. n. to over-swell.

rigore, —gŏ'rĕ, m. rigour.   [to puff up.

rigorista, —gŏris'tă, m. rigorist.

rigoro, rĕ'gŏrŏ, m. rivulet, streamlet.

rigorosità, rĭgŏrŏsĭtă', f. severity, rigour.

rigoroso, —rŏ'sŏ, a. rigorous.

riguardare, —gŭārdā'rĕ, v. a. & n. to look at, to behold; to regard, to concern; to aim at, to take aim at.

riguardato, —dā'tŏ, a. circumspect.

riguardevole, —gŭārdā'vŏlĕ, a. considerable, remarkable.

riguardo, —gŭār'dŏ, m. look, regard, view; sight; aim; consideration.

riguarire, —gŭārĕ'rĕ, v. n. to get well again, to recover.

rigurgitare, —gŭrjĭtā'rĕ, v. a. to regurgitate; to overflow.

rigurgito, —gŭr'jĭtŏ, m. bubbling up; overflowing.   [let free.

rilasciare, —lāsshā'rĕ, v. a. to release, to relax, to slacken.

rilassare, —lāssā'rĕ, v. a. to relax, to slacken.

rilasso, —lāss'ŏ, a. slack, wearied; weak.

rilente, —lĕn'tĕ, a —, adv. softly, gently, slowly; cautiously.

rilevare, —lĕvā'rĕ, v. a. to raise up again; to erect; to comfort; to establish; to nurse; to suckle; to educate; rilevarsi, —vār'sĕ, to get on one's feet again; to recover.

rilievo, —liĕ'vŏ, m. leavings, remains, pl., refuse; relief; importance.

rilucere. —lŏ'dshĕrĕ, v. n. ir. to shine, to glitter.

rima, rĭ'mă, f. rhyme; verse; song.

rimanere, rĭmānĕ'rĕ, v. n. ir. to remain, to stay; to cease, to abstain.

rimare, —mā'rĕ, v. a. & n. to rhyme.

rimasuglio, —māsŭl'yŏ, m. remainder, residue.   [to jump.

rimbalzare, rĭmbāltzā'rĕ, v. n. to rebound, to jump.

rimbalzo, —bāl'tzŏ, m. rebound.

rimboccare, —bŏkkā'rĕ, v. a. to turn upside down; to discharge; to empty; to overflow.   [to boom.

rimbombare, —bŏmbā'rĕ, v. n. to resound.

rimborsare, —bŏrsā'rĕ, v. a. to reimburse; to repay.   [repayment.

rimborso, —bŏr'sŏ, m. re-imbursement.

rimbrottare, —brŏttā'rĕ, v. a. to reproach, to scold.   [ugly.

rimbruttire, —brŭttĕ'rĕ, v. n. to become ugly.

rimbucare, —būkā'rĕ, v. n. to hide in a hole.   [cure.

rimediare, rĭmĕdiā'rĕ, v. a. to remedy, to cure.

rimedio, —mā'diŏ, m. remedy; medicine.

rimembranza, —mĕmbrăn'tză, f. remembrance, memory.

rimembrare, —brā'rĕ, rimemorare, —mŏrā'rĕ, v. a. to remind, to remember.

rimenare, —mĕnā'rĕ, v. a. to bring back; to handle; to stir.   [repair.

rimerdare, —mĕndā'rĕ, v. a. to mend, to repair.

rimenio, —mĕnĕ'ŏ, m. shaking.

rimeno, —mā'nŏ, m. return, repayment; profit.

rimeritare, —mĕrĭtā'rĕ, v. a. to recompense.

rimessa, —mĕs'să, f. remission, remittance; return of money; coach-house.

rimesso, —mĕs'sŏ, a. subdued, dispirited; weak, low, faint.

rimettere, —mĕt'tĕrĕ, v. a. ir. to replace, to set again; to remit, to pardon; to restrain; to drive back; to restore; to commit; to consign; to deliver up; rimettersi, —mĕt'tĕrsĕ, to yield; to refer to.

rimirare, —mirā'rĕ, v. a. to look at intently.

rimondare, —mŏndā'rĕ, v. a. to clean, to purge; to prune; to expiate.

rimorso, —mŏr'sŏ, m. remorse; contrition, repentance.

rimorchiare, —mŏrkiā'rĕ, v. a. to tow.

rimosso, —mŏs'sŏ, a. removed, distant.

rimostranza, —mŏstrăn'tză, f. remonstrance.   [to represent.

rimostrare, —trā'rĕ, v. a. to remonstrate; to represent.

rimpatriare, rĭmpātriā'rĕ, v. n. to return to one's country.   [proud.

rimpettito, —pĕttĭ'tŏ, a. high-breasted, proud.

rimpetto, —pĕt'tŏ, pr. over against, opposite, facing.   [conceal.

rimpiattare, —piāttā'rĕ, v. a. to hide, to conceal.

rimpiazzare, —piātzā'rĕ, v. a. to replace; to fill the place of, to surrogate.

rimproverare, —prŏvĕrā'rĕ, v. a. to reprove, to reprimand.

rimprovero, —prŏ'vĕrŏ, m. reproach.

rimuginare, rĭmŭjĭnā'rĕ, v. a. to make a diligent search.

rimunerare, —mŭnĕrā'rĕ, v. a. to remunerate, to reward.

rimunerazione, —tziŏ'nĕ, f. remuneration, reward.

rimuovere, –mŏŏ'vĕrĕ, v. a. ir. to remove.

rinascere, –nässh'ĕrĕ, v. n. ir. to be born again, to revive.

rincagnarsi, rĕnkänyär'sĕ, v. r. to frown, [to knit one's brows.

rincagnato, –känyä'tŏ, a. flat-nosed.

rincalzare, –kältsä'rĕ, v. a. to pursue hotly, to urge, to press; to lay new mould about the roots of trees &c. ; to prop up.

rincarare, –kärä'rĕ, v. a. & n. to raise the price; to grow dearer.

rinchiudere, –kiŏŏ'dĕrĕ, v. a. ir. to shut [in, to enclose.

rincontra, –kŏn'trä, pr. facing, over against; **andare alla –**, to go to meet.

rincontrare, –trä'rĕ, v. a. to meet.

rincontro, –kŏn'trŏ, m. rencounter, meeting; **di –**, opposite.

rincorare, –kŏrä'rĕ, v. a. to encourage.

rincrescere, –krĕssh'ĕrĕ, v. n. ir. to grow again; to be tired; to be disagreeable.

rinculare, –kŭlä'rĕ, v. a. to recoil, to withdraw, to retire, to recede.

rinfacciare, –fätshä'rĕ, v. a. to reproach.

rinfamare, –fämä'rĕ, v. n. to restore to fame. [reform.

rinformare, –fŏrmä'rĕ, v. a. to form, to

rinforzamento, –fŏrtzämĕn'tŏ, m. reinforcement; succour.

rinforzare, –tzä'rĕ, v. a. to reinforce; to strengthen, to recover one's strength.

rinforzo, –fŏr'tzŏ, m. reinforcement; reinforcements, pl.

rinfrancare, –fränkä'rĕ, v. a. to free; to embolden; to strengthen.

rinfrescare, –frĕskä'rĕ, v. a. to refresh, to cool; to renew. [growl; to neigh.

ringhiare, rĕnghiä'rĕ, v. n. to snarl, to

ringhiera, –ghiĕ'rä, f. hustings, pl.; rostrum.

ringhio, rĕn'ghiŏ, m. neighing.

ringiovanire, –jŏvänĕ'rĕ, v. n. to grow young again.

ringraziamento, –grätzämĕn'tŏ, m. thanks, returning of thanks.

ringraziare, –grätziä'rĕ, v. a. to return thanks, to thank. [raise higher.

rinnalzare, –ältzä'rĕ, v. a. to raise, to

rinnegare, –nĕgä'rĕ, v. a. to deny, to abjure, to abnegate.

rinnegato, –gä'tŏ, m. renegade. [jure.

rinnovare, –nŏvä'rĕ, v. a. to renew; to renovate, to restore.

rinnovatore, –tŏ'rĕ, m. renewer, restorer.

rinnovazione, –tziŏ'nĕ, f. renewing, renewal. [to begin again.

rinnovellare, –nŏvĕllä'rĕ, v. a. to renew,

rinoceronte, rĕnŏdshĕrŏn'tĕ, m. rhinoceros.

rinomanza, –nŏmän'tzä, f. renown, fame.

rinomare, –mä'rĕ, v. a. to make famous.

rinominare, –nŏminä'rĕ, v. a. to praise, to celebrate.

rintegrare, see **reintegrare.**

rinterzare, –tĕrtzä'rĕ, v. a. to triplicate, to treble, to fold three times.

rintoppare, –tŏppä'rĕ, v. a. to mend, to botch; to repair; –, v. n. to meet with.

rintoppo, –tŏp'pŏ, m. meeting; encounter, shock; obstacle.

rintracciare, –trätshä'rĕ, v. a. to investigate, to explore.

rintronare, –trŏnä'rĕ, v. n. to resound.

rintronare, –trŏ'närĕ, m. resounding.

rintuzzare, –tŭtzä'rĕ, v. a. to blunt; to abate. [port, relation.

rinunzia, rĕnŭn'tziä, f. renunciation; re-

rinunziare, –nŭntziä'rĕ, v. a. to renounce; to relate, to tell.

rinunziazione, see **rinunzia.**

rinverdire, –vĕrdĕ'rĕ, v. a. & n. to make green again; to grow green again.

rinvergare, –vĕrgä'rĕ, v. a. to discover, to find out.

rinvertire, –vĕrtĕ'rĕ, v. a. to exchange; to convert; –, v. n. to return.

rinverzare, –vĕrtzä'rĕ, v. a. to stop up, to wedge up.

rinvestire, –vĕstĕ'rĕ, v. a. to invest.

rinviare, –viä'rĕ, v. a. to send back; to dismiss.

rinvitare, –vitä'rĕ, v. a. to invite again.

rinvolto, –vŏl'tŏ, m. parcel, packet.

rio, rĕ'ŏ, m. brook, rivulet; –, a. wicked, guilty.

riotta, rĕŏt'tä, f. quarrel, dispute; uproar.

ripa, see **riva.**

riparamento, rĕpärämĕn'tŏ, m. repair; rampart.

riparare, –pärä'rĕ, v. a. to repair; to remedy; to shelter, to defend; to restore, to comfort; to oppose; to hinder.

riparazione, –tziŏ'nĕ, f. reparation.

riparo, –pä'rŏ, m. remedy, expedient; resource; defence.

ripartimento, –pärtimĕn'tŏ, m. distribution; portion, share.

ripartire, –pärtĕ'rĕ, v. a. to distribute, to share.

ripentirsi, –pĕntĕr'sĕ, v. r. to repent, to regret.

ripercuotere, –pĕrkŏŏ'tĕrĕ, v. a. ir. to repercuss.

ripercussione, –kŭssiŏ'nĕ, f. repercussion, reflection.

ripestare, –pĕstä'rĕ, v. a. to pound again.

ripetere, –pä'tĕrĕ, v. a. to repeat.

ripetio, –pĕtĕ'ŏ, m. dispute, quarrel; regret, sadness.

ripetizione, –tĭtziŏ'nĕ, f. repetition.

ripezzare, –pĕtzä'rĕ, v. a. to mend, to patch up. [staircase.

ripiano, –piä'nŏ, m. landing-place of a

ripido, rĕ'pidŏ, a. steep, precipitous.

ripiegare, rĕpiĕgä'rĕ, v. a. to fold, to plait, to blunt.

ripiego, –piĕ'gŏ, m. expedient, means

ripieno, –piĕ'nŏ, m. stuffing; –, a. full.

riporre, –pŏr'rĕ, v. a. ir. to put again, to place again; to rebuild; to restore; to hide; to bury.

riportare, –pŏrtä'rĕ, v. a. to carry back; to carry off; to report, to relate; to gain.

riporto, –pŏr'tŏ, report, information.

riposare, –pŏsä'rĕ, v. n. to repose, to rest oneself, to sleep; to pause.

riposo, –pŏ'sŏ, m. repose, rest; tranquillity.

riprendere, *–prĕn'dĕrĕ,* v. a. ir. to retake, to recover, to reprove, to chide.

riprensibile, *–sĕ'blĕ,* a. reprehensibile.

riprensione, *–sĭō'nĕ,* f. reprehension, reproof, reprimand, check, rebuke.

ripresa, *–prā'sā,* f. repetition ; reprimand.

ripresentare, *–presĕntā'rĕ,* v. a. to re-present ; to expose.

riprodurre, *–prōdŭr'rĕ,* v. a. ir. to reproduce.

riproduzione, *–tzĭō'nĕ,* f. reproduction.

riprova, *–prō'vā,* f. proof, evidence.

riprovare, *–prōvā'rĕ,* v. a. to reprobate ; to reject.

riprovazione, *–tzĭō'nĕ,* f. reprobation.

ripudiare, *–pŭdĭā'rĕ,* v. a. to repudiate ; to divorce.

ripudio, *–pō'dĭō,* m. repudiation ; divorce.

ripugnare, *–pŭnyā'rĕ,* v. a. & n. to repugn, to resist, to be contrary to.

ripulsa, *–pŭl'sā,* f. repulse, refusal.

ripulsare, *–pŭlsā'rĕ,* v. a. to repulse, to refuse, to deny ; [attribute.

riputare, *–pŭtā'rĕ,* v. a. to repute, to reputation.

riputazione, *–tzĭō'nĕ,* f. reputation, fame.

risa, *–rĕ'sā,* f. laughter, derision.

risaia, *risā'ā,* f. rice-field.

risaldare, *–sāldā'rĕ,* v. a. to solder again ; to heal up.

risaltare, *–sāltā'rĕ,* v. n. to leap again, to rebound ; to jut out ; to excel.

risalto, *–sāl'tō,* m. rebound ; projection.

risanare, *–sānā'rĕ,* v. a. to cure.

risapere, *–sāpā'rĕ,* v. a. ir. to know by hearsay.

risarcire, *–sārdshĭ'rĕ,* v. a. to mend, to repair, to compensate.

risata, *see* **risa.**

riscaldare, *riskāldā'rĕ,* v. a. to warm *or* to heat (again).

riscappare, *–skāppā'rĕ,* v. n. to escape again.

riscattare, *–skāttā'rĕ,* v. a. to redeem.

riscatto, *–skāt'tō,* m. redemption, ransom.

rischiarare, *–skĭārā'rĕ,* v. a. rischiarire, *–kĭārĕ'rĕ,* v. a. & n. to clear, to illustrate, to explain.

rischio, *rĭs'kĭō,* m. risk, peril, hazard.

rischioso, *–kĭō'sō,* a. hazardous.

risciacquare, *rĭsshākŭā'rĕ,* v. a. to rinse, to wash. [to abate.

riscontare, *–skōntā'rĕ,* v. a. to discount,

riscontrare, *–skōntrā'rĕ,* v. a. to compare, to collate ; to abate ; –, v. n. to meet (by chance) ; **riscontrarsi nelle parole,** to say the same thing. [ing ; comparing.

riscontro, *–skōn'trō,* m. rencounter, meet-

riscossione, *–skŏssĭō'nĕ,* f. exaction ; receipt of money.

riscuotere, *–skŭō'tĕrĕ,* v. a. ir. to rescue, to exact, to dun ; to recover ; **riscuotersi,** *–skŭō'tĕrsĭ,* to be revenged, to regain, to be quits ; to shiver.

risdegnarsi, *risdĕnyā'rsĭ,* v. r. to fly into a passion again.

risecare, *see* **resecare.**

risegnare, *–sĕnyā'rĕ,* v. a. to resign, to renounce. [submission.

risegnazione, *–tzĭō'nĕ,* f. resignation ;

riseguire, *–sĕgŭĕ'rĕ,* v. a. to continue.

risensare, *–sĕnsā'rĕ,* v. n. to recover one's senses.

risentire, *–sĕntĕ'rĕ,* v. a. & n. to hear again ; to resound ; **risentirsi,** *–tĭr'sĭ,* to recover one's senses ; to wake up.

risentito, *–sĕntĕ'tō,* a. sensible ; keen.

riserbare, *–sĕrbā'rĕ,* v. a. to reserve ; to preserve.

riserbo, *–sĕr'bō,* m. reservation, reserve.

riserrare, *–sĕrrā'rĕ,* v. a. to shut again, to shut in.

riservare, *see* **riserbare.** [to shut in.

risguardare, *risgŭārdā'rĕ,* v. a. to look, to regard ; to observe. [be in danger.

risicare, *rĭsĭkā'rĕ,* v. a. & n. to risk ; to danger.

risico, *rĕ'sĭkō,* m. risk, hazard, peril, danger.

risicoso, *rĭsĭkō'sō,* a. hazardous, dangerous.

risma, *rĭs'mā,* f. ream of paper ; faction, party.

riso, *rĕ'sō,* m. (risa, f.pl.) laugh, laughter.

riso, *rĕ'sō,* m. rice.

risolvere, *rĭsōl'vĕrĕ,* v. a. ir. to dissolve, to melt ; to reduce ; to resolve, to determine ; [solutely, determinately.

risolutamente, *–sōlŭtāmĕn'tĕ,* ad. resolutely, determinately.

risoluto, *–sōlŭ'tō,* a. dissolved ; resolute.

risoluzione, *–lŭtzĭō'nĕ,* f. resolution ; decision. [semble.

risomigliare, *–sōmĭlyā'rĕ,* v. a. to resemble.

risonanza, *–sōnān'tzā,* f. resounding, sound.

risonare, *–nā'rĕ,* v. n. to resound. [tion.

risorto, *–sōr'tō,* m. royal power ; jurisdiction.

risovvenire, *–sōvvĕnĕ'rĕ,* v. n. to remember. [to spare.

risparmiare, *rĭspārmĭā'rĕ,* v. a. to save, to spare.

rispettabile, *–pĕttā'bĭlĕ,* a. respectable, venerable. [honour.

rispettare, *–pĕttā'rĕ,* v. a. to respect, to honour.

rispetto, *–pĕt'tō,* m. respect, regard, consideration ; **a –, in –, per –,** in comparison, as for, as to, on account of ; **per di,** for the sake of.

rispettoso, *–pĕttō'sō,* a. respectful.

risplendere, *rĭsplĕn'dĕrĕ,* v. n. to shine ; to be brilliant. [correspondence.

rispondenza, *rĭspōndĕn'tzā,* f. conformity,

rispondere, *–pōn'dĕrĕ,* v. a. & n. ir. to answer, to reply ; to correspond, to agree, to suit ; to be answerable ; **rispondersi,** *–pōn'dĕrsĭ,* to consent.

risposta, *–pōs'tā,* f. answer.

rissa, *rĭs'sā,* f. strife, dispute.

rissare, *–sā'rĕ,* v. n. to quarrel, to dispute.

ristabilire, *rĭstābĭlĕ'rĕ,* v. a. to restore, to re-establish. [stanch, to stop.

ristagnare, *–stānyā'rĕ,* v. a. to solder ; to stanch, to stop.

ristampa, *–stām'pā,* f. re-impression, new edition.

ristare, *–stā'rĕ,* v. n., **ristarsi,** *–stār'sĭ,* to stop, to cease, to discontinue.

ristaurare, *see* **restaurare.**

ristorare, *–stōrā'rĕ,* v. a. to restore ; to reward. [tion.

ristorazione, *–tzĭō'nĕ,* f. comfort, restoration.

ristretto, *–strĕt'tō,* m. abridgment ; epitome ; –, a. restricted, straitened, compressed ; abridged.

ristringere, *–strĭn′jĕrĕ,* v. a. ir. to restrain; to join, to unite; to force.

ristucco, *–stŭk′kŏ,* a. surfeited; weary.

risultare, *see* **resultare.**

risultato, *see* **resultato.**

ritardamento, *–tărdămĕn′tŏ,* m., **ritardanza,** *–dăn′tză,* f. delay, stop; deferring, hindrance.

ritardare, *–tărdā′rĕ,* v. a. to retard.

ritardazione, *–tzĭō′nĕ,* f. retarding, delay.

ritardo, *–tăr′dŏ,* m. delay; stop; obstruction.

ritegno, *–tĕn′yŏ,* m. reservedness, reserve; self-possession, moderation, discretion; prop; hindrance; support, defence; retentive faculty, memory.

ritenere, *–tĕnĕ′rĕ,* v. a. ir. to retain; to preserve. [mory.

ritenitiva, *–nĭtĕ′vă,* f. retentiveness; me-

ritenuto, *–nŭ′tŏ,* a. retained; reserved; discreet, cautious; self-possessed.

ritirare, *–tĭrā′rĕ,* v. a. to draw back, to take away; to withdraw, to retire; **ritirarsi,** *–răr′sĭ,* to retire, to withdraw.

ritirata, *–tĭrā′tă,* f. retreat; evasion, subterfuge; water-closet.

ritiro, *–tĕ′rŏ,* m. retirement, retreat.

ritmico, *rĭt′mĭkŏ,* a. rhythmical, harmonious.

ritmo, *rĭt′mŏ,* m. rhythm; measure.

rito, *rĕ′tŏ,* m. rite, ceremony; custom.

ritocco, *rĭtŏk′kŏ,* m. retouching; –, a. retouched.

ritornare, *–tŏrnā′rĕ,* v. a. to return, to send back, to restore; –, v. n. to come back. [chorus.

ritornello, *–nĕl′lŏ,* m. (mus.) burden,

ritorno, *–tŏr′nŏ,* m. return; net gain.

ritorre, *–tŏr′rĕ,* v. a. to remove, to retake.

ritorta, *–tŏr′tă,* f. tie, band.

ritrarre, *–trăr′rĕ,* v. a. ir. to draw, to extract; to take a portrait; to take off; to withdraw; **egli ritrae dal padre,** he takes after his father; **ritrarsi,** *–trăr′sĭ,* to retire; to disengage oneself from; to change one's mind; to repent; to be disheartened.

ritratta, *–trăt′tă,* f. retreat.

ritrattare, *–tă′rĕ,* v. a. to discourse upon again; to retract. [profit.

ritratto, *–trăt′tŏ,* m. portrait; description;

ritrosa, *–trŏ′să,* f. fowling-net; snare; entanglement; channel.

ritroso, *–trŏ′sŏ,* m. whirlpool; –, a. stubborn; peevish; a –, against the grain; in an opposite sense.

ritrovare, *–trŏvā′rĕ,* v. a. to find again; to find out, to invent. [sembly.

ritrovo, *–trŏ′vŏ,* m. meeting; circle, as-

ritto, *rĭt′tŏ,* a. right; straight; upright; just; **ritto ritto,** quite straight; –, ad. straight, directly.

rituale, *rĭtŭā′lĕ,* m. ritual.

riunione, *–ŭnĭō′nĕ,* f. renewal of friendship.

riunire, *–ŭnē′rĕ,* v. a. to reunite; to reconcile.

riuscire, *–ŭsshē′rĕ,* v. n. to succeed, to prosper; to come to an end.

riuscita, *–ŭsshē′tă,* f. success, issue, progress.

riva, *rē′vă,* f. seashore, bank.

rivale, *rĭvā′lĕ,* m. rival, competitor.

rivalità, *–nălĭtă′,* f. rivalry, competition.

rivalsa, *–văl′să,* f. (com.) reimbursement.

rivangare, *–vāngā′rĕ,* v. a. to hoe again; (fig.) to investigate. [again.

rivarcare, *–vărkā′rĕ,* v. n. to pass over

rivedere, *–vĕdē′rĕ,* v. a. ir. to see again; to revise, to review.

rivelare, *–vĕlā′rĕ,* v. a. to reveal.

rivelazione, *–tzĭō′nĕ,* f. revelation.

rivendere, *–vĕn′dĕrĕ,* v. a. to sell again, to retail.

rivendita, *–dē′tă,* f. exchange, truck.

rivendicare, *–dĭkā′rĕ,* v. a. to revenge.

rivenire, *–vĕnē′rĕ,* v. n. ir. to come again, to return.

riverberare, *see* **reverberare.**

riverenza, *–vĕrĕn′tză,* f. veneration; reverence, bow. [to salute.

riverire, *–rē′rĕ,* v. a. to revere, to respect;

riversare, *–vĕrsā′rĕ,* v. a. & n. to pour out, to overset; to overflow.

riverso, *–vĕr′sŏ,* m. reverse; wrong side; overflow; misfortune.

riviera, *–vĭē′ră,* f. coast, sea-shore; river.

rivincita, *–vĭn′dshĭtă,* f. reconquering.

rivista, *–vĭs′tă,* f. review.

rivo, *rē′vŏ,* m. brook, stream.

rivocare, *rĭvŏkā′rĕ,* v. a. to recall, to repeal; to annul.

rivocazione, *–tzĭō′nĕ,* f. revocation, recall, repeal.

rivolgere, *–vŏl′jĕrĕ,* v. a. ir. to revolve; to wrap up; to engage; **rivolgersi,** *–vŏl′jĕrsĭ,* to turn against; to change one's mind. [bellion.

rivolta, *–vŏl′tă,* f. turning; change; re-

rivoltare, *–tā′rĕ,* v. a. & n. to turn, to invert; to revolt; **rivoltarsi,** *–tăr′sĭ,* to revolt.

rivoltella, *–vŏltĕl′lă,* f. revolver.

rivoluzionario, *–vŏlŭtzĭŏnā′rĭŏ,* m. revolutionist; –, a. revolutionary.

rivoluzione, *–tzĭō′nĕ,* f. revolution, rebellion; change. [erect.

rizzare, *rĭtzā′rĕ,* v. a. to hoist, to raise, to

roba, *rŏ′bă,* f. goods, articles, victuals, chattels, pl.; stuff; robe, gown.

robaccia, *rŏbăt′shă,* f. trash, trifles, pl.;

robbia, *rŏb′bĭă,* f. madder. [slut.

robustezza, *rŏbŭstĕt′ză,* f. sturdiness, vigour. [sturdy.

robusto, *–bŭs′tŏ,* a. robust, vigorous,

rocaggine, *–kăd′jĭnĕ,* f. hoarseness.

rocca, *rŏk′kă,* f. rock; fortress.

roccetto, *rŏtshĕt′tŏ,* m. rochet, surplice.

rocchetto, *rŏkkĕt′tŏ,* m. surplice; bobbin.

rocchio, *rŏk′kĭŏ,* m. piece of wood; block of stone. [dirt.

roccia, *rŏt′shă,* f. rock; precipice; filth,

rocco, *rŏk′kŏ,* m. crosier; rook (at chess).

roco, *rŏ′kŏ,* a. hoarse; uncouth.

rodere, *rŏ′dĕrĕ,* v. a. ir. to gnaw, to nibble.

Rodomonte, *rŏdŏmŏn′tĕ,* m. Rodomont, bully.

rogare, *rŏgä′rĕ*, v. a. (law) to draw up a deed, to contract, to subscribe.

rogna, *rŏn′yä*, f. scab, mange.

rognoso, *rŏnyŏ′sŏ*, a. scabby, leprous.

rogo, *rŏ′gŏ*, m. funeral pile; −, *rŏ′gŏ*, m. brier; bramble.

romaiuolo, *rŏmäïŭŏ′lŏ*, m. ladle.

romano, *mä′nŏ*, m. steel-yard.

romanticismo, *−mäntïdshïs′mŏ*, m. romanticism.

romantico, *−män′tïkä*, a. romantic.

romanzesco, *−tzĕs′kŏ*, a. romantic.

romanziere, *−tzïĕ′rĕ*, m. romancer.

romanzo, *−mān′tzŏ*, m. romance, novel.

rombo, *rŏm′bŏ*, m, humming, rumbling, whizzing; turbot; rhombus.

romeo, *rŏmä′ŏ*, m. pilgrim (going to Rome).

romitaggio, *−mïtä′jŏ*, m. hermitage, solitude.

romito, *−mï′tŏ*, m. hermit; −, a. solitary.

romitorio, *−mï′tŏ*, m. hermitage.

romore, *−mŏ′rĕ*, m. noise, uproar.

romoreggiare, *−rĕdjä′rĕ*, v. n. to make a noise.

romorio, *−mŏ′rĭŏ*, m. noise, clatter.

rompere, *rŏm′pĕrĕ*, v. a. ir. to break; to interrupt; to stop; to hinder; − **il capo a**, to teaze.

rompicapo, *−pïkä′pŏ*, m. tiresome person.

rompicollo, *−kŏl′lŏ*, m. break-neck; precipice; dangerous man.

ronca, *rŏn′kä*, f. hedging-bill. [thistles.

roncare, *−kä′rĕ*, v. a. to weed, to clear of

ronchione, *−kïŏ′nĕ*, m. block, log.

ronciglio, *−tshïl′yŏ*, m. hook, harpoon.

ronda, *rŏn′dä*, f. round, patrol.

rondine, *rŏn′dïnĕ*, f. (poet.) swallow.

ronzare, *−tzä′rĕ*, v. n. to buzz; to hum; to ramble.

ronzino, *−tzē′nŏ*, m. nag, pony.

ronzio, *rŏntzē′ŏ*, m. buzzing, humming.

ronzone, *−tzŏ′nĕ*, m. stallion; humble-

rorido, *rŏ′rïdŏ*, a. (poet.) dewy. [bee.

rosa, *rŏ′sä*, f. rose; − **canina**, sweet briar.

rosaceo, *rŏsä′dshĕŏ*, a. rosy.

rosaio, *−sä′ŏ*, m. rose-bush; rosary.

rosario, *−sä′rïŏ*, m. rosary.

roseo, *rŏ′sĕŏ*, a. (poet.) rosy.

roseto, *rŏsä′tŏ*, m. bed of roses; garden of roses. [monds &c.

rosetta, *−sĕt′tä*, f. little rose, rose of diamonds &c.

rosicare, *−sïkä′rĕ*, v. a. to gnaw, to nibble.

rosignuolo, *−sïnyŭŏ′lŏ*, m. nightingale.

rosmarino, *rŏsmärē′nŏ*, m. rosemary.

rosolare, *rŏsŏlä′rĕ*, v. a. to fry, to roast.

rosolia, *−sŏlï′ä*, f. measles, pl.

rosolio, *−sŏ′lïŏ*, m. rosolis.

rospo, *rŏs′pŏ*, m. toad.

rossastro, *−säs′trŏ*, a. reddish.

rossiccio, *−sït′shŏ*, **rossigno**, *−sïn′yŏ*, a. reddish.

rosso, *rŏs′sŏ*, m. red colour; −, a. red.

rossore, *−sŏ′rĕ*, m. blush, redness.

rosta, *rŏs′tä*, f. fan.

rostro, *rŏs′trŏ*, m. beak, bill.

rota, *rŏ′tä*, f. wheel.

rotaia, *rŏtä′ä*, f. cart-rut, track of a wheel.

rotare, *−tä′rĕ*, v. a. & n. to break upon the wheel; to wheel, to go round like a wheel; to rotate.

rotazione, *−tzïŏ′nĕ*, f. rotation, turning.

rotella, *−tĕl′lä*, f. buckler; small wheel; knee-pan.

rotolare, *−tŏlä′rĕ*, v. a. to roll.

rotolo, *rŏ′tŏlŏ*, m. roll, scroll.

rotondare, *rŏtŏndä′rĕ*, v.a.to (make)round.

rotondità, *−dïtä′*, f. roundness.

rotondo, *−tŏn′dŏ*, a. round, circular.

rotta, *rŏt′tä*, f. rupture, breach; rout; consternation.

rottame, *−tä′mĕ*, m. crumbs, pl.; rubbish.

rotto, *rŏt′tŏ*, m. break, rupture.

rottura, *−tŏ′rä*, f. rupture, fracture; rent, cleft, gap, opening, breach; hernia.

rovaio, *rŏvä′ŏ*, m. northwind.

rovello, *−vĕl′lŏ*, m. rage, fury.

rovente, *−vĕn′tĕ*, a. red-hot.

rovere, *rŏ′vĕrĕ*, m. holm-oak.

rovesciare, *rŏvĕsshä′rĕ*, v.a. to overthrow, to overturn, to spill.

rovescio, *−vĕssh′ŏ*, m. wrong side, reverse; heavy shower; reprimand.

roveto, *−vä′tŏ*, m. hedge of thorns.

rovina, *−vē′nä*, f. ruin, decay, destruction.

rovinare, *−vïnä′rĕ*, v. a. to ruin, to demolish; −, v. n. to fall headlong; to fall into ruins.

rovinio, *−vïnï′ŏ*, m. great noise; precipice.

rovinoso, *−vïnŏ′sŏ*, a. impetuous, furious.

rovistare, *−vïstä′rĕ*, v. a. to rummage.

rozza, *rŏt′zä*, f. jade. [clownish, rude.

rozzo, *rŏt′zŏ*, a. rugged, coarse, raw,

ruba, *rŏ′bä*, f. robbery, rapine.

rubacchiare, *rŭbäkkïä′rĕ*, v. a. to pilfer.

rubacuori, *−kŭŏ′rï*, f. coquette.

rubare, *rŭbä′rĕ*, v. a. to steal, to rob.

rubesto, *−bĕs′tŏ*, a. fierce; horrible.

rubicondo, *−bïkŏn′dŏ*, a. ruddy, rubicund.

rubido, *rŏ′bïdŏ*, a. rugged, rough.

rubigine, *rŭbĕ′jïnĕ*, f. (poet.) rust.

rubino, *rŭbē′nŏ*, m. ruby.

rubizzo, *−bï′zŏ*, a. robust, strong, stout.

rubo, *rŏ′bŏ*, m. (poet.) bramble.

rubrica, *rŭbrē′kä*, f. rubric; −, *rŏ′brïkä*, f. red chalk; rubric. [(poet.) red.

rubro, *rŏ′brŏ*, m. briar, bramble; −, a.

rude, *rŏ′dĕ*, a. rude, rough, coarse.

rudimento, *rŭdïmĕn′tŏ*, m. rudiment, principle.

ruffa, *rŭf′fä*, f. throng, crowd.

ruffianesimo, *−fïänä′sïmŏ*, m. cunning, pimping.

ruffiano, *−fïä′nŏ*, m. pimp, go-between.

ruga, *rŏ′gä*, f. wrinkle.

rugghiare, *rŭgghïä′rĕ*, v. n. to roar.

ruggine, *rŭd′jïnĕ*, f. rust; mildew; grudge,

rugginoso, *−djïnŏ′sŏ*, a. rusty. [hatred.

ruggire, *−djï′rĕ*, v. n. to roar.

ruggito, *−djï′tŏ*, m. roar, roaring.

rugiada, *rŏjä′dä*, f. dew; comfort; help.

rugumare, *−gŭmä′rĕ*, v. a. to chew, to ruminate; to consider.

ruina, *see* **rovina**.

ruinare, *see* **rovinare**.

rullare, rŭllā'rĕ, v. a. to roll, to whirl.
rullo, rŭl'lŏ, m. roller.
ruminare, rŭmīnā'rĕ, v. a. & n. to ruminate; to consider.
rumore, see romore.
ruolo, rŭō'lŏ, m. roll, catalogue, register.
ruota, rŭō'tă, f. wheel; turn.
ruotare, -tā'rĕ, v. a. to wheel; to rotate.
rupe, rō'pĕ, f. rock, cliff.
rurale, rĭrā'lĕ, a. rural, rustic.
ruscello, rŭsshĕl'lŏ, m. brook, rivulet.
ruspo, rŭs'pŏ, m. sequin.
russare, rŭssā'rĕ, v. n. to snore.
rusticità, -tĭshĭtā', f. rusticity, rudeness.
rustico, rŭs'tĭkŏ, a. rustic; clownish; **legare alla -a,** to sew, to stitch (books).
ruta, rō'tă, f. rue.
rutilare, rŭtĭlā'rĕ, v. n. (poet.) to shine, to glitter.
ruttare, rŭttā'rĕ, v. n. to belch, to vomit.
rutto, rŭt'tŏ, m. belching, ructation.
ruvidezza, -vĭdĕt'ză, **ruvidità,** -dĭtā', f. roughness, coarseness; rudeness.
ruvido, rō'vĭdŏ, a. rough, rugged; rude.
ruzzare, rŭdză'rĕ, v. n. to play the fool, to toy.
ruzzo, rŭd'zŏ, m. playfulness; wantonness.
ruzzola, rŭd'zŏlă, f. spinning-top.
ruzzolare, -dzŏlā'rĕ, v. a. & n. to play with a top; to sink a ship.

S.

sabato, să'bătŏ, m. Saturday.
sabbia, săb'biă, f. sand, gravel.
sabbione, -bĭō'nĕ, m. sandy ground.
sabbioso, -bĭō'sŏ, a. sandy.
saccardo, săkkăr'dŏ, m. soldier's boy; blackguard. [insolent.
saccente, sătshĕn'tĕ, a. learned; cunning; self-conceit.
saccenteria, -tĕrī'ă, f. self-conceit.
saccheggiare, săkkĕdjā'rĕ, v. a. to sack, to pillage. [ing, pillage.
saccheggio, -kĕd'jŏ, m. sacking, plundering, pillage.
sacchetto, -kĕt'tŏ, m. small bag; satchel.
sacco, săk'kŏ, m. sack, large bag; sackcloth; plundering. [plunder.
saccomanno, -măn'nŏ, m. soldier's scrub; plunder.
sacerdotale, sădshĕrdŏtā'lĕ, a. sacerdotal, priestly.
sacerdote, -dŏ'tĕ, m. priest.
sacerdotessa, -dŏtĕs'să, f. priestess.
sacerdozio, -dŏ'tzĭŏ, m. priesthood.
sacra, să'kră, f. consecration.
sacramentale, -mĕntā'lĕ, a. sacramental.
sacramentare, -tā'rĕ, v. a. to administer the sacrament; **sacramentarsi,** -tăr'sĭ, to receive the sacrament.
sacramento, -mĕn'tŏ, m. sacrament; oath; Lord's supper.
sacrare, săkrā'rĕ, v. a. to consecrate.
sacrificare, -krĭfĭkā'rĕ, v. a. to sacrifice; to slay. [sacrifice.
sacrificio, -fĭ'djŏ, **sacrifizio,** -ĭzĭŏ, m. sacrifice.
sacrilegio, -lĕ'djŏ, m. sacrilege.

sacrilego, -krĕ'lĕgŏ, a. sacrilegious; impious, infidel.
sacro, să'krŏ, a. sacred, consecrated; execrable; **– morbo,** m. falling-sickness.
sacrosanto, -săn'tŏ, a. sacred, holy.
saetta, săĕt'tă, f. arrow; dart; lancet; thunderbolt. [from a bow.
saettare, -tā'rĕ, v. a. to dart; to shoot
sagace, săgā'dshĕ, a. sagacious.
sagacità, -dshĭtā', **sagacia,** -gā'dshĭă, f. sagacity.
saggezza, sădjĕt'ză, f. wisdom, prudence.
saggiare, -djā'rĕ, v. a. to try, to taste.
saggina, -djē'nă, f. millet; Turkey wheat.
saggio, săd'jŏ, m. wise man; assay, trial; proof; taste; sample; –, a. wise, prudent.
sagittario, săjĭttā'rĭŏ, m. archer.
sagliente, săljĕn'tĕ, a. ascending.
sagra, să'gră, f. consecration.
sagrestia, -grĕstē'ă, f. sacristy, vestry.
saia, să'ĭă, f. fine thin serge.
saio, să'ĭŏ, **saione,** săĭō'nĕ, m. long robe; cassock; coat of mail.
sala, să'lă, f. hall; dining-room; parlour.
salace, -lā'dshĕ, a. salacious, salty; libidinous.
salame, -lā'mĕ, m. salt-meat; salt-pork.
salamistro, -mĭs'trŏ, m. would-be wit, ignorant.
salamoia, -mŏ'ĭă, f. brine, pickle.
salare, -lā'rĕ, v. a. to salt, to pickle.
salariare, -rĭā'rĕ, v. n. to pay a salary.
salario, -lā'rĭŏ, m. salary. [blood.
salassare, -lăssā'rĕ, v. a. to bleed, to let
salasso, -lăs'sŏ, m. blood-letting.
salceto, săldshĕ'tŏ, m. willow-plot; intricate affair. [wood.
salcigno, -dshĭn'yŏ, a. knotty, scragged (of
salcio, săl'dshŏ, m. willow-tree.
salda, săl'dă, f. solder; paste; starch.
saldare, -dā'rĕ, v. a. to solder; to heal up; to close an account.
saldatura, -tō'ră, f. soldering; healing up; seam; settling of an account.
saldo, săl'dŏ, m. balance, settling of an account; –, a. sound, whole; solid, massive.
sale, să'lĕ, m. salt; wit. [stout; healthy.
salgemma, -djĕm'mă, f. mineral salt.
saliare, săltā'rĕ, a. sumptuous, splendid.
salice, să'lĭdshĕ, m. willow-tree.
saliera, săltĕ'ră, f. salt-pit; salt-box.
salina, -lē'nă, f. salt-pit; salt-meat; salt
salino, -lē'nŏ, a. saline; saltish. [fish.
salire, -lē'rĕ, v. n. to ascend.
saliscendi, săltsshĕn'dĭ, m. latch of a door.
salita, -lē'tă, f. ascent, rising ground.
saliva, -lē'vă, f. saliva, spittle.
salma, săl'mă, f. (poet.) burden, weight; spoil. [psalms; to praise.
salmeggiare, -mĕdjā'rĕ, v. a. to sing
salmeria, -mĕrī'ă, f. baggage.
salmista, -mĭs'tă, m. psalmist.
salmo, săl'mŏ, m. psalm.
salmodia, -mŏdī'ă, f. psalmody.
salnitro, -nē'trŏ, m. nitre, saltpetre.
salone, săl'ō'nĕ, m. saloon. [ment.
salsa, săl'să, f. sauce; seasoning; chastise-
salsedine, -sĕ'dĭnĕ, f. saltness.

salsedinoso, –sĕdĭnŏ' sŏ, a. salty.
salsiccia, –sĭt' shă, f. sausage.
salso, săl' sŏ, a. briny; biting.
saltabeccare, săltăbĕkkă' rĕ, saltabel-
lare, –bĕllă' rĕ, v. n. to gambol; to leap
about.   [man's jacket.
saltambarco, –tămbăr' kŏ, m. country-
saltare, –tă' rĕ, v. n. to jump, to leap, to
dance, to hop, to skip.
saltellare, –tĕllă' rĕ, salterellare, –tĕ-
rĕllă' rĕ, v. n. to skip, to gambol; to go
tripping along.   [book; nun's veil.
salterio, –tĕ' rĭŏ, saltero, –rŏ, m. psalm-
saltimbanco, –tĭmbăn' kŏ,m. mountebank;
ballad-singer.
salto, săl' tŏ, m. leap; jump, skip, bound.
saluberrimo, –sălŭbĕr' rĭmŏ, a. very salubrious.
salubre, –lŏ' brĕ, a. salubrious, wholesome.
salubrità, –lăbrĭtă', f. salubrity.
salume, –lŏ' mĕ, m. salt-meat, fish, &c.;
salt-pit.
salutare, –lŭtă' rĕ, v. a. to salute, to greet,
to hail; –, a. salutary, wholesome. [ing.
salutazione, –tzĭŏ' nĕ, f. salutation, greet-
salute, –lŏ' tĕ, f. health; salutation, safety.
saluto, –lŏ' tŏ, m. salute, salutation.
salva, săl' vă, f. volley, discharge.
salvacondotto, –kŏndŏt' tŏ, m. safe-conduct.
salvadanaio, –dănă' ŏ,m. money-box.
salvaguardia, –găr' dĭă, f. safeguard.
salvare, sălvă' rĕ, v. a. to save.
salvatico, –vă' tĭkŏ, m. wild forest; –, a.
wild, savage.
Salvatore, –tŏ' rĕ, m. Saviour.
salvazione, –tzĭŏ' nĕ, f. salvation; preservation.
salvezza, –vĕt' ză, f. safety; salvation.
salvia, săl' vĭă, f. (bot.) sage.
salvietta, –vĭĕt' tă, f. napkin.
salvo, săl' vŏ, m. agreement, contract; –, a.
safe; sure; –, pr. besides, except; –che,
provided that.
sambuca, sămbŏ' kă, f. sackbut.
sambuco, –bŏ' kŏ, m. elder-tree.
sampogna, –pŏn' yă, f. pipe, flageolet.
san, săn, for santo.
sanare, sănă' rĕ, v. a. & n. to cure, to
heal; to get cured, to heal.
sandalo, săn' dălŏ, m. sandal-wood; sandal.
sangue, săn' gŭĕ, m. blood; race.
sanguigna, –gŭĭn' yă, f. red lead.
sanguigno, –gŭĭn' yŏ, a. sanguine; bloody;
plethoric; blood-coloured.   [ding.
sanguinaccio, –nă' shŏ, m. black-pud-
sanguinario, –nă' rĭŏ, a. sanguinary;
cruel.   [coloured.
sanguineo, –gŭ' nĕŏ, a. sanguine; blood-
sanguinolente, –nŏlĕn' tĕ, a. bloody;
blood-thirsty.
sanguinoso, –nŏ' sŏ, a. bloody, sanguinary.
sanguisuga, –sŏ' gă, f. leech; blood-sucker.
sanie, să' nĭĕ, f. sanies; (poet.) matter, pus.
sanità, sănĭtă', f. health.
sanna, săn' nă, f. wild boar's tusk.

sano, să' nŏ, a. sound, healthy; entire,
whole.
sansa, săn' să, f. chestnut-skin.   [whole.
santificare, săntĭfĭkă' rĕ, v. a. to sanctify,
to canonize.
santificazione, –tzĭŏ' nĕ, f. sanctification.
santimonia, –mŏ' nĭă, santità, –tĭtă', f.
holiness; sua –, His Holiness.
santo, săn' tŏ, m. saint; –, a. holy, sacred,
santoccio, –tŏt' shŏ, m. dunce. [blessed.
santolo, săn' tŏlŏ, m. godfather.
santuario, –tŭă' rĭŏ, m. relic; sanctuary.
sanzionare, –tzĭŏnă' rĕ, v. a. to sanction.
sanzione, –tzĭŏ' nĕ, f. sanction; confirmation.
sapere, săpĕ' rĕ, m. knowledge, science,
erudition; –, v. a. ir. to know, to understand; to smack, to smell of; – a mente,
to know by heart.
sapiente, –pĭĕn' tĕ, a. knowing, well informed, skilful.   [wisely.
sapientemente, –mĕn' tĕ, ad. learnedly,
sapienza, –pĭĕn' tză, f. wisdom.
saponaio, săpŏnă' ŏ, m. soap-boiler.
sapone, –pŏ' nĕ, m. soap.
saponeria, –nĕrĭ' ă, f. soap-manufactory.
saporare, –pŏră' rĕ, v. n. to taste, to
savour, to relish.
sapore, –pŏ' rĕ, m. savour, taste, relish.
saporito, –rĭ' tŏ. saporoso, –rŏ' sŏ, a.
savoury; agreeable.
saprosità, –rŏsĭtă', f. savouriness.
saputa, –pŏ' tă, f. knowledge, science.
saputo, –pŏ' tŏ, a. known, wise; cautious.
saracinesca, sărădshĭnĕs' kă, f. portcullis.
sarcasmo, sărkăs' mŏ, m. sarcasm.
sarcastico, –kăs' tĭkŏ, a. sarcastic.
sarchiare, săr̆kĭă' rĕ, v. a. to weed.
sarchio, săr̆ kĭŏ, m. weeding-hook.
sardella, –dĕl' lă, sardina, –dĕ' nă, f.
sardine, pilchard.
sargia, săr' jă, f. serge (stuff).
sarmento, sărmĕn' tŏ, m. vine-branch.
sarte, săr' tĕ, f. sartiame, –tĭă' mĕ, m.
(mar.) cordage, shrouds, pl.
sarto, săr' tŏ, sartore, –tŏ' rĕ, m. tailor.
sasso, săs' sŏ, m. stone; rock; tomb.
Satana, să' tănă, Satanasso, –năs' sŏ, m.
Satan, evil spirit.
satanico, –tă' nĭkŏ, a. satanic, diabolical.
satira, să' tĭră, f. satire, lampoon.
satireggiare, –tĭrĕdjă' rĕ, v. a. to satirise.
satirico, –tĭ' rĭkŏ, a. & m.satirical; satirist.
satiro, să' tĭrŏ, m. satyr; satirist.
satisfare, see soddisfare.
sativo, sătĭ' vŏ, a. fit for sowing.
satollare, –tŏllă' rĕ, v. a. to satiate.
satollo, –tŏl' lŏ, a. satiated, glutted.
satrapo, –tră' pŏ, m. satrap.
saturare, –tŭră' rĕ, v.a. to saturate, to cloy.
saturità, –tŭrĭtă', f. saturity.
saturnale, –tŭrnă' lĕ, a. saturnal; noisy.
saturnino, –tŭrnă' nŏ, saturnio, –tăr' nĭŏ,
a. saturnine, gloomy.
saturo, să' tŭrŏ, see satollo.
saviezza, săvĭĕt' ză, f. wisdom.

savio, *să´vĭŏ*, m. wise man, philosopher;
　—, a. sage, wise; learned.

savore, *–vō´rĕ*, m. savour, relish; sauce.

savorra, *–vŏr´rä*, f. ballast; cargo

sauro, *săŭ´rŏ*, a. sorrel; light bay.

saziare, *sätzĭä´rĕ*, v.a. to satiate, to satisfy.

sazietà, *säzĭĕtä´*, f. satiety.

sazio, *să´tzĭŏ*, a. satiated, cloyed.

sbaccellare, *sbätshĕllä´rĕ*, v. a. to shell,
　husk.　　　　　　　　　　　　[inattention.

sbadataggine, *–dätä´jĭnĕ*, f. listlessness,

sbadato, *–dä´tŏ*, a. inattentive, negligent.

sbadigliare, *–dĭlyĭä´rĕ*, v. n. to yawn; to
　gape.

sbadiglio, *–dĭl´yĭŏ*, m. yawn; gaping.

sbagliare, *sbälyä´rĕ*, v. n. to mistake, to
　be mistaken.

sbaglio, *sbäl´yŏ*, m. mistake, blunder.

sbaldanzire, *–däntzĭ´rĕ*, v.a. to despond.

sbalestrare, *–lĕsträ´rĕ*, v. a. to miss the
　mark.　　　　　　　　　　　　　[falsehoods.

sballare, *sbällä´rĕ*, v. a. to unpack; to tell

sballone, *–lō´nĕ*, m. story-teller, romancer.

sbalordimento, *sbälŏrdĭmĕn´tŏ*, m. be-
　wilderment, amazement.

sbalordire, *–dī´rĕ*, v. a. to bewilder, to
　confound; —, v. n. to be amazed.

sbalzare, *sbältzä´rĕ*, v. a. & n. to throw,
　to fling; to leap; to rush.

sbalzo, *sbäl´tzŏ*, m. bound, bounce, somerset.

sbandire, *sbändī´rĕ*, v. a. to dismiss, to
　disband.　　　　　　　　　　　　　[disperse.

sbaragliare, *sbärälyä´rĕ*, v.a. to rout, to

sbaraglio, *–räl´yŏ*, m. rout, disorder.

sbarattare, *–rättä´rĕ*, v. a. to rout, to
　disperse.　　　　　　　　　　　　[rass.

sbarazzare, *–rätzä´rĕ*, v. n. to disembar-

sbarbare, *sbärbä´rĕ*, v. a. to eradicate, to
　bereave.

sbarbato, *–bä´tŏ*, a. beardless; uprooted.

sbarcare, *–kä´rĕ*, v. a. to disembark.

sbarco, *sbär´kŏ*, m. disembarking, landing.

sbarra, *sbär´rä*,f. bar, rail; stop; barricade.

sbarrare, *–rä´rĕ*, v. a. to bar, to barri-
　cade; to unbar.

sbassare, *sbässä´rĕ*, v.a. to lower, to abate.

sbattere, *sbät´tĕrĕ*, v. a. to beat, to toss,
　to abate; to refute.

sbattezzare, *–tĕdzä´rĕ*, v. a. to force to
　renounce the Christan faith.

sbattimento, *–tĭmĕn´tŏ*, m. tossing, shak-
　ing; agitation.

sbeffare, *sbĕffä´rĕ*, sbeffeggiare, *–fĕ-
　djä´rĕ*, v. a. to laugh at, to ridicule.

sbendare, *sbĕndä´rĕ*, v. a. to unband, to
　unveil.　　　　　　　　　　　　　[wry face.

sberleffo, *sbĕrlĕf´fŏ*,m.gash,scar; grimace,

sbertare, *–tä´rĕ*, v. a. to scoff, to mock.

sbiadito, *sbĭädī´tŏ*, a. light blue.

sbiancato, *sbĭänkä´tŏ*, a. whitish, pale.

sbieco, *sbĭĕ´kŏ*, a. awry, slant; crooked.

sbigottimento, *sbĭgŏttĭmĕn´tŏ*, m. dis-
　may, alarm.

sbigottire, *–gŏttī´rĕ*, v. a. & n. to terrify;
　to be frightened.

sbilanciamento, *–länchämĕn´tŏ*, m. out-
　weighing; bending downwards.

sbilanciare, *–dshä´rĕ*, v. a. to outweigh,
　to incline the scale.

sbilancio, *see* sbilanciamento.

sbilenco, *–lĕn´kŏ*, a. crooked, bow-legged.

sbirciare, *sbĭrdshä´rĕ*, v. a. to leer, to ogle.

sbirro, *see* birro.

sboccare, *sbŏkkä´rĕ*, v. n. to disembogue,
　to rush out, to overflow; to break off the
　neck of a bottle.

sboccatura, *–tō´rä*, f. mouth (of a river).

sbocciare, *–tshä´rĕ*, v. n. to open, to ex-
　pand (of flowers.)

sbocco, *sbŏk´kŏ*, m. mouth; irruption.

sbonzolare, *sbŏntzŏlä´rĕ*, v. n. to fall
　down; to crack.　　　　　　　[lay out money.

sborsare, *sbŏrsä´rĕ*, v. a. to disburse, to

sborso, *sbŏr´sŏ*, m. disbursement; sum
　paid.　　　　[button; to insult; to reproach.

sbottonare, *sbŏttŏnä´rĕ*, v. a. to un-

sbottoneggiare, *–nĕdjä´rĕ*, v. a. to sa-
　tirize, to ridicule; to iquz.

sbozzare, *sbŏtzä´rĕ*, v. a. to sketch; to
　rough-draw.

sbozzo, *sbŏt´zŏ*, m. sketch, rough draught.

sbracato, *sbräkä´tŏ*, a. without one's
　small-clothes; easy, delightful; immense.

sbraciare, *–dshä´rĕ*, v. a. & n. to stir the
　fire; to waste; to boast.

sbramare, *–mä´rĕ*, v. a. to sate one's ap-
　petite; to satisfy desire.

sbranare, *–nä´rĕ*, v. a. to tear in pieces.

sbrancare, *sbränkä´rĕ*, v. a. to lop off.

sbrano, *sbrä´nŏ*, m. tearing, rending.

sbrattare, *sbrättä´rĕ*, v. a. to clean, to
　empty; to disengage.

sbricio, *sbrē´dshĭŏ*, a. vile, wretched.

sbriciolare, *sbrĭdshŏlä´rĕ*, v.a. to crumble,
　to grind, to pulverize.

sbrigare, *sbrĭgä´rĕ*, v.a. to expedite, to
　despatch, to hasten.

sbrigliare, *sbrĭlyä´rĕ*, v.a. to unbridle.

sbrigliato, *–yä´tŏ*, a. unbridled, loose,
　impetuous.　　　　　　　[speak at random.

sbroccare, *sbrŏkkä´rĕ*, v. n. to vomit; to

sbrogliare, *sbrŏlyä´rĕ*, v.a. to disentangle.

sbruffare, *sbrŭffä´rĕ*, v. a. to spirt out; to
　besprinkle.

sbruffo, *sbrŭf´fŏ*, m. besputtering, gulp.

sbucare, *sbŭkä´rĕ*, v. a. & n. to come out
　of a hole; to draw out.

sbucciare, *–dshä´rĕ*, v. a. to bark, to
　skin.　　　　　　　　　　　　　[to rage.

sbuffare, *sbŭffä´rĕ*, v. n. to fume, to pant.

scabbia, *skäb´bĭä*, f. scab, itch.

scabro, *skä´brŏ*, scabroso, *–brŏ´sŏ*, a.
　scabby, rough, rugged, scraggy.　　　[ness.

scabrosità, *–brŏsĭtä´*, f. ruggedness; hard-

scabroso, *–brŏ´sŏ*, a. scabby, rugged,
　scraggy; hard.　　　　　　　　　　　[idly.

scacazzare, *–kätzä´rĕ*, v. a. to squander

scacchi, *skäk´kĭ*, m. pl. chess.

scacchiere, *–kĭä´rĕ*, m. chess-board.

scacciare, *skätshä´rĕ*, v. a. to drive away,
　to expel.

scacco, *skäk´kŏ*, m. square in a chess-
　board; — matto, check-mate.

scadere, skådä'rĕ, v. n. ir. to decay; to devolve.
scafo, skä'fŏ, m. hulk, skeleton of a ship.
scagionare, –igně're, v. a. to excuse.
scaglia, skäl'yä, f. scale of a fish or snake; sling; bark, shell. [to recount wonders.
scagliare, –yä're, v. a. to scale; to fling;
scaglione, –yŏ'nĕ, m. step; stairs, pl.; degree, progression.
scala, skä'lä, f.staircase, stairs; step; scale; ladder; (rail.) perron. [to scale.
scalare, –lä're, v. a. to take by escalade.
scalata, –lä'tä, f. escalade, storming.
scalcare, skälkä're, v. a. to tread upon, to
scalciare, –dshä'rĕ, v. a. to kick. [crush.
scalco, skäl'kŏ, m. steward, carver of meat.
scaldare, –dä'rĕ, v. a. to warm, to heat; to excite.
scaldatojo, –dätŏ'ŏ, m. warming-place.
scalea, see scala.
scaleo, see scala. [sacrifice.
scalfire, –fĕ'rĕ, v. a. to skin lightly, to
scalfittura, –fittŏ'rä, f. scratch.
scalino, skä'lĭnŏ, m. step, stair.
scalmana, skälmä'nä, f. pleurisy.
scalogno, skälŏŋ'yŏ, m. scallion, shalot.
scalpicciare, –pĭtshä're, scalpitare, –pĭtä'rĕ, v. a. to stamp upon, to trample under foot; to scorn.
scalpore, –pŏ'rĕ, m. noisy complaint, lamentation.
scaltrito, –trĭ'tŏ, scaltro, skäl'trŏ, a. cunning, crafty, sagacious.
scalzo, skäl'zŏ, a. unshod, bare; unarmed.
scambiare, skämbĭä'rĕ, v. a. to exchange; to truck. [frequent change.
scambietto, –bĭĕt'tŏ, m. caper, gambol;
scambievole, –bĭĕ'vŏlĕ, a. mutual, reciprocal.
scambio, skäm'bĭŏ, m. exchange, barter.
scamosciare, –mŏsshä'rĕ, v. a. to dress shammy leather. [save, to preserve.
scampare, skämpä'rĕ, v. a. to deliver, to
scampo, skäm'pŏ, m. escape, flight, refuge; safety; evasion. [cloth &c.).
scampolo, skäm'pŏlŏ, m. remnant (of
scamuzzolo, –mät'zŏlŏ, m. little bit.
scancellare, see cancellare.
scancio, –dshŏ'ŏ, a. slanting, sloping.
scandaglio, –däl'yŏ, m. plummet; examination.
scandalizzare, –lĭtzä'rĕ, v. a. to scandalise, to occasion scandal; scandalizzarsi, –tzär'sĭ, to be scandalised, to take
scandalo, skän'dälŏ, m.scandal. [offence.
scandaloso, –dälŏ'sŏ, a. scandalous.
scandella, –dĕl'lä, f. oats, pl.
scannafosso, skännäfŏs'sŏ, m. (mil.) kind of fortification. [to oppress.
scannare, –nä'rĕ, v. a. to cut the throat;
scannellare, –nĕllä'rĕ, v. a. to wind off.
scannello, –nĕl'lŏ, m. bureau, writing-desk; small bench. [bank.
scanno, skän'nŏ, m. seat, bench; sand-
scansare, –sä'rĕ, v. a. to remove out of the way; to avoid.
scansia, skänsĭ'ä, f. book-shelf.

scantonare, –tŏně'rĕ, v. a. to break off the concerns; to avoid. [flax.
scapecchiare, skäpĕkkĭä'rĕ, v. a. to card
scapestrato, –pĕsträ'tŏ, a. debauched.
scapezzare, –pĕtzä'rĕ, v. a. to lop off, to behead.
scapigliare, –pĭlyä'rĕ, v. a. & n. to ruffle, to dishevel; to lead a dissolute life.
scapitare, –pĭtä'rĕ, v. a. & n. to suffer loss.
scapito, skä'pĭtŏ, m. loss, damage.
scapolare, –pŏlä're, v. a. & n. to liberate, to rescue; to escape. [married.
scapolo, skä'pŏlŏ, a. free, disengaged; un-
scappare, skäppä'rĕ, v. n. to escape.
scappata, –pä'tä, f. escape, flight.
scappino, –pĕ'nŏ, m. sock.
scappucciare, –pätshä'rĕ, v. n. to stumble.
scappuccio, –pät'shŏ, m. fault, blunder.
scarabeo, skäräbä'ŏ, m. black beetle.
scarabocchiare, –bŏkkĭä're, v. a. to scribble, to scrawl. [scrawl.
scarabocchio, –bŏk'kĭŏ, m. scribbling,
scaracchiare, –räkkĭä'rĕ, v. a. to banter, to mock.
scarafaggio, –fäd'jŏ, m. scarabæus, beetle.
scaramazzo, –mät'zŏ, a. imperfectly round (of pearls); bunchy; irregular.
scaramuccia, –mät'shä, f. skirmish.
scaramucciare, –mätshä'rĕ, v. n. to skirmish.
scaraventare, –vĕntä'rĕ, v. a. to sling, to throw with great force.
scarco, skär'kŏ, m. (poet.) unloading, discharging. [(wool); to slander.
scardassare, –dässä're, v. a. to card
scardasso, –däs'sŏ, m. combing-card.
scarica, skä'rĭkä, f. unloading, landing; volley. [charge.
scaricare, –rĭkä're, v. a. to unload, to dis-
scarico, skä'rĭkŏ, m. unloading, discharge; –, a. unloaded, discharged, eased; free.
scarificare, –rĭfĭkä'rĕ, v. a. to scarify.
scarlattina, skärlättĭ'nä, f. scarlet-fever.
scarlatto, –lät'tŏ, m. scarlet.
scarmigliare, –mĭlyä'rĕ, v. a. to rumple, to ruffle, to entangle.
scarnire, skärnĕ'rĕ, v. a. to scarify, to slash; to flay.
scarno, skär'nŏ, a. emaciated, lean.
scarpa, skär'pä, f. shoe; scarp of a wall.
scarpellare, –pĕllä'rĕ, v. a. to chisel, to carve.
scarpello, –pĕl'lŏ, m. chisel. [carve.
scarpino, –pĕ'nŏ, m. small light shoe.
scarseggiare, –sĕdjä'rĕ, v. n. to be short of, to want; to be stingy. [penury.
scarsità, skärsĭtä', f. scarcity, sparingness;
scarso, skär'sŏ, a. scarcity; want; –, a. scarce, stingy, niggardly. [to set aside.
scartare, –tä'rĕ, v. a. to reject, to discard;
scassinare, skässĭnä'rĕ, v. a. to smash, to
scatola, skä'tŏlä, f. box, case. [destroy.
scattare, skättä'rĕ, v. a. & n. to dart, to let off; to pass; to escape.
scatto, skät'tŏ, m. discrepancy.
scaturigine, skätŭrĭ'jĭnĕ, f. source, spring.
scaturire, –rĕ'rĕ, v. n. to spring, to spout out; to rise, to issue.

scavalcare, *-vălkă'rĕ*, v. a. to dismount, to unhorse; (fig.) to supplant; —, v. n. to dismount.

scavallare, *-văllă'rĕ*, v. n. to play the wanton, to get frolicsome. *see* **scavalcare**; —, v. n. to play the wanton, to get frolicsome.

scavare, *skăvă'rĕ*, v. a. to excavate, to dig.

scavezzare, *-vĕtză'rĕ*, v. a. to break, to crack, to split.

scavo, *skă'vŏ*, m. hollow. | overstrain.

sceda, *sshă'dă*, f. nonsense, mockery, trifles.

scegliere, *sshĕl' yĕrĕ*, v. a. ir. to choose, to select; to pick out.

scelleraggine, *sshĕllĕrăd' jĭnĕ*, **scelleratezza**, *-tĕt' ză*, f. wickedness, villany.

scellerato, *-lĕră' tŏ*, m. scoundrel; —, a. wicked, villanous.

scellino, *-lĕ' nŏ*, m. shilling.

scelta, *sshĕl' tă*, f. selectness, exquisiteness.

sceltume, *-tŏ' mĕ*, m. refuse, trash.

scemare, *sshĕmă' rĕ*, v. a. & n. to diminish; to decay. | silly; foolish.

scemo, *sshă' mŏ*, a. diminished; deficient;

scempiaggine, *sshĕmpiăd' jĭnĕ*, **scem- piataggine**, *-piătăd' jĭnĕ*, f. foolishness.

scempiare, *-pĭă' rĕ*, v. a. to unfold, to explain. | a. simple; silly, imbecile.

scempiato, *-pĭă' tŏ*, **scempio**, *sshĕm' pĭŏ*, a. simple; silly, imbecile.

scena, *sshă' nă*, f. scene, stage, theatre.

scenario, *sshĕnă' rĭŏ*, m. actor's guide-book; play-bill; side-scenes, pl.

scendere, *sshĕn' dĕrĕ*, v. a. ir. to descend; to be descended.

sceneggiare, *sshĕnĕdjă' rĕ*, v. a. to re-present by scenery, to represent upon the stage; to declaim.

scenico, *sshă' nĭkŏ*, a. scenic, theatrical.

scernere, *sshĕr' nĕrĕ*, v. a. to discern; to choose, to select, to pick out.

scerpellone, *-pĕllŏ' nĕ*, m. great blunder.

scerre, *see* **scegliere**.

scesa, *sshă' să*, f. descent, declivity; rheum.

sceso, *sshă' sŏ*, a. descended, issued.

scetticismo, *sshĕttĭdshĭs' mŏ*, m. scepticism. | sceptic.

scettico, *sshĕt' tĭkŏ*, a. & m. sceptical;

scettro, *sshĕt' rŏ*, m. sceptre.

sceverare, *sshĕvĕră' rĕ*, v. a. to sever, to set apart; to wean.

scheda, *skă' dă*, f. note, billet, poll-ticket.

schedula, *skĕ' dălă*, f. little note.

scheggia, *skĕd' jă*, f. chip, splinter, crag.

scheggiare, *-djă' rĕ*, v. a. to cleave, to shatter, to shiver; —, v. n. to burst in pieces.

scheggio, *skĕd' jŏ*, m. cliff, rock; splinter.

scheletro, *skĕ' lĕtrŏ*, m. skeleton.

schema, *skă' mă*, m. scheme.

scherano, *skĕră' nŏ*, m. assassin, brigand.

schermo, *skĕr' mŏ*, m. defence; weapons, pl.

schernire, *-nĕ' rĕ*, v. a. to scorn, to deride.

scherno, *skĕr' nŏ*, m. scorn, derision; affront. | to jest, to joke, to banter.

scherzare, *-tză' rĕ*, v. n. to dally, to play, to jest, sport.

scherzevole, *see* **scherzoso**.

scherzo, *skĕr' tzŏ*, m. pleasantry, raillery, jest, sport.

scherzoso, *-tzŏ' sŏ*, a. playful, jocular.

schiaccia, *skĭăt' shă*, f. trap; wooden leg.

schiacciare, *-tshă' rĕ*, v. a. to crush, to bruise. | ears.

schiaffare, *skĭăffă' rĕ*, v. a. to box one's

schiaffo, *skĭăf' fŏ*, m. slap, box on the ear.

schiamazzare, *skĭămătză' rĕ*, v. n. to cackle; to cry out, to clamour. | lure.

schiamazzo, *-măt' zŏ*, m. noise; bird-call;

schiantare, *skĭăntă' rĕ*, v. a. to rend, to crack, to split.

schianto, *skĭăn' tŏ*, m. cut, cleft, crack, fracture; noise; passion; torment.

schiarare, *skĭără' rĕ*, v. a. to clear up, to elucidate, to explain.

schiarire, *-rĕ' rĕ*, v. n. to clear up, to illustrate, to explain; —, v. n. to get clear, to get thin; to appear.

schiatta, *skĭăt' tă*, f. race, progeny; species.

schiattare, *-tă' rĕ*, v. n. to burst.

schiattire, *-tĕ' rĕ*, v. n. to yelp, to squeak.

schiava, *skĭă' vă*, f. female slave.

schiavitù, *skĭăvĭtŭ'*, f. slavery.

schiavo, *skĭă' vŏ*, m. slave.

schiccherare, *skĭkkĕră' rĕ*, v. a. to daub, to scribble.

schidione, *skĭdĭŏ' nĕ*, m. spit, broach.

schiena, *skĭă' nă*, f. back-bone; croup, ridge.

schiera, *skĭă' ră*, f. legion, battalion, company, squadron; band; rank, file.

schierare, *skĭĕră' rĕ*, v. a. to draw up in line of battle. | rightness.

schiettezza, *skĭĕttĕt' ză*, f. frankness, up-

schietto, *skĭĕt' tŏ*, a. pure, plain, level; clean, neat; honest; frank.

schifare, *skĭfă' rĕ*, v. a. & n. to shun, to avoid; to loathe, to abhor.

schifo, *skĕ' fŏ*, m. skiff; —, a. nasty; disgusting; coy, shy, reluctant.

schifoso, *skĭfŏ' sŏ*, a. nasty, disgusting.

schiodare, *skĭŏdă' rĕ*, v. a. to unnail.

schioppo, *skĭŏp' pŏ*, m. gun, musket.

schisto, *skĭs' tŏ*, m. schist, cleaving-stone.

schivare, *skĭvă' rĕ*, v. a. & n. to avoid, to shun.

schiudere, *skĭŭ' dĕrĕ*, v. a. ir. to disclose, to open; to exclude; —, v. n. to expand (of flowers), to blow. | scum.

schiuma, *skĭŭ' mă*, f. froth, foam, dross,

schiumare, *skĭŭmă' rĕ*, v. a. to skim, to cream; —, v. n. to froth, to foam.

schivo, *skĭ' vŏ*, a. shy, reserved, modest; sorrowful. | spout, to squirt.

schizzare, *skĭtză' rĕ*, v. a. to sketch; to

schizzatoio, *-tŏ' ŏ*, m. syringe; squirt.

schizzinoso, *-tzĭnŏ' sŏ*, a. disdainful, haughty. | sketch.

schizzo, *skĭt' zŏ*, m. splash, spouting;

sciacquare, *sshăkŭă' rĕ*, v. a. to rinse, to wash. | shuffle; to rinse; to jumble.

sciaguattare, *sshăgŭăttă' rĕ*, v. a. to

sciagura, *sshăgŏ' ră*, f. misfortune, disaster.

sciagurato, *-gŭră' tŏ*, a. wretched, un-fortunate, miserable; wicked.

scialacquare, *sshălăkŭă' rĕ*, v. a. to lavish, to squander.

scialare, *sshălă' rĕ*, v. a. to exhale; to eva-porate.

scialbare, sshálbä´rĕ, v. a. to whitewash.
scialbo, sshál´bŏ, a. whitewashed; pale.
scialo, sshä´lŏ, m. exhalation.
scialuppa, –lüp´pä, f. shallop.   [ward.
sciamannato, –mánnä´tŏ, a. ill-built; awk-
sciamare, –mä´rĕ, v. n. to swarm (of bees).
sciame, sshä´mĕ, m. swarm of bees.
sciamito, –mĭ´tŏ, m. calimanco; (bot.)
amaranth.
sciancato, sshänkä´tŏ, a. hip-shot, lame.
sciarpa, sshär´pä, f. scarf.
sciarrada, sshärrä´dä, f. routing, defeat;
strife, quarrel.
sciatica, sshä´tĭkä, f. hip-gout.
sciatto, sshät´tŏ, a. slovenly; simple.
sciaura, see **sciagura.**
sciaurato, see **sciagurato.**
sciente, sshĭen´tĕ, a. knowing, learned.
scientifico, –tĕ´fĭkŏ, a. scientific, learned.
scienza, sshĭen´tzä, f. science, knowledge;
letters, pl.
scilinguare, sshĭlĭngüä´rĕ, v. n. to stammer, to lisp.
scilla, sshĭl´lä, f. sea-onion.
sciloma, sshĭlŏ´mä, m. tiresome verbiage.
scimmia, sshĭm´mĭä, f. ape, monkey.
scimmiotto, –mĭŏt´tŏ, m. young ape.
scimunito, –münĭ´tŏ, a. foolish, imbecile.
scingere, sshĭn´jĕrĕ, v. a. ir. to ungird, to
untie.
scintilla, sshĭntĭl´lä, f. spark.   [twinkle.
scintillare, –tĭlä´rĕ, v. n. to sparkle, to
sciocchezza, sshŏkkĕt´zä, f. foolishness;
folly.
sciocco, sshŏk´kŏ, a. insipid, silly, foolish.
sciocciere, sshŏl´yĕrĕ, v. a. ir. to untie.
sciolo, sshĕ´ŏlŏ, a. sciolous; arrogant.
sciolto, sshŏl´tŏ, a. untied, ungirded; independent, free; agile, nimble; easy.
scioperare, sshŏpĕrä´rĕ, v. a. to hinder
from working; **scioperarsi,** –rär´sĭ, to
loiter, to do nothing.
scioperato, –pĕrä´tŏ, a. idle, sluggish,
unoccupied.   [time.
sciopero, sshŏ´pĕrŏ, m. idleness, losing
sciorinare, sshŏrĭnä´rĕ, v. a. to air
(linen &c.); to display; to divulge.
sciorre, see **sciogliere.**
scipito, sshĭpĭ´tŏ, a. insipid; tiresome.
scirocco, sshĭrŏk´kŏ, m. southeast wind,
sciroppo, –rŏp´pŏ, m. syrup.   [sirocco.
scirro, sshĭr´rŏ, m. (med.) scirrhus.
scisma, sshĭs´mä, f. schism, dissension.
scissione, sshĭssĭŏ´nĕ, f. scission; separation.
scissura, –sŏ´rä, f. cleft, rent, chink.
sciupare, sshäpä´rĕ, v. a. to consume; to
wear out; to spoil, to destroy.
sclamare, see **esclamare.**
scoccare, skŏkkä´rĕ, v. a. to let fly, to
shoot off; –, v. n. to escape; to burst
forth.
scodella, skŏdĕl´lä, f. porringer; porridge.
scodellino, –dĕllĭ´nŏ, m. small porringer;
saucer.   [to squash, to crush.
scofacciare, –fätshä´rĕ, v. a. to make flat;
scoglio, skŏl´yŏ, m. rock, reef, shelf, sand-
bank.

scoiare, skŏĭä´rĕ, v. a. to flay, to skin.
scoiattolo, skŏĭät´tŏlŏ, m. squirrel.
scolare, skŏlä´rĕ, m. scholar; –, v. n. to
flow, to drop, to drain, to trickle.
scolastico, –lás´tĭkŏ, a. scholastic.
scolatoio, –lätŏ´ŏ, m. strainer, drain, sewer.
scolio, skŏ´lĭŏ, m. scholion, commentary.
scollare, skŏllä´rĕ, v. a. to unglue; to
disjoin.
scollegare, skŏllĕgä´rĕ, v. a. to disunite.
scolo, skŏ´lŏ, m. running, course.
scolorare, skŏlŏrä´rĕ, v. a. to discolour.
scolorire, –rĕ´rĕ, v. n. to lose one's colour;
to grow pale.   [justify.
scolpare, skŏlpä´rĕ, v. a. to exculpate, to
scolpire, –pĕ´rĕ, v. a. to engrave, to carve;
to pronounce distinctly.
scoltura, –püŏ´rä, f. sculpture; engraving, print.
scolta, skŏl´tä, f. sentinel, watch.
scombuiare, skŏmbüä´rĕ, scombusso-
lare, –büssŏlä´rĕ, v. a. to disperse, to
scatter, to rout.
scommessa, skŏmmĕs´sä, f. wager, bet.
scommettere, –mĕt´tĕrĕ, v. a. ir. to disjoin; to excite discord.
scommuovere, –müŏ´vĕrĕ, v. a. ir. to excite to revolt, to raise.
scomodare, skŏmŏdä´rĕ, v. a. to trouble,
to incommode.
scomodità, –mŏdĭtä´, f. inconvenience,
trouble.   [commodious.
scomodo, skŏ´mŏdŏ, a. inconvenient, in-
scompagnare, skŏmpänyä´rĕ, v. a. to separate, to uncouple.
scompartimento, –pärtĭmĕn´tŏ, m. partition, compartment.
scompartire, –pärtĕ´rĕ, v. a. to divide
into compartments, to distribute.
scompigliare, –pĭlyä´rĕ, v. a. to embroil,
to disorder, to disturb.   [order.
scompiglio, –pĭl´yŏ, m. confusion, dis-
scomporre, –pŏr´rĕ, v. a. & n. ir. to discompose, to disorder.   [position.
scomposizione, –pŏsĭtzĭŏ´nĕ, f. decom-
scomunare, skŏmünä´rĕ, v. a. to break
the community.   [tion, curse.
scomunica, –mŏ´nĭkä, f. excommunica-
scomunicare, –münĭkä´rĕ, v. a. to excommunicate.   [cation.
scomunicazione, –tzĭŏ´nĕ, f. excommuni-
sconcertare, skŏndshĕrtä´rĕ, v. a. to disconcert, to disturb.   [agreement.
sconcerto, –dshĕr´tŏ, m. discord; dis-
sconciare, –dshä´rĕ, v. a. to spoil, to derange, to embroil, to confound.
sconciatura, –tŏ´rä, f. abortion, miscarriage; dwarf.
sconcio, skŏn´dshŏ, m. inconvenience,
damage; –, a. unbecoming, indecent;
deformed; strange; dishonest.
sconcordia, –kŏr´dĭä, f. discord, variance.
sconfessare, –fĕssä´rĕ, v. a. to disown, to
deny.   [fit; to ruin.
sconfiggere, –fĭd´jĕrĕ, v. a. ir. to discom-
sconfitta, –fĭt´tä, f. discomfiture, ruin.
sconfortare, –fŏrtä´rĕ, v. a. to dissuade;
sconfortarsi, –tär´sĭ, to be discouraged.

sconforto, –*fŏr'tŏ,* m. discomfort.

scongiurare, –*jūr'ā'rĕ,* v. a. to conjure; to entreat.

sconnettere, –*nĕt'tĕrĕ,* v. a. & n. ir. to disunite; to be incoherent.   [ful.

sconoscente, *skŏnŏsshĕn'tĕ,* a. ungrate-

sconoscenza, –*sshĕn'tzā,* f. ingratitude.

sconoscere, *skŏnŏssh'ĕrĕ,* v. n. ir. to be ungrateful.

sconosciuto, –*sshū'tŏ,* a. unknown.

sconsiderato, *skŏnsīdĕrā'tŏ,* a. inconsiderate.

sconsigliare, –*sīlyā'rĕ,* v. a. to dissuade.

sconsolato, *skŏnsŏlā'tŏ,* a. disconsolate.

scontare, *skŏntā'rĕ,* v. a. to abate; to discount.   [tent, to disgust.

scontentare, –*tĕntā'rĕ,* v. a. to discon-

scontento, –*tĕn'tŏ,* a. discontented, sad.

sconto, *skŏn'tŏ,* m. discount.   [tort.

scontorcere, –*tŏr'dshĕrĕ,* v. a. ir. to con-

scontrare, *skŏntrā'rĕ,* v. a. to meet with, to encounter; to check an account.

scontro, *skŏn'trŏ,* m. meeting; shock; adversary; mark.

scontroso, –*trŏ'sŏ,* a. capricious; wilful; peevish.

sconvenevole, –*vĕnā'vŏlĕ,* **sconveniente,** –*vĕnĭĕn'tĕ,* a. unsuitable, unbecoming, indecent.

sconvenienza, –*vĕnĭĕn'tzā,* f. unbecomingness.   [suitable.

sconvenire, –*vĕnē'rĕ,* v. n. ir. to be un-

sconvolgere, –*vŏl'jĕrĕ,* v. a. ir. to turn upside down; to confound; to dissuade.

sconvolgimento, –*vŏljĭmĕn'tŏ,* m. convulsion; disorder.   [crooked.

sconvolto, –*vŏl'tŏ,* a. overturned, upset;

scopa, *skŏ'pā,* f. birch-tree; broom, besom.

scopare, *skŏpā'rĕ,* v. a. to sweep; to scourge (criminals); to wander through.

scoperchiare, –*pĕrkĭā'rĕ,* v. a. to uncover; to raise the lid.

scoperta, –*pĕr'tā,* f. discovery.

scoperto, –*pĕr'tŏ,* a. uncovered, open;

scopetta, –*pĕt'tā,* f. brush.   [bare.

scopettare, –*pĕttā'rĕ,* v. a. to brush.

scopo, *skŏ'pŏ,* m. aim, mark; intent, design, purpose.

scoppiare, *skŏppĭā'rĕ,* v. n. to burst, to crack; to come forth.

scoppio, *skŏp'pĭŏ,* m. crack, crash; explosion; light gun.

scoprimento, *skŏprĭmĕn'tŏ,* m. discovery.

scoprire, *skŏprē'rĕ,* v. a. ir. to uncover, to discover.

scoraggiamento, *skŏrādjāmĕn'tŏ,* **scoraggimento,** –*rādjĭmĕn'tŏ,* m. discouragement.

scoraggiare, *skŏrādjā'rĕ,* **scoraggire,** –*djē'rĕ,* **scorare,** –*rā'rĕ,* v. a. to dishearten, to discourage.

scorbacchiare, *skŏrbākkĭā'rĕ,* v. a. to defame, to dishonour.   [on paper.

scorbiare, *skŏrbĭā'rĕ,* v. a. to make blots

scorbio, *skŏr'bĭŏ,* m. blot, spot; defect.

scorbuto, *skŏrbū'tŏ,* m. scurvy.

scorciare, *skŏrdshā'rĕ,* **scorcire,** –*dshē'rĕ,* v. a. to shorten, to curtail.

scorciatoia, –*tŏ'ā,* f. cross-way; by-path.

scorcio, *skŏr'dshŏ,* m. foreshortening; last; end.

scordare, *skŏrdā'rĕ,* v. a. to put out of tune; (fig.) to cause discord; –, v. n. to be discordant, to disagree.

scorgere, *skŏr'jĕrĕ,* v. a. ir. to perceive, to discern; to escort, to accompany.

scoria, *skŏ'rĭā,* f. scoria, dross, scum

scornacchiare, *skŏrnākkĭā'rĕ,* v. a. to rally, to banter; to slander.

scornare, *skŏrnā'rĕ,* v. a. to break off the horns; to affront, to scorn; to defame.

scorno, *skŏr'nŏ,* m. affront, shame.

scorpione, *skŏrpĭŏ'nĕ,* m. scorpion (also as sign of the zodiac).

scorporare, *skŏrpŏrā'rĕ,* v. a. to disembody; to take out of the capital stock.

scorporo, *skŏr'pŏrŏ,* m. disembodying.

scorrazzare, *skŏrrātzā'rĕ,* v. a. to make excursions.

scorrere, *skŏr'rĕrĕ,* v. n. to run away, to slip away; to glide; to make incursions.

scorretto, –*rĕt'tŏ,* a. incorrect, faulty; dissolute.   [gliding.

scorrevole, –*rā'vŏlĕ,* a. running, flowing,

scorribanda, –*rībān'dā,* f. little excursion.

scorsa, *skŏr'sā,* f. course, run; incursion.

scorso, *skŏr'sŏ,* m. oversight, mistake, fault; –, a. run out; past over; spoiled.

scorta, *skŏr'tā,* f. escort, convoy.

scortare, *skŏrtā'rĕ,* v. a. to shorten, to abridge; to escort.

scortese, *skŏrtā'sĕ,* a. disobliging, impolite.

scortesia, *skŏrtĕsē'ā,* f. incivility.

scorticare, *skŏrtĭkā'rĕ,* v. a. to skin, to flay.

scortichino, *skŏrtĭkē'nŏ,* m. slaughtering-knife; boiling water used for scalding.

scorto, *skŏr'tŏ,* m. abridgment; –, a. shortened, abridged; perceived; intelligible; prudent; clever.

scorza, *skŏr'tzā,* f. bark, peel; (fig.) outside, appearance.   [to plunder; to forsake.

scorzare, –*tzā'rĕ,* v. a. to bark; to skin;

scoscio, *skŏssh'ŏ,* m. precipice, downfall.

scossa, *skŏs'sā,* f. shake, toss; leap, sudden shower.

scostare, *skŏstā'rĕ,* v. a. to remove; to drive away; **scostarsi,** –*tār'sĭ,* to go from; to forsake.

scostumatezza, *skŏstūmātĕt'zā,* f. impoliteness; indecency; libertinage.

scostumato, –*tūmā'tŏ,* a. impolite; lewd.

scotimento, *skŏtĭmĕn'tŏ,* m. shaking, shake; shock.

scotola, *skŏt'ŏlā,* f. brake (to beat flax).

scotolare, *skŏtŏlā'rĕ,* v. a. to beat flax.

scottare, *skŏttā'rĕ,* v. a. to scald; to burn; to nettle; to harm.

scotto, *skŏt'tŏ,* m. bill, reckoning; scot.

scozzonare, *skŏtzŏnā'rĕ,* v. a. to break in a horse.   [stool.

scranna, *skrān'nā,* f. folding-stool, camp-

screanzato, *skrĕāntzā'tŏ,* a. coarse, unmannerly.   [split, to burst.

screpolare, *skrĕpŏlā'rĕ,* v. n. to crack, to

screpolatura, –tō′rȧ, f. crevice, chink, cleft, slit, gap, fissure; crack.

scriba, skrē′bȧ, m. writer, copyist.

scricchiolare, skrĭkkĭōlä′rē, v. n. to creak, to rattle, to crack. [box.

scrigno, skrēn′yō, m. bunch; casket; strongbox.

scrinare, skrēnä′rē, v. a. to unknot or to uncurl the hair.

scritta, skrĭt′tȧ, f. scritto, –tō; m. writing; inscription; bond. [inkstand.

scrittoio, –tō′ō, m. writing-desk; study;

scrittore, –tō′rē, m. writer, author; copyist, copier, transcriber.

scrittrice, –trē′dshē, f. authoress.

scrittura, –tū′rȧ, f. writing; Holy Scripture, Bible; document.

scritturale, –tūrä′lē, a. scriptural.

scrivania, skrĭvänē′ȧ, f. large writing-desk. [book-keeper.

scrivano, skrĭvä′nō, m. scrivener, writer;

scrivere, skrē′vērē, v. a. ir. to write.

scroccare, skrōkkä′rē, v. a. to cheat, to swindle; to spunge upon.

scrocchio, skrōk′kĭō, m. usury.

scroccone, –kō′nē, m. swindler, sharper.

scrofa, skrō′fȧ, f. sow; concubine.

scrofola, skrō′fōlȧ, f. scrofula, king's evil.

scrollare, skrōllä′rē, v. a. to shake, to toss.

scrosciare, skrōsshä′rē, v. n. to crackle, to crash; to boil up, to bubble, to wallop.

scroscio, skrōssh′ō, m. rattling, clatter, crash.

scrostare, skrōstä′rē, v. a. to take off the crust, to peel; to chip (bread).

scrostatura, –tō′rȧ, f. taking off the crust; peeling off; chipping. [difficulty.

scrupolo, skrō′pōlō, m. scruple, doubt;

scrupoloso, skrūpōlō′sō, a. scrupulous, over-nice; captious, risky.

scrutare, skrūtä′rē, scrutinare, –tĭnä′rē, v. a. to scrutinize, to examine.

scrutinio, –tē′nĭō, m. scrutiny, inquiry.

scucire, skūdshē′rē, v. a. ir. to unsew, to unstitch, to rip up; to undo.

scuderia, skūdērē′ȧ, f. stable; stud.

scudetto, –dēt′tō, scudicciuolo, –dĭtshūō′lō, m. small shield, small scutcheon.

scudiere, skūdĭē′rē, m. esquire.

scudiscio, –dĭssh′ō, m. switch, rod, twig.

scudo, skō′dō, m. shield, buckler, scutcheon, coat of arms; defence, protection; crown (coin). [dress.

scuffia, skūf′fĭȧ, f. woman's cap, coif, headdress.

scuffiare, –fĭä′rē, v. a. to devour.

scuffina, –fē′nȧ, f. rasp.

scultore, skūltō′rē, m. sculptor; engraver.

scultura, –tō′rȧ, f. sculpture.

scuoiare, skūōĭä′rē, v. a. to flay, to fleece.

scuola, skūō′lȧ, f. school, college.

scuorare, skūōrä′rē, v. a. to dishearten.

scuotere, skūō′tērē, v. a. ir. to shake, to throw off; to toss; to deprive.

scure, skō′rē, f. hatchet, axe.

scuriada, skūrĭä′dȧ, f. scourging, whipping; coachman's whip.

scurità, skūrĭtä′, f. darkness, obscurity.

Italian and English.

scuro, skō′rō, a. obscure, dark; retired; mysterious, obscure. [like.

scurrile, skūrrē′lē, a. scurrilous, buffoon-

scurrilità, –lĭtä′, f. scurrility, buffoonery.

scusa, skō′sȧ, f. excuse; pretext.

scusabile, skūsä′bĭlē, a. excusable.

scusare, skūsä′rē, v. a. to excuse; to justify; to pardon. [reaved.

scusso, skŭs′sō, a. shaken; stripped, bereaved.

sdarsi, sdär′sĭ, v. r. to grow idle.

sdaziare, sdätzĭä′rē, v. a. to tax, to lay a duty on.

sdegnare, sdēnyä′rē, v. a. to disdain, to despise; sdegnarsi, –yär′sĭ, to be or to get angry. [scorn; wrath.

sdegno, sdēn′yō, m. indignation, disdain,

sdegnoso, –yō′sō, a. disdainful, scornful, angry, wrathful, irate.

sdimenticare, see dimenticare.

sdoganare, sdōgänä′rē, v. a. to redeem from the custom-house. [to lie down.

sdraiarsi, sdräär′sĭ, v. r. to lie stretched,

sdrucciolare, sdrūtshōlä′rē, v. n. to slip, to glide; to stumble.

sdrucciolevole, –tshōlä′vōlē, a. slippery.

sdrucciolo, sdrūt′shōlō, a. sliding, lubric; transitory; swift.

sdrucio, strō′dshō, m. unseaming; cleft, crack. [unsew, to rip up.

sdrucire, strūdshē′rē, v. a. to unstitch, to

sdrucito, –dshē′tō, m. rent, chink.

se, sē, c. if, provided that, unless; thus; – bene, although; – non, except; se′ (= se i, se gli), if the; se′ (= sei), thou art; –, sè, pn. oneself, himself, herself, itself, themselves.

sebaceo, sēbä′dshēō, a. sebaceous.

sebbene, sēbbē′nē, c. although, though.

secante, sēkän′tē, f. secant.

secare, sēkä′rē, v. a. (poet.) to cut.

secca, sēk′kȧ, seccagna, –kän′yȧ, f. shallow, sand-bank.

seccare, sēkkä′rē, v. a. to dry up, to drain; to waste, to tease, to importune.

seccatura, –tō′rȧ, f. tiresomeness; importunity, tedious thing.

secchereccio, sēkkērē′tshō, a. half dry, withered. [bucket, pail.

secchia, sēk′kĭȧ, f. secchio, –kĭō, m.

seccia, sēt′shȧ, f. stubble.

secco, sēk′kō, a. dry, arid; slender, thin, meagre; stingy. [fruit.

seccume, sēkkō′mē, m. dried leaves; dried

secento, sēdshēn′tō, a. six hundred.

seco, sē′kō, pn. with him, with her; with oneself.

secolare, sēkōlä′rē, secolaresco, –lärēs′kō, a. secular, worldly, profane.

secolarizzare, –lärĭdzä′rē, v. a. to secularize. [tion.

secolarizzazione, –tzĭō′nē, f. seculariza-

secolo, sē′kōlō, m. century; the age.

seconda, sēkōn′dȧ, f. after-birth; following.

secondare, –kōndä′rē, v. a. to second, to assist, to support.

secondario, –dä′rĭō, a. secondary, accessory; –, ad. in the second place.

secondina, –dē′nȧ, f. after-birth.

secondo, *–kŏn'dŏ,* m. second; **–,** a. second, inferior; propitious; **–,** ad. secondly; **–,** pr. according to.

secondochè, *–kĕ',* c. as, according as.

secondogenito, *–jă'nĭtŏ,* m. second-born, second son.

sedano, *sĕ'dănŏ,* m. celery.   [pease.

sedare, *sĕdā'rĕ,* v. a. to assuage, to appease.

sedato, *–dā'tŏ,* a. sedate, peaceful, quiet.

sede, *sĕ'dĕ,* f. seat.

sedentario, *sĕdĕntā'rĭŏ,* a. sedentary.

sedere, *sĕdā'rĕ,* m. sitting down, seat, bottom; **–,** v. n. ir. to sit down, to be seated; **to be situated.**   [bishop.

sedia, *sĕ'dĭa,* f. chair, seat; see (of a

sedicesimo, *sĕdĭdshă'sĭmŏ,* a. sixteenth.

sedici, *sĕ'dĭdshĭ,* a. sixteen.

sedile, *sĕdĭ'lĕ,* m. seat, bench, chair.

sedimento, *–dĭmĕn'tŏ,* m. sediment.

sedizione, *–tzĭŏ'nĕ,* f. sedition, tumult.

sedizioso, *–tzĭŏ'sŏ,* a. seditious.

sedurre, *–dūr'rĕ,* v. a. ir. to seduce, to corrupt, to debauch.

seduzione, *–dūtzĭŏ'nĕ,* f. seduction.

sega, *sĕ'gă,* f. saw.

segale, *sĕgā'lĕ,* f. rye.

segaligno, *–lĭn'yŏ,* a. slender, lank.

segare, *sĕgā'rĕ,* v. a. to saw; to cut; to reap, to mow.

segatura, *–tă'ră,* f. saw-dust, sawing; reaping; hay-making; harvest.

seggetta, *sĕdjĕt'tă,* f. porter's chair; close-stool.   [seat; see.

seggia, *sĕd'jă,* f., **seggio,** *–jŏ,* m. chair,

segmento, *sĕgmĕn'tŏ,* m. segment.

segnacolo, *sĕnyā'kŏlŏ,* m. mark, sign, token; signet, book-mark.

segnalare, *sĕnyălā'rĕ,* v. a. to signalise.

segnale, *–yā'lĕ,* m. signal, sign, token; omen, prognostic, foretoken.

segnare, *–yā'rĕ,* v. a. to mark, to note, to stamp; to bleed; **segnarsi,** *–ār'sĭ,* to make the sign of the cross; to be amazed.

segnato, *–yā'tŏ,* a. marked, noted, evident; engraved, imprinted, beaten (path), cited, quoted; designed.   [blance.

segnatura, *–yātŏ'ră,* f. signature, resem-

segno, *sĕn'yŏ,* m. sign, mark, token, wonder, ensign, seal, trace.

sego, *sĕ'gŏ,* m. tallow, suet.   [set apart.

segregare, *sĕgrĕgā'rĕ,* v. a. to separate, to

segregazione, *–tzĭŏ'nĕ,* f. separation.

segreta, *sĕgrĕ'tă,* f. secret place.

segretariato, *–grĕtārĭā'tŏ,* m. secretary-ship.   [desk.

segretario, *–tā'rĭŏ,* m. secretary; writing-

segreto, *–grĕ'tŏ,* m. secret, mystery, inmost soul, confidant; **–,** a. secret, hidden.

seguente, *sĕgŭĕn'tĕ,* a. following, succeeding.   [suite, consequence.

seguenza, *–gŭĕn'tză,* f. sequence, series,

segugio, *sĕgŭ'jŏ,* m. blood-hound.

seguire, *sĕgŭĭ'rĕ,* **seguitare,** *–gŭĭtā'rĕ,* v. a. & n. to follow, to pursue, to yield; to succeed.

seguito, *sĕ'gŭĭtŏ,* m. retinue, suite, continuation; issue, event, success.

sei, *sĕ'ĭ,* a. six.

seicento, *sĕĭdshĕn'tŏ,* a. six hundred.

selce, *sĕl'dshĕ,* f. flint-stone; paving-stone.

selciare, *–dshă'rĕ,* v. a. to pave (with pebbles).

sella, *sĕl'lă,* f. saddle; seat; stool.

sellaio, *sĕllā'ŏ,* m. saddler.

sellare, *sĕllā'rĕ,* v. a. to saddle.

selva, *sĕl'vă,* f. wood, forest.

selvaggio, *–văd'jŏ,* a. savage, **wild,** uncultivated; rude, unpolished.

selvatico, *–vā'tĭkŏ,* a. wild, savage.

selvetta, *–vĕt'tă,* f. grove, boscage.

sembiante, *sĕmbĭăn'tĕ,* m. countenance, look; air, mien, semblance, appearance, colour, show; **–,** a. resembling, like.

sembianza, *–bĭăn'tză,* f. face, countenance, appearance, resemblance.   [appear.

sembrare, *sĕmbră'rĕ,* v. n. to seem, to

seme, *sĕ'mĕ,* m. seed; origin, sowing-time; cause; race; extraction.   [race.

sementa, *sĕmĕn'tă,* f. seed, sowing; cause;

sementare, *–mĕntā'rĕ,* v. a. to sow.

semenza, *–mĕn'tză,* f. seed; sown field; race, extraction, cause.

semenzaio, *–tză'ŏ,* m. seed-plot.

semestrale, *sĕmĕstră'lĕ,* a. of six months.

semestre, *–mĕs'trĕ,* m. space of six months.   [months.

semi, *sĕ'mĭ,* a. half.

semicroma, *sĕmĭkrŏ'mă,* f. (mus.) semi-quaver.

semila, *sĕmĭ'lă,* a. six thousand.

seminare, *sĕmĭnā'rĕ,* v. a. to sow; to propagate, to diffuse.   [school.

seminario, *–nā'rĭŏ,* m. nursery; boarding-

semola, *sĕ'mŏlă,* f. bran, pollard.

sempiterno, *sĕmpĭtĕr'nŏ,* a. eternal; **in –,** for ever and ever.

semplice, *sĕm'plĭdshĕ,* a. simple; pure, unmixed; single, plain, honest; silly.

semplicemente, *–mĕn'tĕ,* ad. simply; sincerely.

semplicità, *–plĭdshĭtă',* f. simplicity.

sempre, *sĕm'prĕ,* ad. always, ever; **– che,** as often as; **– mai,** for ever.

senapa, *sĕ'năpă,* **senape,** *–năp'ĕ,* f. mustard-seed, mustard.   [mustard.

senapismo, *sĕnăpĭs'mŏ,* m. cataplasm of

senato, *sĕnā'tŏ,* m. senate; senate-house.

senatore, *–tŏ'rĕ,* m. senator.

senile, *sĕnĭ'lĕ,* a. senile, decrepit.

senio, *sĕ'nĭŏ,* m. old age, decrepitude.

seniore, *sĕnĭŏ'rĕ,* a. senior, older.

senno, *sĕn'nŏ,* m. sense, wisdom, judgment; intelligence; cleverness, cunning; trick; meaning, opinion, sentiment; **a mio –,** at my pleasure; **con –,** wisely; **da –,** in earnest.

seno, *sĕ'nŏ,* m. bosom, breast; heart; cleverness, creek, little bay.

sensale, *sĕnsā'lĕ,* m. broker, agent.

sensato, *–sā'tŏ,* a. sensible, judicious, prudent, intelligent.

sensazione, *–tzĭŏ'nĕ,* f. sensation.

sensibile, *–sĭ'bĭlĕ,* a. sensible, perceptible.

sensibilità, *–sĭbĭlĭtă',* f. sensibility, tenderness.   [(bot.) sensitive plant.

sensitiva, *–sĭtĭ'vă,* f. perceptive faculty;

sensitivo, –*sĕtĕ'vŏ*, a. sensitve, ticklish; touchy, irritable.

senso, *sĕn'sŏ*, m. sense; sentiment, feeling; meaning, signification, acception; understanding, judgment.   [sense.

sensorio, –*sŏ'rĭŏ*, m. sensorium, seat of

sensuale, *sĕnsŭa'lĕ*, a. sensual: carnal.

sensualità, –*sŭalĭtā'*, f. sensuality.

sentenza, *sĕntĕn'tzā*, f. sentence, judgment, decision; saying.   [to decide.

sentenziare, –*tzĭā'rĕ*, v. n. to sentence,

sentenzioso, –*tzĭŏ'sŏ*, a. sententious.

sentiero, *sĕntĭĕ'rŏ*, m. path, by-way.

sentimentale, *sĕntĭmĕntā'lĕ*, a. sentimental.   [mentality.

sentimentalismo, –*tālĭs'mŏ*, m. sentimentalism.

sentimento, –*mĕn'tŏ*, m. sentiment, feeling; judgment, understanding; opinion.

sentina, *sĕntĭ'nā*, f. sink-well of a ship; common sewer.

sentinella, *sĕntĭnĕl'lā*, f. sentry, sentinel.

sentire, *sĕntĭ'rĕ*, v. a. & n. to feel; to hear; to smell; to taste; to perceive; to be sensible of; to esteem, to think.

sentita, –*tĭ'tā*, f. feeling, sense; sagacity.

sentito, –*tĭ'tŏ*, a. judicious; prudent.

sentore, –*tŏ'rĕ*, m. smell, scent, odour; hint, advice; noise.

senza, *sĕn'tzā*, pr. without; **senz' altro,** without doubt; – **che,** besides, except, moreover; – **più,** without anything else; simply, only; – **modo,** excessively.

sepalo. *sĕpā'lŏ*, m. (bot.) hedge.   [part.

separare, *sĕpārā'rĕ*, v. a. to separate, to

separazione, –*tzĭŏ'nĕ*, f. separation.

sepolcrale, *sĕpŏlkrā'lĕ*, a. sepulchral.

sepolcreto, –*krĕ'tŏ*, m. place full of ancient tombs.

sepolcro, *sĕpŏl'krŏ*, m. sepulchre, tomb.

sepoltura, –*tŏ'rā*, f. burial.

seppellimento, *sĕppĕllĭmĕn'tŏ*, m. burial.

seppellire, *sĕppĕllĭ'rĕ*, v. a. to bury, to inter; to hide.

seppia, *sĕp'pĭā*, f. cuttle-fish, sepia.

sequela, *sĕkŭĕ'lā*, f. sequel, consequence.

sequestrare, *sĕkŭĕstrā'rĕ*, v. a. to sequester; to set aside.

sequestro, –*kŭĕs'trŏ*, m. sequestration.

sera, *sĕ'rā*, f. evening; night; **buona –,** good evening.

serafico, *sĕrā'fĭkŏ*, a. seraphic.   [seraph.

serafino, *sĕrā'fĭnŏ*, **serafo,** –*rā'fŏ*, m.

serale, *sĕrā'lĕ*, a. of the evening.

seralmente, –*rālmĕn'tĕ*, ad. every evening.

serata, –*rā'tā*, f. (the whole) evening.

serbare, *sĕrbā'rĕ*, v. a. to keep, to preserve; to reserve, to guard.   [pond; coop.

serbatoio, –*bātŏ'ŏ*, m. preserve; fish-

serbo, *sĕr'bŏ*, m. keeping, deposit, custody.

sere, *sĕ'rĕ*, m. Sir, my Lord.

serenare, *sĕrĕnā'rĕ*, v. a. to make clear; to brighten up; (fig.) to calm.

serenata, –*nā'tā*, f. (mus.) serenade.

serenità, *sĕrĕnĭtā'*, f. serenity; Serene Highness (title).

sereno, *sĕrā'nŏ*, a. serene, clear, bright; calm; smooth.

sergente, *sĕrjĕn'tĕ*, m. sergeant; constable.

serico, *sĕ'rĭkŏ*, a. silken, silky.

serie, *sĕ'rĭĕ*, f. series; succession.

serietà, *sĕrĭĕtā'*, f. seriousness, gravity.

serio, *sĕ'rĭŏ*, a. serious, grave; important.

sermento, *sĕrmĕn'tŏ*, m. vine-tendril.

sermocinare, *sĕrmŏchĭnā'rĕ*, v. n. to harangue; to preach.

sermone, *sĕrmŏ'nĕ*, m. sermon, speech; discourse; dialect.

serotino, *sĕrŏtĭ'nŏ*, a. late in the day or season; lingering; tardy.

serpe, *sĕr'pĕ*, f. & m. serpent, snake.

serpeggiare, –*pĕdjā'rĕ*, v. n. to wind, to meander.

serpentino, –*pĕntĭ'nŏ*, m. serpentine stone (a fine dark-green marble); –, a. serpentine.   [creep.

serpere, *sĕr'pĕrĕ*, v. n. to wind about, to

serra, *sĕr'rā*, f. saw; defile; crowd.

serraglio, *sĕrrāl'yŏ*, m. enclosure of palisades, wall; harem, seraglio.

serrame, *sĕrrā'mĕ*, m. lock.

serrare, *sĕrrā'rĕ*, v. a. to shut up; to contain; to press; to pursue closely.

serrato, –*rā'tŏ*, a. close, pressed together.

serratura, –*tŏ'rā*, f. lock; accomplishment.   [ment.

serto, *sĕr'tŏ*, m. garland.

serva, *sĕr'vā*, f. servant-maid.

servaggio, –*vād'jŏ*, m. servitude, slavery.

servare, *sĕrvā'rĕ*, v. a. to keep, to preserve.

servente, –*vĕn'tĕ*, m. servant, footman; –, a. serving.

servigio, –*vĕ'jŏ*, m. service; kind office.

servile, –*vĕ'lĕ*, a. servile, slavish, mean.

servilmente, –*vĭlmĕn'tĕ*, ad. servilely, meanly.

servilità, –*vĭlĭtā'*, f. servility.

servire, *sĕrvĭ'rĕ*, v. a. to serve; to wait on; to help at table; to deserve, to merit; **servirsi,** –*vĭr'sĭ*, to employ.

servitore, –*vĭtŏ'rĕ*, m. servant, valet.

servitù, –*vĭtŭ'*, f. servitude; servants, pl.

servizio, see **servigio.**

servo, *sĕr'vŏ*, a. slavish; subject; –, m. slave; servant.   [one and a half.

sesquialtero, *sĕskŭĭāl'tĕrŏ*, a. containing

sesquipedale, –*pĕdā'lĕ*, a. a foot and a half.

sessagesima, *sĕssājĕ'sĭmā*, a. sixtieth.

sessanta, *sĕssān'tā*, a. sixty.

sessantesimo, –*tĕ'sĭmŏ*, sixtieth.

sessantina, –*tĕ'nā*, f. sixty, threescore.

sessennale, *sĕssĕnnā'lĕ*, a. sixty years old.

sessennio, *sĕssĕn'nĭŏ*, m. space of six years.

sessione, *sĕssĭŏ'nĕ*, f. session, sitting.

sesso, *sĕs'sŏ*, m. sex; **bel –,** the fair sex.

sessuale, *sĕssŭā'lĕ*, a. sexual.

sestante, *sĕstān'tĕ*, m. sextant.   [order.

sestare, *sĕstā'rĕ*, v. a. to adjust, to set in

sestina, *sĕstĭ'nā*, f. six-lined stanza.

sesto, *sĕs'tŏ*, m. order, rule; –, a. sixth.

sestodecimo, –*dĕ'dshĭmŏ*, a. sixteenth.

seta, *sĕ'tā*, f. silk.

setaceo, *sĕtā'dshĕŏ*, a. setaceous.

setaiuolo, *sĕtăĭŭŏ'lŏ*, m. silk-manufac-
turer; silk-mercer, dealer in silks.
sete, *sā'tĕ*, f. thirst; eagerness.
seteria, *sĕtĕrē'ă*, f. silk-stuff; silk-manu-
factory; silk-mercery.
setola, *sā'tŏlă*, f. hog's bristle; brush.
setoloso, *sĕtŏlŏ'sŏ*, a. bristly.
setone, *sĕtŏ'nĕ*, m. hair-rope.
setta, *sĕt'tă*, f. sect, faction; plot.
settanta, *sĕttăn'tă*, a. seventy.
settantesimo, *−tā'sĭmŏ*, a. seventieth.
settario, *sĕttā'rĭŏ*, **settatore**, *−tŏ'rĕ*, m.
sectary, follower, partisan.
sette, *sĕt'tĕ*, a. seven. [a sect.
setteggiare, *sĕttĕdjā'rĕ*, v. n. to enter
settembre, *sĕttĕm'brĕ*, m. September.
settentrionale, *sĕttĕntrĭŏnā'lĕ*,a.northern.
settentrione, *−trĭŏ'nĕ*, m. north.
settimana, *sĕttĭmā'nă*, f. week.
settimanale, *−nā'lĕ*, a. weekly
settimanalmente, *−mĕn'tĕ*, ad. every
settimo, *sĕt'tĭmŏ*, a. seventh. [week.
setto, *sĕt'tŏ*, a. (poet.) divided, cut.
severamente, *sĕvĕrămĕn'tĕ*, ad. severely.
severità, *−vĕrĭtā'*, f. severity, rigour.
severo, *−vā'rŏ*, a. severe, rigorous.
sevizia, *−vĕ'tzĭă*, f. cruelty, inhumanity.
sevo, *sā'vŏ*, m. tallow, suet. [sections.
sezionare, *sĕtzĭŏnā'rĕ*, v. a. to divide in
sezione, *sĕtzĭŏ'nĕ*, f. section. [idle.
sfaccendato, *sfătchĕndā'tŏ*, a. unoccupied;
sfacciataggine, *−tshătād'jĭnĕ*, f. effron-
sfacciato, *−tshā'tŏ*, a. impudent. [tery.
sfaldare, *sfăldā'rĕ*, v. a. to cut in slices;
to exfoliate. [to enclose.
sfaldellare, *−dĕllā'rĕ*, v. a. to pack up,
sfamare, *sfămā'rĕ*, v. a. to satiate.
sfare, *sfā'rĕ*, v. a. to cut asunder, to destroy.
sfarinare, *sfărĭnā'rĕ*, v. a. to pulverise.
sfarzo, *sfăr'tzŏ*, m. pomp, magnificence.
sfarzoso, *−tzŏ'sŏ*, a. pompous.
sfasciare, *sfăsshā'rĕ*, v. a. to unswathe; to
pull down (walls.) [pl.
sfasciume, *−sshŏ'mĕ*, m. rubbish, ruins,
sfatare, *sfătā'rĕ*, v. a. to scorn, to disdain.
sfavillare, *−vĭllā'rĕ*, v. n. to sparkle, to
glitter.
sfendere, *sfĕn'dĕrĕ*, v. a. ir. to cleave.
sfera, *sfā'ră*, f. sphere, globe, circle,
sfericità, *sfĕrĭtshĭtā'*, f. sphericity.
sferico, *sfā'rĭkŏ*, a. spherical.
sferza, *sfĕr'tză*, f. whip, lash, scourge.
sferzare, *sfĕrtzā'rĕ*, v. a. to whip; to
chastise. [to evaporate.
sfiatare, *sfĭătā'rĕ*, v. n. to breathe; to toil;
sfibbiare, *sfĭbbĭā'rĕ*, v. a. to unbuckle.
sfibrare, *sfĭbrā'rĕ*, v. a. to enervate.
sfida, *sfē'dă*, f. challenge, provocation.
sfidare, *sfĭdā'rĕ*, v. a. to defy, to challenge; to dishearten. [deform.
sfigurare, *sfĭgŭrā'rĕ*, v. a. to disfigure, to
sfinge, *sfĭn'jĕ*, f. sphynx.
sfinimento, *sfĭnĭmĕn'tŏ*, m. faint, faint-
ing-fit, swoon.
sfinire, *sfĭnē'rĕ*, v. a. to finish, to perfect.

sfiorire, *sfĭŏrē'rĕ*, v. n. to lose the flowers;
to wither, to fade.
sfogare, *sfŏgā'rĕ*, v. n. to evaporate.
sfogatoio, *−gătŏ'ŏ*, m. air-hole, vent.
sfoggiare, *sfŏdjā'rĕ*, v. n. to be ostentatious in one's attire; to exaggerate.
sfoggio, *sfŏd'jŏ*, m. pomp, luxury.
sfoglia, *sfŏl'yă*, f. spangle, foil; lamina.
sfogliare, *sfŏlyā'rĕ*, v. a. to strip off leaves.
sfogo, *sfŏ'gŏ*, m. exhaling, evaporation;
issue, relief, ease. [ning, blasting.
sfolgoramento, *sfŏlgŏrămĕn'tŏ*, m. light-
sfolgorare, *−gŏrā'rĕ*, v. a. to blast; to
hasten; to scatter; to destroy; −, v. n. to
glitter; to lighten, to flash.
sfondare, *sfŏndā'rĕ*,v.a. & n. to pull down;
to sink in. [ground of a painting.
sfondo, *sfŏn'dŏ*, m. hollow; bottom; back-
sfondolare, *see* **sfondare**.
sformare, *sfŏrmā'rĕ*, v. a. to disfigure.
sfornire, *sfŏrnē'rĕ*, v. a. to unfurnish; to
deprive, to bereave.
sfortuna, *sfŏrtŏ'nă*, f. misfortune.
sfortunato, *−tŭnā'tŏ*, a. unhappy.
sforzare, *sfŏrtzā'rĕ*, v. a. to force, to constrain; to violate, to weaken, to enervate.
sforzo, *sfŏr'tzŏ*, m. effort, strain; attempt,
trial. [to shatter, to demolish.
sfracellare, *sfrădshĕllā'rĕ*, v. a. to smash,
sfratto, *sfrăt'tŏ*, m. flight, evasion; expulsion, banishment.
sfregare, *sfrĕgā'rĕ*, v. a. to rub; to scour.
sfregiare, *sfrĕjā'rĕ*, v. a. to dishonour;
to slash in the face. [affront.
sfregio, *sfrā'jŏ*, m. gash, scar; blot,
sfrenato, *sfrĕnā'tŏ*, a. unbridled; dissolute. [to cast stones.
sfrombolare, *sfrŏmbŏlā'rĕ*, v. a. to fling,
sfrontatezza, *sfrŏntătĕt'ză*, f. effrontery.
sfrontato, *−tā'tŏ*, a. brazenfaced, impudent. [flying away, slippery.
sfuggevole, *sfŭdjē'vŏlĕ*, a. transitory,
sfuggire, *sfŭdjē'rĕ*, v. a. to avoid, to
escape from; **alla sfuggita**, by stealth.
sgabellare, *sgăbĕllā'rĕ*, v. a. to redeem
out of a custom-house, to pay duty on.
sgabello, *sgăbĕl'lŏ*, m. joint-stool.
sgambarsi, *sgămbăr'sĭ*, v. r. to walk
quickly; to get tired.
sgangherare, *sgănghĕrā'rĕ*, v. a. to unhinge; to disorder; to dislocate.
sgannare, *sgănnā'rĕ*, v. a. to undeceive.
sgarbatamente, *sgărbătămĕn'tĕ*, ad. im-
politely, in a disobliging way.
sgarbatezza, *−tĕt'ză*, f. impoliteness.
sgarbato, *−bā'tŏ*, a. impolite; awkward.
sgarbo, *sgăr'bŏ*, m. impoliteness; awkwardness. [be mistaken.
sgarrare, *sgărrā'rĕ*, v. n. to mistake, to
sghembo, *sghĕm'bŏ*, a. crooked, tortuous,
oblique, wry.
sgherro, *sghĕr'rŏ*, m. bully, cut-throat.
sghignare, *sghĭnyā'rĕ*, v. a. to laugh at,
to deride. [into loud laughter.
sghignazzare, *−yătză'rĕ*, v. n. to burst

sgocciolare, *sgŏtshŏlā' rĕ,* v. a. to distil, to drop. [ping.
sgocciolo, *sgŏt' shŏlŏ,* m. draining, drop-
sgomberare, *sgŏmbĕrā' rĕ,* **sgombrare,** *–brā' rĕ,* v. a. to remove; to carry off; to disburden; –, v. n. to go away.
sgombero, *sgŏm' bĕrŏ,* **sgombro,** *–brŏ,* m. removal; deliverance; –, a. disencumbered, disengaged; empty.
sgomentare, *sgŏmĕntā' rĕ,* v. a. to discourage, to terrify.
sgomento, *–mĕn' tŏ,* m. fright, amazement.
sgominare, *–mĭnā' rĕ,* v. a. to disorder, to throw into disorder, to derange.
sgominio, *–mĭ' nĭŏ,* m. disorder, confusion.
sgorgare, *sgŏrgā' rĕ,* v. n. to disgorge.
sgradire, *sgrādē' rĕ,* v. a. to displease, to disgust. [etch.
sgraffiare, *sgrāffiā' rĕ,* v. a. to scratch; to
sgraffio, *sgrāf' fiŏ,* m. scratch, fresco.
sgranchiare, *sgrānkiā' rĕ,* **sgranchire,** *–kē' rĕ,* v. a. to stretch one's limbs.
sgravare, *sgrāvā' rĕ,* v. a. to unload; to alleviate, to ease.
sgravio, *sgrā' vĭŏ,* m. ease, relief.
sgraziato, *–tziā' tŏ,* a. awkward, clumsy; unfortunate, unhappy. [prove.
sgridare, *sgrĭdā' rĕ,* v. a. to scold; to re-
sgridata, *–dā' tā,* f. scolding; reprimand.
sgrigiolare, *–jŏlā' rĕ,* v. n. to clash, to crackle, to crack.
sgroppare, *sgrŏppā' rĕ,* **sgruppare,** *sgrŭppā' rĕ,* v. a. to untie a knot.
sguaiataggine, *sgŭāiātā' jĭnĕ,* f. awkwardness, stupidness.
sguaiato, *sgŭāiā' tŏ,* a. awkward, stupid.
sguancio, *sgŭān' dshŏ,* (a –,) ad. awry, athwart. [regard; to value.
sguardare, *sgŭārdā' rĕ,* v. a. to look at; to
sguardo, *sgŭār' dŏ,* m. look, countenance; aspect. [to deprive.
sguarnire, *sgŭārnē' rĕ,* v. a. to disgarnish.
sguazzare, *sgŭātzā' rĕ,* v. a. & n. to ford over; to squander. [to divest.
sguernire, *sgŭĕrnē' rĕ,* v. a. to unfurnish.
sguisciare, *sgŭisshā' rĕ,* v. n. to swim; to skip. [slide away.
sguizzare, *–īzā' rĕ,* v. n. to slip off, to
sgusciare, *sgŭsshā' rĕ,* v. a. to shell, to husk.
si, *sē',* ad. yes, truly; **– bene,** yes indeed; **si ...si ...,** as well ... as, both ... and.
si, *sē,* pn. one, people, they; **– dice,** they say. [hiss, to whistle.
sibilare, *sĭbĭlā' rĕ,* v. a. & n. to incite; to
sibilla, *–bēl' lā,* f. sybil, prophetess.
sicario, *–kā' rĭŏ,* m. hired assassin.
sicchè, *sĭkkē',* ad. thus; therefore.
siccità, *sĭtshĭtā',* f. dryness.
siccome, *sĭkkō' mĕ,* ad. as, so; as soon as; **– se,** as if. [surely.
sicuramente, *–kūrāmĕn' tĕ,* ad. certainly.
sicurezza, *–kūrĕt' zā,* f. security, safety; assurance, confidence; boldness; faith, trust; guarantee, bail.
sicuro, *–kū' rŏ,* a. safe, sure; assured; firm; clever; practised.

sicurtà, *sĭkūrtā',* f. security; bail.
sidro, *sē' drŏ,* m. cider.
sieda, *see* **sedia.** [hedge.
siepare, *sĭĕpā' rĕ,* v. a. to enclose with a
siepe, *sĭĕ' pĕ,* f. hedge; enclosure; obstacle
siero, *sĭĕ' rŏ,* m. whey.
sieroso, *sĭĕrō' sŏ,* a. serous, watery.
siesta, *sĭĕs' tā,* f. afternoon's nap.
siffatto, *sĭffāt' tŏ,* a. such, just so.
sifilide, *–fē' lĭdĕ,* f. syphilis.
sifone, *–fō' nĕ,* m. syphon; conduit-pipe.
sigillare, *–jĭllā' rĕ,* v. a. to seal; to con-
sigillo, *–jĭl' lŏ,* m. seal). [firm.
significare, *sĭnyĭfĭkā' rĕ,* v. a. to signify, to mean. [significant.
significativo, *–kātē' vŏ,* a. significative,
significato, *–kā' tŏ,* m. signification, meaning, import, purport.
significazione, *–tzĭō' nĕ,* f. signification.
signora, *sĭnyō' rā,* f. Madam, mistress, lady.
signore, *–yō' rĕ,* m. Sir, gentleman.
signoreggiare, *–rĕdjā' rĕ,* v. a. & n. to domineer, to govern, to command.
signoresco, *–rĕs' kŏ,* a. of a lord, gentlemanlike. [the court-officers.
signoria, *–rē' ā,* f. lordship; sovereignty;
signorile, *–rē' lĕ,* a. noble, illustrious.
signorilmente, *–rĭlmĕn' tĕ,* ad. nobly, magnificently.
signorina, *–rē' nā,* f. young lady, miss.
signorino, *–rē' nŏ,* m. young gentleman.
silenzio, *sĭlĕn' tzĭŏ,* m. silence, stillness; pause, stop.
silenzioso, *–tzĭō' sŏ,* a. silent, still.
silice, *sē' lĭtshĕ* m. pebble.
siliqua, *sē' lĭkŭā,* f. husk, shell (of peas &c.).
sillaba, *sĭl' lābā,* f. syllable.
sillabare, *–lābā' rĕ,* v. a. to spell.
sillabico, *–lā' bĭkŏ,* a. syllabic.
silografia, *sĭlŏgrāfē' ā,* f. xylography.
silvano, *sĭlvā' nŏ,* a. sylvan; foreign.
silvestre, *–vĕs' trĕ,* a. woody; wild.
simboleggiare, *sĭmbŏllĕdjā' rĕ,* v. a. to symbolise.
simbolico, *–bŏ' lĭkŏ,* a. symbolical.
simbolo, *sĭm' bŏlŏ,* m. symbol, allegory; similare, *sĭmĭlā' rĕ,* a. similar. [creed.
simile, *sē' mĭlĕ,* a. & ad. similar, like; in like manner. [resemblance, analogy.
similitudine, *sĭmĭlĭtū' dĭnĕ,* f. similitude.
similmente, *–mĕn' tĕ,* ad. likewise.
simmetria, *sĭmmĕtrē' ā,* f. symmetry, proportion.
simmetrico, *–mā' trĭkŏ,* a. symmetrical.
simo, *sē' mŏ,* a. flat-nosed.
simpatia, *sĭmpātē' ā,* a. sympathy.
simpatico, *–pā' tĭkŏ,* a. sympathetic; congenial; prepossessing. [pathise.
simpatizzare, *–tĭtzā' rĕ,* v. n. to sym-
simposio, *–pō' sĭŏ,* m. great feast. [idol.
simulacro, *sĭmŭlā' krŏ,* m. image, likeness.
simulare, *–lā' rĕ,* v. a. to simulate, to dissemble, to feign.
simulazione, *–tzĭō' nĕ,* f. dissimulation.
simultaneità, *sĭmŭltānĕĭtā',* f. simultaneousness.

simultaneo, _-tä'nĕŏ,_ a. simultaneous.

sinagoga, _sĭnăgŏ'gă,_ f. synagogue.

sinceramente, _sĭnshĕrämĕn'tĕ,_ ad. sincerely.

sincerare, _-dshĕrä'rĕ,_ v. a. to exculpate, to justify; **sincerarsi,** _-rär'sĭ,_ to clear up; to ascertain.

sincerità, _-dsherĭtä',_ f. sincerity, candour.

sincero, _-dshä'rŏ,_ a. sincere.

sindaco, _sĭn'däkŏ,_ m. syndic; mayor; burgomaster.

sinfonia, _-fŏnĕ'ă,_ f. symphony; concert.

singhiozzare, _-ghĭŏtzä'rĕ,_ v. n. to sob; to hiccup.   [cough.

singhiozzo, _-ghĭŏt'zŏ,_ m. 'sobbing; hic-

singolare, _sĕngŏlä'rĕ,_ a. singular, peculiar, particular; rare, excellent.

singolarità, _-lărĭtä',_ f. singularity, rarity.

singolarizzare, _-lărĭdzä'rĕ,_ v. a. to particularise.   [singularly.

singolarmente, _-mĕn'tĕ,_ ad. particularly,

singolo, _sĭn'gŏlŏ,_ a. single, each single one, one by one.

singulto, _-gŭl'tŏ,_ m. (poet.) sob, sigh.

siniscalco, _sĭnĭskäl'kŏ,_ m. seneschal; steward.   [the left hand.

sinistra, _-nĭs'trä,_ f. left hand; **da —,** on

sinistrare, _-trä'rĕ,_ v. n. to go across; to stumble; to rage.

sinistro, _-nĭs'trŏ,_ m. inconvenience, misfortune; —, a. left, left-handed; unlucky.

sino, _sĕ'nŏ,_ pr. till, until; even to, as far as; **sin adesso,** till now, hitherto; **— a che,** till, until (that); **— a tanto che,** until, as long as; **sin dove?** how far? **sin qui,** hither.

sinodale, _sĭnŏdä'lĕ,_ a. synodal.

sinodo, _sĕ'nŏdŏ,_ m. synod.

sinonimo, _sĭnŏ'nĭmŏ,_ m. synonym; —, a. synonymous.

sinuosità, _sĭnŏŏsĭtä',_ f. sinuosity.

sinuoso, _-nŏŏ'sŏ,_ a. sinuous, tortuous

sirena, _sĭrä'nä,_ f. siren, mermaid.

siringa, _-rĭn'gä,_ f. syringe; siphon.

siringare, _-gä'rĕ,_ v. a. to spurt, to squirt.

Sirio, _sĕ'rĭŏ,_ m. Sirius, dog-star.

sirocchia, _sĭrŏk'kĭä,_ f. sister.

siroppo, _-rŏp'pŏ,_ m. syrup.

sistema, _sĭstä'mä,_ m. system.

sistemare, _-tĕmä'rĕ,_ v. a. to systematise.

sistematico, _-mä'tĭkŏ,_ a. systematic.

sistro, _sĕs'trŏ,_ m. cithern.   [smell.

sitare, _sĭtä'rĕ,_ v. n. to emit an offensive

sitibondo, _sĭtĭbŏn'dŏ,_ a. very thirsty, covetous.   [(poet.) to long for.

sitire, _sĭtĭ'rĕ,_ v. a. & n. to be thirsty;

sito, _sĕ'tŏ,_ m. site, situation; house; stink.

situare, _sĭtŭä'rĕ,_ v. a. to situate, to place.

situazione, _-tzĭŏ'nĕ,_ f. situation, position.

slacciare, _slätshä'rĕ,_ v. a. to unlace.

slanciare, _slandshä'rĕ,_ v. a. to fling, to launch.   [launching of a ship.

slancio, _slän'dshŏ,_ m. casting, throwing;

slargare, _slärgä'rĕ,_ v. a. to widen, to enlarge, to stretch.

sleale, _slĕä'lĕ,_ a. disloyal, perfidious.

slealtà, _slĕältä',_ f. disloyalty, perfidy

slegare, _slĕgä'rĕ,_ v. a. to untie.

slitta, _slĕt'tä,_ f. sledge, sleigh.

slogare, _slŏgä'rĕ,_ v. a. to put out of joint.

slogatura, _-tŏ'rä,_ f. dislocating.

sloggiare, _slŏdjä'rĕ,_ v. a. & n. to dislodge; to remove.

slungare, _slŭngä'rĕ,_ v. a. to lengthen.

smacco, _smäk'kŏ,_ m. affront, insult.

smagliare, _smälyä'rĕ,_ v. a. to break the meshes; to excite, to spur on.

smagrare, _smägrä'rĕ,_ **smagrire,** _-grĕ'rĕ,_ v. n. to grow thin, to fall off.

smallare, _smällä'rĕ,_ v. a. to peel.

smaltare, _smältä'rĕ,_ v. a. to enamel.

smaltire, _-tĕ'rĕ,_ v. a. to digest; to sell off by retail.

smaltitoio, _-tĭtŏ'ŏ,_ m. drain, sewer.

smalto, _smäl'tŏ,_ m. cement, mortar; enamel: basis, foundation; floor; mosaic.

smania, _smä'nĭä,_ f. madness.   [a passion.

smaniare, _-nĭä'rĕ,_ v. n. to rage, to fly into

smaniglia, _-nĭl'yä,_ f. bracelet.

smanioso, _-nĭŏ'sŏ,_ a. furious, rabid.

smargiassata, _smärjässä'tä,_ f. brag, boast, puff, braggardism.

smargiasso, _-jäs'sŏ,_ m. hector, bully.

smarrimento, _-rĭmĕn'tŏ,_ m. error, fault, fainting, swoon, miscarriage.

smarrire, _-rĕ'rĕ,_ v. a. to mislay; to miss, to lose; to disorder, to confound.

smembrare, _smĕmbrä'rĕ,_ v. a. to dismember.

smemorare, _smĕmŏrä'rĕ,_ v. n., **smemorarsi,** _-rär'sĭ,_ to grow forgetful.

smeraldo, _smĕräl'dŏ,_ m. emerald.

smergo, _smĕr'gŏ,_ m. plungeon.

smerigliare, _smĕrĭlyä'rĕ,_ v. a. to polish with emery.

smeriglio, _-rĕl'yŏ,_ m. emery.

smettere, _smĕt'tĕrĕ,_ v. a. ir. to lay aside.

smilzo, _smĕl'tzŏ,_ a. thin, slender; spare.

sminuire, _see_ **diminuire** &c.

sminuzzare, _smĭnŭtzä'rĕ,_ v. a. to hash, to mince; to detail.   [boundless.

smisurato, _-sŭrä'tŏ,_ a. unmeasured,

smoccolare, _smŏkkŏlä'rĕ,_ v. a. to snuff a candle; to behead.   [moderateness.

smoderatezza, _smŏdĕrätĕt'zä,_ f. immoderatezza,

smoderato, _-rä'tŏ,_ a. immoderate; excessive.   [alight.

smontare, _smŏntä'rĕ,_ v. n. to descend; to

smorfia, _smŏr'fĭä,_ f. grimace.

smorto, _smŏr'tŏ,_ a. pale as death.

smorzare, _smŏrtzä'rĕ,_ v. a. to extinguish.

smotta, _smŏt'tä,_ f. landslip, landslide.

smottare, _-tä'rĕ,_ v. n. to tumble down.

smozzicare, _smŏtzĭkä'rĕ,_ v. a. to cut off, to mutilate.   [away, to dry up.

smungere, _smŭn'jĕrĕ,_ v. a. ir. to suck

smuovere, _smŏŏ'vĕrĕ,_ v. a. ir. to move, to shake; to excite; to persuade.

smussare, _smŏssä'rĕ,_ v. a. to break off the corners or angles; to truncate.

snaturare, _snätŏrä'rĕ,_ v. a. to change one's nature.

snellezza, _snĕllĕt'zä,_ f. nimbleness.

snello, _snĕl'lŏ,_ a. nimble, alert, swift.

snervare, _snĕrvä'rĕ,_ v. a. to enervate.

snocciolare, *snòtshōlä′rĕ*, v. a. to take out the kernels; to explain.

snodare, *snōdä′rĕ*, v. a. to untie.

snudare, *snūdä′rĕ*, v. a. to strip naked.

soave, *sō̄ä′vĕ*, a. sweet, pleasant, gentle, delicate, delicious; soft; calm.

soavità, *sōävitä′*, f. sweetness; kindness.

sobborgo, *sōbbōr′gŏ*, subborgo, *sŭbbōr′gŏ*, m. suburb.

sobillare, *sōbillä′rĕ*, v. a. to seduce.

sobrietà, *–brĭĕtä′*, f. sobriety, temperance.

sobrio, *sō′brĭŏ*, a. sober, moderate.

socchiudere, *sōkkĭō′dĕrĕ*, v. a. to leave ajar; to shut. [tragedy.

socco, *sōk′kŏ*, m. (poet.) buskin; (fig.)

soccorrere, *–kōr′rĕrĕ*, v. a. ir. to succour, to assist. [relief.

soccorso, *–kōr′sŏ*, m. succour, assistance;

sociabile, *sōdshä′bĭlĕ*, sociale, *–dshä′lĕ*, a. sociable, social. [ship.

società, *–dshĭĕtä′*, f. society; club; partnership.

socio, *sō′dshŏ*, m. companion; partner.

soda, *sō′dä*, f. soda, kali.

sodalizio, *sōdälĭ′tzĭŏ*, m. company, fellowship, fraternity.

sodare, *–dä′rĕ*, v. a. to strengthen; to promise; to bail, to guarantee.

soddisfare, *sōddĭsfä′rĕ*, v. a. ir. to satisfy, to give satisfaction.

soddisfazione, *–fätzĭō′nĕ*, f. satisfaction.

sodo, *sō′dŏ*, m. basement, foundation; bail; –, a. firm, solid, compact; stout;

sofa, *sō′fä*, m. sofa. [strong.

sofferenza, *sōffĕrĕn′tzä*, f. sufferance, endurance.

sofferire, *see* soffrire. [durance.

soffiare, *–fĭä′rĕ*, v. a. & n. to blow; to excite, to incite.

soffice, *sōf′fĭdshĕ*, a. soft, downy.

soffietto, *–fĭĕt′tŏ*, m. bellows, pl.

soffio, *sōf′fĭŏ*, m. blowing, puff; breath.

soffione, *–fĭō′nĕ*, m. bellows; –, a. proud.

soffitta, *–fĭt′tä*, f., soffitto, *–tŏ*, m. garret, entablature.

soffittare, *–fĭttä′rĕ*, v. a. to vault, to ceil.

soffitto, *–fĭt′tŏ*, a. hidden, occult.

soffocare, *–fōkä′rĕ*, soffogare, *–gä′rĕ*, v. a. to suffocate, to stifle.

soffocazione, *–tzĭō′nĕ*, f. suffocation.

soffrire, *sōffrĭ′rĕ*, v.a. to suffer, to undergo.

soffritto, *–frĭt′tŏ*, m. fricassee.

sofisma, *sōfĭs′mä*, f., sofismo, *–mŏ*, m.

sofista, *–fĭs′tä*, m. sophist. [sophism.

sofisticare, *–ĭtkä′rĕ*, v. a. to sophisticate.

sofisticheria, *–ĭtkĕrĭ′ä*, f. sophistry.

sofistico, *–fĭs′tĭkŏ*, a. sophistical.

soggettare, *sōdjĕttä′rĕ*, v. a. to subject, to subdue. [matter.

soggetto, *–djĕt′tŏ*, m. subject; object,

sogghignare, *sōgghĭnyä′rĕ*, v. n. to smile.

soggiacere, *sōdjädshä′rĕ*, v. n. ir. to be subject to. [jugate; to surpass.

soggiogare, *–djŏgä′rĕ*, v. a. & n. to subjugate.

soggiornare, *–djōrnä′rĕ*, v. a. & n. to keep; to sojourn, to live; to labour.

soggiorno, *–djōr′nŏ*, m. sojourn, abode; care. [join, to add.

soggiungere, *–djŭn′jĕrĕ*, v. a. ir. to subjoin.

soggiuntivo, *–tĭ′vŏ*, m. (gr.) subjunctive

soglia, *sōl′yä*, f. threshold. [mood.

soglio, *sōl′yŏ*, m. throne; threshold.

sognare, *sōnyä′rĕ*, v. n. to dream, to fancy, to imagine.

sogno, *sōn′yŏ*, m. dream; reverie.

soia, *sō′ä*, f. flattery, wheedling.

solaio, *sōlä′ŏ*, m. floor, ceiling. [solely.

solamente, *sōlämĕn′tĕ*, ad. only, merely,

solare, *–lä′rĕ*, a. solar; –, v. a. to new-sole.

solata, *–lä′tä*, f. sunshine.

solcare, *sōlkä′rĕ*, v. a. to furrow, to plough; to sail.

solco, *sōl′kŏ*, m. furrow, track; wrinkle.

Soldano, *sōldä′nŏ*, m. Sultan.

soldare, *–dä′rĕ*, v. a. to recruit, to enlist (soldiers); to raise (soldiers).

soldatesca, *–tĕs′kä*, f. soldiery.

soldatesco, *–tĕs′kŏ*, a. soldierly, military.

soldato, *–dä′tŏ*, m. soldier. [salary.

soldo, *sōl′dŏ*, m. penny; soldier's pay,

sole, *sō′lĕ*, m. sun; (poet.) year.

solecchio, *sōlĕk′kĭŏ*, m. parasol; canopy.

soleggiare, *–lĕdjä′rĕ*, v. a. to expose to the sun. [famous.

solenne, *–lĕn′nĕ*, a. solemn; splendid;

solennità, *–lĕnnĭtä′*, f. solemnity, celebration. [to celebrate.

solennizzare, *–nĭtzä′rĕ*, v.a. to solemnize,

solennizzazione, *–tzĭō′nĕ*, f. celebration.

solere, *sōlĕ′rĕ*, v. n. ir. to be accustomed; to use; –, m. use, custom, habit. [ful.

solerte, *–lĕr′tĕ*, a. careful, diligent, watchful.

solerzia, *sōlĕr′tzĭä*, f. diligence, care.

soletta, *–lĕt′tä*, f. sole for a stocking.

solfa, *sōl′fä*, f. (mus.) gamut.

solfanello, *–fänĕl′lŏ*, m. match; vesta.

solfeggiare, *–fĕdjä′rĕ*, v. n. (mus.) to sing the gamut. [the gamut.

solfeggio, *–fĕd′jŏ*, m. (mus.) singing of

solfo, *see* zolfo.

solidario, *sōlĭdä′rĭŏ*, a. bound *or* answerable for the whole.

solidità, *–dĭtä′*, f. solidity.

solido, *sō′lĭdŏ*, a. solid, consistent, durable.

solingo, *sōlĭn′gŏ*, a. solitary, desert, lonely, retired.

solio, *sō′lĭŏ*, m. royal seat, throne.

solitario, *sōlĭtä′rĭŏ*, a. solitary, retired, lonely, secluded.

solito, *sō′lĭtŏ*, a. accustomed, usual.

solitudine, *sōlĭtō′dĭnĕ*, f. solitude; retreat, retirement. [divert.

sollazzare, *sōllätzä′rĕ*, v. a. to amuse, to

sollazzo, *–lät′zŏ*, m. amusement.

sollecitare, *–lĕdshĭtä′rĕ*, v. a. to solicit, to urge; –, v. n. to make haste.

sollecitazione, *–tzĭō′nĕ*, f. solicitation, entreaty, request.

sollecito, *–lĕ′dshĭtŏ*, a. solicitous, anxious, careful; diligent, quick.

sollecitudine, *–lĕdshĭtō′dĭnĕ*, f. solicitude; haste, diligence; commission, order.

solleticare, *–lĕtĭkä′rĕ*, v. a. to tickle.

sollevare, *–lĕvä′rĕ*, v. a. to raise, to heave up; to excite, to alleviate, to ease.

sollievo, *–lĭĕ′vŏ*, m. relief, ease, comfort.

sollione, *–lĭō′nĕ*, m. dog-days, pl.

sollo, *sŏl'lŏ,* a. soft, tender, flabby; infirm.
solo, *sŏ'lŏ,* a. only, alone; —, ad. solely, only, but; **— che,** provided that.
solstiziale, *sŏlstĭtzĭä'lĕ,* a. solstitial.
solsizio, *sŏl'tzĭŏ,* m. solstice.
soltanto, *—tän'tŏ,* ad. solely, only, but; **— che,** provided.
solubile, *sŏlŏ'bĭlĕ,* a. soluble; separable.
solubilità, *—lŭbĭlĭtä',* f. solubility; separableness.
solvere, *sŏl'vĕrĕ,* v. a. ir. to untie, to melt; to resolve; to disjoin; to absolve, to deliver; to explain; to pay.
soluzione, *sŏlŭtzĭŏ'nĕ,* f. solution; explanation.
soma, *sŏ'mä,* f. back-load, weight, burden.
somaro, *sŏmä'rŏ,* somiere, *—mĭä'rĕ,* m. beast of burden.
somigliante, *sŏmĭlyän'tĕ,* a. resembling.
somiglianza, *—yän'tzä,* f. likeness, resemblance.
somigliare, *—yä'rĕ,* v. a. to compare; —, v. n. to resemble, to be like.
somma, *sŏm'mä,* f. sum, quantity; height; extremity; conclusion; result; sum; **in —,** in short.
sommamente, *—mĕn'tĕ,* ad. extremely.
sommare, *—mä'rĕ,* v. a. to sum up.
sommario, *—mä'rĭŏ,* a. & m. summary.
sommergere, *—mĕr'jĕrĕ,* v. a. ir. to submerge, to sink. [sinking.
sommersione, *—mĕrsĭŏ'nĕ,* f. submersion.
sommessione, *—mĕssĭŏ'nĕ,* f. submission, obedience. [humble.
sommessivo, *—sĕ'vŏ,* a. submissive.
sommettere, *—mĕt'tĕrĕ,* v. a. ir. to submit, to subdue.
somministrare, *—mĭnĭsträ'rĕ,* v. a. to supply, to afford.
somministrazione, *—tzĭŏ'nĕ,* f. providcommission, *see* **sommessione.**
sommità, *—mĭtä',* f. summit, top; height; sublimity.
sommo, *sŏm'mŏ,* a. supreme, highest.
sommossa, *—mŏs'sä,* f. commotion, instigation.
sommuovere, *—mŭŏ'vĕrĕ,* v. a. ir. to move; to stir up, to stimulate; to induce.
sonaglio, *sŏnäl'yŏ,* m. little bell; airbubble.
sonare, *—nä'rĕ,* v. a. & n. to sound; to play upon; to strike; to ring (the bells); to blow (a horn).
sonata, *—nä'tä,* f. (mus.) sonata.
sonetto, *—nĕt'tŏ,* m. sonnet.
sonnambulismo, *sŏnnämbŭlĭs'mŏ,* m. somnambulism.
sonnambulo, *—näm'bŭlŏ,* m. somnambulist.
sonnecchiare, *—nĕkkĭä'rĕ,* v. n. to slumber, to doze.
sonno, *sŏn'nŏ,* m. sleep, slumber; rest.
sonnolento, *—nŏlĕn'tŏ,* a. sleepy, drowsy.
sonnolenza, *—nŏlĕn'tzä,* f. somnolency, somnolence, great drowsiness.
sonorità, *—nŏrĭtä',* f. sonorousness.
sonoro, *sŏnŏ'rŏ,* a. sonorous; resounding.
sontuosità, *sŏntŭŏsĭtä',* f. sumptuousness.
sontuoso, *—tŭŏ'sŏ,* a. sumptuous, splendid.

soperchiare, *sŏpĕrkĭä'rĕ,* v. a. & n. to surpass, to outdo; to impose upon; to affront.
soperchio, *—pĕr'kĭŏ,* m. excess; insult; —, a. excessive: —, ad. overmuch, excessively. [quench, to suppress.
sopire, *sŏpĭ'rĕ,* v. a. to lull, to calm; to
sopore, *sŏpŏ'rĕ,* m. drowsiness, lethargy.
soporifero, *—rĭ'fĕrŏ,* a. soporific.
soppestare, *sŏppĕstä'rĕ,* v. a. to pound, to bruise, to crush, to squash.
soppiantare, *—pĭäntä'rĕ,* v. a. to supplant
sopportabile, *—pŏrtä'bĭlĕ,* a. sufferable.
sopportare, *—pŏrtä'rĕ,* v. a. to support, to endure; to bear.
soppressa, *—prĕs'sä,* f. press; mangle.
soppressare, *—sä'rĕ,* v. a. to press, to mangle; to oppress. [pression.
soppressione, *—sĭŏ'nĕ,* f. oppression, suppression.
sopprimere, *—prĭ'mĕrĕ,* v. a. ir. to suppress, to oppress.
sopra, *sŏ'prä,* pr. on, upon, above, over, beyond, about, towards.
soprabbondanza, *sŏpräbbŏndän'tzä,* f. superabundance. [abound.
soprabbondare, *—bŏndä'rĕ,* v. n. to super-
sopracciglio, *—tshĭl'yŏ,* m. eye-brow.
sopracciò, *—tshŏ'* m. superintendent, director.
sopraddetto, *—dĕt'tŏ,* a. above-said.
sopraffare, *—fä'rĕ,* v. a. to overcharge.
sopraffine, *—fĕ'nĕ,* **sopraffino,** *—nŏ,* a. superfine, very fine.
sopraggiungere, *—djŭn'jĕrĕ,* v. a. ir. to surprise, to take unawares; to add; —, v. n. to come unexpectedly, to happen.
soprammano, *—mä'nŏ,* a. extraordinary, excellent; invariable.
sopranimo, *sŏprä'nĭmŏ,* ad. with animosity.
soprannaturale, *sŏprännätŭrä'lĕ,* a. supernatural.
soprannome, *—nŏ'mĕ,* m. surname; family-
soprannumerario, *—nŭmĕrä'rĭŏ,* a. supernumerary. [prano; —, a. superior.
soprano, *sŏprä'nŏ,* m. counter-tenor, so-
soprappiù, *sŏpräppĭŭ',* m. overplus; addition; **di —,** into the bargain; —, ad. besides. [take unawares.
soprapprendere, *—prĕn'dĕrĕ,* v. a. ir. to
soprascritta, *sŏpräskrĭt'tä,* f. inscription, superscription; direction, address.
soprascrivere, *—skrĕ'vĕrĕ,* v. a. ir. to write the address; to superscribe.
soprascrizione, *—skrĭtzĭŏ'nĕ,* f. superscription, title.
soprastare, *—stä'rĕ,* v. a. & n. to stand above, to be higher, to be superior; to overcome; to domineer; to rule; to put off, to delay; to be imminent.
soprattenere, *sŏprättĕnĕ'rĕ,* v. a. ir. to hold back, to detain; to stop.
soprattieni, *—tĭä'nĕ,* m. delay (of payment), respite. [cipally.
soprattutto, *—tŭt'tŏ,* ad. above all, prin-
sopravvenire, *sŏprävvĕnĕ'rĕ,* v. n. ir. to happen unexpectedly.
sopravvivere, *—vĕ'vĕrĕ,* v. n. ir. to survive, to outlive.

soprintendere, *sŏprĭntĕn'dĕrĕ,* v. a. ir. to superintend.

sopruso, *sŏprō'sŏ,* m. injury. [throw.

soqquadrare, *sŏkkŭádrā'rĕ,* v. a. to over-

soqquadro, *–kŭá'drŏ,* m. ruin; confusion.

sorbetto, *sŏrbĕt'tŏ,* m. sherbet, ice-cream.

sorbire, *–bĭ'rĕ,* v. a. to sip up, to swallow.

sorbo, *sŏr'bŏ,* m. sorb apple-tree.

sorcio, *sŏr'dshŏ,* m. mouse, rat.

sorcolo, *sŏr'kŏlŏ,* m. graft, scion.

sordidezza, *sŏrdĭdĕt'zā,* f. filthiness.

sordido, *sŏr'dĭdŏ,* a. sordid, filthy, niggardly, stingy.

sordità, *sŏrdĭtā',* f. deafness.

sordo, *sŏr'dŏ,* a. deaf; dull; (fig.) inexorable; **lanterna sorda,** f. dark-lantern. [tern.

sorella, *sŏrĕl'lā,* f. sister; nun.

sorgente, *sŏrjĕn'tĕ,* f. source, origin.

sorgere, *sŏr'jĕrĕ,* v. n. ir. to arise, to rise, to get up, to ascend; to issue.

sorgozzone, *–gŏtzŏ'nĕ,* m. prop, stay; strut; blow. [to overcome.

sormontare, *–mŏntā'rĕ,* v. a. to surmount,

soro, *sŏ'rŏ,* a. sorrel; stupid.

sorpassare, *sŏrpássā'rĕ,* v. a. to surpass; to excel, to outdo.

sorprendere, *–prĕn'dĕrĕ,* v. a. ir. to surprise, to astonish; to deceive.

sorpresa, *–prā'sā,* f. surprise, astonishment; deceit, trick. [to support.

sorreggere, *–rĕj'jĕrĕ,* v. a. ir. to bear up,

sorridere, *–rĭ'dĕrĕ,* v. n. ir. to smile.

sorriso, *–rĭ'sŏ,* m. smile. [pose.

sorso, *sŏr'sŏ,* m. sip, gulp, draught; re-

sorta, *sŏr'tā,* f. sort, kind; manner, way; capital, stock, fund.

sorte, *sŏr'tĕ,* f. fate, destiny, fortune, luck; chance, hazard; condition, state; sorcery.

sortilegio, *–tĭlĕ'jŏ,* m. sorcery, witchcraft.

sortire, *sŏrtĭ'rĕ,* v. a. to draw by lots; to share, to deal out; –, v. n. (mil.) to sally; to go out. [sally.

sortita, *–tĭ'tā,* f. choice, assortment; (mil.)

soscrittore, *sŏskrĭttŏ'rĕ,* m. subscriber.

soscrivere, *–skrĭ'vĕrĕ,* v. a. ir. to subscribe, to sign. [signature.

soscrizione, *–skrĭtzĭŏ'nĕ,* f. subscription,

sospendere, *sŏspĕn'dĕrĕ,* v. a. ir. to suspend, to keep in suspense, to defer.

sospensione, *–pĕnsĭŏ'nĕ,* f. suspension.

sospensivo, *–sĭ'vŏ,* a. ambiguous, suspensory, doubtful.

sospensorio, *–sŏ'rĭŏ,* m. suspensory.

sospettare, *sŏspĕttā'rĕ,* v. a. to suspect, to mistrust; to smell a rat.

sospetto, *sŏspĕt'tŏ,* m. suspicion, mistrust.

sospingere, *–spĭn'jĕrĕ,* v. a. ir. to push with force, to stimulate, to press on.

sospirare, *–spĭrā'rĕ,* v. a. & n. to sigh, to groan; to long for.

sospiro, *–spĭ'rŏ,* m. sigh; moan.

sossopra, *sŏssŏ'prā,* ad. upside down.

sosta, *sŏs'tā,* f. peace, rest; burning wish.

sostantivo, *sŏstántĭ'vŏ,* m. (gr.) substantive.

sostanza, *–tán'tzā,* f. substance. [tive.

sostanziale, *–tzĭā'lĕ,* a. substantial.

sostanzialità, *–tzĭālĭtā',* f. substantiality.

sostare, *sŏstā'rĕ,* v. a. & n. to stop, to suspend; to appease; to pause.

sostegno, *–tĕn'yŏ,* m. prop; assistance, aid, support.

sostenere, *–tĕnĕ'rĕ,* v. a. ir. to support, to suffer; to sustain, to maintain, to nourish; to protect.

sostentare, *–tĕntā'rĕ,* v. a. to support, to prop; to nourish, to keep.

sostituire, *–tĭtŭĭ'rĕ,* v. a. to substitute.

sostituto, *–tĭtŭ'tŏ,* m. substitute.

sostituzione, *–tzĭŏ'nĕ,* f. substitution.

sottana, *sŏttā'nā,* f. petticoat; priest's cassock. [stealth, secretly.

sottecchi, *–tĕk'kĭ,* **sottecco,** *–kŏ,* ad. by stealth, secretly.

sottentrare, *sŏttĕntrā'rĕ,* v. n. to creep under; to steal in. [evasion.

sotterfugio, *sŏttĕrfŭ'jŏ,* m. subterfuge,

sotterraneo, *–tĕrrā'nĕŏ,* a. subterranean.

sotterrare, *–tĕrrā'rĕ,* v.a. to inter, to bury.

sottile, *–tĭ'lĕ,* m. misery, extreme need; –, a. subtil, thin; fine, delicate; poor; witty, ingenious.

sottilità, *–tĭlĭtā',* f. subtilty; sagacity.

sottinteso, *–ĭntĕ'sŏ,* a. understood, left out.

sotto, *sŏt'tŏ,* pr. under, with; –, ad. down, beneath. [secretly.

sottomano, *sŏttŏmā'nŏ,* ad. underhand.

sottomettere, *–mĕt'tĕrĕ,* v. a. ir. to submit, to subdue. [sion, subjection.

sottomissione, *–mĭssĭŏ'nĕ,* f. submission, subjection.

sottoporre, *–pŏr'rĕ,* v. a. ir. to put under; to subject, to subdue.

sottoscrivere, *–skrĭ'vĕrĕ,* v. a. ir. to subscribe. [tion.

sottoscrizione, *–skrĭtzĭŏ'nĕ,* f. subscription.

sottoveste, *–vĕs'tĕ,* f. under-waistcoat.

sottrarre, *sŏttrār'rĕ,* v. a. ir. to subtract; to take away; to detract from.

sottratto, *–trāt'tŏ,* m. allurement.

sottrazione, *–trātzĭŏ'nĕ,* f. subtraction.

sovente, *sŏvĕn'tĕ,* a. frequent; –, ad. often.

soverchiare, *–vĕrkĭā'rĕ,* v. n. to tumble down, to fall to ruin.

soverchio, *–vĕr'kĭŏ,* m. overplus, excess, superfluity, superabundance; –, a. superfluous, excessive.

sovra, *see* **sopra.**

sovraneggiare, *sŏvránĕdjā'rĕ,* v. a. & n. to domineer.

sovranità, *–vránĭtā',* f. sovereignty.

sovrano, *–vrā'nŏ,* m. sovereign; (mus.) soprano; –, a. sovereign, chief.

sovvenire, *sŏvvĕnĭ'rĕ,* v. a. ir. to aid, to assist; to relieve, to supply.

sovvenzione, *–vĕntzĭŏ'nĕ,* f. subsidy.

sovvertire, *–vĕrtĭ'rĕ,* v. a. ir. to overthrow, to overturn, to upset; to ruin.

sozio, *sŏ'tzĭŏ,* m. companion, partner.

sozzare, *sŏtzā'rĕ,* v. a. to soil, to stain.

sozzo, *sŏt'zŏ,* a. nasty; profligate.

spaccare, *spákkā'rĕ,* v. a. to split, to cleave; **spaccarsi,** *–kār'sĭ,* to chap, to crack.

spacciare, *spátshā'rĕ,* v. a. to sell off; to despatch; to hasten; to make an end of; to ruin, to demolish; to put to death.

spaccio, *spät'shŏ*, m. sale; course; despatch, expedition.

spaccone, *späkkŏ'nĕ*, m. braggart, boaster.

spada, *spä'dä*, f. sword; swordsman; punishment; spade (at cards).

spago, *spä'gŏ*, m. pack-thread. [parate.

spaiare, *späiä'rĕ*, v. a. to unmatch; to separate.

spalancare, *spälänkä'rĕ*, v. a. to open wide; to speak openly.

spalla, *späl'lä*, f. shoulder.

spalletta, *-lĕt'tä*, f. parapet, railings, pl.

spalliera, *-liĕ'rä*, f. back of a chair; espalier; first bench of rowers in a galley.

spallino, *-lē'nŏ*, m. epaulette; scarf.

spalmare, *spälmä'rĕ*, v. a. to tar, to careen a ship, to keel-haul.

spalto, *späl'tŏ*, m. floor, pavement.

spampanata, *spämpänä'tä*, f. boasting; ostentation. [pour out.

spandere, *spän'dĕrĕ*, v. a. ir. to shed, to

spanna, *spän'nä*, f. span, palm. [pous.

spanto, *spän'tŏ*, a. spread, extended; pom-

sparagio, *spärä'giŏ*, m. asparagus.

sparagnare, *-rängä'rĕ*, v. a. to spare, to save, to lay by, to lay up.

sparagno, *-rän'yŏ*, m. saving; frugality.

sparare, *-rä'rĕ*, v. a. to unlearn; to unfurnish (a house); to fire; to fling.

sparata, *-rä'tä*, f. great promises, pl.; boasting. [table.

sparecchiare, *-rĕkkiä'rĕ*, v. a. to clear the

spareggio, *-rĕd'jŏ*, m. disparity, disproportion. [to scatter; to extend.

spargere, *spär'jĕrĕ*, v. a. ir. to pour out;

sparire, *spärē'rĕ*, v. n. to disappear.

sparizione, *-rĭtziŏ'nĕ*, f. disappearance.

sparlare, *spärlä'rĕ*, v. a. to speak ill of, to slander. [to dissipate; to waste.

sparnazzare, *-nätsä'rĕ*, v. a. to scatter,

sparo, *spä'rŏ*, m. discharge, volley.

sparpagliare, *spärpälyä'rĕ*, v. a. to scatter here and there, to disperse, to sprinkle.

spartire, *spärtē'rĕ*, v. a. to separate, to divide; to allot. [hawk.

sparviere, *-viĕ'rĕ*, **sparviero**, *-rŏ*, m.

sparuto, *spärŭ'tŏ*, a. spare, meagre.

spasimo, *spä'sĭmŏ*, m. spasm, convulsion.

spassare, *spässä'rĕ*, v. n. to amuse or recreate oneself. [walk.

spasseggiare, *-sĕdjä'rĕ*, v. n. to take a

spassionatezza, *spässiŏnätĕt'zä*, f. apathy, indifference. [different.

spassionato, *-nä'tŏ*, a. dispassionate, inspasso**, *späs'sŏ*, m. pastime; pleasure, sport.

spastare, *spästä'rĕ*, v. a. to unpaste; to clean, to efface.

spatola, *spä'tŏlä*, f. spatula, spattle.

spauracchio, *späŭräk'kiŏ*, m. scarecrow; phantom; fright.

spaurire, *-rē'rĕ*, v. a. to frighten, to terrify, to alarm.

spavalderia, *spävälderē'ä*, a. effrontery.

spavaldo, *-väl'dŏ*, a. bold, impudent.

spaventare, *-vĕntä'rĕ*, v. a. &n. to frighten, to terrify, to daunt, to fear.

spavento, *-vĕn'tŏ*, m. fright, dread; alarm.

spaventoso, *-tŏ'sŏ*, a. frightful, fearful.

spazio, *spä'tziŏ*, m. space; interval of time.

spazioso, *spätziŏ'sŏ*, a. spacious, roomy.

spazzare, *spätzä'rĕ*, v. a. to sweep, to mop; to empty, to void; to disengage from.

spazzatura, *-tŏ'rä*, f. sweepings, pl.

spazzino, *-tzē'nŏ*, m. sweeper.

spazzola, *spät'zŏlä*, f. clothes-brush.

spezzolare, *-tzŏlä'rĕ*, y. a. to brush.

specchiare, *spĕkkiä'rĕ*, v. a. to look in a glass; to examine. [glass.

specchietto, *-kiĕt'tŏ*, m. small looking-

specchio, *spĕk'kiŏ*, m. looking-glass.

speciale, *spĕshä'lĕ*, a. special, particular.

specialità, *-dshälitä'*, f. speciality, peculiarity; province, line. [cially.

specialmente, *-dshälmĕn'tĕ*, ad. spe-

specie, *spĕ'dshĕ*, f. species, kind; image; far —, to make a strange impression; to surprise. [to particularise.

specificare, *spĕdshĭfĭkä'rĕ*, v. a. to specify,

specificazione, *-fĭkätziŏ'nĕ*, f. specification, distinction. [cular.

specifico, *-dshĕ'fĭkŏ*, a. specific, parti-

speciosità, *-dshiŏsĭtä'*, f. beauty.

specioso, *-dshiŏ'sŏ*, a. fair, pretty.

speco, *spĕ'kŏ*, m. cave, cavern, den, grotto.

specolare, see speculare &c.

specula, *spĕ'kŭlä*, f. observatory.

speculare, *spĕkŭlä'rĕ*, v. n. to speculate, to meditate. [retical.

speculativo, *-tĭ'vŏ*, a. speculative, theo-

speculazione, *-tziŏ'nĕ*, f. speculation, meditation; theory.

spedale, *spĕdä'lĕ*, m. hospital.

spediente, *spĕdiĕn'tĕ*, a. suitable, proper; necessary. [send; to finish; to hasten.

spedire, *-dē'rĕ*, y. a. to despatch, to

spedito, *-dē'tŏ*, a. prompt, swift; ready.

spedizione, *-tziŏ'nĕ*, f. expedition, despatch; (mil.) campaign, inroad.

spelare, *spĕlä'rĕ*, v. a. to pluck out the hair. [to excoriate.

spellare, *spĕllä'rĕ*, v. a. to tear the skin,

spelonca, *spĕlŏn'kä*, f. cave, cavern; re-

spelta, *spĕl'tä*, f. spelt. [treat, shelter.

speme, *spĕ'mĕ*, f. (poet.) hope, expectation.

spendere, *spĕn'dĕrĕ*, v. a. ir. to spend; to employ.

spengere, *spĕn'jĕrĕ*, v. a. ir. to extinguish;

spengersi, *spĕn'jĕrsĭ*, to be extinguished.

spennare, *spĕnnä'rĕ*, v. a. to pluck out the feathers. [thoughtless.

spensierato, *-siĕrä'tŏ*, a. reckless,

spenzolare, *-tzŏlä'rĕ*, v. n. to dangle.

spera, *spĕ'rä*, f. (poet.) sphere, globe.

speranza, *spĕrän'tzä*, f. hope; confidence.

sperare, *spĕrä'rĕ*, v. a. & n. to hope; to think. [dissipate, to destroy.

sperdere, *spĕr'dĕrĕ*, v. a. ir. to lose; to

spergere, *spĕr'jĕrĕ*, v. a. ir. to scatter, to sprinkle. [oneself.

spergiurare, *-jŭrä'rĕ*, v. n. to forswear

sperico, *spĕ'rĭkŏ*, a. spherical, globular.

spericolarsi, *spĕrĭkŏlär'sĭ*, v. r. to expose oneself to danger.

spericolato, *-kŏlä'tŏ*, a. fearful.

sperienza, *spĕriĕn'tzä*, **sperimento**,

—*mĕn' tŏ*, m. experience; experiment, trial; proof. [perience, to try.
sperimentare, —*mĕntă' rĕ*, v. a. to experiment.
sperma, *spĕr' mă*, f. sperm; seed; spermaceti.
sperperare, —*pĕră' rĕ*, v. a. to dissipate; to ravage, to destroy, to lay waste.
sperpero, *spĕr' pĕrŏ*, m. wasting; riot.
sperto, *spĕr' tŏ*, a. expert, experienced.
spesa, *spă' să*, f. expense, cost, charges, pl.
spesare, *spĕsă' rĕ*, v. a. to defray.
spessare, *spĕssă' rĕ*, v. a. to thicken, to condense. [to repeat.
spesseggiare, —*sĕdjă' rĕ*, v. a. to reiterate.
spesso, *spĕs' sŏ*, m. thickness, bigness; 'size; —, a. thick, dense; close, compact; frequent; —, ad. often, frequently; **spesso spesso**, very often.
spettabile, *spĕttă' bĭlĕ*, a. remarkable, [notable.
spettacolo, —*tă' kŏlŏ*, m. spectacle, public exhibition. [concern.
spettare, *spĕttă' rĕ*, v. n. to belong to, to
spettro, *spĕt' trŏ*, m. spectre, apparition.
speziale, *spĕtzĭă' lĕ*, m. apothecary; —, a. special, particular, peculiar; —, ad. especially.
spezie, *spă' tzĭĕ*, f. species, sort, kind.
spezieria, *spĕtzĭĕrĭ' ă*, f. apothecary's shop.
spezzare, *spĕtză' rĕ*, v. a. to dash to pieces, to split.
spia, *spĕ' ă*, f. spy, emissary.
spiacere, *spĭădshă' rĕ*, v. n. ir. to displease.
spiacevole, —*dshă' vŏlĕ*, a. unpleasant, disagreeable. [region.
spiaggia, *spĭăd' jă*, f. sea-shore, coast;
spianare, *spĭănă' rĕ*, v. a. to level; to raze; to explain.
spianata, —*nă' tă*, f.; **spianato** —*tŏ*, **spiano** *spĭă' nŏ*, m. explanade; plainness, evenness.
spiantare, *spĭăntă' rĕ*, v. a. to root out; to raze; to undo; to destroy.
spiare, *spĭă' rĕ*, v. a. to spy, to seek out.
spiattellare, *spĭăttĕllă' rĕ*, v. n. to speak the plain truth.
spica, *spĕ' kă*, f. ear of corn.
spiccare, *spĭkkă' rĕ*, v. a. to detach, to unhook; to lop off; —, v. n. to be prominent; to shine; to excel.
spicciare, *spĭtshă' rĕ*, v. a. to utter; to despatch; —, v. n. to spout, to rush out.
spicco, *spĭk' kŏ*, m. splendour, lustre.
spicilegio, *spĭdshĭlĕ' jŏ*, m. collection of literary scraps. [boar-spear.
spiede, *spĭă' dĕ*, **spiedo**, —*dŏ*, m. spit,
spiegare, *spĭĕgă' rĕ*, v. a. to unfold, to explain.
spietato, —*tă' tŏ*, a. inhuman, cruel.
spiga, *spĕ' gă*, f. ear of corn.
spigo, *spĕ' gŏ*, m. lavender.
spigolare, *spĭgŏlă' rĕ*, v. a. to glean.
spilla, *spĭl' lă*, f. pin, breast-pin.
spillare, —*lă' rĕ*, v. a. to drop, to distil.
spillo, *spĭl' lŏ*, **spillone**, —*lŏ' nĕ*, m. pin; breast-pin.
spilorcio, *spĭlŏr' dshŏ*, a. niggardly.
spina, *spĕ' nă*, f. thorn; goad; fish-bone; backbone; awl.

spinace, *spĭnă' dshĕ*, m. spinach.
spinale, —*nă' lĕ*, a. spinal.
spinare, —*nă' rĕ*, v. a. to prick with thorns.
spingare, *spĭngă' rĕ*, v. a. to jog one's feet.
spingere, *spĭn' jĕrĕ*, v. a. ir. to push, to thrust; to spur on. [bone.
spino, *spĕ' nŏ*, m. thorn, hawthorn; back-
spinoso, *spĭnŏ' sŏ*, m. hedge-hog; —, a. thorny; spinous, spiny; difficult.
spinta, *spĭn' tă*, f. push, thrust.
spione, *spĭŏ' nĕ*, m. spy; scout.
spira, *spĕ' ră*, f. spiral line.
spiraglio, *spĭră' lyŏ*, m. air-hole, vent.
spirale, —*ră' lĕ*, a. & f. spiral; spiral line.
spirare, —*ră' rĕ*, v. a. to exhale, to breathe; to inspire; —, v. n. to respire, to breathe; to blow; to expire.
spiritale, see **spirituale**. [the devil.
spiritare, —*rĭtă' rĕ*, v. n. to be possessed by
spirito, *spĕ' rĭtŏ*, m. spirit; ghost; genius; demon; sense, mind; judgment; wit; piety. [fiery; ingenious, witty.
spiritoso, *spĭrĭtŏ' sŏ*, a. spirited; lively,
spirituale, —*tŭă' lĕ*, a. spiritual; pious.
spiro, *spĕ' rŏ*, m. (poet.) breath, respiration; spirit. [pluck off feathers.
spiumare, *spĭŭmă' rĕ*, v. a. to pick off; to
splendere, *splĕn' dĕrĕ*, v. n. to shine, to sparkle. [ficent.
splendido, *splĕn' dĭdŏ*, a. splendid, magnificent.
splendore, —*dŏ' rĕ*, m. splendour, brightness. [petuous.
spodestato, *spŏdĕstă' tŏ*, a. powerless; im-
spoglia, *spŏl' yă*, f. cast-off skin; cast-off clothes, pl.; spoil, booty.
spogliare, —*yă' rĕ*, v. a. to strip naked, to divest; to dispossess, to rob, to plunder.
spoglio, *spŏl' yŏ*, m. spoil, booty; furniture; chattels, pl.
spola, *spŏ' lă*, f. weaver's shuttle.
spolpare, *spŏlpă' rĕ*, v. a. to pick the flesh off the bone; to deprive.
spolpo, *spŏl' pŏ*, a. emaciated, very lean.
sponda, *spŏn' dă*, f. edge; bank, strand; parapet.
spongioso, —*jŏ' sŏ*, a. spongy, fungous.
spontaneità, —*tănĕĭtă'*, f. spontaneousness, voluntariness.
spontaneo, —*tă' nĕŏ*, a. spontaneous, voluntary.
spopolare, *spŏpŏlă' rĕ*, v. a. to depopulate.
spoppare, *spŏppă' rĕ*, v. a. to wean.
sporcare, *spŏrkă' rĕ*, v. a. to soil, to dirty, to spot. [scene.
sporco, *spŏr' kŏ*, a. filthy, impure; ob-
sporgere, *spŏr' jĕrĕ*, v. a. ir. to put forward, to stretch out; —, v. n. to project, to come forth.
sporre, *spŏr' rĕ*, v. a. ir. to explain; to lay down; to bring forth; to hazard.
sporta, *spŏr' tă*, f. hand-basket; pudenda.
sportare, —*tă' rĕ*, v. n. to project.
sporto, *spŏr' tŏ*, m. projection; balcony.
sportula, *spŏr' tŭlă*, f. fee or bribe to a judge; present.
sposa, *spŏ' să*, f. spouse; bride.
sposalizio, *spŏsă' tzĭŏ*, m. espousals, pl.

sposare, *-sā'rě,* v. a. to marry.
sposereccio, *-ěrět'shŏ,* a. marital, conjugal.　　　　　　　　　[planation.
sposizione, *-sītzīŏ'ně,* f. exposition, explanation.
sposo, *spŏ'sŏ,* m. spouse; bridegroom.
spossare, *spŏssā'rě,* v. a. to weaken, to enervate.
spranga, *sprān'gā,* f. bar, cross-piece, cross-bar; holdfast; dove-tail.
sprangare, *-gā'rě,* v. a. to cross-bar; to thump.　　　　　　　[squander.
sprecare, *sprěkā'rě,* v. a. to waste, to
spreco, *sprě'kŏ,* m. waste, prodigality.
sprecone, *sprěkŏ'ně,* a. prodigal, lavish.
spregiare, *sprějā'rě,* v. a. to disdain, to despise, to scorn.
spregio, *sprě'jŏ,* m. contempt, disdain.
spremere, *sprě'měrě,* v. a. to squeeze out, to express.　　　　　　　[disdain.
sprezzare, *sprětzā'rě,* v. a. to despise, to
sprezzo, *sprět'zŏ,* m. contempt, scorn.
sprizzare, *sprītzā'rě,* v. a. & n. to irrigate; to spout out.
sprocco, *sprŏk'kŏ,* m. scion, sucker.
spromettere, *sprŏmět'těrě,* v. a. ir. to retract one's promise.　　　　　[stimulate.
spronare, *sprŏnā'rě,* v. a. to spur; to
spropiare, *see* **spropriare &c.**
sproporzione, *sprŏpŏrtzīŏ'ně,* f. disproportion.　　　　　　　[do foolish things.
spropositare, *-pŏsītā'rě,* v. n. to say or
sproposito, *-pŏ'sītŏ,* m. awkward error, blunder; silliness; a—, rashly, heedlessly.
spropriare, *-prīā'rě,* v. a. to dispossess; to expropriate.
spropriazione, *-tzīŏ'ně,* f. expropriation.
sprovvedere, *sprŏvvědā'rě,* v. a. ir. to destitute, to strip naked.
spruzzare, *sprŭtzā'rě,* v. a. to sprinkle; to powder.　　　　　　[to sprinkle slightly.
spruzzolare, *-tzŏlā'rě,* v. n. to drizzle;
spugna, *spŏn'yā,* f. sponge.
spugnoso, *-yŏ'sŏ,* a. a spongy, porous.
spulezzare, *spŭlětzā'rě,* v. n. to run away.
spulezzo, *-lět'zŏ,* m. precipitate flight.
spuma, *spŏ'mā,* f. foam, froth; dross.
spumare, *spŭmā'rě,* v. **spumeggiare,** *-mědjā'rě,* v. n. to foam, to spume, to froth.
spuntare, *spŭntā'rě,* v. a. to blunt; to break off the point; to erase; —, v. n. to shoot; to burst forth.
spunto, *spŭn'tŏ,* a. pale, wan.　　[cleanse.
spurgare, *spŭrgā'rě,* v. a. to purge, to
spurgo, *spŭr'gŏ,* m. spitting, spittle.
spurio, *spŏ'rīŏ,* a. a spurious, bastard.
sputacchiare, *spŭtākkīā'rě,* v. a. to spit continually; to bespit.
sputacchio, *-tāk'kīŏ,* m. spittle.
sputare, *-tā'rě,* v. a. to spit out.
sputo, *spŏ'tŏ,* m. spittle; spitting.
squadernare, *skŭāděrnā'rě,* v. a. to show openly, to manifest; to examine; to peruse (a book).
squadra, *skŭā'drā,* f. square; squadron.
squadrare, *-drā'rě,* v. a. to square; to rule; to quarter; to tear, to rend.

squadrone, *-drŏ'ně,* m. squadron, troop, band.　　　　　　　　　[liquefy.
squagliare, *skŭālyā'rě,* v. a. to melt, to
squallido, *skŭāl'līdŏ,* a. squalid; wan, pale; sad.
squama, *skŭā'mā,* f. scale (of fish); mail.
squamoso, *-mŏ'sŏ,* a. scaly.　　　　[rend.
squarciare, *skŭārdshā'rě,* v. a. to tear, to
squarciata, *-āshā'tā,* f. rending stroke, cutting blow.　　　　　　　　　[gash.
squarcio, *skŭār'dshŏ,* m. great rent, great
squarcione, *-dshŏ'ně,* m. boaster.
squarquoio, *-kŭŏ'ŏ,* a. filthy.
squartare, *-tā'rě,* v. a. to quarter; to reprimand.　　　　　　　　　[jog.
squassare, *skŭāssā'rě,* v. a. to shake, to
squilla, *skŭīl'lā,* f. little bell; sea-onion.
squillare, *-lā'rě,* v. n. to sound loud and shrill.
squillo, *skŭīl'lŏ,* m. sound.　　　　　[shrill.
squisitezza, *skŭīsītět'zā,* f. exquisiteness.
squisito, *skŭīsī'tŏ,* a. exquisite, excellent.
squittire, *skŭīttī'rě,* v. n. to yelp, to squeak.　　　　　　　　　[extirpate.
sradicare, *srādīkā'rě,* v. a. to root out; to
scragionevole, *srājŏnā'vŏlě,* a. unreasonable.　　　　　　　　　[debauchery.
sregolatezza, *srěgŏlātět'zā,* f. irregularity.
sregolato, *-gŏlā'tŏ,* a. irregular, disorderly; excessive, licentious.
sta, *stā,* for: **questa.**　　　　　[to manure.
stabbiare, *stābbīā'rě,* v. a. to fold (sheep);
stabbio, *stāb'bīŏ,* m. manure.
stabile, *stā'bīlě,* a. stable, durable.
stabilire, *-bīlī'rě,* v. a. to establish; to appoint, to settle; to place.
stabilità, *-bīlītā',* f. stability, firmness.
stabilmente, *-bīlměn'tě,* ad. firmly, constantly.　　　　　　　　　[ostler.
stabulario, *-bŭlā'rīŏ,* m. stable-boy,
staccare, *stākkā'rě,* v. a. to detach, to separate; to unhook.
stacciare, *stātshā'rě,* v. a. to bolt, to sift.
staccio, *stāt'shŏ,* m. sieve.
stadera, *stādā'rā,* f. steel-yard.
stadio, *stā'dīŏ,* m. stadium.
staffa, *stāf'fā,* f. stirrup; mould; cymbal.
staffiere, *-fīā'rě,* m. groom, lackey.
staffilare, *-fīlā'rě,* v. a. to whip.
staffile, *-fī'lě,* m. stirrup-strap; whip.
staggire, *stādjě'rě,* v. a. to seize, to sequestrate.
stagionare, *stājŏnā'rě,* v. a. to season, to ripen; to mitigate.
stagione, *-jŏ'ně,* f. season, fit time; time.
stagliare, *stālyā'rě,* v. a. to hack, to chop; to compute in the gross.　　　[quickly.
stagliato, *-yā'tŏ,* ad. shortly; distinctly
stagnare, *stānyā'rě,* v. a. to stanch, to stop; to solder; —, v. n. to be stagnant.
stagno, *stān'yŏ,* m. pool, marsh; tin.
staio, *stā'ŏ,* m. bushel.　　　　　　[pewter.
stalla, *stāl'lā,* f. stable; stall; rest; repose.
stallaggio, *-lād'jŏ,* m. stabling; stables, pl.
stalliere, *-līā'rě,* m. stable-boy, ostler.
stallo, *stāl'lŏ,* m. dwelling, habitation.
stallone, *-lŏ'ně,* m. stallion; ostler.

stamane, stămă'nĕ, stamani, –nĕ, ad. this morning.

stambecco, stămbĕk'kŏ, m. wild goat.

stamburare, –būrā'rĕ, v. n. to beat the drum.

stame, stă'mĕ, m. thread.

stampa, stăm'pā, f. press; impression, printing; print, stamp; image; mould; kind, sort.   [print, to impress.

stampare, –pā'rĕ, v. a. to stamp, to

stampatore, –pātŏ'rĕ, m. printer; – in cotone, calico-printer; – di zecca, coiner.

stampella, –pĕl'lā, f. crutch.

stamperia, –pĕrē'ā, f. printing-office.

stampita, –pē'tā, f. song; tiresome discourse.

stampo, stăm'pŏ, m. puncheon, punch.

stancare, stănkā'rĕ, v. a. to tire, to fatigue; –, v. n.; stancarsi, –kār'sĭ, to be exhausted; to tire oneself.   [tude.

stanchezza, –kĕt'zā, f. weariness, lassi-

stanco, stăn'kŏ, a. tired, fatigued; harassed.

stanga, stăn'gā, f. bar, spar, peg

stangare, –gā'rĕ, v. a. to bar, to barricade.

stanghetta, –ghĕt'tā, f. small bar; bolt.

stanotte, stănŏt'tĕ, ad. this night.

stante, stăn'tĕ, ad. & pr. since, afterwards; during; immediately.   [spoiled; rotten.

stantio, –tē'ŏ, a. stale; flat; useless;

stanza, stăn'tsā, f. room, apartment; habitation, abode, residence; strophe, instance, entreaty.   [tionary.

stanziale, –tsiā'lĕ, a. permanent, stationary.

stanziare, –tsiā'rĕ, v. a. to order, to command; to fix, to establish; to locate; to judge; –, v. n. to dwell, to reside.

stare, stā'rĕ, v. n. ir. to stand, to stop, to be, to be placed; to reside, to lodge, to dwell; to live, to remain; to last, to hold out, to continue; to cost; come state? how do you do?

starnutare, stărnŭtā'rĕ, starnutire, –tē'rĕ, v. n. to sneeze.

stasare, stāsā'rĕ, v. a. to unstop, to open.

stasera, –sĕ'rā, ad. this evening.

state, stă'tĕ, f. summer.

statico, stă'tĭkŏ, m. hostage; pledge.

statista, –tĭs'tā, m. statesman.

statistica, –tĭs'tĭkā, f. statistics, pl.

statistico, –tĭs'tĭkŏ, a. statistical.

stato, stă'tŏ, m. state; rank, condition; – maggiore, (mil.) staff.

statua, stă'tŭā, f. statue.

statuaria, –tŭā'rĭā, f. sculpture.

statuario, –tŭā'rĭŏ, m. statuary, sculptor.

statura, –tŭ'rā, f. stature, posture; size.

statuto, –tŭ'tŏ, m. statute.

stazionario, stătziŏnā'rĭŏ, a. stationary.

stazione, –tziŏ'nĕ, f. station; habitation; railway-station.

stazzonare, stădzŏn'ārĕ, v. a. to handle, to

stecca, stĕk'kā, f. splinter; paper-knife; cue.

steccare, –kā'rĕ, v. a. to palisade, to rail, to fence.   [pl.

stecccato, –kā'tŏ, m. palisade, fence; lists,

stecchire, –kē'rĕ, v. n. to dry up; to grow lean.

stella, stĕl'lā, f. star; rowel (of a spur); eye; destiny.

stellato, –lā'tŏ, a. starry.

stelletta, –lĕt'tā, f. asterisk.

stelo, stă'lŏ, m. stem, stalk; pivot.

stemp(e)rare, stămp(ĕ)rā'rĕ, v. dilute, to dissolve; to soften; to destroy;

stemp(e)rarsi, –rār'sĭ, to melt, to rot.

stemperato, –pĕrā'tŏ, a. dilated; adulterated, blunted; distempered, dissolute.

stempiato, –piā'tŏ, a. absurd, ridiculous.

stendardo, stĕndār'dŏ, m. standard, ensign.

stendere, stĕn'dĕrĕ, v. a. & n. ir. to extend, to stretch out, to spread; to enlarge, to lengthen.   [nate.

stenebrare, stĕnĕbrā'rĕ, v. a. to illumi-

stenografia, stĕnŏgrāfē'ā, f. stenography.

stenografico, –grā'fĭkŏ, a. stenographical.

stenografo, –nŏ'grăfŏ, m. stenograph.

stentare, stĕntā'rĕ, v. a. to toil hard; to labour; to delay; to vex; –, v. n. to want; to be needy; to suffer, to be in pain.

stento, stĕn'tŏ, m. toil, drudgery; misery, suffering, hardship, adversity.

stenuare, stĕnŭā'rĕ, v. a. to extenuate, to emaciate, to exhaust; to lessen.

sterco, stĕr'kŏ, m. dung, ordure; excrement.

stercorare, –kŏrā'rĕ, v. a. to manure.

sterile, stă'rĭlĕ, a. sterile, barren.

sterilità, stĕrĭlĭtā', f. sterility.

sterlina, stĕrlē'nā, f. sterling coin, standard rate (of coin.).   [nate.

sterminare, stĕrmĭnā'rĕ, v. a. to extermi-

sterminato, –nā'tŏ, a. immense, excessive.   [root out.

sterpare, stĕrpā'rĕ, v. a. to extirpate, to

sterrare, stĕrrā'rĕ, v. a. to dig up.

sterrato, stĕrrā'tŏ, m. place dug out, ditch.

stesso, stĕs'sŏ, a. self, same; egli –, himself; lo –, the same.

stia, stă'ā, f. hen-coop, mew.

stiacciare, stiătshā'rĕ, v. a. & n. to squeeze; to storm.   [cake.

stiacciata, –tshā'tā, f. bannock, thin

stiappa, stiăp'pā, f. shiver, splinter.

stidione, stiădŏ'nĕ, m. spit.

stigma, stĭg'mā, f. mark, stamp; brand.

stilare, stilā'rĕ, v. a. & n. to bring into use; to be usual.   [manner.

stile, stĕ'lĕ, m. style; gnomon; fescue;

stiletto, stilĕt'tŏ, m. small dagger; graver.

stilla, stĭl'lā, f. drop; tear.

stillare, –lā'rĕ, v. a. to distil, to instil; –, v. n. to drop; to drizzle.

stillato, –lā'tŏ, m. jelly-broth.

stima, stĕ'mā, f. esteem; regard.

stimabile, stĭmă'bĭlĕ, a. estimable, valuable.

stimare, –mā'rĕ, v. a. & n. to esteem, to value; to think, to consider, to judge.

stimolare, –mŏlā'rĕ, v. a. to stimulate, to provoke.   [incitement.

stimolo, stĕ'mŏlŏ, m. goad, spur; stimulus,

stinco, stĭn'kŏ, m. shin-bone.

stingere, stĭn'jĕrĕ, v. a. ir. to extinguish.

stioppo, _see_ schioppo.   [quantity.
stipa, _stē'pä_, f. small fire-wood; heap,
stipare, _stīpä'rē_, v. a. to condensate; to
stop; to pile, to heap up.   [give wages.
stipendiare, _–pēndīä'rē_, v. a. to hire, to
stipendiario, _–dīä'riō_, m. stipendiary;
pensioner.   [hire.
stipendio, _–pēn'dīō_, m. stipend, wage;
stipite, _stē'pītē_, m. trunk of a tree; pole,
door-post.
stipo, _stē'pō_, m. chest of drawers.
stipulare, _stīpōlä'rē_, v. n. to stipulate.
stipulazione, _–tzīō'nē_, f. stipulation.
stiracchiare, _stīräkkīä'rē_, v. n. to pull;
to overstrain; to cavil.   [to strain.
stirare, _–rä'rē_, v. a. to pull out, to stretch,
stirpe, _stēr'pē_, f. race, extraction, lineage.
stitico, _stē'tīkō_, a. costive; astringent;
close-fisted; peevish. ill-humoured; insipid.
stivale, _stīvä'lē_, m. boot; simpleton.
stivaletto, _–lēt'tō_, m. half-boot, buskin.
stivare, _stīvä'rē_, v. a. to stow, to crowd
together.
stizza, _stīt'zä_, f. anger, wrath, passion.
stizzirsi, _stītzīr'sī_, v. r. to get angry.
stizzo, _stīt'zō_, m. fire-brand.
stizzoso, _–tzō'sō_, a. irascible, passionate.
stoccata, _stōkkä'tä_, f. sword(etc.)-thrust.
stocco, _stōk'kō_, m. rapier; pole, stake;
stoffa, _stōf'fä_, f. stuff.   [stock, race.
stoia, _stō'ä_, f. mat, hassock; portico.
stoicamente, _stōīkämēn'tē_, ad. stoically.
stoico, _stō'īkō_, a. stoical.
stola, _stō'lä_, f. stole, long vest.
stolidità, _stōlīdītä'_, f. stolidity, stupidity.
stolido, _stō'līdō_, a. silly, foolish.
stoltezza, _stōltēt'zä_, f. stupidity.
stolto, _stōl'tō_, a. foolish, infatuated.
stomacare, _stōmäkä'rē_, v. n. to disgust;
to loathe, to abominate.
stomaco, _stō'mäkō_, m. stomach; loathing.
stoppa, _stōp'pä_, f. tow.   [to stopple.
stoppare, _–pä'rē_, v. a. to stop with tow;
stoppia, _stōp'pīä_, f. stubble; stubble-field.
stoppino, _–pē'nō_, m. wick; rush-light.
storcere, _stōr'dshērē_, v. a. ir. to wrest, to
twist, to distort.
stordimento, _–dīmēn'tō_, m. stunning.
stordire, _–dē'rē_, v. a. & n. to stun, to
astound; to be amazed.
storia, _stō'rīä_, f. history, tale.   [torical.
storico, _stō'rīkō_, m. historian; –, a. his-
storietta, _stōrīēt'tä_, f. short story, novel.
storione, _–rīō'nē_, m. sturgeon.
stormire, _stōrmē'rē_, v. a. to make a noise,
to rustle.   [troop.
stormo, _stōr'mō_, m. flight of birds; throng,
stornare, _–nä'rē_, v. a. to turn aside; to
deter, to dissuade; –, v. n. to fall back.
stornello, _–nēl'lō_, m. starling; peg-top.
storno, _stōr'nō_, m. starling.
storpiare, _–pīä'rē_, v. a. to maim, to lame.
storpio, _stōr'pīō_, m. hindrance; lame
person.   [tort.
storta, _stōr'tä_, f. twisting; scimitar; re-
stovigliaio, _stōvīlyä'ō_, m. potter.

stoviglie, _–vēl'yē_, f. pl. kitchen-utensils,
pots and pans, pl.
strabiliare, _strābīlīä'rē_, v. n. to be astonished, to wonder.
straboccare, _–bōkkä'rē_, v. n. to overflow,
to rush over; to dash down, to tumble
headlong.   [weary.
straccare, _strākkä'rē_, v. a. to tire, to
stracciare, _strätshä'rē_, v. a. to tear, to
rend.
straccio, _strät'shō_, m. rag, tatter; rent.
stracco, _strāk'kō_, a. weary, fatigued.
strada, _strä'dä_, f. road, way; – ferrata,
railroad, railway; – laterale, branch-
railway, branch-line; – maestra, main
road, highway; – vicinale, by-way.
stradare, _–dä'rē_, v. a. to put on the way,
to show the way.
stradiere, _–dīē'rē_, m. exciseman.
stradone, _–dō'nē_, m. large street; broad
alley.   [der.
strafalcione, _–fäldshō'nē_, m. error, blun-
strafare, _–fä'rē_, v. a. ir. to do more than
necessary.
strage, _strä'jē_, f. carnage, butchery.
strale, _strä'lē_, m. arrow, dart; misfortune.
stramazzare, _–mätzä'rē_, v. a. to strike
down; to frighten; –, v. n. to fall like a
log.
strambo, _strām'bō_, a. band-legged, crooked.
strame, _strä'mē_, m. straw; litter, lair.
strangolare, _strängōlä'rē_, v.a. to strangle,
to suffocate.
straniare, _strānīä'rē_, v. a. to estrange, to
alienate.   [–, a. foreign, strange.
straniero, _–nīē'rō_, m. foreigner, stranger;
strano, _strä'nō_, a. strange, foreign; odd,
unusual; rude; pale; –, ad. strangely,
rudely.   [ordinary, unusual.
straordinario, _strāōrdīnä'rīō_, a. extra-
strapazzare, _sträpätzä'rē_, v. a. to disdain;
to insult; to work coarsely; to harass.
strapazzo, _–pät'zō_, m. ill-usage, insult,
drudgery; fool.
strappare, _sträppä'rē_, v. a. to pluck off,
to tear off; to wrest, to wrench.
strappo, _sträp'pō_, m. jerk, wrench, pull.
strascicare, _strāsshīkä'rē_, **strascinare**,
_–nä'rē_, v. a. to drag along, to trail.
strascico, _strāssh'īkō_, m. dragging along;
train of a gown.   [floor.
strato, _strä'tō_, m. couch, bed; pavement,
stratto, _strät'tō_, a. strange; sprung, ex-
tracted; prone; addicted.
stravagante, _strävägän'tē_, a.extravagant.
stravaganza, _–gän'tzä_, f. extravagance,
eccentricity.   [to feast.
straviziare, _–vītzīä'rē_, v. n. to banquet,
stravizio, _–vē'tzīō_, m. feast, merry-
making; debauch, debauchery.
stravolgere, _–vōl'jērē_, v. a. ir. to wrest
aside, to twist round; to dislocate.
straziare, _strätsīä'rē_, v. a. to tear; to
squander; to abuse, to outrage, to torment.
strazio, _strä'tzīō_, m. slaughter; outrage,
insult.
strebbiare, _strēbbīä'rē_, v. a. to rub, to
polish; to paint one's face.

strega, strĕ'gā, f. sorceress, witch.

stregare, strĕgā'rĕ, v. a. to bewitch, to fascinate, to captivate.

stregghia, see **striglia**.

stregone, strĕgŏ'nĕ, m. sorcerer, magician.

stregua, strĕ'gŭā, f. share, scot; reckoning.

stremare, strĕmā'rĕ, v. a. to diminish.

strenna, strĕn'nā, f. New Year's gift.

strenuità, strĕnūĭtā', f. strenuousness.

strenuo, strĕ'nŭŏ, a. strenuous; brave.

strepitare, strĕpĭtā'rĕ, v. n. to make a noise; to speak loudly.

strepito, strĕ'pĭtŏ, m. noise, bustle.

stretta, strĕt'tā, f. throng, crowd; distress; strait, defile.

stretto, strĕt'tŏ, m. strait; defile; difficulty; distress; —, a. pressed; strict, strait, close, narrow, intimate; secret.

strettoio, —tŏ'ŏ, m. wine-press; ligature.

stria, strĕ'ā, f. chamfering, fluting.

striato, strĭā'tŏ, a. channelled, chamfered.

stridere, strĕ'dĕrĕ, v. n. to scream, to shriek; to crackle.

strido, strĕ'dŏ, **stridore**, strĭdŏ'rĕ, m. shrill cry, shriek; excessive cold; chattering of the teeth.

stridulo, strĕ'dŭlŏ, a. shrill, sharp, piercing, acute.

strigare, strĭgā'rĕ, v. a. to disentangle, to unravel, to undo.

striglia, strĭl'yā, f. curry-comb.

strillare, strĭllā'rĕ, v. n. to scream, to roar.

strillo, strĭl'lŏ, m. shriek, shrill cry.

stringa, strĭn'gā, f. lace, tag.

stringare, —gā'rĕ, v. a. to restrain; to compel.

stringere, strĭn'jĕrĕ, v. a. ir. to bind fast, to urge, to force.

strione, strĭŏ'nĕ, m. actor, comedian.

striscia, strĭssh'ā, f. band; streamer; stream (of light); serpent; scimitar.

strisciare, —sshā'rĕ, v. n. & a. to go trailing along; to slide, to crawl; to graze, to touch slightly.

stritolare, strĭtŏlā'rĕ, v. a. to grind, to pound, to triturate.

strofa, strŏ'fā, **strofe**, —fĕ, f. strophe, stanza.

strofinaccio, strŏfĭnāt'shŏ, m. duster; dish-cloth.

strofinare, —fĭnā'rĕ, v. a. to rub, to polish.

strombettare, strŏmbĕttā'rĕ, v. a. to sound the trumpet.

stroncare, strŏnkā'rĕ, v. a. to cut off, to break off.

stropicciare, strŏpĭtshā'rĕ, v. a. to rub; to scour; to strike against; to fatigue.

stroppiare, strŏppĭā'rĕ, v. a. to lame.

stroppio, strŏp'pĭŏ, m. hindrance.

stroscio, strŏssh'ŏ, m. murmur of waters; rushing noise; fall.

strozza, strŏt'zā, f. wind-pipe, throat.

struggere, strŭd'jĕrĕ, v. a. ir. to melt, to dissolve.

struma, strŏ'mā, f. king's evil.

strumento, strŭmĕn'tŏ, m. instrument.

strutto, strŭt'tŏ, m. lard, bacon.

struttura, —tŏ'rā, f. structure; disposition.

struzzo, strŭt'zŏ, m. ostrich.

stuccare, stŭkkā'rĕ, v. a. to do over with stucco; to surfeit.

stucchevole, —kĕ'vŏlĕ, a. troublesome,

stucco, stŭk'kŏ, m. stucco, fine plaster; —, a. satiated; tired.

studente, stŭdĕn'tĕ, m. student.

studiare, —dĭā'rĕ, v. a. to study, to attend to; to mind, to cultivate; to hasten.

studio, stŏ'dĭŏ, m. study; diligence; industry; school; school-room; model.

studiolo, stŭdĭŏ'lŏ, m. study; application.

studioso, —dĭŏ'sŏ, a. studious, diligent; quick, prompt.

stufa, stŏ'fā, f. hot-house, steam-bath.

stufare, stŭfā'rĕ, v. a. & n. to stew slowly; to keep a bagno; **stufarsi**, —fār'sĭ, to sweat; to be weary.

stufato, —fā'tŏ, a. stewed; wearied.

stufo, stŏ'fŏ, a. disgusted, weary, tired.

stummia, stŭm'mĭā, f. froth.

stummiare, —mĭā'rĕ, v. a. to scum.

stuoia, stŭŏ'ā, f. mat, matting.

stuolo, stŭŏ'lŏ, m. troop, band, quantity.

stuonare, —nā'rĕ, v. n. to be or sing out of tune.

stupefare, stŭpĕfā'rĕ, v. a. ir. to stupefy, to astonish; **stupefarsi**, —fār'sĭ, to be astonished.

stupendo, —pĕn'dŏ, a. surprising, wonderful; exquisite.

stupidire, —pĭdĕ'rĕ, v. n. to be amazed; to grow stupid.

stupidità, —pĭdĭtā', f. stupidity.

stupido, stŏ'pĭdŏ, a. stupid, dull; surprised.

stupire, stŭpĕ'rĕ, v. n. to be amazed or surprised.

stupore, —pŏ'rĕ, m. stupor, amazement.

stuprare, stŭprā'rĕ, v. a. to violate, to deflower, to ravish.

stupro, stŏ'prŏ, m. violation, ravishment.

sturare, stŭrā'rĕ, v. a. to unstop, to uncork.

sturbare, stŭrbā'rĕ, v. a. to disturb, to vex.

stuzzicadenti, stŭtzĭkādĕn'tĭ, m. toothpick.

stuzzicare, —kā'rĕ, v. a. & n. to poke, to stir up; to stimulate; to tickle.

stuzzicorecchi, —kŏrĕk'kĭ, m. ear-pick.

su, sŭ, ad. & pr. up, upon, above, over; near; — **e giù**, up and down; **su su!** courage! come on!

subalterno, sŭbāltĕr'nŏ, m. subaltern, subordinate.

subbuglio, sŭbbŭl'yŏ, m. tumult, uproar.

subissare, sŭbĭssā'rĕ, v. a. to overthrow; to submerge; —, v. n. to sink down; to perish.

subisso, —bĭs'sŏ, m. overthrow, destruction; at once.

subietto, see **soggetto**.

subitamente, —bĭtāmĕn'tĕ, ad. suddenly.

subitaneo, —tā'nĕŏ, a. sudden, unlooked for; —, ad. suddenly.

subito, sŏ'bĭtŏ, a. sudden, quick; hasty; —, ad. suddenly.

sublimare, sŭblĭmā'rĕ, v. a. to sublimate; to exalt.

sublimato, —mā'tŏ, m. (chem.) sublimate.

sublime, —blē'mĕ, a. sublime, eminent.

sublimità, —blĭmĭtā', f. sublimity.

subordinare, sŭbŏrdĭnā'rĕ, v. a. to subordinate; tion.

subordinazione, —tzĭŏ'nĕ, f. subordina-

subornare, —ŏrnā'rĕ, v. a. to suborn, to bribe, to corrupt.

subornazione, –tzïŏ'nĕ, f. subornation, bribery, corruption.

suburbano, sŭbŭrbă'nŏ, a. suburban.

succedaneo, sŭtshĕdă'nĕŏ, a. succedaneous.

succedere, –tshă'dĕrĕ, v. a. & n. to succeed; to inherit; to happen; to prosper.

successione, –tshĕssĭŏ'nĕ, f. succession; inheritance.

successivo, –sĕ'vŏ, a. (& ad.) successive(ly).

successo, –tshĕs'sŏ, m. success, event, issue, end, conclusion.

successore, –sŏ'rĕ, m. successor, inheritor.

succhiare, sŭkkĭă'rĕ, v. a. & n. to suck, to swallow. [pierce.

succhiellare, –kĭĕllă'rĕ, v. a. to bore, to

succhio, sŭk'kĭŏ, m. auger, wimble; juice.

succiare, sŭtshă'rĕ, v. n. to suck. [sap.

succino, sŭt'shĭnŏ, m. yellow amber.

succinto, sŭtshĭn'tŏ, a. tucked up; succinct, short, concise.

succo, sŭk'kŏ, m. juice, sap; moisture.

succoso, –kŏ'sŏ, a. juicy, full of sap.

succubo, sŭk'kŭbŏ, m. incubus, nightmare.

suco, see **sugo**.

sudacchiare, sŭdăkkĭă'rĕ, v. n. to perspire

sudare, sŭdă'rĕ, v. n. to sweat. [a little.

suddetto, sŭddĕt'tŏ, a. above-mentioned.

sudditanza, –dĭtăn'tză, f. quality of subject. [liable.

suddito, sŭd'dĭtŏ, a. subject, dependant.

sudicio, sŭd'dĭshŏ, a. filthy, nasty.

sudiciume, –dĭshŏ'mĕ, m. nastiness.

sudore, –dŏ'rĕ, m. sweat; toil, labour.

sufficiente, sŭffĭdshĕn'tĕ, a. sufficient, enough; qualified, able.

sufficienza, –dshĕn'tză, f. sufficiency; capacity, ability; plenty, abundance.

suffraganeo, sŭffrăgă'nĕŏ, a. suffragan.

suffragare, –gă'rĕ, v. a. to help, to favour.

suffragio, –fră'jŏ, m. suffrage, vote, help.

suffumicare, –fŭmĭkă'rĕ, **suffumigare**, –gă'rĕ, v. a. to suffumigate.

sufolare, sŭfŏlă'rĕ, v. a. to hiss, to whisper.

sugare, sŭgă'rĕ, v. a. to suck up.

suggellare, sŭdjĕllă'rĕ, v. a. to seal.

suggello, –djĕl'lŏ, m. seal; mark, sign.

suggere, see **succiare**.

suggerire, –djĕrĕ'rĕ, v. a. to suggest.

suggezione, –djĕtzĭŏ'nĕ, f. subjection.

sughero, sŭ'ghĕrŏ, m. cork; cork-tree.

sugna, sŭn'yă, f. hog's lard, grease.

sugnoso, –yŏ'sŏ, a. greasy, fat.

sugo, sŏ'gŏ, m. juice, sap.

sugoso, sŭgŏ'sŏ, a. juicy, succulent.

suicida, sŭĭdshĕ'dă, m. suicide (murderer).

suicidio, –dshe'dĭŏ, m. suicide (murder).

sul, sŭl, for : **su il**.

sulfureo, sŭlfŏ'rĕŏ, a. sulphureous.

sulla, sŭl'lă, for : **su la**.

sultana, sŭltă'nă, f. Sultaness.

sultano, –tă'nŏ, m. Sultan.

sunto, sŭn'tŏ, m. epitome, extract, abridgment.

suntuoso, –tŭŏ'sŏ, a. sumptuous. [its.

suo, sŏ'ŏ, m. his property; –, pn. his, her,

suocera, sŭŏ'dshĕră, f. mother-in-law.

suocero, sŭŏ'dshĕrŏ, m. father-in-law.

---

suolo, sŭŏ'lŏ, m. ground, pavement; sole, hoof.

suonare, sŭŏnă'rĕ, v. a. & n. to sound.

suono, sŭŏ'nŏ, m. sound, noise; tune; air; fame, report.

suora, sŭŏ'ră, f. (poet.) sister; nun.

superare, sŭpĕră'rĕ, v. a. to surmount, to surpass; to excel. [tily; nobly.

superbamente, sŭpĕrbămĕn'tĕ, ad. haughtily; nobly.

superbia, –pĕr'bĭă, f. haughtiness, pride.

superbire, –pĕrbĕ'rĕ, v. n. to become proud. [magnificent, glorious.

superbo, –pĕr'bŏ, a. proud, haughty; stately,

superficie, sŭpĕrfĭ'dshĕ, f. superficies, surface; outside. [cess.

superfluità, –flŭĭtă', f. superfluity; excess.

superfluo, –pĕr'flŭŏ, a. superfluous.

superiore, –pĕrĭŏ'rĕ, m. superior; –, a. superior.

superiorità, –rĭŏrĭtă', f. superiority.

superno, –pĕr'nŏ, a. supreme, divine.

superstite, –pĕr'stĭtĕ, a. surviving, remaining.

superstizione, –stĭtzĭŏ'nĕ, f. superstition.

superstizioso, –stĭzĭŏ'sŏ, a. superstitious; over-nice.

supino, sŭpĭ'nŏ, m. (gr.) supine; –, a. supine, on one's back; lazy; –, ad. supinely.

suppa, sŭp'pă, f. soup, pottage.

suppellettile, –pĕllĕt'tĭlĕ, f. chattels, moveables, pl., furniture. [to deceive.

supplantare, –plăntă'rĕ, v. a. to supplant;

supplica, sŭp'plĭkă, f. petition, memorial.

supplicare, –plĭkă'rĕ, v. a. to supplicate.

supplice, –sŭp'plĭdshĕ, a. suppliant, submissive, humble.

supplimento, –plĭmĕn'tŏ, m. supplement, addition. [stitute.

supplire, –plĕ'rĕ, v. a. to supply; to substitute.

supplizio, –plĕ'tzĭŏ, m. torture; punishment.

supporre, –pŏr'rĕ, v. a. ir. to suppose, to substitute. [tion, hypothesis.

supposizione, –pŏsĭtzĭŏ'nĕ, f. supposition.

suppurare, –pŭră'rĕ, v. n. to suppurate.

suppurazione, –tzĭŏ'nĕ, f. suppuration.

supputare, –pŭtă'rĕ, v. a. to suppute, to compute, to calculate, to estimate.

supremazia, sŭprĕmătzĭ'ă, f. supremacy.

supremo, –prĕ'mŏ, a. supreme.

sur, sŭr, for : **su, sopra**.

surrettizio, sŭrrĕttĭ'tzĭŏ, a. surreptitious.

surrogare, –rŏgă'rĕ, v. a. to surrogate, to substitute. [substitution.

surrogazione, –tzĭŏ'nĕ, f. surrogation.

suscettibile, sŭshĕttĭ'bĭlĕ, a. susceptible.

suscettibilità, –tĭtă', f. susceptibility.

suscitare, sŭshĭtă'rĕ, v. a. to raise up, to rouse; to revivify; to excite.

susina, sŭsĭ'nă, f. plum.

susino, sŭsĕ'nŏ, m. plum-tree.

susseguente, sŭssĕgŭĕn'tĕ, a. subsequent, consecutive. [auxiliary.

sussidiario, –sĭdĭă'rĭŏ, a. subsidiary,

sussidio, –sĕ'dĭŏ, m. subsidy, help; suggestion.

sussistenza, *–sĭstĕn' tzå*, f. subsistence.
sussistere, *–sĭs' tĕrĕ*, v. n. ir. to subsist;
· to exist, to be.
susta, *sŭs' tå*, f. packing-cord; spring.
susurrare, *sŭsŭrrå' rĕ*, v. n. to murmur,
to whisper; to coo.   [calumny.
susurro, *–sŭr' rŏ*, m. murmur, whisper;
sutura, *sŭtū' rå*, f. suture (of the skull).
suzzare, *sŭdzå' rĕ*, v. a. & n. to dry up, to
wither; to waste.
svagare, *svågå' rĕ*, v. a. to divert from, to
distract; to dissuade; svagarsi, *–går' sĭ*,
to rest one's mind; to take relaxation.
svago, *svå' gŏ*, m. distraction.
svanire, *svånē' rĕ*, v. n. to vanish, to disappear; to fade away, to fail.
svantaggio, *svåntåd' jŏ*, m. disadvantage,
detriment.
svaporare, *svåpŏrå' rĕ*, v. a. to evaporate.
svariare, *svårĭå' rĕ*, v. n. to vary, to
change, to differ.   [different.
svario, *svå' rĭŏ*, m. difference; –, a. various.
svecchiare, *svĕkkĭå' rĕ*, v. a. to renew, to
reform.   [arouse; to stimulate.
svegliare, *svĕlyå' rĕ*, v. a. to awake, to
arouse; to stimulate.
svelare, *–lå' rĕ*, v. a. to unveil, to discover.
svelenire, *–lĕnē' rĕ*, v. a. to appease, to
mitigate.   [root out.
svellere, *svĕl' lĕrĕ*, v. a. ir. to pull up, to
svelto, *svĕl' tŏ*, a, torn away; easy, nimble;
quick.   [odious.
svenevole, *svĕnĕ' vŏlĕ*, a. disagreeable.
svenevolezza, *–nĕvŏlĕt' zå*, f. ungainliness.
svenire, *svĕnē' rĕ*, v. n. ir. to faint away,
to swoon.   [winnow.
sventare, *svĕntå' rĕ*, v. a. to ventilate; to
sventura, *–tō' rå*, f. misfortune.
sventurato, *–rå' tŏ*, a. unfortunate, fatal.
sverginare, *svĕrjĭnå' rĕ*, v. a. to deflower.
svergognare, *–gŏnyå' rĕ*, v.a. to disgrace,
to shame, to violate.
svergognato, *–yå' tŏ*, a. disgraced; bold.
svernare, *–nå' rĕ*, v. n. to (pass the) winter.
sverre, see svellere.   [cabbage.
sverza, *svĕr' dzå*, f. splinter of wood; green
sverzare, *–dzå' rĕ*, v. a. to cut to chips.
svestire, *svĕstē' rĕ*, v. a. to undress.
svettare, *svĕttå' rĕ*, v. a. & n. to lop off the
tops of trees; to shake.
svezzare, *svĕtzå' rĕ*, v. a. to disaccustom.
sviare, *svĭå' rĕ*, v. a. to lead astray.
svigorire, *svĭgŏrē' rĕ*, v. a. to enervate.
svilire, *svĭlē' rĕ*, v. a. to abase; to undervalue.   [insult, to abuse.
svillaneggiare, *svĭllånĕdjå' rĕ*, v. a. to
sviluppare, *svĭlŭppå' rĕ*, v. a. to unfold.
svincolare, *svĭnkŏlå' rĕ*, v. a. to untie.
sviscerare, *svĭsshĕrå' rĕ*, v. a. to dis-
embowel, to eviscerate.
svista, *svĭs' tå*, f. oversight, mistake.
svitare, *svĭtå' rĕ*, v. a. to unscrew.
sviticchiare, *–tĭkkĭå' rĕ*,v.a. to disentwine.
svituperare, *–tŭpĕrå' rĕ*, v. a. to blame.
svogliatezza, *svŏlyåtĕt' zå*, f. disgust,
ennui, weariness.
svogliato, *–yå' tŏ*, a. disgusted, loathing.

svolazzare, *svŏlåtzå' rĕ*, v. n. to flutter, to
fly about.   [dissuade.
svolgere, *svŏl' jĕrĕ*, v. a. ir. to unfold; to
svolta, *svŏl' tå*, f. turn, turning, bending.
svoltare, *–tå' rĕ*, v. a. to bend, to unwrap;
to turn aside, to dissuade.

T.

tabaccaio, *tåbåkkå' ŏ*, m. tobacconist.
tabacchiera, *–kĭĕ' rå*, f. snuff-box.
tabacco, *–båk' kŏ*, m. tobacco; snuff;
presa di –, pinch of snuff.
tabano, *–bå' nŏ*, a. slanderous.
tabarro, *–bår' rŏ*, m. cloak, great coat.
tabe, *tå' bĕ*, f. rottenness, putrefaction.
tabefatto, *–fåt' tŏ*, a. rotten; putrid.
tabella, *–bĕl' lå*, f. rattle, clapper; (fig.)
chatterer.   [chapel.
tabernacolo, *–bĕrnå' kŏlŏ*, m. tabernacle.
tabido, *tå' bĭdŏ*, a. tabid; consumptive.
tacca, *tåk' kå*, f. notch; gap; blemish, spot;
size, stature, cut.
taccagno, *–kån' yŏ*, a. sordid, covetous.
taccherella, *–kĕrĕl' lå*, f. little notch; little
stain; little defect.   [defect.
taccia, *tåt' shå*, f. stain, blot, spot; blemish,
tacciare, *–tshå' rĕ*, v. a. to tax; to blame,
to accuse.   [chatterer; trick, trifle.
taccola, *tåk' kŏlå*, f. jack-daw, magpie;
taccolare, *–lå' rĕ*, v. n. to chatter, to prate.
taccuino, *–kŭĕ' nŏ*, m. pocket-book.
tacere, *tåtshå' rĕ*, v. a. ir. to conceal, to
pass over in silence; to hide; –, v. n. to
be silent, to keep silence; to be quiet.
tacitamente, *–shĭtåmĕn' tĕ*, ad. tacitly.
tacito, *tå' tshĭtŏ*, a. tacit, silent.
taciturnità, *–tŭrnĭtå'*, f. taciturnity.
taciturno, *–tŭr' nŏ*, a. taciturn, silent;
pensive.   [posterior, pl.
tafanario, *–fånå' rĭŏ*, m. (fam.) backside,
tafano, *–få' nŏ*, m. ox-fly, gad-fly.
tafferuglio, *–fĕrŭl' yŏ*, m. uproar, quarrel.
taffettà, *–fĕttå'*, m. taffetas.
taglia, *tål' yå*, f. cutting; slaughter, carnage;
tax, impost; ransom; alliance; stature,
size, form; condition.   [pocket.
tagliaborse, *–bŏr' sĕ*, m. cut-purse, pick-
tagliacantoni, *–kåntŏ' nĭ*, m. cut-throat.
tagliare, *–yå' rĕ*, v. a. to cut, to cut off;
to carve, to fell; to part, to divide; to
cheat, to deceive.
tagliata, *–yå' tå*, f. cut; slaughter; boast.
tagliato, *–yå' tŏ*, a. well-shaped.   [slash.
tagliatura, *–tō' rå*, f. cutting; incision,
tagliente, *–yĕn' tĕ*, a. cutting, sharp; keen;
satirical.   [size, figure; opportunity.
taglio, *tål' yŏ*, m. edge; cut; wound; shape,
taglione, *–yŏ' nĕ*, m. retaliation; tax.
tagliuola, *–yŭō' lå*, f. trap, snare.   [hash.
tagliuzzare, *–yŭtzå' rĕ*, v. a. to mince, to
talamo, *tå' låmŏ*, m. (poet.) nuptial bed.
talchè, *tålkĕ'*, c. so that.
tale, *tå' lĕ*, a. such; like; il Signor –,
such a one; so-and-so.   [be agreeable,
talentare, *tålĕntå' rĕ*, v. n. to please, to

talento, –lĕn'tŏ, m. inclination; wish, desire; fancy; talent, gift, ability; mal – de, in spite of.

talismano, –lĭsmä'nŏ, m. talisman.

tallire, tăllē'rē, v. n. to run to seed.

tallo, tăl'lŏ, m. stalk, sprout; graft; slip.

tallone, –lō'nē, m. heel, heel-bone.

talmente, –mĕn'tē, ad. so, so much, in such a manner.   [times, now and then.

talora, tălŏ'rä, talotta, –ŏt'tä, ad. sometalpa, tăl'pä, talpe, –pē, f. mole.

taluno, tălŏ'nŏ, pn. somebody, some.

talvolta, –vŏl'tä, ad. sometimes, now and then.   [dolt.

tambellone, tămbĕllŏ'nē, m. large brick;

tamburare, –bŭrä'rē, v. a. to accuse, to impeach.

tamburello, –rĕl'lŏ, m. tabour, tabret.

tamburetto, –rĕt'tŏ, m. tambourine.

tamburino, –rē'nŏ, m. small drum; drummer, drummer-boy.

tamburo, –bŏ'rŏ, m. drum; trunk; barrel (of a watch).   [thump, to strike.

tambussare, –bŭssä'rē, v. a. to bang, to

tampoco, –pŏ'kŏ, ad. no more, not even, nor yet, neither.

tana, tä'nä, f. den, cave; eye-hole; socket.

tanaglia, –näl'yä, f. pincers, tweezers, pl.

tanfo, tän'fŏ, m. mouldy taste, mouldy smell.

tanghero, –ghĕ'rŏ, a. rude, coarse.

tantino, –tē'nŏ, m. very little bit; –, a. very little, least.

tanto, tän'tŏ, a. so much, as much, so many, as many; – o quanto, ever so little; da –, so capable; so clever; essere –, to be sufficient; –, ad. so much, to that degree; only, but; a –, di –, so, to such a degree; di – in –, from time to time; in –, in the mean time; non –, not only, notwithstanding; per –, however, nevertheless; a – per –, at this rate; – per uno, so much each.

tantochè, –kē', c. as long as, so that, insomuch that, until.

tantosto, –tŏs'tŏ, ad. immediately.

tapinare, tăpĭnä'rē, v. n. to lead a dog's life; tapinarsi, –när'sĭ, to fret, to repine.

tapino, –pē'nŏ, a. wretched, miserable.

tappeto, tăppē'tŏ, m. carpet, cover.

tappezzare, –tzä'rē, v. a. to hang with tapestry.   [ings, pl.

tappezzeria, –tzĕrē'ä, f. tapestry, hang-

tappezziere, –tzĭē'rē, m. upholsterer; paper-hanger.

tara, tä'rä, f. tare, waste (of goods).

tarabuso, tărăbŏ'sŏ, m. bittern.

tarantella, tărăntĕl'lä, f. tarantula.

tarantello, –tĕl'lŏ, m. overweight.

tarantola, –răn'tŏlä, f. tarantula.

tarantolato, –lä'tŏ, a. bit by a tarantula.

tarchiato, tărkĭä'tŏ, a. strong-limbed, sturdy.

tardare, tărdä'rē, v. a. to retard, to put off, to delay; to arrest; to hinder; –, v. n. to tarry, to stay, to loiter; to grow late; il mio oriuolo tarda, my watch goes too slow.

tardi, tär'dĭ, ad. late; slowly.   [too slow.

tardità, tărdĭtä', f. slowness, indolence.

tardivo, –dē'vŏ, tardo, –tär'dŏ, a. slow, lazy; late, tardy; dull, heavy.

tarlare, –lä'rē, v. n. to get worm-eaten

tarlo, tär'lŏ, m. wood-worm, moth.

tarma, tär'mä, f. wood-louse, centipede.

taroccare, tărŏkkä'rē, v. n. to bluster; to fume, to rage.   [stutter, to stammer.

tartagliare, tărtălyä'rē, v. a. & n. to

tartareo, –tä'rēŏ, a. hellish, infernal.

tartaro, tär'tärŏ, m. Tartarus, hell; tartar.

tartaruga, –tärŏ'gä, f. tortoise, tortoise-shell.   [thrash; to harass, to abuse.

tartassare, –tässä'rē, v. a. to beat, to

tartufo, –tŭ'fŏ, m. truffle.

tasca, täs'kä, f. pocket, satchel, wallet.

tassa, täs'sä, f. tax, duty, impost; assessment, rate.

tassare, tässä'rē, v. a. to tax, to rate, to assess; to charge with, to accuse; to blame.

tasso, täs'sŏ, m. yew-tree; badger; anvil.

tasta, täs'tä, f. probe; tent, lint; chagrin, ennui.

tastare, –tä'rē, v. a. to touch, to handle; to probe, to sound; to try, to taste.

tastatura, –tŏ'rä, f. finger-board; keys of an organ, pl.   [feel, to handle.

tasteggiare, –tĕdjä'rē, v. a. to touch, to

tasto, täs'tŏ, m. touch, feeling; tact; key of an organ or piano-forte.

tattamella, tăttämĕl'lä, f. chat, tittle-tattle.

tattica, tät'tĭkä, f. tactics, pl.

tattico, tät'tĭkŏ, a. tactical.

tatto, tät'tŏ, m. sense of feeling; touch. tact; finesse.

tauro, tää'rŏ, m. bull; Taurus.

tautologia, –tŏlŏjē'ä, f. tautology.

taverna, tävĕr'nä, f. pot-house.

taverniere, –vĕrnĭē'rē, m. pot-house keeper; drunkard.

tavola, tä'vŏlä, f. table, board; counter; roll, register, fare; index; chess-board; – danzante, turning table.

tavoletta, –lĕt'tä, f. small table, toilet; (paint.) pallet.

tavoliere, –lĭä'rē, m. chess-board, draught board, card-table; gamester's bank; banker, dealer in money.

tazza, tät'zä, f. cup; cup-full; flat tumbler.

tazzetta, –zĕt'tä, f. small cup; daffodil, narcissus; foundation.

te, tē, pn. thee.

teatrale, tĕäträ'lē, a. theatrical.

teatro, tĕä'trŏ, m. theatre.

teccola, tĕk'kŏlä, f. very small spot.

tecnico, tĕk'nĭkŏ, a. technical.

teco, tĕ'kŏ, pn. with thee.

teda, tĕ'dä, f. nuptial torch; larch-tree.

tediare, tĕdĭä'rē, v. n. to tire, to tease, to annoy.

tedio, tĕ'dĭŏ, m. tediousness, weariness.

tedioso, tĕdĭŏ'sŏ, a. tedious, tiresome.

tegame, tĕgä'mē, m. earthen stew-pan.

tegnente, tĕnyĕn'tē, a. tenacious, viscous; stingy, sordid, mean.

tegola, –gŏlä, f., tegolo, –gŏlŏ, m. tile

tela, *tā′lă,* f. cloth; linen; canvass; picture; – **d' oro,** gold-leaf; – **di ragno,** cobweb.

telaio, *tĕlā′ŏ,* m. weaver's loom; painter's frame; printer's chase.

telefono, *tĕlĕ′fŏnŏ,* m. telephone.

telegrafare, *–grā′fā′rĕ,* v.a. to telegraphize.

telegrafia, *–grā′jĕ′ă,* f. telegraphy.

telegrafico, *–grā′fĭkŏ,* a. telegraphic.

telegrafo, *–tă′grāfŏ,* m. telegraph.

teleria, *tĕlĕrĕ′ă,* f. linen-trade; quantity of linen. [glass.

telescopio, *tĕlĕskŏ′pĭŏ,* m. telescope, spy-glass; toll-booth.

telo, *tă′lŏ,* m. breadth of cloth; extension; (poet.) dart, arrow; dash of lightning.

telonio, *tĕlŏ′nĭŏ,* m. money-changer's counter; toll-booth.

tema, *tā′mă,* f. fear, apprehension; alarm.

tema, *tā′mă,* m. theme, thesis.

temerario, *tĕmĕrā′rĭŏ,* a. rash, imprudent, inconsiderate. [hesitate.

temere, *tĕmā′rĕ,* v.a. to fear, to dread; to

temerità, *–mĕrĭtă′,* f. temerity, rashness.

tempellare, *tĕmpĕllă′rĕ,* v.a. to shake, to toss; to stir; –, v.n. to vacillate, to waver; to hesitate.

tempera, *tĕm′pĕrā,* f. temper; humour; disposition, character; way; kind, sort; accord, harmony; **a –,** in water-colours.

temperamento, *–pĕrămĕn′tŏ,* m. temperament, temper. [sober.

temperante, *–pĕrăn′tĕ,* a. tempering;

temperanza, *–pĕrăn′tză,* f. temperance, moderation.

temperare, *–pĕrā′rĕ,* v.a. to temper; to mix; to moderate; to prepare, to regulate; – **una penna,** to make a pen.

temperato, *–pĕrā′tŏ,* a. tempered; temperate, sober. [temper.

temperatura, *–rătŏ′ră,* f. temperature.

temperino, *–rĕ′nŏ,* m. pen-knife.

tempesta, *–pĕs′tă,* f. tempest, hail-storm.

tempestare, *–pĕstā′rĕ,* v.a. to trouble, to harass, to annoy; –, v.n. to storm, to rage, to foam, to be tempestuous.

tempestivo, *–tĕ′vŏ,* a. timely, opportune, seasonable; suitable, advantageous.

tempestoso, *–tŏ′sŏ,* a. tempestuous, stormy.

tempio, *tĕm′pĭŏ,* m. temple; church.

tempo, *tĕm′pŏ,* m. time; weather; leisure, opportunity; season; **a –,** in good time, opportunely; **col –,** in time; **di – in –,** now and then; **per –,** early, betimes; **già –,** long since, a long while ago; **a suo –,** at the fitting moment; **un –,** formerly, for some time.

tempone, *–pŏ′nĕ,* m. long time; feasting, joy; amusement.

temporale, *–pŏrā′lĕ,* a. temporal, transitory; perishable; secular, wordly.

temporaneo, *–pŏrā′nĕŏ,* a. temporary.

temporeggiare, *–pŏrĕdjā′rĕ,* v.a. & n. to temporise; to put off, to delay.

tempra, *tĕm′pră,* f. temper; humour.

temprare &c., *see* **temperare &c.**

tenace, *tĕnā′dshĕ,* a. tenacious, viscous; persevering, firm; close-fisted.

tenacità, *–nădshĭtă′,* f. clamminess; avarice. [hangings, pl.; awning.

tenda, *tĕn′dă,* f. tent; curtain; bed-curtain,

tendenza, *–dĕn′tză,* f. tendency, propensity; direction.

tender, *tĕn′dĕr,* m. tender of a locomotive.

tendere, *tĕn′dĕrĕ,* v.a. to extend, to stretch; to spread.

tendine, *tĕn′dĭnĕ,* f. tendon. [to spread.

tendinoso, *–dĭnŏ′sŏ,* a. sinewy.

tenebre, *tĕ′nĕbrĕ,* f. pl. darkness, obscurity.

tenebrare, *tĕnĕbrā′rĕ,* v.n. to darken; to grow gloomy.

tenebroso, *–brŏ′sŏ,* a. dark; gloomy.

tenente, *tĕnĕn′tĕ,* m. lieutenant.

tenere, *tĕnā′rĕ,* v.a. ir. to hold; to keep; to take; to direct; to shelter; to judge, to believe; –, v.n. to dwell, to live; to be firm; to set off; **tenersi,** –nĕr′sĕ, to think oneself; to forbear; –, m. handle, hold; dominion.

tenero, *tă′nĕrŏ,* a. tender, soft; delicate, sensible; ticklish, captious; zealous.

tenerume, *tĕnĕrŏ′mĕ,* m. cartilages, tendrils, pl.; shoots, pl.

tenia, *tā′nĭă,* m. tenia, tape-worm.

tenimento, *tĕnĭmĕn′tŏ,* m. stay, prop, support; property, holding; obligation, duty.

tenitorio, *–tŏ′rĭŏ,* m. territory.

tenore, *tĕnŏ′rĕ,* m. tenor, contents; true intent, substance; meaning; manner; accord, harmony; (mus.) tenor, tenor-singer.

tenta, *tĕn′tă,* f. probe; trial, experiment.

tentare, *–tā′rĕ,* v.a. to attempt, to try; to probe, to touch lightly; to urge, to instigate. [experiment.

tentativo, *–tātĕ′vŏ,* m. attempt, trial,

tentennare, *–tĕnnā′rĕ,* v.a. & n. to shake, to toss; to waver, to vacillate; to nod; to knock at the door, to rap.

tentennino, *–nĕ′nŏ,* m. restless man.

tentone, *–tŏ′nĕ,* **tentoni,** *–nĕ,* ad. groping along, in the dark.

tenue, *tă′nŭĕ,* a. slender, thin, slight; poor.

tenuità, *tĕnŭĭtă′,* f. tenuity; thinness, smallness. [pacity.

tenuta, *tĕnŭ′tă,* f. possession, estate; capacity.

tenzonare, *tĕntzŏnā′rĕ,* v.a. to dispute, to contest, to quarrel; to battle, to combat.

tenzone, *–tzŏ′nĕ,* f. dispute, contest; fight, single combat.

teologia, *tĕŏlŏjĕ′ă,* f. theology.

teologico, *–lŏ′jĭkŏ,* a. theological.

teologo, *tĕŏ′lŏgŏ,* m. theologian; professor of divinity.

teorema, *tĕŏrā′mă,* m. theorem.

teoretico, *–rā′tĭkŏ,* a. theoretical; speculative. [speculation.

teoria, *–rĕ′ă,* **teorica,** *tĕŏ′rĭkă,* f. theory;

teorico, *tĕŏ′rĭkŏ,* m. theorist; –, a. theoretical, speculative.

tepidezza, *tĕpĭdĕt′ză,* tepidity, **tepidità,** *–dĭtă′,* f. lukewarmness; indifference.

tepido, *tă′pĭdŏ,* a. lukewarm; indifferent.

tergere, *tĕr′jĕrĕ,* v.a. ir. to clean, to scour; to dry. [versate, to shuffle.

tergiversare, *–jĭvĕrsā′rĕ,* v.n. to tergiversate, to shuffle.

tergo, *tĕr′gŏ,* m. back; **a –,** behind.

teriaca, *tĕrīä′ kä,* f. treacle.

terme, *tĕr′mĕ,* f. pl. hot-baths, pl.

terminare, *—mīnä′rĕ,* v. a. to limit; to conclude, to finish, to close.

terminazione, *—tzīō′nĕ,* f. termination; end, term; (gr.) ending.

termine, *tĕr′mīnĕ,* m. term, limit; end; aim; state, condition; **– tecnico,** technical term; **termini,** pl. words, terms, expressions, pl.

termometro, *—mō′mĕtrō,* m. thermometer.

ternario, *—nä′rīō,* a. triple, threefold.

terno, *tĕr′nō,* m. six (at dice).

terra, *tĕr′rä,* f. earth; land, ground; world; country, province; estate, landed property, farm.

terracotta, *—kŏt′tä,* f. baked clay.

torragno, *—rän′yō,* a. creeping; low.

terrapienare, *tĕrräpīĕnä′rĕ,* v. a. to terrace.

terrapieno, *—pīĕ′nō,* m. platform, terrace.

terrazza, *—rät′zä,* f. terrace.

terrazzo, *—rät′zō,* m. belvedere.

terremoto, *tĕrrĕmō′tō,* m. earthquake.

terreno, *tĕrrä′nō,* m. land, ground; territory; district; vestibule; **pian –,** ground-floor.   [terrestrial, earthly.

terreno, *—rä′nō,* **terrestre,** *—rĕs′trĕ,* a.

terribile, *tĕrrē′bĭlĕ,* a. terrible.

terribilità, *—rĭbĭlĭtä′,* f. terribleness, dread.   [dreadfully.

terribilmente, *—bĭlmĕn′tĕ,* ad. terribly,

territorio, *—rĭtō′rĭō,* m. territory, district.

terrore, *tĕrrō′rĕ,* m. terror, dread.

terso, *tĕr′sō,* a. clean; bright, neat, spruce; terse.   [(nar.) foresail

terzeruolo, *—tzĕrŭō′lō,* m. holster-pistol.

terzetta, *—zĕt′tä,* f. pocket-pistol.

terzetto, *—zĕt′tō,* m., **terzina,** *—tzĭ′nä,* f. triplet (verse).   [neuter.

terzo, *tĕr′tzō,* m. third part; **–,** a. third;

tesa, *tä′sä,* f. tension; brim (of a hat).

tesaurizzare, *tĕsäŭrĭdzä′rĕ,* v. a. to treasure up, to amass, to hoard.

tesi, *tä′sĭ,* f. thesis, position.   [rership.

tesoreria, *tĕsōrĕrē′ä,* f. treasury, treasu-

tesoriere, *—rĭä′rĕ,* m. treasurer.

tesoro, *tĕsō′rō,* m. treasure, riches; stock.

tessera, *tĕs′sĕrä,* f. tally; mark, sign; **tesserandolo,** see **tessitore.**   [pledge.

tessere, *tĕs′sĕrĕ,* v. a. to weave, to inter-weave; (fig.) to plot; to contrive.

tessitore, *—sĭtō′rĕ,* m. weaver; contriver.

tessitura, *—tō′rä,* f. weaving; web; texture; framework.

testa, *tĕs′tä,* f. head; chief; person; mind, judgment; top; front, extremity.

testamentare, *—tämĕntä′rĕ,* v. a. to make one's will.   [tary.

testamentario, *—mĕntä′rĭō,* a. testamen-

testamento, *—mĕn′tō,* m. testament, will; Holy Scripture.

testare, *tĕstä′rĕ,* v. n. to bequeath, to leave by will; **–,** v. n. to make one's will.

testatore, *—tō′rĕ,* m. testator.

testatrice, *—trē′dshĕ,* f. testatrix.

testè, *tĕstĕ′,* ad. just now, lately.

testereccio, *tĕstĕrĕt′shō,* a. headstrong,

testicolo, *—tĕ′kŏlō,* m. testicle.   [obstinate.

testificare, *—tĭfīkä′rĕ,* v. a. to testify, to attest, to certify.

testimone, *—tĭmō′nĕ,* m. (poet.) witness.

testimoniare, *—mōnĭä′rĕ,* v. a. to testify, to give evidence, to affirm upon oath.

testimonio, *—mō′nĭō,* m. witness, eye-witness; evidence.   [pan; earthen pot-lid.

testo, *tĕs′tō,* m. text; flower-pot; baking-

testore, *tĕstō′rĕ,* m. weaver.

testudineo, *—tŭdĭnä′ō,* a. idle, lazy, slow.

testuggine, *—tŭd′jĭnĕ,* f. tortoise; testudo (war-engine).

testura, *—tō′rä,* f. weaving; texture, tissue.

tetano, *tä′tänō,* m. tetanus, cramp; stiffness.   [ness, horror.

tetraggine, *tĕträd′jĭnĕ,* f. obscurity; dreari-

tetro, *tä′trō,* a. dark.

tetta, *tĕt′tä,* f. nipple, teat.   [breast.

tettare, *—tä′rĕ,* v. a. to suck, to draw the

tetto, *tĕt′tō,* m. roof; (fig.) house.

tettoia, *—tō′ä,* f. penthouse.

ti, *tĭ,* pn. thee, to thee; thyself.

tiara, *tĭä′rä,* f. tiara, mitre.

tibia, *tĭ′bĭä,* f. flute, flageolet; shank, shin.

ticchio, *tĭk′kĭō,* m. whim, caprice; ridiculousness.   [ous habit.

tiepido, *see* **tepido.**

tiglio, *tĭl′yō,* m. linden-tree; fibre; vein in stones, streak.

tiglioso, *—yō′sō,* a. tough; fibrous.

tigna, *tĕn′yä,* f. scurf, scab; trouble.

tignuola, *—yŭō′lä,* f. moth, weevil.

tigra, *tĭ′grä,* f. tigress.

tigre, *tĭ′grĕ,* **tigro,** *—grō,* m. tiger.

timballo, *tĭmbäl′lō,* m. tymbal, kettle-drum.

timidità, *—mĭdĭtä′,* f. timidity, fear.

timido, *tĭ′mĭdō,* a. timid, fearful; bashful,

timo, *tĭ′mō,* m. thyme.

timone, *tĭmō′nĕ,* m. rudder, helm; carriage-pole; guide; hand-gearing, regulator.

timoniere, *—mōnĭä′rĕ,* m. steersman, pilot,

timorato, *tĭmōrä′tō,* a. godly, pious.

timore, *—mō′rĕ,* m. fear; apprehension, alarm.

timoroso, *—mōrō′sō,* a. fearful, timid.

timpano, *tĭm′pänō,* m. tabour, tympanum; wheel.

tinca, *tĭn′kä,* f. tench (fish).

tinella, *tĭnĕl′lä,* f. small vat.   [stain.

tingere, *tĭn′jĕrĕ,* v. a. to tinge, to dye; to

tino, *tĭ′nō,* m. large vat; wine-press; wine-cask; bathing-tub.   [tub.

tinozza, *tĭnŏt′zä,* f. washing-tub; bathing-

tinta, *tĭn′tä,* f. tint, colour; dye-house.

tintinno, *—tĭn′nō,* m. tinkling.

tintinnare, *—tĭnnä′rĕ,* v. a. & n. to tinkle

tintore, *—tō′rĕ,* m. dyer.   [to resound.

tintoria, *—tōrē′ä,* f. dye-house.   [tract.

tintura, *—tō′rä,* f. dye, tint; tincture, extipico, *tĭ′pĭkō,* a. typical.

tipo, *tĭ′pō,* m. type, model.   [printig-house.

tipografia, *tĭpōgräfē′ä,* f. typography;

tipografico, *—grä′fĭkō,* a. typographical.

tipografo, *—pō′gräfō,* m. typographer, printer.

tiranneggiare, *tĭrănĕdjă'rĕ,* v. a. to tyrannize over.
tirannico, *tĭrăn'nĭtŏ,* a. tyrannical.
tirannia, *–rănnĕ'ŭ,* f. tyranny, cruelty.
tiranno, *–răn'nŏ,* m. tyrant, oppressor.
tirare, *tĭră'rĕ,* v. a. to draw, to pull, to drag; to extend; to allure; to throw, to shoot; to aim at; to print; –, v. n. to advance towards, to approach.
tirata, *tĭră'tă,* f. drawing; draught; way.
tirato, *–ră'tŏ,* a. drawn, stretched; clear, limpid, light, bright.
tiro, *tĕ'rŏ,* m. throw, shot; reach; draught; trick; viper; yoke (of oxen); – **a sei,** a coach and six.   [education.
tirocinio, *tĭrŏdshĕ'nĭŏ,* m. novitiate; [education.
tirone, *–rŏ'nĕ,* m. novice, apprentice.
tirso, *tĭr'sŏ,* m. thyrsus.
tisi, *tĭ'sĭ,* **tisichezza,** *tĭsĭkĕt'ză,* f. phthisis, consumption.
tisico, *tĭ'sĭkŏ,* a. consumptive; emaciated.
titillare, *tĭtĭllă'rĕ,* v. a. to tickle; to please.
titolare, *–tŏlă'rĕ,* a. titular; –, v. a. to give a title, to name, to call.
titolo, *tĭ'tŏlŏ,* m. title; dignity; plea; title-page.   [stagger; to hesitate.
titubare, *tĭtŭbă'rĕ,* v. n. to waver, to
tizzone, *tĭtzŏ'nĕ,* m. brand, firebrand.
toccare, *tŏkkă'rĕ,* v. a. to touch, to feel; to excite, to drive on; to strike, to offend; to receive; to play upon; to concern; to mention; to obtain.
toccato, *–kă'tŏ,* m. touch, feeling.
tocco, *tŏk'kŏ,* m. touch, feeling; stroke; little bit.
toeletta, *tŏĕlĕt'tă,* f. toilet, dressing-table.
togliere, *tŏl'yĕrĕ,* v. a. ir. to take (away); to carry off; to seize; to deliver; to dissuade; to undertake; to borrow; to hinder; to try.
tollerante, *tŏllĕrăn'tĕ,* a. tolerant. [tion.
tolleranza, *–răn'tză,* f. tolerance, tolera-
tollerare, *–ră'rĕ,* v. a. to tolerate.
tomba, *tŏm'bă,* f. tomb; granary; farmhouse.
tomo, *tŏ'mŏ,* m. volume, tome.
tonare, *tŏnă'rĕ,* v. a. & n. to thunder; to
tonchio, *tŏn'kĭŏ,* m. weevil, mite. [roar.
tondino, *–dĕ'nŏ,* m. small plate; hoop.
tondo, *tŏn'dŏ,* m. sphere, globe; plate; –, a. round, circular; heavy, coarse.
tonno, *tŏn'nŏ,* m. tunny (fish).
tonsura, *–sŏ'ră,* f. tonsure.
tontina, *–tĕ'nă,* f. life-rent.
topaia, *tŏpăŭ'ă,* f. rat's nest.
topo, *tŏ'pŏ,* m, rat; mouse.
toppa, *tŏp'pă,* f. door-lock.
toppo, *tŏp'pŏ,* m. log of wood, block, trunk.
torace, *tŏră̆'shĕ,* m. thorax, chest.
torba, *tŏr'bă,* f. turf (fuel).
torbido, *tŏr'bĭdŏ,* a. troubled; turbulent.
torbo, *tŏr'bŏ,* a. thick, muddy.
torcere, *tŏr'dshĕrĕ,* v. a. ir. to twist, to writhe, to turn, to wring.
torchio, *tŏr'kĭŏ,* m. torch.
torcia, *tŏr'dshă,* f. torch; taper.
torcolo, *tŏr'kŏlŏ,* m. press.

tordo, *tŏr'dŏ,* m. thrush; simpleton.
torello, *tŏrĕl'lŏ,* m. young bull.
torlo, see **tuorlo.**
torma, *tŏr'mă,* f. troop, multitude, crowd.
tormentare, *–mĕntă'rĕ,* v. a. to torment.
tormento, *–mĕn'tŏ,* m. torment, torture.
tornare, *tŏrnă'rĕ,* v. a. & n. to return; to come back; to begin again; to be just; to remember; to happen.
tornasole, *–sŏ'lĕ,* m. sun-flower.
tornata, *–nă'tă,* f. return; session, meeting.
torneare, *–nĕă'rĕ,* v. a. to enclose, to fence; –, v. n. to joust, to tilt.
torneo, *–nĕ'ŏ,* m. tournament, tilt; turn.
torniaio, *–nĭă̆'ŏ,* m. turner.
tornio, *tŏr'nĭŏ,* m. turner's wheel or lath.
torno, *tŏr'nŏ,* m. turn; turning-lath; –, ad. about, nearly.
toro, *tŏ'rŏ,* m. bull; Taurus; nuptial bed.
toroso, *tŏrŏ'sŏ,* a. nervous, fleshy.
torpedine, *tŏrpĕ'dĭnĕ,* f. torpedo (fish); laziness; torpidity.   [pidity.
torpidezza, *–pĭdĕt'ză,* f. torpidness, tor-
torpido, *tŏr'pĭdŏ,* a. torpid.   [ness.
torpore, *–pŏ'rĕ,* m. numbness; sluggish-
torre see **togliere.**
torre, *tŏr'rĕ,* f. tower, dungeon.
torreggiare, *–rĕdjă'rĕ,* v. n. to tower; to soar aloft.
torrente, *–rĕn'tĕ,* m. torrent.   [f. turret.
torretta, *–rĕt'tă,* **torricella,** *–rĭdshĕl'lă,*
torrido, *tŏr'rĭdŏ,* a. torrid, parched.
torsello, *–sĕl'lŏ,* m. small bale of goods; punch.
torso, *tŏr'sŏ,* m. stump, trunk; torso.
torsolo, see **torso.**
torta, *tŏr'tă,* f. tart.
tortellino, *–tĕllĕ'nŏ,* m. little tart.
torto, *tŏr'tŏ,* m. wrong, injury, insult; falsity; –, a. twisted; bent; unjust.
tortola, *tŏr'tŏlă,* **tortora,** *–tŏră,* f. turtledove; turtle.
tortuoso, *–tŭŏ'sŏ,* a. tortuous, crooked:
tortura, *–tŏ'ră,* f. twistedness; iniquity; wickedness; torture, pain.   [torment.
torturare, *–tŭră'rĕ,* v. a. to torture, to
torvo, *tŏr'vŏ,* a. surly, grim, stern.
tosa, *tŏ'să,* f. girl, maid, lass.   [prune.
tosare, *tŏsă'rĕ,* v. a. to shear, to shave; to
tosco, *tŏs'kŏ,* m. poison; –, a. poisoned;
toso, *tŏ'sŏ,* m. boy, lad.   [malignant.
tosone, *tŏsŏ'nĕ,* m. order of the golden tosse,** *tŏs'sĕ,* f. cough.   [fleece.
tossicare, *–sĭkă'rĕ,* v. a. to poison.
tossico, *tŏs'sĭkŏ,* m. poison.
tossire, *–sĕ'rĕ,* v. n. to cough.
tosto, *tŏs'tŏ,* a. quick; bold; –, ad. soon, quickly; – **che,** as soon as. ▾
totale, *tŏtă'lĕ,* a. total, whole; complete.
totalità, *–tălĭtă',* f. totality, sum total.
totalmente, *–tălmĕn'tĕ,* ad. totally, quite.
tovaglia, *tŏvăl'yă,* f. table-cloth; napkin.
tovagliuolo, *–yŭŏ'lŏ,* m. napkin; small table-cloth.
tozzetto, *tŏtzĕt'tŏ,* m. small bit.
tozzo, *tŏt'zŏ,* m. bit, morsel; –, a. **thick** and short.

tra, *trä* ad. & pr. between, betwixt, among, in the course of; besides. moreover.

trabacca, *träbäk' kä,* f. pavilion, tent.

traballare, *–bällä' rě,* v. n. to stagger, to vacillate.

traboccare, *–bŏkkä' rě,* v. a. to inundate; to throw, to hurl; to precipitate; –, v. n. to overflow, to superabound; to exceed.

trabocchetto, *–bŏkkět' tŏ,* m. snare, pitfall.

traboccherole, *–kd' vŏlě,* a. huge, immense; fatal; inconsiderate; immoderate.

trabocco, *–bŏk' kŏ,* m. downfall; overflow; ruin; pitfall.

tracannare, *–kännä' rě,* v. a. to drink hard.

traccia, *trät' shä,* f. trace, track, footstep; mark, sign; treaty.

tracciare, *–tshä' rě,* v. a. to trace.

tracollare, *träkŏllä' rě,* v. n. to tumble; to fall headlong; to nod.

tracorrere, *–kŏr' rěrě,* v. a. & n. ir. to forget, to omit; to run swiftly.

tracotante, *–kŏtăn' tě,* a. haughty, overbearing.　　　　　[sumption; insolence.

tracotanza, *–tăn' tzä,* f. haughtiness, presumption.

tradimento, *trădĭměn' tŏ,* m. treason.

tradire, *–dě' rě,* v. a. to betray, to deceive.

traditore, *–dǐtŏ' rě,* m. traitor.

tradizione, *–tsĭd' ně,* f. tradition.

tradotto, *–dŏt' tŏ,* a. translated.

tradurre, *–dŭr' rě,* v. a. ir. to translate; to transfer; to extend.

traduttore, *–dŭttŏ' rě,* m. translater.

traduzione, *–dŭtzĭŏ' ně,* f. translation, version.　　　　　[to languish, to pant.

trafelare, *–fělä' rě,* v. n. to be out of breath;

trafficare, *träffĭkä' rě,* v. a. & n. to handle, to finger; to trade, to traffic.　　　[merce.

traffico, *träf' fěkŏ,* m. traffic, trade, commerce.

trafiggere, *trăfĭd' jěrě,* v. a. ir. to transpierce; to vex.　　　　　[ture; vexation.

trafitta, *–fĭt' tä,* f. wound; sting, puncture.

traforare, *–fŏrä' rě,* v. a. & n. to pierce through; to run through.

traforo, *–fŏ' rŏ,* m. open-work lace; nook, cranny.　　　　　[with; to conceal.

trafugare, *–fŭgä' rě,* v. a. to run away

trafurello, *–fŭrěl' lŏ,* m. little rogue.

tragedia, *trăjě' dĭä,* f. tragedy.

tragedo, *–jä' dŏ,* m. writer of tragedics.

tragettare, *träjěttä' rě,* v. a. & n. to toss up and down; to pass over.　　　[path.

traghetto, *trăghět' tŏ,* m. passage; footway, *trä' jtkŏ,* a. tragical.

tragico, *trä' jtkŏ,* a. tragical.

tragicomico, *–kŏ' mĭkŏ,* a. tragi-comic.

tragicommedia, *–kŏmmě' dĭä,* f. tragicomedy.　　　　　[comedy.

tragittare, *see* **tragettare.**

tragittatore, *träjĭttătŏ' rě,* m. archer;

traguardo, *trăgŭär' dŏ,* m. level.　[slinger.

trainare, *träĭnä' rě,* v. a. to drag along, to haul.

traino, *trä' ĭnŏ (trä' ĭnŏ),* m. train, carriage; sledge; float; trot; waggon-load; railwaytrain; baggage.　　　[to cease, to omit.

tralasciare, *trălăsshä' rě,* v. a. to desist,

tralcio, *träl' dshŏ,* m. shoot; twig.

tralignare, *trălĭnyä' rě,* v. n. to degenerate.

tralucere, *–lŏ' dshěrě,* v. n. ir. to shine through, to be transparent.

trama, *trä' mä,* f. woof, weft; conspiracy.

tramaglio, *–mäl' yŏ,* m. drag-net, trammel.

tramare, *–mä' rě,* v. a. to weave; to machinate.　　　　　[order.

trambusto, *trämbŭs' tŏ,* m. confusion, disorder.

tramenare, *trăměnä' rě,* v. a. to manage.

tramezza, *–měz' zä,* f. partition-wall.

tramezzare, *–mětzä' rě,* v. a. & n. to put between; to be interposed.

tramezzo, *–mět' zŏ,* m. partition-wall; interval; diaphragm.

tramite, *trä' mĭtě,* m.(poet.)cross-way, path.

tramoggia, *trămŏd' jä,* f. feeder (of machines).

tramontana, *–mŏntä' nä,* f., **tramontano,** *–nŏ,* m. north-wind, North; north or polar-star.　　　　　[to set (of stars).

tramontare, *–mŏntä' rě,* v. n. to go down;

tramortire, *–mŏrtě' rě,* v. n. to faint, to swoon.　　　　　[pl. stilts, pl.

trampali, *trăm' pălĭ,* **trampoli,** *–pŏlĭ,* m.

tramutare, *trămŭtä' rě,* v. a. to remove, to transplant; to change; to exchange.

trangugiare, *trăngŭjä' rě,* v. a. to swallow up, to devour.　　　　　[quillise, to appease.

tranquillare, *–kĭllä' rě,* v. a. to tranquillise.

tranquillità, *–kĭllĭtä',* f. tranquillity.

tranquillo, *–kĭl' lŏ,* a. tranquil, quiet.

transazione, *trănsătzĭŏ' ně,* f. transition; transaction.

transitivo, *trănsĭtě' vŏ,* a. transitive.

transito, *trăn' sĭtŏ,* m. passage; transit; decease; (rail.) crossing; death.

transizione, *–sĭtzĭŏ' ně,* f. transition.

trapassare, *trăpăssä' rě,* v. a. to surpass; to transgress; to omit; to pierce; –, v. n. to cross over; to cease; to pass away; to die.　　　　　[pass, digression.

trapasso, *–păs' sŏ,* m. passing over; tres-

trapelare, *–pělä' rě,* v. n. to drop, to distil.

trappola, *trăp' pŏlä,* f. trap, snare; ambush; deceit.　　　　　[cheat.

trappolare, *–pŏlä' rě,* v. a. to ensnare; to

trapuntare, *trăpŭntä' rě,* v. a. to quilt, to stitch.

trapunto, *–pŭn' tŏ,* a. emaciated, lean.

traripare, *–rĭpä' rě,* v. a. to precipitate.

trarre, *trăr' rě,* v. a. ir. to draw, to pull; to pluck; to take out; to reap.

trascegliere, *trăsshěl' yěrě,* v. a. ir. to choose; to pick.　　　　[dent; excellent.

trascendente, *–sshěnděn' tě,* a. transcen-

trascendere, *–sshěn' děrě,* v. a. ir. to surpass, to exceed, to excel.

trascerre, *see* **trascegliere.**

trascorso, *trăskŏr' sŏ,* m. oversight, mistake, fault.　　　　　[scribe, to copy.

trascrivere, *–skrě' věrě,* v. a. to tran-

trascuraggine, *–kŭrăd' jĭně,* m. disregard, negligence.　　　　　[to neglect.

trascurare, *–kŭrä' rě,* v. a. to pass over;

trascuratezza, *–tăt' zä,* f. disregard.

trascurato, *–kŭrä' t.,* a. neglected, negligent, careless.　　　　　[convey.

trasferire, *–fěrě' rě,* v. a. to transfer, to

trasfigurare, *–fĭgŭrä' rě,* v. a. & n. to transfigure, to transform.

trasfigurato, _–rä'tŏ_, a. transformed, changed. [tion, change.

trasfigurazione, _–tzĭŏ'nĕ_, f. transforma-

trasfondere, _–fŏn'dĕrĕ_, v. a. ir. to transfuse, to decant; to communicate.

trasformare, _–fŏrmä'rĕ_, v. a. to transform.

trasformazione, _–tzĭŏ'nĕ_, f. transformation; change. [to trespass.

trasgredire, _–grĕdĭ'rĕ_, v. a. to transgress,

trasgressione, _–grĕssĭŏ'nĕ_, f. transgression; digression.

traslatare, _–lätä'rĕ_, v. a. to translate; to transfer.

traslativo, _–lätĭ'vŏ_, **traslato**, _–lä'tŏ_, a. translated; figurative, allegorical.

traslatore, _–lätŏ'rĕ_, m. translator.

traslazione, _–lätzĭŏ'nĕ_, f. translation.

trasmarino, _–märĭ'nŏ_, a. beyond sea.

trasmettere, _–mĕt'tĕrĕ_, v. a. ir. to send over, to transmit. [migrate.

trasmigrare, _–mĭgrä'rĕ_, v. n. to trans-

trasmissione, _–mĭssĭŏ'nĕ_, f. transmission.

trasmutare, _–mŭtä'rĕ_, v. a. to transform.

trasognare, _–sŏnyä'rĕ_, v. n. to dote, to rave; to dream.

trasparente, _träspärĕn'tĕ_, a. transparent.

trasparenza, _–pärĕn'tzä_, f. transparency.

traspirare, _träspĭrä'rĕ_, v. n. to transpire.

traspirazione, _–pĭrätzĭŏ'nĕ_, f. transpiration, perspiration.

trasporre, _träspŏr'rĕ_, v. a. ir. to transport; to transplant.

trasportabile, _–pŏrtä'bĭlĕ_, a. transportable. [to transfer; to convey.

trasportare, _–pŏrtä'rĕ_, v. a. to transport,

trasporto, _–pŏr'tŏ_, m. transport; ecstasy.

trassinare, _–sĭnä'rĕ_, v. a. to handle, to touch; to ill-use.

trastullare, _–tŭllä'rĕ_, v. a. to divert, to amuse; **trastullarsi**, _–lär'sĭ_, to take one's pleasure.

trastullo, _–tŭl'lŏ_, m. amusement, pastime.

trasversale, _–vĕrsä'lĕ_, **trasverso**, _–vĕr'sŏ_, a. transverse, crossing; oblique.

trasversalmente, _–mĕn'tĕ_, ad. transversely.

tratta, _trät'tä_, f. throw, shot; space, distance; permit; drawing of lots; crowd; (com.) draft, bill. [affable.

trattabile, _–tä'bĭlĕ_, a. tractable, gentle,

trattabilità, _–bĭlĭtä'_, f. tractableness; gentleness. [ment.

trattamento, _–mĕn'tŏ_, m. treatise, treat-

trattare, _–tä'rĕ_, v. a. to treat; to negotiate, to contract; to handle; to manage; to use.

trattato, _–tä'tŏ_, m. treatise; discourse; dissertation; negotiation; plot.

trattenere, _–tĕnĕ'rĕ_, v. a. ir. to entertain, to amuse; to keep waiting.

tratto, _trät'tŏ_, m. throw, pull; draught; stroke with a pen; space, extent; manner, behaviour; trick; saying; **ad un –**, at once; **ad ogni –**, every moment; **di primo –**, at first; **tratto tratto**, from time to time.

trattore, _–tŏ'rĕ_, m. tavern-keeper; restaurant.

trattoria, _–tŏrĕ'ä_, f. eating-house, tavern; (mil.) trajectory.

travagliare, _trävälyä'rĕ_, v. a. to work; to torment; to afflict. [labour; pain.

travaglio, _–väl'yŏ_, m. trouble, affliction.

travaglioso, _–yŏ'sŏ_, a. painful, afflictive.

travalicare, _–välĭkä'rĕ_, v. a. to pass over; to transgress. [transfuse.

travasare, _–väsä'rĕ_, v. a. to decant, to

trave, _trä'vĕ_, m. beam; roof-beam.

travedere, _–vĕdĕ'rĕ_, v. a. ir. to see indistinctly or double.

traversa, _–vĕr'sä_, f. cross-piece (of timber); iron-bar; dam; cross-road, traverse; width, breadth; cross, accident; (rail.) sleeper; **alla –**, across.

traversare, _–vĕrsä'rĕ_, v. a. to traverse, to pass over.

traversia, _–vĕrsĭ'ä_, f. contrary wind, tempest; (fig.) cross-accident, misfortune.

traverso, _–vĕr'sŏ_ a. cross, oblique; adverse; **a –**, across, through.

travestimento, _–vĕstĭmĕn'tŏ_, m. disguise; hypocrisy, dissembling.

travestire, _–vĕstĭ'rĕ_, v. a. to disguise.

traviare, _–vĭä'rĕ_, v. a. to mislead, to turn aside; **–**, v. n., **traviarsi**, _–vĭär'sĭ_, to go astray, to deviate. [deceive.

travisare, _–vĭsä'rĕ_, v. a. to disguise, to

travolgere, _–vŏl'jĕrĕ_, v. a. ir. to disorder, tre, _trĕ'_, a. three; third. [to overturn.

trebbia, _trĕb'bĭä_, f. flail.

trebbiare, _–bĭä'rĕ_, v. a. to thrash.

trebbio, _trĕb'bĭŏ_, m. sport, pastime.

trecca, _trĕk'kä_, f. huckster.

treccia, _trĕt'shä_, f. lock of hair; curl.

treccone, _trĕkkŏ'nĕ_, m. fruiterer, huckster.

trecentesimo, _trĕshĕntĕ'sĭmŏ_, a. three hundredth.

trecento, _–dshĕn'tŏ_, a. three hundred.

tredicesimo, _–dĭshä'sĭmŏ_, a. thirteenth.

tredici, _trä'dĭdshĕ_, a. thirteen.

treggea, _trĕdjä'ä_, f. sugar-plum.

treggia, _trĕd'jä_, f. sledge, dray. [shiver.

tremare, _trĕmä'rĕ_, v. n. to tremble, to

tremendo, _–mĕn'dŏ_, a. tremendous, terrible.

trementina, _–mĕntĭ'nä_, f. turpentine.

tremila, _–mĕ'lä_, a. three thousand.

tremolare, _–mŏlä'rĕ_, v. n. to tremble, to shake; to sparkle.

tremolo, _trä'mŏlŏ_, a. tremulous, shaking.

tremore, _trĕmŏ'rĕ_, m. tremor, trembling, fear, fright.

tremuoto, _–mŭŏ'tŏ_, m. earthquake.

treno, _trä'nŏ_, m. train, equipage; sledge; load; (rail.) railway-train; **– diretto**, _–dĭrĕt'tŏ_ fast train.

trenta, _trĕn'tä_, a. thirty.

trentesimo, _–tä'sĭmŏ_, a. thirtieth.

trentina, _–tĕ'nä_, f. thirty pieces.

trepidare, _trĕpĭdä'rĕ_, v. n. to tremble.

trepido, _trä'pĭdŏ_, a. trembling, fearful.

treppiè, _trĕppĭĕ'_, **treppiede**, _–pĭĕ'dĕ_, m. tripod. [trifles.

tresca, _trĕs'kä_, f. cheerful company; riot;

trespolo, _trĕs'pŏlŏ_, m. trestle, prop.

triangolare, _trĭängŏlä'rĕ_, a. triangular.

triangolo, _trĭän'gŏlŏ_, m. triangle.

tribbiare, *tríbbiä′rĕ*, v. a. to pound, to bruise; to thrash.

tribolare, *tríbŏlä′rĕ*, v. a. to afflict; to trouble, to torment.   [trouble, sorrow.

tribolo, *trĕ′bŏlŏ*, m. bramble; mourning.

tribù, *tríbŭ′*, f. tribe, clan.

tribuna, *–bŏ′nä*, f. tribune, gallery.

tribunale, *–bŭnä′lĕ*, m. tribunal, court of justice.

tribuno, *–bŏ′nŏ*, m. tribune.   [justice.

tributario, *–bŭtä′rĭŏ*, a. tributary.

tributo, *–bŭ′tŏ*, m. tribute, duty.

tridente, *–dĕn′tĕ*, m. trident.

} **triegua**, *see* **tregua**.

triennale, *trĭĕnnä′lĕ*, a. of three years.

triennio, *–ĕn′nĭŏ*, m. space of three years.

trifoglio, *–fŏl′yŏ*, m. trefoil.

trigesimo, *–jĕ′sĭmŏ*, a. thirtieth.

trillare, *trĭllä′rĕ*, v. a. & n. to trill, to quaver.

trillo, *trĭl′lŏ*, m. trill, shake, quaver.

trimestre, *trĭmĕs′trĕ*, a. of three months.

trina, *trĕ′nä*, f. galoon, lace, fringe.

trincare, *trĭnkä′rĕ*, v. n. to tipple.

trincea, *–dshä′ä*, f. trench, intrenchment; (rail.) cutting.

trincerare, *–dshĕrä′rĕ*, v. a. to entrench.

trinciare, *–dshä′rĕ*, v. a. to carve (at table); to cut capers; to indent.

trincone, *–kŏ′nĕ*, m. great drunkard.

Trinità, *trĭnĭtä′*, f. Trinity.

trio, *trĕ′ŏ*, m. trio; glee.

triocco, *trĭŏk′kŏ*, m. tumultuous assembly.

trionfare, *trĭŏnfä′rĕ*, v. a. & n. to triumph; to subdue; to conquer.   [cards.

trionfo, *trĭŏn′fŏ*, m. triumph; trump (at

triplice, *trĕ′plĭdshĕ*, **triplo**, *trĭp′lŏ*, a. triple, threefold.

tripode, *trĕ′pŏdĕ*, m. tripod, trivet.

trippa, *trĭp′pä*, f. tripe, belly.

tripudiare, *trĭpŭdĭä′rĕ*, v. n. to dance and skip for joy, to exult.

tripudio, *–pŏ′dĭŏ*, m. capering for joy.

tristezza, *trĭstĕt′zä*, **tristizia**, *–tĕ′tzĭä*, f. sadness, melancholy, grief; wickedness.

tristo, *trĭs′tŏ*, a. sad, afflicted; wretched; wicked.   [to scrutinize.

tritare, *trĭtä′rĕ*, v. n. to grind, to pound;

tritello, *–tĕl′lŏ*, m. fine bran.

trito, *trĕ′tŏ*, a. pounded, minced; beaten, common, trite, every-day.

tritume, *–tŏ′mĕ*, m. crumbs, trifles, pl.

tritura, *–tŏ′rä*, f. pounding; affliction.

triturare, *–tŭrä′rĕ*, v. a. to grind, to pound,

trivella, *–vĕl′lä*, f. borer.   [to bruise.

trivellare, *–vĕllä′rĕ*, v. a. to bore, to pierce.

triviale, *–vĭä′lĕ*, a. trivial.

trivialità, *–vĭälĭtä′*, f. triviality.

trivio, *trĕ′vĭŏ*, m. cross-road.

trofeo, *trŏfĕ′ŏ*, m. trophy.

troglio, *trŏ′lyŏ*, a. stammering

troia, *trŏ′ä*, f. sow, swine.

tromba, *trŏm′bä*, f. trumpet; water-pump; trunk of an elephant, proboscis; shell; — **parlante**, speaking-trumpet; **vendere alla —**, to sell by auction.   [to proclaim.

trombare, *–bä′rĕ*, v. a. & n. to trumpet;

trombetta, *–bĕt′tä*, f. small trumpet; trumpeter.

trombettare, *–bĕttä′rĕ*, v. a. to trumpet; to proclaim, to divulge.

trombone, *–bŏ′nĕ*, m. sackbut.

troncare, *trŏnkä′rĕ*, v. a. to cut off; to mutilate, to mangle.

troncato, *–kä′tŏ*, a. cut off; unfinished.

tronco, *trŏn′kŏ*, m. trunk; stem, race, line-age; —, a. cut off, docked; unfinished, imperfect.

troncone, *–kŏ′nĕ*, m. large trunk.

tronfio, *trŏn′fĭŏ*, a. haughty; angry.

trono, *trŏ′nŏ*, m. throne; thunder.

troppo, *trŏp′pŏ*, ad. too much.

troscia, *trŏssh′ä*, f. furrow of the water.

trota, *trŏ′tä*, f. trout.   [fast.

trottare, *trŏttä′rĕ*, v. n. to trot, to walk

trotto, *trŏt′tŏ*, m. trot.

trovare, *trŏvä′rĕ*, v. a. to find, to meet with; to discover, to invent; to observe, to remark; **trovarsi**, *–vär′sĭ*, to find oneself; to be present.

trovato, *–vä′tŏ*, m. device, discovery, invention; —, a. found, met with; discovered.

trovatore, *–tŏ′rĕ*, m. finder, inventor; troubadour.

trucidare, *trŭdshĭdä′rĕ*, v. a. to murder.

truciolo, *trŏ′dshŏlŏ*, m. chip; bit.

truculento, *trŭkŭlĕn′tŏ*, a. cruel, barbarous.

truffa, *trŭf′fä*, f. cheat, fraud, sharping; nonsense, trifle.

truffare, *–fä′rĕ*, v. a. to cheat, to defraud, to dupe, to make a fool of.

trufferia, *–fĕrĕ′ä*, f. cheat, roguish trick.

trullo, *trŭl′lŏ*, m. fart; blockhead.

truogolo, *trŭŏ′gŏlŏ*, m. trough.

truppa, *trŭp′pä*, f. troop, band.

tu, *tŏ*, pn. thou.

tuba, *tŏ′bä*, f. (poet.) trumpet.

tubercolo, *tŭbĕr′kŏlŏ*, m. tubercle.

tubero, *tŏ′bĕrŏ*, m. medlar-tree.   [pipe.

tubo, *tŏ′bŏ*, m. tube, syphon; socket; gas-

tuffare, *tŭffä′rĕ*, v. a. to plunge into the water, to steep; **tuffarsi**, *–fär′sĭ*, to plunge into, to rush into.

tuffo, *tŭf′fŏ*, m. plunging; ruin, loss.

tugurio, *tŭgŏ′rĭŏ*, m. (poet.) cottage.

tulipano, *tŭlĭpä′nŏ*, m. tulip.

tumido, *tŏ′mĭdŏ*, a. tumid, puffed up.

tumore, *tŭmŏ′rĕ*, m. tumour, swelling; haughtiness, pride.

tumulare, *–mŭlä′rĕ*, v. a. (poet.) to bury.

tumulo, *tŏ′mŭlŏ*, m. (poet.) grave, tomb.

tumulto, *tŭmŭl′tŏ*, m. tumult.

tumultuoso, *–tŭŏ′sŏ*, a. tumultuous.

tunnelle, *tŭn′nĕllĕ*, m. (rail.) tunnel.

tuo, *tŏ′ŏ*, pn. thy, thine; **il —**, thy property.

tuono, *tŭŏ′nŏ*, m. thunder; rumour; tone; noise, bustle, alarm.

tuorlo, *tŭŏr′lŏ*, m. yolk of an egg; middle.

tura, *tŏ′rä*, f. dam, dike.

turaccio, *tŭrät′shŏ*, m. cork, stopple, bung.

turare, *–rä′rĕ*, v. a. to stop up.

turba, *tŭr′bä*, f. crowd; populace.

turbare, *–bä′rĕ*, v. a. to disturb; to trouble, to disquiet.   [wind.

turbine, *tŭr′bĭnĕ*, **turbo**, *tŭr′bŏ*, m. whirl-

turbinoso, *–vĭnŏ'ſŏ,* a. turbulent, tempestuous. [turquoise.

turchina, *–kĭ'nă,* **turchese,** *–kā'ſĕ,* f.

turchino, *–kĭ'nŏ,* a. & m. azure, sky-blue.

turcimanno, *–dshĭmăn'nŏ,* m. interpreter.

turgidezza, *–jŭdĕt'ză,* f. turgidity.

turgido, *tŭr'jĭdŏ,* a. turgid, swoln; bombastic. [pan.

turibolo, *tŭrĕ'bŏlŏ,* m. censer, perfuming-pan.

turma, *tŭr'mă,* f. flock, crowd.

turno, *tŭr'nŏ,* m. turn, change.

turpe, *tŭr'pĕ,* a. villanous, infamous; deformed.

turpemente, *–mĕn'tĕ,* ad. basely, meanly.

turpitudine, *–ptŭ'dĭnĕ,* f. turpitude, baseness, infamy.

tutela, *tŭtă'lă,* f. tutelage; guardianship.

tutelare, *–tĕlă'rĕ,* a. tutelar.

tutore, *–tŏ'rĕ,* m. guardian, trustee.

tuttavia, *tŭttăvĕ'ă,* **tuttavolta,** *–vŏl'tă,* ad. & c. always, incessantly, as often as; whenever, however, nevertheless.

tutto, *tŭt'tŏ,* a. all, whole; every; –, ad. wholly, entirely, quite; **per –,** everywhere; **– che,** almost, although; **– a un tempo,** all of a sudden; **tutt' uno,** entirely the same.

tuttora, *tŭttŏ'ră,* ad. always.

U.

ubbidire, *ŭbbĭdĕ'rĕ,* v. a. & n. to obey.

ubbriaco, *–brĭă'kŏ,* a. drunk, tipsy.

ubertà, *ŭbĕrtă',* f. fertility; abundance.

ubriaco, *see* **ubbriaco.**

uccellare, *ŭtshĕllă'rĕ,* v. a. to fowl, to go bird-catching; to banter; –, m. aviary.

uccello, *ŭtshĕl'lŏ,* m. bird; simpleton.

uccidere, *ŭtshĕ'dĕrĕ,* v. a. ir. to kill.

udienza, *ŭdĭĕn'tză,* f. audience, auditory; interrogation; **(sala d'–),** audience-chamber.

udire, *ŭdĕ'rĕ,* v. a. ir. to hear, to listen.

udito, *ŭdĕ'tŏ,* m. hearing, sense of hearing.

uditore, *–tŏ'rĕ,* m. auditor, hearer.

uditorio, *–tŏ'rĭŏ,* m. auditory.

ufficiale, *ŭffĭdshă'lĕ,* **uffiziale,** *–tzĭă'lĕ,* m. official; officer. [office, function.

ufficio, *ŭffĭdsh'ŏ,* **uffizio,** *ŭffĕ'tzĭŏ,* m.

ufficioso, *–dshŏ'ſŏ,* a. officious, obliging.

uggia, *ŭd'jă,* f. shade; bad presage; aversion.

uggioso, *ŭdjŏ'ſŏ,* a. shaded, shady; chilling, blighting; damp, cloudy; tiresome; mistrustful.

ugna, *ŭn'yă,* f. nail, claw. [anoint.

ugnere, *ŭn'yĕrĕ,* v. a. ir. to grease, to

ugnone, *–yŏ'nĕ,* m. great claw, great nail.

uguagliare, *ŭgŭălyă'rĕ,* v. a. to make equal.

uguale, *ŭgŭă'lĕ,* a. equal, like, even.

ugualità, *ŭgŭălĭtă',* f. equality.

uh ! *ŭ,* int. oh ! ah !

ulcera, *ŭl'dshĕră,* f. ulcer, sore. [fester.

ulcerare, *–dshără'rĕ,* v. n. to ulcerate, to

ulcerazione, *–tzĭŏ'nĕ,* f. ulceration.

uliva, *ŭlĕ'vă,* f. olive.

ulivo, *ŭlĕ'vŏ,* m. olive-tree; olive-branch.

ulteriore, *ŭltĕrĭŏ'rĕ,* a. ulterior, further.

ultimamente, *–tĭmămĕn'tĕ,* ad. lastly, latterly, finally.

ultimare, *–mă'rĕ,* v. a. to bring to an end.

ultimo, *ŭl'tĭmŏ,* a. last, utmost.

ululare, *ŭlŭlă'rĕ,* v. n. to howl.

ululo, *ŏ'lŭlŏ,* m. howling.

umanista, *ŭmănĭs'tă,* m. humanist.

umanità, *–mănĭtă',* f. humanity; kindness.

umano, *–mă'nŏ,* a. human; humane, kind.

umbilico, *ŭmbĭlĕ'kŏ,* m. navel; centre.

umettare, *ŭmĕttă'rĕ,* v. a. to moisten, to wet. [damp.

umidità, *ŭmĭdĭtă',* f. humidity, moisture.

umido, *ŏ'mĭdŏ,* a. humid, moist.

umile, *ŏ'mĭlĕ,* a. humble, submissive; vile.

umiliare, *ŭmĭlĭă'rĕ,* v. a. to humble, appease; to subdue.

umiliazione, *–tzĭŏ'nĕ,* f. humiliation.

umiltà, *ŭmĭltă',* f. humbleness, respect.

umilmente, *ŭmĭlmĕn'tĕ,* ad. humbly.

umore, *ŭmŏ'rĕ,* m. humour, moisture; phlegm; temper; whim; peevishness.

umorista, *–rĭs'tă,* m. humourist.

umoroso, *–rŏ'ſŏ,* a. damp, moist; humorous.

un, *ŭn,* for: uno.

una, *ŏ'nă,* ad. together (with).

unanime, *ŭnă'nĭmĕ,* a. unanimous.

unanimemente, *–nĭmĕmĕn'tĕ,* ad. unanimously.

unanimità, *–nĭmĭtă',* f. unanimity.

uncinare, *ŭndshĭnă'rĕ,* v. a. to hook on; to snatch.

uncino, *–dshĭ'nŏ,* m. hook, grappling-iron.

undecimo, *–dĕ'dshĭmŏ,* **undicesimo,** *–dĭdshă'ſĭmŏ,* a. eleventh.

undici, *ŭn'dĭdshĭ,* a. eleven. [oily.

ungente, *ŭnjĕn'tĕ,* a. unctuous, greasy,

ungere, *see* **ugnere.** [claw.

unghia, *ŭn'ghĭă,* f. nail; hoof; talon,

unghione, *–ghĭŏ'nĕ,* m. great crooked talon, great claw.

unguentare, *–gŭĕntă'rĕ,* v. a. to anoint.

unguento, *–gŭĕn'tŏ,* m. ointment, salve.

unico, *ŏ'nĭkŏ,* a. unique, only.

unicorno, *ŭnĭkŏr'nŏ,* m. unicorn.

uniforme, *–fŏr'mĕ,* a. uniform; equal.

uniformità, *–fŏrmĭtă',* f. uniformity.

unigenito, *–jĕ'nĭtŏ,* m. only son; Christ.

unigeno, *ŭnĕ'jĕnŏ,* m. only child.

unione, *ŭnĭŏ'nĕ,* f. union. [birth.

uniparo, *ŭnĕ'părŏ,* a. bringing one at a

unire, *ŭnĕ'rĕ,* v. a. to unite, to join; to dishonour.

unisono, *ŭnĕ'ſŏnŏ,* m. unison, concord.

unità, *ŭnĭtă',* f. unity, union; concord.

universale, *–vĕrſă'lĕ,* a. universal.

universalità, *–sălĭtă',* f. universality.

universalmente, *–sălmĕn'tĕ,* ad. universally.

università, *–vĕrſĭtă',* f. universality, generality; commonalty; university.

universo, *–vĕr'ſŏ,* m. universe, whole world; –, a. universal. [meaning.

univoco, *ŭnĕ'vŏkŏ,* a. univocal, of one

uno, *ŏ'nŏ,* art. & a. a, an, one; — ad —, one by one; in —, together.
untare, *ŭntă'rĕ,* v. a. to anoint.
unto, *ŭn'tŏ,* a. greasy; soiled.
untume, *—tŏ'mĕ,* m. unctuous matter; — delle ruote, cart-grease.
untuoso, *—tŭŏ'sŏ,* a. oily, greasy.
unzione, *—tzĭŏ'nĕ,* f. unction, ointment.
uomo, *ŭŏ'mŏ,* m. (**uomini,** pl.) man; husband; subject.   [want.
uopo, *ŭŏ'pŏ,* m. advantage, profit; need,
uovo, *ŭŏ'vŏ,* m. (**nova,** f. pl.) egg.
upupa, *ŭ'pŭpă,* f. lapwing.
urbanità, *ŭrbănĭtă',* f. urbanity, politeness.
urbano, *—bă'nŏ,* a. polite.
urente, *ŭrĕn'tĕ,* a. burning.
uretra, *ŭ'rĕtră,* f. urethra.
urgente, *ŭrjĕn'tĕ,* a. urgent, pressing.
urgenza, *—jĕn'tză,* a. urgency, pressing necessity.
urgere, *ŭr'jĕrĕ,* v. a. to urge, to press.
urlare, *ŭrlă'rĕ,* v. n. to howl.
urlo, *ŭr'lŏ,* m. howl; moan.
urna, *ŭr'nă,* f. urn; ballot-box.
urtare, *—tă'rĕ,* v. a. & n. to dash against, to shock, to hit.
urtata, *ŭrtă'tă,* f. shock, clash, hurt.
urto, *ŭr'tŏ,* m. shock, clash; hit, knock, hurt.
usanza, *ŭsăn'tză,* f. use, custom, habit; manner, fashion; intercourse, intimacy.
usare, *ŭsă'rĕ,* v. a. to use, to make use of; to frequent; —, v. n. to be accustomed.
usato, *ŭsă'tŏ,* m. use, custom, habit; —, a. accustomed, used, practised; frequented; worn out.
usatti, *ŭsăt'tĕ,* m. pl. boots, pl.
usbergo, *ŭsbĕr'gŏ,* m. cuirass.
usciere, *ŭsshĭĕ'rĕ,* m. door-keeper, usher.
uscio, *ŭssh'ŏ,* m. outside door, entrance.
uscire, *ŭsshĕ'rĕ,* v. n. ir. to go out, to issue.
uscita, *ŭsshē'tă,* f. going out, issue; egress; mischance; door; diarrhœa; end, term; success.   [ment.
uscito, *ŭsshē'tŏ,* m. exile, outlaw; excre-
usignuolo, *ŭsĭnyŭŏ'lŏ,* m. nightingale.
usitato, *ŭsĭtă'tŏ,* a. used, employed; usual; wont, accustomed.
uso, *ŏ'sŏ,* m. use, usage, custom, habit; exercise; —, a. used; accustomed.
ussaro, *ŭs'sărŏ,* m. hussar.
ustolare, *ŭstŏlă'rĕ,* v. n. to wish ardently.
usuale, *ŭsŭă'lĕ,* a. usual, common, ordinary.
usufrutto, *ŭsŭfrŭt'tŏ,* m. use, profit, advantage.   [vantage.
usura, *ŭsŭ'ră,* f. usury.
usuraio, *ŭsŭrăĭ'ŏ,* **usuriere,** *—rĭĕ'rĕ,* m. usurer.
usurpare, *ŭsŭrpă'rĕ,* v. a. to usurp.
usurpatore, *—pătŏ'rĕ,* m. usurper.
usurpazione, *—tzĭŏ'nĕ,* f. usurpation.
utensili, *ŭtĕnsē'lĕ,* m. pl. kitchen-utensils.
utero, *ŏ'tĕrŏ,* m. uterus, womb.   [pl.
utile, *ŏ'tĭlĕ,* m. utility, profit; —, a. useful, profitable.
utilità, *ŭtĭlĭtă',* f. utility.

utilizzare, *—lĭdză'rĕ,* v. a. & n. to make use of; to profit, to gain; to be of advantage.
uva, *ŏ'vă,* f. grape; — spina, gooseberry; — secca, raisin.   [wish.
uzzolo, *ŭd'zŏlŏ,* m. intense desire, ardent

V.

vacante, *văkăn'tĕ,* a. vacant, empty, void.
vacanza, *—kăn'tză,* f. vacancy, vacation; school-holidays, pl.
vacare, *—kă'rĕ,* v. a. to want; to attend, to apply to; —, v. n. to be vacant, to be free; to cease, to end; to repose; to want, not to have.
vacca, *văk'kă,* f. cow.
vaccaro, *—kă'rŏ,* m. cow-keeper.
vacchetta, *—kĕt'tă,* f. little cow; Russian leather.
vaccina, *vătshē'nă,* f. beef; cow-pox.
vacillare, *vădshĭllă'rĕ,* v. n. to vacillate, to waver, to stagger.
vacuità, *—kŭĭtă',* f. vacuity, emptiness.
vacuo, *vă'kŭŏ,* m. vacuum; —, a. void, empty; free; lazy.   [to ramble.
vagabondare, *văgăbŏndă'rĕ,* v. n. to stroll,
vagabondo, *—bŏn'dŏ,* a. vagabond, vagrant.
vagamente, *—găměn'tĕ,* ad. handsomely, pleasingly.   [about; to extravagate.
vagare, *—gă'rĕ,* v. n. to rove, to ramble
vaghezza, *—ghĕt'ză,* f. desire; pleasure, delight.
vagina, *—jē'nă,* f. sheath, scabbard.
vagire, *—jē'rĕ,* v. n. to cry (as a babe).
vagito, *—jē'tŏ,* m. cry of a babe.
vaglia, *văl'yă,* f. valour, worth.
vagliare, *—yă'rĕ,* v. a. to sift, to winnow; to pick.
vagliatura, *—tŏ'ră,* f. siftings, pl.
vaglio, *văl'yŏ,* m. corn-sieve.
vago, *vă'gŏ,* m. lover, gallant; —, a. vague, indeterminate; roving, rambling; inconstant; attractive; beautiful; desirous.
vagolare, see **vagare.**
vagone, *—gŏ'nĕ,* m. (rail.) waggon.
vaiaio, *văĭăĭ'ŏ,* m. furrier.
vaio, *văĭ'ŏ,* a. blackish, spotted.
vaiuolo, *—ĭŭ'lŏ,* m. small-pox.   [brave.
valente, *vălĕn'tĕ,* a. able, skilful; valiant,
valere, *vălĕ'rĕ,* m. value, worth, price; valour, force; —, v. n. & n. to be worth, to cost; to be equal to; to deserve, to merit; to suffice; to be able; vale a dire, that is to say.
valeriana, *—lĕrĭă'nă,* f. valerian.
valetudinario, *—lĕtŭdĭnă'rĭŏ,* a. valetudinarian.   [fit.
valevole, *—lă'vŏlĕ,* a. useful, profitable.
valicare, *—lĭkă'rĕ,* v. a. to pass over..
valico, *vă'lĭkŏ,* m. passage, entry.
validità, *—lĭdĭtă'* f. validity.   [ful; legal.
valido, *vă'lĭdŏ,* a. valid, vigorous; power-
valigia, *—lē'jă,* f. valise, portmanteau.
vallare, *văllă'rĕ,* v. a. to entrench.
vallata, *—lă'tă,* f. valley; trench.

valle, *văl'lĕ*, f. valley, dale.

valletto, *-lĕt'tŏ*, m. page, gentleman's

vallo, *văl'lŏ*, m. rampart. [servant.

valore, *-lō'rĕ*, m. value, worth; price; valour; might, force.

valoroso, *-lōrō'sŏ*, a. valiant.

valsente, *-sĕn'tĕ*, m. value; price.

valvola, *văl'vōlă*, f. valve.

valuta, *vălū'tă*, f. value, worth, price; stock; coin, money. [estimate.

valutare, *-lūtā'rĕ*, v. a. to value, to

vampa, *văm'pă*, f. flame; passion.

vampiro, *-pē'rŏ*, m. vampire. [ardour.

vampo, *văm'pŏ*, m. flame; lightning;

vanagloria, *vănăglō'riă*, f. vainglory.

vanaglorioso, *-glōriō'sŏ*, a. vainglorious.

vanamente, *-mĕn'tĕ*, ad. vainly.

vaneggiare, *-nĕdjă'rĕ*, v. n. to imagine wildly; to rave, to talk nonsense; to be empty.

vanga, *văn'gă*, f. mattock, spade.

vangare, *-gă'rĕ*, v. a. to dig up with a spade.

vangelo, *-jĕ'lŏ*, m. the Gospel.

vanguardia, *-gŭăr'diă*, f. vanguard.

vanire, *vănē'rĕ*, v. n. to disappear.

vanità, *vănitā'*, f. vanity; futility.

vano, *vă'nŏ*, a. vain, empty; useless; vain-glorious, proud; **in —**, in vain.

vantaggiare, *văntădjă'rĕ*, v.a. to have the advantage over. [good fortune.

vantaggio, *-tăd'jŏ*, m. advantage; profit;

vantaggioso, *-djō'sŏ*, a. advantageous.

vantare, *-tă'rĕ*, v. a. to praise. [tage.

vanto, *văn'tŏ*, m. boasting; praise; advan-

vaporare, *văpōră'rĕ*, v. a. & n. to evaporate, to exhale; **vaporarsi**, *-răr'si*, to steam, to fume off. [melancholy.

vapore, *-pō'rĕ*, m. vapour, steam; (fig.)

varcare, *vărkă'rĕ*, v. a. to pass over.

varco, *văr'kŏ*, m. passage, opening; ford.

variabile, *văriă'bilĕ*, a. variable.

variabilità, *-bilitā'*, f. variableness.

variare, *-riă'rĕ*, v. a. & n. to vary; to differ, to disagree. [ference.

variazione, *-tziō'nĕ*, f. variation; dif-

varietà, *-riĕtā'*, f. variety, diversity.

vario, *vă'riŏ*, a. various, different, change-able; speckled.

vasaio, *văsă'ŏ*, m. potter.

vasca, *văs'kă*, f. basin, tub.

vascello, *văshĕl'lŏ*, m. vessel.

vasellaio, *văsĕllă'ŏ*, **vaselliere**, *-liĕ'rĕ*, m. potter.

vasello, *-sĕl'lŏ*, m. small vase.

vaso, *vă'sŏ*, m. vase; vessel; **— da fiori**, flower-pot.

vassallo, *văssăl'lŏ*, m. vassal.

vastità, *văstitā'*, f. vastness.

vasto, *văs'tŏ*, a. vast, immense.

vate, *vă'tĕ*, m. (poet.) bard, poet.

vaticinare, *-tăshĭnă'rĕ*, v. a. to prophecy. to foretell. [where.

ve, *vĕ*, pn. |you|; to you; —, ad. there.

vecchia, *vĕk'kiă*, f. old woman.

vecchiaia, *-kiă'iă*, f. old age.

vecchiezza, *-kiĕt'ză*, f. old age.

vecchio, *vĕk'kiŏ*, a. old, ancient.

vecchiume, *-kiŏ'mĕ*, m. old rags &c.

veccia, *-vĕt'shă*, f. vetch, fitch.

vece, *vă'dshĕ*, f. place, room; subsitute; **in —**, instead of; **prender** or **tener le veci**, to represent; (in comp.) **vece ...**, **vice ...**

vedere, *vĕdā'rĕ*, v. a. ir. to see, to per-ceive; —. m. sight, appearance; figure.

vedetta, *-dĕt'tă*, f. horse-sentry, outpost.

vedova, *vă'dōvă*, f. widow. [deprive.

vedovare, *vĕdōvă'rĕ*, v. a. to widow, to

vedovezza, *-vĕt'ză*, f. widowhood.

vedovo, *vă'dōvŏ*, m. widower; —, a. widowed, isolated; deprived.

veduta, *vĕdū'tă*, f. sight, view; prospect.

veduto, *-dū'tŏ*, p. seen; **far —**, to make believe; to feign.

veemente, *vĕĕmĕn'tĕ*, a. vehement, violent.

veemenza, *-mĕn'tză*, f. vehemence.

vegetabile, *vĕjĕtă'bĭlĕ*, **vegetale**, *-tă'lĕ*, a. vegetable; **vegetali**, s. pl. vegetables.

vegetare, *-tă'rĕ*, v. n. to vegetate. [pl.

vegetazione, *-tziō'nĕ*, f.vegetation,growth.

vegeto, *vă'jĕtŏ*, a. vigorous, stout.

veggente, *vĕdjĕn'tĕ*, p. seeing; **a mio —**, before my eyes.

veglia, *vĕl'yă*, f. watching; vigil; evening, evening-party; midnight-taper.

vegliardo, *-yăr'dŏ*, m. old man.

vegliare, *-yă'rĕ*, v. a. & n. to observe; to watch, to sit up; to prosper.

veglio, *vĕl'yŏ*, a. (poet.) old, ancient.

vegnente, *vĕnyĕn'tĕ*, a. coming, next: thriving.

veicolo, *vĕĭ'kōlŏ*, m. vehicle.

vela, *vă'lă*, f. sail; **vele**, pl., ships, pl.

velame, *vĕlă'mĕ*, m. veil, covering.

velare, *-lă'rĕ*, v. a. to veil, to cover, to hide. [sail, to sail.

veleggiare, *-lĕdjă'rĕ*, v. a. & n. to set

veleno, *-lă'nŏ*, m. poison; venom; anger;

velenoso, *-lĕnō'sŏ*, a. venomous. [malice.

veletta, *-lĕt'tă*, f. vedette, sentry.

vellicare, *vĕllĭkă'rĕ*, v. a. to prick, to stimulate.

vello, *vĕl'lŏ*, m. fleece; wool; tuft.

velloso, *-lō'sŏ*, a. woolly, shaggy, rough.

vellutato, *-lūtă'tŏ*, a. velvety.

velluto, *-lū'tŏ*, m. velvet; —, a. shaggy.

velo, *vă'lŏ*, m. veil, crape, shin; bark; crust; cover, pretext.

veloce, *vĕlō'dshĕ*, a. swift, quick, nimble.

velocemente, *-mĕn'tĕ*, ad. swiftly.

velocipede, *-lōdshĕ'pĕdĕ*, m. velocipede; —, a. swift-footed.

velocità, *-dshitā'*, f. velocity, swiftness.

veltro, *vĕl'trŏ*, m. greyhound.

vena, *vă'nă*, f. vein; (fig.) abundance.

venale, *vĕnă'lĕ*, a. to be sold; mercenary.

vendemmia, *vĕndĕm'miă*, f. vintage; vin-tage-time.

vendemmiare, *-miă'rĕ*, v. a. to gather the grapes; to acquire money.

vendere, *vēn'dĕrĕ,* v. a. to sell, to vend; — all' asta, to sell by auction; — a contanti, to sell for ready money.

vendetta, *–dĕt'tā,* f. vengeance.

vendicare, *–dīkā'rĕ,* v. a. to revenge, to vindicate.

vendicativo, *–tē'vŏ,* a. revengeful.

vendita, *vēn'dītā,* f. sale, selling.

venditore, *–dītō'rĕ,* m. seller, vender.

venerabile, *vĕnĕrā'bīlĕ,* a. venerable.

venerabilità, *–bīlītā',* f. venerableness.

venerare, *–rā'rĕ,* v. a. to venerate, to revere. [Good Friday.

venerdì, *vĕnĕrdī',* m. Friday; — santo,

venereo, *–nĕrŏ'ŏ,* a. venereal; lustful.

venia, *vā'nīā,* f. forgiveness; permission.

veniale, *vēn'ī'lĕ,* a. pardonable.

venire, *vēnē'rĕ,* v. n. ir. to come, to arrive; to happen.

ventaglio, *vēntāl'yŏ,* m. fan.

ventare, *–tā'rĕ,* v. n. to be windy, to blow. [fire-fan.

ventaruola, *–rāŏ'lā,* f. weather-cock;

ventesimo, *–tā'sīmŏ,* a. twentieth.

venti, *vēn'tī,* a. twenty.

ventilare, *–tīlā'rĕ,* v. a. to ventilate, to fan; to discuss; —, v. n. to flutter.

vento, *vēn'tŏ,* m. wind; (fig.) hint; vanity.

ventola, *[vēn'tōlā,]* f. fan; chandelier; screen of a table-lamp.

ventolare, *–tōlā'rĕ,* v. a. to winnow; to float in the wind.

ventosa, *–tō'sā,* f. cupping-glass.

ventoso, *–tŏ'sŏ,* a. windy, flatulent; proud.

ventraia, *–trāī'ā,* f. paunch, belly.

ventre, *vēn'trĕ,* m. belly; womb.

ventriloquo, *–trē'lōkŭŏ,* m. ventriloquist.

ventura, *–tōō'rā,* f. fortune, adventure, chance; a —, by chance; alla —, at random; buona —, good luck; far la —, to tell fortunes.

venturiere, *–tūrī'ĕ'rĕ,* [m. volunteer; adventurer. [—, next year.

venturo, *–tōō'rŏ,* a. future, to come; l'anno

venturoso, *–tūrō'sŏ,* a. lucky, favourable.

venusto, *vēnŭs'tŏ,* a. graceful, lovely, handsome, fine.

venuta, *vēnōō'tā,* f. arrival.

venuto, *vēnōō'tŏ,* p. come; ben —, welcome.

ver, *vēr,* pr. (poet.) towards, against.

verace, *vērā'dshĕ,* a. true, sincere; trusty.

veracità, *–rādshītā',* f. veracity.

veramente, *–mēn'tĕ,* ad. truly, indeed.

veranda, *–rān'dā,* f. veranda.

verbale, *–bā'lĕ,* a. verbal; literal.

verbo, *vēr'bŏ,* m. verb; word, saying; — a —, word for word.

verbosità, *–bōsītā',* f. verbiage, prattle.

verboso, *–bŏ'sŏ,* a. talkative.

verdastro, *–dās'trŏ,* a. greenish.

verde, *vēr'dĕ,* m. verdure, green; vigour; —, a. green; fresh, young; tender; unripe; sour. [dant; to become green.

verdeggiare, *–dēdjā'rĕ,* v. n. to be verdant.

verderame, *–dĕrā'mĕ,* m. verdigris.

verdetto, *–dĕt'tŏ,* a. greenish; sourish.

verdone, *–dŏ'nĕ,* m. green-finch.

verdura, *–dŏ'rā,* f. greenness.

verecondia, *vĕrēkŏn'dīā,* f. modesty, bashfulness.

verecondo, *–kŏn'dŏ,* a. modest, bashful, chaste.

verga, *vēr'gā,* f. rod, switch, wand.

vergare, *–gā'rĕ,* v. a. to stripe, to streak; to trace.

verghetta, *–ghĕt'tā,* f. little rod.

vergine, *vēr'jīnĕ,* f. virgin, maid; Virgin Mary. [hood.

verginità, *–jīnītā',* f. virginity, maiden-

vergogna, *–gŏn'yā,* f. shame, bashfulness; infamy.

vergognare, *–yā'rĕ,* v. a. to shame; vergognarsi, *–yār'sī,* to be ashamed.

vergognoso, *–yŏ'sŏ,* a. modest; shameful.

vergola, *vēr'gŏlā,* f. small switch.

veridicità, *–rīdīdshītā',* f. veracity.

veridico, *–rē'dīkŏ,* a. frank, speaking truth.

verificare, *–rīfīkā'rĕ,* v. a. to verify, to prove.

verificatore, *–tō'rĕ,* m. verifier; examiner.

verificazione, *–tzīō'nĕ,* f. verification; examination. [bability, likelihood.

verisimiglianza, *–sīmīlyān'tzā,* f. pro-

verisimile, *–sĕ'mīlĕ,* a. probable, likely.

verità, *vērītā',* f. truth, verity.

veritiere, *–rītī'ĕ'rĕ,* veritiero, *–rŏ,* a. [true, sincere.

verme, *vēr'mĕ,* m. worm.

vermena, *–mā'nā,* f. sprig, sucker.

vermicelli, *–mīdshĕl'lī,* m. pl. vermicelli, pl. (rolled paste).

vermiglio, *–mīl'yŏ,* a. vermil.

vermiglione, *–yŏ'nĕ,* m. vermilion.

vernacolo, *–nā'kŏlŏ,* a. vernacular.

vernare, *vērnā'rĕ,* v. n. to winter; to be in winter; to be chilled with cold.

vernata, *–nā'tā,* f. winter-season.

vernice, *–nē'dshĕ,* m. varnish.

verniciare, *–nīdshā'rĕ,* v. a. to varnish.

verno, *vēr'nŏ,* m. winter.

vero, *vā'rŏ,* a. true, sure, certain; real.

verone, *vērō'nĕ,* m. terrace, open gallery.

verre, *vēr'rĕ,* m. boar, boar-pig.

verruca, *–rŏ'kā,* f. wart.

versare, *vērsā'rĕ,* v. a. to pour out, to diffuse; to dissipate; to overturn; (— lacrime), to shed (tears); versarsi, *–sār'sī,* to fly into a passion.

versatile, *–sā'tīlĕ,* a. versatile.

versato, *–sā'tŏ,* a. versed; expert; skilful.

verseggiare, *–sēdjā'rĕ,* versificare, *–sīfīkā'rĕ,* v. a. to versify.

versione, *–sīō'nĕ,* f. version, translation.

versipelle, *–sīpĕl'lĕ,* a. crafty, deceitful.

verso, *vēr'sŏ,* m. verse, tune; song; expedient, way; versi sciolti, pl. blank verse; —, pr. towards, against; about; with regard to; in comparison with.

vertere, *vēr'tĕrĕ,* v. n. to concern, to relate to. [cular.

verticale, *–tīkā'lĕ,* a. vertical, perpendi-

verticalmente, *–tīkālmen'tĕ,* ad. vertically. [mit, height.

vertice, *vēr'tīdshĕ,* m. vertex, top, sum-

vertigine, *–tī'jīnĕ,* f. vertigo, dizziness.

vertiginoso, _-tĭjĭnŏ'sŏ,_ a. giddy.

veruno, _vĕrŏ'nŏ,_ a. nobody, no one.

verzicare, _vĕrzēkă'rĕ,_ v. n. to be or to grow green, to flourish.

verziere, _-tzĭĕ'rĕ,_ m. kitchen-garden.

verzotto, _-tzŏt'tŏ,_ m. cabbage.

verzura, _-tzŏ'rŭ,_ f. greenness; grass-plot.

vescia, _vĕssh'ă,_ f. puff-ball; idle talk.

vescica, _vĕsshĕ'kă,_ f. bladder; blister; alembic; idle talk.

vescovile, _vĕskŏvē'lĕ,_ a. episcopal, of a bishop.

vescovo, _vĕs'kŏvŏ,_ m. bishop. [bishop.

vespa, _vĕs'pă,_ f. wasp.

vespaio, _-pā'ŏ,_ m. wasp's nest; attire; ceiling. [pers, pl.

vespero, _vĕs'pĕrŏ,_ m. (poet.) evening, vespertino, _-pĕrtĭ'nŏ,_ a. of the evening.

vespro, see vespero.

vessare, _vĕssā'rĕ,_ v. a. to vex, to harass.

vessazione, _-tzĭŏ'nĕ,_ f. vexation.

vessica, _vĕssĕ'kă,_ f. urine-bladder.

vessicatorio, _-sĭkătŏ'rĭŏ,_ m. vesicatory.

vesta, _vĕs'tă,_ f. coat, gown, robe; dress.

vestale, _vĕstă'lĕ,_ f. vestal.

veste, see vesta.

vestibulo, _-tĕ'bŭlŏ,_ m. vestibule, hall.

vestigio, _-tĕ'jŏ,_ m. vestige, trace.

vestimento, _-tĭmĕn'tŏ,_ m. dress, clothes, pl.; vestment.

vestire, _vĕstĕ'rĕ,_ v. a. to dress, to vest.

veterano, _vĕtĕrā'nŏ,_ a. & m. veteran.

vetraio, _-trā'ŏ,_ m. glazier.

vetrata, _-trā'tă,_ f. glass-window.

vetrice, _vă'trĭshĕ,_ f. osier.

vetriolo, _vĕtrĭŏ'lŏ,_ m. vitriol.

vetro, _vă'trŏ,_ m. glass; pane of glass; drinking-glass.

vetta, _vĕt'tă,_ f. summit, top; twig; handle.

vettina, _-tĕ'nă,_ f. water-pipe, duct, canal.

vettovaglia, _-tŏvă'yă,_ f. victuals, provisions, pl.

vettovagliare, _-yă'rĕ,_ v. a. to victual.

vettura, _-tŏ'ră,_ f. carriage, vehicle; coach-hire; freight.

vetturale, _-tŭrā'lĕ,_ vetturino, _-rĕ'nŏ,_ m. driver of a hackney-coach.

vetustà, _vĕtŭstă',_ f. (poet.) antiquity.

vetusto, _-tŭs'tŏ,_ a. old, ancient.

vezzeggiare, _vĕtzĕdjă'rĕ,_ v. a. to caress, to fondle, to flatter.

vezzo, _vĕt'zŏ,_ m. sport, diversion, amusement; habit, custom; necklace.

vezzoso, _-tzŏ'sŏ,_ a. charming, pleasing; nice, prim. [you, you.

vi, _vĭ,_ ad. there, in that place; —, pn. to

via, _vĕ'ă,_ f. way, road, street; course; manner, means; —. ad. away; —, i. come on! courage!

viadotto, _vĭădŏt'tŏ,_ m. viaduct.

viaggiare, _-djă'rĕ,_ v. n. to travel. to journey.

viaggiatore, _-tŏ'rĕ,_ m. traveller.

viaggio, _vĭăd'jŏ,_ m. journey, voyage, travel.

viale, _vĭă'lĕ,_ m. avenue, alley.

viatico, _vĭă'tĭkŏ,_ m. viaticum; travelling-charges, pl.

viatore, _-tŏ'rĕ,_ viatrice, _-trĕ'dshĕ,_ f. traveller, passenger. [brandish.

vibrare, _vĭbră'rĕ,_ v. a. & n. to vibrate, to brandish.

vibrazione, _-tzĭŏ'nĕ,_ f. vibration.

vicario, _vĭkă'rĭŏ,_ m. vicar, curate; substitute, chief.

vicenda, _-dshĕn'dă,_ f. vicissitude, change; intercourse; requital, return; event; affair, business; place. [alternate.

vicendevole, _-dĕ'vŏlĕ,_ a. reciprocal,

vicinale, _-dshĕnă'lĕ,_ a. neighbouring.

vicinanza, _-năn'tză,_ f. neighbourhood; neighbours, pl.

vicinità, _-dshĕnĭtă',_ f. vicinity.

vicino, _-dshĕ'nŏ,_ m. neighbour; —, a. near, neighbouring; —, pr. near, close to, just by.

vicissitudine, _-dshĭssĭtŏ'dĭnĕ,_ f. vicissitude.

vico, _vĕ'kŏ,_ m. narrow lane. [tude.

vie, _vĕ'ĕ,_ ad. much, by far; vie via, immediately. [hibit, to forbid.

vietare, _vĭĕtă'rĕ,_ v. a. to avoid; to pro-

vieto, _vĭĕ'tŏ,_ a. old; obsolete.

vietume, _vĭĕtŏ'mĕ,_ m. old thing or stuff.

vigesimo, _vĭjĕ'sĭmŏ,_ a. twentieth.

vigilare, _-jĭlă'rĕ,_ v. a. & n. to watch, to be vigilant, to sit up.

vigile, _-jĕ'lĕ,_ a. vigilant.

vigilia, _-jĕ'lĭă,_ f. watching, watch; eve.

vigliaccheria, _vĭlyăkkĕrĕ'ă,_ f. cowardice.

vigliacco, _vĭlyăk'kŏ,_ a. cowardly, timorous.

viglietto, _-yĕt'tŏ,_ m. note, billet.

vigna, _vĭn'yă,_ f. vineyard, vine.

vignaiuolo, _-yăŭŏ'lŏ,_ m. vine-dresser.

vigneto, _-yĕ'tŏ,_ m. vineyard.

vigore, _vĭgŏ'rĕ,_ m. vigour, strength.

vigoreggiare, _-rĕdjă'rĕ,_ v. a. to invigorate; to encourage.

vigoria, _-gŏrĕ'ă,_ f. vigour, force.

vigoroso, _-gŏrŏ'sŏ,_ a. vigorous.

vile, _vĕ'lĕ,_ a. vile, low, abject; despicable.

vilia, _vĕ'lĭă,_ f. vigil, eve; watching.

vilipendere, _vĭlĭpĕn'dĕrĕ,_ v. a. ir. to despise, to scorn.

vilipendio, _-pĕn'dĭŏ,_ m. contempt.

vilipeso, _-pă'sŏ,_ a. despised, vile.

villa, _vĭl'lă,_ f. villa, country-seat.

villaggio, _-lăd'jŏ,_ m. village.

villanesco, _-lănĕs'kŏ,_ a. rustic, coarse.

villania, _-lănĕ'ă,_ f. insult, injury; filthiness; obscenity. [—, a. rustic, coarse.

villano, _-lă'nŏ,_ m. countryman, peasant;

villeggiare, _-lĕdjă'rĕ,_ v. n. to stay at one's country-seat; to enjoy the country.

villeggiatura, _-lĕdjătŏ'ră,_ f. enjoyments of the country, pl.; country-season.

villoso, _-lŏ'sŏ,_ a. hairy, woolly, shaggy.

vilmente, _vĭlmĕn'tĕ,_ ad. vilely, meanly.

viltà, _vĭltă',_ f. cowardice, vileness; cheapness. [disorder.

viluppo, _vĭlŭp'pŏ,_ m. packet, parcel; crowd,

vimine, _vĕ'mĭnĕ,_ m. willow-twig; tie.

vinaio, _vĭnā'ŏ,_ vinattiere, _-năttĭĕ'rĕ,_ m. vintner; wine-merchant.

vincastro, _vĭnkăs'trŏ,_ m. switch, rod.

vincere, _vĭn'dshĕrĕ,_ v. a. ir. to vanquish, to conquer; to outdo; to win (at cards &c.).

vincheto, *–kǎ'tŏ*, m. osier-plot.
vincido, *vin'dshĭdŏ*, a. soft, flabby.
vincita, *vin'dshĭtǎ*, f. gain.
vincitore, *–dshĭtŏ're*, m. victor, conqueror.
vinco, *vin'kŏ*, m. osier, willow, tie.
vincolare, *–kŏlǎ're*, v. a. to bind by contract.
vincolo, *vĭn'kŏlŏ*, m. tie, band; chain.
vindice, *vin'dĭdshĕ*, m. revenger; punisher.
vino, *vē'nŏ*, m. wine.
vinolento, *vinŏlĕn'tŏ*, a. given to wine.
viola, *vĭŏ'lǎ*, f. stock-gilliflower; violet; (mus.) viol.
violaceo, *vĭŏlǎ'dshĕŏ*, a. violet-coloured.
violare, *–lǎ're*, v. a. to violate. [colour.
violato, *–lǎ'tŏ*, a. violated; of a violet-
violatore, *–lǎtŏ're*, m. violator, infringer.
violazione, *–tzĭŏ'nĕ*, f. violation, infringement. [constrain.
violentare, *–lĕntǎ're*, v. a. to force, to
violento, *–lĕn'tŏ*, a. violent, impetuous.
violentemente, *–tĕmĕn'tĕ*, ad. violently.
violenza, *–lĕn'tzǎ*, f. violence.
violinista, *–lĭnĭs'tǎ*, m. violin-player.
violino, *–lē'nŏ*, m. violin.
violoncello, *–lŏndshĕl'lŏ*, m. violoncello.
violone, *–lē'nĕ*, m. bass-viol.
viottola, *vĭŏt'tŏlǎ*, **viottolo**, *–tŏlŏ*, m. narrow path, avenue; garden-walk.
vipera, *vē'pĕrǎ*, f. viper.
virginale, *virjĭnǎ'lĕ*, a. virginal.
virginità, see **verginità**.
virgola, *vĭr'gŏlǎ*, f. comma.
virgulto, *–gŭl'tŏ*, m. young shoot.
virile, *vĭrē'lĕ*, a. virile, manly, brave.
virilità, *–rĭlĭtǎ'*, f. virility, manhood.
virilmente, *–rĭlmĕn'tĕ*, ad. in a manly manner.
virtù, *vĭrtŭ'*, f. virtue; power, efficacy.
virtuale, *–tŭǎ'lĕ*, a. virtual.
virtuoso, *–tŭŏ'sŏ*, a. virtuous; efficacious.
virulento, *vĭrŭlĕn'tŏ*, a. virulent; malig-
virulenza, *–lĕn'tzǎ*, f. virulence. [nant.
viscere, *vĭssh'ĕrĕ*, f. entrails, bowels, pl.
vischio, *vĭs'kĭŏ*, m. bird-lime, snare; mistletoe. [viscous, glutinous.
vischioso, *–kĭŏ'sŏ*, **viscido**, *vĭssh'ĭdŏ*, a.
visciola, *vĭssh'ŏlǎ*, f. egriot, sour-cherry.
visconte, *vĭskŏn'tĕ*, m. viscount.
viscoso, *vĭskŏ'sŏ*, a. viscous, glutinous.
visibile, *vĭsē'bĭlĕ*, a. visible.
visibilità, *–sĭbĭlĭtǎ'*, f. visibility.
visiera, *–sĭǎ'rǎ*, f. vizor; mask.
visione, *–sĭŏ'nĕ*, f. vision, apparition.
visita, *vē'sĭtǎ*, f. visit. [visit.
visitare, *vĭsĭtǎ're*, v. a. to visit, to pay a
visitatore, *–tŏ're*, m. visitor; examiner.
visitazione, *–tzĭŏ'nĕ*, f. visitation.
visivo, *vĭsē'vŏ*, a. visual, visible.
viso, *vē'sŏ*, m. visage, face, countenance; – a –, face to face; a – aperto, boldly.
vispezza, *vĭspĕt'zǎ*, f. briskness, agility; sharpness.
vispo, *vĭs'pŏ*, a. brisk, lively, nimble.
vista, *vĭs'tǎ*, f. sight, eye-sight; view, prospect; appearance, show; a –, at sight; within sight; a prima –, at first sight.

visto, see **vispo**.
vistoso, *–tŏ'sŏ*, a. handsome, pleasing.
vita, *vē'tǎ*, f. life; living; waist, shape.
vitale, *vĭtǎ'lĕ*, a. vital, living.
vitalità, *–tǎlĭtǎ'*, f. vitality.
vite, *vē'tĕ*, f. vine; screw, vice.
vitello, *vĭtĕl'lŏ*, m. calf; veal.
viticchio, *–tĭk'kĭŏ*, m. hedge-weed.
vitreo, *–vē'trĕŏ*, a. vitreous, glassy.
vittima, *vĭt'tĭmǎ*, f. victim; sacrifice.
vitto, *vĭt'tŏ*, m. food, livelihood.
vittoria, *vĭttŏ'rĭǎ*, f. victory. [phant.
vittorioso, *–tŏrĭŏ'sŏ*, a. victorious, trium-
vituperare, *vĭtŭpĕrǎ're*, v.a. to vituperate, to blame. [tion.
vituperazione, *–pĕrǎtzĭŏ'nĕ*, f. vitupera-
vitupero, *–tǎpĕ'rŏ*, m. disgrace, dishonour; infamy. [alley.
viuzza, *vĕǎt'zǎ*, **viuzzo**, *–zŏ*, m. lane,
viva, *vē'vǎ*, i. vivat!
vivace, *vĭvǎ'dshĕ*, a. sprightly, lively.
vivacità, *–vǎdshĭtǎ'*, f. vivacity.
vivagno, *–vǎn'yŏ*, m. edge; list of cloth.
vivaio, *–vǎ'ŏ*, m. fish-pond; nursery. [ter.
vivanda, *–vǎn'dǎ*, f. food, victuals, dishes,
vivandiere, *–dĭĕ'rĕ*, m. sutler; caterer.
vivere, *vē'vĕrĕ*, v. n. to live, to be alive.
vivido, *vē'vĭdŏ*, a. vivid, lively, vivacious.
viviparo, *vĭvē'pǎrŏ*, a. viviparous.
vivo, *vē'vŏ*, a. alive, living; lively, sprightly.
viziare, *vĭtzĭǎ're*, v. a. to vitiate, to spoil; to defile. [desire.
vizio, *vē'tzĭŏ*, m. vice, defect; blemish;
vizioso, *vĭtzĭŏ'sŏ*, a. vicious, wicked, faulty.
vizzo, *vĭt'zŏ*, a. flaccid, withered, dry.
vocabolario, *vŏkǎbŏlǎ'rĭŏ*, m. vocabulary, dictionary.
vocabolo, *–kǎ'bŏlŏ*, m. word, term.
vocale, *–kǎ'lĕ*, a. & f. vocal; vowel.
vocativo, *–kǎtē'vŏ*, m. (gr.) vocative.
vocazione, *–tzĭŏ'nĕ*, f. vocation; calling.
voce, *vŏ'dshĕ*, f. voice; word, vote, sentence; a–, a viva –, by word of mouth: sotto –, in a low voice.
vociferare, *–dshĭfĕrǎ're*, v. n. to bawl.
vociferazione, *–tzĭŏ'nĕ*, f. clamour; rumour. [ardour.
voga, *vŏ'gǎ*, f. rowing, course; vogue;
vogare, *vŏgǎ're*, v. a. to row. [petite.
voglia, *vŏl'yǎ*, f. will, wish, desire; appetite;
voglioso, *vŏlyŏ'sŏ*, a. desirous, eager.
voi, *vŏ'ĕ*, pn. pl. you.
volare, *vŏlǎ're*, v. n. to fly; –, m. flight; rapid course. [volley.
volata, *–lǎ'tǎ*, f. flight; **volato**, *–tŏ*, m. flight;
volatile, *–lǎ'tĭlĕ*, a. volatile, flying.
volatili, *–lǎ'tĭlĭ*, m. pl. birds, fowls, pl.
volatilità, *–tĭlĭtǎ'*, f. volatility.
volatilizzare, *–lĭdzǎ're*, v. a. to volatilize.
volcanico, *vŏlkǎ'nĭkŏ*, a. volcanic.
volcano, *vŏlkǎ'nŏ*, m. volcano
volentieri, *vŏlĕntĭĕ're*, ad. willingly.
volentieroso, *–tĭĕrŏ'sŏ*, a. willing; desirous.
volere, *vŏlē're*, v. a. & n. ir. to will; to wish, to desire; to bid; to consent; –

bene, to wish well; to love; **– dire,** to mean, to signify.

volgare, *vŏlgä′rĕ,* a. vulgar, common.

volgarità, *–gärïtä′,* f. vulgarity; simplicity.

volgarmente, *–gärmĕn′tĕ,* ad. vulgarly.

Volgata, *–gä′tä,* f. Vulgate.

volgere, *vŏl′jerä′,* v. a. ir. to turn, to revolve; to cross; to bend, to incline; to turn aside, to persuade; to alter, to change, to address, to direct.

volgo, *vŏl′gŏ,* m. common people, multitude.

volo, *vŏ′lŏ,* m. flight; soaring.

volontà, *vŏlŏntä′,* f. will, desire, wish.

volontario, *–tä′rïŏ,* a. & m. voluntary; volunteer.

volpe, *vŏl′pĕ,* f. fox; (fig.) cunning man.

volpone, *–pŏ′nĕ,* m. old fox.

volta, *vŏl′tä,* f. turn, turning, revolving, whirl; vault; winding, direction; way, road; lapse; **alla –,** towards; **alcune volte, alle volte,** sometimes; **una –,** once; **altre volte,** formerly; **due volte,** twice.

voltare, *–tä′rĕ,* v. a. to turn, to turn round; to change; to wallow; to apply to.

volteggiare, *–tĕdjä′rĕ,* v. n. to flutter about; to fly about; to tumble.

volto, *vŏl′tŏ,* m. vault, arch; –, m. face, visage.   [tumble; to wallow.

voltolare, *–tŏlä′rĕ,* v. a. & n. to roll; to wallow.

volubile, *vŏlŏ′bïlĕ,* a. voluble; variable.

volubilità, *–lïbïlïtä′,* f. volubility, fickleness.

volvere, *see* **volgere.**   [ness.

volume, *vŏlŏ′mĕ,* m. volume, book; mass.

voluminoso, *–lŭmïnŏ′sŏ,* a. voluminous; bulky.

voluta, *–lŏ′tä,* f. volute.

voluttuario, *–lŭttŭä′rïŏ,* **voluttuoso,** *–tŭŏ′sŏ,* a. voluptuous.

vomere, *vŏ′merĕ,* m. plough-share.

vomitare, *vŏmïtä′rĕ,* v. a. to vomit.

vorace, *vŏrä′dshĕ,* a. voracious.

voracità, *–rädshïtä′,* f. voracity.

voragine, *–rä′jïnĕ,* f. gulf, whirlpool; abyss; ruin.

vortice, *vŏr′tïdshĕ,* m. vortex; whirlpool.

Vossignoria, *vŏssïnyŏrĕ′ä,* f. (you) Sir.

vostro, *vŏs′trŏ,* pn. your, yours.

votare, *vŏtä′rĕ,* v. a. to empty, to clear; to abolish; to dedicate; **–,** v. n. to give

votivo, *–tĕ′vŏ,* a. votive.   [one's vote.

voto, *vŏ′tŏ,* m. vow, vote, wish; **–,** a. empty, void; deprived, inane.

vulcano, *see* **volcano.**   [hurt.

vulnerare, *vŭlnerä′rĕ,* v. a. to wound, to

Z.

zacchera, *tzäk′kerä,* f. splash of dirt; (fig.) trouble, embarrassment; trifle.   [satirp.

zaffata, *tzäffä′tä,* f. outburst on uncorking;

zafferano, *dzäfferä′nŏ,* m. saffron.

zaffiro, *–fĕ′rŏ,* m. sapphire.

zaffo, *tzäf′fŏ,* m. bung, stopper; bailiff.

zagaglia, *tzägäl′yä,* f. javelin (of the Moors).

zaino, *dzä′ïnŏ,* m. bag of a shepherd.

zampa, *tzäm′pä,* f. paw, talon.

zampillare, *tzämpïllä′rĕ,* v. n. to gush or to spout out.

zampillo, *–pïl′lŏ,* m. water-spout.

zampino, *tzämpĕ′nŏ,* m. little paw.

zampogna, *–pŏn′yä,* f. shepherd's pipe.

zana, *tzä′nä,* f. basket; cradle; trick.

zanca, *tzän′kä,* f. leg, shank.

zangola, *tzän′gŏlä,* f. churn.

zanna, *tzän′nä,* f. tusk, tooth; fang.

zannare, *–nä′rĕ,* v. a. to polish.

zanni, *tzän′nĭ,* m. buffoon.

zanzara, *dzändzä′rä,* f. gnat.

zanzariere, *–rïä′rĕ,* m. mosquito-guard, gauze bed-curtain.

zappa, *tzäp′pä,* f. mattock; spade.   [ruin.

zappare, *–pä′rĕ,* v. a. to hoe, to dig; to

zappone, *–pŏ′nĕ,* m. mattock.

zara, *dzä′rä,* f. hazard; risk, danger.

zattera, *tzät′terä,* f. raft.

zavorra, *dzävŏr′rä,* f. ballast.

zazzera, *tzät′zerä,* f. long hanging hair.

zecca, *tzĕk′kä,* f. mint; tick.

zecchino, *–kĕ′nŏ,* m. sequin.

zeffiro, *dzĕf′fïrŏ,* m. zephyr.

zelare, *dzĕlä′rĕ,* v. n. to be zealous.

zelo, *dzĕ′lŏ,* m. zeal, fervency, ardour

zeppa, *tzĕp′pä,* f. wedge.

zeppare, *–pä′rĕ,* v. a. to fill up, to cram.

zeppo, *tzĕp′pŏ,* a. quite full, crammed.

zerbino, *dzärbĕ′nŏ,* m. fop, dandy.

zero, *dzä′rŏ,* m. zero; cypher, nothing.

zia, *tzĕ′ä,* f. aunt.

zibaldone, *dzïbäldŏ′nĕ,* m. mixture, medley.

zibellino, *–bĕllĕ′nŏ,* m. sable; fur of the

zibetto, *–bĕt′tŏ,* m. civet-cat.   [sable.

zibibbo, *–bĕb′bŏ,* m. dry red-raisin.

zigomo, *tzïgŏ′mŏ,* m. check-bone.

zimbellare, *dzïmbĕllä′rĕ,* v. a. to allure (birds by a bird-call).   [bird; lure, bait.

zimbello, *–bĕl′lŏ,* m. bird-call; decoy-

zinale, *tzïnä′lĕ,* m. apron.

zinco, *tzïn′kŏ,* m. zinc.   [gipsy.

zingano, *tzïn′gänŏ,* **zingaro,** *–gärŏ,* m.

zinna, *tzïn′nä,* f. nipple, breast; neck of a

zinnale, *–nä′lĕ,* m. breast-cloth.   [bottle.

zinzino, *–tzĕ′nŏ,* m. sip, small draught,

zio, *tzä′ŏ,* m. uncle.   [rest of drink.

zitella, *tzïtĕl′lä,* f. young girl, spinster.

zitto, *dzït′tŏ,* m. silence, hush, peace.

zizzania, *dzïdzä′nïä,* f. darnel; discord.

zoccolo, *tzŏk′kŏlŏ,* m. wooden shoe; plinth; clod, turf; ninny.

zodiaco, *dzŏdï′äkŏ,* m. zodiac.

zolfa, *tzŏl′fä,* f. (mus.) gamut.

zolfanello, *–fänĕl′lŏ,* m. match, vesta; **– volcanico,** lucifer-match.

zolfata, *–fä′tä,* **zolfatara,** *–tä′rä,* f. sulphur-mine.

zolfino, *–fĕ′nŏ,* a. sulphureous.

zolfo, *tzŏl′fŏ,* m. sulphur, brimstone.

zolla, *dzŏl′lä,* f. clod, glebe.   [to thump

zombare, *dzŏmbä′rĕ,* v. a. to beat, to bang

zona, *dzŏ′nä,* f. girdle; zone.

zoofito, *dzŏŏfĕ′tŏ,* m. zoophyte.

zoologia, *–lŏjĕ′ä,* f. zoology.

zoologico, –*tŏ' jĭkŏ,* a. zoological.
zoppicare, *dżŏppĭkä' rĕ,* v. n. to limp, to go lame.
zoppo, *dżŏp' pŏ,* a. lame; defective.
zotichezza, *dżŏtĭkĕt' zä,* f. awkwardness.
zotico, *dżŏ' tĭkŏ,* a. clownish, boorish, rude.
zucca, *tzŭk' kä,* f. gourd, pumpkin; cucumber; noddle, pate.
zuccaiuola, –*käĭŭŏ' lä,* f. mole-cricket.
zucoherare, –*kĕrä' rĕ,* v. a. to sugar.
zucchero, *tzŭk' kĕrŏ,* m. sugar; **– candito,** sugar-candy.
zuccheroso, –*kĕrŏ' sŏ,* a. saccharine; sweet.
zucchetta, –*kĕt' tä,* f. small gourd; small pumpkin.

zucconare, –*kŏnä' rĕ,* v. a. to cut the hair.
zuccone, –*kŏ' nĕ,* m. bald head.
zuccotto, –*kŏt' tŏ,* m. head-piece.
zuffa, *tzŭf' fä,* f. strife, quarrel.
zufolare, *dżŭfŏlä' rĕ,* v. n. to whistle, to flute; to whisper.
zufolo, *dżŏ' fŏlŏ,* m. whistle, flageolet.
zuppa, *tzŭp' pä,* f. soaked bread, sop.
zuppiero, –*pĭä' rŏ,* m. soup-dish, porringer, tureen.
zuppo, *tzŭp' pŏ,* a. soaked, saturated.
zurlare, *dżŭrlä' rĕ,* v. n. to sport, to joke, to jest.
zurlo, *dżŭr' lŏ,* m. gaiety, good humour, playfulness; immoderate desire.

Scelta de' Nomi di Paesi, di Nazioni &c.

Proper Names of Countries, Towns and People.

Abissinia, *ăbissĕ'nĭă,* Abyssinia. [sinian.
abissinio, *–sĕ'nĭŏ,* Abys-
Abuchiro, *ăbŭkē'rŏ,* 'Abu-kir.
Acaia, *ăkä'ă,* Achaia.
Affrica, *ăf'frĭkă,* Africa.
affricano, *–kă'nŏ,* African.
Aia, *ä'ă,* the Hague.
albanese, *ălbănā'sĕ,* Alba-nian.
Aibione, *–bĭŏ'nĕ,* Albion.
Alemagna, *ălĕmăn'yă,* Germany. [Alexandria.
Alessandria, *ălĕssăn'drĭă,*
Algeri, *ăljĕ'rĭ,* Algiers.
Alpi, *ăl'pĭ,* Alps.
Alsazia, *–să'tsĭă,* Alsace.
alsaziano, *–tsĭă'nŏ,* Alsa-tian.
Altona, *ăl'tŏnă,* Altona.
Alvernia, *–vĕr'nĭă,* Au-vergne.
amburghese, *ămbŭrghā'-sĕ,* Hamburghese. [burg.
Amburgo, *–bŭr'gŏ,* Ham-
americano, *ămĕrĭkă'nŏ,* American. [Amsterdam.
Amsterdam, *ămstĕrdăm',*
andalusiano, *ăndălŭsĭă'-nŏ,* Andalusian.
Ande, *ăn'dĕ,* Andes.
Angiò, *ănjŏ',* Anjou.
Annover, *ănnŏ'vĕr,* Hanover. [Caribee Islands.
Antille, *–tĭl'lĕ,* Antilles.
antiocheno, *ăntĭŏkā'nŏ,* habitant of Antioch.
Antiochia, *–tĭŏ'kĭă,* An-tioch. [werp.
Anversa, *–vĕr'să,* Ant-
Appennini, *ăppĕnnē'nĭ,* Apennines.
Aquisgrana, *ăkŭĭsgră'nă,* Aix-la-Chapelle.
arabico, *ără'bĭkŏ,* **arabo,** *ă'răbŏ,* Arab.
Arcangelo, *ărkăn'jĕlŏ,* Archangel. [Strasburg.
Argentina, *–jĕntē'nă,*
armeno, *–mĕ'nŏ,* Armenian.
Asia, *ă'sĭă,* Asia.
asiatico, *ăsĭă'tĭkŏ,* Asiatic.

Assia, *ăs'sĭă,* Hesse.
assiano, *–sĭă'nŏ,* Hessian.
Atene, *ătā'nĕ,* Athens.
ateniese, *ătĕnĭā'sĕ,* ate-niense,** *–nĭĕn'sĕ,* Athenian.
Atlante, *ătlăn'tĕ,* Atlas.
atlantico, *–lăn'tĭkŏ,* At-lantic. [burg.
Augusta, *ăŭgŭs'tă,* Augs-
Australia, *ăŭstră'lĭă,* Australia.
Austria, *ăŭs'trĭă,* Austria.
austriaco, *ăŭstrĭ'ăkŏ,* Au-strian.
Avana, *ăvă'nă,* Hayannah.
Avignone, *ăvĭnyŏ'nĕ,* Avignon.
Azzorre, *ădzŏr'rĕ,* Azores.

Babilonia, *băbĭlŏ'nĭă,* Ba-bylon. [nă, Baden.
Bada, *bă'dă,* **Badena,** *–dā'-*
Balcano, *bălkă'nŏ,* Balkan.
Baleari, *bălĕă'rĭ,* Baleares.
Baltico, *băl'tĭkŏ,* **Mare –,** Baltic. [does.
Barbada, *băr'bădă,* Barba-
Barberia, *–bĕrē'ă,* Barbary.
Basilea, *băsĭlā'ă,* Basle.
batavo, *bă'tăvŏ,* Batavian.
bavarese, *–vără'sĕ,* ba-varo,** *bă'vărŏ,* Bavarian.
Baviera, *–vĭĕ'ră,* Bavaria.
belgico, *bĕl'jĭkŏ,* **belga,** *–gă,* Belgian.
Belgio, *bĕl'jŏ,* Belgium.
Bellisola, *bĕllĕ'sŏlă,* Bell-isle.
Bengala, *bĕngă'lă,* Bengal.
Beozia, *bĕŏ'tsĭă,* Beotia.
berlinese, *bĕrlĭnā'sĕ,* Ber-linian.
Berlino, *–lē'nŏ,* Berlin.
Bermude, *–mŏ'dĕ,* Bermu-das. [das.
Berna, *bĕr'nă,* Bern. [das.
Besanzone, *bĕsăntsŏ'nĕ,* Besançon. [lehem.
Betlemme, *bĕtlĕm'mĕ,* Beth-
Bisanzio, *bĭsăn'tsĭŏ,* By-zantium.
Biscaglia, *bĭskăl'yă,* **Bis-caia,** *–kăĭ'ă,* Biscay.

Boemia, *bŏā'mĭă,* Bohemia.
boemo, *bŏā'mŏ,* Bohemian.
Bolzano, *bŏlză'nŏ,* Botzen.
Bordò, *bŏrdŏ',* Bordeaux.
Borgogna, *bŏrgŏn'yă,* Bur-gundy. [gundian.
borgognone, *–yŏ'nĕ,* Bur-
Bosforo, *bŏs'fŏrŏ,* Bos-phorus. [bant.
Brabante, *brăbăn'tĕ,* Bra-brabanzese,** *–dză'sĕ,* Bra-bantine.
Brandemburgo, *brăndĕm-bŭr'gŏ,* Brandenburg.
Brasile, *bră sē'lĕ,* Brazil.
brasiliano, *–sĭlĭă'nŏ,* Bra-zilian.
Brema, *brā'mă,* Bremen.
Breslavia, *brĕslă'vĭă,* Bres-lau. [Britain.
Bretagna, *brĕtăn'yă,* Great
bretone, *–tŏ'nĕ,* Briton.
Brunsvig, *brŭns'vĭg,* Brunswick. [sels.
Brusselle, *brŭssĕl'lĕ,* Brus-
brussellese, *–sĕllā'sĕ,* Brusselian. [charest.
Bucarest, *bŭkărĕst',* Bu-
Bulgaria, *bŭlgă'rĭă,* Bul-garia. [rian.
bulgaro, *bŭl'gărŏ,* Bulga-

Cadice, *kă'dĭshĕ,* Cadiz
caffro, *kăf'frŏ,* Kaffir.
calabrese, *kălăbrā'sĕ,* Ca-labrian. [bria.
Calabria, *kălă'brĭă,* Cala-
californese, *–lĭfŏrnā'sĕ,* Californian. [fornia.
California, *–fŏr'nĭă,* Cali-
calmucco, *kălmăk'kŏ,* Cal-muck. [Campania.
Campania, *kămpă'nĭă,*
Canarie (isole), *kănă'rĭĕ,* Canary-Islands. [diot.
candiotto, *kăndĭŏt'tŏ,* Can-
Cannibali, *–nĭbă'lĭ,* **isole de' –,** Caribbee-Islands.
Cantorberì, *–tŏrbĕrē',* Can-terbury.
Capo, *kă'pŏ,* **– di Buona Speranza,** Cape of Good-Hope.

Cariddi, *–rĭd'dĭ,* Charybdis. [thia.

Carintia, *–rĭn'tĭä,* Carinthians.

Carmelo, *kärmā'lŏ,* Carmel.

Carpati, *–pä'tĭ,* Carpathians. [thage.

Cartagine, *–tä'jĭnĕ,* Carthaginian.

cartaginese, *–jĭnä'sĕ,* Carthaginian. [Sea.

Caspio, *käs'pĭŏ,* Caspian

Castiglia, *–tĭl'yä,* Castile.

castigliano, *–yä'nŏ,* Castilian. [talonia.

Catalogna, *kätälōn'yä,* Catalonia.

Caucaso, *käu'käsŏ,* Caucasus.

caucaseo, *käu kä'sĕŏ,* belonging to the Caucasus.

Ceilan, *dshā'län,* Ceylon.

Cevenne, *dshĕvĕn'nĕ,* Cevennes. [tĕ, Clermont.

Chiaramonte, *kĭäramōn'–*

China, *kī'nä,* China.

chinese, *kĭnä'sĕ,* Chinese.

Cipro, *dshē'prŏ,* Cyprus.

circasso, *dshĭrkäs'sŏ,* Circassian. [blentz.

Coblenza, *kŏblĕn'tzä,* Co-

Colonia, *kŏlō'nĭä,* Cologne.

Copenaghen, *kŏpĕnä'–ghĕn,* Copenhagen.

Cordigliere, *kŏrdĭlyä'rĕ,* Cordilliers. [thian.

corintio, *kŏrĭn'tĭŏ,* Corinthian.

Corinto, *kŏrĭn'tŏ,* Corinth.

Cornovaglia, *kŏrnŏväl'yä,* Cornwall.

cosacco, *kŏsäk'kŏ,* Cossack.

Costantinopoli, *kŏstäntĭ–nŏ'pŏlĭ,* Constantinople.

Costanza, *–tän'tzä,* Constance. [cow.

Cracovia, *kräkŏ'vĭä,* Cracow.

Creta, *krä'tä,* Crete.

cretese, *krĕtä'sĕ,* Cretan.

Crimea, *krĭmä'ä,* Crimea.

croato, *krŏä'tŏ,* Croatian.

Croazia, *krŏä'tzĭä,* Croatia.

Cumberlandia, *kŭmbĕr–län'dĭä,* Cumberland.

Curlandia, *kŭrlän'dĭä,* Courland. [landian.

curlandese, *–dä'sĕ,* Cour-

Dalmazia, *dälmä'tzĭä,* Dalmatia. [mascus.

Damasco, *dämäs'kŏ,* Da-

danese, *dänä'sĕ,* Dane; Danish. [Denmark.

Danimarca, *–nĭmär'kä,*

Danubio, *–nŏ'bĭŏ,* Danube.

Dardanelli, *därdänĕl'lĭ,* Dardanelles.

Delfinato, *dĕlfĭnä'tŏ,* Dauphiny, Dauphinate.

Delfo, *dĕl'fŏ,* Delphos, Delphi.

Digione, *dĭjŏ'nĕ,* Dijon.

Dresda, *drĕs'dä,* Dresden.

Dublino, *dŭblĭ'nŏ,* Dublin.

Due-Ponti, *dŭĕ pŏn'tĭ,* Deux-ponts. [Dunkirk.

Duncherche, *dŭnkĕr'kĕ,*

Dune, *dŏ'nĕ,* Downs.

Edimburgo, *ĕdĭmbŭr'gŏ,* Edinburgh.

Efeso, *ĕ'fĕsŏ,* Ephesus.

Egitto, *ĕjĭt'tŏ,* Egypt.

egiziano, *–tzĭä'nŏ,* Egyptian.

Eidelberga, *ĕĭdĕlbĕr'gä,* Heidelberg.

Elba, *ĕl'bä,* Elba; Elbe.

Ellesponto, *ĕllĕspŏn'tŏ,* Hellespont.

Erzegovina, *ĕrtzĕgŏvä'nä,* Herzegovina. [tes.

Eufrate, *ĕŭfrä'tĕ,* Euphrates.

Europa, *ĕŭrŏ'pä,* Europe.

europeo, *–rŏpä'ŏ,* European.

Faenza, *fäĕn'dzä,* Fayence.

Fenicia, *fĕnĭ'dshä,* Phœnicia. [ders.

Fiandra, *fĭän'drä,* Flanders.

finlandese, *fĭnländä'sĕ,* Finlander. [land.

Finlandia, *–län'dĭä,* Finland.

fiorentino, *fĭŏrĕntĭ'nŏ,* Florentine.

Firenze, *fĭrĕn'tzĕ,* Florence.

Fontanablò, *fŏntänäblŏ',* Fontainebleau. [French.

francese, *frändshä'sĕ,* French.

Francia, *frän'dshä,* France.

Francoforte, *–kŏfŏr'tĕ,* Frankfort. [burg.

Friburgo, *frĭbŭr'gŏ,* Friburg.

Frigia, *frē'jä,* Phrygia.

Frisia, *frē'sĭä,* Friesland.

frisio, *frē'sĭŏ,* Frieslander.

Galilea, *gälĭlä'ä,* Galilee.

galizio, *–lĭ'tzĭŏ,* Galician.

Galles, *gäl'lĕs,* Wales.

Gand, *gänd,* Ghent.

Gange, *gän'jĕ,* Ganges.

Genova, *jä'nŏvä,* Genoa.

genovese, *jĕnŏvä'sĕ,* Genoese. [gian.

georgiano, *jŏrjä'nŏ,* Georgian.

Gerico, *jä'rĭkŏ,* Jericho.

Germania, *jĕrmä'nĭä,* Germany.

germano, *–mä'nŏ,* German.

Gerusalemme, *–rŭsälĕm'–mĕ,* Jerusalem. [Jamaica.

Giammaica, *jämmä'ĭkä,*

Giappone, *jäppŏ'nĕ,* Japan.

giapponese, *–pŏnä'sĕ,* Japanese.

Giava, *jä'vä,* Java.

Gibilterra, *jĭbĭltĕr'rä,* Gibraltar.

Ginevra, *–nä'vrä,* Geneva.

ginevrino, *–nĕvrĭ'nŏ,* Genevese. [dan.

Giordano, *jŏrdä'nŏ,* Jordan.

Giudea, *jŭdä'ä,* Judea.

Glasgovia, *gläsgŏ'vĭä,* Glasgow. [Gothland.

Gotlandia, *gŏtlän'dĭä,*

Gottardo, *gŏttär'dŏ,* **Monte San –,** St. Gothard.

Granata, *gränä'tä,* Granada.

Grecia, *grä'tshä,* Greece.

greco, *grä'kŏ,* Grecian, Greek. [wich.

Grenvik, *grĕnvĭk',* Greenwich.

Grigioni, *grĭjŏ'nĭ,* Grisons.

groenlandese, *grŏĕnlän–dä'sĕ,* Greenlander.

Groenlandia, *–län'dĭä,* Greenland.

Guascogna, *gŭäskŏn'yä,* Gascony.

guascone, *–kŏ'nĕ,* Gascon

Guienna, *gŭĕn'nä,* Guienne.

Ibernia, *ĭbĕr'nĭä,* Hibernia.

ibero, *ĭbä'rŏ,* Iberian.

Illiria, *ĭllĭ'rĭä,* **Illirica,** *–rĭkä,* Illyricum.

illirico, *–lĭ'rĭkŏ,* Illyrian.

India, *ĭn'dĭä,* India, Indies.

indiano, *–dĭä'nŏ,* Indian.

Indo, *ĭn'dŏ,* Indus.

Indostan, *–dŏstän',* Hindostan. [män'nĭä, Ingria.

Inghermannia, *–ghĕr–*

Inghilterra, *–ghĭltĕr'rä,* England. [Englishman.

inglese, *–glä'sĕ,* English;

Ionico, *ĭŏ'nĭkŏ,* Ionian.

Iorca, *ĭŏr'kä,* York.

Ipra, *ē'prä,* Ypres.

Irlanda, *ĭrlän'dä,* Ireland.

irlandese, *–dä'sĕ,* Irish; Irishman.

Islanda, *ĭslän'dä,* Iceland.

islandese, *–dä'sĕ,* Icelander. [lite.

israelita, *ĭsräĕlī'tä,* Israelite.

istriano, *ĭstrĭä'nŏ,* Istrian.

Italia, *ĭtä'lyä,* Italy.

italiano, *–lĭä'nŏ,* Italian.

lacedemone, *lädshĕdä'mŏ–nĕ,* Lacedæmonian.

Lancastro, *län'kästrŏ,* Lancaster.

lappone, *läppŏ'nĕ,* Laplander, *–nä'sĕ,* Laplander. [land.

Lapponia, *–pŏ'nĭä,* Lapland.

latino, *lätĭ'nŏ,* Latin.

Lazio, *lä'tzĭŏ,* Latium.

Lemano, lĕmă′ nŏ, Lake of Geneva.
Lemno, lĕm′ nŏ, Lemnos.
Lesbo, lĕs′ bŏ, Lesbos.
Libano, lĕ′ bănŏ, Lebanon.
Liegi, lĭă′ jĭ, Liege. [burg.
Limburgo, lĭmbŭr′ gŏ, Lim-
Lione, lĭŏ′ nĕ, Lyons.
Lipsia, lĭp′ sĭă, Leipsic.
Lisbona, lĭsbŏ′ nă, Lisbon.
lisbonese, –bŏnă′ sĕ, Lis-
bonian. [thuany.
Lituania, lĭtŭă′ nĭă, Li-
lituano, lĭtŭă′ nŏ, Lithua-
nian. [pool.
Liverpul, lĭvĕrpŏl′, Liver-
Livorno, –vŏr′ nŏ, Leghorn.
Loira, lŏĕ′ră, Loire.
Lombardia, lŏmbăr′ dĭă,
Lombardy. [bard.
lombardo, –băr′ dŏ, Lom-
londinese, lŏndĭnă′ sĕ, Lon-
doner.
Londra, lŏn′ dră, London.
Lorena, lŏră′ nă, Lorraine.
Losanna, lŏsăn′ nă, Lau-
sanne.
Lubecca, lŭbĕk′ kă, Lubeck.
Lucemburgo, lŭdshĕm-
bŭr′ gŏ, Lussemburgo,
lŭssĕmbŭr′ gŏ, Luxemburg.
Lucerna, –dshĕr′ nă, Lu-
cern. [siana.
Luigiana, lŭĭjă′ nă, Loui-

macedone, mădshă′ dŏnĕ,
Macedonian. [Macedonia.
Macedonia, –dshĕdŏ′ nĭă,
Maddeburgo, măddĕbŭr′
gŏ, Magdeburg, Maidenburg.
Madera, mădă′ ră, Madeira.
Madrid, –drĭd′, Madrid-
de, –drĭd′ dĕ, Madrid.
madrileno, –lă′ nŏ, inhabi-
tant of Madrid.
Magonza, –gŏn′ tză, Mentz.
Malines, –lĕ′ nĕs, Mechlin.
Manica (la), mă′ nĭkă, Bri-
tish Channel. [tua.
Mantova, măn′ tŏvă, Man-
mantovano, –tŏvă′ nŏ,
Mantuan. [rathon.
Maratona, mărătŏ′ nă, Ma-
Marca, măr′ kă, Marchia,
–kĭă, March. [seilles.
Marsiglia, mărsĕl′ yă, Mar-
Martinicca, –tĭnĭk′ kă,
Martinique.
Maurizio (San), măŭrĕ′
tzĭŏ, St. Maurice.
Meclemburgo, mĕklĕnbŭr′-
gŏ, Mecklenburg.
medo, mă′ dŏ, Mede.
Menfi, mĕn′ fĭ, Memphis.
Meno, mă′ nŏ, Mein.
messicano, mĕssĭkă′ nŏ,
Mexican.

Messico, mĕs′ sĭkŏ, Mexico.
Milano, mĭlă′ nŏ, Milan.
Mileto, –lă′ tŏ, Miletus.
Mitavia, –tă′ vĭă, Mitau.
Moldo, mŏl′ dŏ, Moldau.
Molucche (isole), mŏlŭk′-
kĕ, Molucca Islands.
Monaco, mŏ′ năkŏ, Munich.
Monbianco, mŏnbĭăn′ kŏ,
Montblanc. [Montauban.
Montalbano, mŏntălbă′ nŏ,
Montenegro, –tĕnă′ grŏ,
Black Mountains.
Montereale, –rĕă′ lĕ, Kö-
nigsberg.
moro, mŏ′ rŏ, Moor.
Mosa, mŏ′ să, Mœse, Mœsa.
Mosca, mŏs′ kă, Moscow.
Moscovia, –kŏ′ vĭă, Mus-
covy. [covite.
moscovita, –kŏvĭ′ tă, Mus-
Mosella, mŏsĕl′ lă, Mosella.
Mozambico, mŏdzămbĕ′ kŏ,
Mozambique.

Nanchino, nănkĕ′ nŏ, Nan-
kin.
Nansì, nănsĕ′, Nancy.
napoletano, năpŏlĕtă′ nŏ,
Neapolitan.
Napoli, nă′ pŏlĭ, Naples.
Narbona, nărbŏ′ nă, Nar-
bonne.
Nasso, năs′ sŏ, Naxus.
Navarra, năvăr′ ră, Na-
varre. [reth.
Nazaret, nă′ tzărĕt, Naza-
Nieper, nĭĕ′ pĕr, Dnieper.
Niester, nĭĕs′ tĕr, Dniester.
Nilo, nĕ′ lŏ, Nile.
Ninive, nĭ′ nĭvĕ, Nineveh.
Nizza, nĭt′ză, Nice.
Norimberga, nŏrĭmbĕr′ gă,
Nuremberg. [Normandy.
Normandia, nŏrmăndă′ ă,
normanno, –măn′ nŏ, Nor-
man.
Norvegia, –vă′ jă, Norway.
norvegese, –vĕjă′ sĕ, Nor-
wegian. [Nottingham.
Nottingam, nŏttĭngăm′,
Nubia, nŏ′ bĭă, Nubia.
nubio, nŏ′ bĭŏ, Nubian.
numantino, nŭmăntĕ′ nŏ,
Numantian.
Numida, –mĕ′ dă, Numidia.

Oder, ŏ′ dĕr, Oder.
Olanda, ŏlăn′ dă, Holland.
olandese, –dă′ sĕ, Hollan-
der, Dutchman.
Oldemburgo, ŏldĕmbŭr′ gŏ,
Oldenburg.
Olimpo, ŏlĭm′ pŏ, Olympus.
Oporto, ŏpŏr′ tŏ, Porto.
Orcadi (isole), ŏrkă′ dĭ,
Orkneys.

Orebbe, ŏrĕ′ bĕ, Horeb.
orleanese, ŏrlĕănă′ sĕ, Orleanese.
Osford, ŏsfŏră′, Oxford.
Ostenda, ŏstĕn′ dă, Ostend.
otentotti, ŏtĕntŏt′ tĭ, Hot-
tentots.
Ottomana, ŏttŏmă′ nă, La
Porta –, the Ottoman Port.
ottomani, –mă′ nĭ, Otto-
mans.

Pacifico, pădshĕ′ fĭkŏ, Pa-
cific. [derborn.
Paderborn, –dĕrbŏrn′, Pa-
Padova, pă′ dŏvă, Padua.
padovano, –dŏvă′ nŏ, Pa-
duan.
Paesi Bassi, păĕ′ sĕ băs′ sĕ,
Low Countries, Netherlands.
Palatinato, pălătĭnă′ tŏ,
Palatinate. [nian.
palatino, –tĕ′ nŏ, Palati-
Palestina, –lĕstĕ′ nă, Pa-
lestine. [Pampeluna.
Pamplona, –pămplŏ′ nă,
Parigi, pără′ jĭ, Paris.
parigino, –rĭjă′ nŏ, Pari-
sian.
partico, păr′ tĭkŏ, Parthian.
Passo di Calè, păs′ sŏ dĭ
kălă′, the Straits of Dover.
Patmo, păt′ mŏ, Patmos.
Patrasso, pătrăs′ sŏ, Patras.
Pechino, pĕkĕ′ nŏ, Peking.
Peloponneso, pĕlŏpŏnnă′-
sŏ, Peloponnesus.
Pensilvania, pĕnsĭlvă′ nĭă,
Pensylvania.
pensilvano, –vă′ nŏ, Pen-
sylvanian. [gamus.
Pergamo, pĕr′ gămŏ, Per-
Perpignano, –pĭnyă′ nŏ,
Perpignan.
Persia, pĕr′ sĭă, Persia.
persiano, –sĭă′ nŏ, perso,
pĕr′ sŏ, Persian.
Perugia, pĕrŏ′ jĭă, Perusia.
perugino, –rŭjă′ nŏ, Peru-
sian. [vian.
peruviano, –vĭă′ nŏ, Peru-
Pest, pĕst, Pesth.
Piacenza, pĭădshĕn′ tză,
Piacenza, Placentia.
Piccardia, pĭkkărdĕ′ ă, Pi-
cardy. [mont.
Piemonte, pĭĕmŏn′ tĕ, Pied-
piemontese, –tă′ sĕ, Pied-
montese.
Pietroburgo, pĭĕtrŏbŭr′-
gŏ, Petersburg.
Pindo, pĭn′ dŏ, Pindus.
Pirenei, pĭrĕnĕ′ ĭ, Pyrenean
Mountains.
polacco, see polonese.
Polonia, pŏlŏ′ nĭă, Poland.
polonese, –lŏnă′ sĕ, Pole.

Pomerania, *pŏmĕrä'nĭă,* Pomerania.

Ponto, *pŏn'tŏ,* Pontus.

Portogallo, *pŏrtŏgäl'lŏ,* Portugal. [tuguese.

portoghese, *-ghĕ'sĕ,* Por-

Porto Reale, *-rĕä'lĕ,* Port-Royal. [na, Posen.

Posnania, *pŏsnä'nĭă,* Pos-

Potsdam, *pŏtsdäm',* Potsdam.

Praga, *prä'gä,* Prague.

Presburgo, *presbŏr'gŏ,* Pressburg. [yence.

Provenza, *prŏvĕn'tzä,* Pro-

Province Unite, *-vĭn'dshĕ ŏnt'tĕ,* United Provinces.

Prussia, *prŭs'sĭä,* Prussia.

prussiano, *-sĭä'nŏ,* Prussian.

Puglia, *pŭl'yä,* Apulia.

Ratisbona, *rätĭsbŏ'nă,* Ratisbon.

Reims, *rĕ'ĭms,* Rheims.

Reno, *rĕ'nŏ,* Rhine.

Rezia, *rĕ'tzĭä,* Rhætia.

Rezie, *rĕ'tzĭĕ,* **Alpi -,** Rhætian Alps.

Roano, *rŏä'nŏ,* Rouen.

Roccella, *rŏtshĕl'lă,* Rochelle.

Rodano, *rŏ'dänŏ,* Rhone.

Rodi, *rŏ'dĭ,* Rhodes.

rodiano, *rŏdĭä'nŏ,* Rhodian.

Roma, *rŏ'mä,* Rome.

romanesco, *rŏmänĕs'kŏ,* Romanian.

Romania, *-mänĭ'ä,* Roumania. [Roumanian.

romanian, *-mä'nĭän,*

romano, *-mä'nŏ,* Roman.

Rossiglione, *rŏssĭlyŏ'nĕ,* Roussillon. [Rotterdam.

Rotterdam, *rŏttĕrdäm',*

rumeno, *rŭmä'nŏ,* Roumanian.

Russia, *rŭs'sĭä,* Russia.

russo, *rŭs'sŏ,* Russian.

Sabina, *säbĭ'nä,* Sabina.

sabino, *-bĭ'nŏ,* Sabine.

Salamina, *-lämĭ'nä,* Salamis. [Saltzburg.

Salisburgo, *-lĭsbŏr'gŏ,*

Salisburi, *-bŭr'ĕ,* Salisbury. [salonica.

Salonico, *-lŏn'ĭ kŏ,* Thes-

Samaria, *sämä'rĭä,* Samaria.

samaritano, *-märĭtä'nŏ,* Samaritan. [moid.

samoiade, *-mŏ'ĭä'dĕ,* Sa-

Samo, *sä'mŏ,* Samos.

Samotracia, *-trä'dshĭä,* Samothrace.

sannita, *sännĭ'tä,* Samnite.

Saona, *sŏ'nä,* Saone.

saracino, *särädshĕ'nŏ,* Saracen. [dinia.

Sardegna, *särdĕn'yä,* Sar-

sardo, *sär'dŏ,* Sardinian.

sarmate, *-mä'tĕ,* Sarmatian.

sassone, *sässŏ'nĕ,* Saxon.

Sassonia, *-sŏ'nĭä,* Saxony.

Sava, *sä'vä,* Save.

Savoia, *-vŏ'ĭä,* Savoy.

savoiardo, *-vŏĭär'dŏ,* Savoyard.

Scandinavia, *skändĭnä'vĭä,* Scandinavia.

Scania, *skä'nĭä,* Schonen.

Schelda, *skĕl'dä,* Scheld.

Schiaffusa, *skĭäffŏ'sä,* Schaffhausen. [nian.

schiavone, *-vŏ'nĕ,* Sclavo-

Schiavonia, *-vŏ'nĭä,* Sclavonia.

Scilla, *sshĭl'lä,* Scylla.

Scozia, *skŏ'tzĭä,* Scotland.

scozzese, *skŏtzä'sĕ,* Scotch, Scotchman. [land.

Selandia, *sĕlän'dĭä,* Zealand.

Sempione, *sĕmpĭŏ'nĕ,* Simplon. [Senegal.

Senegallia, *sĕnĕgäl'lĭä,*

senese, *sĕnä'sĕ,* Senese.

Senna, *sĕn'nä,* Seine.

Siberia, *sĭbĕ'rĭä,* Siberia.

Sicilia, *sĭdshĭ'lĭä,* Sicily.

siciliano, *-dshĭlĭä'nŏ,* Sicilian.

Sidone, *sĭdŏ'nĕ,* Sidon.

Siena, *sĭä'nä,* Sienna.

Sinigaglia, *sĭnĭgäl'yä,* Senegallia. [cuse.

Siracusa, *säräkŏ'sä,* Syra-

siracusano, *-käsä'nŏ,* Syracusan.

Siria, *sĕ'rĭä,* Syria.

sirio, *sĕ'rĭŏ,* Syrian.

Siviglia, *sĭvĭl'yä,* Sevilla.

Slesia, *slä'sĭä,* Silesia.

slesiano, *släsĭä'nŏ,* Silesian.

Slesvich, *slĕs'vĭk,* Slesvic.

Smirne, *smĭr'nĕ,* Smyrna.

Solura, *sŏlŏ'rä,* Soleure.

Spagna, *spän'yä,* Spain.

spagnuolo, *-yä'ŏ'lŏ,* Spaniard.

Sparta, *spär'tä,* Sparta.

spartano, *spärtä'nŏ,* Spartan. [tan.

Spira, *spĕ'rä,* Spire,

Stati Uniti, *stä'tĭ ŏnĭ'tĭ,* United States.

Stettino, *stĕttĕ'nŏ,* Stettin.

Stiria, *stĕ'rĭä,* Styria.

stiriano, *stĭrĭä'nŏ,* **stirio,** *stĕ'rĭŏ,* Stirian.

Stoccolma, *stŏkkŏl'mä,* Stockholm.

Strasburgo, *sträsbŏr'gŏ,* Strasburg. [gart.

Stutgard, *stätgärd',* Stut-

svedese, *svĕdä'sĕ,* Swede.

Svevia, *svä'vĭä,* Suabia.

svevo, *svä'vŏ,* Suabian.

Svezia, *svä'tzĭä,* Sweden.

Svizzera, *svĭt'zĕrä,* Switzerland.

svizzero, *svĭtzĕ'rŏ,* Swiss.

Sund, *sŭnd,* The Sound.

Suterlandia, *sŭtĕrlän'dĭä,* Sutherland.

Tago, *tä'gŏ,* Tagus.

Tamigi, *tämĕ'jĭ,* Thames.

Tartaria, *tärtä'rĭä,* Tartary.

tartaro, *tär'tärŏ,* Tartar.

tebano, *tĕbä'nŏ,* Theban.

Tebe, *tĕ'bĕ,* Thebes.

Termopili, *tĕrmŏ'pĭlĭ,* Thermopylae.

Terra Nuova, *tĕr'rä nŭŏ'vä,* New-Found]land.

Tessaglia, *tĕssäl'yä,* Thessaly. [salonian.

tessalico, *-sä'lĭkŏ,* Thes-

Tevere, *tĕ'vĕrĕ,* Tiber.

Tigri, *tĕ'grĭ,* Tigris.

Tiro, *tĕ'rŏ,* Tyre.

tirolese, *tĕrŏlä'sĕ,* Tyrolese.

Tirolo, *tĭrŏ'lŏ,* Tyrol.

Tobolska, *tŏbŏl'skä,* Tobolsk.

Tolone, *tŏlŏ'nĕ,* Toulon.

Tolosa, *tŏlŏ'sä,* Toulouse.

Tonchino, *tŏnkĕ'nŏ,* Tonkin.

Torino, *tŏrĕ'nŏ,* Turin.

Toscana, *tŏskä'nä,* Tuscany.

toscano, *-kä'nŏ,* Tuscan.

trace, *trä'dshĕ,* Thracian.

Tracia, *trä'dshĭä,* Thrace.

Transilvania, *tränsĭlvä'nĭä,* Transylvania.

transilvano, *-vä'nŏ,* Transylvanian. [tine.

trentino, *trĕntĕ'nŏ,* Tren-

Trento, *trĕn'tŏ,* Trent.

Treviri, *trä'vĭrĭ,* Treves.

Trieste, *trĭĕs'tĕ,* Triest.

Tripoli, *trĕ'pŏlĭ,* Tripoli.

Troia, *trŏ'ĭä,* Troy.

troiano, *-ĭä'nŏ,* Trojan.

Tubinga, *tŭbĭn'gä,* Tubingen.

Tunisi, *tŭnĕ'sĕ,* Tunis.

Turchia, *tŭrkĕ'ä,* Turkey.

turco, *tŭr'kŏ,* Turk.

Turgovia, *tŭrgŏ'vĭä,* Turgovia. [ringia.

Turingia, *tŭrĭn'jĭä,* Thuringia.

turingiano, *-jĭä'nŏ,* Thuringian.

Tusculo, *tŭs' kŭlŏ*, Tusculum.

Ucrania, *ūkră' nĭă*, Ukraine.
Ulma, *ŭl' mă*, Ulm.
Ungheria, *ănghĕr' ă*, Hungary. [garian.
ungherese, *—r' ĕ*, Hungarian.
Upsala, *ŭp' sălă*, Upsal.

Valacchia, *vălăk' kĭă*, Wallachia. [lachian.
valacco, *vălăk' kŏ*, Wallachian.
Valenza, *—lĕn' tsă*, Valence, Valencia.
Valesia, *lă' sĭă*, Valais.
Valchiusa, *vălkĭŏ' să*, Vaucluse.

vallese, *văllă' sĕ*, Vaudese.
Vandea, *văndă' ă*, Vendee.
Varsavia, *vărsă' vĭă*, Varsovia, *—sŏ' vĭă*, Warsaw.
veneto, *see* **veneziano**.
Venezia, *vĕnă' tsĭă*, Venice.
veneziano, *—nĕtsĭă' nŏ*, Venetian.
Venosa, *—nŏ' să*, Venusium.
Verona, *vĕrŏ' nă*, Verona.
Versaglia, *vĕrsăl' yă*, Versailles.
Veser, *vă' sĕr*, Weser.
Vestfalia, *vĕstfă' lĭă*, Westphalia. [vius.
Vesuvio, *vĕsŏ' vĭŏ*, Vesuvius.
Vienna, *vĭĕn' nă*, Vienna.

viennese, *—nd' sĕ*, Viennese.
Villafranca, *vĭllăfrăn' kă*, Villefranche. [nia.
Virginia, *vĭrjă' nĭă*, Virginia.
Virtemberga, *vĭrtĕmbĕr' gă*, Wurtemberg. [goth.
visigoto, *vĭsĭgŏ' tŏ*, Visigoto.
Vistola, *vĭs' tŏlă*, Vistula.
Volinia, *vŏlĭ' nĭă*, Volhynia.
Vormes, *vŏr' mĕs*, Worms.
Vosgi, *vŏs' jĭ*, Vosges.
Vurtsburgo, *vŭrtsbŭr' gŏ*, Würzburg.

Zelanda, *dzĕlăn' dă*, Zealand. [landian.
zelandese, *—lăndă' sĕ*, Zealandian.
Zurigo, *dzŭrĭ' gŏ*, Zurich.

Scelta de' Nomi Propri d' Uomini e di Donne.

Christian Names of Men and Women.

Abelardo, *ăbĕlăr' dŏ*, Abelard.
Abele, *ăbă' lĕ*, Abel. [lard.
Abramo, *ăbră' mŏ*, Abraham.
Achille, *ăkĭl' lĕ*, Achilles.
Adamo, *ădă' mŏ*, Adam.
Adolfo, *ădŏl' fŏ*, Adolphus.
Agata, *ăgă' tă*, Agatha.
Agnese, *ănyă' sĕ*, Agnes.
Agostino, *ăgŏstĭ' nŏ*, Austin.
Alberto, *ălbĕr' tŏ*, Albert.
Alessandro, *ălĕssăn' drŏ*, Alexander.
Alessio, *ălĕs' sĭŏ*, Alexis.
Alfonso, *ălfŏn' sŏ*, Alphonsus. [philus.
Amadeo, *ămădă' ŏ*, Theodore [stasius.
Ambrogio, *ămbrŏ' jŏ*, Ambrose.
Anastasio, *ănăstă' sĭŏ*, Anastasio.
Andrea, *ăndră' ă*, Andrew.
Angelica, *—jĕ' lĭkă*, Angelina, *—jĕlĕ' nă*, Angelica.
Anna, *ăn' nă*, Ana, Anne.
Annina, *—nĕ' nă*, Nancy, Nanny, Janet.
Anselmo, *ănsĕl' mŏ*, Anselm.

Antonietta, *—tŏnĭĕt' tă*, Antonia. [Tony.
Antonio, *—tŏ' nĭŏ*, Anthony.
Arnoldo, *ărnŏl' dŏ*, Arnold.
Arrigo, *—rĭ' gŏ*, Henry, Harry, Hal. [nasius.
Atanasio, *ătănă' sĭŏ*, Athanasius.
Augusto, *ăŭgŭs' tŏ*, Augustus.

Baldassare, *băldăssă' rĕ*, Balthasar. [naby.
Barnaba, *băr' năbă*, Barnabas.
Bartolommeo, *—tŏlŏmmă' ŏ*, Bartholomew.
Basilio, *băsĭ' lĭŏ*, Basil.
Battista, *băttĭs' tă*, Baptist.
Beatrice, *bĕătrĭ' dshĕ*, Beatrice, Trixie. [nedicta.
Benedetta, *bĕnĕdĕt' tă*, Benedetto, *—dĕt' tŏ*, Benedict, Bennet.
Beniamino, *bĕnĭămĕ' nŏ*, Benjamin, Ben. [nard.
Bernardo, *bĕrnăr' dŏ*, Bertha, *bĕr' tă*, Bertha.
Bertrando, *—trăn' dŏ*, Bertrand.
Bianca, *bĭăn' kă*, Blanche.

Biagio, *bĭă' jŏ*, Blase.
Bonifazio, *bŏnĭfă' tsĭŏ*, Boniface.
Brigida, *brĕ' jĭdă*, **Brigita**, *—jĭtă*, Bridget, Biddy.
Brunone, *brŭnŏ' nĕ*, Bruno.

Carlo, *kăr' lŏ*, Charles.
Carlotta, *—lŏt' tă*, Charlotte.
Carolina, *kărŏlĕ' nă*, Caroline, Carry. [simir.
Casimirro, *kăsĭmĕr' rŏ*, Casimir.
Caterina, *—tĕrĕ' nă*, Catharine, Kate, Kitty.
Cecilia, *dshĕdshĕ' lĭă*, Cecily, Cissy.
Cesare, *dshă' sărĕ*, Cæsar.
Chiara, *kĭă' ră*, Clara.
Cipriano, *dshĭprĭă' nŏ*, Cyprian.
Cirillo, *dshĕrĭl' lŏ*, Cyril.
Claudio, *klăŭ' dĭŏ*, Claudius.
Clemente, *klĕmĕn' tĕ*, Clement. [lius.
Cornelio, *kŏrnă' lĭŏ*, Cornelius.
Corrado, *kŏrră' dŏ*, Conrad.
Cosimo, *kŏ' sĭmŏ*, Cosmus.

Costantino, kŏstăntĕ́ nŏ, Constantine. [stance.
Costanza, –tăn' tză, Constance.
Crisostomo, krĭsŏs' tŏmŏ, Chrysostom. [pin.
Crispino, krĭspĕ' nŏ, Crispin.
Cristiano, –tiă' nŏ, Christian.
Cristina, –tĕ' nă, Christina.
Cristoforo, –tŏ' fŏrŏ, Christopher, Kit.

Damiano, dămiă' nŏ, Damian.
Daniele, –niĕ' lĕ, Daniel.
Davide, –vĕ' dĕ, David, Davy. [tus.
Diodato, diŏdă' tŏ, Deodatus.
Dionigi, –nĕ' jĕ, Dionysius.
Domenico, dŏmĕ' nĭkŏ, Dominic. [Dolly.
Dorotea, dŏrŏtĕ' ă, Dorothy,

Edmondo, ĕdmŏn' dŏ, Edmund. [ward, Ned.
Edoardo, ĕdŏăr' dŏ, Edward.
Edvige, ĕdvĕ' jĕ, Edwiga.
Elena, ĕlĕ' nă, Helen, Nell, Nelly. [nor, Ellen.
Eleonora, ĕlĕŏnŏ' ră, Eleanora.
Elisabetta, ĕlĭsăbĕt' tă, Elizabeth, Eliza, Betty, Bess, Bessy.
Emanuele, ĕmănŭĕ' lĕ,
Emanuello, –nŭĕl' lŏ, Emanuel. [Emmy.
Emilia, ĕmĕ' liă, Emily,
Emilio, ĕmĕ' liŏ, Emilius.
Enrichetta, ĕnrĭkĕt' tă, Henrietta, Harriet.
Enrico, ĕnrĕ' kŏ, Henry.
Erasmo, ĕrăs' mŏ, Erasmus.
Ernesto, ĕrnĕs' tŏ, Ernest.
Everardo, ĕvĕrăr' dŏ, Everard.
Eugenio, ĕdjĕ' niŏ, Eugene.

Fabiano, făbiă' nŏ, Fabian.
Fabrizio, –brĕ' tziŏ, Fabricius.
Fausto, fă' ŭstŏ, Faustus.
Federico, fĕdĕrĕ' kŏ, Frederick. [rica.
Federiga, –rĕ' gă, Frederica.
Federigo, see Federico.
Felice, fĕlĕ' dshĕ, Felix.
Felicita, –lădshĕ' tă, Felicity. [Ferdinand.
Ferdinando, fĕrdĭnăn' dŏ,
Filippina, fĭlĭppĕ' nă, Philippa.
Filippo, –lĭp' pŏ, Philip.
Fiorentina, fiŏrĕntĕ' nă, Florence.
Francesca, frăndshĕs' kă,
Franceschina, –kĕ' nă, Frances, Fanny.

Francesco, –dshĕs' kŏ, Francis, Frank.

Gabriele, găbrĕă' lĕ, Gabriel.
Gabriella, –brĕĕ' lă, Gabriela.
Gaetano, gătă' nŏ, Cajetan.
Gaspare, găspă' rĕ, **Gasparo,** –rŏ, **Gasparre,** –păr' rĕ, Jasper.
Gastone, –tŏ' nĕ, Gaston.
Genovieffa, jĕnŏvĕĕf' fă, Genoveva. [trude.
Gertrude, jĕrtrŏ' dĕ, Germ.
Gerardo, jĕrăr' dŏ, Gerard.
Geremia, –rĕmĕ' ă, Jeremy.
Germano, jĕrmă' nŏ, German. [gueline.
Giacomina, jăkŏmĕ' nă, Jaqueline.
Giacomo, jă' kŏmŏ, James, Jem, Jimmy.
Giannetta, jănnĕt' tă,
Giannina, –nĕ' nă, Jenny.
Gioacchino, jŏăkkĕ' nŏ, Joachim.
Giobbe, jŏb' bĕ, Job.
Giorgina, jŏrjĕ' nă, Georgiana.
Giorgio, jŏr' jŏ, George.
Giosuè, jŏsŭ̀ĕ', Joshua, Josh. [Jenny, Joan.
Giovanna, jŏvăn' nă, Jane.
Giovanni, –văn' nĭ, John, Jack. [ome.
Girolamo, jĭrŏ' lămŏ, Jerome.
Giuditta, jŭdĕt' tă, Judith.
Giulia, jŏ' liă, Julia.
Giuliana, jŭlĭă' nă, Juliana.
Giuliano, –liă' nŏ, Julian.
Giulio, jŏ' liŏ, Julius.
Giuseppe, jŭsĕp' pĕ, Joseph.
Giuseppina, –pĕ' nă, Josephine.
Giustina, jŭstĕ' nă, Justina.
Giustino, –tĕ' nŏ, Justinus.
Giusto, jŭs' tŏ, Just.
Goffredo, gŏffrĕ' dŏ, Geoffrey, Godfrey.
Gregorio, grĕgŏ' riŏ, Gregory. [selda, Grissel.
Griseldis, grĭsĕl' dĭs, Grissel.
Gualtieri, gŭăltĭĕ' rĭ, Walter, Wat. [Wilhelmina.
Guglielmina, gŭlyĕlmĕ' nă,
Guglielmo, –yĕl' mŏ, William, Will, Bill.
Guido, gŭĕ' dŏ, Guy. [vus.
Gustavo, gŭstă' vŏ, Gustavus.

Ignazio, ĭnyă' tziŏ, Ignatius.
Ilario, ĭlă' riŏ, Hilary.
Innocenzo, ĭnnŏdshĕn' tzŏ, Innocent.
Isabella, ĭsăbĕl' lă, Isabel, Isabella.
Isacco, ĭsăk' kŏ, Isaac.
Isidoro, ĭsĭdŏ' rŏ, Isidorus.

Lattanzio, lăttăn' tziŏ, Lactantius.
Leandro, lĕăn' drŏ, Leander.
Leonardo, lĕŏnăr' dŏ, Leonard.
Leone, lĕŏ' nĕ, Leo. [nard.
Leonora, –nŏ' ră, Eleanor.
Leopoldo, –pŏl' dŏ, Leopold. [Lizzy.
Lisetta, lĭsĕt' tă, Lizzie.
Livio, lĕ' viŏ, Livy.
Lodovico, lŏdŏvĕ' kŏ, Lewis, Louis. [rence.
Lorenzo, –rĕn' tzŏ, Lawrence.
Luca, lŏ' kă, Luke.
Lucia, lădshĕ' ă, Lucy.
Luciano, –dshiă' nŏ, Lucian.
Lucio, lŏ' dshŏ, Lucius.
Lucrezia, lăkrĕ' tziă, Lucretia.
Luigi, lŭĕ' jĕ, Lewis, Louis.
Luigia, –lŭĕ' jă, **Luisa,** –să, Louisa, Louise.

Maddalena, măddălĕ' nă, Magdalen, Madeline.
Marcello, mărdshĕl' lŏ, Marcellus. [Mark.
Marco, măr' kŏ, Marcus.
Margherita, –ghĕrĕ' tă, Margaret, Margery, Meg, Peggy.
Maria, mărĕ' ă, Mary.
Marianna, –riăn' nă, Marian.
Marietta, –rĕĕ' tă, **Mariuccia,** –rĕŭt' shă, Molly, Polly. [Patty.
Marta, măr' tă, Martha.
Martino, –tĕ' nŏ, Martin.
Massimiliano, măssĭmĭliă' nŏ, Maximilian. [mus.
Massimo, măs' sĭmŏ, Maximilian.
Matilde, mătĭl' dĕ, Matilda, Patty. [Mat.
Matteo, măttĕ' ŏ, Matthew.
Mattia, –tĕ' ă, Matthias.
Maurizio, măŭrĕ' tziŏ, Morris. [Melchior.
Melchiorre, mĕlkiŏr' rĕ,
Michele, mĭkĕ' lĕ, Michael, Mike. [sĕ', Moses.
Moisè, mŏĭsĕ', **Mosè,** mŏ-

Nerone, nĕrŏ' nĕ, Nero.
Nicodemo, nĭkŏdĕ' mŏ, Nicodemus. [Nick.
Nicolò, nĭkŏlŏ', Nicholaus.
Noè, nŏĕ', Noah.

Oliviero, ŏlĭvĭĕ' rŏ, Oliver.
Onofrio, ŏnŏ' friŏ, Humphrey. [land.
Orlando, ŏrlăn' dŏ, Rowland.
Orsola, ŏr' sŏlă, Ursula.
Ortensia, –tĕn' siă, Hortense.
Ottavia, ŏttă' viă, Octavia.

Ottavio, ŏttă' vĭŏ, Octavius.
Ottone, ŏttŏ' nĕ, Otto.

Paola, păŏ' lă, Paolina, păŏlĕ' nă, Paulina.
Paolino, păŏlĕ' nŏ, Paulinus.
Paolo, păŏ' lŏ, Paul.
Patrizio, pătrĕ' tzĭŏ, Patrick, Pat.
Petronilla, pĕtrŏnĭl' lă, Petronella. [nius.
Petronio, —trŏ' nĭŏ, Petro-
Pietro, pĭĕ' trŏ, Peter.
Pio, pĕ' ŏ, Pius.
Pompeo, pŏmpĕ' ŏ, Pompey.
Prisco, prĭs' kŏ, Priscus.
Prospero, prŏs' pĕrŏ, Prospe.

Rachele, răkĕ' lĕ, Rachel.
Rafaelle, —făĕl' lĕ, Raffaello, —lŏ, Raphael.
Raimondo, răimŏn' dŏ, Reymund.
Remigio, rĕmĕ' jŏ, Remy.
Renato, —nă' tŏ, Renatus.
Riccardo, rĭkkăr' dŏ, Richard, Dick.
Rinaldo, rĭnăl' dŏ, Reynold.
Roberto, rŏbĕr' tŏ, Robert, Robin, Bob. [derick, Rory.
Roderico, —dĕrĕ' kŏ, Rodolfo, —dŏl' jŏ, Ralph.
Rolando, —lăn' dŏ, Rowland. [nus.
Romano, —mă' nŏ, Roma-
Romualdo, —mŭăl' dŏ, Ro-

Rosa, rŏ' să, Rosa.
Rosmunda, rŏsmŭn' dă, Rosamond.
Rosaura, rŏsăŭ' ră, Rosary.
Rosetta, —sĕt' tă, Rose.
Ruggero, rŭdjă' rŏ, Roger, Hodge.

Salomone, sălŏmŏ' nĕ, Solomon. [Sam.
Samuele, sămŭĕl' lĕ, Samuel,
Sansone, sănsŏ' nĕ, Simson.
Sara, să' ră, Sarah, Sally.
Saverio, —vă' rĭŏ, Xaverius.
Sebastiano, sĕbăstĭă' nŏ, Sebastian.
Sempronio, sĕmprŏ' nĭŏ, Sempronius.
Serafino, sĕră̆fĕ' nŏ, Seraphinus.
Severino, —vĕrĕ' nŏ, Severinus.
Severo, —vă' rŏ, Severus.
Sigismondo, sĭjĭsmŏn' dŏ, Sigismund.
Silvano, sĭlvă' nŏ, Sylvanus. [vester.
Silvestro, —vĕs' trŏ, Sylvio, sĭl' vĭŏ, Sylvius.
Simone, sĭmŏ' nĕ, Simon, Sim.
Sisto, sĭs' tŏ, Sixtus.
Sofia, sŏfĕ' ă, Sophia, Sophy.
Stanislao, stănĭslă' ŏ, Stanislaus.
Stefano, stĕ' fănŏ, Stephen.

Susanna, sŭsăn' nă, Susan, Sue, Suzy.

Tacito, tă' dshĭtŏ, Tacitus.
Tancredi, tănkrĕ' dĕ, Tancred. [bald.
Tebaldo, tĕbăl' dŏ, Theo-
Teodoro, tĕŏdŏ' rŏ, Theodore. [dosius.
Teodosia, —dŏ' sĭŏ, Theo-
Teofilo, tĕŏ' fĭlŏ, Theophilus.
Teresa, tĕrĕ' să, Theresa.
Timoteo, tĭmŏ' tĕŏ, Timothy, Tim.
Tito, tĕ' tŏ, Titus.
Tobia, tŏbĕ' ă, Tobias, Toby.
Tommaso, tŏmmă' sŏ, Thomas, Tommy, Tom.

Ubaldo, ŭbăl' dŏ, Hubaldus.
Ugo, ŏ' gŏ, Ugone, —gŏnĕ, Hugh.
Udelrica, ŭdĕlrĕ' kă, Ulrica.
Udelrico, —rĕ' kŏ, Ulric.
Urbano, ŭrbă' nŏ, Urban.

Valentino, vălĕntĕ' nŏ, Valentine. [rian.
Valeriano, —lĕrĭă' nŏ, Valerio, —lă' rĭŏ, Valerius.
Vincenzo, vĭndshĕn' dzŏ, Vincent. [Wenceslaus.
Vinceslao, vĭndshĕslă' ŏ,

Zaccaria, dzăkkără' ă, Zachary, Zachariah.

Infinitivo.	Indicativo Presente.	Congiuntivo Presente.	Condizionale presente.	Correlativo present?.
accadere	—	—	—	—
accedere	—	—	—	—
accendere	—	—	—	—
accignersi	accingo	—	—	—
accogliere	accolgo	—	—	—
accorgersi		—		
accorrere			—	
accrescere	vedi	crescere		
addurre	—	—		
adempire	adempisco	—		
affigere	vedi	figgere		
affliggere	—	—	—	
aggiugnere	—	—	—	
alludere	—	—		
ammettere	vedi	mettere		
andare	vo (vado), vai, va, andiamo, andate, vanno	ch'io vada, che tu vada (vadi), ch'egli vada, che noi andiamo, che voi andiate, ch'eglino vadano		irei, iresti irebbe &c
annettare				
anteporre	vedi	porre		
antivedere	vedi	vedere		
apparire	apparisco (appaio), apparisci, apparisce (appare), appariamo, apparite, appariscono (appaiono)	ch'io apparisca (appaia), — tu apparisca, — apparisca, — appariamo, — appariate, appariscano (appaiano)		
appartenere	vedi	tenere	—	—
appendere	—	—	—	—
apporre	vedi	porre	—	—
apprendere	—	—	—	—
aprire	apro	—	—	—
ardere	—	—	—	—
arrendersi	—	—	—	—
arridere	—	—	—	—
ascendere	—	—	—	—
ascondere	vedi	nascondere	—	—
ascrivere	vedi	scrivere	—	—
aspergere	—	—	—	—
assalire	vedi	salire	—	—
assidere	—	—	—	—
assistere	—	—	—	—
assolvere	—	—	—	—
assorbere	—	—	—	—
assumere	—	—	—	—
astenersi	vedi	tenere	—	—
astergere	—	—	—	—
astrarre	vedi	trarre	—	—
attendere	—	—	—	—
attenere	vedi	tenere	—	—

1) The tenses and moods n o t given in this table are declined r e g u l a r l y.

irregolari[1]).

Imperfetto.	Definito.	Futuro.	Gerundio.	Participio passato.	Imperativo.
—	accadde	—	—	accaduto	
—	accedei	—	—	acceduto	
—	accesi	—	—	acceso	
—	accinsi	—	—	accinto	
—	accolsi	accoglierò (accorrò)	—	accolto	
—	m'accorsi	—	—	accorto	
—	accorsi	—	—	accorso	
—	addussi	—	—	addutto	
—	—	—	—	adempito	
—	afflissi	—	—	afflitto	
—	aggiunsi	—	—	aggiunto	
—	allusi	—	—	alluso	
iva &c., ivano (irono)	—	andrò, andrai &c. (erò; erai &c.)	—	—	va', vada, andiamo, andate, vadano
—	annessi	—	—	annesse	
—	—	—	—	apparso	
—	appesi	—	—	appeso	
—	appresi	—	—	appreso	
—	aprii	aprirò	—	aperto	
—	arsi	—	—	arso	
—	arresi	—	—	arreso	
—	arrisi	—	—	arriso	
—	ascesi	—	—	asceso	
—	aspersi	—	—	asperso	
—	assisi	—	—	assiso	
—	—	—	—	assistito	
—	assolsi	—	—	assolto	
—	assorsi	—	—	assorto	
—	assunsi	—	—	assunto	
—	astersi	—	—	asterso	
—	attesi	—	—	atteso	

Infinitivo.	Indicativo Presente.	Congiuntivo Presente.	Condizionale presente.	Correlativo presente.
attignere (attin- gere)	—	—	—	—
attorcere		—	—	—
attrarre	*vedi*	trarre		
avvenire	*vedi*	venire		
avvolgere	*vedi*	volgere		
benedire	*vedi*	dicere, dire		
bere (bevere)	beo (bevo), bei (bevi), bee (beve), beviamo, beete (bevete), beono (bevono)	ch'io bea (beva)	—	—
cadere	cado, cadi &c.	—	—	cadrei, ca- dresti &c
cedere	—	—	-	—
chiedere	—	—	-	—
chiudere	—	—	-	—
cingere	cingo, cingi, cinge, cin- giamo, cingete, cingono	—	-	—
circoncidere		—	-	
circonscrivere	*vedi*	scrivere		
cogliere	colgo, cogli, coglie, cogliamo, cogliete, col- gono	ch'io colga &c., che noi cogliamo, - - cogliate, - - colgano	-	correi &c.
commettere	*vedi*	mettere		
commuovere	*vedi*	muovere		
comparire	*vedi*	apparire		
compiacere	*vedi*	piacere		
compiangere (compiagnere)	—	—		
compire, com- piere	compio			
comporre	*vedi*	porre		
compromettere	*vedi*	promettere		
comprendere	—	—	-	—
comprimere	—	—	-	—
compugnere (compungere)	—	—		
concedere	*vedi*	cedere		
conchiudere (concludere)	—	—		—
concorrere	—	—	-	—
condiscendere	—	—	-	—
condolere (–si)	*vedi*	dolere		
conducere (con- durre)	—	—	—	
configgere	*vedi*	figgere		
confondere	*vedi*	fondere		
congiungere (congiugnere)	—	—	—	—
connettere	—	—	-	—
conoscere	conosco &c.	—	-	—
conquidere	—	—	-	—
consistere	—	—	-	—
consumere	—	—	-	—
contendere	—	—		
contenere	*vedi*	tenere	—	—
contorcere	—			
contraddire	*vedi*	dire		
contraffare	*vedi*	fare		
contrarre	*vedi*	trarre		
convenire	*vedi*	venire		
convincere	*vedi*	vincere		
convolgere	—		—	—
coprire	copro &c.	—	—	—
correggere		—	—	—

Imperfetto.	Definito.	Futuro.	Gerundio.	Participio passato.	Imperativo.
—	attinsi	—.	—	attinto	
—	attorsi	—	—	attorto	
beeva &c.	bevvi, bevesti, beve, bevemmo, beveste, bevvero	berò (bevero), berei &c.	beendo	bevuto	bei, bea, beviamo, beete, beano
—	caddi, cadesti, cadde, cademmo, cadeste, caddero	cadrò, cadrai &c.	—	caduto	
—	cessi (cedei)	=	—	ceduto (cesso)	
—	chiesi	=	—	chiesto	
—	chiusi	=	—	chiuso	
—	cinsi	=	—	cinto	
—	circoncisi	—	—	circonciso	
—	colsi, cogliesti &c.	corrò, corrai &c.	—	colto	cogli, coglia (colga), cogliamo, cogliete, cogliano
—	compiansi	—	—	compianto	
—.	compii (compiei)		—	compiuto	
—|	compresi	=	—	compreso	
—|	compressi	=	—	compresso	
—|	compunsi	=	—	compunto	
—|	concniusi	=		conchiuso	
—|	concorsi	=	—	concorso	
—|	condiscesi	=		condisceso	
—|	condussi	=		condotto	
—	congiunsi	—	—	congiunto	
—	connessi		—	connesso	
—	conobbi	conoscerò	—	conosciuto	
—	conquisi	=	—	conquiso	
—	consistett	=	—	consistito	
—	consunsi	=	—	consunto	
—	contesi	=	—	conteso	
—	contorsi		—	contorto	
—	convolsi	—	—	convolto	
—	copersi	coprirò	—	coperto	
—	corressi		—	corretto	

Infinitivo.	Indicativo Presente.	Congiuntivo Presente.	Condizionale presente.	Correlativo presente.
correre		—	—	—
corrispondere	*vedi*	rispondere	—	—
corrodere		—	—	—
costringere	*vedi*	stringere	—	—
crescere	cresco		—	—
crocifiggere	*vedi*	figgere	—	—
cucire	cucio		—	—
cuocere			—	—
dare	do, dai, dà, diamo, date, danno	ch'io dia, – – dia, – – dia, – – diamo, – – diate, – – diano	se io dessi, se tu dessi &c.	—
decadere	*vedi*	cadere	—	—
decidere		—	—	—
dedurre	deduco, deduci		—	—
deludere		—	—	—
deporre	*vedi*	porre	—	—
deprimere		—	—	—
descrivere	*vedi*	scrivere	—	—
detenere	*vedi*	tenere	—	—
detrarre	*vedi*	trarre	—	—
difendere		—	—	—
dipignere (dipingere)		—	—	—
dire	dico, dici, dice, diciamo, dite, dicono	ch'io dica, – – dica, – – dica, – – diciamo, – – diciate, – – dicano	se io dicessi &c.	direi &c.
dirigere	dirigo		—	—
discendere		—	—	—
discorrere	*vedi*	correre	—	—
discutere		—	—	—
disdire	*vedi*	dire	—	—
disfare	*vedi*	fare	—	—
disgiungere	*vedi*	giungere	—	—
dispergere	*vedi*	spergere	—	—
dispiacere	*vedi*	piacere	—	—
disporre	*vedi*	porre	—	—
dissuadere	—	—	—	—
distendere	—		—	—
distinguere			—	—
distogliere	distolgo		—	—
distruggere		—	—	—
divenire	*vedi*	venire	—	—
dividere		—	—	—
dolersi	mi dolgo, ti duoli, si duole, ci dolghiamo, vi dolete, si dolgono	ch'io mi dolga, – – doglia, – – dogliamo, – – dogliate, – – dolgano)	—	dorrei &c.
dovere	devo (debbo, deggio), devi (debbi, dei), deve (debbe, dee), dobbiamo, deggiamo, dovete, devono (debbono, deggiono)	ch'io debba, – – debba, – – debba, – – dobbiamo, – – dobbiate, – – debbano	—	dovrei &c.
eleggere		—	—	—
elidere	—	—	—	—
eludere	—	—	—	—
emergere	⌐	—	—	—
empiere (empire)	empisco	—	—	—
equivalere	*vedi*	valere	—	—
ergere (ereggere)	—	—	—	—
escludere	—	—	—	—
espellere	—	—	—	—
esigere	—	—	—	—
esporre	*vedi*	porre	—	—
esprimere	—	—	—	—

Imperfetto.	Definito.	Futuro.	Gerundio.	Participio passato.	Imperativo.
—	corsi	—	—	corso	
—	corrosi	—	—	corroso	
—	crebbi	crescerò	—	cresciuto	
—	cucii	cucirò	—	cucito	
—	cossi	—	—	cotto	
—	diedi (detti), desti, diede, demmo, deste, diedero (dettero)	darò, darai &c.	—	—	da', dia, diamo, date, diano
—	decisi	—	—	deciso	
—	dedussi, deducesti	—	—	dedotto	
—	delusi	—	—	deluso	
—	depressi	—.	—	depresso	
—	difesi	—	—	difeso	
—	dipinsi	—	—	dipinto	
diceva &c.	dissi, dicesti, disse, dicemmo, diceste, dissero	dirò, dirai &c.	dicendo	detto	di', dica, diciamo, dite, dicano
—	diressi	—	—	diretto	
—	discesi	—	—	disceso	
—	discussi	—	—	discusso	
✓	dissuasi	—	—	dissuaso	
—	distesi	—	—	disteso	
—	distinsi	—	—	distinto	
✓	distolsi	distoglierò	—	distolto	
✓	distrussi	—	—	distrutto	
—	divisi	—	—	diviso	
✓	(mi) dolsi, dolesti, dolse, dolemmo, doleste, dolsero	mi dorrò, dorrai &c.	—	dolutosi	duoliti, dolgasi, dogliamoci, doletevi, dolgansi
—	—	dovrò, dovrai &c.	—	—	debbi, debba (deggia), dobbiamo, dobbiate, debbano (deggiano)
—	elessi	—	—	eletto	
—	elisi	—	—	eliso	
—	elusi	—	—	eluso	
—	emersi	—	—	emerso	
—	—	—	—	empiuto (empito)	
—	ersi (eressi)	—	—	eretto	
—	esclusi	—	—	escluso	
—	espulsi	—	—	espulso	
—	—	—	—	esatto	
—	espressi	—	—	espresso	

Infinitivo.	Indicativo Presente.	Congiuntivo Presente.	Condizionale presente.	Correlativo presente.
estendere	—	—	· —	—
estinguere		—	—	
estrarre	*vedi*	trarre		
evadere		—	—	
fare	fo (faccio), fai, fa, facciamo, fate, fanno	ch'io faccia, — — faccia, — — faccia, — — facciamo, — — facciate, — — facciano	se io facessi, se tu facessi&c.	—
fendere	—	—	—	—
figgere	—	—	—	—
fingere	—	—	—	—
fondere	—	—	—	—
frammettere	*vedi*	mettere	—	—
frangere	—	—	—	—
friggere	—	—	—	—
genuflettere	—	—	—	—
giacere	giaccio, giaci, giace, giacciamo, giacete, giacciono	ch'io giaccia &c.	—	—
giugnere (giungere)	—	—	—	—
immergere	—	—	—	—
imporre	*vedi*	porre	—	—
imprendere	—	—	—	—
incendere	—	—	—	—
inchiudere	—	—	—	—
includere	—	—	—	—
incidere	—	—	—	—
incorrere	—	—	—	—
increscere	*vedi*	crescere	—	—
inducere (indurre)	—	—	—	—
indulgere	—	—	—	—
infignere (infingere)	—	—	—	—
infliggere	infliggo	—	—	—
influere	influisco	—	—	—
infrangere	—	—	—	—
ingiugnere (ingiungere)	—	—	—	—
inscrivere	—	—	—	—
insistere	—	—	.	—
interrompere	*vedi*	rompere	—	—
insorgere	—	—	—	—
intendere	—	—	—	—
intraprendere	—	—	—	—
introducere (introdurre)	—	—	—	—
intrudere	—	—	—	—
invadere	—	—	—	—
involgere	—	—	—	—
ledere	—	—	—	—
leggere	—	—	—	—
licere	—	—	—	—
lucere	—	—	—	—
maledire	*vedi*	dire	—	—
mantenere	*vedi*	tenere	—	—
mescere	—	—	—	—
mettere	—	—	—	—
mordere	—	—	—	—
morire	muoio, muori, muore, moriamo, morite, muoiono	ch'io muoia, — — muoia, — — muoia, — — moriamo, — — moriate, — — muoiano	—	morrei &c.

Imper- fetto.	Definito.	Futuro.	Ge- rundio.	Participio passato.	Imperativo.
—	estesi	—	—	esteso	
—	estinsi	—	—	estinto	
—	evasi	—	—	evaso	
faceva, facevi &c.	feci, facesti, fece, facemmo, faceste, fecero	farò, farai &c.	facendo	fatto	fa', faccia, facciamo, fate, facciano
—	fendei	—	—	feso	
—	fissi	—	—	fisso	
—	finsi	—	—	finto	
—	fusi	—	—	fuso	
—	fransi	—	—	franto	
—	frissi	—	—	fritto	
—	genuflessi	—	—	genuflesso	
—	giacqui, giacesti, giacque, giacemmo, giaceste, giacquero	—	—	giaciuto	giaci, giaccia, giaccia- mo, giacete, giaccia- no
—	giunsi	—	—	giunto	
—	immersi	—	—	immerso	
—	impresi	—	—	impreso	
—	incesi	—	—	inceso	
—	inchiusi	—	—	inchiuso	
—	inclusi	—	—	incluso	
—	incisi	—	—	inciso	
—	incorsi	—	—	incorso	
—	indussi	—	—	indotto	
—	indulsi	—	—	indulto	
—	infinsi	—	—	infinto	
—	inflissi	—	—	inflitto	
—	influssi	—	—	influito	
—	infransi	—	—	infranto	
—	ingiunsi	—	—	ingiunto	
—	inscrissi	—	—	inscritto	
—	insistetti (insistei)	—	—	—	
—	insorsi	—	—	insorto	
—	intesi	—	—	inteso	
—	intrapresi	—	—	intrapreso	
—	introdussi	—	—	introdotto	
—	intrusi	—	—	intruso	
—	invasi	—	—	invaso	
—	involsi	—	—	involto	
—	lesi	—	—	leso	
—	lessi	—	—	letto	
—	—	—	—	lecito	
—	—	—	—	*is wanting*	
—	misi	—	—	misto	
—	morsi	—	—	messo	
—	morii &c.	morrò (mori- rò), morrai &c.	—	morso morto	muori, muoia, mo- riamo, morite, muo- iano

Infinitivo.	Indicativo Presente.	Congiuntivo Presente.	Condizionale presente.	Correlativo present
mugnere (mungere)	—	—	—	—
muovere	—	—	—	—
nascere	nasco	—	—	—
nascondere	—	—	—	—
nuocere	nuoco	—	—	—
occorrere	—	—	—	—
offendere	—	—	—	—
offrire	offro	—	—	—
ommettere	*vedi*	mettere	—	—
opprimere	—	—	—	—
parere	paio, pari, pare, paiamo, parete, paiono	ch'io paia, — — paia &c.	—	parrei &c.
percorrere	*vedi*	correre	—	—
percuotere	—	—	—	—
perdere	—	—	—	—
permettere	*vedi*	mettere	—	—
persistere	—	—	—	—
persuadere	—	—	—	—
piacere	piaccio, piaci, piace, piacciamo, piacete, piacciono	ch'io piaccia, — — piaccia &c.	—	—
piagnere (piangere)	—	—	—	—
pignere (pingere)	—	—	—	—
piovere	piove	—	—	—
ponere	*vedi*	porre	—	—
porgere	—	—	—	—
porre	pongo, poni, pone, ponghiamo, ponete, pongono	ch'io ponga, che tu ponga &c.	—	porrei &c.
possedere	possiedo (posseggo) &c.	—	—	—
potere	posso, puoi, può, possiamo, potete, possono	ch'io possa, — — possa (possi), — — possa, — — possiamo, — — possiate, — — possano	—	potrei, potresti &c.
precludere	*vedi*	includere		
predire	*vedi*	dire		
prefiggere	*vedi*	figgere		
premettere	*vedi*	mettere		
prendere	—	—		
prescrivere	*vedi*	scrivere		
presumere	—	—	—	—
pretendere	—	—	—	—
pretendere	*vedi*	tendere		
prevalere	*vedi*	valere		
prevedere	*vedi*	vedere		
prevenire	*vedi*	venire		
produrre (produrre)	*vedi*	—	—	—
promettere	*vedi*	mettere		
promuovere	*vedi*	muovere		
proponere, proporre	*vedi*	ponere, porre		
prorompere	*vedi*	rompere		
proteggere	—	—	—	—
protrarre	*vedi*	trarre		
provedere, provenire	*vedi*	vedere, venire		
pugnere (pungere)	—	—	—	—
racchiudere	*vedi*	chiudere		

Imperfetto.	Definito.	Futuro.	Gerundio.	Participio passato.	Imperativo.
—	munsi	—	—	munto	
—	mossi	—	—	mosso	
—	nacqui	nascerò	—	nato	
—	nascosi	—	—	nascosto	
—	nocqui	nocerò	—	nociuto	
—	occorsi	—	—	occorso	
—	offesi	—	—	offeso	
—	offersi	—	—	offerto	
—	oppressi	—	—	oppresso	
	parvi, paresti, parve, paremmo, pareste, parvero	—	—	—	pari, paia, paiamo, parete, paiono
—	percossi	—	—	percosso	
—	perdei, persi	—	—	perduto	
—	persistetti	—	—	persistito	
—	persuasi	—	—	persuaso	
	piacqui, piacesti, piacque, piacemmo, piaceste, piacquero	—	—	piaciuto	piaci, piaccia, piacciamo, piacete, piacciano
—	piansi	—	—	pianto	
—	pinsi	—	—	pinto	
—	piove (piovette)	pioverà	—	piovuto	
—	porgei, porsi	—	—	porto	
	posi, ponesti, pose, ponemmo, poneste, posero	porrò, porrai &c.	—	posto	poni, ponga, ponghiamo, ponete, pongano
—	possedei, possedetti &c.	—	—	posseduto	
—	—	potrò, potrai &c.	—	—	
—	presi	—	—	preso	
—	presunsi	—	—	presunto	
—	pretesi	—	—	preteso	
—	produssi	—	—	prodotto	
—	protessi	—	—	protetto	
—	punsi	—	—	punto	

Italian and English.

Infinitivo.	Indicativo Presente.	Congiuntivo Presente.	Condizionale presente.	Correlativo presente.
raccogliere	*vedi*	cogliere	—	—
rattorcere	—	—	—	—
ravvedersi	mi ravvedo (ravveggo)	—	—	—
ravvolgere	—	—	—	—
recidere	—	—	—	—
redimere	—	—	—	—
reggere	—	—	—	—
rendere	—	—	—	—
reprimere	—	—	—	—
resistere	—	—	—	—
respignere (re-spingere)	*vedi*	spingere	—	—
ricadere	*vedi*	cadere	—	—
riconoscere	*vedi*	conoscere	—	—
ridere	—	—	—	—
rilucere	—	—	—	—
rimanere	rimango, rimani, rimane, rimanghiamo, rimanete, rimangano	ch'io rimanga &c.	—	rimarrei&c.
rimettere	*vedi*	mettere	—	—
rispondere	—	—	—	—
rodere	—	—	—	—
rompere	—	—	—	—
salire	salgo, sali, sale, salghiamo, salite, salgono	ch'io salga &c., che noi salghiamo, — — salghiate, — — salgano	—	—
sapere	so, sai, sa, sappiamo, sapete, sanno	ch'io sappia, — — sappi (sappia) &c.	—	saprei &c.
scadere	*vedi*	cadere	—	—
scegliere	scelgo, scegli, sceglie, scegliamo, scegliete, scelgono	ch'io scelga &c., che noi scegliamo, — — scelgliate, — — scelgano	—	—
scendere	—	—	—	—
schiudere	*vedi*	chiudere	—	—
sciogliere (sci-orre)	sciolgo, sciogli, scioglie, sciogliamo, sciogliete, sciolgono	ch'io sciolga &c., che noi sciogliamo, — — sciogliate, — — sciolgano	—	sciorrei &c.
scomporre	*vedi*	porre	—	—
scommettere	*vedi*	mettere	—	—
sconnetter·	—	—	—	—
scorgere	—	—	—	—
scorrere	—	—	—	—
scuotere	—	—	—	—
sedere	seggo (siedo), siedi, siede, sediamo (seggiamo), sedete, seggono (siedono)	ch'io sieda (segga), — — segga, — — segga, che noi sediamo (seggiamo), — — sediate, — — siedano (seggano)	—	—
sedurre	—	—	—	—
seppellire	seppelisco	—	—	—
socorrere	*vedi*	correre	—	—
soddisfare	*vedi*	fare	—	—
soffrire	—	—	—	—
soggiacere	*vedi*	giacere	—	—
soggiungere	*vedi*	giungere	—	—
solere	soglio, suoli, suole, sogliamo, solete, sogliano	—	—	—
solvere	—	—	—	—
sopra . . .	*vedi*	giungere, prendere,	scrivere,	venire,
sopprimere	—	—	—	—
sorgere	—	—	—	—
sorprendere	*vedi*	prendere	—	—
sorreggere	—	—	—	—

Imperfetto.	Definito.	Futuro.	Gerundio.	Participio passato.	Imperativo.
—	rattorsi		—	rattorto	
—	ravvidi	ravvedrò	—	ravvedutosi	
—	ravvolsi	—	—	ravvolto	
—	recisi	—	—	reciso	
—	redensi	—	—	redento	
—	ressi	—	—	retto	
—	resi	—	—	reso	
—	repressi	—	—	represso	
—	resistetti (resistei)		—		
—	risi, ridesti &c.	—	—	riso	
—	rilucei	—		—	
—	rimasi, rimanesti, rimase, rimanemmo, rimaneste, rimasero	rimarrò, rimarrai &c.	—	rimasto (rimaso)	rimani, rimanga, rimanghiamo, rimanete, rimangano
—	risposi	—	—	risposto	
—	rosi	—	—	roso	
—	ruppi	—	—	rotto	
—	salsi	—	—	—	sali, saiga, sagliamo, salite, salgano
—	seppi, sapesti, seppe, sapemmo, sapeste, seppero	saprò, saprai &c.	—	saputo	sappi, sappia, sappiamo, sappiate, sappiano
—	scelsi, scegliesti, scelse, scegliemmo, sceglieste, scelsero	—	—	scelto	scegli, scelga, scegliamo, scegliete, scelgano
—	scesi	—	—	seeso	
—	sciolsi, sciogliesti, sciolse, sciogliemmo, scioglieste, sciolsero	sciorrò, sciorrai &c.	—	sciolto	sciogli, sciolga, sciogliamo, sciogliete, sciolgano
—	sconnessi	—	—	sconnesso	
—	scorsi	—	—	scorto	
—	scôrsi	—	—	scorso	
—	scossi	—	—	scosso	
—	sedei	—	—	seduto	
—	sedussi	—	—	sedotto	
—	—	—	—	seppoltr	
—	soffersi	—	—	sofferto	
—	*def.*	*def.*	*def.*	solito	
vivere	solsi	—	—	solto (soluto)	
—	soppressi	—	—	soppresso	
—	sorsi	—	—	sorto	
—	sorressi	—	—	sorretto	

Infinitivo.	Indicativo Presente.	Congiuntivo Presente.	Condizionale presente.	Correlativo presente.
sorridere	—	—	—	—
sospendere	—	—	—	—
sospignere (sospingere)				
sostenere	*vedi*	tenere		
sotto ...	*vedi*	mettere, porre, ridere,	scrivere	
sottrarre	*vedi*	trarre		
sovvenire	*vedi*	venire		
spandere	—	—	—	—
spargere	—	—	—	—
sparire	sparisco	—		
spendere	—	—	—	—
spengere	spengo, spengi, spenge, spengiamo, spengete, spengono	ch'io spenga, — — spenga, — — spenga, — — spengiamo, — — spengiate, — — spengano		
spergere	—	—	—	—
spiacere	*vedi*	piacere		
spignere (spingere)	—	—	—	—
sporgere	—	—	—	—
sporre	*vedi*	porre		
stare	sto, stai, sta, stiamo, state, stanno	ch'io stia, — — stia, — — stia, che noi stiamo, — — state, — — stiano (stieno)	se io stessi, se tu stessi &c.	—
stendere	—	—	—	—
storcere	—	—	—	—
stravolgere	—	—	—	—
stringere (stringere)	—	—	—	—
struggere	—	—	—	—
succedere	—	—	—	—
supporre	*vedi*	porre		
surgere	sorgo	—	—	—
svellere	—	—	—	—
svolgere	*vedi*	volgere		
tacere	taccio, taci, tace, tacciamo, tacete, tacciono	ch'io taccia &c.	—	—
tendere	—	—	—	—
tenere	tengo, tieni, tiene, tenghiamo, tenete, tengono	ch'io tenga, — — tenghi (tenga), — — tenga, — — tenghiamo, — — tenghiate, — — tengano	—	terrei &c.
tergere	—	—	—	—
tignere (tingere)	—	—	—	—
togliere	tolgo, togli, toglie, togliamo, togliete, tolgono	ch'io tolga &c., che noi togliamo, — — togliate, — — tolgano	—	torrei &c.
torcere	—	—	—	—
tòrre	*vedi*	togliere		
tradurre	traduco, traduci &c.	—	—	—
traffiggere	—	—	—	—
tra ...	*vedi*	scegliere, scendere,	scrivere	
trarre (traere)	traggo, trai, trae, traiamo, traete, traggono	ch'io tragga &c., che noi traiamo, — — traiate, — — traggano	se io trassi &c.	trarrei &c.
tras ...	*vedi*	mettere, ponere, volgere		
uccidere	—	—	—	—
udire	odo, odi, ode, udiamo, udite, odono	ch'io oda &c., che noi udiamo, — — udiate, — — odano	—	—
ungere	—	—	—	—

Imperfetto.	Definito.	Futuro.	Gerundio.	Participio passato.	Imperativo.
—	sorrisi	—	—	sorriso	
—	sospesi	—	—	sospeso	
—	sospinsi	—	—	sospinto	
—	—	—	—	spanto	
—	sparsi	—	—	sparso	
—	—	—	—	sparito	
—	spesi	—	—	speso	
—	spensi, spegnesti, spense, spegnemmo, spegneste, spensero	—	—	spento	spengi, spenga, spengiamo, spengete, spengano
—	spersi	—	—	sperso	
—	spinsi	—	—	spinto	
—	sporsi	—	—	sporto	
—	stetti, stesti, stette, stemmo, steste, stettero	—	—	—	sta', stia, stiamo, state, stiano
—	stesi	—	—	steso	
—	storsi	—	—	storto	
—	stravolsi	—	—	stravolto	
—	strinsi	—	—	strinto	
—	strussi	—	—	strutto	
—	successi	—	—	successo	
—	sursi	—	—	surto	
—	svelsi	—	—	svelto	
	tacqui, tacesti, tacque, tacemmo, taceste, tacquero	—	—	taciuto	taci, taccia, tacciamo, tacete, tacciano
—	tesi (tendei)	—	—	teso	
—	tenni, tenesti, tenne, tenemmo, teneste, tennero	—	—	tenuto	tieni, tenga, tenghiamo, tenete, tengano
—	tersi	—	—	terso	
—	tinsi	—	—	tinto	
—	tolsi, togliesti, tolse, togliemmo, toglieste, tolsero	—	—	tolto	togli, tolga, tolghiamo, togliete, tolgano
—	torsi	—	—	torto	
—	tradussi	—	—·	tradotto	
—	traffissi	—	—	traffitto	
traeva &c.	trassi, traesti, trasse, traemmo, traeste, trassero	—	—	tratto	trai, tragga, traiamo, traete, traggano
—	uccisi	—	—	ucciso	
—	udii, udisti, ude &c.	ud(i)rò)	—	udito	odi, oda, udiamo, udite, odano
—	unsi	—	—	unto	

Infinitivo.	Indicativo Presente.	Congiuntivo Presente.	Con-dizionale presente.	Correlativo presente.
uscire	esco, esci, esce, usciamo, uscite, escono	ch'io esca &c., che noi usciamo, — — usciate, — — escano	—	—
valere	valgo (vaglio), vali, vale, vagliamo (valghiamo), valete, valgono (vagliono)	ch'io vaglia (valga) &c., che noi vagliamo, — — vagliate, — — vagliano (valgano)	—	varrei &c.
vedere	vedo (veggo), vedi, vede, vediamo (veggiamo), vedete, vedono (veggono)	ch'io veda (vegga) &c., che noi vediamo (veggiamo), — — vediate (veggiate), — — vedano (veggano)	—	vedrei &c.
venire	vengo, vieni, viene, veniamo, venite, vengono	ch'io venga, — — venga (venghi) &c., che noi venghiamo, — — venghiate, — — vengano	—	verrei &c.
vilipendere	—			—
vincere	vinco	—	—	—
vivere	—	—	—	—
volere	voglio (vo'), vuoi, vuole, vogliamo, volete, vogliono	ch'io voglia, — — voglia &c., che .noi vogliamo, — — vogliate, — — vogliano	—	vorrei, vorresti, vorrebbe &c.
volgere	—		—	—

Imperfetto.	Definito.	Futuro.	Gerundio.	Participio passato.	Imperativo.
—	—	—	—	—	esci, esca, usciamo, uscite, escano
—	valsi, valesti, valse, valemmo, valeste, valsero	varrò, varrai &c.	—	valuto	vagli, vaglia, vagliamo, valete, vagliano
—	vidi, vedesti, vide, vedemmo, vedeste, videro	vedrò, vedrai &c.	—	veduto	vedi, veda (vegga), vediamo(veggiamo), vedete, vedano (veggano)
—	venni, venisti, venne, venimmo, veniste, vennero	verrò, verrai &c.	—	venuto	vieni, venga, veniamo, venite, vengano
—	vilipesi	—	—	vilipeso	
—	vinsi	—	—	vinto	
—	vissi	—	—	vissuto to)	
	volli, volesti, volle, volemmo, voleste, vollero	vorrò, vorrai &c.		voluto	
—	volsi	—	—	volto	

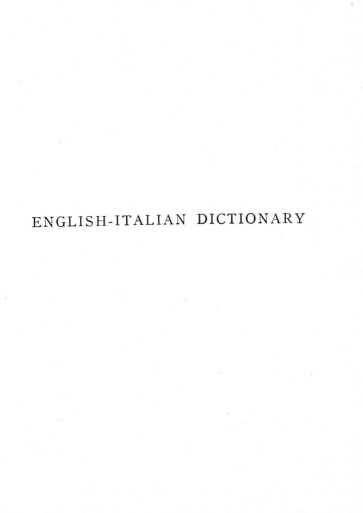

ENGLISH-ITALIAN DICTIONARY

ENGLISH-ITALIAN DICTIONARY

A.

a, ă, an, ăn, art. uno, una.
aback, ăbăk', ad. (mar.) dietro, indietro; to be taken —, essere spaventato.
abacus, ăb'ăkăs, s. abbaco, m.; tavola numeraria, f.
abaft, ăbăft', ad. (mar.) a poppa.
abandon, ăbăn'dăn, v. a. abbandonare; lasciare.
abandonment, —mĕnt, s. abbandono, m.
abase, ăbăs', v. n. abbassare; deprimere.
abasement, —mĕnt, s. abbassamento, m.; umiliazione, f. [rossore; confondere.
abash, ăbăsh', v. a. svergognare, far arabashment, —mĕnt, s. vergogna, confusione, f., rossore, m.
abate, ăbăt', v. a. abbassare, diminuire; annullare; —, v. n. diminuirsi.
abatement, —mĕnt, s. abbassamento, m.; diminuzione, f.
abature, ăbă'tăr, s. traccia, f. (d' un cervo,
abb, ăb, s, ordito, m. [&c.).
abbacy, ăb'băsĭ, s. badia, f.
abbess, ăb'bĕs, s. badessa, 1.
abb(e)y, ăb'bĭ, s. badia, f.; monastero, m.
abbot, ăb'băt, s. abate, m.; prete, m.
abbotship, —shĭp, s. dignità d' abbate, f.
abbreviate, ăbbrē'vĭăt, v. a. abbreviare; scorciare; compendiare. [f.
abbreviation, —vĭă'shăn, s. abbreviazione,
abdicate, ăb'dĭkăt, v. a. abdicare; rinunziare. [rinunzia, f.
abdication, —kă'shăn, s. abdicazione, f.;
abdomen, —dō'mĕn, s. abdome, m.
abdominal, —dŏm'ĭnăl, a. abdominale.
abduct, —dăkt', v. a. rubare; rapire.
abduction, —dăk'shăn, s. rubatura, f.; rapimento, m. [tore, m.
abductor, —dăk'tăr, s. rubatore, m.; rapiabed, ăbĕd', ad. a letto, in letto.
aberration, —ĕrră'shăn, s. sviamento, m.; smarrimento, m.; errore, sbaglio, m.
abet, ăbĕt', v. a. incoraggiare; proteggere; assistere; favorire. [stimolo, m.
abetment, —mĕnt, s. incoraggiamento, m.
abetter, abettor, —tăr, s. instigatore, m.; instigatrice, f.
abeyance, ăbă'ăns, s. aspettativa, f.; (law) lands in —, pl. terre giacenti, f. pl.
abhor, ăbhŏr', v. a. aborrire; detestare.
abhorrence (-cy), —rĕnsĭ (-sĭ), aborrimento, m.; odio, m. [nemico.
abhorrent, —rĕnt, a. aborrente; contrario,

abide, ăbĭd', v. n. ir. abitare, dimorare; aspettare; tollerare, soffrire.
abigail, ă'bĭgăl, s. cameriera, f.; pettegola, f.
ability, ăbĭl'ĭtĭ, s. abilità, capacità, f.; forza, f.; abilities, pl. ricchezza, f.; talento, dono, m.
abject, ăb'jĕkt, a. abietto, basso, vile; —, ăbjĕkt', v. a. gittare via, scagliare.
abjectness, —jĕkt'nĕs, abjection, —jĕk'-shăn, s. bassezza, miseria, povertà, viltà, f.; abiezione, f. [mente; poveramente.
abjectly, ăb'jĕktlĭ, ad. bassamente, vilabjuration, —jŭră'shăn, s. abiura, f.
abjure, ăbjŏr', v. a. abiurare; rinunziare.
ablactate, —lăk'tăt, v.a. slattare, spoppare.
ablactation, —tă'shăn, s. spoppamento, m.
ablation, —lă'shăn, s. privazione, f.
ablative, ăb'lătĭv, s. ablativo, m.
ablaze, ăblăz', a. fiammeggiante.
able, ă'bl, a. abile, capace; robusto; to be —, potere.
able-bodied, —bŏd'ĭd, a. robusto, vigoroso.
ablegate, ăb'lēgăt, v. a. delegare.
ablegation, —lēgă'shăn, s. deputazione, delegazione, f.
allocate, ăb'lŏkăt, v. a. dare in affitto.
allocation, —kă'shăn, s. affitto, m.; locazione, f. [ficazione, f.
ablution, —lŭ'shăn, s. abluzione, f.; puriably, ă'blĭ, ad. abilmente. [ziare.
abnegate, ăb'nĕgăt, v. a. negare; rinunabnegation, —nĕgă'shăn, s. rinunzia, f.
abnormal, —nŏr'măl, a. irregolare, difforme; anormale.
abnormity, —nŏr'mĭtĭ, s. difformità, f.
aboard, ăbŏrd', ad. a bordo; to go —, imbarcarsi.
abode, ăbŏd', s. dimora, f.; abitazione, f.
abolish, ăbŏl'ĭsh, v. a. abolire; cassare; annullare. [rogazione, f.
abolition, ăbŏlĭsh'ăn, s. abolizione, f.; abolitionist, —ĭnĭst, s. partigiano dell' abolizione della schiavitù, m.
abominable, ăbŏm'ĭnăbl, a. abominabile, abominevole; detestabile. [flezza, f.
abominableness, —nĕs, s. abominevoabominably, —năbli, ad. abominevolmente.
abominate, —năt, v. a. abominare; detestare. [detestamento, m.
abomination, —nă'shăn, s. abominio, m.;
aboriginal, —ŏrĭj'ĭnăl, a. primitivo.

aborigines, _-ĭnēz,_ s. pl. aborigeni, primi abitatori d' un paese, m. pl.

abort, _ăbŏrt',_ v. n. abortire.

abortion, _ăbŏr'shŭn,_ s. aborto, m.

abortive, _-bŏr'tĭv,_ a. abortivo; prematuro; **-ly,** ad. immaturamente.

abortment, _-bŏrt'mĕnt,_ s. l' abortire, m.

abound, _ăbŏŭnd',_ v. n. abbondare.

about, _ăbŏŭt',_ ad. & pr. intorno, circolarmente; verso; **all –,** da per tutto; **round –,** in giro; **I have no money – me,** non ho danari addosso; **to be – to,** stare per.

above, _ăbŭv',_ ad. & pr. su, sopra; oltre; in su; più; **over and –,** soprappiù, di più; **to be –,** superare; **– all,** sopra tutto, principalmente.   [detto.

above-mentioned, _-mĕnshŏnd,_ a. sopradetto.

abrade, _ăbrăd',_ v. a. radere, raschiare.

abrasion, _-rā'zhŭn,_ s. raschiatura, f.

abreast, _ăbrĕst',_ ad. a lato; (mar.) a traverso, in faccia.   [diare.

abridge, _ăbrĭj',_ v. a. abbreviare, compendiare.

abridgment, _-mĕnt,_ s. abbreviamento, m.; compendio, m.

abroad, _ăbrăd',_ ad. fuora; fuori di casa; fuor di paese; **to go –,** uscire; **to set –,** divolgare; **to walk –,** spasseggiare.

abrogate, _ăb'rŏgăt,_ v. a. abolire; annullare.

abrogation, _-gā'shŭn,_ s. abrogazione, f.

abrupt, _ăbrŭpt',_ a. subitaneo, repentino, improvviso; dirupato; **-ly,** ad. di subito.

abruptness, _-nĕs,_ s. subitezza, f.; ruvidezza, scortesia, f.   [f.

abscess, _ăb'sĕs,_ s. ascesso, m.; postema, m.

abscind, _ăbsĭnd',_ v. a. tagliare; spartire.

abscission, _-sĭsh'ŭn,_ s. taglio, m.

abscond, _-skŏnd',_ v. n. nascondersi, celarsi.

absconder, _-ĕr,_ s. nascondente, nasconditore, m.; fuggitore, m.

absence, _ăb'sĕns,_ s. assenza, f.; lontananza, f.; **– of mind,** distrazione, f.

absent, _ăb'sĕnt,_ a. assente; lontano; distratto; **–,** _ăbsĕnt',_ v. n. assentarsi, fuggir via, discostarsi.   [assente, m. & f.

absentee, _-sĕntē',_ **absenter,** _-sĕn'tĕr,_ s. assenzio, m.

absinth, _ăb'sĭnth,_ s. assenzio, m.

absolute, _ăb'sŏlŭt,_ a. assoluto; illimitato; arbitrario; **-ly,** ad. assolutamente.

absoluteness, _-nĕs,_ s. potere assoluto, m.; indipendenza, f.; despotismo, m.

absolution, _-lŏ'shŭn,_ s. assoluzione, f.; remissione di colpa, f.

absolutism, _ăb'sŏlŭtĭzm,_ s. assolutismo, m.

absolutist, _-sŏlŭtĭst,_ s. assolutista, m.

absolutory, _-lŭtŭrĭ,_ a. assolutorio.

absolve, _-zŏlv',_ v. a. assolvere; dispensare, esentare, liberare.

absonant, _ăb'sŏnănt,_ **absonous,** _-sŏnŭs,_ a. assurdo; discordante, dissonante.

absorb, _-sŏrb',_ v. a. assorbire; inghiottire; consumare; rovinare.

absorbent, _-ĕnt,_ s. (med.) assorbente, m.

absorption, _-sŏrp'shŭn,_ s. assorbimento, m.

abstain, _-stăn',_ v. n. astenersi; privarsi. [m.

abstemious, _-stē'mŭs,_ a. astemio, temperato, sobrio; **-ly,** ad. temperatamente.

abstemiousness, _-nĕs,_ s. temperanza, f.; sobrietà, f.

abstention, _-tĕn'shŭn,_ s. astensione, f.

absterge, _-tŭrj',_ v. a. astergere, lavare; purgare, nettare.

abstergent, _-ĕnt,_ a. astergente; astersivo; **-s,** pl. medicine astersive, f. pl.

abstersion, _-tŭr'shŭn,_ s. astersione, f.; nettamento, m.   [peranza, f.

abstinence, _ăb'stĭnĕns,_ s. astinenza, temperanza, f.

abstinent, _ăb'stĭnĕnt,_ a. astinente; sobrio; **-ly,** ad. sobriamente.

abstract, _ăb'străct,_ s. astratto, m.; sommario, m.; **in the –,** ad. in astratto; **–,** a. astratto; **–,** _-străkt',_ v. a. astrarre.

abstracted, _-trăk'tĕd,_ a. astratto; separato; **-ly,** ad. astrattamente.

abstracter, _-tĕr,_ s. autore d' un sommario, m.; ladro, m.

abstracting, _-tĭng,_ pr. (**– from**) separato.

abstraction, _-shŭn,_ s. astrazione, f.; separazione, f.   [astratto.

abstractly, _-tlĭ,_ ad. astrattamente, in astruse, _ăbstrŏs',_ a. astruso, recondito; **-ly,** ad. astrusamente, in modo astruso.

abstruseness, _-nĕs,_ s. oscurità, f.; difficoltà, f.; senso recondito, m.

absurd, _ăbsŭrd',_ a. assurdo, incongruo, stravagante; **-ly,** ad. assurdamente.

absurdity, _-dĭtĭ,_ s. assurdità, f.; stravaganza, f.   [copia, f.

abundance, _ăbŭn'dăns,_ s. abbondanza, f.;

abundant, _-dănt,_ a. abbondante; copioso; **-ly,** ad. abbondantemente, in gran copia.

abuse, _ăbūz',_ v. a. abusare; ingiuriare, maltrattare, ingannare, deflorare.

abuse, _ăbŭs',_ s. abuso, m.; affronto, m., ingiuria, f.; seduzione, f.

abusive, _ăbŭ'sĭv,_ a. ingiurioso, oltraggioso; **-ly,** ad. abusivamente, ingiuriosamente.

abusiveness, _-nĕs,_ s. ingiuria, f., oltraggio, m.   [tiguo.

abut, _ăbŭt',_ v. n. confinare, essere contiguo.

abutment, _-mĕnt,_ s. confine, limite, m.; contiguità, vicinanza, prossimità, f.

abuttals, _-tălz,_ s. pl. confini, m. pl.

abysmal, _ăbĭz'măl,_ a. senza fondo.

abyss, _ăbĭs',_ s. abisso, m.; golfo, inferno, m.

acacia, _ăkăsh'ĭă,_ s. acacia, f.

academic(al), _ăkădĕm'ĭk(ăl),_ a. accademico, d' accademia.

academician, _-mĭsh'ăn,_ s. membro d' un' università, accademico, m.

academy, _ăkăd'ĕmĭ,_ s. accademia, università, f.; società di belle arti, f.; maneggio, m.

accede, _ăksēd',_ v. n. accedere; concorrere.

accedence, _-sē'dĕns,_ s. assenso, m.

accelerate, _-sĕl'ĕrăt,_ v. a. accelerare.

acceleration, _-lĕrā'shŭn,_ s. acceleramento, m., fretta, f.

accelerative, _-sĕl'ĕrătĭv,_ a. accelerativo.

accent, _ăk'sĕnt,_ s. accento, m.; tuono, m.; **–,** _-sĕnt',_ v. a. notare con accento, accentare; pronunziare.

accentuate, _-sĕn'tŭăt,_ v. a. accentare. [f.

accentuation, _-tŭā'shŭn,_ s. accentuazione, f.

accept, _ăksĕpt',_ v. a. accettare; aggradire; comprendere.

acceptability, *–tăbĭl'ĭtĭ*, s. qualità accettevole, f.

acceptable, *–sĕp'tăbl*, a. accettevole.

acceptableness, *–tăblnĕs,* s. accoglimento, m.; grazia, f., favore, m.

acceptably, *–tăbĭt*, ad. accettevolmente; gradevolmente, gratamente.

acceptance, *–tăns*, acceptation, *–tĕ'shăn*, s. accettazione, f.

accepter, *–tŭr*, s. accettatore, m.; accettatrice, f.   [sicazione, accezione, f.

acception, *–shăn*, s. significato, m., signi-

access, *ăksĕs'*, s. accesso, m.; adito, m., entrata, f.; entratura, f.; (med.) accessione, f.

accessary, *ăk'sĕssărĭ*, s. accessorio, m.; complice, m.; –, a. accessorio.   [bile.

accessible, *–sĕs'sĭbl*, a. accessibile; affa-

accession, *–sĕsh'ŭn*, s. accessione, f.; adizione, f.; avvenimento, m., venuta, f.

accessory, *ăk'sĕssărĭ*, a. accessorio.

accidence, *ăk'sĭdĕns*, s. rudimenti della grammatica, m. pl.

accident, *–sĭdĕnt*, s. accidente, caso, avvenimento, m.; disgrazia, f., infortunio, m.

accidental, *–dĕn'tăl*, a. casuale, fortuito; –ly, ad. per accidente, casualmente.

acclaim, *–klăm'*, v. a. acclamare.

acclamation, *–klămā'shăn*, s. acclamazione, f.; applauso, m.

acclimatise, *–klī'mătĭz*, v. a. acclimare.

acclivity, *–klīv'ĭtĭ*, s. acclività, f.; chino, m.

acclivous, *–klī'vŭs*, a. acclive.   [dabile.

accommodable, *–kŏm'mŏdăbl*, a. accomo-

accommodate, *–kŏm'mŏdăt*, v. a. accomodare, adattare, acconciare.

accommodating, *–dătĭng*, a. convenevole; proprio; –ly, ad. convenevolmente, comodamente, bene.

accommodation, *–mŏdā'shăn*, s. accomodamento, m.; comodità, f.; accordo, m.

accommodation-bill, *–bĭl*, s. cambio finto, m.   [compagnamento, m.

accompaniment, *–kŭm'pănĭmĕnt*, s. ac-

accompanist, *–kŭm'pănĭst*, s. accompagnatore, m.   [nare.

accompany, *–kŭm'pănĭ*, v. a. accompag-

accomplice, *–kŏm'plĭs*, s. complice, m. & f.

accomplish, *–kŏm'plĭsh*, v. a. compire; finire; perfezionare, adempire.

accomplished, *–kŏm'plĭsht*, a. compito, finito; perfetto.

accomplishment, *–plĭshmĕnt*, s. compimento, m.; finimento, m.; perfezione, f.

accord, *–kŏrd'*, s. accordo, m., convenzione, f.; unione, f.; with one –, unanimemente; –, v. a. accordare; conciliare; –, v. n. accordarsi; convenire.

accordance, *–ăns*, s. accomodamento, m.; unione, conformità, f.   [vole.

accordant, *–ănt*, a. accordante, convene-

according, *–ĭng*, pr. secondo; conforme; – as, secondo che, come; –ly, ad. conformemente, conseguentemente.

accost, *–kŏst'*, v. a. accostare; approdare; avvicinarsi.   [tricante, raccoglitore, m.

accoucheur, *ăkkūshăr'*, s. ostetrico, oste-

account, *–kŏŭnt'*, s. conto, m.; calcolo, m.; valore, pregio, m.; distinzione, stima, f.; ragione, f.; on –, a conto; on – of, a cagione di; on no –, in niun modo; to call to –, chieder ragione; –, v. a. contare; stimare; credere.

accountability, *–kŏŭntăbĭl'ĭtĭ*, s. responsabilità, f.

accountable, *–ăbl*, a. obbligato, tenuto.

accountant, *–ănt*, s. calcolatore, m.

account-book, *–bŭk*, s. libro de' conti, m.

accouple, *–kŭp'l*, v. a. accoppiare; congiugnere; unire.

accoutre, *–kŏ'tŭr*, v. a. aggiustare; parare.

accoutrement, *–mĕnt*, s. guarnimento, m.; vestimento, m.

accredit, *–krĕd'ĭt*, v. a. accreditare.

accrue, *–krŏ'*, v. n. derivare; provenire.

accumu'ate, *–kū'mŭlăt*, v. a. accumulare; amassare; –, v. n. accumularsi.

accumulation, *–lā'shăn*, s. accumulazione, f.; cumulo, m.

accumulative, *–lā'tĭv*, a. accumulativo.

accuracy, *ăk'kŭrăsĭ*, s. accuratezza, esattezza, puntualità, f.

accurate, *ăk'kŭrăt*, a. accurato, esatto; –ly, ad. accuratamente, esattamente.

accurateness, *–kŭrătnĕs*, s. accuratezza, esatezza, diligenza, f.

accurse, *–kŭrs'*, v. a. maledire, esecrare.

accursed, *–kŭr'sĕd*, a. maledetto; –, *–kŭrst'*, scomunicato; riprovato.

accusation, *–kŭzā'shăn*, s. accusa, f.

accusative, *–kū'zătĭv*, s. accusativo, m.

accusatory, *–zătŭrĭ*, a. accusatorio.

accuse, *ăkkŭz'*, v. a. accusare, incolpare.

accuser, *–zŭr*, s. accusatore, m.; accusatrice, f.   [assuefare.

accustom, *ăkkŭs'tŭm*, v. a. accostumare;

accustomarily, *–ărĭlĭ*, ad. ordinariamente, comunemente.   [comune.

accustomed, *–tŭmd*, a. ordinario; usuale,

ace, *ăs*, s. asso, m.   [severità, f.

acerbity, *ăsĕr'bĭtĭ*, s. acerbità, durezza,

acetate, *ăs'ĕtăt*, s. (chem.) acetato, m.

acetous, *ăsĕ'tŭs*, a. acetoso, acerbo.

ache, *ăk*, s. male, m.; dolore, m.; –, v. n. fare male; dolere.   [acquistare.

achieve, *ăchĕv'*, v. a. eseguire, effettuare;

achievement, *–mĕnt*, s. adempimento, m.; fatto, m.; prodezza, f.; impresa, f.

achiever, *–ŭr*, s. esecutore, m.; facitore, m.

aching, *ā'kĭng*, s. pena, f., dolore, m.

achromatic, *ăkrŏmăt'ĭk*, a. acromatico.

acid, *ăs'ĭd*, a. acido, agro.

acidity, *ăsĭd'ĭtĭ*, s. acidità, f.; agrezza, f.

acidulae, *ăsĭd'ŭlĕ*, s. pl. acque minerali acidette, f. pl.

acidulate, *ăsĭd'ŭlăt*, v. a. fare acido.

acknowledge, *ăknŏl'ĕj*, v. a. riconoscere; confessare.   [grato.

acknowledging, *–ĕjĭng*, a. riconoscente;

acknowledgment, *–mĕnt*, s. riconoscimento, m.

acme, *ăk'mĕ*, s. cima, punta, vetta, f.

acolyte, *ăk'ŏlīt*, s. accolito, m.

aconite, *ăk'ŏnĭt*, s. aconito, m.

acorn, *ā'kŏrn*, s. ghianda, f.

acoustics, ăkŏŏ'stĭks, s. acustica, teoria
de' suoni, f,   [visare, informare.
acquaint, ăkkwānt', v. a. avvertire, av-
acquaintance, –āns, s. conoscenza, f.;
familiarità, f.; amico, m.
acquiesce, –kwĕs', v. n. consentire; con-
tentarsi; sottomettersi.   [assenso, m.
acquiescence, –sĕns, s. acquiescenza, f.;
acquiescent, –sĕnt, a. consenziente.
acquirable, –kwīr'ăbl, a. acquistabile.
acquire, –kwīr', v. a. acquistare; guadagnare; arrivare.
acquirement, –mĕnt, s. acquisto, m.   [f.
acquisition, –kwĭzĭsh'ŭn, s. acquisizione
acquit, –kwĭt', v. a. assolvere; essentare,
liberare; **to – a debt,** pagare un debito;
to – oneself, compire.
acquitment, –mĕnt, **acquittal,** –tăl, s.
assoluzione, f.; liberazione, f.
acquittance, –tăns, s. quietanza, f.
acre, ā'kŭr, s. jugero, m.
acrid, ăk'rĭd, a. acre; mordace.
acridity, ăkrĭd'ĭtĭ, s. agrezza, acidità, f.
acrimonious, –mō'nĭŭs, a. acre, corrosivo.
acrimony, ăk'rĭmŭnĭ, **acrity,** ăk'rĭtĭ, s.
acrimonia, f.; agrezza, f.
across, ăkrŏs', ad. a scancio, a sgembo;
to come –, scoprire; incontrare.
acrostic, ăkrŏs'tĭk, s. acrostico, m.
act, ăkt, s. atto, m., azione, f.; fatto, m.;
decreto, m.; **in the very –,** in fragranti;
–, v. a. rappresentare; operare; –, v. n.
fare, agire; **– of Parliament,** decreto
del parlamento; **–s,** pl. atti.
acting, ăkt'ĭng, s. azione, recitazione, f.
action, ăk'shŭn, s. azione, operazione, f.;
lite, processo, m.; **–s,** pl. (com.) aziones,
pl., fondi, m.pl.
actionable, –ăbl, a. esposto a un' azione.
actionary, –ārĭ, s. (com.) azionario, m.
action-taking, –tā'kĭng, a. litigioso.
active, ăk'tĭv, a. attivo; agile; destro;
lesto; **–ly,** ad. attivamente; agilmente.
activeness, –nĕs, **activity,** –tĭv'ĭtĭ, s.
attività, f.; vivacità, f.; agilità, f.; prontezza, f.
actor, ăk'tŭr, s. attore, m.; commediante, m.
actress, ăk'trĕs, s. attrice, f.
actual, ăk'tŭăl, a. attuale; effettivo; **–ly,**
ad. attualmente, effettivamente; presente-
mente.
actuality, –tŭăl'ĭtĭ, s. attualità, f.   [m.
actuary, ăk'tŭărĭ, s. attuario, m.; notaio,
actuate, ăk'tŭāt, v. a. effettuare; incitare;
puntare, affilare.
aculeate, ăk'lĕăt, a. acuminato.   [f.
acumen, ăkū'mĕn, s. acume, m.; acutezza,
acuminate, –mĭnāt, v. a. aguzzare, ap-
acute, ăkūt', a. aguzzo; sagace; –, s.
accento acuto, m.; **– angle,** angolo
acuto.   [sagacemente.
acutely, –lĭ, ad. acutamente; sottilmente;
acuteness, –nĕs, s. acutezza, f.; sagacità, f.
adage, ăd'āj, s. adagio, proverbio, m.
adagio, ădā'jĭō, s. & ad. (mus.) adagio.
adamant, ăd'dmănt, s. diamante, adamante,
m.   [crudele.
adamantine, –măn'tĭn, a. adamantino;

adapt, ădăpt', v. a. adattare, accomodare,
aggiustare.   [lità, f.
adaptability, ădăptăbĭl'ĭtĭ, s. adattabi-
adaptable, –ăbl, a. adattabile, aggiusta-
bile, applicabile.
adaptation, –tā'shŭn, s. aggiustamento,
accomodamento, m., conformità, f.
add, ăd, v. a. aggiugnere; unire; **to – up,**
sommare.   [pendice, f.
addendum, ădĕn'dŭm, s. aggiunta, ap-
adder, ăd'dŭr, s. aspide, m.
addict, –dĭkt' (oneself), v. n. addarsi;
applicarsi; abbandonarsi.
addictedness, –ĕdnĕs, **addiction,** –dĭk'-
shŭn, s. propensione; applicazione.
addition, –dĭsh'ŭm, s. addizione, f.; aggiunta, f.; raddoppiamento, m.
additional, –ŭl, a. di soprappiù; **–ly,** ad.
in modo che accresce.
addle, ăd'dl, a. vuoto, vano; sterile; **–**
egg, uovo sterile, m.; **––headed,** discervellato; **––pated,** sciocco; –, v.a. rendere sterile.
address, ăddrĕs', s. indirizzo, m.; sagacità, f.; arte, f.; rifugio, m.; lettera dedica-
toria, f.; supplica, f.; –, v. a. indirizzare;
presentare; mandare, inviare una lettera.
adduce, –dūs', v. a. addurre; aggiugnere.
ademption, ădĕm'shŭn, f. privazione.
adept, ădĕpt', s. alchimista, m.
adequacy, ăd'ĕkwăsĭ, s. corrispondenza,
proporzione, f.
adequate, ăd'ĕkwăt, a. adeguato, proporzionato, conforme; **–ly,** ad. adeguatamente.   [proporzione, f.
adequateness, –nĕs, s. adeguamento, m.,
adhere, ădhēr', v. n. attaccarsi, aderire;
favorire.   [m.
adherence, –rĕns, s. aderenza, f.; favore,
adherent, –rĕnt, a. attaccato, unito; –, s.
aderente; fautore, m.   [vore, m.
adhesion, –hē'zhŭn, s. adesione, f.; fa-
adhesive, –hē'sĭv, a. viscoso, tenace.
adhesiveness, –nĕs, s. viscosità, f.
adieu, ădū', ad. addio.
adipose, ăd'ĭpōs, a. adiposo, grasso.
adit, ăd'ĭt, s. adito, m., entrata, f.
adjacence, ădjā'sĕns, **adjacency,** –jā'-
sĕnsĭ, s. adiacenza, f.; contiguità, f.
adjacent, –jā'sĕnt, a. adiacente; contiguo.
adjective, ăd'jĕktĭv, s. (gr.) adiettivo, m.;
–ly, ad. adiettivamente.
adjoin, –jŏĭn', v. a. aggiugnere; accrescere;
–, v. n. essere contiguo.
adjourn, –jŭrn', v. a. differire; rimettere.
adjournment, –mĕnt, s. dilazione, f.; ritardamento, m.
adjudge, –jŭj', **adjudicate,** –jŏ'dĭkāt,
v. a. aggiudicare; decretare, condannare.
adjudication, –jōdĭkā'shŭn, s. aggiudicazione, f.; condanna, f.
adjunct, ăd'jŭnkt, s. aggiunto, m.
adjuration, –jŏră'shŭn, s. il giurare, m.
adjure, ădjōr', v. a. giurare; scongiurare.
adjust, ădjŭst', v. a. aggiustare; acconciare; regolare.
adjuster, –jŭst'ŭr, s. aggiustatore, m.

adjustment, *–mĕnt,* s. aggiustamento, acconciamento, m.; accordo, m.   [m.

adjutancy, *ăd'jŭtănsĭ,* s. uffizio d'ajutante,

adjutant, *ăd'jŭtănt,* a. ajutante, m.

adjute, *ădjōt',* v. a. aiutare, soccorrere.

admeasurement, *–mĕzh'ŭrmĕnt,* s. misuramento, m.

administer, *–mĭn'ĭstŭr,* v. a. amministrare; governare; aiutare; **to – an oath,** dare il giuramento.

administration, *–nĭstrā'shŭn,* s. amministrazione, f., governo, m.

administrative, *–mĭn'ĭstrātĭv,* a. amministrante.   [stratore, m.

administrator, *–nĭstrā'tŭr,* s. amministrability,

admirability, *–mĭrăbĭl'ĭtĭ,* s. ammirabilità, f.   [maraviglioso.

admirable, *ăd'mĭrăbl,* a. ammirabile;

admirably, *–răblĭ,* ad. ammirabilmente.

admiral, *ăd'mĭrăl,* s. ammiraglio, m.; **Lord High –,** grande ammiraglio, m.

admiralship, *–shĭp,* s. almirante, m. (vascello); carico dell' ammiraglio, m.

admiralty, *ăd'mĭrăltĭ,* s. ammiragliato, m.

admiration, *–mĭrā'shŭn,* s. ammirazione, f.; maraviglia, f.; **note** *or* **sign of –,** (gr.) segno d'esclamazione, m.

admire, *ădmīr',* v. a. ammirare; maravigliarsi; amare.   [ratrice, f.

admirer, *–rŭr,* s. ammiratore, m.; ammiringly,

admiringly, *–rĭnglĭ,* ad. con maraviglia.

admissible, *–mĭs'sĭbl,* a. ammissibile, accettabile.   [entratura, f.

admission, *–mĭsh'ŭn,* s. ammissione, f.;

admit, *–mĭt',* v. a. ammettere, introdurre; ricevere; accettare; permettere.

admittance, *–tăns,* s. entrata, entratura, f.

admittedly, *–tĕdlĭ,* ad. per ammissione.

admixture, *–mĭks'tŭr,* s. mischiamento, m., mistione, f.

admonish, *–mŏn'ĭsh,* v. a. ammonire, avvertire; riprendere.

admonishment, *–mĕnt,* **admonition,** *–nĭsh'ŭn,* s. ammonizione, f., avviso, m.; consiglio, m.

admonitory, *–mŏn'ĭtărĭ,* a. ammonitorio.

ado, *ădō',* s. strepito, rumore, m.; difficoltà, fatica, f.

adolescence, *(–cy) ădōlĕs'sĕns (sĭ),* s. adolescenza, f.   [m.

adolescent, *–lĕs'sĕnt,* a. & s. adolescente,

adopt, *ădŏpt',* v. a. adottare; ricevere.

adoption, *ădŏp'shŭn,* s. adozione, f.

adoptive, *ădŏp'tĭv,* a. adottivo.

adorable, *ădōr'ăbl,* a. adorabile; sommamente amabile.   [beltà, f.

adorableness, *–ăblnĕs,* s. eccellenza, f.;

adorably, *–ăblĭ,* ad. adorabilmente.

adoration, *ădōrā'shŭn,* s. adorazione, f.

adore, *ădōr',* v. a. adorare; venerare.

adorer, *ădō'rŭr,* s. adoratore, amante, m.; adoratrice, f.

adorn, *ădōrn',* v. a. adornare; abbellire.

adornment, *–mĕnt,* s. adornamento, m.; abbellimento, m.

adrift, *ădrĭft',* ad. all' avventura; in balia; (mar.) in deriva.

adroit, *ădrŏĭt',* a. destro, svelto; abile.

adroitness, *–nĕs,* s. destrezza, f.

adulation, *ădŭlā'shŭn,* f. adulazione, lusinga, leccatura, moina, f.

adulatory, *ăd'ŭlătărĭ,* a. adulatorio.

adult, *ădălt',* s. adulto, m.; adolescenza, f.; –, a. adulto, cresciuto.

adulterate, *ădŭl'tĕrāt,* v. a. adulterare; falsificare, corrompere; –, a. adulterato, falsificato.   [f.; corruzione, f.

adulteration, *–răshŭn,* f. adulterazione,

adulterer, *–tŭrŭr,* s. adultero, m.

adulteress, *–tŭrĕs,* s. adultera, f.

adulterine, *–tŭrĭn,* **adulterous,** *–tŭrŭs,* a. adulterino; d' adulterio.

adultery, *–tŭrĭ,* s. adulterio, m.

advance, *ădvāns',* s. avanzo,|m.; anticipazione, f.; **––money,** s. pagamento anticipato, m.; –, v. a. promuovere; anticipare; –, v. n. avanzare; andar innanzi.

advancement, *–mĕnt,* s. avanzamento, aggrandimento, m.; progresso, m.

advantage, *–văn'tăj,* s. vantaggio, m.; sopprapiù, m.; profitto, m.; utilità, f.; –, v. a. acquistare; beneficare; promovere; **to take – of,** valersi, servirsi.

advantage-ground, *–grŏŭnd,* s. posizione vantaggiosa, f.; preminenza, f.

advantageous, *–tā'jŭs,* a. vantaggioso, profittevole; **–ly,** ad. vantaggiosamente.

advantageousness, *–nĕs,* s. vantaggio, m., utilità, f.; profitto, m.

advent, *ăd'vĕnt,* s. avvenimento, m.

Advent, –, Avvento, m.

adventitious, *–tĭsh'ŭs,* a. avventizio, casuale.

adventure, *–vĕn'tŭr,* s. avventura, f.; accidente, m.; pericolo, m.; **by –,** a caso; **at all –s,** alla ventura; –, v. a. avventurare, intraprendere; azzardare.

adventurer, *–tŭrŭr,* s. avventuriere, m.

adventuresome, *–tŭrsŭm,* a. ardito, temerario, azzardoso.

adventurous, *–tŭrŭs,* a. ardito; coraggioso; **–ly,** ad. arditamente.

adverb, *ăd'vŭrb,* s. (gr.) avverbio, m.

adverbial, *–vŭr'bĭăl,* a. avverbiale; **–ly,** ad. avverbialmente.   [nemico, m.

adversary, *ăd'vŭrsărĭ,* s. avversario, m.;

adverse, *ăd'vŭrs,* a. avverso, contrario; **–ly,** ad. contrariamente, in modo contrario.   [fortunio, m.; calamità, f.

adversity, *–vŭr'sĭtĭ,* s. avversità, f., in-

advert, *ădvŭrt',* v. n. considerare, riflettere, deliberare; osservare.

advertence, *–vŭr'tĕns,* s. avvertenza, f.

advertise, *ăd'vŭrtĭz,* v. a. avvisare, avvertire, ammonire.

advertisement, *–vŭr'tĭzmĕnt,* s. avvertimento, avviso, m.; informazione, f.

advertising, *–tĭ'zĭng,* s. informazione, f.

advice, *ădvĭs',* s. avviso, m.; consiglio, m.; **––boat,** s. nave di procaccio, f.

advisability, *–vĭzăbĭl'ĭtĭ,* s. prudenza, sagacità, f.   [dente.

advisable, *–vī'zăbl,* a. convenevole; prudente.

advisableness, *–nĕs,* s. convenevolezza, f.; utilità, f.; prudenza, f.

advise, *ădvīz'*, v. a. avvisare; consigliare;
—, v.n. consultare, deliberare; considerare.
advised, *—vīzd'*, a. avvisato, avvertito;
-ly, ad. cautamente, con prudenza.
advisedness, *—zĕdnĕs*, s. considerazione,
prudenza, f. [f.
advocacy, *ăd' vŏkăsĭ*, s. difesa, f.; apologia
advocate, *ăd' vŏkăt*, s. avvocato, m.; inter-
cessore, m.; fautore, m.; —, v. a. difendere. [avvocato, m.
advocateship, *—shĭp*, s. uffizio dell'
advowee, *—vŏŭ'*, s. padrone, m.; presen-
tatore, m. [presentazione, f.
advowson, *—vŏŭ'săn*, s. padronato, m.;
ægis, *ē'jĭs*, s. egida, f.
æon, *ē'ŏn*, s. era, eternità, f.
æra, *ē'ră*, s. era, epoca, f.
aerial, *āē'rĭăl*, a. aereo, d'aria.
aerie, *ē'rĭ*, s. nido (di falconi &c.), m.
aerometer, *ārŏm'ĕtăr*, s. aerometro, m.
aeronaut, *ăr'ŏnăt*, s. aeronauta, m.
aerostat, *ăr'ŏstăt*, s. aerostato, m.
aerostatics, *—stă'tĭks*, aerostation,
—stă'shăn, aerostatica, f.
afar, *ăfăr'*, ad. lontano, lungi. [viltà, f.
affability, *ăffăbĭl'ĭtĭ*, s. affabilità, f.; ci-
affable, *ăf'făbl*, a. affabile; civile, cortese.
affably, *—făblĭ*, a. affabilmente, cortesemente. [m.; faccenda, f.
affair, *ăffăr'*, s. affare, fatto, m.; negozio,
affect, *ăffĕkt'*, v. a. muovere; affettare,
pretendere. [artificio, m.
affectation, *—tă'shăn*, s. affettazione, f.;
affected, *—tĕd*, a. affettato, inclinato;
studiato; -ly, ad. con affettazione.
affecting, *—tĭng*, a. patetico; -ly, adv.
pateticamente. [amore, m.
affection, *—fĕk'shăn*, s. affezione, f.;
affectionate, *—shănăt*, a. affezionato, affettuoso; -ly, ad. affettuosamente.
affectionateness, *—nătnĕss*, s. affetto,
m., tenerezza, f.
affiance, *—fĭ'ăns*, s. sposalizio, m.; confidenza, f.; —, v. a. sposare; fidanzare.
affidavit, *—fĭdă'vĭt*, s. deposizione fatta
con giuramento, f.
affiliate, *—fĭl'ĭăt*, v. a. adottare.
affiliation, *—ĭlĭ'shăn*, s. affiliazione, f.
affinity, *—fĭn'ĭtĭ*, s. affinità, f.; conformità, f. [care; approvare.
affirm, *—fărm'*, v. a. confermare, ratifi-
affirmation, *—mă'shăn*, s. affermazione, f.
affirmative, *—fărm'ătĭv*, a. affermativo;
-ly, ad. affermativamente; —, s. afferma-
tiva, f. [v. a. affiggere; attaccare.
affix, *ăf'fĭks*, s. (gr.) affisso, m.; —, *—fĭks'*,
afflict, *—flĭkt'*, v. a. affliggere; tormentare.
afflictedness, *—tĕdnĕs*, s. afflizione, f.;
desolazione, ambascia, doglia, f.
afflicter, *—tăr*, s. che affligge, che tormenta.
affliction, *—flĭk'shăn*, s. afflizione, f.; dolore, m.; tormento, m. [bondanza, f.
affluence, *ăf'flŭĕns*, s. affluenza, f.; ab-
affluent, *—ănt*, a. affluente; abbondante.
afflux, *ăf'flŭks*, affluxion, *—flŭk'shăn*,
s. afflusso, m.

afford, *—fŏrd'*, v. a. dare; provvedere;
produrre. [muccia, f.; tumulto, m.
affray, *—fră'*, s. combattimento, m.; scara-
affright, *—frīt'*, v. a. spaventare; im-
paurare; —, s. vedi fright.
affront, *—frănt'*, s. affronto, m.; ingiuria,
f.; —, v. a. affrontare; insultare, oltraggiare.
affrontive, *—tĭv*, a. oltraggioso, ingiurioso.
afield, *ăfēld'*, ad. in campo; da lunga.
afire, *ăfīr'*, aflame, *ăflăm'*, a. in incendio,
in fiamme.
afloat, *ănŏt'*, ad. a galla, galleggiante.
afoot, *ăfŭt'*, ad. a piede. [innanzi.
afore, *ăfōr'*, ad. & pr. prima; avanti;
afraid, *ăfrăd'*, a. spaventato.
afresh, *ăfrĕsh'*, ad. di nuovo, da capo.
aft, *ăft*, adv. (mar.) verso poppa; fore
and —, (mar.) su e giù.
after, *ăf'tăr*, ad. & pr. dopo; secondo;
dietro, poi; one — another, un dopo
l'altro; — all, in somma.
after-ages, *—ājĭz*, s. pl. secoli futuri, m.
pl., posterità, f.
after-birth, *—bărth*, s. secondina, f.
after-cost, *—kŏst*, s. spesa di soprappiù, f.
after-crop, *—krŏp*, s. seconda raccolta, f.
after-days, *—dāz*, s. pl. avvenire, m.
after-game, *—gām*, s. nuovo espediente,
m.; rivincita, f. [roventimento, m.
afterglow, *—glō*, s. roventezza, f., ar-
after-hours, *—ărz*, afterlife, *—līf*, s.
pl. avvenire, m.
after-math, *—măth*, s. guaime, m.
afternoon, *—nōn*, s. dopo pranzo, m.
after-piece, *—pēs*, s. farsa, f.
after-reckoning, *—rĕk'nĭng*, s. revisione
d'un conto, f. [nente, m.
after-taste, *—tăst*, s. cattivo sapore rima-
after-thought, *—thăt*, s. intenzione oc-
culta, restrizione mentale, f.
afterward(s), *—wărd(z)*, ad. dopo, dipoi.
after-wit, *—wĭt*, s. senno fuor di stagione,
m. [altra volta.
again, *ăgĕn'*, ad. di nuovo, ancora, un'
against, *ăgĕnst'*, pr. contro; in faccia;
— the grain, contra pelo; contra voglia.
age, *āj*, s. età, f.; secolo, m.; old —, età
avanzata, f.; full —, adolescenza, f.; to
be of —, esser maggiore; under —,
minore; over —, troppo vecchio(of horses).
aged, *ā'jĕd*, a. vecchio, attempato.
agency, *ā'jĕnsĭ*, s. azienda, f.; azione, f.
agent, *ā'jĕnt*, a. agente; operante; —, s.
agente, m.; ministro, presidente, m.
agglomerate, *ăgglŏm'ărăt*, v. a. aggomitolare; ammassare; adunare; —, v. n.
aggomitolarsi; adunarsi.
agglomeration, *—mără'shăn*, s. agglo-
merazione, f., ammasso, m.
agglutinate, *—glŭ'tĭnăt*, v. a. conglutinare, unire. [accrescere, aumentare.
aggrandise, *ăg'grăndīz*, v. a. aggrandire;
aggrandisement, *ăg'grăndĭzment*, s.
grandimento, m. [aumentare.
aggravate, *ăg'grăvăt*, v. a. aggravare;

aggravation, –vā'shăn, s. aggravazione, f.; aggravamento, m.; **enormità**, f.

aggregate, ăg'grĕgăt, a. aggregato; –, s. aggregato, m.; unione, f.; –, v. a. aggregare; unire. [f.; l' aggregare, m.

aggregation, –gă'shăn, s. aggregazione, f.

aggress, –grĕs', v. n. assalire; attaccare.

aggression, –grĕsh'ăn, s. aggressione, assalita, f.; assalto, assalimento, m.

aggressive, –grĕs'sĭv, a. aggressivo, offensivo. [tore, m.

aggressor, –grĕs'ăr, s. aggressore, assali-

aggrieve, –grēv', v. a. affliggere, tra-vagliare; danneggiare.

aghast, ăgăst', a. spaventato, impaurito.

agile, ăj'ĭt, a. agile; snello, destro.

agility, ăjĭt'ĭtĭ, s. agilità, f.; destrezza, f.

agitate, ăj'ĭtăt, v. a. agitare; smuovere.

agitation, –tă'shăn, s. agitazione, f.; agi-tamento, m.; turbazione, f. [agente, m.

agitator, –tă'tăr, s. maneggiatore, m.;

agnail, ăg'năl, s. panereccio, m.

agnate, ăg'năt, s. agnato, parente, m.

agnation, ăgnă'shăn, s. agnazione, f.; pa-rentela, f. [long – ? quanto tempo è ?

ago, ăgŏ', ad. dopo; tempo fa; da; **how**

agog, ăgŏg', ad. to **set –**, far venir de-siderio. [atto; to **be –**, andare.

agoing, ăgŏ'ĭng, ad. in movimento, in

agonize, ăg'ŏnĭz, v. n. agonizzare; soffrire.

agony, ăg'ŏnĭ, s. agonia, f.; angoscia, f.

agrarian, ăgră'rĭăn, a. agrario.

agree, ăgrĕ', v. a. metter d' accordo; quie-tare; –, v. n. accordarsi; convenire.

agreeable, –ăbl, a. convenevole; pia-cevole, ameno, grato.

agreeableness, –ăblnĕs, s. convenevo-lezza, f.; congruità, f.; grazia, f.

agreeably, –ăblĭ, ad. convenevolmente; piacevolmente; vagamente; **– with**, adv. secondo; [siamo intesi, toppa.

agreed, ăgrĕd', a. fisso, aggiustato; –, ad.

agreement, ăgrĕ'mĕnt, s. accordo, m.; conformità, f.; concento, m,

agricultural, ăgrĭkŭl'tŭrăl, a. appar-tenente all' agricoltura.

agriculture, –kŭl'tŭr, s. agricoltura, f.

agrimony, ăg'rĭmănĭ, acrimonia, f.

aground, ăgrŏŭnd', ad. in terra; sventu-ratamente. [di febbre, m.

ague, ă'gū, s. febbre, f.; **fit of –**, accesso

aguish, ă'gūĭsh, a. febbrile.

ah! ā, i. ah! ahimè! ahi!

aha! ăhă', i. ben! bene! [a prua.

ahead, ăhĕd', ad. innanzi, davanti; (mar.)

ahoy! ăhŏĭ', (mar.) ohi!

aid, ăd, s. aiuto, soccorso, m.; –, v. a. aiutare, soccorrere.

aid-de-camp, – dĕ kŏng, s. (mil.) aiu-tante di campo, m.

aider, ăd'ăr, s. aiutatore, m.; **– and abettor**, complice, m.

ail, ăl, v. a. appensare; tormentare; **what ails you?** che male avete?

ailing, ăl'ĭng, a. indisposto, incomodato.

ailment, –mĕnt, s. male, m.; indisposi-zione, f.

aim, ăm, s. mira, f.; bersaglio, m.; disegno, m.; –, v. a. mirare; aspirare, tendere.

aimless, –lĕs, a. senza mira.

ain't, ănt, non sono, non è.

air, ăr, s. aria, f.; apparenza, f.; aspetto, m.; cantata, f., canto, m.; –, v. a. mettere all' aria, sventolare; seccare.

air-balloon, –băllŏn', s. pallone aerosta-tico volante, m. [d'aria, m.

air-cushion, – kăsh'ăn, s. cuscino

air-gun, –găn, s. archibugio ad aria, m.

air-hole, –hŏl, s. sfogatoio, m.; spiraglio, m.; ventilatore, m. [leggerezza, f.

airiness, ăr'ĭnĕs, s. l'esporre all' aria, m.;

airing, ăr'ĭng, s. passeggiata, f.

airless, –lĕs, a. senz' aria. [f.

air-pump, –pămp, s. tromba pneumatica,

air-shaft, –shăft, s. spiraglio, m.

air-tight, –tĭt, a. imperme–bile all' aria.

air-vessel, –vĕssl, s. recipiente, m.

airy, ăr'ĭ, a. d' aria, aereo.

aisle, ĭl, s. navata (d' una chiesa), f.

ajar, ăjăr', a. socchiuso.

akin, ăkĭn', a. imparentato, consanguineo.

alabaster, ălăbăs'tăr, s. alabastro, m.; –, a. alabastrino. [misero me!

alack! ălăk', –(-a-day)! –ă dă, i. ohimè!

alacrity, ălăk'rĭtĭ, s. vivacità, allegrezza, f.

alarm, ălărm', s. allarme, m.; spavento, m.; –, v. a. allarmare; spaventare. [f.

alarm-bell, –bĕl, s. campana dello stormo,

alarmist, ălărm'ĭst, s. allarmista, m.

alarm-post, –pŏst, s. piazza della riunione delle truppe, f.; luogo del appuntamento,

alarm-watch, –wŏch, s. sveglia, f. [m.

alarum, vedi alarm. [oimè!

alas, ălăs', alas-a-day, –ă dă, i. ohimè!

alb(e), ălb, s. camice, m.

albeit, ălbĕ'ĭt, c. frattanto; benchè.

albugo, ălbŭ'gŏ, s. albugine, f.

album, ăl'băm, s. album, m.

alchemic(al), ălkĕm'ĭk(ăl), a. alchimico.

alchemist, ăl'kĕmĭst, s. alchimista, m.

alchemy, ăl'kĕmĭ, s. alchimia, f.

alcohol, ăl'kŏhŏl, s. alcool, m.

alcoholic, –kŏhŏl'ĭk, a. alcoolico.

alcove, ălkŏv', s. alcova, f.

alder, ăl'dăr, s. ontano, m. [scabino, m.

alderman, –măn, s. assessore aggiunto,

ale, ăl, s. birra forte, f.

alehouse, –hŏŭs, s. osteria, f.

alehouse-keeper, –kēpăr, s. oste, m.

alembic, ălĕm'bĭk, s. lambicco, m.

alert, ălărt', a. vigilante; lesto, agile, vivace.

alertness, –nĕs, s. vigilanza, f.; destrezza, f.; petulanza, f. [birra, f.

ale-silver, ăl'sĭlvăr, s. imposizione sulla

ale-stake, –stăk, s. insegna di birreria, f.

ale-wife, –wĭf, s. ostessa, f.

alga, ăl'gă, s. alga, alga, erba marina, f.

algebra, ăl'jĕbră, s. algebra, f.

algebraic(al), –brā'ĭk(ăl), a. algebraico, d' algebra.

algebraist, ăl'jĕbrăĭst, s. algebrista, m.

alias, ă'lĭăs, ad. altrimenti.

alibi, ăl'ĭbĭ, s. (law) alibi, in altro luogo, m.

alien, ăl'yĕn, s. forestiere, m. & f.; –, a. alieno, straniero.

alienable –*yēnăbl*, a. alienabile.

alienate, –*yĕnăt*, v. a. alienare; trasferire, vendere.

alienation, –*yĕnă'shăn*, s. alienazione, f.; **– of mind**, s. alienazione di mente, f.

alight, *ălīt'*, v. n. smontare; mettere piè a terra.   [parimente.

alike, *ălīk'*, a. & ad. simile; similmente.

aliment, *ăl'ĭmĕnt*, s. alimento, m.; cibo, m.

alimental, –*mĕn'tăl*, **alimentary**, –*tări*, a. alimentario, nutritivo.

alimentation, –*tă'shăn*, s. alimentazione, f., nutricamento, m.   [f.

alimony, *ăl'ĭmŏnĭ*, s. pensione alimentaria, f.

aliquot, *ăl'ĭkwŏt*, a. aliquoto.

alive, *ălīv'*, a. vivente, vivo; attivo.

alkali, *ăl'kălī*, s. alcali, m.

alkaline, *ăl'kălīn*, a. alcaline.

all, *ăl*, s. tutto, totale, m.; –, a. tutto, ciascuno; **– of a sudden**, **– at once**, subitamente; **– over**, da per tutto; **not at –**, no certo; **– the better**, tanto meglio; **– the same**, nondimeno; **once for –**, una volta per sempre; –, ad. in tutto, interamente.   [allegare; mescolare.

allay, *ălā'*, s. lega, f.; misura, f.; –, v. a.

allayment, –*mĕnt*, s. alleviamento, m.; conforto, m.   [chiarazione, f.

allegation, –*lĕgă'shăn*, s. allegazione, f.;

allege, –*lĕj'*, v. a. allegare; dichiarare.

allegiance, –*lĕ'jăns*, s. lealtà, fedeltà, f.

allegoric(al), –*lĕgŏr'ĭk(ăl)*, a. allegorico;

–ly, ad. allegoricamente.

allegorise, *ăl'lĕgŏrīz*, v. a. allegorizzare.

allegory, *ăl'lĕgŏrĭ*, s. allegoria, f.

allegro, –*lĕ'grō*, s. (mus.) allegro, m.

alleviate, –*lĕ'vĭăt*, v. a. alleviare; mitigare.

alleviation, –*lĕvĭā'shăn*, s. alleviamento, m.; conforto, m.   [m.

alley, *ăl'lĭ*, s. viale di giardino, m.; chiasso,

All-hallowmass, *ăl hăl'lōmăs*, **All-hallowtide**, –*tĭd*, s. primo di Novembre, m.

alliance, –*lī'ăns*, s. alleanza, f.; affinità, f.

allied, *ăllīd'*, a. alleato, confederato.

alligate, *ăl'lĭgăt*, a. collegare.

alligator, *ăl'lĭgătŏr*, s. alligatore, m.

alliteration, –*lĭtŭră'shăn*, s. allitterazione, f.

allocation, –*lŏkă'shăn*, s. allogazione, f.

allocution, –*lŏkū'shăn*, s. allocuzione, f.

allodium, –*lō'dĭăm*, s. allodio, m.

allot, –*lŏt'*, v. a. assegnare; aggiudicare.

allotment, –*mĕnt*, s. assegnazione, f.; distribuzione, f.   [cedere; permettere.

allow, –*lŏŭ'*, v. a. dare; accordare, concedere; permettere; con-

allowable, –*ăbl*, a. ammissibile; permesso, giusto.   [concessione, f.; (mar.) razione, f.

allowance, –*ăns*, s. mantenimento, m.; –, v. a. legare.

alloy, –*lŏĭ'*, s. lega, f.; –, v. a. legare.

All-souls-day, *ăl sōls' dā*, s. festa di tutti i Santi, f.

allspice, *ăl'spĭs*, s. pigmento, m.

allude, *ăllūd'*, v. n. alludere; sottintendere.

allure, –*lōr'*, v. a. adescare, allettare.

allurement, –*mĕnt*, s. adescamento, allettamento, m., lusinga, f.

alluring, –*lō'rĭng*, s. allettamento, m.;

–, a. lusinghevole; fallace; **–ly**, ad. lusinghevolmente.

allusion, –*lō'zhăn*, s. allusione, f.

allusive, –*sĭv*, a. allusivo; **–ly**, ad. in modo allusivo.

alluvial, –*lō'vĭăl*, a. alluvionale.

alluvion, –*lō'vĭăn*, s. alluvione, f.

all-wise, *ăl'wĭs*, a. onnisciente.

ally, *ăllī'*, s. alleato, m.; parente, m.; –, v. a. associare; legare.

almanac, *ăl'mănăk*, s. almanacco, m.

almightiness, *ălmīt'ĭnĕs*, s. onnipotenza, f.

almighty, –*mīt'ĭ*, a. onnipotente.   [f.

almond, *ā' mănd*, s. mandorla, f.; **–s**, pl. glandule, f. pl.

almond-milk, –*mĭlk*, s. lattata, f.

almond-tree, –*trē*, s. mandorlo, m.

almoner, *ăl' mŏnăr*, s. elemosiniere, m.; cappellano, m.   [siniere, m.

almonry, *ăl' mŏnrĭ*, s. ufficio dell' elemosina, m.

almost, *ăl' mŏst*, ad. quasi; pressochè.

alms, *ămz*, s. pl. elemosina, f.

alms-house, –*hŏŭs*, s. spedale, m.

alnage, *ăl'năj*, s. misura delle stoffe, f.

alnager, –*năjăr*, s. misuratore, m.

alnight, *ăl'nĭt*, s. candela di cera, f.;

aloes, *ăl'ōz*, s. aloè, m.   [lumicina, f.

aloft, *ălŏft'*, ad. & pr. su; in alto.

alone, *ălōn'*, a. & ad. solo, solitario; **to let –**, lasciare, abbandonare.

along, *ălŏng'*, ad. & pr. pur via; alla lunga, lungo; accosto, appresso.

alongside, –*sĭd*, adv. lungo la banda.

aloof, *ălōf'*, ad. di lungi; da lontano; (mar.) al vento.

aloud, *ălŏŭd'*, ad. ad alta voce; forte.

alphabet, *ăl'făbĕt*, s. alfabeto, m.

alphabetic(al), –*bĕt'ĭk(ăl)*, a. alfabetico; **–ly**, ad. alfabeticamente.

alpine, *ăl'pīn*, a. alpestre.

already, *ăltrĕd'ĭ*, ad. già, di già, innanzi.

also, *ăl'sō*, c. anche, ancora; oltre.

altar, *ăl'tăr*, s. altare, m.; **high –**, altare maggiore, m.

altar-piece, –*pēs*, s. paliotto, m.

alter, *ăl'tăr*, v. a. alterare; cangiare; rifare; –, v. n. cambiare, variare; corrompersi.

alterable, –*tărăbl*, a. alterabile.

alterably, –*tărăblĭ*, ad. in modo alterabile.

alteration, –*tŭră'shăn*, s. alterazione, f.

alterative, –*tărătĭv*, a. alterativo.

altercate, –*tŭrkăt*, v. n. altercare, litigare.

altercation, –*kā'shăn*, s. altercazione, contesa, f., alterco, m.

alternate, –*tŭr'năt*, a. alternativo, reciproco; –, v. a. alternare; avvicendare.

alternately, –*nătlĭ*, ad. a vicenda.

alternation, –*nā'shăn*, s. alternazione, f.

alternative, –*tŭr'nătĭv*, s. alternativa, f.; –, a. alternativo; **–ly**, ad. alternativamente.   [corchè.

although, *ăltho'*, *ălthō'*, c. benchè, an-

altitude, *ăl'tĭtŭd*, s. altitudine, altezza, f.

altogether, *ăltŭgĕth'ăr*, ad. affatto, interamente.   [ramente.

alum, *ăl'ăm*, s. allume, m.

aluminium, *ălŭmĭn'ĭăm*, s. alluminio, m.

aluminous, *ălō'mĭnăs*, a. alluminoso.

alum-salt, ăl'ŭm sălt, s. salgemma, m.

always, ăl'wăz, ad. sempre, continuamente.

amain, ămān', ad. vigorosamente; di tutta forza.

amalgam, ămăl'găm, s. amalgama, m.

amalgamate, –gămāt, v. a. & n. amalgamare; amalgamarsi.   [zione, f.

amalgamation, –mă'shŭn, s. amalgamamanuensis, ămănŭĕn'sĭs, s. amanuense, copista, segretario, m.   [m.

amaranth, ăm'ărănth, s. (bot.) amaranto,

amaryllis, –rĭl'lĭs, s. (bot.) amarilli, m.

amass, ămăs', v.a. ammassare, accumulare.

amateur, ăm'ătūr, s. amatore, dilettante, m.

amativeness, ăm'ătĭvnĕs, s. disposizione all' amore, f.

amatory, –ătūrĭ, a. amatorio.

amaze, ămāz', v. a. stordire; sorprendere.

amazedly, –zĕdlĭ, ad. in modo sorprendente.   [stupore, m.

amazement, ămāz'mĕnt, s. sorpresa, f.,

amazing, –zĭng, a. stupendo, miracoloso.

amazingly, –zĭnglĭ, ad. maravigliosamente.

amazon, ăm'ăzŏn, s. amazone, f.   [mente.

ambassador, ămbăs'sădūr, s. ambasciatore, m.   [f.

ambassadress, –sădrĕs, s. ambasciatrice,

amber, ăm'bŭr, s. ambra, f.; –, a. ambrato, d' ambra.   [destro.

ambidextrous, ămbĭdĕks'trŭs, a. ambi-

ambient, ăm'bĭĕnt, a. ambiente.

ambiguity, –bĭgū'ĭtĭ, s. ambiguità, f.; dubbiezza, f.; irresoluzione, f.

ambiguous, –bĭg'ŭŭs, a. ambiguo, equivoco; **–ly,** ad. ambiguamente, equivocamente.   [f.

ambit, ăm'bĭt, s. circuito, m., circonferenza,

ambition, –bĭsh'ŭn, s. ambizione, f.

ambitious, –bĭsh'ŭs, s. ambizioso; **–ly,** ad. ambiziosamente.   [l' ambio.

amble, ăm'bl, s. ambio, m.; –, v. n. andar

ambler, –blŭr, s. cavallo che va d' ambio,

ambrosial, ămbrō'zhăl, a. ambrosio. [m.

ambs-ace, ămz'ăz, s. ambassi, m. pl.

ambulance, ăm'būlăns, s. ambulanza, f., spedale che segue un' armata, m.

ambuscade, –băskād', **ambush,** ăm'bŭsh, s. imboscata, f.; agguato, inganno, m.;
to lie in –, tender un agguato.

ameliorate, ămēl'yŏrāt, v. a. migliorare.

amelioration, –yŏrā'shŭn, s. miglioramento, m.   [tenuto.

amenable, ămē'năbl, a. responsabile;

amend, ămĕnd', v. a. amendare; –, v. n. ammendarsi; correggersi; tornare in salute.

amendable, –ăbl, a. ammendabile, che può racconciarsi.   [riforma, f.

amendment, –mĕnt, s. ammendamento, m.;

amends, ămĕndz', s. ammenda, f.; ricompensa, f.   [volezza, f.

amenity, ămĕn'ĭtĭ, s. amenità, f.; piacearmerce, ămărs', v. a. imporre una multa.

amercement, –mĕnt, s. ammenda, multa, f.

amethyst, ăm'ĕthĭst, s. ametista, f.

amiability, vedi amiableness.

amiable, ā'mĭăbl, a. amabile; affezionato, affabile, benigno.   [bilità, f.; grazia, f.

amiableness, –nĕs, s. amabilità, f.; affa-

amiably, –blĭ, ad. amabilmente; benignamente; con amorevolezza.

amianth, ăm'ĭănth, s. amianto, m.

amicable, ăm'ĭkăbl, a. amichevole, piacevole, da amico.

amicably, –ĭkăblĭ, ad. amichevolmente.

amice, ăm'ĭs, s. amitto, m.

amid(st), ămĭd(st'), pr. fra; nel mezzo.

amidships, –shĭps, ad. dirimpetto.

amiss, ămĭs', ad. male; a male, in mala parte.

amity, ăm'ĭtĭ, s. amicizia, concordia, f.

ammonia, ămmō'nĭă, s. ammoniaca, f.

ammunition, –mŭnĭsh'ŭn, s. munizione, f.; – **bread,** s. pane di munizione, m.

amnesty, ăm'nĕstĭ, s. amnistia, f., perdono generale, m.

among(st), ămŭng(st'), pr. fra, tra, infra.

amorous, ăm'ŏrŭs, a. amoroso; **–ly,** ad. amorosamente, con amore.

amorousness, –nĕs, s. amorevolezza, affabilità, f.   [fezione, f.

amorphous, ămŏr'fŭs, a. amorfo.

amount, ămŏŭnt', s. montante, m.; somma totale, f.; –, v. n. montare; arrivare; ascendere.

amour, ămōr', s. intrigo amoroso, m.

amphibian, ămfĭb'ĭăn, s. anfibio, animale che vive in terra ed in acqua, m.

amphibious, –fĭb'ĭŭs, a. anfibio.

amphitheatre, –fĭthē'ătŭr, s. anfiteatro,

ample, ăm'pl, a. ampio, largo.   [m.

ampleness, –nĕs, s. ampiezza, f.; grandezza, f.   [cazione, f.

amplification, –plĭfĭkā'shŭn, s. amplifi-

amplify, ăm'plĭfī, v. a. amplificare; esagerare; –, v. n. diffondersi; distendersi.

amplitude, ăm'plĭtūd, s. ampiezza, f.

amply, ăm'plĭ, ad. ampiamente, copiosamente, abbondantemente.

amputate, ăm'pŭtāt, v. a. amputare.

amputation, –tā'shŭn, s. amputazione, f.

amuck, ămŭk', ad. furiosamente.

amulet, ăm'ŭlĕt, s. amuleto, m.

amuse, ămūz', v. a. trattenere, divertire.

amusement, –mĕnt, s. trattenimento, m.; passatempo, spasso, m.

amusing, –zĭng, **amusive,** –sĭv, a. dilettevole; **–ly,** ad. piacevolmente.

an, ăn, art. uno, una.   [anabattisti, f.

anabaptism, ănăbăp'tĭzm, s. eresia degli

anabaptist, –tĭst, s. anabattista, m.

anachronism, ănăk'rŏnĭzm, s. anacronismo, m.   [ad. per analogia.

analogical, ănălŏj'ĭkăl, a. analogico; **–ly,**

analogous, ănăl'ŏgŭs, a. analogo, simile.

analogy, ănăl'ŏjĭ, s. analogia, conformità, f.

analyse, ăn'ălĭz, v. a. analizzare.

analysis, ănăl'ĭsĭs, s. analisi, f.

analyst, ăn'ălĭst, s. analista, m.

analytic(al), –lĭt'ĭk(ăl), a. analitico; **–ly,** ad. per via d' analisi.

anarchic(al), ănăr'kĭk(ăl), a. anarchico.

anarchy, ăn'ărkĭ, s. anarchia, f.

anathema, ănăth'ĕmă, s. anatema, f.; scomunica, f.   [scomunicare.

anathematize, –mătīz, v.a. anatemizzare,

anatomical, –tŏm'ĭkăl, a. anatomico; **–ly,** ad. anatomicamente.

anatomist, *ănăt'ŏmĭst,* s. anatomista, anatomico m.

anatomize, *ănăt'ŏmīz,* v. a. anotomizzare.

anatomy, *ănăt'ŏmĭ,* s. anatomia, f.

ancestor, *ăn'sĕstŭr,* s. antenato, m.; predecessore, m. [tario.

ancestral, *ănsĕs'trăl,* a. d' antenati, eredi-

ancestry, *ăn'sĕstrĭ,* s. schiatta; razza, f.

anchor, *ăng'kŭr,* s. ancora, f.; –, v. n. gittar l' ancora, ancorare.

anchorage, *–kŭrăj,* s. ancoramento, m.

anchorite, *ăn'kŏrīt,* s. anacoreta, eremita,

anchovy, *–chŏ'vĭ,* s. acciuga, f. [m.

ancient, *ăn'shĕnt,* a. antico, vecchio; **–ly,** ad. anticamente.

ancientness, *–shĕntnĕs,* s. anzianità, f.

ancientry, *–shĕntrĭ,* s. il lustro d' un' and, *ănd,* c, c, ed. [antica stirpe.

andiron, *ăn'dīrn,* s. alare, m.

anecdote, *ăn'ĕkdōt,* s. aneddoto, m.

anemone, *ănĕm'ŏnĕ,* s. anemone, m.

anent, *ănĕnt',* pr. concernente.

anew, *ănū',* ad. di nuovo, ancora.

angel, *ăn'jĕl,* s. angiolo, m.

angelic(al), *ănjĕl'ĭk(ăl),* a. angelico.

anger, *ăng'gŭr,* s. collera, ira, f.; stizza, f.; –, v. a. adirare, irritare; stizzare.

angle, *ăng'gl,* s. amo (da pigliar pesci), m.; angolo, m.; –, v. a. pescare coll' amo;

angled, *–gld,* a. angoloso. [allettare.

angler, *–glŭr,* s. pescatore coll' amo, m.

anglicism, *ăng'glĭsĭzm,* s. anglicismo, m.

angling-line, *ăng'glĭng lĭn,* s. lenza, f.

angling-rod, *–rŏd,* s. verga, alla quale s' appica la lenza, f. [mente.

angrily, *ăng'grĭlĭ,* ad. con collera, irata-

angry, *ăng'grĭ,* a. irato, collerico. [m.

anguish, *ăng'gwĭsh,* s. angoscia, f., affanno,

angular, *ăn'gŭlăr,* a. angolare, angoloso.

angularity, *–lăr'ĭtĭ,* s. angolarità, f.

anigh, *ănī',* pr. da vicino. [notte.

anight(s), *ănīt('s),* ad. di notte, in tempo di

anil, *ăn'ĭl,* s. pianta onde si cava l' indaco.

animadversion, *ănĭmădvŭr'shŭn,* s. osservazione, f.; biasimo, m.

animadvert, *–mădvŭrt',* v. a. osservare, considerare; notare; censurare. [malc.

animal, *ăn'ĭmăl,* s. animale, m.; –, a. ani-

animalcule, *–măl'kŭl,* s. animaletto, m.

animality, *–ĭtĭ,* s. animalità, f.

animate, *ăn'ĭmăt,* v. a. animare; incoraggiare; –, a. animato, brioso.

animation, *–mā'shŭn,* s. animazione, f.; vivacità, f. [core, m.

animosity, *–mŏs'ĭtĭ,* s. animosità. f.; ran-

animus, *ăn'ĭmŭs,* s. animo, m.; volontà, f.

anise, *ăn'ĭs,* s. anice, m. [intenzione, f.

aniseed, *ăn'ĭsĕd,* s. anice, f.; anisetto, m.

ankle, *ăng'kl,* s. collo del piede, m.

ankle-bone, *–bōn,* s. caviglia del piede, f.

annals, *ăn'nălz,* s. pl. annali, m. pl.

anneal, *ănnēl',* v. a. temporare (il vetro).

annex, *–nĕks',* v. a. giugnere, unire; –, s. annesso, m. [connessione, f.

annexation, *–nĕksă'shŭn,* s. aggiunzione, f.

annihilate, *–nī'hĭlāt,* v. a. annichiliare,

annihilation, *–hĭl'shŭn,* s. annichilimento; distruzione, f.

anniversary, *–nĭvŭr'sări,* a. annuale; –, s. anniversario, m.

annotate, *ăn'nŏtāt,* v. a. annotare.

annotation, *–tă'shŭn,* s. annotazione, f.; osservazione, f.

announce, *–nŏŭns',* v. a. annunziare, avvisare, avvertire; pubblicare. [f.

announcement, *–mĕnt,* s. annunziazione,

annoy, *ănnŏ',* v. a. annoiare, molestare.

annoyance, *–ăns,* s. annoio, m.

annoying, *–ĭng,* a. molesto, importuno.

annual, *ăn'nŭăl,* a. annuale; **–ly,** ad. annualmente, d' anno in anno.

annuitant, *–nū'ĭtănt,* s. pensionante, m.

annuity, *–nū'ĭtĭ,* s. rendita annuale, f.

annul, *ănnŭl',* v. a. annullare, estinguere.

annular, *ăn'nŭlăr,* a. annulare.

annulet, *ăn'nŭlĕt,* s. piccolo anello, m.

annulment, *–nŭl'mĕnt,* s. annullazione, f.

annunciation, *–nŭnshĭă'shŭn,* s. annunziazione, f.; annunzio del angelo, m.

anodyne, *ăn'ŏdīn,* a. (med.) anodino.

anoint, *ănŏĭnt',* v. a. ugnere, unguentare; (vulg.) bastonare, randellare.

anomalous, *ănŏm'ălăs,* a. anomalo, irregolare; **–ly,** ad. irregolarmente.

anomaly, *ănŏm'ălĭ,* s. anomalia, irregolarità, f.

anon, *ănŏn',* ad. adesso adesso, fra poco; subito; **ever and –,** ad ogni momento.

anonymous, *ănŏn'ĭmŭs,* a. anonimo; **–ly,** ad. anonimamente.

another, *ănŭth'ŭr,* a. altro; differente; **one** – l' un l' altro.

answer, *ăn'sŭr,* v. n. risposta, replica, f.; –, v. a. & n. rispondere, replicare; corrispondere; essere mallevadore; (com.) soddisfare. [veniente, conforme.

answerable, *–ăbl,* a. corrispondente, con-

answerableness, *–ăblnĕs,* s. convenienza, f.; conformità, f.; responsabilità, f.

ant, *ănt,* s. formica, f. [m.

antagonism, *ăntăg'ŏnĭsm,* s. antagonismo,

antagonist, *–ŏnĭst,* s. antagonista, m.; rivale, avversario, emulo, m.

antarctic, *ăntărk'tĭk,* a. antartico.

ant-bear, *ănt'băr,* **ant-eater,** *–ētŭr,* s. formichiere, m. [priorità, f.

antecedence, *ăntĕsē'dĕns,* s. precedenza,

antecedent, *–sē'dĕnt,* a. antecedente, precedente; **–ly,** ad. antecedentemente, precedentemente, innanzi. [f.

antechamber, *–tshām'bŭr,* s. anticamera,

antedate, *ăn'tĕdāt,* v. a. antidatare.

antediluvian, *–dĭlū'vĭăn,* a. antidiluviano.

antelope, *ăn'tĕlōp,* s. antilope, m., gazzella, f. [diano.

antemeridian, *–mĕrĭd'ĭăn,* s. antemeri-

antennae, *–tĕn'nē,* s. pl. antenne, f. pl., tentacoli di alcuni insetti, m. pl.

antepenultimate, *–pĕnŭl'tĭmăt,* a. (gr.) antepenultimo. [dente.

anterior, *ăntē'rĭŭr,* a. anteriore, prece-

anteriority, *–rĭ'ĭtĭ,* s. anteriorità, priorità, f.

anthem, *ăn'thĕm,* s. antifona, f.

anther, ăn' thŭr, s. antera, f.
ant-hill, ănt' hĭl, s. formicaio, m.
anthology, ănthŏl' ŏjĭ, s. antologia, f.
Anthony's-fire (St.), ăn' tŏnĭs jĭr, s. risipola, eresipola, f.
anthracite, ăn' thrăsĭt, s. antracite, f.
anthropology, —thrŏpŏl' ŏjĭ, s. antropologia, f. [zanni, giullare, m.
antic, ăn' tĭk, a. grottesco; —, s. buffone,
antichrist, ăn' tĭkrĭst, s. anticristo, m.
anticipate, ăntĭs' ĭpăt, v. a. anticipare,
prevenire. [prevenzione, f.
anticipation, —sĭpā' shăn, s. anticipazione,
anticipatory, —tĭs' ĭpătŭrĭ, a. anticipato.
antidote, ăn' tĭdŏt, s. antidoto, m.
antimony, ăn' tĭmŏnĭ, s. antimonio, m.
antipathy, ăntĭp' ăthĭ, s. antipatia, avversione, repugnanza, f.
antipodes, ăn' tĭpōdz, s. pl. antipodi, m.pl.
antipope, ăn' tĭpōp, s. antipapa, m.
antiquarian, ăntĭkwā' rĭăn, antiquary,
ăn' tĭkwărĭ, s. antiquario, m.
antiquated, ăn' tĭkwătĕd, a. antiquato.
antique, ăntēk', s. anticaglia, f.; —, a.
antico.
antiquity, —tĭk' kwĭtĭ, s. antichità, f.
antiseptic, —sĕp' tĭk, a. antisettico.
antithesis, ăntĭth' ĕsĭs, s. antitesi, f.
antler, ănt' lŭr, s. pugnale delle corna del
anvil, ăn' vĭl, s. incudine, f. [cervo, m.
anxiety, ăngzī' ĭtĭ, s. ansietà, f.; affanno, m.
anxious, ăngk' shŭs, a. ansioso; —ly, ad.
con ansietà, con ansia.
any, ĕn' nĭ, a. & pn. ogni, ognuno, chiunque, qualunque; —how, come si voglia;
— longer, più lungo tempo; —one, —
body, qualcuno, ciascheduno, ognuno;
—more, più; —thing, ogni cosa, che che
si sia; —where, altrove. [forte.
apace, ăpās', ad. presto, prestamente,
apart, ăpärt', ad. da parte, da canto.
apartment, —mĕnt, s. appartamento, m.
apathetic, ăpăthĕt' ĭk, a. apatico.
apathy, ăp' ăthĭ, s. apatia, f.; indolenza, f.
ape, ăp, s. scimia, f.; babbuino, m.
ape, —, v. a. contraffare, imitare.
apeak, ăpēk', ad. a piombo; perpendicolarmente. [aperitivo.
aperient, ăpē' rĭĕnt, a. (med.) aperiente,
aperture, ăp' ărtŭr, s. apertura, f.
apery, ā' pŭrĭ, s. scimmieria, zannata, f.
apex, ā' pĕks, s. colmo, m., sommità, f.;
cima, f. [sima, f.
aphorism, ăf' ŏrĭzm, s. aforismo, m.; mas-
aphoristic, —rĭs' tĭk, a. aforistico.
apiary, ā' pĭărĭ, s. arnia, f.; alveare, m.
apiece, ăpēs', ad. a testa, per ciascuno.
apish, ā' pĭsh, a. di scimmia; giullaresco;
—ly, ad. da scimmia; buffonescamente.
apishness, —nĕs, s. buffoneria, f.; giul-
leria, zannata, f.
Apocalypse, ăpŏk' ălĭps, s. apocalissi.
apocrypha, —rĭfă, s. pl. libri apocrifi, m.pl.
apocryphal, —rĭfăl, a. apocrifo, non autentico, sospetto.
apologetic, ăpŏlŏjĕt' ĭk, a. apologetico.
apologise, ăpŏl' ŏĭz, v. n. far un' apologia.

apologist, —ŏjĭst, s. apologista, m.
apology, —ŏjĭ, s. apologia, difesa, f.
apophthegm, ăp' ŏthĕm, s. apoftemma, f.
apoplectic, ăpŏplĕk' tĭk, a. apoplettico.
apoplexy, ăp' ŏplĕksĭ, s. apoplessia, f.
apostasy, ăpŏs' tăsĭ, s. apostasia, f.
apostate, —tăt, s. apostata, rinnegato, m.
apostatise, —tătĭz, v. n. apostatare.
apostle, ăpŏs' sl, s. apostolo, m.
apostleship, —shĭp, s. apostolato, m.
apostolic, ăpŏstŏl' ĭk, a. apostolico.
apostrophe, ăpŏs' trŏfĕ, s. (gr.) apostrofo,
m.; apostrofe (retorica), f.
apostrophise, —trŏfĭz, v. a. apostrofare;
indirizzare la parola ad altra persona.
apothecary, ăpŏth' ĕkărĭ, s. speziale, m.;
—'s shop, spezieria, f.
apotheosis, ăpŏthē' ŏsĭs, s. apoteosi, f.
appal, ăppăl', v. a. stupefare; spaventare.
appanage, ăp' pănăj, s. appanaggio, m.
apparatus, ăppărā' tŭs, s. apparato, m.;
apparecchio, m.
apparel, —păr' ĕl, s. addobbo, m.; vestimento, vestito, m.; —, v. a. addobbare,
abbellire; vestire.
apparent, —pā' rĕnt, a. apparente, evidente;
—ly, ad. apparentemente, chiaramente.
apparition, —părĭsh' ăn, s. apparizione,
visione, f. [dello, m.
apparitor, —păr' ĭtŭr, s. cursore, m.; bi-
appeal, ăppēl', s. appellazione, f.; accusa,
f.; —, v. n. appellare; accusare.
appear, ăppēr', v. n. apparire; comparire;
farsi vedere.
appearance, —ăns, s. apparenza, f.; probabilità, f.; first—, apparenza, presenza,
f.; at first —, a prima vista.
appeasable, —pē' zăbl, a. placabile.
appease, —pēz', v. a. placare; quietare.
appellant, —pĕl' lănt, s. appellante, m.
appellation, —lā' shăn, s. appellazione, f.
appellative, —pĕl' lătĭv, s. (gr.) appellativo, m.
appellee, —pĕllē', s. accusato, m.
appellor, —pĕl' lŭr, s. appellante, m.
append, —pĕnd', v. a. appendere, sospendere. [m.
appendage, —ĭdj, s. accessorio, intimato,
appendix, —dĭks, s. appendice, f.; dipendenza, f. [convenirsi.
appertain, —pŭrtăn', v. n. appartenere;
appetence, ăp' pĕtĕns, s. appetenza, f.;
brama, f.
appetite, ăp' pĕtĭt, s. appetito, m.; avidità,
appetiser, —pĕtĭzăr, s. stimolante l' appetito, m. [f.
appetite, ăp' pĕtĭt, s. appetito, m.; avidità,
applaud, —plăd', v. a. applaudire, approvare. [mante, m.
applauder, —dŭr, s. applauditore, accla-
applause, —plăz', s. applauso, m.; acclamazione, f.
apple, ăp' pl, s. pomo, m., mela, f.
apple-tree, —trē, s. melo, pomo, m.
appliance, —plī' ăns, s. adattamento, m.
applicability, —plĭkăbĭl' ĭtĭ, s. aderenza,
convenienza, f.

applicable, *ăp' plĭkăbl,* a. applicabile; convenevole.
applicably, *-kăblĕ,* ad. convenevolmente.
applicant, *ăp' plĭkănt,* s. applicatore, m.;
applicatrice, f.
application, *-kă' shăn,* s. applicazione,
f.; ricorso, rifugio, m.
apply, *ăpplī',* v. a. applicare, adattare;
—, v. n. applicarsi ; impiegarsi.
appoint, *-pŏint',* v. a. ordinare ; regolare;
destinare, assegnare.   [nario, m.
appointee, *-pŏintē',* s. nominato, funzio-
appointment, *-pŏint'mĕnt,* s. decreto,
mandato, m.; assegnamento, m.
apportion, *-pŏr' shăn,* v. a. proporzionare.
apportionment, *-mĕnt,* s. distribuzione
eguale, f.   [esaminare.
appose, *ăppōz',* v. a. (jur.) interrogare,
apposite, *ăp' pŏzĭt,* a. proprio, congruo;
—ly, ad. propriamente, convenevolmente.
appositeness, *-nĕs,* s. proprietà, f.; convenienza, f.
apposition, *-zĭsh' ŭn,* s. apposizione, f.
appraise, *ăpprāz',* v. a. apprezzare, stimare.
appraisement, *-mĕnt,* s. estimazione, f.,
apprezzamento, m.   [tore, m.
appraiser, *-ăr,* s. apprezzatore, estima-
appreciable, *-prē' shĭăbl,* a. apprezzabile,
estimabile.   [tare, pregiare.
appreciate, *-shĭāt,* v. a. stimare, valu-
appreciation, *-shĭā' shăn,* s. apprezzamento, m., stima, f.   [tivo.
appreciative, *-prē' shĭătĭv,* a. apprezza-
apprehend, *-prĕhĕnd',* v. a. prendere,
catturare; intendere, conoscere ; temere.
apprehension, *-hĕn' shăn,* s. cattura, f.;
concezione, f.; comprendimento, intelletto,
m.; paura, f., timore, m.   [pauroso.
apprehensive, *-hĕn' sĭv,* a. apprensivo;
apprentice, *-prĕn' tĭs,* s. apprendista, m.;
fattorino, m.; —, v. a. prendere per fattorino.   [m.
apprenticeship, *-shĭp,* s. apprendistato,
apprise, *-prīz',* v. a. informare.
approach, *-prōch',* s. avvicinamento, m.;
accesso, m.; —, v. a. avvicinare ; approssimare; —, v. n. avvicinarsi, accostarsi.
approachable, *-ăbl,* a. accessibile.
approbation, *-prŏbā' shăn,* s. approvazione, f.   [tivo, approvante.
approbatory, *ăp' prŏbătărĭ,* a. approva-
appropriate, *-prō' prĭăt,* v. a. appropriare; —, a. appropriato ; convenevole,
idoneo, acconcio.
approval, *-prō' văl,* s. approvazione, f.
approve, *-prōv',* v. a. approvare; avere
per buono; accettare, ricevere.
approximate, *-prŏks'ĭmăt,* v. n. approssimarsi, accostarsi ; —, a. prossimo, vicino.
approximation, *-mă' shăn,* s. approssimazione, f.   [nenza, attenenza, f.
appurtenance, *-păr' tĕnăns,* s. apparte-
apricot, *ā' prĭkŏt,* s. albicocca, f.
April, *ā' prĭl,* s. aprile, m.
April-fool, *-fōl,* s. uno a cui si ficca una
grossa fandonia il primo giorno d' aprile,
m.

apron, *ā' prŭn (-prŏn),* s. grembiale, m.
apsis, *ăp' sĭs,* s. abside, f.
apt, *ăpt',* a. atto, idoneo, acconcio; —ly,
ad. attamente, acconciamente.
aptitude, *ăp' tĭtūd,* s. attitudine, naturale
disposizione, f.   [conformità, f.
aptness, *ăpt' nĕs,* s. attezza, convenienza, f.;
aqua-fortis, *ăkwăfŏr' tĭs,* s. acquaforte, f.
aquatic, *ăkwăt' ĭk,* a. aquatico.
aqueduct, *ăk' wĕdŭkt,* s. acquedotto, m.;
canale, m.
aqueous, *ā' kwĕŭs,* a. acquoso.
aquiline, *ăk' wĭlĭn,* a. aquilino, d' aquila.
arabesque, *ăr' ăbĕsk,* a. (a)rabesco.
arable, *ăr' ăbl,* a. arabile.
arbalist, *ăr' bălĭst,* s. balestra, f.
arbiter, *-bĭtăr,* s. arbitro, m.
arbitrament, *-bĭ' rămĕnt,* s. arbitrio, m.
arbitrarily, *ăr' bĭtrărĭlĭ,* ad. arbitraria-
mente.   [luta, f.
arbitrariness, *-trărĭnĕs,* s. autorità asso-
arbitrary, *-trărĭ,* a. arbitrario ; dispotico.
arbitrate, *-bĭtrāt,* v a. arbitrare, giudicare como arbitro.
arbitration, *-trā' shăn,* arbitrement,
-bĭt' rĕmĕnt, s. arbitrato, compromesso, m.
arbitrator, *-trā' tăr,* s. arbitro, m.
arborescent, *-bŏrĕs' sĕnt,* a. arborescente,
simile ad un albero.   [m.
arbour, *ăr' băr,* s. pergola, f., pergolato,
arbute, *ăr' bŭt,* s. corbezzolo, m.   [m.
arc, *ărk,* s. arco, m.; segmento (d' un cerchio),
arcade, *ărkād',* s. arco, m., volta, f.
arcanum, *-kă' năm,* s. arcano, segreto, m.
arch, *ărch,* s. volta, f.; arco, m.; capo, m.;
—, v. a. archeggiare.
arch, —, a. astuto: (in comp.) arci . .
archæological, *ărkĕŏlŏj' ĭkăl,* a. archeo-
logico.
archæology, *-kĕŏl' ŏjĕ,* s. archeologia, f.
archangel, *ărkānj' ĕl,* s. arcangelo, m.
archbishop, *ărchbĭsh' ŏp,* s. arcivescovo,
m.   [m.
archbishopric, *-prĭk,* s. arcivescovato,
archduchess, *-dăch' ĕs,* s. arciduchessa, f.
archduke, *-dăk,* s. arciduca, m.
archdukedom, *-dŏm,* s. arciducato, m.
archer, *ărch' ăr,* s. arciere, m.
archery, *-ărĭ,* s. arte di tirare l' arco, m.
archiepiscopal, *ărkĭĕpĭs' kŏpăl,* a. d' arcivescovo.
architect, *ăr' kĭtĕkt,* s. architetto, m.
architectural, *-tĕk' tărăl,* a. architettonico.   [f.
architecture, *ăr' kĭtĕktăr,* s. architettura,
archives, *ăr' kīvz,* s. pl. archivio, m.
archivist, *-kĭvĭst,* s. archivista, m.
archly, *ărch' lĕ,* ad. giocosamente.
archness, *-nĕs,* s. malizietta, astuzia, f.
archpriest, *-prēst',* s. arciprete, m.
arch-stone, *-stōn,* s. peduccio di volta, m.
archway, *-wā,* s. volta, f.; porticina, f.
arctic, *ărk' tĭk,* a. artico, settentrionale.
ardency, *ăr' dĕnsĭ,* ardour, *ăr' dăr,* s. ardore, m.; fervore, m.; passione, f.
ardent, *-dĕnt,* a. ardente; appassionato
—ly, ad. ardentemente; con passione.
arduous, *-dŭăs,* a. arduo; difficile.

area, *d'rĕă,* s. area, f.; spazio, m.

arenaceous, *ărĕnă'shŭs,* a. sabbioso.

argentation, *ărjĕntă'shŭn,* s. l' inargentare, m. [argento.

argentiferous, *-tĭf'ărŭs,* a. producente

argil, *ăr'jĭl,* s. argilla, argiglia, f.

argillaceous, *-lă'shŭs,* a. argilloso.

argue, *ăr'gŭ,* v. n. arguire; disputare, contestare; accusare.

argument, *-gŭmĕnt,* s. argomento, m.; indizio, m.; controversia, f. [tazione, f.

argumentation,—*mĕntă'shŭn,* s.argomen-

argumentative, *-mĕn'tătĭv,* a. dimostrativo.

arid, *ăr'ĭd,* a. arido, secco; sterile.

aridity, *ărĭd'ĭtĭ,* s. aridità, f.

aright, *ărīt',* ad. dirittamente; precisamente; sanamente; **to set –,** aggiustare.

arise, *ărīz',* v. n. ir. levarsi; venire, derivare, procedere.

aristocracy, *ărĭstŏk'răsī,* s. aristocrazia, f.

aristocrat, *ăr'ĭstŏkrăt (ărĭs'tŏkrăt),* s. aristocratico, m.

aristocratical, *-krăt'ĭkăl,* a. aristocratico; **-ly,** ad. aristocraticamente.

arithmetic, *ărĭth'mĕtĭk,* s. aritmetica, f.

arithmetical, *-mĕt'ĭkăl,* a. aritmetico; **-ly,** ad. aritmeticamente.

arithmetician,—*tĭsh'ăn,* s. aritmetico, m.

ark, *ărk,* s. arca, f.; **– of the Covenant,** arca dell' alleanza, f.

arm, *ărm,* s. braccio, m.; ramo, m.; potere, m.; arme, arma, f.; –, v. a. armare; munire; guernire; –, v. n. armarsi; munirsi.

armament, *ăr'mămĕnt,* s. armamento, m.

arm-chair, *ărm'chăr,* s. sedia a bracciuoli, f.

armful, *-fŭl,* s. bracciata, f. [f.

arm-hole, *-hŏl,* s. ascella, f.

armistice, *ăr'mĭstĭs,* s. armistizio, m.

armlet, *ărm'lĕt,* s. braccialetto, bracciale, m.

armour, *ăr'mŭr,* s. armatura, f.; armi, f. pl.

armour-bearer, *-bărăr,* s. scudiere, m.

armourer, *ăr'mŭrăr,* s. armaiuolo, m.

armoury, *-mŭrī,* s. armatura, f.; arsenale, m.

arm-pit, *ărm'pĭt,* s. ascella, f. [m.

army, *ăr'mĭ,* s. esercito, m.; armata, f.

aroma, *ărŏ'mă,* s. aroma, m.

aromatic, *-măt'ĭk,* a. aromatico.

around, *ărŏŭnd',* ad. & pr. intorno, all' intorno, attorno, d' attorno.

arouse, *ărŏŭz',* v. a. svegliare; stimolare.

arquebuse, *ăr'kĕbŭz,* s. archibuso, m.

arquebusier, *-băzăr',* s. archibusiere, m.

arraign, *ărrān',* v. a. assettare; dinunziare. [cesso, m.

arraignment, *-mĕnt,* s. accusa, f.; processo, m.

arrange, *-rănj',* v. a. porre in ordine; assettare, aggiustare. [m.

arrangement, *-mĕnt,* s. ordine, m.; assetto.

arrant, *ăr'rănt,* a. mero, vero, di prima riga; **-ly,** ad. perversamente, corrotta- [mente.

arras, *ăr'răz,* s. arazzo, m. (panno).

array, *ărrā',* s. vestito, abito, m.; schiera, f.; –, v. a. vestire, abbigliare; schierare.

arrear, *ărrēr',* s. debito, m.; retroguardia (d' un esercito), f.; **to be in –s,** restar debitore.

arrest, *ărrĕst',* s. arresto, m., cattura, f.; –, v. a. arrestare, catturare.

arrival, *ărrī'văl,* s. arrivo, m., venuta, f.

arrive, *ărrīv',* v. n. arrivare; venire; accadere. [sunzione, f.; temerità, f.

arrogance, *ăr'rŏgăns,* s. arroganza, presunzione, f.

arrogant, *-rŏgănt,* a. arrogante, presuntuoso; **-ly,** ad. arrogantemente, orgogliosamente. [garsi.

arrogate, *-rŏgăt,* v. n. presumere; arrogare.

arrogation, *-gă'shŭn,* s. pretensione, f.

arrow, *ăr'rŏ,* s. saetta, freccia, f.; dardo,

arsenal, *ăr'sĕnăl,* s. arsenale, m. [m.

arsenic, *ăr'sĕnĭk,* s. arsenico, m.

arson, *ăr'sŏn,* s. incendiario, m.

art, *ărt,* s. arte, f.; professione, f.; industria, f.; **black –,** negromanzia, f.

arterial, *ărtē'rĭăl,* a. arterioso.

artery, *ăr'tărĭ,* s. arteria, f.

artful, *ărt'fŭl,* a. artificioso; abile; **-ly,** ad. con arte, maestramente. [f.; astuzia, f.

artfulness, *-nĕs,* s. maestria, destrezza,

artichoke, *ăr'tĭchŏk,* s. carciofo, m.

article, *ăr'tĭkl,* s. articulo, m.; –, v. n. stipulare, patteggiare.

articulate, *-tĭk'ŭlăt,* a. articolato, distinto; **-ly,** ad. distintamente; –, v. a. articolare; pronunziare distintamente.

articulation, *-lă'shŭn,* s. articolazione; giuntura, f.

artifice, *ăr'tĭfĭs,* s. artificio, m., astuzia, f.

artificer, *-tĭf'ĭsăr,* s. artifice, artista, m.; artigiano, m.

artificial, *-fĭsh'ăl,* a. artificiale, artificioso; **-ly,** ad. artificialmente, con artificio.

artillery, *-tĭl'lărī,* s. artiglieria, f. [ficio.

artillery-man, *-măn,* s. artigliere, m.

artillery-practice, *-prăktĭs,* s. cannonata, f.

artisan, *ăr'tĭzăn,* s. artigiano, artifice, **m.**

artist, *ăr'tĭst,* s. artista, artefice, m.

artistic, *-tĭs'tĭk,* a. artistico.

artless, *ărt'lĕs,* a. fatto senz' arte; semplice; –, ad. senz' arte, naturalmente.

artlessness, *-nĕs,* s. naturalezza, innocenza, f.

as, *ăz,* ad. & c. mentre, come; così; quale; pressochè; perchè, poichè; **– for,** come per; **– for to,** in quanto a; **– it were,** per così dire.

asbestos, *ăsbĕs'tŭs,* s. amianto, m.

ascend, *ăssĕnd',* v. a. & n. ascendere, montare. [nante; –, s. ascendente, m.

ascendant, *-ănt,* a. superiore, predominante.

ascendency, *-dĕnsī,* s. influenza, f.; potere, m., facoltà, f. [ascendimento, m.

ascension, *-sĕn'shŭn,* s. ascensione, f.,

ascent, *-sĕnt',* s. salita, montata, f.; eminenza, f.; (rail.) salita, f.

ascertain, *-sărtān',* v. a. accertare; fissare; tassare, apprezzare.

ascetic, *ăssĕt'ĭk,* s. ascetico, m.

ascribe, *ăskrĭb',* v. a. ascrivere, attribuire; [imputare.

ash, *ăsh,* s. frassino, m.

ashamed, *ăshāmd',* a. vergognoso.

ash-coloured, *ăsh'kŭlŭrd,* a. cenericcio,

ashen, *ăsh'ĕn,* a. di frassino.

ashes, *ăsh'ŏz*, s. pl. cenere, f., ceneri, f. pl.
ash-hole, *-hŏl*, **ash-pan**, *-păn*, s. vaso cinerario, m.
ashore, *ăshŏr'*, ad. a terra, a riva; **to go** **—**, (mar.) prender terra, sbarcare.
Ash-Wednesday, *—wĕnz'dā*. s. mercoledì delle ceneri, m.
ashy, *ăsh'ĭ*, a. ceneroso.
aside, *ăsīd'*, ad. da parte, da banda.
ask, *ăsk*, v. a. domandare; chiedere; **to —** **out**, invitare;   [traverso; biccante.
askance, *ăskăns'*, **askant**, *-kănt'*, ad. a
askew, *ăskū'*, ad. biecamente, stortamente.
aslant, *ăslănt'*, ad. obliquamente.
asleep, *ăslēp'*, a. sonnacchioso; **to fall** **—**, addormentarsi.
asp, *ăsp*, s. aspide, m.
asparagus, *ăspăr'ăgăs*, s. sparagio, m.
aspect, *ăs'pĕkt*, s. aspetto, m.; vista, f.; aria, f.; apparenza, presenza, f.
aspen, *ăs'pĕn*, a. di aspide; **—**, s. aspide, f.
asperity, *-pĕr'ĭtĭ*, s. asprezza, ruvidezza, f.; severità, f,   [diffamare.
asperse, *-părs'*, v. a. aspergere; (fig.)
aspersion, *-păr'shăn*, s. aspersione, f.; (fig.) calunnia, diffamazione, f.
asphalt, *ăsfălt'*, s. asfalto, m.
asphyxia, *ăsfĭks'ĭă*, s. asfissia, f.
asphyxiate, *-fĭks'ĭăt*, v. a. asfissiare, soffocare.
aspirant, *ăspĭ'rănt*, s. aspirante, candidato, m.   [dato, m.
aspirate, *ăs'pĭrăt*, v. a. aspirare, pronunziare con aspirazione.   [bramosia.
aspiration, *-ră'shăn*, s. aspirazione, f.;
aspire, *ăspīr'*, v. n. aspirare; bramare.
asquint, *ăskwĭnt'*, ad. biecamente, di traverso.   [asina, f.
ass, *ăs*, s. asino. m.; miuchione, m.; **she —**,
assail, *ăssāl'*, v. a. assalire, attaccare.
assailable, *-ăbl*, a. che può esser assalito.
assailant, *-ănt*, **assailer**, *-ăr*, s. assalitore, aggressore, m.
assassin, *ăsăs'sĭn*, s. assassino, m.
assassinate, *-sĭnāt*, v. a. assassinare.
assassination, *-sĭnă'shăn*, s. assassinamento, assassinio, m.
assault, *ăssălt'*, s. assalto, m.; ingiuria, f.; **—**, v. a. assaltare, attaccare.
assay, *ăssā'*, s. prova, f.; sperimento, m.; **—**, v. a. provare; assaggiare; **—**, v. n. tentare; provarsi.
assayer, *-ăr*, s. saggiatore, m.
ass-driver, *ăs'drīvăr*, s. asinaio, m.
assemblage, *ăssĕm'blăj*, s. adunamento, m.; concorso, m.
assemble, *-sĕm'bl*, v. a. adunare, riunire; **—**, v. n. adunarsi; unirsi.
assembly, *-sĕm'blĭ*, s. assemblea, f.; adunata, f.
assent, *-sĕnt'*, s. assenso, m.; consenso, m.; **—**, v. n. assentire, consentire.
assert, *-sŭrt'*, v. a. asserire; mantenere, sostenere, affermare.
assertion, *-sŭr'shăn*, s. asserzione, f.
assertive, *-sŭr'tĭv*, a. assertivo.
assess, *ăsĕs'*, v. a. tassare.
assessed, *-sĕst'*, a. diretto.

assessment, *-sĕs'mĕnt*, s. tassare, m.; tassa, f.; tassagione, f.
assessor, *-săr*, s. assessore, m.; tassatore, m.   [m. pl.
assets, *ăs'sĕts*, s. pl. (jur.) beni sufficienti,
asseverate, *-sĕv'ărăt*, v. a. asseverare, confermare con giuramento.
asseveration, *-vĕrā'shăn*, s. asseveranza, f.; affermazione, f.   [genza, f.
assiduity, *-sĭd'ŭĭtĭ*, s. assiduità, diligenza; **assiduous**, *-sĭd'ŭăs*, a. assiduo, diligente; **-ly**, ad. assiduamente; continuamente.
assign, *-sīn'*, v. a. assegnare, commettere, delegare.
assignable, *-ăbl*, a. che può assegnarsi.
assignation, *-sĭgnā'shăn*, s. assegnazione, f.; appuntamento, m.
assignee, *-sīnē'*, s. deputato, m.
assigner, *-sīn'ăr*, s. costituitore, m.
assignment, *-sīn'mĕnt*, s. consegnazione, f.; cessione, f.; deposito, m.
assimilate, *-sĭm'ŭlăt*, v. a. assomigliare; comparare.   [mento, paragone, m.
assimilation, *-mĭlă'shăn*, s. assomiglianza, f.
assist, *ăssĭst'*, v. a. assistere, soccorrere, aiutare.   [soccorso, m.
assistance, *-sĭs'tăns*, s. assistenza, f.,
assistant, *-tănt*, s. assistente, aiutatore, m.
assize, *ăssīz'* s. assise, f.; tariffa, f.; **—**, v. a. tassare; regolare.
associate, *-sō'shăăt*, s. associato, m.; compagno, m.: **—**, v. a. associare; accompagnare; praticare.
association, *-shă'shăn*, s. associazione, unione, f.; società, f.; taglia, f.
assonance, *ăs'sŏnăns*, s. assonanza, f.
assort, *ăssŏrt'*, v. a. assortire; classificare.
assortment, *-mĕnt*, s. assortimento, m.
assuage, *ăsswāj'*, v. a. alleviare; **—**, v. n. alleviarsi.   [conforto, m.
assuagement, *-mĕnt*, s. addolcimento, m.;
assume, *ăssūm'*, v. a. assumere, prendere; presumere, arrogarsi.
assuming, *-sū'mĭng*, a. presuntuoso.
assumption, *-săm'shăn*, s. presunzione, arroganza, f.   [danza, f.; costanza, f.
assurance, *ăshŏ'răns*, s. sicurezza, f.; fi-
assure, *ăshŏr'*, v. a. assicurare; affermare.
assuredly, *-rēdlĭ*, ad. sicuramente, certamente, per verità, senza dubbio.
asterisk, *ăs'tĕrĭsk*, s. asterisco, m.
astern, *ăstŭrn'*, ad. (mar.) per la poppa, in poppa.
asthma, *ăst'mă*, s. asma, f.
asthmatic, *-măt'ĭk*, a. asmatico.
astir, *ăstŭr'*, ad. in agitazione.
astonish, *ăstŏn'ĭsh*, v. a. stupire; stordire.
astonishingly, *-ĭnglĭ*, ad. maravigliosamente.   [sorpresa, f.
astonishment, *-mĕnt*, s. stupore, m.,
astound, *ăstŏŭnd'*, v. a. stordire, coster-
astral, *ăs'trăl*, a. astrale.   [nare.
astray, *ăstră'*, ad. fuor di via; **to lead —**, sviare.   [m.
astriction, *ăstrĭk'shăn*, s. astringimento,
astride, *ăstrīd'*, adv. a cavalcioni.
astringent, *ăstrĭn'jĕnt*, a. astringente, costrittivo.

astrologer, -trŏl'ŏjẽr, s. astrologo, m.
astrological, -trŏlŏj'ĭkăl, a. astrologico.
astrology, -trŏl'ŏjĭ, s. astrologia, f.
astronomer, -trŏn'ŏmẽr, s. astronomo, m.   [nomico.
astronomic(al), -trŏnŏm'ĭk(ăl), a. astro-
astronomy, -trŏn'ŏmĭ, s. astronomia, f.
astute, ăstūt', a. astuto, fino, accorto.
asunder, ăsŭn'dẽr, ad. separatamente; in due parti.
asylum, ăsī'lŭm, s. asilo, m. ; rifugio, m.
at, ăt, pr. a, ad ; da ; in ; per ; al, alla, agli, alle ; – first, alla prima ; – hand, appresso ; – home, a casa ; – last, in fine, finalmente ; – leisure, a bell' agio ; – once, subito, alla prima ; – least, almeno ; – present, per adesso ; – sea, sul mare ; – an end, finito ; – all, punto.
atheism, d'thēĭzm, s. ateismo, m.
atheist, ā'thēĭst, s. ateista, ateo, m.
atheistical, -ĭs'tĭkăl, a. ateistico.
athirst, ăthŭrst', a. assetato, sitibondo ;
–, ad. sitibondamente.
athlete, ăth'lēt, s. atleta, m.
athletic, -lĕt'ĭk, a. atletico, vigoroso.
athwart, -wărt', ad. & pr. a traverso, a
atilt, ătĭlt', ad. con botta.   [sghembo.
atlas, ăt'lăs, s. atlante, m.
atmosphere, ăt'mŏsfẽr, s. atmosfera, f.
atmospheric, -fĕr'ĭk, a. atmosferico.
atom, ăt'ŏm, s. atomo, m.   [d'atomi.
atomic(al), ătŏm'ĭk(ăl), a. consistente
atone, ătōn', v. a. espiare ; purgare.
atonement, -mĕnt, s. espiazione, f. ; placamento, m.
atop, ătŏp', ad. in alto ; sulla sommità.
atrabilious, ătrăbĭl'ĭŭs, a. atrabiliare, malinconico.
atrocious, ătrō'shŭs, a. atroce, orribile, enorme ; –ly, ad. atrocemente ; orribilmente.   [leratezza, f.
atrocity, ătrŏs'ĭtĭ, s. atrocità, f. ; scel-
attach, ătăch', v. a. arrestare, catturare ; guadagnare ; sequestrare. [d'ambasciata,m.
attaché, ătăshā', s. applicato, m. ; addetto
attachment, -tăch'mĕnt, s. aderenza, f., affetto, m. ; sequestro, m.
attack, ătăk', s. attacco, assalto, m. ; –, v. a. attaccare, assalire.   [acquistare.
attain, ătăn', v. a. ottenere, conseguire,
attainable, -ăbl, a. acquistabile.
attainder, -dẽr, s. (jur.) convinzione, f.
attainment, -mĕnt, s. acquisto, m.
attaint, -tănt', v. a. macchiare ; corrom-
pere ; disonorare ; infettare ; accusare ; –, s. macchia, f. ; ignominia, f.
attar, ăt'tăr, s. olio rosato, m.
attempt, -tĕmt', s. tentativa, f. ; sperimento, m.; intrapresa, f. ; –, v. a. provare, tentare ; intraprendere.
attend, -tĕnd', v. a. accompagnare ; –, v. n. stare attento, attendere ; osservare.
attendance, -dns, s. servizio, f. ; assi-
duità, f. ; cura, f. ; corteggio, m.; to
dance –, far spalliera.   [m.
attendant, -dnt, s. servitore, m.; seguace,

attention, -tĕn'shŭn, s. attenzione, f. ; to
give –, to pay –, far attenzione.
attentive, -tĕn'tĭv, a. attento, ufficioso ;
–ly, ad. attentamente, con cura.
attenuate, -tĕn'ādt, v. a. attenuare, affievolire ; diminuire.   [f.
attenuation, -năd'shŭn, s. attenuazione,
attest, -tĕst', v. a. attestare, certificare.
attestation, -td'shŭn, s. attestazione, testimonianza, f.
attic, ăt'tĭk, a. elegante ; delicato ; –, s. abbaino, m.; soffita, f.
attire, ăttīr', s. abbigliamento, m.; –, v. a. acconciare ; abbellire, ornare.
attitude, ăt'tĭtăd, s. attitudine, f. ; posa-
tura, f.   [la posatura.
attitudinarian, -dĭnă'rĭăn, s. chi dirige
attitudinise, -tă'dĭnĭz, v. a. posare.   [m.
attorney, -tăr'nĭ, s. notaro, procuratore,
attract, -trăkt', v. a. attrarre ; allettare.
attraction, -trăk'shŭn, s. attrazione, f. ; allettamento, m.   [per attrazione.
attractive, -tĭv, a. attrattivo ; –ly, ad.
attributable, -trĭb'ŭtăbl, a. imputabile.
attribute, ăt'trĭbūt, s. attributo, m.; proprietà, f. ; –, -trĭb'ŭt, v. a. attribuire, imputare, ascrivere.   [commendazione, f.
attribution, -bū'shŭn, s. attribuzione, f.
attrition, -trĭsh'ŭn, s. attrizione, f. ; tri-
tamento, m.   [cordare.
attune, -tūn', v. a. render armonioso, ac-
auburn, ă'bŭrn, a. bruno.
auction, ăk'shŭn, s. incanto, m.
auctioneer, -shănẽr', s. venditore all' incanto, m.
audacious, ădā'shŭs, a. audace, temerario ;
–ly, ad. audacemente ; arditamente.
audacity, ădăs'ĭtĭ, s. audacia, f.; baldanza, arditezza, f.
audible, ă'dĭbl, a. udibile ; alto, sonoro.
audibly, -dĭblĭ, ad. ad alta voce.   [m.
audience, ă'dĭĕns, s. udienza, f. ; uditorio,
audit, ă'dĭt, s. esame d'un conto, m.; –, v. a. esaminare conti.
auditor, ă'dĭtăr, s. uditore, m.   [f.
auditory, ă'dĭtărĭ, s. uditorio, m.; udienza,
auger, ă'găr, s. succhiello, m.
aught, ăt, pn. checchessia.
augment, ăgmĕnt', v. a. aumentare ; accrescere ; –, v. n. aumentarsi.
augmentation, -mĕntă'shŭn, s. incremento, m. ; accrescimento, m.   [tivo.
augmentative, -mĕn'tătĭv, a. aumenta-
augur, ă'găr, v. n. augurare ; congetturare.
augury, ă'gŭrĭ, s. augurio, presagio, m.
August, ă'gŭst, s. agosto, m. (mese).
august, ăgăst', a. augusto ; nobile.
aulic, ă'lĭk, a. aulico.
aunt, ănt, s. zia, f.
aureola, ărĕ'ŏlă, s. aureola, f.
auricular, ărĭk'ŭlăr, a. auricolare ; –ly, ad. all' orecchio, segretamente ; by –
evidence, quanto si sa per bocca altrui.
auriferous, ărĭf'ărŭs, a. aurifero.
aurora, ărō'ră, s. aurora, f. ; – borealis, s. aurora boreale, f.   [zione, f.
auscultation, ăskăltă'shŭn, s. ascolta-

auspices, *ås'pĭsĕz,* s. pl. auspicio, m.; grazia, f.
anspicious, *åspĭsh'ŭs,* a. favorevole; fausto; **-ly,** ad. favorevolmente.
austere, *åstêr',* a. austero, rigido; severo; **-ly,** ad. austeramente; severamente.
austerity, *åstêr'ĭtĭ,* s. austerità, f.; mortificazione, f.
austral, *ås'trål,* a. australe, meridionale.
authentic(al), *åthĕn'tĭk(ål),* a. autentico, valido; **-ly,** ad. autenticamente.
authenticate, *–tĭkåt,* v. a. autenticare; convalidare.
authenticity, *–tĭs'ĭtĭ,* s. autenticità, f.
author, *å'thŏr,* s. autore, m.; inventore, m.
authoress, *–ĕs,* s. autrice, f. [zione, f.
authorisation, *åthŏrĭzå'shŭn,* s. autorizzazione, f.
authorise, *å'thŏrĭz,* v. a. autorizzare, dare facoltà, autorità.
authoritative, *åthŏr'ĭtåtĭv,* a. autorevole, d'autorità; **-ly,** ad. in maniera autorevole, con autorità. [imperiosa, f.
authoritativeness, *–nĕs,* s. aria o maniera
authority, *åthŏr'ĭtĭ,* s. autorità, f.; stima, f.; credito m. [f.
authorship, *å'thŭrshĭp,* s. qualità d' autore, f.
autocracy, *åtŏk'råsĭ,* s. autocrazia, f.
autocrat, *å'tŏkråt,* s. sovrano assoluto, m.
autocratic(al), *–kråt'ĭk(ål),* a. autocratico.
autograph, *å'tŏgråf,* s. autografo, m.
autography, *åtŏg'råfĭ,* s. autografia, f.
automatic, *åtŏmåt'ĭk,* a. automatico.
automaton, *åtŏm'åtŏn,* s. automa, m.
autonomy, *åtŏn'ŏmĭ,* s. autonomia, f.
autopsy, *å'tŏpsĭ,* s. autopsia, f.
autumn, *å'tŭm,* s. autunno m.
autumnal, *åtŭm'nål,* a. autunnale.
auxiliary, *ågzĭl'ĭårĭ,* a. ausiliario; **auxiliaries,** s. pl. truppe ausiliarie, f. pl.
avail, *åvål',* s. profitto, vantaggio, m., –, v. a. & n. giovare; valere; servire; esser profittevole.
available, *–åbl,* a. utile, giovevole.
avalanche, *åv'ålånsh,* s. valanga, f.
avarice, *åv'årĭs,* s. avarizia, cupidità, f.
avaricious, *–rĭsh'ŭs,* a. avaro, cupido; **-ly,** ad. avaramente, cupidamente.
avast, *åvåst',* i. basta! fermate!
avaunt! *åvånt',* i. vattene! addietro!
avenge, *åvĕnj',* v. a. vendicare.
avenue, *åv'ĕnŭ,* s. passaggio, m.; viale d'alberi, m.
aver, *åvêr',* v. a. avverare, verificare.
average, *åv'ĕråj,* s. (mar.) avaria, f.; tributo, m.; ragguaglio, m.
averse, *åvêrs',* a. repugnante; contrario; **-ly,** ad. repugnantemente, malvolentieri.
aversion, *åvêr'shŭn,* s. avversione, repugnanza, f.; antipatia, f.
avert, *åvêrt',* v. a. allontanare.
aviary, *å'vĭårĭ,* s. uccelliera, f.
avidity, *åvĭd'ĭtĭ,* s. avidità, f.; cupidigia, f.
avocation, *åvŏkå'shŭn,* s. impiego, m.; faccenda, f.
avoid, *åvŏĭd',* v. a. evitare, schivare; sfuggire; –, v. n. essere vacante.

avoidable, *–åbl,* a. evitabile.
avoidance, *–åns,* s. evitazione, f.; vacanza, f.; scampo, m. [dici once per libbra, m.
avoirdupois, *åvâr'dŭpŏz',* s. peso di se-
avouch, *åvŏuch',* v a. affermare, mantenere, asseverare.
avow, *åvŏu',* v. a. confessare.
avowal, *–ål,* s. confessione, dichiarazione, f.; giustificazione, f. [mente.
avowedly, *–ĕdlĭ,* ad. apertamente, schietta-
await, *åwåt',* s. aguato, m.; insidia, f.; –, v. a. aspettare.
awake, *åwåk',* v. a. ir. svegliare; ravvivare; –, v. n. svegliarsi, destarsi; –, a. svegliato, destato.
awaken, *–kĕn,* v. n. svegliarsi.
awakening, *–nĭng,* s. svegliamento, m.
award, *åwård',* s. giudizio, m.; sentenza, f.; –, v. a. aggiudicare, sentenziare; de-
awarder, *–ŭr,* s. arbitro, m. [terminare.
aware, *åwår',* a. avveduto, avvertito.
away, *åwå',* ad. via; **to go –,** andar via; **to run –,** fuggirsene.
awe, *å,* s. timore, m.; riverenza, f., rispetto, m.; –, v. a. tenere in timore, inspirare tema.
awful, *å'fŭl,* a. terribile; maestoso; **-ly,** ad. in modo terribile.
awfulness, *–nĕs,* s. terrore, m.; solennità, f. [qualche tempo fù.
awhile, *åhwĭl',* ad. qualche tempo; **– ago,**
awkward, *åk'wård,* a. goffo, sgraziato; **-ly,** ad. goffamente, sgraziatamente.
awkwardness, *–nĕs,* s. goffaggine, sgra-
awl, *ål,* s. lesina, f. [ziataggine, f.
awless, *å'lĕs,* a. sfrontato; senza rispetto.
awning, *ån'ĭng,* s. tenda, f.; padiglione, m.
awry, *årĭ',* a. storto, sconvolto, distorto; –, ad. di traverso, obliquamente.
axe, *åks,* s. accetta, scure, f.
axiom, *åk'sĭŭm,* s. assioma, m.
axis, *åk'sĭs,* s. asse, f.
axle(tree), *åk'sl(trē),* s. asse, sala del carro, f.; perno, m.
ay, *å'ĭ,* ad. sì; –, i. ohime! infelice me!
azalea, *åzå'lĕå,* s. (bot.) azalea, f.
azure, *å'zhŭr,* s. azzurro, m.; –, a. azzurro, turchino.

B.

baa, *bå (bå),* s. belato, m.; –, v. n. belare.
babble, *båb'bl,* s. ciarla, f.; cicalamento, m.; –, v. n. ciarlare, cicalare.
babbler, *–blŭr,* s. ciarlone, cicalone, m.; cicalona, f.
babe, *båb,* **baby,** *bå'bĭ,* s. bambino, m.
baboon, *båbŏn',* s. babbuino, m.
babyhood, *bå'bĭhŭd,* s. infanzia, f.
babyish, *–ĭsh,* a. infantile.
baby-linen, *–lĭnĕn,* s. fasce e biancherie per un neonato, f. pl.
bacchanalian, *båkånå'lĭån,* a. bacchico.
bachelor, *båch'ĕlŭr,* s. baccelliere, m.; celibe, m. [celibato, m
bachelorship, *–shĭp,* s. baccellierato, m.;

back, *băk*, s. dorso, dosso, m.; schiena, f.;
to turn one's - upon, voltar le spalle a;
—, v. a. montare (a cavallo); secondare;
—, ad. dietro, in dietro; di nuovo; **a year**
—, un anno prima.
backbite, *-bīt*, v. a. calunniare, diffamare.
backbiter, *-bītăr*, s. calunniatore, maldicente, m.   [lancia, m.
back-board, *-bōrd*, s. dossiere d' una
backbone, *-bōn*, s. spina, f.
back-door, *-dōr*, s. porta di dietro, f.;
sotterfugio, m.
backer, *-băk'ăr*, s. partigiano, m.
backfriend, *-frĕnd*, s. amico falso, m.;
amica falsa, f.
backgammon, *-găm'măn*, s. tavoliere, m.
background, *-grŏŭnd*, s. sfondo, m.
back-handed, *-hăndĕd*, a. colla mano in-
versa.
back-rent, *-rĕnt*, s. resto di pigione, m.
backslide, *-slīd*, v. n. tergiversare.
backslider, *-slīdăr*, s. apostata, m.
backstairs, *-stărs*, s. scala segreta, f.
backward, *-wărd*, a. restio, tardivo, tardo;
repugnante; **-wards**, *-wărdz*, ad. in
dietro, di dietro; **-ly**, ad. con repugnanza,
mal volentieri.   [pugnanza, f.
backwardness, *-nĕs*, s. tardità, f.; re-
backwoods, *-wŭds*, s. pl. terre incolte, f. pl.
backwoodsman, *-măn*, s. abitante delle
foreste occidentali dell' America settentrionale, m.
bacon, *bă'kăn*, s. lardone, lardo, m.
bad, *băd*, a. cattivo, vizioso, dannoso.
badge, *băj*, s. segno, m.; indizio, m.; —,
v. a. segnare, marcare.
badger, *băj'ăr*, s. tasso, m.; incettatore, m.
badly, *băd'lĭ*, ad. male, malamente.
badness, *-nĕs*, s. cattiva qualità, f.; difetto, m.   [schernire; rovinare.
baffle, *băf'fl*, v. a. eludere; frustrare,
bag, *băg*, s. sacco, sacchetto, m.; borsa, f.;
—, v. a. insaccare, mettere in sacco.   [f.
baggage, *băg'ăĭj*, s. bagaglio, m.; bagascia,
bagging, *-gĭng*, s. tela grossolana, f.
bagman, *-măn*, s. merciaiulo ambulante, m.
bagnio, *băn'yŏ*, s. bagno, m.; stufa, f.
bagpipe, *băg'pīp*, s. cornamusa, piva, f.
bail, *băl*, s. sicurtà, f.; mallevadore, m.;
—, v. a. mallevare, dare sicurtà.
bailee, *bālē*, s. depositario, m.
bailiff, *băl'ĭf*, s. balivo, sergente, m.
bait, *băt*, s. esca, f.; inganno, m., lusinga,
f.; —, v. a. adescare; allettare, lusingare;
—, v. n. battere l' ali.
baize, *băz*, s. baietta, f.   [il pane.
bake, *băk*, v. a. ir. cuocere al forno; fare
bakehouse, *-hŏŭs*, **bakery**, *-bā'kărĭ*, s.
panatteria, f., forno, m.
baker, *bā'kăr*, s. fornaio, panattiere, m.;
-'s dozen, tredici.
baking, *-kĭng*, s. cocitura, f.; fornata, f.
balance, *băl'ăns*, s. bilancia, f.; contrappeso, m.; —, v. a. bilanciare; contrappesare,
aggiustare; esaminare; —, v. n. esitare,
fluttuare.
balance-sheet, *-shēt*, s. bilancio, m.
balance-wheel, *-hwēl*, s. rota motrice, f.

balancing-pole, *-lănsĭng pōl*, s. bilanciere,
balcony, *băl'kŏnĭ*, s. balcone, m.   [m.
bald, *băld*, a. calvo; spelato; usato.
baldness, *-nĕs*, s. calvizie, f.
bale, *băl*, s. balla, f.; fascio, m.; mazzo,
m.; —, v. a. imballare.   [fausto.
baleful, *-fŭl*, a. triste, lamentevole; in-
balk, *băk*, s. trave, f.; solco, m.; contrattempo, m.; mancanza, f.; danno, pregiudizio, m.; —, v. a. tralasciare, omettere;
frustrare; mancare di parola.   [ballo, m.
ball, *băl*, s. palla, f.; globo, m.; bilia, f.;
ballad, *băl'lăd*, s. ballata, f.; canzone a
ballo, f.   [canzoni, m.
ballad-singer, *-sĭngăr*, s. cantatore di
ballast, *băl'lăst*, s. (mar.) zavorra, stiva,
f.; —, v. a. (mar.) stivare.
ballet, *băl'lĕt*, s. balletto, m.
ballet-dancer, *-dăn'săr*, s. ballerina, f.
balloon, *băllŏn'*, s. pallone, m.
ballot, *băl'lŏt*, s. voto, suffragio, m.; —,
v. n. ballottare; dare il voto.
ballot-box, *-bŏks*, s. urna d' elezione, f.
balm, *băm*, **balsam**, *băl'săm*, s. balsamo,
m.; (fig.) addolcimento, lenimento, m.;
—, v. a. imbalsamare; (fig.) addolcire,
lenire.   [balsamico; lenitivo.
balmy, *băm'ĭ*, **balsamic**, *bălsăm'ĭk*, a.
baluster, *băl'ăstăr*, s. balaustro, m.
balustrade, *bălăstrăd'*, s. balaustrata,
colonnata di balaustri, f.   [f.
bamboo, *băm'bŏ*, s. canna nodosa (d' India),
bamboozle, *-bŏ'zl*, v. a. minchionare, ingannare, gabbare.   [munica, f.
ban, *băn*, s. bando, m., proclama, f.; sco-
band, *bănd*, s. vincolo, m.; legame, m.;
banda, f.; compagnia, truppa, f.; —, v. a.
legare, fasciare; radunare.   [m.
bandage, *băn'dăj*, s. vincolo, m.; legame,
bandbox, *-bŏks*, s. scatola per biancherie, f.
bandit, *băn'dĭt*, s. bandito, m.; ladrone, m.
band-master, *-măstăr*, s. (mil.) maestro
di cappella, m.
bandy, *băn'dĭ*, a. torto, storto, curvo; —,
v. a. ballottare; palleggiare; discutere.
bandy-legged, *-lĕggĕd*, a. strambo,
storto di gambe.
bane, *băn*, s. veleno, m.; rovina, f.; **rat's**
—, arsenico, m.; —, v. a. avvelenare; corrompere.
baneful, *-fŭl*, a. velenoso; pernicioso.
bang, *băng*, s. colpo, m.; percossa, f.; —,
v. a. battere.   [argento, f.
bangle, *băng'gl*, s. piccola armilla d'
banish, *băn'ĭsh*, v. a. bandire, esiliare.
banishment, *-mĕnt*, s. esilio, m.; sbandi-
mento, m.
banjo, *băn'jŏ*, s. chitarra dei negri, f.
bank, *băngk*, s. sponda, riva, f.; lido, m.;
scoglio, m.; banco, m.; **- of circulation**, banco di giro; **to keep the** —, far
banco; —, v. a. arginare; mettere denari nel
banco.   [banco.
banker, *băngk'ăr*, s. banchiere, m.
banknote, *-nōt*, s. biglietto di banca, m.
bankrupt, *-răpt*, s. mercante fallito, m.
bankruptcy, *-răptsĭ*, s. fallimento, m.,
bancarotta, f.

English and Italian.

banner, *băn'nŭr*, s. bandiera, insegna, f.
bannister, *vedi* baluster.
banquet, *băng'kwĕt*, s. banchetto, m.; convito, m.; —, v. n. banchettare, fare banchetti.
bantam, *băn'tăm*, s. gallina di Java, f.
banter, *băn'tŭr*, s. burla, beffa, f.; scherno, m.; —, v. a. burlare, beffare.
bantling, *bănt'ling*, s. bambino, m.
baptise, *băp'tīz*, v. a. battezzare.
baptism, *băp'tizm*, s. battesimo, m.
baptismal, *–tiz'măl*, a. battesimale; — record, s. fede di battesimo, f.   [m.
baptistery, *băp'tistŭri*, s. fonte battesimale.
bar, *băr*, s. barra, sbarra, stanga, f.; ostacolo, impedimento, m.; —, v. a. sbarrare, stangare; escludere; interdire.
barb, *bărb*, s. barba, f.; cavallo barbero, m.; —, v. a. fare la barba; intagliare. [m.
barbarian, *bărbā'riăn*, s. barbaro, villano.
barbarism, *băr'bărizm*, s. barbarismo, m.
barbarity, *–băr'iti*, s. barbarie, f.; inumanità, f.
barbarous, *băr'bărŭs*, a. barbaro; inumano; —ly, ad. barbaramente; crudelmente.
barber, *băr'bŭr*, s. barbiere, m.
bard, *bărd*, s. bardo, m.
bare, *băr*, a. nudo, ignudo, scoperto; puro; privo; —, v. a. nudare, scoprire; privare.
barebone, *–bōn*, s. magro, scheletro, m.
barefaced, *–fāst*, a. sfacciato; aperto.
barefoot(ed), *–fŭt(ĕd)*, v. a. piedi nudi, scalzo.   [perta.
bareheaded, *–hĕdĕd*, a. colla testa scoperta.
barelegged, *–lĕggĕd*, a. colle gambe nude.
barely, *–li*, ad. solamente; poveramente.
bareness, *–nĕs*, s. nudità, f.; povertà, f.
bargain, *băr'gĕn*, s. patto, accordo, m.; mercato, m.; a – is a –, 'tis a –, quel che è fatto è fatto; —, v. n. patteggiare, pattuire; stiracchiare il prezzo.
barge, *bărj*, s. barca, barchetta, f.
bargeman, *–măn*, bargee, *bărgē'*, s. barcaiuolo, m.; nocchiere, m.
bar-iron, *băr'īrn*, s. ferro in verga, m.
baritone, *bă'rītōn*, s. baritono, m.
bark, *bărk*, s. scorza, corteccia, f.; barca, f.; —, v. a. scorzare, scortecciare; —, v. n. abbaiare; gridare.
barley, *băr'li*, s. orzo, m.; —sick, a. ebbro.
bar-maid, *băr'măd*, s. serva in una taverna, f.   [s. pl. pollame, m.
barn, *bărn*, s. capanna, f.; —door fowls,
barnfloor, *–flōr*, s. aia, f.
barometer, *bărŏm'ĕtŭr*, s. barometro, m.
baron, *băr'ŏn*, s. barone, m.; giudice, m.
baronage, *–ŏnăj*, s. baronia, f.
baroness, *–ŏnĕs*, s. baronessa, f.
baronet, *–ĕt*, s. baronetto, m.   [barone.
baronial, *bărō'niăl*, a. appartenente a
barony, *–ŏni*, s. baronia, f.   [caserma, f.
barrack, *băr'răk*, s. baracca, f.; —s, pl.
barratry, *băr'rătri*, s. (mar.) baratteria, f.; truffa, f.; inganno, m.
barrel, *băr'rĕl*, s. barile, m.; cilindro, m.; canna (d' un archibuso), f.; —, v. a. imbottare.   [(of roads) fatto convesso.
barrelled, *–rĕld*, a. (of fire-arms) a canna;

barrel-organ, *–ŏrgăn*, s. ghironda, f.
barren, *băr'rĕn*, a. sterile, infruttuoso; arido, magro; —ly, ad. sterilmente; aridamente.
barrenness, *–nĕs*, s. sterilità, f.; aridità, f.
barricade, *bărrĭkād'*, s. barricata, f.; ostacolo, m.; —, v. a. barricare, sbarrare.
barrier, *băr'riŭr*, s. barriera, f.; ostacolo, m.
barring, *băr'ing*, ad. eccetto.   [m.
barrister, *băr'ristŭr*, s. avvocato patrocinante, difensore, m.
bar-room, *băr'rŏm*, s. taverna, f.
barrow, *băr'rō*, s. barella, f.
barter, *băr'tŭr*, v. a. barattare, cambiare.
basalt, *băsălt'*, s. basaltite, m.
base, *bās*, s. base, f.; piedestallo, m.; (mus.) basso, m.; —, v. a. vile, basso, abietto.
baseless, *–lĕs*, a. senza fondamento.
basely, *–li*, ad. bassamente, abiettamente, vilmente.   [dazione, f.
basement, *–mĕnt*, s. fondamento, m.; fonbaseness, *–nĕs*, s. bassezza, viltà, f.; indegnità, f.; pussillanimità, f.
bashful, *băsh'fŭl*, a. timido, vergognoso; —, ad. vergognosamente; modestamente.
basilisk, *băs'ilisk*, s. basilisco, m.
basin, *bā'sn*, s. bacino, m.   [sostegno, m.
basis, *bā'sis*, s. base, f., fondamento, m.
bask, *băsk*, v. n. scaldarsi al sole.
basket, *băs'kĕt*, s. canestro, paniere, m.
basrelief, *băs'rĕlĭf*, s. bassorilievo, m.
bass, *bās*, s. basso, contrabbasso, m.; stoia, m.
bassoon, *băssōn'*, s. bassone, m.   [f.
bass-viol, *băs'vīŏl*, s. viola, f.
bastard, *băs'tŭrd*, s. bastardo, m.; bastarda, f.; –, a. bastardo, illegittimo.
bastardy, *–di*, s. bastardigia, f.
baste, *băst*, v. a. bastonare; imbastire; spruzzare.   [v. a. bastonare.
bastinado, *băstinā'dō*, s. bastonata, f.; –,
basting, *bā'sting*, s. colpi di bastone, m. pl.; pillottare, m.
bastion, *băst'yŏn*, s. (mil.) bastione, m.
bat, *băt*, s. mazza, f.; pipistrello, m.
batch, *băch*, s. fornata di pane, f.
bate, *băt*, v. a. sbattere; diminuire.
bath, *băth*, s. bagno, m.; stufa, f.
bathe, *băth*, v. a. bagnare; innaffiare; –, v. n. bagnarsi.   [toio, m.
bathing-gown, *bā'thing gŏun*, s. accappabathing-machine, *–măshēn'*, s. carretta da bagno, f.
bathos, *bā'thŏs*, s. filastrocca, f.   [f.
bath-tub, *băth'tŭb*, s. tinozza da bagnarsi,
battalion, *băttăl'yăn*, s. battaglione, m.
batten, *băt'n*, v. a. ingrassare; –, v. n. ingrassarsi, impinguarsi.
batter, *băt'tŭr*, s. farinata, f.; frittella, f.; –, v. a. abbattere; demolire, rovinare.
battering-ram, *–ring răm*, s. ariete, m.
battery, *–tări*, s. (mil.) batteria, f.
battle, *băt'tl*, s. combattimento, m.; battaglia, f.; –, v. a. combattere, pugnare.
battle-array, *–ărrā'*, s. ordine di battaglia, f.
battledoor, *–dōr*, s. racchetta, f.
battlement, *–mĕnt*, s. merlo, m.

bauble, *bȧ' bl*, s. bagattella, cosa da nulla,
f.   [mare ad alta voce.
bawl, *bȧl*, v. n. gridare; strillare; procla-
bay, *bȧ*, s. baia, f.; golfo, m.; belamento,
m.; –, a. baio, castagnino; –, v. n. abbaiare; belare.
bayonet, *bȧ' ȧnĕt*, s. baionetta, f.; –, v. a.
traffiggere con una baionetta.
bay-tree, –*trē*, s. lauro, alloro, m.
bay-window, –*windō*, s. finestra tonda, f.
be, *bē*, v. n. ir. essere, esistere; trovarsi;
stare.
beach, *bēch*, s. lido, m., riva; sponda, f.
beacon, *bē' kn*, s. faro, fanale, m.; lanterna, f.
bead, *bēd*, s. perla, f.; –s, pl. rosario, m.
beadle, *bē' dl*, s. bidello, m.
beagle, *bē' gl*, s. bracco, m.
beak, *bēk*, s. becco, rostro; sprone, m.
beaker, –*ȧr*, s. tazza, ciotola, f.
beam, *bēm*, s. trave, f.; timone, m.; bilanciere, m.; stilo, m.; raggio, m.; –, v. n.
bean, *bēn*, s. fava, f.   [raggiare.
bear, *bȧr*, s. orso, m.; –, v. a. ir. portare;
produrre; –, v. n. ir. sofferire; comportarsi.   [tabile.
bearable, *bȧr' ȧbl*, a. tollerabile, compor-
beard, *bērd*, s. barba, f.; –, v. a. strappare
la barba; affrontare.
bearded, –*ĕd*, a. barbato, pennuto.
beardless, –*lĕs*, a. sbarbato, imberbe.
bearer, *bȧr' ȧr*, s. portatore, m.
bearing, *bȧr' ĭng*, s. portamento, m.; situazione, f.; patimento, m., afflizione, f.,
dolore, m.   [burden, bestia da soma, f.
beast, *bēst*, s. bestia, f., bruto, m.; – of
beastliness, –*lĭnĕs*, s. brutalità, f.
beastly, –*lĭ*, a. bestiale, brutale.
beat, *bēt*, v. a. ir. battere; percuotere; –,
v. n. ir. palpitare; –, s. colpo, m.; percossa, f.   [berta, f.
beater, –*tȧr*, s. battitore, m.; pestello, m.
beatific, *bēȧtĭf' ĭk*, a. beatifico.
beatify, *bēȧt' ĭfȳ*, v. a. beatificare.
beating, *bēt' ĭng*, s. battito, palpito, m.
beatitude, *bēȧt' ĭtȳd*, s. beatitudine, feli-
beau, *bō*, s. zerbinotto, m.   [cità, f.
beauteous, *bū' tĭȧs*, a. bello, vago; –ly,
ad. bellamente.
beautiful, *bū' tĭfȧl*, a. bello, leggiadro,
vago; –ly, ad. bellamente, vezzosamente.
beautify, *bū' tĭfȳ*, v. a. ornare, abbellire;
–, v. n. ornarsi, abbellirsi.
beauty, *bū' tĭ*, s. beltà, f.; vaghezza, f.;
– spot, mosca, f.
beaver, *bē' vȧr*, s. castore, castoro, m.; cappello di castoro, m.
becalm, *bēkȧm'*, v. a. calmare; moderare;
(mar.) togliere il vento.
because, *bēkȧs'*, c. perchè, perciocchè.
beck, *bēk*, s. segno, m.; cenno, m.
beck(on), –*('n)*, v. n. fare cenno, accennare; assentire.   [bene; divenire.
become, *bēkȧm'*, v. n. ir. convenire; stare
becoming, –*kȧm' ĭng*, a. convenevole, decente; –ly, ad. convenevolmente.
becomingness, –*nĕs*, s. convenevolezza,
convenenza, f.; proprietà, f.

bed, *bĕd*, s. letto, m.; matrimonio, m.;
quadro, m.; –, v. a. mettere in letto.
bedaub, *bĕdȧb'*, v. a. macchiare, bruttare;
scarabocchiare.   [letto, f.
bed-chamber, *bĕd' chȧmbȧr*, s. camera da
bed-clothes, –*klōthz*, s. pl. coperte del
letto, f. pl.
bedding, –*dĭng*, s. biancheria da letto, f.
bedew, *bĕdū'*, v. a. umettare, innaffiare.
bedevil, –*dĕv' l*, v. a. ammaliare, affatturare, affascinare.
bedim, –*dĭm'*, v. a. oscurare, offuscare.
bedlam, *bĕd' lȧm*, s. ospedale dei pazzi, m.
bedlamite, –*ĭt*, s. pazzo, forsennato, m.
bed-post, *bĕd' pōst*, s. piede della lettiera,f.
bedrid(den), –*rĭd(dn)*, a. obbligato a star
bedstead, –*stĕd*, s. lettiera, f.   [in letto.
bed-time, –*tĭm*, s. ora d' andare a letto, f.
bee, *bē*, s. ape, f.; pecchia, f.
beech, *bēch*, s. faggio, m.
beechen, *bēch'n*, a. di faggio.
beech-nut, –*nȧt*, s. faggiuola, f.
beef, *bēf*, s. vaccina, f.; carne di bue, f.;
beeves, pl. bestiame bovino, m.
beef-eaters, –*ētȧrz*, s.pl. nome degli an-
tichi alabardieri dei re inglesi, dei quali
sono tuttavia alcuni a Londra, con una
speciale devisa.   [bistecca, f.
beef-steak, –*stēk*, s. carbonata di vaccina,
beef-tea, –*tē*, s. bolla, f., brodo, m.
bee-hive, *bē' hĭv*, s. alveare, m.
bee-line, –*lĭn*, s. linea retta, f.
bee-master, –*mȧstȧr*, s. apicultore, m.
beer, *bēr*, s. birra, f.; small –, birra
leggiera, f.
beeswax, *bēs' wȧks*, s. cera, f.
beet, *bēt*, s. bietola, f.
beetle, *bē' tl*, s. scarafaggio, m.; maglio, m.
beet-root, *bēt' rōt*, s. barbabietola, f.
befall, *bēfȧl'*, v. n. ir. accadere, avvenire.
befit, –*fĭt'*, v. n. convenire, essere convene-
befool, –*fōl'*, v. a. infatuare.   [vole.
before, –*fōr'*, ad. & pr. avanti, prima, innanzi; primieramente.
beforehand, –*hȧnd*, ad. avanti tratto, anticipatamente.   [volte; un tiempo.
beforetime, –*tĭm*, ad. anticamente, altre
befoul, –*fȯl'*, v. a. sporcare, imbrattare.
befriend, –*frĕnd'*, v. a. favorire, proteggere.   [v. n. mendicare, limosinare.
beg, *bĕg*, v. a. domandare; pregare; –,
beget, –*gĕt'*, v. a. ir. generare.
beggar, *bĕg' gȧr*, s. mendicante, m.; –, v. a.
impoverire; spogliare.
beggarliness, –*lĭnĕs*, s. mendicità, povertà, f.; miseria, f.
beggarly, –*lĭ*, a. povero; miserabile; –,
ad. poveramente; meschinamente.
beggary, –*gȧrĭ*, s. mendicità, f.; miseria,
indigenza, f.
begin, *bēgĭn'*, v. a. ir. cominciare, principiare, dar principio.   [m.
beginner, –*nȧr*, s. principiante, novizio,
beginning, –*nĭng*, s. principio, m.; origine,
f.; –s, pl. elementi, rudimenti, m. pl.
begone, –*gȯn'*, i. vanne via! vattene!
begrime, –*grĭm'*, v. a. annerare.
begrudge, –*grȧj'*, v. a. invidiare.

beguile, *–gīl'*, v. a. ingannare, truffare.
behalf, *–hāf'*, s. favore, m.; causa, f.; difesa, f.; **in your –,** per amor vostro.
behave, *–hāv'*, v. n. ir. comportarsi, condursi. [condotto, m.
behaviour, *–hāv'yŭr*, s. portamento, m.;
behead, *–hĕd'*, v. a. decapitare.
behest, *–hĕst'*, s. comando, ordine, m.
behind, *–hīnd'*, ad. & pr. dietro, in dietro, addietro, di dietro. [tivo stato.
behindhand, *–hīnd*, ad. in dietro; in cattivo stato.
behold, *–hōld'*, v. a. ir. riguardare; osservare; vedere; **– I** i. ecco!
beholden, *–ĕn*, a. obbligato; debitore.
beholder, *–ŭr*, s. spettatore, m.
behoof, *–hōf'*, s. profitto, m.; comodo, m.; utilità, f. [prio.
behove, *–hŏv*, v. n. bisognare; essere probeing, *bē'ing*, s. essere, m.; esistenza, f.; **–,** c. posto che, poichè, giacchè.
belabour, *bĕlā'bŭr*, v. a. bastonare, battere.
belated, *–lā'tĕd*, a. sorpreso dalla notte.
belch, *bĕlch*, s. rutto, m., eruttazione, f.; fazzoletto di seta delle Indie di più colori m.; **–,** v. n. ruttare.
beldam(e), *bĕl'dăm*, s. vecchiaccia, f.
beleager, *bĕlē'gŭr*, v. a. assediare, bloccare.
belfry, *bĕl'frī*, s. campanile, m. [care.
belie, *bĕlī'*, v. a. imitare; calunniare.
belief, *–lĕf'*, s. fede, fidanza, f.; credenza, f.
believe, *–lēv'*, v. a. credere; prestar fede; **–,** v. n. pensare; immaginarsi.
believer, *–ŭr*, s. credente, m.; fedele, m.; cristiano, m.
bell, *bĕl*, s. campana, f.; **little –,** campanella, f.; **to bear the –,** essere vittore; **–,** v. n. fiorire in forma di campana; bramire, gridare come i cervi. [m.
bell-cord, *–kŏrd*, s. cordone di sonaglio.
bell-founder, *–fōŭndŭr*, s. fonditore di campane, m.
bellicose, *bĕl'lĭkŏs*, a. bellicoso, guerriero.
belligerent, *bĕllĭj'ŭrĕnt*, a. belligerante.
bell-man, *bĕl'măn*, s. campanaro, m.
bellow, *bĕl'lŏ*, v. n. mugghiare, muggire.
bellows, *bĕl'lŏz* (vulg. *bĕl'lŭs*), s. pl. soffietto, m.
bell-pull, bell-rope, *vedi* **bell-cord.**
bell-wether, *–wĕthŭr*, s. montone che porta il campanaccio, m.
belly, *bĕl'lī*, s. ventre, m.; pancia, f.; **–,** v. n. divenir panciuto, ingrassare.
bellyful, *–fūl*, s. scorpacciata, f.; sazietà, f.
belong, *bĕlŏng'*, v. n. appartenere; aspettarsi. [pl.
belongings, *–ĭngz*, s. pl. effetti, beni, m.
beloved, *–lŭv'ĕd*, a. amato, diletto.
below, *bĕlō'* ad. & pr. sotto; giù: a basso; quaggiù.
belt, *bĕlt*, s. pendaglio, m. [rare.
bemoan, *bĕmŏn'*, v. a. compiagnere, deplobench, *bĕnsh*, s. scanno, banco, m.; corte, f.; **King's –,** consiglio aulico, m.; prigione in Londra, f.
bencher, *–ŭr*, s. giureconsulto, m.
bend, *bĕnd*, v. a. ir. tendere; curvare, piegare; (mar.) dar volta; **–,** v. n. ir. curvarsi, piegarsi; sommettersi; **–,** s. piegavira, cu vità, f.; costole della nave, f. pl.

beneath, *bĕnēth'*, ad. & pr. sotto, di sotto; giù; a basso.
benediction, *bĕnēdĭk'shŭn*, s. benedizione, f.; grazia, f. [favore, m.
benefaction, *–fāk'shŭn*, s. benefizio, m.;
benefactor, *–fāk'tŭr*, s. benefattore, m.
benefactress, *–fāk'trĕs*, s. benefattrice, f.
benefice, *bĕn'ĕfĭs*, s. beneficio, m.; parrocchia, f. [liberalità, f.
beneficence, *bĕnĕf'ĭsĕns*, s. beneficenza,
beneficent, *–nĕf'ĭsĕnt*, a. beneficente; liberale.
beneficial, *–fĭsh'ăl*, a. profittevole, vantaggioso, utile; **–ly,** ad. profittevolmente, utilmente.
beneficiary, *–fĭsh'ĭărĭ*, s. beneficiario, m.
benefit, *bĕn'ĕfĭt*, s. benefizio, m.; profitto, vantaggio, m.; **–,** v. a. beneficare; **–,** v. n. profittare.
benefit-night, *–nĭt*, s. rappresentazione teatrale a vantaggio d'un attore o d'un' attrice, beneficiata, f.
benevolence, *–nĕv'ŏlĕns*, s. benevolenza, f.; liberalità, f. [fico.
benevolent, *–ŏlĕnt*, a. benevolo, benebenighted,** *–nīt'ĕd*, a. sorpreso dalla notte.
benign, *bĕnīn'*, a. benigno, m.; **–ly,** ad. benigno, favorevole, liberale.
benignity, *–nĭg'nĭtĭ*, s. benignità, bontà, affabilità, f. [mente.
benignly, *–nīn'lĭ*, ad. benignamente; dolcebent,** *bĕnt*, s. piega, f.; inclinazione, f.
benumb, *bĕnŭm'*, v. a. intirizzire, agghiacciare, stupire.
benzine, *bĕn'zĕn*, s. belzuino, m.
bepraise, *bĕprāz'*, v. a. lodare.
bequeath, *–kwēth'*, v. a. legare, lasciare in testamento.
bequest, *–kwĕst'*, s. legato, m.
bereave, *–rēv'*, v. a. ir. privare; spogliare.
bereavement, *–mĕnt*, s. derelizione, f.; privazione, f.
berlin, *bŭrlĭn'*, s. berlina, f. (carrozza).
berry, *bĕr'rĭ*, s. bacca, coccola, f.
berth, *bŭrth*, s. (mar.) posto, m.; letto, m.; luogo, m.
beseech, *bĕsēch'*, v. a. ir. supplicare; scongiurare. [proprio.
beseem, *–sēm'*, v. n. convenire, essere
beseeming, *–ĭng*, s. decenza, leggiadria, f.
beset, *–sĕt'*, v. a. ir. (mil.) assediare; circondare.
besetting, *–tĭng*, a. abituale, consueto.
beside(s), *–sīd(z)*, pr. & ad. oltre, eccetto; più innanzi; di più. [care.
besiege, *–sēj'*, v. a. (mil.) assediare, bloccare.
besmear, *–smēr'*, v. a. sporcare, lordare.
besot, *–sŏt'*, v. a. infatuare. [pagliuole.
bespangle, *–spăng'gl*, v. a. ornare di
bespatter, *–spăt'tŭr*, v. a. spruzzare; bruttare di fango; calunniare.
bespeak, *–spēk'*, v. a. ir. ordinare; ingaggiare. [aspergere.
besprinkle, *–sprĭngk'l*, v. a. spruzzare.
best, *bĕst*, a. ottimo, migliore; **–,** ad. il miglior modo ; **–,** s. il migliore.
bestial, *bĕst'yăl*, a. bestiale, brutale; **–ly,** ad. bestialmente, brutalmente.

bestiality, -yǎl'ĭtĭ, s. bestialità, brutalità, f.

bestir, běstûr', v. n. ingegnarsi, adoperarsi.

bestow, -stō', v. a. dare, presentare; spendere; dare in matrimonio; to - oneself, trattenersi; impiegarsi.

bestowal, -stō'ǎl, s. dono, m.

bestrew, -strō', v. a. ir. sparpagliare; dispergere.

bestride, -strīd', v. a. ir. accavalciare; attraversare; oltrepassare. [mettere.

bet, bět, s. scommessa, f.; -, v. a. scombetake, bětāk', v. a. ir. consegnare; to - oneself, applicarsi; impiegarsi.

bethink, -thĭngk', v. a. ir. considerare; riflettere; -, v. n. ricordarsi.

betide, -tīd', v. n. accadere, avvenire; woe - thee! guai a te!

betime(s), -tīm(z), ad. di buon' ora, per tempo. [gire.

betoken, -tō'kn, v. a. significare, presabetray, -trā', v. a. tradire; divulgare.

betrayal, -trā'ǎl, s. tradizione, f.

betroth, -trōth', v. a. fidanzare; impalmare.

betrothal, -trōth'ǎl, s. sposalizio, m.

better, bět'tûr, a. & ad. migliore; meglio, in miglior modo; so much the -, tanto meglio; - and -, di bene in meglio; our -s, s. pl. i nostri superiori, m. pl.; -, v. a. migliorare, emendare.

bettor, bět'tûr, s. scommettitore, m.

between, bětwēn', betwixt, -twĭkst', pr. fra; in mezzo; -whiles, di tempo in tempo; betwixt and -, d' una mezza età.

bevel, běv'ěl, s. squadra, f.; -, v. a. & n. afaccettare; sbiecare. [vanda, f.

beverage, běv'ârĭj, s. beveraggio, m.; bevy, běv'ĭ, s. stuolo, m.; nuvolo, m.

bewail, běwāl', v. a. deplorare, piangere.

beware, -wâr', v. n. guardarsi, avere cura.

bewilder, -wĭl'dûr, v. a. sviare; imbrogliare; intrigare.

bewilderment, -měnt, s. imbroglio, m.

bewitch, -wĭch', v. a. ammaliare, affascinare.

bewitchingly, -ĭnglĭ, ad. d' una maniera incantevole.

beyond, -yǒnd', pr. di là, oltre, sopra; - measure, fuor di modo, oltremodo.

bias, bī'ǎs, s. sgembo, m.; inclinazione, f.; -, v. a. inclinare; preoccupare, persuadere.

bib, bĭb, s. bavaglio, m.; -, s. pl. ogni sorta d' ornamento donnesco.

bibacious, bĭbā'shǔs, a. bibace.

bibber, bĭb'bûr, s. bevitore, beone, m.

Bible, bī'bl, s. Bibbia, f.

biblical, bĭb'lĭkǎl, a. biblico.

bibliography, -lĭŏg'râfĭ, s. bibliografia, f.

bibulous, bĭb'ūlǎs, a. spongioso, assorbente.

bicker, bĭk'ûr, v. n. disputare, contendere.

bid, bĭd, v. a. ir. dire, ordinare, comandare; commettere; invitare; offerire; to - adieu, dire addio.

bidding, bĭd'dĭng, s. comando, m.

bide, vedi abide.

biennial, bĭěn'nĭǎl, a. di due anni.

bier, bēr, s. bara, f.; cataletto, m.

biffin, bĭf'fĭn, s. pomo seccato in forno, m.

bifurcated, bĭfûr'kātěd, a. biforcato.

big, bĭg, a. grande; grosso, gravido.

bigamist, bĭg'ǎmĭst, s. bigamo, m.

bigamy, bĭg'ǎmĭ, s. bigamia, f.

bight, bĭt, s. baia, f., golfo, m. [dezza, f.

bigness, bĭg'něs, s. grossezza, f.; granbigot, bĭg'ŏt, s. bacchettone, m.

bigoted, -ātěd, a. dedito al bacchettonismo; -ly, ad. da bacchettone.

bigotry, -ŏtrĭ, s. bacchettoneria, f.

bilberry, bĭl'běrrĭ, s. mirtillo, m.

bilbo, bĭl'bō, s. spadaccia, f.; -es, -bōz, pl. ceppi, m. pl.

bile, bĭl, s. bile, f.; collera, f.

bilge, bĭlj, s. piano della nave, m.; --water, s. (mar.) acqua di fondo della nave, f.; -, v. n. (mar.) far acqua.

bilious, bĭl'yǎs, a. bilioso.

bilk, bĭlk, v. a. ingannare, truffare, beffare.

bill, bĭl, s. becco, rostro, m.; conto, m.; biglietto, m., cedola, f.; lista, f., catalogo, m.; - of divorce, lettera di divorzio, f.: - of fare, nota delle vivande, f.; - of health, patente di sanità, m.; - of exchange, s. lettera di cambio, f.; - of lading, s. polizza di carico, f.; -, v. n. baciarsi l'un l'altro.

bill-broker, -brōkâr, s. sensale, m.

billet, bĭl'lět, s. biglietto, m.; ceppo, m.; -, v. a. alloggiare soldati.

billiard-ball, bĭl'yârd bǎl, s. palla, f.

billiard-pocket, -pŏkět, s. buca del biliardo, biliã, f.

billiards, -yârds, s. biliardo, trucco, m.

billingsgate, bĭl'lĭngsgât, s. ribalderia, f.

billion, bĭl'yǎn, s. bilione, f.

billow, bĭl'lō, s. onda, f., flutto, m.

billowy, -lō, a. tempio, enfiato.

bill-poster, bĭl'pōstûr, bill-sticker, -stĭkâr, s. chi attacca i cartelli.

bin, bĭn, s. cofano, m.; buffetto, m., arca, f.

bind, bīnd, v. a. ir. legare; obbligare; contrarre; -, v. n. impegnarsi, obbligarsi.

binder, -âr, s. legatore, m.

binding, -ĭng, s. legamento, m.; legatura, f.

binnacle, bĭn'ǎkl, s. (mar.) chiesola, f.

binocular, bĭnŏk'ūlâr, a. binocolo.

biographer, bĭŏg'râfûr, s. biografo, m.

biographical, bĭŏgrâf'ĭkǎl, a. biografico.

biography, bĭŏg'râfĭ, s. biografia, f.

biped, bī'pěd, s. bipede, m.

birch, bûrch, s. betulla, scopa, f.

birchen, bûrch'n, a. di betulla.

bird, bûrd, s. uccello, m.; to kill two -s with one stone, batter due chiodi ad un caldo; -, v. n. prendere uccelli, uccelbird-cage, -kâj, s. gabbia, f. [lare.

bird-call, -kâl, s. richiamo, m.; fistio, m.

bird-catcher, -kâtshâr, s. uccellatore, m.

bird-lime, -lĭm, s. vischio, m.

bird's eye-view, bârdz'ĭvū, s. vista avuta dall' alto, non circostanziata, f.

birth, bûrth, s. nascita, natività, f.; stirpe, f.; origine, f.; parto, m.; ventrata, f.; (mar.) luogo, posto, m.

birthday, –*dā*, s. giorno ai nascita, natale.
birth-place,–*plās*, s. luogo natale. m. [m.
birth-right, –*rīt*, s. primogenitura, f.
biscuit, *bīs'kīt*, s. biscotto, biscottino, m.
bisect, *bīsĕkt'*, v. a. dividere in due parti.
bishop, *bīsh'ŏp*, s. vescovo, m.
bishopric, –*rīk*, s. vescovato, m.
bismuth, *bīz'mŭth*, s. bismuto, m.
bison, *bī'zŏn*, s. bisonte, m.
bit, *bīt*, s. pezzo, m.; boccone, m.; freno, morso, m.; **not a** –, **never a** –, niente
bitch, *bītch*, s. cagna, f.   [affatto.
bite, *bīt*, s. morso, m.; –, v. a. ir. mordere, morsicare; pizzicare; ingannare, trappolare; **to – the dust,** mordere la polvere.
bitter, *bīt'tŭr*, a. amaro, aspro; piccante; crudele; –**ly,** ad. amaramente; acutamente; severamente.
bittern, –*tŭrn*, s. tarabuso, m.
bitterness, –*tŭrnĕs*, s. amarezza, f.; rancore, m.; afflizione, f., cordoglio, m.
bitumen, *bītă'mĕn*, s. bitume, m.
bituminous, –*mĭnŭs*, a. bituminoso.
bivouac, *bīv'ăāk*, s. bivacco, m.; –, v. n. passar la notte all' aria.   [chiacchierare.
blab, *blăb*, s. ciarlone, m.; –, v. a. ciarlare,
black, *blăk*, s. color nero, m.; –, a. nero; funesto, triste; cattivo; –**and blue,** livido.
blackamoor, –*ămōr*, s. nero, m.
black-ball, –*băl*, s. pallottola nera, f.; –, v. a. escludere, ributtare.
blackberry, –*bĕrrī*, s. mora di rovo, f.
black-bird, –*bŭrd*, s. merlo, m.   [m.
black-cattle, –*kăttl*, s. bestiame vaccino,
blacken, *blăk'n*, v. a. annerire, far nero; –, v. n. divenir nero.   [sul occhio, m.
black-eye, –*ī*, s. occhio pesto, m.; pugno
blackguard, –*gārd*, s. birbone, briccone, m.
black-lead, –*lĕd*, s. piombaggine, f. [m.
blackleg, –*lĕg*, s. scrocco, m.
black-letter, –*lĕttŭr*, s. lettera gotica, f.
blackmail, –*māl*, s. estorsione, f.
blackness, –*nĕs*, s. nerezza, f.; atrocità, f.
black-pudding, –*pŭdđīng*, s. sanguinaccio, m.
black-sheep, –*shĕp*, s. pecora rognosa, f.
blacksmith, –*smĭth*, s. fabbro, m.   [m.
black-thorn, –*thŏrn*, s. prugno salvatico,
bladder, *blăd'dŭr*, s. vescica, f.
blade, *blād*, s. lama, f.; fusto, m.; stelo, m.; bravaccio, m.
blade-bone, –*bŏn*, s. osso della spalla, m.
blamable, –*blā'măbl*, a. biasimevole; colpevole.
blamably, –*măblī*, ad. biasimevolmente.
blame, *blām*, s. biasimo, m.; obbrobrio, m.; colpa, f.; –, v. a. biasimare, censurare; condannare.   [–**ly,** ad. innocentemente.
blameless, –*lĕs*, a. incolpabile, innocente;
blanch, *blănsh*, v. a. bianchire; mondare; dissimulare.   [placido.
bland, *blănd*, a. dolce; blando; piacevole.
blandishment, –*ĭshmĕnt*, s. blandimento, m., carezze, moine, f. pl., vezzi, m. pl.
blank, *blăngk*, s. spazio vuoto, m.; bianco, m.; bersaglio, m.: –, a. bianco; pallido; confuso; sciolto; –, v. a. confondere, sgomentare.

blanket, –*ĕt*, s. coperta da letto, f.; pera. f.
blaspheme, *blăsfĕm'*, v. a. & n. bestemmiare, ingiurare.
blasphemous, *blăs'fĕmŭs*, a. esecrabile, empio; –**ly,** ad. esecrabilmente, in modo empio.
blasphemy, *blăs'fĕmĭ*, s. bestemmia, f.
blast, *blăst*, s. soffio di vento, m.; bruma, f.; golpe, f.; –, v. a. annebbiare; ingiuriare.
blast-furnace, –*fŭrnăs*, s. fornace grande, f.
blaze, *blāz*, s. fiamma, vampa, f.; –, v. a. allumare; pubblicare, divulgare; –, v. n. scintillare; splendere.   [divulgare.
blazon, *blā'zn*, v. a. blasonare; divisare;
blazonry, –*znrī*, s. blasone, m.
bleach, *blĕch*, v. a. imbiancare al sole; –, v. n. bianchire.   [freddo.
bleak, *blĕk*, a. pallido; smorto; aspro,
bleakness, –*nĕs*, s. pallidezza, f.; freddura, f., freddo, m.
blear, *blēr*, a. oscuro; cisposo, lippo.
bleat, *blĕt*, s. belato, m.; –, v. n. belare.
bleb, *blĕb*, s. pustula, f.; bolla, f.
bleed, *blĕd*, v. a. ir. cavare sangue; –, v. n. gettare sangue.
bleeding, –*ĭng*, s. cavata di sangue, f.
blemish, *blĕm'ĭsh*, s. macchia, f.; disonore, m., infamia, f.; –, v. a. macchiare; diffamare.   [bruttare.
blend, *blĕnd*, v. a. mescolare, mischiare;
bless, *blĕs*, v. a. benedire; glorificare;
God – you! Dio vi benedica!   [cità, f.
blessedness, –*sĕdnĕs*, s. beatitudine, felicità, f.
blessing, –*ĭng*, s. benedizione, f.; grazia di Dio, f.   [biare; guastare.
blight, *blīt*, s. nebbia, f.; –, v. a. annebbiare;
blind, *blĭnd*, a. cieco; nascoso, oscuro; –, v. a. accecare; ingannare; –**(Venetian –),** s. persiana, f.; – **alley,** strada cieca, f.; ronco, m.
blind-fold, –*fōld*, a. cogli occhi bendati; –, v. a. bendare gli occhi.
blindly, –*lī*, ad. ciecamente, alla cieca.
blindman's buff, –*măns bŭf*, s. giuoco della cieca, m.   [m.
blindness, –*nĕs*, s. cecità, f.; accecamento.
blind-side, –*sīd*, s. debolezza, f.; difetto,
blindworm, –*wŭrm*, s. cicigna, f. [m.
blink, *blĭngk*, s. occhiata, f.; –, v. n. accennar cogli occhi.
blinkers, –*ărz*, s. pl. paraocchi, m. pl.
bliss, *blĭs*, s. felicità, beatitudine, f.
blissful, –*fŭl*, a. felice, beato; –**ly,** ad. felicemente, beatamente.   [dine, f.
blissfulness, –*fŭlnĕs*, s. felicità, beatitu-
blister, *blĭs'tŭr*, s. vescia, f.; bolla, f.; vescicante, m.; –, v. a. applicare un vescicante; –, v. n. formarsi in vesciche.
blithe, *blĭth*, a. gioioso, giocondo, lieto.
bloat, *blōt*, v. a. enfiare; gonfiare; –, v. n. gonfiarsi; –, a. enfiato, gonfio.
bloatedness, –*ĕdnĕs*, s. enfiagione, gonfiatura, f.
bloater, –*ŭr*, s. buffone, m.   [fiezza, f.
block, *blŏk*, s. ceppo, m.; forma, f.; testa di moro, f.; ostacolo, intoppo, m.; –, v. a. bloccare, assediare.
blockade, *blŏkkād'*, s. blocco, m.; –, v. a. bloccare, assediare.   [m.
blockhead, –*hĕd*, s. babbaccione, sciocco,

block-house, *–hō̆ŭs*, s. (mil.) luogo fortificato, forte, m.; fortezza, f.

blood, *blŭd*, s. sangue, m.; famiglia, f.; stirpe, f.; ira, collera, f.; **to let –**, cavar sangue; **–**, v. a. insanguinare; esasperare.

bloodguiltiness, *–gŭ̆iltnĕ̆s*, s. omicidio, assassinamento, m.

blood-hound, *–hōŭnd*, s. limiero, m.

bloodily, *–ĭlĭ*, ad. sanguinosamente; crudelmente.   [nità, f.

bloodiness, *–ĭnĕ̆s*, s. crudeltà, inumanità, f.

bloodless, *–lĕ̆s*, a. esangue.

blood-letter, *–lĕtlăr , s*. salassatore, m.

blood-letting, *–lĕ̆tĭng*, s. cavata di sangue, f.   [sangue, m.

bloodshed, *–shĕ̆d*, s. spargimento di

bloodshot, *–shŏ̆t*, a. stravasato.

blood-sucker, *–sŭkăr*, a. sanguisuga, f.

bloodthirsty, *–thărstĭ*, a. sanguinolente.

blood-vessel, *–vĕ̆ssl*, s. vaso sanguigno, m.

bloody, *blŭd'ĭ*, a. sanguinoso, sanguinario; crudele; **– flux**, s. flusso di sangue, m.

bloom, *blōm*, s. fiore, m.; **–**, v. n. fiorire.

blossom *vedi* **bloom**.

blot, *blŏ̆t*, s. macchia, f.; cancellatura, f.; infamia, f.; **–**, v. a. macchiare; cassare, scancellare; disonorare.

blotch, *blŏ̆ch*, s. pustula, f.; macchia, f.

blotting-case, *blŏ̆t'tĭng kăs*, **blotting-pad**, *–păd*, s. scartafaccio, m.

blotting-paper, *–păpăr*, s. carta sugante, f.; straccia, f.

blow, *blō*, v. a. ir. soffiare; sonare; **–**, v. n. ir, ansare; aprirsi, dilatarsi; **–**, s. colpo, m.

blow-pipe, *–pĭp*, s. canna da soffiare, f.

blubber, *blŭb'băr*, s. la parte untuosa della balena, f.; **–**, v. n. gonfiarsi le guance.

bluchers, *blōōchărz*, s.pl. stivaletti, m.pl.

bludgeon, *blŭj'ŭn*, s. bastone impiombato, m., mazza, f.

blue, *blō*, a. turchino, azzurro; **–**, v. a. tingere di turchino.   [m.

blue-bottle, *–bŏ̆ttl*, s. fioraliso; moscone,

blue-devils, *–dĕvlz*, **blues**, *blōz*, s. pl. cattivo umore, m.

blueness, *–nĕ̆s*, s. colore azzurro, m.

blue-peter, *–pĕtăr*, s. (mar.) bandiera di partenza, f.   [scrittrice, f.

blue-stocking, *–stŏkĭng*, s. pedantessa,

bluff, *blŭf*, a. rustico, grossolano.

bluffness, *–nĕ̆s*, s. rusticità, f.

bluish, *blō'ĭsh*, a, azzurrino.

blunder, *blăn'dăr*, s. errore, m.; fallo, m.; **–**, v. a. confondere; imbrogliare; **–**, v. n. sbagliare, ingannarsi.

blunderbuss, *–bŭs*, s. moschettone, m.

blunderer, *–dărăr*, s. sciocco, balordo, m.

blunderhead, *–hĕ̆d*, s. pecorone, babbaccione, m. [–, v. a. spuntare; reprimere.

blunt, *blŭnt*, a. ottuso, grossolano, rozzo;

bluntly, *–lĭ*, ad, bruscamente, rozzamente.

bluntness, *–nĕ̆s*, s. ottusità, f.; rozzezza, f.   [–, v. a. macchiare; disonorare.

blur, *blăr*, s. macchia, f.; disonore, m.;

blurt (out), *blărt*, v. a. parlare inconsideratamente.

blush, *blŭsh*, s. rossore, m.; vergogna, f.; **–**, v. n. arrossire; essere confuso.

bluster, *blŭs'tăr*, s. fracasso, m.; millanteria, f.; **–**, v. n. strepitare; tempestare.

blusterer, *–tărăr*, s. bravaccio, m.

blusterous, *–ŭs*, a. tumultuoso, turbulento.

boa, *bō'ă*, s. boa, m.; pelliccia da collo, f.

boar, *bōr*, s. verro, m.; **wild –**, cignale, cinghiale, m.

board, *bōrd*, s. asse, f.; tavola, f.; sala del consiglio, f.; bordo, m.; **–**, v. a. intavolare; abbordare; **–**, v. n. tenere a dozzina; stare a dozzina.

boarder, *–ăr*, s. dozzinante, m.   [f.

boarding-house, *–ĭng hōŭs*, s. pensione,

board-school, *–skōl*, s. scuola dove i fanciulli stanno a pensione, f.

board-wages, *–wŏ̆jĕz*, s. pl. salario di vitto, m.   [–, v. a. vantare.

boast, *bōst*, s. jattanza, millanteria, f.;

boastful, *–fŭl*, a. vanaglorioso.

boat, *bōt*, s. battello, m., barca, f.

boat-hook, *–hōk*, s. uncino, gancio di lancia, m.

boatman, *–măn*, s. barcaiuolo, m.

boating, *–ĭng*, s. il remare e la navigazione.

boatswain, *bō'sn*, s. nostromo, m.

bob, *bŏ̆b*, s. ciondolo, m.; motto, detto satirico, m.; botta, f.; (cant) scellino, m.; **–**, v. a. battere; ingannare; **–**, v. n. ciondolare; pendere.

bobbin, *bŏ̆b'bĭn*, s. cannello, m.

bobtail, *bŏ̆b'tăl*, s. coda corta, f.

bode, *bōd*, v. a. presagire, prognosticare.

bodice, *bŏ̆d'ĭs*, s. busto, m.; corsaletto, m.; giubbettino, cintino, m.

bodied, *bŏ̆d'ĭd*, a. con corpore.

bodiless, *–dĭlĕ̆s*, a. incorporeo.

bodily, *–dĭlĭ*, a. corporeo; **–**, ad. corporeamente.   [m.

bodkin, *bŏ̆d'kĭn*, s. ponteruolo,m.; stiletto,

body, *bŏ̆d'ĭ*, s. corpo, m.; guscio (d'una carrozza), m.; sostanza, f.; società, f.; **any –**, **every –**, ognuno, chiunque.

body-clothes, *–klŏ̆thz*, s. pl. gualdrappa, copertina, f.   [colore, f.

body-colour, *–kŭlăr*, s. prima mano di

body-guard, *–gărd*, s. guardie del corpo, f. pl.   [cadaveri, m.

body-snatcher, *–snăchăr*, s. rubatore di

bog, *bŏ̆g*, s. palude, pantano, m.

boggle, *bŏ̆g'gl*, v. n. esitare, bilanciare.

boggy, *bŏ̆g'gĭ*, a. paludoso, pantanoso.

bogus, *bō'gŭs*, a. fraudolento.   [nero, m.

bohea(tea), *bŏhē'(tē)*, s. tè seccato, tè

boil, *bŏ̆il*, s. fignolo, m.; ciccione, m., ulcera, f.; **–**, v. a. lessare, bollire, cuocere; **–**, v. n. bollire; ondeggiare.

boiler, *–ăr*, s. caldaia, f.; calderone a vapore, m.

boisterous, *bŏ̆is'tărŭs*, a. furioso, tempestoso, violento; **-ly**, ad. furiosamente, violentemente.

bold, *bōld*, a. ardito, bravo, coraggioso; impudente; **-ly**, ad. arditamente, con bravura.   [temerità, f.; coraggio, m.

boldness, *–nĕ̆s*, s. arditezza, intrepidità,

bole, *bôl*, s. tronco, m.

bolster, *bôl'stâr*, s. piumaccio, m.; –, v. a. appoggiare; avvolgere con banda.

bolt, *bôlt*, s. freccia, f.; dardo, m.; catenaccio, m.; –, v. a. incatenacciare; abburattare. [f., buratto, m.

bolting-cloth, *–ĭng klôth*, s. stamigna,

bolus, *bô'lŭs*, s. bolo, m.; pillola, f.

bomb, *bŏm*, s. (mil.) bomba, f.

bombard, *–bârd*, v. a. bombardare.

bombardier, *–dêr'*, s. bombardiere, m.

bombardment, *–bârd'měnt*, s. bombardamento, m. [franamento, m.

bombast, *bŭm'băst*, ampollosità, f., an-

bombastic, *–băs'tĭk*, a. ampolloso, gonfio.

bond, *bŏnd*, s. nodo, legame, m.; obbligazione, promessa, f.; –, v. a. porre merci in deposito.

bondage, *–dj*, s. schiavitù, f.; servitù, f.

bond-holder, *–hôldâr*, s. possessore d'una obbligazione, m. [depositeria, f.

bonding-warehouse, *–ĭng wârhôŭs*, s.

bondman, *–măn*, s. schiavo, m.

bondsman, *–z'măn*, s. mallevadore, m.; sicurtà, f.

bone, *bŏn*, s. osso, m.; –, v. a. disossare.

bonelace, *–lâs*, s. merletto, m.

bonesetter, *–sěttâr*, s. chirurgo che rimette le ossa dislogate, m.

bonfire, *bŏn'fīr*, s. fuoco d'allegrezza, m.

bonnet, *bŏn'nět*, s. berretta, f.

bonny, *bŏn'nĭ*, a. leggiadro; grazioso.

bonus, *bô'nŭs*, s. premio, m.

bony, *bô'nĭ*, a. ossuto.

booby, *bô'bĭ*, s. balordo, sciocco, m.

book, *bŭk*, s. libro, m.; tomo, m.; –, v. a. allibrare, scrivere nel libro. [m.

book-binder, *–bĭndâr*, s. legatore di libri,

book-case, *–kâs*, s. scaffale, m.

book-debt, *–dět*, s. debito attivo, m.

booking-office, *–ĭng ŏffĭs*, s. uffizio delle diligenze, m. [banco, m.

book-keeper, *–kêpâr*, s. giovane di

book-keeping, *–kêpĭng*, s. (com.) il tenere i libri, m.

book-marker, *–mâr'kâr*, s. segnacolo, m.

bookseller, *–sĕllâr*, s. libraio, m.

bookworm, *–wûrm*, s, tarlo, m., tignola, f.; uomo troppo studioso, m.

boom, *bŏm*, s. (mar.) boma, f., polo (di vela), m.; –, v. n. sbalzare; lanciarsi.

boon, *bŏn*, s. dono, m.; favore, m., grazia, f.; –, a. buono; lieto, gioviale.

boor, *bŏr*, s. rustico, villano, m.

boorish, *–ĭsh*, a. rustico, villano, **rozzo**; **–ly**, ad. rusticamente, rozzamente.

boorishness, *–ĭshnĕs*, s. rusticità, f.

boot, *bŏt*, s. stivale, m.; profitto, guadagno, m.; **to** –, per soprappiù; –, v. a. mettersi gli stivali.

booted, *–ĕd*, a. stivalato.

booth, *bŏth*, s. capanna, f.

boot-jack, *–bŏt'jăk*, s. tirastivali, m.

bootless, *–lĕs*, a. inutile, svantaggioso.

boot-maker, *–mâkâr*, s. calzolaio, m.

boots, *bŏts*, s. lustrastivali, m.

booty, *bô'tĭ*, s. bottino, m., preda, f.

border, *bôr'dâr*, s. orlo, lembo, m.; estremità, f.; –, v. a. orlare; confinare; –, v. n. essere contiguo.

borderer, *–dârâr*, s. confinante, m.

bore, *bôr*, s. bocca (d'un arme), f.; calibro, m.; succhiello; uomo noioso, m.; –, v. a. forare, bucare; annoiare.

boreal, *bôr'ĕdl*, a. boreale, settentrionale.

Boreas, *bôr'ĕds*, s. borea, m.

born, *bôrn*, a. nato; destinato.

borough, *bŭr'ŏ*, s. borgo, m.; villaggio, m.

borrow, *bôr'rŏ*, v. a. pigliare in prestito.

borrower, *–âr*, s. prenditore in prestito.

boscage, *bŏs'kâj*, s. boschetto, m. [m.

bosh, *bŏsh*, s. filastrocca, f.

bosom, *bŭz'âm*, s. seno, grembo, m.; cuore, m.; desiderio, m.; golfo, m.; – **a shirt**, s. sparato (d'una camicia), m.; –, v. a. chiudere in seno, insenare. [m.

bosom-friend, *–frĕnd*, s. amico intimo,

boss, *bŏs*, s. gobba, f.; borchia, f.; figura (di rilievo), f.; –, *bŏs*, (am.) padrone, m.

botanic(al), *bŏtăn'ĭk(ăl)*, a. botanico.

botanist, *bŏt'ănĭst*, s. botanico, m.

botany, *bŏt'ănĭ*, s. botanica, f.

botch, *bŏch*, s. enfiato, m., pustula, f.; –, v. a. rappezzare, rattoppare.

botcher, *–âr*, s. rappezzatore, m.

both, *bŏth*, a. ambo, ambe; l'uno e l'altro, ambedue; c. egualmente che.

bother, *bŏth'âr*, v. a. imbarrazzare, confondere.

bottle, *bŏt'tl*, s. fiasco, m.; balla (di fieno), f.; –, v. a. infiascare, affastellare.

bottom, *bŏt'tŏm*, s. fondo, m.; valle, f.; fine, f.; vascello, m.; –, v. a. fondare, fare fondo.

bottomless, *–lĕs*, a. senza fondo; imperscrutabile.

bottomry, *–rĭ*, s. (mar.) prestito a rischio e avventura, m.; cambio marittimo, m.

bough, *bŏŭ*, s. ramo, m.

boulder, *bŏl'dâr*, s. ciottolo, m.

bounce, *bŏŭns*, s. strepito, fracasso, m.; bravata, f.; –, v. n. strepitare; vantarsi.

bouncer, *–âr*, s. vantatore, m.; bubbola, panzana, f.

bound, *bŏŭnd*, s. limite, m.; salto, sbalzo, m.; –, v. a. limitare, terminare; destinare, obbligare; reprimere; –, v. n. sbalzare. [fine, m.

boundary, *bŏŭn'dârĭ*, s. termine, m.; confine, m.

bounden, *–dĕn*, a. obbligato, tenuto.

boundless, *–lĕs*, a. immenso, infinito.

bounteous, *bŏŭn'tĭŭs*, **bountiful**, *–tĭfŭl*, a. buono, benigno; liberale; **–ly**, ad. benignamente, liberalmente.

bounty, *bŏŭn'tĭ*, s. bontà, f.; liberalità, f.

bouquet, *bô'kâ*, s. mazzetto di fiori, mazzo, m.; confine, limite, m. [m.

bourn, *bôrn*, s. confine, m.; tratto, m.

bout, *bŏŭt*, s. volta, fiata, f.; tratto, m.

bow, *bŏ*, s. arco, m.; inchino, m., riverenza, f.; –, *bŏŭ*, v. a. curvare, piegare; deprimere; –, v. n. inchinarsi.

bowels, *bŏŭ'ĕlz*, s. pl. viscere, budella, f. pl.; compassione, tenerezza, f.

bower, *bŏŭ'âr*, s. pergola, f.; (mar.) ancora di posta, f.

bowie-knife, *bō'ĭ nīf,* s. lungo e largo pugnale, m.

bowl, *bōl,* s. ampiattazza, f.; boccia, pallottola, f.; –, v. a. giuocar alle bocce.

bowline, *bō'lĭn (bōō'lĭn),* s. (mar.) bolina, f.

bowling-green, *bōl'ĭng grēn,* s. carriera del giuoco di bocce, f. [m.

bowsprit, *bō'sprĭt,* s. (mar.) bompresso,

bowstring, *–strĭng,* s. la corda dell' arco, f.

bow-window, *–wĭndō,* s. finestra tonda, o fatta a volta, f. [dato ai cani, m.

bow-wow, *bōŭ'wōŭ,* s. nome vezzeggiativo

box, *bŏks,* s. scatola, cassetta, f.; bossolo (árbol), m.; palco (in teatro), m.; **– on the ear,** schiaffo, m.; –, v. a. chiudere in una scatola; –, v. n. battersi a pugni.

boxer, *bŏks'ŭr,* s. pugilatore, m.

boxing-day, *–ĭng dā,* **boxing-night,** *–nīt,* s. il domani della festa del Natale.

box-office, *–ŏfĭs,* s. uffizio dove si addomanda biglietti d' entrata in un palco, m.

boy, *bŏĭ,* s. giovanetto, ragazzo, m.; servo, m.

boycot, *bŏĭ'kŏt,* v. a. bandire; mandare in bando.

boyhood, *–hŭd,* s. puerizia, infanzia, f.

boyish, *–ĭsh,* a. puerile, fanciullesco; **–ly,** ad. fanciullescamente. [laggine, f.

boyishness, *–nĕs,* s. puerilità, fanciullaggine, f.

brace, *brās,* s. coppia, f., paio, m.; cintura, f., cignone, m.; (mar.) cordame, m.; –, v. a. legare, bendare; ristringere; (mar.) bracciare; dar forza, vigore.

bracelet, *–lĕt,* s. braccialetto, m.

bracket, *brăk'ĕt,* s. beccatello, m.; **–s,** pl. (mar.) candelieri, m. pl.

brackish, *brăk'ĭsh,* a. salmastro.

brad, *brăd,* s. chiodo senza capo, m.

brad-awl, *–äl,* s. lesina, f.

brag, *brăg,* s. vantamento, m., millanteria, f.; –, v. n. vantarsi, millantarsi.

braggadocio, *–gădō'shĭō,* **braggart,** *brăg'gŭrt,* s. bravaccio, vantatore, millantatore, m. [m.; –, v. a. intrecciare.

braid, *brăd,* s. tessitura, f.; intrecciamento,

brain, *brăn,* s. cervello, m.; giudizio, senno, m.; –, v. a. ammazzare; discervellare.

brainless, *–lĕs,* a. scervellato, sciocco.

brainpan, *–păn,* s. cranio, m.

brainsick, *–sĭk,* a. sciocco, frenetico.

brake, *brāk,* s. maciulla, f.; briglione, m., morsa, f.; madia, f.; spine, f. pl.; (rail.) freno, m.; **to apply the –,** frenare.

brakesman, *–s'măn,* s. l' impiegato che sulle locomotive è incaricato di serrare i freni, frenatore.

bramble, *brăm'bl,* s. rovo, m.

bran, *brăn,* s. crusca, f.

branch, *brănsh,* s. ramo, m.; progenie, f.; –, v. a. dividere, separare; –, v. n. ramificare; spargersi in rami.

branch-house, *–hŏŭs,* s. accommandita, società mercantile, f. [dario, ramo, m.

branch-line, *–lĭn,* s. (rail.) tronco secondario.

brand, *brănd,* s. tizzone, brando, m.; fulmine, m.; –, v. a. suggellare con ferro infocato; diffamare. [treppiede, m.

brand-iron, *–īrn,* s. ferro infocato, m.;

brandish, *brăn'dĭsh,* v. a. brandire; vibrare.

brandy, *brăn'dĭ,* s. acquavite, f. [brare.

brangle, *brăn'gl,* s. querela, rissa, f.; –, v. n. contendere, disputare, rissare.

brass, *brăs,* s. rame, bronzo, m.; sfacciataggine, f.; **red –,** rame, m.

brass-founder, *–fŏŭndŭr,* s. ottonaio, m.

brass-ware, *–wăr,* s. ottoname, m.

brat, *brăt,* s. bambino, babbuino, m.

bravado, *brăvā'dō,* s. bravata, smargiassata, millanteria, f.

brave, *brāv,* s. bravaccio, millantatore, m.; –, a. bravo, coraggioso; nobile; –, v. a. bravare; insultare.

bravely, *–lĭ,* ad. coraggiosamente.

bravery, *brā'vŭrĭ,* s. bravura, f., coraggio, m.; magnificenza, f. [m.

bravo, *brā'vō,* s. satellite prezzolato, bravo.

brawl, *brăl,* s. querela, rissa, f.; contrasto, m.; –, v. n. rissare; contendere. [m.

brawler, *–ŭr,* s. gridatore, m.; litigatore.

brawn, *brăn,* s. polpa, f.; forza, f.; carne di verro, f. [forza, f.; vigore, m.

brawniness, *–ĭnĕs,* s. parte carnosa, f.;

brawny, *–ĭ,* a. carnoso; robusto, forte.

bray, *brā,* s. raglio, m.; strepito, m.; –, v. n. ragliare, ragghiare.

braze, *brāz,* v. a. coprire di rame; saldare.

brazen, *brā'zn,* a. di bronzo; impudente; –, v. n. esser impudente. [dente.

brazen-faced, *–fāst,* a. sfrontato, impu-

brazier, *brā'zŭr,* s. calderaio, m.; stufa, f.

breach, *brēch,* s. breccia, f.; apertura, f.; mancanza, f.; violazione, f.

bread, *brĕd,* s. pane, m.; sussistenza, f.; **brown –,** pane nero, m.; **household –,** pane casereccio, m. [nestro da pane, m.

bread-basket, *–băskĕt,* s. pancia, f., ca-

breadstuff, *–stŭf,* s. frumento, m.

breadth, *brĕdth,* s. larghezza, ampiezza, f.

break, *brāk,* s. rompimento, m.; (rail.) freno, m.; **– of day,** spuntar del giorno, m.; –, v. a. ir. rompere; spezzare; fracassare, rovinare; debilitare; violare; vincere, sottomettere; proporre, offerire; –, v. n. ir. rompersi; spezzarsi, spaccarsi; (com.) fallire.

breakage, *–āj,* s. rompimento, m.

breakfast, *brĕk'făst,* s. colazione, f., asciolvere, m.; –, v. n. far colazione.

breaking, *brāk'ĭng,* s. rompimento, m.; frattura, crepatura, f.; **–up,** vacanze, f. pl.

breakwater, *–wātŭr,* s. molo, m., diga, f.

breast, *brĕst,* s. seno, petto, m.; coscienza, f.; (mar.) fianco, n.

breastbone, *–bōn,* s. sterno, m.

breast-high, *–hī,* a. dell' altezza di parapetto.

breast-plate, *–plāt,* s. pettabbotta, f.

breast-work, *–wŭrk,* s. parapetto, m.; sponda, f. [soffio, m.

breath, *brĕth,* s. lena, f., fiato, respiro, m.;

breathe, *brĕth,* v. a. esalare; –, v. n. respirare; prender ristoro.

breathing, *–ĭng,* s. respiro, m.; riposo, m.

breathless, *brĕth'lĕs,* a. anelante; trafelato.

breech, *brĕch*, s. deretano, m.; **- of a gun,** culatta di cannone, f.; **-es,** pl. calzoni, m. pl. brache, f. pl.

breech-loader, *-lōdăr*, s. schioppo *o* cannone che si carica dalla culatta, m.

breed, *brĕd*, s. razza, f.; ventrata, f.; **-,** v. a. ir. produrre, generare; allevare; **-,** v. n. generarsi; partorire.

breeder, *-ăr*, s. allevatore di bestiame, m.; cavalla da razza, f.

breeding, *-ing*, s. educazione, f.; buona creanza, f.; civiltà, f.

breeze, *brēz*, s. aura, f., venticello, m., brezza, f.; tafano, m.; **-,** v. n. (mar.) soffiare, far vento.

breezy, *brē zĭ*, a. rinfrescante, refrigerante.

brethren, *brĕth'rĕn*, s. pl. fratelli, m. pl.

brevet, *brĕ vĕt*, s. brevetto, m.

breviary, *brĕ vĭărĭ*, s. breviario, m.   [f.

brevity, *brĕv'ĭtĭ*, s. brevità, f.; precisione, f.

brew, *brō*, v. a. mescolare; tramare; **-,** v. n. far la birra *o* cervogia; **-,** s. misura, f.; quantità di birra che si fa in una volta, f.

brewer, *-ăr*, s. birraio, m.   [f.

brewery, *-ărĭ*, **brew-house,** *-hŏŭs*, s.

briar, *vedi* **brier.** |birreria, f.

bribe, *brīb*, s. donativo per corrompere, m.; **-,** v. a. corrompere.   [m.

briber, *brī băr*, s. corruttore, subornatore.

bribery, *brī bărĭ*, s. corrompimento, subornamento, m. |imitare i mattoni.

brick, *brĭk*, s. mattone, m.; pane, m.; **-,** v. a.

brick-bat, *-băt*, s. pezzo di mattone, m.

brick-kiln, *-kĭl*, s. fornace da mattoni, f.

bricklayer, *-lāăr*, s. muratore, m.

brickwork, *-wŭrk*, s. ammattonato, m.

bridal, *brī'dăl*, a. nuziale; **-,** s. sposalizio, m.

bride, *brīd*, s. sposa, f.

bridegroom, *-grōm*, s. sposo, m.

bridesmaid, *-z' măd*, s. fanciulla che accompagna per onore la sposa, paraninfa, f.

bridge, *brĭj*, s. ponte, m.; rialto (del naso), m.

bridle, *brī dl*, s. briglia, f., freno, m.; **-,** v. a. imbrigliare; raffrenare, ristringere.

brief, *brēf*, s. breve, m.; compendio, m.; **-,** a. breve; succinto, conciso.

briefly, *-lĭ*, ad. brevemente, in poche parole.

brier, *brī ăr*, s. rovo, pruno, m.; spine, f. pl.

brig, *brĭg*, **brigantine,** *-ăntēn*, s. brigantino, m.

brigade, *brĭgād'*, s. brigata, f.   [tino, m.

brigadier, *-gădēr'*, s. brigadiere, m. [m.

brigand, *brĭg'ănd*, s. ladrone, masnadiere, m.

bright, *brīt*, a. lucido; brillante; **-ly,** ad. chiaramente, splendidamente.

brighten, *-n*, v. a. lustrare; pulire; **-,** v. n. diventare lucido.

brightness, *-nĕs*, s. splendore, lustro, m.; chiarezza, f.; acutezza, f. [splendore, m.

brilliancy, *brĭl'yănsĭ*, s. lucidezza, f.;

brilliant, *-yănt*, s. brillante, diamante, m.; **-,** a. brillante; risplendente; **-ly,** ad. splendidamente.

brim, *brĭm*, s. orlo, m.; margine, f.; estremità, f.; **-,** v. a. empire fino all' orlo; **-,** v. n. esser pieno.

brimful, *-fŭl*, a. colmo, pieno fino all' orlo.

brimstone, *-stōn*, s. zolfo, m.

brindled, *brĭn'dld*, a. macchiato.   [f. pl.

brine, *brīn*, s. salamoia, f.; (fig.) lagrime,

bring, *brĭng*, v. a. ir. portare; trasferire; menare; condurre; ridurre; **to - forth,** produrre; partorire; **to - up,** allevare.

brink, *brĭngk*, s. orlo, lembo, m.; ripa, f.

briny, *brī'nĭ*, a. salino, salso.

brisk, *brĭsk*, a. vivace, lieto, giocoso, spiritoso; **- (up),** v. n. rallegrarsi.

brisket, *brĭs'kĕt*, s. petto d' un animale, m.

briskly, *brĭsk'lĭ*, ad. vivacemente; lietamente, giovialmente, briosamente.

briskness, *-nĕs*, s. vivacità, allegria, f.

bristle, *brĭs'sl*, s. setola, f.; **-,** v. n. arricciarsi.

bristly, *-lĭ*, ad. setoloso; arricciato.

brittle, *brĭt'l*, a. fragile, frale, fievole.

brittleness, *-nĕs*, s. fragilità, fralezza, f.

broach, *brōch*, s. spiedo, schidone, m.; **-,** v. a. infilzare nello stidione; spillare; divulgare, pubblicare.

broad, *brād*, a. largo, esteso; aperto; osceno; **- daylight,** s. giorno chiaro, m.; **at - noon,** in sul mezzo giorno.

broadcloth, *-klōth*, s. panno largo, m.

broaden, *brād'n*, v. n. allargarsi, dilatarsi, crescere in larghezza.

broadly, *-lĭ*, ad. largamente; ampiamente.

broadness, *-nĕs*, s. larghezza, ampiezza, f.; rozzezza, f.

broad-side, *-sīd*, s. (mar.) sparo, m., bordata, f.

broadsword, *-sŏrd*, s. spada tagliente, f.

broadwise, *-wīs*, ad. secondo la larghezza.

brocade, *brōkād'*, s. broccato, m.

brogue, *brōg*, s. scarpa di legno, f.; cattivo dialetto, m.

broider, *vedi* **embroider.** |dialetto, m.

broil, *brŏil*, s. rissa, f.; disputa, f.; rumore, m.; **-,** v. a. arrostire; **-,** v. n. ardere.

broken, *brō'kn*, a. rotto, spezzato; **- meat,** s. minuzzoli, m. pl.; bricioli (di carne), m. pl.; **- week,** s. settimana nella quale cade uno giorno di festa, f.   [tico.

broken-winded, *-wĭndĕd*, a. bolso, asmatico.

broker, *brō kăr*, s. sensale, m.; rigattiere, m.

brokerage, *-ĭj*, s. senseria, f.   [m.

bronchial, *brŏng'kĭăl*, a. bronchiale.

bronchitis, *-kī'tĭs*, s. bronchite, f.

bronze, *brŏnz*, s. bronzo, m.; medaglia, f.; **-,** v. a. dar il color del bronzo.

brooch, *brōch*, s. gioiello, m.; ornamento di gioielli, m.; **-,** v. a. adornare di gioie.

brood, *brōd*, s. covata, f.; razza, f.; schiatta, f.; **-,** v. a. & n. covare, maturare.

brood-hen, *-hĕn*, s. chioccia, f.

brook, *brōk*, s. ruscello, m.; **-,** v. a. & n. sofferire, tollerare.   [nestra, f.

broom, *brōm*, s. ginestra, f.; scopa di ginestra, f.; acutezza, f.

broomstick, *-stĭk*, s. manico della scopa, m.

broth, *brōth*, s. brodo, m.   [m.

brothel, *brŏth'ĕl*, s. bordello, m.

brother, *brŭth'ăr*, s. fratello, m.   [nita, f.

brotherhood, *-hŭd*, s. fratellanza, fraternità, f.

brother-in-law, *-in lā*, s. cognato, m.

brotherly, *-lĭ*, a. & ad. fraterno, fraternamente. |chiusa, f.

brougham, *brō'ăm (brŏm),* s. carozza

brow, *brŏŭ*, s. ciglio, m.; fronte, f.; cima (d' un monte), f. [piglio.

browbeat, *–bēt*, v. a. guardare con ci-

brown, *brŏŭn*, a. bruno, nereggiante; **to be in a – study**, star pensoso, meditare di cose triste; – **paper**, s. carta straccia, f.; – **sugar**, s. zucchero rottame, m.; –, v. a. imbrunire.

brownness, *–nĕs*, s. brunezza, f.

browse, *brŏŭz*, s. messa, f.; pollone, m.; –, v. n. mangiare foglie; pascolare.

bruin, *brŏŭ'în*, s. orso, m.; orsa, f.

bruise, *brŏz*, s. ammaccamento, m.; schiacciatura, f.; contusione, f.; –, v. a. ammaccare; schiacciare; rompere, pestare.

bruit, *brŏt*, s. rumore, m.; fama, f.

brunt, *brănt*, s. urto, m.; impeto, m.; disastro, m.

brush, *brăsh*, s. spazzola, f.; granata, f.; impeto, incontro, m.; –, v. a. spazzolare; toccare leggermente; –, v. n. muoversi o passare in fretta; **to – off**, portare via, fuggire.

brushwood, *–wŭd*, s. bosco basso, m.

brushy, *–i*, a. setoloso, peloso.

brutal, *brŏ'tăl*, a. brutale; crudele; **–ly**, ad. brutalmente, crudelmente.

brutality, *–tăl'ĭtĭ*, s. brutalità, f.; crudeltà, f.

brutalize, *–tălĭz*, v. a. rendere brutale o salvatico; –, v. n. diventare brutale.

brute, *brŏt*, a. feroce; irragionevole; –, s. brnto, m., bestia, f.

brutish, *brŏ'tĭsh*, a. brutale, bestiale; feroce; **–ly**, ad. bestialmente; ferocemente.

bubble, *băb'bl*, s. bubbola, f.; bagattella, f.; sciocco, goffo, m.; –, v. a. & n. bollire; ingannare. [m.

buccaneer, *băkănēr'*, s. flibustiere, pirata,

buck, *băk*, s. daino maschio, m. [m.

bucket, *băk'ĕt*, s. secchia, f.; (mar.) bugliolo,

buckle, *băk'l*, s. fibbia, f., fermaglio, m.; riccio, m.; –, v. a. affibbiare; chiudere; inannellare; –, v. n. piegare; applicarsi.

buckler, *–lăr*, s. scudo, m.

buckram, *băk'răm*, s. bugrane, f.

buckskin, *–skĭn*, s. pelle caprina, pelle di caprone, f. [mentone, m.; miglio, m.

buck-wheat, *–hwĕt*, s. granoturco, for-

bucolic, *băkŏl'ĭk*, a. bucolico, pastorale.

bud, *băd*, s. bottone germoglio, m.; –, v. a. & n. innestare; pullulare.

budge, *băj*, v. n. muoversi, cangiare sito.

budget, *băj'ĕt*, s. valigia, f.; provvisione, f.; bilancio dello Stato, m.

buff, *băf*, s. cuoio di bufalo, m.; –, a. di cuoio di bufalo; –, v. n. battersi con

buffalo, *băf'fălô*, s. bufalo, m. [pugni.

buffer(-head), *băf'făr(hĕd)*, s. (rail.) cuscino da urto, m.

buffet, *băf'fĕt*, s. schiaffo, m.; guanciata, f.; –, v. a. schiaffeggiare; –, v. n. giocare alle pugna.

buffoon, *băfŏn'*, s. buffone, m.

buffoonery, *–ărĭ*, s. buffoneria, f.

bug, *băg*, s. cimice, m.

bugbear, *–bār*, s. spauracchio, m.

buggy, *băg'gĭ*, a. pieno di cimici.

bugle(-horn), *bū'gl(hŏrn)*, s. corno da

buhl, *bŭl*, s. tarsia, f. [caccia, m.

build, *bĭld*, v. a. ir. edificare; costruire; –, v. n. fidarsi. [tore, m.

builder, *–ăr*, s. edificatore, m.; fabbrica-

building, *–ĭng*, s. edificio, m.; fabbrica, f.; costruzione, f.

bulb, *bălb*, s. bulbo, m.; cipolla, f.; **– of the eye**, pupilla, f.

bulbous, *–ŭs*, a. bulboso. [darsi.

bulge, *bălj*, v. a. (mar.) far acqua; affon-

bulk, *bălk*, s. massa, f.; grossezza, f.; grosso, m.; tronco, busto, m.; (mar.) scaffo, m.; **by the –**, all' ingrosso. [f.

bulkiness, *–inĕs*, s. grossezza, f.; larghezza,

bulky, *–ĭ*, a. grosso, massiccio. [dità, f.

bull, *bŭl*, s. toro, m.; sbaglio, m.; assur-

bull-baiting, *–bătĭng*, s. combattimento di cani con tori, m. [m.

bull-dog, *–dŏg*, s. alano, cane da presa,

bullet, *bŭl'lĕt*, s. palla (di moschetto o di cannone), f. [m.

bull-fight, *bŭl'fĭt*, s. combattimento di tori,

bull-finch, *–fĭnch*, s. fringuello marino, m.

bullion, *–yŭn*, s. verga d' oro o d' argento, f.

bullock, *–ŏk*, s. torello, bue giovine, m.

bully, *bŭl'lĭ*, s. bravo, sgherro, m.; –, v. n. fare il bravaccio.

bulrush, *bŭl'rŭsh*, s. giunco, m.

bulwark, *–wărk*, s. baluardo, bastione, m.; –, v. a. fortificare.

bumble-bee, *băm'bl bē*, s. bordone, m.

bum-boat, *–bôt*, s. battello da provvisioni, m.

bump, *bămp*, s. tumore, m.; protuberanza, f.; colpo, m.; –, v. a. strepitare.

bumper, *–ăr*, s. bicchiere traboccante, m.

bumpkin, *–kĭn*, s. contadinaccio, m.

bumptious, *–shŭs*, a. presuntuoso.

bun, *băn*, s. focaccia fatta con burro e uova, f.

bunch, *bănsh*, s. gobba, f.; tumore, m.; fascio, m.; nodo, m.; **– of grapes**, grappolo d' uva, m.; –, v. a. far convesso.

bunchy, *bănsh'ĭ*, a. crescente in grappoli; gobbo, gibboso.

bundle, *băn'dl*, s. fardello, fagotto, m.; –, v. a. fare un fardello.

bung, *băng*, s. turacciolo, cocchiume, m.; –, v. a. turare, stoppare.

bungalow, *băng'gălô*, s. villa d' India d' un sol piano, f.

bung-hole, *–hôl*, s. foro della botte, m.

bungle, *băng'gl*, s. sbaglio, errore, m.; –, v. a. acciarpare, acciabattare.

bungler, *–glăr*, s. acciarpone, m.

bunnion, *băn'yăn*, s. occhio pollino, callo a' piedi, m. [f., buratto, m.

bunting, *–tĭng*, s. stoffa da far bandiere.

buoy, *băŏĭ* (*bŏĭ*), s. (mar.) gavitello, m.; segnale dell' ancora, m.; –, v. a. galleggiare; nuotare.

buoyancy, *–ănsĭ*, s. leggerezza, f.

buoyant, *–ănt*, a. galleggiante; leggiero.

bur, *băr*, s. (bot.) bardana, f.

burden, *băr'dn*, s. soma, f., carico, m.;

ritornello, m.; —, v. a. caricare; imbarazzare. [molesto.

burdensome,—*săm*, a. grave; oppressivo;

burdock, *bŭr'dŏk*, s. lappola, f.

bureau, *bŭ'rō (bŭrō')*, s. segreteria, f.; scrittoio, armario, m.

bureaucrat,—*krăt*, s. burocratico, m.

burgess, *bŭr'jĕs*, s. borghese, cittadino, m.

burgher, *bŭrg'ŭr*, s. borghese, m.

burglar, *bŭrg'lăr*, s. ladro domestico, rubatore per rottura, m. [m.

burglary,—*lări*, s. el rubare per rottura,

burgomaster, *bŭr'gŏmăstŭr*, s. borgomastro, m. [m. pl.

burial, *bĕr'ĭăl*, s. sepoltura, f.; funerali,

burial-place,—*plās*, s. cimitero, m. •

burlesque, *bŭrlĕsk'*, a. burlesco; faceto; —, s. discesso burlesco, m.; —, v. a. burlare, beffare.

burly, *bŭr'lĭ*, a. grosso, corpacciuto.

burn, *bărn*, s. scottatura, f., abbruciamento, m.; —, v. a. ir. abbruciare, bruciare; —, v. n. ir. ardere. [m.

burner,—*ăr*, s. incendiario, m.; bocciuolo,

burning-glass, —*ĭng glăs*, s. lente ustoria, f., vetro ardente, m.

burnish, *bŭr'nĭsh*, v. a. brunire; dare il lustro; —, v. n. diventare lucido.

burr, *bŭr*, s. timpano dell'orecchio, m.

burrow, *bŭr'rō*, s. borgo, m.; tana di coniglio, f.; —, v. n. nascondersi.

bursar, *bŭr'săr*, s. tesoriere, m.

burse, *bŭrs*, s. borsa, f.; banco, m.

burst, *bŭrst*, s. crepatura, f., fracasso, m.; —, v. n. ir. crepare; aprirsi; to — into tears, pianger dirottamente; to — with laughing, morire dalle risa.

bury, *bĕr'ĭ*, v. a. sotterrare, seppellire.

burying-ground, —*ĭng grŏŭnd*, s. cimi-'bus, *bŭs*, s. omnibus, m. [tero, m.

busby, *bŭs'bĭ*, s. elmo d' un ussaro Inglese, m. [coda di volpe, f.

bush, *bŭsh*, s. cespuglio m.; frasca, f.

bushel,—*ĕl*, s. staio, m.

bushy,—*ĭ*, a. cespuglioso; folto, fronzuto.

busily, *bĭz'ĭlĭ*, ad. attivamente; diligentemente; arditamente. [faccenda, f.

business, *bĭz'nĕs*, s. affare, negozio, m.,

busk, *bŭsk*, s. stecca, f.; cespuglio, m.

buskin, *bŭs'kĭn*, s. stivaletto, m.

buss, *bŭs*, s. bacio, m.; omnibus, m.

bust, *bŭst*, s. busto, m. [dia, m.

bustard, *bŭs'tărd*, s. gallo salvatico d' Indie.

bustle, *bŭs'l*, s. tumulto, m.; rumore, m.; —, v. n. far strepito; affrettarsi.

bustler,—*lăr*, s. faccendiere, affannone, m.

busy, *bĭz'ĭ*, a. affaccendato, occupato; —, v. a. occupare; —, v. n. occuparsi; intromettersi.

busybody,—*bŏdĭ*, s. affannone, m.

but, *bŭt*, c. ma, però; fuorchè, eccetto; solamente.

butcher, *bŭch'ŭr*, s. macellaio, m.; —'s shop, s. macello, m.; —, v. a. macellare; uccidere.

butchery,—*ărĭ*, s. macello, m.

butler, *bŭt'lăr*, s. dispensiere, canovaio, m.

butt, *bŭt*, s. scopo, m.; mira, f.; segno,

m.; fine, m.; botte, f.; —, v. a. cozzare; urtare, spingere.

butter, *bŭt'tăr*, s. burro, m.; —, v. a. condire con burro, ungere con burro; truffare; —ed egg, s. uovo condito di burro, m. [*flŏŭr*, s. fioretto giallo, m.

butter-cup, —*kŭp*, butter-flower, —

butterfly, —*flĭ*, s. farfalla, f.

buttermilk, —*mĭlk*, s. siero, m.

buttery, —*tŭrĭ*, a. burroso; —, s. bettola, f.

buttock, *bŭt'tŏk*, s. chiappa, natica, f.

button, *bŭt'n*, s. bottone, m.; boccia, f.; —, v. a. abbottonare.

button-hole, —*hōl*, s. occhiello, m.

button-hook, —*hŏk*, s. uncino per abbottonare, m.

buttress, *bŭt'trĕs*, s. barbacane, m.; sostegno, m.; —, v. a. sostenere, appoggiare.

buxom, *bŭk'săm*, a. obbediente; allegro, giocondo, lieto; —ly, ad. amorosamente.

buy, *bĭ*, v. a. ir. comprare. [lietamente.

buzz, *bŭz*, s. ronzio, susurro, m.; —, v. n. ronzare, susurrare.

buzzard, *bŭz'zărd*, s. abozzago, m.

by, bye, *bĭ*, pr. per; da: al; vicino; appresso; — and —, adesso adesso; — the bye, di volo; — much, di molto; — hard —, qui vicino; — chance, a caso; — degrees, gradamente, poco a poco; — all means, in ogni modo, certamente; — no means, in conto nessuno; — oneself, solo; — one o'clock, a un' ora.

by-gone, —*gŏn*, a. passato.

by-lane, —*lān*, s. vicolo, m.

by-law, —*lā*, s. regolamento, statuto, m.

by-name, —*năm*, s. soprannome, m. [f.

by-path, —*păth*, s. strada poco frequentata,

by-road, —*rōd*, s. sentiero discosto, m.

by-speech, —*spēch*, s. orazione occasionale, f.

by-stander, —*stăndăr*, s. spettatore, m.

by-street, —*strēt*, s. strada fuor di mano, f.

by-way, —*wā*, s. traversa, f. [sima, f.

by-word, —*wărd*, s. proverbio, m.; mas-

C.

cab, *kăb*, s. calessino, m.; carozza d' affitto, f. [zione, f.; —, v. n. tramare, cospirare.

cabal, *kăbăl'*, s. cabala, f.; trama, cospira-

cabalistic, —*lĭs'tĭk*, a. cabalistico.

cabbage, *kăb'băj*, s. cavolo, m.; —, v. a. & n. rubare i ritagli. [puccia, f.

cabbage-lettuce, —*lĕtŭs*, s. lattuga cap-

cabin, *kăb'ĭn*, s. camerino, m.; gabinetto, m.; —, v. a. chiudere in un luogo ristretto; —, v. n. vivere in un luogo ristretto.

cabin-boy, —*bŏĭ*, s. mozzo, m.

cabin-passenger, —*păssĕnjăr*, s. passeggiero di prima classe, m. [dio, m.

cabinet, *kăb'ĭnĕt*, s. gabinetto, m.; arma-

cabinet-council, —*kŏŭnsĭl*, s. gabinetto della corte, m.

cabinet-maker, —*măkŭr*, s. ebanista, m.

cable, *kā'bl*, s. (mar.) gomena, f., cavo, m.; —'s length, s. lunghezza della gomena, f.

cabman, *kăb′măn*, s. cocchiere, m.
caboose, *kăbōz′*, s. (mar.) cucina, m.
cabstand, *kăb′stănd*, s. luogo dove stanno le carozze d' affitto, m.
cackle, *kăk′l*, s. il chiocciare (dell' oca), m.; –, v. n. chiocciare.
cackler, *–lăr*, s. chiacchierone, m. [m.
cad, *kăd*, s. cocchiere, m.; ragazzo di piazza,
cadaverous, *kădăv′ărŭs*, a. cadaverico.
caddy, *kăd′dĭ*, s. scatola da tè, f.
cade, *kăd*, s. barile, m.
cadence, *kā′dĕns*, s. (mus.) cadenza, f.
cadet, *kădĕt′*, s. cadetto, m.; volontario, m.
cage, *kădj*, s. gabbia, f.; prigione, f.; –, v. n. chiudere in gabbia; imprigionare.
cairn, *kărn*, s. tumulo, m. [adulare.
cajole, *kăjōl′*, v. a. lusingare, vezzeggiare;
cajolery, *–jō′lărĭ*, s. adulazione, carezza, f.
cake, *kăk*, s. focaccia, f.; –, v. n. incrostarsi, rappigliarsi.
calamitous, *kălăm′ĭtŭs*, a. calamitoso.
calamity, *–ĭtĭ*, s. calamità, miseria, f.
calcareous, *kălkā′rĭŭs*, a. di calcina.
calcine, *kăl′sĭn*, v. a. calcinare. [lare.
calculable, *kăl′kŭlăbl*, a. che si può calco-
calculate, *–kŭlăt*, v. a. calcolare, computare.
calculation, *–lă′shăn*, s. computo, m.
calculus, *–kŭlŭs*, s. calcolo, m.; computo, m.
caldron, *kăl′drŏn*, s. caldaia, f. [m.
calendar, *kăl′ĕndăr*, s. calendario, almanacco, m. [manganare.
calender, *–*, s. mangano, m.; –, v. a.
calf, *kăf*, s. vitello, m.; vitella, f.; polpa delle gambe, f.
calibre, *kăl′ĭbăr*, s. calibro, m.
calico, *kăl′ĭkō*, s. calicot, m. (tela;di cotone).
calisthenics, *kălĭsthĕn′ĭks*, s. pl. esercizi ginnastici igienici, m. pl.
calk, *kăk*, v. a. (mar.) calafatare.
calker, *–ăr*, s. (mar.) calfato, m.
call, *kăl*, s. chiamata, f.; vocazione, f.; invito, m.; (mar.) fischio, m.; –, v. a. chiamare; appellare; convocare, radunare; comandare; **to – names**, ingiuriare; **to – for**, domandare, cercare; **to – upon**, visitare; **to – out**, chiamar uno a duello, sfidarlo.
call-bell, *–bĕl*, s. campanello a martello, m.
call-boy, *–bŏĭ*, s. garzone, servitore, m.
caller, *–ăr*, s. visitatore, m.
calligraphy, *kălĭg′răfĭ*, s. calligrafia, f.
calling, *kăl′lĭng*, s. vocazione, f.; mestiere, uffizio, impiego, m.
callosity, *kăllŏs′ĭtĭ*, s. callosità, f.
callous, *kăl′lŭs*, a. calloso; insensibile.
callow, *kăl′lō*, a. spiumato, nudo.
calm, *kăm*, s. calma, f.; tranquillità, f.; –, a. calmo, tranquillo, quieto; –, v. a. calmare; abbonacciare; quietare; placare.
calmly, *–lĭ*, ad. tranquillamente, quietamente, placabilmente.
calmness, *–nĕs*, s. calma, tranquillità, f.
calomel, *kăl′ŏmĕl*, s. calomelano, m.
caloric, *kălŏr′ĭk*, s. calorico, m.
calumniate, *kălăm′nĭăt*, v. a. calunniare, diffamare, sparlare. [f.
calumniation, *–nĭă′shăn*, s. diffamazione,

calumnious, *–lăm′nŭŭs*, a. calunnioso, diffamatorio. [zione, f.
calumny, *kăl′ămnĭ*, s. calunnia, diffama-
Calvary, *kăl′vărĭ*, s. Calvario, m.
calve, *kăv*, v. n. fare un vitello; figliare.
Calvinist, *kăl′vĭnĭst*, s. Calvinista, m.
cambric, *kăm′brĭk*, s. cambraia, f.
camel, *kăm′ĕl*, s. cammello, m.
camelopard, *kămĕl′ŏpărd*, s. camellopardalo, m. [figura intagliata, f.
cameo, *kăm′ĕŏ*, s. cammeo, m., pietra e
camera, *kăm′ĕră*, s. apparato fotografico, m.
camomile, *kăm′ŏmĭl*, s. camomilla, f.
camp, *kămp*, s. campo, m.; –, v. n. accamparsi, porsi a campo.
campaign, *kămpăn′*, s. campagna, f.; –, v. n. participare a una campagna.
campaigner, *–ăr*, s. veterano, m.
camphor, *kăm′făr*, s. canfora, f.
camp-meeting, *kămp′mĕtĭng*, s. uffizio divino di campagna, m. [ripiegarsi, f.
camp-stool, *–stōl*, s. scranna, seggiola da
can, *kăn*, s. sorta di barile, f.; –, v. n. ir. potere.
canal, *kănăl′*, s. canale, condotto, m.
canary-bird, *kănā′rĕ bărd*, s. canarino, m.
cancel, *kăn′sĕl*, v. a. cancellare, annullare.
cancer, *kăn′săr*, s. granchio, m.; cancro, m.
Cancer, *–*, Cancro, m. (sign of the zodiac).
cancerous, *–ŭs*, a. cancroso.
candid, *kăn′dĭd*, a. candido, ingenuo, sincero; **-ly**, ad. candidamente.
candidate, *kăn′dĭdăt*, s. candidato; competitore, m.
candied, *kăn′dĭd*, a. candito, confetto.
candle, *kăn′dl*, s. candela, f.
candle-end, *–ĕnd*, s. moccolo, m.
candle-light, *–lĭt*, s. lume di candela, m.; **by –**, alla candela.
Candlemas, *–măs*, s. Candelaia, f. [m.
candle-snuffer, *–snăffăr*, s. smoccolatoio,
candle-stick, *–stĭk*, s. candeliere, m.; **branched –**, candelabro, m.
candour, *kăn′dăr*, s. candore, m.; ingenuità, f.; sincerità, f.
candy, *kăn′dĭ*, s. zucchero candito, m.; –, v. a. candire, confettare.
cane, *kăn*, s. canna; bastone, m.; –, v. a. bastonare. [s. sedia intrecciata, f.
cane-bottom(ed) chair, *–bŏttăm(d)tshăr*,
cane-mill, *–mĭl*, s. fabbrica di zucchero.
canicular, *kănĭk′ŭlăr*, a. canicolare. [m.
canine, *kănĭn′*, a. canino; **– hunger**, s. fame canina, f. [panierina, f.
canister, *kăn′ĭstăr*, s. scatola da tè, f.;
canister-shot, *–shŏt*, s. mitraglia, f.
canker, *kăng′kăr*, s. canchero, m.; –, v. a. corrompere, corrodere; –, v. n. corrompersi.
cannibal, *kăn′nĭbăl*, s. cannibale, m.
cannibalism, *–ĭzm*, s. antropofagia, f.
cannon, *kăn′nŏn*, s. cannone, m.
cannonade, *–nŏnād′*, s. cannonata, f.; –, v. a. cannoneggiare, cannonare.
cannon-ball, *–băl*, s. palla da cannone, f.
cannonier, *–nēr′*, s. cannoniere, m.
canoe, *kănŏ′*, s. canoa, f., canotto, m.

canon, *kăn'ŏn,* s. canone, m.; regola, f.;
  – **law,** s. legge canonica, f.

canoness, *–nŏnĕs,* s. canonichessa, f.

canonical, *–nŏn'ĭkăl,* a. canonicale, canonico; **–s,** s. pl. apparecchio d'uno
canonico, m.   [zione, f.

canonization, *–nĭzd'shăn,* s. canonizza-

canonize, *kăn'ŏnĭz,* v. a. canonizzare,
dichiarare santo.

canonry, *kăn'ŏnrĭ,* s. canonicato, m.

canopy, *kăn'ŏpĭ,* s. baldacchino, m.

cant, *kănt,* s. gergo, m.; vendita, f.; –, v. a.
gettare via, rigettare; –, v. n. parlar in
gergo.

cantankerous, *–tăng'kărŭs,* a. fastidioso.

canteen, *kăntēn',* s. cantina, f.

canter, *kănt'ăr,* s. galloppo piccolo, m.;
ipocrito, m.   [f. pl.

cantharides, *kănthăr'ĭdĕz,* s. pl. cantaridi,

canticle, *kăn'tĭkl,* s. cantica, f.

canton, *kăn'tŏn,* s. cantone, m.; –, v. a.
dividere in cantoni; stare a quartiere.

cantonment, *–mĕnt,* s. (mil.) alloggiamento militare, m.

canvass, *kăn'văs,* s. canovaccio, m.;
ricerca di suffragi, f.; –, v. a. esaminare,
consultare; –, v. n. brigare, sollecitare.

canvasser, *–văsăr,* s. sollecitatore, m.

caoutchouc, *kŏŏ'chŭk,* s. gomma elastica, f.

cap, *kăp,* s. berretta, f.; cappello, m.; testa,
f., capo, m.; saluto, m.; –, v. a. sberret-
tare.   [neità, f.

capability, *kăpăbĭl'ĭtĭ,* s. capacità, ido-

capable, *kă'păbl,* a. capace; atto, idoneo.

capacious, *kăpă'shŭs,* a. capace, ampio,
spazioso, vasto.

capacitate, *–păs'ĭtāt,* v. a. rendere capace.

capacity, *–tĭt,* s. capacità, f.; abilità, f.;
disposizione, f.

caparison, *–păr'ĭsŭn,* s. copertina, gualdrappa, f.; –, v. a. porre la copertina (ad
un cavallo).   [lare, m.

cape, *kăp,* s. capo, promontorio, m.; col-

caper, *kă'păr,* s. capriola, f.; cappero, m.;
pirata, m.; **to cut –s,** fare delle capriole;
–, v. n. capriolare.

capillary, *kăp'ĭllărĭ,* a. capillare.

capital, *kăp'ĭtăl,* a. capitale; principale;
–ly, ad. capitalmente; mortalmente; –,
s. fondo, m.; metropoli, f.; capitello, m.

capitalise, *–tălĭz,* v. a. capitalizzare.

capitalist, *–ĭst,* s. capitalista, m.

capitation, *–tă'shăn,* s. tassa per testa, f.,
testatico, m.

Capitol, *kăp'ĭtŏl,* s. Campidoglio, m.

capitulary, *kăpĭt'ŭlărĭ,* s. membro d' un
capitolo, m.   [convenzioni.

capitulate, *–ălăt,* v. n. capitolare, fare

capitulation, *–lă'shăn,* s. capitolazione,
convenzione, f.

capon, *kă'pn,* s. cappone, m.

capot, *kăpŏt',* s. cappotto, mantello, m.

caprice, *kăprēs',* s. capriccio, m., fantasia, f.

capricious, *–prĭsh'ŭs,* a. capriccioso; **–ly,**
ad. capricciosamente.

Capricorn, *kăp'rĭkŏrn,* s. Capricorno, m.
(sign of the zodiac).

capsize, *kăp'sĭz,* v. a. rovesciarsi.

---

capstan, *kăp'stăn,* **capstern,** *–stĕrn,* s.
(mar.) argano di vascello, m.

capsule, *kăp'sŭl,* s. capsula, f.

captain, *kăp'tĭn,* s. capitano, m.; capo, m.;
– of foot, capitano d' infanteria, m.; –
of horse, capitano di cavalleria, m.

captaincy, *–sĭ,* **captainship,** *–shĭp,* s.
grado, ufficio di capitano, m.

captious, *kăp'shŭs,* a. cavilloso, insidioso;
critico, sofistico; **–ly,** ad. cavillosamente;
criticamente.   [beria, f.

captiousness, *–nĕs,* s. cavillazione, fur-

captivate, *kăp'tĭvăt,* v. a. cattivare; soggiogare.

captive, *kăp'tĭv,* s. captivo, schiavo, m.

captivity, *–tĭv'ĭtĭ,* s. captività, schiavitù, f.

captor, *kăp'tăr,* s. che fa una preda.

capture, *kăp'tŭr,* s. cattura, f.; –, v. a.
catturare.   [donna), m.

capuchin, *kăpŭshĕn',* s. cappuccio (da

car, *kăr,* s. carretta, f.; carro, m.

carabine, *kăr'bĭn,* s. carabina, f.

carabinier, *–bĭnēr',* s. carabiniere, m.

caravan, *kărăvăn',* s. carovana, f.

caravansary, *–sărĭ,* s. albergo delle caro-

caraway, *kăr'ăwă,* s. carvi, m.   [vane, m.

carbine, *vedi* **carabine.**

carbon, *kăr'bŏn,* s. carbonio, m.

carbonize, *–bŏnĭz,* v. a. carbonizzare.

carbuncle, *–bŭngkl,* s. carboncello, carbonchio, m.   [f.

carcass, *kăr'kăs,* s. carcame, m.; carcassa,

card, *kărd,* s. carta, f.; cardo, m.; **pack
of –s,** s. mazzo di carte, m.; **visiting –,**
biglietto di visita, m.; –, v. a. cardare;
giocare alle carte.

cardboard, *–bŏrd,* s. cartone, m.

carder, *–ăr,* s. cardatore, m.

cardiac, *kăr'dĭăk,* a. cardiaco.

cardinal, *kăr'dĭnăl,* a. cardinale, principale; –, s. cardinale, m.

card-table, *–tăbl,* s. tavola da giuoco, f.

care, *kăr,* s. cura, f.; sollecitudine, f.; –,
v. n. curare, aver cura; apprezzare,
stimare; **what do I –?** che importa
a me?

careen, *kărēn',* v. a. (mar.) carenare.

career, *kărēr',* s. carriera, f.; corso, m.;
–, v. n. correre con velocità.

careful, *kăr'fŭl,* a. sollecito, cauto, prudente; **–ly,** ad. cautamente, prudentemente.   [zione, f.; cautela, prudenza, f.

carefulness, *–fŭlnĕs,* s. cura, f.; atten-

careless, *–lĕs,* a. negligente, trascurato;
–ly, ad. senza cura, negligentemente.

carelessness, *–lĕsnĕs,* s. negligenza,
trascuranza, f.   [–, v. a. accarezzare.

caress, *kărĕs',* s. carezza, amorevolezza, f.;

cargo, *kăr'gō,* s. (mar.) carico, m.

caricature, *kărĭkătŭr',* s. caricatura, f.;
–, v. a. mettere in ridicolo.

caricaturist, *–tŭ'rĭst,* s. caricaturista, m.

caries, *kă'rĭĕz,* s. carie, m.; putrefazione, f.

cark, *kărk,* v. n. essere ansioso, sollecito.

carman, *kăr'măn,* s. carrettiere, m.

Carmelite, *kăr'mĕlĭt,* s. Carmelitano, m.

carmine, *kăr'mĭn,* s. carminio, m.

carnage, *kăr'năj,* s. macello, m.; strage, f.

carnal, kăr'năl, a. carnale, sensuale; -ly, ad. carnalmente, sensualmente.

carnality, -năl'ĭtĭ, s. sensualità, incontinenza, f. [incarnato, m.; garofano, m.

carnation, -nā'shŭn, s. carnagione, f.;

carnival, kăr'nĭvăl, s. carnovale, m.

carnivorous, -nĭv'ŏrŭs, a. carnivoro, vorace, ingordo, mangione.

carol, kăr'ŏl, s. carola, f., canto divoto, m.; canto d' allegrezza, m.; -, v. a. carolare; celebrare. [carotidi, f. pl.

carotid arteries, kărŏt'ĭd ăr'tĕrēz, s. pl.

carousal, -rŏŭl'zăl, s. gozzoviglia, crapula, f.

carouse, -rŏŭz', v. a. & n. gozzovigliare.

carp, kărp, s. carpione, m.; -, v. n. criticare; censurare.

carpenter, kăr'pĕntăr, s. legnaiuolo, falegname, m.; (mar.) carpentiere, m.; -'s bench, banco da artiere, m.

carpentry, -pĕntrĭ, s. arte del legnaiuolo, f.; legname, m. [censore, m.

carper, -păr, s. cavillatore, biasimatore,

carpet, kăr'pĕt, s. tappeto, m.; -, v. a. coprire d' un tappeto.

carpet-bag, -băg, s. sacco da viaggio, m.

carping, kăr'pĭng, a. critico, litigioso; -ly, ad. criticamente.

carriage, kăr'rĭj, s. porto, m.; carriaggio, m., vettura, f.; carretta, f.; portamento, m.; a - and four, carrozza con tiro a quattro. [-păd, a. franco di porto.

carriage-free, -frē, carriage-paid,

carriage-house, -hŏŭs, s. (rail.) loggia da vagoni, f.

carrier, kăr'rĭăr, s. vetturino, m.; portatore, m.; -pigeon, colomba postale, f., piccione che porta lettere, m.

carrion, kăr'rŭn, s. carogna, f.

carronade, -rŏnād', s. (mar.) carrata, f.

carrot, kăr'rŏt, s. carota, f.

carroty, -rŏtĭ, a. rosso, rossigno.

carry, kăr'rĭ, v. a. portare; condurre; guadagnare; -, v. n. comportarsi; procedere; to - the day, ottenere la vittoria; to - it high, procedere con alterigia.

carry-all, -ăl, s. omnibus, m.

cart, kărt, s. carretta, f.; carro, m.; -, v. a. & n. esporre sur un carro; condurre

cartage, kăr'tăj, s. nolo, m. [col carro.

cartel, kăr'tĕl, s. cartello, m., disfida, f.

carter, kăr'tăr, s. carrettiere, m.

cart-horse, -hŏrs, s. cavallo di carretta, m. [tosino, m.

Carthusian, kărthū'zhăn, s. frate Certosino, m.

cartilage, kăr'tĭlăj, s. cartilagine, f.

carting, kăr'tĭng, s. nolo, m.

cart-load, -lŏd, s. carrettata, carrata, f.

cartoon, kărtŏn', s. cartone, m.

cartridge, kăr'trĭj, s. cartoccio, m.; ball -, cartoccio con balla; blank -, cartoccio senza balla.

cartridge-box, -bŏks, s. giberna, f.

cart-rut, kărt'rŭt, s. rotaia, f.

cartwright, -rīt, s. carradore, carraio, m.

carve, kărv, v. a. tagliare, scolpire; trinciare; -, v. n. intagliare. [trinciante, m.

carver, kăr'văr, s. scultore; intagliatore;

carving, -vĭng, s. scultura, f., el scolpire,

carving-knife, -nīf, s. trinciante, m. [m.

case, kăs, s. caso, m.; stato, m., condizione, f.; scatola, f.; guaina, f., astuccio, m.; to put the -, supporre una cosa.

case-knife, -nīf, s. coltellaccio da cucina, m.

casemate, -māt, s. casamatta, f. [m.

casement, -mĕnt, s. finestra, f.

case-shot, -shŏt, s. mitraglia, f.

cash, kăsh, s. danaro contante, m., cassa, f.

cash-box, -bŏks, s. cassa, f. [f.

cashier, kăshēr', s. cassiere, banchiere, m.; -, v. a. cassare; congedare. [chiere, m.

cash-keeper, -kēpăr, s. cassiere, banchashmire, kăsh'mēr, m. casimirra, f.

casing, kā'sĭng, s. intonaco, m.; incassatura, f.

cask, kăsk, s. botte, f.; barile, m.

casket, -ĕt, s. cassetta, f.; -, v. a. riporre nella cassetta.

cassation, kăssā'shŭn, s. cassazione, f.

cassock, kăs'sŏk, s. sottana, f.

cassowary, kăs'sŏwărĭ, s. casuare, m.

cast, kăst, s. tiro, m.; colpo, m.; tirata, f., getto, m.; aspetto, m.; forma, f.; estremità, f.; maniera, f.; - of the eyes, occhiata, f.; -, v. a. ir. gettare; lanciare; guadagnare; condannare; -, v. n. ir. ruminare; pensare, considerare; piegarsi; to - an account, fare un conto; to - lots, tirar le sorti.

castanet, kăs'tănĕt, s. castagnetta, f.

castaway, kăst'ăwā, s. reprobo, malvagio,

castellan, kăs'tĕllăn, s. castellano, m. [m.

caster, kăst'ăr, s. calcolatore, m.; pepaiuola, f.; rotella, f. [punire.

castigate, kăs'tĭgăt, v. a. gastigare,

castigation, -gā'shŭn, s. gastigamento, m., punizione, f. [m.

castings, kăst'ĭngs, s. pl. lavoro di getto,

casting-vote, -vōt, s. suffragio decisivo,

cast-iron, kăst'īrn, s. ferro fuso, m. [m.

castle, kăs'sl, s. castello, m., fortezza, f.; -, v. n. fare rocco.

castled, -sld, a. munito di castelli.

castor, kăs'tăr, s. castoro, m.; cappello di castoro, m.

castor-oil, -ŏĭl, s. olio di ricino, m.

castrate, kăs'trăt, v. a. castrare; mutilare.

castration, -trā'shŭn, s. castratura, f.

cast steel, kăst'stēl, s. acciaio fuso, m.

casual, kăzh'ŭăl, a. casuale, fortuito; -ly, ad. casualmente, fortuitamente.

casualty, -tĭ, s. caso fortuito, caso, accidente, m.

casuist, kăsh'ŭĭst, s. casista, m.

casuistical, -ĭs'tĭkăl, a. casistico.

cat, kăt, s. gatto, m.; gatta, f.; - of nine tails, disciplina, sferza, f.; -'s paw, venticello regolare, m.; merlotto, m.

cataclysm, kăt'ăklĭzm, s. diluvio, m.

catacombs, -ăkŏmz, s. pl. catacombe, f. pl.

catalepsy, -ălĕpsĭ, s. catalessia, f.

catalogue, -ălŏg, s. catalogo, registro, m.

cataplasm, -ăplăsm, s. cataplasma, m.

catapult, -ăpŭlt, s. catapulta, f.

cataract, *–ărăkt,* s. cateratta, f.; cascata, f.; **to couch the –,** operare la cateratta.
catarrh, *kătăr',* s. catarro, m.
catarrhal, *–răl,* a. catarroso.
catastrophe, *kătăs'trŏfĕ,* s. catastrofe, f.
cat-call, *kăt'kăl,* s. fischio, m.; zufolo, m.
catch, *kăch,* v. a. ir. prendere; chiappare, pigliare; rapire; –, v. n. ir. essere contagioso; comunicarsi; arrivare; **to – cold,** infreddarsi, raffreddarsi; **to – fire,** accendersi; infocarsi; –, s. presa, cattura, f.; bottino, m.; profitto, m.; ritornello, m.; annello, m.
catcher, *–ŭr,* s. ingannatore, m.
catching, *–ĭng,* a. contagioso.
catch-word, *–wŭrd,* s. rimando, m.
catechise, *kăt'ĕkĭz,* v. a. catechizzare; interrogare.
catechism, *–ĕkĭzm,* s. catechismo, m.
catechist, *–ĕkĭst,* s. catechista, m.
categorical, *–gŏr'ĭkăl,* a. categorico; **–ly,** ad. categoricamente.
category, *kăt'ĕgŏrĭ,* s. categoria, f.
cater, *kā'tŭr,* v. n. provvedere, far le provvisioni; procacciare.
caterpillar, *kăt'ărpĭllăr,* s. bruco, m.
caterwaul, *–wăl,* v. n. miagolare, gnaulare; –, s. chiasso, frastuono, m.
cat-gut, *kăt'gŭt,* s. corda di minugia, f.
cathedral, *kăthē'drăl,* s. cattedrale, f.
cat-hole, *kăt'hōl,* s. gattaiuola, f.
Catholic, *kăth'ŏlĭk,* s. Cattolico, m.; –, a. cattolico. [m.
catholizism, *–thŏl'ĭzĭzm,* s. cattolicismo, m.
catkin, *kăt'kĭn,* s. (bot.) fiocchi, m. pl.
catsup, *kăts'ŭp,* s. salamoia da funghi, f.
cattle, *kăt'tl,* s. bestiame, m.; pecore, f. pl.; **black –,** bestie bovine, f. pl.
cattle-plague, *–plāg,* s. morbo contagioso delle bestie bovine, m.
cattle-show, *–shō,* s. esposizione di bestiame, f.
caul, *kăl,* s. caffia, f.; integumento, m.
cauliflower, *kăl'ĭflŏŭr,* s. cavolo fiore, m.
cause, *kăz,* s. causa, f.; ragione, f., motivo, m.; processo, m.; –, v. a. causare, cagionare; eccitare.
causeless, *–lĕs,* a. che è senza causa; ingiusto; **–ly,** ad. senza causa.
causeway, *–wā,* **causey,** *kă'zĭ,* s. via, strada, f. [caustico, corrosivo.
caustic, *kăs'tĭk,* s. caustico, m.; –, a.
cauterise, *kă'tŭrĭz,* v. a. cauterizzare.
cautery, *kă'tŭrĭ,* s. cuuterio, m.
caution, *kă'shŭn,* s. prudenza, f.; circospezione, sagacità, f.; avvertimento, avviso, m.; –, v. a. avvertire, ammonire.
cautionary, *–ărĭ,* a. d'ostaggio.
cautious, *kă'shŭs,* a. prudente, accorto; **–ly,** ad. accortamente; sagacemente.
cavalcade, *kăvălkād',* s. cavalcata, f.
cavalier, *kăvălēr',* s. cavaliere, m.
cavalry, *kăv'ălrĭ,* s. cavalleria, f.
cave, *kāv,* s. cava, spelonca, f., antro, m.
caveat, *kă'vēăt,* s. avvertenza, f.; ammonizione, f., avviso, m. [f.
cavern, *kăv'ŭrn,* s. caverna, f.; spelonca,

cavernous, *–ŭs,* a. cavernoso, cavo.
caviar, *kăvĭăr',* s. caviale, m.
cavil, *kăv'ĭl,* s. cavillazione, f., sofisma, m.; –, v. a. cavillare; sofisticare, criticare.
caviller, *–lăr,* s. cavillatore, sofistico, m.
caw, *kă,* v. n. crocitare, gracchiare.
cease, *sēs,* v. a. cessare; discontinuare; –, v. n. desistere.
ceaseless, *–lĕs,* a. continuo, incessante; **–ly,** ad. incessantemente, continuamente.
cedar, *sē'dăr,* s. cedro, m.
cede, *sēd,* v. a. cedere; abbandonare.
ceil, *sēl,* v. a. soffittare.
ceiling, *–ĭng,* s. soffitta, f., soffitto, m.
celebrate, *sĕl'ĕbrăt,* v. a. celebrare; esaltare. [f.; lode, f.
celebration, *–brā'shŭn,* s. celebrazione, f.
celebrity, *–lĕb'rĭtĭ,* s. celebrità, fama, f.
celerity, *–lĕr'ĭtĭ,* s. celerità, f.
celery, *sĕl'ărĭ,* s. appio, m.
celestial, *sĕlĕst'yăl,* a. celestiale, celeste; –, s. celestiale, beato, m.
celibacy, *sĕl'ĭbăsĭ,* s. celibato, m.
celibate, *sĕl'ĭbăt,* a. celibato.
cell, *sĕl,* s. cella, cellula, f.
cellar, *–lăr,* s. cantina, canova, f.
cellarage, *–lărĕj,* s. cantine, f. pl.
cellaret, *–lărĕt,* s. bottiglieria, f.
cellular, *–lŭlăr,* a. cellulare.
cellule, *–lŭl,* s. cellula, f.
cement, *sĕmĕnt',* s. cemento, smalto, m.; –, v. a. assodare, saldare; –, v. n. affermarsi, unirsi.
cemetery, *sĕm'ĕtărĭ,* s. cimitero, m.
cenotaph, *sĕn'ŏtăf,* s. cenotafio, m.
censer, *sĕn'sŭr,* s. incensiere, turribolo, m.
censor, *sĕn'sŏr,* s. censore, critico, m.
censorious, *–sō'rĭŭs,* a. censorio, severo; **–ly,** ad. da censore; in modo severo.
censorship, *sĕn'sŏrshĭp,* s. dignità di censore, censura, f. [biasimevole.
censurable, *sĕn'shŭrăbl,* a. censurabile; f.
censure, *sĕn'shŭr,* s. censura, f.; riprensione, f.; –, v. a. censurare, criticare; biasimare.
census, *sĕn'sŭs,* s. censo, m. [per cento.
cent, *sĕnt,* s. cento, m.; **five per –,** cinque
centenarian, *sĕntĕnā'rĭăn,* s. centenario, m. [cent'anni; –, s. centinaio, m.
centenary, *sĕn'tĕnărĭ,* a. centenario, di
centennial, *–tĕn'nĭăl,* a. centenario.
centipede, *sĕn'tĭpĕd,* s. centopede, centogambe, m.
central, *sĕn'trăl,* a. centrale, centrico; **–ly,** ad. centralmente, nel centro.
centralize, *–ĭz,* v. a. centralizzare.
centre, *sĕn'tŭr,* s. centro, m.; cuore, m.; –, v. a. & n. concentrare; concentrarsi.
centrifugal, *–trĭf'ŭgăl,* a. centrifugo.
centripetal, *–trĭp'ĕtăl,* a. centripeto.
centuple, *sĕn'tŭpl,* s. centuplo; –, v. a. centuplicare. [m.
century, *sĕn'tŭrĭ,* s. centuria, f.; secolo, m.
cereals, *sē'rĭălz,* s. pl. cereali, m. pl.
cerecloth, *sēr'klŏth,* **cerement,** *–mĕnt,* s. incerato, m.; tela incerata, f.
ceremonial, *sĕrĕmō'nĭăl,* a. cerimoniale; –, s. cerimoniale, m.; rito, m;

ceremonious, −mŏ′nĭăs, a. cerimonioso; −ly, ad. con cerimonia.

ceremony, sĕr′ĕmŏnĭ, s. cerimonia, formalità, f.; complimento, m.

certain, săr′tĭn, a. certo, sicuro; evidente; for−, di certo, per certo; −ly, ad. certamente, senza dubbio.

certainty, −tĭ, certitude, săr′tĭtūd, s. certezza, sicurezza, f.

certificate, −ĭf′ĭkăt, s. certificato, m., attestazione, f.   [zione, attestazione, f.

certification, −fĭkā′shŭn, s. certificazione, f.

certify, săr′tĭfĭ, v. a. certificare, render certo; confermare.

cerulean, sĕrū′lăn, a. ceruleo, turchino.

cerumen, sĕrū′mĕn, s. cerume, m.

cessation, sĕssā′shŭn, s. cessazione, f.; − of arms, armistizio, m.   [zione, f.

cession, sĕs′shŭn, s. cessione, f.; rassegnacesspool, sĕs′pŏl, s. smaltitoio, pozzo nero, m., cloaca, f.

chafe, chāf, s. ardore, furore, m., rabbia, f.; −, v. a. scaldare; irritare, stizzire, mettere in collera; −, v. n. adirarsi, incollerirsi.

chafer, chā′făr, s. scarafaggio, m.

chaff, chăf, s. lolla, loppa, f.

chaff-cutter, −kăttăr, s. tritapaglia, f.

chaffer, −făr, v. n. trafficare; stiracchiare, mettere a prezzo; trattare.

chafferer, −fărăr, s. mercante, m.

chaffinch, −fĭnsh, s. fringuello, m.

chagrin, shăgrĕn′, s. malumore, affanno, m.; stizza, f.

chain, chăn, s. catena, f.; serie, f.; −s, pl. catene, f. pl., schiavitù, f.; −, v. a. incatenare, mettere alla catena, legare con catena.

chain-bridge, −brĭj, s. ponte di catene, ponte pensile, m.   [f. pl.

chain-shot, −shŏt, s. palle incatenate, chair, chăr, s. sedia, f.; sedia portatile, f.; −, v. a. condurre in trionfo.   [m.

chair-bottomer, −bŏttămăr, s. seggiolaio, chairman, −măn, s. presidente, m.; portantino, m.

chaise, chāz, s. calessino, m.

chalice, chăl′ĭs, s. calice, m., coppa, f.

chalk, chăk, s. creta, f., gesso, m., marna, f.; French −, pietra da sarti, steatite, f.; −, v. a. segnare col gesso; schizzare.

chalk-pit, −pĭt, s. cava di marna, f.

chalky, chăk′ĭ, a. cretoso.

challenge, chăl′lĕnj, s. disfida, f.; pretensione, f.; rigettamento, rifiuto, m.; −, v. a. sfidare; recusare.

challenger, −lĕnjăr, s. sfidatore, m.

chamber, chăm′băr, s. camera, f.; stanza, f.   [colpi.

chambered, −bărd, a. (of revolvers) da...

chamberlain, −bărlĭn, s. camarlingo, m.

chamber-maid, −mād, s. cameriera, f.

chamber-pot, −pŏt, s. orinale, m.

chameleon, kămē′lĕăn, s. camaleonte, m.

chamois-leather, shăm′wă lĕthăr, s. camoscio, m.   [rodere.

champ, chămp, v. a. & n. masticare,

champagne, shămpān′, s. vino di Sciampagna, m.   [aperto, m.

champaign, −, s. campagna, f., paese

champion, chăm′pĭŏn, s. campione, eroe, m.; −, v. a. sfidare a singolar certame.

chance, chăns, s. azzardo, m., ventura, f., caso, m., sorte, f.; −, v. n. accadere, avvenire, occorrere.

chancel, chăn′sĕl, s. santuario, m.

chancellor, −lŭr, s. cancelliere, m.; Lord High−, Gran Cancelliere (d'Inghilterra).

chancery, chăn′sŭrĭ, s. cancelleria, f.

chancre, shăng′kŭr, s. canchero, cancro, m.

chandelier, shăndĕlēr′, s. candelabro, m.; lumiera, f.

chandler, chănd′lŭr, s. candelaio, m.

change, chănj, s. cambiamento, m.; mutazione, vicenda, f.; varietà, f.; moneta, f.; −, v. a. cambiare; mutare, alterare; −, v. n. cangiarsi; mutarsi.

changeable, −ăbl, changeful, −fŭl, a. mutabile; instabile, variabile.

changeableness, −ăblnĕs, s. incostanza, mutabilità, f.

changeably, −ăblĭ, ad. incostantemente.

changeless, −lĕs, a. invariabile, costante.

changeling, −lĭng, s. parto supposto, m.; sciocco, m.

channel, chăn′nĕl, s. canale, m; letto (d' un fiume), m.; scanalatura, f.; −, v. a. scanalare.   [tare; celebrare.

chant, chănt, s. canto, m.; −, v. a. can-

chanter, −ăr, s. cantatore, cantore, m.

chanticleer, −ĭklăr, s. gallo, m.

chaos, kā′ŏs, s. caos, m.; confusione, f.

chaotic, kăŏt′ĭk, a. confuso.

chap, chăp, s. fessura, f.; crepatura, f., fesso, m.; −, v. n. crepare; fendersi.

chape, chāp, s. puntale, m.; fermaglio, m.

chapel, chăp′ĕl, s. cappella, chiesetta, f.

chaplain, chăp′lĭn, s. cappellano, m.; limosiniere, m.

chaplet, −lĕt, s. corona, f.; rosario, m.

chapman, −măn, s. compratore, m.; mercante, m.   [imboccatura, f.

chaps, chăps, s. bocca (d' un' animale), f.;

chapter, chăp′tăr, s. capitolo, m.; capo, m.

char, chăr, s. giornata, f.; −, v. a. ridurre in carbone; −, v. n. lavorare alla giornata.

character, kăr′ăktăr, s. carattere, m.; segno, m.; lettera, f.; descrizione, f.; dignità, f.; −, v. a. intagliare; inscrivere.

characteristic, −tărĭs′tĭk, a. caratteristico.

characterize, kăr′ăktărĭz, v. a. caratterizzare.

charade, shărād′, s. sciarrada, f.

charcoal, chăr′kōl, s. carbone di legna, m.

charge, chărj, s. carico, m., carica, f., peso, m.; cura, incombenza, f.; uffizio, impiego, m.; accusa, imputazione, f.; deposito, m.; spesa, f.; assalto, m.; −, v. a. caricare; comandare, imporre; accusare, incolpare.   [dioso.

chargeable, −ăbl, a. imputabile; dispen-

charger, −ăr, s. cavallo da guerra, m.; gran piatto, m.

charily, chăr′ĭlĭ, ad. accortamente.

chariness, −ĭnĕs, s. cura, f.; esitazione, f.

English and Italian.

chariot, *chăr'ĭŏt,* s. carro, m., carrozza, f.; −, v. n. condurre in carrozza.

charioteer, −*ēr',* s. cocchiere, conduttor del carro, m.

charitable, *chăr'ĭtăbl,* a. caritatevole, beneficente, benefico.

charitableness, −*nĕs,* s. beneficenza, f.

charitably, −*ĭ,* ad. caritatevolmente.

charity, *chăr'ĭtĭ,* s. carità, f.; beneficenza, limosina, f.   [veri infanti, f.

charity-school, −*skŏl,* s. scuola pei poveri.

charlatan, *shăr'lătăn,* s. ciarlatano, saltimbanco, f.   [barreria, f.

charlatanry, −*lătănrĭ,* s. ciarlataneria, f.

Charles's-Wain, *chărlz'ĕz wān,* s. Orsa maggiore (costellazione), f.

charlock, *chăr'lŏk,* s. senape, m.

charm, *chărm,* s. incanto, m.; allettamento, m.; −, v. a. incantare, ammaliare, allettare, rapire.   [trice, f.

charmer, −*ăr,* s. incantatore, m.; incantatrice, f.

charmingly, −*ĭnglĭ,* ad. vagamente, piacevolmente, vezzosamente.   [m.

charnel-house, *chăr'nĕl hŏŭs,* s. carnaio, m.

chart, *chărt,* s. carta da navigare, f.

charter, *chăr'tŭr,* s. patente, m.; privilegio, m.; −, v. a. noleggiare.

charwoman, *chăr'wŭmăn,* s. donna che lavora a giornata, f.

chary, *chăr'ĭ,* a. accorto, prudente.

chase, *chās,* s. caccia, f.; foresta, f.; −, v. a. cacciare; mandar via.

chasing, *chā'sĭng,* s. cesellatura, f.

chasm, *kăzm,* s. fessura, f.; apertura, f.; vacuo, m.   [puro.

chaste, *chāst,* a. casto, pudico; onesto;

chasten, *chās'n,* v. a. gastigare, punire; correggere.   [f.; modestia, f.

chasteness, *chāst'nĕs,* s. castità, pudicizia,

chastise, *chăstīz',* v. a. gastigare, punire.

chastisement, *chăs'tĭzmĕnt,* s. gastigo, m.

chastity, *chăs'tĭtĭ,* s. castità, f.; purità, f.

chat, *chăt,* s. ciarla, f., cicaleccio, m.; −, v. n. ciarlare, chiachierare.

chattel, *chăt'tl,* s. mobile, m.

chatter, −*tăr,* s. ciarla, f., el cicalare, m.; −, v. n. ciarlare; battere i denti.

chatterer, −*tărŭr,* **chatter-box,** −*tărbŏks,* s. ciarliero, ciarlatore, m.

chatty, −*tĭ,* a. loquace, ciarlone.

chaw, *chă,* v. a. masticare; ruminare.

cheap, *chēp,* (−**ly**), a. (& ad.) a buon mercato, a buon prezzo.

cheapen, *chēp'n,* v. a. prezzolare, mercatare.

cheapness, −*nĕs,* s. buon mercato, vil prezzo, m.

cheat, *chēt,* s. frode, furberia, f., inganno, m.; furbo, m.; barattiere, m.; giuntatore, m.; −, v. a. far fraude, ingannare, truffare; giuntare.

check, *chĕk,* s. scacco, m.; ostacolo, impedimento, m.; rimprovero, m., riprensione, f.; −, v. a. frenare, reprimere; riprendere; −, v. n. fermarsi; opporsi.

checker, −*ăr,* v. a. far a scacchi; intarsiare; screziare.

checker-board, −*bŏrd,* s. scacchiere, m.

checker-work, −*wŭrk,* s. tarsia, f.; screzio, m.

check-mate, −*māt,* s. scaccomatto, m.

cheek, *chĕk,* s. guancia, f.; gota, f.; (fam.) impudenza, f.; − **by jowl,** testa a testa.

cheek-bone, −*bōn,* s. mascella, f.

cheer, *chēr,* s. pasto, m.; banchetto, m., allegrezza, f., umore, coraggio, m.; volto, m.; −, v. a. rallegrare; animare; −, v. n. rallegrarsi, incoraggiarsi, farsi animo.

cheerful, −*fŭl,* a. gaio, allegro, lieto, gioioso; −**ly,** ad. allegramente, lietamente.

cheerfulness, −*fŭlnĕs,* **cheeriness,** −*ĭnĕs,* s. gioia, allegrezza, f.

cheering, −*ĭng,* s. approvazione, f., applauso, m.

cheerless, −*lĕs,* a. triste, malinconico.

cheese, *chēz,* s. formaggio, cacio, m.

cheese-dairy, −*dărĭ,* s. fabbrica di formaggio, f.

cheese-hopper, −*hŏppăr,* s. baco del cacio, m.

cheesemonger, −*mŭnggăr,* s. caciaiuolo, m.; pizzicagnolo, m.

chemical, *kĕm'ĭkăl,* a. chimico.

chemist, *kĕm'ĭst,* s. chimico, m.

chemistry *kĕm'ĭstrĭ,* s. chimica, f.

cherish, *chĕr'ĭsh,* v. a. amare teneramente; mantenere; allevare.

cheroot, *shĕrŏt',* s. maniglia (cigar), f.

cherry, *chĕr'rĭ,* s. ciliegia, f.; **wild** −, agriotta, f.; −, a. rosso, vermiglio.

cherry-stone, −*stōn,* s. nocciolo di ciliegia, m.

cherry-tree, −*trē,* s. ciliegio, m.

cherub, *chĕr'ŭb,* s. cherubino, m.

chesnut, *vedi* chestnut.

chess, *chĕs,* s. scacchi, m. pl.   [liere, m.

chess-board, −*bŏrd,* s. scacchiere, tavoliere, m.

chess-man, −*măn,* s. pedina, f.; scacco, m.

chest, *chĕst,* s. cassa, f.; casso, cassero (del corpo), m.; −**of drawers,** s. armadio, m.

chestnut, *chĕs'nŭt,* s. castagna, f.; **horse** −, ippocastano, m.   [nino.

chestnut-coloured, −*kŭlŭrd,* a. castagnino.

chestnut-tree, −*trē,* s. castagno, m.

cheval-glass, *shĕvăl'glăs,* s. specchio mobile, m.   [siderare, meditare.

chew, *chŏ,* v. a. masticare; ruminare; considerare.

chicane, *shĭkān',* s. cavillo, inganno, raggiro, m.; −, v. n. cavillare; sofisticare.

chicaner, −*nŭr,* s. cavillatore, m.

chicanery, −*nărĭ,* s. cavillo, m., raggiri, m. pl.; sofisticheria, f.

chick(en), *chĭk('ĕn),* s. pollastro, m.

chicken-hearted, −*hărtĕd,* a. timido, pauroso; pusillanime.

chicken-pox, −*pŏks,* s. morbiglione, m.

chick-pea, *chĭk'pē,* s. cece, m.

chick-weed, −*wēd,* s. (bot.) centonchio, m.

chide, *chīd,* v. a. ir. biasimare; riprendere; −, v. n. disputare, schiamazzare.

chief, *chēf,* a. primo, principale; −**ly,** ad. principalmente; −, s. capo, comandante, m.; **the Lord − Justice,** primo giudice (in Inghilterra), m.   [tano, m.

chieftain, −*tĭn,* s. comandante, m.; capitano, m.

chilblain, *chĭl'blăn,* s. pedignone, f.

child, *chīld,* s. fanciullo, m.; figlio, figliuolo,

m.; **from a –**, dall' infanzia, dalla culla;
to be with –, essere gravida.
child-bed, –*bĕd*, s. letto della partoriente,
m.; puerperio, m. [lezza, f.
childhood, –*hŭd*, s. infanzia, f.; fanciul-
childish, –*ĭsh*, a. bambinesco, fanciullesco; –**ly**, ad. a modo di fanciullo. [f.
childishness, –*ĭshnĕs*,s.infanzia,puerizia,
childless, –*lĕs*, a. che è senza figliuoli.
childlike, –*lĭk*, a. fanciullesco, bambi-
children, *chĭl'drĕn*, pl. di **child**. [nesco.
chill, *chĭl*, a. freddo, freddoloso; –, s.
freddo, m., freddura, f.; –, v. a. freddare;
gelare. [m.
chilliness, –*lĭnĕs*, s. freddura, f.; brivido,
chilly, –*lĭ*, a. freddoloso.
chime, *chīm*, s. scampanata, f.; accordo,
m., armonia, f.; –, v. n. scampanare;
accordarsi, unirsi.
chimera, *kĭmē'rȧ*, s. chimera, f.
chimerical, –*mĕr'ĭkȧl*, a. chimerico; –**ly**,
ad. chimericamente.
chimney, *chĭm'nĭ*, s. camino, m.
chimney-corner, –*kŏrnŭr*, s. luogo de'
ciarloni, m. [mino, f.
chimney-piece, –*pēs*, s. cornice del ca-
chimney-sweeper, –*swēpŭr*, s. spazza-
chin, *chĭn*, s. mento, m. [camino, m.
china (ware), *chī'nȧ (wȧr)*, s. porcellana,
f.; maiolica, f.
chine, *chīn*, s. schiena, f.; spina, f.
chink, *chĭngk*, s. fessura, crepatura, f.;
–, v. a. & n. tintinnare; spaccarsi.
chintz, *chĭnts*, s. indiana (tela dipinta), f.
chip, *chĭp*, s. scheggia, f.; truciolo, m.;
–**s**, pl. croste (di pane), f. pl.; –, v. a.
truciolare, sbriciolare, sminuzzare.
chirographer, *kīrŏg'rȧfŭr*, s. scrivano
publico, m. [f.
chiromancy, *kī'rōmȧnsĭ*, s. chiromanzia,
chiropodist, *kīrŏp'ŏdĭst*, s. callista, m.
chirp, *chŭrp*, s. garrito, m.; pigolare, m.;
–, v. a. garrire; pigolare, piare.
chirping, –*ĭng*, s. garrito, m.; canto (d'
uccelli), m. [scalpellare, intagliare.
chisel, *chīz'ĕl*, s. scalpello, m.; –, v. a.
chit, *chĭt*, s. bambino, m.; stipite, m.
chit-chat, –*chăt*, s. ciarla, f.
chitterlings, –*tŭrlĭngz*, s. pl. budella,
minuge, f. pl. [fanciullesco.
chitty, –*tĭ*, a. lentigginoso; bambinesco,
chivalrous,*shĭv'ȧlrŭs*,**chivalric**,–*ălrĭk*,
a. cavalleresco. [cavaliere, m.
chivalry, –*ȧlrĭ*, s. dignità di cavaliere, f.
chives, *chīvz*, s. pl. cipolletta, f.
chloral, *klō'rȧl*, s. cloral, m.
chloroform, *klō'rōfŏrm*, s. cloroformio, m.
chocolate, *chŏk'ŏlȧt*, s. cioccolata, f.
chocolate-drop, –*drŏp*, s. pastiglia di
cioccolata, f.
chocolate-stick, –*stĭk*, s. frullo, m.
choice, *chŏĭs*, s. scelta, elezione, f.; varietà,
f.; –, a. scelto, squisito, raro.
choiceless, –*lĕs*, a. senza il potere di
scegliere; indifferente.
choicely, –*lĭ*, ad. caramente. [f.
choiceness, –*nĕs*, s. rarità, f.; delicatezza,
choir, *kwīr*, s. coro (d' una chiesa), m.

choke, *chōk*, v. a. soffocare, strangolare;
turare, stoppare.
choker, *chō'kŭr*, s. (fam.) cravatta, f.
choky, *chō'kĭ*, a. soffocante. [f.
choler, *kŏl'ŭr*, s. collera, f.; bile, f.; stizza,
cholera, *kŏl'ȧrȧ*, s. colera, m.
choleric, –*ĭk*, a. collerico; stizzoso.
choose, *chōz*, v. a. ir. scegliere, eleggere;
–, v. n. ir. potere scegliere.
chop, *chŏp*, s. fetta, f.; crepatura, f.; braciuola, f.; –**s**, pl. mascelle, f. pl.; bocca,
m.; imboccatura (d' un fiume), m.; –, v. a.
tagliare; sminuzzare; –, v. n. cambiare,
barattare; disputare.
chopper, *chŏp'pŭr*, s. coltellaccio, m.
chopping-knife, –*pĭng nĭf*, s. coltello da
beccaio, m. [mente.
choral, *kō'rȧl*, a. corale; –**ly**, ad. coral-
chord, *kŏrd*, s. corda, f.; –, v. a. metter
corde ad istrumenti a corda. [m.
chorister, *kwĭr'ĭstŭr*, s. corista, cantore,
chorus, *kō'rŭs*, s. coro, m.
chouse, *chŏŭs*, v. a. ingannare, truffare.
chrism, *krĭzm*, s. cresima, f.
Christ, *krĭst*, s. Cristo.
christen, *krĭs'n*, v. a. battezzare.
Christendom, –*dŏm*, s. cristianità, f.
christening, *krĭst'nĭng*, s. battesimo, m.
Christian, *krĭst'yȧn*, a. cristiano; –
name, s. nome di battesimo, m.; –, s.
Cristiano, m.; Cristiana, f. [tiano.
christianise, *krĭst'yȧnĭz*, v. a. fare Cris-
Christianity,*krĭstĭȧn'ĭtĭ*,s.Cristianesimo,
m.; Cristianità, f. [mente.
christianly, *krĭst'yȧnlĭ*, ad. cristiana-
Christmas, *krĭs'mȧs*, s. natale, m.; natività (del Signore), f. [m., strenna, f.
Christmas-box, –*bŏks*, s. salvadanaio,
chromatic, *krōmȧt'ĭk*, a. cromatico.
chromolithography,*krōmōlĭth'ŏgrȧfĭ*, s.
cromolitografia, f.
chronic(al), *krŏn'ĭk(ȧl)*, a. cronico.
chronicle, *krŏn'ĭkl*, s. cronaca, f.; –, v. a.
scrivere le cronache. [cronista, m.
chronicler, –*klŭr*, s. scrittore di cronache.
chronological, *krŏnŏlŏj'ĭkȧl*, a. cronologico; –**ly**, ad. in modo cronologico.
chronology, *krŏnŏl'ŏjĭ*, s. cronologia, f.
chronometer, *krŏnŏm'ĕtŭr*, s. cronometro, m.
chrysalis, *krĭs'ȧlĭs*, s. crisalide, m.
chrysanthemum, *krĭsȧn'thĕmŭm*, s. (bot.)
crisantemo, m.
chub, *chŭb*, s. ghiozzo, m.
chubby, *chŭb'bĭ*, a. paffuto.
chuck, *chŭk*, s. sorgozzone, m.; –, v. a.
chiocciare; dare un sorgozzone.
chuckle, *chŭk'l*, v. a. chiocciare; car-
reggiare; –, v. n. sganasciare.
chum, *chŭm*, s. compagno di camera, m.
chump, *chŭmp*, **chunk**, *chŭngk*, s. pezzo,
m.; tronco di legno, m.
church, *chŭrch*, s. chiesa, f.; –, v. a. andare in chiesa; –, v. n. render grazie dopo
il parto. [zione, f.
church-ale, –*ăl*, s. festa della consacra-
churching, –*ĭng*, s. cerimonia della purificazione, f.

church-law, –lâ, s. diritto canonico, m.
churchman, –mân, s. ecclesiastico, prete, m.
church-warden, –wârdn, s. santese, m.
churchyard, –yârd, s. cimitero, m. [m.
churl, chârl, s. villano, rustico, m.; avaro,
churlish, –ish, a. rustico, zotico, taccagno;
  –ly, ad. rozzamente, zoticamente.
churn, chârn, s. zangola, f.; –, v. a. far il
  burro.
cicatrice, sïk' âtrïs, s. cicatrice, f.
cider, sï' dâr, s. sidro, m.
cigar, sïgâr', s. sigaro, m.
cigarette, sïg' ârĕt, s. sigaretta, f.
cigar-holder, –hôldâr, s. bocchino, m.
cimeter, sïm' ëtâr, s. scimitarra, f.
cincture, sïngk' châr, s. cintura, fascia, f.
cinder, sïn' dâr, s. cenere, f.
cinnabar, sïn' nâbâr, s. cinabro, vermiglione, m,   [cannella, f.
cinnamon, sïn' nâmôn, s. cinnamomo, m.,
cipher, sï' fâr, s. cifra, f.; –, v. a. & n. calcolare, computare.
circle, sâr' kl, s. circolo, cerchio, m.; società, f.; –, v. a. cerchiare; limitare; –,
  v. n. muovere in giro, girare.   [m.
circlet, sâr' klĕt, s. cerchietto, cerchiello,
circuit, sâr' kït, s. circuito, m.; contorno, m.
circuitous, –kû' ïtâs, a. circolare; –ly, ad.
  circolarmente.   [–, s. lettera circolare, f.
circular, sâr' kûlâr, a. circolare, rotondo;
circulate, sâr' kûlât, v. n. circolare; girare,
  volgersi intorno.
circulating-library, –lâtïng lïbrârï, s.
  gabinetto di lettura, f.
circulation, –lâ' shân, s. circolazione, f.
circulatory, sâr' kûlâtârï, a. circolatorio,
  circolare; –decimal, s. frazione decimale
  periodica, f.
circumcise, sâr' kâmsïz, v. a. circoncidere.
circumcision, –sïzh' ân, s. circoncisione, f.
circumference, –kâm' fĕrĕns, s. circonferenza, f.; circuito, m,   [confiesso, m.
circumflex, sâr' kâmflĕks, s. accento cir-
circumjacent, –jâ' sĕnt, a. contiguo, cir-
  convicino.   [locuzione, f.
circumlocution, –lôkû' shân, s. circon-
circumlocutory, –lôk' ûtârï, a. perifra-
  stico.   [intorno.
circumnavigate, –nâv' ïgât, v. n. navigare
circumnavigation, –nâvïgâ' shân, s. cir-
  cumnavigazione, f.   [limitare.
circumscribe, –skrïb', v. a. circoscrivere;
circumscription, –skrïp' shân, s. circo-
  scrizione, f.
circumspect, –spĕkt, a. circospetto, considerato, cauto; prudente.
circumspection, –spĕk' shân, s. circospezione, f.; prudenza, f.
circumstance, –stâns, s. circostanza, f.;
  evento, m.; condizione, f., stato, m.
circumstanced, –stânst, a. circostanziato,
  specificato.
circumstantial, –stân' shâl, a. accidentale,
  casuale; –ly, ad. secondo le circostanze,
  casualmente.   [stanziare, specificare.
circumstantiate, –stân' shiât, v. a. circo-
circumvent, –vĕnt, v. a. circonvenire, ingannare.

circumvention, –vĕn' shân, s. circonven-
  zione, f., inganno, m.; insidia, f.
circus, sâr' kâs, s. circo, m.
cistern, sïs' târn, s. cisterna, f.
citadel, sït' âdĕl, s. cittadella, fortezza, f.
citation, sïtâ' shân, s. (jur.) citazione, f.;
  allegazione, f.   [allegare.
cite, sït, v. a. (jur.) citare, assegnare;
cithern, sïth' ârn, s. sistro, m.
citizen, sït' ïzĕn, s. borghese, cittadino, m.
citizenship, –shïp, s. cittadinanza, f.
citron, sït' rôn, s. cedrato, m.
citron-tree, –trĕ, s. cedro, m.
citron-water, –wâtâr, s. acqua cedrata, f.
city, sït' ï, s. città, f.
civet, sïv' ĕt, s. zibetto, m.
civet-cat, –kât, s. zibetto, m. (animale).
civic, sïv' ïk, a. civico, da cittadino.
civil, sïv' ïl, a. civile; politico; cortese.
civilian, sïvïl' yân, s. giureconsulto, m.
civilisation, –ïzâ' shân, s. civilizzazione,
  f.; stato civilizzato, m.
civilise, sïv' ïlïz, v. a. civilizzare, coltivare,
  dirozzare.   [cortesia, f.
civility, –vïl' ïtï, s. civiltà, f.; urbanità,
civilly, sïv' ïllï, ad. civilmente, cortesemente.
clack, klâk, s. strepito, m.; nottolino d'
  molino, m.; –, v. n. strepitare; scoppiare.
clad, klâd, a. vestito, coperto.
claim, klâm, s. diritto, m.; pretensione, f.;
  to lay a – to, pretendere aver diritto a;
  –, v. a. richiamare; pretendere; arrogarsi.
claimant, –ânt, s. pretendente, m.
clam, klâm, v. a. invescare, impaniare.
clamber, klâm' bâr, v. n. rampicarsi.
clamminess, –mïnĕs, s. viscosità, f.; tenacità, f.
clammy, –mï, a. viscoso; tenace.
clamorous, klâm' ârâs, a. clamoroso, strepitoso, tumultuoso; –ly, ad. strepitosa-
  mente.
clamour, –âr, s. clamore, m.; strepito, m.;
  grido, m.; –, v. n. strepitare; gridare.
clamp, klâmp, s. mezza puleggia, f.; in-
  castro, m.; –, v. a. incastrare.
clan, klân, s. famiglia, razza, f.; tribù, f.
clandestine, klândĕs' tïn, a. clandestino;
  –ly, ad. in modo clandestino.
clang, klâng, s. suono acuto, m.; rumore,
  m.; –, v. n. strepitare; sonare.
clangorous, –gârâs, a. strepitoso.
clangour, –gâr, s. strombettata, f.
clank, klângk, s. suono acuto, strepito, m.;
  –, v. n. sonare, strepitare.
clap, klâp, s. strepito, m.; colpo, m.; fracasso, m.; –, v. a. battere; applaudire;
  applicare.
clapper, –pâr, s. applauditore, approva-
  tore, m.; battaglio (di campana), m.; martello (d' una porta), m.; battente (di mulino), m.
clapping, –pïng, s. plauso, m.
clap-trap, –trâp, s. colpo di teatro, m.
clare-obscure, klâr ôbskûr', s. chiar-
claret, klâr' ĕt, s. claretto, m. [oscuro, m.

clarification, *-rĭfĭkă'shŭn,* s. chiarificazione, f.

clarify, *klăr'ĭfī,* v. a. chiarificare, chiarire; conciare con colla (il vino); –, v. n. chiariarsi.

clarinet, *klăr'ĭnĕt,* s. chiarina, f. [rirsi.

clarion, *klăr'ĭŏn,* s. clarino. m.

clash, *klăsh,* s. urto, m.; fracasso, m.; contrasto, m.; differenza, contesa, f.; –, v. n. urtarsi; scontrarsi, dibattersi, disputare.

clasp, *klăsp,* s. fermaglio, m.; ganghero, m.; abbracciamento, amplesso, m.; –, v. a. affibbiare; abbracciare.

clasp-knife, *-nīf,* s. coltello da tasca, m.

class, *klăs,* s. classe, f.; ordine, m.; –, v. a. classificare. [classico, m.

classic(al), *-sĭk(ăl),* a. classico; –, s. autore classico, m.

classification, *-sĭfĭkă'shŭn,* s. classificazione, f.

classify, *-sĭfī,* v. a. classificare.

clatter, *klăt'tŭr,* s. strepito, fracasso, m.; –, v. a. & n. strepitare; cicalare.

clause, *klăz,* s. clausola, f.; articolo, m.; stipolazione, condizione, f.

claustral, *klăz'trăl,* a. claustrale.

clavicle, *klăv'ĭkl,* s. clavicola, f.

claw, *klă,* s. artiglio, m.; branca, f.; rampa, f.; –, v. a. (s)graffiare; adulare, lusingare.

clawed, *klăd,* a. unguiculato.

clay, *klă,* s. creta, f.; argilla, ı.

clayey, *-ĭ,* **clayish,** *-ĭsh,* a. argilloso.

clay-pit, *-pĭt,* s. cava d' argilla, f.

clean, *klēn,* a. & ad. netto, puro, bianco; affatto, intieramente; –, v. a. nettare; lavare, pulire. [pulitezza, f.; purità, f.

cleanliness, *klĕn'lĭnĕs,* s. nettezza, f.

cleanly, *klĕn'lĭ,* a. & ad. puro, netto, pulito; elegante; pulitamente; elegantemente. [f.

cleanness, *klĕn'nĕs,* s. nettezza, f.; purità.

cleanse, *klĕnz,* v. a. purgare, purificare.

clear, *klēr,* a. chiaro, puro; innocente; evidente; –, ad. affatto, intieramente; **to get – of,** uscire di; –, v. a. chiarire; purgare; giustificare, assolvere; –, v. n. divenire chiaro; **to – accounts,** liquidare conti.

clearage, *-āj,* s. sgombero, m.

clearance, *-ăns,* s. bulletta di passaporto, f., certificato, m.; (mar.) spedizioni di dogana, f. pl. [mente.

clearly, *-lĭ,* ad. chiaramente, evidentemente.

clearness, *-nĕs,* s. chiarezza, f.; splendore, m.; nettezza, f.; purità, f.; innocenza, f. [dizioso.

clear-sighted, *-sītĕd,* a. perspicace, giudizioso.

clearstarch, *-stărch,* v. a. inamidare.

cleave, *klēv,* v. a. ir. fendere; spaccare; –, v. n. ir. fendersi. [caio, m.

cleaver, *klē'vŭr,* s. coltellaccio da beccaio, m.

cleft, *klĕft,* s. fessura, f.; apertura, f.

clematis, *klĕm'ătĭs,* s. (bot.) clematide, vincapervinca, f. [nignità, f.

clemency, *klĕm'ĕnsĭ,* s. clemenza, f.; benignità, f.

clement, *klĕm'ĕnt,* a. clemente; benigno.

clench, *klĕnsh,* v. a. serrare.

clergy, *klŭr'jĭ,* s. clero, m., ecclesiastici, m. pl. [m.

clergyman, *-măn,* s. ecclesiastico, prete,

clerical, *klĕr'ĭkăl,* a. chericale.

clerk, *klărk,* s. cherico, chierico, m.; sagrestano, m.; scrivano, m.; segretario, m.

clerkship, *-shĭp,* s. chericato, m.; carica di scrivano, f.; dottrina, f.

clever, *klĕv'ŭr,* a. abile, destro; disposto; **-ly,** ad. abilmente, destramente.

cleverness, *-nĕs,* s. abilità, destrezza, f.

clew, *klū,* s. gomitolo, m.; guida, f.

click, *klĭk,* s. saliscendi, m.; –, v. n. tintinnare; scricchiolare.

client, *klī'ĕnt,* s. cliente, m.

cliff, *klĭf,* s. scoglio, scheggio, m.

climacteric, *klĭmăk'tĕrĭk,* a. climaterico.

climate, *klī'măt,* s. clima, m.; regione, f.

climatic, *-măt'ĭk,* a. climatico.

climax, *klī'măks,* s. clima, m.

climb, *klĭm,* v. a. ir. rampicare; montare; –, v. n. ir. arrampicarsi; salire.

climber, *-ŭr,* s. (bot.) viburno, m.

clinch, *klĭnsh,* s. equivoco, m.; –, v. a. impugnare; serrare; ribardire; **to – an argument,** confermare un argomento.

clincher, *-ŭr,* s. rampone, m. [parsi.

cling, *klĭng,* v. n. ir. appiccarsi; aggrapparsi.

clinical, *klĭn'ĭkăl,* a. clinico.

clink, *klĭngk,* s. tintinnio, m.; –, v. a. fare sonare; –, v. n. tintinnire; risonare.

clinker, *-ŭr,* s. mattone invetriato, m.

clip, *klĭp,* s. colpo, m.; abbracciamento, m.; –, v. a. tosare; abbracciare.

clipper, *-pŭr,* s. tosatore, m.; cimatore, m.; nave spedita, f.

clippings, *-pĭngz,* s. pl. tosatura, f.

cloak, *klōk,* s. mantello, m.; pretesto, m.; –, v. a. mantellare; palliare.

cloak-room, *-rōm,* s. scaricatoio, m.

clock, *klŏk,* s. orologio, oriuolo, m.; **what o' – is it?** che ora fa? [f.

clock-dial, *-dīăl,* s. mostra d' un oriuolo,

clock-maker, *-mākŭr,* s. orologiaio, m.

clock-work, *-wŭrk,* s. congegno, m., struttura d' un oriuolo, f.

clod, *klŏd,* s. zolla (di terra), f.; sciocco, babbuasso, m.; –, v. n. coagularsi.

clog, *klŏg,* s. ostacolo, m.; zoccolo, m.; –, v. a. imbarazzare; caricare; –, v. n. coagularsi; unirsi.

clogginess, *-gĭnĕs,* s. imbarazzo, m.; confusione, f. [m.

cloister, *klŏis'tŭr,* s. chiostro, monastero,

close, *klōz,* a. & ad. serrato, stretto; contiguo, vicino; conciso; celato, segreto; riserbato; fosco, oscuro; **– by,** molto vicino; –, s. conclusione, f.; fine, m. & f.; chiusura, f.; –, v. a. serrare; chiudere; terminare; –, v. n. chiudersi; scaldarsi; riunirsi; accordarsi; **to – an account,** saldare un conto.

closefight, *-fĭt,* s. zuffa rabbiosa, f.

close-fisted, *-fĭstĕd,* **close-handed,** *-hăndĕd,* a. spilorcio. [mente.

closely, *-lĭ,* ad. segretamente; nascosamente.

closeness, *-nĕs,* s. spessezza, densità, f.; chiusura, f.; riserbatezza, f.; cautela, f.

closet, *klŏz'ĕt,* s. gabinetto, camerino, m.; –, v. a. chiudere nel gabinetto.

closure, *klō'zhŭr*, s. chiusura, f.; conclusione, f. [-, v. n. coagularsi.
clot, *klŏt*, s. concrezione, coagulazione, f.;
cloth, *klŏth*, s. tela, f.; panno, |m.; to-vaglia, f.; **to lay the –**, apparecchiare la tavola.
clothe, *klōth*, v. a. ir. vestire; coprire.
clothes, *klōthz*, s.pl. abito, m.; vestimento, m.; panni, m. pl.; biancherie, f. pl.: **suit of –**, vestito, m.; **bed–**, coperte del letto, f. pl. [biancheria, m.
clothes-basket,–*băskĕt*, s. canestro della
cloth-horse, *klŏth' hŏrs*, s. seccatoio, m.
clothes-peg, *klŏthz' pĕg*, s. portamantelli,
clothier, *klŏth'yĕr*, s. pannaiuolo, m. [m.
clothing, *klō'thĭng*, s. vestimento, vestito, m.
cloth-press, *klŏth' prĕs*, s. armadio, m.
cloud, *klŏŭd*, s. nube, nuvola, f.; macchia, f.; avversità, f.; –, v. a. annuvolare; offuscare; –, v. n. annuvolarsi, oscurarsi.
cloudily, –*lĭ*, ad. oscuramente.
cloudiness, –*ĭnĕs*, s. oscurità, f.; offuscamento, m.
cloudless, –*lĕs*, a. senza nubi; chiaro.
cloudy, *klŏŭd'ĭ*, a. nuvoloso; malinconico, mesto. [rappezzare, rattoppare.
clout, *klŏŭt*, s. cencio, straccio, m.; –, v. a.
clove, *klōv*, s. garofano, m.
clover, *klō'vŭr*, s. trifoglio, m.; **to live in –**, vivere lussurioso. [m.; arlecchino, m.
clown, *klŏŭn*, s. contadino, m.; villano,
clownish, –*ĭsh*, a. rustico, zotico; –**ly**, ad. rusticamente, zoticamente.
cloy, *klŏĭ*, v. a. satollare, saziare; inchiodare; turare, stoppare.
club, *klŭb*, s. mazza, clava, f.; società, f.; parte, f., scotto, m.; –, v. n. andar di metà.
club-law, –*lă*, s. diritto del più forte, m.
club-room, –*rōm*, s. sala d' assemblea, f.
cluck, *klŭk*, v. n. chiocciare.
clue, *klŭ*, s. traccia, guida, norma, f.
clump, *klŭmp*, s. pezzacolo di legno, m.; gruppo d' alberi, m.
clumsily, *klŭm'zĭlĭ*, ad. rozzamente. [f.
clumsiness, –*zĭnĕs*, s. rozzezza, rusticità,
clumsy, *klŭm'zĭ*, a. rozzo, rustico.
cluster, *klŭs'tŭr*, s. gruppo, m.; grappolo, m.; sciame, m.; –, v. a. raccogliere in sieme; –, v. n. crescere in grappoli.
clutch, *klŭch*, s. artiglio, m.; unghia, f.; –, v. a. impugnare; serrare.
coach, *kōch*, s. carrozza, f.; **a – and six**, una carrozza a sei cavalli; –, v. a. & n. scarrozzare, andar in carrozza. [m.
coach-box, –*bŏks*, s. sedile del cocchiere, f.
coach-hire, –*hĭr*, s. affitto di carrozza, m.
coach-house, –*hŏŭs*, s. rimessa di carrozza, f.; (rail.) loggia da vagoni, f. [m.
coachman, –*măn*, s. cocchiere, carrozziere,
coach-office, –*ŏffĭs*, s. uffizio delle diligenze, m. [strignimento, m.
coaction, *kōăk'shŭn*, f. coazione, f.; co-
coadjutor, –*ădjō'tŭr*, s. coadiutore, m.
coagulate, –*ăg'ŭlăt*, v. a. & n. coagulare.
coagulation, –*ăgŭlā'shŭn*, s. coagulazione, f., coaguo, m.

coal, *kōl*, s. carbone fossile, m. [m.
coal-dust, –*dŭst*, s. carbone po_verizzato,
coalesce, *kōalĕs'*, v. n. collegar_i, unirsi.
coalescence, –*ĕns*, s. coalescenza, f.
coal-heaver, *kōl' hēvŭr*, s. facchino che porta carbone, m.
coal-hole, –*hōl*, **coal-house**, –*hŏŭs*, s. carbonaia, f.
coalition, *kōălĭsh'ŭn*, s. unione, connessione, f. [miniera di carbone, f.
coal-mine, *kōl' mĭn*, **coal-pit**, –*pĭt*, s.
coarse, *kōrs*, a. grosso, grossolano; –**ly**, ad. grossolanamente, rozzamente.
coarseness, –*nĕs*, s. ruvidezza, rozzezza, f.
coast, *kōst*, s. costa, f., lido, m.; –, v. n. (mar.) costeggiare; andar lungo le coste.
coaster, –*ŭr*, s. (mar.) costeggiatore, m.; pilota costiere, m.
coasting, –*ĭng*, s. (mar.) cabottaggio, m.
coasting-pilot, –*ĭng pĭlăt*, s. (mar.) piloto costiere, m
coat, *kōt*, s. vestito, abito, m.; gonnella, f.; saio, m.; tosone, vello, m.; – **of mail**, s. giaco, m.; – **of arms**, s. stemma, arme gentilizia, f.; –, v. a. vestire, coprire.
coating, –*ĭng*, s. copertura, f.
coax, *kōks*, v. a. lusingare, accarezzare.
coaxer, –*ŭr*, s. lusingatore, adulatore, m.
cob, *kŏb*, s. gabbiano, m.; cavallo intero, m.
cobble, –*bl*, v. a. rappezzare, rattoppare.
cobbler, –*blŭr*, s. ciabattino, m.; rappezzatore, m. [pola, f.
cobweb, –*wĕb*, s. tela del ragno, m.; trap-
cochineal, *kŏch'ĭnĕl*, s. cocciniglia, f.
cock, *kŏk*, s. gallo, m.; canna (di condotti), f.; forma (d' un cappello), f.; ago della bilancia, m.; gnomone, m.; stilo, m.; cane (d' uno schioppo), m.; –, v. a. inalzare; montare; –, v. n. fare del grande; gonfiarsi.
cockade, –*kăd'*, s. fiocco, m.; coccarda, f.
cock-a-doodle-doo, –*ă dō̆ dl dō̆*, s. cuccurucù, canto del gallo, m.
cockatrice, *kŏk'ătrĭs*, s. basilisco, m.
cock-chafer, –*chăfŭr*, s. scarabeo, m.
cock-crow, –*krō*, s. alba, f. [m.
cock-crowing, –*krōĭng*, s. canto del gallo,
cocked, *kŏkt*, a. angoloso, ripiegato.
cocker, *kŏk'ŭr*, v. a. accarezzare.
cockerel, *kŏk'ĕrĕl*, s. gallo giovine, m.
cockfight, –*fĭt*, s. battaglia di galli, f.
cockle, *kŏk'l*, s. chiocciola, f. (pesce); (bot.) loglio, m.; –, v. a. piegare; raggrinzare; –, v. n. piegarsi; raggrinzarsi.
cock-loft, –*lŏft*, s. solaio, m.; granaio, m.
cockney, –*nĕ*, s. goffo, m.; uno nato in Londra, m.
cock-pit, –*pĭt*, s. arena dove si fanno combattere i galli, f.; (mar.) ospedale, m.
cock's-comb, –*s'kŏm*, s. cresta di gallo, f.; civettino, m.
cocoa, *kō'kō*, s. cacao, m.
cocoon, *kŏkōn'*, s. bozzolo,
cod, *kŏd*, s. guscio, baccello, m.; merluzzo, m.
coddle, *kŏd'dl*, v. a. far bollire; lusingare.
code, *kōd*, s. codice, m.
codicil, *kŏd'ĭsĭl*, s. codicillo, m.
codify, *kŏd'ĭfĭ*, v. a. far un codice.

codling, *kŏd'lĭng*, s. piccolo merluzzo, m.; mela da cuocere, f. [m.

cod-liver oil, *–lĭvăr ŏĭl*, s. olio di pesce,

coefficient, *kŏŭf'fĭsh'ĕnt*, s. cooperazione, f.; (math.) coefficiente, m.

coequal, *kŏŭ kwŏl*, a. coeguale.

coerce, *kŏŭrs'*, v. a. restringere, reprimere.

coercion, *kŏăr'shăn*, s. costrignimento, raffrenamento, m.

coercive, *kŏăr'sĭv*, a. coercitivo.

coeval, *kŏŭ'văl*, a. &s. contemporaneo (m.).

coexistence, *–ĕgzĭs'tĕns*, s. coesistenza, f.

coffee, *kŏf'fĭ*, s. caffè, m. [s. caffè, m.

coffee-berry, *–bĕrrĭ*, coffee-bean, *–bĕn*,

coffee-grounds, *–grŏŭnds*, s. pl. fondata del caffè, f. [da caffè, f.

coffee-house, *–hŏŭs*, s. caffè, m., bottega

coffee-man, *–măn*, s. caffettiere, m.

coffee-pot, *–pŏt*, s. caffettiera, f.

coffee-roaster, *–rŏstăr*, s. tamburo da arrostire il caffè, m.

coffee-set, *–sĕt*, s. vasellame da caffè, m.

coffee-tree, *–trĕ*, s. caffè, m.

coffer, *kŏf'făr*, s. cofano, m., cassa, f., forziere, m. [–, v. a. porre nel cataletto.

coffin, *kŏf'fĭn*, s. bara, f., cataletto, m.;

cog, *kŏg*, s. dente (d' una ruota), m.; –, v. a. adulare; lusingare; to – the dice, impiombare i dadi.

cogency, *kŏ'jĕnsĭ*, s. forza, f.; ragione, f.

cogent, *kŏ'jĕnt*, a. potente; energico; –ly, ad. irresistibilmente.

cogitate, *kŏj'ĭtăt*, v. n. pensare, meditare.

cogitation, *–tă'shăn*, s. cogitazione, meditazione, riflessione, f.

cognate, *kŏg'năt*, a. cognato.

cognation, *–nă'shăn*, s. cognazione, f.; parentela, affinità, f. [vincimento, m.

cognition, *–nĭsh'ăn*, s. conoscenza, f.; con-

cognizance, *kŏg'nĭzăns*, s. conoscenza, notizia, f.; marca, f.; competenza, f.

cognizant, *–zănt*, a. informato; (jur.) competente.

cog-wheel, *kŏg'hwĕl*, s. ruota dentata, f.

cohabit, *kŏhăb'ĭt*, v. n. coabitare, vivere insieme. [f.

cohabitation, *–tă'shăn*, s. coabitazione,

coheir, *kŏăr'*, s. coerede, m.

coheiress, *–ĕs*, s. coerede, f.

cohere, *kŏhĕr'*, v. n. aderire; esser conforme, convenire; affarsi. [f.

coherence, *–rĕns*, s. coerenza, connessione,

coherent, *–rĕnt*, a. coerente; consistente.

cohesion, *kŏhĕ'zhăn*, s. coesione, f.

cohesive, *–sĭv*, a. aderente.

coif, *kŏĭf*, s. cuffia, f., berrettino, m.

coil, *kŏĭl*, s. strepito, rumore, garbuglio, m.; –, v. a. raggomitolare.

coin, *kŏĭn*, s. moneta, f., denaro, m.; conio, m.; angolo, m.; –, v. a. battere moneta, coniare.

coinage, *–dj*, s. monetaggio, m. [rere.

coincide, *kŏĭnsĭd'*, v. n. coincidere, concor-

coincidence, *kŏĭn'sĭdĕns*, s. coincidenza, f.; riscontro, m.

coincident, *–sĭdĕnt*, a. coincidente.

coiner, *kŏĭn'ăr*, s. monetiere, m.

coining, *–ĭng*, s. monetaggio, m.

coke, *kŏk*, s. carbon fossile da cui si è estratto il bitume, coch, m. [m.

colander, *kŭl'ăndăr*, s. colatoio, setaccio,

cold, *kŏld*, a. freddo; indifferente; riserbato; –ly, ad. freddamente; –, s. freddo, m., freddezza, f.

cold-blooded, *–blŭdĕd*, a. di sangue freddo.

coldness, *–nĕs*, s. freddezza, f.; indifferenza,

cole, *kŏl*, s. cavolo, m. [f.

colewort, *–wărt*, s. cavolo verzotto, m.

colic, *kŏl'ĭk*, s. colica, f.

collaborate, *kŏllăb'ŏrăt*, v. a. collaborare.

collaboration, *–ră'shăn*, s. collaborazione, f. [rovinare.

collapse, *kŏllăps'*, v. n. cadere insieme;

collar, *kŏl'lăr*, s. collare, m.; collaretto, m.; –, v. a. prendere al collare.

collar-bone, *–bŏn*, s. clavicola, f.

collate, *kŏllăt'*, v. a. conferire; confrontare.

collateral, *–lăt'ărăl*, a. collaterale; –ly, ad. in linea collaterale.

collation, *–lă'shăn*, s. collazione, f.; collezione, f.

colleague, *kŏl'lĕg*, s. collega, compagno, m.

collect, *kŏl'lĕkt*, s. colletta, f.; –, *kŏllĕkt'*, v. a. raccogliere, far una colletta; compilare. [raccolta, f.; estratto, m.

collection, *–lĕk'shăn*, s. collezione, f.;

collective, *–lĕk'tĭv*, a. collettivo, aggregato; –ly, ad. collettivamente.

collector, *–lĕk'tăr*, s. collettore, m.; cassiere, m. [zione, f.

college, *kŏl'lĕj*, s. collegio, m.; congrega-

collegian, *–lĕ'jĭăn*, s. membro d'un collegio, m. [collegio.

collegiate, *–lĕ'jĭăt*, a. collegiato, d'un

collide, *kŏllĭd'*, v. n. collidersi.

collier, *kŏl'yăr*, s. carbonaio, m.; barca carbonaia, f.

colliery, *–yărĭ*, s. miniera di carbone, f.

collision, *–lĭzh'ăn*, s. collisione, f.; concorso, m.

collop, *kŏl'lŏp*, s. fetta di carne, f.

colloquial, *–lŏ'kwĭăl*, a. della o nella lingua di conversazione; intimo, familiare; –ly, ad. nella conversazione, familiarmente.

colloquy, *kŏl'lŏkwĭ*, s. colloquio, m.; conferenza, f. [ganno, m.

collusion, *–lŏ'zhăn*, s. collusione, f.; in-

collusive, *–lŏ'sĭv*, a. collusivo; –ly, ad. collusivamente.

colonel, *kăr'nĕl*, s. colonnello, m.

coloneley, *–sĭ*, colonelship, *–shĭp*, s. grado di colonnello, m.

colonial, *kŏlŏ'nĭăl*, a. coloniale.

colonise, *kŏl'ŏnĭz*, v. a. formare colonie, popolare di abitanti.

colonist, *kŏl'ŏnĭst*, s. colono, m.

colony, *kŏl'ŏnĭ*, s. colonia, f.

colossal, *kŏlŏs'săl*, a. colossale.

colossus, *kŏlŏs'săs*, s. colosso, m.

colour, *kŭl'ăr*, s. colore, m.; pretesto, m., apparenza, f.; –s, pl. insegna, bandiera, f.; to change –, cambiar colore, impallidire; –, v. a. colorare; scusare; –, v. n. divenire rosso.

colourable, *–ăbl*, a. specioso; plausibile.

colouring, *–ĭng,* s. colorito, m.
colourist, *–ĭst,* s. colorista, m.   [rente.
colourless, *–lĕs,* a. senza colore; traspa-
colours, *–ʒ,* s. pl. bandiera, f.; **water–,**
   acquerelli, m. pl.; **with flying –,** (mil.)
   a bandiera spiegata.
colt, *kŏlt,* s. puledro, m.; pazzerello, m.
colter, *kŏl'tŭr,* s. coltro m.; vomere, m.
columbine, *kŏl'ŭmbĭn,* a. colombino.
column, *kŏl'ŭm,* s. colonna, f.
columnar, *kŏlŭm'năr,* a. di colonne.
coma, *kŏ'mă,* s. (med.) coma, letargo, m.
comatose, *kŏ'mătōs,* a. letargico.
comb, *kŏm,* s. pettine, m.; striglia, f.;
   favo, m.; **–,** v. a. pettinare; strigliare;
   scardassare, cardare.
combat, *kŭm'băt,* s. combattimento, m.,
   battaglia, f.; **single** or **private –,** duello,
   m.; **–,** v. a. & n. combattere; oppugnare.
combatant, *–bătănt,* s. combattente, m.
combative, *–bătĭv,* a. inclinato a contendere.   [dassiere, cardatore, m.
comber, *kŏm'ăr,* s. pettinatore, m.; scar-
combination, *kŏmbĭnă'shŭn,* s. combinazione, f.; trama, f.
combine, *kŏmbĭn',* v. a. combinare; unire;
   –, v. n. associarsi, unirsi.   [tellina, f.
combing-cloth, *kŏm'ĭng klŏth,* s. man-
combustible, *kŏmbŭs'tĭbl,* a. combustibile.
combustion, *–bŭst'yŭn,* s. combustione,
   f., abbruciamento, m.
come, *kŭm,* v. n. ir. venire; pervenire;
   avvenire, arrivare; **–,** i. su! via! animo!
comedian, *kŏmē'dĭăn,* s. commediante, m.;
   attore, m.
comedy, *kŏm'ĕdĭ,* s. commedia, f.   [f.
comeliness, *kŭm'lĭnĕs,* s. grazia, vaghezza,
comely, *kŭm'lĭ,* a. grazioso, decente;
   gentile; **–ly,** ad. graziosamente, decente-
   mente; gentilmente.   [–, s. forestiere, m.
comer, *kŭm'ăr,* s. uno che viene; **new
comet,** *kŏm'ĕt,* s. cometa, f.
comfit, *kŭm'fĭt,* s. confetto, m., conserva, f.
comfort, *kŭm'fărt,* s. conforto, m.; aiuto,
   m.; consolazione, f.; ricreazione, f.; **–,** v. a.
   confortare; ristorare.
comfortable, *–ăbl,* a. confortevole; grato.
comfortableness, *–ăblnĕs,* s. conforta-
   zione, f., conforto, ristoro, m.
comfortably, *–ăblĭ,* ad. in modo conforta-
   tivo, lietamente.   [sciallo, m.
comforter, *–ăr,* s. consolatore, m.; piccolo
comfortless, *–lĕs,* a. senza conforto, desolato.   [–ly, ad. facetamente.
comic(al), *kŏm'ĭk(ăl),* a. comico, faceto;
comicalness, *–ălnĕs,* s. facezia, f.; piacevolezza, f.   [–, s. venuta, f., arrivo, m.
coming, *kŭm'ĭng,* a. vegnente; futuro;
coming-in, *–ĭn,* s. entrata, rendita, f.
comma, *kŏm'mă,* s. (gr.) virgola, f.
command, *kŏmmănd',* s. comando, m.;
   ordine, m.; **–,** v. a. comandare; ordinare;
   –, v. n. aver il comando.   [m.; capo, m.
commander, *–măn'dăr,* s. comandante.
commandment, *–mĕnt,* s. comandimento,
m.   [morare; celebrare.
commemorate, *–mĕm'ōrăt,* v. a. comme-

commemoration, *–rā'shŭn,* s. comme-
   morazione, f.; ricordanza, f.; celebrazione,
   solennità, f.   [entrare; avviare.
commence, *–mĕns',* v. a. & n. cominciare;
commencement, *–mĕnt,* s. principio,
   cominciamento, m., origine, f.
commend, *–mĕnd',* v. a. commendare, raccomandare, lodare; approvare.
commendable, *–mĕn'dăbl,* a. commenda-
   bile, lodevole.   [mente.
commendably, *–dăblĭ,* ad. commendevol-
commendation, *–dā'shŭn,* s. commenda-
   zione, f.; raccomandazione, f.   [datizio.
commendatory, *–mĕn'dătărĭ,* a. commen-
commender, *–mĕn'dăr,* s. lodatore, m.
commensurable, *–mĕn'sŭrăbl,* a. commensurabile.
commensurate, *–mĕn'sŭrăt,* a. proporzionato, eguale; **–,** v. a. commensurare,
   proporzionare.
comment, *kŏm'mĕnt,* s. commento, m.,
   glossa, f.; **–,** *kŏmmĕnt',* v. n. commentare,
   glossare.   [f.; annotazione, f.
commentary, *kŏm'mĕntărĭ,* s. esposizione,
commentator, *–tā'tŭr,* s. commentatore,
   glossatore, m.   [gozio, m.
commerce, *kŏm'mărs,* s. commercio, ne-
commercial, *–măr'shăl,* a. di commercio,
   commerciale; **– directory,** s. almanacco
   di banco, m.
comminatory, *–mĭn'ătărĭ,* a. minacciante.
commingle, *–mĭng'gl,* v. a. mischiare,
   mescolare; **–,** v. n. mischiarsi; unirsi.
commiserate, *–mĭz'ŭrăt,* v. a. commiserare, compatire.   [zione, pietà, f.
commiseration, *–rā'shŭn,* s. commisera-
commissariat, *–mĭssā'rĭăt,* s. commis-
   sariato, m.   [m.
commissary, *kŏm'mĭssărĭ,* s. commissario,
commission, *–mĭsh'ŭn,* s. commissione,
   f.; uffizio, m.; brevetto, m.; **–,** v. a. commettere; delegare, autorizzare.
commissioner, *–ănăr,* s. commissario, m.;
   magistrato, m.   [dare in custodia.
commit, *–mĭt',* v. a. commettere; affidare;
commitment, *–mĕnt,* s. committal, *–tăl,* s.
   imprigionamento, arresto, m.
committee, *–tē,* s. delegazione, f.; com-
   missari, m. pl.
commode, *–mōd',* s. seggetta, f.
commodious, *–mō'dĭŭs,* a. comodo, convenevole, agevole; **–ly,** ad. comodamente.
commodity, *–mŏd'ĭtĭ,* s. comodo, m.; vantaggio, profitto, m.; mercanzia, f.
commodore, *kŏm'mŏdōr,* s. (mar.) com-
   modoro, m., comandante d' una squadra
   navale.
common, *kŏm'mŏn,* a. comune; ordinario,
   volgare; **–,** s. pascolo comune, m.; **in –,**
   in comunità; **– sense,** senso comune, m.
commonage, *–dj,* s. diritto di pascere, m.
commonalty, *–ăltĭ,* s. comunanza, comunità, f.; popolazzo, m., plebe, f.
common-council, *kŏănsĭl,* s. consiglio
   della città, m.
commoner, *–ăr,* s. membro de' Comuni, m.
common-hall, *–hăl,* s. palazzo della città,
   m.

common-law, -lā, s. leggi municipali, f. pl.

commonly, -lĭ, ad. comunemente, usualmente. [quenza, f.

commonness, -nĕs, s. comunanza, f.; frecommonplace, -plās, s. soggetto ordinario, m.; cose trite e ritrite, f. pl.; —, a. triviale.

commons, kŏm'mŏnz, s. camera bassa, camera de' Comuni, f.; plebe, f.

commonweal, -wēl, commonwealth, -wĕlth, s. repubblica, f.

commotion, -mŏ'shăn, s. commovimento, m.; tumulto, m. [scorrere.

commune, -mūn', v. n. conferire; di-communicable, -mū'nĭkăbl, a. comunicabile. [cante, m.

communicant, -mū'nĭkănt, s. comunicommunicate, -mū'nĭkāt, v. a. comunicare, far partecipe; —, v. n. comunicarsi.

communication, -kā'shŭn, s. comunicazione, f.; conferenza, f.; commercio, m.

communicative, -mū'nĭkātĭv, a. comunicativo, familiare.

communicativeness, -nĕs, s. natura comunicativa, f.; franchezza, f.

communion, -mūn'yŭn, s. comunione, f.; società, f.; corrispondenza, f.

communion-table, -tăbl, s. tavola della comunione, f.

communism, kŏm'mănĭzm, s. comunismo, m., comunità di beni, f.

communist, -ĭst, s. comunista, m.

community, -mū'nĭtĭ, s. comunità, f.

commutable, -mū'tăbl, a. commutabile.

commutation, -mūtā'shăn, s. commutazione, f.

commute, -mūt', v. a. commutare.

compact, kŏmpăkt', a. compatto, denso, connesso; —, kŏm'păkt, s. patto, m., convenzione, f. [dezza, f.

compactness, -păkt'nĕs, s. sodezza, salcompactly, -păkt'lĭ, ad. saldamente; fortemente, con precisione. [m.

companion, -păn'yŭn, s. compagno, socio, companionable, -ăbl, a. di buona compagnia, sociabile. [pagnia, f.; seguito, m.

companionship, -shĭp, s. società, comcompany, kăm'pănĭ, s. compagnia, f.; società, assemblea, f.; truppa, f.

comparable, kŏm'părăbl, a. comparabile.

comparative, -păr'ătĭv, a. comparativo; -ly, ad. a comparazione, rispettivamente; —, s. (gr.) comparativo, m.

compare, -păr', s. comparazione, f.; agguaglio, m., somiglianza, f.; —, v. a. comparare; assomigliare.

comparison, -păr'ĭsŭn s. comparazione, f.; analogia, f.; in – with, in paragone di.

compartment, -părt'mĕnt, s. compartimento, m.

compass, kăm'păs, s. circuito, m.; giro, m.; spazio, m.; bussola, f.; compasso, m.; —, v. a. circondare; cignere; —, v. n. venire a capo, ottenere; riuscire.

compass-card, -kărd, s. carta marina, f.

compasses, -ĕz, s. pl. compasso, m.

compassion, -păsh'ŭn, s. compassione, pietà, f. [compatire.

compassionate, -ănăt, v. a. commiserare,

compatibility, -pătĭbĭl'ĭtĭ, s. compatibilità, convenienza, attezza, f. [venevole.

compatible, -păt'ĭbl, a. compatibile, concompatriot, -pā'trĭŏt, s. compatriota, m.

compeer, kŏmpēr', s. compagno, collega, m.

compel, kŏmpĕl', v. a. costrignere, forzare, obbligare. [viamento, m.

compend, kŏm'pĕnd, s. compendio, abbrecompendious, -pĕn'dŭs, a. compendioso, succinto, conciso; -ly, ad. in compendio.

compendium, -dĭŭm, s. compendio, m.

compensate, -pĕn'sāt, v. a. compensare; rimunerare. [zione, f.

compensation, -sā'shŭn, s. compensacompete, kŏmpēt', v. n. competere.

competence, kŏm'pĕtĕns, s. competenza, sufficienza, f.

competent, -pĕtĕnt, a. competente, sufficiente; -ly, ad. competentemente.

competition, -tĭsh'ăn, s. competenza, concorrenza, f. [corrente, m.

competitor, -pĕt'ĭtŭr, s. competitore, concompilation, -pĭlā'shăn, s. compilazione, collezione, f. [comporre.

compile, -pĭl', v. a. compilare; ordinare.

complacence, -plā'sĕns, s. compiacenza, f.

complacent, -sĕnt, a. compiacente; civile.

complain, kŏmplān', v. n. compiagnere, lamentarsi. [f.; lamento, m.; affanno, m.

complaint, -plānt', s. doglianza, querela, complaisance, -plāzăns', s. compiacenza, gentilezza, f. [cortese.

complaisant, -zănt', a. compiacente, complement, kŏm'plĕmĕnt, s. compimento, m.; complemento, m.

complete, -plēt', a. compiuto, perfetto; -ly, ad. compiutamente, perfettamente; —, v. a. compire; finire. [m.; colmo, m.

completion, -plē'shŭn, s. adempimento, complex, kŏm'plĕks, a. complesso, composto.

complexion, -plĕk'shŭn, s. complessione, costituzione, f., stato del corpo, m.

complexioned, -shŭnd, a. complesso; d'una costituzione.

complexity, -plĕks'ĭtĭ, s. complicazione, f.

compliance, -plĭ'ăns, s. compiacenza, f.

compliant, -plĭ'ănt, a. condiscendente.

complicate, kŏm'plĭkăt, v. a. imbrogliare, intrecciare.

complication, kŏmplĭkā'shăn, s. complicazione, unione, f.; aggregazione, f.

complier, -plĭ'ăr, s. che compiace facilmente, compiacente, m.

compliment, kŏm'plĭmĕnt, s. complimento, m.; —, v. a. complimentare.

complimentary, -mĕn'tări, a. complimentoso. [formarsi, adattarsi.

comply, kŏmplī', v. n. condiscendere; concomponent, -pŏ'nĕnt, a. componente, costituente.

comport, -pŏrt', v. a. soffrire; —, v. n. convenire; comportarsi, accomodarsi.

compose, -pōz', v. a. comporre; ordinare, regolare; accomodare.

composed, -pŏ'zĕd, a. composto, quieto, grave; -ly, ad. compostamente, seriamente. [m.

composer, -zăr, s. compositore, m.; autore,

composing-stick, *–zĭng stĭk,* s. compositoio, m.

composite, *kŏm'pŏzĭt,* a. composto.

composition, *–pŏzĭsh'ăn,* s. composizione, f.; composto, m.; aggiustamento, m.

compositor, *–pŏz'ĭtăr,* s. compositore, m.; stampatore, m.

compost, *kŏm'pŏst,* s. letame, concime, m.

composure, *–pō'zhŭr,* s. compositura, f.; quiete, tranquillità, f.

compound, *kŏmpŏŭnd',* a. & s. composto (m.); –, *kŏm'pŏŭnd,* v. a. comporre, combinare; –, v. n. aggiustarsi; accordarsi, convenire. [dere, intendere; contenere.

comprehend, *–prĕhĕnd',* v. a. comprendere.

comprehensible, *–hĕn'sĭbl,* a. comprensibile, intelligibile. [comprensibile.

comprehensibly, *–sĭblĭ,* ad. in modo comprensibile.

comprehension, *–hĕn'shăn,* s. comprensione, f.; intelligenza, f.

comprehensive, *–hĕn'sĭv,* a. che comprende molto; succinto; **–ly,** ad. comprensivamente. [f.

comprehensiveness, *–nĕs,* s. precisione, f.

compress, *kŏm'prĕs,* s. piumacciuolo, m.; –, *kŏmprĕs',* v. a. comprimere, ristringere.

compressible, *–prĕs'ĭbl,* a. che può essere compresso, compressibile. [f.

compression, *–prĕsh'ăn,* s. compressione, –prĭz, v. a. comprendere, contenere; capire.

comprise, *kŏm'prŏmĭz,* s. compromesso, m.; –, v. a. compromettere.

compulsion, *kŏmpŭl'shăn,* s. costringimento, m.; violenza, forza, f.

compulsory, *–pŭl'sŭrĭ,* a. coercitivo; **–ly,** ad. forzatamente, per forza.

compunction, *–pŭngk'shăn,* s. compunzione, f., pentimento, m.

computation, *–pŭtā'shăn,* s. computo, calcolo, m. [colare.

compute, *–pŭt',* v. a. computare; calcolare.

comrade, *kŏm'rād,* s. compagno, socio, m.

con, *kŏn,* ad. contro.

concatenation, *–kătĕnā'shăn,* s. concatenazione, f.; serie, f.

concave, *kŏn'kāv,* a, concavo.

concavity, *–kāv'ĭtĭ,* s. concavità, f.

conceal, *kŏnsēl',* v. a. celare, nascondere.

concealment, *–mĕnt,* s. celamento, m.; nascondimento, m.

concede, *–sēd',* v. a. concedere, permettere; acconsentire.

conceit, *–sēt',* s. concetto, pensiero, m.; fantasia, f.; voglia, f.; –, v. n. immaginarsi; figurarsi.

conceited, *–ĕd,* a. affettato, vano; **–ly,** ad. in modo affettato; fantasticamente, vanamente. [pirsi, concepibile.

conceivable, *–sē'văbl,* a. che può concepire.

conceive, *–sēv',* A. a. concepire, comprendere; –, v. n. pensare, figurarsi, immaginarsi.

concentrate, *–sĕn'trāt,* v. a. concentrare.

concentration, *–trā'shăn,* s. concentrazione, f. [v. n. concentrarsi.

concentre, *–sĕn'tŭr,* v. a. concentrare; –,

concentric(al), *–trĭk(ăl),* a. concentrico.

conception, *–sĕp'shăn,* s. concezione, f.; concepimento, f.; concetto, pensiero, m.

concern, *–sŭrn',* s. affare, m.; negozio, m.; interesse, m.; importanza, conseguenza, f.; –, v. a. concernere; appartenere; risguardare; importare.

concerned, *–sŭrnd',* a. interessato; afflitto, inquieto. [intorno.

concerning, *–sŭrn'ĭng,* pr. concernente.

concert, *kŏn'sŭrt,* s. concerto, m.; accordo, m.; –, *kŏnsŭrt',* v. a. concertare; stabilire, insieme.

concession, *–sĕsh'ăn,* s. concessione, f.

conch, *kŏngk,* s. conca, f. [accordare.

conciliate, *–sĭl'ĭāt,* v. a. conciliare; unire,

conciliation, *–lĭā'shăn,* s. conciliazione, f.; pacificamento, m. [paciere, m.

conciliator, *–sĭl'ĭātăr,* s. conciliatore,

conciliatory, *–ātărĭ,* a. conciliatorio, che concilia.

concise, *–sīs',* a. conciso, succinto; **–ly,** ad. concisamente, con brevità.

conciseness, *–nĕs,* s. brevità, f.; concisione, f. [minare; risolvere, decidere.

conclude, *–klōd',* v. a. conchiudere; terminare; risolvere, decidere.

conclusion, *–klō'zhăn,* s. conchiusione, f.; fine, m. & f.; decisione, f.

conclusive, *–sĭv,* a. conclusivo, decisivo; **–ly,** ad. conclusivamente. [rire.

concoct, *–kŏkt',* v. a. concuocere; digoconcoction, *kŏk'shăn,* s. concozione, f.

concomitant, *–kŏm'ĭtănt,* a. & s. concomitante, m.; compagnone, m.

concord, *kŏng'kŏrd,* s. concordia, f.; armonia, f. [accordo, m.

concordance, *–kŏr'dăns,* s. concordanza, f.;

concordant, *–dănt,* a. concordante; conforme. [venzione, f.

concordat, *–dăt,* s. concordato, m., concorso, m.; moltitudine, f.

concourse, *kŏng'kŏrs,* s. concorso, m.; moltitudine, f.

concrete, *kŏn'krĕt,* a. concreto, coagulato; –, *kŏnkrĕt',* v. n. congelarsi, coagularsi.

concretion, *–krē'shăn,* s. concrezione, f.; coalescenza, f. [m.

concubinage, *–kū'bĭnĕj,* s. concubinato,

concubine, *kŏng'kūbĭn,* s. concubina, f.

concupiscence, *–kū'pĭsĕns,* s. concupiscenza, f.

concur, *–kŭr',* v. n. concorrere; cooperare;

concurrence, *–rĕns,* s. concorrenza, f.; unione, f.; assistenza, f.

concussion, *–kŭsh'ăn,* s. concussione, f.

condemn, *–dĕm',* v. a. condannare; disapprovare, biasimare.

condemnation, *–nā'shăn,* s. condanna, f.; gastigo, m. [torio.

condemnatory, *–nătŭrĭ,* a. condanna-

condensation, *–dĕnsā'shăn,* s. condensamento, m. [stringere.

condense, *–dĕns',* v. a. condensare, ricondere; acconsentire. [denza, f.

condescend, *–dĕsĕnd',* v. n. condiscendere; acconsentire. [denza, f.

condescension, *–sĕn'shăn,* s. condiscendign, *–dīn',* a. condegno, meritato.

condign, *–dīn',* a. condegno, meritato.

condiment, *kŏn'dĭmĕnt,* s. condimento, m.; salsa, f.

condition, –*dĭsh'ŭn,* s. condizione, f.; stato, m.; grado, m.; umore, m., tempra, f.

conditional, –*ăl,* a. condizionale; **–ly,** ad. condizionalmente, con patto.

condolatory, –*dō'lătărĭ,* a. di condoglianza. [condolersi.

condole, –*dōl',* v. a. lamentare; **–,** v. n.

condolence, –*dō'lĕns,* s. condoglianza, f.

condonation, –*dōnā'shŭn,* s. condonazione, f., perdono, m.

condone, –*dōn',* v. a. condonare.

conduce (to), –*dūs',* v. a. contribuire a, condurre a. [ducevole.

conducive, –*dū'sĭv,* a. acconcio, conduct, –*dŭkt',* v. a. condurre, guidare.

conductor, –*dŭk'tŭr,* s. conduttore, [m.; direttore, m.; (rail.) conduttore, m.

conduit, –*kŭn'dĭt,* s. condotto, m.; acquecone, *kŏn,* s. cono, m. [dotto, m.

coney, *kō'nĭ,* s. coniglio, m.

confabulate, –*ăb'ŭlāt,* v. n. confabulare.

confection, –*fĕk'shŭn,* s. confezione, f. confettura, f.

confectioner, –*ăr,* s. confetturiere, m.

confederacy, –*fĕd'ărăsĭ,* s. confederazione, lega, f.

confederate, –*fĕd'ărăt,* a. & s. confederato, m.; **–,** v. n. confederarsi, collegarsi.

confederation, –*fĕdărā'shŭn,* s. confederazione, f. [conferire; discorrere.

confer, –*fŭr',* v. a. comparare; **–,** v. n.

conference, *kŏn'fărĕns,* s. conferenza, f.

confess, –*fĕs',* v. a. & n. confessare; confessarsi. [certamente.

confessedly, –*sĕdlĭ,* ad. indubitamente,

confession, –*fĕsh'ŭn,* s. confessione, affermazione, f.

confessional, –*ăl,* a. confessionale.

confessor, –*fĕs'sŭr,* s. confessore, m.

confidant, –*fĭdănt',* s. confidente, m.; familiare, m.

confide, –*fīd',* v. n. confidare; confidarsi.

confidence, *kŏn'fĭdĕns,* s. confidenza, fiducia, f.

confident, *kŏn'fĭdĕnt,* a. sicuro, sfacciato, temerario; **–,** s. confidente, m.; amico, m.

confidential, –*dĕn'shăl,* a. confidenziale; **–ly,** ad. confidenzialmente.

confine, *kŏn'fīn,* s. confine, limite, m.; **–,** *kŏnfīn',* v. a. limitare; imprigionare; **–,** v. n. confinare, essere contiguo.

confinement, –*fīn'mĕnt,* s. costringimento, m.; prigione, f. [ficare.

confirm, –*fŭrm',* v. a. confermare; ratificare.

confirmation, –*mā'shŭn,* s. confermazione, f.; ratificazione, f.; prova, f.

confirmatory, –*fŭrm'ătĭv,* a. confermatory, –*ătărĭ,* a. confermativo.

confiscate, –*fĭs'kăt,* v. a. confiscare.

confiscation, –*kā'shŭn,* s. confisca, f.

conflagration, –*flăgrā'shŭn,* s. conflagrazione, f.

conflict, *kŏn'flĭkt,* s. conflitto, combattimento, m.; **–,** *kŏnflĭkt',* v. n. contendere; combattere. [concorso, m.

confluence, *kŏn'flŭĕns,* s. confluenza, f.;

confluent, –*flŭĕnt,* a. confluente; concorrente.

conform, –*fŏrm',* v. a. conformare, concordare; **–,** v. n. conformarsi.

conformable, –*ăbl,* conformabile.

conformably, –*ăblĭ,* ad. in conformità.

conformation, –*mā'shŭn,* s. conformazione, f. [miglianza, f.

conformity, –*fŏrm'ĭtĭ,* s. conformità, soconfound, –*fŏŭnd',* v. a. confondere; distruggere. [ternità, f.; società, f.

confraternity, –*frătăr'nĭtĭ,* s. confraconfront, –*frŭnt',* v. a. confrontare; comparare, paragonare. [ordinare.

confuse, –*fūz',* v. a. confondere. disconfusedly, –*zĕd'lĭ,* ad. confusamente.

confusion, –*fū'zhŭn,* s. confusione, f.; perturbamento, m., distruzione, f.

confute, –*fūt',* v. a. confutare; riprovare.

congeal, –*jēl',* v. a. congelare; rappigliare. [larsi.

congealable, –*jĕl'ăbl,* a. che può congecongelation, –*jĕld'shŭn,* s. congelamento, m.; congelazione, f. [gruente.

congenial, –*jē'nĭăl,* a. congenere; conconger, *kŏng'gŭr,* s. gongro, m. (pesce).

congestion, –*jĕst'yŭn,* s. amasso, m.; (med.) congestione, f.

conglomerate, –*glŏm'ărăt,* v. a. conglobare, aggomitolare. [razione, f.

conglomeration, –*ră'shŭn,* s. conglomecongratulate, –*grăt'ŭlāt,* v. a. felicitare.

congratulation, –*lā'shŭn,* s. congratulazione, f. [gratulatorio.

congratulatory, –*grăt'ŭlătărĭ,* a. con**congregate,** *kŏn'grĕgăt,* v. a. congregare; adunare, unire.

congregation, –*grĕgā'shŭn,* s. congregazione, f.; adunanza, f.

congress, *kŏng'grĕs,* s. congresso, m.; conferenza, f. [convenienza, f.

congruity, *kŏngrŏ'ĭtĭ,* s. congruenza, f.;

congruous, –*grŏŭs,* a. congruo; conveniente; **–ly,** ad. in modo congruo.

conic(al), *kŏn'ĭk(ăl),* a. conico; **–ly,** ad. a maniera di cono.

coniferous, *kŏnĭf'ărŭs,* a. (bot.) conifero.

conjectural, *kŏnjĕk'tŭrăl,* a. congetturale; **–ly,** ad. per via di congettura.

conjecture, –*tŭr,* s. congettura, f.; **–,** v. a. congetturare; augurare.

conjoin, –*jŏĭn',* v. a. & n. congiugnere; unire; unirsi.

conjoint, –*jŏĭnt',* a. congiunto, unito.

conjugal, *kŏn'jŭgăl,* a. coniugale, maritale; **–ly,** ad. maritalmente.

conjugate, *kŏn'jŭgăt,* v. a. coniugare.

conjugation, –*gā'shŭn,* s. coniugazione, f.

conjunction, –*jŭnk'shŭn,* s. unione f.; (gr.) congiunzione, f.

conjunctive, –*tĭv,* a. congiuntivo.

conjuncture, –*tŭr,* s. congiuntura, f.; occasione, f.; caso, m.

conjuration, –*jŭrā'shŭn,* s. incanto, m.; cospirazione, congiura, f.

conjure, *kŏnjŏr',* v. a. & n. cospirare, congiurare; **–,** *kŭn'jŭr,* esorcizzare.

conjurer, -jŏ'rŭr, s. congiuratore, m.;
–, kŭn'jŭrŭr, mago, m.

connect, -nĕkt', v. a. connettere, congiugnere, unire.

connexion, -nĕk'shŭn, s. connessione, f.

connivance, -nĭ'vŭns, s. connivenza, f.

connive, nĭv', v. n. usar connivenza, tollerare.   [m.; guidice, m.

connoisseur, kŏn'nĭssŭr, s. conoscitore,

connubial, -nŭ'bĭl, a. coniugale, matrimoniale.   [vincere.

conquer, kŏng'kŭr, v. a. conquistare.

conqueror, -ŭr, s. conquistatore, vincitore, m,   [vittoria, f.

conquest, kŏng'kwĕst, s. conquista, f.;

consanguineous, -sănggwĭn'ĭŭs, a. consanguineo.   [parentela, f.

consanguinity, -ĭtĭ, s. consanguineità,

conscience, kŏn'shĕns, s. coscienza, f.; scrupolo, m.

conscientious, -shĭĕn'shŭs, a. coscienzioso, scrupoloso; -ly, ad. coscienziosamente.

conscious, kŏn'shŭs, a. consapevole; persuaso; -ly, ad. consapevolmente.

conscript, kŏn'skrĭpt, a. co(n)scritto.

conscription, -skrĭp'shŭn, s. coscrizione, f., arrolamento, m.   [dedicare.

consecrate, kŏn'sĕkrāt, v. a. consacrare;

consecration, -krā'shŭn, s. consacrazione, f.

consecutive, -sĕk'ūtĭv, a. consecutivo; -ly, ad. consecutivamente.

consent, -sĕnt', s. consenso, m.; consentimento, m., approvazione, f.; –, v. n. consentire, approvare.

consentient, -sĕn'shĭĕnt, a. consenziente.

consequence, kŏn'sĕkwĕns, s. conseguenza, f.; importanza, f.

consequent, -sĕkwĕnt, consequential, -kwĕn'shăl, a. conseguente; conclusivo; -ly, ad. conseguentemente.   [zione, f.

conservation, -sŭrvā'shŭn, s. conservazione, f.

conservative, -sŭr'vătĭv, a. conservativo.

conservator, -vā'tŭr, s. conservatore, m.; difensore, m.

conservatory, -sŭr'vătŭrĭ, a. conservante; –, s. conservatorio, m.

consider, -sĭd'ŭr, v. a. considerare; esaminare; –, v. n. pensare; riflettere, meditare; stimare.

considerable, -ăbl, a. considerabile.

considerably, -ăblĭ, ad. considerabilmente.

considerate, -sĭd'ărăt, a. considerato, discreto, prudente; -ly, ad. con considerazione, prudentemente.

consideration, -rā'shŭn, s. considerazione, f.; attenzione, f.; riflessione, f.; valore, pregio, m.; importanza, f.

considering, -ĭng, c. atteso, stante; – that, atteso che, perchè.   [custodia.

consign, -sĭn', v. a. consegnare; dare in

consignee, kŏn'sĭnē, s. commissionario, m.

consignment, -sĭn'mĕnt, s. consegna, f.; deposito, m.   [fondamento; accordarsi.

consist, -sĭst', v. n. consistere; avere il

consistence(-cy), -tĕns(ĕ), s. consistenza, f.; densità, f.

consistent, -tĕnt, a. consistente; coerente; conforme, convenevole, proporzionato; -ly, ad. coerentemente.

consistory, kŏn'sĭstŭrĭ, s. concistorio, m.

consolable, -sŏ'lăbl, a. consolabile.

consolation, -lă'shŭn, s. consolazione, f., conforto, m.   [consolante.

consolatory, -sŏl'ătŭrĭ, a. consolatorio,

console, -sōl', v. a. consolare; –, kŏn'sōl, s. mensola, f.   [lidare; consolidarsi.

consolidate, -sŏl'ĭdāt, v. a. & n. consolidation, -dă'shŭn, s. consolidazione, f.

consonance, kŏn'sŏnăns, s. consonanza, f.

consonant, -sŏnănt, a. consonante; conforme; –, s. (gr.) consonante, f.

consort, kŏn'sŏrt, s. consorte, compagno, m.; moglie, f.; concorso, m.; –, kŏnsŏrt', v. n. consociarsi.

conspicuous, -spĭk'ŭŭs, a. cospicuo, evidente; -ly, ad. notabilmente, splendidamente.

conspiracy, kŏn'ăsĭ, s. cospirazione, f.

conspirator, -ătŭr, s. cospiratore, congiuratore, m.   [giurare, tramare.

conspire, -spĭr', v. n. cospirare, congiurare, tramare.

constable, kŭn'stăbl, s. conestabile, m.; commissario, m.   [f.

constabulary, -stăb'ŭlărĭ, s. gendarmeria,

constancy, kŏn'stănsĭ, s. costanza, perseveranza, f.; sofferenza, f.

constant, -stănt, a. costante, perseverante; -ly, ad. costantemente, perseverantemente.   [zione, f.

constellation, -stĕllă'shŭn, s. costellaconsternation, -stĕrnā'shŭn, s. costernazione, f.   [densare; ristringere.

constipate, kŏn'stĭpăt, v. a. costipare; condconstituency, -stĭt'ŭĕnsĭ, s. i commettenti, m. pl.   [–, s. che costituisce.

constituent, -stĭt'ŭĕnt, a. costituente;

constitute, kŏn'stĭtūt, v. a. costituire, stabilire; ordinare; statuire.

constitution, -tū'shŭn, s. costituzione, f., statuto, m.; stato, m.; temperamento, m.

constitutional, -ăl, a. costituzionale; legale.   [sforzare; arrestare.

constrain, -strān', v. a. costringere;

constrainedly, -ĕdlĭ, ad. per forza.

constraint, -strānt', s. costringimento, m., forza, violenza, f.

constrict, -strĭkt', v. a. contrarre; condensare, comprimere.

constrictor, -ŭr, s. costrittore, m.

constringent, -strĭn'jĕnt, a. costringente.

construct, -strŭkt', v. a. costruire; fabbricare, edificare.

construction, -strŭk'shŭn, s. costruzione, costruttura, f.; fabbricazione, f.; interpretazione, f.   [per induzione.

constructively, -tĭvlĭ, ad. implicitamente,

construe, kŏn'strŏ, v. a. costruire; ordinare; interpretare.

consul, kŏn'sŭl, s. console, m.

consular, -sŭlăr, a. consolare.

consulate, *–sŭlăt,* **consulship,** *–sŭlshĭp,* s. consolato, m., dignità di console, f.

consult, *–sŭlt',* v. a. esaminare; –, v. n. consultare, deliberare.

consultation, *–tă'shăn,* s. consultazione, consulta, f.; consiglio, m.

consumable, *–sū'măbl,* a. consumabile.

consume, *–sūm',* v. a. consumare; spendere; –, v. n. consumarsi. |tore, m.

consumer, *–sū'măr,* s. consumatore, guasta-

consummate, *–sŭm'măt,* v. a. perfezionare; terminare, finire.

consummation, *–mă'shăn,* s. complimento, m.; perfezione, f.

consumption, *–sŭm'shăn,* s. consunzione, f.; dissipamento, m.; (med.) etica, f.

consumptive, *–tĭv,* a. consuntivo, etico.

contact, *kŏn'tăkt,* s. contatto, toccamento, m.

contagion, *–tă'jŭn,* s. contagio, m.; peste, f. |ziale.

contagious, *–jŭs,* a. contagioso, pestilen-

contain, *–tăn',* v. a. contenere; comprendere; raffrenare, reprimere; temperare.

contaminate, *–tăm'măt,* v. a. contaminare; corrompere; –, a. contaminato, corrotto. |zione, f.; bruttura, f.

contamination, *–nă'shăn,* s. contamina-

contemn, *–tĕm',* v. a. disprezzare.

contemplate, *–tĕm'plăt,* v. a. contemplare, considerare. |zione, f.

contemplation, *–plă'shăn,* s. contemplazione.

contemplative, *–tĕm'plătĭv,* a. contemplativo; **-ly,** ad. per contemplazione.

contemporaneous, *–tĕmpŏră'nŭs,* **contemporary,** *–tĕm'pŏrări,* a. contemporaneo. |m.

contempt, *–tĕmt',* s. dispregio, m.; scherno,

contemptible, *–tĭbl,* a. spregevole; **to make –,** avvilire. |mente.

contemptibly, *–tĭblĭ,* ad. dispregevol-

contemptuous, *–tŭŭs,* a. sprezzante; sdegnoso; **-ly,** ad. fieramente, sdegnosamente. |contrastare; sforzarsi.

contend, *–tĕnd',* v. a. contendere; –, v. n.

content, *–tĕnt',* a. contento, sodisfatto; –, s. contento, m.; sodisfazione, f.; **–s,** pl. contenuto, contenimento, m.; –, v. a. contentare; sodisfare. |lietamente.

contentedly, *–ĕdlĭ,* ad. con sodisfazione.

contentedness, *–ĕdnĕs,* s. contentezza, f.; sodisfazione, f. |disputa, f.

contention, *–tĕn'shăn,* s. contenzione, f.;

contentious, *–shŭs,* a. contenzioso, litigioso; **-ly,** ad. contenziosamente, litigiosamente.

contentment, *–tĕnt'mĕnt,* s. contentamento, m., sodisfazione, f.; piacere, m.

contest, *kŏn'tĕst,* s., contesa, rissa, f.; quistione, f.; –, *kŏntĕst',* v. a. contestare, quistionare; disputare. |traditore.

contestant, *–tĕs'tănt,* a. contestante, con-

context, *kŏn'tĕkst,* s. tessitura, f.; contesto, m. |suto, m.

contexture, *–tĕks'tăr,* s. tessitura, f., tessuto, m.

contiguity, *–tĭgū'ĭtĭ,* s. contiguità, vicinanza, f.

contiguous, *–tĭg'ŭăs,* a. contiguo, vicino.

continence, *kŏn'tĭnĕns,* s. continenza, f.; castità, f.

continent, *–tĭnĕnt,* a. continente; casto; **-ly,** ad. continentemente; –, s. continente, m., terra ferma, f.

continental, *–nĕn'tăl,* a. continentale.

contingency, *–tĭn'jĕnsĭ,* s. contingenza, f., accidente, m.

contingent, *–jĕnt,* a. contingente, casuale; **-ly,** ad. casualmente; –, s. contingente, m., parte, porzione, f.

continual, *–tĭn'ŭăl,* a. continuo, perpetuo; **-ly,** ad. continuamente, di continuo, sempre. |zione, permanenza, f.

continuance, *–ăns,* s. continuità, f.; dura-

continuation, *–nŭă'shăn,* s. continuazione, f.; serie, f.

continue, *–tĭn'ū,* v. a. continuare; –, v. n. perseverare, persistere, durare; dimorare.

continuity, *–nŭ'ĭtĭ,* s. continuità, f.; serie, f.

continuous, *–tĭn'ŭăs,* a. continuo, unito insieme. |cigliare.

contort, *–tŏrt',* v. a. contorcere, attor-

contortion, *–tŏr'shăn,* s. contorsione, f., contorcimento, m.

contour, *–tŏr',* s. contorno, m.; circonferenza, f.; delineamento, m.

contraband, *kŏn'trăbănd,* s. & a. contrabbando, m.; di contrabbando; proibito, illegale. |m.

contrabandist, *–dĭst,* s. contrabbandiere,

contract, *kŏn'trăkt,* s. contratto, accordo, m.; –, *kŏntrăkt',* v. a. contrattare; contrarre; ritirare; –, v. n. contrarsi, ristringersi.

contraction, *–trăk'shăn,* s. contrazione, f.; raccorciamento, m.; abbreviazione, f.

contractor, *–trăk'tăr,* s. contraente, m.

contradict, *kŏntrădĭkt',* v. a. contraddire.

contradiction, *–dĭk'shăn,* s. contraddizione, opposizione, f.; ostacolo, m.

contradictorily, *–tărĭlĭ,* ad. contraddittoriamente. |dizione, f.

contradictoriness, *–tărĭnĕs,* s. contrad-

contradictory, *–tărĭ,* a. contraddittorio; –, s. contraddicimento, m.

contrariety, *–rī'ĭtĭ,* **contrariness,** *kŏn'trărĭnĕs,* s. contrarietà, f.; opposizione, f.

contrarily, *kŏn'trărĭlĭ,* ad. contrariamente.

contrary, *–trărĭ,* a. contrario, opposto; –, s. contrario, m., contrarietà, f.; **on the –,** al contrario.

contrast, *kŏn'trăst,* s. contrasto, m.; opposizione, f.; –, *kŏntrăst',* v. a. fare un contrasto; porre all'incontro.

contravention, *–vĕn'shăn,* s. contravvenzione, f. |contribuente.

contributary, *–trĭb'dtărĭ,* a. tributario,

contribute, *–trĭb'ŭt,* v. a. contribuire.

contribution, *–bŭ'shăn,* s. contribuzione, f.

contributive, *–trĭb'ŭtĭv,* a. che può contribuire, contributivo.

contributor, *–ŭtăr,* s. contribuente, m.

contributory, *–ŭtărĭ,* a. contribuente, m.

contrite, *kŏn'trĭt,* a. contrito, compunto; **-ly,** ad. con contrizione.

contrition, *–trĭsh'ăn,* s. contrizione, f.; pentimento, m.

contrivance, *–trĭ'văns,* s. invenzione, f.; progetto, m.; pratiche segrete, f. pl.

contrive, *–trĭv',* v. a. inventare, tramare, macchinare.

control, *–trŏl',* s. registro, m.; ristringimento, m.; autorità, f.; –, v. a. raffrenare; restrignere; governare; confutare.

controller, *–lăr,* s. registratore, verificatore, m.   [troversia.

controversial, *kŏntrŏvăr'shăl,* a. di con-

controversy, *kŏn'trŏvărsĭ,* s. controversia, f.; contesa, disputa, f.

controvert, *–trŏvărt,* v. a. controvertere, contendere, disputare.

controvertible, *–văr'tĭbl,* a. controvertibile, disputabile.

contumacious, *–tămĭ'shăs,* a. contumace; **–ly,** ad. contumacemente.

contumacy, *kŏn'tămăsĭ,* s. contumacia, f.; ostinazione, f.

contumelious, *–tămĭ'lĭăs,* a. contumelioso, ingiurioso; **–ly,** ad. contumeliosamente, ingiuriosamente.   [giuria, f.

contumely, *kŏn'tămĕlĭ,* s. contumelia, in-

contusion, *–tŭ'zhăn,* s. contusione, f., ammaccamento, m.

conundrum, *kŏnŭn'drŭm,* s. facezia plebea, f., bisticcio, m.   [scenza, f.

convalescence, *kŏnvălĕs'sĕns,* s. convalescenza, f.

convalescent, *–sĕnt,* a. convalescente.

convene, *–vēn',* v. a. convocare; adunare; –, v. n. adunarsi, ragunarsi.

convenience, *–vē'nĭĕns,* s. convenienza, comodità, f.; proporzione, f.

convenient, *–nĭĕnt,* a. conveniente, convenevole, comodo, atto; ragionevole; **–ly,** ad. convenientemente, comodamente.

convent, *kŏn'vĕnt,* s. monastero, m.

conventicle, *–vĕn'tĭkl,* s. conventicola, f.

convention, *–shăn,* s. convenzione, f.; patto, accordo, m.

conventional, *–ăl,* a. convenzionale; **–ly,** ad. convenzionalmente, per patto.

conventionalism, *–ălĭzm,* **conventionality,** *–ăl'ĭtĭ,* s. frase di convenzione, f.

conventual, *–vĕn'tăăl,* a. conventuale.

converge, *–vărj',* v. n. convergere.

convergence, *–văr'jĕns,* s. convergenza, f.

convergent, *–jĕnt,* a. convergente.

conversable, *–văr'săbl,* a. conversevole, socievole.

conversation, *–să'shăn,* s. conversazione, f.; familiarità, f.; commercio, m.

conversational, *–ăl,* a. conversevole.

conversationalist, *–ălĭst,* s. buon parlatore, m.

converse, *kŏn'vărs,* s. società, f.; familiarità, f.; commercio, m.; pratica, f.; –, *kŏnvărs',* v. n. conversare; praticare; bazzicare.   [cenda.

conversely, *–lĭ,* ad. reciprocamente, a vi-

conversion, *–văr'shăn,* s. conversione, f.; rivolgimento, m.

convert, *kŏn'vărt,* s. convertito, m.; –, *kŏnvărt',* v. a. & n. convertire; convertirsi.

convertible, *–văr'tĭbl,* a. convertibile.

convex, *kŏn'vĕks,* a. convesso.

convexity, *–vĕks'ĭtĭ,* s. convessità, f.

convey, *–vā',* v. a. trasportare, trasmettere; condurre; comunicare; mandare.

conveyance, *–ăns,* s. trasporto, m.; vettura, f.; cessione, f.

conveyancer, *–ănsăr,* s. notaro, m.

convict, *kŏn'vĭkt,* s. bandito, m.; fuoruscito, m.; –, *kŏnvĭkt',* v. a. convincere, provare reo.   [tĭshmĕnt, s. colonia dei rei.

convict-establishment, *kŏn'vĭkt ĕstăb-*

conviction, *–vĭk'shăn,* s. convinzione, f.; confutazione, f.; condannazione, f.

convince, *–vĭns',* v. a. convincere; provare.   [vincente, evidentemente.

convincingly, *–sĭnglĭ,* ad. in modo convincente.

convivial, *–vĭ'vĭăl,* a. festivo; sociabile.

conviviality, *–vĭvĭăl'ĭtĭ,* s. buon umore, m., festevolezza, allegria, f.

convocation, *–vŏkă'shăn,* s. convocazione, f.; assemblea, f.   [radunare.

convoke, *–vŏk',* v. a. convocare; adunare.

convoy, *kŏn'vŏĭ,* s. convoglio, m., scorta, accompagnatura, f.; –, *kŏnvŏĭ',* v. a. convogliare, accompagnare.

convulse, *–văls',* v. a. convellere, sconvolgere.

convulsion, *–văl'shăn,* s. convulsione, f.; commozione, f.; turbulenza, f.

convulsive, *–sĭv,* a. convulsivo; **–ly,** ad. in modo convulsivo.

coo, *kŏ,* v. n. susurrare; gemere.

cook, *kŭk,* s. cuoco, m.; cuoca, f.; –, v. a. fare la cucina, cucinare.

cookery, *–ărĭ,* s. arte del cuoco, cucina, f.

cool, *kŏl,* a. fresco, freddo; –, s. fresco, freddo, m.; –, v. a. rinfrescare, raffreddare; moderare, sminuire; –, v. n. rinfrescarsi, raffreddarsi.   [m.

cooler, *–ăr,* s. refrigerativo, refrigerante, m.

coolly, *–lĭ,* ad. freddamente; indifferentemente.   [m.

coolness, *–nĕs,* s. freschezza, f., fresco, m.

coom, *kŏm,* s. untume delle ruote, m.

coop, *kŏp,* s. stia, f.; barile, m.; –, v. n. rinchiudere; ingabbiare.

cooper, *kŏp'ăr,* s. bottaio, m.

cooperate, *kŏŏp'ărăt,* v. a. cooperare.

cooperation, *–ră'shăn,* s. cooperazione, f.; concorrenza, f.   [cooperante.

cooperative, *–ŏp'ărătĭv,* a. cooperativo,

cooperator, *–ărătăr,* s. cooperatore, m.

coordination, *–ŏrdĭnă'shăn,* s. coordinazione, f.; egualità, f.   [m.

copartner, *kŏpărt'năr,* s. socio, compagno,

copartnership, *–shĭp,* s. società, compagnia, f.

cope, *kŏp,* s. pianeta da prete, f.; –, v. a. barattare; –, v. n. contendere; battersi.

copier, *kŏp'ĭăr,* s. copista, copiatore, m.

coping, *kŏ'pĭng,* s. comignolo, m., cima, f.

copious, *kŏ'pĭăs,* a. copioso, abbondante; **–ly,** ad. copiosamente; abbondantemente.

copiousness, *–nĕs,* s. abbondanza, ricchezza, dovizia, f.

copper, *kŏp'păr,* s. rame, m.; numerario di rame, m.; calderone, m.; **–s,** pl. vassellami da cucina, m. pl.

copperas, *–părăs,* s. vetriuolo, m.

copper-plate, –plắt, s. stampa di rame,
f.; lastra di rame, f.
copper-smith, –smĭth, s. calderaio, m.
copper-work, –wŭrk, s. manifattura di
rame, fucina del rame, f.
coppery, –pŭrĭ, a. che contiene del rame.
coppice, kŏp'pĭs, copse, kŏps, s. macchia,
f.; bosco ceduo, m.
copy, kŏp'ĭ, s. copia, f.; esemplare, m.;
originale, m.; –, v. a. copiare; trascrivere;
imitare.   [copie, m.
copy-book, –bŭk, s. quaderno, libro delle
copying-clerk, –ĭng klărk, s. spedizio-
niere, m.   [graio, m.
copying-machine, –măshĕn', s. panto-
copyist, –ĭst, s. copista, m.
copyright, –rĭt, s. diritto di proprietà let-
teraria, m.; manoscritto, m.
coquet, kŏkĕt', v. n. civettare.
coquetry, kŏ'kĕtrĭ, s. civetteria, f.
coquettish, –kĕt'tĭsh, a. da civetta.
coral, kŏr'ăl, s. corallo, m.
coralline, –lĭn, s. corallina, f.
cord, kŏrd, s. corda, f.; tendine, f.; – of
wood, s. catasta, misura di legna, f.; –,
v. a. legare con corde.   [m.
cordage, kŏr'dăj, s. cordame, m,: sartiame,
cordial, kŏr'dĭăl, a. cordiale; affettuoso;
–ly, ad. cordialmente; –, s. cordiale
(brodo da bere), m.   [cordiale, m.
cordiality, –dăl'ĭtĭ, s. cordialità, f., affetto
corduroy, kŏr'dŭrŏĭ, s. specie di stoffa di
cotone, f.   [ciume, m.
core, kŏr, s. torso, m.; interiore, m.; mar-
cork, kŏrk, s. sughero, turacciolo, m.; –,
v. a. turare.
corkscrew, –skrŏ s. rampino, m.; –
staircase, scala a chiocciola, f.
cormorant, kŏr'mŏrănt, s. cormorante
(uccello acquatico), m.; ghiottone, m.
corn, kŏrn, s. frumento, m.; grano m.; –,
v. a. saleggiare; macinare in polvere.
cornelian, kŏrnē'lĭăn, s. cornalina, f.
corner, kŏr'năr, s. angolo, m.; canto, cantone, m.; cantonata, f.; estremità, f.
corner-house, –hŏŭs, s. casa di canto-
nata, f.   [cantone, m.
corner-stone, –stŏn, s. pietra angolare, f.,
cornet, kŏr'nĕt, s. cornetta, m. & f.; corno,
cornetcy, –sĭ, s. grado di cornetta, m. [m.
corn-exchange, kŏrn'ĕkschănj, s. borsa
delle biade, f.
corn-field, –fĕld, s. seminato, m.
corn-flower, –flŏŭr, s. fioraliso, m.,
battisegola, f.
cornice, kŏr'nĭs, s. cornice, f.
corn-loft, kŏrn'lŏft, s. granaio, m.
corn-rose, –rŏs, s. nigella, f.   [f.
corn-salad, –sălăd, s. valeriana domestica,
corn-trade, –trăd, s. traffico di biade, m.
corollary, kŏr'ŏllărĭ, s. corollario, m.
coronation, kŏrŏnā'shŭn, s. corona-
mento, m., coronazione, f.
coronet, kŏr'ŏnĕt, s. piccola corona, f.
corporal, kŏr'pŏrăl, a. corporale; materiale; –ly, ad. corporalmente; –, s. corporale, m.

corporate, kŏr'pŏrăt, a. unite in un corpo.
corporation, –rā'shăn, s. corpo municipale, m.; comunità, f.
corporeal, –pŏ'rĭăl, a. corporeo, corpo-
rale; materiale.   [reggimento, m.
corps, kŏr, s. (mil.) corpo di forze, m.;
corpse, kŏrps, s. cadavere, corpo morto, m.
corpulence, kŏr'pŭlĕns, s. corpulenza, f.
corpulent, –pŭlĕnt, a. corpulento, corpacciuto, grasso.
Corpus-Christi-Day, kŏr'pŭs krĭstĭ dā,
s. Corpus Dominj, m. (festa).   [m.
corpuscle, kŏr'păskl, s. corpuscolo, atomo,
correct, kŏrrĕkt', a. corretto, esatto; –,
v. a. correggere; punire, gastigare; temperare, moderare.
correction, –rĕk'shŭn, s. correzione, f.;
emenda, f.; gastigo, m.; riprensione, f.
corrective, –rĕk'tĭv, a. correttivo; –, s.
correttivo, m.; restrizione, f.
correctly, –rĕkt'lĭ, ad. correttamente,
esattamente.   [tezza, f.
correctness, –nĕs, s. accuratezza, esat-
correlative, kŏrrĕl'ătĭv, a. correlativo, re-
ciproco.   [dere, essere proporzione.
correspond, kŏr'rĕspŏnd, v. n. corrispon-
correspondence, –spŏn'dĕns, s. corrispondenza, f.; intesa, f.
correspondent, –dĕnt, a. corrispondente;
conforme, proporzionato; –, s. corrispondente, m.
corroborate, kŏrrŏb'ŏrāt, v. a. corroborare.
corroboration, –rā'shăn, s. corrobora-
zione, f.   [tivo.
corroborative, –rŏb'ŏrătĭv, a. corrobora-
corrode, kŏrrŏd', v. a. corrodere; consumare a poco a poco.
corrosion, –rŏ'zhăn, s. corrosione, f.
corrosive, –rŏ'sĭv, s. (med.) corrosivo, m.
corrupt, –răpt', a. corrotto, guasto, depravato; cattivo; –, v. a. corrompere,
guastare, depravare; –, v. n. corrompersi; guastarsi.
corruptible, –răp'tĭbl, a. corruttibile.
corruption, –răp'shăn, s. corruzione, f.;
depravazione, f.
corruptive, –răp'tĭv, a. corruttivo.
corruptly, –răpt'lĭ, ad. corrottamente.
corruptness, –nĕs, s. corruzione, corruttela, f.; imputidimento, m.   [mare, m.
corsair, kŏr'săr, s. corsaro, ladrone di
corset, kŏr'sĕt, s. fascetta, f.; busto, m.
coruscation, kŏrŭskā'shăn, s. corrusca-
zione, f.
corvette, kŏrvĕt', s. (mar.) corvetta, f.
cosily, kŏ'zĭlĭ, ad. a bell' agio; senza
stento.
cosmetic, kŏzmĕt'ĭk, a. & s. cosmetico (m.).
cosmopolitan, –mŏpŏl'ĭtăn, cosmopolite, –mŏp'ŏlĭt, s. cosmopolita, cittadino
del mondo, m.
cossack, kŏs'săk, s. Cosacco, m.
cosset, kŏs'sĕt, v. a. allevare senza madre.
cost, kŏst, s. spesa, f.; costo, m.; prezzo,
valore, m.; –, v. a. & n. ir. costare, valere.
coster, kŏs'tăr, coster-monger, –măng'-
găr, s. colui che vende per le strade, m.
costive, kŏs'tĭv, a. costipativo.

costiveness, *–nĕs*, s. costipamento, m.

costliness, *kŏst′lĭnĕs*, s. suntuosità, f.; spesa grande, f.   [dioso; splendido.

costly, *–lĭ*, a. caro, suntuoso, dispen-

costume, *kŏstăm′* (*kŏs′tŭm*), s. costume, m.; modo di vestire, m.

cosy, *kŏ′zĭ*, a. comodo.

cot, *kŏt*, s. capanna, f.

co-trustee, *kŏ trŭstē′*, s. curatore, m.

cottage, *kŏt′tĭj*, s. capanna, f., tugurio, m.; villa, f.   [panna, m.

cottager, *–tĭjâr*, s. che abita in una ca-

cotton, *kŏt′tn*, s. cotone, m., bambagia, f.; **explosive** *–*, s. cotone explosivo, m.; *–*, v. n. adattarsi; convenire.

cotton-mill, *–mĭl*, s. filatura di cotone.

cotton-tree, *–trē*, s. pianta del cotone, m.

cotton-wool, *–wŭl*, s. bambagia, ovatta,f.

couch, *kŏŭch*, s. lettuccio, lettucciuolo, m.; *–*, v. a. coricare; stendere; *–*, v. n. coricarsi; distendersi.

cough, *kŏf*, s. tossa, tosse, f.; *–*, v. n. tossire; **to – out,** espettorare.

council, *kŏŭn′sĭl*, s. consiglio, m.; avvocato, m.; **privy –,** consigliere intimo, m.

council-board, *–bŏrd*, s. tavola del consiglio, f.; i consiglieri, m. pl.

councillor, *kŏŭn′sĭllâr*, s. consigliere, m.; membro del consiglio, m.

counsel, *kŏŭn′sĕl*, s. consiglio, m.; avviso, m.; avvocato, m.

counsellor, *–lâr*, s. consigliere, m.; avvocato, m.; **privy –,** consigliere di stato, m.

count, *kŏŭnt*, s. numero, m.; conto, computo, m.; conte, m.; *–*, v. a. contare, computare, calcolare; stimare.

countenance, *kŏŭn′tĕnâns*, s. aria, f., viso, m.; aspetto, m.; favore, m., protezione, f.; aiuto, m.; *–*, v. a. favorire; proteggere, difendere.

counter, *kŏŭn′târ*, s. banco, m.; gettone, m.; *–*, ad. contro, a rimpetto.   [trariare.

counteract, *–ăkt′*, v. a. attraversare, con-

counteraction, *–ăk′shŭn*, s. opposizione,f.

counterbalance, *–bălâns′*, s. contrappeso, m.; *–*, *–băl′ăns*, v. a. contrappesare; adeguare, aggiustare.

counterfeit, *–fĭt*, a. contraffatto, imitato, falso; supposto; *–*, s. falsificazione, f.; impostore, ingannatore, m.; *–*, v. a. imitare; falsificare.

counterfeiter, *–fĭtâr*, s. contraffattore, m.; falsario, m.; **– of coin,** falso monetario, m.

counterfoil, *–fŏĭl*, s. contra-taglia, f.

counterjumper, *–jŭmpâr*, s. giovane di bottega, m.

countermand, *–mănd′*, v. a. contrammandare; (com.) rivocare una commissione.

counterpane, *–pān*, s. coltre, m.; coperta da letto, f.   [parte opposta, f.

counterpart, *–pârt*, s. copia, f.; (mus.)

counterplot, *–plŏt*, s. artifizio opposto ad artifizio.

counterpoise, *–pŏĭz*, s. contrappeso, m.; *–*, *–pŏĭz*, v. a. contrappesare.

counterscarp, *–skârp*, s. controscarpa, f.

countersign, *–sīn′*, v. a. contrassegnare.

countervail, *–văl*, v. n. valere altrettanto, equivalere.

countess, *kŏŭn′tĕs*, s. contessa, f.

counting-house, *kŏŭnt′ĭng hŏŭs*, s. banco (de′ mercanti), m.; fattoria, f.

countless, *kŏŭnt′lĕs*, a. innumerabile.

countrified, *kŭn′trĭfĭd*, a. campestre, rustico, grossolano.

country, *kŭn′trĭ*, s. regione, f.; campagna, f.; provincia, paese, f.; *–*, a. rustico, campestre.   [f.

country-dance, *–dăns*, s. contraddanza,

country-house, *–hŏŭs*, s. villa, casa di campagna, f.

country-life, *–lĭf*, s. vita campestre, f.

countryman, *–măn*, s. contadino, villano, m.

country-seat, *vedi* **country-house.**

country-squire, *–skwīr*, s. gentiluomo di provincia, m.

countrywoman, *–wŭmăn*, s. contadina, f.

county, *kŏŭn′tĭ*, s. contea, f.; provincia, f.

couple, *kŭp′l*, s. coppia, f.; paio, m.; *–*, v. a. accoppiare; maritare; *–*, v. n. copularsi, congiungersi.

couplet, *kŭp′lĕt*, s. paio, m.; distico, m.

couplings, *kŭp′lĭngs*, s. pl. (rail.) accoppiamento, m.   [m.; bravura, f.

courage, *kŭr′ĭj*, s. coraggio, m.; animo,

courageous, *kŭrā′jŭs*, a. coraggioso, bravo; **–ly,** ad. coraggiosamente.   [m.

courier, *kŭr′âr*, s. corriere, messaggiere,

course, *kŏrs*, s. corso, m.; carriera, f.; ordine, m.; viaggio, m.; cammino, m.; metodo, m., maniera, f.; usanza, f.; servizio (di tavola), m.; **–s,** pl. menstruo, m.; (mar.) vele basse, f. pl.; **of –,** necessariamente; comunemente, ordinariamente; *–*, v. a. cacciare, dare la caccia; *–*, v. n. vagare.   [m.

courser, *kŏr′sâr*, s. corsiere, m.; destriero,

court, *kŏrt*, s. corte, f.; cortile, m.; tribunale, m.; i giudici, m. pl.; *–*, v. a. corteggiare; brigare; sollecitare.

court-day, *–dā*, s. giorno curiale, m.

court-dresser, *–drĕssâr*,s.lusingatore, m.

courteous, *kŭrt′yŭs*, a. cortese, gentile; **–ly,** ad. cortesemente.

courtier, *kŏr′târ*, s. cortigiano, m.

courtesan, *kŭr′tĭzăn*, s. cortigiana, f.

courtesy, *kŭr′tĕsĭ*, s. riverenza (di donna), f.; civiltà, f.; *–*, v. n. fare la riverenza.

court-house, *kŏrt′hŏŭs*, s. curia, f., foro, m.   [cortese, m.

courtier, *kŏrt′yâr*, s. cortigiano, m.; uomo

courtlike, *–lĭk*, a. civile; elegante.

courtliness, *–lĭnĕs*, s. affabilità, compiacenza, f.; eleganza, f.

courtly, *–lĭ*, a. civile; grazioso.

court-martial, *–mărshâl*, s. corte marziale, f., consiglio di guerra, m.

court-plaster, *–plăstâr*, s.cerotto anglico, impiastro d′Inghilterra, m.

courtship, *–shĭp*, s. civiltà, complacenza, pulitezza, f.; galanteria, f.

court-yard, *–yârd*, s. anticorte, f.

cousin, *kŭz′n*, s. cugino, m.; cugina, f.; **first –, – german,** cugino germano, m.

cove, *kōv,* s. cala piccola, f.; rifugio, m.

covenant, *kŭv'ĕnănt,* s. patto, contratto, m.; –, v. n. pattuire, trattare.

cover, *kŭv'ŭr,* s. coperchio, m.; rifugio, m.; pretesto, m., scusa, f.; –, v. a. coprire; celare, palliare. [mento, m.

covering, *–ĭng,* s. coprimento, m.; vestimento, m.

coverlet, *–lĕt,* **coverlid,** *–lĭd,* s. copertura, coperta, f.

covert, *kŭv'ŭrt,* a. coperto, nascosto, segreto; **–ly,** ad. segretamente, m.; –, s. luogo coperto, nascondiglio, m.; rifugio, m.

coverture, *–tŭr,* s. copertura, f.; protezione, f.; condizione di donna maritata, f.

covet, *kŭv'ĕt,* v. a. bramare, desiderare.

covetous, *–tŭs,* a. avido, avaro; sordido; **–ly,** ad. avaramente; sordidamente.

covetousness, *–nĕs,* s. avarizia, f.; cupidità, cupidigia, f.

cov(e)y, *kŭv'ĭ,* s. covata, f.; nidiata, f.

cow, *kōŭ,* s. vacca, f.; –, v. a. intimorire; spaventare. [m.

coward, *kōŭ'ărd,* s. codardo, m.; poltrone, m.

cowardice, *–dĭs,* s. codardia, vigliaccheria, pusillanimità, f.

cowardly, *–dlĭ,* a. codardo, vigliacco, pusillanimo; –, ad. poltronescamente; vilmente.

cower, *kōŭ'ŭr,* v. n. appiattarsi; chinarsi.

cow-herd, *–hĕrd,* s. vaccaro, m.

cow-house, *–hōŭs,* s. stalla da vacche, f.

cow-keeper, *–kēpŭr,* s. vaccaro, m.

cowl, *kōŭl,* s. cappuccio, m.

cowslip, *kōŭ'slĭp,* s. primavera, f.

coxcomb, *kŏks'kōm,* s. cresta d'un gallo, f.; sciocco, farfallino, m.

coy(ish), *kōĭ'ĭsh,* a. contegnoso; timido; modesto; **–ly,** ad. contegnosamente.

coyness, *–nĕs,* s. contegno, m.; modestia affettata, f.

coz, *kŭz,* s. (fam.) cugino, m.

cozen, *–zn,* v. a. ingannare, truffare. [m.

cozenage, *kŭz'ĕnāj,* s. truffa, f., inganno, m.

cozener, *–ĕnŭr,* s. ingannatore, giuntatore, m. [mela salvatica, f.

crab, *krăb,* s. granchio, m.; cancro, m.;

crab-apple-tree, *–ăppl trē,* s. melo salvatico, m.

crabbed, *–bĕd,* a. aspro; arcigno; **–ly,** ad. aspramente; arcignamente.

crabbedness, *–nĕs,* s. asprezza, f.; arcignezza, f.; viso arcigno, m.; difficoltà, f.

crack, *krăk,* s. crepatura, fessura, f.; scoppio, fracasso, m.; millantatore, m.; –, v. a. crepare, fendere; schiacciare; rompere; –, v. n. fendersi, scoppiare; vantarsi, millantarsi.

crack-brained, *–brānd,* a. discervellato.

cracker, *–ŭr,* s. salterello, m.; petardo, m.; diavolone (sweetmeat), m.; millantatore, m. [chiolare.

crackle, *krăk'l,* v. n. scoppiettare, scricchiolare.

crackling, *–lĭng,* s. schioppetata, f.

cracknel, *–nĕl,* s. ciambella, f. [cullare.

cradle, *krā'dl,* s. culla, cuna, f.; –, v. a. cullare.

craft, *krăft,* s. mestiere, m., professione, f.; astuzia, f., artificio, m.; barca, f., battello, m., chiatta, f.

English and Italian.

craftily, *krăf'tĭlĭ,* ad. astutamente, con astuzia.

craftiness, *–tĭnĕs,* s. astuzia, f.; stratagemma, f. [fice, m.

craftsman, *krăfts'măn,* s. artigiano, artefice, m.

crafty, *–tĭ,* a. astuto, scaltro, volpino.

crag, *krăg,* s. rupe, f.; collottola, nuca, f.

cragged, *–gĕd,* a. aspro, erto, scosceso.

cragginess, *–gĭnĕs,* s. asprezza, f.; ertezza, f.

craggy, *vedi* **cragged.** [f.

cram, *krăm,* v. a. impinzare; ficcare; –, v. n. impinzarsi di carne &c.

cramp, *krămp,* s. granchio, m.; ritiramento di muscoli, m.; ostacolo, m.; –, v. a. uncinare; costringere.

cramp-fish, *–fĭsh,* s. torpedine, f.

cramp-iron, *–ĭrn,* s. rampicone, m.; graffio, m. [sifone, m.

crane, *krān,* s. grù, grue, f.; argano, m.;

crank, *krăngk,* a. robusto, vigoroso; allegro; –, s. lieva, f.; sinuosità, f.

crannied, *krăn'nĭd,* a. crepato, screpolato.

cranny, *–nĭ,* s. crepatura, fenditura, f.

crape, *krāp,* s. velo, m.

crash, *krăsh,* s. fracasso, f. [strepito, m.; –, v. n. strepitare.

crass, *krăs,* a. crasso, spesso.

crate, *krāt,* s. cesto, paniere, m.

crater, *krā'tŭr,* s. cratere, m.

cravat, *krăvăt',* s. cravatta, f.

crave, *krāv,* v. a. pregare, implorare.

craven, *krā'vn,* s. gallo scorato, m.; codardo, m. [s. desiderio ardente, m.

craving, *–vĭng,* a. insaziabile; avido; –,

craw, *krā,* s. gozzo, m.

crawfish, *–fĭsh,* s. granchio, gambero, m.

crawl, *krăl,* v. n. strascinare, rampicare; umiliarsi; **to – with,** brulicare; formicolare. [colare.

crayfish, *vedi* **crawfish.**

crayon, *krā'ŏn,* s. pastello, m.

craze, *krāz,* v. a. fracassare, rompere; dimentare. [cillità, f.

craziness, *krā'zĭnĕs,* s. infermità, imbecillità, f.

crazy, *–zĭ,* a. decrepito; debile, malsano.

creak, *krēk,* v. n. scricchiolare; cigolare.

cream, *krēm,* s. crema, f., fiore di latte, m.; –, v. a. schiumare; –, v. a. rappigliarsi.

creamy, *krēm'ĭ,* a. pieno di crema.

crease, *krēs,* s. piega, crespa, ruga, f.; –, v. a. piegare, increspare.

create, *krēăt',* v. a. creare, causare. [f.

creation, *–d'shăn,* s. creazione, f.; elezione, f.

creative, *–d'ĭv,* a. creativo, generativo.

creator, *–d'tŭr,* s. creatore, m.

creature, *krē'tŭr (krē'chŭr),* s. creatura, f.; animale, m. [f.; fama, f.

credence, *krē'dĕns,* s. credenza, f.; fede,

credentials, *krēdĕn'shălz,* s. pl. lettere credenziali, f. pl.

credibility, *–dĭbĭl'ĭtĭ,* s. credibilità, probabilità, f. [fede.

credible, *krĕd'ĭbl,* a. credibile, degno di

credibly, *–ĭblĭ,* ad. credibilmente.

credit, *krĕd'ĭt,* s. credito, m.; fede, f.; riputazione, fama, stima, f.; autorità, f.; –, v. a. credere, prestar fede; far onore; fidarsi.

creditable, *–ăbl,* a. onorevole; stimabile.

creditableness, *–nĕs*, s. onorevolezza, f.; riputazione, f.   [volmente.

creditably, *–ăblĭ*, ad. con credito, onore-

creditor, *–ĭtăr*, s. creditore, m.

credulity, *–dŭ'lĭtĭ*, s. credulità, f.

credulous, *krĕd'dŭlŭs*, a. credulo, facile a credere; **–ly**, ad. da credulo.

creed, *krēd*, s. credo, m.

creek, *krĕk*, s. piccolo seno di mare; (am.) ruscello, m.; **–**, v. n. scricchiolare.

creep, *krēp*, v. n. ir. rampicare, strisciare; abbassarsi, umiliarsi.   [tile, m.

creeper, *–ăr*, s. pianta strisciante, f.; ret-

creephole, *–hŏl*, s. buco per scampare, m.; pretesto, m.

crenelated, *krĕn'ĕldtĕd*, a. merlatto.

crepuscular, *krĕpŭs'kŭlăr*, a. tra 'l dì e la notte.   [–, 'a. crescente.

crescent, *krĕs'sĕnt*, s. luna crescente, f.;

cress, *krĕs*, s. crescione, m.

crest, *krĕst*, s. cresta, f.; pennacchio, m.; orgoglio, m.; animo, m.

crested, *–ĕd*, a. crestuto.   [tito.

crestfallen, *–făln*, a. sgomentato, sbigot-

cretaceous, *krĕtă'shŭs*, a. cretaceo, cretoso.

crevice, *krĕv'ĭs*, s. creptura, fenditura, f.

crew, *krŏ*, s. banda, f.; torma, f.; mano, f.; (mar.) equipaggio (d'un vascello), m.

crewel, *krŏ'ŭl*, s. lana filata, f.

crib, *krĭb*, s. mangiatoia, f.; capanna, f.

crick, *krĭk*, s. scricchiolata, f.

cricket, *–ĕt*, s. grillo, m.; sgabello, m.; giuoco alla palla, m.

crier, *krĭ'ăr*, s. banditore, m.

crime, *krĭm*, s. delitto, m.; colpa, f.

criminal, *krĭm'ĭnăl*, a. colpevole; **–ly**, ad. colpevolmente; **–**, s. delinquente, malfattore, m.

criminality, *–nălĭtĭ*, s. criminalità, f.

criminate, *krĭm'ĭnăt*, v. a. incolpare.

crimination, *–nă'shăn*, s. incolpazione, accusa, f.

crimp, *krĭmp*, s. commissionario, m.; (mil.) arrolatore, ingaggiatore, m.; –(le), v. a. increspare, aggrinzire.   [chermisì, m.

crimson, *krĭmz'n*, a. chermisino; **–**, s.

cringe, *krĭnj*, s. ossequio servile, m.; **–**, v. n. adulare vilmente.

crinkle, *krĭng'gl*, s. piega, grinza, f.; sinuosità, f.; **–**, v. n. serpeggiare, volteggiare.

crinoline, *krĭn'ŏlĕn*, s. faldiglia, f.

cripple, *krĭp'pl*, a. zoppo, mutilato; **–**, v. a. storpiare, mutilare.   [crisi, m.

crisis, *krĭ'sĭs*, s. crisi, f.; periodo decisivo,

crisp, *krĭsp*, a. crespo; **–**, v. a. increspare; inanellare, arricciare.

crispness, *–nĕs*, s. arricciatura, increspatura, f.; fragilità, f.

criterion, *krĭtĕ'rĭŏn*, s. criterio, m.

critic, *krĭt'ĭk*, a. critico; **–**. s. critico, m.; censore, m.

critical, *–ĭkăl*, a. critico; esatto, accurato; **–ly**, ad. criticamente; da critico; esattamente.

criticise, *–ĭsĭz*, v. a. criticare, censurare.

criticism, *–ĭsĭzm*, s. criticismo, m.; critica, f.   [tica, f.

croak, *krŏk*, v. n. gracidare.

crockery, *krŏk'ărĭ*, s. stoviglie, f. pl., maiolica, f.

crocodile, *krŏ'kŏdĭl*, s. coccodrillo, m.

crone, *krŏn'*, s. vecchia, vecchiaccia, f.

crony, *krŏ'nĭ*, s. amico vecchio, m.; conoscenza vecchia, f.

croo, *krŏ*, v. a. tubare.

crook, *krŏk*, s. uncino, m.; crocco, m.; rocco, m.; **–**, v. a. & n. incurvare; piegarsi.

crooked, *krŏ'kĕd*, a. incurvato, curvato.

crookedly, *–ĕdlĭ*, ad. tortamente; malvolentieri,

croon, *krŏn'*, v. n. sussurare; gèmire.

crop, *krŏp*, s. gozzo (d'uccello), m.; raccolta, f.; cavallo scodato, m.; **–**, v. a. scortare; tosare; **–**, v. n. fare la raccolta; mietere.

cropper, *–păr*, s. miettitore, m.

croquet, *krŏ'kĕ*, s. giuoco di bocce percosse, m.   [vescovile, m.

crosier, *krŏ'zhăr*, s. pastorale, bastone

cross, *krŏs*, s. croce, f.; afflizione, pena, f., tormento, m.; infortunio, m.; **–**, a. traverso, contrario, opposto; perverso; **–**, pr. & ad. alla traversa; attraverso; **–**, v. a. attraversare; impedire; **to – over**, passare.

cross-bar, *–băr*, **cross-beam**, *–bĕm*, s. sbarra, f.; trave traversa, f.

cross-bow, *–bŏ*, s. balestra, f.

cross-breed, *–brĕd*, s. razza incrociata, f.

cross-examine, *–ĕgzăm'ĭn*, v. a. esaminare artatamente.

cross-grained, *–grănd*, a. bisbetico.

crossing, *krŏs'sĭng*, **cross-line**, *–lĭn*, s. (rail.) transito, passaggio, m.

crossing-sweeper, *—swĕ'păr*, s. spazzino di crocevie, m.

crossly, *krŏs'lĭ*, ad. attraverso; in modo opposto; sventuratamente.

crossness, *–nĕs*, s. intersecazione, f.; perversità, f.; mal umore, m.

cross-purpose, *–părpăs*, s. proposito non riuscito o sconcertato, m.

cross-road, *–rŏd*, **cross-way**, *–wă*, s. crociechio, m.

crotch, *krŏch*, s. uncinetto, m.; amo, m.

crotchet, *–ĕt*, s. croma, f.; fantasia, f., capriccio, m.; parentesi, f.   [liarsi.

crouch, *krŏŭch*, v. n. appiattarsi; umiliarsi.

croup, *krŏp*, s. groppa, f.; groppone, m.

crow, *krŏ*, s. cornacchia, f.; lieva, f.; stanga, f.; canto del gallo, m.; **–**, v. n. ir. cantare; vantarsi, millantarsi.

crowd, *krŏŭd*, s. folla, f.; calca, f.; moltitudine, f.; **–**, v. a. affollare; stringere; **–**, v. n. stringersi nella calca; **to – sail**, far forza di vele.

crown, *krŏŭn*, s. corona, f.; ghirlanda, f.; cima, sommità, f.; ornamento, m.; fine, m.; forma (d'un cappello), f.; **–**, v. a. coronare; ricompensare; damare (una pedina.)

crown-glass, *–glăs*, s. vetro bianco, m.

crown-land, *–lănd*, s. dominio della corona, m.

crown-prince, _prĭns_, s. principe ereditario, m. [tormentoso.

crucial, _krŏʹshĭȧl_, a. trasversale; penoso,

crucible, _krŏʹsĭbl_, s. crogiuolo, m.

crucifix, _krŏʹsĭfĭks_, s. crocifisso, m.

crucifixion, _-fĭkʹshȧn_, s. crocifissione, f.

cruciform, _krŏʹsĭfŏrm_, a. in forma di croce. [mentare.

crucify, _krŏʹsĭfī_, v. a. crocifiggere; tormentare.

crude, _krŏd_, a. crudo, aspro; acerbo; immaturo; imperfetto; _-ly_. ad. immaturamente. [turità, f.; indigestione, f.

crudity, _krŏʹdĭt_, s. crudezza, f.; immaturità, f.; indigestione, f.

cruel, _krŏʹĕl_, a. crudele; inumano; _-ly_, ad. crudelmente, inumanamente, barbaramente.

cruelty, _-ĕltĭ_, s. crudeltà, f.; inumanità, f.

cruet, _krŏʹĕt_, cruet-stand, _-stȧnd_, s. stagnata, ampollina (per l'oglio o l'aceto), f.

cruise, _krŏz_, s. (mar.) crociera, f.; _-_, v. n. incrociare, correr la marina.

cruiser, _krŏʹzȧr_, s. legno di crociera, m.

crumb, _krăm_, s. midolla; mica, f.

crumble, _krămʹbl_, v. a. sminuzzare; tritare; _-_, v. n. sminuzzarsi; stritolarsi.;

crumple, _krămʹpl_, v. a. raggrinzare.

crusade, _krŏsādʹ_, s. crociata, f. [m.

crusader, _sŏʹdȧr_, s. soldato della crociata,

crush, _krŭsh_, v. a. schiacciare, ammaccare; premere, opprimere; _-_, s. ammaccamento, schiacciamento, m.

crushing-mill, _-ĭng mĭl_, s. macchina con cui si trita il minerale, f.

crust, _krŭst_, s. crosta, f.; incrostatura, f.; _-_, v. a. & n. incrostare; incrostarsi, formarsi in crosta. [crostuto.

crustaceous, _krŭstāʹshȧs_, s. crostaceo,

crustily, _-tĭlĭ_, ad. di cattivo umore.

crustiness, _-tĭnĕs_, s. crosta, f.; cattivo umore, m.

crusty, _-tĭ_, a. crostuto; bisbetico.

crutch, _krŭch_, s. gruccia, stampella, f.

cry, _krī_, v. a. chiamare; promulgare; _-_, v. n. gridare; strepitare; piangere; _-_, s. grido, clamore, m.; pianto, m.; muta (di cani), f.

crying out, _-ĭng ŏŭt_, s. esclamazione, f.

crypt, _krĭpt_, s. cripta, f.

crystal, _krĭsʹtȧl_, s. cristallo, m.

crystalline, _-lĭn_, a. cristallino.

crystallisation, _-lĭzāʹshȧn_, s. cristallizzazione, f. [lizzare.

crystallise, _krĭsʹtȧllĭz_, v. a. & n. cristallizzare, partorire.

cub, _kŭb_, s. orso giovane, m.; _-_, v. a. figliare, partorire.

cube, _kūb_, s. cubo, m. [liare, partorire.

cubic(al), _kūʹbĭk(ȧl)_, a. cubico.

cubiform, _kūʹbĭfŏrm_, a. cubiforme.

cubit, _kūʹbĭt_, s. cubito, gomito, m.

cuckoo, _kŭkʹkŏ_, s. cuculo, m.

cucumber, _kūʹkŭmbȧr_, s. cetriuolo, m.

cud, _kŭd_, s. cibo ruminato, m.

cuddle, _kŭdʹl_, v. n. appiatarsi, stare appiatato, covigliarsi.

cuddy, _kŭdʹdĭ_, s. cameretta a prua d'una navicella, f. [v. a. bastonare.

cudgel, _kŭjʹĕl_, s. bacchio, bastone, m.; _-_,

cudgelling, _-lĭng_, s. bastonata, f.

cudgel-player, _-plāʹŭr_, s. che sa tirar di bastone, m.

cue, _kū_, s. coda, f.; fine, f.; indizio, m.; avviso, m.; umore, m.; stecca da biliardo, f.

cuff, _kŭf_, s. manichino, m.; guanciata, f.; _-_, v. a. schiaffeggiare; _-_, v. n. far alle pugne. [busto, f.

cuirass, _kwĭrȧsʹ_, s. corazza, armadura del

cuirassier, _-sēr_, s. soldato armato di corazzo, corazziere, m.

culinary, _kūʹlĭnȧrĭ_, a. di cucina.

cull, _kŭl_, v. a. scegliere, cogliere.

culminate, _kŭlʹmĭnāt_, v. n. culminare.

culpability, _-pȧbĭlʹĭtĭ_, s. delitto, misfatto,

culpable, _kŭlʹpȧbl_, a. colpevole. [m.

culpably, _-blĭ_, ad. reamente, biasimevolmente, colpevolmente.

culprit, _kŭlʹprĭt_, s. accusato, reo, m.

cultivate, _kŭlʹtĭvāt_, v. a. coltivare; migliorare, perfezionare.

cultivation, _-vāʹshȧn_, s. coltivamento, m., coltura, f.; miglioramento, m.

culture, _kŭlʹtȧr (kŭlʹchŭr)_, s. coltura, f.; coltivamento, m. [brogliare.

cumber, _kŭmʹbȧr_, v. n. imbarazzare; impacciare

cumbersome. _-sȧm_, cumbrous, _kŭmʹbrȧs_, a. scomodo, molesto, affannoso.

cumulative, _kŭmūlāʹtĭv_, a. cumulativo.

cunning, _kŭnʹnĭng_, a. astuto, scaltrito, fino, esperto; _-ly_, ad. astutamente; destramente; _-_, s. astuzia, f.; sagacità, f.

cup, _kŭp_, s. coppa, tazza, f.; bicchiere, m.; (bot.) boccia, f.; _-_, v. a. appiccare le ventose.

cupboard, _-bŏrd_, s. credenza, f.

cupidity, _kūpĭdʹĭtĭ_, s. cupidità, cupidigia,

cupola, _kūʹpŏlȧ_, s. cupola, f. [f.

cupping-glass, _kŭpʹpĭng glȧs_, s. ventosa, coppetta, f. [m.

cur, _kŭr_, s. cane degenerato, m.; furfante,

curable, _kūʹrȧbl_, a. curabile, sanabile.

curacy, _kūʹrȧsĭ_, s. ufficio di curato, f.

curate, _kūʹrȧt_, s. curato, parroco, m.

curative, _kūʹrȧtĭv_, a. curativo.

curator, _-rȧʹtŭr_, s. curatore, m.; amministratore, m.

curb, _kŭrb_, s. freno, morso, m.; ristringimento, m., proibizione, f.; _-_, v. a. frenare, tener a freno; rintuzzare, ristringere.

curd, _kŭrd_, s. latte rappreso, m.; _-_, v. a. coagulare.

curdle, _kŭrdʹl_, v. a. & n. coagulare, rappigliare; coagularsi, rappigliarsi.

cure, _kŭr_, s. cura, f.; parrocchia, f.; _-_, v. a. curare, guarire.

curfew, _kŭrʹfū_, s. coperchio del fuoco, m.

curing, _kūʹrĭng_, s. curare, guarire, m. [f.

curiosity, _kūrĭŏsʹĭtĭ_, s. curiosità, f.; rarità,.

curious, _kūʹrĭȧs_, a. curioso; squisito, raro, delicato; esatto; _-ly_, ad. curiosamente; con esattezza.

curl, _kŭrl_, s. riccio, m.; sinuosità, f.; _-_, v. a. arricciare, inanellare; _-_, v. n. arricciarsi.

curling-irons, _-ĭng īrns_, s. calamistro,

curling-paper, _-pȧpȧr_, s. carta da ricci, f.

curling-tongs, –*tŏngz,* s. pl. calamistro, ferro da arricciare, m.

curly, *kŭr'lĭ,* a. riccio, ricciuto.

curmudgeon, *kŭrmŭdj'ăn,* s. avaro, spilorcio, m.   [f.

currant, *kŭr'rănt,* s. ribes, m., uva spina, f.

currency, *kŭr'rĕnsĭ,* s. corso, m.; circolazione, f.; continuità, f.; carta monetata, f.

current, *kŭr'rĕnt,* a. corrente; comune; –, s. corrente, f.   [m.

current-price, –*prĭs,* s. prezzo corrente.

currently, –*lĭ,* ad. correntemente; generalmente.

curricle, *kŭr'rĭkl,* s. barroccio, m.

currier, *kŭr'rĭjr,* s. conciatore di pelli, m.

currish, *kŭr'rĭsh,* a. cagnesco; brutale; –ly, ad. brutalmente.   [strigliare.

curry, *kŭr'rĭ,* v. a. lustrare il cuoio;

currycomb, –*kŏm,* s. striglia, f.

curse, *kŭrs,* s. maledizione, imprecazione, f.; –, v. a. maledire; –, v. n. giurare; bestemmiare.   [miseramente, odiosamente.

cursedly, *kŭrs'ĕdlĭ,* ad. pessimamente.

cursive, *kŭr'sĭv,* a. corsivo.   [giera.

cursorily, –*sŏrĭlĭ,* ad. in fretta; alla leggiera.

cursory, –*sŭrĭ,* a. leggiero, frettoloso.

curt, *kŭrt,* a. corto; breve.

curtail, *kŭrtăl',* v. a. mozzare, troncare.

curtain, *kŭr'tĭn,* s. cortina, f.; cortinaggio di letto, m.; –, v. a. incortinare, chiudere con cortine.   [(in letto), m.

curtain-lecture, –*lĕkchŭr,* s. rabbuffo

curtain-rod, –*rŏd,* s. verga di ferro, f.

curtsey, *kŭrt'sĭ,* s. inchino, m., riverenza, f.

curvated, *kŭr'vătĕd,* a. curvato, piegato.

curvature, *kŭr'vătŭr,* s. incurvatura, f.

curve, *kŭrv,* a. curvo, storto; –, s. linea curva, f.; incurvatura, f.; –, v. a. curvare, piegare.

curvet, *kŭr'vĕt,* s. corvetta, f.; salto, m.; –, v. a. fare le corvette, corvettare; saltare.

cushion, *kŭsh'ŭn,* s. cuscino, m.; guanciale, origliere, m.

cusp, *kŭsp,* s. corna della mezzaluna, f. pl.

custard, *kŭs'tărd,* s. berlingozzo, m.

custodian, *kŭstō'dĭăn,* s. custode, m.

custody, *kŭs'tŏdĭ,* s. custodia, f.; prigione, f.

custom, *kŭs'tăm,* s. costume, f.; usanza, f.; uso, rito, m.; dogana, f.; avventore, m.

customarily, –*ărĭlĭ,* ad. abitualmente, ordinariamente.   [comune.

customary, –*ărĭ,* a. abituale, ordinario,

customer, –*ăr,* s. avventore, compratore, m.

custom-free, –*frē,* a. franco di dogana.

custom-house, –*hŏŭs,* s. dogana, f.

custom-house officer, –*ŏffĭsăr,* s. dogane re, m.

cut, *kŭt,* v. a. ir. tagliare; mozzare; ferire; dividere, separare; –, v. n. ir. tagliarsi, intersecarsi; penetrare; traversare; **to capers,** fare delle capriuole; **to teeth,** far i denti; **to short,** farla finita; abbreviare; –, s. taglio, m.; pezzo, m.; (rail.) intaglio, m.; stampa, f.; **and dry,** a. taffatto pronto, in punto.

cutaneous, *kŭtā'nĕŭs,* a. cutaneo.

---

cutaway, *kŭt'ăwā,* s. frac, marzino, m.

cuticle, *kŭt'ĭkl,* s. cuticola, pellicola, f.

cutlass, *kŭt'lăs,* s. scimitarra, f.

cutler, *kŭt'lăr,* s. coltellinaio, m.

cutlery, –*lărĭ,* s. arte del coltellinaio, f.

cutlet, *kŭt'lĕt,* s. braciuola, f.

cutpurse, –*pŭrs,* s. tagliaborse, borsaiuolo, m.   [cutter, m.; scialuppa, f.

cutter, *kŭt'tăr,* s. tagliatore, m.; (mar.)

cut-throat, –*thrŏt,* s. assassino, tagliacantoni, m.; luogo periglioso, m.

cutting, *kŭt'tĭng,* s. ritaglio, m., tagliata, f.; (rail.) intaglio, m., trincea, f.   [f. pl.

cutting-nippers, –*nĭppărs,* s. pl. pinzette,

cutwater, *kŭt'wătăr,* s. (mar.) tagliamare, m., polen, f.

cyclopædia, *sĭklŏpē'dĭă,* s. enciclopedia, f.

cygnet, *sĭg'nĕt,* s. cigno giovane, m.

cylinder, *sĭl'ĭndăr,* s. cilindro, m.

cylindric(al), –*lĭn'drĭk(ăl),* a. cilindrico.

cymbal, *sĭm'băl,* s. cembalo, m.

cynic, *sĭn'ĭk,* s. cinico, m., **cynical,** –*ĭkăl,* –, a. cinico; brutale.   [(costellazione).

cynosure, *sĭ'nŏzhŭr,* s. Orsa minore, f.

cypress(-tree), *sĭ'prĕs(trē),* s. cipresso, m.

czar, *zăr,* s. czar, imperatore della Russia, m.

czarina, *zărē'nă,* s. imperadrice della Russia, f.

D.

dab, *dăb,* v. a. percuotere leggermente; –, s. piccolo schiaffo, m.; zacchera, f.

dabble, *dăb'l,* v. a. imbrattare; schiccherare; –, v. n. sporcarsi.

dabbler, –*lăr,* s. guastamestiere, m.

dace, *dăs,* s. ghiozzo, m. (pesce).

dad, *dăd,* s. babbo, padre, m.

daddy, *vedi* dad.   [falangio, m.

daddy-longlegs, –*dĭ lŏnglĕgs,* s. ragno

daffodil, *dăf'dĭl,* s. asfodillo, m.

dagger, *dăg'găr,* s. pugnale, m., daga, f.

daggle, *dăg'l,* v. a. & n. imbrattare, sporcare; imbrattarsi.   [ogni giorno.

daily, *dă'lĭ,* a. quotidiano, diurno; –, ad.

daintily, *dăn'tĭlĭ,* ad. delicatamente.

daintiness, –*tĭnĕs,* s. delicatezza, f.

dainty, *dăn'tĭ,* a. delicato, squisito; elegante; –, s. delicatezza, f.

dairy, *dā'rĭ,* s. cascina, f.; latticini, m. pl.

dairy-maid, –*mād,* s. fante che fa i latticini.   [cini, f.

daisy, *dā'zĭ,* s. margheritina, f.

dale, *dăl,* s. valle, valletta, f.

dalliance, *dăl'lĭăns,* s. amorevolezza, f., trastullo, m.; ritardo, m.

dally, *dăl'lĭ,* v. n. scherzare; accarezzare; dimorare, indugiare.   [turare, murare.

dam, *dăm,* s. molo, m.; –, v. a. stoppare,

damage, *dăm'ĭj,* s. danno, detrimento, m.; –s, pl. compenso, risarcimento, m.; (mar.) avaria, f.; –, v. a. danneggiare.

damageable, –*ăbl,* a. dannoso, pernicioso.

damask, *dăm'ăsk,* s. damasco, m.; –, a. damaschino, di damasco.

damaskeen, *dăm'ăskēn,* v. a. damascare.

dame, *dăm,* s. dama, signora, f.

damn, *dăm*, v. a. dannare, condannare; fischiare.

damnable, *-năbl*, s. dannabile.

damnably, *-năblĭ*, ad. dannabilmente; orribilmente.

damnation, *-nd'shăn*, s. dannazione, f.

damp, *dămp*, a. umido; depresso, tristo; —, s. umidità, f.; afflizione, f.; —, v. a. inumidire; sgomentare, scoraggiare.

dampen, *dămp'n*, v. a. inumidire.

damper, *dăm'păr*, s. (mus.) sordina, f.; guastafeste, m.

dampness, *dămp'nĕs*, s. umidità, f.

damsel, *dăm'zĕl*, s. damigella, f.

damson, *dăm'zn*, s. pruna di Damasco, f.

dance, *dăns*, s. ballo, m., danza, f.; —, v. n. ballare, danzare; to - attendance, aspettar lungo tempo invano; fare spaldancer, *dăn'săr*, s. ballerino, m. [liera.

dancing-master, *-sĭng măstăr*, s. maestro di ballo, m.

dandle, *dăn'dl*, v. a. dondolare; accarezzare.

dandriff, *dăn'drĭf*, s. forfora, f.

dandy, *dăn'dĭ*, s. damerino, m.

danger, *dăn'jăr*, s. pericolo, m.; rischio, m.

dangerous, *-jărăs*, a. pericoloso; -ly, ad. periglsiosamente. [corteggiare vilmente.

dangle, *dăng'gl*, v. n. pendere, dondolare;

dangler, *-glăr*, s. galante, m.; innamorato, dank, *dăngk*, a. umido, molle. [m.

dapper, *dăp'păr*, a. lesto, attivo, vivace.

dapple, *dăp'l*, v. a. strisciare; —, a. pomato.

dare, *dăr*, v. a. ir. sfidare; provocare; —, v. n. osare, arrischiarsi.

daring, *dăr'ĭng*, a. ardito; audace; -ly, ad. arditamente; coraggiosamente.

dark, *dărk*, a. oscuro, fosco; ignorante; —, oscurità, f.; tenebre, f. pl.; ignoranza, f.

darken, *dărk'n*, v. a. & n. oscurare; render tetro; oscurarsi. [f.

dark-lantern, *-lăn'tărn*, s. lanterna cieca,

darkly, *-lĭ*, ad. oscuramente; ciecamente.

darkness, *-nĕs*, s. oscurità, f., tenebre, f. pl.

darksome, *-săm*, a. oscuro, fosco, nero.

darling, *dăr'lĭng*, a. favorito, diletto, caro; —, s. favorito, m. [pezzare.

darn, *dărn*, v. a. cucire, rimendare, rap-

darnel, *dăr'nĕl*, s. loglio, m., zizzania, f.

darner, *dăr'năr*, s. racconciatore, rimendatore, rapezzatore, m.

dart, *dărt*, s. dardo, m.; —, v. a. dardegiare; lanciare; —, v. n. andar velocemente.

dash, *dăsh*, s. collisione, f.; tratto, m.; colpo, m.; - of the pen, pennata, f.; —, v. a. colpire; urtare; spruzzare; percuotere; fracassare; cancellare; confondere; —, v. n. lanciarsi; sgorgare; —, i. ad un tratto.

dash-board, *-bŏrd*, s. manteletta, f.

dashing, *-ĭng*, a. brillante, attillato; [focoso, impetuoso.

dastard, *dăs'tărd*, s. codardo, poltrone, m.

dastardly, *-lĭ*, a. codardamente.

date, *dăt*, s. data, f.; conclusione, f.; dattero, m.; out of -, fuor d' uso, vecchio; —, v. a. mettere la data, datare.

date-tree, *-trē*, s. palma, f.

dative, *dă'tĭv*, a. & s. (gr.) dativo (m.).

daub, *dăb*, s. pitturaccia, f.; —, v. a. imbrattare; scombiccherare; piaggiare; —, v. n. far l' ipocrita.

dauber, *dăb'ăr*, s. pittoraccio, m.

daughter, *dă'tăr*, s. figliuola, f.; --in-law, figliastra, f.

daunt, *dănt*, v. a. intimidire; spaventare.

dauntless, *-lĕs*, a. intrepido, coraggioso.

davenport, *dăv'ĕnpŏrt*, s. leggio, scrittoio, f.

daw, *dă*, s. cornacchia, f. [m.

dawdle, *dă'dl*, v. n. indugiare.

dawdler, *-dlăr*, s. indugiatore, m.

dawn, *dăn*, s. alba, f., lo spuntare del giorno, m.; —, v. n. spuntare; cominciare a nascere, apparire.

day, *dă*, s. giorno, m.; dl, m.; lume, m.; giornata, f.; -s, pl. tempo, m.; secolo, m.; -s of grace, giorni di grazia, m. pl.; - by -, ogni giorno; by -, di giorno, per giorno. [pensione.

day-boarder, *-bŏrdăr*, s. scolare in mezza

day-book, *-bŭk*, s. giornale, diario, m.

daybreak, *-brăk*, s. lo spuntare del giorno, m. [giornata, m.

day-labourer, *-lăbŭrăr*, s. operaio alla

day-light, *-lĭt*, s. giorno chiaro, m.; luce del giorno, f. [s. scolare esterno. m.

day-pupil, *-pŭpĭl*, day-scholar, *-skŏlăr*, day-spring, *-sprĭng*, s. alba, f., lo spuntare del giorno, m.

day-star, *-stăr*, s. stella mattutina, f.

day-time, *-tĭm*, s. giorno, m.; chiarezza del sole, f. [m.

day-waiter, *-wătăr*, s. servitore di piazza,

dazed, *dăz'd*, a. abbagliato.

dazzle, *dăz'l*, v. a. abbagliare.

deacon, *dē'kn*, s. diacono, m.

dead, *dĕd*, a. morto; stupefatto; vano; malinconico; insensibile; inabitato; bianco; pesante; (of sounds) sordo; (of liquors) sventato; (of letters) che non può esser recapitata; - wood, s. legno secco, m.; —, ad. grandemente, affatto; —, s. silenzio profondo, m.; (of night, winter) mezzo, m.; the -, s. pl i morti, m. pl.

dead-born, *-bŏrn*, a. nato morto.

dead-drunk, *-drăngk*, a. ebbrissimo.

deaden, *dĕd'n*, v. a. rallentare; addormentare, affievolire. [beri, f.

dead-heat, *-hĕt*, s. corsa sforzata de' bar-

dead-house, *-hŏŭs*, s. stanza mortuaria, f.

deadly, *-lĭ*, a. mortale, periglioso, fatale; violento; implacabile; —, ad. mortalmente; estremamente.

dead-march, *-mărch*, s. marcia funebre, f.

deadness, *-nĕs*, s. addormentamento, m.; scipidezza, f. [f.

dead-nettle, *-nĕttl*, s. (bot.)-ortica morta,

deaf, *dĕf*, a. sordo; insensibile.

deafen, *dĕf'n*, v. a. assordare; produrre sordità.

deafness, *-nĕs*, s. sordità, sordaggine, f.

deal, *dēl*, s. quantità, abbondanza, f.; abete, m.; a great -, a good -, molto, assai; —, v. a. ir. distribuire; dare; —, v. n. negoziare, trafficare; to - at cards, fare le carte; to - with, avere a fare con,

dealer, –*ŭr*, s. mercante, trafficatore, m.; colui che distribuisce le carte.

dealing, –*lĭng*, s. traffico, negozio, commercio, m.; affari, m. pl.

dean, *dēn*, s. decano, m.   [decano, m.

deanery, –*ŭrĭ*, s. decanato, m.; grado del

dear, *dēr*, a. diletto, caro, amato; prezioso; **–ly,** ad. caramente; teneramente.

dearness, –*nĕs*, s. amore, m.; scarsità, carestia, f.

dearth, *dŭrth*, s. scarsezza, carestia, f.

death, *dĕth*, s. morte, f.; trapasso, m.

death-bed, –*bĕd*, s. agonia, f.

death-bell, –*bĕl*, s. rintocco funebre, m.

death-blow, –*blō*, s. colpo mortale, m.

death-dealing, –*dēlĭng*, a. mortale; letale.

deathlike, –*līk*, a. inanimato; letargico.

death-penalty, –*pĕnăltĭ*, s. pena di morte.

death-throe, –*thrō*, s. agonia, f.   [f.

death-warrant, –*wŏrrănt*, s. sentenza di morte, f.

death-watch, –*wŏch*, s. grillo, m.

debar, *dēbär'*, v. a. escludere; proibire; prevenire; derubare.

debarkation, –*bärkā'shŭn*, s. sbarco, m.

debase, –*bās'*, v. a. avvilire; disprezzare; falsificare, adulterare.

debasement, –*mĕnt*, s. abbassamento, avvilimento, m.; dispregio, m.   [putabile.

debatable, –*bā'tăbl*, a. contestabile, dis-

debate, –*bāt'*, s. contesa, f.; disputa, discussione, f.; –, v. a. discutere; esaminare; –, v. n. deliberare, meditare; contendere, disputare, litigare.

debater, –*ŭr*, s. disputatore, m.

debauch, –*bŏch'*, s. gozzoviglia, dissolutezza, f.; –, v. a. corrompere; sedurre; frastornare.   [tezza, f.

debauchery, –*ŭrĭ*, s. dissolutezza, sirena-

debenture, –*bĕn'tŭr*, s. restante d' un debito, obbligo, m.   [volire.

debilitate, –*bĭl'ĭtāt*, v. a. debilitare, affie-

debility, –*bĭl'ĭtĭ*, s. debilità, debolezza, f.

debit, *dĕb'ĭt*, s. debito, m.; –, v. a. vendere.

debouch, *dĕbōōch'*, v. a. uscire; sboccare.

debt, *dĕt*, s. debito, obbligo, m.; **to run into –s,** contrarre debiti, indebitirsi.

debtor, *dĕt'tŭr*, s. debitore, m.

decade, *dĕk'ăd*, s. decade, deca, f.

decadency, –*kā'dĕnsĭ*, s. decadenza, f.

Decalogue, *dĕk'ălŏg*, s. Decalogo, m.

decamp, *dēkămp'*, v. n. (mil.) levare il campo; fuggire.   [m.

decampment, –*mĕnt*, s. decampamento,

decant, –*kănt'*, v. a. decantare, travasare.

decanter, –*kăn'tŭr*, s. guastada, caraffa, f.

decapitation, –*kăpĭtā'shŭn*, s. decapitazione, decollazione, f.

decay, –*kā'*, s. decadenza, f., decadimento, declino, m., rovina, f.; –, v. n. consumarsi; decadere; declinare; diminuire.

decease, –*sēs'*, s. morte, f., trapasso, m.

deceit, –*sēt'*, s. inganno, m.; fraude, f.; furberia, baratteria, f.

deceitful, –*fŭl*, a. ingannevole, fraudolento, fallace; **–ly,** ad. ingannevolmente, fraudolentemente.

deceive, –*sēv'*, v. a. ingannare.

December, –*sĕm'bŭr*, s. dicembre, m.

decency, *dē'sĕnsĭ*, s. decenza, f.; modestia, f.   [dieci anni.

decennial, *dēsĕn'nĭăl*, a. decennale, di

decent, *dē'sĕnt*, a. decente, decoroso, dicevole; convenevole; **–ly,** ad. con decenza.

deception, *dēsĕp'shŭn*, s. fraude, f.; inganno, m.   [fallace.

deceptive, –*tĭv*, a. ingannevole; falso,

decide, –*sīd'*, v. a. decidere; determinare, risolvere, stabilire.

decidedly, –*ĕdlĭ*, ad. decisivamente.

deciduous, –*sĭd'ŭs*, a. deciduo, caduco.

decimal, *dĕs'ĭmăl*, a. decimale.

decimate, *dĕs'ĭmāt*, v. a. decimare, levare la decima.

decimation, –*mā'shŭn*, s. decimazione, f.

decipher, *dēsī'fŭr*, v. a. decifrare.

decision, –*sĭzh'ŭn*, s. decisione, f.; determinazione, f.

decisive, –*sī'sĭv*, a. decisivo, ultimo; **–ly,** ad. decisivamente, ultimamente.

deck, *dĕk*, s. bordo, m.; ponte (di nave), m.

deck-hand, –*hănd*, s. (mar.) marinaio di tolda, m.   [gare.

declaim, *dēklām'*, v. n. declamare; arrin-

declamation, –*klămā'shŭn*, s. declamazione, f.

declamatory, –*klăm'ătŏrĭ*, a. declamatorio.

declaration, –*klără'shŭn*, s. dichiarazione, f.; spiegazione, f.

declare, –*klār'*, v. a. dichiarare; manifestare; –, v. n. dichiararsi; manifestarsi.

declension, –*klĕn'shŭn*, s. (gr.) declinazione, f.

declination, –*klĭnā'shŭn*, s. declinazione, f., declinamento, m.; scemamento, m.

decline, –*klīn'*, s. declinazione, f.; decadenza, rovina, f.; marasmo, m.; –, v. a. declinare; evitare, scansare; eludere; –, v. n. decadere, calare; abbassarsi.

declivity, –*klĭv'ĭtĭ*, a. declività, f.; pendio, m.; (rail.) discesa, f.   [inante.

declivous, –*klĭ'vŭs*, a. a pendio; decli-

decoction, –*kŏk'shŭn*, s. decozione, f.; cotto, m.   [analizzare.

decompose, –*kŏmpōz'*, v. a. scomporre;

decomposition, –*pŏzĭsh'ŭn*, s. discioglimento, m.; analisi, f.

decorate, *dĕk'ŏrāt*, v. a. decorare, ornare.

decoration, –*rā'shŭn*, s. decorazione, f., ornamento, m.; abbellimento, m.

decorative, *dĕk'ŏrătĭv*, a. decorativo.

decorator, *dĕk'ŏrātŭr*, s. adornatore, m.

decorous, –*kŏ'rŭs*, a. decente; decoroso; **–ly,** ad. decorosamente; convenevolmente.

decorum, –*kŏ'rŭm*, s. decoro, m.; decenza, f.

decoy, –*kŏ'*, s. allettamento, m.; zimbello, m.; seduzione, f.; –, v. a. allettare, zimbellare; sedurre.

decoy-bird, –*bŭrd*, s. zimbello, m.

decrease, –*krēs'*, s. decrescimento, m.; scemamento, m.; diminuzione, f.; –, v. a. diminuire; –, v. n. sminuire, declinare.

decree, –*krē'*, s. decreto, m.; statuto, m.; –, v. a. decretare; statuire, ordinare.

decrepit, –*krĕp'ĭt*, a. decrepito.

decrial, –*krī'ăl*, s. censura strepitosa, f.

decrier, *–krī'ǎr,* s. detrattore, m.
decry, *–krī',* v. a. screditare; biasimare.
dedicate, *dĕd'ĭkǎt,* v. a. dedicare; consecrare.
dedication, *–kā'shǎn,* s. dedicazione, f.
dedicatory, *dĕd'ĭkǎtŭrĭ,* a. dedicatorio; –
epistle, s. dedica, f.   [conchiudere.
deduce, *–dūs',* v. a. dedurre; inferire;
deduct, *–dŭkt',* v. a. dedurre; sottrarre.
deduction, *–dŭk'shǎn,* s. sottraimento, m.,
deduzione, conseguenza, f.
deductively, *–tĭvlĭ,* ad. conseguentemente.
deed, *dēd,* s. fatto, atto, m.; azione, f.; contratto, m.; **in the very –,** su 'l fatto.
deem, *dēm,* v. n. ir. giudicare; pensare.
deep, *dēp,* a. profondo; alto, sommo;
grave; sagace; segreto, nascosto; astuto;
fino; **(of colours)** carico; –, s. abisso,
m.; mare, m.; silenzio oscuro, m.
deepen, *dēp'n,* v. a. affondare, cavare;
oscurare.
deeply, *–lĭ,* ad. profondamente; seriamente, gravemente; tristamente.
deep-laid, *–lād,* a. occulto, celato
deepness, *–nĕs,* s. profondità, f.; profondo, m.; fondo, m.
deer, *dēr,* s. cervo, m.; daino, m.
deer-stalking, *–stāking,* s. caccia di salvaggina, f.
deface, *dĕfās',* v. a. sfigurare; guastare,
rovinare; cancellare.
defacement, *–mĕnt,* s. disfigurazione, f.
defalcate, *–fǎl'kāt,* v. a. difalcare; sottrarre.   [calunnia, f.
defamation, *–fǎmā'shǎn,* s. diffamazione,
defamatory, *–fǎm'ǎtŭrĭ,* a. diffamatorio;
calunnioso.   [niare.
defame, *–fām',* v. a. diffamare; calunniare.
default, *–fǎlt',* s. diffalta, f.; mancanza,
f.; colpa, f., vizio, m.; –, v. a. scemare.
defaulter, *–ǎr,* s. reo di peculato, m.; concussionario, m.
defeat, *–fēt',* s. sconfitta, f.; rotta, f.; –,
v. a. sconfiggere; frustrare, deludere.
defect, *–fĕkt',* s. difetto, m.; vizio, m.
defection, *–fĕk'shǎn,* s. defezione, f.; apostasia, f.
defective, *–fĕk'tĭv,* a. difettivo, imperfetto.
defence, *–fĕns',* s. difesa, f.; protezione, f.
defenceless, *–lĕs,* a. senza difesa, senza
guardia; impotente.   [proibire.
defend, *–fĕnd',* v. a. difendere; proteggere;
defendant, *–fĕn'dǎnt,* s. difensore, m.;
reo convenuto, m.   [difendibile.
defensible, *–sĭbl,* a. che può essere difeso,
defensive, *–sĭv* a. difensivo; **–ly,** ad.
sulla difesa; –, s. difesa, f.
defer, *–fǎr',* v. a. differire; prolungare;
–, v. n. indugiare.
deference, *dĕf'ǎrĕns,* s. rispetto, riguardo,
m.; considerazione, f.   [deferente.
deferential, *–rĕn'shǎl,* a. di deferenza;
defiance, *–fī'ǎns,* s. disfida, f.; chiamata, f.
defiant, *–fī'ǎnt,* a. diffidente.
deficiency, *–fĭsh'ĕnsĭ,* s. diffalta, f.; mancamento, difetto, m.   [imperfetto,
deficient, *–ĕnt,* a. deficiente; difettivo,
deficit, *dĕf'ĭsĭt,* s. deficit, m.; mancanza, f.

defile, *–fīl',* s. passaggio stretto, m.; –,
v. a. macchiare; contaminare; –, v. n.
marciare alla sfilata.   [definibile.
definable, *–fī'nǎbl,* a. che si può definire,
define, *–fīn',* v. a. definire; limitare; –,
v. n. determinare; decidere.
definite, *dĕf'ĭnĭt,* a. definito, determinato;
esatto, preciso.
definition, *–nĭsh'ǎn,* s. definizione, f.
definitive, *–fĭn'ĭtĭv,* a. definitivo, positivo; **–ly,** ad. definitamente, precisamente.   [via.
deflect, *–flĕkt',* v. n. deviare; uscire della
deflection, *–flĕk'shǎn,* s. deviazione, f.,
deviamento, m.
deflower, *–flŏŭr',* v. a. deflorare.
defoliation, *–fōlĭā'shǎn,* s. sfoliazione, f.
deform, *–fōrm',* v. a. sformare, sfigurare.
deformation, *–fōrmā'shǎn,* s. deformazione, f.
deformity, *–fōr'mĭtĭ,* s. difformità, f.
defraud, *–frǎd',* v. a. defraudare; truffare.
defray, *–frā',* v. a. spesare, dare la spesa.
deft, *dĕft,* a. abile, destro.
deftly, *–lĭ,* ad. abilmente, destramente.
defunct, *dĕfŭngkt',* a. defunto, morto.
defy, *–fī',* v. a. sfidare; sdegnare, bravare.
degeneracy, *–jĕn'ǎrǎsĭ,* s. degenerazione,
depravazione, f.; bassezza, f.
degenerate, *–jĕn'ǎrǎt,* v. n. degenerare;
–, a. degenerato.   [f.
degeneration, *–rǎ'shǎn,* s. depravazione,
degradation, *–grǎd'shǎn,* s. degradazione, f.; avvilimento, m.
degrade, *–grǎd',* v. a. degradare; avvilire.
degree, *–grē',* s. grado, m.; ordine, m.;
condizione, f.; **by –s,** a grado a grado,
successivamente.   [apoteosi, f.
deification, *dēĭfĭkā'shǎn,* s. deificazione,
deify, *dē'ĭfī,* v. a. deificare, divinizzare.
deign, *dān,* v. n. degnarsi.
deism, *dē'ĭzm,* s. deismo, m.
deist, *dē'ĭst,* s. deista, m.
Deity, *dē'ĭtĭ,* s. Deità, Divinità, f.
deject, *dĕjĕkt',* v. a. abbattere, sgomentare;
affliggere.
dejection, *–jĕk'shǎn,* s. afflizione, tristezza, f.; (med.) defecazione, f.
delay, *–lā',* v. a. ritardare, differire; –. s.
ritardo, indugio, m.
delectable, *–lĕk'tǎbl,* ad. dilettevole.
delegate, *dĕl'ĕgǎt,* v. a. delegare, deputare; –, s. delegato, m.   [commissione, f.
delegation, *–gǎ'shǎn,* s. delegazione, f.;
delf(t), *dĕlf(t),* s. miniera, f.; maiolica, f.
deliberate, *dĕlĭb'ǎrǎt,* v. a. deliberare,
ponderare, considerare; –, a. cauto, accorto; **–ly,** ad. deliberatamente, cautamente.   [prudenza, f.
deliberateness, *–nĕs,* s. circospezione,
deliberation, *–rǎ'shǎn,* s. deliberazione, f.
deliberative, *–ĭb'ǎrǎtĭv,* a. deliberativo.
delicacy, *dĕl'ĭkǎsĭ,* s. delicatezza, f.; squisitezza, f.; mollezza, f.
delicate, *dĕl'ĭkǎt,* a. delicato; squisito;
effeminato, molle; **–ly,** ad. delicatamente;
debolmente.

delicious, –lĭsh'ŭs, a. delizioso, squisito; **-ly**, ad. deliziosamente.

deliciousness, –nĕs, s. squisitezza, f.; diletto, piacere, m.

delight, –līt', s. diletto, piacere, m.; delizia, f.; divertimento, m.; –, v. a. & n. dilettare; dilettarsi.

delightful, –fŭl, a. dilettevole, delizioso; **-ly**, ad. dilettevolmente, deliziosamente.

delineate, –lĭn'ĕāt, v. a. delineare; disegnare.   [m.; schizzo, m.

delineation, –nĕā'shŭn, s. delineamento,

delinquency, –lĭng'kwĕnsĭ, s. delitto, m.

delinquent, –kwĕnt, s. delinquente, malfattore, reo, m.

delirious, –lĭr'ĭŭs, a. delirante.

delirium, –lĭr'ĭŭm, s. delirio, m.

deliver, –lĭv'ŭr, v. a. dare, commettere; presentare; liberare; restituire; assistere nel parto.

deliverance, –ŭrăns, s. liberazione, f.

delivery, –ŭrĭ, s. liberazione, m.; parto, m.

delude, –lūd', v. a. deludere; ingannare.

deluge, dĕl'ūj, s. diluvio, m., inondazione, f.; –, v. a. inondare.   [ganno, m.

delusion, –lū'zhŭn, s. delusione, f., in-

delusive, –sĭv, a. ingannevole, fallace.

delve, dĕlv, v. a. zappare, scavare.

demagogic(al), dĕmăgŏj'ĭk(ăl), a. demagogico.   [popolare, demagogo, m.

demagogue, dĕm'ăgŏg, s. capo di fazione

demand, –dĕmănd', s. domanda, f.; richiesta, f.; quistione, f.; vendita, f.; –, v. a. domandare; esigere; quistionare; fare istanze.

demarcate, dĕm'ărkāt, v. a. demarcare.

demarcation, –mărkā'shŭn, s. demarcazione, f.   [portarsi.

demean, –mēn' (to – oneself), v. r. com-

demeanour, –ŭr, s. portamento, contegno, m.; condotta, f.   [m.

demented, –mĕn'tĕd, a. demente.

demerit, –mĕr'ĭt, s. demerito, m.   [m.

demesne, –mēn', s. dominio, patrimonio,

demise, –mīz', s. trapasso, m., morte, f.; –, v. a. lasciare in testamento, legare.

demisemiquaver, dĕm'ĭsĕmĭkwāvŭr, s. (mus.) biscroma, f.

demission, –mĭsh'ŭn, s. congedo, m.

democracy, dĕm'ŏkrăt, s. governo popolare, m., democrazia, f.

democrat, dĕm'ŏkrăt, m. democratico, m.

democratic(al), –krăt'ĭk(ăl), a. democratico.   [battere, distruggere.

demolish, –mŏl'ĭsh, v. a. demolire; ab-

demolition, –lĭsh'ŭn, s. demolizione, distruzione, rovina, f.

demon, dē'mŏn, s. dimonio, m.

demoniac, dēmō'nĭăk, a. & s. demoniaco, m.; diabolico.   [bile; ostensibile.

demonstrable, –mŏn'străbl, a. dimostra-

demonstrably, –blĭ, ad. demostrativamente; evidentemente.   [provare.

demonstrate, –strāt, v. a. dimostrare;

demonstration, –strā'shŭn, s. dimostrazione, f.; prova, f.

demonstrative, –mŏn'strătĭv, a. dimostrativo; **-ly**, ad. dimostrativamente.

demoralization, –mŏrălīzā'shŭn, s. demoralizzazione, corruzione della morale, f.

demoralize, –mŏr'ălīz, v. a. demoralizzare.

demur, –mŭr', v. a. sospettare; dubitare; –, v. n. differire; esitare; –, s. dubitazione, f.   [-ly, ad. modestamente.

demure, –mŭr', a. ritroso; grave; decente;

demureness, –nĕs, s. contegno, m.; discrezione, f.; gravità, serietà, f.

demurrer, –mŭr'rŭr, s. (jur.) dilazione, sospensione, f., indugio, m.

den, dĕn, s. caverna, spelonca, f.

deniable, dĕnī'ăbl, a. negabile.

denial, –nī'ăl, s. diniego, m.; rifiuto, m.

denizen, dĕn'ĭzn, s. forestiere matricolato, m.; –, v. a. francheggiare.

denominate, dĕnŏm'ĭnăt, v. a. denominare.

denomination, –nā'shŭn, s. denominazione, f.   [tivo.

denominative, –nŏm'ĭnătĭv, a. denomina-

denominator, –nŏm'ĭnătŭr, s. (ar.) denominatore, m.

denote, –nōt', v. a. denotare; indicare.

denounce, –nŏŭns', v. a. denunziare, notificare; dichiarare.

dense, dĕns, a. denso, condensato.

density, dĕn'sĭtĭ, s. densità, f.; spessezza, f.

dent, dĕnt, s. dente, m., tacca, f.; –, v. a. dentare.   [dentale, f.

dental, dĕn'tăl, a. & s. dentale, f.; lettera

dentifrice, –tĭfrĭs, s. dentifricio, m.; polvere da nettare i denti, f.

dentist, –tĭst, s. dentista, cavadenti, m.

dentistry, –rĭ, s. arte del dentista, f.

dentition, –tĭsh'ŭn, s. dentizione, f.

denudation, –nūdā'shŭn, s. spogliamento, f.   [m.

denude, dēnūd', v. a. denudare.

denunciation, –nŭnsĭā'shŭn, s. denunziamento, m.; minaccia, f.

deny, –nī', v. a. negare; rifiutare, ricusare, rinunziare.

deodorize, –ō'dŭrīz, v. a. disinfettare.

depart, dēpărt', v. n. partire; morire; rinunziare.

department, –mĕnt, s. dipartimento, m.

departure, –pār'tŭr, s. partenza, f.; abbandono, m.   [dipendere; confidarsi.

depend, –pĕnd', v. n. dipendere; essere

dependant, –pĕn'dănt, **dependent**, –dĕnt, a. & s. dipendente, m.

dependence (**-cy**), –dĕns(ĭ), s. dipendenza, f.; fidanza, f.   [vere.

depict, –pĭkt', v. a. dipingere; descri-

depilation, –pĭlā'shŭn, s. depilazione, f.

depletion, –plē'shŭn, s. votamento, m., evacuazione, f.   [mentabile.

deplorable, –plŏ'răbl, a. deplorabile, la-

deplorably, –blĭ, ad. in modo lamentevole.

deploration, –rā'shŭn, s. lamentazione, f., compianto, m.   [tare.

deplore, –plŏr', v. a. compiangere, lamen-

deploy, –plŏĭ', v. a. sviluppare.

deponent, –pō'nĕnt, s. testimonio, m.

depopulate, –pŏp'ūlāt, v. a. spopolare; devastare.   [m.; devastamento, m.

depopulation, –lā'shŭn, s. spopolamento,

deportation, _-pŏrtă'shăn_, s. deportazione, f.   [m.; condotta, f.
deportment, _-pŏrt'mĕnt_, s. portamento,
deposal, _-pŏ'zăl_, s. deposizione, f.
depose, _-pŏz'_, v. a. deporre; testificare,
attestare; destituire.
deposit, _-pŏz'ĭt_, s. deposito, m.; pegno, m.;
-, v. a. depositare; impegnare.
depositary, _-ĭtăr'_, s. depositario, m.
deposition, _-pŏzĭsh'ăn_, s. deposizione, f.;
testimonianza, f.   [depositeria, f.
depository, _-pŏz'ĭtăr'_, s. deposito, m.;
depravation, _-prăvă'shăn_, s. depravazione, corruzione, f.   [pere.
deprave, _-prăv'_, v. a. depravare, corrom-
depravity, _-prăv'ĭtĭ_, s. depravazione, f.
deprecate, _dĕp'rĕkăt_, v. a. allontanare da
sè pregando un male; supplicare.
deprecation, _-kă'shăn_, s. supplica, preghiera, f.   [supplichevole.
deprecatory, _dĕp'rĕkătărĭ_, a. deprecativo,
depreciate, _-prē'shĭăt_, v. a. deprezzare,
abbassare il prezzo, avvilire.
depreciation, _-shĭă'shăn_, s. abbassamento di prezzo, m.
depredate, _dĕp'rĕdăt_, v. a. depredare.
depredation, _dĕprĕdă'shăn_, s. depredamento, saccheggio, m.   [sare, avvilire.
depress, _-prĕs'_, v. a. deprimere; abbas-
depressed, _-prĕst'_, a. costernato, abbattuto.   [avvilimento, m.
depression, _-prĕsh'ăn_, s. depressione, f.;
deprivation, _-prĭvă'shăn_, s. privazione,
(jur.) deposizione, f.
deprive, _-prĭv'_, v. a. privare; deporre.
depth, _dĕpth_, s. profondità, f.; abisso, m.;
oscurità, f.; mezzo, m.; in the - of
winter, nel cuor del verno.
deputation, _dĕpŭtă'shăn_, s. deputazione, f.
depute, _-pŭt'_, v. a. deputare, delegare.
deputy, _dĕp'ŭtĭ_, s. deputato, delegato, m.
derange, _dĕrănj'_, v. a. disordinare. [m.
derangement, _-mĕnt_, s. disordinamento,
derelict, _dĕr'ĕlĭkt_, s. merce abbandonata, f.
dereliction, _-lĭk'shăn_, s. abbandonamento, abbandono, m.
deride, _-rīd'_, v. a. deridere; beffare. [m.
derision, _-rĭzh'ăn_, s. derisione, f.; scherno,
derisive, _-rī'sĭv_, a. derisivo, ridicolo.
derivable, _-rī'văbl_, a. che si può derivare.
derivation, _-rĭvă'shăn_, s. derivazione,
f.; etimologia, f.   [dere, trarre origine.
derive, _-rīv'_, v. a. & n. derivare; proce-
derogate, _dĕr'ōgăt_, v. a. derogare; -, v. n.
disdirsi.   [deroga, f.
derogation, _-gă'shăn_, s. derogazione,
derogatory, _-rŏg'ătărĭ_, a. derogatorio.
derrick, _dĕr'rĭk_, s. lieva, f.
dervis, _dăr'vĭs_, s. dervis, m.
descant, _dĕs'kănt_, s. canto, m.; lungo
discorso, m.; -, v. n. arringare; interpretare, commentare.   [origine; calure.
descend, _dĕsĕnd'_, v. n. discendere; trarre
descendent, _-sĕn'dĕnt_, a. & s. nato, m.;
discendente, m.   [nascita, f.; posterità, f.
descent, _-sĕnt'_, discesa, f.; invasione, f.;

describe, _-skrīb'_, v. a. descrivere.
description, _-skrĭp'shăn_, s. descrizione, f.
descriptive, _-tĭv_, a. descrittivo.
descry, _dĕskrī'_, v. a. scoprire; discernere.
desecrate, _dĕs'ĕkrăt_, v. a. dissacrare.
desecration, _-kră'shăn_, s. profanazione, f.
desert, _dĕz'ărt_, a. deserto, solitario; -, s.
deserto, m.; solitudine, f.
desert, _dĕzărt'_, s. merito, m.; pospasto, m.;
-, v. a. disertare; abbandonare; lasciare.
deserter, _-ăr_, s. (mil.) disertore, m.
desertion, _-zăr'shăn_, s. (mil.) diserzione,
f.; (fig.) abbandono, m.   [degno.
deserve, _-zărv'_, v. a. meritare; essere
deservedly, _-zăr'vĕdlĭ_, ad. meritamente,
degnamente.   [degno.
deserving, _-vĭng_, a. meritevole, meritorio,
desideratum, _-sĭdără'tŭm_, s. cosa desiderabile, f.; cosa che manca, f.
design, _-zīn'_, s. disegno, m.; progetto, m.;
intenzione, f, pensiero, m.; intrapresa, f.;
-, v. a. disegnare; premeditare; tramare.
designate, _dĕs'ĭgnăt_, v. a. disegnare, indicare, designare; distinguere.
designation, _-nă'shăn_, s. designazione,
destinazione, f.; indicazione, f.
designedly, _-zīnĕd'lĭ_, ad. con disegno,
intenzionalmente, a posta.
designing, _-zīn'ĭng_, a. insidioso, ingannevole.   [siderabile, m.
desirability, _-zīrăbĭl'ĭtĭ_, s. l' esser de-
desirable, _-zī'răbl_, a. desiderabile.
desire, _-zīr'_, s. desiderio, m., brama, f.;
cupidità, f.; domanda, f.; -, v. a. desiderare, bramare.   [-ly, ad. cupidamente.
desirous, _-zī'răs_, a. desideroso, avido;
desist, _-zīst'_, v. n. desistere; tralasciare.
desk, _dĕsk_, s. leggio, scrittoio, m.
desolate, _dĕs'ōlăt_, v. a. desolare; spopolare; -, a. desolato; solitario; tristo.
desolation, _-lă'shăn_, s. distruzione, f.;
rovina, f.   [disperare.
despair, _dĕspăr'_, s. disperazione, f.; -, v. n.
despairingly, _-ĭnglĭ_, ad. disperatamente.
despatch, _-spăch'_, s. dispaccio, m.; espresso m.; -, v. a. dispacciare.
despatch-boat, _-bŏt_, s. corriera, f.
despatch-box, _-bŏks_, s. scrittoio portatile, m.   [biato, m.
desperado, _dĕspĕrā'dō_, s. disperato, arrab-
desperate, _dĕs'părăt_, a. disperato, furioso;
-ly, ad. disperatamente; terribilmente;
alla cieca.
desperation, _-ră'shăn_, s. disperazione, f.
despicable, _dĕs'pĭkăbl_, a. disprezzabile,
spreggevole; basso.
despise, _dĕspīz'_, v. a. dispregiare, sdegnare.
despite, _-spīt'_, s. dispetto, sdegno, m.;
malizia, f.; in - of, malgrado, a marcio
dispetto.
despoil, _-spŏĭl'_, v. a. spogliare, privare.
despond, _-spŏnd'_, v. n. disperare; sbigottirsi, perdersi d' animo. [zione, f.
despondency, _-spŏn'dĕnsĭ_, s. dispera-
despot, _dĕs'pŏt_, s. despota, m.
despotic(al), _-pŏt'ĭk(ăl)_, a. dispotico;
-ly, ad. dispoticamente.

despotism, dĕs'pŏtĭzm, s. dispotismo, m.

dessert, dĕzzûrt', s. frutta, f. pl. [f.

destination, dĕstīnā'shŭn, s. destinazione,

destine, dĕs'tĭn, v. a. destinare, assegnare; stabilire. [sorte, f.

destiny, dĕs'tĭnī, s. destino, fato, m.;

destitute, dĕs'tĭtūt, a. destituto, abbandonato, derelitto; privo.

destitution, –tū'shŭn, s. mancamento, m.; abbandono, m. [nare.

destroy, dĕstrŏī', y. a. distruggere, rovi-

destruction, –strŭk'shŭn, s. distruzione, rovina, f.

destructive, –tĭv, a. distruttivo, pernicioso; –ly, ad, distruttivamente.

desultorily, dĕs'ŭltŏrĭlī, ad. leggermente.

desultoriness, dĕs'ŭltŏrĭnĕs, s. leggerezza, incostanza, f.

desultory, dĕs'ŭltŏrī, a. leggero, incostante; senza metodo.

detach, dĕtăch', v. a. (mil.) distaccare.

detachment, –mĕnt, s. (mil.) distaccamento, m.; divisione, f.

detail, –tāl', s. dettaglio, m.; particolarità, f.; (am.) reclutamento, m.; in –, a minuto; –, v. a. raccontare; circostanziare.

detain, –tān', v. a. ritenere; impedire; fermare.

detect, dĕtĕkt', v. a. scoprire; svelare.

detection, –tĕk'shŭn, s. scoperta, f.

detective, –tĭv, s. uffiziale della polizia segreta, m.

detention, –tĕn'shŭn, s. detenzione, ritenzione, f.; carcerazione, f.

deter, –tŭr', v. a. atterrire; dissuadere;

deterge, –tŭrj', v. a. detergere; purgare.

deteriorate, –tē'rĭŏrāt, v. a. deteriorare.

deterioration, –rā'shŭn, s. deterioramento, m. [determinare.

determinable, –tŭr'mĭnăbl, a. che si può

determinate, –mĭnāt, a. determinato, preciso; –ly, ad. determinatamente, precisamente. [zione, f.; decisione, f.

determination, –nā'shŭn, s. determinazione, f.

determinative, –tŭr'mĭnătĭv, a. determinativo, decisivo,

determine, –mĭn, v. a. determinare; decidere; –, v. n. conchiudere, finire.

detest, –tĕst', v. a. detestare; abborrire.

detestable, –tĕs'tăbl, a. detestabile, abominevole.

detestably, –tăblī, ad. detestabilmente.

detestation, –tā'shŭn, s. detestazione, abominazione, f. [detronizzare.

dethrone, –thrōn', v. a. privare del trono,

dethronement, –mĕnt, s. privazione del trono, detronizzazione, f.

detonate, dĕt'ŏnāt, v. a. (chem.) esplodere.

detonation, –nā'shŭn, s. detonazione, f.

detract, –trăkt', v. a. detrarre; sminuire; derogare.

detraction, –trăk'shŭn, s. detrazione, f.

detriment, dĕt'rĭmĕnt, s. danno, detrimento, m. [nocivo.

detrimental, –mĕn'tăl, a. pregiudizievole,

deuce, dūs, s. due, m.; diavolo, m.; –, i. diamine!

devastate, dĕv'ăstāt, v. a. devastare.

devastation, –tā'shŭn, s. devastazione, f.

develop, –vĕl'ŏp, v. a. sviluppare.

development, –ŏpmĕnt, s. sviluppo, m.

deviate, dē'vĭāt, v. a. deviare.

deviation, dēvĭā'shŭn, s. deviazione, f.; smarrimento, m. [spediente, m.

device, dēvīs', s. invenzione, f.; motto, m.;

devil, dĕv'l, s. diavolo, m.

devilish, –lĭsh, a. diabolico; –ly, ad. diabolicamente. [lestia, f.

devilment, –lmĕnt, s. importunità, mo-

devilry, –lrī, s. diavoleria, f.

devious, dē'vĭŭs, a. remoto, sviato.

devise, dēvīz', s. legato, lascito, m.; –, v. a. & n. immaginare, deliberare, inventare; far un lascito o un legato.

deviser, –vī'zŭr, s. inventore, m.

devisor, –vī'sŭr, s. testatore, m.

devoid, –vŏĭd', a. spogliato (delle cose necessarie). [f., acquisto, m.

devolution, –vŏlō'shŭn, s. devoluzione, f.

devolve, –vŏlv', v. a. & n. svolgere; tramandare; scadere, toccare in sorte.

devote, –vōt', v. a. dedicare, esecrare.

devotedness, –vō'tĕdnĕs, s. divozione, f.

devotee, dĕv'ŏtē, s. bacchettone, devoto, m.

devotion, –vō'shŭn, s. divozione, f.; disposizione, f.

devotional, –ăl, a. divoto, pio.

devour, –vŏŭr', v. a. divorare; assorbire; dissipare. [divotamente.

devout, –vŏŭt', a. divoto, pio; –ly, ad.

devoutness, –nĕs, s. divozione, f.

dew, dū, s. rugiada, f.

dew-lap, –lăp, s. giogaia, f.

dew-worm, –wŭrm, s. lombrico, m.

dewy, dū'ī, a. rugiadoso.

dexterity, dĕkstĕr'ĭtī, s. destrezza, f.

dexterous, dĕks'tŭrŭs, a. destro, abile; –ly, ad. destramente.

diabetes, dīăbē'tēz, s. diabete, m.

diabolic(al), –bŏl'ĭk(ăl), a. diabolico; –ly, ad. diabolicamente.

diadem, dī'ădĕm, s. diadema, m.

diagnosis, –ŏgnō'sĭs, s. diagnosi, f.

diagnostic, –ŏgnŏs'tĭk, a. & m. diagnostico (m.); –s, pl. diagnostica, f.

diagonal, –ăg'ŏnăl, a. diagonale; –ly, ad. diagonalmente.

diagram, dī'ăgrăm, s. diagramma, m.

dial, dī'ăl, s. mostra d' orologio, f.; orologio a sole, m.

dialect, dī'ălĕkt, s. dialetto, m.

dialogue, dī'ălŏg, s. dialogo, m.

diameter, dīăm'ĕtŭr, s. diametro, m.

diametrical, –mĕt'rĭkăl, a. diametrale; –ly, ad. diametralmente.

diamond, dī'ămŏnd, s. diamante, m.; (at cards) quadri, m.pl.; –cut into angles, brillante, m.

diamond-cutter, –kŭttŭr, s. gioielliere, m.

diaper, dī'ăpŭr, s. biancheria damascata, f.; –, v. a. damascare.

diapason, dīăpā'zŏn, s. diapason, m.

diaphragm, dī'ăfrăm, s. diaframma, tramezzo, m.

diarrhœa, dīărrē'ă, s. diarrea, f.

diary, dī'ărĭ, s. diario, m.
dibble, dĭb'l, v. a. piantare col foraterra.
dice, dīs, s. pl. (of die) dadi, m. pl.
dice-box, –bŏks, s. bossolo, m.
dickens, dĭk'nz, i. diamine!
dictate, dĭk'tāt, s. precetto, m., regola, f.;
–, v. a. dettare. [tura, f.
dictation, –tā'shŭn, s. dettato, m., detta-
dictatorial, –tātō'rĭăl, a. dittatorio; magistrale.
dictatorship, –tā'tŭrshĭp, s. dittatura, f.
diction, dĭk'shŭn, s. dizione, f., stile, m.
dictionary, –ărĭ, s. dizionario, m.
didactic(al), dĭdăk'tĭk(ăl), a. didattico,
istruttivo.
diddle, dĭd'l, v. n. vacillare.
die, dī, s. dado, m.; conio, m.; tintura, f.;
tinta, f., colore, m.; –, v. n. morire; svaporare; –, v. a. tingere; colorare.
diet, dī'ĕt, s. nutrimento, m.; dieta, f.; assemblea, f.; –, v. a. nutrire; –, v. n. fare
dieta. [f.
dietary, –ărĭ, a. dietetico; –, s. dietetica,
differ, dĭf'fŭr, v. n. differire, esser dissimile, diverso. [f.
difference, –ĕns, s. differenza, f.; disputa,
different, –ĕnt, a. differente; dissimile;
–ly, ad. differentemente.
differentiate, –ĕn'shĭāt, v.a. differenziare.
difficult, dĭf'fĭkŭlt, a. difficile; faticoso;
–ly, ad. difficilmente, con difficoltà.
difficulty, –tĭ, s. difficoltà, f.; dubbio,
m.; ostacolo, m. [sospetto, m.
diffidence, dĭf'fĭdĕns, s. diffidenza, f.,
diffident, –fĭdĕnt, a. diffidente, sospettoso;
–ly, ad. con diffidenza. [luce, f.
diffraction, –frăk'shŭn, s. diffrazione della
diffuse, dĭffūz', v. a. diffondere; spargere;
–, a. diffuso, prolisso; –ly, ad. diffusamente.
diffusion, –fū'zhŭn, s. diffusione, f.;
spargimento, m.; copiosità, f.
diffusive, –sĭv, a. diffusivo, prolisso.
dig, dĭg, v. a. zappare, vangare; scavare.
digest, dĭjĕst', v. a. digerire; ordinare; –,
v. n. suppurare.
digestible, –jĕs'tĭbl, a. digestibile.
digestion, –jĕst'yŭn, s. digestione, f.
digestive, –jĕs'tĭv, s. rimedio digestivo, m.
digger, dĭg'gŭr, s. zappatore, vangatore, m.
digit, dĭj'ĭt, s. dito, m. (misura); numero
(o cifra, f.) semplice, m.
dignify, dĭg'nĭfī, v. a. elevare; esaltare.
dignitary, dĭg'nĭtărĭ, s. prelato, m.
dignity, dĭg'nĭtĭ, s. dignità, f.; grado d'
onore, m.
digress, dĭgrĕs', v. n. fare digressione.
digression, –grĕsh'ŭn, s. digressione, f.,
sviamento, m.
digressive, –grĕs'sĭv, a. digressivo.
dike, dīk, s. fosso, m.; canale, m.; vallo, m.
dilapidate, dĭlăp'ĭdāt, v. a. dilapidare.
dilapidation, –dā'shŭn, s. dilapidamento,
m.; rovina, f.
dilatation, –lătā'shŭn, s. dilatazione, f.
dilate, –lāt', v. a. dilatare; stendere; –,
v. n. dilatarsi, distendersi, diffondersi.

dilatory, dĭl'ătărĭ, a. dilatorio, tardo.
dilemma, –lĕm'mă, s. dilemma, m.; alternativa, f. [f.
diligence, dĭl'ĭjĕns, s. diligenza, prontezza,
diligent, dĭl'ĭjĕnt, a. diligente; assiduo;
–ly, ad. diligentemente. [fastidire.
dilly-dally, dĭl'lĭdăl'lĭ, v. n. stare a bada,
dilucid, dĭlū'sĭd, a. lucido.
diluent, dĭl'ūĕnt, a. diluente, dissolvente.
dilute, –lōt', v. a. stemperare; mescolare.
dilution, –lū'shŭn, s. stemperamento, m.
diluvial, –vĭăl, a. diluviano.
dim, dĭm, a. oscuro, fosco; stupido; –, v.
a. oscurare; offuscare. [estensione, f.
dimension, dĭmĕn'shŭn, s. dimensione,
diminish, –mĭn'ĭsh, v. a. & n. diminuire;
–, v. n. diminuirsi. [discredito, m.
diminution, –mĭsh'ŭn, s. diminuzione, f.;
diminutive, –mĭn'ŭtĭv, a. & s. diminutivo (m.); –ly, ad. in modo diminutivo.
dimissory, –mĭs'sărĭ, a. dimissorio, di-
missoriale.
dimity, dĭm'ĭtĭ, s. dimito, m.
dimly, dĭm'lĭ, ad. oscuramente.
dimness, –nĕs, s. oscuramento, m.; stupidità, f.
dimple, dĭm'pl, s. piccola fossetta, f.
din, dĭn, s. strepito, fracasso, m.; –, v. a.
stordire; chiamazzare.
dine, dīn, v. a. invitare a desinare; –, v. n.
desinare; pranzare.
diner-out, dī'năr ŏŭt, s. che desina in
una trattoria, m.; parassita, m.
dingy, dĭn'jĭ, a. oscuro; bruno.
dining-hall, dī'nĭng hăl, dining-room,
–rōm, s. sala da mangiare, f.
dinner, dĭn'năr, s. desinare, m.; pranzo, m.
dinner-time, –tĭm, s. ora di pranzo, f.
dinner-waggon, –wăggŏn, s. guattero, m.
dint, dĭnt, s. impressione, f., vestigio, m.;
segno, m.; colpo, m.; forza, f.
diocese, dī'ŏsĕs, s. diocesi, f.
dip, dĭp, v. s. smergo, m.; (of the needle)
inclinazione, pennata, f.; –, v. a. ir. intingere, immollare; –, v. n. ir. immer-
gersi; penetrare.
diphtheria, dĭfthē'rĭă, s. difteria, f.
diphthong, dĭp'thŏng, s. dittongo, m.
diploma, dĭplō'mă, s. diploma, m., lettera
patente, f.
diplomacy, –măsĭ, s. diplomatia, f.
diplomatic, –măt'ĭk, a. diplomatico; –s,
s. pl. arte diplomatica, f. [m.
diplomatist, –plō'mătĭst, s. diplomatico,
dipper, dĭp'păr, s. tuffatore, m.
dire, dīr, a. orrendo
direct, dĭrĕkt', a. retto, diretto; chiaro; –,
v. a. dirigere; indirizzare; regolare, ordinare.
direction, –rĕk'shŭn, s. direzione, f.; soprascritta, f.; incombenza, f.; ordine, m.
directly, –rĕkt'lĭ, ad. direttamente; immediatamente.
director, –rĕk'tăr, s. direttore, m.
directory, –tărĭ, s. direttorio, m.
dirge, dŭrj, s. canzone funebre, f.
dirigent, dīr'ĕ jĕnt, a. dirigente.

dirt, *dŭrt*, s. fango, m.; loto, m.; –, v. a. sporcare; infangare.   [mente; vilmente.
dirtily, *dŭr'tĭlĭ*, ad. sporcamente; sordida-
dirtiness, *–tĭnĕs*, s. sporchezza, f.; bassezza, vilezza, f.
dirty, *–tĭ*, a. sporco, sordido; vile, infame.
disability, *dĭsăbĭl'ĭtĭ*, s. incapacità, inabilità, f.; impotenza, f.
disable, *–ā'bl*, v. a. rendere incapace; (mar.) disarmare.   [abilità, f.
disablement, *–mĕnt*, s. incapacità, inabilità, f.
disabuse, *–ābūz'*, v. a. disingannare.
disaccustom, *–ăkkŭstŭm'*, v. a. disusare, disvezzare.
disacknowledge, *–ăknŏl'ĕj*, v. a. negare.
disadvantage, *–ădvăn'tāj*, s. disavvantaggio, danno, m.; –, v. a. disavvantaggiare.
disadvantageous, *–id'jŭs*, a. svantaggioso; **–ly**, ad. con isvantaggio.
disaffect, *–ăffĕkt'*, v. a. disaffezionare; scontentare; odiare.
disaffection, *–fĕk'shŭn*, s. malevolenza, f.
disagree, *–ăgrē'*, v. n. differire; discordare.   [vole.
disagreeable, *–ăbl*, a. contrario, disdice-
disagreeableness, *–nĕs*, s. spiacevolezza, contrarietà, f.
disagreeably, *–ăblĭ*, ad. spiacevolmente.
disagreement, *–mĕnt*, s. differenza, f.; discordanza, f.   [v. n. rifiutare.
disallow, *–ăllŏu'*, v. a. disapprovare; –,
disappear, *–ăppēr'*, v. a. sparire, svanire
disappearance, *–ăns*, s. svanimento, m.
disappoint, *–ăppŏĭnt'*, v. a. mancar di parola; deludere.
disappointment, *–mĕnt*, s. mancamento di parola, m.; traversia, f.
disapprobation, *–ăpprŏbā'shŭn*, disapproval, *–prō'văl*, s. censura, f.; biasimo, m.; riprovazione, f.   [f.
disapproval, *–prō'văl*, s. disapprovazione,
disapprove, *–prōv'*, v. a. disapprovare.
disarm, *–ārm'*, v. a. disarmare.
disarmament, *–ăr'mămĕnt*, s. disarmamento, m.
disarray, *–ărrā'*, s. disordine, m.; confusione, f.; –, v. a. svestire; spogliare.
disaster, *dĭzăs'tăr*, s. disastro, m.; infortunio, m., calamità, f.
disastrous, *–trŭs*, a. disastroso, calamitoso, funesto; **–ly**, ad. sventuratamente, funestamente.
disavow, *dĭsăvŏŭ'*, v. a. negare; disdire.
disavowal, *–ăl*, s. disapprovazione, f.
disband, *–bănd'*, v. a. sbandare; congediare.
disbelief, *–bēlēf'*, s. incredulità, f.
disbelieve, *–bēlēv'*, v. a. discredere; diffidare.   [miscredente, m.
disbeliever, *–lē'văr*, s. incredulo, m.;
disburden, *–bŭr'dn*, v. a. scaricare; sgravare; sbarazzare.
disburse, *–bŭrs'*, v. a. sborsare; spendere.
disbursement, *–mĕnt*, s. sborso, pagamento, m.; **–s**, pl. danaro sborsato, m.
discard, *–kārd'*, v. a. scartare; licenziare.

discern, *dĭszŭrn'*, v. a. discernere; differenziare; distinguere.   [tibile.
discernible, *–ĭbl*, a. discernibile, percettibile.
discerning, *–ĭng*, a. giudizioso; perspicace; **–ly**, ad. giudiziosamente.
discharge, *–chārj'*, s. sparo, m.; licenza, libertà, f.; quietanza, ricevuta, f.; discolpa, f.; assoluzione, f.; –, v. a. scaricare; liberare, licenziare; sprigionare; assolvere; adempire; –, v. n. scaricarsi; dissiparsi; fare il suo debito; tener la promessa; spedire un affare; dimettere (un ufficiale).
disciple, *dĭssī'pl* pl, s. discepolo, scolare, m.
disciplinarian, *–sĭplĭnā'rĭăn*, a. di disciplina; –, s. (mil.) che insegna la disciplina, m.; presbiteriano, m.
discipline, *dĭs'sĭplĭn*, s. disciplina, f.; insegnamento, m.; educazione, f.; sommissione, f.; –, v. a. disciplinare; insegnare.
disclaim, *–klām'*, v. a. rifiutare, negare; rinunziare.
disclaimer, *–ăr*, s. rifiuto, m.
disclose, *–klōz'*, v. a. scoprire, palesare.
disclosure, *–klō'zhŭr*, s. scoperta, f.; rivelamento, m.
discoloration, *–kŭlŭrā'shŭn*, s. discolorazione, f., scoloramento, m.
discolour, *–kŭl'ăr*, v. a. discolorare.
discomfit, *–kŭm'fĭt*, v. a. disfare; sconfiggere; vincere.   [f.
discomfiture, *–ŭr*, s. sconfitta, f.; strage,
discomfort, *–fŭrt*, s. sconforto, m.; afflizione, f.
discommode, *–kŏmmōd'*, v. a. incomodare, importunare, disagiare.
discompose, *–kŏmpōz'*, v. a. scomporre; disordinare, disturbare.
discomposure, *–pō'zhŭr*, s. disordine, m.; perturbamento, m.; travaglio, m.
disconcert, *–kŏnsŭrt'*, v. a. sconcertare; disordinare; confondere.
disconnect, *–kŏnnĕkt'*, v. a. disunire.
disconnexion, *–nĕk'shŭn*, s. disunione, f.
disconsolate, *–kŏn'sŏlăt*, a. inconsolabile; **–ly**, ad. sconsolatamente.
discontent, *–kŏntĕnt'*, a. scontento, dispiaciente; –, s. scontento, m.; dolore, m.; –, v. a. scontentare.
discontinuation, *–kŏntĭnŭā'shŭn*, s. discontinuazione, intermissione, interruzione, f.   [interrompere; cessare.
discontinue, *–tĭn'ū*, v. a. discontinuare,
discord, *dĭs'kŏrd*, discordance, *–kŏr'dăns*, s. discordanza, f.; discordia, dissensione, f.; dissenso, m.
discordant, *–kŏr'dănt*, a. discordante; **–ly**, ad. con discordanza.
discount, *dĭs'kŏŭnt*, s. sconto, m.; sottrazione, f.; –, *–kŏŭnt'*, v. a. scontare; dedurre, sottrarre.
discountenance, *–kŏŭn'tĕnăns*, v. a. turbare, far rimanere confuso, far perdere il contegno, sconcertare; disapprovare.
discourage, *–kŭr'ĭj*, v. a. scoraggiare; dissuadere, scoraggiamento, m.
discouragement, *–mĕnt*, s. sgomento,
discourse, *–kŏrs'*, s. discorso, m.; ragiona-

mento, m.; trattato, m.; —, v. a. discorrere; ragionare; discutere; esaminare.

discoursive, –kŏr' sĭv, a. discorsivo,

discourteous, –kûrt' yŭs, a. scortese, incivile; **-ly,** ad. scortesemente.

discourtesy, –kûr' tĕsĭ, s. scortesia, inciviltà, f. [manifestare; trovare.

discover, –kŭv' ûr, v. a. scoprire; rivelare;

discoverer, –ûr, s. scopritore, m.; esploratore, m. [mento, m.

discovery, –ûrĭ, s. scoperta, f., scopridiscredit, –krĕd' ĭt, s. discredito, m.; disonore, m.; —, v. a. discreditare; disonorare.

discreditable, –ăbl, a. disonorevole.

discreet, –krēt', a. discreto, circospetto; prudente, savio; **-ly,** ad. discretamente; prudentemente, saviamente.

discrepancy, –krĕp' ănsĭ, s. differenza, f.; contrarietà, f. [rente; contrario.

discrepant, –ănt, a. discrepante, differente, –krĕsh' ŭn, s. discrezione, f.

discretionary, –ărĭ, a. illimitato.

discriminate, –krĭm' ĭnāt, v. a. distinguere; separare; **-ly,** ad. distintamente.

discrimination, –nā' shŭn, s. differenza, f.; distinzione, f.

discriminative, –krĭm' ĭnătĭv, a. distintivo; caratteristico.

discursive, –kûr' sĭv, a. vagante; discorsivo; **-ly,** ad. in modo discorsivo.

discuss, –kŭs', v. a. discutere, esaminare.

discussion, –kŭsh' ŭn, s. discussione, f.

disdain, –dān', s. disprezzo, disdegno, m.; —, v. a. disdegnare, disprezzare.

disdainful, –fŭl, a. sdegnoso; **-ly,** ad. sdegnosamente.

disease, –dĭzĕ', s. malattia, f., morbo, m.

diseased, –dĭzĕzd', a. ammalato.

disembark, –dĭsĕmbărk', v. a. & n. sbarcare. [m.

disembarkation, –bărkā' shŭn, s. sbarco,

disembarrass, –bâr' râs, v. a. sbarazzare. [smembrane.

disembody, –ĕmbŏd' ĭ, v. a. scorporare,

disembogue, –ĕmbŏg', v. n. sboccare.

disenchant, –ĕnchănt', v. s. levare l'incanto. [m., disillusione, f.

disenchantment, –mĕnt, s. disinganno,

disencumber, –ĕnkŭm' bûr, v. a. sbarazzare, liberare [bramento, sbarazzare, m.

disencumbrance, –kŭm' brăns, s. sgombramento, m.

disengage, –ĕngāj', v. a. liberare; —, v. n. liberarsi; sbrigarsi.

disengagement, –mĕnt, s. disimpegno, m.; disoccupazione, f.; libertà, f.

disentangle, –ĕntăng' gl, v. a. sviluppare, d'sempegnare; separare.

disentanglement, –mĕnt, s. sviluppo, sviluppamento, m.

disentomb, –ĕntōm', v. a. risuscitare.

disestablish, –ĕstăb' lĭsh, v. a. rinuovere; scavalcare.

disfavour, –fă' vûr, s. disfavore, m., disgrazia, f.; disgusto, m.; —, v. a. disfavorire.

disfiguration, –fĭgûrā' shŭn, **disfigurement,** –fĭg' ûrmĕnt, s. sfiguramento,

m., bruttezza, f.; disfigurazione, f.; deformità, f. [formare.

disfigure, –fĭg' ûr, v. a. sfigurare, difformare.

disfranchise, –frăn' chĭz, v. a. privare della franchigia.

disgorge, –gŏrj', v. a. vomitare; recere.

disgrace, –grās', s. disonore, m.; disgrazia, f., disfavore, m.; ignominia, f.; —, v. a. disonorare.

disgraceful, –fŭl, a. disonorevole, ignominioso; **-ly,** ad. ignominiosamente, disonorevolmente.

disguise, –gīz', s. travestimento, m.; —, v. a. travestire; fingere; simulare.

disgust, –gŭst', s. disgusto, m.; fastidio, m.; —, v. a. disgustare.

dish, dĭsh, s. piatto, m.; vivanda, f.; tazza, f.; —, v. a. mettere nel piatto; minestrare.

dish-clout, –klŏŭt, s. strofinacciolo, m.

dish-cover, –kŭvûr, s. coperchio da piatto, m. [intimorire.

dishearten, dĭs hârt' n, v. a. scoraggiare;

dishevel, dĭshĕv' ĕl, v. a. scapigliare.

dishonest, dĭs ŏn' ĕst, a. disonesto, ignominioso, infame; **-ly,** ad. disonestamente. [zia, f.

dishonesty, –tĭ, s. disonestà, f.; impudicizia, f.

dishonour, –ŏn' ûr, s. disonore, m.; infamia, f.; —, v. a. disonorare; svergognare.

dishonourable, –ăbl, a. disonorevole.

dishonourably, –ăblĭ, ad. disonorevolmente. [vande, m.

dish-warmer, dĭsh' wârmûr, s. scaldavivande, m.

dish-water, –wătûr, a. lavatura di scodelle, f. [disinganno, m.

disillusion, dĭsĭllō' shŭn, s. disillusione, f.,

disillusionize, –zhănĭz, v. a. disingannare.

disinclination, –ĭnklĭnā' shŭn, s. indifferenza, f.; disgusto, f.; disprezzo, m.

disincline, –ĭnklīn', v. a. produrre disgusto, disgustare.

disinfect, –ĭnfĕkt', v. a. disinfettare.

disingenuous, –ĭnjĕn' ŭŭs, a. simulato, finto, artificioso.

disinherit, –ĭnhĕr' ĭt, v. a. diseredare.

disinter, –ĭntûr', v. a. disseppellire.

disinterested, –ĭn' tărĕstĕd, a. disinteressato; **-ly,** ad. disinteressatamente.

disinterestedness, –nĕs, s. disinteresse, m. [mento, m.

disinterment, –ĭntûr' mĕnt, s. dissotterramento, m.

disjoin, –jŏĭn', v. a. disgiungere.

disjoint, –jŏĭnt', v. a. slogare; smembrare; —, v. n. disgiungersi.

disjunction, –jăngk' shŭn, s. disgiunzione, f.; separamento, m.

disjunctive, –tĭv, a. (gr.) disgiuntivo.

disk, dĭsk, s. disco, m.

dislike, dĭslīk', s. disgusto, m.; avversione, f.; —, v. a. disapprovare, dispiacere, disamare.

dislocate, dĭs' lŏkāt, v. a. slogare.

dislocation, –kă' shŭn, s. slogamento, m.; scommettitura, f.

dislodge, –lŏj', v. a. sloggiare; scacciare; —, v. n. mutar casa.

disloyal, *-lŏï'ăl,* a. sleale, infedele; perfido; **-ly,** ad. slealmente, infidamente.

disloyalty, *-ălti,* s. slealtà, infedeltà, f.; perfidia, f.

dismal, *diz'măl,* a. tristo, misero, funesto; orribile; **-s,** s. pl. affanno, m.; cordoglio, m.   [spogliare.

dismantle, *dĭsmăn'tl,* v. a. smantellare;

dismast, *-măst',* v. a. (mar.) disalberare.

dismay, *-mă',* s. smarrimento d' animo, m.; terrore, m.; **–,** v. a. spaventare, scoraggiare.   [sbranare, dilaniare.

dismember, *-mĕm'bĕr,* v. a. smembrare,

dismiss, *-mĭs',* v. a. congedare, licenziare; ripudiare.

dismissal, *-săl,* **dismission,** *-mĭsh'ăn,* s. licenziamento, congedo, m.

dismount, *-mŏūnt',* v. a. scavalcare, smontare; imboccare; **–,** v. n. smontare; scendere.   [dienza, f.

disobedience, *-ŏbė'dĭēns,* s. disubbi-

disobedient, *-dĭēnt,* a. disubbidiente; **-ly,** ad. disubbidientemente.

disobey, *-ŏbė',* v. a. disubbidire.

disoblige, *-ŏblĭj',* v. a. disobligare, dispiacere, offendere.   [incivilmente.

disobliging, *-ŏblĭj'ĭng,* ad. scortesemente,

disobligingness, *-jĭngnĕs,* s. scortesia, inciviltà, f.

disorder, *-ŏr'dĕr,* s. disordine, m., irregolarità, f.; confusione, f.; indisposizione, f.; **–,** v. a. disordinare; perturbare; sconcertare.

disorderly, *-lĭ,* a. confuso, tumultuoso; **–,** ad. senza ordine, confusamente.

disorganization, *-ŏr'gănĭzā'shăn,* s. disorganizzazione, f.   [zare.

disorganize, *-ŏr'gănz,* v. a. disorganiz-

disown, *-ŏn',* v. a. non confessare, negare; rinunziare.   [vilire.

disparage, *-păr'dj,* v. a. sprezzare; avvilire.

disparagement, *-mĕnt,* s. sprezzamento, scherno, disonore, m.

disparity, *-ĭtĭ,* s. disparità, f.; disuguaglianza, f.; differenza, f.   [nato, quieto.

dispassionate, *-păsh'ănăt,* a. spassio-

dispel, *-pĕl',* v. a. espellere; scacciare.

dispensable, *-pĕn'săbl,* a. dispensabile.

dispensary, *-sărĭ,* s. dispensario di medicinali, m.; spezieria, f.

dispensation, *-pĕnsā'shăn,* s. dispensa, distribuzione, f.   [m., farmacopea, f.

dispensatory, *-pĕn'sătŭrĭ,* s. ricettario,

dispense, *-pĕns',* v. a. dispensare; distribuire; esentare.   [pagliare.

disperse, *-pĕrs',* v. a. dispergere; spar-

dispersion, *-pĕr'shăn,* s. dispersione, f.; dispergimento, m.   [mentare.

dispirit, *dĭspĭr'ĭt,* v. a. scoraggiare, sgo-

displace, *-plăs',* v. a. dislogare; disordinare.   [dicare.

displant, *-plănt',* v. a. spiantare; sra-

display, *-plă',* v. a. esposizione, mostra, f.; **–,** v. a. esporre; spiegare; far mostra.

displease, *-plĕz',* v. a. dispiacere; offendere.

displeasure, *-plĕsh'ŭr,* s. dispiacere, m.; disgusto, m.; scontento, m.; noia, f.

disport, *-pōrt',* v. a. & n. divertire; divertirsi.

disposable, *-pō'zăbl,* a. disponibile.

disposal, *-pō'zăl,* s. disposizione, f., potere, m.

dispose, *-pōz',* v. a. disporre; preparare; dare; assettare; **–,** v. n. prevalersi; disfarsi; contrattare; **-ed,** disposto, inclinato; **to be -ed of,** da vendere.

disposition, *-pōzĭsh'ăn,* s. disposizione, inclinazione, f.; ordine, m.; talento, m.; carattere, m.   [spogliare.

dispossess, *-pŏzzĕs',* v. a. possessare;

dispraise, *-prāz,* v. a. biasimare; criticare, censurare.

disproof, *-prŏf',* s. confutazione, f.

disproportion, *-prŏpōr'shăn,* s. disproporzione, disparità, f.

disproportionate, *-ăt,* a. sproporzionato.

disprove, *-prŏv',* v. a. disapprovare, riprovare, confutare; convincere.

disputable, *-pū'tăbl,* a. disputabile.

disputant, *dĭs'pūtănt,* s. disputatore, m.; controversista, m.

disputation, *-tā'shăn,* s. disputazione, f.; controversia, f.

disputatious, *-shăs,* a. disputativo, contenzioso.

dispute, *-pūt',* s. disputa, contesa, controversia, f.; **–,** v. a. & u. disputare, dibattere.   [settitudine, inabilità, f.

disqualification, *-kwŏlĭfĭkā'shăn,* s. in-

disqualify, *-kwŏl'ĭfĭ,* v. a. rendere inetto.

disquiet, *-kwī'ĕt,* s. inquietudine, tribolazione, f.; travaglio, m.; **–,** v. a. inquietare, tribolare.   [ansietà, f.

disquietude, *-ětŭd,* s. inquietudine,

disquisition, *-kwĭzĭsh'ăn,* s. disquisizione, f.; esame, m.

disregard, *-rēgărd',* s. trascuraggine; indifferenza, f.; neglezanza, f.; **–,** v. a. trascurare; disprezzare.

disregardful, *-fŭl,* a. trascurante, negligente; disprezzante; **-ly,** ad. dispregevolmente.

disrelish, *-rĕl'ĭsh,* s. cattivo gusto, disgusto, m.; **–,** v. a. disapprovare, non approvare.   [ricordarsi.

disremember, *-rĕmĕm'bĕr,* v. a. non

disrepair, *-rēpăr',* s. cattivo, stato, disfacimento, m.

disreputable, *-rĕp'ŭtăbl,* a. vergognoso.

disrepute, *-rēpūt',* s. disonore, discredito, f.; disgrazia, f.

disrespect, *-rĕspĕkt',* s. mancanza di rispetto, irriverenza, f.

disrespectful, *-fŭl,* a. irriverente; incivile; **-ly,** ad. senza rispetto.

disrobe, *-rŏb',* v. a. svestire; spogliare.

disruption, *-răp'shăn,* s. dirompimento, m., rottura, f.; crepatura, f.

dissatisfaction, *-sătĭsfăk'shăn,* s. scontento, m.; disgusto, dispiacere, m.

dissatisfactory, *-făk'tŭrĭ,* a. spiacevole; molesto.   [disgustato.

dissatisfied, *-săt'ĭsfīd,* a. malcontento,

dissatisfy, *-săt'ĭsfĭ,* v. a. scontentare; dispiacere.

dissect, –sĕkt', v.a. notomizzare, sezionare.

dissecting-room, –ĭng rŏm, s. sala di notomia, f. [analisi, f.; notomia, f.

dissection, –sĕk'shăn, s. dissezione, f.;

dissemble' –sĕm'bl, v. a. simulare; –, v. n. far l' ipocrita. [tamente.

dissemblingly, –blĭnglĭ, ad. dissimula-

disseminate, –sĕm'ĭnāt, v. a. disseminare; spargere; propagare. [discordia, f.

dissension, –sĕn'shăn, s. dissensione, f.;

dissent, –sĕnt', s. sentimento contrario, m., opinione contraria, f.; –, v. n. dissentire, differire.

Dissenter, –ŭr, s. discordante, m.

Dissentient, –sĕn'shĕnt, s. dissenziente, m. [zione, f.; discorso, m.

dissertation, –sŭrtā'shăn, s. disserta-

dissever, –sĕv'ŭr, v. a. sceverare; separare. [diverso.

dissimilar, –sĭm'tlăr, a. dissimile;

dissimilarity, –lăr'ĭtĭ, s. dissimilitudine, f. [mulare.

dissimulate, –sĭm'ŭlāt, v. a. & n. dissi-

dissimulation, –mŭlā'shăn, s. dissimulazione, f. [sumare.

dissipate, dĭs'sĭpāt, v.a. dissipare; con-

dissipation, –pā'shăn, s. dissipazione, f.; distruzione, f.

dissoluble, dĭs'sŏlŭbl, a. dissolubile.

dissolute, dĭs'sŏlŏt, a. dissoluto, licenzioso; –ly, ad. dissolutamente.

dissolution, –lō'shăn, s. dissoluzione, f.; liquefazione, f.; licenza, f. [dissiparsi.

dissolve, dĭzzŏlv', v. a. dissolvere; –, v. n.

dissolving scenes, –sŏl'vĭng sēns, dissolving views, –vāz, s. pl. giochi di lanterna magica, m. pl. [scordanza, f.

dissonance, dĭs'sŏnăns, s. dissonanza, di-

dissonant, –sŏnănt, a. dissonante; differente. [gliare.

dissuade, –swād', v. a. dissuadere; sconsi-

dissuasion, –swā'zhăn, s. dissuasione, f.

dissuasive, dĭsswā'sĭv, a. dissuasivo.

dissylable, –sĭl'ĭdbl, s. dissillabo, di due sillabe, m.

distaff, dĭs'tăf, s. conocchia, rocca, f.

distance, dĭs'tăns, s. distanza, f., intervallo, m.; decoro, m.; rispetto, m.; at a –, in lontananza; out of –, a perdita d' occhio; –, v. a. discostare; lasciare in dietro.

distant, dĭs'tănt, a. distante, discosto.

distaste, –tāst', s. disgusto, m.; dispiacere, m.; tedio, m. [ingrato; offensivo.

distasteful, –fŭl, a. fastidioso, tedioso;

distemper, –tĕm'pŭr, s. malattia, f., morbo, m.; disordine, imbroglio, m.; –, v. a. disturbare; far ammalato.

distend, –tĕnd', v. a. stendere; allargare.

distension, –tĕn'shăn, s. distendimento, m., estensione, f.

distich, dĭs'tĭk, s. distico, m.

distil, dĭstĭl', v. a. & n. distillare.

distillation, –lā'shăn, s. distillazione, f.

distillery, –lăr'ĭ, s. distilleria, f.

distinct, –tĭngkt', a. distinto, chiaro; separato; dissimile, differente.

distinction, –tĭngk'shăn, s. distinzione, f.; differenza, f.

distinctive, –tĭv, a. distintivo; –ly, ad. in modo distintivo, per distinzione.

distinctly, –tĭngkt'lĭ, ad. distintamente; chiaramente. [dezza, f.

distinctness, –nĕs, s. chiarezza, luci-

distinguish, –tĭng'gwĭsh, v. a. distinguere; separare; notare. [guere.

distinguishable, –ăbl, a. che si può distin-

distinguishingly, –ĭnglĭ, ad. con distinzione, onorevolmente.

distort, –tŏrt', v. a. contorcere; rivolgere; stralunare.

distortion, –tŏr'shăn, s. contorsione, f., storcimento, m.

distract, –trăkt', v. a. ir. distrarre; separare; impazzare; molestare; –ed, distratto, pazzo. [smaniosamente.

distractedly, –ĕdlĭ, ad. forsennatamente.

distractedness, –ĕdnĕs, s. smania, f.

distraction, –trăk'shăn, s. distrazione, f.; confusione, f.; smania, f. [fiscare.

distrain, –trān', v. a. sequestrare, con-

distraint, –trānt', s. staggina, f., sequestro, staggimento, m.

distress, –trĕs, s. staggina, f.; calamità, miseria, estremità, f.; –, v. a. staggire; tribolare, vessare.

distribute, –trĭb'ŭt, v. a. distribuire.

distribution, –bŭ'shăn, s. distribuzione, f.

distributive, –trĭb'ŭtĭv, a. distributivo.

district, dĭs'trĭkt, s. distretto, m.; regione, f.; giurisdizione, f.

distrust, –trŭst', s. diffidenza, f.; sospetto, m.; –, v. a. non fidarsi.

distrustful, –fŭl, a. diffidente; sospettoso; –ly, ad. sospettosamente.

disturb, –tŭrb', v. a. disturbare; inquietare; impedire.

disturbance, –tŭr'băns, s. disturbo, m.; confusione, f.; tumulto, m.

disunion, –ū'nĭăn, s. disunione, f.; dissensione, f.; controversia, f.

disunite, –ănĭt', v. a. disunire, disgiugnere; –, v. n. disunirsi, disgiungersi.

disuse, –ūz', s. disuso, m.; –, v. n. disusarsi; lasciar l'uso. [fare un fosso.

ditch, dĭch, s. fosso, m., fossa, f.; –, v. a.

ditty, dĭt'ĭ, s. canzone, f. [aperitivo.

diuretic, dĭūrĕt'ĭk, a. (med.) diuretico,

diurnal, dĭŭr'năl, a. diurno, giornale; –, s. giornale, m. [v. n. tuffarsi; penetrare.

dive, dĭv, v. a. immergere; esplorare; –,

diver, dĭ'vŭr, s. tuffatore, m.; investigatore, m.; tagliaborse, m. [divergente.

diverge, –vĕrj', v. n. divergere; essere

divergence, –ēns, s. divergenza, f.

divergent, –ĕnt, a. divergente.

divers, dĭ'vŭrz, a. diversi; parecchi.

diverse, dĭvĕrs', a. diverso, differente, vario; –ly, ad. differentemente.

diversification, dĭvĕrstfĭkā'shăn, s. diversificazione, f.; varietà, f. [variare.

diversify, –vŭr'sĭfĭ, v. a. diversificare;

diversion, –shăn, s. divertimento, m., ricreazione, f.

diversity, –sĭtĭ, s. diversità, differenza, f.

divert, *−vûrt',* v. a. distornare; divertire, ricreare. [mento, m.

divertisement, *−vûr'tizmĕnt,* s. divertimento, m.

divest, *−vĕst',* v. a. svestire; spogliare, privare. [spoglio, m.; privazione, f.

divestiture, *−vĕs'titûr,* s. spogliamento, m.

divide, *−vīd',* v. a. dividere; disunire; −, v. n. dividersi; disunirsi.

dividend, *dĭv'ĭdĕnd,* s. (ar.) dividendo, m.

divination, *−vĭnā'shŭn,* s. divinazione, f., indovinamento, m.

divine, *−vīn',* s. ecclesiastico, **m.;** teologo, m.; −, a. divino; eccellente; −, v. a. indovinare; presagire; presentire.

divinely, *−lĭ,* ad. divinamente.

diving-bell, *dĭ'vĭng bĕl,* s. campana di marangone, f. [divinatoria, f.

divining-rod, *dĭvĭ'nĭng rŏd,* s. bacchetta

divinity, *dĭvĭn'ĭtĭ,* s. divinità, f.; teologia, f.

divisibility, *−vĭzĭbĭl'ĭtĭ,* s. divisibilità, f.

divisible, *−vĭz'ĭbl,* a. divisibile.

division, *−vĭzh'ŭn,* s. divisione, f.; disunione, f.

divisor, *−vī'zŭr,* s. (ar.) divisore, m.

divorce, *−vōrs',* s. divorzio, m.; −, v. a. far divorzio. [care.

divulge, *−vŭlj',* v. a. divulgare, pubblicare.

dizziness, *dĭz'zĭnĕs,* s. vertigine, f., capogiro, m.

dizzy, *dĭz'zĭ,* a. vertiginoso, sventato.

do, *dō,* s. fracasso, strepito, chiasso, m.; −, v. a. ir. fare; effettuare, finire; cuocere; cucinare; −, v. n. ir. stare, portarsi.

docile, *dŏs'ĭl,* a. docile; disciplinabile.

docility, *−sĭl'ĭtĭ,* s. docilità, f.

dock, *dŏk,* s. darsena, f., bacino, cantiere, m.; coda troncata, f.; lapazio, m.; −, v. a. scortare, racconciare.

docket, *−ĕt,* s. cedola, f.; estratto, m.; −, v. a. notare, segnare.

dockyard, *−yârd,* s. cantiere, m.

doctor, *dŏk'tŭr,* s. dottore, m.; medico, m.; −, v. a. medicare.

doctoress, *−ĕs,* s. dottoressa, f.

doctorship, *−shĭp,* s. dottorato, m., dignità di dottore, f.

doctrinal, *−trīnăl,* a. dottrinale, istruttivo.

doctrine, *−trĭn,* s. [dottrina, scienza, f.; istruzione, f. [precetto, m.

document, *−kŭmĕnt,* s. documento, m.;

documentary, *−mĕn'tărĭ,* a. giustificativo.

dodge, *dŏj,* s. usar furberia, operare con astuzia.

dodger, *−ŭr,* s. intrigante, m.

doe, *dō,* s. daina, f. [diare; spiare.

dog, *dŏg,* s. cane, m.; Sirio, m.; −, v. a. codog-cheap, *−chēp,* v. a. buon mercato, a vil prezzo. [canicolari, m. pl.

dog-days, *−dāz,* s. pl. canicola, f., giorni

doge, *dōj,* s. doge, m. [(pesce).

dog-fish, *dŏg'fĭsh,* s. cane di mare, m.

dogged, *dŏg'gĕd,* a. cagnesco; arcigno, burbero, aspro; **−ly,** ad. d' un' aria arcigna.

doggedness, *−nĕs,* s. umore arcigno, m.

doggerel, *dŏg'grĕl,* s. cattivi versi, m. pl.

dog-hole, *dŏg'hōl,* **dog-kennel,** *−kĕnnĕl,* s. canile, m.

dog-latin, *−lătĭn,* s. latino barbaro, m.

dogmatic(al), *dŏgmăt'ĭk(ăl),* a. dogmatico; **−ly,** ad. in maniera dogmatica.

dog-rose, *dŏg'rōs,* s. rosa canina, f.

dog's ear, *−s'ĕr,* s. canto ripiegato d'una pagina, cornetto, m.

dog-star, *−stâr,* s. canicola, f.; Sirio, m.

dog-weary, *−wērĭ,* a. stracco come un cane, stanchissimo. [fatti, eventi, m. pl.

doing, *dō'ĭng,* s. azione, fatto, m.; **−s,** pl.

dole, *dŏl,* s. distribuzione f.; porzione, f.; elemosina, f.; −, v. a. distribuire; dare.

doleful, *−fŭl,* a. tristo, doloroso, mesto, lugubre, afflitto.

doll, *dŏl,* s. bambola, f., bamboccio, m.

dollar, *dŏl'lăr,* s. tallero, m.; dollaro, m.

dolphin, *dŏl'fĭn,* s. delfino, m.

dolt, *dŏlt,* s. minchione, balordo, m.

domain, *dōmān',* s. dominio, m.

dome, *dōm,* s. cupola, volta, f.; edifizio, m.

domestic, *dōmĕs'tĭk,* a. domestico, familiare. [dimesticare.

domesticate, *−tĭkāt,* v. a. domesticare,

domestication, *−kā'shăn,* s. dimesticamento, m.; ritiro, m. [domestichezza, f.

domesticity, *−tĭs'ĭtĭ,* s. domesticità, f.

domicile, *dŏm'ĭsĭl,* s. domicilio, m.; albergo, m.

domiciliary, *−ĭărĭ,* a. domiciliario.

domiciliary-visit, *−vĭzĭt,* s. (jur.) visita domiciliare, f. [valere.

dominate, *dŏm'ĭnāt,* v. a. dominare, prevalere.

domination, *−nā'shăn,* s. dominio, impero, m., signoria, f. [reggiare.

domineer, *−nēr',* v. a. dominare; signoreggiare.

dominion, *dŏmĭn'yăn,* s. dominio, m.; territorio, m.; giurisdizione, f.

domino, *dŏmĭnō',* s. dominò, m.; specie di veste da maschera, dominò, m. [su.

don, *dŏn,* s. don, signore, m.; −, v. a. metter

donate, *dŏnāt',* v. a. donare. [m.

donation, *dŏnā'shăn,* s. donazione, f., dono.

done, *dŭn,* a. fatto; conchiuso; cotto.

donee, *dŏnē',* s. (jur.) donatario, m.

donkey, *dŏng'kĭ,* s. asinello, m.

donor, *dŏ'năr,* s. donatore, m.

doodle, *dŏŏ'l,* s. ozioso, sfaccendato, m.

doom, *dōm,* s. sentenza, f.; condanna, f.; −, v. a. sentenziare; condannare. [m.

doomsday, *−z'dā,* s. giudizio universale,

door, *dōr,* s. porta, f.; entrata, f.; **within −s,** in casa. [carceriere, m.

door-keeper, *−kēpăr,* s. portinaio, m.;

door-plate, *−plăt,* s. lastro di metallo, f.

door-scraper, *−skrăpăr,* s. lamina di ferro per pulire le scarpe del fango, f.

door-way, *−wā,* s. portone, m.

dormant, *dŏr'mănt,* a. dormiente; segreto.

dormer-window, *−măr wĭndō,* s. spiraglio, abbaino, m.

dormitory, *−mĭtărĭ,* s. dormitorio, m.

dormouse, *−mŏŭs,* s. ghiro, m. [niera, f.

dorsel, *−sĕl,* **dorser,** *−sŭr,* s. cesta, paniera, f.

dose, *dōs,* s. dose, f.; presa, f.; −, v. a. (med.) dosare. [porre i punti.

dot, *dŏt,* s. punto, m.; −, v. n. puntare;

dotage, *dō'tăj,* s. perdita d'intelletto, m.; imbecillità, f.; vaneggiamento, m.

dotard, *−tărd,* s. vecchio rimbambito, m.

dotation, _-tā'shăn_, s. dotazione, f.
dote, _dōt_, v. n. vaneggiare, bamboleggiare, amare soverchiamente.
dotingly, _dō'tĭnglĭ_, ad. con soverchio amore, appassionatamente.
double, _dăb'l_, a. doppio; simulato; –, s. doppio, m.; artificio, inganno, m.; –, v. a. raddoppiare; dissimulare; piegare.
double-chin, _-chĭn_, s. doppio mento, m.
double-dealer, _-dēlăr_, s. furfante, furbo.
double-edged, _-ĕjd_, a. a due tagli. [m.
double-entry, _-ĕntrĭ_, s. scrittura doppia, f.
double-lock, _-lŏk_, v. a. serrare a doppia chiave. [tato.
double-quick, _-kwĭk_, a. con passo affrettato.
doublet, _dăb'lĕt_, s. giubbone, m.
double-tongued, _dăb'l tăngd_, a. doppio, furbo, ingannevole.
doubloon, _dăblōn'_, s. doppione, m.
doubly, _dăb'lĭ_, ad. doppiamente, a doppio.
doubt, _dŏŭt_, s. dubbio, m.; –, v. a. sospettare; –, v. n. dubitare.
doubtful, _-fŭl_, a. dubbioso, incerto; **-ly**, ad. dubbiosamente. [–, ad. senza dubbio.
doubtless, _-lĕs_, a. indubitabile, certo;
dough, _dō_, s. pasta, f.
doughty, _dŏŭ'tĭ_, a. valoroso, coraggioso.
doughy, _dō'ĭ_, a. pastoso.
douse, _dŏŭs_, v. a. immergere all' improvviso; –, v. n. cascare nell' acqua improvviso.
dove, _dăv_, s. colomba, f. [visamente.
dove-cot, _-kŏt_, s. colombaia, f.
dove-like, _-lĭk_, a. simile ad una colomba.
dove-tail, _-tāl_, s. coda di rondine, f.
dowager, _dŏŭ'ăjăr_, s. vedova, f.
dowdy, _dŏŭ'dĭ_, s. donnaccia, f.
dower, _dŏŭ'ăr_, s. dote, f.; pensione, f.
dowered, _-ărd_, a. dotato.
down, _dŏŭn_, s. penna matta, f.; lanugine, f.
down, –, pr. & ad. giù; a basso, abbasso; a secondo; **– the stream**, a seconda della corrente; **up and –**, qua e là; **upside –**, sossopra; **to sit –**, sedersi.
down-cast, _-kăst_, a. abbattuto.
downer, _-ăr_, s. caso infelice, m.
down-fall, _-fāl_, s. traboccamento, m.; rovina, f. [m., china, f., pendio, m.
down-hill, _-hĭl_, s. discesa, f.; declivio.
downright, _-rĭt_, a. evidente; franco; –, ad. giù a piombo. [m.
down-train, _-trăn_, s. treno di partenza.
downward, _-wărd_, a. declive; abbattuto, afflitto; **-(s)**, ad. giù, abbasso.
downy, _dŏŭn'ĭ_, a. lanuginoso; molle.
doze, _dōz_, v. a. addormentare; rendere stupido; –, v. n. essere sonnoglioso.
dozen, _dăz'n_, s. dozzina, f.
drab, _drăb_, s. specie di panno, f.; prostituta, f.; –, a. rossiccio.
drachm, _drăm_, s. dramma, f.
draft, _drăft_, s. disegno, m.; copia, f.; tratta, f.; –, v. a. disegnare; (mil.) distaccare.
drag, _drăg_, s. uncino, m.; grancio, m.; tramuglio, m.; –, v. a. & n. tirare per forza; strascinare.
drag-chain, _-chăn_, s. catena da fermare, f.
draggle, _drăg'l_, v. a. & n. infangare; infangarsi.

drag-net, _-nĕt_, s. tramaglio, m.
dragoman, _-ŏmăn_, s. dragomanno, m.
dragon, _-ŏn_, s. dragone, m.
dragon-fly, _-flī_, s. tulipida, f.
dragoon, _drăgōn'_, s. dragone, m.
drain, _drăn_, s. fogna, f., condotto sotterraneo, m.; –, v. a. seccare; fognare.
drainage, _-ăj_, s. scolo, flusso, m.
drake, _drăk_, s. anitra, f.; cannoncino, m.
dram, _drăm_, s. dramma, f.; sorso (di qualche liquore), m.; –, v. n. bere liquori distillati.
drama, _drăm'ă_, s. dramma, m.
dramatic(al), _drămăt'ĭk(ăl)_, a. drammatico; **-ally**, ad. a modo di dramma.
dramatise, _drăm'ătĭz_, v. n. comporre drammi. [m.
dramatist, _-ătĭst_, s. autore drammatico, m.
draper, _drā'păr_, s. mercante di panni, pannaiuolo, m. [tura di panni, f.
drapery, _-părĭ_, s. drapperia, f.; manifattura di panni, f.
drastic, _drăs'tĭk_, a. (med.) vigoroso.
draught, _drăft_, s. pl. sorso, m.; piano, m.; disegno, m.; copia, f.; tratta, f.; tiro (d'acqua), m.; biglietto, m.; sommario, m.; **at one –**, ad un sorso.
draught-board, _-bōrd_, s. tavoliere, m.; scacchiere, m. [m.
draught-horse, _-hŏrs_, s. cavallo da tiro.
draughts, _-s_, s. pl. giuoco della dama, m.
draughty, _drăf'tĭ_, a. ventoso.
draw, _drā_, v. a. ir. tirare, trainare; attrarre, allettare; disegnare; strascinare; –, v. n. ir. accorciarsi, ristringersi; ritirarsi; **to – nigh**, avvicinarsi, avanzare. [f.
draw-back, _-băk_, s. sconto, m.; ritirata.
draw-bridge, _-brĭj_, s. ponte levatoio, m.
drawer, _-ăr_, s. tiratore, m.; disegnatore, m.; tiratoio, m.; **-s**, s. pl. mutande, f. pl.
drawing, _-ĭng_, s. delineamento, disegno, schizzo, m. [disegnare, f.
drawing-board, _-ĭng bōrd_, s. tavola da disegno, m.
drawing-master, _-măstăr_, s. maestro di disegno, m. [segnare, f.
drawing-paper, _-păpăr_, s. carta da disegno, m.
drawing-pen, _-pĕn_, s. tiralinee, m.
drawing-room, _-rōm_, s. anticamera, f.; assemblea, f.
drawl, _drāl_, v. n. strascinare (le parole).
draw-well, _-wĕl_, s. pozzo profondo, m.
dray(cart), _drā('kărt)_, s. carro, m.; slitta, treggia, f.
drayman, _-măn_, s. carrettiere, m.
dread, _drĕd_, a. terribile; –, s. terrore, m., paura, f.; –, v. a. & n. ir. temere, paventare.
dreadful, _-fŭl_, a. terribile, spaventevole.
dream, _drĕm_, s. sogno, m.; stravaganza, f.; –, v. n. ir. sognare; immaginarsi. [so.
dreamer, _-ăr_, s. sognatore, m.; pensieroso.
dreaminess, _drĕm'ĭnĕs_, s. meditazione, f.; sonnolenza, f.
dreamy, _drĕm'ĭ_, a. chimerico. [mente.
drearily, _drē'rĭlĭ_, ad. orribilmente; tristamente.
dreary, _drē'rĭ_, a. orribile; tristo, penoso.
dredge, _drĕj_, s. tramaglio, m. [m.
dredger, _-ăr_, s. pescatore con un tramaglio.
dredging-machine, _-ĭng măshĕn_, s. scorticatoio, m.

dregs, *drĕgz*, s. pl. feccia, f., sedimento, m.

drench, *drĕnsh*, s. beveraggio, m. (medicina d'animale); –, v. a. abbeverare; bagnare; innaffiare, umettare.

dress, *drĕs*, s. abito, vestimento, m.; addobbamento, ornamento, m.; cuffia, f.; –, v. a. vestire; addobbare, adornare; acconciare; cucinare, cuocere; –, v. n. aggiustarsi; acconciarsi; **to – a vine**, potare una vigna; **to – a wound**, medicare una ferita.

dresser, *–sŭr*, s. acconciatore, m.; cameriere, m.; tavola di cucina, f.

dressing, *drĕs'sĭng*, s. vestimento, m.; addobbo, m.; apparato, m.; fascia, f.

dressing-gown, *–gŏŭn*, s. veste da camera, f.   [vestirsi, f.

dressing-room, *–rŏm*, s. camera da

dressing-table, *–tăbl*, s. (tavola da) toe-

dressy, *drĕs'sĭ*, a. acconciato.   [letta, f.

dribble, *drĭb'bl*, v. a. stillare; –, v. n. gocciolare; fare bava.   [tuccio, m.

dribblet, *drĭb'lĕt*, s. piccol debito, debi-

drift, *drĭft*, s. impulso, m.; corso, m.; obietto, m.; maneggio, m.; **– of ice**, pezzo di ghiaccio, m.; **– of sand**, alzamento di rena mobile, m.; **– of snow**, caduta di neve, f.; –, v. a. spingere; cacciare; –, v. n. accumularsi.

drill, *drĭl*, s. succhiello, spillo, m.; babbuino, m.; –, v. a. forare; disciplinare.

drink, *drĭngk*, v. a. ir. bere, bevere; assorbire;   v. n. innebriarsi; –, s. bevanda, f., beveraggio, m.

drinkable, *–ăbl*, a. potabile.

drinking-bout, *–ĭng bŏŭt*, s. beveria, f.

drinking-cup, *–kŭp*, s. tazza, coppa, f.

drip, *drĭp*, s. goccia, gocciola, f.; –, v. a. & n. spruzzare, gocciolare.

dripping, *–pĭng*, s. unto, m.   [f.

dripping-pan, *–păn*, s. ghiotta, leccarda,

drive, *drĭv*, v. a. ir. condurre, guidare, menare; cacciare; impellere, forzare; –, v. n. ir. aver in mira, tendere; avanzare; –, s. passeggiata in carrozza, f.

drivel, *drĭv'l*, s. bava, saliva, f.; –, v. n. bavare; esser bavoso.

driver, *drĭv'ŭr*, s. conduttore, m.; cocchiere, m.; zeppa, f.; (am.) ispettore di schiavi, m.   [ciolare.

drizzle, *drĭz'l*, v. a. & n. spruzzolare, goc-

drizzling-rain, *–lĭng răn*, s. spruzzaglia, f.

droll, *drŏl*, a. comico, burlevole; –, s. buffone, m.   [farsa, f.

drollery, *–lărĕ*, s. buffoneria, facezia, f.;

dromedary, *drŏm'ĕdărĕ*, s. dromedario, m.; (cant) ladro goffo, m.

drone, *drŏn*, s. pecchione, m.; infingardaccio, m.; –, v. n. ronzare; tentennare, cincischiare.   [affliggersi, esser tristo.

droop, *drŏp*, v. n. languire; infievolire;

drooping, *–ĭng*, s. languore, m.

drop, *drŏp*, s. goccia, f.; orecchino, m.; **by –s**, a goccia a goccia; –, v. a. lasciare cascare; abbandonare; cessare; metter da bando; –, v. n. gocciolare; cascare; svenire, sparire; morire.   [f.

drop-scene, *–sĕn*, s. cortina d' intermezzo,

dropsical, *–sĭkăl*, a. idropico.

dropsy, *–sĭ*, s. idropisia, f.   [m.

dross, *drŏs*, s. scoria, f.; feccia, f.; rifiuto,

drought, *drŏŭt*, s. secchezza, f.; sete, f.

drove, *drŏv*, s. branco, m.; gregge, f.; folla,

drover, *drŏ'vŭr*, s. bifolco, m.   [f.

drown, *drŏŭn*, v. a. annegare; immergere; –, v. n. annegarsi.

drowse, *drŏŭz*, v. a. addormentare, render sonnacchioso; –, v. n. dormire.

drowsily, *–zĭlĭ*, ad. in modo sonnacchioso, lentamente.   [dolenza, f.; pigrizia, f.

drowsiness, *–zĭnĕs*, s. sonnolenza, f.; in-

drowsy, *–zĭ*, a. sonnolento; stupido.

drub, *drŭb*, s. colpo, m.; botta, f.; –, v. a. bastonare.   [faticarsi; stentare.

drudge, *drŭj*, s. facchino, m.; –, v. n. affaticarsi.

drudgery, *–ărĕ*, s. servigio vile, m.

drug, *drŭg*, s. droga, f.; –, v. a. mescolare con ingredienti medicinali.

drugget, *–gĕt*, s. droghetta, m.

druggist, *–gĭst*, s. droghiere, m.

drum, *drŭm*, s. tamburo, m.; timpano, m.; –, v. a. battere il tamburo; (am.) far avventori.   [giore, m.

drum-major, *–mĕjăr*, s. tamburo mag-

drummer, *–mŭr*, s. tamburo, m.; (am.) che fa avventori, m.

drumming, *–mĭng*, s. battimento del tamburo, m.   [buro, f.

drum-stick, *–stĭk*, s. bacchetta di tam-

drunk, *drŭngk*, a. ubbriaco.

drunkard, *–ărd*, s. briacone, trincone, m.

drunken, *drŭngk'n*, a. ubbriaco, inebriato.

drunkenness, *–nĕs*, s. ubriachezza, f.

dry, *drĭ*, a. secco, arido; sitibondo, assetato; insipido; –, v. a. seccare, inaridire; asciugare; –, v. n. seccarsi, inaridirsi.

dry-goods, *–gŭds*, s. pl. mercanzie a minuto, f. pl.   [poveramente.

dryly, *–lĭ*, a. senza umidità, aridamente;

dryness, *–nĕs*, s. siccità, f.; freddezza, f.; insipidezza, f.

drynurse, *–nŭrs*, s. nutrice non lattante, f.; –, v. a. allevare senza lattare.

dry-rot, *–rŏt*, s. albume, m. (mallattia del legname).

dry-shod, *–shŏd*, a. a secco; a piè secco.

dual, *dŭ'ăl*, a. duale.   [cavaliere).

dub, *dŭb*, v. a. fare; creare; armare (un

dubious, *dŭ'bĭŭs*, a. dubbioso; **-ly**, ad. dubbiosamente, con dubbio.

ducal, *dŭ'kăl*, a. di duca o da duca.

ducat, *dŭk'ăt*, s. ducato, m.

duchess, *dŭch'ĕs*, s. duchessa, f.

duchy, *dŭch'ĭ*, s. ducato, m.

duck, *dŭk*, s. anitra, f.; (fig.) caro, m., cara, f.; tela di vele, f.; –, v. a. tuffare, immergere; –, v. n. tuffarsi.

duckling, *–lĭng*, s. anitrina, f.

duck-weed, *–wĕd*, s. lente palusre, f.

ductile, *dŭk'tĭl*, a. duttile; flessibile; trattevole.   [lità, docilità, f.

ductility, *–tĭl'ĭtĕ*, s. duttilità, f.; flessibi-

dudgeon, *dŭj'ŭn*, s. mala parte, f., cattivo umore, m.

duds, *dŭds*, s. abiti, arnesi, m. pl.

due, *dú,* a. debito, dovuto; –, ad. debitamente; esattamente; –, s. debito, m.; tributo, m.; imposta, f. [fare duello.

duel, *dú'ĕl,* s. duello, m.; –, v. n. duellare,

duellist, *–lĭst,* s. duellante, m.

duet, *dú'ĕt,* s. (mus.) duetto, duo, m.

duffer, *dŭf'fŭr,* s. uomo stupido, m.

dug, *dŭg,* s. mammella, f., capezzolo, m.

dug-out, *–ŏŭt,* s. (am.) piroga, f.

duke, *dúk,* s. duca, m.

dukedom, *–dŭm,* s. ducato, m.

dulcimer, *dŭl'sĭmŭr,* s. saltero, m.

dull, *dŭl,* a. stupido, goffo; ottuso; tristo, mesto; tedioso; – (of hearing), duro d' orecchio; –, v. a. stupidire; render ottuso; offuscare.

dullard, *–lărd,* s. babbuasso, m.

dully, *–lĭ,* ad. stupidamente; lentamente.

dulness, *–nĕs,* s. stupidezza, balordaggine, f.; pigrizia, lentezza, f.; sonnolenza, f.

duly, *dú'lĭ,* ad. debitamente, convenevolmente.

dumb, *dŭm,* a. muto. [mente.

dumb-bell, *–bĕl,* s. peso per far esercizi ginnastici, m. [confondere.

dumbfound, *–fŏŭnd,* v. a. render muto; confondere.

dumbness, *–nĕs,* s. mutezza, f.; silenzio, m.

dumb-show, *–shŏ,* s. pantomima, f.

dumb-waiter, *–wătŭr,* s. trespolo per porvi i piatti sulla tavola, m.

dummy, *dŭm'mĭ,* s. muto, m.; prestanome, m.; marionetta, f.

dump, *dŭmp,* s. cordoglio, m.; malinconia,

dumpy, *–ĭ,* a. corto e grosso, tozzo. [f.

dun, *dŭn,* a. bruno, fosco; tanè; –, s. creditore importuno, m.; –, v. a. importunare, molestare.

dunce, *dŭns,* s. goffo, babbuasso, m.

dung, *dŭng,* s. concime, letame, m.; sterco, m.; –, v. a. concimare, letamare. [f,

dungeon, *dŭn'jŭn,* s. prigione sotterranea,

dung-hill, *dŭng'hĭl,* s. mucchio di letame, m. [libro in duodecimo, m.

duodecimo, *dŭŏdĕs'ĭmŏ,* s. in dodici, m.;

dupe, *dúp,* s. merlotto, gonzo, m.; –, v. a. ingannare, truffare. [copia, f.

duplicate, *dú'plĭkăt,* s. duplicato, m.,

duplicity, *–plĭs'ĭtĭ,* s. duplicità, f.; doppiezza, f.

durability, *–răbĭl'ĭtĭ,* s. durabilità, f.

durable, *dú'răbl,* a. durabile; solido.

durably, *–răblĭ,* ad. durabilmente, durevolmente. [f.

durance, *dú'răns,* s. prigionia, f.; durata,

duration, *–rā'shăn,* s. durata, f.

during, *dú'rĭng,* pr. & c. per, durante.

dusk, *dŭsk,* a. oscuro, fosco, bruno, buio; –, s. crepuscolo, bruzzo, bruzzolo, m.; –, v. a. oscurare; –, v. n. oscurarsi; divenire bruno.

duskily, *–ĭlĭ,* ad. oscuramente, foscamente.

duskiness, *–ĭnĕs,* s. oscurità, f.

dusky, *dŭsk'ĭ,* a. oscuro, fosco; negriccio.

dust, *dŭst,* s. polvere, f.; –, v. a. coprire di polvere; nettare da polvere.

dust-cart, *–kărt,* s. carretta di trasporre il letame, f.

duster, *–ŭr,* s. cencio, strofinaccio, m.

dust-hole, *–hŏl,* s. letamaio, m.

dustman, *–măn,* s. paladino, m.

dust-pan, *–păn,* s. pala da spazzatura, f.

dust-shot, *–shŏt,* s. migliarola, f. [vere.

dusty, *dŭst'ĭ,* a. polveroso, coperto di pol-

duteous, *dú'tĭăs,* **dutiful,** *dú'tĭfŭl,* a. ubbidiente, ossequioso; rispettoso; –ly, ad. ossequiosamente, sommessamente.

dutifulness, *–nĕs,* s. ubbidienza, f.; sommessione, f., omaggio, m.

duty, *dú'tĭ,* s. dovere, debito, m.; funzione, f.; uffizio, m.; tassa, f.; dogana, gabella, f.; on –, in funzione. [dire dal crescere.

dwarf, *dwărf,* s. nano, m.; –, v. a. impe-

dwarfish, *–ĭsh,* a. piccoletto, piccino.

dwell, *dwĕl,* v. n. ir. abitare, dimorare; dilatarsi.

dwelling, *–lĭng,* s. abitazione, dimora, f.

dwindle, *dwĭn'dl,* v. n. impiccolire, diminuire; consumarsi; peggiorare. [f.

dye, *dĭ,* v. a. tignere; colorire; –, s. tintura,

dyeing, *–ĭng,* s. tintura, f.

dye-works, *–wŭrks,* s. pl. tintoria, f.

dying, *–ĭng,* a. moriente; moribondo; –, s. morte, f.

dynamics, *dĭnăm'ĭks,* s. pl. dinamica, f.

dynamite, *dĭn'ămĭt,* s. dinamite, f.

dynamo, *dĭ'nămŏ,* s. dinamo, m. [f.

dynasty, *dĭn'ăstĭ,* s. dinastia, f.; sovranità,

dysentery, *dĭs'ĕntărĭ,* s. (med.) dissenteria, f.

dyspepsy, *dĭspĕp'sĭ,* s. dispepsia, f.

dyspeptic, *–tĭk,* a. malato di dispepsia.

E.

each, *ĕch,* pn. ciascheduno, ciascuno; on – side, dalle due bande; – other, l' un l' altro.

eager, *ē'găr,* a. desideroso, bramoso, fervente, ardente; veemente; –ly, ad. ferventemente, ardentemente; veementemente.

eagerness, *–nĕs,* s. premura, f., fervore, ardore, m.; passione, f.; veemenza, f.

eagle, *ē'gl,* s. aquila, f.; moneta d' oro, f. (10 dollars).

eagle-eyed, *–ĭd,* a. di vista acuta.

eaglet, *ē'glĕt,* s. aquila piccola, f.

ear, *ēr,* s. orecchio, m.; spiga, f.; –, v. n. spighire, fare la spiga.

ear-ache, *–āk,* s. otalgia, f.

eared, *ērd,* a. che ha degli orecchi; spighito.

earl, *ŭrl,* s. conte, m.

ear-lap, *–lăp,* s. oreglia, f.

earldom, *ŭrl'dăm,* s. contea, f.

earless, *ēr'lĕs,* s. senza orecchi.

earliness, *ŭr'lĭnĕs,* s. prontezza, fretta, f.; diligenza, f. [di buon' ora.

early, *ŭr'lĭ,* a. mattutino; pronto; –, ad.

earn, *ŭrn,* v. a. guadagnare; meritare, lucrare, acquistare.

earnest, *ŭr'nĕst,* a. ardente; zelante, fervido; –, s. serio, m.; caparra, f., pegno, m.; in good –, seriosamente, da vero.

earnestly, *–lĭ,* ad. seriamente; istanti-mente.

earnest-money, *–mănĭ,* s. caparra, f.

earnestness, *–nĕs,* s. ardore, m.; premura, veemenza, f.; diligenza, f.

earnings, *ăr´nĭngs,* s. pl. mercede delle fatiche, m.

ear-ring, *ĕr´rĭng,* s. orecchino, m.

earth, *ărth,* s. terra, f.; suolo, mondo, m.; –, v. a. coprire di terra; –, v. n. nascondersi sotto terra.   [scita.

earth-born, *–bŏrn,* a. terrestre; di vil natura.

earthen, *ăr´thn,* a. di terra; argilloso; – **ware,** s. vasellame, m.

earthiness, *ărth´ĭnĕs,* **earthliness,** *–lĭnĕs,* s. qualità terrestre, natura terrena, f.

earthly, *–lĭ,* a. terrestre, del mondo, corporeo.

earthquake, *–kwăk,* s. terremoto, m.

earthwork, *–wŭrk,* s. (mil.) terrazzo, m.

earthworm, *–wŭrm,* s. lombrico, m.

earthy, *ărth´ĭ,* a. di terra, terrestre, terreno; grossolano.   [stica, f.

ear-trumpet, *ĕr´trŭmpĕt,* s. tromba acustica.

ear-wax, *–wăks,* s. cerume, m.

ear-witness, *–wĭtnĕs,* s. testimonio auriculare, m.

ease, *ēz,* s. agio, m.; comodo, alleggiamento, m.; conforto, m.; riposo, m.; tranquillità, f.; facilità, f.; –, a. a bell' agio; –, v. a. alleviare; mitigare.

easel, *ē´zl,* s. telaio, m.   [m.; conforto, m.

easement, *ēz´mĕnt,* s. sollievo, m.; aiuto,

easily, *ē´zĭlĭ,* ad. agevolmente; facilmente.

easiness, *ē´zĭnĕs,* s. agevolezza, f.; facilità, f.; condiscendenza, f.; riposo, m.

east, *ēst,* s. levante, oriente, est, m.; –, a.

Easter, *–ăr,* s. Pasqua, f.   [orientale.

easterly, *–ărlĭ,* **eastern,** *–ărn,* a. di levante, orientale.   [oriente.

eastward, *–wărd,* a. verso l' oriente, all'

easy, *ē´zĭ,* a. agevole; facile; quieto; libero; trattabile, sociabile; benigno, piacevole; **– of belief,** credulo.

eat, *ēt,* v. a. ir. mangiare; rodere; –, v. n. ir. pascolare.

eatable, *ē´tăbl,* a. da mangiare; **–s,** s. pl. vivande, f. pl.; viveri, m. pl.

eating-house, *–ĭng hŏŭs,* s. bettola, f.; taverna, trattoria, f.

eaves, *ēvz,* s. gronda, grondaia, f.

eavesdrop, *–drŏp,* v. n. ascoltare presso la finestra.

ebb, *ĕb,* s. riflusso, m., bassa marea, f.; scemamento, m.; –, v. n. rifluire; calare; decrescere, scemare.

ebony, *ĕb´ŏnĭ,* s. ebano, m.; **to deal in –,** esercitar la tratta dei negri.

ebullition, *ĕbŭlĭsh´ŭn,* s. ebollizione, f.; effervescenza, f.

eccentric(al), *ĕksĕn´trĭk(ăl),* a. eccentrico.

eccentricity, *–trĭs´ĭtĭ,* s. eccentricità, f.

ecclesiastic, *ĕkklēzĭăs´tĭk,* a. & s. ecclesiastico, m.; chierico, m.   [eco.

echo, *ĕk´ō,* s. eco, m.; –, v. a. risonare per

eclectic, *ĕklĕk´tĭk,* a. scelto.

eclipse, *ĕklĭps´,* s. eclisse, eclissi, f.; –, v. n. oscurarsi.

ecliptic, *ĕklĭp´tĭk,* s. eclittica, f.

economic(al), *ĕkŏnŏm´ĭk(ăl),* a. economico; frugale.

economist, *ĕkŏn´ŏmĭst,* s. economo, m.

economize, *–nŏmīz,* v. a. economizzare.

economy, *–nŏmĭ,* s. economia, f.; frugaecstasy, *ĕk´stăsĭ,* s. estasi, f.   [lità, f.

ecstatic(al), *–stăt´ĭk(ăl),* a. estatico.

eddy, *ĕd´dĭ,* s. gorgo, m.; riflusso impetuoso, m.; –, v. n. girare, aggirarsi.

edge, *ĕj,* s. taglio, m.; filo, m.; orlo, m.; sponda, spiaggia, f.; (fig.) estremità, f.; sagacità, f.; –, v. a. affilare, aguzzare; orlare; eccitare, irritare; –, v. n. opporsi.

edge-tool, *–tōl,* s. strumento tagliente, m.

edgeways, *–wāz,* **edgewise,** *–wīz,* ad. dalla parte del taglio; per fianco.

edging, *ĕj´ĭng,* s. orlo, m., frangia, f.

edible, *ĕd´ĭbl,* a. da mangiare.

edict, *ē´dĭkt,* s. editto, bando, m.

edification, *ĕdĭfĭkā´shŭn,* s. edificazione, f.

edifice, *ĕd´ĭfĭs,* s. edifizio, m.; fabbrica, f.

edify, *ĕd´ĭfĭ,* v. a. edificare; fabbricare; istruire.   [pubblicare]

edit, *ĕd´ĭt,* v. a. preparare un' edizione,

edition, *ĕdĭsh´ŭn,* s. edizione, f.; pubblicazione, f.; stampa, f.

editor, *ĕd´ĭtăr,* s. editore, m.

editorial, *–tō´rĭăl,* s. articolo di fondo d' una gazzetta, m.

educate, *ĕd´ŭkāt,* v. a. educare; istruire.

education, *–kā´shŭn,* s. educazione, f.; istruzione, f.

educe, *ĕdūs´,* v. a. estrarre; cavare.

eel, *ēl,* s. anguilla, f.

eel-pout, *–pōŭt,* s. gavoncho, m.

efface, *ĕffās´,* v. a. cancellare; cassare.

effect, *ĕffĕkt´,* s. effetto, m.; successo, m.; realità, f.; **–s,** pl. effetti, m.; beni, m. pl.; –, v. s. effettuare, eseguire.

effective, *–ĕk´tĭv,* a. effettivo; attivo; **–ly,** ad. effettivamente, con effetto; **–s,** s. pl. truppe di guerra, f. pl.

effectual, *–tŭăl,* a. effettuale, effettivo; **–ly,** ad. effettualmente, con effetto.

effeminacy, *–fĕm´ĭnăsĭ,* s. effeminatezza, f.

effeminate, *–mĭnăt,* v. a. effeminare; ammollire; –, v. n. divenire effeminato; –, a. effeminato.   [vescenza.

effervesce, *–fŭrvĕs´,* v. n. essere in effer-

effervescence, *–sĕns,* s. effervescenza, f.

effete, *ĕffēt´,* a. sterile.   [fervore.

efficacious, *–fĭkā´shŭs,* a. efficace, efficiente; **–ly,** ad. efficacemente.

efficacy, *ĕf´fĭkăsĭ,* s. efficacia, f.; forza, f.; virtù, f.   [f.

efficiency, *–fĭsh´ĕnsĭ,* s. virtù, f.; potenza,

efficient, *–ĕnt,* a. efficace.   [ritratto, m.

effigy, *ĕf´fĭjĭ,* s. effigie, f.; immagine, f.,

efflorescence, *–flōrĕs´sĕns,* s. fioritura, f.; efflorescenza, f.

effluvium, *–flō´vĭăm,* s. evaporazione, f.

effort, *ĕf´fōrt,* s. sforzo, m.; violenza, f.

effrontery, *–frŏn´tărĭ,* s. sfacciataggine, impudenza, f.   [lucidezza, f.

effulgence, *–fŭl´jĕns,* s. splendore, m.;

effulgent, *–jĕnt,* a. rifulgente, splendente.

effusion, *-fū'zhŭn,* s. effusione, f., versamento, m.; spargimento, m.

eft, *ĕft,* s. stellione, m. (lucertola).

egg, *ĕg,* s. uovo, m.; **poached -s,** pl. uova affogate, f. pl.

egg-cup, *-kŭp,* s. ovaiuolo, m.

egg-flip, *-flĭp,* s. latte di gallina, m.

egg-shell, *-shĕl,* s. guscio d' uovo, m.

eglantine, *ĕg'lăntīn,* s. rosa salvatica, f.

egotism, *ĕg'ŏtizm,* s. egoismo, m.

egotist, *ĕg'ŏtĭst,* s. egoista, m.

egotistical, *-tĭs'tĭkăl,* a. da egoista.

egregious, *ĕgrē'jŭs,* a. egregio, eccellente, insigne; **-ly,** ad. eccellentemente.

egress, *ē'grĕs,* **egression,** *ĕgrĕsh'ăn,* s. esito, m., uscita, f. [peluria, f.

eiderdown, *ī'dărdŏŭn,* s. piumino, m., [una eiaculazione.

eight, *āt,* a. otto.

eighteen, *ā'tēn,* a. diciotto.

eighteenth, *ā'tēnth,* a. diciottesimo.

eighth, *ātth,* a. ottavo; **-ly,** ad. in ottavo luogo.

eightieth, *ā'tĭĕth,* a. ottantesimo.

eighty, *ā'tī,* a. ottanta.

either, *ē'thăr,* pn. l' uno o l' altro, ciascuno, qualunque; **-,** c. sia, sia che; ovvero che; o.

ejaculate, *ĕjăk'ŭlāt,* v. a. eiaculare, fare

ejaculation, *-lā'shŭn,* s. giaculatoria, corta e fervente preghiera, f.

eject, *ĕjĕkt',* v. a. gettare; mandare fuora.

ejection, *ĕjĕk'shŭn,* s. espulsione, f.; (med.) evacuazione, f.; egestione, f.

eke, *ēk,* v. a. allungare; dilatare, aumentare, accrescere.

elaborate, *ĕlăb'ŏrăt,* v. a. elaborare; limare, perfezionare; **-,** a. elaborato, perfetto; **-ly,** ad. con esattezza.

elaboration, *-rā'shŭn,* s. squisita diligenza, f., perfezionamento, m. [passare.

elapse, *ĕlăps',* v. n. scorrer via, svanire,

elastic(al), *ĕlăs'tĭk(ăl),* a. elastico. [f.

elasticity, *-tĭs'ĭtī,* s. elasticità, f.; molla,

elate, *ĕlāt',* a. orgoglioso; **-,** v. a. insuperbire; esaltare, inalzare. [bia, f.

elation, *ĕlā'shŭn,* s. orgoglio, m., superbia, f.

elbow, *ĕl'bŏ,* s. gomito, cubito, m.; angolo, m.; **-,** v. a. spingere col gomito; **-,** v. n. fare un angolo.

elbow-chair, *-chăr,* s. sedia d'appoggio, f.

elbow-room, *-rōm,* s. agio, m.; spazio, m.; libertà, f. [**-,** s. sambuco, m.

elder, *ĕl'dăr,* a. maggiore; maggiornato;

elderly, *-lī,* a. attempato. [m. pl.

elders, *ĕl'dărz,* s. pl. maggiori, anziani,

eldership, *ĕl'dărshĭp,* s. primogenitura, f.; anzianità, f.

elder-tree, *-trē,* s. sambuco, m.

eldest, *ĕl'dĕst,* a. primogenito, maggiornato.

elect, *ĕlĕkt',* v. a. eleggere, scegliere; **-,** a. eletto, scelto.

election, *ĕlĕk'shŭn,* s. elezione, scelta, f.

electioneering, *-shănēr'ĭng,* s. broglio nell' elezione dei membri del Parlamento, m. [eleggere; **-ly,** ad. per elezione.

elective, *ĕlĕk'tĭv,* a. elettivo, che si può

elector, *ĕlĕk'tăr,* s. elettore, m.

electoral, *-tărăl,* a. elettorale, di elettore.

electorate, *-tărāt,* s. elettorato, m.

electric(al), *ĕlĕk'trĭk(ăl),* a. elettrico.

electrician, *-trĭsh'ăn,* s. chi si occupa di elettricismo, m.

electricity, *-trĭs'ĭtī,* s. elettricità, f.

electrification, *-fĭkā'shŭn,* s. elettrizzazione, f.

electrify, *ĕlĕk'trĭfī,* v. a. elettrizzare.

electro-gilding, *-trŏ gĭldĭng,* s. doratura galvanica, f. [solvere per l' elettricità.

electrolyze, *-līz,* v. a. scomporre o dissolvere

electuary, *-tŭărī,* s. elettuario, m.

eleemosinary, *ĕlĕmŏz'ĭnărī,* a. che vive d' elemosina. [bellezza, f.

elegance, *ĕl'ĕgăns,* s. eleganza, f.; grazia,

elegant, *ĕl'ĕgănt,* a. elegante; grazioso; **-ly,** ad. elegantemente; con grazia.

elegiac(al), *ĕlĕjī'ăk(ăl),* a. elegiaco, lugubre.

elegy, *ĕl'ĕjī,* s. elegia, f.

element, *ĕl'ĕmĕnt,* s. elemento, m.; principio, fondamento, m.

elemental, *ĕlĕmĕn'tăl,* **elementary,** *-tărī,* a. elementario.

elephant, *ĕl'ĕfănt,* s. elefante, m.

elephantine, *-făn'tīn,* a. elefantino, elefantesco. [inalzare; rallegrare.

elevate, *ĕl'ĕvāt,* v. a. elevare; esaltare,

elevation, *-vā'shŭn,* s. elevamento, m.; esaltazione, f.; sublimità, f.

eleven, *ĕlĕv'n,* a. undici. [simo.

eleventh, *ĕlĕv'nth,* a. undecimo, undice-

elf, *ĕlf,* s. spirito folletto, m.; **-,** v. a. arruffare. [tato.

elfin, *ĕl'fĭn,* a. di spirito folletto; incan-

eligibility, *ĕlĭjĭbĭl'ĭtī,* s. eligibilità, capacità d' essere eletto, f.

eligible, *ĕl'ĭjĭbl,* a. eligibile; preferibile.

eliminate, *ĕlĭm'ĭnāt,* v. a. rilegare, esiliare.

elk, *ĕlk,* s. alce, m.

ell, *ĕl,* s. auna, f.; canna, f.

ellipsis, *ĕllĭp'sĭs,* s. elisse, elissi, f.

elliptic(al), *-tĭk(ăl),* a. elittico, d' elissi.

elm(-tree), *ĕlm(trē),* s. olmo, m.

elocution, *ĕlŏkū'shŭn,* s. elocuzione, f.; facondia, f. [zione, m.

elocutionist, *-ĭst,* s. professore di elocu-

elongate, *ĕlŏng'gāt,* v. a. allungare, prolungare; stendere; **-,** v. n. allungarsi, allontanarsi; stendersi. [varsi.

elope, *ĕlŏp',* v. n. scappare, fuggire; sal-

elopement, *-mĕnt,* s. scappata, f.; fuga, f.

eloquence, *ĕl'ŏkwĕns,* s. eloquenza, f.

eloquent, *ĕl'ŏkwĕnt,* a. eloquente; **-ly,** ad. eloquentemente.

else, *ĕls,* pn. altro; oltre; altrove; **-,** ad. altrimente, altramente. [luogo.

elsewhere, *ĕls'hwăr,* ad. altrove, in altro

elucidate, *ĕlŏ'sĭdāt,* v. a. dichiarare; manifestare.

elucidation, *-dā'shŭn,* s. dichiarazione, esposizione, spiegazione, f.

elude, *ĕlŏd',* v. a. eludere, schifare; scansare, sfuggire. [m., fraude, f.

elusion, *ĕlŏ'zhŭn,* s. elusione, f.; artificio,

elusive, *-sĭv,* **elusory,** *-sărī,* a. che elude; ingannevole.

emaciate, ĕmăsh'ĭăt, v. a. estenuare; indebolire; —, v. n. dimagrare.

emaciation, -ăsh'shăn, s. emaciazione, f.

emanate, ĕm'ănăt, v. a. emanare.

emanation, -nă'shăn, s. emanazione, f.; origine, f. [affrancare.

emancipate, ĕmăn'sĭpăt, v. a. emancipare;

emancipation, -pă'shăn, s. emancipazione, f.

embalm, ĕmbäm', v. a. imbalsamare.

embank, -băngk', v. a. interrare. [m.

embankment, -mĕnt, s. (rail.) terrapieno,

embargo, -bär'gō, s. serramento del porto, embargo, m.

embarcation, -kă'shăn, embarkment, -bärk'mĕnt, s. imbarcamento, imbarco, m.

embarrass, -băr'răs, v. a. imbarazzare, imbrogliare. [broglio, m.

embarrassment, -mĕnt, s. imbarazzo, imbroglio, m.

embassy, ĕm'băssĭ, s. ambasceria, ambasciata, legazione, f.

embattle, -băt'l, v. a. metter in battaglia.

embellish, -bĕl'lĭsh, v. a. abbellire, addobbare. [m.

embellishment, -mĕnt, s. abbellimento,

Ember-days, ĕm'bŭr dăz, s. pl. Quattro Tempora, f. pl.

embers, ĕm'bŭrz, s. pl. ceneri calde, f. pl.

Ember-week, ĕm'bŭr wĕk, s. settimana delle quattro tempora, f.

embezzle, -bĕz'l, v. a. guastare, corrompere; appropriarsi.

embezzlement, -mĕnt, s. malversazione, f.

embitter, -bĭt'tŭr, v. a. far amare; (fig.) amareggiare.

emblazon, -blă'zn, v. a. blasonare.

emblem, ĕm'blĕm, s. emblema, simbolo, m.

emblematic(al), -mät'ĭk(ăl), a. emblematico, figurativo. [mento, m.

embodiment, -bŏd'ĭmĕnt, s. incorporamento, m.

embody, -bŏd'ĭ, v. a. incorporare.

embolden, -bŏl'dn, v. a. incoraggiare, animare. [tagliare.

emboss, -bŏs', v. a. fare di rilievo, in-

embrace, -brăs', v. a. abbracciare; comprendere. [tura, f.

embrasure, -brä'shŭr, s. cannoniera, apertura, f.

embrocation, -brōkă'shăn, s. embroca, docciatura, f.

embroidery, -brŏĭdŭrĭ, s. ricamo, m.

embroil, -brŏĭl', v. a. imbrogliare, confondere. [m.

embryo, ĕm'brĭō, s. embrione, m.; abbozzo,

emendation, ĕmĕndă'shăn, s. emenda, correzione, f.

emerald, ĕm'ĕrăld, s. smeraldo, m.

emerge, ĕmŭrj', v. n. emergere; levarsi.

emergency, ĕmŭr'jĕnsĭ, s. emergenza, f.; accidente, m., occorrenza, f.

emery, ĕm'ŭrĭ, s. smeriglio, m.

emetic, ĕmĕt'ĭk, s. emetico, m.

emigrant, ĕm'ĭgrănt, s. emigrante, m.; emigrato, m.

emigrate, ĕm'ĭgrăt, v. n. emigrare.

emigration, -gră'shăn, s. emigrazione, f.

eminence, ĕm'ĭnĕns, s. eminenza, eccellenza, celebrità, f.

eminent, ĕm'ĭnĕnt, a. eminente; alto; celebre, famoso; -ly, ad. eminentemente.

emissary, ĕm'ĭssărĭ, s. emissario, m.; spia, f.

emission, ĕmĭsh'ăn, s. emissione, f.

emit, ĕmĭt', v. a. mandare fuora; rilasciare; scaricare; svaporare.

emmet, ĕm'mĕt, s. formica, f.

emollient, ĕmŏl'lĭĕnt, a. lenitivo; —, s. medicina emolliente, f.

emolument, ĕmŏl'ŭmĕnt, s. emolumento, profitto, vantaggio, m. [zione, f.

emotion, ĕmŏ'shăn, s. emozione, agitazione, f.

emotional, -năl, a. commovente, affettivo.

emperor, ĕm'pŭrŭr, s. imperadore, m.

emphasis, ĕm'făsĭs, s. enfasi, energia, f. con enfasi; accentuare.

emphasise, ĕm'făsĭz, v. a. pronunziare con enfasi; accentuare.

emphatic(al), -făt'ĭk(ăl), a. enfatico, energico; -ally, ad. con enfasi.

empire, ĕm'pĭr, s. impero, m.

empirical, -pĭr'ĭkăl, a. empirico; ciarlatanesco; -ly, ad. in modo empirico.

empiricism, -pĭr'ĭsĭzm, s. empirismo, m.

employ, ĕmplŏĭ', s. impiego, uffizio, m.; occupazione, f.; —, v. a. impiegare, mettere in uso; occupare. [commettente, m.

employer, -ŭr, s. che impiega, m.; (com.)

employment, -mĕnt, s. impiego, uffizio, m.; funzione, f.; occupazione, f.

emporium, -pŏ'rĭŭm, s. mercato grande, m.; piazza mercantile, f. [potere.

empower, -pŏw'ŭr, v. a. autorizzare, dar

empress, ĕm'prĕs, s. imperatrice, f.

emptiness, ĕm'tĭnĕs, s. vuoto, vacuo, m.; incapacità, f.; ignoranza, f.

empty, ĕm'tĭ, a. vacuo; vano, ignorante; —, v. a. vuotare, evacuare.

empyrean, -pĭrē'ăn, a. empireo.

emulate, ĕm'ŭlăt, v. a. emulare; imitare; concorrere. [lità, concorrenza, f.

emulation, -lă'shăn, s. emulazione, rivalità, concorrenza, f.

emulgent, ĕmŭl'jĕnt, a. emulgente.

emulous, ĕm'ŭlŭs, a. emulo, rivale; ambizioso; -ly, ad. a gara. [f.

emulsion, ĕmŭl'shăn, s. (med.) emulsione;

enable, ĕnā'bl, v. a. abilitare, rendere abile.

enact, ĕnăkt', v. n. decretare; stabilire.

enactment, -mĕnt, s. decreto, m.; ordinanza, f. [smaltare.

enamel, ĕnăm'ĕl, s. smalto, m.; —, v. a.

enamour, ĕnăm'ŭr, v. a. innamorare, accender d'amore. [nare.

encage, ĕnkăj', v. a. ingabbiare; imprigionare.

encamp, -kămp', v. n. accamparsi. [m.

encampment, -mĕnt, s. accampamento,

encase, -kăs', v. a. incassare.

encaustic, -kăs'tĭk, a. encaustico; — painting, s. encaustica, f.

enchain, -chăn', v. a. incatenare.

enchant, -chănt', v. a. incantare.

enchantingly, -ĭnglĭ, ad. in modo incantevole.

enchantment, -mĕnt, s. incanto, m.

enchantress, -rĕs, s. incantatrice, ammaliatrice, f. [dare, cingere.

encircle, -sŭr'kl, v. a. cerchiare, circon-

enclose, –klōz′, v. a. chiudere, inchiudere; comprendere; circondare.

enclosure, –klō′zhŭr, s. ricinto, m.; circuito, m.; chiuso, m. [m.

encomium, –kō′mĭŭm, s. encomio, elogio, attorniare. [v. a. ridomandare.

encompass, –kŭm′pŭs, v. a. circondare;

encore, ăngkŏr′, ad. ancora, di nuovo; –,

encounter, ĕnkŏŭn′tŭr, s. scontro, conflitto, duello, m., scaramuccia, f.; –, v. a. incontrare; –, v. n. scontrarsi, combattere.

encourage, –kŭr′ĭj, v. a. incoraggiare, animare. [mento, m.

encouragement, –mĕnt, s. incoraggiamento.

encroach, –krŏch′, v. n. usurpare a poco a poco. [a poco, m.

encroachment, –mĕnt, s. l'usurpare a poco

encrust, –krŭst′, v. a. incrostare.

encumber, –kŭm′bŭr, v. a. imbarazzare, impedire; caricare.

encumbrance, –kŭm′brăns, s. imbarazzo, m.; impedimento, m. [lare.

encyclical, –sĭk′lĭkăl, a. enciclico, circolare.

end, ĕnd, s. fine, m.; estremità, f.; disegno, m.; avvenimento, evento, m.; termine, m.; to no –, in vano; to the – that, affinchè; to be at one's wit's –, non saper che fare; on –, ritto; arricciato; –, v. a. finire; –, v. n. cessare.

endanger, –dăn′jŭr, v. a. esporre a pericolo, arrischiare.

endear, –dēr′, v. a. rendere caro.

endearment, –mĕnt, s. tenerezza, f.; affezione, f.

endeavour, –dĕv′ŭr, s. sforzo, m.; –, –, v. a. tentare; –, v. n. sforzarsi, affaticarsi. [carsi.

endemic, –dĕm′ĭk, a. endemico.

ending, ĕnd′ĭng, s. fine, conclusione, f.

endive, ĕn′dĭv, s. indivia, f.

endless, ĕnd′lĕs, a. infinito, perpetuo; –ly, ad. senza fine, perpetuamente.

endorse, –dŏrs′, v. a. indossare.

endorsee, –dŏrsē′, s. portatore, m.

endorsement, –dŏrs′mĕnt, s. girata, f.

endorser, –dŏr′sŭr, s. giratario, m.

endow, –dŏŭ′, v. a. dotare; arricchire.

endowment, –mĕnt, s. dote, f.; dono, m., fondazione, f. [fribile.

endurable, –dŭr′ăbl, a. sopportabile, sofferenza, f.; pa-

endurance, –răns, s. durazione, f.; pacienza, sofferenza, f. [–, v. n. durare.

endure, –dŭr′, v. a. sopportare, soffrire;

endways, ĕnd′wāz, endwise, –wīz, ad. a perpendicolo.

enemy, ĕn′ĕmĭ, s. nemico, avversario, m.

energetic, ĕnărjĕt′ĭk, a. energico, vigoroso; efficace.

energy, ĕn′ărjĭ, s. energia, f.; efficacia, f.

enervate, ĕnŭr′vāt, v. a. snervare.

enfeeble, –fē′bl, v. a. indebolire, debilitare.

enfilade, –fĭlād′, s. (mil.) passaggio stretto, m.; –, v. a. infilare, traversare.

enfold, –fōld′, v. a. involgere; (in one's arms) abbracciare, stringere al seno.

enforce, –fōrs, v. a. assodare; fortificare; invigorire; –, v. n. provare.

enforcement, –mĕnt, s. costringimento, m., violenza, f.; approvazione, sanzione, f.

enfranchise, –frăn′chĭz, v. a. affrancare; naturalizzare.

engage, –gāj′, v. a. impegnare, obbligare; attaccare; indurre; –, v. n. impegnarsi; combattere.

engagement, –mĕnt, s. impegno, m.; obbligo, m.; occupazione, f.; conflitto, combattimento, m. [tivo.

engagingly, –ĭnglĭ, ad. in modo attrat-

engender, –jĕn′dŭr, v. a. generare, produrre; –, v. n. prodursi.

engine, ĕn′jĭn, s. ingegno, m.; macchina, f.; congegno, m.; artificio, stratagemma, m.

engine-driver, –drĭvŭr, s. conduttore di locomotiva, m. [nacchinista, m.

engineer, –jĭnēr′, s. ingegnere, m.; (rail,) engineering, –ĭng, enginery, ĕn′jĭnrĭ, s. artiglieria, f. [pire.

engrave, –grāv′, v. a. ir. intagliare, scolengraver, –grā′vŭr, s. intagliatore, scultore, m.

engraving, –vĭng, s. intaglio, m.

engross, –grōs′, v. a. ingrossare, spessire; incettare.

engulf, –gŭlf′, v. a. ingolfare.

enhance, –hăns′, v. a. alzare il prezzo, rincarare; aumentare; encomiare.

enigma, ĕnĭg′mă, s. enimma, m.

enigmatic(al), –măt′ĭk(ăl), a. enimmatico; –ly, ad. in modo enimmatico.

enjoin, –jŏĭn′, v. a. ingiungere; ordinare, prescrivere.

enjoy, –jŏĭ′, v. a. godere, sentir piacere; possedere; –, v. n. rallegrarsi.

enjoyment, –mĕnt, s. godimento, m., gioia, f.; possesso, m.

enlarge, –lärj′, v. a. distendere, dilatare; aggrandire; liberare; –, v. n. distendersi, dilatarsi.

enlargement, –mĕnt, s. ampliazione, aumentazione, f.; liberamento, m.

enlighten, –lĭ′tn, v. a. schiarire; istruire, insegnare.

enlightenment, –mĕnt, s. lumi, m. pl., dottrina, f.; sapere, m. [per soldato.

enlist, –lĭst′, v. a. & n. arrolare; arrolarsi

enlistment, –mĕnt, s. arrolamento, m.

enliven, –lĭv′n, v. a. animare, avvivare; esilarare.

enmesh, –mĕsh, v. a. accalappiare, irretire.

enmity, ĕn′mĭtĭ, s. inimicizia, f.; odio, m. [tare.

ennoble, –nō′bl, v. a. annobilire, nobilienormity, ĕnŏr′mĭtĭ, s. enormità, f.; atrocità, f.

enormous, –mŭs, a. enorme; –ly, ad. enormemente, eccessivamente.

enough, ĕnŭf′, ad. assai, abbastanza; –, s. sufficienza, bastevolezza, f.

enounce, ĕnŏŭns′, v. a. enunciare.

enquire, ĕnkwīr′, v. a. informarsi, ricercare. [zione, f.

enquiry, –kwī′rĭ, s. questione, investigazione, f.

enrage, –rāj′, v. a. fare arrabbiare; irritare. [cantare.

enrapture, ĕnrăp′tŭr, v. a. rapire, incantare.

enrich, –rĭch′, v. a. arricchire; ornare.

enrichment, –mĕnt, s. arricchimento, m.

enroll, –*rōl'*, v. a. arrolare, registrare.

ensconce, –*skŏns'*, v. a. difendere; proteggere; assicurare. [vare.

enshrine, –*shrīn'*, v. a. incassare; preservare.

ensign, *ĕn'sīn*, s. insegna, bandiera, f., stendardo, m.; segno, m. [segna, m.

ensign-bearer, –*bărŭr*, s. alfiere, insegna, m.

ensigncy, *ĕn'sīnsī*, s. carica d'alfiere, f.

enslave, –*slāv'*, v. a. render schiavo, fare servo, sottomettere.

ensnare, –*snār'*, v. a. prendere colla trappola; sedurre; imbarazzare. [cedere.

ensue, –*sū'*, v. n. provenire, nascere, procedere.

entablature, –*tăb'lătŭr*, s. cornicione, m.

entail, –*tāl'*, s. sostituzione, f.; –, v. a. (jur.) sostituire.

entangle, –*tăng'gl*, v. a. imbarazzare, intralciare; avviluppare. [confusione, f.

entanglement, –*mĕnt*, s. imbarazzo, m.;

enter, *ĕn'tŭr*, v. a. iniziare; ammettere; registrare; –, v. n. andar dentro, entrare; impegnarsi; cominciare, intraprendere.

entering, –*īng*, s. entrata, f. [intentare.

enterprise, –*prīz*, s. impresa, f.

entertain, –*tān'*, v. a. trattenere; intrattenere; ricevere; regalare.

entertainer, –*ŭr*, s. mantenitore, m.; trattenitore, m.

entertainment, –*mĕnt*, s. conversazione, f.; trattenimento, banchetto, divertimento, passatempo, m. [mettere.

enthral, –*thrăl'*, v. a. assoggettare, sottomettere.

enthrone, –*thrōn'*, v. a. esaltare al trono.

enthusiasm, –*thū'zĭăzm*, s. entusiasmo, m.; immaginazione, f.; stravaganza, f.

enthusiast, –*zĭăst*, s. entusiaste, m.

enthusiastic(al), –*ăs'tĭk(ăl)*, a. entusiastico; –ally, ad. con entusiasmo.

entice, –*tīs'*, v. a. allettare, adescare; indurre, instigare.

enticement, –*mĕnt*, s. allettamento, adescamento, m.; incitamento, istigamento, m.

entire, –*tīr'*, a. intero, compiuto, perfetto; fermo, solido; –ly, ad. interamente, affatto.

entireness, –*nĕs*, entirety, –*tī*, s. interezza, f.; integrità, totalità, f.

entitle, –*tī'tl*, v. a. intitolare; dare diritto.

entity, *ĕn'tĭtī*, s. entità, f.

entomb, –*tōm'*, v. a. mettere nel sepolcro, seppellire. [logo, m.

entomologist, –*tŏmŏl'ŏjĕst*, s. entomologo.

entomology, –*ŏjī*, s. entomologia, f.

entrails, *ĕn'trālz*, s. pl. intestini, m. pl., viscere, f. pl.

entrance, *ĕn'trăns*, s. entrata, f.; ammissione, f.; accesso, m.; cominciamento, m.; l'esordire, m.

entrance-hall, –*hăl*, s. vestibolo, m.

entrance-money, –*mŭnī*, s. entrata, f.

entrap, –*trăp'*, v. a. irretire, ingannare, truffare. [rare.

entreat, –*trēt'*, v. a. supplicare, scongiurare.

entreaty, –*trē'tī*, s. sollecitamento, m., preghiera, f.; supplica, f.; istanza, f.

entrust, –*trŭst'*, v. a. confidare; affidare.

entry, *ĕn'trī*, s. entrata, f., passaggio, m.; introito, m.; accesso (al possesso), m.; registratura, f. [viluppare.

entwine, –*wīn'*, v. a. intrecciare, avviluppare.

enumerate, *ĕnū'mĕrăt*, v. a. enumerare.

enumeration, –*rā'shŭn*, s. enumerazione, f., novero, m. [dichiarare.

enunciate, *ĕnŭn'sĭăt*, v. a. enunciare.

enunciation, –*sĭā'shŭn*, s. enunciazione, f. [volgere.

envelope, *ĕnvĕl'ŏp*, v. a. inviluppare, involvere.

envelope, *ĕn'vĕlŏp*, s. coperta, f., involto, m. [attossicare.

envenom, –*vĕn'ŏm*, v. a. avvelenare.

enviable, *ĕn'vĭăbl*, a. invidiabile.

envious, *ĕn'vĭŭs*, a. invidioso; –ly, ad. con invidia. [vicinanze, f. pl.

environs, –*vī'rŏnz*, s.pl. contorni, m. pl., vicinanze, f. pl.

envoy, *ĕn'vŏī*, s. inviato, delegato, m.

envy, *ĕn'vī*, s. invidia, f.; rivalità, f.; –, v. a. invidiare.

epaulet, *ĕp'ălĕt*, s. spalletta, f.

ephemeral, *ĕfĕm'ĕrăl*, a. effimero, d'un giorno.

epic, *ĕp'ĭk*, a. epico, eroico. [giorno.

epicure, *ĕp'ĭkŭr*, s. epicureo, m.

epicurean, –*kŭrē'ăn*, a. epicureo.

epidemic, *ĕpĭdĕm'ĭk*, s. epidemia, f.; –, a. epidemico.

epigram, *ĕp'ĭgrăm*, s. epigramma, m.

epigrammatic, –*măt'ĭk*, a. epigrammatico. [duco, m.

epilepsy, *ĕp'ĭlĕpsī*, s. epilessia, f., mal caduco, m.

epileptic, –*lĕp'tĭk*, a. epilettico.

epilogue, *ĕp'ĭlŏg*, s. epilogo, m.

Epiphany, *ĕpĭf'ănī*, s. Epifania, f.

episcopacy, *ĕpĭs'kŏpăsī*, s. episcopato, vescovado, m.

episcopal, –*kŏpăl*, a. episcopale.

episode, *ĕp'ĭsŏd*, s. episodio, m.

epistle, *ĕpĭs'l*, s. epistola, lettera, f.

epistolary, –*tŏlărī*, a. epistolare.

epitaph, *ĕp'ĭtăf*, s. epitaffio, m.

epithet, *ĕp'ĭthĕt*, s. epiteto, m.

epitome, *ĕpĭt'ŏmē*, s. epitome, m.; sommario, m. [breviare.

epitomize, –*tŏmīz*, v. a. epitomare, abbreviare.

epoch, *ĕp'ŏk*, s. epoca, era, f.

equable, *ĕk'wăbl*, a. equabile.

equal, *ē'kwŏl*, s. uguale, m.; simigliante, m.; compagno, m.; –, a. uguale, pari; uniforme; simile, simigliante; imparziale; –, v. a. agguagliare; compensare; corrispondere.

equalisation, –*īză'shŭn*, s. agguagliamento, m. [uguale; aggiustare.

equalize, *ē'kwŏlīz*, v. a. agguagliare, far uguale; aggiustare.

equality, *ēkwŏl'ĭtī*, s. egualità, parità, f.; uniformità, f.

equally, *ē'kwŏlī*, ad. ugualmente.

equanimity, *ēkwănĭm'ĭtī*, s. equanimità, tranquillità d'animo, f.; moderazione, f.

equation, *ēkwā'shŭn*, s. aggiustamento, m.

equator, –*tŭr*, s. equatore, m.

equatorial, *ēkwătō'rĭăl*, a. equatoriale.

equerry, *ĕk'wĕrī*, s. scudiere d'un principe, m.

equestrian, ĕkwĕs'trĭăn, a. equestre, di
cavaliere; – performer, s. voltegiattore
a cavallo, m.

equilateral, ĕkwĭlăt'ărăl, a. equilatero.

equilibrist, ĕkwĭlĭb'rĭst, s. chi sta in
equilibrio, m.; fattucchiero, m. [m.

equilibrium, ĕkwĭlĭb'rĭăm. s. equilibrio,

equine, ĕ'kwĭn, a. equino, cavallino.

equinoctial, ĕkwĭnŏk'shăl, a. equinoziale.

equinox, ĕ'kwĭnŏks, s. equinozio, m.

equip, ĕkwĭp', v. a. fornire; apparecchiare;
(mar.) equipaggiare.

equipage, ĕk'wĭpăj, s. fornimento, apparecchio, m.; equipaggio, m.; arnese, m.;
vassoio, m.

equipment, ĕkwĭp'mĕnt, s. armamento,
m.; acconciamento, m.; equipaggiamento,
m. [trappeso, m.

equipoise, ĕ'kwĭpŏĭz, s. equilibrio, con-

equitable, ĕk'wĭtăbl, a. equo, ragionevole.

equitably, –tăblĭ, ad. con equità, guista-
mente. [giustizia, f.

equity, ĕk'wĭtĭ, s. equità, imparzialità,

equivalence, ĕkwĭv'ălĕns, s. equivalenza,
f. [valore uguale; –, s. equivalente, m.

equivalent, –lĕnt, a. equivalente, di

equivocal, –ŏkăl, a. equivoco, ambiguo;
dubbio; –ly, ad. equivocamente; dub-
biamente.

equivocate, –ŏkăt, v. a. equivocare.

equivocation, –kā'shŭn, s. equivocazione,

era, ĕ'ră, s. era, epoca, f. [f.

eradicate, ĕrăd'ĭkăt, v. a. sradicare;
estirpare; sbarbare. [estirpamento, m.

eradication, –kā'shŭn, s. sradicare, m.;

erase, ĕrās', v. a. raschiare. cancellare.

eraser, ĕră'săr, s. raschiatoio, m.

erasure, ĕră'shŭr, cancellatura, f.

ere, ăr, ad. prima, prima che, più tosto,
anziche. [–, v. a. ergere, inalzare.

erect, ĕrĕkt', a. eretto, inalzato; dritto;

erection, ĕrĕk'shŭn, s. stabilimento, m.;
struttura, f.

ermine, ăr'mĭn, s. ermellino, m.

erotic, ĕrŏt'ĭk, a. erotico, amoroso.

err, ăr, v. n. errare, traviare; ingannarsi.

errand, ĕr'rănd, s. messaggio, m.; ambasciata, f.

errand-boy, –bŏĭ, s. servitorino, servito-
rello, m.; messaggiere, m.

errant, ĕr'rănt, a. errante; vagabondo.

errantry, –rĭ, s. il vagare, m.

errata, ĕrră'tă, s. pl. errori di stampa, m. pl.

erratic, –răt'ĭk, a. erratico, errante;
irregolare.

erring, ăr'rĭng, s. traviamento, m.

erroneous, –rō'nĭăs, a. erroneo, falso;
–ly, ad. erroneamente, con errore.

error, ĕr'rŭr, s. errore, traviamento, m.;
sbaglio, m.; mancamento, m.

eructation, ĕrăkt'ăshŭn, s. eruttazione. f.

erudite, ĕr'ŭdĭt, a. erudito.

erudition, –dĭsh'ŭn, s. erudizione. f., ammaestramento, m.; dottrina. f.

eruption, ĕrŭp'shŭn, s. eruzione, f.; sortita impetuosa, f. [f.

erysipelas, ĕrĭsĭp'ĕlăs, s. (med.) risipola,

escalade, ĕskălād', v. a. scalare, dar la
scalata.

escape, ĕskāp', s. fuga, f., scampo, m.;
errore, sbaglio, m.; –, v. a. evitare;
schivare: –, v. n. scampare, fuggire.

escarpment, –kărp'mĕnt, s. scarpa, f.,
pendio, m., china, f.

eschalot, ĕshălŏt', s. cipollina. f.

escheat, ĕschĕt', s. profitto casuale, m.;
diritto, m.; –, v. n. scadere in diritto.

eschew, ĕschŏ', v. a. evitare; sfuggire.

escort, ĕs'kŏrt, s. scorta, guida, f., convoglio, m.; –, ĕskŏrt', v. a. scortare, accompagnare, convioare. [fnaio, m.

escritoire, ĕskrĭt'wăr, s. scrittoio, cala-

esculent, ĕs'kŭlĕnt, a. esculento, mange-
reccio; –, s. alimento, m.

escutcheon, kăch'ăn, s. scudo, m.; arme,
insegne, f. pl.

especial, –pĕsh'ăl, a. speciale.

especially, –ălĭ, ad. specialmente; principalmente.

espial, –pĭ'ăl, espionage, ĕs'pĭŏnăj, s.
spia, f.; scoperta, f.; spiagone, f.

esplanade, –plănăd', s. spianata, f.

espousals, –pŏw'zălz, s. pl. sposalizia, f.,
sposamento, m.

espouse, –pŏw'z', v. a. sposare; difendere.

espy, ĕspĭ', v. a. spiare; osservare, scoprire.

esquire, –kwĭr', s. scudiere, m.; (on
letters) signore, m.

essay, ĕs'să, s. sperimento, saggio, m.,
prova, f.; –, ĕssă', v. a. tentare, assaggiare. [m.

essence, ĕs'sĕns, s. essenza, f.; profumo,

essential, –sĕn'shăl, a. essenziale, principale; –, s. essenziale, m.

essentially, –lĭ, ad. essenzialmente.

establish, –tăb'lĭsh, v. a. stabilire, fermare, fissare; fondare.

establishment, –mĕnt, s. stabilimento,
fondamento, istituto, m.; approvazione,
f.; modello, m.

estate, ĕstăt', s. stato, m.; condizione, f.;
fortuna, f., beni, m. pl.

esteem, ĕstĕm', s. stima, considerazione,
f.; conto, m.; –, v. a. stimare, apprezzare; pensare. [s. pl. estetica, f.

esthetic(al), –thĕt'ĭk(ăl), a. estetico: –s,

estimable, ĕs'tĭmăbl, a. stimabile, apprezzabile. [zare; valutare.

estimate, –tĭmăt, v. a. stimare, apprez-

estimation, –mā'shŭn, s. estimazione,
stima; opinione, f.; conto, m.

estrange, ĕstrănj', v. a. alienare; allontanare: dissudare.

estrangement, –mĕnt, s. alienazione,
f.; separazione, f.; distanza, f.

estuary, ĕs'tŭărĭ, s. braccio (di mare), m.,
bocca, f.; bagno a vapore, m.

etch, ĕch, v. a. incidere con acqua forte.

etching, –ĭng, s. intaglio con acqua forte,
m. [ad. in eterno.

eternal, ĕtăr'năl, a. eterno, perpetuo; –ly,

eternity, –nĭtĭ, s. eternità, perpetuità, f.

eternize, –nĭz, v. a. eternare.

ether, ĕ'thăr, s. aria, f.; cielo, etere, m.

ethereal, *ĕthĕ'rĭăl,* a. etereo, dell' etere, celeste.

ethic(al), *ĕth'ĭk(ăl),* a. etico, morale, **-ly,** ad. eticamente, moralmente; **-s,** s. pl. etica, f.

etymological, *ĕtĭmŏlŏj'ĭkăl,* a. etimologico.

etymology, *-mŏl'ŏjĭ,* s. etimologia, f.

Eucharist, *ū'kărĭst,* s. Eucaristia, f.

eulogize, *ū'lŏjĭz,* v. a. lodare, encomiare.

eulogy, *ū'lŏjĭ,* s. elogio, m., lode, f.

eunuch, *ū'nŭk,* s. eunuco, m.

euphemism, *ū'fĕmĭzm,* s. eufemismo, m.

euphonic, *ūfŏn'ĭk,* a. eufonico, armonioso.

euphony, *ū'fŏnĭ,* s. eufonia, f.

evacuate, *ĕvăk'ŭăt,* v. a. evacuare.

evacuation, *-ā'shŭn,* s. evacuazione, f., evacuamento, m.   [—, v. n. evadere.

evade, *ĕvād',* v. a. scampare, scappare; fugitivo.   [-ly, ad. evangelicamente.

evanescent, *ĕvănĕs'ĕnt,* a. che svanisce,

evangelic(al), *ĕvănjĕl'ĭk(ăl),* a. evangelico;

evangelist, *ĕvăn'jĕlĭst,* s. evangelista, m.

evaporate, *ĕvăp'ŏrăt,* v. a. svaporare; dissipare; —, v. n. evaporare; dissiparsi.

evaporation, *-rā'shŭn,* s. evaporazione, f.

evasion, *ĕvā'zhŭn,* s. scappata, f.; sotterfugio, pretesto, m.   [camente.

evasive, *-sĭv,* a. evasivo; **-ly,** ad. sofisti-

eve, *ĕv,* s. vigilia, f.; sera, f.

even, *ĕ'vn,* a. uguale, pari, simile; uniforme; —, ad. anche, anzi, ancora; quasi; fino, infino; **- as,** come, come se; **- now,** or' ora; **- on,** dirittamente; **- so,** giusto così; —, v. a. appianare, agguagliare.

even-handed, *-hăndĕd,* a. imparziale; equo, retto.

evening, *ĕv'nĭng,* s. sera, serata, f.

evenly, *-lĭ,* ad. ugualmente, uniformemente.   [imparzialità, f.; livello, m.

evenness, *-nĕs,* s. ugualità, uniformità, f.;

event, *ĕvĕnt',* s. evento, avvenimento, m.; esito, m.

eventful, *-fŭl,* a. pieno d'avvenimenti.

eventual, *ĕvĕn'tŭăl,* a. eventuale, casuale, fortuito; **-ly,** ad. eventualmente.

eventuality, *-tŭăl'ĭtĭ,* s. eventualità, f.

ever, *ĕv'ăr,* ad. sempre, sempremai, tuttavia; **for - (and -),** per sempre, eternamente; **- and anon,** di quando in quando.

evergreen, *-grēn,* a. sempreverde; —, s. sempreviva, barba di Giove, f.   [nità, f.

everlasting, *-lăs'tĭng,* a. eterno; —, s. eter-

evermore, *-mōr',* ad. sempre; eternamente.

every, *ĕv'ărĭ,* a. ogni, ciascheduno; **- one,** **-body,** ciascuno, ognuno; **-where,** da per tutto; **-thing,** ogni cosa.

evict, *ĕvĭkt',* v. a. spossessare.

eviction, *ĕvĭk'shŭn,* s. evizione, f.

evidence, *ĕv'ĭdĕns,* s. evidenza, f.; prova, f.; testimonio, m.; —, v. a. provare, mostrare.

evident, *-ĭdĕnt,* a. evidente, manifesto, chiaro; **-ly,** ad. evidentemente.

evil, *ĕ'vĭ,* a. cattivo, malo, perverso; —, ad. male; —, s. male, m.; malvagità, f.; calamità, f.

evil-doer, *-dŏ'ăr,* s. malfattore, m.

evilly, *ĕ'vĭlĭ,* ad. male, malamente.

evil-minded, *-mĭndĕd,* a. maldisposto, malizioso, maligno.   [calunnia, f.

evil-speaking, *-spēkĭng,* s. maldicenza,

evince, *ĕvĭns',* v. a. convincere; provare; dimostrare.   [m.

evocation, *ĕvŏkā'shŭn,* s. songiuramento,

evoke, *ĕvŏk',* v. a. evocare.

evolution, *ĕvŏlū'shŭn,* s. sviluppo, m.; rivolgimento, m.; (mil.) evoluzione, f.

evolve, *ĕvŏlv',* v. a. & n. sviluppare; sviewe, *ŭ, s.* pecora, f.   [lupparsi.

ewer, *ū'ăr,* s. mesciroba, f.   [inasprire.

exacerbate, *ĕgzăsăr'băt,* v. a. esacerbare,

exact, *ĕgzăkt',* a. esatto, puntuale; diligente; giusto; —, v. a. esigere; strappare.

exaction, *-ăk'shŭn,* s. esazione, f.

exactly, *-ăkt'lĭ,* ad. esattamente, accuratamente.   [lità, f.

exactness, *-nĕs,* s. esattezza, f.; puntua-

exaggerate, *-ăj'ărăt,* v. a. esagerare, amplificare.   [amplificazione, f.

exaggeration, *-rā'shŭn,* s. esagerazione, f.

exalt, *ĕgzălt',* v. a. esaltare, alzare; lodare, vantare.   [elevamento, m.

exaltation, *-ā'shŭn,* s. esaltazione, f.;

examination, *ĕgzămĭnā'shŭn,* s. esame, m.

examine, *ĕgzăm'ĭn,* v. a. esaminare, interrogare; pesare, considerare; discutere.

example, *ĕgzăm'pl,* s. esempio, m.; esemplare, m.; modello, m.; **for -,** per esempio.

exasperate, *-ăs'părăt,* v. a. esasperare; irritare, provocare.   [f., irritamento, m.

exasperation, *-rā'shŭn,* s. esasperazione, f.

excavate, *ĕks'kăvăt,* v. a. scavare, cavare.

excavation, *-vā'shŭn,* s. scavamento, m.; cavità, f.; (rail.) intaglio, m., trincea, f.

exceed, *ĕksēd',* v. a. eccedere; trapassare, superare; —, v. n. oltrepassare; uscir del convenevole.

exceeding, *-ĭng,* a. eccessivo; **-ly,** ad. eccessivamente; perfettamente.

excel, *ĕksĕl',* v. a. eccellere, sorpassare.

excellence, *ĕk'sĕlĕns,* s. eccellenza, eccellenzia, preeminenza, superiorità, f.

excellent, *-sĕllĕnt,* a. **-ly,** a. eccellente (mente).

except, *ĕksĕpt',* v. a. eccettuare, escludere; —, v. n. ricusare; **-(ing),** pr. eccetto, fuorchè.   [esclusione, f.

exception, *-sĕp'shŭn,* s. eccezione, f.;

exceptionable, *-ăbl,* a. che si può obiettare; a cui si può dare eccezione.

exceptional, *-ăl,* a. **-ly,** ad. eccezionale; in via d'eccezione.

excerpt, *ĕksŭrpt',* v. a. scegliere.   [f.

excess, *ĕksĕs',* s. eccesso, m.; intemperanza,

excessive, *-sĭv,* a. eccessivo; **-ly,** ad. eccessivamente.

exchange, *-chănj',* s. cambio, m.; baratto, m.; borsa, f.; —, v. a. cambiare, barattare; permutare.   [biare.

exchangeable, *-ăbl,* a. che si può cam-

exchange-office, *-ŏffĭs,* s. banco, m.

exchequer, *-chĕk'ăr,* s. erario, tesoro pubblico, m.   [dello Stato, m.

exchequer-bill, *-bĭl,* s. buono di cassa

excise, *ĕksĭz',* s. assisa, f.   [m.

exciseman, *-măn,* s. uffiziale delle assise,

excitability, *ĕksĭtăbĭl'ĭtĭ*, s. eccitabilità, f.
excitable, *-sĭt'ăbl*, a. facile ad esser ec-
citato, irritabile.
excite, *-sīt'*, v. a. eccitare, stimolare.
excitement,*-mĕnt*,s.eccitamento,stimolo,
m. [ad alta voce.
exclaim, *-klām'*, v. n. esclamare; gridare
exclamation, *-klămă'shŭn*, s. esclamazione, f., esclamare, m. [tuare.
exclude, *-klōd'*, v. a. escludere; eccet-
exclusion, *-klō'shŭn*, s. esclusione, esclu-
siva, f.; eccezione, f. [esclusivamente.
exclusive, *-sĭv*, a. esclusivo; *-ly*, ad.
excommunicate, *-kŏmmū'nĭkāt*, v. a.
scommunicare. [munica, f.
excommunication, *-kā'shŭn*, s. sco-
excoriation, *-kōrĭā'shŭn*, s. escoriazione, scalfittura, f.
excrement, *ĕks'krĕmĕnt*, s. escremento, m.
excrescence, *-krĕs'ĕns*, s. escrescenza, f.;
tumore, m.
excruciating, *-krō'shĭāiĭng*, a. atroce.
exculpate, *-kŭl'pāt*, v. a. scolpare, scusare, giustificare. [giustificazione, f.
exculpation, *-pā'shŭn*, s. discolpa, f.;
exculpatory, *-kŭl'pătŭrĭ*, a. scusante,
giustificante. [digressione, f.
excursion, *-kŭr'shŭn*, s. sviamento, m.,
excursionist, *-ĭst*, s. chi fa escursioni, m.
excusable, *-kū'zăbl*, a. scusabile.
excuse, *-kūz'*, s. scusa, f.; *-*, v. a. scusare,
scolpare.
execrable, *ĕks'ĕkrăbl*, a. esecrabile.
execrably, *-blĭ*, ad. esecrabilmente.
execrate, *ĕks'ĕkrāt*, v. a. esecrare, detestare. [maledizione, f.
execration, *-krā'shŭn*, s. esecrazione,
execute, *ĕks'ĕkūt*, v. a. eseguire, effettuare;
esercitare; giustiziare (un malfattore).
execution, *-kū'shŭn*, s. esecuzione, f.;
sequestro, m.
executioner, *-ĕr*, s. carnefice, m.
executive, *ĕgzĕk'ūtĭv*, a. esecutivo.
executor, *ĕgzĕk'ūtŭr*, s. esecutore testamentario, m. [taria, f.
executrix, *-ūtrĭks*, s. esecutrice testamen-
exemplary, *ĕg'zĕmplărĭ*, a. esemplare.
exemplification, *-plĭfĭkā'shŭn*, s. esemplificazione, f.; copia, f.
exemplify, *ĕgzĕm'plĭfī*, v. a. esemplificare; provare con esempi.
exempt, *ĕgzĕmpt'*, a. esente, privilegiato.
exemption, *-ĕm'shŭn*, s. esenzione, f.;
privilegio, m.
exercise, *ĕks'ĕrsīz*, s. esercizio, m.; travaglio, lavoro, m.; tema, m.; *-*, v. a. esercitare; practicare; *-*, v. n. esercitarsi;
applicarsi, |self, adoprarsi, sforzarsi.
exert, *ĕgzŭrt'*, v. a. impiegare; to *- one's*
exertion, *-ŭr'shŭn*, s. adoperamento, m.;
sforzo, m.; potere, m.
exfoliate, *ĕksfō'lĭāt*, v. n. sfaldarsi.
exfoliation, *-ā'shŭn*, s. sfaldatura, f.
exhalation, *ĕkzhălā'shŭn*, s. esalazione, f.,
evaporamento, m.; vapore, m.
exhale, *ĕgzhāl'*, v. a. esalare, evaporare.
exhaust, *-hāst'*, v. a. esaurire; rasciugare.
exhaustion, *-yŭn*, s. disseccamento, m.

exhaustive, *-ĭv*, a. che esaurisce, esau-
riente. [produrre.
exhibit, *-hĭb'ĭt*, v. a. esibire; mostrare,
exhibition, *ĕkzhĭbĭsh'ŭn*, s. esibizione, f.;
presentazione, f.; borsa, f.
exhibitioner, *-ĕr*, s. borsaio, m.
exhibitor, *ĕgzhĭb'ĭtŭr*, s. esponente, m.
exhilarate, *-hĭl'ărāt*, v. a. rallegrare,
rasserenare; divertire.
exhilaration, *-rā'shŭn*, s. gioia, allegrezza, giocondità, f.; piacere, m.
exhort, *-hŏrt'*, v. a. esortare; incitare.
exhortation, *-tā'shŭn*, s. esortazione, f.
exhumation, *ĕkshūmā'shŭn*, s. esuma-
zione, f. [lire.
exhume, *-hūm'*, v. a. esumare, disseppel-
exigency, *ĕks'ĭjĕnsĭ*, s. esigenza, necessità,
f., bisogno, m.
exile, *ĕg'zīl*, s. esilio, sbandeggiamento,
m.; *-*, v. a. esiliare, sbandeggiare.
exist, *ĕgzĭst'*, v. n. esistere, essere.
existence, *-tĕns*, s. esistenza, f.
existent, *-tĕnt*, a. esistente.
existing, *-tĭng*, a. attuale, reale.
exit, *ĕks'ĭt*, s. esito, m., uscita, f.; partita, f.
exonerate, *ĕgzŏn'ĕrāt*, v. a. sgravare,
discaricare. [m.
exoneration, *-rā'shŭn*, s. scaricamento,
exorbitance, *-ŏr'bĭtăns*, s. esorbitanza,
enormità, f. [cessivo.
exorbitant, *-bĭtănt*, a. esorbitante, ec-
exorcise, *ĕks'ŏrsīz*, v. a. esorcizzare, scongiurare.
exorcism, *-ŏrsĭzm*, s. esorcismo, m.
exordium, *ĕgzŏr'dĭŭm*, s. esordio, m.;
prologo, m. [pianta esotica, f.
exotic, *ĕgzŏt'ĭk*, a. esotico, straniero; *-*, s.
expand, *ĕkspănd'*, v. a. spandere. [f.
expanse, *-păns'*, s. espansione, estensione.
expansion, *-păn'shŭn*, f. espansione, f.
expansive, *-sĭv*, a. espansivo.
expatiate, *-pā'shĭāt*, v. n. distendersi.
expatriate, *-pā'trĭāt*, v. a. spatriare.
expect, *-pĕkt'*, v. a. aspettare, attendere;
sperare. [s. aspettazione, f.; speranza, f.
expectance, *-tăns*, expectancy, *-tănsĭ*,
expectant, *-tănt*, s. aspettatore, m.
expectation, *-tā'shŭn*, s. aspettazione,
aspettativa, speranza, f. [espurgare.
expectorate, *-pĕk'tŏrāt*, v. a. espettorare,
expectoration, *-rā'shŭn*, s. espettora-
zione, f.
expediency, *-pē'dĭĕnsĭ*, s. convenevolezza,
convenienza, f.; proprietà, f.; spedizione, f.
expedient, *-dĭĕnt*, a. convenevole; utile;
-, s. espediente, m.; mezzo, m.; *-ly*, ad.
convenevolmente.
expedite, *ĕks'pĕdīt*, v. a. spedire, accelerare.
expedition, *-dĭsh'ŭn*, s. spedizione, f.;
prestezza, fretta, f.
expeditious, *-dĭsh'ŭs*, a. speditivo,
pronto; *-ly*, ad. affrettatamente.
expel, *-pĕl'*, v. a. espellere, scacciare.
expend, *-pĕnd'*, v. a. spendere, sborsare.
expenditure, *-dĭtŭr*, s. spesa, f., costo, m.
expense, *-pĕns'*, s. spesa, f.; sborso, sbor-
samento, m.

expensive,' *-siv*, a. dispendioso, prodigo; **-ly**, ad. dispendiosamente, con grande spesa.

experience, *-pe'riĕns*, s. esperienza, f.; cognizione, f.; practica, usanza, f.; **-**, v. a. sperimentare, provare.

experiment, *-pĕr'ĕmĕnt*, s. esperimento, m., prova, f.; **-**, v. a. sperimentare, provare.

experimental, *-mĕn'tăl*, a. sperimentale; **-ly**, ad. sperimentalmente.

expert, *-pŭrt'*, a. esperto, sperimentato, versato, pratico; **-ly**, ad. espertamente.

expertness, *-nĕs*, s. abilità, destrezza, f.

expiate, *ĕks'pĭăt*, v. a. espiare; riparare.

expiation, *-pĭ'shăn*, s. espiazione, f.; riparazione, f.

expiatory, *-pĭd'tări*, a. espiatorio.

expiration, *-pĭrd'shăn*, s. espirazione, esalazione, f.; respirazione, f.; morte, f.

expire, *-spĭr'*, v. n. spirare, esalare; morire.   [interpretare.

explain, *-plān'*, v. a. esplicare, spiegare;

explanation, *-plănd'shăn*, s. esplicazione, interpretazione, f.

explanatory, *-plăn'ătări*, a. esplicativo.

expletive, *ĕks'plĕtĭv*, a. espletivo.

explicable, *ĕks'plĭkăbl*, a. spiegabile.

explication, *-kd'shăn*, s. esplicazione, spiegazione, f.

explicit, *-plĭs'ĭt*, a. espresso, distinto, chiaro, manifesto; **-ly**, ad. espressamente.

explode, *-plōd'*, v. a. rigettare, disapprovare, condannare.   [illustre, m.

exploit, *-plŏĭt'*, s. fatto d' arme, fatto

exploration, *-plŏrd'shăn*, s. investigazione, f.; ricerca, f.

explore, *-plōr'*, v. a. esplorare, investigare, ricercare; esaminare.

explosion, *-plŏ'zhŭn*, s. esplosione, f.

explosive, *-sĭv*, a. esplodente; **- cotton**, s. cotone esplosivo, m.

exponent, *-pō'nĕnt*, s. esponente, m.

export, *-pōrt'*, v. a. esportare, trasportare.

export, *ĕks'pōrt*, **exportation,** *-td'shăn*, s. esportazione, f., trasporto, m.

export-duty, *-dătĭ*, s. dazio, m.

expose, *-pōz'*, v. a. esporre; mostrare; scoprire; abbandonare.

exposition, *-zĭsh'ăn*, s. esposizione, f.; interpretazione, f.   [disputare.

expostulate, *-pŏs'tŭlăt*, v. a. contendere,

expostulation, *-ld'shăn*, s. discussione, disputa, f.   [situazione, f.

exposure, *-pō'zhŭr*, s. esposizione, f.

expound, *-pōŭnd'*, v. a. spiegare, interpretare.

express, *-prĕs'*, a. espresso, preciso, distinto; simile; **-**, s. espresso, corriere mandato, m.; **-**, v. a. esprimere; rappresentare.   [locuzione, f.

expression, *-prĕsh'ăn*, s. espressione, f.;

expressionless, *-lĕs*, a. che è senza espressione.   [ad. con modo espressivo.

expressive, *-prĕs'sĭv*, a. espressivo; **-ly**,

expressly, *-lĭ*, ad. espressamente, direttamente; a bella posta.

expropriate, *-prō'prĭāt*, v. a. espropriare,

expropriation, *-d'shăn*, s. espropriazione, f.   [scacciamento, m.

expulsion, *-păl'shăn*, s. espulsione, f., cellare.

expunge, *-pănj'*, v. a. espungere, can

expurgate, *-pŭr'găt*, v. a. espurgare.

expurgation, *-gd'shăn*, s. espurgazione, f.

exquisite, *ĕks'kwĭzĭt*, a. squisito, eccellente, perfetto; **-ly**, ad. squisitamente; **-**, s. elegante, m.

exquisiteness, *-nĕs*, s. squisitezza, f.

extant, *ĕks'tănt*, a. esistente, sussistente.

extemporary, *-tĕm'pŏrări*, s. estemporaneo; improvviso.

extempore, *-pŏrĕ*, ad. all' improvviso.

extemporize, *-pŏrĭz*, v. n. improvvisare.

extend, *-tĕnd'*, v. a. stendere; dilatare; **-**, v. n. (di)stendersi.   [allungamento, m.

extension, *-tĕn'shăn*, s. estensione, f.;

extensive, *-sĭv*, a. estensivo, largo; **-ly**, ad. estensivamente, ampiamente.

extent, *-tĕnt'*, s. estensione, f.; portato, m.; sequestro, m.   [nuire, scemare.

extenuate, *-tĕn'ŭăt*, v. a. stenuare; smi

extenuation, *-d'shăn*, s. estenuazione, f.; mitigazione, f.; magrezza, f.

exterior, *-tē'rĭŭr*, a. esteriore, esterno; **-**, s. esteriore, m.

exteriority, *-rĭŏr'ĭtĭ*, s. esteriorità, f.

exterminate, *-tŭr'mĭnăt*, v.a. sterminare, stirpare.   [zione, f.

extermination, *-nd'shăn*, s. stermina

external, *-năl*, a. esterno, esteriore; visibile; **-ly**, ad. esternamente, nell' esterno; **-s**, s. pl. apparenze, f. pl.

extinct, *-tĭngkt'*, a. estinto; morto.

extinction, *-tĭngk'shăn*, s. estinzione, f.; abolizione, f.   [smorzare.

extinguish, *-tĭng'gwĭsh*, v. a. estinguere;

extinguisher, *-ŭr*, s. spegnitoio, m.

extirpate, *-tŭr'păt*, v. a. estirpare.

extirpation, *-pd'shăn*, s. estirpazione, f., estirpamento, m.; distruzione, f.

extol, *-tōl'*, v. a. estollere, esaltare, lodare.

extort, *-tōrt'*, v. a. estorcere; torre per forza.   [zione violenta, f.

extortion, *-tōr'shăn*, s. estorsione, f.; esazione, f.

extortioner, *-ŭr*, s. esattore, m.; oppressore, m.

extra, *ĕks'trd*, s. scrittura unita, f., allegato, m.; **- super**, a. sopraffino.

extract, *ĕks'trăkt*, s. estratto, m.; sommario, m.; **-**, *-trăkt'*, v. a. estrarre; scegliere.   [nascita, f.

extraction, *-trăk'shăn*, s. estrazione, f.;

extradition, *-trădĭsh'ăn*, s. estradizione, f.

extraneous, *-trd'nĭŭs*, a. estraneo.

extraordinarily, *-trŏr'dĭnărĭlĭ*, ad. straordinariamente.

extraordinary, *-dĭnărĭ*, a. straordinario.

extravagance, *-trăv'ăgăns*, s. stravaganza, f.; pazzia, f.

extravagant, *-ăgănt*, a. stravagante, eccessivo, esorbitante; fantastico, bizarro; **-ly**, ad. stravagantemente.

extreme, *-trēm'*, a. estremo, ultimo; grandissimo; **-ly**, ad. estremamente; **-**, s. estremità, f.

extremity, *–trĕm'ĭtĭ*, s. estremità, estrema parte, f.; fine, f.; miseria, f.

extricate, *ĕks'trĭkăt*, v. a. distrigare, sviluppare. |m.

extrication, *–trĭkă'shăn*, s. disimpaccio, m.

extrinsic, *–trĭn'sĭk*, a. estrinseco, esteriore. |soprabbondanza, f.

exuberance, *ĕgzū'bărăns*, s. esuberanza,

exuberant, *–bărănt*, a. esuberante, soprabbondante.

exude, *ĕksūd'*, v. n. sudare, traspirare.

exult, *ĕgzŭlt'*, v. n. esultare. |gioia, f.

exultation, *–tă'shăn*, s. esultanza, f.;

exultingly, *–tĭnglĭ*, ad. con gioia.

eye, *ĭ*, s. occhio, m.; (bot.) rampollo, m., gemma, f., bottone, m.; viso, aspetto, m.; foro dell' ago, m.; –, v. a. considerare, guardare; osservare; adocchiare.

eye-ball, *–băl*, s. pupilla, f.

eye-brow, *–brŏŭ*, s. sopracciglio, m.

eye-glass, *–glăs*, s. occhiale, m.

eye-lash, *–lăsh*, s. ciglio, m.

eyeless, *–lĕs*, a. senz' occhi, cieco.

eyelet, *–lĕt*, s. occhiello, m.

eye-lid, *–lĭd*, s. palpebra, f.

eye-sight, *–sĭt*, s. vista, f.; occhi, m. pl.

eye-sore, *–sŏr*, s. fastidio, m.

eye-tooth, *–tŏth*, s. dente occhiale, m.

eye-wash, *–wŏsh*, s. collirio, m.

eye-witness, *–wĭtnĕs*, s. testimonio oculare, m.

eyry, *ā'rĕ*, s. nido d' uccello di rapina, m.

F.

fable, *fā'bl*, s. favola, f.; finzione, f.

fabric, *făb'rĭk*, s. fabbrica, f.; edifizio, m.; tessuto, m. |edificare.

fabricate, *făb'rĭkăt*, v. a. fabbricare;

fabrication, *–kă'shăn*, s. fabbricazione, f., facimento, m.

fabulous, *făb'ŭlăs*, a. favoloso, controvato; **-ly**, ad. favolosamente.

face, *făs*, s. faccia, f.; viso, volto, m.; cera, f.; aria, f.; fronte, m.; prospetto, aspetto, m.; facciata, f.; superficie, f.; apparenza, f.; esteriore, m.; stato, m.; confidenza, f.; assicuranza, f.; **in my –**, in presenza mia; –, v. a. guardare nel viso; voltare (una pagina); –, v. n. far faccia, fare fronte; far delle smorfie; affrontare, bravare; **to – (it) out**, mantenere.

face-ache, *–āk*, s. tic doloroso, m.

facet, *făs'ĕt*, s. faccetta f.

facetious, *făsē'shăs*, a. faceto, giocoso, burlesco; **-ly**, ad. facetamente, burlescamente, piacevolmente.

facial, *fā'sĭăl*, a. faciale.

facile, *făs'ĭl*, a. facile; pieghevole, trattabile; compiacente.

facilitate, *făsĭl'ĭtăt*, v. a. rendere facile.

facility, *făsĭl'ĭtĭ*, s. facilità, f.; agevolezza, destrezza, f.; affabilità, f.

facing, *fā'sĭng*, s. fronte, m.; facciata, f.; mostra, f.; guernitura, f.; –, pr. in faccia, rimpetto.

fac-simile, *făk sĭm'ĭlĕ*, s. facsimile, m.

fact, *făkt*, s. fatto, m.; atto, m.; in –, effettivamente; **matter of –**, s. cosa di fatto, f.

faction, *făk'shăn*, s. fazione, f.; discordia,

factionist, *–ĭst*, s. fazioso, m. |f.

factious, *făk'shăs*, a. fazioso; **-ly**, ad. in modo sedizioso.

factiousness, *–nĕs*, s. spirito di fazione, spirito di partito, m. |ciale.

factitious, *făktĭsh'ăs*, a. fattizio, artificale.

factor, *făk'tŭr*, s. fattore, m.; agente, m.

factory, *–tŭrĭ*, s. fattoria, f.; società (di mercanti), f.

factotum, *–tŏ'tăm*, s. faccendiere, m.

faculty, *făk'ŭltĭ*, s. facoltà, potenza, f.: podestà, f.; privilegio, m.

fad, *făd*, s. capriccio, ghiribizzo, m.; singolarità, f.

fade, *făd*, v. n. sfiorire; languire.

fag, *făg*, s. schiavo, m.; groppo (di panno), m.; –, v. n. affaticarsi; dimenarsi.

fag-end, *–ĕnd*, s. punta, f.; estremità, f.

fagot, *făg'ŏt*, s. fagotto, m.

fail, *făl*, s. fallo, m.; errore, m.; mancamento, m.; omissione, f.; –, v. a. abbandonare, cessare; omettere, negligere; –, v. n. fallare, errare; mancare; perire, morire.

failing, *–ĭng*, s. fallo, errore, m.; colpa, mancanza, f. |f.; fallimento, m.

failure, *–ŭr*, s. deficienza, f.; mancanza, f.

fain, *făn*, a. obbligato, sforzato, costretto; –, ad. volentieri; pure.

faint, *fănt*, a. languido, debole, fiacco, timido; –, v. n. divenir languido; svenire; tramortire.

faint-hearted, *–hărtĕd*, a. timido, pusillanimo; **-ly**, ad. timidamente.

fainting(-fit), *–ĭng(fĭt)*, s. deliquio, svenimento, m. |mente.

faintly, *–lĭ*, ad. debolmente, languidamente.

faintness, *–nĕs*, s. debolezza, fiacchezza, f.; languore, m.

fair, *făr*, a. bello, vezzoso, buono; chiaro, sereno; sincero, candido, franco; onesto; favorevole; biondo; **– sex**, bel sesso, m.; –, ad. pian piano; civilmente; –, s. fiera, f., mercato pubblico, m.

fair-complexioned, *–kŏmplĕk'shănd*, a. biondo; di carnagione bianca. |fiera, f.

fairing, *–ĭng*, s. donativo di fiera, m.

fairly, *–lĭ*, ad. vagamente; bene, di buona fede, sinceramente; piacevolmente.

fairness, *–nĕs*, s. beltà, f.; probità, onestà, f.; candore, m.

fair-spoken, *–spŏkn*, a. affabile, elegante, cortese. |fate, incantevole.

fairy, *fā'rĕ*, s. fata, maga, f.; –, a. di

faith, *făth*, s. fede, f.; credenza, f.; lealtà, sincerità, veracità, f. |ad. fedelmente.

faithful, *–fŭl*, a. fedele; candido; **-ly**,

faithfulness, *–nĕs*, s. fedeltà, lealtà, costanza, f. |dulo.

faithless, *–lĕs*, a. perfido, infido; incredulo.

falchion, *făl'shăn*, s. falcione, m., scimitarra, f.

falcon, *fă'kn*, s. falcone, m. |tarra, f.

falconer, *–ŭr*, s. falconiere, m.

falconery, *-rĭ*, s. caccia del falcone, f.

fall, *fål*, v. a. ir. abbassare; abbattere; scemare; –, v. n. ir. cadere, cascare; perire; **to – asleep**, addormentarsi; **to – short**, non venire a fine, mancare; **to – sick**, ammalarsi; **to – off**, cascare da; disdirsi; separarsi; apostatare; **to – out**, accadere; avvenire, succedere; venire alle mani; **to – upon**, avventarsi; lanciarsi, attaccare; –, s. caduta, f.; cascata, f.; (rail.) discesa, f.

fallacious, *fållå'shŭs*, a. fallace, falso; **-ly**, ad. fallacemente.   [falsità, f.

fallacy, *fål'låsŭ*, s. fallacia, f.; sofisma, m.,

fallibility, *-lĭbĭl'ĭtĭ*, s. fallibilità, f.

fallible, *fål'ĭbl*, a. fallibile.

falling, *fål'lĭng*, s. caduta, f.; decadenza, f.; (mar.) **– off**, s. abbrivo, m.; **– out**, s. dissensione, f.; disputa, f.

falling-sickness, *-sĭknĕs*, s. mal caduco, m., epilessia, f.

falling-star, *-står*, s. stella cadente, f.

fallow, *fål'lŏ*, a. rossigno; incolto.

false, *fåls*, a. falso, contraffatto; perfido; **-ly**, ad. falsamente; perfidamente.

falsehood, *-hŭd*, **falseness**, *-nĕs*, s. falsità, f.; perfidia, f.   [zione, f.

falsification, *-sĭfĭkå'shŭn*, s. falsifica-

falsify, *fål'sĭfĭ*, v. a. falsificare.

falsity, *-sĭtĭ*, s. falsità, f.; errore, m.

falter, *-tăr*, v. n. balbettare, esitare; mancare, fallire.   [f.

faltering, *-ĭng*, s. balbuzie, f.; esitazione,

falteringly, *-lĭ*, ad. con esitazione, con difficoltà.   [rumore, m.

fame, *fåm*, s. fama, f.; rinomanza, f.;

famed, *fåmd'*, a. rinomato, famoso, celebre.

familiar, *fåmĭl'yăr*, a. familiare; domestico; **-ly**, ad. familiarmente, –, s. intimo amico, m.

familiarity, *-lĭăr'ĭtĭ*, s. familiarità, f.

familiarize, *-mĭl'yărĭz*, v. a. render familiare, dimesticare.

family, *fåm'ĭlĭ*, s. famiglia, f.; schiatta, f.; spece, f.; **in the-way**, incinta, gravida.

famine, *fåm'ĭn*, s. penuria di viveri, f.; carestia, f.   [essere affamato.

famish, *-ĭsh*, v. a. affamare; –, v. n.

famous, *få'mŭs*, a. famoso, rinomato; **-ly**, ad. famosamente.   [brità, f.

famousness, *-nĕs*, s. rinomanza, f.; cele-

fan, *fån*, s. ventaglio, m.; vaglio, m.; –, v. a. ventilare; vagliare.

fanatic, *fånăt'ĭk*, a. & s. fanatico (m.).

fanaticism, *-ĭsĭzm*, s. fanatismo, m.

fanciful, *fån'sĭfŭl*, a. fantastico, bizzarro; **-ly**, ad. fantasticamente.

fancy, *-sĭ*, s. fantasia, immaginazione, f.; fantasma, f.; capriccio, m.; –, v. a. & n. amare; figurarsi, immaginarsi; pensare, credere.

fancy-articles, *-ărtĭkls*, **fancy-goods**, *-gŭds*, s. pl. mercanzie, robe di moda, f. pl.; lavori d' ebanista, m. pl

fancy-ball, *-bål*, s. ballo in maschera, m.

fancy-fair, *-får*, s. bazar, m.

fancy-sick, *-sĭk*, a. ipocondrico.

fang, *fång*, s. zanna, branca, f.; artiglio, dente, m.   [nuto.

fanged, *fångd'*, a. fornito di zanne, zan-

fantastic, *fåntås'tĭk*, a. fantastico, bizzarro; **-ally**, ad. fantasticamente.

fantasticalness, *-ălnĕs*, s. fantasticheria, f.   [ad. lontano.

far, *får*, a. lontano, remoto, distante; –,

farce, *fårs*, s. farsa, f.

farcical, *får'sĭkål*, a. burlesco.   [f.

farcy, *-sĭ*, s. scabbia, f.; rogna de' cavalli,

fardel, *-dĕl*, s. fardello, involto, m.

fare, *får*, s. cera, f., mangiare, m., viveri, m. pl.; nolo, passaggio, m.; prezzo, m.; –, v. n. andare, stare; mangiare; vivere.

farewell, *-wĕl*, ad. addio; –, s. addio, congedo, m.

farinaceous, *fårĭnå'shŭs*, a. farinaceo.

farm, *fårm*, s. masseria, possessione, f.; –, v. a. prendere a fitto; coltivare.

farmer, *får'măr*, s. fittaiuolo, castaldo, m.

farming, *-ĭng*, s. affitto a censo, m.

farm-yard, *-yård*, s. pollaio, m.

farrago, *fårrå'gŏ*, s. farragine, f.

farrier, *får'rĭăr*, s. manescalco, m.

farriery, *-rĭărĭ*, s. mascalcia, f.

farrow, *får'rŏ*, s. porcello, porchetto, m.; –, v. a. fare i porcelli.   [vista, presbite.

far-seeing, *får'sĕĭng*, a. che è di lunga

farther, *får'thăr*, a. ulteriore, più lontano; –, ad. avanti, innanzi, oltre.

farthest, *-thĕst*, a. lo più lungo.

farthing, *får'thĭng*, s. fardino, m.

fascinate, *fås'sĭnåt*, v. a. ammaliare.

fascination, *-nå'shăn*, s. fascino, m., malia, f.

fascine, *fåssĕn'*, s. fascina, f., fagotto, m.

fashion, *fåsh'ăn*, s. maniera, forma, f.; usanza, moda, f.; condizione, f.; guisa, sorte, f.; aria, apparenza, f.; **people of –**, s. gente distinta, nobiltà, f.; **out of –**, fuor di moda; –, v. n. formare.

fashionable, *-åbl*, a. alla moda; elegante.

fashionably, *-åblĭ*, ad. alla moda; elegantemente, di buon tuono.

fast, *fåst*, a. fermo, saldo, stretto; stabile, fisso; –, ad. fermamente; fermo, stretto; saldamente; subitamente, subito; –, s. digiuno, m., astinenza da cibi, f.; –, v. n. digiunare.

fasten, *fås'n*, v. a. legare; attaccare, fissare, serrare, fermare; –, v. n. appiccarsi; attaccarsi.

faster, *fås'tăr*, s. digiunatore, m.

fastidious, *-tĭd'ĭŭs*, a. sdegnoso; **-ly**, ad. fastidiosamente.   [forte, m.

fastness, *fåst'nĕs*, s. fermezza, f.; luogo

fat, *fåt*, a. grasso, carnoso, pingue; –, s. grasso, m.; sugna, f.   [fatalmente.

fatal, *få'tăl*, a. fatale; funesto; **-ly**, ad.

fatalism, *-ĭzm*, s. fatalismo, m.

fatalist, *-ĭst*, s. fatalista, m.

fatality, *fåtăl'ĭtĭ*, s. fatalità, f.; predestinazione, f.   [f. pl.

fate, *fåt*, s. fato, destino, m.; **-s**, pl. Parche,

fated, *få'tĕd*, a. fatato, decreto.

fateful, *fåt'fŭl*, a. fatale.

father, *fâth' ăr*, s. padre, m.
fatherhood, *–hŭd*, s. paternità, f.
father-in-law, *–ĭn lå*, s. suocero, m.
fatherland, *–lånd*, s. patria, f.
fatherless, *–lĕs*, a. senza padre.
fatherly, *–lĭ*, a. & ad. paternale, paterno ; a modo di padre.
fathom, *fâth' ăm*, s. braccio, m. (misura) ;
—, v. a. scandagliare, affondare ; penetrare.
fathomless, *–lĕs*, a. non misurabile, immenso ; impenetrabile.
fatigue, *fåtēg'*, s. fatica, pena, f. ; —, v. a. affaticare, stancare. [f., servizio, m.
fatigue-party, *–pårtĭ*, s. (mil.) funzione,
fatling, *fåt'lĭng*, s. bestia grassa, f.
fatness, *–nĕs*, s. grassezza, f. ; untuosità, f.
fatten, *fåt'n*, v. a. ingrassare ; —, v. n. divenir grasso, ingrassare.
fattening, *–nĭng*, s. ingrassamento, m.
fatty, *fåt'ĭ*, a. grasso ; untuoso, oleoso.
fatuity, *fåtū'ĭtĭ*, s. fatuità, stupidezza, f.
fatuous, *fåt'ūŭs*, a. fatuo, sciocco.
fault, *fålt*, s. fallo, difetto, errore, m.; colpa, f. ; offesa, f. [m.
fault-finder, *–fīndăr*, s. censore, critico,
faultily, *fål'tĭlĭ*, ad. impropriamente.
faultiness, *–tĭnĕs*, s. difetto, m.; delitto, m.
faultless, *–lĕs*, a. senza errori ; perfetto, eccellente.
faulty, *–tĭ*, a. colpevole ; difettoso.
faun, *fån*, s. fauno, m.
favour, *fā'văr*, s. favore, f.; protezione, f.; grazia, cortesia, f.; credito, m.; cera, aria, f.; fiocco di nastri, m.; **under (with) your —,** con vostra licenza ; —, v. a. favorire, proteggere.
favourable, *–âbl*, a. favorevole, propizio.
favourably, *–âblĭ*, ad. favorevolmente.
favoured, *–vård*, a. favorito, appoggiato ; **ill —,** malfatto, brutto, deforme.
favourite, *–vŭrĭt*, s. favorito, m.
fawn, *fån*, s. daino giovine, m.; —, v. a. figliare ; corteggiare servilmente.
fawningly, *–ĭnglĭ*, ad. lusinghevolmente, servilmente.
fay, *fā*, s. fata, incantatrice, f.
fealty, *fē'ăltĭ*, s. fedeltà, lealtà, f.
fear, *fēr*, s. timore, m., paura, f. ; —, v. a. & n. temere ; avere paura.
fearful, *–fŭl*, a. timido, timoroso ; terribile ;
–ly, ad. timidamente ; terribilmente.
fearless, *–lĕs*, a. intrepido, coraggioso ;
–ly, ad. senza timore. [coraggio, m.
fearlessness, *–nĕs*, s. intrepidezza, f.,
feasibility, *fēzĭbŭ'ĭtĭ*, s. agevolezza a farsi, possibilità, f. [farsi.
feasible, *fē'zĭbl*, a. fattibile, agevole a
feast, *fēst*, s. banchetto, m.; festa, festività, f.; —, v. a. regalare ; —, v. n. festeggiare, banchettare.
feaster, *–ăr*, s. ghiotto, m.; che ordina banchetti, f.; festeggiante, m.
feat, *fēt*, s. fatto, atto, m., azione, f.
feather, *fĕth' ăr*, s. piuma, penna, f.; ornamento, m.; bagattella, f.; —, v. a. coprire di piume ; ornare ; arricchire.
feather-bed, *–bĕd*, s. letto di piume, m., coltrice, f.

feather-broom, *–brŏm*, s. mazzo di piume, m.
feathery, *–ărĭ*, a. coperto di piume. [f.
feature, *fē'tŭr*, s. lineamento, m.; faccia.
febrifuge, *fĕb' rĭfūj*, s. febbrifugo, m.
febrile, *fĕb' rĭl*, a. febbrile, di febbre.
February, *fĕb' rŏårĭ*, s. febbraio, m.
fecund, *fĕk' ŭnd*, a. fecondo, fertile.
fecundity, *–kŭn' dĭtĭ*, s. fecondità, fertilità, f.; copia, f.
federal, *fĕd' ărăl*, a. alleato, federato.
federalist, *–ĭst*, s. federalista, m.
federate, *–ărăt*, a. confederato, collegato.
federation, *–rā' shŭn*, s. confederazione, f.
fee, *fē*, s. feudo, m.; mercede, paga, f., salario, m.; —, v. a. pagare, remunerare ;
feeble, *fē' bl*, a. debole. [corrompere
feebleness, *–nĕs*, s. debolezza, f.
feebly, *–blĭ*, ad. debolmente, fievolmente.
feed, *fēd*, s. nutrimento, m.; pastura, f.; —, v. a. ir. nutrire, pascere ; alimentare ; conservare ; —, v. n. ir. nutrirsi ; divenir grasso. [bavaglio, m.
feeder, *–ăr*, s. nutritore, m.; ghiottone, m.;
feeding-bottle, *–ĭng bŏttl*, s. zampilletto, m.
feel, *fēl*, v. a. ir. palpare, toccare, tastare, palpeggiare ; sentire ; —, v. n. ir. essere sensibile o sensitivo ; —, s. tatto, tocco, m.
feeler, *–ăr*, s. antenna, f.; (fig.) toccare il polso, m. [sensibilità, f.
feeling, *–ĭng*, s. tatto, m.; sentimento, m.;
feelingly, *–lĭ*, ad. sensibilmente.
feet (pl. di foot), *fēt*, s. fanteria, f.
feign, *fān*, v. a. fingere, simulare ; inventare ; —, v. n. immaginarsi.
feint, *fānt*, s. finzione, f.; finta, f.
felicitate, *fĕlĭs' ĭtăt*, v. a. felicitare ; congratularsi. [congratulazione, f.
felicitation, *–tā' shŭn*, s. felicitazione.
felicitous, *–lĭs' ĭtŭs*, a. felicissimo.
felicity, *–ĭtĭ*, s. felicità, prosperità, f.
feline, *fē' lĭn*, a. felino ; di gatto.
fell, *fĕl*, a. barbaro, inumano ; —, s. pelle, pelliccia, f.; cuoio, m.
fellow, *fĕl' lō*, s. compagno, camerata, collega, m.; membro (d' un collegio), m. [m.
fellow-citizen, *–sĭtĭzĕn*, s. concittadino,
fellow-creature, *–krētăr*, s. simile, m.
fellow-feeling, *–fēlĭng*, s. simpatia, f.
fellow-prisoner, *–prĭzŏnăr*, s. compagno di prigione, m. [f.
fellowship, *–shĭp*, s. compagnia, società,
fellow-soldier, *–sŏljăr*, s. compagno d' armi, commilitone, m. [m.
fellow-student, *–stŭdĕnt*, s. condiscepolo,
fellow-sufferer, *–sŭffărăr*, s. compagno in miseria, m. [di viaggio, m.
fellow-traveller, *–trăvĕllăr*, s. compagno
felly, *fĕl' lĭ*, s. razzo di ruota, m.
felon, *fĕl' ŏn*, s. fellone, ribaldo, m.
felonious, *–lō' nĭŭs*, a. fellonesco, crudele, inumano.
feloniously, *–lĭ*, ad. fellonescamente.
felony, *fĕl' ŏnĭ*, s. fellonia, f.; scelleratezza,
felt, *fĕlt*, s. feltro, m.; borra, f. [f.
felucca, *fĕlŭk' kå*, s. feluca, f.

female, *fĕ'māl,* a. femminino, di femmina; –, s. femmina, f.   [nato, dolce.
feminine, *fĕm'ĭnĭn,* a. femminino; effemi-
fen, *fĕn,* s. palude, m., maremma, f.
fence, *fĕns,* s. siepe, chiusura, f.; difesa, f.;
    schermo, m.; palizzata, f.; –, v. a. chiu-
    dere; palifizzare; difendere; –, v. n.
    schermire.
fenceless, *–lĕs,* a. senza chiusura, aperto.
fencer, *–ăr,* s. schermitore, m.
fencing, *fĕn'sĭng,* s. chiusura, f.; scherma,
    arte della scherma, f.   [scherma, m.
fencing-master, *–māstăr,* s. maestro di
fencing-school, *–skŏl,* s. sala d' armi, f.
fend, *fĕnd,* v. a. parare, schivare; –, v. n.
fender, *–ăr,* s. gardata, f.   [difendersi.
fennel, *fĕn'nĕl,* s. finocchio, m.
ferment, *fărmĕnt',* v. a. & n. fermentare,
    lievitare; –, făr'mĕnt, s. fermento, lievito,
    m.   [zione, f.
fermentation, *–tā'shŭn,* s. fermenta-
fern, *fărn,* s. felce, f.   [felcaia, f.
fernery, *fărn'ărĭ, fern-plot, –plŏt,* s.
ferocious, *fĕrō'shŭs,* a. feroce, fiero; **-ly,**
    ad. ferocemente.
ferocity, *–rŏs'ĭtĭ,* s. ferocità, f.
ferret, *fĕr'rĕt,* s. furetto, fioretto, m.; –,
    v. a. cacciare col furetto; investigare.
ferreter, *–ăr,* s. cacciatore col furetto, m.;
    investigatore, indagatore, m.
ferruginous, *fĕrrō'jĭnŭs,* a. ferruginoso.
ferrule, *fĕr'rŭl,* s. ghiera, viera, f.
ferry, *fĕr'rĭ,* s. chiatta, f.; passaggio, m.;
    –, v. a. passare col barchetto.
ferryman, *–măn,* s. barcaiuolo, m.
fertile, *făr'tĭl,* a. fertile, fecondo.
fertilise, *–tĭlīz,* v. a. fertilizzare, fecon-
    dare.
fertility, *–tĭl'ĭtĭ,* s. fertilità, fecondità, f.
ferule, *făr'ŭl,* s. sferza, f., staffile, m.
fervency, *–vĕnsĭ,* s. fervore, m.; zelo,
    affetto, m.   [ad. con fervore.
fervent, *–vĕnt,* a. fervente, fervido; **-ly,**
fervid, *–vĭd,* a. fervido, ardente.
fervour, *–văr,* s. fervore, affetto, m.
fescue, *fĕs'kū,* s. tocco, m.
fester, *–tăr,* v. n. suppurare, impostemire.
festival, *–tĭvăl,* a. festivo; –, s. giorno
    festivo, m.   [festivo, m.
festivity, *–tĭv'ĭtĭ,* s. giubilo, m.; giorno
festoon, *–tŏn',* s. festone, m.; –, v. a.
    tagliare a festone.
fetch, *fĕch,* s. artificio, m.; pretesto, m.;
    astuzia, f.; –, v. a. andare a cercare; por-
    tare; produrre.
fetid, *fĕt'ĭd,* a. fetido, puzzolente.
fetidness, *–nĕs,* s. fetore, puzzo, m.   [f.
fetlock, *fĕt'lŏk,* s. barbetta della pastoia,
fetter, *–tăr,* v. a. mettere in catene.
fetters, *–tărz,* s. pl. catene, f. pl.; ferri,
    ceppi, m. pl.
feud, *fūd,* s. feudo, m.; contesa, rissa, f.
feudal, *fū'dăl,* a. feudale.
feudalism, *–ĭzm,* s. feudalità, f.
feudatory, *–dătărĭ,* s. feudatario, m.
fever, *fē'văr,* s. febbre, f.
feverish, *–ĭsh,* a. febbricitante.

few, *fū,* a. poco; **a –,** alcuni; **– and far
    between,** scarso, raro, a lunghi inter-
fewer, *–ăr,* a. meno.   [valli.
fewness, *–nĕs,* s. piccol numero, m.;
    scarsità, f.
fiat, *fī'ăt,* s. decreto, m.   [mentire.
fib, *fĭb,* s. bugia, menzogna, f.; –, v. n.
fibre, *fī'băr,* s. fibra, f., filamento, m.
fibrine, *–brĭn,* s. fibrina, f.
fibrous, *–brŭs,* a. fibroso.
fickle, *fĭk'l,* a. mutabile, incostante.
fickleness, *–nĕs,* s. mutabilità, incon-
    stanza, f.   [zione, f.
fiction, *fĭk'shŭn,* s. finzione, f.; inven-
fictitious, *–tĭsh'ŭs,* a. fittizio, finto; **-ly,**
    ad. fintamente.
fiddle, *fĭd'l,* s. violino, m.; –, v. n. suo-
    nare il violino; baloccare.
fiddler, *–ăr,* s. violinista, m.
fiddlesticks ! *–stĭks,* i. follie! pazzie!
fidelity, *fĭdĕl'ĭtĭ,* s. fedeltà, lealtà,
    onestà, f.
fidget, *fĭj'ĕt,* s. agitazione, inquietezza,
    impazienza, f.; –, v. n. agitarsi, dime-
    narsi, muoversi.
fidgety, *–ĕtĭ,* a. inquieto, impaziente.
fie, *fī,* i. eh via, puh!
fief, *fĕf,* s. feudo, m.   [spazio, m.
field, *fēld,* s. campo, m.; campagna, f.
field-book, *–bŭk,* s. catasto, m.
field-day, *–dā,* s. giorno di rivista, m.
field-fare, *–făr,* s. tordela, f.
field-marshal, *–mărshăl,* s. maresciallo
    di campo, m.   [pagna, m.
field-mouse, *–mŏŭs,* s. sorcio di cam-
field-officer, *–ŏf'ĭsăr,* s. ufficiale dello
    stato maggiore, m.   [m.
field-piece, *–pēs,* s. pezzo d' artiglieria,
field-practice, *–prăktĭs,* s. esercizio mili-
    tare, m.
field-sports, *–spŏrts,* s. pl. caccia, f.
fiend, *fēnd,* s. nemico, m.; demonio, spirito
    maligno, m.
fiendish, *–ĭsh,* a. diabolico, infernale.
fierce, *fērs,* a. fiero, furioso; feroce; cru-
    dele; **-ly,** ad. furiosamente.
fierceness, *–nĕs,* s. fierezza, ferocità, f.;
    crudeltà, f.   [impeto, m.
fieriness, *fī'ărĭnĕs,* s. ardore, fervore, m.;
fiery, *–ărĭ,* a. collerico, furioso, focoso.
fife, *fĭf,* s. piffero, m.
fifteen, *fĭf'tēn,* a. quindici.
fifteenth, *–tēnth,* a. quindecimo.   [luogo.
fifth, *fĭfth,* a. quinto; **-ly,** ad. in quinto
fiftieth, *fĭf'tĭĕth,* a. cinquantesimo.
fifty, *fĭf'tĭ,* a. cinquanta.
fig, *fĭg,* s. fico, m.; bagattella, f.
fight, *fīt,* s. combattimento, m., battaglia,
    f.; conflitto, m., zuffa, mischia, f.; –, v.
    a. ir. contrastare; –, v. n. ir. combattere,
    far battaglia.
fig-leaf, *fĭg'lĕf,* s. foglia di fico, f.
figment, *–mĕnt,* s. finzione, f., inven-
    zione, f.
fig-pecker, *–pĕkăr,* s. beccafico, **m.**
fig-tree, *–trē,* s. fico (albero), m.
figurative, *–gŭrătĭv,* a. figurativo, alle-
    gorico; **-ly,** ad. figurativamente.

figure, *fĭg'ûr,* s. figura, forma, f.; immagine, f.; apparenza, f.; cifra, f.; —, v. a. figurare. [prua, f.
figure-head, *—hĕd,* s. (mar.) figura di
filament, *fĭl'âmĕnt,* s. filamento, m., fibra, f.
filbert, *—bûrt,* s. avellana, f. [dare.
filch, *fĭlch,* v. a. truffare, ingannare, frau-
filcher, *—ûr,* s. truffatore, furbo, m.
file, *fĭl,* s. filo, m.; fila, f.; lista, linea, f.; ordine, m.; lima, f.; —, v. a. infilare; limare; pulire; **to — off,** marciare alla sfilata, sfilare.
file-cutter, *—kûttŭr,* s. fabbro di lime, m.
filial, *fĭl'yăl,* a. filiale, di figliuolo; **—ly,** ad. in modo filiale.
filibuster, *fĭlĭbŭs'tûr,* s. filibustiere, m.
filigree, *fĭl'ĭgrē,* s. filigrana, f.
filings, *fĭl'lĭngz,* s. pl. limatura, f.
fill, *fĭl,* v. a. empire; saziare; versare; —, v. n. riempirsi; —, s. sufficienza, f.
fillet, *fĭl'lĕt,* s. banda, f.; striscia, f.; coscia di vitello, f.
fillip, *fĭl'lĭp,* s. buffetto, biscottino, m.
filly, *fĭl'lĭ,* s. cavallo giovane, puledro, m.
film, *fĭlm,* s. membrana, pellicola, f.
filter, *fĭl'tûr,* s. filtro, colatoio, m.; —, v. a. colare, filtrare. [bruttura, f.
filth(iness), *fĭlth('ĭnĕs),* s. sporcheria,
filthily, *—lĭ,* ad. sporcamente.
filthy, *—ĭ,* a. sporco, sordido.
filtration, *fĭltrā'shŭn,* s. filtrazione, f.
fin, *fĭn,* s. ala, f.; pinna (de' pesci), f.
final, *fĭ'nâl,* a. finale, ultimo; **—ly,** ad. finalmente.
finance, *fĭnâns',* s. finanza, f.
financial, *—năn'shăl,* a. relativo alle finanze.
finanzier, *—sēr',* s. finanziere, m.
finch, *fĭnsh,* s. fringuello, m.
find, *fĭnd,* v. a. ir. trovare; scoprire; fornire; provvedere; —, v. n. avvedersi, accorgersi; **to — oneself,** trovarsi, essere; stare (di salute).
fine, *fĭn,* a. fino, sottile; pulito; bello, elegante; puro; lucido, chiaro, trasparente; acuto; squisito; destro; —, s. multa, f.; **in —,** in somma; —, v. a. affinare; purgare; condannare all' ammenda.
finedraw, *—drā,* v. a. cucire, risarcire.
finedrawer, *—drāŭr,* s. racconciatore, m.
finely, *—lĭ,* ad. elegantemente.
fineness, *—nĕs,* s. finezza, f.; delicatezza, f.; bellezza, f. [mento, m.
finery, *fĭ'nârĭ,* s. ornamento, m.; aggiusta-
fine-spun, *—spŭn,* a. (fig.) delicato; sottile.
finger, *fĭng'gŭr,* s. dito, m.; —, v. a. maneggiare, toccare; (mus.) muover le dita sullo strumento.
finger-board, *—bōrd,* s. tastiera, f.
finger-glass, *—glăs,* s. bicchiere pel vino di sciampagna, m.
fingering, *—ĭng,* s. maneggiamento, toccamento, m.; portamento delle mani sullo strumento, m. [f.
finger-post, *—pōst,* s. colonna milliaria,
finger-stall, *—stăl,* s. ditale, m.

finical, *fĭn'ĭkăl,* a. affettato.
finicalness, *—nĕs,* s. affettazione, f.
finish, *fĭn'ĭsh,* v. a. finire, terminare, conchiudere, compire.
finite, *fĭ'nĭt,* a. limitato, determinato.
finny, *fĭn'nĭ,* a. fornito di pinne.
fir, *fûr,* s. abete, m.
fire, *fîr,* s. fuoco, m.; incendio, m.; abbruciamento, m.; —, v. a. mettere il fuoco; infiammare; —, v. n. tirare; dar fuoco.
fire-arms, *—ārms,* s. pl. arme da fuoco, f. pl. [teora, f.
fire-ball, *—băl,* s. granata, bomba, f.; me-
fire-brand, *—brănd,* s. tizzone, m.
fire-brigade, *—brĭgăd,* s. pompieri, m. pl.
fire-damp, *—dămp,* s. earburo, m.
fire-eater, *—ētŭr,* s. sacripante, spaccamonti, m. [cendi, f.
fire-engine, *—ĕnjĭn,* s. tromba per gl' in-
fire-escape, *—ĕskăp,* s. apparato per salvarsi d' un incendio, m.
fire-fly, *—flĭ,* s. mosca lucente, f.
fire-lock, *—lŏk,* s. schioppo, m.
fireman, *—măn,* s. estintore d' incendi, m.; (rail.) fochista, m.
fire-office, *—ŏfĭs,* s. uffizio d' assicurazione contro gl'incendi, m.
fire-place, *—plăs,* s. focolare, m.
fire-plug, *—plŭg,* s. otre d' una tromba, m.
fire-proof, *—prŏf,* a. resistente al fuoco.
fire-shovel, *—shŭvl,* s. paletta da fuoco, f.
fire-side, *—sĭd,* s. focolare, m.; camino, m.
fire-water, *—wătŭr,* s. acquavite, m.
fire-wood, *—wŭd,* s. legna, f.
firing, *fĭr'ĭng,* s. legna, f.; (mil.) tiro, m.
firkin, *fûr'kĭn,* s. quarteruolo, m. (misura).
firm, *fûrm,* a. fermo, stabile, costante; **the — land,** il continente; —, s. firma, f.
firmament, *fûr'mâmĕnt,* s. firmamento, m.; cielo, m.
firmly, *—lĭ,* ad. fermamente.
firmness, *—nĕs,* s. fermezza, f.; costanza, f.
first, *fûrst,* a. primo; principale; —, ad. primieramente; **at —,** alla prima.
firstling, *—lĭng,* s. primogenito, m.
fiscal, *fĭs'kăl,* a. fiscale.
fish, *fĭsh,* s. pesce, m.; —, v. a. pescare.
fish-bone, *—bŏn,* s. spina di pesce, f.
fisher, *—ûr,* **fisherman,** *—ûrmăn,* s. pescatore, m.
fishery, *—ûrĭ,* s. pesca, f.; pescare, m.
fish-hook, *—hŏk,* s. amo, m.
fishing, *—ĭng,* s. pesca, pescagione, f.
fishing-boat, *—bŏt,* s. barca da pescatore.
fishing-line, *—lĭn,* s. lenza, f. [f.
fishing-rod, *—rŏd,* s. canna dell' amo, f.
fish-market, *—mărkĕt,* s. pescheria, f. [m.
fish-monger, *—mŭnggûr,* s. pescivendolo,
fish-pond, *—pŏnd,* s. vivaio, m., peschiera, f.
fish-wife, *—wĭf,* s. pescivendola, f. [f.
fishy, *—ĭ,* a. abbondante di pesci.
fissure, *fĭsh'ûr,* s. fessura, spaccatura, f.; screpatura, f.; fesso, m. [serrato, m.
fist, *fĭst,* s. pugno, m.; **clinched —,** pugno
fistula, *fĭs'tŭlâ,* s. fistola, f.
fit, *fĭt,* a. idoneo, atto, capace; convenevole; —, s. accesso, attacco, parossismo;

capriccio, m.; **by −s and starts**, a stento, a spilluzzico; −, v. a. aggiustare, adattare, accomodare; −, v. n. accomodarsi; **to − out**, provvedere, fornire.

fitful, −*fŭl*, a. variabile; irregolare; bizzarro, fantastico.   [mente.

fitly, −*lĭ*, ad. convenevolmente, giusta-

fitness, −*nĕs*, s. convenienza, convenevolezza, f.; proporzione, f.

fitting, −*tĭng*, a. convenevole; giusto, idoneo; −, s. attezza, f.; convenevolezza, f.

five, *fĭv*, a. cinque.   [f.

fiver, *fĭ' văr*, s. cinque lire sterling, m.

fives, *fĭvz*, s. pl. vivole, f. pl.

fix, *fĭks*, v. a. (af)fissare; piantare; stabilire; −, v. n. fissarsi; determinarsi; stabilire la sua dimora.

fixed, *fĭkst*, a. fisso; destinato **−ly**, ad. fissamente; certamente.

fixedness, −*ĕdnĕs*, **fixity**, −*ĭtĭ*, s. stabilità, fermezza, f.   [zioni, f. pl.

fixings, −*ĭngs*, s. pl. masserizie, decorafixture, −*tŭr*, s. fermezza, f.; mobile, m.

fizz(le), *fĭz (fĭz'l)*, v. n. fischiare.

flabbiness, *flăb'bĭnĕs*, s. flacidità, f.

flabby, −*bĭ*, a. floscio, vizzo, moscio.

flaccid, *flăk'sĭd*, a. flacido.

flag, *flăg*, s. bandiera, insegna, f.; giaggiuolo, m.; −, v. a. lasciare cadere; lastricare; −, v. n. cadere; sgomentarsi; avvilirsi; languidire.

flagellate, *flăj'ĕllăt*, v. a. flagellare.

flageolet, *flăj'ĕlĕt*, s. zufolo, m.   [lerato.

flagitious, *flăjĭsh'ŭs*, a. flagizioso, scelflagman, *flăg'măn*, s. (rail.) bandieraio, m.

flag-officer, −*ŏffĭsăr*, s. caposquadra, m.

flagon, *flăg'ŏn*, s. fiasco, m., boccetta, f.

flagrancy, *flă' grănst*, s. fervore, fuoco, m.; notorietà, f.   [festo.

flagrant, −*grănt*, a. ardente, focoso; maniflag-ship, *flăg'shĭp*, s. ammiraglio, m. (nave).

flag-staff, −*stăff*, s. albero di nave, m.

flag-stone, −*stŏn*, s. lastra, f.

flag-union, −*ănĭän*, s. bandiera d' artiflail, *flăl*, s. correggiato, m.   [mone, f.

flake, *flăk*, s. fiocco, m.; scintilla, f.; lamina, f.; giaggiuolo, m.; −, v. n. rompersi in lamine, spelarsi.

flaky, *flă'kĭ*, a. fioccoso, laminoso.

flame, *flăm*, fiamma, f.; fervore, m.; amore, m.; −, v. n. fiammeggiare.

flaming, *flă'mĭng*, a. fiammante; ardente.

flange, *flănj*, s. orlo, risalto, m.; sponda, f.

flank, *flăngk*, s. fianco, lato, m.; −, v. a. fiancheggiare, fiancare.

flannel, *flăn'nĕl*, s. flanella, f.

flap, *flăp*, s. lembo, m.; botta, percossa, f., colpo, m.; falda d' un vestito, f.; **− of the ear**, oreglia, f.; −, v. a. battere, percuotere.

flare, *flăr*, s. fiamma, f.; −, v. n. splendere momentaneamente.

flash, *flăsh*, s. fiamma subita, f.; vampa, f.; baleno, lampo, m.; **− of wit**, concetto spirito so, m.; −, v. a. spruzzare, schizzare; −, v. n. lampeggiare, scintillare; −, a. falso, contrafatto.

flashy, −*ĭ*, a. frivolo, insipido; pomposo.

flask, *flăsk*, s. fiasco, m., fiaschetta, f.

flat, *flăt*, a. piatto, spianato; insipido; franco; −, s. pianura, f.; paese piano, m.; (mar.) basso fondo, m.; (mus.) bimmolle, m.; −, v. a. spianare, appianare; sventare; −, v. n. appianarsi; insipidire.

flatly, −*lĭ*, ad. in piano, sulla terra; schiettamente.   [f.; debolezza, f.

flatness, −*nĕs*, s. pianezza, f.; insipidezza, f.

flatten, *flăt'n*, v. a. appianare; abbattere; −, v. n. appianarsi; insipidire.

flatter, *flăt'tăr*, v. a. adulare, lusingare; −, s. laminatoio, m.

flattery, −*tărĭ*, s. lusinga, adulazione, f.

flatting-mill, −*ĭng mĭl*, s. laminatoio, m.

flatulency, *flăt'dlĕnsĭ*, s. (med.) flatuosità, f.   [frivolo.

flatulent, −*dlĕnt*, a. flatuoso, ventoso;

flatwise, −*wĭz*, ad. in piano, sulla terra.

flaunt, *flănt*, s. pompa, f.; −, v. n. pompeggiare, pavoneggiarsi.

flavour, *flă'văr*, s. sapore gustoso, gusto gradevole, odore, m.; −, v. a. far odoroso o gustoso.

flavourless, −*lĕs*, a. insipido, senza sapore.

flaw, *flă*, s. fessura, crepatura, f.; difetto, errore, m.; buffo di vento, m.; −, v. a. rompere.

flawless, −*lĕs*, a. senza difetto.

flax, *flăks*, s. lino, m.; **to dress −**, scotolare il lino.

flax-comb, −*kŏm*, s. scotola, f.

flaxen, −*ĕn*, a. di lino; biondo.

flay, *flă*, v. a. scorticare.

flea, *flĕ*, s. pulce, f.

flea-bite, −*bĭt*, s. morsicatura di pulce, f.

fledge, *flĕj*, v. a. coprire di piume; dar penne.   [delle ale.

flee, *flĕ*, v. n. ir. fuggire

fleece, *flĕs*, s. tosone, vello, m.; −, v. a. tondere; scorticare.

fleecy, *flĕ'sĭ*, a. lanoso.   [flotta, f.

fleet, *flĕt*, a. presto, veloce; leggiero; −, s.

fleeting, −*ĭng*, a. passeggiero.

fleetness, −*nĕs*, s. velocità, prestezza, f.

flesh, *flĕsh*, s. carne, f.; polpa, f.; (fig.) carnalità, f.; −, v. a. ingrassare; incitare; **−ed**, a. incarnato.   [gare, f.

flesh-brush, −*brŭsh*, s. spazzola da frefleshings, −*ĭngz*, s. pl. lavoro a maglia,

fleshless, −*lĕs*, a. magro, smunto.   [m.

fleshy, −*ĭ*, a. carnoso; polposo.

flexibility, *flĕksĭbĭl'ĭtĭ*, s. flessibilità, f.

flexible, *flĕks'ĭbl*, a. flessibile.   [tura, f.

flexion, *flĕk'shăn*, s. flessione, f.; piegarsi.

flick, *flĭk*, v. a. chiacchierare.   [narsi.

flicker, *flĭk'ăr*, v. n. svolazzare, dime-

flier, *flĭ'ăr*, s. fuggitivo, m.

flight, *flĭt*, s. fuga, f.; volata, f.; covata, f.; scarica, f.; stormo, m.; impeto, slancio, m.; **(of steps)** terrazzo, m.

flight-time, −*tĭm*, s. tempo del passo degli uccelli, m.

flighty, −*ĭ*, a. fuggitivo, fuggevole; veloce.

flimsiness, *flĭm'zĭnĕs*, s. leggerezza, trivialità, futilità, f.

flimsy, −*zĭ*, a. fiacco, floscio; triviale.

flinch, *flĭnsh*, v. n. sbigottirsi; ritirarsi; tralasciare, desistere.

fling, *flĭng*, v. a. ir. gettare, buttare; vibrare; lanciare; —, v. n. ir. calcitrare; —, s. colpo, m., botta, f.; burla, f.

flint, *flĭnt*, s. pietra focaia, selce, f.; ciottolo, m.

flint-glass, *—glås*, s. cristallo di rocca, m.

flinty, *—ĭ*, a. selcioso; (fig.) inesorabile.

flip, *flĭp*, v. a. cicalare, cinguettare.

flippancy, *—pånsĭ*, s. leggerezza, f.; ciarleria, f. [gliato, ciarliero.

flippant, *—pånt*, a. vivace, allegro; sveflirt, *flûrt*, s. civetta. f.; —, v. a. lanciare, gettare; —, v. n. beffeggiare; civettare.

flirtation, *flûrtå'shŭn*, s. civetteria, f.

flit, *flĭt*, v. n. svolazzare, fuggire.

flitch, *flĭtch*, s. lardone, m.; costereccio di porco, m.

float, *flôt*, s. fodero di legname, m.; zatta, f.; sughero, m.; —, v. a. immergere, inondare; —, v. n. fiottare, ondeggiare, galleggiare, fluttuare. [m.

floating-bridge, *—ĭng brĭj*, s. pontone,

floating-capital, *—kåp'ĭtål*, s. fondo circolante, m. [m.

floating-debt, *—dĕt*, s. debito fluttuante, flock, *flŏk*, s. gregge, mandra, f.; fiocco, m.; bioccolo di lana, m.; —, v. n. affollarsi.

floe, *flô*, s. ghiacciuolo, m.

flog, *flŏg*, v. a. frustare, sferzare.

flogging, *—gĭng*, s. frustata, staffilata, f.

flood, *flŭd*, s. inondazione, f., diluvio, m.; flusso, m.; —, v. a. inondare.

floor, *flôr*, s. palco, m.; pavimento, suolo, m.; piano, appartamento, m.; —, v. a. impalcare con tavole; gettare a terra.

flooring, *—ĭng*, s. impalcamento, m.

floral, *flô'rål*, a. florale.

florid, *flŏr'ĭd*, a. floridob.

florin, *flŏr'ĭn*, s. fiorino, m.

florist, *flôr'ĭst*, s. dilettante di fiori, m.

floss-silk, *flŏs'sĭlk*, s. filaticcio, m.

flossy, *flŏs'sĭ*, a. serico, di seta.

flotilla, *flŏtĭl'lå*, s. flottiglia, f.

flounce, *flŏŭns*, s. guarnizione, balzana, f.; —, v. a. guarnire di balzane; —, v. n. tuffarsi; dimenarsi.

flour, *flŏŭr*, s. farina, f., fiore del grano, m.

flourish, *flŭr'ĭsh*, s. ornamento, m.; tratto di penna, m.; (of a trumpet) trombata, f.; —, v. a. ornare, adornare, abbellire; —, v. n. fiorire; prosperare; vantarsi; suonare di trombe.

flout, *flŏŭt*, s. scherzo, m., beffa, burla, f.; —, v. n. schernire, beffare, burlare.

flow, *flô*, s. flusso, m.; abbondanza, f.; fiume d'eloquenza, m.; —, v. a, & n. inondare; colare.

flower, *flŏŭr*, s. fiore, m.; ornamento, m., farina, f.; (fig.) scelta, f.; —, v. a. & n. ornare di fiori; fiorire.

flower-bed, *—bĕd*, s. aiuola, f.

floweret, *—rĕt*, s. fiorellino, m.

flower-girl, *—gŭrl*, s. fioraia, f.

flower-pot, *—pŏt*, s. vaso per i fiori, m.

flower-show, *—shô*, s. esposizione di fiori,

flowery, *—rĭ*, a. pieno di fiori. [f.

fluctuate, *flŭk'tûåt*, v. n. fluttuare; bilanciare; esitare.

fluctuation, *—d'shŭn*, s. ondeggiamento, m.

flue, *flô*, s. tubo, m.; calugine, f.

fluency, *flô'ĕnsĭ*, s. fluidità, volubilità, f.

fluent, *—ĕnt*, a. fluente; abbondante; eloquente; -ly, ad. con facilità.

fluid, *—ĭd*, a. & s. fluido (m.).

fluidity, *—ĭd'ĭtĭ*, s. fluidità, liquidità, f.

fluke, *flôk*, s. marra, f., raffio dell' ancora, m.

flummery, *flŭm'ŭrĭ*, s. pappa d' avena cotta, f.; sciocchezza, inezia, f.; adulazione, f. [m.

flunkey, *flŭngk'ĭ*, s. lacchè, m.; staffiere,

flurry, *flŭr'rĭ*, s. colpo di vento, m., raffica, f.; burrasca, f.; agitazione, fretta, f.; —, v. a. agitare; spaventare.

flush, *flŭsh*, a. fresco, vigoroso; (am.) liberale; —, s. affluenza subita, f.; flusso, rossore subito, m.; —, v. a. alzare; —, v.n. arrossire; scorrere con impeto.

fluster, *flŭs'tŭr*, v. a. turbare; incitare; stordire. [—, v. a. scanalare.

flute, *flôt*, s. flauto, m.; scanalatura, f.;

flutist, *flô'tĭst*, s. sonatore di flauto, m.

flutter, *flŭt'tŭr*, s. ondulazione, f.; dimenamento, m.; confusione, f.; —, v. a. sconcertare; turbare; —, v. n. svolazzare; agitarsi. [dissenteria, f.

flux, *flŭks*, s. flusso, m.; concorso, m.;

fly, *flĭ*, s. mosca, f.; ala, f.; volante, m.; bilanciere, m.; Spanish —, cantaride, f.; —, v. a. ir. sfuggire; —, v. n. ir. volare; scappare; svanire; passare.

fly-blow, *—blô*, s. cacatura di mosche, f.

fly-catcher, *—kåchŭr*, s. mangiamosche,

fly-flap, *—flåp*, s. cacciamosche, m. [m.

flying-fish, *—ĭng fĭsh*, s. pesce volante, m.

fly-man, *—mån*, s. cocchiere, m.

fly-wheel, *—whĕl*, s. volante, m.

foal, *fôl*, s. puledro, m.; cavallina, f.; —, v. a. fare un puledro.

foam, *fôm*, s. spuma, schiuma, f.; —, v. n. spumare, schiumare.

foamy, *fô'mĭ*, a. spumoso.

fob, *fŏb*, s. bersellino, m.

focus, *fô'kŭs*, s. fuoco, m.; centro, m.

fodder, *fŏd'dår*, s. foraggio, m.

foe, *fô*, s. nemico, avversario, m.

fog, *fŏg*, s. nebbia, f.

fogey, *fô'gĭ*, s. un vecchio benigno, m.; goffo, m.; crostino di pane, m.

foggy, *fŏg'gĭ*, a. nebuloso, nebbioso.

foible, *fŏĭ'bl*, s. debolezza, f.

foil, *fŏĭl*, s. fioretto, m.; disfatta, f.; foglia, f.; ripulsa, f.; —, v. a. superare; vincere; frustrare; scoprire la traccia.

foist, *fŏĭst*, v. a. inserire; ficcare.

fold, *fôld*, s. ovile, m.; piega, crespa, f.; (of doors) battente, m.; —, v. a. chiudere nell' ovile; piegare.

folder, *—ŭr*, s. piegatoio, m., stecca, f. [f.

folding, *—ĭng*, s. piegatura, f.; doppiatura,

folding-bed, –*běd,* s. letto da campagna,

folding-chair, –*chăr,* s. ciscranna, f. |m.

folding-door, –*dŏr,* s. porta a due impòste o battenti, f.

folding-screen, –*skrēn,* s. paravento, m.

foliage, *fŏ'lĭăj,* s. fogliame, m.; frondi,f.pl.

folio, *fŏ'lĭŏ,* s. libro in folio, m.

folk, *fŏk,* s. gente, popolo, m.

follow, *fŏl'lŏ,* v. a. seguire; accompagnare; imitare; –, v. n. seguire, provenire, procedere. |imitatore, settatore, m.

follower, –*ăr,* s. seguace, m.; aderente, m.;

folly, *fŏl'lĭ,* s. pazzia, f.; stravaganza, f.

foment, *fŏměnt',* v. a. fomentare; incoraggiare.   [fomento, m.

fomentation, –*tă'shŭn,* s. fomentazione,f.;

fond, *fŏnd,* a. appassionato, indulgente, benigno; **–ly,** ad. teneramente, appassionatamente.   [giare.

fondle, *fŏnd'l,* v. a. accarezzare, vezzeg-

fondling, –*lĭng,* s. mignone, favorito, m.

fondness, –*nĕs,* s. tenerezza, f.; debolezza, f.; affetto, amore, m.

font, *fŏnt,* s. fonte battesimale, m.

food, *fŏd,* s. cibo, pasto, nutrimento, m.; esca, f.; allettamento, m.

fool, *fŏl,* s. sciocco, pazzo, matto, m.; buffone, m.; –, v. a. frustrare; ingannare; –, v. n. fare il pazzo, scherzare, ruzzare;

foolery, –*ărĭ,* s. pazzia, follia, f.; impertinenza, f.; bagattella, f.

foolhardiness, –*hărdĭnĕs,* s. temerità, f.

foolhardy, –*hărdĭ,* a. temerario.

foolish, –*ĭsh,* a. pazzo, stolto; ridicolo; **–ly,** ad. follemente, stoltamente.

foolishness, *vedi* **folly.**

foolscap, –*s'kăp,* s. carta da petizione, f.

foot, *fŭt,* s. piede, m.; passo, m.; base, f.; fanteria, f.; **– by –,** a poco a poco; –, v. a. calcitrare; calpestare; –, v. n. andar a piedi; camminare; ballare, saltellare.

foot-ball, –*băl,* s. pallone, m.

foot-bath, –*băth,* s. pediluvio, m.

foot-board, –*bŏrd,* s. predella, f., sgabello, m.

foot-bridge, –*brĭj,* s. ponticello, m.

foot-hold, –*hŏld,* s. pedata, f.

footing, –*ĭng,* s. pedata, traccia, f.; passo, m.; sentiero, m.; fondamento, m.; principio, m.; stato, m., condizione, f.

footman, –*măn,* s. staffiere, m.; (mil.) fantaccino, m.

foot-note, –*nŏt,* s. annotazione, nota, f.

foot-pace, –*păs,* s. passo lento, m.; pianerottolo, m.

foot-pad, –*păd,* s. ladrone di strada, m.

foot-path, –*păth,* s. sentiero, m.; marciapiede, m.   [piede, m.

foot-pavement, –*păvmĕnt,* s. marcia-

foot-post, –*pŏst,* s. procaccia, m.   [m.

foot-print, –*prĭnt,* s. pedata, f., vestigio,

foot-soldier, –*sŏljăr,* s. soldato di fanteria, m.   [m.

foot-stall, –*stăl,* s. base, f.; piedestallo,

foot-step, –*stĕp,* s. vestigio, m., traccia, f.

foot-stool, –*stŏl,* s. predella, f., sgabello, m.

foot-warmer, –*wărmăr,* s. caldanino, m.

foot-way, –*wă,* s. sentiero, m.

fop, *fŏp,* s. zerbino, damerino, m.

foppery, *fŏp'ĕr,* s. inpertinenza, f.; affettazione, f.   [sciocco.

foppish, –*pĭsh,* a. attillato, affettato,

for, *fŏr,* pr. & c. per, in luogo di, perchè, perciocchè; a cagione che; **as – me,** in quanto a me; **– example,** per esempio; **what –?** perchè?

forage, *fŏr'ăj,* s. foraggio, m.; –, v. a. foraggiare, saccheggiare.

forager, –*ăr,* s. foraggiere, m.

forasmuch (as), *fŏr ăs mŭch (ăs),* c. avvegnachè, perciocchè, a cagione che.

forbear, *fŏrbăr',* v. a. ir. evitare; sopportare, tollerare; –, v. n. cessare; astenersi, raffrenarsi.   [f.

forbearance, –*ăns,* s. pazienza, indulgenza,

forbid, –*bĭd',* v. a. ir. proibire; impedire; vietare; **God –,** Iddio non voglia.

force, *fŏrs,* s. forza, f.; violenza, f.; potere, m.; necessità, f.; **–s,** pl. truppe, f. pl.; –, v. a. forzare, sforzare; costringere; superare; violare, stuprare; –, v. n. sforzarsi; **forced march,** s. marcia affrettata, f.

forcedly, –*ĕdlĭ,* ad. per forza.

forcemeat-balls, –*mēt bălz,* s. pl. gnocchi d'ammorsellato o di carne trita, m. pl.

forcible, *fŏr'sĭbl,* a. forte; potente, vigoroso; efficace; prevalente.

forcibly, –*sĭblĭ,* ad. per forza, fortemente.

forcing-house, –*sĭng hăŭs,* s. serbatoio, m.

ford, –*fŏrd,* s. guado, m.; –, v. a. guadere.

fordable, –*ăbl,* a. guadabile.

fore, *fŏr,* a. anteriore; –, ad. anteriormente; **– and aft,** (mar.) da prua a poppa.

forebode, –*bŏd',* v. a. presagire, pronosticare.

forecast, *fŏr'kăst,* s. prevedimento, m.; preconoscenza, f.; –, *kăst',* v. n. ir. prevedere, considerare innanzi, concertare.

foreclose, –*klŏz',* v. a. escludere, impedire, impedimento, m.

foredoom, –*dŏm',* v. a. predestinare.

forefathers, *fŏr'făthărz,* s. pl. predecessori, antenati, m. pl.

forefend, *vedi* **forebid.**   [sori, m. pl.

forefinger, *fŏr'fĭngăr,* s. dito indice, m.

forego, –*gŏ',* v. a. ir. precedere; cedere; abbandonare.

foregone, –*gŏn',* a. passato; anticipato.

foreground, *fŏr'grŏŭnd,* s. parte inferiore d'una pittura, f.

forehead, –*hĕd,* s. fronte, f.; impudenza, f.

foreign, *fŏr'ĕn,* a. forestiere, straniero.

foreigner, –*ăr,* s. forestiere, straniero, m.

foreknowledge, –*nŏl'ĕj,* s. prescienza, f.

foreland, *fŏr'lănd,* s. capo, promontorio, m.

forelock, –*lŏk,* s. capelli d'avanti, m. pl., ciuffo, m.

foreman, –*măn,* s. capo, condottiere, m.; capo de' giurati, m.; proto, m.

foremast, –*măst,* s. (mar.) albero di trinchetto, m.

forementioned, –*mĕn'shănd,* a. predetto.

foremost, –*mŏst,* a. primo in ordine.

forenoon, –*nŏn,* s. mattina, f.

forensic, *fŏrĕn'sĭk,* a. forense.

forepart, *fōr'pȧrt*, s. parte d'avanti, f.
forerunner, *–rŭnn'ŭr*, s. precursore, m.; foriere, m.
foresail, *–sȧl*, s. trinchetto, m.
foresee, *–sē'*, v. a. ir. prevedere, presentire.
foreshadow, *–shȧd'ō*, v. a. presagire.
foreshorten, *–shŏrt'n*, v. a. raccorciare.
foresight, *fōr'sīt*, s. prevedimento, m.; prescienza, f.
forest, *fōr'ĕst*, s. foresta, selva, f.
forestall, *fōrstȧl'*, v. a. anticipare, preoccupare; incettare.
forester, *fōr'ĕstŭr*, s. guardaboschi, m.
foretaste, *fōr'tȧst*, s. sapore predominante, m.; –, *–tȧst'*, v. a. pregustare, assaggiare.
foretell, *–tĕl'*, v. a. ir. predire; profetizzare.
foreteller, *–tĕl'lŭr*, s. pronosticatore, profeta, m. [f.
forethought, *fōr'thȧt*, s. premeditazione, f.
foretop, *–tŏp*, s. ciuffo, m.
forewarn, *–wȧrn'*, v. a. avertire avanti, dar avvisi.
forfeit, *fōr'fĭt*, a. confiscato, sequestrato; –, s. ammenda, f.; trasgressione, f.; delitto, m.; –, v. a. perdere per sequestro, pena, f.
forfeiture, *–ŭr*, s. confisca, f.; multa, pena, f.
forge, *fōrj*, s. fucina, ferriera, f.; fabbrica, f.; –, v. a. fabbricare; contraffare; macchinare, inventare.
forger, *–ŭr*, s. fabbro, m.; inventore, macchinatore, m.; falsario, m.
forgery, *–ŭrī*, s. lavoro di fabbro, m.; falsificazione, f. [bliare.
forget, *fōrgĕt'*, v. a. ir. dimenticare, obbligare.
forgetful, *–fŭl*, a. dimenticchevole, negligente. [obblio, m.; negligenza, f.
forgetfulness, *–nĕs*, s. dimenticanza, f.,
forget-me-not, *–mē'nŏt*, s. miosotto, m.
forgive, *–gĭv'*, v. a. ir. perdonare; rimettere. [sione, f.
forgiveness, *–nĕs*, s. perdono, m.; remissione, f.
fork, *fōrk*, s. forca, forchetta, f.
forked, *fōrkt*, **forky**, *fōr'kī*, a. forcuto, biforcato.
forlorn, *fōrlōrn'*, a. abbandonato, derelitto; **– hope**, s. soldati esposti in un' assalto, m. pl. [tudine, f.; miseria, f.
forlornness, *–nĕs*, s. abbandono, m.; solitudine, f.
form, *fōrm*, s. forma, figura, f.; foggia, f.; maniera, f.; moda, f.; formalità, f.; banco, m.; covo, m.; –, v. a. formare.
formal, *fōr'mȧl*, a. formale; affettato; –ly, ad. formalmente. [monia, f.
formality, *–mȧl'ĭtĭ*, s. formalità, f.; cerimonia, f.
formation, *–mȧ'shȧn*, s. formazione, f.
former, *fōr'mŭr*, a. primiero, passato; –ly, ad. tempo fù, altre volte. [ribile.
formidable, *–mĭdȧbl*, a. formidabile, terribile.
formula, *–mŭlȧ*, s. formula, f.
formulary, *–mŭlȧrī*, s. formulario, m.
formulate, *–mŭlȧt*, v. a. formulare.
forsake, *–sȧk'*, v. a. ir. lasciare, abbandonare.
forsooth, *–sōth'*, ad. in verità, veramente.
forswear, *–swȧr'*, v. a. ir. spergiurare.
fort, *fōrt*, s. forte, m.

forth, *fōrth*, a. & ad. avanti; fuor fuori; affatto; **and so –**, eccetera. [parire.
forthcoming, *–kȧmĭng*, a. sul punto d'apparire.
forthwith, *–wĭth'*, ad. incontinente, subito.
fortieth, *fōr'tĭĕth*, a. quarantesimo.
fortification, *–tĭfĭkȧ'shȧn*, s. (mil.) fortificazione, f.; cittadella, f.
fortify, *fōr'tĭfī*, v. a. fortificare; munire.
fortitude, *–tĭtŭd*, s. fortezza, f., coraggio, m.
fortnight, *fōrt'nĭt*, s. quindici giorni, m. pl.
fortress, *fōr'trĕs* s. fortezza, f.; bastita, f.
fortuitous, *fōrtū'ĭtŭs*, a. fortuito, casuale; –ly, ad. fortuitamente.
fortunate, *fōr'tŭnȧt*, a. fortunato; –ly, ad. fortunatamente.
fortune, *fōr'tŭn (–chŭn)*, s. fortuna, f.; sorte, m.; caso, evento, m.; stato, m., condizione, f.; beni, m, pl.; ricchezze, f. pl.
fortune-hunter, *–hȧntŭr*, s. che va a caccia di donne ricche.
fortune-teller, *–tĕllŭr*, s. dicitore di buona fortuna, indovino, m.
forty, *fōr'tĭ*, a. quaranta.
forward, *–wȧrd*, a. anticipato; presto; attivo; presuntuoso; pronto, disposto; –, ad. avanti; innanzi; –, v. a. avanzare; accelerare, favorire.
forwarder, *–ŭr*, s. promotore, fautore, m.; (am.) commissionario, m.
forwardness, *–nĕs*, s. prontezza, f.; premura, f., ardore, m.; progresso, m.; sollecitudine, f.
forwards, *–wȧrdz*, ad. avanti.
foss, *fŏs*, s. fosso, m.
fossil, *fŏs'sĭl*, a. & s. fossile (m.).
foster, *fŏs'tŭr*, v. a. nutrire; allevare; governare; educare. [latte, m.
foster-brother, *–brȧthŭr*, s. fratello di latte, m.
foster-child, *–chĭld*, s. allievo, m.
foster-father, *–fȧthŭr*, s. balio, m.
foster-mother, *–mȧthŭr*, s. balia, f.; nutrice, f. [f.
foster-sister, *–sĭstŭr*, s. sorella di latte,
foster-son, *–sȧn*, s. allievo, m.
foul, *fȧul*, a. sporco, impuro; cattivo; vergognoso; **– copy**, s. stracciafogli, m.; –ly, ad. bruttamente, bassamente, vergognosamente; –, v. a. sporcare; diffamare.
foulness, *–nĕs*, s. sporcizia, bruttezza, deformità, f. [ficare.
found, *fȧund*, v. a. fondare; stabilire, edificare.
foundation, *–dȧ'shȧn*, s. fondamento, m., base, f.
foundationer, *–ŭr*, s. borsaio, m.
foundation-stone, *–stōn*, s. pietra fondamentale, f.
founder, *–dȧr*, s. fondatore, fonditore, m.; –, v. a. render incordato; –, v. n. affondare, andar a fondo.
foundery, *fȧun'drĭ*, s. fonderia, f. [m.
foundling, *fȧund'lĭng*, s. fanciullo esposto,
foundress, *fȧun'drĕs*, s. fondatrice, f.
fount, *fȧunt*, **fountain**, *fȧun'tĭn*, s. fonte, m., fontana, f.; –s, pl. acque minerali, f. pl.
fountain-head, *–hĕd*, s. sorgente, f.
four, *fōr*, a. quattro.
fourfold, *–fōld*, a. quadruplo.
four-footed, *–fūtĕd*, a. quadrupede.

four-score, *–skôr*, a. ottanta.
fourteen, *–tên*, a. quattordici.
fourteenth, *–tênth*, a. quartodecimo.
fourth, *–th*, a. quarto; **–ly**, ad. in quarto luogo.
fowl, *fôûl*, s. uccello, m.; pollame, m.
fowler, *–ûr*, s. uccellatore, m.
fowling, *–ĭng*, s. uccellagione, f.
fowling-piece, *–ĭng pês*, s. schioppetto da uccelli, m.　　　　　[m.
fox, *fôks*, s. volpe, f.; (fig.) uomo astuto, m.
fox-brush, *–brûsh*, s. coda di volpe, f.
fox-glove, *–glâv*, s. (bot.) bacchera, f.
fraction, *frăk'shŭn*, s. frazione, f.
fractional, *–shŭnăl*, a. (ar.) frazionario.
fractious, *–shŭs*, a. perverso; litigioso, stizzoso, rissoso.
fracture, *–tûr*, s. frattura, f.; –, v. a. rompere con violenza, frangere.
fragile, *frăj'ĭl*, a. fragile, debole.
fragility, *–jĭl'ĭtĭ*, s. fragilità, f.; fralezza, debolezza, f.
fragment, *frăg'mênt*, s. frammento, m.
fragmentary, *–ărĭ*, a. frammentato.
fragrance, *frā'grăns*, s. fragranza, f., odore soave, m,
fragrant, *–grănt*, a. odoroso; **–ly**, ad. soavemente.
frail, *frāl*, a. frale, fragile; –, s. paniera, f.
frailty, *–tĭ*, s. fragilità, debolezza, f.
frame, *frām*, s. forma, figura, f.; struttura, f.; fabbrica, f.; quadro, m.; impannata, f.; cassa, f.; disposizione, f.; –, v. a. formare; costruire, fabbricare; controvare, inventare.　[tura, f.; scheletro di legname, m.
framework, *–wûrk*, s. ossatura, intelaiatura.
franchise, *frăn'chĭz*, s. franchigia, f.; privilegio, m.
frangible, *frăn'jĭbl*, a. fragile.
frank, *frăngk*, a. franco, libero; sincero, generoso, liberale; –, s. franco, m.; lettera privilegiata, f.; –, v. a. privilegiare (lettere).
frankincense, *–ĭnsêns*, s. incenso, m.
frankly, *–lĭ*, ad. francamente.
frankness, *–nês*, s. franchezza, f.; sincerità, f.
frantic, *frăn'tĭk*, a. frenetico, furioso.
fraternal, *frătûr'năl*, a. fraterno; **–ly**, ad. fraternamente.
fraternity, *–nĭtĭ*, s. fraternita, f.
fraternize, *frăt'ûrnĭz*, v. a. istituire una fratellanza, affratellarsi.
fratricide, *–rĭsĭd*, s. (murder) fratricidio, m.; (murderer) fratricida, m. & f.
fraud, *frăd*, s. fraude, trufferia, f.
fraudulent, *frā'dŭlênt*, a. **–ly**, ad. fraudolente (mente).
fraught, *frăt*, p. & a. caricato; empiuto.
fray, *frā*, s. rissa, contesa, f.; zuffa, f.; –, v. a. & n. spaventare; usarsi.
freak, *frêk*, s. capriccio, m.; fantasia, f.
freckle, *frêk'l*, s. lentiggine, f.; macchia
freckled, *–ld*, a. lentigginoso.　[rossa, f.
free, *frê*, a. libero, franco; liberale; immune; ingenuo, sincero; naturale; –, v. a. liberare, esentare; francare.　[m.
freebooter, *–bôtûr*, s. rubatore, filibustiere.
freedman, *–d'măn*, s. liberto, m.

freedom, *–dŭm*, s. libertà, f.; immunità, f.
freehearted, *–hărtêd*, a. liberale, generoso.
freehold, *–hôld*, s. feudo, m.
freely, *–lĭ*, ad. liberamente, volentieri.
freeman, *–măn*, s. uomo libero, m.
freemason, *–mă'sn*, s. frammassone, m.
freemasonry, *–mă'snrĭ*, s. frammassoneria, f., ordine de' frammassoni, m.
freeschool, *–skôl*, s. scuola pubblica, f.
freespoken, *–spôkn*, a. franco, candido, ingenuo.
freestone, *–stôn*, s. pietra macigna, f.
freethinker, *–thĭnkûr*, s. spirito forte, libertino, m.
freethinking, *–thĭnkĭng*, freethought, *–thôt*, s. libertinaggio, m.; incredulità, irreligiosità, f.
free-trade, *–trăd*, s. franchigia di commercio, f.
freewill, *–wĭl*, s. libero arbitrio, m.
freeze, *frêz*, v. n. ir. gelare, congelare; gelarsi.　　　　　　[ciaia, f.
freezing-machine, *–ĭng măshên*, s. ghiacfreight, *frăt*, s. noleggio, m.; carica, f.; –, v. a. (mar.) noleggiare; caricare.
freighter, *–ûr*, s. noleggiatore, m.
freighting, *–ĭng*, s. nolo, m.
frenchify, *frênsh'ĭfĭ*, v. a. dare le maniere Francesi, far divenir Francese.
frenzied, *frên'zĭd*, a. frenetico, insano.
frenzy, *frên'zĭ*, s. frenesia, pazzia, f., furore, m.　　　　　　　[moltitudine, f.
frequency, *frê'kwênsĭ*, s. frequenza, f.;
frequent, *–kwênt*, a. **–ly**, ad. frequente (mente); –, v. a. frequentare.　[tivo.
frequentative, *–kwên'tătĭv*, a. frequentafrequenter, *–kwênt'ûr*, s. frequentatore, m.
fresco, *frês'kô*, s. pittura a fresco, f.
fresh, *frêsh*, a. fresco, nuovo, recente; – water, s. acqua dolce, f.　　[frescarsi.
freshen, *frêsh'n*, v. a. & n. rinfrescare; rinfreshet, *–êt*, s. laghetto d' acqua dolce, m.
freshly, *–lĭ*, ad. frescamente; novellamente; recentemente.
freshman, *–măn*, s. inesperto, novizio, m.
freshness, *–nês*, s. freschezza, f., fresco, m.
fret, *frêt*, s. fermentazione, f.; agitazione, f.; tasto, m.; stretto, m.; –, v. a. fregare; vessare, irritare, crucciare; –, v. n. agitarsi, alterarsi, adirarsi.
fretful, *–fŭl*, a. stizzoso, cruccioso; **–ly**, ad. in modo stizzoso.
fretfulness, *–fŭlnês*, s. umore stizzoso, m.
fret-work, *–wûrk*, s. lavoro in relievo, intaglio, m.; stria, f.
fretting, *–ĭng*, s. agitazione, f.
friability, *frĭăbĭl'ĭtĭ*, s. friabilità, f.
friable, *frĭ'ăbl*, a. friabile, polverizzabile.
friar, *frĭ'ûr*, s. monaco, frate, m.
friary, *–ărĭ*, s. monastero, m.
friction, *frĭk'shŭn*, s. fregamento, m.
Friday, *frĭ'dă*, s. venerdì, m.; **Good –**, venerdì santo, m.　[s. pl. parenti, m. pl.
friend, *frênd*, s. amico, m.; amica, f.; **–s**,
friendless, *–lês*, a. senza amici.
friendliness, *–lĭnês*, s. amicizia, benevolenza, f.　　　　　[ad. amichevolmente.
friendly, *–lĭ*, a. amichevole, benevolo; –,

friendship, *–shĭp*, s. amicizia, f.

frieze, *frēz*, s. fregio, m.

frigate, *frĭg'ăt*, s. fregata, f.

fright, *frĭt*, s. paura, f., spavento, m.

frighten, *frĭt'tn*, v. a. impaurire, spaventare.

frightful, *frĭt'fŭl*, a. spaventevole, terribile; **-ly**, ad. spaventevolmente.

frigid, *frĭj'ĭd*, a. frigido, freddo; **-ly**, ad. freddamente.   [impotenza, f.

frigidity, *–jĭd'ĭtĭ*, s. frigidità, freddezza,f.;

frill, *frĭl*, s. collare increspato, m.

fringe, *frĭnj*, s. frangia, f.; **–**, v. a. guarnire di frange.   [f.; ciarpe, f. pl.

frippery, *frĭp'părĭ*, s. strada de' rigattieri,

frisk, *frĭsk*, s. salto, m.; **–**, v. n. salterellare.

frisky, *frĭs'kĭ*, a. gaio, vivace, spiritoso.

frith, *frĭth*, s. stretto, braccio di mare, m.

fritter, *frĭt'tăr*, s. frittella, f.; **–**, v. a. tritare, sminuzzare; consumare.

frivolity, *frĭvŏl'ĭtĭ*, s. frivolezza, f.

frivolous, *frĭv'ŏlŭs*, a. frivolo, vano; **-ly**, ad. frivolmente; di poca importanza.

frizz(le), *frĭz'l*, v. a. arricciare, inanellare.

fro, *frō*, ad. quà e là; indietro; **to go to and –**, andare e venire.

frock, *frŏk*, s. giubbetta di tela, f.; tonaca, f.

frog, *frŏg*, s. rannochia, rana, f.

frolic, *frŏl'ĭk*, a. gaio, lieto; **–**, s. ghiribizzo, m., fantasia, f.; **–**, v. n. burlare, beffare.

frolicsome, *–săm*, a. scherzoso, gaio.

from, *frŏm*, pr. da, dal, di. [pianta), m.

frond, *frŏnd*, s. stelo, gambo (di una

front, *frŭnt*, s. fronte, f.; frontispizio, m.; parte d' avanti, f.; ciuffo, m.; **–**, v. a. fronteggiare.   [m.; benda, striscia, f.

frontal, *–tăl*, s. frontale, m.; frontispizio,

frontier, *frŏn'tēr*, s. frontiera, f., limite, m.

frontispiece, *–tĭspēs*, s. frontispizio, m.; facciata, f.   [f.

frontlet, *frŭnt'lĕt*, s. frontale, m., benda,

frost, *frŏst*, s. gelata, f.; ghiaccio, m.

frostbitten, *–bĭttn*, a. attaccato dal ghiaccio, gelato.

frosty, *frŏs'tĭ*, a. ghiacciato, gelato.

froth, *frŏth*, s. schiuma, spuma, f.; **–**, v. n. schiumare, spumare.

frothy, *frŏth'ĭ*, a. spumoso; frivolo, vano.

froward, *frō'wărd*, a. stizzoso, arcigno, ostinato; **-ly**, ad. ostinatamente.

frowardness, *–nĕs*, s. cattivo umore, m.

frown, *frŏŭn*, s. raggrinzamento della fronte, m.; disprezzo, m.; **–**, v. n. ringhiare; increspare le ciglia.

frozen, *frō'zn*, a. gelato, gelato.

frugal, *frō'găl*, a. frugale, parco, economo; **-ly**, ad. frugalmente.   [ranza, f.

frugality, *–găl'ĭtĭ*, s. frugalità, f.; moderuit, *frūt*, s. frutto, m.; rendita, f. [m.

fruiterer, *–ărăr*, s. fruttaiolo, fruttaiuolo, f.

fruitful, *–fŭl*, a. fertile; fecondo; profittabile, utile; **-ly**, ad. fertilmente.

fruitfulness, *–fŭlnĕs*, s. fertilità, f.

fruitless, *–lĕs*, a. sterile; inutile; **-ly**, ad. inutilmente; vanamente.

fruit-tree, *–trē*, s. albero fruttifero, m.

frump, *frŭmp*, s. vecchia stizzosa, f.

frustrate, *frŭs'trăt*, v. a. frustrare; annullare.   [disiacimento, m.

frustration, *–trā'shŭn*, s. delusione, f.,

fry, *frĭ*, s. fregola, f.; presciolini, m. pl.; frittura, f.; **–**, v. a. friggere.

frying-pan, *–ĭng păn*, s. padella, f.

fuddle, *fŭd'l*, v. a. & n. ubriacare, imbriacarsi.

fudge, *fŭj*, i. minchioneria! son frottole!

fuel, *fū'ĕl*, s. provvisione di legna, carboni, &., f.

fugacity, *fūgăs'ĭtĭ*, s. fugacità, f.; fuga, f.

fugitive, *fū'jĭtĭv*, a. & s. fugitivo (m.).

fugue, *fūg*, s. (mus.) fuga, f.

fulcrum, *fŭl'krŭm*, s. punto di bilico, m.

fulfil, *fŭlfĭl'*, v. a. adempire, compire.

fulfilment, *–mĕnt*, s. compimento, m.

full, *fŭl*, a. pieno, compito; intero, totale; **–**, s. tutto, compimento, m.; **–**, ad. interamente, affatto; **–**, v. a. sodare; follare, calpestare.

full-blown, *–blōn*, a. nel più bello del fiore, gonfiato.

full-dress, *–drĕs*, s. abito di gala, m.

fuller, *fŭl'lăr*, s. fullone, m.   [naturale.

full-length, *–lĕngth*, a, di o in grandezza

fulling-mill, *–lĭng mĭl*, s. mulino da sodare i panni, m.; gualchiera, f.

full-moon, *–mōn*, s. luna piena, f.

fully, *–lĭ*, ad. interamente, pienamente, ampiamente.

fulminant, *–mĭnănt*, a. fulminante.

fulminate, *–mĭnăt*, v. a. & n. fulminare.

fulmination, *–nă'shŭn*, s. fulminazione, f.   [danza, f.

fulness, *–nĕs*, s. ripienezza, f.; abbon-

fulsome, *–săm*, a. dispiacevole, fastidioso.

fumble, *fŭm'bl*, v. n. maneggiare con mala grazia, malmenare; balbettare.

fume, *fūm*, s. fumo, vapore, m., chimera, f.; **–**, v. a. seccare al fumo, affumicare; esalare; **–**, v. n. svaporarsi; adirarsi.

fumigate, *fū'mĭgăt*, v. a. suffumicare, profumare; fumigare.

fumigation, *–gă'shŭn*, s. fumigazione, f.

fumy, *fū'mĭ*, a. fumoso, vaporoso.

fun, *fŭn*, s. divertimento, m.; baia, burla, f.

function, *fŭngk'shŭn*, s. funzione, f.; impiego, m.

functionary, *–ărĭ*, s. impiegato, m.

fund, *fŭnd*, s. fondo, m.; capitale, m.; **–**, v. a. collocare i denari.   [m.

fundament, *fŭn'dămĕnt*, s. fondamento, f.

fundamental, *–mĕn'tăl*, a. fondamentale; **-ly**, ad. fondamentalmente.

funeral, *fū'nĕrăl*, s. funerale, m.; esequie, f. pl.; **–**, a. funerale.   [lugubre.

funereal, *–nē'rĭăl*, a. funereo, funebre,

fungosity, *fŭnggŏs'ĭtĭ*, s. escrescenza carnosa, f.

fungous, *fŭng'gŭs*, a. fungoso, spugnoso.

fungus, *–*, s. fungo, m.; escrescenza di carne, f.

funk, *fŭngk*, s. fetore, m.; tanfo, m.

funnel, *fŭn'nĕl*, s. imbuto, m., pevera, f.

funny, *fŭn'nĭ*, a. buffonesco, giocoso.

fur, *fŭr*, s. pelliccia, f.; **–**, v. a. impellicare.

furbelow, –*bĕlŏ*, s. falbalà, f.
furbish, –*bĭsh*, v. a. forbire, pulire.
furious, *fū′rĭăs*, a. furioso, frenetico;
–**ly**, ad. con furia. [miglio, f.
furlong, *fŭr′lŏng*, s. ottava parte d' un
furlough, –*lŏ*, s. permissione d' assenza,
f., congedo, m. [m.
furnace, –*năs*, s. fornace, f., forno grande,
furnish, –*nĭsh*, v. a. fornire; provvedere;
addobbare (una casa).
furnisher, –*ăr*, s. provveditore, m.
furniture, –*nĭtŭr* (–*nĭchŭr*), s. guarnitura,
f.; mobili, m. pl.
furniture-broker, –*brŏkŭr*, s. rigattiere,
furrier, *fŭr′ĭŭr*, s. pellicciaio, pellicciere,
m. [–, v. a. solcare, rugare.
furrow, *fŭr′rŏ*, s. solco, m.; fossatello, m.;
furry, *fŭr′rĭ*, a. coperto di pelliccia.
further, *fŭr′thăr*, a. & ad. ulteriore; di
là; di più, più avanti, più innanzi, più
oltre; –, v. a. avanzare, aiutare; pro-
nuovere. [mento, progresso, m.
furtherance, –*ăns*, s. aiuto, m.; avanza-
furthermore, –*mŏr*, ad. di più, oltre;
oltre a ciò. [rimotissimo.
furthest, *fŭr′thĕst*, a. il più lontano,
furtive, *fŭr′tĭv*, a. furtivo, segreto; –**ly**,
ad. furtivamente; segretamente.
fury, *fū′rĭ*, s. furia, frenesia, f.; ira, f.;
furze, *fŭrz*, s. (bot.) erica, f. [furore, m.
fuse, *fŭz*, v. a. & n. fondere; liquefarsi.
fusee, *fŭzĕ′*, s. fuso, m.; scoppietto, m.;
(of a watch) piramide, f.
fusibility, –*ĭbĭl′ĭtĭ*, s. fusibilità, f.
fusible, –*zĭbl*, a. fusibile.
fusilier, *fŭzĭlēr′*, s. fusiliere, m.
fusion, *fŭ′zhŭn*, s. fusione, liquefazione, f.
fuss, *fŭs*, s. fracasso, strepito, m.
fussy, *fŭs′ĭ*, a. faccendiere.
fustian, *fŭs′tĭăn*, s. frustagno, m., ampollosità, f. [f.; tanfo, m.
fustiness, –*tĭnĕs*, s. mucidezza, muffa,
fusty, *fŭs′tĭ*, a. mucido, muffato.
futile, *fū′tĭl*, a. futile, frivolo.
futility, –*tĭl′ĭtĭ*, s. leggerezza, f.; vanità, f.
future, *fū′tŭr*, a. futuro; –, s. futuro, avvenire, m. [venire, m.
futurity, –*tū′rĭtĭ*, s. tempo futuro, av-
fy, *fĭ*, i. oibò! – **for shame**! deh vergo-
gnatevi!

G.

gab, *găb*, s. muso, ceffo, m.; cicalio, m.
gabble, *găb′l*, s. chiacchiera, ciarla, f.; –,
v. n. cicalare.
gabbler, –*lăr*, s. ciarlone, ciarliero, m.
gable(-end), *gā′bl(ĕnd)*, s. gronda, f.;
gaby, *gā′bĭ*, s. allocco, m. [tetto, m.
gad, *găd*, s. pezzo d' acciaio; bulino, m.;
–, v. n. andare qua e là.
gad-fly, –*flī*, s. tafano, m.
gaff, *găf*, s. rampone, m.; fiocina, f.
gag, *găg*, s. sbarra, f.; –, v. a. porre in
bocca una sbarra. [misura, f.
gage, *gāj*, s. pegno, m.; guanto, m.;

gaiety, *gā′ĭtĭ*, s. gaiezza, f.
gaily, –*lĭ*, ad. gaiamente.
gain, *gān*, s. guadagno, lucro, profitto, m.;
–, v. a. & n. guadagnare; avvanzarsi.
gainer, –*ăr*, s. guadagnatore, m.
gainings, –*ĭngz*, s. pl. guadagno, m.
gainless, –*lĕs*, a. inutile.
gainsay, –*sā*, v. a. contraddire; opporsi,
contrariare, contrastare. [aria, f.
gait, *gāt*, s. andamento, portamento, m.;
gaiters, *gā′tărz*, s. pl. uose, f. pl.
galaxy, *găl′ăksĭ*, s. via lattea, f.
gale, *gāl*, s. (mar.) vento fresco, m.
galiot, *găl′ĭŏt*, s. (mar.) galeotta, f.
gall, *găl*, s. fiele, m.; (fig.) odio, m.; rancore, m.; –, v. a. & n. scorticare; affliggersi.
gallant, *găl′lănt*, a. galante; elegante;
bravo; –, *găllănt′*, s. galantuomo, m.;
zerbino, m.; amante, m. [bravamente;
gallantly, *găl′lăntlĭ*, ad. galantemente;
gallantry, –*rĭ*, s. galanteria, f.; bravura,
f.; valore, m.
galleon, *găl′lĕŏn*, s. galeone, m.
gallery, *găl′lĕrĭ*, s. galleria, f.; loggia, f.;
andito, m.
galley, *găl′lĭ*, s. (mar.) galera, f. [m.
galley-slave, –*slāv*, s. galeotto, forzato
gallinaceous, *găllĭnā′shŭs*, a. gallinaceo.
gallipot, *găl′lĭpŏt*, s. albarello, vasetto, m.
gall-nut, *găl′nŭt*, s. noce di galla, f.
gallon, *găl′lŭn*, s. misura di quattro boc-
cali, gallone, f. [galoppare.
gallop, *găl′ŭp*, s. galoppo, m.; –, v. n.
gallows, *găl′lŏz*, s. pl. patibolo, m.
galvanic, *gălvăn′ĭk*, a. galvanico.
galvanise, *găl′vănĭz*, v. a. galvanizzare.
galvanism, *găl′vănĭzm*, s. galvanismo, m.
gambit, *găm′bĭt*, s. gambetto, m.
gamble, *găm′bl*, v. n. giocare.
gambler, –*blăr*, s. giocatorone, m.
gambling-house, –*blĭng hŏŭs*, s. casino
da giocare, m.
gamboge, *gămbŏj′*, s. gommagutte, m.
gambol, *găm′bŏl*, s. salto, scambietto, m.;
–, v. n. salterellare.
game, *găm*, s. giuoco, m.; scherzo, passatempo, m.; salvaggine, f.; –, v. n. giocare.
game-bag, –*băg*, s. tasca da cacciatori, f.
game-cock, –*kŏk*, s. gallo di combattimento, m. [m.
game-keeper, –*kēpăr*, s. guardacaccia,
gamesome, –*săm*, a. giocoso, giocondo;
–**ly**, ad. scherzevolmente.
gamester, –*stăr*, s. giocatore, m.
gaming, *găm′ĭng*, s. giuoco, giocare, m.
gammon, *găm′măn*, s. sbaraglino, m.; –,
v. a. beffare.
gamut, *găm′ŭt*, s. (mus.) zolfa, f.
gander, *găn′dăr*, s. maschio dell' oca, m.
gang, *găng*, s. truppa, banda, f.
gangrene, –*grēn*, s. (med.) cancrena, f.
gangway, –*wā*, s. (mar.) passavanti, f.;
una nave da guerra, corridore, m.
gaol, *jăl*, s. prigione, f.; carcere, m.
gaoler, –*ăr*, s. guardiano delle prigioni, m.

gap, *găp,* s. apertura, crepatura, f.; lacuna, f.; breccia, f.; deficienza, f.

gape, *găp,* v. n. sbadigliare; creparsi, spaccarsi, aprirsi.

gaping, *gā'ping,* s. sbadigliamento, m.

gap-toothed, *găp'töthd,* a. sdentato.

garb, *gărb,* s. vestimento, abito, m.: aria, f.; maniera, f.; portamento, m.

garbage, *găr'bāj,* s. tripple.f.pl. [separare.

garble, *găr'bl,* v. n. scegliere; scernere.

garden, *găr'dn,* s. giardino, m.; —, v. n. coltivare un giardino. [diniera, f.

gardener, *—dnār,* s. giardiniere, m.; giar-

gardening, *—dning,* s. il coltivare un giardino, m. [un giardinaggio, m.

garden-plot, *—plŏt,* s. spartimento d'

gargle, *găr'gl,* s. gargarismo, m.; —, v. n. gargarizzare.

gargoyle, *găr'gŏil,* s. doccia della gronda.

garish, *găr'ish,* a. splendido, pomposo.

garland, *găr'länd,* s. ghirlanda, f.

garlic, *găr'lik,* s. aglio, m. [mento, m.

garment, *găr'měnt,* s. abito, vestito, vesti-

garner, *găr'nār,* s. granaio, m.; —, v. a. mettere nel granaio; ammassare.

garnet, *găr'nět,* s. granato, m.; (mar.) carrucola, f.

garnish, *găr'nish,* s. ornamento, m.; —, v.a. guarnire, ornare, abbellire.

garret, *găr'rět,* s. solaio, f.; soffitta, stanza a tetto, f.

garrison, *găr'risn,* s. guarnigione, f.; —, v. a. mettere guarnigione.

garrotter, *gărŏt'ār,* s. strangolatore; ladro che pone ad altrui in bocca una sbarra, m.

garrulity, *gărrŭ'lĭtĭ,* s. garrulità, loquacità, f.; ciarla, f. [ciarliero.

garrulous, *găr'rŭlăs,* a. garrulo, loquace;

garter, *găr'tār,* s. giarrettiera, f.

gas, *găs,* s. gas, gaz, m.

gasalier, *—ālēr',* s. lampadario a gas, m.

gas-burner, *găs'būrnār,* s. becco, m.

gaseous, *gā'zēăs,* a. gassoso, gazoso.

gash, *găsh,* s. sfregio, m.; cicatrice, f.; —, v. a. sfregiare, tagliare.

gas-jet, *găs'jět,* s. fiamma (di gas), f.

gas-lamp, *—lămp,* s. lampada di gas, f.

gaslight, *—līt,* s. lume a gas, m.; luce del gas, f. [di gas, f.

gas-lighting, *—līting,* s. illuminazione

gasometer, *găsŏm'ĕtār,* s. gassometro, m.

gasp, *găsp,* s. anelito, respiro, m.; —, v. n. anelare, respirare con affanno.

gastric, *găs'trĭk,* a. gastrico. [mico.

gastronomic, *—trŏnŏm'ĭk,* a. gastrono-

gas-works, *găs'wŭrks,* s. pl. luogo ove si genera il gas, m.

gate, *găt,* s. porta, f.; portone, m.

gate-way, *—wā,* s. portone, passaggio, m.

gather, *găth'ār,* v. a. cogliere, raccogliere; rincrespare, piegare; conchiudere, inferire: —, v. n. accumularsi, assembrarsi, condensarsi; suppurare.

gathering, *—ing,* s. collezione, f.

gaudily, *gā'dĭlĭ,* ad. fastosamente; sfoggiatamente. [zione, f.

gaudiness, *—dĭněs,* s. fasto, m.; ostenta-

gaudy, *—dĭ,* a. pomposo, fastoso; —, s. festa, f.; festeggiamento, m.

gauffer, *găf'fār,* v. a. imprimere le stoffe.

gauge, *găj,* s. stazza, f.; —, v. a. stazzare; misurare.

gauger, *găg'jār,* s. misuratore di liquidi, m.

gauging, *—jing,* s. stazzatura, f.

gaunt, *gănt,* a. magro, affilato, smunto.

gauntlet, *—lět,* s. guanto di ferro, m.; gastigo militare, m.

gauze, *găz,* s. velo, m.; tocca, f.

gawky, *gā'kĭ,* a. sciocco, bafocco.

gay, *gā,* a. gaio, gioioso, lieto.

gaze, *găz,* s. sguardo fisso, m.; —, v. n. guardare fissamente.

gazelle, *găzěl',* s. gazzella, f.

gazer, *gā'zār,* s. spettatore, m.

gazette, *găzět',* s. gazzetta, f.

gazetteer, *găzěttēr',* s. gazzettiere, m.; dizionario di gazzetta, m.; scrittore di novelle, m. [m. pl.; roba, f.

gear, *gēr,* s. vestimenti, m. pl.; mobili,

gelatin(e), *jěl'ătin,* s. gelatina, f.

gelatinous, *—lăt'ĭnăs,* a. gelatinoso.

geld, *gěld,* v. a. castrare.

gelding, *—ing,* s. cavallo castrato, m.

gem, *jěm,* s. gemma, f.; bottone, m.; —, v. a. & n. adornare di gemme; germogliare.

gender, *jěn'dār,* s. genere, m. [gliare.

genealogical, *jěněălŏj'ĭkăl,* a. genealogico.

genealogy, *—ŏj't,* s. genealogia, f.

general, *jěn'ěrăl,* a. generale, universale; comune; —ly, ad. generalmente; —, s. generale; suono di tamburi per dar l'allarme, m. [mento ad un genere, m.

generalisation, *—īsā'shăn,* s. riduci-

generalise, *jěn'ěrălĭz,* v. a. generalizzare.

generality, *—āl'ĭtĭ,* s. generalità, f.; maggiore parte, f.

generalship, *jěn'ěrălshĭp,* s. generalato, m.

generate, *jěn'ěrăt,* v. a. generare; produrre; cagionare.

generation, *—rā'shăn,* s. generazione, f.; produzione, f.; razza, f.

generator, *—rā'tār,* s. generatore, creatore, m.; principio, m.

generic, *—něr'ĭk,* a. generico.

generosity, *—ŏs'ĭtĭ,* s. generosità, f.; liberalità, f. [generosamente.

generous, *jěn'ěrăs,* a. generoso; —ly, ad.

genet, *jěn'ět,* s. ginnetto, m.

genial, *jē'nĭăl,* a. geniale; naturale; giocondo; —ly, ad. in modo geniale; naturalmente. [grezza, f.

geniality, *jěnĭăl'ĭtĭ,* s. genio, m.; alle-

genitive, *—ĭtĭv,* s. (gr.) genitivo, m.

genius, *jē'nĭăs,* s. genio, m.; spirito, m.; talento, m.

genteel, *jěntēl',* a. gentile, grazioso, elegante; cortese; —ly, ad. gentilmente, elegantemente.

gentian, *jěn'shăn,* s. genziana, f.

gentile, *jěn'tĭl,* s. gentile, m.; pagano, m.

gentility, *—tĭl'ĭtĭ,* s. gentilità, f.; gentilezza, f.; nobiltà, f.

gentle, *jěn'tl,* a. dolce; piacevole; benigno; domestico, mansueto.

gentlefolks,–*fóks,* s. gente nobile, nobilità, f.

gentleman, –*măn,* s. gentiluomo, m. [f.

gentlemanlike, –*mănlĭk,* a. da gentiluomo. [dolcezza, f.

gentleness, –*nês,* s. gentilezza, cortesia, f.;

gentlewoman, –*wŭmăn,* s. gentildonna, damigella, f. [mente.

gently, –*lĭ,* ad. gentilmente; benigna-

gentry, –*trĭ,* s. persone qualificate, f. pl.

genuflexion, *jĕnŭflĕk'shăn,* s. genuflessione, f.

genuine, *jĕn'dĭn,* a. vero, naturale; **–ly,** ad. veramente; naturalmente.

genuineness, –*nês,* s. purità, f.; realità, f.; autenticità, f.

genus, *jē'nŭs,* s. genere, m.

geographer, *jĕŏg'răfăr,* s. geografo, m.

geographical, *jĕŏgrŏf'ĭkăl,* a. geografico.

geography, *jĕŏg'răfĭ,* s. geografia, f.

geological, *jĕŏlŏj'ĭkăl,* a. geologico.

geologist, *jĕŏl'ŏjĭst,* s. geologo, m.

geology, –*ŏjĭ,* s. geologia, f.

geometric(al), *jĕŏmĕt'rĭk(ăl),* a. geometrico. [m.

geometrician, *jĕŏmĕtrĭsh'ăn,* s. geometra,

geometry, *jĕŏm'ĕtrĭ,* s. geometria, f.

germ, *jărm,* s. germe, germoglio, m.

german, *jăr'măn,* s. cugino germano, m.; cugina germana, f.

germinal, *jăr'mĭnăl,* a. di germe.

germinate, –*mĭnăt,* v. n. germogliare.

gesticulate, *jĕstĭk'ŭlăt,* v. n. gesticolare.

gesticulation, –*lā'shăn,* s. gesticolazione, f., gesteggiare, m. [tura, f.

gesture, *jĕs'tŭr* (–*chăr*), s. gesto, m.; posi-

get, *gĕt,* v. a. ir. guadagnare; ottenere, acquistare; impetrare, ricevere; meritare; impadronirsi, prendere, pigliare; impegnare; **–,** v. n. ir. venire; arrivare; aver ricorso; **to – the better,** aver la superiorità; **to – by heart,** imparare a mente; **to – with child,** far divenir gravida.

getter-up, –*tŭr ŭp,* s. promotore, m.

gewgaw, *gŭ'gă,* s. bubbola, f.; cose da nulla, f. pl. [landa, gaiser, m.

Geyser, *gī'zăr,* s. Geiser, sorgente d'Islanda, gaiser, m.

ghastliness, *găst'lĭnês,* s. viso spaventoso, m.; vista orrenda, f.; squallidezza, f.; pallore estremo, m.; orrore, m.

ghastly, –*lĭ,* a. squallido, orrendo.

gherkin, *găr'kĭn,* s. cetriuolo conservato con aceto, m. [f.

ghost, *gŏst,* s. spirito, m.; anima de' morti,

ghostly, –*lĭ,* a. spirituale.

giant, *jĭ'ănt,* s. gigante, m.

giantess, –*ês,* s. gigantessa, f.

gibberish, *gĭb'bărĭsh,* s. gergo, m.

gibbet, *jĭb'bĕt,* s. forca, f.; **–,** v. a. impiccare; appendere.

gibe, *jĭb,* s. beffa, burla, f.; **–,** v. a. & n. beffare, burlare; schernire. [ecc.), f. pl.

giblets, *jĭb'lĕts,* s. pl. frattaglie (delle oche,

giddily, *gĭd'dĭlĭ,* ad. inconsideratamente.

giddiness, –*dĭnês,* s. capogiro, m., vertigine, f.; incostanza, f.

giddy, –*dĭ,* a. vertiginoso; incostante.

gift, *gĭft,* s. dono, m.; talento, m.

gig, *gĭg,* s. ruzzola, trottola, f.; paleo, m.; biroccio, m.

gigantic, *jĭgăn'tĭk,* a. gigantesco.

giggle, *gĭg'gl,* v. n. sogghignare.

gild, *gĭld,* v. a. dorare.

gilding, –*ĭng,* s. doratura, f.

gill, *jĭl,* s. branchie (di pesci), f. pl.

gillyflower, *jĭl'ĭflŏur,* s. leucoio, m.

gilt, *gĭlt,* a. dorato.

gimcrack, *jĭm'krăk,* s. meccanismo vol? gare, m.; ciappola, f.

gimlet, *jĭm'lĕt,* s. succhiello, m.

gin, *jĭn,* s. trappola, f.; stiaccia, f.; ginepro, liquore, m.

ginger, *jĭn'jăr,* s. zenzero, gengiovo, m.

gingerbread, –*brĕd,* s. confortino, m.

gipsy, *jĭp'sĭ,* s. zingaro, m.; zingara, f.

giraffe, *jĭrăf',* s. giraffa, f.

gird, *gŭrd,* v. a. & n. ir. cingere, circondare; beffare, burlare.

girder, –*ŭr,* s. trave maestra, f.

girdle, *gŭr'dl,* s. cintura, zona, f.; **–,** v. a. cingere.

girl, *gŭrl,* s. ragazza, zittella, f. [m.

girlhood, –*hŭd,* s. stato d'una giovinetta,

girlish, *gŭr'lĭsh,* a. di ragazza.

girth, *gŭrth,* s. cinghia, cintura, f.

gist, *jĭst,* s. punto principale d'una accusa, m.

give, *gĭv,* v. a. ir. dare; donare; conferire; vendere; **–,** v. n. ir. liquefarsi; animollirsi; rilasciare; consentire.

gizzard, *gĭz'zărd,* s. ventriglio, m.

glacial, *glā'shăl,* a. glaciale.

glacier, *glā'sĭăr* (–*shtŭr*), s. ghiacciaio, m.

glad, *glăd,* a. contento, lieto, allegro.

gladden, *glăd'n,* v. a. rallegrare.

glade, *glăd,* s. viale d'alberi, f.; (am.) gelicidio, m.

gladiator, *glăd'ĭă'tăr,* s. gladiatore, m.

gladness, *glăd'nês,* s. gioia, gaiezza, f.

gladsome, –*săm,* a. gioioso, giocondo.

glamour, *glăm'ăr,* s. incanto, m.

glance, *glăns,* s. occhiata, f.; raggio di luce, m.; baleno, m.; **–,** v. n. raggiare; occhiare; scalfire; rasentare, strisciare.

gland, *glănd,* s. glandula, f.

glanders, *glăn'dărz,* s. pl. stranguglioni (de' cavalli), m. pl.

glare, *glăr,* s. luce soverchia, f.; occhiata feroce, f.; **–,** v. n. splendere; scintillare, abbagliare; occhiare.

glaring, *glă'rĭng,* a. abbagliante; splendente.

glass, *glăs,* s. vetro, m.; bicchiere, m.; specchio, m.; telescopio, m.; occhialino, m.; barometro, m.; oriuolo a polvere, m.; **–es,** pl. occhiali, m. pl.; **–,** a. di vetro, m.

glass-blower, –*blŏăr,* s. soffiatore, m.

glass-case, –*kăs,* s. vetrina, f.

glass-door, –*dŏr,* s. vetrata, f.

glass-house, –*hŏăs,* s. vetraia, fabbrica de' vetri, f.

glass-maker, –*măkăr,* s. vetraio, m.

glass-shade, –*shăd*, s. globo di vetro, m.
glass-work, –*wûrk*, s. vetreria, fabbrica di vetro, f.
glassy, *glăs'sĭ*, a. vitreo; invetriato.
glaze, *glāz*, v. a. invetriare; verniciare; lisciare.
glazier, *glā'zhär*, s. vetraio, m.
glazing, –*zĭng*, s. invetriamento, m.
gleam, *glēm*, s. raggio, m.; fulmine, n₁.; –, v. n. risplendere, scintillare.
gleamy, *glē'mĭ*, a. scintillante.
glean, *glēn*, v. a. spigolare; raccogliere.
glebe, *glēb*, s. zolla, gleba, f.; terreno, suolo, m.
glee, *glē*, s. gioia, f.; canzone gioiale, f.
gleeful, –*fŭl*, a. gioioso, gaio.
gleet, *glēt*, s. puzza, f.; marciume, m.
glen, *glēn*, s. valle, vallata, f.
glib, *glĭb*, a. liscio, lubrico; **–ly,** ad. correntemente; con facilità. [mente.
glide, *glīd*, v. n. scorrere; passare leggiermente.
glim, *glĭm*, s. lanterna cieca, f.
glimmer, –*mär*, s. luce debole, f.; mica, f.; –, v. n. tralucere, trasparire.
glimpse, *glĭmps*, s. barlume, m.; –, v. a. (am.) scorgere. [lucere; brillare.
glisten, *glĭs'n*, **glitter,** *glĭt'tär*, v. n. rilucere; brillare.
gloaming, *glōm'ĭng*, s. crepuscolo, m.
gloat, *glōt*, v. n. guardar sottecchi.
globe, *glōb*, s. globo, m.; sfera, f.
globular, *glŏb'dlär*, a. globuloso.
globule, *glŏb'ŭl*, s. globetto, m.
gloom, *glŏm*, **gloominess,** –*ĭnĕs*, s. oscurità, f.; tristezza, malinconia, f.
gloomy, *glŏ'mĭ*, a. oscuro, nuvoloso; triste, malinconico. [zione, f.
glorification, *glŏrĭfĭkă'shăn*, s. glorificazione, f.
glorify, *glŏ'rĭfĭ*, v. a. glorificare; vantarsi.
glorious, –*rŭs*, a. glorioso, famoso; **–ly,** ad gloriosamente.
glory, –*rĭ*, s. gloria, f.; fama, rinominanza, celebrità, f.; aureola, f.; –, v. n. gloriarsi, vantarsi.
gloss, *glŏs*, s. glossa, f.; commento, m.; lustro, liscio, m.; –, v. a. glossare, lustrare, pulire.
glossary, *glŏs'ărĭ*, s. glossario, m. [m.
glosser, –*är*, s. glossatore, m.; interprete, m.
glossy, –*sĭ*, a. liscio, pulito, lucido.
glove, *glŭv*, s. guanto, m.; **to be hand and – with one,** essere amicissimi.
glover, –*är*, s. guantaio, m.
glow, *glŏ*, s. ardore, m.; splendore, m.; vivezza, f.; –, v. n. rosseggiare; esser infocato, esser infiammato.
glowworm, –*wŭrm*, s. lucciola, f.
glue, *glŭ*, s. colla, f.; cemento, m.; –, v. a. appiccare con colla.
gluey, *glŭ'ĭ*, a. tenace, viscoso, glutinoso.
glum, *glăm*, a. arcigno, ritroso.
glut, *glăt*, s. saturità, f.; abbondanza, f.; –, v. a. inghiottire; satollare, saziare.
gluten, *glŭ'tĕn*, s. glutino, m.
glutinous, –*tĭnŭs*, a. viscoso; tenace.
glutton, *glăt'n*, s. ghiotto, goloso, m.
gluttonous, –*nŭs*, a. ghiotto, goloso; **–ly,** ad. golosamente; avidamente.

gluttony, –*nĭ*, ingordigia, f.
glycerine, *glĭs'ărĭn*, s. glicerina, f.
glycose, *glĭkŏs'*, s. zucchero d' amido, m.
gnarled, *närld*, a. nodoso. [ringhiare.
gnash, *năsh*, v. a. & n. digrignare i denti
gnat, *năt*, s. moscerino, m.
gnaw, *nä*, v. a. & n. rodere, rosicchiare.
gnome, *nŏm*, s. gnome, m.
go, *gŏ*, v. n. ir. andare, camminare; passare; partirsi; **– to I coraggio! –,** s. corso del mondo, m.; energia, f.
goad, *gŏd*, s. pungiglione, m.; stimolo, m.; –, v. a. punzecchiare, pungere; stimolare, eccitare.
goal, *gŏl*, s. termine, m., meta, f.
goat, *gŏt*, s. capra, f.; **he––,** s. becco, m.
goat-herd, –*hèrd*, s. capraio, m.
gobble, *gŏb'bl*, v. a. ingozzare.
gobbler, –*blär*, s. ghiottone, m.
go-between, *gŏ'bëtwèn'*, s. mediatore, mezzano, m. [m.
goblet, *gŏb'lĕt*, s. ciotola, tazza, f., bicchiere,
goblin, *gŏb'lĭn*, s. larva, f.; ombra, f., spirito, fantasma, m.
God, *gŏd*, s. Dio, Iddio, m. [cia, f.
god-child,–*chĭld*, s. figlioccio, m.; figlioccia, f.
god-daughter, –*dätär*, s. figlioccia, f.
goddess, –*dĕs*, s. dea, f. [m.
god-father, –*fäthär*, s. padrino, compare,
Godhead, –*hĕd*, s. Divinità, f., Dio, m.
godless, –*lĕs*, a. ateo, empio.
god-like, –*lĭk*, a. divino.
godliness, –*lĭnĕs*, s. divozione, f.; pietà, f.
godly, –*lĭ*, a. divoto, pio; –, ad. divotamente. [tola, f.
god-mother, –*mäthär*, s. madrina, f., santa.
godson, –*săn*, s. figlioccio, m.
goer, *gŏ'är*, s. camminatore, m.; cavallo che ha il passo sicuro, m.
goggle, *gŏg'gl*, v. n. guardare biecamente.
goggle-eyed, –*ĭd*, a. guercio, bieco, stralunato. [passo, m.
going, *gŏ'ĭng*, s. andare, m., andatura, f.;
gold, *gŏld*, s. oro, m.; moneta, f.
gold-beater, –*bĕtär*, s. battiloro, m.
gold-bound, –*bĕnd*, a. fregiato d' oro.
golden, –*n*, a. d'oro; eccellente; **– rule,** s. regola del tre, f.
gold-fish, –*fĭsh*, s. orata, f.
gold-leaf, –*lĕf*, s. foglia d' oro, f.
goldsmith, –*smĭth*, s. orefice, m.
golosh, *gŏlŏsh'*, s. calosce, f. pl.
gondolier, *gŏndŏlĕr'*, s. gondoliere, m.
gone, *gŏn*, p. & a. passato; morto; avanzato (in età). |
gong, *gŏng*, s. cembalo, m.
good, *gŭd*, a. buono, benigno; favorevole; convenevole; **–by(e),** addio; –, ad. bene; –, s. bene, vantaggio, profitto, m.; **–s,** pl. beni, effetti, m. pl.; mercanzie, f. pl.
good-humour, –*ămär*, s. buon umore, m.
good-humoured, –*ămărd*, a. di buon umore.
goodies, –*ĭz*, s. confetto, m. [f.
goodliness, –*lĭnĕs*, s. bellezza, f.; eleganza,
goodly, –*lĭ*, a. bello, vago; splendido.
good-nature, –*năchär*, s. indole dolce, f.
good-natured, –*năchärd*, a. d'indole dolce.

goodness, *–něs,* s. bontà, benignità, f.
good-will, *–wǐl,* s. benevolenza, bontà, f.
goose, *gōs,* s. oca, f.; quadrello, m.
gooseberry, *–běrǐ,* s. uva spina, f.
goose-step, *–stěp,* s. passi d'oca, m. pl.
gore, *gōr,* s. sangue accagliato, m.; –, v. a. stilettare; trafiggere.
gorge, *gōrj,* s. gola, f.; gozzo, m.; sorso, m.; –, v. a. satollare, impinzare; saziare.
gorgeous, *–jǔs,* a. fastoso, pomposo; **–ly,** ad. fastosamente; suntuosamente.
gorget, *–jět,* s. gorgiera, f.
gorgon, *–gŏn,* s. gorgone, f.
gormandize, *–mǎndǐz,* v. n. mangiare avidamente; esser dedito alla gola.
gormandizer, *–ǎr,* s. ghiotto, ghiottone, m.
gory, *gō'rǐ,* a. coperto di sangue.
goshawk, *gŏs'hǎk,* s. avvoltoio, m.
gosling, *gŏz'lǐng,* s. papero, m.
Gospel, *gŏs'pěl,* s. Evangelo, m.
gossamer, *gŏs'sǎmǎr,* s. filamenti di S. Maria, m. pl.
gossip, *gŏs'sǐp,* s. compare, m.; comare, f.; pettegolezzo, m.; –, v. n. ciarlare.
gothic, *gŏth'ǐk,* a. gotico.
gouge, *gŏj,* s. scarpello a doccia, m.
gourd, *gōrd,* s. zucca, f.
gout, *gŏŭt,* s. gotta, f.; podagra, f.; **– in the hips,** sciatica, f.
gouty, *gŏŭ'tǐ,* a. gottoso; podagroso.
govern, *gǔv'ǔrn,* v. a. & n. governare; regolare; reggere.
governable, *–ǎbl,* a. trattabile.
governess, *–ěs,* s. direttrice, insegnatrice.
government, *–mčnt,* **governance,** *–ǎns,* s. governo, m.; amministrazione, f.
governor, *–ǎr,* s. governatore, direttore, m.
gown, *gŏŭn,* s. veste, roba, toga, f.
gownsman, *–s'mǎn,* s. uomo togato, m.
grab(ble), *grǎb'(bl),* v. a. palpare, palpeggiare.
grace, *grās,* s. grazia, f.; bontà, f.; favore, m.; perdono, m.; leggiadria, f.; **to say –s,** benedire la tavola; –, v. a. ornare; favorire.
graceful, *–fǔl,* a. grazioso, leggiadro, elegante; amabile; **–ly,** ad. con grazia, elegantemente.
graceless, *–lěs,* a. sgraziato; sfacciato; [scellerato.
gracious, *grā'shǔs,* a. grazioso, favorevole; **–ly,** ad. graziosamente.
graciousness, *–něs,* s. gentilezza, grazia, f.
gradation, *grǎdǎ'shǎn,* s. gradazione, f.
grade, *grǎd,* s. grado, m. [cesa), f.
gradient, *grā'dǐčnt,* s. (rail.) salita (e disgradual,** *grā'dǔǎl,* a. graduale; **–ly,** ad. gradualmente; [addottorare; inalzare.
graduate, *–ǔǎt,* v. a. conferire un grado, s. innesto, m. [innesti, f.
graduation, *–ǎ'shǎn,* s. graduazione, f.
graft, *grǎft,* v. a. annestare, innestare; –, s. innesto, m. [innesti, f.
grafting-knife, *–ǐng nǐf,* s. coltello da grain,** *grān,* s. grano, m.; seme, m., semenza, f.; disposizione, f.; **against the –,** a malincuore; **–s,** pl. feccia dell'orzo dopo fatta la birra, f.
grained, *grānd,* a. granato, granito.
gram, *grǎm,* s. grammo, m.

grammar, *grǎm'mǎr,* s. grammatica, f.
grammarian, *–mǎ'rǐǎn,* s. grammatico, m.
grammatical, *–mǎt'ǐkǎl,* a. grammaticale; **–ly,** ad. grammaticalmente.
grampus, *grǎm'pǔs,* s. orca, f.
granary, *grǎn'ǎrǐ,* s. granaio, m.
grand, *grǎnd,* a. grande; nobile, illustre.
grandam, *grǎn'dǎm,* s. ava, nonna, f.; vecchia, f. [tina, f.
grandchild, *–chǐld,* s. nipote, m.; nipotina, f.
granddaughter, *–dǎtǎr,* s. nipotina, f.; **great –,** pronipote, f.
grandee, *grǎndē',* s. grande di Spagna, m.
grandeur, *grǎn'd'yǔr,* s. grandezza, f.; magnificenza, f. [bisavo, m.
grandfather, *–fǎthǔr,* s. avo, m.; **great –,** grandiloquent,** *–dǐl'ǒkwěnt,* a. grandiloquente.
grandiose, *grǎn'd'ǐǒs,* a. grandioso.
grandly, *–lǐ,* ad. grandemente.
grand-mother, *–mǔthǔr,* s. ava, avola, f.; **great –,** bisava, f.
grand-sire, *–sǐr,* s. avo, m.
grand-son, *–sǔn,* s. nipotino, m.; **great –,** pronipote, m.
grange, *grǎnj,* s. masseria, f.
granite, *grǎn'ǐt,* s. granito, m.
granny, *grǎn'nǐ,* s. ava, buona madre, f.
grant, *grǎnt,* v. a. concedere, permettere, accordare; **to take for granted,** tener per certo; –, s. concessione, f. [granire.
granulate, *grǎn'ǔlǎt,* v. a. granulare;
grape, *grāp,* s. uva, f.; **bunch of –s,** s. grappolo d'uva, m.
grape-shot, *–shŏt,* s. mitraglia, f. [m.
grape-stone, *–stŏn,* s. granello dell'uva, m.
graphic, *grǎf'ǐk,* a. grafico; pittoresco; **–ally,** ad. in modo grafico.
grapnel *grǎp'nčl,* s. grappino, m.
grapple, *grǎp'pl,* v. a. afferrare, aggrappare; –, v. n. azzuffarsi, attaccarsi; –, s. grappino, m.
grasp, *grǎsp,* v. a. & n. impugnare; grappare; sforzarsi di prendere; –, s. impugnatura, f.
grass, *grǎs,* s. erba, f.; pastura, f.
grass-hopper, *–hŏppǎr,* s. grillo, m. [f.
grass-plot, *–plŏt,* s. terra coperta d'erba,
grass-widow, *–wǐdō,* s. consorte vedova,
grassy, *–sǐ,* a. erboso, coperto d'erba. [f.
grate, *grāt,* s. graticola, gratella, f.; ferrata, f.; –, v. a. grattugiare; fregare; offendere. [ad. con gratitudine.
grateful, *–fǔl,* a. grato, riconoscente; **–ly,**
gratefulness, *–něs,* s. gratitudine, f.
grater, *grāt'ǎr,* s. grattugia, raspa, f.
gratification. *grǎtǐfǐkǎ'shǎn,* s. gratificazione, f. [sare; contentare.
gratify, *grǎt'ǐfǐ,* v. a. gratificare, compen-
grating, *grǎt'ǐng,* a. aspro, offensivo; –, s. cancello, m., ferrata, f.
gratis, *grā'tǐs,* ad. gratis, gratuitamente, per nulla.
gratitude, *grǎt'ǐtǔd,* s. gratitudine, f.
gratuitous, *–tǔ'ǐtǔs,* a. gratuito, volontario; **–ly,** ad. gratuitamente.

gratuity, *–ŭĭ*, s. dono, presente, m.; liberalità, f. [f.

gratulation, *–lā' shăn*, s. congratulazione, grave, *grāv*, a. grave, serio, solenne; **–ly**, ad. con gravità; **–**, s. sepolcro, m., fossa, f.; **–**, v. a. ir. intagliare, scolpire.

grave-clothes, *–klōthz*, s. pl. vestimento de' morti, m.

grave-digger, *–dĭggŭr*, s. beccamorti, m.

gravel, *grāv' ĕl*, s. ghiaia, f.; rena, f.; (med.) renella, f.; **–**, v. a. coprire di ghiaia; imbarazzare.

graveless, *grāv' lĕs*, a. insepolto.

gravelly, *grāv' ĕllĭ*, a. ghiaioso, renoso.

gravel-pit, *grāv' ĕt pĭt*, s. renaio, m.; cava di sabbione, f.

gravel-walk, *–wăk*, s. viale ghiaiato, m.

graven, *grā' vĕn*, a. scolpito, inciso.

graver, *grā' vŭr*, s. intagliatore, scultore, m.; bulino, m. [tomba, f., tumulo, m.

grave-stone, *grāv' stōn*, s. lapida, f.;

gravitate, *grāv' ĭtăt*, v. n. gravitare.

gravitation, *–tā' shăn*, s. gravitazione, f., peso, m. [portanza, f.

gravity, *grāv' ĭtĭ*, s. gravità, serietà, f.; importanza, f.

gravy, *grā' vĭ*, a. sugo (della carne), m.

gray, *grā*, a. bigio, grigio, canuto.

gray-beard, *–bĕrd*, s. barbabianca, vecchione, m.

gray-haired, *–hărd*, a. canuto.

grayish, *–ĭsh*, a. alquanto bigio.

grayling, *–lĭng*, s. ombrina, f. (pesce).

grayness, *–nĕs*, s. colore bigio, m.

graze, *grāz*, v. a. & n. pascere, pascolare; rasentare. [stiame, m.

grazier, *grā' zhŭr*, s. ingrassatore di bestiame.

grease, *grēs*, s. grasso, m.; untume, m.; **–**, v. a. ungere.

greasiness, *grē' zĭnĕs*, s. untuosità, f.

greasy, *–zĭ*, a. grasso, untuoso; sporco.

great, *grāt*, a. grande; illustre, nobile; generoso; **–ly**, ad. molto; grandemente.

great-coat, *–kōt*, s. soprabito, m.

greatness, *–nĕs*, s. grandezza, f.; dignità, f.; potere, m.; magnificenza, f.

greed, *grēd*, greediness, *grē' dĭnĕs*, s. ghiottoneria, golosità, f.; avidità, f.

greedily, *–dĭlĭ*, ad. golosamente; avidamente.

greedy, *–dĭ*, a. goloso, vorace; avido.

Greek, *grēk*, s. lingua greca, f.

green, *grēn*, a. verde; fresco; immaturo; nuovo; giovane; **–**, s. color verde, m.; verdura, f.; **–s**, pl. legumi, mm. pl.

greenback, *–băk*, s. rana arborea, f.; **–s**, pl. (am.) carta monetata, f. [f.

greengage, *–gāj*, s. susina di color verde.

greengrocer, *–grōsŭr*, s. fruttaiuolo, m.

greenhorn, *–hŏrn*, s. sbarbatello, m.

greenhouse, *–hŏŭs*, s. stufa (per le piante),

greenish, *–ĭsh*, a. verdiccio, glauco. [f.

greenness, *–nĕs*, s. verdura, f., verdume, m.; immaturità, f.; vigore, m.

green-room, *–rōm*, s. stanza del camino ne' teatri, f.

green-sickness, *–sĭknĕs*, s. clorosi, f. [m.

green-stall, *–stăl*, s. mercato di legumi,

greensward, *–swărd*, s. pianura verde, f.

greenwood, *–wŭd*, s. legname verde; bosco,

green-yard, *–yărd*, s. legnaia, f. [m.

greet, *grēt*, v. a. & n. salutare; felicitare.

greeting, *–ĭng*, s. saluto, m.; complimento,

gregarious, *grĕgā' rĭŭs*, a. di gregge. [m.

grenade, *grĕnăd'*, s. granata, f.

grenadier, *–nădēr'*, s. granatiere, m.

grey, *vedi* gray.

greyhound, *grā' hŏŭnd*, s. levriere, m.

gridiron, *grĭd' ĭrn*, s. graticola, f.

grief, *grēf*, s. cordoglio, m.; afflizione, f., affanno, m.; angoscia, f.

grievance, *grē' văns*, s. gravamento, gravame, m., querela, f.; torto, m.

grieve, *grēv*, v. a. & n. attristare; attristarsi.

grievous, *grē' ŭs*, a. doglioso; enorme, orribile; **–ly**, ad. dolorosamente; crudelmente.

griffin, *grĭf' fĭn*, s. griffo, grifone, m.

grig, *grĭg*, s. anguilla piccola, cieca, f.; buon compagno, m.

grill, *grĭl*, v. a. arrostire sulla gratella.

grim, *grĭm*, a. orrido, rigido; arcigno; **–ly**, ad. orridamente; arcignamente.

grimace, *grĭmăs'*, s. smorfia, f.; affettazione, f. [strega, f.

grimalkin, *–măl' kĭn*, s. gatto vecchio, m.;

grime, *grĭm*, s. sporcizia, f.; **–**, v. a. sporcare. [torvo, m.

grimness, *grĭm' nĕs*, s. orrore, m.; viso grimy, *grĭ' mĭ*, a. lordo, sporco, sudicio.

grin, *grĭn*, s. morfia, f.; stridore de' denti, m.; **–**, v. n. fare morfie; digrignare i denti.

grind, *grĭnd*, v. a. ir. macinare, tritare; masticare; digrignare i denti; **(students)** preparare.

grinder, *–ŭr*, s. arrotino, m.; mulino, m.; ripetitore, m.; **–s**, pl. denti mascellari, m.

grindstone, *–stōn*, s. mola, f. [pl.

grip, *grĭp*, s. elsa della spada, f.

gripe, *grĭp*, s. pugnello, m.; manata, f.; presa, f.; oppressione, f.; afflizione, f.; **–s**, pl. colica, f.; **–**, v. a. impugnare; premere; **–**, v. n. causare dolori colici.

griskin, *grĭs' kĭn*, s. braciuola di porco, f.

grisly, *grĭz' lĭ*, a. orribile, terribile.

grist, *grĭst*, s. macinamento, m.; farina, f.; provvedimento, m.

gristle, *grĭs' l*, s. cartilagine, f.

gristly, *–lĭ*, a. cartilaginoso.

grit, *grĭt*, s. crusca, f.; sabbia, f.; limatura (di metallo), f.

gritty, *grĭt' tĭ*, a. arenoso.

grizzle, *grĭz' l*, s. color grigio, m.

grizzled, *–ld*, grizzly, *–lĭ*, a. alquanto grigio, bigiccio.

groan, *grōn*, s. gemito, m.; sospiro, m.; **–**, v. n. gemere; sospirare.

groat, *grōt*, s. quattro soldi, m. pl.

groats, *grōts*, s. farina d' avena, f.

grocer, *grō' sŭr*, s. droghiere, m. [f. pl.

grocery, *–sŭrĭ*, s. drogheria, f.; droghe,

grog, *grŏg*, s. bibita di rum e acqua calda,

groggy, *–gĭ*, a. ebbro, ubriaco. [f.

groin, *grŏĭn*, s. anguinaia, f.

groom, *grōm*, s. palafreniere, m.; sposo, m.; cameriere, m.; –, v. a. governare un cavallo.

groomsman, *–s' măn*, s. paraninfo, m.

groove, *grōv*, s. antro profondo, m.; scanalatura, f.; –, v. a. scanalare. [cercare.

grope, *grōp*, v. a. palpare, toccare, tastare;

gross, *grōs*, a. grosso, spesso; rozzo, basso; stolto, ignorante; **–ly**, ad. rozzamente, –, s. grosso, m.; parte maggiore, f.

grossness, *–nĕs*, s. grossezza, f.; rozzezza

grot(to), *grŏt('tŏ)*, s. grotta, f. [f.

grotesque, *grŏtĕsk'*, a. grottesco.

ground, *grăănd*, s. terra, f.; terreno, m.; paese, campo, m.; fondamento, m.; soggetto, m.; ragione, f.; **–s**, pl. feccia, f.; residuo, m.; principii, m.pl.; –, v. a. stabilire, fondare; insegnare; (mar.) mettere a secco. [m.

ground-floor, *–flōr*, s. quartiere a terreno, m.

ground-ivy, *–ivĭ*, s. edera terrestre, f.

groundless, *–lĕs*, a. malfondato; senza ragione; **–ly**, ad. senza fondamento; senza ragione. [fondamento, m.

groundlessness, *–lĕsnĕs*, s. mancanza di

ground-plot, *–plŏt*, s. base, f., fondamento, principio, m.

ground-rent, *–rĕnt*, s. terratico, m.

groundsel, *–sĕl*, s. soglia, f.

ground-work, *–wŭrk*, s. fondo, fondamento, m. [aggroppare.

group, *grōp*, s. gruppo, groppo, m.; –, v. a.

grouse, *grŏŭs*, s. francolino, m.

grout, *grŏŭt*, s. farina d' avena, f.; sedimento, m. [m.

grove, *grōv*, s. boschetto, m.; viale d' alberi,

grovel, *grŏv'l*, v. n. rampicare; avvilirsi.

grow, *grō*, v. a. coltivare; –, v. n. ir. crescere; divenire grande; divenir, farsi; parvenire; arrivare.

grower, *–ŭr*, s. coltivatore, m.

growl, *grŏŭl*, s. borbottamento, m.; –, v. n. grugnare, borbottare.

growth, *grōth*, s. crescimento, m.

grub, *grŭb*, s. lombrico, m.; nano, m.; caramogio, m.; –, v. a. sarchiare.

grudge, *grŭj*, s. odio, rancore, m.; ira, f.; –, v. a. portare invidia, invidiare; confutare. [a malincuore.

grudgingly, *–ĭnglĭ*, ad. invidiosamente,

gruel, *grō'ĕl*, s. polenda, f.

gruff, *grŭf*, a. arcigno; rozzo; **–ly**, ad. arcignamente.

gruffness, *–nĕs*, s. arcignezza, f.

grumble, *grŭm'bl*, v. n. borbottare, mormorare. [morare.

grumpy, *–pĭ*, a. di gola, aspro. |morare.

grunt, *grŭnt*, v. n. grugnire, grugnare.

guarantee, *gărăntĕ'*, **guaranty**, *găr'-ăntĕ*, s. sicurtà, f.; mallevadore, m.; –, v. a. mallevare; guarantire.

guard, *gărd*, s. guardia, custodia, f.; difesa, f.; elsa, f.; (rail.) conduttore, m.; –, v. a. guardare; proteggere; –, v. n. stare in guardia; preservarsi.

guarded, *găr'dĕd*, a. cauto.

guard-house, *gărd' hŏŭs*, **guard-room**, *–rŏm*, s. (mil.) stanza di guardia, f.

guardian, *găr' dĭăn*, a. tutelare; –, s. guardiano, m.; curatore, protettore, m.

guardianship, *–shĭp*, s. carica del guardiano, f. [coste, m.

guard-ship, *gărd' shĭp*, s. (mar.) guardacoste, m.

gudgeon, *gŭj'ăn*, s. ghiozzo (pesce), m.; affronto, m. [compensa.

guerdon, *găr' dŏn*, s. guiderdone, m.; ribond, m.

guess, *gĕs*, s. congettura, f.; supposizione, f.; –, v. a. & n. congetturare; indovinare.

guest, *gĕst*, s. convivale, m.; forestiere, m.

guffaw, *gŭf' fŭ'*, s. scoppio di risa, m.

guidance, *gī'dăns*, s. condotta, f.

guide, *gīd*, s. guida, f.; scorta, f.; condottore, m.; –, v. a. guidare; dirigere; accompagnare.

guide-book, *–bŭk*, s. itinerario, m.

guide-post, *–pŏst*, s. colonna milliaria, f.

guild, *gĭld*, s. società, compagnia, f.

guild-hall, *–hăl*, s. casa della città, f.

guile, *gĭl*, s. inganno, m.; furberia, f.

guileful, *–fŭl*, a. ingannevole, furbo.

guileless, *–lĕs*, a. senza frode.

guillotine, *gĭl'ŏtĕn*, s. ghigliottina, f.; *găllŏtĕn'*, v. a. ghigliottinare.

guilt, *gĭlt*, s. delitto, misfatto, m.; colpa, f.

guiltless, *–lĕs*, a. netto di colpa, innocente.

guilty, *gĭl'tĭ*, a. colpevole; scellerato.

guinea, *gĭn'ĭ*, s. ghinea, f.

guinea-hen, *–hĕn*, s. gallina di faraone, f.

guise, *gīz*, s. guisa, foggia, f.; maniera, f.

guitar, *gĭtăr'*, s. chitarra, f.

gulch, *gălch*, s. borro, m.

gulf, *gŭlf*, s. golfo, m.; abisso, m.

gull, *gŭl*, s. gabbiano, m.; furbo, m.; balordo, m.; –, v. a. ingannare, truffare.

guller, *–lăr*, s. ingannatore, furbo, m.

gullet, *–lĕt*, s. gola, strozza, f.; collo, m.

gullibility, *găllĭbĭl'ĭtĭ*, s. credulità, f.

gullible, *găl'ĭbl*, a. credulo.

gully, *găl'lĭ*, v. n. correre rumorosamente, mormoreggiare. [toio, m.

gully-hole, *–hŏl*, s. chiavica, f., smaltigulp, gălp, s. gorgo, m.; sorso, tratto, m.; –, v. a. inghiottire.

gum, *găm*, s. gomma, f.; gengiva, f.; –, v. a. ingommare; (am.) indentare.

gummy, *–mĭ*, a. gommoso, viscoso.

gumption, *–shăn*, s. destrezza, f.; intelligenza, f.

gum-tree, *–trĕ*, s. albero gommifero, m.

gun, *găn*, s. schioppo, fucile, m.; **(great –)** cannone, m. |f.

gun-boat, *–bŏt*, s. scialuppa cannoniera,

gun-carriage, *–kărrĭj*, s. affusto, m.

gunnel, *–nĕl*, s. (mar.) parapetto, orlo, m.

gunner, *–năr*, s. cannoniere, artigliere m.

gunnery, *–nărĭ*, s. arte del cannoniere, f.

gunpowder, *–pŏŭdăr*, s. polvere da cannone, f. |f.

gun-room, *–rŏm*, s. (mar.) Santa Barbera,

gun-shot, *–shŏt*, s. tiro di moschetto o cannone, m.; portata, f.

gunsmith, *–smĭth*, s. armaiuolo, fabbricatore d' armi, m. |f.

gun-stock, *–stŏk*, s. cassa dello schioppo,

gurgle, *gûr'gl,* v. n. gorgogliare.
gush, *gŭsh,* s. sgorgamento. m.; trabocco, m.; –, v. n. sgorgare, sboccare.
gusset, *gŭs'sĕt,* s. gherone, m.
gust, *gŭst,* s. gusto, m.; colpo di vento, m.
gusty, *gŭs'tĭ,* a. tempestoso.
gut, *gŭt,* s. budello, intestino, m.; ghiottornia, f.; –, v. a. sviscerare.
gutter, *gŭt'tŭr,* s. gronda, grondaia, f.; –, v. a. scanalare; –, v. n. scolare.
guttural, *–tŭrăl,* a. gutturale.
guy, *gĭ,* s. fantoccio, burattino, m.; caricatura, f. [lare.
guzzle, *gŭz'zl,* v. n. gozzovigliare, crapulare.
gymnasium, *jĭmnā'stŭm,* s. ginnasio, m.
gymnastic, *–năs'tĭk,* a. ginnastico; –s, s. pl. ginnastica, f.
gypsum, *jĭp'sŭm,* s. gesso, m.
gyrate, *jĭrāt',* v. n. girare.

H.

ha! *hä!* i. ah! ahi! [m.
haberdasher, *hăb'ŭrdăshŭr,* s. merciaio,
haberdashery, *–dăshări,* s. merceria, f.
habiliment, *hăbĭl'ĭmĕnt,* s. abbigliamento, abito, m.; vestito, m.
habilitate, *vedi* abilitare.
habit, *hăb'ĭt,* s. abitudine, f., uso, m.; abito, vestimento, m.; disposizione (del corpo), f.; **by** –, per abito.
habitable, *–ăbl,* a. abitabile. [f.
habitation, *–tă'shăn,* s. abitazione, f.; casa,
habitual, *–bĭt'ŭăl,* a. abituale; ordinario; **–ly,** ad. abitualmente. [costumare.
habituate, *–bĭt'ŭāt,* v. a. abituare; ac-
habitude, *hăb'ĭtŭd,* s. abitudine, f.; uso, m.
hack, *hăk,* s. marra, zappa, f.; cavallo d' affitto, m.; –, v. a. sminuzzare, tritare; stroppiare (una lingua). [gluzzare.
hackle, *hăk'l,* s. seta cruda, f.; –, v. a. ta-
hackney, *–nĭ,* s. cavallo d' affitto, m.; carogna, f. [affitto, f.
hackney-coach, *–kōch,* s. carrozza d'
hackneyed, *–nĭd,* a. comune, trito.
haddock, *hăd'dŏk,* s. baccalà, f.
haft, *hăft,* s. manico, m.; –, v. a. mettere
hag, *hăg,* s. strega, maga, f. [il manico.
haggard, *–gărd,* a. selvaggio; fiero.
haggle, *hăg'gl,* v. a. tagliuzzare; mutilare; –, v. n. stiracchiare nel prezzo. [m.
haggler, *–glŭr,* s. che stiracchia il prezzo,
ha-ha, *hä'hä,* f. fosso di chiusura, m.
hail, *hăl,* s. grandine, gragnuola, f.; –, v. a. salutare; –, v. imp. grandinare; **–! i.** Iddio vi salvi! ave!
hail-fellow, *–fĕllō,* s. amico intimo, m.
hailstone, *–stōn,* s. grano di gragnuola, m.
hair, *hăr,* s. capello, m.; pelo, m.; crino (d' un cavallo), m. [sima distanza, f.
hair-breadth, *–brĕdth,* s. (fig.) minutis-
hair-cloth, *–klŏth,* s. cilicio, m.
hair-dresser, *–drĕssŭr,* s. parrucchiere, pettinatore, m.
hairless, *–lĕs,* a. senza capelli, calvo.

hair-mattress, *–măttrĕs,* s. saccone elastico, m.
hair-pin, *–pĭn,* s. forcella, f. [f.
hair-powder, *–pŏŭdăr,* s. polvere di Cipro,
hair-sieve, *–sĕv,* s. setaccio, m.
hair-splitting, *–splĭttĭng,* s. puntiglio, m., cavillazione, f.
hairy, *hă'rĭ,* a. capelluto, peloso, crinito.
halberd, *hăl'bŭrd,* s. alabarda, f.
halberdier, *–dĕr,* s. alabardiere, lanzo, m.
halcyon, *hăl'sĭŏn,* s. alcione, m.; –, a. quieto, tranquillo.
hale, *hăl,* a. sano, vigoroso; gagliardo.
half, *hăf,* a. mezzo; –, ad. a metà, di pari; **in parte;** –, s. metà, f.
half-blood, *–blŭd,* s. fratello (m.) o sorella (f.) da un lato. [meticcio.
half-bred, *–brĕd,* **half-caste,** *–kăst,* a.
half-moon, *–mōn,* s. mezza luna, f.
half-penny, *hă'pĕnnĭ,* s. mezzo soldo, m.
halfway, *hăf'wă,* a. a mezza strada. [m.
hall, *hăl,* s. sala, f., palazzo, m.; vestibulo,
halliard, *hăl'yărd,* s. (mar.) drizza, f.
halloo, *hăllō',* v. a. incoraggiare (i cani); chiamare. [crare.
hallow, *hăl'lō,* v. a. santificare, consa-
hallucination, *–lōsĭnă'shăn,* s. allucinazione, f.; abbaglio, m.
halo, *hă'lō,* s. aureola, f.
halt, *hălt,* a. zoppo, azzoppito; –, s. posa, fermata, f.; (mil.) alto, m.; –, v. n. fare alto, fermarsi; zoppicare; stare in dubbio.
halter, *hăl'tŭr,* s. cavezza, f.; corda, f.
halve, *hăv,* v. a. dividere in due, dimezzare.
ham, *hăm,* s. garretto, m.; prosciutto, m.
hamlet, *–lĕt,* s. borghetto, m.
hammer, *hăm'măr,* s. martello, m.; cane dello schioppo, m.; –, v. a. martellare; inventare, immaginare; –, v. n. occuparsi; balbutire.
hammer-cloth, *–klŏth,* s. gualdrappa, f.
hammock, *–mŏk,* s. branda, f.
hamper, *–pŭr,* s. paniere grande, m.; –, v. a. imbarazzare; allettare.
hamstring, *–strĭng,* s. tendine del garretto, m.; –, v. a. tagliare i tendini del garretto.
hand, *hănd,* s. mano, f.; palma, f.; scrittura, soscrizione, f.; lato, m.; ago (d' un oriuolo), m.; (mar.) marinaio, m.; **at –,** qui vicino; **– in –,** insieme; –, v. a. dar la mano; dare di mano in mano; menare.
hand-barrow, *–bărrō,* s. barella, f.
hand-basket, *–băskĕt,* s. canestro a manico, m., cesta a manico, f.
hand-bell, *–bĕl,* s. campanello, m.
hand-bill, *–bĭl,* s. biglietto, m.
hand-book, *–bŭk,* s. manuale, m.
handcuff, *–kŭf,* s. manette, f. pl.
handed, *–ĕd,* a. dato di mano in mano.
handful, *–fŭl,* s. pugno, m.; manata, f. [m.
hand-gallop, *–găllăp,* s. piccolo galoppo,
handicap, *hăn'dĭkăp,* s. corso con vantaggio, m.; –, v. a. impedire, mettere ostacoli. [fessione, f.
handicraft, *–dĭkrăft,* s. mestiere, m., pro-
handicraftsman, *–smăn,* s. artigiano, m.; artefice, m.

handily, *–dĭlĭ,* ad. con destrezza.

handiness, *–dĭnĕs,* s. destrezza, abilità, f.

handiwork, *–dĭwărk,* s. opera manuale, f.; manifattura, f. [m.

handkerchief, *hăn'kŭrchĭf,* s. fazzoletto,

handle, *hăn'dl,* s. manico; orecchio, m.; impugnatura, f.; –, v. a. maneggiare; trattare. [toccamento, m.

handling, *hănd'lĭng,* s. maneggiamento, m.

hand-mill, *–mĭl,* s. molinello, m.

hand-rail, *–răl,* s. parapetto d'un ponte, &c. m., spalletta, f.

hand-saw, *–sŭ,* s. sega piccola, f.

handsel, *hăn'sĕl,* s. prima vendita, f.; –, v. a. comprar il primo; far uso per la prima volta.

handsome, *–sŭm,* a. bello, elegante; grazioso; –ly, ad. elegantemente, bellamente.

hand-spike, *hănd'spĭk,* s. (mar.) intrecciatoio, m. [scrittura, f.; mano, f.

hand-writing, *–rlĭng,* s. manoscritto, m.

handy, *hăn'dĭ,* a. destro, abile; convenevole.

hang, *hăng,* v. a. ir. appendere, appiccare; piegare; –, v. n. ir. pendere; stare sospeso; contrappesare. [m.

hanger, *–ŭr,* s. scimitarra, f.; coltellaccio,

hanger-on, *–ŏn,* s. parassito, scroccone, m.

hangings, *hăng'ĭngz,* s. pl. tapezzeria, f.

hangman, *–măn,* s. carnefice, m.

hangnail, *–năl,* s. chiodo ribadito, m.

hank, *hăngk,* s. matassa, f.; inclinazione, voglia, f.

hanker, *–ŭr,* v. n. desiderare ardentemente.

hansom, *hăn'sŭm,* s. calessino m.

hap-hazard, *hăp'hăzŭrd,* s. accidente, evento casuale, m. [disgraziato.

hapless, *–lĕs,* a. sfortunato, sventurato.

haply, *–lĭ,* ad. per accidente, a caso.

happen, *hăp'n,* v. n. avvenire, accadere.

happily, *–pĭlĭ,* ad. fortunatamente, per sorte. [ventura, f.

happiness, *–pĭnĕs,* s. felicità, f.; buona

happy, *–pĭ,* a. felice, fortunato.

harangue, *hărăng',* s. aringa, f.; –, v. a. aringare; perorare. [tribolare.

harass, *hăr'ăs,* v. a. stancare, faticare;

harbinger, *hăr'bĭnjŭr,* s. foriere; precursore, presagio, m.

harbour, *–bŭr,* s. alloggio, m.; rifugio, m.; porto, m.; –, v. a. alloggiare, albergare; –, v. n. soggiornare.

hard, *hărd,* a. duro; fermo; rigoroso; faticoso, molesto; difficile; oneroso; **– of hearing,** quasi sordo; –, ad. presso a poco; fortemente; difficilmente; **– by,** presso. [nire duro.

harden, *hăr'dn,* v. a. & n. indurare; divenir duro.

hard-hearted, *hărd'hărtĕd,* a. crudele, inumano. [vura, f.

hardihood, *hăr'dĭhŭd,* s. intrepidità, bravura, f.

hardily, *–dĭlĭ,* ad. coraggiosamente, arditamente. [arditezza, f.

hardiness, *–dĭnĕs,* s. pena, difficoltà, f.;

hardly, *hărd'lĭ,* ad. appena; severamente.

hardness, *–nĕs,* s. durezza, f.; difficoltà, f.; severità, f. [fatica, f., travaglio, m.

hardship, *–shĭp,* s. durezza, f.; difficoltà, f.

hard-ware, *–wăr,* s. chincaglia, f.

hardy, *hăr'dĭ,* a. ardito, coraggioso, bravo.

hare, *hăr,* s. lepre, f. [robusto, forte.

harebell, *–bĕl,* s. campanella, turchina, f.

hare-brained, *–brănd,* a. discervellato, pazzesco.

hare-lip, *–lĭp,* s. labbro fesso, m.

hark, *hărk,* i. odi! sta attento!

harlequin, *hăr'lĕkwĭn,* s. arlecchino, m.

harlot, *–lŏt,* s. cortigiana, f.

harm, *hărm,* s. male, m.; danno, pregiudizio, m.; delitto, m.; –, v. a. nuocere; far torto, pregiudiziare.

harmful, *–fŭl,* a. nocevole, dannoso; –ly, ad. nocevolmente. [centemente.

harmless, *–lĕs,* a. innocente; –ly, ad. innocentemente.

harmonic, *–mŏn'ĭk,* a. armonico.

harmonious, *–mo'nĭŭs,* a. armonioso; –ly, ad. con armonia; dolcemente.

harmonize, *hăr'mŏnĭz,* v. a. far armonioso; aggiustare; –, v. n. esser d' accordo.

harmony, *–mŏnĭ,* s. armonia, f.

harness, *–nĕs,* s. arnese, m.; –, v. a. mettere in arnese. [suonare l' arpa.

harp, *hărp,* s. arpa, f.; –, v. n. arpeggiare.

harpist, *–ĭst,* s. sonatore d' arpa, arpista,

harpoon, *hărpŏn',* s. arpone, m. [m.

harpsichord, *hărp'sĭkŏrd,* s. gravicembalo, m., spinetta, f.

harpy, *hăr'pĭ,* s. arpia, f.

harridan, *hăr'rĭdăn,* s. rozza, r.

harrier, *–rĭŭr,* s. levrierino, m. [care.

harrow, *–rŏ,* s. erpice, f.; –, v. a. erpicare; –, v. a. tormentare.

harry, *–rĭ,* v. a. tormentare.

harsh, *hărsh,* a. aspro, austero, rigido, duro; severo; –ly, ad. aspramente, severamente. [durezza; severità, f.

harshness, *–nĕs,* s. asprezza, rigidità,

hart, *hărt,* s. cervo, m. [vollato; in aria.

harum-scarum, *hă'răm skă'răm,* a. discervellato.

harvest, *hăr'vĕst,* s. messe, raccolta, f.; mietitura, f.; –, v. a. mietere, raccogliere.

harvester, *–tŭr,* **harvest-man,** *–măn,* s. mietitore, segatore, m. [tura, f.

harvest-home, *–hŏm,* s. festa della mietitura; s. ammorsellato, m.; –, v. a. sminuzzare. [biare con fermaglio.

hash, *hăsh,* s. ammorsellato, m.; –, v. a. sminuzzare.

hasp, *hăsp,* s. fermaglio, m.; –, v. a. affibbiare con fermaglio.

hassock, *hăs'ŏk,* s. inginocchiatoio, m.

haste, *hăst,* s. fretta, prestezza, f.; **in –,** in fretta, in furia. [–, v. n. affrettarsi.

hasten, *hă'sn,* v. a. affrettare; sollecitare;

hastily, *–stĭlĭ,* ad. in fretta; iratamente.

hastiness, *–stĭnĕs,* s. fretta, prestezza, f.; stizza, collera, f. [maturo.

hasty, *–stĭ,* a. presto, pronto, stizzoso, precipitoso.

hasty-pudding, *–pŭddĭng,* s. pappa, f.

hat, *hăt,* s. cappello, m.; **–s off !** giù col cappello ! [m.

hat-band, *–bănd,* s. nastro del cappello,

hat-box, *–bŏks,* **hat-case,** *–kăs,* s. cappelliera, f.

hatch, *hăch,* s. covata, f.; scoperta, f.; (mar.) boccaporto, m.; –, v. a. covare; tramare, far pratiche; tratteggiare.

hatchet, *–ĕt,* s. accetta, scure, f.

hatchment, *–mĕnt,* s. scudo funebre, m.; arme della famiglia, f. pl.

hatchway, *–wă,* s. (mar.) boccaporto, m.

hate, *hāt*, s. odio, rancore, m.; —, v. a. odiare, detestare. [mente.

hateful, *—fūl*, a. odioso; —ly, ad. odiosa-

hater, *hā'tŭr*, s. nemico, m.

hatred, *—trĕd*, s. odio, m.; aborrimento, m.

hatter, *hăt'tŭr*, s. cappellaio, m.

haughtily, *hă'tĭlĭ*, ad. orgogliosamente.

haughtiness, *—tĭnĕs*, s. alterigia, super-bia, f., orgoglio, m.

haughty, *—tĭ*, a. orgoglioso, superbo.

haul, *hăl*, s. tiramento, m.; strascinamento, m.; —, v. a. tirare a braccia, strascinare.

haunch, *hănsh*, s. anca, coscia, f.

haunt, *hănt*, s. rifugio, m.; dimora, f.; frequentazione, f.; —, v. a. frequentare; molestare.

haunter, *—ŭr*, s. frequentatore, m.

hautboy, *hŏ'bŏĕ (ā'bŏĕ)*, s. (mus.) oboè, m.

have, *hăv*, v. a. ir. avere; possedere; sapere; to — rather, voler più tosto.

haven, *hā'vn*, s. porto, m.

havoc, *hăv'ŏk*, s. rovina, f.; guasto, m.

haw, *hă*, s. siepe, f.; orticello, m.; —, v. n. balbutire. [conare; rivendere; sputare.

hawk, *hăk*, s. falcone, m.; —, v. a. fal-

hawker, *—ŭr*, s. merciaiuolo, m.

haw-thorn, *hă'thŏrn*, s. spino bianco, m.

hay, *hā*, s. fieno, m.

hay-cock, *—kŏk*, s. bica di fieno, f.

hay-loft, *—lŏft*, s. fienile, m. [m.

hay-maker, *—măkŭr*, s. segatore di fieno,

hay-rick, *—rĭk*, hay-stack, *—stăk*, s. mucchio di fieno, m.

hazard, *hăz'ărd*, s. rischio, m.; pericolo, m.; accidente, m.; sorte, f.; to run a —, arrischiare; —, v. a. arrischiare, avven-turare. [—ly, ad. pericolosamente.

hazardous, *—ŭs*, a. rischioso, pericoloso;

haze, *hāz*, s. nebbia, f., vapore denso, m.

hazel, *hā'zĕl*, s. nocciuolo, m.; —(ly), a. del colore delle nocciuole.

hazel-nut, *—nŭt*, s. nocciuola, f.

hazy, *hā'zĭ*, a. nebbioso, fosco, oscuro.

he, *hē*, pn. egli, esso, colui.

head, *hĕd*, s. testa, f.; capo, m.; teschio (d' un cinghiale), m.; sommità, f.; titolo, frontispizio, m.; intelletto, m.; pomo (d' una canna), m.; sorgente (d' un fiume), f.; — and ears, interamente, estrema-mente; —, v. a. guidare, comandare; con-durre; decapitare; levare la cima.

head-ache, *—āk*, s. mal di capo, m.

head-dress, *—drĕs*, s. acconciatura (di capo), f. [f.

headiness, *—ĭnĕs*, s. pertinacia, f.; temerità,

head-land, *—lănd*, s. promontorio, m.

headless, *—lĕs*, a. discervellato.

headlong, *—lŏng*, a. temerario, incon-siderato; —, ad. inconsideratamente; teme-rariamente.

head-master, *—măstŭr*, head-pro-fessor, *—prŏfĕssŭr*, s. rettore, m.

headmost, *—mŏst*, a. primo.

head-piece, *—pēs*, s. caschetto, m.; in-telletto, m. [quartiere generale, m.

head-quarters, *—kwărtŭrs*, s. pl. (mil.)

headship, *—shĭp*, s. primato, m.; autorità, f.

headsman, *—s'măn*, s. boia, m.

head-stall, *—stăl*, s. testiera (d' una briglia), f.

headstrong, *—strŏng*, a. ostinato, caparbio.

headway, *—wā*, s. (mar.) cammino, pro-gresso, m.; strada, f. [lento.

heady, *hĕd'ĭ*, a. ostinato, temerario; vio-

heal, *hēl*, v. a. & n. guarire, sanare.

health, *hĕlth*, s. salute, f.; sanità, f.; pro-sperità, f.

healthiness, *—ĭnĕs*, s. stato di salute, m.

healthy, *hĕlth'ĭ*, a. sano; vigoroso.

heap, *hēp*, s. mucchio, cumulo, m.; bica, f.; —, v. a. accumulare, ammassare.

hear, *hēr*, v. a. ir. intendere; ascoltare; —, v. n. ir. udire; imparare.

hearer, *—ŭr*, s. uditore, ascoltatore, m.

hearing, *—ĭng*, s. udito, m.; udienza, f.

hearken, *hăr'kn*, v. n. ascoltare, stare ad udire, origliare.

hearsay, *hēr'sā*, s. fama, f., rumore, m.

hearse, *hērs*, s. carro funebre, m.; cata-falco, m.

heart, *hărt*, s. cuore, m.; coraggio, m.; vigore, m.; centro, m.; amore, m.; by —, a mente, a memoria; with all my —, di tutto cuore. [—, s. crepacuore, m.

heart-breaking, *—brăking*, a. afflittivo;

heart-burning, *—bŭrning*, s. (med.) car-dialgia, f.; odio, m.

heart-felt, *—fĕlt*, a. sensitivo, sensibile.

hearth, *hărth*, s. focolare, camino, m.

heartily, *hăr'tĭlĭ*, ad. cordialmente.

heartiness, *—tĭnĕs*, a. inumano; —, s. cor-dialità, sincerità, f. [timidamente.

heartless, *hărt'lĕs*, a. timido; —ly, ad.

heart's-ease, *—s'ēz*, s. viola, f.

heart-sick, *—sĭk*, a. pieno d' afflizione.

heart-whole, *—hōl*, a. nonspento per l' amore; indomabile.

hearty, *hăr'tĭ*, a. sincero; sano, vigoroso.

heat, *hēt*, s. calore, m.; vivacità, animosità, f.; —, v. a. r. scaldare, riscaldare; infiam-mare. [m.

heater, *—ŭr*, s. ferro da stirare (i pannilini).

heath, *hēth*, heather, *hĕth'ŭr*, s. erica, f.; terreno incolto, m.

heathen, *hē'thn*, a. & s. pagano (m.).

heathenish, *—thnish*, a. pagano; —ly, ad. da pagano.

heathenism, *—ĭzm*, s. paganesimo, m.

heave, *hēv*, s. alzata con forza, f.; solleva-mento, m.; sospiro, m.; —, v. a. r. & ir. alzare, sollevare; elevare; (mar.) virare; —, v. n. r. & ir. sollevarsi; enfiarsi; palpi-tare; respirare; nauseare.

heaven, *hĕv'n*, s. cielo, m.; firmamento, m.

heavenly, *—lĭ*, a. celeste; divino; —ly, ad. divinamente.

heavily, *hĕv'ĭlĭ*, ad. pesantemente.

heaviness, *—ĭnĕs*, s. gravezza, f.; sonno-lenza, f.; depressione, f.

heavy, *hĕv'ĭ*, a. grave; pesante; triste, afflittivo; balocco, insensato.

hebrew, *hē'brō*, s. ebreo, giudeo, m.

hecatomb, *hĕk'ŏtŏm*, s. ecatombe, f.

hectic(al), *hĕk'tĭk(ăl)*, a. etico, tisico.

hector, *hĕk'tŭr*, s. ammazzasette, m.; —, v. a. millantarsi, bravare.

hedge, *hĕj,* s. siepe, f.; –, v. a. cingere di siepe.

hedge-hog, *–hŏg,* s. riccio, m.; spinoso, m.

hedge-row, *–rō,* s. filare d' alberi, m.

heed, *hēd,* s. cura, guardia, f.; attenzione, f.; –, v. a. attendere, osservare.

heedful, *–fŭl,* a. attento, circospetto; **-ly,** ad. cautamente.

heedless, *–lĕs,* a. disattento, trascurato; **-ly,** ad. trascuratamente.

heel, *hēl,* s. calcagno, m.; **to take to one's –s,** fuggire; –, v. n. ballare; rattaccare. [conare.

heifer, *hĕf'ăr,* s. giovenca, f.

height, *hīt,* s. altezza, f.; elevazione, f.; sommità, f.; grandezza, f. [migliorare.

heighten, *hī'tn,* v. a. alzare; aumentare;

heinous, *hā'nŭs,* a. odioso; atroce; **-ly,** ad. odiosamente.

heir, *ār,* s. erede, m.; **– apparent,** erede presuntivo in linea diretta; **– presumptive,** erede presuntivo in linea collaterale.

heirdom, *–dŭm,* **heirship,** *–shĭp,* s. diritto d' erede, m.

heiress, *ār'ĕs,* s. erede, f. [m. pl.

heirloom, *–lŭm,* s. mobili non alienabili,

heliograph, *hē'lĭŏgrăf,* s. eliografo, m

hell, *hĕl,* s. inferno, m.

hell-cat, *–kăt,* s. furia, f.

hellenism, *hĕl'lĕnĭzm,* s. ellenismo, m.

hellenist, *–lĕnĭst,* s. ellenista, m.

hell-hound, *hĕl'hŏŭnd,* s. Cerbero, m.; tizzone d' inferno, m.

hellish, *–lĭsh,* a. infernale, diabolico; **-ly,** ad. in maniera infernale.

helm, *hĕlm,* s. (mar.) timone, m.

helmet, *–ĕt,* s. elmo, casco, m.

helmsman, *–s'măn,* s. (mar.) timoniere, m.

help, *hĕlp,* s. aiuto, soccorso, m.; –, v. a. aiutare, assistere, sovvenire; servire (a tavola); **I cannot – it,** non è mia colpa.

helper, *–ăr,* **helpmate,** *–māt,* **helpmeet,** *–mēt,* s. aiutatore, m.

helpful, *–fŭl,* a. utile; salutevole.

helpless, *–lĕs,* a. inutile; impotente; **-ly,** ad. senza aiuto. [abilità, f.

helplessness, *–nĕs,* s. impotenza, in-

helter-skelter, *hĕl'tŭr skĕl'tŭr,* ad. in gran fretta, scompigliatamente.

helve, *hĕlv,* s. manico, m.

hem, *hĕm,* s. orlo, m.; –, v. a. orlare, fregiare; –, v. n. spurgarsi; **– ! i,** ehi! vedi!

hemisphere, *hĕm'ĭsfēr,* s. emisfero, m.

hemlock, *hĕm'lŏk,* s. (bot.) cicuta, f.

hemorrhage, *hĕm'ŏrăj,* s. emorragia, f.

hemorrhoids, *hĕm'ŏrŏĭdz,* s. pl. emorroide, f. pl.

hemp, *hĕmp,* s. canapa, f.

hempen, *hĕm'pn,* a. di canapa.

hen, *hĕn,* s. gallina, f.; femmina (degli uccelli), f.

hence, *hĕns,* ad. da qui; perciò, dunque.

henceforth, *–fŏrth,* **henceforward,** *–fŏr'wŭrd,* ad. di qui innanzi, all' avvenire.

hen-house, *hĕn'hŏŭs,* **hen-coop,** *–kōp,* s. pollaio, m.

hen-pecked, *–pĕkd,* a. governato dalla moglie. [moglie.

hen-roost, *–rŏst,* s. pollaio, m.

---

her, *hăr,* pn. lei, la, le; di lei, **a lei;** il suo, la sua, i suoi, le sue.

herald, *hĕr'ăld,* s. araldo, m.

heraldic, *hĕrăl'dĭk,* a. araldico.

heraldry, *hĕr'ăldrĭ,* s. araldica, f.

herb, *hărb,* s. erba, f.; **-s,** pl. legumi, m. pl.

herbaceous, *–bā'shŭs,* a. erbaceo. [f.

herbage, *hăr'băj,* s. erbaggio, m.; pastura,

herbal, *–băl,* s. erbario, m. [botanico, m.

herbalist, *–bălĭst,* s. raccoglitore d' erbe,

herbivorous, *–bĭv'ŏrăs,* a. erbivoro.

herd, *hărd,* s. gregge, f.; truppa, f.; –, v. n. andare in truppa; associarsi.

herdsman, *–z'măn,* s. pastore, m.

here, *hēr,* ad. qui, in questo luogo.

hereabout(s), *–ăbŏŭt'(z),* ad. qui vicino; qui all' intorno.

hereafter, *–ăf'tŭr,* ad. da qui innanzi, da qui avanti, all' avvenire. [mentre.

hereat, *–ăt',* ad. a questo, a ciò; in questo

hereby, *–bī',* ad. per questo mezzo.

hereditary, *hĕrĕd'ĭtărĭ,* a. ereditario, d' eredità. [f.

heredity, *–tĭ,* s. trasmissione per eredità,

herefrom, *hērfrŏm',* ad. da qui.

herein, *–ĭn',* ad. in questo mentre, in ciò.

hereof, *–ŏf',* ad. di questo, di quello.

heresy, *hĕr'ĕsĭ,* s. eresia, f.

heretic, *–ĕtĭk,* s. & a. eretico (m.).

heretofore, *hĕrtŏfōr',* ad. altre volte, un tempo; a' tempi andati, per lo passato.

hereupon, *–ăpŏn',* ad. in questo mezzo.

herewith, *–wĭth',* ad. con ciò; per questo mezzo. [eredità, f.

heritage, *hĕr'ĭtăj,* **heritance,** *–ĭtăns,* s.

hermetic(al), *hărmĕt'ĭk(ăl),* a. ermetico; **-ly,** ad. ermeticamente.

hermit, *hăr'mĭt,* s. eremita, romito, m.

hermitage, *–mĭtăj,* s. eremitaggio, eremo,

hermitical, *–mĭt'ĭkăl,* a. eremitico. [m.

hernia, *hăr'nĭă,* s. ernia, f.

hero, *hē'rō,* s. eroe, m. [ad. eroicamente.

heroic(al), *hērŏ'ĭk(ăl),* a. eroico; **-ally,**

heroine, *hĕr'ŏĭn,* s. eroina, f.

heroism, *–ŏĭzm,* s. eroismo, m.

heron, *hĕr'ŭn,* s. airone, m.

heronry, *–rĭ,* s. uccelliera d' aironi, f.

herring, *hĕr'rĭng,* s. aringa, f.

hers, *hărz,* pn. suo, sua; suoi, sue.

herself, *hărsĕlf',* pn. se stessa, essa stessa.

hesitate, *hĕz'ĭtāt,* v. n. esitare, star dubbioso, essere incerto. [dubitazione, f.

hesitation, *–tā'shŭn,* s. esitazione, f.;

heterodox, *hĕt'ĕrŏdŏks,* a. eterodosso.

heterodoxy, *–dŏksĭ,* s. eterodossia, f.

heterogeneous, *–jĕ'nĭŭs,* a. eterogeneo, dissimile.

hew, *hū,* v. a. ir. sminuzzare; tagliare.

hewer, *–ăr,* s. taglialegna, m.; abbattitore, f.

hey, *hā,* i. ah! olà !

heyday, *–dā,* s. gaiezza, f.; **– ! i,** oh! oh!

hiatus, *hĭă'tŭs,* s. apertura, lacuna, f.

hibernate, *hĭ'bŭrnāt,* v. n. svernare, passar l' inverno.

hiccough, *hĭk'ăp,* s. singhiozzo, singulto, m.; –, v. n. singhiozzare. [m.

hickory, *hĭk'ŏrĭ,* s. noce americano (albero),

hide, *hīd*, s. pelle, f., cuoio, m.; —, v. n. ir. nascondere, (vulg.) battere.
hideous, *hīd'ŭs*, a. orribile; —ly, ad. orribilmente. [diglio, m.
hiding-place, *hī'dĭng plās*, s. nasconhierarchy, *hī'ărārkĭ*, s. gerarchia, f.
hieroglyph, *hī'ĕrŏglĭf*, s. geroglifico, m.
higgle, *hĭg'l*, v. n. rivendere.
higgledy-piggledy, —*dĭ pĭgldĭ*, ad. confusamente, alla rinfusa.
higgler, —*glăr*, s. rivenditore, m.
high, *hī*, a. alto, elevato; sublime; eccessivo; altiero, arrogante; nobile, illustre; violento.
high-altar, —*āltăr*, s. altare maggiore, m.
high-born, —*bŏrn*, a. d' alta nascita, bennato. [vivido.
high-coloured, —*kŭlŏrd*, a. di colore
high-flown, —*flōn*, a. orgoglioso.
highland, —*lănd*, s. paese montuoso, m.
highlander, —*lăndăr*, s. montanaro, m.
highly, —*lī*, ad. in alto; molto, grandemente; altieramente.
high-minded, —*mĭndĕd*, a. magnanimo, generoso. [f.
highness, —*nĕs*, s. altezza, f.; grandezza,
high-water, —*wătăr*, s. marea alta, f., acque piene, f. pl.
highway, —*wā*, s. strada maestra, f.
highwayman, —*wămăn*, s. malandrino, rubatore, m. [festoso.
hilarious, *hĭlā'rĭŭs*, a. ilare, giulivo.
hilarity, —*lăr'ĭtĭ*, s. allegria, allegrezza, giocondità, f.; gaiezza, f.
hill, *hĭl*, s. collina, f. [m.
hillock, —*lŏk*, s. collinetta, f.; monticello.
hill-tribes, —*trĭbz*, s. pl. montagnuoli, hilly, —*lī*, a. montagnoso. [m. pl.
hilt, *hĭlt*, s. manico (della spada), m.
him, *hĭm*, pn. lui, lo.
himself, —*sĕlf*, pn. se stesso, egli stesso, si.
hind, *hīnd*, s. cerva, damma, f.; rustico, m.; —(er), a. posteriore; deretano.
hinder, *hĭn'dăr*, v. a. impedire; imbarazzare.
hinder, *hĭn'dăr*, a. di dietro, posteriore.
hind(e)rance, *hĭn'd(ă)răns*, s. impedimento, ostacolo, m.
hind(er)most, *hĭn'd(ŭr)mŏst*, a. ultimo.
hind-quarter, *hĭnd'kwărtăr*, s. piede di dietro, m.
hinge, *hĭnj*, s. arpione, cardine, m.; punto principale, m.; —, v. a. gangherare.
hint, *hĭnt*, s. indizio, avviso, sentore, m.; cenno, m.; barlume, m.; —, v. a. insinuare, dare un indizio, accennare; alludere.
hip, *hĭp*, s. anca, f.
hip-bath, —*bāth*, s. insesso, m.
hippodrome, *hĭp'pŏdrŏm*, s. ippodromo, m. [tamo, m.
hippopotamus, —*pŏt'ămŭs*, s. ippopohip-shot, *hĭp'shŏt*, a. sciancato, zoppo.
hire, *hīr*, s. affitto, m., pigione, m., nolo, m.; salario, m.; —, v. a. affittare, appigionare. [nario (m.)
hireling, —*lĭng*, a. & s. venale (m.); merce
hirsute, *hŭrsŭt*, a. irsuto, ruvido.

his, *hĭz*, pn. suo, sua; suoi, sue.
hiss, *hĭs*, v. a. & n. fischiare; sibilare;
hist, *hĭst*, i. silenzio! zitto! [scoppiare.
historian, *hĭstŏ'rĭăn*, s. scrittore di storie, istorico, m. [ad. istoricamente.
historic(al), —*stŏr'ĭk(ăl)*, a. istorico; —ly,
history, *hĭs'tŏrĭ*, s. storia, istoria, f.
histrionic, —*trĭŏn'ĭk*, a. istrionico.
hit, *hĭt*, s. colpo, m., percossa, botta, f.; azzardo, m.; —, v. a. ir. bastonare, percuotere; —, v. n. ir. pervenire; incontrare; urtarsi.
hitch, *hĭch*, v. n. dimenarsi; (mar.) annodare; —, s. uncino, m.; rampone, m.; (mar.) nodo, m.; difficoltà, f.
hither, *hĭth'ăr*, a. citeriore; —, ad. qui, quà; —, to, fin qui, fino a quest' ora,
hive, *hĭv*, s. arnia, f., alveare, m.; —, v. a. fare entrare nell' arnia; —, v. n. raccohoar, *hŏr*, a. bianco, canuto. [gliersi.
hoard, *hŏrd*, s. mucchio segreto m.; tesoro, m.; —, v. a. ammassare.
hoar-frost, *hŏr'frŏst*, s. brina, f
hoariness, *hŏr'ĭnĕs*, s. bianchezza, 1.; canutezza, f. [rauca.
hoarse, *hŏrs*, a. rauco; —ly, ad. con voce
hoarseness, —*nĕs*, s. fiocaggine, f.
hoary, *hŏ'rĭ*, a. bianco, bigio, canuto.
hoax, *hōks*, s. burla, beffa, f.; —, v. a. minchionare.
hob, *hŏb*, s. villano, rustico, m.
hobble, *hŏb'bl*, v. n. zoppicare; mancare.
hobby, —*bĭ*, s. cavallino, m.; sciocco, m.
hobby-horse, —*hŏrs*, s. cavalluccio di legno, m.; (fig.) trastullo, m., cosa prediletta, f. [tasma, m.
hobgoblin, —*gŏblĭn*, s. folletto, m.; fanhobnail, —*nāl*, s. chiodo da ferrare un cavallo, m.
hob-nob, *hŏb'nŏb*, v. n. portare brindisi.
Hobson's choice, *hŏb'sŏnz chŏĭs*, s. scelta forzata, f.
hock, *hŏk*, s. garetto, m.; vecchio vino del Reno, m.; —(le), y. a. tagliare i tendini delle gambe.
hockey, *hŏk'ĭ*, s. giuoco di palla, m.
hocus, *hŏ'kŭs*, v. n. truffare.
hocus-pocus, —*pŏkŭs*, s. gherminella, f.
hodge-podge, *hŏj'pŏj*, s. manicaretto, m.; ammorsellato, m. [m.
hodman, *hŏd'măn*, s. manovale, operaio,
hoe, *hŏ*, s. zappa, marra, f.; —, v. a. zappare.
hog, *hŏg*, s. porco, m. [pare; scavare.
hoggish, —*gĭsh*, a. porcino, di porco; ingordo; —ly, ad. da porco; ingordamente.
hogshead, *hŏgz'hĕd*, s. botte, f.
hoiden, *hŏĭ'dn*, s. ragazza grossolana, f.
hoist, *hŏĭst*, v. a. alzare; (mar.) spiegare (le vele).
hold, *hōld*, s. presa, cattura, f.; prigione, f.; fortezza, f.; influsso, m.; influenza, f.; —, i. olà! fermate! —, v. a. ir. tenere; pigliare, prendere; contenere; ritenere; possedere; fruire; convocare; celebrare; —, v. n. ir. continuare, durare; credere, pensare; attaccarsi, rappigliarsi; fermarsi.

7*

holder, *hŏl′dăr*, s. tenitore, m,; vassallo,
holdfast, *hŏld′făst*, s. rampone, m.   [m.
holding, *-ĭng*, s. feudo, m.; affitto, m.
hole, *hŏl*, s. buco, forame, m.; caverna, f.
holiday, *hŏl′ĭdâ*, s. giorno di festa; anni-
     versario, m.
holiness, *hŏ′lĭnĕs*, s. santità, f.
hollow, *hŏl′lŏ*, a. cavo, vuoto; finto,
     doppio; –. s. cavo, m.; cavità, f.; fossa,
     f.; –, v. a. scavare; vuotare.
hollowness, *-nĕs*, s. cavità, f.; dissimu-
holly, *hŏl′lĭ*, s. agrifoglio, m.   [lazione, f.
holly-hock, *-hŏk*, s. (bot.) bismalva, f.
holster, *hŏl′stăr*, s. fodera della pistola, f.
holy, *hŏ′lĭ*, a. santo, sacrato, pio.
holy-water, *–wâtăr*, s. acqua benedetta, f.
holy-week, *–wĕk*, s. settimana santa, f.
homage, *hŏm′âj*, s. omaggio, m.; –, v. a.
     render omaggio.
home, *hŏm*, s. casa, f.; dimora, stanza,
     f.; patria, f.; –, ad. in casa, in patria.
home-born, *–bŏrn*, home-bred, *–brĕd*,
     a. del paese, nativo.
homeless, *–lĕs*, a. senza ricovero. [città, f.
homeliness, *–lĭnĕs*, s. rozzezza, rusti-
homely, *–lĭ*, a. rozzo, grossolano, incolto.
home-made, *–mâd*, a. fatto nella casa.
home-rule, *–rŏl*, s. amministrazione in-
     dipendente, m.
home-ruler, *–ăr*, s. partigiano dell'
     amministrazione indipendente, m.
home-sick, *–sĭk*, a. nostalgico.
home-sickness, *–sĭknĕs*, s. nostalgia, f.
home-spun, *–spŭn*, a. casalingo.
homeward, *–wărd*, ad. verso casa.
homicidal, *hŏmĭs′ĭdăl*, a. micidiale.
homicide, *hŏm′ĭsĭd*, s. omicida, m.
homily, *hŏm′ĭlĭ*, s. omelia, f.
homœopathist, *hŏmĕŏp′athĭst*, s. medico
     omeopatico, m.
homœopathy, *–ăthĭ*, s. omeopatia, f.
homogeneous, *hŏmŏjĕ′nĭăs*, a. della stessa
hone, *hŏn*, s. cote, f.   [natura.
honest, *ŏn′ĕst*, a. onesto, giusto, sincero;
     casto; –ly, ad. onestamente, giustamente.
honesty, *ŏn′ĕstĭ*, s. onestà, f.; sincerità, f.
honey, *hŭn′ĭ*, s. miele, m.; dolcezza, f.;
     my –, amor mio, anima mia.
honey-comb, *–kŏm*, s. favo, m.   [f.
honey-dew, *–dû*, s. manna, rugiada dolce,
honey-moon, *–mŏn*, s. primo mese del
     matrimonio, m.   [m.
honeysuckle, *–sŭkl*, s. (bot.) caprifoglio,
honied, *hŭn′ĭd*, a. condito di miele, dolce.
honorary, *ŏn′ărârĭ*, a. d'onore, per onore;
     –, s. onorario, salario, m.
honour, *ŏn′ŭr*, s. onore, m.; rispetto, m.;
     fama, f.; –, v. a. onorare, riverire, rispet-
     tare.
honourable, *–ăbl*, a. onorevole, illustre.
honourably, *–ăblĭ*, ad. onorevolmente,
     nobilmente.   [v. a. incappucciare.
hood, *hŭd*, s. cappuccio, m.; cuffia, f.; –,
hoodman-blind, *–mănblĭnd*, s. mosca
     cieca, f. (giuoco).   [occhi; ingannare.
hoodwink, *hŭd′wĭnk*, v. a. bendare gli
hoof, *hŏf*, s. unghia, f.

hoof-bound, *–bŏŭnd*, a. incastellato.
hook, *hŭk*, s. uncino, m.; fermaglio, m.;
     amo, m.; by – or by crook, o di ruffa
     o di raffa; –, v. a. uncinare; aggraffare;
     adescare.
hooked, *hŭkt*, a. curvo, curvato.
hook-nosed, *hŭk′nŏzd*, a. che ha il naso
     aquilino.
hoop, *hŏp*, s. cerchio, m.; guardinfante,
     m.; upupa, f.; –, v. a. & n. cerchiare;
hooper, *–ăr*, s. bottaio, m.   [gridare.
hooping-cough, *hŏp′ĭng kŏf*, s. tosse
hoopoo, *hŏ′pŏ*, s. upupa, f. [convulsa, f.
hoot, *hŏt*, s. schiamazzo, m.; –, v. n.
     schiamazzare
hop, *hŏp*, s. luppolo, m.; salto, m.; –,
     v. a. conciare la birra co' luppoli; –, v. n.
     saltellare.   [aspettare.
hope, *hŏp*, s. speranza, f.; –, v. n. sperare;
hopeful, *–fŭl*, a. di grand' aspettazione;
     –ly, ad. con speranza.   [f.
hopefulness, *–fŭlnĕs*, s. buona speranza,
hopeless, *–lĕs*, a. senza speranza, dispe-
     rato; –ly, ad. che è senza speranza.
hopelessness, *–lĕsnĕs*, s. disperazione, f.
hop-garden, *hŏp′gărdn*, hop-ground,
     –grŏŭnd, s. campo di luppoli, m.
hopper, *hŏp′păr*, s. saltatore, m.; tra-
     moggia, f.   [luppoli, m.
hop-pole, *–pŏl*, s. palo da sostenere i
horary, *hŏ′rărĭ*, a. d' un' ora.
horde, *hŏrd*, s. truppa vagante, f.
horizon, *hŏrĭ′zn*, s. orizzonte, m.
horizontal, *hŏrĭzŏn′tăl*, a. orizzontale;
     –ly, ad. orizzontalmente.
horn, *hŏrn*, s. corno, m.; cornetta, f.
horn-beetle, *–bĕtl*, s. cervo volante, m.
horned, *hŏrnd*, a. cornuto.
hornet, *hŏr′nĕt*, s. calabrone, m. (mosca
     pungente).
horned-owl, *hŏrnd′ŏŭl*, s. allocco, m.
horn-pipe, *hŏrn′pĭp*, s. cornamusa, f.
horny, *hŏr′nĭ*, a. incallito, indurito.
horrible, *hŏr′rĭbl*, a. orribile.
horribly, *–rĭblĭ*, ad. orribilmente.
horrid, *–rĭd*, a. orrido, orribile.
horrific, *–rĭf′ĭk*, a. spaventevole.
horror, *hŏr′răr*, s. orrore, terrore, m.
horse, *hŏrs*, s. cavallo, m.; cavalleria, f.;
     cavalletto, m.; –, v. a. montare una ca-
horseback, *–băk*, ad. a cavallo.   [valla.
horse-block, *–blŏk*, s. montatoio, m.
horse-breaker, *–brĕkăr*, s. cozzone, m.;
     cavallerizzo, m.
horse-chestnut, *–chĕsnŭt*, s. hippo-
     castano, marrone d' India, m.
horse-cloth, *–klŏth*, s. gualdrappa, f.
horse-fly, *–flĭ*, s. tafano, m.   [f.
horse-guard, *–gărd*, s. guardia a cavallo
horse-hair, *–hăr*, s. crine di cavallo, m.
horse-laugh, *–lâf*, s. riso smoderato, m.
horse-leech, *–lĕch*, s. veterinario, m.;
     manescalco, m.; sanguisuga maggiore, f.
horseman, *–măn*, s. cavaliere, cavalca-
     tore, m.   [m.
horsemanship, *–mănshĭp*, s. maneggio,
horse-meat, *–mĕt*, s. foraggio, m.
horse-play, *–plâ*, s. trastullo rozzo, m,

horse-pond, *-pŏnd*, s. abbeveratoio, m.
horse-power, *-pōŭŭr*, s. forza di cavallo,
  f.   [*-rāsĭng*, s. corsa di cavalli, f.
horse-race, *-rās*, horse-racing,
horse-radish, *-rădĭsh*, s. rafano, m.
horse-shoe, *-shō*, s. ferro di cavallo, m.
horse-whip, *-hwĭp*, s. bacchetta, frusta,
  sferza, f.   [f.
horsewoman, *-wŭmăn*, s. cavalieressa,
horticulture, *hŏrtĭkŭl'tŭr*, s.orticultura,f.
horticulturist, *-tŭrĭst*, s. giardiniere,
  orticultore, m.   [brache, f. pl.
hose, *hŏz*, s. calzetta, f.; calzoni, m. pl.,
hosier, *hŏ'zhŭr*, s. calzettaio, m.
hosiery. *-zhŭrĭ*, s. mercanzie del calzettaio, f. pl.
hospitable, *hŏs'pĭtăbl*, a. ospitale.
hospitably, *-ăblĭ*, ad. con ospitalità.
hospital, *-pĭtăl*, s. spedale, m.
hospitality, *-tăl'ĭtĭ*, s. ospitalità, f.;
  ospizio, m.   [cito, m.; ostia, f.
host, *hŏst*, s. oste, albergatore, m.; escr-
hostage, *hŏs'tăj*, s. ostaggio, m.
hostess, *hŏst'ĕs*, s. ostessa, albergatrice, f.
hostile, *hŏs'tĭl*, a. ostile, nemico.
hostility, *-tĭl'ĭtĭ*, s. ostilità, f.
hot, *hŏt*, a. caldo, fervido; veemente.
hot-bed, *-bĕd*, s. letto di concime, m.
hotel, *hŏtĕl'*, s. locanda, f.
hot-house, *hŏt'hŏŭs*, s. bagno caldo, m.;
  stufa, serra, f.
hotly, *-lĭ*, ad. caldamente; vivamente.
hotpress, *-prĕs*, v. a. cilindrare, lustrare.
hotspur, *-spŭr*, s. uomo caparbio o violento, m.   [i garetti.
hough, *hŏk*, s. garetto, m.; –, v. a. tagliare
hound, *hŏŭnd*, s. cane da caccia, m.
hour, *ŏŭr*, s. ora, f.
hour-glass, *-glăs*, s. oriuolo a polvere, m.
hour-hand, *-hănd*, s. lancetta dell' oriuolo, f.
hourly, *-lĭ*, a. & ad. d' ora in ora.   [f.
hour-plate, *-plăt*, s. mostra d'oriuolo, f.
house, *hŏŭs*, s. casa, f.; abitazione, f.; alloggiamento, m.; famiglia, f.; –, v. a. ricevere in casa, alloggiare; raccogliere; –,
  v. n. abitare.
house-breaker, *-brăkŭr*, s. ladro domestico, m.   [m.
house-dog, *-dŏg*, s. cane da casa, mastino,
household, *-hŏld*, s. famiglia, f.; governo
  domestico, m.   [m.
householder, *-hŏldŭr*, s. padrone di casa,
house-keeper, *-kēpŭr*, s. padrone di casa,
  m.; massaia, f.
house-keeping, *-kēpĭng*, s. governo domestico, m.; economia, f.
houseless, *-lĕs*, a. senza ricovero.
housemaid, *-măd*, s. serva di casa, f.
house-warming, *-wărmĭng*, s. festino
  allegro, m.   [f.
housewife, *-wĭf*, s. massaia, f.; economa,
housewifery, *-rĭ*, s. economia, f.; governo domestico, m.
housing, *hŏŭzĭng*, s. gualdrappa, f.
hovel, *hŏv'ĕl*, s. capanna, casuccia, f.
hover, *hŏv'ŭr*, v. n. svolazzare.
how, *hŏŭ*, ad. come, quanto; in che ma-

niera? – much, per quanto; – do you
do? come sta?
howitzer, *hŏŭ'ĭtsŭr*, s. (mil.) obice, m.
howl, *hŏŭl*, s. urlo, m.; –, v. n. urlare.
how(so)ever, *-(sŏ)ĕv'ŭr*, ad. con tutto
  ciò, pure, benchè.
hubbub, *hŭb'bŭb*, s. tumulto, fracasso, m.;
  romore, m.; confusione, f.
huckaback, *hŭk'ăbăk*, s. traliccio, m.;
  tela da sacchi, f.
huckle, *hŭk'kl*, s. anca, coscia, f.
huckster, *hŭk'stŭr*, s. rivenditore, m.
huddle, *hŭd'dl*, s. fretta, f.; confusione,
  f.; –, v. a. rimescolare.
hue, *hŭ*, s. colore, m.; grido, m.; – and
  cry, grido pubblico, m.
huff, *hŭf*, s. impeto di collera, f.; vantatore, m.; –, v. a. soffiare; insultare; bravare; –, v. n. strepitare.
huffish, *hŭf'fĭsh*, a. insolente, arrogante;
  –ly, ad. insolentemente, arrogantemente.
hug, *hŭg*, s. abbracciamento, m.; –, v. a.
  abbracciare; careggiare.   [mente.
huge, *hŭj*, a. vasto, enorme; –ly, ad. vasta-
hugeness, *-nĕs*, s. vastità, f.
hulk, *hŭlk*, s. carena (d' un naviglio), f.;
  mazza pesante, f.   [f.
hull, *hŭl*, s. baccello, m.; guscio, m.; pelle,
hum, *hŭm*, s. rombo, m.; mormorio, m.;
  –, v. n. rombare; mormoreggiare; bor-
  bogliare.
human, *hŭ'măn*, a. umano; mortale.
humane, *hŭmăn'*, a. umano; benigno;
  –ly, ad. umanamente.
humanise, *hŭ'mănĭz*, v. a. render umano;
  render affabile.   [logo, m.
humanist, *-mănĭst*, s. umanista, m.; filo-
humanity, *-măn'ĭtĭ*, s. umanità, f.   [m.
humankind, *hŭ'mănkĭnd*, s. genere umano,
humanly, *-mănlĭ*, ad. benignamente, affabilmente.
humble, *hŭm'bl*, a. umile; modesto; vile;
  –, v. a. umiliare, abbassare. [brone, m.
humble-bee, *-bē*, s. pecchione, m.; cala-
humbleness, *-nĕs*, s. umiltà, f.
humbly, *hŭm'blĭ*, ad. umilmente.
humbug, *hŭm'bŭg*, s. ciarlataneria, trappola, f.; –, v. a. trappolare; corbellare.
humdrum, *hŭm'drŭm*, a. stolto, sciocco,
  infingardo.
humid, *hŭ'mĭd*, a. umido, inumidito.
humidity, *-mĭd'ĭtĭ*, s. umidità, f.
humiliate, *-mĭl'ĭăt*, v. a. umiliare, mortificare.
humiliation, *-lĭă'shăn*, s. umiliazione, f.
humility, *-mĭl'ĭtĭ*, s. umiltà, f.   [m.
humming-bird, *hŭm'mĭng bŭrd*,s.colibrì,
humming-top, *-tŏp*, s. paleo, m.
humorist, *ŭ'mŭrĭst*,s. uomo fantastico, m.
humorous, *ŭ'mŭrŭs*, a. fantastico, capriccioso; –ly, ad. capricciosamente.
humorsome, *ŭ'mŭrsŭm*, a. fantastico, bisbetico.
humour, *ŭ'mŭr*, s. umore, m., disposizione dell' animo, f.; capriccio, m.; fantasia, f.; –, v. a. contentare, compiacere,
hump, *hŭmp*, s. gobba, f.; scrigno, m.
humpback, *-băk*, s. gobbo, m.

hunch, *hŭnsh,* s. gomitata, f.

hunchback, *vedi* **humpback.**

hundred, *hŭn'drĕd,* a. cento; **–,** s. centinaio, m.; cantone, m.

hundredfold, *–fōld,* a. centuplo.

hundredth, *–drĕdth,* a. centesimo.

hundred-weight, *hŭn'drĕd wāt,* s. quintale, m. [aver fame.

hunger, *hŭng'gŭr,* s. fame, f.; **–,** v. n.

hungrily, *–grĭlĭ,* ad. con gran fame, con appetito grande.

hungry, *–grĭ,* a. affamato.

hunks, *hŭnks,* s. avaro, spilorcio, m.

hunt, *hŭnt,* v. a. & n. cacciare; perseguire.

hunter, *–ŭr,* s. cacciatore, m.; cavallo di caccia, m.; cane da caccia, m.

hunting, *–ĭng,* s. caccia, f.; **to go a –,** andare alla caccia. [tori, m.

hunting-box, *–bŏks,* s. ritrovo de' caccia-

hunting-crop, *–krŏp,* s. canna dei cacciatori con laccio all' estremità, f. [m.

hunting-horn, *–hŏrn,* s. corno da caccia,

hunting-watch, *–wŏch,* s. oriuolo da caccia, m.

huntress, *hŭn'trĕs,* s. cacciatrice, f.

huntsman, *hŭnts'măn,* s. cacciatore, m.; capocaccia, m.

hurdle, *hŭr'dl,* s. graticcio, canniccio, m.

hurdy-gurdy, *hŭr'dĭ gŭr'dĭ,* s. viola da cieco, f.

hurl, *hŭrl,* v. a. lanciare; scagliare.

hurly-burly, *hŭr'lĭ bŭr'lĭ,* s. tumulto, garbuglio, m. [burrasca, f.

hurricane, *hŭr'rĭkān,* s. uragano, m.,

hurry, *hŭr'rĭ,* s. precipitazione, fretta, f.; tumulto, m.; **in a –,** in fretta; **–,** v. a. affrettare; precipitare; **–,** v. n. affrettarsi.

hurt, *hŭrt,* s. ferita, f.; detrimento, danno, pregiudizio, m.; sconcio, m.; **–,** v. a. ir. ferire; fare male; danneggiare.

hurtful, *–fŭl,* a. nocivo, dannoso, pernicioso; **–ly,** ad. perniciosamente. [m.

hurtfulness, *–nĕs,* s. danno, pregiudizio.

husband, *hŭz'bănd,* s. marito, sposo, m.; agricoltore, m.; **–,** v. a. maritare; coltivare. [bifolco, m.

husbandman, *–măn,* s. agricoltore, m.,

husbandry, *–rĭ,* s. agricoltura, f.; economia, f. [tacere; **– i.** silenzio! zitto!

hush, *hŭsh,* v. a. & n. imporre silenzio;

hush-money, *–mŭnĭ,* s. subornazione, guadagno illecito, m.

husk, *hŭsk,* s. baccello, m.; guscio, m.; loppa, f.; pelle, f.; **–,** v. a. sgusciare.

huskiness, *hŭs'kĭnĕs,* s. raucedine, f.

husky, *hŭs'kĭ,* a. pieno di loppa.

hussar, *hŭzzăr',* s. (mil.) ussaro, m.

hussy, *hŭz'zĭ,* s. buona roba, f.

hustings, *hŭs'tĭngz,* s. pl. luogo da eleggere, m.; consiglio, m. [tate.

hustle, *hŭs'l,* v. a. rovesciare, dar gomi-

hut, *hŭt,* s. capanna, baracca, f.

hutch, *hŭch,* s. madia, f.; cassa, f.; arca, f.

hyacinth, *hī'ăsĭnth,* s. giacinto, m.

hydrant, *hī'drănt,* s. idrante, m.

hydraulic, *–drä'lĭk,* a. idraulico; **–s,** s. pl. idraulica, f.

hydrogen, *hī'drŏjĕn,* s. idrogeno, m.

hydrophobia, *–drŏf'bĭă,* s. idrofobia, f.

hydrostatics, *–stăt'ĭks,* s. pl. idrostatica, f.

hyena, *hī'ēnă,* s. iena, f. [f.

hygiena, *hī'jĭĕn (hī'jĕn),* s. igiene, f.

hymeneal, *–mĕnē'ăl,* a. nuziale; maritale.

hymn, *hĭm,* s. inno, m.; cantico, m.

hyperbole, *hĭpŭr'bŏlē,* s. iperbole, f.; esagerazione, f.

hyperbolic, *–bŏl'ĭk,* a. iperbolico; **–ally,** ad. iperbolicamente.

hypercritic, *–krĭt'ĭk,* s. critico severo, m.

hypochondria, *hĭpŏkŏn'drĭă,* s. ipocondria, f.

hypochondriac, *–kŏn'drĭăk,* s. ipocondrio, m.; **–,** a. ipocondriaco.

hypocrisy, *–pŏk'rĭsĭ,* s. ipocrisia, f.

hypocrite, *hĭp'ŏkrĭt,* s. ipocrita, m.

hypocritical, *–krĭt'ĭkăl,* a. ipocrita.

hypothesis, *–pŏth'ĕsĭs,* s. ipotesi, f.

hypothetical, *–thĕt'ĭkăl,* a. ipotetico; **–ly,** ad. per ipotesi.

hyssop, *hĭs'sŭp,* s. issopo, m.

hysteric(al), *hĭstĕr'ĭk(ăl),* a. isterico, uterino. [m. pl.

hysterics, *hĭstĕr'ĭks,* s. pl. dolori isterici,

I.

I, *ī,* pn. io.

ice, *īs,* s. ghiaccio, m.; **–,** v. a. ghiacciare.

ice-bound, *–bōŭnd,* a. serrato di ghiaccio.

ice-box, *–bŏks,* **ice-cellar,** *–sĭllăr,* **ice-house,** *–hōŭs,* **ice-safe,** *–sāf,* s. ghiacciaia, f.

icicle, *ī'sĭkl,* s. ghiacciuolo, m.

iciness, *ī'sĭnĕs,* s. gelidezza, f., stato di ghiaccio, m.

iconoclast, *īkŏn'ŏklăst,* s. iconoclasta, m.

icy, *ī'sĭ,* a. agghiacciato; frigido.

idea, *īdē'ă,* s. idea, f.; immaginazione, f.

ideal, *īdē'ăl,* a. ideale; intellettuale; **–ly,** ad. idealmente. [simo.

identic(al), *īdĕn'tĭk(ăl),* a. identico, mede-

identify, *īdĕn'tĭfī,* v. a. identificare.

identity, *īdĕn'tĭtĭ,* s. identità, f.

idiocy, *ĭd'ĭŏsĭ,* **idiotcy,** *ĭd'ĭŏtsĭ,* s. idiotismo, m., imbecillità, f.

idiom, *ĭd'ĭŭm,* s. idioma, m.

idiomatic, *ĭdĭŏm'ătĭk,* a. idiomatico.

idiosyncrasy, *–sĭng'krăsĭ,* s. idiosincrazia, f. [m.

idiot, *ĭd'ĭŏt,* s. idiota, ignorante, sciocco,

idiotic, *ĭdĭŏt'ĭk,* a. idiotico.

idle, *ī'dl,* a. pigro, ozioso; inutile, frivolo, vano; **–,** v. n. consumare il tempo in vano.

idleness, *–nĕs,* s. pigrizia, f., ozio, m.

idler, *ī'dlŭr,* s. poltrone, m.; infingardo, m.; staccendato, m. [–, vaneggiare.

idly, *ī'dlĭ,* ad. in ozio; vanamente; **to talk**

idol, *ī'dŏl,* s. idolo, m., immagine, f.

idolater, *īdŏl'ătŭr,* s. idolatra, m.

idolatrous, *īdŏl'ătrŭs,* a. idolatrico.

idolatry, *īdŏl'ătrĭ,* s, idolatria, f.

idolise, *ī'dŏlīz,* v. a. idolatrare.

idyl, *ĭ'dĭl*, s. jdillio, m.
idyllic, *ĭdĭl'lĭk*, a. idillico.
if, *ĭf*, c. se; purchè, benchè.
igneous, *ĭg'nĭăs*, a. igneo.   [tuo, m.
ignis-fatuus, *ĭg'nĭs făt'ŭăs*, s. fuoco fa-
ignite, *ĭgnīt'*, v. a. accendere, infiammare.
ignitible, *-nĭt'ĭbl*, a. infiammabile.
ignition, *ĭgnĭsh'ăn*, s. infocamento, m.
ignoble, *ĭgnō'bl*, a. ignobile; basso.
ignobly, *-blĭ*, ad. ignobilmente; bassamente, vilmente.
ignominious, *-mĭn'ĭăs*, a. ignominioso,
infamante; *-lĭy*, ad. ignominiosamente.
ignominy, *ĭg'nŏmĭnĭ*, s. ignominia, infamia, f.   [m.
ignoramus, *-ĭg'răm'ŭs*, s. ignorante, sciocco,
ignorance, *ĭg'nŏrăns*, s. ignoranza, f.
ignorant, *-rănt*, a. ignorante; *-lĭy*, .d.
ignorantemente.
ignore, *ĭgnōr'*, v. a. ignorare, non sapere.
ill, *ĭl*, a. malo, cattivo; ammalato; *-*, ad.
male, malamente; *-*, s. male, infortunio,
m.   [galmente.
illegal, *ĭllē'găl*, a. illegale; *-lĭy*, ad. ille-
illegality, *-lēgăl'ĭtĭ*, s. cosa non legale,
m.; ingiustizia, f.
illegible, *-lĕj'ĭbl*, a. che non si può leggere,
illeggibile.   [f.
illegitimacy, *-jĭt'ĭmăsĭ*, s. illegittimità.
illegitimate, *-jĭt'ĭmăt*, a. illegittimo;
-lĭy, ad. illegittimamente.
illiberal, *-lĭb'ărăl*, a. illiberale; sordido;
-lĭy, ad. in modo illiberale.   [teria, f.
illiberality, *-răl'ĭtĭ*, s. illiberalità, gret-
illicit, *-lĭs'ĭt*, a. illecito, proibito.
illimited, *ĭllĭm'ĭtĭd*, a. illimitato, senza
limiti.
illiterate, *-lĭt'ărăt*, a. illetterato; ignorante.   [f.
illness, *ĭl'nĕs*, s. malattia, f.; indisposizione,
illogical, *-lŏj'ĭkăl*, a. senza ragionamento.
ill-shaped, *ĭl'shāpt*, a. mal fatto, deforme.
ill-timed, *-tīmd*, a. inopportuno; mal a
proposito.   [trattare.
ill-treat, *ĭl'trēt*, ill-use, *-ăz*, v. a. mal-
illuminate, *-lū'mĭnăt*, v. a. illuminare.
illumination, *-nā'shăn*, s. illuminazione,
illumine, *-lū'mĭn*, v. a. illuminare.   [f.
illusion, *-lū'zhăn*, s. illusione, f., errore, m.
illusive, *-sĭv*, illusory, *-sŭrĭ*, a. illu-
sorio.   [cidare, schiarire.
illustrate, *-lŭs'trăt*, v. a. illustrare; dilu-
illustration, *-trā'shăn*, s. dichiarazione,
f., spiegamento, m.
illustrative, *-lŭs'trătĭv*, a. illustrante.
illustrious, *-lŭs'trĭăs*, a. illustre, celebre;
nobile; *-lĭy*, ad. illustremente; nobilmente.
ill-will, *ĭl'wĭl*, s. malevolenza, f.
image, *ĭm'ĕj*, s. immagine, f.; statua, f.;
-, v. a. immaginare; rappresentarsi.
imagery, *-ărĭ*, s. idee chimeriche, f. pl.
imaginable, *ĭmăj'ĭnăbl*, a. immaginabile;
concepibile.   [merico.
imaginary, *-ĭnărĭ*, a. immaginario, chi-
imagination, *-nă'shăn*, s. immaginazione,
f.; idea, f.   [tivo.
imaginative, *ĭmăj'ĭnătĭv*, a. immagina-

imagine, *ĭmăj'ĭn*, v. a. immaginare; inventare, disegnare, ideare.
imbecile, *ĭm'bĕsĭl*, a. imbecille; sciocco.
imbecility, *-sĭl'ĭtĭ*, s. imbecillità, f.; debolezza, f.
imbed, *ĭmbĕd'*, v. a. porre, profondare.
imbibe, *-bīb'*, v. a. imbevere; succiare.
imbroglio, *-brō'lĭō*, s. imbroglio, m.
imbrue, *-brō'*, v. a. immollare; inzuppare.
imbue, *-bŭ'*, v. a. imbevere; inspirare.
imitate, *ĭm'ĭtăt*, v. a. imitare.   [f.
imitation, *-tă'shăn*, s. imitazione, copia,
imitative, *ĭm'ĭtătĭv*, a. imitativo.
immaculate, *-măk'ŭlăt*, a. immaculato,
puro.   [incorporale.
immaterial, *-mătĕ'rĭăl*, a. immateriale.
immature, *-mătŭr'*, a. immaturo, imper-
fetto.   [surabile, immenso.
immeasurable, *-mĕzh'ŭrăbl*, a. immen-
immeasurably, *-răblĭ*, ad. immensamente.
immediate, *-mē'dĭăt*, a. immediato; *-lĭy*,
ad. immediatamente, subitamente.   [bile.
immemorial, *-mĕmō'rĭăl*, a. immemora-
immense, *-mĕns'*, a. immenso, vasto;
-lĭy, ad. immensamente.
immensity, *-mĕn'sĭtĭ*, s. immensità, f.
immerge, *-mărj'*, immerse, *-mărs'*, v. a.
immergere, attuffare.
immersion, *-măr'shăn*, s. immersione, f.
immigrant, *ĭm'mĭgrănt*, s. immigrante,
m. & f.   [prastante.
imminent, *ĭm'mĭnĕnt*, a. imminente, so-
immobile, *ĭm'mŏbĭl*, a. immobile.
immobility, *-mŏbĭl'ĭtĭ*, s. immobilità, f.
immoderate, *-mŏd'ărăt*, a. immoderato,
eccessivo; *-lĭy*, ad. eccessivamente.
immodest, *-mŏd'ĕst*, a. immodesto; *-lĭy*,
ad. immodestamente.
immodesty, *-ĕstĭ*, s. immodestia, f.
immolate, *ĭm'mŏlăt*, v. a. immolare, sacrificare.   [f.
immolation, *-mŏlă'shăn*, s. immolazione,
immoral, *-mŏr'ăl*, a. immorale; disonesto.
immorality, *-mŏrăl'ĭtĭ*, s. immoralità, f.;
disonestà, f.   [ad. immortalmente.
immortal, *-mŏr'tăl*, a. immortale; *-lĭy*,
immortalise, *-mŏr'tălĭz*, v. a. immortalare; eternare.
immortality, *-tăl'ĭtĭ*, s. immortalità, f.
immovable, *-mōv'ăbl*, a. immobile; *-s*,
s. pl. beni immobili, m. pl.
immovably, *-ăblĭ*, ad. immobilmente.
immunity, *-mŭ'nĭtĭ*, s. immunità, f.; esenzione, f.   [con muro.
immure, *-mŭr'*, v. a. murare, circondare
immutability, *-mŭtăbĭl'ĭtĭ*, s. immutabilità, f.
immutable, *-mŭ'tăbl*, a. immutabile.
immutably, *-tăblĭ*, ad. immutabilmente;
per sempre.
imp, *ĭmp*, s. innesto, m.; folletto, diavo-
letto, m.   [m.
impact, *ĭm'păkt*, s. contatto, m.; impulso,
impair, *-păr'*, v. a. sminuire; peggiorare.
impale, *-pāl'*, v. a. palificare.
impalpable, *-păl'păbl*, a. impalpabile,
intangibile.

impannel, –păn'něl, v. a. inscrivere i nomi
dei giurati. [nicare.

impart, –pärt', v. a. far partecipe; comu-

impartial, –pär'shăl, a. imparziale; –ly,
ad. senza parzialità.

impartiality, –shăl'ĭtĭ, s. imparzialità, f.

impassable, –pȧs'săbl, a. che non può
passarsi. [f.

impassibility, –sĭbĭl'ĭtĭ, s. impassibilità, f.

impassive, –păs'sĭv, a. insensibile.

impatience, –pă'shĕns, s. impazienza, f.

impatient, –pă'shĕnt, a. impaziente; –ly,
ad. impazientemente.

impeach, –pēch', v. a. accusare.

impeachable, –ăbl, a. che può esser de-
nunziato. [f.

impeachment, –mĕnt, s. accusa, denunzia.

impecunious, –pēkū'nĭŭs, a. povero.

impede, –pēd', v. a. impedire; proibire.

impediment, –pĕd'ĭmĕnt, s. impedimento,
ostacolo, m.

impel, –pĕl', v. a. impellere, spingere.

impend, –pĕnd', v. n. soprastare.

impenetrability, –pĕnĕtrăbĭl'ĭtĭ, s. im-
penetrabilità, f.

impenetrable, –pĕn'ĕtrăbl, a. impenetrabile. [mente.

impenetrably, –trăblĭ, ad. impenetrabil-

impenitence, –pĕn'ĭtĕns, s. impenitenza, f.

impenitent, –tĕnt, a. impenitente; –ly,
ad. senza penitenza.

imperative, –pĕr'ătĭv, a. imperativo;
–ly, ad. imperativamente; –, s. (gr.)
modo imperativo, m. [tibile.

imperceptible, –pär sĕp'tĭbl, a. impercet-

imperceptibly, –tĭblĭ, ad. impercettibil-
mente.

imperfect, –pär'fĕkt, a. imperfetto, difettoso; –ly, ad. imperfettamente; –, s. (gr.)
imperfetto, m.

imperfection, –fĕk'shŭn, s. imperfezione,
f.; difetto, m.

imperial, ĭmpē'rĭăl, a. imperiale; –, s.
imperiale (barba), f.; cielo della carrozza, m.

imperil, –pĕr'ĭl, v. a. perigliare, cimentare.

imperious, ĭmpē'rĭŭs, a. imperioso; arrogante; –ly, ad. imperiosamente; arrogantemente. [bile, immarcessibile.

imperishable, –pĕr'ĭshăbl, a. incorrutti-

impermeable, –pär'mĕbl, a. impenetrabile. [–ly, ad. impersonalmente.

impersonal, –pär'sŏndl, a. impersonale;

impersonate, –pär'sŏndt, v. a. personifi-
care. [tazione, f.

impersonation, –sŏnd'shŭn, s. rappresen-

impertinence, –pär'tĭnĕns, s. impertinenza, f.

impertinent, –tĭnĕnt, a. impertinente; incongruo; –ly, ad. impertinentemente.

imperturbable, –pärtŭrb'dbl, a. imperturbabile. [mente.

imperturbably, –dblĭ, ad. imperturbabil-

impervious, –pär'vĭŭs, a. impenetrabile;
inaccessibile. [f.; violenza, f.

impetuosity, –pĕtŭŏs'ĭtĭ, s. impetuosità,

impetuous, –pĕt'ŭăs, a. impetuoso; –ly,
ad. con impeto o violenza.

impetus, ĭm'pĕtŭs, s. impeto, m.; sforzo
violento, m.

impiety, –pī'ĕtĭ, s. empietà, irreligiosità, f.

impinge (on), –pĭnj'(ŏn), v. a. urtar (contro).

impious, ĭm'pĭŭs, a. empio, irreligioso;
–ly, ad. profanamente.

implacable, –plā'kăbl, a. implacabile.

implacably, –kăblĭ, ad. implacabilmente.

implant, –plănt', v. a. piantare; imprimere, inculcare.

implement, ĭm'plĕmĕnt, s. strumento, m.;
–s, pl. mobili (di casa), m. pl.

implicate, ĭm'plĭkăt, v. a. implicare.

implication, –kā'shŭn, s. implicazione, f.

implicit, –plĭs'ĭt, a. implicito; –ly, ad.
implicitamente. [care.

implore, –plōr', v. a. implorare, suppli-

imply, –plī', v. a. implicare; comprendere.

impolicy, –pŏl'ĭsĭ, s. imprudenza, indiscrezione, f.

impolite, –pŏlīt', a. incivile, villano.

impoliteness, –nĕs, s. rozzezza, f.

impolitic, –pŏl'ĭtĭk, impolitical, –pŏlĭt'-
ĭkăl, a. impolitico; imprudente.

import, ĭm'pŏrt, s. importazione, f.; conto,
m.; senso, m., significazione, f.; conseguenza, f.; – duty, dazio d' introduzione, m. –, ĭmpŏrt', v. a. importare;
significare; portare.

importance, –pŏr'tăns, s. importanza, f.

important, –tănt, a. importante, di conseguenza. [entrata, f.

importation, –tā'shŭn, s. importazione, f.

importer, –tär, s. che introduce (le merce
straniere), m.

importunate, –pŏr'tŭnăt, a. importuno;
–ly, ad. importunamente. [noiare.

importune, –pŏrtūn', v. a. importunare,

importunity, –tū'nĭtĭ, s. importunità, f.

impose, –pōz', v. a. ingannare.

imposing, –zĭng, a. imponente.

imposition, –zĭsh'ŭn, s. ordine, m.; imposta, f. [bilità, f.

impossibility, –pŏssĭbĭl'ĭtĭ, s. impossi-

impossible, –pŏs'sĭbl, a. impossibile.

impost, ĭm'pōst, s. imposta, imposizione,
gravezza, f.

impostor, –pŏs'tär, s. ingannatore, m.

imposture, –pŏs'tür, s. impostura, f., inganno, m. [capacità, f.

impotence, ĭm'pŏtĕns, s. impotenza, f.; in-

impotent, –pŏtĕnt, a. impotente; incapace; –ly, ad. impotentemente.

impound, ĭmpŏŭnd', v. a. chiudere in un
ovile; rinchiudere.

impoverish, –pŏv'ŭrĭsh, v. a. impoverire.

impoverishment, –mĕnt, s. impoveri-
mento, m. [possibilità, f.

impracticability, –prăktĭkăbĭl'ĭtĭ, s. im-

impracticable, –prăk'tĭkăbl, a. impraticabile; impossibile. [ledire.

imprecate, ĭm'prĕkăt, v. a. imprecare, ma-

imprecation, –kā'shŭn, s. maledizione, f.

impregnable, –prĕg'năbl, a. inespugna-
bile. [satollare.

impregnate, –prĕg'năt, v. a. impregnare;

impregnation, *–nā'shŭn*, s. impregnamento, m.

impress, *–prĕs'*, s. impressione, f.; impronta, f.; sentenza, f., motto, m.; –, v. a. imprimere, improntare; levar gente per forza. [stampa, f.; edizione, f.

impression, *–prĕsh'ŭn*, s. impressione, f.;

impressionable, *–ăbl*, a.impressionabile.

impressive, *–prĕs'sĭv*, a. espressivo, energico; –ly, ad. energicamente. [pare.

imprint, *–prīnt'* v. a. imprimere; stampimprison, *–prĭz'n*, v. a. imprigionare.

imprisonment, –s. imprigionamento, m. [bilità, f.

improbability, *–prŏbăbĭl'ŭĭ*, s. improbaimprobable, *–prŏb'ābl*, a. improbabile.

improbably, *–ăblĭ*, ad. improbabilmente.

impromptu, *–prŏm'tŭ*, a. improvvisato, estemporaneo; –, s. improvvisata, f.

improper, *–prŏp'ăr*, a. improprio; indecente; –ly, ad. impropriamente.

impropriety, *–prŏprĭ'ĕtĭ*, s. improprietà, f.; sconvenevolezza, f.

improve, *–prŏv'*, v. a. migliorare; perfezionare; –, v. n. far progressi; ammendarsi. [m.; avanzamento, progresso, m.

improvement, *–mĕnt*, s. miglioramento,

improvidence, *–prŏv'ĭdĕns*, s. improvidenza, f. [ad. improvidamente.

improvident, *–ĭdĕnt*, a. improvido; –ly,

imprudence, *–prŏ'dĕns*, s. imprudenza, f.

imprudent, *–dĕnt*, a. imprudente; –ly, ad. imprudentemente.

impudence, *ĭm'pŭdĕns*, s. impudenza, f.

impudent, *–pŭdĕnt*, a. impudente; –ly, ad. impudentemente.

impugn, *–pŭn'*, v. a. assaltare, assalire.

impulse, *ĭm'pŭls*, s. impulso, m.

impulsive, *–pŭl'sĭv*, a. impulsivo.

impunity, *–pŭ'nĭtĭ*, s. impunità, f

impure, *–pŭr'*, a. impuro, immondo; impudico; –ly, ad. impuramente. [f.

impurity, *–pŭ'rĭtĭ*, s. impurità,f.; oscenità,

imputation, *–pŭtā'shŭn*, s. imputazione, f.

impute, *–pŭt'*, v. a. imputare, attribuire a colpa, incolpare.

in, *ĭn*, pr. in; nel; entro, dentro. [cità, f.

inability, *–ăbĭl'ĭtĭ*, s. inabilità, incapainaccessible, *–ăksĕs'ĭbl*, a. inaccessibile.

inaccuracy, *–ăk'kŭrăsĭ*, s. inesattezza, negligenza, trascuranza, f. [esatto.

inaccurate, *–kŭrăt*, a. trascurato, poco

inaction, *–ăk'shŭn*, s. inazione, f.; inerzia, f.; disoccupazione, f.

inactive, *–tĭv*, a. non attivo, ozioso, pigro.

inactivity, *–tĭv'ĭtĭ*, s. inerzia, trascuraggine, f. [incompleto.

inadequate, *–ăd'ĕkwăt*, a. sproporzionato,

inadmissible, *–ădmĭs'ĭbl*, a. inammissibile. [tenza, f.

inadvertence, *–ădvăr'tĕns*, s. inavvertinadvertently, *–tĕntlĭ*, ad. trascuratamente.

inalienable, *–āl'yĕnăbl*, a. inalienabile.

inanimate, *–ăn'ĭmăt*, a. inanimato.

inanition, *–ănĭsh'ŭn*, s. inedia, f.; debolezza, f.

inapplicable, *–ăp'plĭkăbl*, a. non applicabile.

inapposite, *–ăp'pŏzĭt*, a. senza ragione; spostato. [zabile.

inappreciable, *–ăpprē'shĭăbl*, a. inapprezinaptitude, *–ăp'tĭtŭd*, s. inabilità, f.

inarticulate, *–ărtĭk'ŭlăt*, a. inarticolato, indistinto; –ly, ad. indistintamente.

inasmuch, *ĭnăzmŭch'*, ad. attesochè.

inattention, *–ăttĕn'shŭn*, s. disattenzione, f.; trascuranza, f. [curato.

inattentive, *–tĕn'tĭv*, a. disattento; trasinaudible, *–ā'dĭbl*, a. inudibile.

inaugural, *–ā'gŭrăl*, a. inaugurale.

inaugurate, *–ā'gŭrăt*, v. a. inaugurare, investire. [f.

inauguration, *–rā'shŭn*,s. inaugurazione,

inauspicious, *–spĭsh'ŭs*, a. malauguroso; –ly, ad. infaustamente.

inborn, *ĭn'bŏrn*, inbred, *ĭn'brĕd*, a. innato; naturale. [bile.

incalculable, *–kăl'kŭlăbl*, a. incalcola-

incandescent, *–kăndĕs'sĕnt*, a. incandescente. [mento, m.

incantation, *–kăntā'shŭn*, s. incanta-

incapability, *–kăpăbĭl'ĭtĭ*, s. incapacità, f.

incapable, *–kā'păbl*, a. incapace; inabile.

incapacitate, *–kăpăs'ĭtăt*, v. a. rendere incapace. [abilità, f.

incapacity, *–păs'ĭtĭ*, s. incapacità, in-

incarcerate, *–kăr'sŭrăt*, v. a. incarcerare, imprigionare.

incarnate, *–kăr'năt*, a. incarnato.

incarnation, *–nā'shŭn*, s. incarnazione, f.

incase, *–kās'*, v. a. incassare; rinchiudere.

incautious, *–kā'shŭs*, a. incauto; –ly, ad. incautamente; imprudentemente.

incendiary, *–sĕn'dĭărĭ*, s. incendiario, m.

incense, *ĭn'sĕns*, s. incenso, m.; –, *ĭnsĕns'*, v. a. inasprire, irritare; provocare.

incentive, *–sĕn'tĭv*, s. incentivo, motivo, m.; incoraggiamento, m.

inception, *–sĕp'shŭn*, s. cominciamento, principio, m. [biezza, f.

incertitude, *–sŭr'tĭtăd*, s. incertezza, dub-

incessant, *–sĕs'sănt*, a. incessante, continuo; –ly, ad. continuamente.

incest, *ĭn'sĕst*, s. incesto, m.

incestuous, *–sĕs'tŭăs*, a. incestuoso.

inch, *ĭnsh*, s. dito, pollice (duodecima parte d' un piede), m.; – by –, a poco per volta.

incidence, *ĭn'sĭdĕns*, s. caso, accidente, m.

incident, *–sĭdĕnt*, a. casuale, fortuito; –, s. accidente, m.

incidental, *–sĭdĕn'tăl*, a. accidentale, fortuito; –ly, ad. incidentemente.

incipient, *–sĭp'ĭĕnt*, a. incipiente.

incise, *–sĭz'*, v. a. incidere, tagliare.

incision, *–sĭzh'ŭn*, s. incisione, f.; taglio,

incisive, *–sĭ'sĭv*, a. incisivo. [m.

incisor, *–sĭ'zăr*, s. dente incisivo, m.

incite, *–sĭt'*, v. a. incitare, eccitare. [f.

incivility, *–sĭvĭl'ĭtĭ*, s. incivilità, rusticità,

inclemency, *–klĕm'ĕnsĭ*, s. inclemenza, f.; rigore, m.; severità, f.

inclement, *–ĕnt*, a. inclemente, severo.

inclination, *–klĭnă'shŭn,* s. inclinazione, f.; propensione, f.; tendenza, f.
incline, *–klīn',* v. a. & n. inclinare; incurvare; tendere.
include, *–klŏd',* v. a. includere; comprendere, contenere.   [inclusivamente.
inclusive, *–klŏ'sĭv,* a. inclusivo; **–ly,** ad.
incognito, *–kŏg'nĭtō,* a. & ad. incognito.
incoherence, *–kŏhē'rĕns,* s. incoerenza, f.
incoherent, *–rĕnt,* a. incoerente; **–ly,** ad. in modo incoerente.   [bustibile.
incombustible, *–kŏmbŭs'tĭbl,* a. incombustibile.
income, *ĭn'kŭm,* s. rendita, entrata, f.
incommensurable, *–kŏmmĕn'shŭrăbl,* a. incommensurabile.
incommode, *–kŏmmŏd',* v. a. incomodare.
incommodious, *–mŏ'dĭŭs,* a. incomodo, inconveniente, importuno.
incomparable, *–kŏm'părăbl,* a. incomparabile; eccellente.   [mente.
incomparably, *–ăblĭ,* ad. incomparabilmente.
incompatibility, *–kŏmpătĭbĭl'ĭtĭ,* s. incompatibilità, f.
incompatible, *–păt'ĭbl,* a. incompatibile; contrario, opposto.   [petenza, f.
incompetence, *–kŏm'pĕtĕns,* s. incompetenza.
incompetent, *–pĕtĕnt,* a. incompetente; **–ly,** ad. incompetentemente.
incomplete, *–kŏmplēt',* a. incompiuto, imperfetto.   [tĭt, s. incomprensibilità, f.
incomprehensibility, *–kŏmprĕhĕnsĭbĭl'*
incomprehensible, *–hĕn'sĭbl,* a. incomprensibile.   [prensibile.
inconceivable, *–kŏnsē'văbl,* a. inconcepibile.
inconclusive, *–kŏnklŏ'sĭv,* a. inconcludente.   [f.
incongruity, *–kŏngrŏ'ĭtĭ,* s. incongruenza.
incongruous, *–kŏn'grŏŭs,* a. incongruo; **–ly,** ad. incongruentemente.
inconsiderable, *–kŏnsĭd'ărăbl,* a. inconsiderabile.
inconsiderate, *–ărăt,* a. inconsiderato; **–ly,** ad. inconsideratamente.
inconsistency, *–kŏnsĭs'tĕnsĭ,* s. incompatibilità, incongruità, f.
inconsistent, *–tĕnt,* a. inconsistente; **–ly,** ad. incongruentemente; assurdamente.
inconsolable, *–kŏnsŏ'lăbl,* a. inconsolabile.
inconstancy, *–kŏn'stănsĭ,* s. incostanza, f.
inconstant, *–stănt,* a. incostante; instabile.   [bile.
incontestable, *–kŏntĕs'tăbl,* a. incontestabile.
incontestably, *–tăblĭ,* ad. incontestabilmente.   [nenza, f.
incontinence, *–kŏn'tĭnĕns,* s. incontinenza.
incontinent, *–tĭnĕnt,* a. incontinente; **–ly,** ad. incontinentemente.
incontrovertible, *–kŏntrŏvŭr'tĭbl,* a. incontrovertibile, incontestabile.
inconvenience, *–kŏnvē'nĭĕns,* s. inconvenienza, f.; **–,** v. a. incomodare.
inconvenient, *–nĭĕnt,* a. inconveniente, incomodo; **–ly,** ad. inconvenientemente.
inconvertible, *–kŏnvŭr'tĭbl,* ad. inalterabile.
incorporate, *–kŏr'pŏrăt,* v. a. & n. incorporare, incorporarsi; **–,** a. incorporato.

incorporation, *–rā'shăn,* s. incorporazione, f., incorporamento, m.
incorporeal, *–pŏ'rĭăl,* a. incorporeo.
incorrect, *–kŏrrĕkt',* a. scorretto; **–ly,** ad. scorrettamente.
incorrigible, *–kŏr'rĭjĭbl,* a. incorreggibile.
incorruptibility, *–kŏrrŭptĭbĭl'ĭtĭ,* s. incorruttibilità, f.   [durabile.
incorruptible, *–rŭp'tĭbl,* a. incorruttibile,
increase, *–krēs',* s. accrescimento, aumento, m.; **–,** v. a. aumentare; **–,** v. n. crescere, aumentarsi.   [lĭtă, f.
incredibility, *–krĕdĭbĭl'ĭtĭ,* s. incredibilità, f.
incredible, *–krĕd'ĭbl,* a. incredibile.
incredibly, *–ĭblĭ,* ad. incredibilmente.
incredulity, *–krĕdū'lĭtĭ,* s. incredulità, miscredenza, f.
incredulous, *–krĕd'ŭlŭs,* a. incredulo.
increment, *ĭn'krĕmĕnt,* s. incremento, m.; prodotto, m.   [accusare.
incriminate, *–krĭm'ĭnăt,* v. a. incolpare,
incrust, *–krŭst',* v. a. incrostare.
incubate, *ĭn'kŭbāt,* v. n. covare.
incubus, *ĭn'kŭbŭs,* s. incubo, m.
inculcate, *–kŭl'kăt,* s. inculcare.
inculpate, *–kŭl'păt,* v. a. incolpare.
incumbency, *–kŭm'bĕnsĭ,* s. possesso d'un beneficio, m.   [beneficiato, m.
incumbent, *–bĕnt,* a. appoggiato; **–,** s.
incur, *–kŭr',* v. n. incorrere; esporsi; attirarsi.   [bile, m.
incurability, *–kŭrăbĭl'ĭtĭ,* s. stato incura-
incurable, *–kŭ'răbl,* a. incurabile, irrimediabile.
incurably, *–răblĭ,* ad. incurabile.
incursion, *–kŭr'shăn,* s. incursione, invasione, f.   [gato.
indebted, *–dĕt'ĕd,* a. indebitato, obbli-
indecency, *–dē'sĕnsĭ,* s. indecenza, sconvenevolezza, f.   [decentemente.
indecent, *–sĕnt,* a. indecente; **–ly,** ad. in-
indecision, *–dĕsĭzh'ăn,* s. irrisoluzione, f.; incertezza, f.
indecisive, *–dĕsī'sĭv,* a. indeciso.
indeclinable, *–dĕklī'năbl,* a. indeclinabile.
indecorous, *–dĕkŏ'rŭs,* a. indecoroso.
indeed, *ĭndēd',* ad. in verità, davvero.
indefatigable, *–dĕfăt'ĭgăbl,* a. infaticabile, indefesso.   [tersi difendere.
indefensible, *–dĕfĕn'sĭbl,* a. da non potersi difendere.
indefinite, *–dĕf'ĭnĭt,* a. indefinito, indeterminato; **–ly,** ad. indefinitamente.
indelible, *–dĕl'ĭbl,* a. indelebile.
indelicacy, *–dĕl'ĭkăsĭ,* s. mancanza di delicatezza, grossezza, f.   [cente.
indelicate, *–ĭkăt,* a. indelicato; indecente.
indemnification, *–dĕmnĭfĭkā'shăn,* s. indennizzazione, f., risarcimento di danno, m.
indemnify, *–dĕm'nĭfī,* v. a. indennizzare.
indemnity, *–dĕm'nĭtĭ,* s. indennità, f.
indent, *–dĕnt',* v. a. intaccare, intagliare.
indentation, *–tā'shăn,* s. intaccatura, f.
indenture, *–dĕn'tŭr,* s. contratto, m.; accordo, m.   [denza, f.
independence, *–dĕpĕn'dĕns,* s. indipen-
independent, *–dĕnt,* a. indipendente; **–ly,** ad. indipendentemente.

indescribable, *–dĕskrī′băbl*, a. indescrivibile, indicibile. [distruggersi.

indestructible, *–dĕstrŭk′tĭbl*, a. da non

indeterminate, *–dĕtŭr′mĭnăt*, a. indeterminato, indeciso; **–ly**, ad. indeterminatamente.

index, *ĭn′dĕks*, s. indice, m.; tavola, f.

Indiaman, *ĭn′dĭămăn*, s. indicoplenta, m.

Indian-summer, *ĭn′dĭăn sŭmmăr*, s. (am.) filamenti della Madonna, [elastica, f.

India-rubber, *ĭn′dĭă rŭbbăr*, s. gomma

indicate, *ĭn′dĭkăt*, v. a. indicare.

indication, *–kā′shăn*, s. indicazione, f.; segno, m.; sintomo, m. [cativo (m.).

indicative, *–dĭk′ătĭv*, a. & s. (gr.) indi-

indictment, *–dīt′mĕnt*, s. accusa, f.

indifference, *–dĭf′fĕrĕns*, s. indifferenza, f.; imparzialità, f.

indifferent, *–fĕrĕnt*, a. indifferente; imparziale; **–ly**, ad. indifferentemente.

indigence, *ĭn′dĭjĕns*, s. indigenza, f.; povertà, f. [paese, indigeno.

indigenous, *–dĭj′ĕnăs*, a. nativo d' un

indigent, *ĭn′dĭjĕnt*, a. indigente; povero.

indigestible, *–dĭjĕs′tĭbl*, a. indigestibile.

indigestion, *–jĕst′yŭn*, s. indigestione, f.; crudità, f. [dignato.

indignant, *–dĭg′nănt*, a. sdegnato, in-

indignation, *–nă′shăn*, s. indignazione, f.; sdegno, m. [traggio, m.

indignity, *–dĭg′nĭtĭ*, s. indegnità, f.; ol-

indigo, *ĭn′dĭgō*, s. indaco, m.

indirect, *–dĭrĕkt′*, a. indiretto; **–ly**, ad. indirettamente.

indiscreet, *–dĭskrēt′*, a. indiscreto, sconsiderato; **–ly**, ad. indiscretamente.

indiscretion, *–dĭskrĕsh′ăn*, s. indiscrezione, imprudenza, f.

indiscriminate, *–dĭskrĭm′ĕnăt*, s. indistinto; **–ly**, ad. senza distinzione.

indispensable, *–dĭspĕn′săbl*, a. indispensabile.

indispensably, *–săbl*, ad. indispensabilmente, necessariamente.

indispose, *–dĭspōz′*, v. a. rendere incapace *od* avverso. [zione, f.

indisposition, *–pŏzĭsh′ăn*, s. indisposizione, f.

indisputable, *–dĭspū′tăbl*, a. incontestabile. [mente.

indisputably, *–tăblĭ*, ad. indisputabil-

indissoluble, *–dĭs′sŏlŭbl*, a. indissolubile.

indistinct, *–dĭstĭngkt′*, a. indistinto, disordinato, confuso; **–ly**, ad. indistintamente. [mente.

indite, *–dīt′*, v. a. redigere.

individual, *–dĭvĭd′ŭăl*, s. individuo, m.; **–**, a. individuale; individuo; **–ly**, ad. individualmente. [lità, f.

individuality, *–ădŭ′ĭtĭ*, s. individualità, f.

indivisible, *–dĭvĭz′ĭbl*, a. indivisibile.

indocility, *–dōsĭl′ĭtĭ*, s. indocilità, f.; caparbietà, f. [f.

indolence, *ĭn′dŏlĕns*, s. indolenza, pigrizia,

indolent, *–lĕnt*, a. indolente; **–ly**, ad. senza curia.

indomitable, *–dŏm′ĭtăbl*, a. indomabile.

indorse, *vedi* endorse.

indubitable, *–dū′bĭtăbl*, a. indubitabile, certissimo.

indubitably, *–tăblĭ*, ad. indubitabilmente

induce, *–dūs′*, v. a. indurre; persuadere.

inducement, *–mĕnt*, s. inducimento, motivo, m., ragione, f.

indue, *–dū′*, v. a. investire; provvedere.

indulge, *–dŭlj′*, v. a. & n. favorire; cor cedere; abbandonarsi.

indulgence, *–dŭl′jĕns*, s. indulgenza, f.

indulgent, *–jĕnt*, a. indulgente; **–ly**, ad. con indulgenza. [m.

induration, *–dŭrā′shăn*, s. indurimento,

industrial, *–dŭs′trĭăl*, a. industriale.

industrious, *–trŭs*, a. industrioso, laborioso; **–ly**, ad. industriosamente.

industry, *ĭn′dăstrĭ*, s. industria, f. [care

inebriate, *–ē′brĭăt*, v. a. inebriare, ubbria

inebriation, *–ĕbrĭā′shăn*, s. ebbrezza, f.

ineffable, *–ĕf′făbl*, a. ineffabile, indicibile.

ineffective, *–ĕffĕk′tĭv*, ineffectual, *–tŭăl*, a. inefficace; inutile; **–ly**, ad. senza effetto, in vano.

inefficacious, *–ĕffĭkā′shăs*, a. inefficace

inefficiency, *–ĕffĭsh′ĕnsĭ*, s. inefficacia, f.

inefficient, *–ĕnt*, a. inefficace; debole.

inelegant, *–ĕl′ĕgănt*, a. inelegante; incolto, rozzo.

ineligibility, *–ĕlĭjĭbĭl′ĭtĭ*, s. ineligibilità, f.

ineptitude, *–ĕp′tĭtŭd*, s. inettitudine, incapacità, f. [renza, f.

inequality, *–ĕkwŏl′ĭtĭ*, s. inegualità, differ-

inert, *–ŭrt′*, a. inerte; **–ly**, ad. pigramente.

inertness, *–nĕs*, s. inerzia, f.

inestimable, *–ĕs′tĭmăbl*, a. inestimabile, inapprezzabile.

inevitable, *–ĕv′ĭtăbl*, a. da non evitarsi.

inexcusable, *–ĕkskū′zăbl*, a. inescusabile.

inexcusably, *–zăblĭ*, ad. inescusabilmente

inexhaustible, *–ĕgzhăst′ĭbl*, a. inesauribile. [implacabile.

inexorable, *–ĕks′ŏrăbl*, a. inesorabile;

inexpediency, *–ĕkspē′dĭĕnsĭ*, s. sconvenevolezza, f.

inexpedient, *–ĕkspē′dĭĕnt*, a. sconvenevole. [pendioso.

inexpensive, *–ĕkspĕn′sĭv*, a. non dis-

inexperience, *–ĕkspē′rĭĕns*, s. inesperienza, imperizia, f. [pratica.

inexpert, *–ĕkspŭrt′*, a. inesperto; senza

inexpiable, *ĭnĕks′pĭăbl*, a. inespiabile.

inexplicable, *–ĕks′plĭkăbl*, a. inesplicabile.

inexpressible, *–ĕksprĕs′ĭbl*, a. ineffabile, indicibile. [m. pl.

inexpressibles, *–s*, s. pl. (fig.) pantaloni,

inextinguishable, *–ĕkstĭng′gwĭshăbl*, a. inestinguibile.

inextricable, *–ĕks′trĭkăbl*, a. inestricabile.

infallibility, *–fălĭbĭl′ĭtĭ*, s. infallibilità, f.

infallible, *–făl′ĭbl*, a. infallibile.

infallibly, *–lĭblĭ*, ad. infallibilmente.

infamous, *ĭn′fămăs*, a. infame; **–ly**, ad. con infamia.

infamy, *ĭn′fămĭ*, s. infamia, f.

infancy, *ĭn′fănsĭ*, s. infanzia, f.

infant, *ĭn′fănt*, s. infante, m.; bambino, m.

infanticide, *–făn′tĭsīd*, s. infanticidio, m.

infantile, *ĭn′făntĭl*, a. infantile.

infantine, *ĭn'făntĭn,* a. infantile.

infantry, *ĭn'făntrĭ,* s. fanteria, f.

infatuate, *-făt'ăăt,* v. a. infatuare; ammaliare. [ganno, m.

infatuation, *-tŭă'shŭn,* s. abbaglio, in-

infect, *-fĕkt',* v. a. infettare. [tagione, f.

infection, *-fĕk'shŭn,* s. infezione, f.; con-

infectious, *-shŭs,* a. infetto, contagioso; -ly, ad. in modo contagioso.

infer, *-fŭr',* v. a. concludere.

inference, *ĭn'fŭrĕns,* s. conclusione, f.

inferior, *-fē'rĭŭr,* a. inferiore; -, s. ufficiale subalterno, m.

inferiority, *-fērĭŏr'ĭtĭ,* s. inferiorità, f.

infernal, *-fŭr'năl,* a. infernale; - stone, s. pietra infernale, f.

infertility, *-fŭrtĭl'ĭtĭ,* s. infecondità, f.

infest, *-fĕst',* v. a. infestare, importunare.

infidel, *ĭn'fĭdĕl,* s. infedele, m.; miscredente, m. [fidia, f.

infidelity, *-fĭdĕl'ĭtĭ,* s. infedeltà, f.; per-

infinite, *ĭn'fĭnĭt,* a. infinito, immenso; -ly, ad. infinitamente.

infinitive, *-fĭn'ĭtĭv,* s. (gr.) infinitivo, m.

infirm, *-fŭrm',* a. infermo, debole.

infirmary, *-fŭr'mărĭ,* s. infermeria, f.

infirmity, *-fŭr'mĭtĭ,* s. infermità, f.; fralezza, f. [infiammarsi.

inflame, *-flām',* v. a. & n. infiammare;

inflammable, *-flăm'măbl,* a. infiammabile, accendibile. [zione, f.

inflammation, *-mă'shŭn,* s. infiammazione, f.

inflammatory, *-flăm'mătŭrĭ,* a. infiammatorio.

inflate, *-flāt',* v. a. enfiare, gonfiare.

inflation, *-flā'shŭn,* s. enfiatura, f.

inflect, *-flĕkt',* v. a. inflettere, piegare; (gr.) coniugare.

inflection, *-flĕk'shŭn,* s. inflessione, f.; variazione, f.; (mus.) modulazione di voce, f. [f.; ostinatezza, f.

inflexibility, *-flĕksĭbĭl'ĭtĭ,* s. inflessibilità,

inflexible, *-flĕks'ĭbl,* a. inflessibile.

inflexibly, *-ĭblĭ,* ad. inflessibilmente.

inflict, *-flĭkt',* v. a. infliggere; condannare.

infliction, *-flĭk'shŭn,* s. punizione, f.

influence, *ĭn'flŭĕns,* s. influenza, f.; -, v. n. influire, causare. [fluente.

influential, *-ĕn'shăl,* a. che influisce, in-

influenza, *-flŭĕn'ză,* s. catarro, in., influenza, f.

influx, *ĭn'flŭks,* s. influsso, m.; sboccamento (d' un fiume), m.; infusione, f.

inform, *-fŏrm',* v. a. informare, insegnare.

informal, *-fŏr'măl,* a. irregolare.

informality, *-măl'ĭtĭ,* s. irregolarità, f.

informant, *-fŏr'mănt,* s. denunziatore, accusatore, m. [f.; istruzione, f.

information, *-mă'shŭn,* s. informazione, f.

infraction, *-frăk'shŭn,* s. infrazione, violazione, f.

infrangible, *-frăn'jĭbl,* a. infrangibile.

infrequent, *-frē'kwĕnt,* a. infrequente, raro.

infringe, *-frĭnj',* v. a. trasgredire; violare.

infuriate, *-fū'rĭăt,* v. a. render furioso.

infuse, *-fūz',* v. a. infondere; ispirare.

infusion, *-fū'zhŭn,* s. infusione, f.; inspirazione, f.

ingathering, *-găth'ŭrĭng,* s. raccolta, f.

ingenious, *-jē'nŭs,* a. ingegnoso, inventivo; -ly, ad. con ingegno.

ingenuity, *-jēnū'ĭtĭ,* s. ingenuità, franchezza, sincerità, f.; destrezza, abilità, f.; genio, m. [-ly, ad. francamente.

ingenuous, *-jĕn'ūs,* a. ingenuo, sincero;

inglorious, *-glō'rĭŭs,* a. inglorioso, disonorevole; -ly, ad. disonorevolmente.

ingot, *ĭn'gŏt,* s. verga (di metallo), f.

ingraft, *-grăft',* v. a. innestare.

ingrained, *-grānd',* a. tinto in grana.

ingrate, *-grāt',* s. ingrato, m.; ingrata, f.

ingratiate, *-grā'shĭăt,* v. n. entrare in grazia, ingraziarsi. [f.

ingratitude, *-grăt'ĭtŭd,* s. ingratitudine,

ingredient, *-grē'dĭĕnt,* s. ingrediente, m.

ingress, *ĭn'grĕs,* s. entrata, f.

ingulf, *-gŭlf',* v. a. inghiottire, divorare.

inhabit, *-hăb'ĭt,* v. a. & n. abitare dimorare; vivere.

inhabitable, *-tăbl,* a. abitabile. [f.

inhabitant, *-tănt,* s. abitante, abitatore,

inhale, *-hāl',* v. a. spirare, respirare.

inharmonious, *-hărmō'nŭs,* a. senza armonia, inherent. [monia.

inherent, *-hē'rĕnt,* a. inerente.

inherit, *-hĕr'ĭt,* v. a. ereditare.

inheritance, *-tăns,* s. eredità, f.

inheritor, *-ĭtŭr,* s. erede, m. & f. [duro.

inhospitable, *-hŏs'pĭtăbl,* a. inospitale;

inhospitality, *-tăl'ĭtĭ,* s. inospitalità, f.

inhuman, *-hū'măn,* a. inumano, barbaro, crudele; -ly, ad. inumanamente. [deltà, f.

inhumanity, *-măn'ĭtĭ,* s. inumanità, crudele...

inimical, *-ĭn'ĭkăl,* a. inimichevole.

inimitable, *-ĭm'ĭtăbl,* a. inimitabile.

iniquitous, *-ĭk'wĭtŭs,* a. iniquo, ingiusto.

iniquity, *-wĭtĭ,* s. iniquità, f.; ingiustizia, f.

initial, *-ĭsh'ăl,* a. cominciante; -, s. lettera maiuscola, iniziale o capitale, f.

initiate, *-ĭsh'ĭăt,* v. a. iniziare.

initiation, *-ĭshĭă'shŭn,* s. iniziazione, f.

inject, *-jĕkt',* v. a. fare un' iniezione, schizzettare.

injection, *-jĕk'shŭn,* s. iniezione, f.

injudicious, *-jōōdĭsh'ŭs,* a. poco giudizioso; -ly, ad. senza giudizio. [dine, m.

injunction, *-jŭngk'shŭn,* s. comando, ordine, m.

injure, *ĭn'jŭr,* v. a. far ingiuria; offendere; danneggiare.

injurious, *-jū'rĭŭs,* a. ingiurioso, ingiusto; -ly, ad. inginriosamente. [danno, m.

injury, *ĭn'jŭrĭ,* s. ingiuria; offesa, f.

injustice, *-jŭs'tĭs,* s. ingiustizia, iniquità, f.

ink, *ĭngk,* s. inchiostro, m. [f.

ink-horn, *-hŏrn,* s. calamaio, m.

inkling, *-lĭng,* s. avviso, m.; sentore, m.

ink-stand, *-stănd,* s. calamaio, m.

inky, *ĭngk'ĭ,* a. d'inchiostro; nero come inchiostro.

inlaid, *-lād',* a. intarsiato. [inchiostro.

inland, *ĭn'lănd,* a. interno; -, s. interiore d'un paese, m.

inlay, *ĭnlā',* s. lavoro a tarsia, m.; -, v. a. ir. intarsiare.

inlet, *in'lĕt,* s. passaggio, m., entrata, f.
inmate, *in'māt,* s. pigionale, m.   [simo.
inmost, *in'mōst,* a. interiore; profondis-
inn, *in,* s. osteria, f.; albergo, m.
innate, *innāt',* a. innato, naturale.
inner, *in'nŭr,* a. interiore, interno; segreto.
innermost, *—mōst,* a. più interno o profondo; intimo.
innocence, *in'nŏsĕns,* s. innocenza, f.
innocent, *—sĕnt,* a. innocente; puro; **—ly,**
ad. innocentemente.
innocuous, *—nŏk'ūŭs,* a. innocente; **—ly,**
ad. innocentemente.
innovate, *in'nŏvāt,* v. a. innovare.
innovation, *—vā'shŭn,* s. innovazione, f.;
novità, f.   [ad. non nocivamente.
innoxius, *—nŏk'shŭs,* a. non nocivo; **—ly,**
innuendo, *—mŭen'dŏ,* s. (jur.) avviso indiretto, m.   [bile.
innumerable, *—nū'mŭrăbl,* a. innumera-
inoculate, *—ŏk'ūlāt,* v. a. inoculare, innestare.
inoculation, *—lā'shăn,* s. inoculazione, f.
inoffensive, *—ŏffĕn'sĭv,* a. non nocivo;
innocente.   [intempestivo.
inopportune, *—ŏppŏrtūn',* a. inopportuno,
inordinate, *—ŏr'dinăt,* a. inordinato; **—ly,**
ad. inordinatamente.
inorganic, *—ŏrgăn'ĭk,* a. senza organi.
inquest, *in'kwĕst,* s. inchiesta, ricerca, f.
inquire, *—kwir',* v. a. ricercare; esaminare;
—, v. n. informarsi.   [esaminazione, f.
inquiry, *—kwī'rĭ,* s. inchiesta, ricerca, f.;
inquisition, *—kwĭzĭsh'ăn,* s. inquisizione,
f.; ricerca, f.
inquisitive, *—kwĭz'ĭtĭv,* a. curioso; **—ly,**
ad. con curiosità, curiosamente.
inquisitor, *—ĭtŭr,* s. inquisitore, m.
inroad, *in'rŏd,* s. incursione, invasione, f.
insane, *insān',* a. insano, pazzo, stolto.
insanity, *—săn'ĭtĭ,* s. insania, pazzia, f.
insatiable, *—sā'shĭăbl,* a. insaziabile.
inscribe, *—skrĭb',* v. a. iscrivere; indirizzare.   [soprascritta, f.
inscription, *—skrĭp'shăn,* s. iscrizione, f.;
inscrutable, *—skrŏ'tăbl,* a. inscrutabile.
insect, *in'sĕkt,* s. insetto, m.
insecure, *—sĕkūr',* a. non sicuro; incerto.
insecurity, *—kŭ'rĭtĭ,* s. rischio, pericolo,
m.; incertezza, f.
insensate, *—sĕn'sāt,* a. insensato.
insensibility, *—sĕnsĭbĭl'ĭtĭ,* s. insensibilità,
f.; stupidezza, f.   [cettibile.
insensible, *—sĕn'sĭbl,* a. insensibile; imper-
insensibly, *—sĭblĭ,* ad. insensibilmente.
inseparable, *—sĕp'ărăbl,* a. inseparabile,
indivisibile.
inseparably, *—ăblĭ,* ad. inseparabilmente.
insert, *—sŭrt',* v. a. inserire.
insertion, *—sŭr'shăn,* s. inserzione, intercalazione, f.   [parte interna, f.
inside, *in'sīd,* s. interiore, interno, m.,
insidious, *—sĭd'ĭŭs,* a. insidioso; **—ly,** ad.
insidiosamente.   [intima, f.
insight, *in'sĭt,* s. ispezione, f.; conoscenza
insignia, *—sĭg'nĭă,* s. pl. insegne, f. pl.
insignificance, *—sĭgnĭf'ĭkăns,* s. poca importanza, f.

insignificant, *—ĭkănt,* a. insignificante;
inutile; **—ly,** ad. in modo insignificante.
insincere, *—sĭnsēr',* a. non sincero, falso.
insincerity, *—sēr'ĭtĭ,* s. dissimulazione,
falsità, infedeltà, f.
insinuate, *—sĭn'ūāt,* v. a. insinuare.
insinuation, *—ā'shăn,* s. insinuazione, f.
insipid, *—sĭp'ĭd,* a. insipido, scipito; **—ly,**
ad. insipidamente.
insipidity, *—pĭd'ĭtĭ,* s. insipidezza, f.
insist, *—sĭst',* v. n. insistere, persistere.
insolence, *in'sŏlĕns,* s. insolenza, f.
insolent, *in'sŏlĕnt,* a. insolente; **—ly,** ad.
insolentemente.   [lubile.
insoluble, *—sŏl'ūbl,* a. insolubile, indisso-
insolvency, *—sŏl'vĕnsĭ,* s. insolvibilità,
incapacità di pagare, f.
insolvent, *—vĕnt,* a. che non può pagare.
insomuch, *insŏmŭch',* c. di modo che,
talmente che,   [osservare; esaminare.
inspect, *—spĕkt',* v. a. aver l' ispezione;
inspection, *—spĕk'shăn,* s. ispezione, f.;
cura, f.   [dente; visitatore, m.
inspector, *—tŭr,* s. ispettore, soprinten-
inspiration, *—spīrā'shăn,* s. ispirazione, f.
inspire, *—spīr',* v. a. ispirare, infondere.
inspirit, *—spĭr'ĭt,* v. a. animare; incoraggiare.   [costanza, f.
instability, *—stăbĭl'ĭtĭ,* s. instabilità, in-
instal, *—stăl',* v. a. installare.
installation, *—lā'shăn,* s. stabilimento in
possesso, m.   [fisso, m.
instalment, *—stăl'mĕnt,* s. pagamento
instance, *in'stăns,* s. istanza, f.; sollecitazione, f.; prova, f.; esempio, m.; **for —,**
per esempio; **—,** v. n. addurre esempi.
instant, *in'stănt,* a. pressante, urgente;
—ly, ad. in un istante; **—,** s. momento, m.
instantaneous, *—tā'nŭs,* a. istantaneo; **—ly,** ad. istantaneamente.
instead, *—stĕd',* pr. in luogo di, in vece di.
instep, *in'stĕp,* s. collo del piede, m.
instigate, *in'stĭgāt,* v. a. stimolare, incitare, eccitare.
instigation, *—stĭgā'shăn,* s. istigazione, f.
instil, *—stĭl',* v. a. istillare, infondere.
instinct, *in'stĭngkt,* s. istinto, m.
instinctive, *—tĭv,* a. fatto per istinto;
naturale; **—ly,** ad. per istinto.
institute, *in'stĭtūt,* s. istituto, m.; precetto, m.; **—,** v. a. istituire, stabilire.
institution, *—tū'shăn,* s. instituzione, f.
instruct, *—strŭkt',* v. a. istruire, insegnare.
instruction, *—strŭk'shăn,* s. insegnamento, m.; dottrina, f.
instructive, *—tĭv,* a. istruttivo.
instructor, *—tŭr,* s. istruttore, insegnante,
m.   [m.; (jur.) contratto, m.
instrument, *in'strŭmĕnt,* s. strumento,
instrumental, *—mĕn'tăl,* a. istrumentale.
insubordinate, *—sŭbŏr'dinăt,* a. insub-
ordinato.   [dienza, f.
insubordination, *—nā'shăn,* s. disubbi-
insufferable, *—sŭf'fărăbl,* a. insopportabile, intollerabile.   [mente.
insufferably, *—ăblĭ,* ad. insopportabil-
insufficiency, *—sŭffĭsh'ĕnsĭ,* s. insufficienza, f.

insufficient, *-ĕnt*, a. insufficiente; incapace; **-ly**, ad. insufficientemente.

insular, *ĭn'sŭlăr*, a. insulare.

insulate, *ĭn'sŭldt*, v. a. isolare.

insult, *ĭn'sălt*, s. insulto, m.; **-**, *ĭnsălt'*, v. a. insultare. [insultante.

insultingly, *-sălt'ĭnglĭ*, ad. d'una maniera insuperabile, *-sŭ'părăbl*, a. insuperabile, invincibile. [superabile.

insuperably, *-ăblĭ*, ad. in maniera insupportable, *-săppŏrt'ăbl*, a. insopportabile. [mente.

insupportably, *-tăblĭ*, ad. insopportabilmente.

insurance, *-shŏ'răns*, s. assicurazione, f.

insure, *-shŏr'*, v. a. assicurare.

insurgent, *-sŭr'jĕnt*, s. insorgente, insorto, ribelle, m.

insurmountable, *-sŭrmŏănt'ăbl*, a. insormontabile. [zione, rivolta, f.

insurrection, *-sŭrrĕk'shăn*, s. insurrectionary, *-ărĭ*, a. ribellante.

intact, *-tăkt'*, a. intatto.

integral, *ĭn'tĕgrăl*, a. integrale, intero; (chem.) integrante; **-**, s. integrale, m.

integrity, *ĭntĕg'rĭtĭ*, s. integrità, f.; probità, onestà, f.

intellect, *ĭn'tĕllĕkt*, s. intelletto, m.

intellectual, *-tĕk'tŭăl*, a. intellettuale.

intelligence, *-tĕl'lĭgĕns*, s. intelligenza, novella, f., avviso, m.; corrispondenza, f.

intelligencer, *-lĭjĕnsăr*, s. novellista, gazzettiere, m.

intelligent, *-lĭjĕnt*, a. intelligente.

intelligible, *-lĭjĭbl*, a. intelligibile; chiaro.

intelligibly, *-jĭblĭ*, ad. intelligibilmente.

intemperance, *-tĕm'părăns*, s. intemperanza, f. [**-ly**, ad. intemperatamente.

intemperate, *-părăt*, a. intemperato;

intend, *-tĕnd'*, v. a. intendere a, proporsi.

intendant, *-tĕn'dănt*, s. intendente, m.

intense, *-tĕns'*, a. intenso, veemente, eccessivo; **-ly**, ad. intensamente. [m.

intensity, *-tĕn'sĭtĭ*, s. eccesso, m.; ardore,

intent, *-*, **intention**, *-tĕn'shăn*, s. intento, m., intenzione, f.; disegno, m.

intent, *-tĕnt'*, a. intento, assiduo; **-ly**, ad. con attenzione.

intentional, *-shănăl*, a. intenzionale; **-ly**, ad. con intenzione.

inter, *-tŭr'*, v. a. sotterrare, seppellire.

intercalation, *-kăld'shăn*, s. intercalazione, f. [mediatore.

intercede, *-sĕd'*, v. n. intercedere; essere

intercept, *-sĕpt'*, v. a. intercettare; arrestare. [mediazione, f.

intercession, *-sĕsh'ăn*, s. intercessione,

intercessor, *-sĕs'săr*, s. mediatore, m.

interchange, *ĭn'tărchănj*, s. cambio, baratto, m.; **-**, v. a. cambiare, cangiare.

intercourse, *ĭn'tărkŏrs*, s. commercio, m.; comunicazione, f.

interdict, *-dĭkt'*, s. interdetto, m.; proibizione, f.; **-**, v. a. interdire, proibire, vietare. [f.; proibizione, f.

interdiction, *-dĭk'shăn*, s. interdizione,

interest, *ĭn'tărĕst*, s. interesse, f.; vantaggio, f.; potere, credito, m.; preten-

denza, f.; **compound -**, interesse composto; **-**, v. a. interessare; impacciare.

interfere, *-fĕr'*, v. n. interporsi; esser opposto. [m.

interference, *-fĕ'rĕns*, s. intervenimento.

interim, *ĭn'tărĭm*, s. interim, m.; intervallo, m.; interstizio, m.

interior, *ĭntĕ'rĭăr*, a. interiore, interno.

interjection, *ĭntŭrjĕk'shăn*, s. interiezione, f. [mettere, m.

interlace, *-lăs'*, v. a. intrecciare, framinterlard, *-lărd'*, v. a. lardellare, lardare. [libro.

interleave, *-lĕv'*, v. a. interfoliare un interline, *-lĭn'*, v. a. scrivere tra linea e linea, interlineare.

interlocution, *-lōkŭ'shăn*, s. interlocuzione, f.; dialogo, m.

interlocutor, *-lŏk'ŭtăr*, s. interlocutore, m.; interlocutrice, f.

interlope, *-lōp'*, v. a. far contrabbandi.

interloper, *-lō'păr*, s. contrabbandiere, m. [f.

interlude, *-lōd'*, s. intermezzo, m.; farsa, intermarriage, *-măr'rĭj*, s. intermatrimonio, m.

intermediate, *-mē'dĭăt*, a. intermedio.

interment, *ĭntŭr'mĕnt*, s. sotterramento, seppellimento, m. [nabile, immenso.

interminable, *ĭntŭr'mĭnăbl*, a. interminintermingle, *-mĭng'gl*, v. a. & n. frammischiare, mescolare.

intermission, *-mĭsh'ăn*, s. intermissione, f., interrompimento, m.

intermit, *-mĭt'*, v. a. discontinuare, tralasciare; cessare.

internal, *ĭntŭr'năl*, a. interno; **-ly**, ad. internamente, di dentro.

international, *-nă'shănăl*, a. internazionale.

interpellation, *-pĕllă'shăn*, s. interpellanza, f.

interpolate, *ĭntŭr'pŏlăt*, v. a. interpolare, inserire. [falsificazione, f.

interpolation, *-pŏlă'shăn*, s. inserzione, f.

interpose, *-pōz'*, v. a. interporre; intramettere; **-**, v. n. interporsi. [zione, f.

interposition, *-pŏzĭsh'ăn*, s. interposizione, f.

interpret, *ĭntŭr'prĕt*, v. a. interpretare.

interpretation, *-prĕtă'shăn*, s. interpretazione, f.

interpreter, *ĭntŭr'prĕtăr*, s. interprete, m.

interregnum, *-rĕg'năm*, s. interregno, m.

interrogate, *ĭntŭr'rŏgăt*, v. a. interrogare, esaminare. [zione, dimanda, f.

interrogation, *-rŏgă'shăn*, s. interrogazione, interrogative, *-rŏg'ătĭv*, **interrogatory**, *-ătŭrĭ*, a. interrogatorio.

interrupt, *-răpt'*, v. a. interrompere.

interruptedly, *-răp'tĕdlĭ*, ad. interrottamente. [f.

interruption, *-răp'shăn*, s. interruzione, intersect, *-sĕkt'*, v. a. incrocicchiare; intersecare; **-**, v. n. intersecarsi. [f.

intersection, *-sĕk'shăn*, s. intersecazione, intersperse, *-spĕrs'*, v. a. spargere qua e là.

interstice, *ĭn'tŭrstĭs,* (*ĭntŭr'stĭs*), s. interstizio, m.; spazio, m.; distanza, f.

intertwine, *-twīn',* v. a. intrecciare.

interval, *ĭn'tŭrvăl,* s. intervallo, m.

intervene, *-vēn',* v. n. intervenire; accadere.

intervention, *-vĕn'shăn,* s. intervento, m.; interponimento, m. [gresso, m.

interview, *ĭn'tŭrvū,* s. conferenza,f., con-

interweave, *-wēv',* v. a. ir. intrecciare, intessere. [intestato.

intestate, *-tĕs'tăt,* a. senza far testamento.

intestinal, *-tĕs'tĭnăl,* a. intestinale, degl' intestini. [-s, s. pl. intestini, m.

intestine, *-tĕs'tĭn,* a. intestino, interno;

intimacy, *ĭn'tĭmăsĭ,* s. intima unione, fratellanza, f.

intimate, *ĭn'tĭmăt,* a. intimo, familiare; **-ly,** ad. intimamente; **-,** s. amico intimo, m.; **-,** v. a. fare intendere.

intimation, *-mă'shăn,* s. sentore, m.

intimidate, *-tĭm'ĭdăt,* v. a. intimorire.

into, *ĭn'tŏ,* pr. in; nel, nello, nella; tra.

intolerable, *-tŏl'ărăbl,* a. intollerabile.

intolerably, *-ăblĭ,* ad. intollerabilmente.

intolerance, *-tŏl'ărăns,* s. intolleranza, f.

intolerant, *-rănt,* a. intollerante.

intonation, *-tŏnă'shăn,* s. intonazione, f.

intoxicate, *-tŏks'ĭkăt,* v. a. inebriare.

intoxication, *-kă'shăn,* s. ebrezza, f.

intractable, *-trăk'tăbl,* a. intrattabile.

intrench, *-trĕnsh',* v. a. trincierare; usurpare. [intrepidamente.

intrepid, *-trĕp'ĭd,* a. intrepido; **-ly,** ad.

intrepidity, *-pĭd'ĭtĭ,* s. intrepidezza, f.; coraggio, m. [razzo, m.; difficoltà, f.

intricacy, *ĭn'trĭkăsĭ,* s. intrigo, m.; imbarazzato, **-ly,** ad. intrigatamente.

intricate, *ĭn'trĭkăt,* a. intrigato; imbarazzato, **-ly,** ad. intrigatamente.

intrigue, *-trēg',* s. intrigo, m.; **-,** v. n. fare intrighi.

intrinsic(al), *-trĭn'sĭk(ăl),* a. intrinseco; **-ly,** ad. intrinsecamente.

introduce, *intrŏdūs',* v. a. introdurre; mettere in uso. [f.

introduction, *-dŭk'shăn,* s. introduzione, f.

introductive, *-dŭk'tĭv,* **introductory,** *intrŏdŭk'tărĭ,* a. introduttivo, introduttorio. [esame interno, m.

introspection, *-spĕk'shăn,* s. introspetto, f.

intrude, *-trŏd',* v. n. intromettersi, introdursi dove non si dovrebbe.

intruder, *-trŏ'dăr,* s. intruso, m.

intrusion, *-shăn,* s. intrusione, f.

intrust, *-trŭst',* v. a. fidare; commettere.

intuition, *-tū'ĭsh'ăn,* s. intuizione, f.

intuitive, *-ĭū'ĭtĭv,* a. intuitivo.

inundate, *-ŭn'dăt,* v. a. inondare.

inundation, *-dă'shăn,* s. inondazione, f.; diluvio, m.

inure, *-ūr',* v. a. accostumare, avvezzare.

inurement, *-mĕnt,* s. abitudine, f.

inutility, *-ătĭl'ĭtĭ,* s. inutilità, f.

invade, *-vād',* v. a. invadere, assaltare.

invader, *-vă'dăr,* s. invasore, m.

invalid, *-vŏl'ĭd,* a. invalido, infermo, debole; **-,** *-văĭ́dă',* s. invalido, m.

invalidate, *-văl'ĭdăt,* v. a. invalidare.

invalidity, *-lĭd'ĭtĭ,* s. invalidità, f.; debolezza, f.

invaluable, *-văl'ŭăbl,* a. inapprezzabile.

invariable, *-vă'rĭăbl,* a. invariabile.

invariably, *-rĭăbĭt,* ad. invariabilmente.

invasion, *-vă'zhăn,* s. invasione, incursione, f.

invective, *-vĕk'tĭv,* s. invettiva, f.

inveigh, *-vā',* v. n. ingiurare, calunniare.

inveigle, *-vē'gl,* v. a. allettare, indurre.

invent, *-vĕnt',* v. a. inventare.

invention, *-vĕn'shăn,* s. invenzione, f.

inventive, *-tĭv,* a. inventivo, ingegnoso.

inventor, *-tăr,* s. inventore, m.

inventory, *ĭn'vĕntărĭ,* s. inventario, m.

inverse, *-vŭrs',* a. inverso, trasposto.

inversion, *-vŭr'shăn,* s. inversione, f.

invert, *-vŭrt',* v. a. invertire, arrovesciare.

invest, *-vĕst',* v. a. investire; conferire.

investigate, *-vĕs'tĭgăt,* v. a. diligentemente cercare, ricercare; esaminare.

investigation, *-gă'shăn,* s. investigazione, inchiesta, f.; ricerca, f.

investiture, *-vĕs'tĭtăr,* s. investitura, f.

investment, *-vĕst'mĕnt,* s. vestimento, abito, m.

inveterate, *-vĕt'ărăt,* a. inveterato.

invidious, *-vĭd'ĭăs,* a. invidio, invidioso; **-ly,** ad. malignamente. [inanimire.

invigorate, *-vĭg'ŏrăt,* v. a. invigorire;

invincible, *-vĭn'sĭbl,* a. invincibile; insuperabile.

invincibly, *-sĭblĭ,* ad. invincibilmente.

inviolable, *-vĭ'ŏlăbl,* a. inviolabile.

inviolate, *-vĭ'ŏlăt,* a. inviolato, puro.

invisibility, *-vĭzĭbĭl'ĭtĭ,* s. invisibilità, f.

invisible, *-vĭz'ĭbl,* a. invisibile.

invisibly, *-ĭblĭ,* ad. invisibilmente.

invitation, *-vĭtă'shăn,* s. invito, m.

invite, *-vīt',* v. a. invitare.

invocation, *-vŏkă'shăn,* s. invocazione, f.

invoice, *ĭn'vŏĭs,* s. (com.) fattura, f.

invoke, *-vŏk',* v. a. invocare.

involuntarily, *-vŏl'ăntărĭlĭ,* ad. involontariamente. [sforzato.

involuntary, *-ăntărĭ,* a. involontario.

involve, *-vŏlv',* v. a. inviluppare; implicare; contenere. [rabile.

invulnerable, *-vŭl'nărăbl,* a. invulnerabile.

inward, *ĭn'wărd,* a. interno, interiore; **-(s), -ly,** ad. al di dentro, internamente.

iodine, *ī'ŏdĭn,* s. iodio, m.

I. O. U. ('I owe you') *ī ō ū,* s. formula di ricevuta per una piccola somma prestata, f.

irascible, *ĭrăs'ĭbl,* a. irascibile, collerico.

irate, *ĭrăt',* a. irato, sdegnato.

ire, *ĭr,* s. ira, collera, f.

iridescence, *ĭrĭdĕs'ĕns,* s. iridescenza, f.

iris, *ī'rĭs,* s. iride, f.; arcobaleno, m.

irk, *ŭrk,* v. a. dispiacere; rincrescere.

irksome, *-sŭm,* a. tedioso, noioso, affannoso.

iron, *ī'rn,* s. ferro, m.; **-s,** pl. ceppi, m. pl.; **-,** a. di ferro; (fig.) severo; **-,** v. a. stirare biancherie; incatenare.

iron-dust, *-dăst,* s. limatura di ferro, f.

ironic(al), *ĭrŏn'ĭk(ăl),* a. ironico; **-ly,** ad. con ironia.

ironing, *ī'rnĭng,* s. lo stirare col ferro.

iron-monger, *—mŭnggŭr,* s. fabbro ferrajo, m.   [f.; pretelle, f. pl.

iron-mould, *—mōld,* s. macchia di ruggine.

iron-ore, *—ōr,* s. minerale di ferro, m.

iron-ware, *—wăr,* s. mercanziuole di ferro, f. pl.   [tura, f.; **-s,** pl. ferriera, f.

iron-work, *—wŭrk,* s. ferri, m. pl., ferratura.

irony, *ī'rŏnĭ,* s. ironia, f.

irradiate, *ĭrrā'dĭăt,* v. a. raggiare, brillare.

irrational, *—răsh'ănăl,* a. irrazionale, irragionevole.   [bile.

irreclaimable, *—rēklăm'ăbl,* a. irreparabile.   [rabile; irreparabile.

irreconcilable, *—rēkŏnsīl'ăbl,* a. implacabile.

irrecoverable, *—rēkŭv'ărăbl,* a. irrecuperabile.

irredeemable, *—rēdēm'ăbl,* a. irredimibile.

irrefragable, *—rĕf'răgăbl,* a. irrefragabile.   [bile.

irrefutable, *—rēfū'tăbl,* a. incontestabile.

irregular, *—rĕg'ŭlăr,* a. irregulare; **-ly,** ad. irregolarmente.   [sregolatezza, f.

irregularity, *—gŭlăr'ĭtĭ,* s. irregolarità, f.

irrelevant, *—rĕl'ĕvănt,* a. irrilevante.

irreligion, *—rēlĭj'ŭn,* s. irreligione, empietà, f.   [irreligiosamente.

irreligious, *—ŭs,* a. irreligioso; **-ly,** ad.

irremediable, *—rēmē'dĭăbl,* a. irremediabile, incurabile.

irreparable, *—rĕp'ărăbl,* a. irreparabile.

irreproachable, *—rēprōch'ăbl,* a. irreprensibile.

irresistible, *—rēzĭs'tĭbl,* a. irresistibile.

irresolute, *—rĕz'ŏlōt,* a. irresoluto; **-ly,** ad. dubbiosamente.   [zione, f.

irresolution, *—rēzŏlō'shŭn,* s. irresoluzione.

irrespective, *—rēspĕk'tĭv,* a. assoluto.

irresponsible, *—rēspŏn'sĭbl,* a. non risponsabile.

irretrievable, *—rētrēv'ăbl,* a. irreparabile.

irretrievably, *—văblĭ,* ad. irreparabilmente.

irreverence, *—rĕv'ŭrĕns,* s. irriverenza, f.

irreverent, *—ărănt,* a. irriverente; **-ly,** ad. senza riverenza.

irrevocable, *—rĕv'ŏkăbl,* a. irrevocabile.

irrigate, *ĭr'rĭgăt,* v. a. irrigare.

irrigation, *—gā'shŭn,* s. irrigazione, f.

irritability, *—tăbĭl'ĭtĭ,* s. irritabilità, f.

irritable, *ĭr'rĭtăbl,* a. irritabile.

irritate, *ĭr'rĭtăt,* v. a. irritare.   [sione, f.

irruption, *—rŭp'shŭn,* s. irruzione, incursione, f.

isinglass, *ī'zĭngglăs,* s. colla di pesce, f.

island, *ī'lănd* s. isola, f.   [lano, m.

islander, *—ăr,* s. abitatore d'isola, m.; isolano, m.

isle, *īl,* s. isola, f.; navata di chiesa), f.

islet, *ī'lĕt,* s. piccola isola, f.

isolate, *ĭ'sŏlăt,* v. a. isolare.

issue, *ĭsh'shū,* s. uscita, f., esito, m.; evento, m.; termine, fine, m.; successo, m.; progenie, prole, f.; cauterio, m., fontanella, f.; **—,** v. a. pubblicare; mandare, comandare; **—,** v. n. uscire; provenire, emanare, discendere.

isthmus, *ĭst'mŭs,* s. istmo, m.

---

it, *ĭt,* pn. il, lo, la; egli, esso.

Italian warehouse, *tăl'yăn wărhōŭs,* s. bottega di ghiottonerie, f.

italics, *ĭtăl'ĭks,* s. caratteri corsivi, m. pl.

itch, *ĭch,* s. rogna, f.; prurigine, f., pizzicore, m.; **—,** v. n. pizzicure.

item, *ī'tĕm,* ad. inoltre, parimente; **—,** s. articolo, m.   [tizione, f.

iteration, *ĭtĕrā'shăn,* s. iterazione, ripetizione, f.

itinerant, *ĭtĭn'ărănt,* a. ambulante; errante.

itinerary, *—ărărĭ,* s. itinerario, m.

its, *ĭts,* pn. suo, sua, suoi, sue.

itself, *ĭtsĕlf',* pn. sé stesso.

ivory, *ī'vŏrĭ,* s. avorio, m.

ivy, *ī'vĭ,* s. edera, ellera, f.

J.

jabber, *jăb'băr,* v. n. cicalare, borbottare.

jabberer, *—ăr,* s. borbottone, cicalone, m.

jack, *jăk,* s. girarrosto, m.; brocca, f.; otre, m.; cavalletto, m.; salterello, m.; cavastivali, m.; giaco, m.; luccio, m.; maschio (d'alcuni animali), m.; giannotto, m.; marinaio, m.: **to be — of all trades,** fare ogni mestiere.

jackal, *jăk'ăl,* s. lupo dorato, m.

jackanapes, *—ănăps,* s. scimmia, f.; sciocco, m.

jackass, *—ăs,* s. asino, m.; goffo, m.

jackboots, *—bōts,* s. pl. stivali grossi, m.vl.

jack-daw, *—dă,* s. cornacchia, f.

jacket, *—ĕt,* s. saione, m., casacca, f.

jade, *jăd,* s. rozza, f.; **—,** v. a. stancare.

jag, *jăg,* s. dentello, m., intaccatura, f.; **—,** v. a. intaccare.

jagged, *jăg'gĕd,* a. dentellato.

jail, *jăl,* s. prigione, f., carcere, m.

jail-bird, *—bŭrd,* s. prigioniere, m.

jailer, *—ăr,* s. carceriere, m.

jam, *jăm,* s. conserva, f.; confettura, f.; **—,** v. a. serrare insieme.

jamb, *jăm,* s. imposta, f., stipite, m.

jangle, *jăng'gl,* v. n. disputare, litigare.

janitor, *jăn'ĭtăr,* s. portinaio, m.

janizary, *jăn'ĭzărĭ,* s. giannizzero, m.

January, *jăn'ŭărĭ,* s. gennaio, m.

Japan, *jăpăn',* s. lavoro verniciato, m.; **—,** v. a. verniciare.

japanner, *—năr,* s. verniciatore, m.

jar, *jăr,* s. discordia, contesa, f.; giara, f.; bottiglia elettrica, f.; **—,** v. n. dissonare, stridere.

jargon, *jăr'gŏn,* s. gergo, m.   [disputare.

jasper, *jăs'păr,* s. diaspro, m.

jaundice, *jăn'dĭs,* s. itterizia, f.

jaundiced, *—dĭst,* a. itterico.

jaunt, *jănt,* s. scorsa, f.; girata, f.; **—,** v. n. andare vagando.

jaunty, *jăn'tĭ,* a. gentile, grazioso, leggiero.

jaw, *jă,* s. mascella, f.

jay, *jă,* s. gazza, f.

jealous, *jĕl'ŭs,* a. geloso.

jealousy, *—ŭsĭ,* s. gelosia, f.

jeer, *jẽr*, s. burla, baia, f.; scherzo, m.; –, v. a. & n. burlare, beffare. [m.

jelly, *jẽl'lĭ*, s. gelatina, f.; sugo premuto,

jelly-broth, *–brŏth*, s. consumato, m.

jelly-fish, *–fĭsh*, s. medusa, f.

jeopard(ize), *jẽp'ãrd(ĭz)*, v. a. arrischiare, avventurare. [sferzare, frustare.

jerk, *jãrk*, s. sferzata, scossa, f.; –, v. a.

jessamine, *jẽs'ãmĭn*, s. gelsomino, m.

jest, *jẽst*, s. burla, f., scherzo, m.

jester, *–ãr*, s. beffatore, burlone, m.

jestingly, *–ĭnglĭ*, ad. in modo scherzevole.

Jesuit, *jẽz'ũĭt*, s. Gesuita, m.; –'s-bark, china, f.

jesuitic(al), *–ũĭt'ĭk(ăl)*, a. gesuitico.

jet, *jẽt*, s. lustrino, m.; zampillo, m.

jetty, *jẽt'tĭ*, s. gettata, f., molo, m.

Jew, *jõ*, s. Giudeo, Ebreo, m.; –'s-harp, scacciapensieri.

jewel, *jõ'ăl*, s. pietra preziosa, f.

jewel-box, *–bŏks*, s. scrigno, m.

jeweller, *–ălăr*, s. gioielliere, m.

jewelry, *–ălrĭ*, s. traffico di gioie, m.

Jewess, *jõ'ĕs*, s. Giudea, Ebrea, f.

Jewish, *jõ'ĭsh*, a. giudaico, ebraico.

Jewry, *jõ'rĭ*, s. ghetto, m.

jib, *jĭb*, s. (mar.) fiocco, m.

jig, *jĭg*, s. giga, f. (ballo). [piantare.

jilt, *jĭlt*, s. civetta, f.; –, v. a. civettare;

jingle, *jĭng'gl*, s. tintinno, m.; –, v. n. tintinnire, risonare.

job, *jŏb*, s. lavoro, m.; colpo (dl pugnale), m.; –, v. a. & n. battere; far agiotaggio.

jobation, *jŏbā'shăn*, s. parole oltraggiose, villanie, f. pl.

jobber, *jŏb'bãr*, s. sensale, m.

job-master, *–mãstãr*, s. affittatore di carrozze o di cavalli, m.

jockey, *jŏk'ĭ*, s. mezzano di cavalli, m.; –, v. a. ingannare, truffare.

jocose, *jŏkōs'*, a. giocoso, faceto; –ly, ad. giocosamente.

jocoseness, *–nĕs*, **jocosity**, *–kŏs'ĭtĭ*, s. giocondità, scherzo, m. [lesco.

jocular, *jŏk'ũlãr*, a. giocoso, faceto, bur-

jog, *jŏg*, s. scossa, f., scotimento, m.; ostacolo, m.; –, v. a. spingere, scuotere, crollare; urtare; –, v. n. avanzare pesantemente.

John Bull, *jŏn bŭll*, s. soprannome del popolo inglese, m.

join, *jōĭn*, v. a. congiungere, unire; –, v. n. unirsi, giugnersi, associarsi, accompagnarsi.

joiner, *–ãr*, s. legnaiuolo, falegname, m.

joinery, *–ãrĭ*, s. lavoro di falegname, m.

joint, *jōĭnt*, a. unito, congiunto; – heir, s. coerede, m.; –, s. giuntura, f.; incastratura, f.; puzzo (di carne), m.; –, v. a. congiugnere; tagliare per le giunture.

jointly, *–lĭ*, ad. congiuntamente.

joint-stock, *–stŏk*, a. (com.) per azioni; anonimo.

jointure, *jōĭn'tãr*, s. rendita, f.

joist, *jōĭst*, s. travicello, m.

joke, *jōk*, s. burla, f., scherzo, m.; –, v. n. scherzare, beffare.

jollity, *jŏl'lĭtĭ*, s. gaiezzs, allegrezza, f.

English and Italian.

jolly, *jŏl'lĭ*, a. gioioso, gaio.

jolly-boat, *–bŏt*, s. piccolo canotto, m.

jolt, *jŏlt*, s. scossa, f.; –, v. a. crollare; scuotere.

jostle, *jŏs'l*, v. n. urtarsi contro; lottare.

jot, *jŏt*, s. iota, punto, m.

journal, *jãr'năl*, s. giornale, diario, m.

journalism, *–ĭzm*, s. giornalismo, m.

journalist, *–ĭst*, s. giornalista, m.

journey, *jãr'nĭ*, s. viaggio, m.; giornata, f.; –, v. n. fare viaggio.

journeyman, *–măn*, s. giornaliere, operaio a giornata, m.

journey-work, *–wãrk*, s. giornata, f.

joust, *jũst (jŏst)*, s. giostra, f., torniamento, m.; –, v. n. giostrare. [mente.

jovial, *jō'vĭăl*, a. gioviale; –ly, ad.gioiosa-

joviality, *–vĭăl'ĭtĭ*, s. gaiezza, f.

joy, *jŏĭ*, s. gioia, f., giubbilo, m.; to give (wish) –, congratulare. [mente.

joyful, *–fŭl*, a. gioioso; –ly, ad. gioiosa-

joyless, *–lĕs*, a. tristo. [fante.

jubilant, *jõ'bĭlănt*, a. giubbilante, trion-

jubilation, *–lā'shăn*, s. giubbilazione, f.

jubilee, *jõ'bĭlē*, s. giubbileo, m.

judaic, *jõdā'ĭk*, a. Giudaico.

Judaism, *jõ'dāĭzm*, s. giudaismo, m.

judge, *jŭj*, s. giudice, m.; –, v. a. & n. giudicare; pensare.

judgment, *–mĕnt*, s. giudizio, m.; sentimento, m., opinione, f.

judicature, *jõ'dĭkătãr*, s. giudicatura, f.

judicial, *jõdĭsh'ăl*, a. giudiziale, giudiziario; –ly, ad. giudizialmente.

judicious, *–ăs*, a. giudizioso, prudente; –ly, ad. giudiziosamente.

jug, *jŭg*, s. brocca, f.; boccale di terra, f.; usignolo, m.

juggle, *jŭg'gl*, s. giuoco di mano, m.; inganno, m.; –, v. n. giocolare.

juggler, *–glãr*, s. giocolatore, m.

juice, *jõs*, s. sugo, succo, m.

juicy, *jõ'sĭ*, a. pieno di succo, succoso.

July, *jõlī'*, s. luglio, m.

jumble, *jŭm'bl*, s. mescuglio confuso, m.; –, v. a. confondere; mescolare.

jump, *jămp*, s. salto, m.; giustacore, m.; –, v. n. saltare; accordarsi.

junction, *jăngk'shăn*, s. congiunzione, unione, f.; railway –, biforcamento (di strada ferrata), m.

juncture, *jăngk'tãr*, s. congiuntura, f.; circostanza, f., caso, stato, m.

June, *jõn*, s. giugno, m.

jungle, *jăng'gl*, s. fitto d'un bosco, m.

junior, *jõ'nĭãr*, a. più giovine (d'un altro).

juniper, *jõ'nĭpãr*, s. ginepro, m.

juniper-berry, *–bĕrrĭ*, s. coccola di ginepro, f.

junket, *jăng'kĕt*, s. festino di nascosto, m.; confettura, f.; –, v. n. gozzovigliare.

junta, *jăn'tă*, **junto**, *–tŏ*, s. assemblea, radunanza, f. [ad. giuridicamente.

juridic(al), *jõrĭd'ĭk(ăl)*, a. giuridico; –ly,

jurisconsult, *jõrĭskŏn'sŭlt*, s. giureconsulto, legista, m. [f.

jurisdiction, *–dĭk'shăn*, s. giurisdizione,

jurisprudence, *–prŏ'dĕns*, s. giurispru-
jurist, *jŏ'rĭst*, s. giurista, m.   [denza, f.
juror, *jŏ'rŭr*, **juryman**, *–măn*, s. giu-
jury, *jŏ'rĭ*, s. giurati, m. pl.   [rato, m.
just, *jăst*, a. giusto, onesto, virtuoso;
  –, – **now**, ad. giustamente, appunto; –
  as if, come se.
justice, *jŭs'tĭs*, s. giustizia, f.; giudice,
  –, v. a. render giustizia.
justifiable, *jŭs'tĭfīăbl*, a. giustificabile.
justifiably, *–ăblĭ*, ad. giustificatamente.
justification, *–fĭkă'shăn*, s. giustificazione, scusa, difesa, f.
justify, *jŭs'tĭfī*, v. a. giustificare.
justle, *jŭs'l*, v. a. & n. urtare; urtarsi.
justly, *jăst'lĭ*, ad. giustamente; esattamente.   [giustezza, esattezza, f.
justness, *–nĕs*, s. giustizia, f.; equità, f.;
jut, *jăt*, v. n. sporgere; uscire di linea.
juvenile, *jŏ'vĕnĭl*. a. giovanile.
juxtaposition, *jăkstăpŏzĭsh'ăn*, s. giusta-
  posizione, f.

K.

kale, *kăl*, s. cavolo riccio, m.   [pio, m.
kaleidoscope, *kălī'dŏskōp*, s. caleidosco-
kangaroo, *kăng'gărō*, s. canguro, m.
keel, *kēl*, s. (mar.) carena, f.; chiglia, f.
keen, *kēn*, a. acuto, affilato; sottile; veemente, severo; mordente, penetrante;
  –ly, ad. acutamente; veementemente,
  aspramente.   [veemenza, f.
keenness, *–nĕs*, s. acutezza, f.; asprezza,
keen-sighted, *–sītĕd*, a. perspicace.
keep, *kēp*, v. a. ir. tenere; mantenere; ritenere; servare, conservare; guardare, proteggere; osservare; celebrare; –, v. n. ir.
  astenersi; fermarsi, fissarsi; restare, dimorare; durare; –, s. guardia, custodia,
  f.; mantenimento, m.; torricella, f.
keeper, *kēp'ŭr*, s. guardiano, m.; custode,
  m.; conservatore, m.; **– of a prison**,
  carceriere, m.
keeping, *–ĭng*, s. guardia, custodia, f.
keepsake, *–sāk*, s. rimembranza, f., dono,
keg, *kĕg*, s. caratello, m.   [m.
ken, *kĕn*, s. vista, f.; prospetto, m.
kennel, *kĕn'nĕl*, s. canaletto, m.; canile,
  m.; muta (di cani), m.; tana, f.   [f.
kerbstone, *kŭrb'stŏn*, s. pietra angolare,
kernel, *kŭr'nĕl*, s. noce, mandorla, f.;
  ghianda, f.; granello, m.
kerosene, *kĕr'ōsĕn*, s. petrolio, m.
ketch, *kĕch*, s. (mar.) nave a due alberi, f.
kettle, *kĕt'tl*, s. caldaia, f., calderone, m.
kettle-drum, *–drăm*, s. timpano, m.
key, *kē*, s. chiave, f.; tasto, m.   [f.
key-board, *–bōrd*, s. registro, m., tastiera,
key-hole, *–hōl*, s. buco della chiave, m.
key-note, *–nŏt*, s. (mus.) tonica, f.
key-ring, *–rĭng*, s. anello per il mazzo
  delle chiavi, m.   [pietra d'un arco).
key-stone, *–stŏn*, s. serraglio, m. (mezza
kick, *kĭk*, s. calcio di cavallo, m.; –, v. a.
  dar de' calci; sprangare calci.
kickshaw, *–shă*, s. frasca, f.

kid, *kĭd*, s. capretto, m.   [ecc.).
kidnap, *kĭd'năp*, v. a. trafugare (figliuoli
kidnapper, *–pŭr*, s. che trafuga (figliuoli
  ecc).   [progenie, f.
kidney, *kĭd'nĭ*, s. arnione, m.; razza,
kilderkin, *kĭl'dărkĭn*, s. barilotto, m.
kill, *kĭl*, v. a. ammazzare, uccidere.
killing, *–lĭng*, a. mortale; (fig.) incante-
kiln, *kĭl*, s. fornace, f.   [vole.
kiln-dry, *–drī*, v. a. seccare al fuoco d'
  una fornace.   [zesi, f.
kilt, *kĭlt*, s. gonnella dei montanari scoz-
kimbo, *kĭm'bŏ*, a. incurvato, piegato.
kin, *kĭn*, s. parente, m., affinità, f.; **next
  of –**, parente stretto, m.
kind, *kīnd*, a. benevolo, benigno; grazioso; cortese, civile; **be so – as**, favo-
  ritemi di; –, s. genere, m., specie, sorta,
  maniera, f., modo, m.; natura, f.
kindle, *kīnd'l*, v. a. & n. accendere; in-
  fiammarsi.
kindliness, *kīnd'lĭnĕs*, s. benevolenza, f.
kindly, *–lĭ*, a. affabile, benigno.
kindness, *–nĕs*, s. benignità, affabilità,
  f.; favore, m., compiacenza, f.
kindred, *kĭn'drĕd*, a. consanguineo; –, s.
  parentato, m.; parenti, m. pl.
king, *kĭng*, s. re, m.
kingdom, *–dăm*, s. regno, reame, m.
kingfisher, *–fĭshŭr*, s. alcione, uccello
  pescatore, m.
kinglike, *–līk*, **kingly**, *–lĭ*, a. (& ad.)
  reale; da re, regalmente.   [f.
kings-evil, *–s'ĕvl*, s. gozzo, m., scrofola,
kinsfolk, *kĭnz'fōk*, s. pl. parenti, m. pl.
kinship, *kĭn'shĭp*, s. parentado, m., consanguinità, f.   [m.
kinsman, *–s'măn*, s. parente, consanguineo,
kinswoman, *–s'wŭmăn*, s. parente, con-
  sanguinea, f.
kirtle, *kŭr'tl*, s. busto, m.; gonnella, f.
kiss, *kĭs*, v. a. baciare; –, s. bacio, m.
kissing, *–sĭng*, s. baciamento, m.
kit, *kĭt*, s. fiasco, m.; secchia, f.. tazzone.
  m.; piccol violino, m.
kitchen, *kĭch'ĕn*, s. cucina, f.
kitchen-dresser, *–drĕssŭr*, s. tavola di
  cucina, f.
kitchen-garden, *–gărdn*, s. orto, m.
kitchen-maid, *–măd*, s. cuoca, f.   [f.
kitchen-range, *–rănj*, s. cucina inglese,
kitchen-stuff, *–stŭf*, s. grascia di cucina,f.
kite, *kīt*, s. nibbio, m.; cervo volante, m.;
  aquilone, m.
kitten, *kĭt'tn*, s. gattino, m.; –, v. n.
  figliare (d'una gatta).
knack, *năk*, s. bagattella, f.; destrezza, f.
knacker, *–ăr*, s. schiaccianoci, m.
knapsack, *năp'săk*, s. bisaccia, tasca (di
  soldato), f.
knave, *năv*, s. furfante, m.; ribaldo, m.;
  fante (al giuoco di carte), m
knavery, *nā'vărĭ*, s. furfanteria, truffa, f.
knavish, *–vĭsh*, a. furbo, ingannoso; **–ly**,
  ad. con furberia.
knead, *nēd*, v. a. impastare, intridere.
kneading-trough, *–ĭng trŏf*, s. madia, f.
knee, *nē*, s. ginocchio, m.; nodo, m.

knee-deep, -dēp, **knee-high**, -hī, a. affondato fin a' ginocchi.

kneel, -nēl, v. n. ir. genuflettersi. [f.

knee-pan, nē'pān, s. rotula del ginocchio.

knell, nēl, s. suono di campana a morto, m.

knickerbockers, nīk'ŭrbŏkŭrz, s. pl. calzoni da cacciatore, m. pl.

knicknacks, nīk'nāks, s. pl. bagattelle, f. pl.

knife, nīf, s. coltello, m. [cavaliere.

knight, nīt, s. cavaliere, m.; –, v. a. creare

knighthood, –hŭd, s. dignità di cavaliere,

knightly, –lī, a. cavalleresco. [f.

knit, nīt, v. a. r. & ir. annodare; unire; –, v. n. r. & ir. lavorare all'ago; (the brow) increspar la fronte.

knitter, –tŭr, s. lavoratore d'ago, m.

knitting-needle, –tīng nēdl, s. ago da lavori a maglia, m. [f.

knob, nŏb, s. tumore, m.; nodo, m.; bozza,

knobby, –bī, a. nodoso, nocchioso; calloso.

knock, nŏk, s. colpo, m., percossa, botta, f.; picchio (alla porta), m.; –, v. a. battere; picchiare; –, v. n. urtarsi; **to-down**, atterrare; ammazzare.

knocker, –ŭr, s. martello (della porta), m.

knoll, nōl, s. poggetto, m.

knot, nŏt, s. nodo, m., banda, brigata, f.; difficoltà, f.; –, v. a. annodare; imbrogliare; –, v. n. germogliare.

knotty, –tī, a. nodoso; difficile.

knout, nŏŭt, s. knout, m., verghe, f. pl.

know, nō, v. a. & n. in sapere, conoscere; essere informato.

knowing, –īng, a. saputo, intelligente.

knowingly, –ī, ad. consapevolmente, a bello studio. [scienza, abilità, f.

knowledge, nŏl'ēj, s. conoscenza, f.;

knuckle, nŭk'l, s. congiuntura, f.; garretto di vitello, m.; –, v. n. sommettersi.

L.

la, lā, là! ecco! vedi!

label, lā'bĕl, s. iscrizione, cartellino, m., etichetta, f.; –, v. a. notare, segnare.

labial, lā'bīăl, a. labiale.

laboratory, lăb'ŏrătŭrī, s. laboratorio, m.

laborious, lăb'ōrŭs, a. laborioso; difficile; **-ly**, ad. laboriosamente.

labour, lā'bŭr, s. lavoro, travaglio, m.; fatica, opera, f.; **to be in** –, aver le doglie; –, v. a. & n. lavorare; affaticarsi; **(with child)** aver le doglie. [m.

labourer, –ŭr, s. lavorante, m.; operaio,

labyrinth, lăb'īrīnth, s. laberinto, m.

lac, lăk, s. lacca, f.

lace, lās, s. stringa, f.; merletto, m.; nastro, m.; –, v. a. allacciare; gallonare, guarnire di merletti.

lacerate, lās'ărāt, v. a. lacerare; stracciare.

lacing, lās'īng, s. l'allacciare, m.

lachrymose, lāk'rīmōz, a. lacrimoso.

lack, lăk, s. mancanza, f., bisogno, m.; –, v. a. & n. mancare, avere bisogno.

lackey, lāk'ī, s. lacchè, m.

laconic, lākŏn'īk, a. laconico.

lacquer, lăk'ŭr, v. a. verniciare.

lad, lăd, s. giovanetto, adolescente, m.; garzone, m.

ladder, lād'dŭr, s. scala a piuoli, f.

lade, lād, v. a. & ir. caricare; colmare.

lading, lā'dĭng, s. caricamento, noleggio, m.; **bill of** –, polizza di carico, f.

ladle, lā'dl, s. cucchiaia, f.; ramaiuolo, m

lady, lā'dī, s. dama, signora, f.; **Our Lady**, la Madonna.

lady-bird, –bŭrd, s. coccinigiia, f. (insetto).

Lady-day, –dā, s. Annunziazione, f.

lady-killer, –kĭllŭr, s. favorito delle donne, m.

ladylike, –līk, a. donnesco; elegante.

lady-love, –lŭv, s. innamorata, f.

ladyship, –shĭp, s. qualità di donna, f.; Signoria, f. [pigramente.

lag, lāg, v. n. restare indietro; muoversi

laggard, –gŭrd, **lagger**, –gŭr, s. pigro, m.; indugiatore, m.

lagoon, lăgōn', s. lacuna, palude, f. [f.

lair, lăr, s. ricettacolo, m.; covile, m.; tana,

laird, lărd, s. signore d'un feudo (in Scozia),

laity, lā'tī, s. laici, secolari, m. pl. [m.

lake, lāk, s. lago, m.; lacca, f. [agnello.

lamb, lăm, s. agnello, m.; –, v. n. far un

lambent, lăm'bĕnt, a. lambente.

lambkin, –kĭn, s. agnelletto, m.

lame, lām, a. zoppo; imperfetto; **-ly**, ad. stortamente; imperfettamente; –, v. a. stroppiare. [fezione, f.

lameness, –nĕs, s. storpiatura, f.; imper-

lament, lămĕnt', v. a. & n. compiangere; lamentarsi; –, s. lamentazione, f.

lamentable, lăm'ĕntăbl, a. lamentevole, deplorabile.

lamentation, –tā'shŭn, s. lamentazione, f.

lamp, lămp, s. lampada, lucerna, f.

lamp-black, –blăk, s. nero di fumo, m.

lamp-lighter, –lītŭr, s. colui che accende le lampade, m. [–, v. a. satireggiare.

lampoon, lămpōn', s. libello satirico, m.;

lamp-post, lămp'pōst, s. lampadario, m.

lamprey, lăm'prī, s. lampreda, f.

lance, lăns, s. lancia, f.; –, v. a. trafiggere; tagliare con lancetta.

lancer, lăn'sŭr, s. lanciere, m.

lancet, lăn'sĕt, s. lancetta, f.

land, lănd, s. terra, f.; regione, f.; paese, m.; –, v. a. & n. sbarcare, prender terra.

landau, lăndō', s. carrozza, f.

landed, lăn'dĕd, a. ricco in possessioni.

land-fall, lănd'fāl, s. eredità inaspettata, f.; luogo da approdare, approdo, m. [f. pl.

land-forces, –fōrsĕz, s. pl. forze terrestri.

land-holder, –hōldŭr, s. padrone del fondo, m. [m.; pianerottolo, m.

landing(-place), –ĭng (plăs), s. sbarcatoio;

landlady, –lādī, s. padrona di terre, f.; ostessa, f. [oste, m.

landlord, –lōrd, s. padrone di poderi, m.;

land-lubber, –lŭbbŭr, s. marinaio disoccupato, m.; vagabondo, m.

land-mark, –mărk, s. limite, m.

landscape, –skāp, s. paesaggio, paese, m.

8 *

landscape-painter, –*pánt̄ar*, s. pittore di paesaggio, paesista, m.   [mento, m.
land-slip, –*slĭp*, s. frana, f., scoscendi-
land-tax, –*tăks*, s. gravezza sopra le terre, f.
landward(s), –*wărd(z)*, ad. verso terra.
lane, *lăn*, s. passaggio, m.; strada stretta, f.
language, *lăng'gwĭj*, s. lingua, f.; linguag-gio, m.   [ad. languidamente; debolmente.
languid, –*gwĭd*, a. languido; debole; –**ly,**
languish, –*gwĭsh*, v. n. languire.
languor, –*gwŭr*, s. languore, m.
lank(y), *lăngk(ĭ)*, a. magro, estenuato, de-bile, languido.
lankness, –*n̄es*, s. magrezza, f.
lansquenet, *lăn'skĕnĕt*, s. lanzichenecco, m.
lantern, *lăn'tŭrn*, s. lanterna, f.; fanale, m.; **dark –,** lanterna cieca, f.; **magic –,** lanterna magica, f.
lap, *lăp*, s. grembo, m.; falda, f.; punta dell' orecchio, f.; –, v. a. inviluppare, in-volgere; leccare, lambire.
lap-dog, –*dŏg*, s. cagnolino, m.
lapful, –*fŭl*, s. grembiata, f., grembiule pieno, m.   [liere, m.
lapidary, *lăp'ĭdărĭ*, s. lapidario, gioiel-
lappet, *lăp'pĕt*, s. falda, f.
lapse, *lăps*, s. cascata, f., scorrimento, m.; piccola colpa, f.; –, v. n. cascare; scor-rere; mancare, errare.
lapwing, *lăp'wĭng*, s. pavoncella, f.
larboard, *lăr'bŏrd*, s. (mar.) babordo (lato sinistro d' una nave), m.
larceny, *lăr'sĕnĭ*, s. furto, latrocinio, m.
larch(-tree), *lărch(trē)*, s. larice, m.
lard, *lărd*, s. lardo, m.; –, v. a. lardare.
larder, *lăr'dŭr*, s. guardavivande, f.
larding-pin, –*dĭng pĭn*, s. lardatoio, m.
large, *lărj*, a. largo, spazioso; liberale; **at –,** ampiamente; –**ly,** ad. largamente; copiosamente; diffusamente.
largeness, –*n̄es*, s. larghezza, grandezza, ampiezza, vastità, f.
largess, *lăr'jĕs*, s. liberalità, f.; larghezza,
lark, *lărk*, s. allodola, f.   [f.
larva, *lăr'vă*, s. larva, f.   [lascivamente.
lascivious, *lăssĭv'ĭŭs*, a. lascivo; –**ly,** ad.
lash, *lăsh*, s. sferzata, f.; cinghia, f.; (fig.) motto pungente, m.; –, v. a. sferzare; cinghiare; censurare aspramente.
lass, *lăs*, s. zittella, ragazza, f.   [f.
lassitude, *lăs'sĭtūd*, s. stanchezza, f.; fatica,
last, *lăst*, a. ultimo; passato; **at –,** in fine; –, ad. ultima volta; –, s. forma (del calzolaio), f.; (mar.) lasto, m.; –, v. n. durare.   [perpetuamente.
lasting, a. permanente; –**ly,** ad.
lastly, *lăst'lĭ*, ad. in fine.
latch, *lăch*, s. saliscendi, m.; –, v. a. chiu-dere con saliscendi.
latch-key, –*kē*, s. chiave comune, f.
late, *lăt*, a. & ad. lento, tardo; ultimo; de-funto; tardi; **of –,** ultimamente; –**ly,** ad. poco fa; poco stante.   [dugio, m.
lateness, –*n̄es*, s. tempo più tardo, m.; in-
latent, *lă'tĕnt*, a. latente, occulto.
lateral, *lăt'ŭrăl*, a. laterale; –**ly,** ad. late-ralmente.

lath, *lăth*, s. panconcello, m., assicella, f. –, v. a. coprire di assicelle.
lathe, *lăth*, s. tornio, m.
lather, *lăth'ăr*, s. schiuma di sapone, f.
latin, *lăt'ĭn*, s. lingua latina, f., latino, m.
latitude, *lăt'ĭtŭd*, s. latitudine, f.; lar-ghezza, f.; spazio, m.   [m.
latitudinarian, –*ăhnd'răăn*, s. spirito forte,
latten, *lăt'tĭn*, s. ottone, m.; latta, f.
latter, *lăt'tăr*, a. ultimo; recente; –**ly,** ad. ultimamente.   [graticciaes; cancellare.
lattice, *lăt'tĭs*, s. graticcio, m.; –, v. a. in-
laudable, *lăd'ăbl*, a. lodevole.
laudably, –*ăblĭ*, ad. lodevolmente, con lode.
laugh, *lăf*, v. n. ridere; –, s. riso, m.
laughable, –*ăbl*, a. ridicolo.   [ridente.
laughingly, –*ĭnglĭ*, ad. con riso, in modo
laughing-stock, –*ĭng stŏk*, s. ludibrio, trastullo, scherno, m.
laughter, *lăf'tăr*, s. riso, m.
launch, *lănsh*, v. a. & n. lanciare; lan-ciarsi; –, s. (mar.) scialuppa, f.
laundress, *lăn'drĕs*, s. lavandaia, f.
laundry, *lăn'drĭ*, s. lavatoio, m.
laureate, *lă'rĕăt*, a. laureato.
laurel, *lŏr'ĕl*, s. laurea, f., lauro, m.
laurelled, –*ĕld*, a. laureato.
lava, *lă'vă*, s. lava, f.
lavender, *lăv'ĕndăr*, s. lavanda, f.
lavish, *lăv'ĭsh*, a. prodigo; –**ly,** ad. pro-digalmente; –, v. a. dissipare.
law, –*lă*, s. legge, f.; giurisprudenza, f.; processo, m.; diritto, m.   [legalmente.
lawful, –*fŭl*, a. legittimo, legale; –**ly,** ad.
law-giver, –*gĭvăr*, s. legislatore, m.
lawless, –*lĕs*, a. senza legge; illegale.
lawlessness, –*n̄es*, s. licenza, f.; illega-
lawn, *lăn*, s. pianura, f.   [lità, f.
law-suit, *lă'sŭt*, s. processo, litigio, m., lite, causa, f.   [legista, m.
lawyer, *lă'yăr*, s. avvocato, m.; giurista,
lax, *lăks*, a. rilassato; fiacco.
laxity, –*ĭtĭ*, s. lassità, f.
lay, *lă*, v. a. ir. mettere, porre; posare; abbonacciare, calmare; disporre; scom-mettere; –, v. n. ir. fare una scommessa; fare le uova; **to – a wager,** fare una scommessa; **to – claim to,** pretendere.
layer, –*ăr*, s. letto, m.; strato, m.; ger-moglio, m.; chioccia, f.   [dello, m.
layman, –*măn*, s. laico, scolare, m.; mo-
lazaretto, *lăzărĕt'tŏ*, **lazar-house,** *lă'zăr hōŭs*, s. lazzeretto, m.
lazily, *lă'zĭlĭ*, ad. lentamente.
laziness, *lă'zĭnĕs*, s. pigrizia, f.
lazy, *lă'zĭ*, a. lento, tardo; pigro.
lea, *lē*, s. prato, m.; pianura, f.
lead, *lēd*, v. a. ir. guidare, condurre; co-mandare; –, v. n. ir. essere il capo; –, s. condotta, f.; cominciamento (nel giuoco), m.; acchito, m.
lead, *lĕd*, s. piombo, m.; –**s,** pl. tetto di piombo, m.; –, v. a. impiombare.
leaden, *lĕd'n*, a. di piombo; pesante, goffo.
leader, *lēd'ăr*, s. conduttore, m.; capi-tano, m.; articolo di fondo, m.; cavallo da sella, m.

leading, *-ĭng*, a. primo, principale; **— article**, s. articolo di fondo, m.; **— hand**, s. mano, m.; **— horse**, s. cavallo da sella, m.
leading-strings, *-strĭngs*, s. pl. stringhe f. pl.; laccio, m. [battitoio, m.
leaf, *lĕf*, s. foglia, f., foglio, m.; battente,
leafless, *-lĕs*, a. sfrondato.
leafy, *lĕf'ĭ*, a. frondoso. [confederarsi.
league, *lĕg*, s. lega, f.; unione, f.; —, v. n.
leaguer, *lĕ'gûr*, s. confederato, m. [acqua.
leak, *lĕk*, s. (mar.) falla, f.; —, v. n. fare
leakage, *-ĝj*, s. colatura, f.; scolo, m
leaky, *lĕk'ĭ*, a. fesso, squarciato.
lean, *lĕn*, a. magro; —, v. n. r. & ir. appoggiarsi; inclinare. [f.
leaning, *-ĭng*, s. pendio, m., inclinazione,
leanness, *-nĕs*, s. magrezza, f.
leap, *lĕp*, v. n. ir. coprire, montare; saltare; lanciarsi; —, s. salto, m.
leap-frog, *-frŏg*, s. salto di rana, m. (giuoco fanciullesco).
leap-year, *-yĕr*, s. anno bisestile, m.
learn, *lûrn*, v. a. & n. insegnare; imparare, apprendere. [-ly, ad. dottamente.
learned, *lûrn'ĕd (lûrnd)*, a. dotto, letterato;
learning, *-ĭng*, s. erudizione, f.; scienza, dottrina, f. [affitto.
lease, *lĕs*, s. affitto, m.; —, v. a. dare in
leasehold, *-hōld*, a. possesso d' un tal lease.
leash, *lĕsh*, s. lassa, f.; —, v. a. legare.
least, *lĕst*, a. & ad. minimo, più piccolo; meno; in minimo modo; **at —**, almeno; **not in the —**, in niun modo.
leather, *lĕth'ûr*, s. cuoio, m., pelle, f.
leather-dresser, *-drĕssûr*, s. conciatore di pelli, m.
leathern, *lĕth'ûrn*, a. di cuoio, di pelle.
leathery, *-ûrĭ*, a. della qualità del cuoio.
leave, *lĕv*, s. permissione, f.; licenza, libertà, f.; congedo, m.; —, v. a. ir. lasciare; abbandonare; finire.
leaven, *lĕv'n*, s. lievito, fermento, m.; —, v. a. lievitare, fermentare.
leavings, *lĕ'vĭngz*, s. pl. rimasugli, m. pl.
lection, *lĕk'shŭn*, s. lezione, lettura, f.
lecture, *lĕk'tûr (-chûr)*, s. lettura, f.; bravata, f., rimprovero, m.; —, v. a. addottrinare; riprendere. [m.
lecturer, *-tûrûr*, s. lettore, m.; professore,
ledge, *lĕj*, s. orlo, lembo, m.; letto, strato, suolo, m.; risalto, m.
ledger, *-jûr*, s. libro maestro (di conti), m.
led-horse, *lĕd'hôrs*, s. cavallo a mano, m.
lee, *lĕ*, s. (mar.) parte opposta al vento, f.
leech, *lĕch*, s. sanguisuga, f.; medico, m.
leek, *lĕk*, s. porro, m.
leer, *lĕr*, s. sguardo di traverso, m.; —, v. a. guardare sottocchio.
lees, *lĕz*, [s. pl. feccia, f., sedimento, m.
lee-side, *lĕ'sīd*, s. (mar.) banda di sottovento, f.
leeward, *-wûrd*, a. (mar.) opposto al vento.
left, *lĕft*, a. sinistro; **on the —**, a sinistra.
left-handed, *-hănded*, a. mancino.
leg, *lĕg*, s. gamba, f.; coscia, f.; quarto di castrato, m.; forma (per le calzette), f.; piede, m.

legacy, *lĕg'âsĭ*, s. legato, lascito, m.
legal, *lĕ'gâl*, a. legale, legittimo; **-ly**, ad. secondo la legge, legalmente.
legality, *lĕgâl'ĭtĭ*, s. legalità, conformità alle leggi, f. [lizzare.
legalize, *lĕ'gâlĭz*, v. a. render legale, legalegate, *lĕg'ât*, s. legato, m.; ambasciatore,
legatee, *lĕg'âtĕ*, s. legatario, m. [m.
legation, *lĕgâ'shŭn*, s. legazione, ambasceria, f.
legend, *lĕj'ĕnd*, s. leggenda, f.
legendary, *-ârĭ*, a. leggendario.
legerdemain, *lĕj'ûrdĕmān*, s. gherminella,
legible, *lĕj'ĭbl*, a. leggibile. [f.
legibly, *-ĭblĭ*, ad. in maniera leggibile.
legion, *lĕ'jŭn*, s. legione, f.
legislate, *lĕj'ĭslāt*, v. a. fare o dar leggi.
legislation, *-lâ'shŭn*, s. legislazione, f.
legislative, *lĕj'ĭslātĭv*, a. legislativo.
legislator, *-lâ'tûr*, s. legislatore, m.
legislature, *-lâtûr*, s. legislatura, legislazione, f.
legitimacy, *lĕjĭt'ĭmâsĭ*, s. legittimità, f.
legitimate, *-ĭmāt*, a. legittimo; **-ly**, ad. legittimamente; —, v. a. legittimare.
legitimation, *-mâ'shŭn*, s. legittimazione, f.
leisure, *lĕ'zhûr*, s. ozio, m.; comodo, m.; **-ly, at —**, ad. a bell' agio.
lemon, *lĕm'ŏn*, s. limone, m.
lemonade, *-ŏnâd*, s. limonata, f.
lemon-tree, *-trĕ*, s. cedro, m.
lend, *lĕnd*, v. a. ir. prestare.
length, *lĕngth*, s. lunghezza, f.; distanza, f.; durazione, f.; **at —**, finalmente.
lengthen, *lĕngth'n*, v. a. allungare; —, v.n. allungarsi; distendersi.
lengthy, *-ĭ*, a. lungo; tirato; tedioso.
leniency, *lĕ'nĭĕnsĭ*, s. lenità, f.
lenient, *-nĭĕnt*, a. leniente; —, s. medicina lenificativa, f. [ficamento, m.
lenitive, *lĕn'ĭtĭv*, a. lenitivo; —, s. lenilenity, *lĕn'ĭtĭ*, s. lenità, f.; umanità, f.
lens, *lĕns*, s. lente, m. (vetro).
Lent, *lĕnt*, s. Quaresima, m.
lenticular, *lĕntĭk'ûlâr*, a. lenticolare.
lentil, *lĕn'tĭl*, s. lente, m.; lenticchia, f.; lentiggine, f.
leonine, *lĕ'ŏnĭn*, a. leonino, di leone.
leopard, *lĕp'ûrd*, s. leopardo, m.
leper, *lĕp'ûr*, s. lebbroso, m.
leprosy, *lĕp'rŏst*, s. lebbra, f.
leprous, *lĕp'rûs*, a. lebbroso.
less, *lĕs*, a. minore; —, ad. meno.
lessee, *lĕssĕ'*, s. pigionale, affittuario, m.
lessen, *lĕs'sn*, v. a. render più piccolo, diminuire; —, v. n. divenire più piccolo.
lesser, *lĕs'sûr*, a. minore, più piccolo.
lesson, *lĕs'sn*, s. lezione, f.; rimprovero, m.
lessor, *lĕs'sûr*, s. affittatore, m.
lest, *lĕst*, c. per paura, per timore di.
let, *lĕt*, v. a. ir. lasciare; permettere; impedire; affittare.
lethal, *lĕ'thâl*, a. letale, mortale.
lethargic, *lĕthâr'jĭk*, a. letargico.
lethargy, *lĕth'ârjĭ*, s. letargo, m.

letter, *lĕt'tŭr,* s. lettera, epistola, f.; carat-
letter-box, *-bŏks,* s. bussola, f. |tere, m.
letter-carrier, *-kărrĭŭr,* s. portalettere,
letter-case, *-kās,* s. portafogli, m. [m.
lettered, *lĕt'tŭrd,* a. letterato, dotto.
lettering, *-ĭng,* s. titolo, m.; carattere, m.
letter-press, *-press,* s. torchio, m.,
    stampa, f.   [poligrafo, m.
letter-writer, *-rĭtŭr,* s. epistolario, m.;
lettuce, *lĕt'tĭs,* s. lattuga, f.
Levant, *lăvănt',* s. levante, oriente, m.
Levantine, *lĕvăn'tĭn,* a. dell' Oriente,
levee, *lĕv'ē,* s. levata, f.   [levantino.
level, *lĕv'ĕl,* a. livello, livellato, piano;
    –, s. livello, piano, m.; livella, f.; –, v. a.
    livellare; appianare.
lever, *lē'vŭr,* s. leva, f.
leveret, *lĕv'ăret,* s. leprettino, m.
Levite, *lē'vĭt,* s. Levita, m.
levity, *lĕv'ĭtĭ,* s. levità, leggerezza, f.;
    volubilità, incostanza, f.
levy, *lĕv'ĭ,* s. leva (di soldati), f.; –, v. a.
    levare; guerreggiare.   [dissolutamente.
lewd, *lōd,* a. dissoluto, lascivo; **-ly,** ad.
lewdness, *-nĕs,* s. dissolutezza, f.
lexicographer, *lĕksĭkŏg'răfŭr,* s. lessico-
    grafo, m.
lexicon, *lĕks'ĭkŏn,* s. lessico, dizionario, m.
liability, *lĭăbĭl'ĭtĭ,* s. obbligazione, respon-
    sabilità, f.   [sabile.
liable, *lĭ'ăbl,* a. soggetto, esposto; respon-
liar, *lĭ'ŭr,* s. mentitore, bugiardo, m.
libation, *lĭbā'shŭn,* s. libazione, f.
libel, *lĭ'bĕl,* s. libello infamatorio, m.;
    satira, f.; –, v. a. diffamare.
libellous, *-lŭs,* a. diffamatorio.
liberal, *lĭb'ărăl,* a. liberale, generoso;
    -ly, ad. liberalmente; generosamente.
liberalism, *-ĭzm,* s. liberalismo, m.
liberality, *-ăl'ĭtĭ,* s. liberalità, generosità,
    magnanimità, f.   [libertà.
liberate, *lĭb'ărāt,* v. a. liberare; dare
liberation, *-rā'shŭn,* s. liberazione, f.,
    liberamento, m.
liberator, *lĭb'ărātŭr,* s. liberatore, m.
libertine, *lĭb'ărtĭn,* a. licenzioso; –, s.
    libertino, m.   [mo.
liberty, *lĭb'ărtĭ,* s. libertà, f.; privilegio,
librarian, *lĭbrā'rĭăn,* s. bibliotecario, m.
library, *lĭ'brărĭ,* s. librerìa, f.; biblioteca, f.
licence, *lĭ'sĕns,* s. licenza, f.; permissione,
    f.   [ad. licenziosamente.
licentious, *lĭsĕn'shŭs,* a. licenzioso; **-ly,**
lichen, *lĭch'ĕn,* *(lĭ'kĕn),* s. (bot.) lichene, m.
lick, *lĭk,* v. n. leccare, lambire; bastonare.
licking, *-ĭng,* s. carica di busse, f.
lictor, *lĭk'tŭr,* s. littore, m.
lid, *lĭd,* s. coperchio, m.; palpebra, f.
lie, *lĭ,* s. bugia, menzogna, f.; –, v. n.
    mentire. [dimorare; **here -s,** qui giace.
lie, –, v. n. ir. giacere; esser situato;
lief, *lĭf,* adv. tanto; volontieri.
liege, *lĭj,* a. ligio, suddito.
lien, *lĭ'ĕn (lēn),* s. diritto da staggimento, m.
lieu, *lŭ,* s. luogo, m.; **in - of,** in vece di.
lieutenancy, *lĕfĕn'ănsĭ,* s. luogotenenza, f.

lieutenant, *-tĕn'ănt,* s. luogotenente, m.
life, *lĭf,* s. vita, f.; esistenza, f.; vivacità, f.;
    condotta, f.; **for -,** a vita; **to the -,** al
    naturale; **high -,** gran mondo, m.
life-belt, *-bĕlt,* **(-boat, -buoy)** s.
    cinghia (scialuppa, f.; gavitello, m.) di
    salvamento, f.   [f.
life-guard, *-gărd,* s. guardia del corpo,
lifeless, *-lĕs,* a. che è senza vita, inanimato.
lifelong, *-lŏng,* a. a vita, vitalizio.
life-office, *-ŏffĭs,* **(-policy)** s. uffizio
    dell' assicurazione sulla vita dell' uomo,
    m.   [di salvamento, m.; rompicapo, m.
life-preserver, *-prĕsĕrvŭr,* s. apparato
life-size, *-sĭz,* s. grandezza naturale, f.
lifetime, *-tĭm,* s. tempo della vita, m.
lift, *lĭft,* s. sforzo (per levar su una cosa),
    m.; alzamento, f.; aiuto, m.; (am.) fer-
    rata, f.; cancello, m.; **at one -,** alla
    prima, in un subito; **to give one a -,**
    assistere alcuno, aiutare alcuno; –, v. a.
    levare, alzare; inalzare; sollevare.
ligament, *lĭg'ăment,* s. ligamento, m.;
    vincolo, m.
ligature, *lĭg'ătŭr,* s. legatura, f.; benda, f.
light, *lĭt,* a. leggiero; facile; agile, veloce;
    frivolo; incostante; chiaro; biondo;
    -(ly), ad. leggiermente; facilmente;
    agilmente.
light, –, s. lume, m.; splendore, m.; faro,
    m.; chiarezza, f.; intelligenza, cono-
    scenza, f.; –, v. a. & n. ir. accendere,
    allumare; dichiarare; scaricare; arrivare;
    scendere, montar da cavallo.
lighten, *lĭt'n,* v. a. illuminare; alleg-
    gerire; –, v. n. lampeggiare.
lighter, *-ŭr,* s. battello, m.
lighterman, *-ŭrmăn,* s. navalestro, m.
light-hearted, *-hărtĕd,* a. gaio, allegro.
light-house, *-hŏŭs,* s. faro, fanale, m.
lighting, *-ĭng,* s. illuminazione, f.
lightly, *-lĭ,* ad. leggermente; facilmente;
    un poco.   [prestezza, f.;
lightness, *-nĕs,* s. leggerezza, agilità, f.;
lightning, *-nĭng,* s. baleno, lampo, m.
lightning-rod, *-nĭng-rŏd,* s. paraful-
    mine, m.   [m. pl.
lights, *lĭts,* s. pl. polmoni (d' un animale),
lightsome, *-sŭm,* a. chiaro; allegro, gaio,
    gioioso, lieto.
ligneous, *lĭg'nĕŭs,* a. di legno, ligneo.
like, *lĭk,* a. simile, somigliante; verisimile;
    –, ad. come, da, alla maniera; –, s. pari-
    glia, f.; somiglianza, f.; cosa simile, f.;
    –, v. a. amare; approvare; –, v. n. avere
    gusto, compiacersi.
likelihood, *-lĭhŭd,* s. probabilità, f.; ap-
    parenza, f.   [probabilmente.
likely, *-lĭ,* a. probabile, verisimile; –, ad.
liken, *lĭ'kn,* v. a. comparare; rassomi-
    gliare.   [glianza, f.; ritratto, m.
likeness, *lĭk'nĕs,* s. sembianza, somi-
likewise, *-wĭs,* ad. parimente, anche.
liking, *lĭk'ĭng,* s. corpulenza, f.; gusto,
lilac, *lĭ'lăk,* s. lilla, m. [m.; senso, m.
lily, *lĭl'ĭ,* s. giglio, m.; **- of the valley,**
    s. mughetto, m.
limb, *lĭmb,* s. membro, m.

limber, *lĭm'bŭr,* a. flessibile, agevole; **—s,** s. pl. stanghe d'una carrozza, f. pl.

lime, *lĭm,* s. calcina, f.; calce, f.; tiglio, m.; **—,** v. a. invischiare.

lime-pit, *—pĭt,* s. buca della calcina, f.

lime-stone, *—stŏn,* s. alberese, m., pietra calcarea, f.

lime-twig, *—twĭg,* s. paniuzza, f.

limit, *lĭm'ĭt,* s. limite, termine, m.; **—,** v. a. ristrignere. [strizione, f.; riserva, f.

limitation, *—tā'shŭn,* s. limitazione, f.; re**limitless,** *lĭm'tĭlĕs,* a. illimitato.

limn, *lĭm,* v. a. disegnare; dipignere con acquarello. [m.

limner, *lĭm'nŭr,* s. miniatore, m.; pittore,

limp, *lĭmp,* a. debole, fiacco; **—,** s. zoppicamento, m.; **—,** v. n. zoppicare.

limpid, *lĭm'pĭd,* a. limpido, chiaro, lucido.

linch-pin, *lĭnsh'pĭn,* s. chiodo (di ruota),

linden, *lĭn'dn,* s. tiglio, m. [m.

line, *lĭn,* s. linea, f.; corda, f.; strada ferrata, f.; lignaggio, m., discendenza, f.; fattezza, f.; tratto, m.; verso, m.; equatore, m.; **—,** v. a. foderare, soppannare; guarnire.

lineage, *lĭn'ĕāj,* s. schiatta, stirpe, f.

lineal, *lĭn'ĕăl,* a. lineare, di linea; **—ly,** ad. linealmente, per linea. [fattezza, .f

lineament, *lĭn'ĕămĕnt,* s. lineamento, m.,

linear, *lĭn'ĕăr,* a. lineare, per linea.

line-keeper, *lĭn'kēpŭr,* s. (rail.) guardiano ferroviario, m.

linen, *lĭn'ĕn,* s. tela, f.; biancherie, f. pl.; **—,** a. fatto di lino, di tela. [tela, m.

linen-draper, *—drāpŭr,* s. mercante di

linen-drapery, *drāpărĭ,* s. teleria, f.

linen-press, *—prĕs,* s. armadio per le biancherie, m.

linger, *lĭng'gŭr,* v. n. languire; esitare.

lingering, *—ĭng,* s. indugio, m., dilazione, f. [lentamente.

lingeringly, *—ĭnglĭ,* ad. tardamente,

linguist, *lĭng'gwĭst,* s. linguista, m.

liniment, *lĭn'ĭmĕnt,* s. lenimento, m.

lining, *lĭn'nĭng,* s. fodera, f.; soppanno, m.; cuffia (d'un cappello), f.

link, *lĭngk,* s. anello (di catena), m.; catena, f.; torcia, f.; **—,** v. a. incatenare; giugnere.

link-boy, *—bŏĭ,* s. ragazzo che porta una linnet, *lĭn'nĕt,* s. fanello, m. [torcia, m.

linseed, *lĭn'sĕd,* s. seme di lino, m.

linseed-oil, *—ŏĭl,* s. olio di lino, m.

linsey-woolsey, *lĭnzĭwŭl'zĭ,* s. mezzalint, *lĭnt,* s. lino, m.; faldella, f. [lana, f.

lintel, *lĭn'tĕl,* s. listello, architrave, m.

lion, *lī'ŏn,* s. leone, m.

lioness, *—ĕs,* s. leonessa, f.

lionise, *—īz,* v. a. trattare come un eroe o una maraviglia; far gran caso di.

lip, *lĭp,* s. labbro, m.; bordo, m.

lip-salve, *—săv,* s. pomata da ungere le labbra, f. [dare; **—,** v. n. fondere.

liquefy, *lĭk'wĕfĭ,* v. a. liquefare; liqui**liqueur,** *lĭkŭr',* s. rosolio, m.

liquid, *lĭk'wĭd,* a. liquido; **—,** s. liquore, m.; (gr.) lettera liquida, f.

liquidate, *—dāt,* v. a. liquidare, pagare un debito.

liquidation, *—dā'shŭn,* s. liquidazione, f.

liquor, *lĭk'ŭr,* s. liquore, m.

liquorice, *lĭk'ărĭs,* s. liquirizia, f.

lisp, *lĭsp,* v. n. scilinguare, balbettare; **—,** s. barbugliamento, m.

list, *lĭst,* s. lista, f.; lizza, f.; corda, f.; voglia, f.; **—,** v. a. arrolare; registrare; **—,** v. n. volere. [orecchio.

listen, *lĭs'n,* v. n. ascoltare, porgere

listless, *lĭst'lĕs,* a. trascurato; indifferente; **—ly,** ad. senza cura.

litany, *lĭt'ănĭ,* s. litanie, f. pl.

literal, *lĭt'ărăl,* a. letterale; **—ly,** ad. letteralmente.

literary, *lĭt'ărărĭ,* a. letterario.

literature, *lĭt'ărătŭr,* s. letteratura, f.

lithe, *lĭth,* a. flessibile, pieghevole.

lithograph, *lĭth'ōgrăf,* s. litografia, f.; **—,** v. a. litografare.

lithographer, *—thŏg'răfŭr,* s. litografo, m.

lithographic, *—thŏgrăf'ĭk,* a. litografico.

lithography, *—thŏg'răfĭ,* s. litografia, f.

litigant, *lĭt'ĭgănt,* s. litigatore, m.

litigate, *lĭt'ĭgāt,* v. a. & n. litigare; contendere.

litigation, *—gā'shŭn,* s. lite, contesa, f.

litigious, *—tĭj'ăs,* a. litigioso, rissoso.

litter, *lĭt'tŭr,* s. lettiga, f.; letto portatile, m.; paglia, f.; ventrata, f.; **—,** v. a. figliare; disordinare.

little, *lĭt'tl,* a. piccolo, poco; **—,** s. poca cosa, f.; **a —,** un poco; **—,** ad. poco, non molto, quasi nulla; **by — and —,** poco a poco.

littleness, *—nĕs,* s. piccolezza, f.

liturgy, *lĭt'ărjĭ,* s. liturgia, f.

live, *lĭv,* v. n. vivere; sussistere; dimorare.

live, *līv,* a. vivo; attivo.

livelihood, *lĭv'lĭhŭd,* s. vita, f.; mestiere,

liveliness, *lĭv'lĭnĕs,* s. vivacità, f. [m.

lively, *lĭv'lĭ,* a. vivace, spiritoso, gaio.

liver, *lĭv'ŭr,* s. vivente, m.; fegato, m.

livery, *lĭv'ărĭ,* s. livrea, f.; **the Livery,** corpo municipale de Londra, m.

Livery-man, *—măn,* s. membro del corpo municipale, m.; **livery-men,** pl. gente di livrea, f. [di cavalli da rimessa, f.

livery-stables, *—stābls,* s. pl. scuderia

livid, *lĭv'ĭd,* a. livido.

living, *lĭv'ĭng,* a. vivente, vivo; **—,** s. vivere, m.; vitto, nutrimento, m.

lizard, *lĭz'ărd,* s. lucertola, f.

lo ! *lō,* i. ecco! ecco qui!

load, *lōd,* v. a. r. & ir. caricare; **—,** s. carica, f.; fardello, m.

loadstar, *—stär,* s. stella polare, f.

loadstone, *—stŏn,* s. calamita, f.

loaf, *lŏf,* s. pane (di zucchero), m.

loafer, *—ŭr,* s. vagabondo, m.

loam, *lŏm,* s. terra grassa, f.; marna, f.

loan, *lŏn,* s. prestito, imprestito, m.

loath, *lŏth,* a. mal disposto; repugnante.

loathe, *lŏth,* v. a. & n. detestare; recare disgusto, nauseare. [m.

loathing, *lŏth'ĭng,* s. disgusto, fastidio,

loathly, *lŏth' lĭ,* **loathsome,** *lŏth' sŭm,* a. fastidioso, nauseoso.

lobby, *lŏb' bĭ,* s. vestibulo, m.

lobe, *lōb,* s. lobo, m.

lobster, *lŏb' stŭr,* s. gambero (di mare), m.

local, *lō' kăl,* a. locale; (med.) esterno.

localise, *lō' kălīz,* v. a. appropriare ad un luogo.

locality, *lōkăl' ĭtĭ,* s. località, f. [luogo.

loch, *lŏk,* s. lago, m.

lock, *lŏk,* s. serratura, f.; serrame, m.; ciocca di capelli, f.; piastra (di pistola), chiusa, f.; fiocco di lana, m.; –, v. a. & n. chiudere a chiave; fermarsi; **to – in,** rinchiudere; serbare; **to – out,** escludere; impedire; **to – up,** rinchiudere, serrare.

locker, *lŏk' ŭr,* s. armadio, m.; credenza, f.

locket, *–ĕt,* s. fermaglio, m. [f.

lock-jaw, *–jă,* s. trisma, m. [f.

lock-out, *–ŏŭt,* s. cessazione dal lavoro.

locksmith, *–smĭth,* s. fabbro (di toppe), magnano, m. [di luogo, m.

locomotion, *lōkōmō' shŭn,* t. cambiamento di luogo in luogo; –(engine), s. locomo-

locomotive, *–mō' tĭv,* a. che si muove di luogo in luogo; –(engine), s. locomo-

locust, *lō' kŭst,* s. locusta, f. [tiva, f.

lodge, *lŏj,* s. loggia, f.; cameretta, f.; covo (d'un cervo), m.; –, v. a. alloggiare; fissare; –, v. n. dimorare, abitare.

lodger, *–ŭr,* s. pigionale, m.

lodging, *lŏj' ĭng,* s. alloggio, m.; locanda, f.

lodging-house, *–hŏŭs,* s. locanda, f.

loft, *lŏft,* s. soffitto, m.; granaio, m.

loftiness, *lŏf' tĭnĕs,* s. altezza, grandezza, f.; sublimità, f.; superbia, f.

lofty, *–tĭ,* a. sublime, alto; superbo.

log, *lŏg,* s. ceppo, toppo, m.; pezzo (di legno, m.; (mar.) lo, m.

log-book, *–bŭk,* s. (mar.) libro di loche, m.

loggerhead, *–gŭrhĕd,* s. minchione, m.

logic, *lŏj' ĭk,* s. logica, f. [sciocco, m.

logical, *–ĭkăl,* a. logicale.

logician, *lŏjĭsh' ăn,* s. logico, dialettico, m.

logwood, *lŏg' wŭd,* s. campeggio, m.

loin, *lŏĭn,* s. lombo, m.; –s, pl. reni, m. pl.

loiter, *lŏĭ' tŭr,* v. n. spender il tempo neghittosamente.

loiterer, *–ŭr,* s. infingardo, m.

loll, *lŏl,* v. a. stendere; –, v. n. appoggiarsi; reggersi.

lonely, *lōn' lĭ,* a. solitario, solo. [m.

loneliness, *–lĭnĕs,* s. solitudine, f.; ritiro, m.

long, *lŏng,* a. & ad. lungo; lungo tempo; –, v. n. desiderare; avere gran voglia.

longevity, *lŏnjĕv' ĭtĭ,* s. longevità, lunga vita, f.

longing, *lŏng' ĭng,* s. desiderio intenso, m.; impazienza, f. [lunghezza, f.

longitude, *lŏn' jĭtūd,* s. longitudine, f.

longitudinal, *–tū' dĭnăl,* a. longitudinale; –ly, ad. in lungo.

loo, *lō,* s. bestia, f. (gioco di carte).

look, *lŏk,* s. guardo, m.; aspetto, n..; occhiata, f.; –, v. a. vedere, guardare; cercare; –, v. n. mirare, considerare; sembrare. [bambola, f.

looking-glass, *–ĭng glăs,* s. specchio, m.;

look-out, *–ŏŭt,* s. vedetta, f.; sentinella, f.; **to keep a –,** stare all' erta.

loom, *lōm,* s. telaio di tessitore, m.; –, v. n. (mar.) apparire in lontananza.

loop, *lōp,* s. trina, f. [noniera, f.

loop-hole, *–hōl,* s. buco, m.; (mil.) can-

loose, *lōs,* a. sciolto, slegato; lento; dissoluto, licenzioso; sviato; –ly, ad. senza fermezza; dissolutamente.

loosen, *lō' sn,* v. a. rilassare.

looseness, *lōs' nĕs,* s. allentamento, m.; flusso di corpo, m.

loot, *lōt,* v. a. saccheggiare. [care.

lop, *lŏp,* v. a. diramare, scapezzare, tron-

lop-eared, *–ĕrd,* a. con le orecchie pendenti. [parte che dall' altra.

lop-sided, *–sīdĕd,* a. più pesante da una

loquacious, *lōkwā' shŭs,* a. loquace; ciarliero. [ciarla, f.

loquacity, *lōkwăs' ĭtĭ,* s. loquacità, f.;

Lord, *lŏrd,* s. signore, m.; Iddio, m.; **Mayor,** Potestà di Londra, m.; **lord,** v. n. dominare.

lordliness, *–lĭnĕs,* s. altezza, f.; alterigia, f.

lordling, *–lĭng,* s. signorello, m.

lordly, *–lĭ,* a. signorile, nobile; altiero, arrogante; –, ad. imperiosamente; arrogantemente.

Lordship, *–shĭp,* s. signoria, f. [f.

lore, *lōr,* s. lezione, dottrina, f.; istruzione,

lose, *lōz,* v. a. ir. perdere; rovinare; dissipare; –, v. n. ir. perdersi, essere perduto; mancare.

loss, *lŏs,* s. perdita, f.; rovina, f.

lot, *lŏt,* s. sorte, f.; fato, m.; porzione, f.;

loth, *vedi* loath. [(am.) terra, f.

lotion, *lō' shŭn,* s. lavatura, f.

lottery, *lŏt' tŭrĭ,* s. lotto, m.

loud, *lŏŭd,* a. alto, forte; grande; –ly, ad. ad alta voce; forte. [m.

loudness, *–nĕs,* s. suono forte, m.; strepito,

lounge, *lŏŭnj,* v. n. infingardire; –, s. oziosità, pigrizia, f.

louse, *lŏŭs,* s. (lice, pl.) pidocchio, m.

lousy, *lŏŭ' zĭ,* a. pidocchioso; abietto.

lout, *lŏŭt,* s. rustico, villano, m.; –, v. a. gabbare, corbellare.

loutish, *–ĭsh,* a. alquanto rustico.

lovable, *lŭv' ăbl,* a. amabile.

love, *lŭv,* s. amore, m.; affetto, m.; **to be in – with one,** esser innamorato d'una persona; –, v. a. amare; dilettarsi.

love-affair, *–ăffăr',* s. intrigo amoroso, m.

love-letter, *–lĕttŭr,* s. biglietto amoroso, m.

loveliness, *–lĭnĕs,* s. amabilità, f. [m.

lovely, *–lĭ,* a. amabile, grazioso.

love-match, *–măch,* s. matrimonio per amore, m.

lover, *–ŭr,* s. amante, m. & f.

love-sick, *–sĭk,* a. malato d'amore.

love-tale, *–tāl,* s. paroline amorose, f. pl.

loving, *lŭv' ĭng,* a. amoroso, affezionato; –ly, ad. affettuosamente.

low, *lō,* a. basso, profondo; piccolo; umile; abietto, vile; –, ad. abbasso; vilmente.

low, –, v. n. mugghiare, muggire.

lower, *lō' ŭr,* a. più basso; inferiore.

lower, *–,* v. a. abbassare, diminuire, uniliare; –, v. n. abbassarsi; –, *lŏŭ' ŭr,* oscurarsi.

lowering, *lōū'ā'rīng*, a. oscuro; arcigno.

lowland, *lō'lănd*, s. pianura, f.; terreno basso, m.

lowliness, *–lĭnĕs*, s. umiltà, bassezza, f.

lowly, *–lĭ*, a. & ad. umile; umilmente, bassamente.

lowness, *–nĕs*, s. bassezza, f.

lowry, *lō'rĕ*, s. (rail.) carro da trasporti, m.

low-water, *–wât'ēr*, s. marea bassa, f.

loyal, *lōĭ'ăl*, a. leale; fedele; **–ly**, ad. lealmente, fedelmente.　　　　[f.

loyalty, *–tĭ*, s. lealtà, fedeltà, f.; aderenza

lozenge, *lŏz'ēnj*, s. rombo, m.; pastiglia, f.

lubber, *lŭb'bēr*, s. rusticone, m.

lubberly, *–lĭ*, a. grossolano, pigro.

lubricate, *lō'brĭkāt*, v. a. lubricare

lucid, *lō'sĭd*, a. lucido, luminoso.　　[f.

lucidity, *–sĭd'ĭtĭ*, s. lucidità, f.; chiarezza,

lucifer match, *lō'sĭfēr măch*, s. zolfanello chimico, lucifero, m.

luck, *lŭk*, s. caso, m.; fortuna, f.

luckily, *–ĭlĭ*, ad. fortunatamente.

luckless, *–lĕs*, a. sfortunato, infelice.

lucky, *lŭk'ĭ*, a. fortunato, benavventurato.

lucrative, *lō'krătĭv*, a. lucrativo, profittevole, vantaggioso.　　　　　[m.

lucre, *lō'kēr*, s. lucro, guadagno, profitto,

lucubration, *–kūbrā'shăn*, s. elucubrazione, f., studio notturno, m.; elaboratezza, f.　　　　[in modo burlesco.

ludicrous, *lō'dĭkrŭs*, a. burlesco; **–ly**, ad.

luff, *lŭf*, v. n. (mar.) tenersi col vento

lug, *lŭg*, v. a. tirare, strascinare.

luggage, *lŭg'gāj*, s. bagaglio, m.

luggage-room, *–rŏm*, s. (rail.) loggia da mercanzie, f.　　　　[bagaglie, m.

luggage-ticket, *–tĭkĕt*, s. biglietto delle

luggage-train, *–trăn*, s. (rail.) convoglio delle mercanzie, m.

luggage-van, *–văn*, s. (rail.) vagone da mercanzie, m.

lugger, *lŭg'gēr*, s. (mar.) trabaccolo, m.

lugubrious, *lōgū'brĭŭs*, a. lugubre, triste.

lukewarm, *lōk'wârm*, a. tiepido; **–ly**, ad. tiepidamente.　　　　[mentare.

lull, *lŭl*, v. a. cullare; quetare; addor-

lullaby, *–lăbĭ*, s. ninnerella, f.

lumbago, *lŭmbā'gŏ*, s. lombagine, f.

lumber, *lŭm'bēr*, s. arnesi inutili, m. pl.

lumber-room, *–rŏm*, s. stanza di robe vecchie, f.　　　　[m.

luminary, *lō'mĭnărĭ*, s. luminare, lume,

luminous, *lō'mĭnŭs*, a. luminoso, fulgido.

lump, *lŭmp*, s. massa, f.; pezzo, m.; grosso, mucchio, m.; **by the –**, all' ingrosso; **–**, v. a. prendere il tutto senza badare.　　　　　[f.

lunacy, *lō'năsĭ*, s. follia, pazzia, frenesia,

lunar, *lō'năr*, a. lunare, della luna; **– caustic**, s. pietra infernale, f.

lunatic, *lō'nătĭk*, a. lunatico.

lunch, *lŭnsh*, **luncheon**, *lŭnsh'ŭn*, s. colazione, f.; **–**, v. n. far colazione. [cola, f.

lunette, *lŭnĕt'*, s. (mil.) mezza luna pic-

lungs, *lŭngz*, s. pl. polmoni, m. pl.

lurch, *lŭrch*, s. stato derelitto, m.

lurcher, *–ēr*, s. bassetto, m.

lure, *lōr*, s. allettamento, m.; **–**, v. a. allettare, adescare.

lurk, *lărk*, v. n. nascondersi, appiattarsi.

lurking-place, *–ĭng plăs*, s. nascondiglio, ripostiglio, riparo, m.

luscious, *lŭsh'ŭs*, a. melato, dolce.

lust, *lŭst*, s. concupiscenza, sensualità, f.; **–**, v. a. concupire.　　[ad. libidinosamente.

lustful, *–fŭl*, a. libidinoso, lascivo; **–ly**,

lustily, *–tĭlĭ*, ad. vigorosamente.

lustiness, *lŭs'tĭnĕs*, s. vigore, m., forza di corpo, robustezza, f.

lustre, *lŭs'tēr*, s. lustro, splendore, m.

lustring, *lŭs'trĭng*, s. lustrino, m. (drappo).

lusty, *lŭs'tĭ*, a. forte, vigoroso.

lute, *lōt*, s. liuto, m.; loto, m.

Lutheran, *lō'thărăn*, s. luterano, m.

luxuriance, *lăgzū'rĭăns*, s. abbondanza, f.; copia, f.　　　　　[superfluo.

luxuriant, *–rĭănt*, a. soprabbondante,

luxuriate, *–rĭăt*, v. n. crescere con esuberanza.

luxurious, *–rĭŭs*, a. lussurioso, voluttuoso; **–ly**, ad. voluttuosamente.

luxury, *lŭks'ŭrĭ*, s. lussuria, f.; esuberanza, f.; voluttà, f.

lyceum, *lĭsē'ăm*, s. liceo, m.

lye(-washing), *lĭ('wŏshĭng)*, s. bucato, m., lisciyia, f.

lying, *lī'ĭng*, s. menzogna, f.; bugia, f.

lying-in, *–ĭn*, s. puerperio, parto, m.

lymph, *lĭmf*, s. linfa, f.

lymphatic, *–făt'ĭk*, a. linfatico, di linfa.

lynch, *lĭnsh*, v. a. punire senza forma di giudizio.

lynx, *lĭngks*, s. lince, m.

lyre, *lĭr*, s. lira, f.

lyric(al), *lĭr'ĭk(ăl)*, a. lirico

M.

macaroon, *măkărōn'*, s. maccherone, m.

mace, *măs*, s. massa, f.; macia, f.

macerate, *măs'ărăt*, v. a. macerare; mortificare.

machinate, *măk'ĭnăt*, v. a. macchinare.

machination, *măkĭnā'shăn*, s. macchinamento, m.; artifizio, m.; trama, f.

machine, *măshēn'*, s. macchina, f.; strumento, m.

machinery, *–ărĭ*, s. meccanismo, m.

machinist, *–ĭst*, s. macchinista, m.

mackerel, *măk'ărĕl*, s. sgombro, m. (pesce).

mackintosh, *măk'ĭntŏsh*, s. abito impermeabile.

mad, *măd*, a. pazzo, forsennato, arrabbiato; appassionato; **–ly**, ad. pazzamente, follemente.

madam, *măd'ăm*, s. madama, signora, f.

mad-cap, *măd'kăp*, s. pazzo, discervellato, matto, m.　　　　　[pazzare.

madden, *măd'dn*, v. a. fare arrabbiare, in-

madder, *–dăr*, s. (bot.) robbia, f.

mad-house, *–hŏûs*, s. spedale de' matti, m.

madly, *–lĭ*, ad. pazzamente.

madman, *–măn,* s. pazzo, matto, m.
madness, *–nĕs,* s. pazzia, follezza, furia, f.
magazine, *măgdzèn',* s. magazzino, m.; giornale, m.; (mar.) Santa Barbara, f.
maggot, *măg'gŏt,* s. baco, bruco, m.; capriccio, m.
magic, *măj'ĭk,* s. magia, f.; –, a. magico.
magically, *–ăllĭ,* ad. magicamente, per magia.   [m.
magician, *–jĭsh'ăn,* s. mago, m.; stregone
magisterial, *–jĭstè'rĭăl,* a. magistrale, imperioso; **–ly,** ad. magistralmente.
magistracy, *măj'ĭstrăsĭ,* s. magistratura, f., magistrato, m.
magistrate, *măj'ĭstrăt,* s. magistrato, m.
magnanimity, *măgnănĭm'ĭtĭ,* s. magnanimità, generosità, f.
magnanimous, *–năn'ĭmŭs,* a. magnanimo; **–ly,** ad. con magnanimità.   [f.
magnet, *măg'nĕt,* s. magnete, m., calamita.
magnetic(al), *–nĕt'ĭk(ăl),* a. magnetico.
magnetism, *măg'nĕtĭzm,* s. magnetismo, m.
magnificence, *–nĭf'ĭsĕns,* s. magnificenza, f.   [**–ly,** ad. con pompa.
magnificent, *–ĭsĕnt,* a. magnificente;
magnify, *măg'nĭfĭ,* v. a. magnificare; esaggerare, esaltare.
magnitude, *măg'nĭtŭd,* s. grandezza, f.
magpie, *măg'pĭ,* s. gazza, f.
mahogany, *măhŏg'ănĭ,* s. mogano, legno d'acaiù, m.
maid, *mad,* s. vergine, zittella, donzella, f.; **– of Morton,** ghigliottina, f.
maiden, *ma'dn,* a. di vergine, virginale; (fig.) fresco; **– speech,** prima aringa d'un oratore, f.   [f.
maidenhood, *–hŭd,* s. verginità, f.; purità.
maidenly, *–lĭ,* a. virginale, pudico; delicato.   [delle lettere, f.
mail, *mal,* s. maglia, f.; valigia, f.; posta
mail-coach, *–kŏch,* s. carrozza di posta, f.
mail-steamer, *–stèmăr,* s. pacchebotto postale, m.
mail-train, *–tran,* s. treno postale, m.
maim, *mam,* s. mutilazione, f.; **–,** v. a. mutilare, storpiare.
main, *man,* a. principale, capitale, essenziale; **–,** s. grosso, totale, m.; oceano, alto mare, m.; forza, f.; **in the –,** in somma.   [nente, m.
main-land, *–lănd,* s. terra ferma, f., continente, m.
main-line, *–lĭn,* s. strada ferrata principale, f.   [tutto.
mainly, *–lĭ,* ad. principalmente, soprattutto.
main-mast, *–măst,* s. (mar.) albero maestro, m.
maintain, *măntăn',* v. a. mantenere, dare il vitto; difendere; **–,** v. n. sostenere.
maintenance, *măn'tĕnăns,* s. mantenimento; sostegno, m.; protezione, difesa, f.
maize, *maz,* s. miglio Indiano, m.
majestic(al), *măjĕs'tĭk(ăl),* a. maestoso, grande; **–ally,** ad. maestosamente con
majesty, *măj'ĕstĭ,* s. maestà, f.   [maestà.
major, *mā'jŭr,* a maggiore; superiore; **–,** s. (mil.) maggiore, m.; prima proposizione d'un sillogismo, f.

major-domo, *–dŏ'mŏ,* s. maggiordomo, maestro di casa, m.
majority, *măjŏr'ĭtĭ,* s. maggiorità, f.; pluralità, f.   [maggiore, f.
majorship, *mā'jŭrshĭp,* s. dignità di
make, *māk,* s. fattura, struttura, f.; forma, f.; compagno, socio, m.
make, *–,* v. a. ir. fare; formare; fabbricare; creare; produrre; costringere, forzare; **–,** v. n. tendere; viaggiare; **to – believe,** far sembiante.   [tore, m.
makepeace, *–pès,* s. conciliatore, mediamaker, *–ăr,* s. facitore, fattore, m.; creatore, m.   [m.
makeshift, *–shĭft,* s. il peggio de' peggi,
makeweight, *–wăt,* s. aggiunta, f.   [f.
making, *–ĭng,* s. foggia, f.; fattura, opera,
malady, *măl'ădĭ,* s. malattia, f., morbo, m.
malapert, *măl'ăpărt,* a. insolente, impudente, sfacciato.
malaria, *mălā'rĭă,* s. aere infetto, m.
malcontent, *măl'kŏntĕnt,* a. & s. malcontento (m.).
male, *māl,* a. maschio, mascolino.
malediction, *mălĕdĭk'shăn,* s. maledizione, f.; esecrazione, f.
malefactor, *–făk'tăr,* s. malfattore, m.
maleficent, *lĕy'ĭsĕnt,* a. malefico, maligno.
malevolence, *–lĕv'ŏlĕns,* s. malevolenza, f.
malevolent, *–lĕnt,* a. malevolo; **–ly,** ad. malignamente.
malice, *măl'ĭs,* s. malizia, perversità, f.
malicious, *–lĭsh'ŭs,* a. malizioso; **–ly,** ad. maliziosamente.
malign, *–lĭn',* a. maligno, nocivo; **–,** v. a. invidiare; nuocere.
malignant, *–lĭg'nănt,* a. maligno; **–ly,** ad. malignamente.
malignity, *–lĭg'nĭtĭ,* s. malignità, f.
malleable, *măl'lĕăbl,* a. malleabile.
mallet, *măl'lĕt,* s. maglio, m.
mallows, *măl'lŏz,* s. malva, f.
malmsey, *măm'zĭ,* s. malvasia, f. (vino).
malpractice, *mălprăk'tĭs,* s. malversazione, f.; azione illecita, f.; maltrattamento, insulto, m.   [birra, m.
malt, *mălt,* s. orzo macinato per far la
malt-liquor, *–lĭkŭr,* s. bevanda d'orzo macinato, f.
maltreat, *mălrtĕt',* v. a. maltrattare.
maltster, *mălt'stăr,* s. mercante d'orzo preparato, m.
mamma, *mămmă',* s. mamma, f.
man, *măn,* s. uomo, m.; individuo, m.; servo, m.; pedina (agli scacchi); dama (alle tavole): **– to –,** l'uno come l'altro; **– of war,** bastimento da guerra, m.; **–,** v. a. fornire d'uomini, armare.
manacle, *măn'ăkl,* v. a. mettere le manette, ammanettare; **–,** s. pl. manette, f. pl.
manage, *măn'dj,* v. a. maneggiare; condurre; governare; **–,** v. n. invigilare.
manageable, *–djăbl,* a. maneggiabile, trattabile.
management, *–mĕnt,* s. maneggiamento, maneggio, m.; condotta, f.; direzione, f.
manager, *–djăr,* s. maneggiatore, direttore, amministratore, m.; economo, m.

managing, *–djĭng,* s. maneggio, m.
mandate, *măn'dăt,* s. mandato, m.; commissione, f.
mandatory, *măn'dătărĭ,* s. mandatario, m.
mandrake, *măn'drăk,* s. (bot.) mandragola, f.
mane, *măn,* s. criniera, giuba, f.
man-eater, *măn'ĕtăr,* s. antropofago, m.
manful, *–fŭl,* a. bravo, coraggioso; **-ly** ad. valorosamente, bravamente.
mange, *mănj,* s. rogna, scabbia (di cane), f.; raspo, m.
manger, *măn'jăr,* s. mangiatoia, f.
mangle, *măng'gl,* s. mangano, m.; – v. a. manganare; stroppiare.
mangy, *măn'jĭ,* a. scabbioso, rognoso.
manhood, *măn'hŭd,* s. virilità, f.; coraggio, m.
mania, *mā'nĭă,* s. mania, pazzia, f.
maniac, *mā'nĭăk,* s. maniaco, pazzo, m.
maniac(al), *–(ăl),* a. maniaco, furioso.
manifest, *măn'ĭfĕst,* a. & s. evidente; manifesto (m.); –, v. a. manifestare.
manifestation, *–fĕstă'shŭn,* s. manifestazione, dimostrazione, f.
manifold, *măn'ĭfŏld,* a. parecchi, diversi.
manikin, *măn'ĭkĭn,* s. piccol uomo, nano, m.
manipulate, *mănĭp'ŭlăt,* v. a. manipolare.
manipulation, *–lă'shŭn,* s. manipolazione, f.
mankind, *măn'kĭnd,* s. genere umano, m.
manlike, *–lĭk,* a. degno d'un uomo, umano; valente.
manliness, *–lĭnĕs,* s. aspetto maschile, m., maschiezza, f.; coraggio, m.
manly, *–lĭ,* a. maschio; nobile; grande.
manner, *măn'năr,* s. maniera, f.; forma, foggia, guisa, f.; specie, sorta, f.; modo, m.; **-s,** pl. civiltà, buona creanza, f.
mannerly, *–lĭ,* a. manieroso; –, ad. con politezza.
manœuvre, *măn'ŏ'văr,* s. manovra, f.; maneggio, m.; –, v. a. manovrare.
manor, *măn'ăr,* s. castello, m.; signoria, f.
manorial, *mănŏ'rĭăl,* a. signorile, signoresco. [f.; stanza, f.
mansion, *măn'shŭn,* s. dimora, abitazione,
mansion-house, *–hŏŭs,* s. villa del padrone, f. [m.
manslaughter, *măn'slătăr,* s. omicidio,
mantle, *măn'tl,* s. mantello, manto, m.; –, v. a. coprire. [f.
mantle-piece, *–pēs,* s. cappa di camino,
manual, *măn'ăl,* a. & s. manuale (m.); libretto, m. [fabbrica, f.
manufactory, *–făk'tărĭ,* s. manifattura,
manufacture, *–făk'tŭr,* s. opera di manifattore, f.; –, v. a. fabbricare.
manufacturer, *–ăr,* s. manifattore, fabbricatore, m.
manumission, *–mĭsh'ŭn,* s. manomissione, liberazione da servitù, manomissione, f.
manure, *mănŭr',* s. letame, concime, m.; –, v. a. ingrassare, concimare. [m.
manuscript, *măn'ŭskrĭpt,* s. manoscritto,
many, *mĕn'ĭ,* a. molti, gran numero di; –

times, molte volte; **how –,** quanto; **as – as,** tanto che.
map, *măp,* s. carta geografica, f.; **– of the world,** mappamondo, m.; –, v. a. delineare, schizzare.
maple, *mā'pl,* s. acero, m.
mar, *măr,* v. a. guastare; corrompere.
marauder, *mără'dăr,* s. predatore, m.
marble, *măr'bl,* s. –, a. marmoreo; –, v. a. marmorizzare.
march, *mărch,* s. marca, m.; marcia, f.; –, v. n. marciare; avanzare.
March, –, s. marzo, m.
marchioness, *măr'shŏnĕs,* s. marchesa, f.
mare, *măr,* s. cavalla, giumenta, f.
margin, *măr'jĭn,* s. margine, f.; orlo, m.; –, v. a. immarginare, scrivere in margine.
marginal, *–năl,* a. marginale.
marigold, *măr'ĭgŏld,* s. fiorrancio, m.
marine, *mărēn',* s. marina, f.; soldato di marina, m.; –, a. marinaresco, di mare.
mariner, *măr'ĭnăr,* s. marinaio, m.; soldato di marina, m.
marital, *măr'ĭtăl,* a. maritale, coniugale.
maritime, *măr'ĭtĭm,* a. marittimo, marino.
marjoram, *măr'jŏrăm,* s. maiorana, f.
mar-joy, *măr'jŏĭ,* s. guastafeste, m.
mark, *mărk,* s. marco, segno, m.; bersaglio, m.; nota, f.; –, v. a. marcare; –, v. n. osservare.
marker, *–ăr,* s. marcatore, m.
market, *măr'kĕt,* s. marcato, m.; piazza del mercato, f.; prezzo, m. [dizionato.
marketable, *–ăbl,* a. vendibile, ben condizionato.
marksman, *mărks'măn,* s. tiratore; cacciatore, m. [cimare colla marna.
marl, *mărl,* s. marna, f.; –, v. a. con-
marl-pit, *–pĭt,* s. cava di marna, f.
marly, *măr'lĭ,* a. pieno di marna.
marmalade, *măr'mălăd,* s. conserva, confettura, f. [scimia, f.; mascherone, m.
marmoset, *măr'mŏzĕt,* s. bertuccione, m.;
marmot, *măr'mŏt,* s. marmotta, f.
maroon, *mărŏn',* s. marrone, m.
mar-plot, *măr'plŏt,* s. uomo turbolento, m. [f.
marquee, *mărkē',* s. tenda d'un ufficiale,
marquesa, *măr'kwĕs,* s. marchesa, f.
marquetry, *măr'kĕtrĭ,* s. tarsia, intarsiatura, f.
marquis, *măr'kwĭs,* s. marchese, m.
marquisate, *măr'kwĭzăt,* s. marchesato, m. [nozze, f. pl.
marriage, *măr'rĭj,* s. matrimonio, m.;
marriageable, *–ăbl,* a. nubile; da marito.
marriage-articles, *–ărtĭklz,* (**–settlement**), s. contratto di matrimonio, m.
married, *măr'rĭd,* a. maritato, coniugale.
marrow, *măr'rŏ,* s. midolla, f.
marrowy, *–rŏĭ,* a. midolloso; pastoso.
marry, *măr'rĭ,* v. a. maritare, sposare; –, v. n. maritarsi.
marsh, *mărsh,* s. palude, pantano, m.
marshal, *măr'shăl,* s. maresciallo, m.
marshy, *–shĭ,* a. paludoso.
mart, *mărt,* s. fiera, f., traffico, m.
marten, *măr'tĕn,* s. martora, f. (animale)

martial, *mȧr'shȧl,* a. marziale; guerresco; - law, s. codice marziale, m.

Martinmas, *mȧr'tinmȧs,* s. festa di San Martino, f.

martyr, *mȧr'tȧr,* s. martire, m.

martyrdom, *–dȯm,* s. martirio, m.

marvel, *mȧr'vĕl,* s. meraviglia, f.; -, v. n. meravigliare.   [ad. meravigliosamente.

marvellous, *–lȧs,* a. meraviglioso; **-ly,**

masculine, *mȧs'kūlin,* a. mascolino; virile.

mash, *mȧsh,* s. mescolanza, mistura, f.; -, v. a. mescolare, mischiare; pestare.

mask, *mȧsk,* s. maschera, f.; mascherata, f.; pretesto, m.; -, v. a. mascherare; velare; -, y. n. mascherarsi.

masker, *–ȧr,* s. che porta la maschera, mascherato, m.

mason, *mȧ'sn,* s. muratore, m.

masonry, *–rī,* s. fabbrica, f.; struttura, f.

masquerade, *mȧskȧrād',* s. mascherata, f.   [m.; messa, f.

mass, *mȧs,* s. massa, f.; pezzo, m.; tutto,

massacre, *mȧs'sȧkȧr,* s. strage, uccisione, f.; -, v. a. fare strage, trucidare.

massive, *mȧs'sĭv,* a. massiccio, solido.

mast, *mȧst,* s. albero (di nave), m.; ghianda, f.; faggiuola, f.; -, v. a. alberare (un bastimento).

master, *mȧs'tȧr,* s. padrone, m.; maestro, m.; signore, m.; (mar.) capitano, m.; -, v. a. dominare, governare; rintuzzare, raffrenare.

master-hand, *–hȧnd,* s. mano maestra, f.

master-key, *–kĕ,* s. chiave maestra, f.

masterly, *–lĭ,* a. da maestro; fatto con arte; -, ad. da maestro.

masterpiece, *–pĕs,* s. capo d' opera, m.

mastership, *–shĭp,* s. maestria, f.; eccellenza, f.   [–tȧch, s. colpo da maestro, m.

master-stroke, *–strŏk,* **master-touch,**

mastery, *mȧs'tȧrĭ,* s. autorità, f.; superiorità, f.   [m.

mastiff, *mȧs'tĭf,* s. mastino, cane da pastore,

mat, *mȧt,* s. stoia, f.; materassa, f.; -, v. a. intrecciare.

match, *mȧch,* s. miccia, f., zolfanello, m.; partito, m.; matrimonio, m.; partita, f.; -, v. a. assortire; pareggiare, uguagliare; maritare; -, v. n. unirsi; esser conforme.

match-box, *–bŏks,* s. scatoletta di zolfanelli, f.   [pari.

matchless, *–lĕs,* a. impareggiabile, senza

matchmaker, *–mākȧr,* s. mezzano di matrimoni, m.

mate, *mȧt,* s. consorte, compagno, m., compagna, f.; assistente, m.; sottopadrone (d'un vascello), piloto, m.; -, v. a. pareggiare; sposare.   [materialmente.

material, *mȧtĕ'rĭȧl,* a. materiale; **-ly,** ad.

materialism, *–ĭzm,* s. materialismo, m.

maternal, *mȧtȧr'nȧl,* a. materno.

maternity, *–tȧr'nĭtĭ,* s. maternità, f.

mathematic(al), *mȧthĕmȧt'ĭk(ȧl),* a. matematico; **-ly,** ad. matematicamente.

mathematician, *–mȧtĭsh'ȧn,* s. matematico, m.   [tica, f.

mathematics, *–mȧt'ĭks,* s. pl. matema-

matins, *mȧt'ĭnz,* s. pl. orazioni del mattutino, f. pl.   [matricida, m.

matricide, *mȧt'rĭsĭd,* s. matricidio, m.;

matriculate, *mȧtrĭk'ŭlȧt,* v. a. registrare alla matricola.   [lare, m.

matriculation, *–kŭlȧ'shȧn,* s. matrico-

matrimonial, *–mȯ'nĭȧl,* a. matrimoniale, di matrimonio.   [connubio, m.

matrimony, *mȧt'rĭmȯnĭ,* s. matrimonio,

matron, *mȧ'trȯn,* s. matrona, f.

matronly, *–lĭ,* a. di matrona; autorevole per età.

matter, *mȧt'tȧr,* s. materia, sostanza, f.; cosa, f.; affare, soggetto, m.; importanza, f.; manoscritto, m.; **no -, it is no -,** non importa; **no such -,** non c' è tal cosa; **what is the -?** che c' è? -, v. n. importare.

matting, *mȧt'tĭng,* s. stoia, f.   [portare.

mattock, *mȧt'tȯk,* s. zappa, marra, f.

mattress, *mȧt'rĕs,* s. materassa, f.

mature, *mȧtūr',* a. maturo; digerito; -, v. a. maturare.

maturity, *–tū'rĭtĭ,* s. maturità, f.

maul, *mȧl,* v. a. tartassare; malmenare; battere.   [tore).

maul-stick, *–stĭk,* s. bacchetta (di, pit-

Maundy-Thursday, *mȧn'dĭthȧrzdȧ,* s. Giovedì santo, m.

mausoleum, *mȧsȯlē'ȧm,* s. mausoleo, m.

maw, *mȧ,* s. stomaco degli animali, m.; gozzo degli uccelli, m.   [vole.

mawkish, *mȧk'ĭsh,* a. nauseoso, stomache-

maxim, *mȧks'ĭm,* s. massima, f.; assioma, m.

may, *mȧ,* v. n. ir. potere; **-be,** forse.   [m.

May, -, s. maggio, m.

may-bug, *–bȧg,* s. bruco, m. (verme).

may-day, *–dȧ,* s. primo giorno di maggio, m.   [potestà, m.

mayor, *mȧ'ȧr,* s. supremo magistrato,

mayoralty, *–ȧltĭ,* s. dignità di potestà, f.

mayoress, *–ĕs,* s. moglie del potestà, f.

may-pole, *mȧ'pȯl,* s. maio, m.

maze, *mȧz,* s. laberinto, m.; perplessità, f.

mazy, *mȧ'zĭ,* a. confuso, imbrogliato.

me, *mĕ,* pn. me, mi.

mead, *mĕd,* s. idromele, m.

meadow, *mĕd'ȯ,* s. prato, m., prateria, f.

meagre, *mĕ'gȧr,* a. magro, smunto; **-ly,** ad. magramente.   [lenza, f.

meagreness, *–nĕs,* s. magrezza, maci-

meal, *mĕl,* s. pasto, m.; farina, f.

mealy, *mĕl'ĭ,* a. farinoso; insipido.

mean, *mĕn,* a. basso, vile, dispregevole; povero; mediocre; **in the - time or while,** frattanto, in questo mentre; -, s. mezzo, m.; espediente, m.; **-s,** pl. mezzo, m., maniera, f.; ricchezze, f. pl.; -, v. a. ir. intendere, proporsi; significare; far conto; -, v. n. ir. volere dire.   [rigiro, m.

meander, *mĕȧn'dȧr,* s. laberinto, m.; giro,

meaning, *mĕn'ĭng,* s. intenzione, f.; significazione, f.; sentimento, m.   [mente.

meanly, *–lĭ,* ad. mediocremente; povera-

meanness, *–nĕs,* s. mediocrità, f.; bassezza, f.; povertà, f.

measless, *mĕ'zlz,* s. pl. rosolia, f.

measurable, *mĕzh'ȧrȧbl,* a. misurabile; moderato.

measure, *mĕzh'ŭr*, s. misura, m.; (mus.) tempo, m., battuta, f.; –, v. a. misurare; aggiustare.
measurement, *–mĕnt*, s. misurazione, f.
measurer, *–ŭr*, s. misuratore, m.; – **of land**, agrimensore, m.
meat, *mēt*, s. carne, f.   [manifattore, m.
mechanic, *mĕkăn'ĭk*, s. meccanico, m.;
mechanical, *–ăl*, a. meccanico; vile; **–ly**, ad. in modo meccanico.
mechanician, *–nĭ'shăn*, s. meccanico, professore di meccanica, m.
mechanics, *–kăn'ĭks*, s. pl. meccanica, f.
mechanism, *mĕk'ănĭzm*, s. meccanismo, m., struttura, f.   [antica, f.
medal, *mĕd'ăl*, s. medaglia, f.; moneta
medallion, *mĕd'yŭn*, s. medaglione, m., medaglia grande, f.   [mettersi.
meddle, *mĕd'l*, v. n. mescolarsi, intromeddler, *–lăr*, s. mezzano, intermediario,
mediate, *mē'dĭăt*, v. n. tramezzare.   [m.
mediation, *–dĭd'shăn*, s. mediazione, interposizione, f.
mediator, *–dĭd'tăr*, s. mediatore, m.
medical, *mĕd'ĭkăl*, a. medico, medicinale.
medicament, *mĕd'ĭkăment*, s. medicamento, rimedio, m.
medicate, *mĕd'ĭkăt*, v. a. medicare.
medicinal, *–dĭs'ĭnăl*, a. medicinale, medico.   [dicamento, m.
medicine, *mĕd'ĭsn*, s. medicina, f.; me-
mediocrity, *mĕdĭŏk'rĭtĭ*, s. mediocrità, f.
meditate, *mĕd'ĭtăt*, v. n. meditare; considerare.   [contemplazione, f.
meditation, *–tă'shăn*, s. meditazione, f.;
meditative, *mĕd'ĭtătĭv*, a. meditativo; meditante.   [raneo.
Mediterranean, *–tĕrră'nĕăn*, a. mediterrmedium, *mē'dĭăm*, s. mezzo, espediente, m.; mediocrità, f.
medlar, *mĕd'lăr*, s. nespola, f. (frutto).
medley, *mĕd'lĭ*, s. mescolanza, f.; miscuglio, m.   [–ly, ad. piacevolmente.
meek, *mēk*, a. dolce; piacevole; placido;
meekness, *–nĕs*, s. dolcezza, f.; modestia, f.   [mare, f.
meerschaum, *mār'shăm*, s. spuma di
meet, *mēt*, v. a. ir. incontrare, adunare, trovare; –, v. n. ir. incontrarsi, adunarsi, trovarsi; –, a. proprio, acconcio.
meeting, *–ĭng*, s. incontro, m.; assemblea, conferenza, adunanza, f.   [mente.
meetly, *–lĭ*, ad. convenevolmente; propria-
melancholy, *mĕl'ăngkŏlĭ*, a. malinconico; –, s. malinconia, f.   [soave.
mellifluous, *mĕlĭf'lŭăs*, a. mellifluo;
mellow, *mĕl'lō*, a. maturo; tenero, molle; –, v. a. maturare; –, v. n. divenir maturo.
mellowness, *–nĕs*, s. maturità, f.
melodious, *mĕlō'dĭăs*, a. melodioso; **–ly**, ad. melodiosamente.
melody, *mĕl'ŏdĭ*, s. melodia, f.
melon, *mĕl'ŏn*, s. popone, ni.
melt, *mĕlt*, v. a. ir. fondere; liquefare; intenerire; –, v. n. ir. fondersi; liquefarsi; intenerirsi.

member, *mĕm'băr*, s. membro, m.; parte, f
membrane, *mĕm'brăn*, s. membrana, f.
memento, *mĕmĕn'tō*, s. ricordo, m.; ricordanza, f.
memoir, *mĕm'wŏr*, s. ricordo (di fatti storici), m., annotazione, f.
memorable, *mĕm'ŏrăbl*, a. memorabile.
memorably, *–răblĭ*, ad. degno di memoria.
memorandum, *–mŏrăn'dăm*, s. annotazione, f.; ricordo, m.
memorial, *–mŏ'rĭăl*, s. memoriale, m., memoria, f.; supplica, f.   [moriale.
memorialise, *–īz*, v. a. presentare un memory, *mĕm'ŏrĭ*, s. memoria, ricordanza, f.; ricordo, m.
menace, *mĕn'ăs*, s. minaccia, f.; –, v. a. minacciare.   [f.
menagerie, *–năj'ŭrĭ*, s. serraglio di bestie.
mend, *mĕnd*, v. a. racconciare, rappezzare, rammendare; migliorare, correggere.
mendacious, *–dā'shăs*, a. mendace.
mendacity, *–dăs'ĭtĭ*, s. menzogna, bugia, f.
mendicant, *mĕn'dĭkănt*, a. & s. mendicante (m.).
mendicate, *mĕn'dĭkăt*, v. n. mendicare.
mendicity, *–dĭs'ĭtĭ*, s. mendicità, f.
menial, *mē'nĭăl*, a. domestico; servile.
mensuration, *mĕnsŭră'shăn*, s. misurazione, f.   [–ly, ad. mentalmente.
mental, *mĕn'tăl*, a. di mente, intellettuale;
mention, *mĕn'shăn*, s. menzione, f.; –, v. a. menzionare, rammemorare.
Mentor, *mĕn'tŏr*, s. mentore, consigliere, m.; direttore, m.
mephitic, *mĕfĭt'ĭk*, a. mefitico.
mercantile, *mŭr'kăntĭl*, a. mercantile.
mercenary, *mŭr'sĕnărĭ*, a. & s. mercenario
mercer, *mŭr'săr*, s. merciaio, m.   [(m.).
mercery, *–sărĭ*, s. merceria, mercanzia a ritaglio, f.   [f.
merchandise, *mŭr'chăndīz*, s. mercanzia, merchant, *mŭr'chănt*, s. mercante, m.
merchant-man, *–măn*, s. vascello mercantile, m.
merciful, *mŭr'sĭfŭl*, a. compassionevole; **–ly**, ad. misericordiosamente.
merciless, *–lĕs*, a. inumano; **–ly**, ad. spietatamente.   [vace.
mercurial, *mŭrkū'rĭăl*, a. mercuriale; vi-
mercury, *mŭr'kŭrĭ*, s. argento vivo, m.
mercy, *mŭr'sĭ*, s. misericordia, f.; perdono, m.   [mente, semplicemente.
mere, *mēr*, a. mero, puro; **–ly**, ad. sola-
meretricious, *mĕrĕtrĭsh'ăs*, a. meretricio, di meretrice.
merge, *mŭrj*, v. a. mergere.
meridian, *mĕrĭd'ĭăn*, s. meridiano, m.; mezzodì, m.
meridional, *–ĭŏnăl*, a. meridionale.
merit, *mĕr'ĭt*, s. merito, m.; –, v. a. meritare.   [ad. meritevolmente.
meritorious, *–tŏ'rĭăs*, a. meritevole; **–ly**,
mermaid, *mŭr'mād*, s. sirena, f.
merrily, *mĕr'rĭlĭ*, ad. gaiamente.
merriment, *mĕr'rĭment*, s. divertimento, festeggiamento, m.
merry, *mĕr'rĭ*, a. giocondo, gioioso, gaio.

mesh, *měsh*, s. maglia, f.　　　[animale, m.
mesmerism, *měs'mărĭzm*, s. magnetismo
mess, *měs*, s. vivanda, f., piatto, m.
message, *měs'ědj*, s. messaggio, m.
messenger, *měs'sěnjăr*, s. messaggiere;
　messaggio, m.　　　　　　　　[merata, m.
mess-mate, *měs'māt*, s. commensale, ca-
messuage, *měs'swdj*, s. podere affittato,
　m.; villa, f.　　　　　　　　　[spirito, m.
metal, *mět'ăl* (*mět'l*), s. metallo, m.; (fig.)
metallic, *-tăl'lĭk*, a. metallico, di metallo.
metallurgy, *mět'ălŭrjĭ*, s. metallurgia, f.
metamorphose, *mětămŏr'fōs*, v. a. tras-
　formare.　　　　　　　　[transformazione, f.
metamorphosis, *-fōsĭs*, s. metamorfosi,
metaphor, *mět'ăfŏr*, s. metafora, f.
metaphoric(al), *-fŏr'ĭk(ăl)*, a. metaforico.
metaphysic(al), *-fĭz'ĭk(ăl)*, a. metafisico.
metaphysics, *-fĭz'ĭks*, s. pl. metafisica, f.
mete, *mět*, v. a. misurare.
meteor, *mē'tĕăr*, s. meteora, f.　[rologico.
meteorological, *mētĕŏrŏlŏj'ĭkăl*, a. meteo-
meteorology, *-ŏl'ŏjĭ*, s. meteorologia, f.
meter, *mē'tăr*, s. misuratore, m.　[penso.
methinks, *měthĭngks'*, v. imp. mi pare, io
method, *měth'ŏd*, s. metodo, m.; maniera, f.
methodic(al), *-thŏd'ĭk(ăl)*, a. metodico;
　-ly, ad. metodicamente.　　　　[versi), f.
metre, *mē'tăr*, s. metro, m.; misura (di
metrical, *mět'rĭkăl*, a. metrico.
metropolis, *mětrŏp'ŏlĭs*, s. metropoli, ca-
　pitale, f.　　　　　　　　　　　[tano, f.
metropolitan, *-pŏl'ĭtăn*, m. metropoli-
mettle, *mět'l*, s. vivacità, foga, f., spirito,
　coraggio, m.　　　　　　　[vivace, spiritoso.
mettled, *mět'ld*, **mettlesome**, *-lsŭm*, a.
mew, *mū*, s. gabbia, f.; **-s**, pl. stalle
　(di cavalli), f. pl.　　　　　　　　[m.
microscope, *mī'krŏskŏp*, s. microscopio,
microscopic(al), *-skŏp'ĭk(ăl)*, a. micro-
　scopico.
mid, *mĭd*, a. mezzo; ugualmente distante.
mid-course, *-kōrs*, s. mezza via, mezza
　strada, f.
midday, *-dă*, s. mezzogiorno, m.
middle, *mĭd'dl*, a. mezzo, mezzano; me-
　diocre; — s. mezzo, centro, m.; cuore, m.
middling, *-dlĭng*, a. mediocre; mezzano.
midland, *-lănd*, a. mediterraneo.
midnight, *-nĭt*, s. mezzanotte, f.
midshipman, *-shĭpmăn*, s. sottotenente
　di nave, m.　　　　　　　　　　　[m.
midst, *mĭdst*, s. mezzo, centro, m.; cuore,
midsummer, *mĭd'sămmăr*, s. mezzo della
　state, m.; festa di San Giovanni, f.
midway, *-wā*, a. & ad. nel mezzo cam-
　mino; — s. mezza strada, f., mezzo cam-
midwife, *-wĭf*, s. levatrice, f.　　[mino, m.
midwifery, *-wĭfrĭ*, s. mestiere di levatrice,
mien, *mēn*, s. aria, cera, f.　　　　　[m.
might, *mĭt*, s. potere, m., potenza, forza, f.
mightily, *-lĭ*, ad. con forza; molto.
mightiness, *-tněs*, s. potenza, possanza,
　f., potere, m.
mighty, *mĭt'ĭ*, a. potente; forte.
mignonette, *mĭn'yŏnět*, s. merletto,
　pizzo m.
migrate, *mĭ'grăt*, v. n. migrare.

migration, *-grā'shăn*, s. migrazione, f.,
　dipartenza, f.　　　　　　　　　　[seggiere.
migratory, *mĭ'grătărĭ*, a. transitorio; pas-
milch, *mĭlch*, a. lattante; lattifero.
mild, *mĭld*, a. dolce; piacevole; moderato;
　indulgente; **-ly**, ad. dolcemente.
mildew, *mĭl'dū*, s. nebbia, f.; golpe, f.,
　carbone, m.　　　　　　　　　　[menza, f.
mildness, *mĭld'něs*, s. dolcezza, f.; cle-
mile, *mĭl*, s. miglio, m.
mileage, *mĭl'dj*, s. prezzo per miglio, m.
mile-stone, *-stŏn*, s. pietra milliare, f.
milfoil, *mĭl'fŏĭl*, s. (bot.) millefoglie, f.
militant, *mĭl'ĭtănt*, a. militante.
military, *mĭl'ĭtărĭ*, a. militare.
militate, *mĭl'ĭtăt*, v. n. combattere.
militia, *mĭlĭsh'ă*, s. milizia, f.; soldati na-
　zionali, m. pl.　　　　　　　　　　[latte.
milk, *mĭlk*, s. latte, m.; —, v. a. trarre il
milkmaid, *-mād*, s. levatrice, f.
milksop, *-sŏp*, s. uomo da nulla, m.
milky, *mĭlk'ĭ*, a. lattifero, latteo; **-way**,
　s. via lattea, f.
mill, *mĭl*, s. mulino, m.; filatura, f.; moli-
　nello, m.; —, v. a. macinare; stampare.
mill-dam, *-dăm*, s. cateratta, chiusa d'un
　mulino, f.　　　　　　　　　　　　[pl.
millennium, *mĭllěn'nĭăm*, s. mille anni, m.
miller, *mĭl'ăr*, s. mugnaio, m.
millet, *mĭl'lět*, s. miglio, m.
mill-hopper, *mĭl'hŏppăr*, s. tramoggia, f.
milliner, *mĭl'lĭnăr*, s. merciaia, f.; mo-
　dista, f.
millinery, *-ărĭ*, s. articoli di moda, m. pl.
million, *mĭl'yăn*, s. milione, m.; **the -**,
　volgo, m.
millionaire, *-yănăr*, s. milionario, m.
millionth, *-yănth*, a. milionesimo.
mill-stone, *mĭl'stŏn*, s. macina, f.　[f.
mime, *mĭm*, s. mimo, buffone, m.; mima,
mimic, *mĭm'ĭk*, v. a. contraffare; imitare.
mimicry, *-ĭkrĭ*, s. imitazione burlesca, f.;
　buffoneria, f.
mince, *mĭns*, v. a. tritare, sminuzzare;
　—, v. n. parlare con affettazione.
mincingly, *mĭn'sĭnglĭ*, ad. in piccole
　parti; affettatamente.
mind, *mĭnd*, s. mente, f., intelletto, m.;
　animo, m.; pensiero, m.; voglia, brama,
　f.; affetto, m.; —, v. a. notare; considerare;
　osservare, riflettere; —, v. n. disegnare;
　applicarsi; proporsi.
minded, *-ěd*, a. inclinato, disposto.
mindful, *-fŭl*, a. attento; diligente; **-ly**,
　ad. attentamente.　　　　　　[negligente.
mindless, *-lěs*, a. disattento, trascurato,
mine, *mĭn*, pn. mio, mia; miei; —, s. mina,
　miniera, f.; —, v. a. scavare, minare, fare
miner, *mĭ'năr*, s. minatore, m.　　[mine.
mineral, *mĭn'ărăl*, a. & s. minerale (m.);
　-spring, sorgente d' acque minerali, f.
mineralogy, *-răl'ŏjĭ*, s. mineralogia, f.
mingle, *mĭng'gl*, v. a. mescolare, mischiare.
miniature, *mĭn'ĭtŭr*, s. miniatura, f.
minim, *mĭn'ĭm*, s. nano, m.; nana, f.
minimise, *mĭn'ĭmĭz*, v. a. sminuire; sce-
　mare.

minimum, *mĭn'ĭmŭm,* s. un minimo, m.

mining, *mīn'ĭng,* s. scavo delle miniere, m.

mining-share, *-shâr,* s. parte che ha alcuno in una miniera, f.

minion, *mĭn'yŭn,* s. mignone, favorito, m.

minister, *mĭn'ĭstâr,* s. ministro, m.; —, v. a. ministrare; somministrare; servire; contribuire.

ministerial, *-tē'rĭăl,* a. ministeriale.

ministration, *-trâ'shăn,* s. amministrazione, f.; ministero, m.

ministry, *mĭn'ĭstrĭ,* s. ministerio, m.; ministri di Stato, m. pl.

minnow, *mĭn'nō,* s. specie di ghiozzo, m.

minor, *mī'nŭr,* a. minore; piccolo; —, s. minore, m.

minority, *mĭnôr'ĭtĭ,* s. minorità, f.; stato di pubertà, m.

minster, *mĭn'stŭr,* s. chiesa cattedrale, f.

minstrel, *mĭn'strĕl,* s. trovatore menestrello, m.; strimpellatore di violino, m.

mint, *mĭnt,* s. (bot.) menta, f.; moneta, f.; zecca, f.; —, v. a. monetare, battere la moneta, coniare.

mintage, *-âj,* s. monetaggio, m.; conio, m.

minuet, *mĭn'ūĕt,* s. minuetto, m.

minus, *mī'nŭs,* ad. meno.

minute, *mĭnūt',* a. minuto, piccolissimo; -ly, ad. esattamente.   [istante, m.

minute, *mĭn'ĭt,* s. minuto, m.; momento, m.

minute-book, *-bŭk,* s. giornale, m.

minuteness, *mĭnūt'nĕs,* s. minutezza, esiguità, f.

minutiæ, *-nū'shĭē,* s. cosa da nulla, f.

minx, *mĭngks,* s. vanarella, civettola, sfacciatella, f.   [viglia, f.

miracle, *mĭr'ăkl,* s. miracolo m., meraviglia, f.

miraculous, *-răk'dlŭs,* a. miracoloso; -ly, ad. miracolosamente.

mirage, *mĭ'râj (mĭrăzh'),* s. miraggio, m.

mire, *mīr,* s. fango, limo, m., melma, f.

mirky, *mŭr'kĭ,* a. tenebroso, oscuro.

mirkiness, *-nĕs,* s. tenebre, f. pl.; oscurità, f.

mirror, *mĭr'rŭr,* s. specchio, m.   [f.

mirth, *mŭrth,* s. gioia, allegria, f.

mirthful, *-fŭl,* a. gioioso, allegro.

miry, *mī'rĭ,* a. fangoso, melmoso, lotoso.

misadventure, *mĭsădvĕn'tŭr,* s. disavventura, f., infortunio, m.

misalliance, *-ăllī'ăns,* s. matrimonio di non pari condizione, m.   [m.

misanthrope, *mĭs'ănthrŏp,* s. misantropo, f.

misanthropy, *-ăn'thrŏpĭ,* s. misantropia, f.   [applicazione, f.

misapplication, *-ăpplĭkâ'shăn,* s. cattiva

misapply, *-ăpplī',* v. a. applicare male.

misapprehend, *-ăpprēhĕnd',* v. a. intendere male, non intendere.

misapprehension, *-hĕn'shăn,* s. errore, m.; sbaglio, m.   [male.

misbehave, *-bēhâv',* v. n. ir. condursi male.

misbehaviour, *-hâv'yŭr,* s. cattiva condotta, f.   [credenza, f.

misbelief, *-bēlēf',* s. miscredenza, mala credenza, f.

misbeliever, *-lē'vŭr,* s. miscredente, m.; infedele, m.

miscalculate, *-kăl'kŭlât,* v. a. calcolare male, computare male.

miscarriage, *-kăr'rĭj,* s. cattiva condotta, f.; cattivo successo, m.; aborto, m.

miscarry, *-kăr'rĭ,* v. n. fallire; abortire; smarrirsi.   [neo.

miscellaneous, *-sĕllâ'nĕŭs,* a. miscellaneo.

miscellany, *mĭs'sĕllănĭ (-sĕl'lănĭ),* s. miscellanea, f.   [tunio, m.

mischance, *-chăns',* s. sventura, f., infortunio, m.

mischief, *mĭs'chĭf,* s. male, m.; danno, m.; infortunio, m.   [male, m.

mischief-maker, *-mâkŭr,* s. commettimale, m.

mischievous, *-chĭvŭs,* a. nocivo, maligno, malizioso; -ly, ad. maliziosamente.

misconceive, *-kŏnsēv',* v. a. intendere male.   [falsa, f.

misconception, *-sĕp'shăn,* s. nozione falsa, f.

misconduct, *-kŏn'dŭkt,* s. cattiva condotta, f.; —, *-dŭkt',* v. a. mal condurre.

misconstruction, *-kŏnstrŭk'shăn,* s. falsa costruzione, f.; cattiva interpretazione, f.   [male.

misconstrue, *-kŏn'strŏ,* v. a. interpretare male.

miscount, *-kŏŭnt',* v. a. calcolare male, contare male.   [fedele, m.

miscreant, *mĭs'krĕănt,* s. miscredente, inmine, m.   [dotta, f.; misfatto, m.

misdeed, *-dēd',* s. misfatto, delitto, crimine, m.

misdemeanour, *-dēmēn'ăr,* s. cattiva condotta, f.; —, *-dăkt',* v. a. mal condurre.

misdirect, *-dĭrĕkt',* v. a. dirigere male.

misdoubt, *-dŏŭt',* v. a. sospettare; diffidare.   [borcio, m.

miser, *mī'zŭr,* s. misero, m.; avaro, spilorcio, m.

miserable, *mĭz'ărăbl,* a. miserabile, meschino; infelice; avaro.   [avaramente.

miserably, *-ăblĭ,* ad. miserabilmente.

miserly, *mī'zŭrlĭ,* a. avaro, da avaro.

misery, *mĭz'ĕrĭ,* s. miseria, f.; indigenza, f.; calamità, f.   [ecc.

misfit, *mĭsfĭt',* s. lo star male di un abito, m.

misfortune, *-fŏr'tŭn,* s. infortunio, m., calamità, f.   [sentire; temere.

misgive, *-gĭv',* v. a. ir. mal presagire, presentimento, m.   [male.

misgiving, *-gĭv'ĭng,* s. sospetto, m.; presentimento, m.

misgovern, *-gŭv'ărn,* v. a. governare male.

misguide, *-gīd',* v. a. guidare male.

mishap, *-hăp',* s. sinistro accidente, m., fatalità, f.   [roneo.

misinform, *-ĭnfŏrm',* v. a. dare avviso erroneo.

misinterpret, *-ĭntâr'prĕt,* v. a. interpretare male.   [falsamente.

misjudge, *-jŭj',* v. a. giudicare male o male.

mislay, *-lâ',* v. a. ir. smarrire; rimuovere.

mislead, *-lēd',* v. a. ir. sviare, traviare; sedurre.   [governare male.

mismanage, *-măn'âj,* v. a. maneggiare o mismanage male.

mismanagement, *-măn'âjmĕnt,* s. cattivo maneggio, m.   [mente.

misname, *-nâm',* v. a. nominare impropriamente.

misnomer, *-nō'mŭr,* s. accusa fatta sotto falso nome, f.   [donne, m.

misogynist, *mĭsŏg'ĭnĭst,* s. odiatore delle donne, m.

misplace, *-plâs',* v. a. slogare, rimuovere; scansare.

misprint, *-prĭnt',* s. errore di stampa, m.; —, v. a. fare errori nella stampa.

misquotation, *-kwōtâ'shăn,* s. citazione falsa, f.

misquote, *–kwŏt'*, v. a. citare falsamente.
misreckon, *–rĕk'n*, v. a. contare male.
misrepresent, *–rĕprĕzĕnt'*, v. a. rappresentare male. [lazione, f.
misrepresentation, *–tă'shŭn*, s. falsa relazione, f.
misrule, *–rōl'*, s. tumulto, m.; confusione, f.
miss, *mĭs*, s. damigella, signorina, f.; sbaglio, errore, fallo, m.; –, v. ₥. mancare; omettere, perdere; –, v. n. errare, abbagliarsi.
missal, *mĭs'săl*, s. missale, m. [gliarsi.
misshape, *mĭsshăp'*, v. a. difformare; disfigurare.
missile, *mĭs'sĭl*, s. proiettile, m.
missing, *mĭs'sĭng*, a. perduto.
mission, *mĭsh'ŭn*, s. missione, f.; ambasciata, f.
missionary, *–ărĭ*, s. missionario, m.
missive, *mĭs'sĭv*, a. missivo; –, s. lettera, epistola, f. [falso, m.
misstatement, *mĭsstăt'mĕnt*, s. rapporto falso, m.
mist, *mĭst*, s. nebbia, f.
mistake, *mĭstăk'*, v. a. ir. non intendere, non comprendere; –, v. n. ir. sbagliare; ingannarsi. [chiamare ,,signore''.
mister, *mĭs'tăr*, s. signore, m.; –, v. a.
mistiness, *mĭs'tĭnĕs*, s. nebbia, oscurità, f.
mistletoe, *mĭz'ltŏ*, s. vischio, m., pania, f.
mistress, *mĭs'trĕs*, s. padrona, f.; innamorata, f.; –, (*mĭs'sĭs*), signora, f.
mistrust, *mĭstrŭst'*, v. a. diffidare; sospettare; –, s. diffidenza, f.
mistrustful, *–fŭl*, a. diffidente; sospettoso.
misty, *mĭst'ĭ*, a. nebbioso; oscuro.
misunderstand, *mĭsŭndărstănd'*, v. a. ir. intendere male. [m.; villania, f.
misusage, *–ā'zdj*, s. cattivo uso, abuso.
misuse, *–ăz*, s. abuso, m.; –, v. a. abusare.
mite, *mīt*, s. tonchio (insetto), m.; ventesima parte d' un grano, f. [cire.
mitigate, *mĭt'ĭgāt*, v. a. mitigare; raddolcire.
mitigation, *–gā'shŭn*, s. mitigazione, f.
mitre, *mī'tăr*, s. mitra, f.
mittens, *mĭt'ns*, s. pl. guanti senza dita, mezzi guanti, m. pl.
mix, *mĭks*, v. a. mischiare, mescolare.
mixture, *mĭks'tăr (–chŭr)*, s. mescolanza, mistura, f.
mizzen, *mĭz'n*, s. (mar.) mezzana, f.
mizzle, *mĭz'l*, v. n. piovigginare, spruzzolare.
moan, *mōn*, v. a. piangere, gemere; –, v. n. dolersi; –, s. pianto, lamento, m.
moanful, *–fŭl*, a. lamentevole; –ly, ad. lamentevolmente.
moat, *mŏt*, s. canale d' acqua per difesa, m.; –, v. a. far un canale d' acqua per difesa.
mob, *mŏb*, s. folla, turba, f.; canaglia, f.; –, v. a. tumultuare.
mobilise, *mŏb'ŭlīz*, v. a. mobilizzare.
mobility, *mŏbĭl'ĭtĭ*, s. mobilità, f.; plebaglia, f.
mock, *mŏk*, a. falso, contraffatto; –, s. derisione, f.; beffa, f., ludibrio, m.; –, v. a. & n. burlare, beffare, deridere.
mockery, *–ărĭ*, s. scherno, m.; burla, f.
mocking-bird, *–ĭng bărd*, s. uccello imitatore, m.

mode, *mōd*, s. modo, m.; costume, m.; moda, f.; forma, f.; maniera, f.
model, *mŏd'ĕl*, s. modello, m.; –, v. ₤. modellare; formare. [tore, m.
modeller, *–lăr*, s. modellatore m.; inventore, m.
moderate, *mŏd'ărāt*, a. moderato · mediocre; –ly, ad. moderatamente; –, v. a. moderare.
moderation, *–rā'shŭn*, s. moderazione, f.
modern, *mŏd'ărn*, a. moderno, recente.
modernise, *mŏd'ărnĭz*, v. a. rimodernare.
modest, *mŏd'ĕst*, a. modesto.
modesty, *–ĕstĭ*, s. modestia, f.; decenza, onestà, f. [zione, f.
modification, *–ĭfĭkā'shŭn*, s. modificazione, f.
modify, *mŏd'ĭfĭ*, v. a. modificare.
modishness, *mō'dĭshnĕs*, s. affettazione di seguire la moda, f. [lare.
modulate, *mŏd'ŭlāt*, v. a. (mus.) modulare.
modulation, *–lā'shŭn*, s. (mus.) modulazione, f. [mello, m.
mohair, *mō'hăr*, s. panno di peli di camoiety, *mŏi'ĕtĭ*, s. metà, f.; mezzo, m.
moist, *mŏĭst*, a. umido.
moisten, *mŏĭ'sn*, v. a. umettare.
moisture, *mŏĭs'tăr*, s. umidità, f.; succo (delle piante), m.; umore, m.
molar, *mŏ'lăr*, a. mascellare.
mole, *mōl*, s. mola, f.; talpa, f.; molo, m.
mole-hill, *–hĭl*, s. topinaia, f. [tare.
molest, *mŏlĕst'*, v. a. moiestare; tormentare.
molestation, *–tā'shŭn*, s. molestamento, m.; fastidio, m. [lire.
mollify, *mŏl'ĭfĭ*, v. a. mollificare, ammollire.
mollusk, *mŏl'lŭsk*, s. mollusco, m.
molten, *mŏl'tn*, a. fuso. [tanza, f.
moment, *mŏ'mĕnt*, s. momento, m.; importanza, f.
momentarily, *–tărĭlĭ*, ad. momentaneamente.
momentary, *–tărĭ*, a. momentaneo.
momentous, *–mĕn'tŭs*, a. importante.
momentum, *–mĕn'tŭm*, s. impeto, m.
monarch, *mŏn'ărk*, s. monarca, m.
monarchic(al), *–ăr'kĭk(ăl)*, a. monarchico.
monarchy, *mŏn'ărkĭ*, s. monarchia, f.
monastery, *mŏn'ăstărĭ*, s. monastero, convento, m. [naco.
monastic, *–năs'tĭk*, a. monastico, da monaco.
Monday, *mŭn'dă*, s. lunedì, f.
monetary, *mŏn'ĕtărĭ*, a. monetario.
money, *mŭn'ĭ*, s. moneta, f., danaro, m.; **ready –, – in hand**, danari contanti, m. pl. [tanti.
moneyed, *–ĭd*, a. danaroso, ricco di contanti.
monger, *mŭng'găr*, s. mercante, venditore, merciaiuolo, m. [spezie.
mongrel, *mŭng'grĕl*, a. generato fra due monition, *mŏnĭsh'ŭn*, s. avvertimento, m.
monitor, *mŏn'ĭtăr*, s. ammonitore, m.; (mar.) monitore, m.
monitory, *–tărĭ*, a. monitorio.
monk, *mŭngk*, s. monaco, m.
monkery, *–ărĭ*, s. monacato, m. [buino, m.
monkey, *mŭng'kĭ*, s. scimmia, f., babmonkish**, *mŭng'kĭsh*, a. monastico, monacale. [niaco, m.
monomaniac, *mŏnŏmă'nĭăk*, s. monoma-

monopolise, –*nŏp'ŏlĭz*, v. a. far monopolio, incettare.
monopolist, –*nŏp'ŏlĭst*, s. monopolista, m.; incettatore, m.
monopoly, –*nŏp'ŏlĭ*, s. monopolio, m.
monosyllabic(al), –*nŏsĭllăb'ĭk(ăl)*, a. monosillabo. [m., monosillaba, f.
monosyllable, –*sĭl'lăbl*, s. monosillabo, m.
monotonous, –*nŏt'ŏnŭs*, a. monotono.
monotony, –*nŏt'ŏnĭ*, s. monotonia, f.
monsoon, *mŏnsōn'*, s. monsone, m.
monster, *mŏn'stăr*, s. mostro, m.
monstrosity, –*strŏs'ĭtĭ*, s. mostruosità, f.
monstrous, *mŏn'strŭs*, a. mostruoso; –ly, ad. mostruosamente.
month, *mŭnth*, s. mese, m.
monthly, –*lĭ*, a. & ad. d' ogni mese, mensuale; una volta il mese, di mese in mese.
monument, *mŏn'ûment*, s. monumento, m.
monumental, –*mĕn'tăl*, a. di monumento, monumentale. [m.
mood, *mōd*, s. modo, m.; umore, capriccio,
moodiness, –*ĭnĕs*, s. cattivo umore, m.
moody, *mōd'ĭ*, a. capriccioso.
moon, *mōn*, s. luna, f.; mese, m. [m.
moon-beam, –*bēm*, s. raggio della luna,
moon-light, –*lĭt*, s. lume di luna, m.
moon-shine, –*shĭn*, s. chiarezza della luna, f.; illusione, f.
moon-struck, –*strŭk*, a. lunatico, pazzo.
moor, *mōr*, s. palude, pantano, m.; moro, m.; –, v. a. (mar.) gettare l' ancora; dare
moorish, *mōr'ĭsh*, a. moresco. [fondo.
moot, *mōt*, v. a. contendere; –, s. controversia, quistione giuridica, f.; –, a. litigioso.
mop, *mŏp*, s. spazzatoio, m.; –, v. a. spazzare; nettare il solaio.
mope, *mōp*, v. n. annoiarsi.
moral, *mŏr'ăl*, a. morale; –ly, ad. moralmente; –, s. dottrina morale, f.; –s, s. pl. buoni costumi, m. pl.
moralise, *mŏr'ălĭz*, v. n. moralizzare.
moralist, –*ălĭst*, s. moralista, m.
morality, *mŏrăl'ĭtĭ*, s. moralità, f.; senso morale, m. [tano, m.
morass, *mŏrăs'*, s. palude, m. & f.; panmorbid, *mŏr'bĭd*, a. malaticcio.
more, *mŏr*, s. & ad. più; maggiore, in maggior numero; – and –, di più in più; once –, ancora una volta; so much the –, tanto più. [ciò, oltre a questo.
moreover, –*ŏ'văr*, ad. & c. di più, oltre a
morning, *mŏrn'ĭng*, s. mattina, f.; good –, buon giorno. [f.
morning-gown, –*gŏn*, s. veste da camera,
morning-star, –*stăr*, s. stella mattutina, f., Lucifero, m. [marrochino, m.
morocco-leather, *mŏrŏk'kŏ lĕthăr*, s.
morose, *mŏrōs'*, a. stizzoso, fastidioso; –ly, ad. stegnosamente.
morrow, *mŏr'rō*, s. domane, m.
morse, *mŏrs*, s. cavallo marino, m. [m.
morsel, *mŏr'sĕl*, s. pezzo, boccone, tozzo,
mortal, *mŏr'tăl*, a. mortale; –, s. uomo, m.; –ly, ad. mortalmente.
mortality, *mŏrtăl'ĭtĭ*, s. mortalità, f.
mortar, *mŏr'tăr*, s. mortaio, m.
mortgage, *mŏr'găj*, s. ipoteca (di beni immobili), f.; –, v. a. ipotecare.

mortgagee, –*găjē'*, s. che ha un' ipoteca.
mortgager, –*găjŭr*, s. che ipoteca i suoi poderi.
mortification, *mŏrtĭfĭkă'shŭn*, s. mortificazione, f.; cancrena, f.
mortify, *mŏr'tĭfĭ*, v. a. mortificare; umiliare; –, v. n. umiliarsi.
mortmain, *mŏrt'măn*, s. (jur.) mano morta, f., beni inalienabili, m. pl.
mortuary, *mŏr'tŭărĭ*, s. sepolcro, m.; –, a. sepolcrale; mortuario.
mosaic, *mŏză'ĭk*, a. mosaico.
mosque, *mŏsk*, s. moschea, f.
mosquito, *mŏskē'tō*, s. zanzara, f.
moss, *mŏs*, s. muschio, musco, m.
mossy, *mŏs'ĭ*, a. muscoso.
most, *mŏst*, a. & ad. il più, la più, i più, le più; molto; –, s. maggior parte, f.; –ly, ad. ordinariamente, per lo più.
mote, *mōt*, s. atomo, m., particella, f.
moth, *mŏth*, s. tignuola, f., tarlo, m.
mother, *mŭth'ŭr*, s. madre, f.; matrice, f.; feccia, f.: – of pearl, madreperla, f.
motherhood, –*hŭd*, s. maternità, f.
mother-in-law, –*ĭn lă'*, s. suocera, f.; matrigna, f.
motherless, –*lĕs*, a. che non ha madre.
motherly, –*lĭ*, a. materno, di madre.
motion, *mō'shŭn*, s. movimento, moto, m.; proposizione, f.; –, v. a. far una proposizione. [bile.
motionless, –*lĕs*, a. senza moto, immomotive, *mō'tĭv*, a. & s. motivo (m.).
motley, *mŏt'lĭ*, mottled, –*tld*, a. variato, di più colori.
motto, *mŏt'tō*, s. motto, m.
mould, *mōld*, s. forma, f., modello, m.; terra, f.; muffa, f.; –, v. a. formare, modellare; gettare in un modello; –, v. n. muffare.
moulder, –*ŭr*, s. fonditore, m.; –, v. a. & n. ridurre in polvere; ridursi in polvere.
mouldiness, –*ĭnĕs*, s. muffa, f. [m.
moulding, –*ĭng*, s. modinatura, f.; getto,
mouldy, *mōld'ĭ*, a. muffato.
moult, *mōlt*, v. n. mudare. [pieno, m.
mound, *mŏŭnd*, s. argine, baluardo, terramount, *mŏŭnt*, s. monte, m., montagna, f.; –, v. a. alzare; caricare.
mountain, *mŏŭn'tĭn*, s. montagna, f.; –, a. di montagna.
mountaineer, –*tĭnē'*, s. montanaro, m.
mountainous, –*tĭnŭs*, a. montagnoso.
mountebank, *mŏŭn'tĕbăngk*, s. ciarlatano, saltimbanco, m.
mourn, *mŏrn*, v. a. piangere, deplorare; –, v. n. portare il bruno; affliggersi.
mourner, –*ăr*, s. piagnone, m.
mournful, –*fŭl*, a. lugubre, tristo; –ly, ad. tristamente. [lamento, m.
mourning, –*ĭng*, s. abito da lutto, m.;
mouse, *mŏŭs*, s. (mice, pl.) sorcio, m.
moustache, *mŭstăsh'*, s. mustacchi, baffi, m. pl., basette, f. pl.
mouth, *mŏŭth*, s. bocca, f.; imboccatura, f.; entrata, f.; –, *mŏŭth*, v. a. masticare; –, v. n. gridare ad alta voce.
mouthful, –*fŭl*, s. boccone, m., boccata, f.

mouth-piece, *-pis,* s. bocchino, m., bocchina, f.; imboccatura, f.

move, *mōv.* v. a. muovere; agitare, commuovere, eccitare, persuadere; disturbare; utenerire, toccare; proporre; —, v. n. muoversi, darsi moto; —, s. mossa, f.; **(at chess)** tiro, m., tirata, f

mcveable, *-ǎbl,* a. mobile; **-s,** s. pl. beni mobili, m. pl.   [m.; mozione, f.

movement, *-mĕnt,* s. moto, movimento, m.

mover, *-ŭr,* s. motore, m.

moving, *-ĭng,* a. movente, toccante; **-ly,** ad. in modo patetico; —, s. movimento, m.

mow, *mōǔ (mō),* s. mucchio, m., bica, f.

mow, *mō,* v. a. & n. ir. segare con falce, mietere; far grugno.

mower, *-ŭr,* s. mietitore, m.

much, *mŭch,* a. & ad. molto, assai; spesso; grandemente.

mucilage, *mū' sĭlǎj,* s. mucillaggine, f.

muck, *mŭk,* s. letame, concime, m.; fimo, m.

mucous, *mū' kŭs,* a. mucoso, mucillagginoso.

mud, *mŭd,* s. fango, m.; limaccio, m.

muddle, *mŭd' l,* v. a. intorbidare; innemuddy, *-dĭ,* a. fangoso, torbido.   [briare.

mudwall, *-wǎl,* s. muro fatto di fango e paglia, m.

muff, *mŭf,* s. manicotto, m.   [rucciare.

muffle, *mŭf' l,* v. a. camuffare, incappemug, *mŭg,* s. ciotola, brocca, f.

muggy, *mŭg' gĭ,* a muffito, umido.

mulberry, *mŭl' bĕrrĭ,* s. mora, f.; **--tree,** s. moro, m.; gelso, m.

mulct, *mŭlkt,* v. a. condannare all' ammule, *mŭl,* s. mulo, m.; mula, f.

mule-driver, *-drīvŭr,* **muleteer,** *mŭlĕ-tĕr',* s. mulattiere, m.

mull, *mŭl,* v. a. riscaldare (del vino); abbruciare; —, s. focaccia fatta con burro e uova, f.

mullet, *mŭl' lĕt,* s. triglia, f. (pesce).

multifarious, *mŭltĭfā' rŭs,* a. vario, differente.   [moltiplicato.

multiple, *mŭl' tĭpl,* a. multiplo, moltiplice;

multiplicand, *-plĭkǎnd',* s. (ar.) moltiplicando, m.

multiplication, *-kā' shŭn,* s. moltiplicazione, f.; **--table,** tavola Pitagorica, f.

multiplicator, *-kā' tŭr,* s. (ar.) moltiplicatore, m.

multiplicity, *-plĭs' ĭtĭ,* s. moltiplicità, f.

multiplier, *mŭl' tĭplŭr,* s. (ar.) moltiplicatore, m.

multiply, *mŭl' tĭplĭ,* v. a. moltiplicare.

multitude, *mŭl' tĭtūd,* s. moltitudine, f.; volgo, m.

multitudinous, *-tū' dĭnŭs,* a. numeroso.

mum! *mŭm,* j. zitto! silenzio!

mumble, *mŭm' bl,* v. a. pronunziare indistintamente; —, v. n. mormorare.

mummer, *mŭm' mŭr,* s. maschera, f.; commediante, m.

mummery, *-mărĭ,* s. mascherata, f.

mummy, *-mĭ,* s. mummia, f.

mumps, *mŭmps,* s. cattivo umore, m.; schinanzia, f.   [gordamente.

munch, *mŭnsh,* v. a. & n. mangiare inmundane, *mŭn' dān,* a. mondano, di mondo.

municipal, *mŭnis' ĭpǎl,* a. municipale.

municipality, *-pǎl' ĭtĭ,* s. municipalità, f.

munificence, *-nĭf' ĭsĕns,* s. munificenza, liberalità, f.

munificent, *-ĭsĕnt,* a. munificente, liberale.

muniment, *mū' nĭmĕnt,* s. (jur.) titolo, m.

munition, *-nĭsh' ŭn,* s. munizione, f.; provmural, *mū' rǎl,* a. murale.   [visione, f.

murder, *mŭr' dŭr,* s. omicidio, m.; assassinio, m.; —, v. a. assassinare; ammazzare.

murderer, *-dŭrŭr,* s. omicida, m.   [zare.

murderess, *-dŭrĕs,* s. omicida, f.

murderous, *-dŭrŭs,* a. micidiale; crudele.

murky, *mŭr' kĭ,* a. oscuro, buio.

murmur, *mŭr' mŭr,* s. mormorio, m.; —, v. a. mormorare; susurrare.

murmuringly, *-ĭnglĭ,* ad. con mormorio.

murrain, *mŭr' rān,* s. mortalità fra' bestiame, f.

muscle, *mŭs' l,* s. muscolo, m.   [colo.

muscular, *mŭs' kŭlǎr,* a. muscolare, di mus-

muse, *mūz,* s. meditazione profonda, f.; Musa, f.; —, v. a meditare; gruminare; pen-

museum, *mūzē' ŭm,* s. museo, m.   [sare.

mushroom, *mŭsh' rŏm,* s. fungo, m.

music, *mū' zĭk,* s. musica, f.; melodia, f.

musical, *-ǎl,* a. musicale; armonioso; **-ly,** ad. in modo musicale.

music-hall, *-hǎl,* s. caffè musicale, m.

musician, *mūzĭsh' ǎn,* s. musico, m.

music-stand, *mū' zĭk stǎnd,* s. leggio da musica, m.

musing, *mū' zĭng,* s. meditazione, f.

musk, *mŭsk,* s. muschio, musco, m.

musket, *mŭs' kĕt,* s. moschetto, schioppo, m.

musketeer, *mŭskĕtēr',* s. moschettiere, m.

musketry, *mŭs' kĕtrĭ,* s. fucilata, f.

muslin, *mŭz' lĭn,* s. mussolina, f.

mussel, *mŭs' ĕl,* s. muscolo, m.

must, *mŭst,* v. n. def. bisogna.

mustard, *mŭs' tǎrd,* s. mostarda, senapa f.

mustard-seed, *-sēd,* s. seme di senapa, m.

muster, *mŭs' tŭr,* s. mostra, rivista, rassegna, f.; —, v. a. mostrare; rassegnare; adunare, ragunare.

musty, *mŭs' tĭ,* a. muffito, rancido.

mutability, *mūtābĭl' ĭtĭ,* s. mutabilità, f.; incostanza, variabilità, f.

mutable, *mū' tǎbl,* a. incostante.

mutation, *-tā' shŭn,* s. mutazione, f.

mute, *mūt,* a. muto, mutolo; **-ly,** ad. in silenzio, senza parlare.

mutilate, *mū' tĭlāt,* v. a. mutilare, mozzare.

mutilation, *-lā' shŭn,* s. mutilazione, f.

mutineer, *-nēr',* s. sedizioso, ribelle, m.

mutinous, *mū' tĭnŭs,* a. sedizioso; **-ly,** ad. sediziosamente.

mutiny, *mū' tĭnĭ,* s. sedizione, f.; ribellione, f.; —, v. n. rivoltarsi, ribellarsi, sollevarsi.

mutter, *mŭt' tŭr,* v. a. & n. borbottare, mormorare; —, s. mormorio, m.

mutton, *mŭt' n,* s. castrato, m.; carne di castrato, f.   [reciprocamente.

mutual, *mū' tŭǎl,* a. reciproco; **-ly,** ad.

muzzle, *mŭz' l,* s. muso, ceffo (d' animale) m.; musoliera, f.; —, v. a. mettere la musoliera.

my, *mī*, pn. mio, mia, mie, miei.
myriad, *mĭr'ĭăd*, s. miriade, f.
myrrh, *mŭr*, s. mirra, f.
myrtle, *mŭrtl*, s. mirto, m.; mortella, f.
myself, *mĭsĕlf'*, pn. io medesimo, io stesso.
mysterious, *mĭstē'rĭŭs*, a. misterioso;
–ly, ad. misteriosamente.
mystery, *mĭs'tărĭ*, s. mistero, m.
mystic(al), *mĭs'tĭk(ăl)*, a. mistico; **–ly**, ad.
in senso mistico.   [f.
mystification,*–kā'shŭn*, s.mistificazione,
mystify, *mĭs'tĭfĭ*, v. a. abusare della credulità di alcuno, burlare alcuno.
myth, *mĭth*, s. mito, m.   [logico.
mythologic(al), *mĭthŏlŏj'ĭk(ăl)*, a. mito-
mythology, *–thŏl'ŏjĭ*, s. mitologia, f.

N.

nab, *năb*, v. a. aggrappare.
nag, *năg*, s. cavallino, m.
nail, *nāl*, s. unghia, f.; branca, f.; chiodo,
m.; **–**, v. a. inchiodare.
nailery, *nā'lărĭ*, s. chioderia, f.
naked, *nā'kĕd*, a. nudo, ignudo; evidente;
–ly, ad. nudamente; semplicemente.
nakedness, *–nĕs*, s. nudità, f.; chiarezza,f.
namby-pamby,*năm'bĭpăm'bĭ*,a.affettato.
name, *nām*, s. nome, m.; fama, riputazione,
f.; **–**, v. a. nomare, appellare.
nameless, *–lĕs*, a. anonimo.
namely, *–lĭ*, ad. specialmente, particolar-
namesake, *–sāk*, s. che ha il medesimo [mente.
nome, omonimo, m.
nankeen, *năngkēn'*, s. anchina, f.
nap, *năp*, s. sonnellino, m.; lanugine, f.
nape, *nāp*, s. nuca, f.
naphtha, *năp'thă*, s. nafta, f.
napkin, *năp'kĭn*, s. salvietta, f.
narcissus, *nărsĭs'sŭs*, s. (bot.) narciso,
m., tazzetta, f.
narcotic(al), *–kŏt'ĭk(ăl)*, a. narcotico.
narrate, *nă'rāt*, v. a. raccontare.
narration, *–rā'shŭn*, s. narrazione, f.;
racconto, m.
narrative, *nă'rătĭv*, a. narrativo.
narrator, *–rā'tăr*, s. raccontatore, m.
narrow, *nă'rō*, a. stretto, angusto; scarso;
avaro; esatto; **–**, v. a. stringere, limitare.
narrowly, *–lĭ*, ad. strettamente.
narrowness, *–nĕs*, s. strettezza, f.; povertà, f.; stitichezza, f.
nasale, *nā'zăl*, a. nasale, del naso.
nastily, *năs'tĭlĭ*, ad. sporcamente.
nastiness, *–tĭnĕs*, s. sporchezza, f.
nasty, *–tĭ*, a. sporco, sordido; osceno.
natal, *nā'tăl*, a. natale, nativo. [polo, m.
nation, *nā'shŭn*, s. nazione, gente, f., po-
national, *năsh'ănăl*, a. nazionale; **–ly**,
ad. di tutta la nazione.   [lizzare.
nationalise, *năsh'ănălĭz*, v. a. naziona-
nationality, *–lĭ'tĭ*, s. nazionalità, f.
native, *nā'tĭv*, a. nativo; **–**, s. originario,
m.; indigeno, m.   [f.
nativity, *nătĭv'ĭtĭ*, s. natività, f.; nascita,
natural, *năt'ărăl* (*năch'ărăl*), a. naturale;

semplice; illegittimo; **–ly**, ad. naturalmente; **–**, s. (mus.) bisquadro, m.
naturalisation, *nătărălĭză'shŭn*, s. diritto di naturalità, f.   [adottare.
naturalise, *năt'ărălĭz*, v. a. naturalizzare;
naturalist, *–lĭst*, s. naturalista, m.
nature, *nā'tăr* (*nā'chăr*), s. natura, f ; proprietà, f.; essenza, f.: temperamento, m. -
naught, *năt*, a. cattivo, malvagio, disonesto; **–**, s. niente, m.
naughtily, *–tĭlĭ*, ad. malamente.
naughtiness, *–tĭnĕs*, s. cattiveria, f.
naughty, *năt'ĭ*, a. cattivo, malvagio.
nausea, *nă'shĭă*, s. nausea, f.
nauseate, *–shĭāt*, v. a. nauseare, disgustare.
nauseous, *–shĭŭs*, a. nauseoso, disgustoso;
–ly, ad. in modo nauseoso.
nautic(al), *nă'tĭk(ăl)*, **naval**, *nā'văl*, a.
nautico, navale.
nave, *nāv*, s. mozzo (d' una ruota), m.;
navata (d' una chiesa), f.
navel, *nā'vl*, s. ombelico, m.
navigable, *năv'ĭgăbl*, a. navigabile.
navigate, *năv'ĭgăt*, v. a. & n. navigare,
veleggiare.
navigation, *–gā'shŭn*, s. navigazione, f.
navigator, *–gā'tăr*, s. navigatore, m.
navvy, *năv'vĭ*, s. lavorante, bracciante, m.
navy, *nā'vĭ*, s. armata navale, flotta, f.
nay, *nā*, ad. no; non solo; di più, inoltre.
near, *nēr*, pr. a. & ad. presso; appresso;
vicino, prossimo; intimo, stretto; pressochè, poco meno, quasi; **to draw –**,
approssimare, accostare.
nearly, *–lĭ*, ad. da vicino; meschinamente.
nearness, *–nĕs*, s. prossimità, f.; meschinità, f.; parentela, affinità, f.
near-sighted, *–sītĕd*, a. miope.
neat, *nēt*, a. netto, puro, pulito; elegante;
–ly, ad. elegantemente; **–**, s. bue, m.,
vacca, f.
neatness, *–nĕs*, s. nettezza, eleganza, f.
nebulous, *nĕb'ŭlŭs*, a. nebuloso.
necessaries, *nĕs'ĕsĕrĭz*, s. pl. necessario,
bisogno, m.
necessarily, *–sĕrĭlĭ*, ad. necessariamente.
necessary, *–sĕrĭ*, s. necessario; indispensabile.
necessitate, *–sĕs'ĭtāt*, v. a. necessitare.
necessitous, *–sĕs'ĭtŭs*, a. indigente.
necessity, *–sĕs'ĭtĭ*, s. necessità, f.
neck, *nĕk*, s. collo, m.; **– of land**, braccio
di terra fra due mari, m.; **– of a violin**,
manico d' un violino, m.   [collo, m.
neckerchief, *–ărchĭf*, s. fazzoletto da
necklace, *–lăs*, s. collana, f.; monile,
vezzo, m.   [zia, f.; magia, f.
necromancy, *nĕk'rōmănsĭ*, s. negroman-
nectar, *nĕk'tăr*, s. nettare, m.
need, *nēd*, s. bisogno, m., necessità, f.; **–**,
v. a. avere bisogno; mancare; **–**, v. n.
esser necessario.
needful, *–fŭl*, a. necessario; requisito;
–ly, ad. necessariamente.
neediness, *–ĭnĕs*, s. povertà, f.; miseria, f.
needle, *nē'dl*, s. ago, m.; guglia, f.
needle-case, *–kās*, s. agoraio, m.
needleful, *–fŭl*, s. gugliata, f.

needle-woman, *–wĭlmăn,* s. cucitrice, f.

needle-work. *–wŭrk,* s. lavoro d' ago, m.

needless, *nĕd'lĕs,* a. inutile; **-ly,** ad. in-utilmente.

needs, *nēdz,* ad. necessariamente.

needy, *nē'dĭ,* a. bisognoso, povero, in-digente.

nefarious, *nẹfā'rĭẹs,* a. abominevole.

negation, *nẹgā'shăn,* s. negazione, f.

negative, *nĕg'ătĭv,* a. negativo; **-ly,** ad. negativamente; **—,** s. negativa, nega-zione, f.   [negligere.

neglect, *nĕglĕkt',* s. negligenza, f.; **—,** v. a.

negligence, *nĕg'lĭjens,* s. negligenza, tra-scuraggine, f.

negligent, *nĕg'lĭjĕnt,* a. negligente, tra-scurato; **-ly,** ad. con negligenza.

negotiable, *nĕgō'shĭăbl,* a. che si può ne-goziare.   [ficare; trattare.

negotiate, *–shĭāt,* v. a. negoziare, traf-

negotiation, *–shĭā'shăn,* s. negoziazione,

Negress, *nē'grĕs,* s. mora, f.   [f.

Negro, *nē'grō,* s. negro, moro, m.

neigh, *nā,* s. nitrito, m.; **—,** v. n. nitrire.

neighbour, *nā'băr,* s. vicino, m.; vicina, f.; **—,** v. a. confinare.

neighbourhood, *–hŭd,* s. vicinanza, f.

neighbourly, *–lĭ,* a. sociabile, amiche-vole; **—,** ad. amichevolmente.

neither, *nē'thăr,* c. nè; nè più; **—,** pn. nè l' uno nè l'altro, nè l' una nè l' altra.

neophyte, *nē'ofĭt,* s. neofito, m.

nephew, *nĕv'ū,* s. nipote, m.

nepotism, *nĕp'ōtĭzm,* s. nipotismo, m.

nerve, *nărv,* s. nervo, nerbo, m.; tendine, m.

nerveless, *–lĕs,* a. snervato, fiacco.

nervous, *năr'vŭs,* a. nervoso, robusto.

nest, *nĕst,* s. nido, m., nidiata, f.; rifugio, asilo, m.   [annidarsi.

nestle, *nĕs'l,* v. a. accarezzare; **—,** v. n.

nestling, *–lĭng,* s. uccello nidiace, m.

net, *nĕt,* s. rete, m., reticella, f.

nether, *nĕth'ăr,* a. basso, inferiore.

netting, *nĕt'ĭng,* s. retame, m.

nettle, *nĕt'l,* s. ortica, f.; **—,** v. a. pungere; esasperare.   [neutrale.

neuter, *nū'tăr,* a. neutro; indifferente.

neutral, *–trăl,* a. neutrale; **-ly,** ad. neu-tralmente.

neutralise, *–trălĭz,* v. a. neutralizzare.

neutrality, *–trăl'ĭtĭ,* s. neutralità, f.

never, *nĕv'ăr,* ad. mai, giammai; **– mind!** non importa!

nevertheless, *–thĕlĕs',* c. nulladimeno.

new, *nū,* a. nuovo, fresco; moderno; **—,** ad. nuovamente; **-ly,** ad. novamente.

new-comer, *–kămăr,* s. forestiero, m.

new-fangled, *–făngld,* a. affettato.

new-fashioned, *–făsh'nd,* a. alla moda.

newness, *–nĕs,* s. novità, f.

news, *nūz,* s. novella, f.; notizia, f.

news-monger, *–mŭnggăr,* s. propaga-tore di nuove, m.

newspaper, *–pāpăr,* s. gazzetta, f.

next, *nĕkst,* a. prossimo; **—,** ad. dopo; in secondo luogo; **the – day,** il giorno se-guente.   [f.; punta, f.

nib, *nĭb,* s. becco, m., bocca (degli uccelli),

nibble, *nĭb'bl,* v. a. mordere; riprendere; **—,** v. n. morsecchiare.

nice, *nĭs,* a. raffinato, delicato, delizioso; esatto, studiato; difficile, scrupoloso; **-ly,** ad. delicatamente; esattamente; dif-ficilmente.

niceness, *–nĕs,* **nicety,** *nī'sĕtĭ,* s. delizia, f.; esattezza, finezza, f.; **niceties,** pl. delicatezze, f. pl.

niche, *nĭch,* s. nicchia, f.

nick, *nĭk,* s. tempo comodo, m.; oppor-tunità, f., taglio, m.; **old –,** diavolo, m.; **—,** v. a. incontrare il tempo.

nickel, *nĭk'ĕl,* s. nichel, m.

nickname, *–năm,* s. soprannome, m.; **—,** v. a. dare un soprannome.

niece, *nēs,* s. nipote, f.   [m.

niggard, *nĭg'gărd,* s. taccagno, spilorcio.

niggardliness, *–lĭnĕs,* s. avarizia, sordi-dezza, f.   [avaramente, sordidamente-

niggardly, *–lĭ,* a. avaro, sordido; **—,** ad.

nigger, *nĭg'găr,* s. negro, m., negra, f.

nigh, *nī,* pr. & ad. vicino, allato; prossimo, contiguo; qui vicino; all' incirca; **-ly,** ad. presso a poco.

night, *nīt,* s. notte, f.; sera, serata, f.

night-fall, *–făl,* s. l' imbrunire, il far della notte, m.

nightingale, *–ĭngāl,* s. rosignuolo, m.

night-light, *–lĭt,* s. lumicina, f.

nightly, *–lĭ,* a. notturno; **—,** ad. di notte tempo, ogni notte.   [sima, f.

night-mare, *–măr,* s. incubo, m.; fanta-

night-shade, *–shăd,* s. (bot.) belladonna, f.

nihilist, *nī'hĭlĭst,* s. nichilista, m.

nimble, *nĭm'bl,* a. agile; lesto, leggiero.

nimbly, *–blĭ,* ad. agilmente.

nimbus, *nĭm'bŭs,* s. nimbo, m.

nine, *nīn,* a. nove.

ninefold, *–fōld,* a. nove volte più.

ninepins, *–pĭnz,* s. pl. birilli, m. pl.

nineteen, *–tēn,* a. diciannove.

nineteenth, *–tēnth,* a. decimonono.

ninetieth, *–tĭĕth,* a. novantesimo.

ninety, *–tĭ,* a. novanta.

ninny, *nĭn'nĭ,* s. sciocco, m.

ninth, *ninth,* s. & a. nono (m); **-ly,** ad. in nono luogo.   [nebbiare.

nip, *nĭp,* v. a. pizzicare; motteggiare; an-

nippers, *nĭp'părz,* s. pl. mollette, f. pl.

nipping, *–pĭng,* a. pungente, mordace.

nipple, *nĭp'pl,* s. capezzolo, m.

nit, *nĭt,* s. lendine, f.

nitre, *nī'tăr,* s. salnitro, m.

no, *nō,* a. nessuno, niuno; **—,** ad. no, non.

nobility, *nōbĭl'ĭtĭ,* s. nobiltà, f.; nobili, m. pl.   [**—,** s. nobile, m.

noble, *nō'bl,* a. nobile, illustre; liberale;

nobleman, *–măn,* s. nobile, gentiluomo, f.

nobleness, *–nĕs,* s. nobiltà, f.

nobly, *–blĭ,* ad. nobilmente; liberalmente.

nobody, *nō'bŏdĭ,* s. nessuno, niuno, veruno, m.   [notte.

nocturnal, *nŏktăr'năl,* a. notturno, di

nod, *nŏd,* s. cenno, segno, m.; **—,** v. n. ac-cennare; dormicchiare.

node, *nōd,* s. nodo, m.; tumore, callo, m.

noise, *nŏiz*, s. strepito, fracasso, m.; –, v. a. divulgare, pubblicare.

noiseless, –*lĕs*, a. silenzioso, tacito.

noisiness, *nŏi'zĭnĕs*, s. grande strepito, tumulto, rumore, m.

noisome, –*sŭm*, a. nauseoso, disgustoso.

noisy, –*zĭ*, a. turbolento, tumultuoso.

nomadic, *nŏmăd'ĭk*, a. nomade, errante.

nomenclature, *nŏmĕnklā'tūr*, s. nomenclatura, f. [–ly, ad. nominatamente.

nominal, *nŏm'ĭnăl*, a. nominale, titolare;

nominate, *nŏm'ĭnāt*, v. a. nominare.

nomination, –*nā'shŭn*, s. nomina, f.; presentazione, f. [tivo, m.

nominative, *nŏm'ĭnătĭv*, s. (gr.) nomina-

nonage, *nŏn'ăj*, s. minorità, f. [f.

non-attendance, –*ătĕn'dăns*, s. incuria,

nondescript, –*dĕskrĭpt'*, a. indefinibile.

none, *nŭn*, a. niuno, nessuno.

nonentity, *nŏnĕn'tĭtĭ*, s. non entità, f.

non-performance, –*pĕrfŏr'măns*, s. mancanza d' effezione, f.

nonplus, *nŏn'plŭs*, s. imbarazzo, m.; –, v. a. confondere, imbarazzare.

non-resistance, –*rĕzĭs'tăns*, s. ubbidienza pronta, f. [mento, m.

nonsense, *nŏn'sĕns*, s. assurdità, f., anfana-

nonsensical, –*sĕn'sĭkăl*, a. assurdo.

nonsuit, *nŏn'sūt*, s. (jur.) desistenza da una lite, f.; –, v. a. condannare per desistenza da una lite. [vermicelli, m., pl.

noodle, *nō'dl*, s. sciocco, gonzo, m.; –s, pl.

nook, *nŏk*, s. angolo, m.; ridotto, m.

noon, *nōn*, s. mezzodì, mezzogiorno, m.

noon-tide, –*tīd*, s. di mezzodì, meridiano, m. [–, v. a. legare, allacciare.

noose, *nōz*, s. nodo scorsoio, m.; laccio, m.;

nor, *nŏr*, c, nè, nè più.

normal, *nŏr'măl*, a. normale.

north, *nŏrth*, s. settentrione, m.

northerly, *nŏr'thŭrlĭ*, northern, –*thŭrn*, a. settentrionale.

north-pole, *nŏrth'pōl*, s. polo artico, m.

north-star, –*stär*, s. stella polare, f.

northward(s), –*wŭrd(z)*, ad. verso settentrione. [m.

nose, *nōz*, s. naso, m.; sentore, m.; tubo,

nose bag, –*băg*, s. musetta, f.

nosegay, –*gā*, s. mazzolino di fiori, m.

nostril, *nŏs'trĭl*, s. narice, f.

nostrum, *nŏs'trŭm*, s. segreto, m.

not, *nŏt*, ad. non, no; – at all, in niun modo, niente affatto.

notable, *nō'tăbl*, a. notabile, considerabile.

notably, –*tăblĭ*, ad. notabilmente.

notarial, *nŏtā'rĭăl*, a. notarile, autenticato da un notaro.

notary, *nō'tărĭ*, s. notaro, m.

notch, *nŏch*, s. tacca, f.; intaccatura, f.; –, v. a. intaccare.

note, *nŏt*, s. nota, annotazione, f.; osservazione, f.; distinzione, f.; merito, m., importanza, f.; biglietto, m.; (mus.) nota, f.; –, v. a. notare; osservare. [taccuino, m.

note-book, –*bŭk*, s. libro di appunti.

noted, *nō'tĕd*, a. notato; rinomato.

nothing, *nŭth'ĭng*, s. niente m.; nullità, f.

notice, *nō'tĭs*, s. notizia, f., avviso, m.;

osservazione, f.; attenzione, f.; –, v. a. osservare.

noticeable, –*ăbl*, a. rimarchevole.

notification, –*tĭfĭkā'shŭn*, s. notificazione, f.

notify, *nō'tĭfī*, v. a. notificare, significare.

notion, *nō'shŭn*, s. nozione, f.; idea, opinione, f. [pubblicità, f.

notoriety, *nŏtŏrī'ĕtĭ*, s. notorietà, f.;

notorious, –*tō'rĭŭs*, a. notorio; –ly, ad. notoriamente. [non ostante, sebbene.

notwithstanding, *nŏtwĭthstănd'ĭng*, c.

nought, *năt*, s. niente, nulla, m.

noun, *nŏŭn*, s. (gr.) nome, m.

nourish, *nŭr'ĭsh*, v. a. nutrire, alimentare.

nourishment, –*mĕnt*, s. nutrimento, m., nutritura, f.; alimento, m. [losa, f.

novel, *nŏv'ĕl*, s. novella, narrazione favo-

novelist, –*ĭst*, s. novelliere, m.

novelty, –*tĭ*, s. novità, f.; cosa nuova, f.

November, *nŏvĕm'bŭr*, s. novembre, m.

novice, *nŏv'ĭs*, s. novizio, m.; novizia, f.

noviciate, *nŏvĭsh'ĭăt*, s. noviziato, m.

now, *nŏŭ*, ad. presente, adesso, ora; – – a-days, d' oggi, al presente; – and then, di quando in quando.

nowadays, *nŏŭ'ddăz*, ad. oggidì, nel tempo presente.

nowhere, *nō'hwăr*, ad. in nessuna parte.

nowise, *nō'wĭz*, ad. in niun modo.

noxious, *nŏk'shŭs*, a. nocivo, pernicioso; –ly, ad. nocivamente. [f.

nozzle, *nŏz'l*, s. capezzolo, naso, m.; punta,

nucleus, *nū'klĕŭs*, s. nocciuolo, m.

nude, *nūd*, a. nudo, ignudo.

nudge, *nŭj*, v. a. tentare, toccare col gomito.

nudity, *nū'dĭtĭ*, s. nudità, f.; semplicità, f.

nugatory, *nū'gătŏrĭ*, a. frivolo.

nuisance, *nū'săns*, s. nocumento, m.; incomodo, m.

null, *nŭl*, a. nullo; invalido.

nullify, *nŭl'lĭfī*, v. a. cancellare, cassare.

nullity, –*lĭtĭ*, s. nullità, f.

numb, *nŭm*, a. torpido, intirizzito; –, v. a. intirizzire; stupefare.

number, *nŭm'bŭr*, s. numero, m., quantità, f.; –, v. a. numerare; contare.

numberless, –*lĕs*, a. innumerabile.

numbness, *nŭm'nĕs*, s. torpore, m.; stupore, m. [numero.

numerale, *nū'mărăl*, s. numerale, di

numeration, –*rā'shŭn*, s. numerazione, f.

numerator, *nū'mŭrātŭr*, s. (ar.) numeratore, m. [merale.

numerical, –*mĕr'ĭkăl*, a. numerico; nu-

numerous, *nū'mărŭs*, a. numeroso; armonioso.

numismatics, *nŭmĭsmăt'ĭks*, s. pl. numismatica, scienza delle monete antiche, f.

numskull, *nŭm'skŭl*, s. minchione, goffo, m.

nun, *nŭn*, s. monaca, f.; religiosa regolare, f.

nuncio, *nŭn'shĭo*, s. nunzio, m.

nunnery, *nŭn'nărĭ*, s. convento (di monache), m. [nozze, f.

nuptial, *nŭp'shăl*, a. nuziale; –s, s. pl.

nurse, *nŭrs*, s. nutrice, balia, f.; –, v. a. nutrire, allevare. [semenzaio, m.

nursery, –*ărĭ*, s. camera della balia, f.;

nursling, _-lĭng_, s. bambino di latte, m.; favorito, m.

nurture, _nŭr'tŭr_, v. a. nutricare, allevare.

nut, _nŭt_, s. noce, nocciuola, f. [m.

nut-cracker, _-krăkŭr_, s. pl. stiaccianoci,

nut-gall, _-gȃl_, s. galla, gallozzola, f.

nutmeg, _-mĕg_, s. noce moscada, f.

nutriment, _nŭ'trĭmĕnt_, s. nutrimento, m.; cibo, m. [trimento, m.

nutrition, _-trĭsh'ŭn_, s. nutrizione, f., nu-

nutritious, _-trĭsh'ŭs_, **nutritive,** _nŭ'-trĭtĭv_, a. nutritivo. [guscio, m.

nut-shell, _nŭt'shĕll_, s. scorza di noce, f.;

nutting, _nŭt'tĭng_, p. **to go a —,** andar a cogliere delle nocciuole. [ciuolo, m.

nut-tree, _-trē_, s. albero del noce, noc-

nymph, _nĭmf_, s. ninfa, f.

O.

oaf, _ōf_, s. merendone, baccellone, m.

oak, _ōk_, s. quercia, f.

oak-apple, _-ăpl_, s. galla, gallozzola, f.

oaken, _ō'kn_, a. di quercia; fatto di quercia.

oakum, _ō'kŭm_, s. (mar.) stoppa, f.

oar, _ōr_, s. remo, m. [tunato, m.

oasis, _ō'ăsĭs_, s. oasi, f.; (fig.) paese for-

oat, _ōt_, s. vena, f.

oath, _ōth_, s. giuramento, m.

obduracy, _ŏb'dŭrăsĭ_, s. durezza di cuore, f. induramento, m.

obdurate, _-dŭrāt_, a. indurito, duro; **-ly,** ad. inflessibilmente.

obedience, _ŏbē'dĭĕns_, s. ubbidienza, f.

obedient, _-dĭĕnt_, a. ubbidiente; sommesso; **-ly,** ad. ubbidientemente.

obeisance, _ŏbā'săns_, s. riverenza, f.; saluto, m. [f.

obelisk, _ŏb'ĕlĭsk_, s. obelisco, m.; aguglia,

obese, _ŏbēs'_, a. obeso, corpulento, eccessivamente pingue.

obesity, _ŏbēs'ĭtĭ_, s. grassezza estrema, f.

obey, _ŏbā'_, v. a. ubbidire.

obituary, _ŏbĭt'ŭărĭ_, s. libro de' morti, mortuario, m.

object, _ŏb'jĕkt_, s. obietto, oggetto, m.; soggetto, m.; **—,** _ŏbjĕkt'_, v. a. obiettare.

objection, _-jĕk'shŭn_, s. obiezione, f.; opposizione, f.; rimprovero, m. [zione.

objectionable, _-ăbl_, a. soggetto ad obiezione.

objective, _-jĕk'tĭv_, a. obiettivo, oggettivo.

oblation, _-lā'shŭn_, s. oblazione, offerta, f.

obligation, _-lĭgā'shŭn_, s. obbligazione, f.

obligatory, _ŏb'lĭgătŭrĭ_, a. obbligatorio.

oblige, _ŏblīj'_, v. a. obbligare, costringere.

obligingly, _ŏblī'jĭnglĭ_, ad. obbligantemente. [compiacenza, f.

obligingness, _-jĭngnĕs_, s. cortesia, f.;

oblique, _ŏblēk'_, a. obliquo; indiretto; **-ly,** ad. obliquamente.

obliquity, _-lĭk'wĭtĭ_, s. obbliquità, f.

obliterate, _-lĭt'ŭrāt_, v. a. obliterare; cancellare. [f.; obliterazione, f.

obliteration, _-rā'shŭn_, s. cancellatura, f.

oblivion, _ŏblĭv'ĭăn_, s. dimenticanza, f.

oblivious, _-lĭv'ĭăs_, a. obbligo.

oblong, _ŏb'lŏng_, a. oblungo, bislungo.

obloquy, _ŏb'lōkwĭ_, s. maldicenza, f.; biasimo, m. [vole.

obnoxious, _-nŏk'shăs_, a. soggetto; colpe-

obscene, _-sēn'_, a. osceno, impudico.

obscenity, _-sĕn'ĭtĭ_, s. oscenità, f.

obscure, _-skŭr'_, a. oscuro; **-ly,** ad. oscuramente; **—,** v. a. oscurare.

obscurity, _-skŭ'rĭtĭ_, s. oscurità, f.

obsequies, _ŏb'sĕkwĭz_, s. pl. esequie, f. pl., mortorio, m.

obsequious, _-sē'kwĭăs_, a. ossequioso; civile; **-ly,** ad. ossequiosamente.

observable, _-zŭr'văbl_, a. osservabile.

observance, _-zŭr'văns_, s. osservanza, f.; riverenza, f.; sommissione, f. [toso.

observant, _-vănt_, a. osservante, rispet-

observation, _-vā'shăn_, s. osservazione, f.; cura, f. [m.

observatory, _-zŭr'vătŭrĭ_, s. osservatorio,

observe, _-zŭrv'_, v. a. osservare; considerare; **—,** v. n. essere attento.

observer, _-zŭr'vŭr_, s. osservatore, m.

observingly, _-vĭnglĭ_, ad. attentamente.

obsolete, _ŏb'sŏlēt_, a. disusato, vecchio.

obstacle, _ŏb'stăkl_, s. ostacolo, m.

obstinacy, _ŏb'stĭnăsĭ_, s. ostinazione, caparbietà, f. **-ly,** ad. ostinatamente.

obstinate, _-stĭnāt_, a. ostinato, caparbio;

obstreperous, _-strĕp'ărŭs_, a. strepitoso, turbulento. [dire.

obstruct, _-strŭkt'_, v. a. ostruire, impe-

obstruction, _-strŭk'shăn_, s. ostruzione, oppilazione, f.; impedimento, m.

obtain, _-tān'_, v. a. ottenere, acquistare; **—,** v. n. stabilirsi. [bile.

obtainable, _-ăbl_, a. ottenibile; consegui-

obtrude, _-trōd'_, v. a. intrudere; imporre.

obtuse, _-tŭs'_, a. ottuso, spuntato; stupido.

obviate, _ŏb'vĭāt_, v. a. ovviare; prevenire.

obvious, _ŏb'vĭăs_, a. aperto; evidente; **-ly,** ad. evidentemente.

occasion, _ŏkkā'zhăn_, s. occasione, opportunità, f.; causa, cagione, f., motivo, m.; **—,** v. a. cagionare, causare.

occasional, _-ăl_, a. occasionale, casuale; **-ly,** ad. occasionalmente. [occidente.

occidental, _ŏksĭdĕn'tăl_, a. occidentale, d'

occult, _ŏkkŭlt'_, a. occulto.

occupancy, _ŏk'kŭpănsĭ_, s. occupazione, f.

occupant, _ŏk'kŭpănt_, **occupier,** _-kŭpĭŭr_, s. occupatore, possessore, m.

occupation, _-pā'shŭn_, s. occupazione, f.; impiego, m. [dere; impiegare.

occupy, _ŏk'kŭpĭ_, v. a. occupare; posse-

occur, _ŏkkŭr'_, v. n. occorrere, accadere; farsi incontro. [m.

occurrence, _-rĕns_, s. occorrenza, f.; evento,

ocean, _ō'shăn_, s. oceano, alto mare, m.

oceanic, _ŏshăn'ĭk_, a. oceanico.

ochre, _ō'kŭr_, s. ocra, f.

octave, _ŏk'tăv_, s. ottava, f. [ottavo, m.

octavo, _-tă'vō_, s. libro in ottavo, m.;

October, _ŏk'tūr_, s. ottobre, m.

ocular, _ŏk'ŭlŭr_, a. oculare, di veduta.

oculist, _ŏk'ŭlĭst_, s. oculista, m.

odd, *ŏd*, a. impari, dispari; bizzarro, fantastico; cattivo; **-ly**, ad. in modo straordinario.   [lità, f.; singolarità, f.

oddity, *-dǐt̮*, oddness, *-nĕs*, s. ineguaoddness, *-nĕs*, s. singolarità, stranezza, f.

odds, *ŏdz*, s. disparità, f.; differenza, f.; vantaggio, m.; superiorità, f.   [mente.

odious, *ŏ'dǐŭs*, a. odioso; **-ly**, ad. odiosaodium, *ŏ'dǐŭm*, s. odio, m.; colpa, f.

odorous, *ŏ'dŭrŭs*, a. odoroso, fragrante.

odour, *ŏ'dŭr*, s. odore, m.; fragranza, f.

of, *ŏv*, pr. di, del, dello, della, dei, delle.

off, *ŏf*, ad. lontano, lunge, lungi; via; **- hand**, immediatamente.

offal, *ŏf'fǎl*, s. rimasuglio, m.; avanzo, m.

offence, *ŏffĕns'*, s. offesa, f.; colpa, f.; affronto, oltraggio, m.

offend, *-fĕnd'*, v. a. offendere; dispiacere; nuocere; **-**, v. n. fallire, peccare.

offender, *-ĕr*, s. offensore, m.

offensive, *-fĕn'sǐv*, a. offensivo; ingiurioso; **-ly**, ad. offensivamente.

offer, *ŏf'fĕr*, v. a. offrire, presentare; tentare; **-**, v n. offrirsi, presentarsi; obbligarsi; **-**, s. offerta, f.   [zione, f.

offering, *-ǐng*, s. offerta, profferta, f.; oblaoffertory, *-tŭr̃*, s. offertorio, m.

office, *ŏf'fǐs*, s. officio, m.; impiego, carica, servizio, m.; cesso, m.; latrina, f.

officer, *-ĕr*, s. ufficiale, m.

official, *-fǐsh'ǎl*, a. uffiziale; **-ly**, ad. ufficialmente; d' uffizio **-**, s. ufficiale, uffiziale, m.   [v. n. uffiziare.

officiate, *-fǐsh'ĕǎt*, v. a. distribuire; **-**, v. n. uffiziare.

officious, *-fǐsh'ŭs*, a. ufficioso; **-ly**, ad. cortesemente, officiosamente.

offing, *ŏf'fǐng*, s. alto mare, m.

offscouring, *ŏf'skŏŭr̃ng*, s. lavatura, f.; fecce, f. pl.

offset, *ŏf'sĕt*, s. germoglio, rampollo, m.

offshoot, *-shŏt*, s. germoglio, rampollo, m.   [scendenti, m. pl.

offspring, *-sprǐng*, s. progenie, f., dioft, *ŏft*, often, *ŏf'n*, ad. spesso, sovente.

oftentimes, *ŏf'ntǐmz*, ad. spesse volte.

ogle, *ŏ'gl*, v. a. occhieggiare; vagheggiare; **-**, s. occhiata, f.

oh ! *ŏ*, i. Oh ! O !

oil, *ŏǐl*, s. olio, m.; **-**, v. a. ungere con olio.

oil-cloth, *-klŏth*, s. tela incerata, f.

oil-colour, *-kŭlŭr*, s. colore a olio, m.

oiliness, *-ǐnĕs*, s. oleosità, f.

oil-man, *-mǎn*, s. oliandolo, m.

oil-painting, *-pǎntǐng*, s. pittura a olio, f.; quadro dipinto a olio, m.

oil-silk, *-sǐlk*, s. taffetà incerato, m.

oily, *ŏǐl'ǐ*, a. oleoso; untuoso.

ointment, *ŏǐnt'mĕnt*, s. untume, m.

old, *ŏld*, a. vecchio; antico; **of -**, anticamente.   [f.

oldness, *-nĕs*, s. antichità, f.; vecchiezza,

oleaginous, *ŏlĕǎdj'ǐnŭs*, a. oleoso

oleander, *ŏlĕǎn'dĕr*, s. oleandro, m.

olfactory, *ŏlfǎk'tŭr̃*, a. olfattorio.

olive, *ŏl'ǐv*, s. uliva, f.

olive-grove, *-grŏv*, s. uliveto, m.

olive-oil, *-ŏǐl*, s. olio d' uliva, m.

olive-tree, *-tṛĕ*, s. ulivo, m.

omelet, *ŏm'ĕlĕt*, s. frittata, f.

omen, *ŏ'mĕn*, s. augurio, presagio, m.

omened, *ŏ'mĕnd*, a. auguroso, di pronostico.

ominous, *ŏm'ǐnŭs*, a. malauguroso; **-ly**, ad. in modo auguroso.

omission, *ŏmǐsh'ŭn*, s. omissione, f., tralasciamento, m.

omit, *ŏmǐt'*, v. a. omettere, tralasciare.

omnibus, *ŏm'nǐbŭs*, s. omnibus, m.

omnipotence, *-nǐp'ŏtĕns*, s. onnipotenza, f.

omnipotent, *-pŏtĕnt*, a. onnipotente.   [f,

omniscience, *-nǐsh'ǐĕns*, s. onniscienza,

on, *ŏn*, pr. & ad. sopra, su; a; al, alla; successivamente; **and so -**, e così del resto; **- the contrary**, al contrario; **to go -**, passare avanti.

once, *wŭns*, ad. una volta, un tempo; **at -**, in un colpo; **all at -**, in un subito; **- for all**, una volta per sempre; **- more**, un' altra volta.

one, *wŭn*, a. & p. uno, una, un; sì; **- by -**, uno ad uno; **- another**, l'un l' altro; **-'s self**, sè stesso, sè stessa.

onerous, *ŏn'ŭrŭs*, a. gravoso; incomodo.

oneself, *wŭnsĕlf'*, s. sè stesso.

onion, *ŭn'yŭn*, s. cipolla, f.

only, *ŏn'lǐ*, a. & ad. solo; solamente.

onset, *ŏn'sĕt*, onslaught, *-slŏt*, s. assalto, attacco, m.

onward(s), *ŏn'wǎrd(z)*, ad. avanti.

ooze, *ŏz*, s. fango, m.; **-**, v. n. trapelare, gemere.

opacity, *ŏpǎs'ǐt̮*, s. opacità, f.; spessezza, f.

opal, *ŏ'pǎl*, s. opale, m.

opaque, *ŏpǎk'*, a. opaco, non diafano.

open, *ŏ'pn*, a. aperto, scoperto; evidente, chiaro; sincero; **-**, v. a. aprire, scoprire; **-**, v. n. aprirsi; fendersi.

opener, *-ĕr*, s. apritore, m.; espositore, m.

open-handed, *-hǎndĕd*, a. generoso, liberale.   [cero; generoso.

open-hearted, *-hǎrtĕd*, a. franco, sinopening, *-ǐng*, s. apertura, f.; principio, m.   [mente.

openly, *-lǐ*, ad. apertamente; francaopenness, *-nĕs*, s. chiarezza, f.; franchezza, sincerità, f.

open-work, *-wŭrk*, s. lavoro traforato, m.

opera, *ŏp'ǎrǎ*, s. opera, f.

opera-glass, *-glǎs*, s. cannocchiale da teatro, m.   [m.

opera-hat, *-hǎt*, s. cappello da ripiegarsi,

operate, *ŏp'ǎrǎt*, v. n. operare; produrre.

operatic(al), *-rǎt'ǐk(ǎl)*, a. di opera.

operation, *-rǎ'shǎn*, s. operazione, f.; effetto, m.   [ficiente.

operative, *ŏp'ǎrǎtǐv*, a. operativo, efoperator, *ŏp'ǎrǎtŭr*, s. operatore, m.

ophthalmy, *ŏf'thǎlmǐ*, s. oftalmia, f.

opiate, *ŏ'pǐǎt*, s. oppiato, m.

opine, *ŏpǐn'*, v. n. opinare.   [mento, m.

opinion, *ŏpǐn'yŭn*, s. opinione, f.; senti-

opinionative, *–di̇v*, a. ostinato, pertinace.   [versario, m.

opponent, *ŏppŏ'ṅĕnt*, s. opponente, av-

opportune, *–pŏrtŭn'*, a. opportuno; **–ly,** ad. opportunamente.

opportunity, *–tû'ṅiti̇*, s. opportunità, f.; occasione, f.   [porsi.

oppose, *–pōz'*, v. a. & n. opporre; op-

opposite, *ŏp'pŏzi̇t*, a. opposito, contrario; **–ly,** ad. dirimpetto; **–,** s. avversario, antagonista, m.   [sistenza, f.

opposition, *–zi̇sh'ăn*, s. opposizione, re-

oppress, *–prĕs'*, v. a. opprimere.

oppression, *–prĕsh'ăn*, s. oppressione, f.; severità, f.

oppressive, *–prĕs'si̇v*, a. oppressivo.

oppressor, *–sŭr*, s. oppressore, m.

opprobrious, *–prŏ'bri̇ŭs*, a. ignominioso.

opprobrium, *–bri̇ŭm*, s. obbrobrio, m.

optic(al), *ŏp'ti̇k(ăl)*, a. ottico, visuale; **–s,** s. pl. ottica, f.

optician, *–ti̇sh'ăn*, s. ottico, m.

optimist, *ŏp'ti̇mi̇st*, s. ottimista, m.

option, *ŏp'shăn*, s. scelta, f.; volontà, f.

optional, *–ăl*, a. libero a scegliersi. [f.

opulence, *ŏp'ûlĕns*, s. opulenza, ricchezza,

opulent, *–ûlĕnt*, a. opulento; **–ly,** ad. opulentemente, riccamente.

or, *ŏr*, c. o, od; **– else,** altrimente.

oracle, *ŏr'ăkl*, s. oracolo, m.

oracular, *ŏrăk'ûlăr*, a. come un oracolo.

oral, *ŏ'răl*, a. vocale, di voce; **–ly,** ad. a viva voce.

orange, *ŏr'ĕnj*, s. arancia, f.

orangeade, *–jād'*, s. aranciata, f.

orange-house, *ŏr'ĕnj hŏûs*, **orangery,** *ŏr'ĕnjŭri̇*, s. stanzone degli agrumi, m.

orange-tree, *–trḗ*, s. arancio, m.

oration, *ŏrā'shăn*, s. orazione, f.

orator, *ŏr'ătŭr*, s. oratore, m.

oratorial, *–tŏ'ri̇ăl*, a. oratorio.

oratory, *ŏr'ătûri̇*, s. eloquenza, f.; oratorio, m. (luogo sagro).

orb, *ŏrb*, s. globo, f.; sfera, spera, f.

orbit, *ŏr'bi̇t*, s. orbita, f.

orchard, *ŏr'chărd*, s. verziere, pomario, m.

orchestra, *ŏr'kĕstră*, s. orchestra, f.

ordain, *ŏrdān'*, v. a. ordinare; stabilire.

ordeal, *ŏr'di̇ăl*, s. prova, f.

order, *ŏr'dŭr*, s. ordine, comando, m.; grado, m.; congregazione di religiosi, f.; **in – to,** ad effetto, per cagione; **–,** v. a. ordinare, regolare; comandare.

ordering, *–i̇ng*, s. disposizione, f.; acconciamento, m.   [mente.

orderly, *–li̇*, a. regolare; **–,** ad. regolar-

ordinance, *ŏr'di̇năns*, s. ordinanza, f.

ordinarily, *–di̇nări̇li̇*, ad. ordinariamente.

ordinary, *–di̇nări̇*, a. ordinario; **–,** s. trattoria, f.

ordination, *–nă'shăn*, s. ordinazione, f.

ordnance, *ŏrd'năns*, s. artiglieria, f.

ore, *ŏr*, s. minerale, fossile, m.

organ, *ŏr'găn*, s. organo, m.

organic(al), *–găn'i̇k(ăl)*, a. organico.

organisation, *–nization'shăn*, s. organizzazione, f.

organise, *ŏr'găni̇z*, v. a. organizzare.

organism, *ŏr'găni̇zm*, s. struttura organica, f.

organist, *ŏr'gănist*, s. organista, m.

organ-pipe, *ŏr'găn pi̇p*, s. canna d'organo, f.   [m.

organ-stop, *–stŏp*, s. giuoco (del organo)

oriental, *ŏri̇ĕn'tăl*, a. orientale.

orifice, *ŏr'i̇fi̇s*, s. orifizio, m.; apertura, f.

origin, *ŏr'i̇ji̇n*, s. origine, principio, m.

original, *ŏri̇j'i̇năl*, a. & s. originale (m.); **–ly,** ad. originalmente.

originality, *–năl'i̇ti̇*, s. originalità, f.

originate, *ŏri̇j'i̇năt*, v. a. & n. originare; derivare.

orison, *ŏr'i̇zŏn*, s. orazione, preghiera, f.

ormolu, *ŏr'mŏlū*, s. foglia trita d'oro, f.

ornament, *ŏr'năment*, s. ornamento, m.; **–,** v. a. ornare, adornare. [d'ornamento.

ornamental, *–mĕn'tăl*, a. ornamentale,

ornate, *ŏr'năt*, a. ornato, abbellito.

orphan, *ŏr'făn*, a. orfano; **–,** s. orfano, m.; orfana, f.

orphanage, *–dj*, s. orfanezza, f.

orphan-asylum, *–ăsi̇'lŭm*, s. casa degli orfani, f.; orfanotrofio, m.

orthodox, *ŏr'thŏdŏks*, a. ortodosso.

orthodoxy, *–thŏdŏksi̇*, s. ortodossia, f.

orthographical, *–thŏgrăf'i̇kăl*, a. ortografico, d'ortografia; **–ly,** ad. in modo ortografico.

orthography, *–thŏg'răfi̇*, s. ortografia, f.

oscillate, *ŏs'si̇lăt*, v. n. oscillare.

oscillation, *–lă'shăn*, s. oscillazione, vibrazione, f., ondeggiamento, m.

osier, *ŏ'zhăr*, s. vinco, vimine, m.

ospray, *ŏs'prā*, s. frusone, m.   [zione.

ossification, *ŏssi̇fi̇kă'shăn*, s. ossifica-

ossify, *ŏs'si̇fi̇*, v. a. fare divenir osso; **–,** v. n. ossificarsi.   [rente.

ostensible, *ŏstĕn'si̇bl*, a. ostensibile, appa-

ostensibly, *–bli̇*, ad. ostensibilmente.

ostentation, *–tă'shăn*, s. ostentazione, f.

ostentatious, *–tă'shăs*, a. pomposo, fastoso; **–ly,** ad. fastosamente.

ostler, *ŏs'lŭr*, s. stalliere, m.

ostracise, *ŏs'trăsi̇z*, v. a. dar l'ostracismo.

ostrich, *ŏs'tri̇ch*, s. struzzo, m.

other, *ŭth'ŭr*, pn. altro, altra.

otherwise, *–wi̇z*, ad. altrimente.

otter, *ŏt'tŭr*, s. lontra, f.

ought, *ăt*, v. n. def. dovere.   [f.

ounce, *ŏûns*, s. oncia, f.; lince, m., pantera,

our, *ŏûr*, **ours,** *–z*, pn. nostro, nostra, nostri, nostre; **–s,** il nostro, la nostra, i nostri.   [noi stesse.

ourselves, *–sĕlvz'*, pn. pl. noi, noi stessi,

oust, *ŏûst*, v. a. togliere; espellere, spodestare; spingere; portare via.

out, *ŏût*, ad. & pr. fuori, fuora, fuor di; **– of casa;** **– ! i.** uscite di qui! **– of doors,** fuori, fuori di casa; **–,** v. a. spogliare, privare.   [preponderare.

outbalance, *–băl'ăns*, v. a. sbilanciare;

outbid, *–bi̇d'*, v. a. ir. alzar il prezzo (all' incanto).   [f.

outbreak, *ŏût'brăk*, s. eruzione, f.; uscita,

outburst, –*bŭrst*, s. esplosione, f.

outcast, –*kăst*, a. esiliato, sbandito; di rifiuto.   [m.; vendita pubblica, f.

outcry, –*krī*, s. rumore, m.; schiamazzo,

outdo, –*dō'*, v. a. ir. superare; soprastare.

outer, *ŏŭt'ăr*, a. esteriore, esterno.

outermost, –*mŏst*, a. estremo, ultimo.

outfit, *ŏŭt'fĭt*, s. approvvigionamento, m.

outfitter, –*tăr*, s. confezioniere, m.

outgoing, –*gōĭng*, s. uscita, f.; spesa, f.

outgrow, –*grō'*, v. a. ir. divenir troppo grande.   [f.

outhouse, –*hŏŭs*, s. rimessa, f.; casipola,

outing, –*ĭng*, s. escursione, f.   [stiero.

outlandish, –*lăndĭsh*, a. straniero, fore-

outlast, –*lăst'*, v. a. durare più lungamente.

outlaw, –*lā*, s. proscritto, bandito, m.; –, v. a. proscrivere, bandire.

outlawry, –*lări*, s. proscrizione, f.

outlay, –*lā*, s. sborso, m.   [saggio, m.

outlet, –*lĕt*, s. uscita, f., esito, m.; pas-

outline, –*lĭn*, s. contorno, m.; schizzo, m.; –, –*lĭn'*, v. a. schizzare.

outlive, –*lĭv'*, v. a. sopravvivere.

outlying, –*lĭĭng*, a. confinante; ulteriore.

outnumber, –*nămbăr*, v. a. sorpassare in numero.

outpost, –*pŏst*, s. guardia avanzata, f.

outrage, –*răj*, s. oltraggio, m.; –, v. a. oltraggiare.

outrageous, –*rā'jăs*, a. oltraggioso, in-giurioso; atroce; –ly, ad. oltraggiosa-mente.

outrider, –*rĭdăr*, s. cavalcante, m.

outright, –*rīt'*, ad. subitamente, incon-tanente.   [rere.

outrun, –*răn'*, v. a. ir. avanzare nel cor-

outset, –*sĕt*, s. cominciamento, principio, m.

outshine, –*shĭn'*, v. a. ir. sorpassare in splendore.

outside, –*sīd*, s. superficie, f., esteriore, m., apparenza, f.; –rs, s. pl. pubblico, m.

outskirt, –*skŭrt*, s. estremità, f., orlo, m.; subborgo, m.

outstep, –*stĕp'*, v. a. oltrepassare.   [dere.

outstretch, –*strĕch'*, v. a. distendere, span-

outstrip, –*strĭp'*, v. a. avanzare, superare; prevenire.

outwall, –*wāl*, s. muro esteriore, m.

outward, –*wărd*, a. esteriore, esterno; –ly, ad. esteriormente.   [ciare.

outweigh, –*wā'*, v. a. pesare di più, sbilan-

outwit, –*wĭt'*, v. a. ingannare, truffare.

outwork, –*wărk*, s. edificio esteriore, m.

oval, *ō'văl*, a. & s. ovale (m.).

ovary, *ō'vărĭ*, s. ovaia, f.

ovation, *ō'vā'shăn*, s. ovazione, f.

oven, *ŭv'n*, s. forno, m.

over, *ō'văr*, pr. & ad. sopra, su, sopra di; troppo, oltre; all –, passato, finito; dap-pertutto; interamente; – and –, molte volte; – and above, oltre; – again, di nuovo, da capo; – against, in faccia, dirimpetto.

overall, –*ăl'*, s. soprabito, m.

overawe, –*ā'*, v. a. tenere in timore o rispetto.

overbalance, –*băl'ăns*, v. a. preponderare, –, s. sovrappiù, m.   [cere.

overbear, –*băr'*, v. a. ir. sormontare; vin-

overbearing, –*băr'ĭng*, a. arrogante, im-perioso.

overboard, *ō'vărbŏrd*, ad. fuori della nave.

overburden, –*băr'dn*, v. a. sopraggravare.

overcast, –*kăst'*, v. a. ir. oscurare; cucire a sopraggetto; valutare troppo.

overcharge, –*chărj'*, v. a. caricare troppo; rincarire; –, s. sopraccarico, m.; rincari-mento, m.   [oscurare.

overcloud, –*klŏŭd'*, v. a. annuvolare,

overcome, –*kăm'*, v. a. ir. superare, sor-montare; vincere.   [dito, presuntuoso,

over-confident, –*kŏn'fĭdĕnt*, a. troppo ar-

overdo, –*dō'*, v. a. ir. fare troppo, ecce-dere.

overdraw, –*drā'*, v. a. fare una tratta che eccede l' ammontare del credito.

overdress, –*drĕs'*, v. a. vestire con troppa pompa.   [troppo.

over-eat, –*ēt'*, v. n. ir. (oneself) mangiar

overflow, *ō'vărflō*, s. inondazione, f.; –, –*flō'*, v. a. & n. ir. inondare, traboccare.

overgrow, –*grō'*, v. a. ir. divenir troppo grande.   [eccessivo, m.

overgrowth, *ō'vărgrōth*, s. accrescimento

overhang, –*hăng'*, v. a. & n. ir. pendere in fuori, aggettare.

overhead, –*hĕd'*, ad. in alto, sopra, in su.

overhear, –*hĕr'*, v. a. ir. udire senza essere osservato.

overheat, –*hĕt'*, v. a. scaldare troppo.

overjoy, –*jŏĭ'*, s. estasi, f., eccesso di gioia, m.   [increstare.

overlay, –*lā'*, v. a. ir. affogare, soffogare, increstare.

overleap, –*lĕp'*, v. a. ir. saltare di là.

overlook, –*lŭk'*, v. a. aver l' ispezione; dominare; invigilare; esaminare; chiudere gli occhi; trascurare; disprezzare.

overmuch, –*mŭch'*, ad. oltremisura, troppo.   [terire, omettere.

overpass, –*păs'*, v. a. trapassare; pre-

overplus, *ō'vărplăs*, s. soprappiù, sover-chio, m.   [prevalere.

overpower, –*pŏŭ'ăr*, v. a. predominare,

overrate, –*rāt'*, v. a. stimare o doman-dare troppo.   [gannare, eludere.

overreach, –*rēch'*, v. a. ir. prevenire; in-

override, –*rīd'*, v. a. ir. strapazzare (un cavallo).

overrule, –*rōl'*, v. a. dominare, governare.

overrun, –*răn'*, v. a. ir. stracorrere; co-prire; inondare; predare; –, v. n. ir. es-sere troppo pieno.   [tere.

oversee, –*sē'*, v. a. ir. soprintendere; omet-

overseer, –*sē'ăr*, s. soprintendente, m.

overset, –*sĕt'*, v. a. ir. rovesciare; –, v. n. ir. demolirsi.   [ombreggiare.

overshadow, –*shăd'ō*, v. a. adombrare,

overshoe, *ō'vărshō*, s. caloscia, f.

overshoot, –*shōt'*, v. a. ir. tirare di là del segno; (oneself) innoltrarsi troppo.

oversight, *ō'vărsĭt*, s. ispezione, cura, f.; errore, sbaglio, m.

oversleep, –*slēp'*, v. n. ir. dormire troppo.

overspread, *–sprĕd'*, v. a. ir. spandere; allargare, dilatare.
overstep, *–stĕp'*, v. a. oltrepassare.
overt, *ŏ'vărt*, a. aperto, pubblico.
overtake, *–tāk'*, v. a. ir. giungere; acchiappare; sorprendere.   [gere troppo.
overtax, *–tăks'*, v. a. tassare troppo, esiovertax, *–tăks'*, v. a. tassare troppo, esioverthrow, *ŏ'vărthrŏ*, s. sovvertimento, m., sconfitta, rovina, rotta, f.; *–, –thrŏ'*, v. a. ir. rovesciare, rovinare, disfare.
overtly, *ŏ'vărtlĭ*, ad. apertamente.
overtop, *–tŏp'*, v. a. soprastare, sorpassare.   [sinfonia di.
overture, *ŏ'vărtăr*, s. apertura, f.; (mus.)
overturn, *–tărn'*, v. a. sovvertire, rovinare; rovesciare.
overvalue, *–văl'ů*, v. a. stimare troppo.
overweening, *–wĕn'ĭng*, a. presuntuoso.
overweight, *ŏ'vărwĕt*, s. preponderanza, f.
overwhelm, *–hwĕlm'*, v. a. sommergere; opprimere; aggravare.
overwork, *–wŭrk'*, v. a. lavorare troppo.
oviparus, *ŏvĭp'ărŭs*, a. oviparo.
owe, *ŏ*, v. a. ir. dovere; essere obbligato.
owing, *–ĭng*, a. debitore; a cagione di.
owl, *ŏŭl*, owlet, *–ĕt*, s. civetta, f.
own, *ŏn*, a. proprio; my *–*, il mio, la mia; *–*, v. a. confessare, concedere; riconoscere; possedere.
owner, *–ăr*, s. proprietario, padrone, m.
ownership, *–shĭp*, s. proprietà, f.; signoria, m.
ox, *ŏks*, s. bue, bove, m.   [f.
oxidise, *ŏks'ĭdĭz*, v. a. ossidare; *–*, v. n. ossidarsi.
oxygen, *ŏks'ĭjĕn*, s. ossigeno, m.
oyster, *ŏĭ'stăr*, s. ostrica, f.

P.

pace, *pās*, s. passo, m.; *–*, v. n. misurare co' passi; *–*, v. n. andare a passo a passo.
pacer, *pā'săr*, s. cavallo ambiante, m.
pacific(al), *păsĭf'ĭk(ăl)*, a. pacifico.   [m.
pacification, *–fĭkā'shăn*, s. pacificamento,
pacify, *păs'ĭfī*, v. a. pacificare; placare.
pack, *păk*, s. balla, f.; fardello, m.; muta (di cani), f.; mazzo di carte, m.; *–*, v. a. imballare; affardellare; imbastare; (cards) accozzare le carte.
package, *păk'ăj*, s. balla, f.
pack-cloth, *–klŏth*, s. tela di sacco, f.
packet, *–ĕt*, s. fardello, m.   [f.
packet-boat, *–bŏt*, s. nave da procaccio,
pack-horse, *păk'hŏrs*, s. cavallo da basto,
packing, *–ĭng*, s. l' imballare, m.   [m.
pack-thread, *–thrĕd*, s. spago, m., cordicina, f.
pact, *păkt*, s. patto, m., convenzione, f.
pad, *păd*, s. strada battuta, f.; sentiero, m.; cavallo portante, m.; ladro, m.; guancialetto, m.; cercine, m.; *–*, v. n. rubare le strade; riempiere di borra.
paddle, *pădĭl*, s. remo corto e largo, m.; *–*, v. n. remigare; guazzare.
paddock, *–ŏk*, s. botta, f.; parco, m.

padlock, *–lŏk*, s. catenaccio, m.
pagan, *pā'găn*, a. & s. pagano (m.).
paganism, *–gănĭzm*, s. paganesimo, m.
page, *pāj*, s. pagina, f.; paggio, m.; *–*, v. a. numerare le pagine.   [f.
pageant, *păj'ĕnt*, s. spettacolo, m., pompa,
pageantry, *–trĭ*, s. fasto, m., pompa, f.
pail, *pāl*, s. secchia, f.
pain, *pān*, s. pena, punizione, f.; dolore, m.; *–*, v. a. dolere, dar pena.   [con pena.
painful, *–fŭl*, a. doloroso, penoso; **-ly**, ad.
painless, *–lĕs*, a. senza pena, senza afflizione; senza dolore.
painstaking, *–z'tāk'ĭng*, a. laborioso.
paint, *pānt*, v. a. dipingere; *–*, v. n. impainter, *–ăr*, s. pittore, m.   [bellettarsi.
painting, *–ĭng*, s. pittura, f.
pair, *păr*, s. paio, m., coppia, f.; *–*, v. a. appaiare; accoppiare; *–*, v. n. accoppiarsi.
palace, *păl'ăs*, s. palazzo, m.   [porito.
palatable, *păl'ătăbl*, a. grato al gusto, sapalate, *păl'ăt*, s. palato, m.; gusto, m.
palatial, *pălā'shăl*, a. magnifico, splendido.
Palatinate, *pălăt'ĭnăt*, s. Palatinato, m.
palatine, *păl'ătĭn*, a. & s. palatino (m.).
palaver, *pălā'văr*, s. ciarla, f.
pale, *pāl*, a. pallido, smorto; *–*, s. palo, m.; palata, f.; *–*, v. a. palizzare.
paleness, *–nĕs*, s. pallidezza, f.
palfrey, *păl'frĭ*, s. palafreno, m.
paling, *pā'lĭng*, palisade, *pălĭsād'*, s. palizzata, f.; *–*, v. a. palizzare.
pall, *păl*, s. palio, panno da morto, m.; *–*, v. a. mantellare; *–*, v. n. mettersi il palio; diventare mucido.   [gliericcio, m.
pallet, *păl'lĕt*, s. piccol letto misero, papalliate, *păl'lĭăt*, v. a. palliare.
palliation, *–lĭā'shăn*, s. palliamento, m.
palliative, *păl'lĭătĭv*, a. & s. palliativo
pallid, *păl'lĭd*, a. pallido, smorto.   [(m.).
pallor, *păl'ăr*, s. pallore, m.
palm, *păm*, s. palma, f.; vittoria, f.; palmo, m.; *–*, v. a. toccare; giuocar di mano.
palmated, *pălmā'tĕd*, a. palmato.
palmistry, *păl'mĭstrĭ*, s. chiromanzia, f.
Palm-Sunday, *păm'sŭndā*, s. domenica delle Palme, f.   [chiaro.
palpable, *păl'păbl*, a. palpabile; evidente,
palpably, *–păblĭ*, ad. in modo palpabile; chiaramente.
palpitate, *păl'pĭtăt*, v. n. palpitare.
palpitation, *–tā'shăn*, s. palpitazione, f.
palsied, *păl'zĭd*, a. paralitico.
palsy, *păl'zĭ*, s. paralisia, f.
paltriness, *păl'trĭnĕs*, s. bassezza, viltà, meschinità, f.
paltry, *–trĭ*, a. vile, abietto, meschino.
pamper, *păm'păr*, v. a. trattare delicatamente; satollare, ingrassare.
pamphlet, *păm'flĕt*, s. libretto, libello, m.; operetta, f.   [bretti, librettista, m.
pampaleteer, *–flĕtĕr'*, s. scrittore di li
pan, *păn*, s. padella, cazzeruola, f.
panacea, *pănăsē'ā*, s. rimedio universale, panacea, m.
pancake, *păn'kāk*, s. fritella, f.

pander, *păn'dăr,* s. ruffiano, m.; –, v. a. ruffianare. [m.
pane, *păn,* s. vetro di finestra, m.; quadrello, m.
panegyric, *pănějĭr'ĭk,* s. panegirico, m.
panel, *păn'ĕt,* s. quadrello, m.; lista de' giurati, f.
pang, *păng,* s. angoscia, f. [giurati, f.
panic, *păn'ĭk,* a. panico; –, s. terrore panico, m.
pannel, *păn'nĕl,* s. basto, m., bardella, f.
pannier, *păn'nĭăr,* s. paniere, m., cesta, f.
panorama, *pănŏrā'mă,* s. panorama, m.
panoply, *păn'ŏplĭ,* s. panoplia, f.
pansy, *păn'zĭ,* s. viola del pensiero, m.
pant, *pănt,* v. n. anelare, ansare; palpitare.
pantaloons, *păntălōōns',* s. pl. calzoni, pantaloni, m. pl. [dei mobili, m.
pantechnicon, *păntĕk'nĭkŏn,* s. magazzino
panther, *păn'thăr,* s. pantera, f.
pantomime, *păn'tŏmĭm,* s. pantomimo, m.
pantry, *păn'trĭ,* s. guardavivande, m.
pap, *păp,* s. papilla, f.; puppa, f., pan cotto, m.
papa, *păpă',* s. babbo, m. (voce fanciullesca).
papacy, *pā'păsĭ,* s. papato, m.
papal, *–păl* a. papale.
paper, *pā'păr,* s. carta, f.; giornale, m.; –s, pl. scritture, f. pl.; fondi di commercio, m. pl.; –, v. a. coprire di carta.
paper-credit, (**--currency**), *–krĕdĭt (kărrĕnsĭ),* s. carta monetata, f.
paper-mill, *–mĭl,* s. cartiera (da fabbricare la carta), f.
paper-weight, *–wăt,* s. calcalettere, f.
Papist, *pā'pĭst,* s. papista, m.
pappy, *păp'pĭ,* a. molle, morbido, sugoso.
par, *păr,* a. & s. pari (m.), ugualità, f.; equivalente (m.); **to be at –,** esser uguale.
parable, *păr'ăbl,* s. parabola, f.
parade, *părăd',* s. parata, f.; ostentazione, mostra, f.; piazza d'arme, f.; –, v. a. far la parata (delle truppe).
Paradise, *păr'ădĭs,* s. paradiso, m.
paradoxical, *–dŏks'ĭkăl,* a. paradosso, strano, bizzarro.
paragon, *păr'ăgŏn,* s. modello perfetto, m.
paragraph, *păr'ăgrăf,* s. paragrafo, m.
parallel, *păr'ăllĕl,* a. parallelo; –, s. linea paralella, f.; –, v. a. paragonare, assomigliare.
paralyse, *păr'ălĭz,* v. a. render paralitico.
paralysis, *părăl'ĭsĭs,* s. paralisi, f.
paralytic, *–lĭt'ĭk,* a. paralitico.
paramount, *păr'ămŏunt,* a. superiore; sovrano, primo; –, s. capo, padrone, m.
paramour, *–mŏr',* s. amante, innamorato, m.
paraphrase, *păr'ăfrăz,* s. parafrasi, f.
parasite, *păr'ăsĭt,* s. parasito, m.
parasitic, *–sĭt'ĭk,* a. parasitico.
parasol, *părăsŏl',* s. parasole, m.; ombrello, m.
parboil, *păr'bŏĭl,* v. a. sobbollire.
parcel, *păr'sĕl,* s. particella, piccola porzione, f.; –, v. a. spartire, sminuzzare.
parcels'-post, *–s pŏst,* s. posta di pacchetti, f.

parch, *părch,* v. a. abbruciare, seccare.
parchment, *–mĕnt,* s. pergamena, carta-pecora, f.
pardon, *păr'dn,* s. perdono, m.; grazia, f.
pardonable, *–ăbl,* a. perdonabile.
pare, *păr,* v. a. pareggiare, scortecciare.
parent, *pā'rĕnl,* s. padre, genitore, m.; madre, f. [stirpe, f.
parentage, *pā'rĕntăj,* s. parentato, m.;
parental, *părĕn'tăl,* a. paterno.
parenthesis, *părĕn'thĕsĭs,* s. parentesi, f.
parenthetical, *–thĕt'ĭkăl,* a. in parentesi.
parish, *păr'ĭsh,* s. parrocchia, f.; –, a. parrocchiale. [m.
parishioner, *păr'ĭsh'ănăr,* s. parrocchiano,
park, *părk,* s. parco, serraglio d'animali, m.; –, v. a. mettere in un parco.
parlance, *păr'lăns,* s. conversazione, f.
parley, *păr'lĭ,* s. conferenza, f.
Parliament, *păr'lĭmĕnt,* s. parlamento, m.; senato, m.
Parliamentary, *–mĕn'tărĭ,* a. parlamentario; **– train,** s. treno lento, m.
parlour, *păr'lăr,* s. sala, f.; parlatorio, m.
parochial, *părŏ'kĭăl,* a. parrocchiale.
parody, *păr'ŏdĭ,* s. parodia, f.; –, v. a. parodiare.
paroquet, *păr'ŏkĕt,* s. pappagallo, m.
parricide, *păr'ĭsĭd,* s. parricida, m.; parricidio, m.
parrot, *păr'rŏt,* s. pappagallo, m.
parry, *păr'rĭ,* v. a. parare; evitare.
parse, *părs,* v. a. (gr.) spiegare le parti d'orazione.
parsimonious, *–sĭmō'nĭăs,* a. parco, economo; **-ly,** ad. con parsimonia.
parsimony, *păr'sĭmŏnĭ,* s. parsimonia, f.
parsley, *părs'lĭ,* s. prezzemolo, m.
parsnip, *părs'nĭp,* s. pastinaca, f.
parson, *păr'sn,* s. curato, m.
parsonage, *–ăj,* s. beneficio (d' una parrocchia), m.
part, *părt,* s. parte, porzione, f.; personaggio, m.; dovere, debito, m.; **–s,** pl. contrade, f. pl.; talento, m.; –, v. a. disunire, separare, dividere; –, v. n. separarsi; partirsi.
partake, *părtăk',* v. a. & n. ir. partecipare, avere parte.
partaker, *–kăr,* s. partecipatore, m.
partial, *păr'shăl,* a. parziale; favorevole; **-ly,** ad. con parzialità, f.
partiality, *–shăl'ĭtĭ,* s. parzialità, f.
participant, *–tĭs'ĭpănt,* a. partecipante.
participate, *–tĭs'ĭpăt,* v. a. partecipare.
participation, *–pā'shăn,* s. partecipazione, f.
participle, *păr'tĭsĭpl,* s. (gr.) participio, m.
particle, *păr'tĭkl,* s. particola, f.; particella, f. [colori.
parti-coloured, *păr'tĭkŭlărd,* a. di più
particular, *–tĭk'ŭlăr,* a. particolare, singolare; **-ly,** ad. particolarmente; –, s. particolare, m., particolarità, f.; **–s,** s. pl. circostanze, particolarità, f. pl.
particularise, *–tĭk'ŭlărĭz,* v. a. particolarizzare.
particularity, *–lăr'ĭtĭ,* s. particolarità, f.

parting, *pȧrt'ĭng,* s. partimento, m.; spartimento dei cappelli, m.; partenza, f.

partisan, *pȧr'tĭzȧn,* s. partigiano, m.

partition, *–tĭsh'ȧn,* s. partizione, f., spartimento, m.; –, v. a. dividere in parti distinte.   [modo.

partly, *pȧrt'lĭ,* ad. in parte, in qualche

partner, *pȧrt'nȧr,* s. associato, socio, compagno, m.   [zione, f.

partnership, *–shĭp,* s. società, f.; associa-

partridge, *pȧr'trĭj,* s. pernice, f.

party, *pȧr'tĭ,* s. parte, f.; fazione, f.; persona, f.; (mil.) distaccamento, m.

party-man, *–mȧn,* s. fazioso, m.; sedi-

paschal, *pȧs'kȧl,* a. pasquale.   [zioso, m.

pass, *pȧs,* s. passo, m.; passaggio, m.; grado, stato, m., situazione, f.; stretto, m.; colpo, m., botta, f.; passaporto, m.; –, v. a. & n. passare, trapassare; trasferire; fuggire; morire.

passable, *–sȧbl,* a. passabile; tollerabile.

passage, *pȧs'sȧj,* s. passaggio, trapasso, m.; evento, caso, accidente, m.; affare, m.

passenger, *pȧs'sĕnjȧr,* s. passeggiere, m.

passenger-train, *–trȧn,* s. treno di persone, m.   [dante, m.

passer-by, *pȧs'sȧr bĭ,* s. passatore, vian-

passing, *pȧs'sĭng,* a. supremo, eminente; passeggiere; –, ad. estremamente.   [f.

passing-bell, *–bĕl,* s. campana da morto, m.

passion, *pȧsh'ȧn,* s. passione, f., affetto, m.; amore, m.; collera, ira, f.

passionate, *–ȧt,* a. appassionato, collerico; *–ly,* ad. iratamente, ardentemente.

Passion-flower, *–flȯȧr,* s. fior di passione, passiflora, f.   [passione, f.

Passion-week, *–wēk,* s. settimana della

passive, *pȧs'sĭv,* a. passivo; *–ly,* ad. passivamente.

pass-key, *pȧs'kē,* s. chiave comune, f.

Passover, *pȧs'ōvȧr,* s. pasqua degli Ebrei,

passport, *pȧs'pȯrt,* s. passaporto, m.   [f.

pass-word, *–wȯrd,* s. parola da segnale, f.

past, *pȧst,* a. passato, scorso, andato; –, pr. al di là, sopra, fuori.

paste, *pȧst,* s. pasta, colla, f.; –, v. a. impastare, incollare.

pasteboard, *–bȯrd,* s. cartone, m.

pastel, *pȧs'tĕl,* s. guado, m.

pastern, *pȧs'tȧrn,* s. pastoia, f.

pastime, *pȧs'tĭm,* s. passatempo, m.

pastor, *pȧs'tȯr,* s. pastore, m.

pastoral, *–tȯrȧl,* a. pastorale.

pastry, *pȧs'trĭ,* s. pasticceria, f.

pasturage, *pȧs'tūrȧj,* s. pastura, f.; pasto, pascolo, m.

pasture, *pȧs'tūr,* s. pastura, f.; –, v. a. pasturare, pascolare; –, v. n. pascere.

pasty, *pȧs'tĭ,* s. pasticcio, m.

pat, *pȧt,* a. convenevole, proprio, opportuno; –, s. piccol colpo, m., botta leggiera, f.; –, v. a. dare una percossa leggiera.

patch, *pȧch,* s. pezza, f.; toppa, f.; pezzo, pezzetto (sul viso), m.; –, v. a. rappezzare; mettere nei sul viso.

patch-work, *–ʋȧrk,* s. rappezzatura, f.

pate, *pȧt,* s. testa, f.; zucca, f.; capo, m., goffo, m.

paten, *pȧt'ĕn,* s. patena, f. (vaso sacro); piatto, m.

patent, *pȧt'ĕnt,* a. patente; privilegiato; –, s. patente, lettera patente, f.   [del re.

patentee, *–tĕntē',* s. che ha una patente

patent-leather, *–lĕthȧr,* s. cuoio verniciato, m.

paternal, *pȧtȧr'nȧl,* a. paterno.

paternity, *–nĭtĭ,* s. paternità, f.

path, *pȧth,* s. sentiero, calle, m.

pathetic, *pȧthĕt'ĭk,* a. patetico; *–ally,* ad. in modo patetico.   [praticabile.

pathless, *pȧth'lĕs,* a. senza sentiero, im-

pathological, *pȧthŏlŏj'ĭkȧl,* a. patologico.

pathology, *–thŏl'ŏjĭ,* s. patologia, f.

pathos, *pȧ'thŏs,* s. passione, f.

patience, *pȧ'shĕns,* s. pazienza, f.

patient, *–shĕnt,* a. & s. paziente (m.); *–ly,* ad. con pazienza.

patriarch, *pȧ'trĭȧrk,* s. patriarca, m.

patriarchal, *–ȧrk'ȧl,* a. patriarcale.

patrician, *pȧtrĭsh'ȧn,* a. patrizio; –, s. patrizio, uomo nobile, m.

patrimony, *pȧt'rĭmȯnĭ,* s. patrimonio, m.

patriot, *pȧ'trĭŏt,* s. patriotto, m.

patriotic, *–ŏtĭk,* a. patriottico.   [m.

patriotism, *pȧ'trĭŏtĭzm,* s. amor di patria,

patrol, *pȧtrŏl',* s. pattuglia, ronda, f.; –, v. n. fare la ronda.

patron, *pȧ'trȯn,* s. patrono, protettore, m.

patronage, *–ȧj,* s. patronato, m.

patroness, *–ĕs,* s. patrona, protettrice, f.

patronise, *–ĭz,* v. a. patrocinare.

patten, *pȧt'tĕn,* s. pattino, m.; zoccolo, m.

patter, *pȧt'tȧr,* v. n. scalpitare.

pattern, *–tȧrn,* s. modello, esempio, m.

patty, *pȧt'tĭ,* s. pasticcetto, m.

paucity, *pȧ'sĭtĭ,* s. pochezza, f., piccolo numero, m.

paunch, *pȧnsh,* s. pancia, f.   [numero, m.

pauper, *pȧ'pȧr,* s. povero, indigente, m.

pauperism, *–ĭzm,* s. povertà, f.

pause, *pȧz,* s. pausa, fermata, f.; –, v. n. pausare; fermarsi, pensare, riflettere.

pave, *pȧv,* v. a. lastricare; appianare.

pavement, *–mĕnt,* s. pavimento, lastricato, selciato, m.

pavilion, *pȧvĭl'yȯn,* s. padiglione, m., tenda, f.; (mar.) stendardo, m.   [lastra, f.

paving-stone, *pȧv'ĭng stȯn,* s. lastrico, m.

paw, *pȧ,* s. zampa, f.; –, v. a. & n. zampettare, zampare; stazzonare, maneggiare; carezzare.

pawn, *pȧn,* s. pegno, gaggio, m.; pedina, f.; –, v. a. impegnare, dare in pegno.

pawn-broker, *–brŏkȧr,* s. che impresta col pegno, prestatore. m.

pay, *pȧ,* s. paga, f., soldo, salario, m.; –, v. a. pagare; rimunerare; soddisfare.

payable, *–ȧbl,* a. pagabile.

pay-day, *–dȧ,* s. giorno di pagamento, m.

payee, *pȧē',* s. a cui si ha da pagare.

pay-master, *pȧ'mȧstȧr,* s. pagatore, m.; tesoriere, m.   [m.

payment, *–mĕnt,* s. pagamento, salario, m.

pea, *pē,* s. (peas and pease, pl.) pisello, m.

peace, *pēs,* s. pace, f.; – ! il silenzio ! tacete !

peaceable, *–ȧbl,* peaceful, *–fȗl,* a. pacifico, tranquillo.

peaceably, -âblǐ, ad. tranquillamente.

peach, pêch, s. pesca, f.; pesco, m.

peach-tree, -trê, s. pesco, m.

peacock, pê'kôk, s. pavone, m.

peahen, -hên, s. pavonessa, f. [f.

peak, pêk, s. sommità, cima, f.; estremità.

peal, pêl, s. scampanata, f.; schiamazzo, m.; -, v. a. assalire con strepito; -, v. n. scampanare.

pear, pâr, s. pera, f. [f.; parigina, f.

pearl, pârl, s. perla, f.; maglia nell'occhio,

pearled, pârld, a. ornato di perle.

pearly, pârl'ǐ, a. pieno di perle; perlato.

pear-tree, pâr'trê, s. pero, m.

peasant, pêz'ânt, s. contadino, m.

peasantlike, -lǐk, a. rustico, rozzo.

pea-shooter, pê'shôtûr, s. cerbottana, f.

peat, pêt, s. terra di torba, f.

pebble, pêb'bl, s. selce, f.

pebbly, -lǐ, a. pieno di selci.

peccadillo, pêkkâdǐl'lô, s. peccatuzzo, m.

peck, pêk, s. profenda, f.; quarto di staio, m.; -, v. a. beccare; percuotere; biasimare, riprendere.

pectoral, pêk'tôrâl, a. pettorale; -, s. rimedio pettorale, m. ǁ pubblico.

peculate, pêk'ûlât, v. n. rubare il danaro

peculation, -lâ'shûn, s. peculato, m.

peculiar, pêkû'lǐûr, a. peculiare, particolare, singolare; -ly, ad. peculiarmente.

peculiarity, -âr'ǐtǐ, s. particolarità, singolarità, f.

pecuniary, pêkû'nǐârǐ, a. pecuniario.

pedagogue, pêd'âgôg, s. pedagogo, pedante, m.

pedal, pêd'âl (pê'dâl), s. pedale, m.

pedant, pêd'ânt, s. pedante, m.

pedantic, -dânt'ǐk, a. pedantesco.

pedantry, pêd'ântrǐ, s. pedanteria, f.

peddle, pêd'dl, v. n. fare il merciaiuolo.

peddling, -dlǐng, a. di poco valore, meschino.

pedestal, pêd'êstâl, s. piedestallo, m.

pedestrian, -dês'trǐân, a. & s. pedestre (m.); pedone, m.

pedigree, pêd'ǐgrê, s. genealogia, f.

pediment, pêd'ǐmênt, s. frontone, m.

pedlar, pêd'lâr, s. merciuolo ambulante, m.

peel, pêl, s. scorza, pelle, f.; pala, f.; -, v. a. scortecciare, scorzare.

peep, pêp, s. spuntare del giorno, m.; occhiata, f.; -, v. n. spuntare; guardare di segreto; pigolare.

peep-hole, -hôl, s. buco da spiare, m.

peer, pêr, s. pari, m.; ottimate, m.; eguale, compagno, m. [nio d'un pari, m.

peerage -âj, s. dignità di pari, f.; dominio.

peeress, -ês, s. moglie d'un pari, f.; donna nobile, f.

peerless, -lês, a. incomparabile.

peevish, pêv'ǐsh, a. bisbetico, ritroso, capriccioso; -ly, ad. ritrosamente; con umore.

peevishness, -nês, s. umor strano, m.

peg, pêg, s. caviglia, f.; pirolo, m.; -, v. a. attaccare con caviglie.

pelf, pêlf, s. ricchezze, f. pl.

pelican, pêl'ǐkân, s. pellicano, m.

pelisse, pêlês', s. pelliccia, f.

pell, pêl, s. pelle, f.

pellet, pêl'lêt, s. pallottola, f.

pellicle, pêl'lǐkl, s. pellicella, f.

pellmell, pêlmêl', ad. confusamente.

pelt, pêlt, s. pelle, f., cuoio, m.; targa, f.

peltry, pêl'trǐ, s. pellicceria, f.

pen, pên, s. penna, f.; stia, f.; -, v. a. scrivere; rinchiudere, ingabbiare.

penal, pê'nâl, a. penale, di penale.

penalty, pên'âltǐ, s. penalità, f.; punizione, f. [f.

penance, pên'âns, s. penitenza, contrizione,

pence, pêns, (pl. di penny).

pencil, pên'sǐl, s. pennello, m.; -, v. a. delineare colla matita; abbozzare.

pencil-case, -kâs, s. matitatoio, m.

pencil-pointer, -pôǐntûr, s. tagliapennelli, m.

pendant, pên'dânt, s. pendente, m.; orecchino, ciondolo, m.; (mar.) pennone, m.

pendent, pên'dênt, a. incerto, irresoluto, indeciso, dubbio.

pending, pênd'ǐng, a. pendente.

pendulum, pên'dûlûm, s. pendolo, m.; oriuolo a tavola, m.

penetrate, pên'êtrât, v. a. & n. penetrare.

penetration, -trâ'shûn, s. acutezza (d'ingegno), f.

pen-holder, pên'hôldûr, s. pennaiuolo, m.

peninsula, pênǐn'sûlâ, s. penisola, f.

penitence, pên'ǐtêns, s. penitenza, f., pentimento, m. [-ly, ad. con penitenza.

penitent, -ǐtênt, n. & s. penitente (m.);

penitential, -tên'shâl, a. penitenziale.

penitentiary, -tên'shârǐ, s. penitenziere.

pen-knife, pên'nǐf, s. temperino, m. [m.

penman, -mân, s. maestro di scrittura, m.; autore, m.

penmanship, -shǐp, s. calligrafia, f.

pennant, pên'ânt, pennon, -nôn, s. pennone, stendardo, m., bandiera, f.

penniless, pên'nǐlês, a. senza un soldo.

penny, pên'nǐ, s. soldo, m. (moneta).

penny-a-liner, -â'lǐnûr, s. corrispondente d'un giornale che riceve un soldo per riga, m.

penny-post, -pôst, s. piccola posta, f.

penny-weight, -wât, s. scrupolo, m., 24 grain.

penny-wise, -wǐz, a. avaro, sordido.

penny-worth, -wûrth, s. prezzo per un soldo, m.

pension, pên'shûn, s. pensione, f.; -, v. a. assegnare una pensione. [pendiato, m.

pensioner, -âr, s. che gode pensione, stipensive, pên'sǐv, a. pensieroso; -ly, ad. pensierosamente. [rito santo, f.

Pentecoste, pên'têkôst, s. festa dello Spi-

penthouse, pênt'hôǔs, s. tettoia, rimessa, f.

penultimate, pênûl'tǐmât, a. penultimo.

penumbra, pênûm'brâ, s. penombra, f.

penurious, pênû'rǐûs, a. avaro, sordido.

penury, pên'ûrǐ, s. penuria, f.

peony, pê'ônǐ, s. peonia, f.

people, pê'pl, s. popolo, m., nazione, gente, f.; -, v a. popolare.

pepper, *pĕp'păr,* s. pepe, m.; –, v. a. impepare; (fig.) battere.
pepper-box, *–bŏks,* **pepper-caster,** *–kăstăr,* s. pepaiuola, f.
pepper-corn, *–kŏrn,* s. seme di pepe, m.
per, *păr,* pr. per.   [ventura, forse.
peradventure, *–ădvĕn'tŭr,* ad. per avventura.
perambulate, *–ăm'bŭlăt,* v. a. andare attorno, girare.
perambulator, *–bŭlătăr,* s. odometro, m.
perceivable, *–sē'văbl,* a. percettibile; sensibile.
perceivably, *–văblĭ,* ad. percettibilmente.
perceive, *–sēv',* v. a. concepire, comprendere; osservare.
percentage, *–sĕnt'dj,* s. commissione, f.; diritto di un tanto per cento, m.
perceptibility, *–sĕptĭbĭl'ĭtĭ,* s. qualità percettibile, percezione, f.   [sibile.
perceptible, *–sĕp'tĭbl,* a. percettibile; sensibile.
perceptibly, *–tĭblĭ,* ad. percettibilmente.
perception, *–sĕp'shŭn,* s. percezione, intelligenza, f.
perch, *părch,* s. pertica, f.; –, v. n. albergare.   [rare.
perchance, *–chăns',* ad. forse, per avventura.
percolate, *păr'kŏlăt,* v. a. filtrare, colare.
percussion, *–kŭsh'ŭn,* s. percussione, percossa, f.
percussion-cap, *–kăp,* s. capsula, fulminante, f.   [f.
perdition, *–dĭsh'ŭn,* s. perdizione, rovina, f.
peremptorily, *pĕr'ĕmtŭrĭlĭ,* ad. perentoriamente, decisivamente.
peremptoriness, *–tărĭnĕs,* s. decisione, determinazione, f.   [cisivo.
peremptory, *–tărĭ,* a. perentorio, decisivo.
perennial, *pĕrĕn'nĭăl,* a. perenne, perpetuo.
perfect, *păr'fĕkt,* a. perfetto, compiuto; puro; –, s. (gr.) perfetto, m.; –, v. a. perfezionare; compire.   [eccellenza, f.
perfection, *–fĕk'shŭn,* s. perfezione, f.; eccellenza, f.
perfectly, *păr'fĕktlĭ,* ad. perfettamente.
perfidious, *–fĭd'ĭăs,* a. perfido, disleale; –ly, ad. perfidamente.
perfidy, *păr'fĭdĭ,* s. perfidia, f.
perforate, *păr'fŏrăt,* v. a. perforare; trafiggere.   [m.
perforation, *–rā'shŭn,* s. perforamento, f.
perforce, *–fōrs',* ad. per forza, a viva forza.
perform, *–fŏrm',* v. a. & n. effettuare, fare, eseguire, compire.
performance, *–ăns,* s. compimento, m.; opera, azione, f.   [attore, m.
performer, *–ăr,* s. esecutore, compitore, attore, m.
perfume, *păr'fŭm,* s. profumo, odore soave, m.; –, *–fŭm',* v. a. profumare.
perfumer, *–fŭ'măr,* s. profumiere, m.; unguentario, m.
perfunctory, *–făngk'tărĭ,* a. negligente.
perhaps, *–hăps',* ad. forse, per avventura.
peril, *pĕr'ĭl,* s. periglio, pericolo, m.
perilous, *–ăs,* a. pericoloso; –ly, ad. pericolosamente.   [tempo, m.
period, *pē'rĭŏd,* s. periodo, m.; spazio di

periodical, *–ŏd'ĭkăl,* a. periodico; –ly, ad. periodicamente; –, s. giornale periodico, m.   [tico (m).
peripatetic, *pĕrĭpătĕt'ĭk,* a. & s. peripatetico, m.
periphrasis, *pĕrĭf'răsĭs,* **periphrase,** *pĕr'ĭfrăz,* s. perifrasi, f.   [dersi.
perish, *pĕr'ĭsh,* v. a. perire; –, v. n. perdersi.
perishable, *–ăbl,* a. caduco, transitorio.
peristyle, *pĕr'ĭstĭl,* s. peristilio, m.; colonnata, f.
periwig, *pĕr'ĭwĭg,* s. parrucca, f.
periwinkle, *–ĭngkl,* s. (bot.) pervinca, f.
perjure, *păr'jŭr,* v. n. spergiurare.
perjurer, *–ăr,* s. spergiuro, m.
perjury, *păr'jărĭ,* s. spergiuro, m.
permanence, *păr'mănĕns,* **permanency,** *–nĕnsĭ,* s. permanenza, f.
permanent, *–nĕnt,* a. permanente; –ly, ad. permanentemente.
permeate, *păr'mĕăt,* v. a. trapassare.
permission, *–mĭsh'ŭn,* s. permissione, licenza, f.
permissive, *–mĭs'sĭv,* a. permissivo.
permit, *păr'mĭt,* s. licenza, f.; polizza di tratta, f.; –, *–mĭt',* v. a. permettere.
permutation, *–mŭtā'shŭn,* s. permutamento, m.   [ad. dannosamente.
pernicious, *–nĭsh'ăs,* a. pernicioso; –ly, ad. dannosamente.
peroration, *pĕrŏrā'shŭn,* s. perorazione, f.
perpendicular, *părpĕndĭk'ŭlăr,* s. perpendicolare, a piombo; –, s. linea perpendicolare, f.; –ly, ad. perpendicolarmente.
perpetrate, *păr'pĕtrăt,* v. a. perpetrare, commettere (un delitto).
perpetration, *–trā'shăn,* s. esecuzione, f., il commettere (d' un' azione), m.
perpetrator, *–trā'tăr,* s. colpevole, delinquente, m.; attore, m.
perpetual, *–pĕt'ŭăl,* a. perpetuo; –ly, ad. perpetuamente.
perpetuate, *–pĕt'ŭăt,* v. a. perpetuare; eternare.   [zione, f.
perpetuation, *–ŭā'shăn,* s. perpetuazione, f.
perpetuity, *–pĕtū'ĭtĭ,* s. perpetuità, f.
perplex, *–plĕks',* v. a. imbrogliare, confondere.   [imbroglio, m.
perplexity, *–plĕks'ĭtĭ,* s. perplessità, f.
perquisite, *păr'kwĭzĭt,* s. profitto, emolumento, guadagno, m.
persecute, *păr'sĕkŭt,* v. a. perseguitare; importunare.   [f.; importunità, f.
persecution, *–kū'shăn,* s. persecuzione, f.
persecutor, *păr'sĕkătăr,* s. persecutore, m.
perseverance, *–sēvērăns,* s. perseveranza, f.   [persistere.
persevere, *–sēvēr',* v. n. perseverare;
perseveringly, *–ĭnglĭ,* ad. perseverantemente.
persist, *–sĭst',* v. a. persistere.   [mente.
persistency, *–ĕnsĭ,* s. persistenza, f.
persistent, *–ĕnt,* a. persistente.
person, *păr'sŏn,* s. persona, f.
personage, *–dj,* s. personaggio, m.
personal, *–ăl,* a. personale; –ly, ad. personalmente; – goods, s. pl. beni mobili, m. pl.   [dividuo, m.
personality, *–ăl'ĭtĭ,* s. personalità, f.; individuo, m.
personalty, *–ăltĭ,* s. beni mobili, m. pl.

personate, *–āt,* v. a. rappresentare, imitare. [zione, f.; carattere, m.
personation, *–ā'shŭn,* s. rappresentazione, f.
personification, *–ĭfĭkā'shŭn,* s. prosopopea, f. [(ad una cosa).
personify, *–sŏn'ĭfĭ,* v. a, dare un corpo
perspective, *–spĕk'tĭv,* a. & s. prospettivo (m.); prospettiva, f. [cace.
perspicacious, *–spĭkā'shŭs,* a. perspicace.
perspicacity, *–kăs'ĭtĭ,* s. perspicacia, f.
perspicuity, *–kū'ĭtĭ,* s. perspicuità, f.
perspiration, *–spĭrā'shŭn,* s. traspirazione, f.
perspire, *–spīr',* v. n. traspirare, sudare.
persuade, *–swād',* v. a. persuadere; convincere. [istigazione, f.
persuasion, *–swā'zhŭn,* s. persuasione, f.;
persuasive, *–sĭv,* a. persuasivo; **–ly,** ad. in modo persuasivo. [impronto.
pert, *pŭrt,* a. lesto, agile; impertinente.
pertain, *–tān',* v. n. appartenere, concernere, spettare.
pertinacious, *–tĭnā'shŭs,* a. pertinace, ostinato; **–ly,** ad. pertinacemente.
pertinacity, *–năs'ĭtĭ,* s. pertinacia, f.
pertinence, *pŭr'tĭnĕns,* s. pertinenza, appartenenza, f.
pertinent, *–tĭnĕnt,* a. pertinente; convenevole; **–ly,** ad. convenevolmente.
pertly, *pŭrt'lĭ,* ad. impertinentemente.
pertness, *pŭrt'nĕs,* s. vivacità, f.; impertinenza, f.
perturb, *–tŭrb',* v. a. perturbare.
perturbation, *–bā'shŭn,* s. perturbazione, f.; alterazione, f.
peruke, *pĕrŏk',* s. parrucca, f.
perusal, *pĕrō'zăl,* s. lettura, f.
peruse, *pĕrōz'* v. a. leggere; esaminare.
Peruvian-bark, *pĕrō'vĭăn bărk,* s. china, f.
pervade, *pŭrvād',* v. a. passare oltre, penetrare. **–ly,** ad. perversamente.
perverse, *–vŭrs',* a. perverso; ostinato;
perversion, *–vŭr'shŭn,* s. pervertimento,
perversity, *–sĭtĭ,* s. perversità, f. [m.
pervert, *–vŭrt',* v. a. pervertire, corrompere. [può passare.
pervious, *pŭr'vĭŭs,* a. pervio, per cui si
pessimist, *pĕs'sĭmĭst,* s. pessimista, m.
pest, *pĕst,* s. peste, pestilenza, f.
pester, *pĕs'tŭr,* v. a. noiare, inquietare.
pest-house, *pĕst'hŏŭs,* s. lazzaretto, spedale, m. [tagioso.
pestiferous, *–tĭf'ĕrŭs,* a. pestifero, contagioso.
pestilence, *pĕs'tĭlĕns,* s. pestilenza, f.
pestilent, *–lĕnt,* **pestilential,** *–lĕn'shăl,* a. pestilenziale.
pestle, *pĕs'tl (pĕs'l),* s. pestello, m.
pet, *pĕt,* s. sdegno, m.; favorito, m.; **–,** v. a. vezzeggiare soverchiamente.
petal, *pĕt'ăl,* s. (bot.) petalo, m.
petard, *pĕtărd',* s. petardo, m.
petition, *–tĭsh'ŭn,* s. supplica, f., memoriale, m.; **–,** v. a. supplicare, pregare.
petitioner, *–ŭr,* s. supplicante, m.
petrel, *pĕt'rĕl,* s. procellaria, f.
petrifaction, *pĕtrĭfăk'shŭn,* s. pietrificazione, f.

petrify, *pĕt'rĭfĭ,* v. a. impietrare; **–,** v. n. divenir pietra.
petroleum, *pĕtrō'lĕăm,* s. petrolio, m.
petticoat, *pĕt'ĭkŏt,* s. gonnella, gonnellina, f. [curatorello, m.
pettifogger, *–fŏggăr,* s. beccalite, procuratorello, m.
pettifogging, *–fŏggĭng,* s. lite, controversia, f.
pettiness, *–nĕs,* s. piccolezza, f.
pettish, *pĕt'tĭsh,* a. stizzoso, stico.
pettitoes, *pĕt'ĭtōz,* s. pl. zampetti di porco, m. pl.
petty, *pĕt'ĭ,* a. piccolo; di poco pregio.
petulance, *pĕt'ūlăns,* s. petulanza, f.
petulant, *–ūlănt,* a. petulante; **–ly,** ad. con petulanza.
pew, *pū,* s. banco di chiesa, m.
pewter, *pū'tŭr,* s. stagno, peltro, m.
pewterer, *–ŭr,* s. stagnaio, m.
phaeton, *fā'tŏn,* s. faeton, m.
phalanx, *făl'ăngks,* s. falange, f.
phantasm, *făn'tăzm,* **phantom,** *–tŏm,* s. fantasma, f.; apparizione, f.
phare, *fār,* s. faro, m.
pharisaical, *fārĭsā'ĭkăl,* a. farisaico.
Pharisee, *fār'ĭsē,* s. fariseo, m.
pharmaceutic(al), *fărmăsū'tĭk(ăl),* a. farmaceutico.
pharmacy, *făr'măsĭ,* s. farmacia, f.
phase, *fāz,* **phasis,** *fā'sĭs,* s. fase, f.
pheasant, *fĕz'ănt,* s. fagiano, m.
phenomenal, *fĕnŏm'ĕnăl,* a. fenomenale, straordinario.
phenomenon, *–ĕnŏn,* s. fenomeno, m.
phial, *fĭ'ăl,* s. fiala, caraffa, f.
philanthropic(al), *fĭlănthrŏp'ĭk(ăl),* a. filantropico. [tropo, m.
philanthropist, *–ăn'thrŏpĭst,* s. filantropo.
philanthropy, *–ăn'thrŏpĭ,* s. filantropia, f.
philological, *fĭlŏlŏj'ĭkăl,* a. filologico, grammaticale.
philologist, *–lŏl'ŏjĭst,* s. filologo, m.
philology, *–ŏjĭ,* s. filologia, f.
philosopher, *fĭlŏs'ŏfŭr,* s. filosofo, m.; **natural –,** fisico, m.; **–'s stone,** s. pietra filosofale, f.
philosophic(al), *–ŏsŏf'ĭk(ăl),* a. filosofico; **–ly,** ad. filosoficamente. [ragionare.
philosophise, *–ŏs'ŏfĭz,* v. n. filosofare;
philosophy, *–ŏs'ŏfĭ,* s. filosofia, f.; **natural –,** fisica, f.
philtre, *fĭl'tŭr,* s. bevanda amorosa, f.
phiz, *fĭz,* s. viso, visaccio, m. [tarro, m.
phlegm, *flĕm,* s. flemma, f.; pituita, f., catarro, m.
phlegmatic, *flĕgmăt'ĭk,* a. flemmatico, pituitoso.
phosphoric, *fŏsfŏr'ĭk,* a. fosforico.
phosphorus, *fŏs'fŭrŭs,* s. fosforo, m.
photograph, *fō'tŏgrăf,* s. fotografo, m.; **–,** v. a. fotografare.
photographer, *–tŏg'răfŭr,* s. fotografo, m.
photographic, *–tŏgrăf'ĭk,* a. fotografico.
photography, *–tŏg'răfĭ,* s. fotografia, f.
phrase, *frāz,* s. frase, f.; espressione, f.; stilo, m.; **–,** v. a. esprimere. [frasi, f.
phraseology, *frăzēŏl'ŏjĭ,* s. collezione di frasi, f.
phrenology, *frĕnŏl'ŏjĭ,* s. frenologia, f.

phthisis, *fthē'ĭs,* s. tisichezza, f.

physic, *fĭz'ĭk,* s. medicina, f.; scienza della medicina, f.; **–s,** s. pl. fisica, f.; **–,** v. a. medicare.　　　　　　　[mente.

physical, *–ĭkăl,* a. fisico; **–ly,** ad. fisica-

physician, *–zĭsh'ăn,* s. medico, m.　　[f.

physiognomy, *fĭzĭog'nŏmĭ,* s. fisionomia,

physiological, *–ĭsĭ'ĭkăl,* a. fisiologico.

physiologist, *–ŏl'ĭst,* s. fisiologico, m.

physiology, *–ŏl'ŏjĭ,* s. fisiologia, f.

pianist, *pĭăn'ĭst,* s. pianista, m. & f.

piano, *pĭă'nō,* s. piano-forte, m.

piaster, *pĭăs'tŭr,* s. piastra, f. (moneta).

picaroon, *pĭkărōn',* s. rubatore, ladro, m.

pick, *pĭk,* s. mazzuolo, m.; scelta, f.; **ear–**, s. stuzzicorecchi, m.; **tooth–,** s. stuzzicadenti, m.

pick, –, v. a. cogliere, scegliere; nettare, mondare; **–,** v. n. mangiare delicatamente; **–,** s. mazzuolo, m.; scelta, f.

pick-axe, *–ăks,* s. zappa, f., piccone, m.

picked, *–ĕd,* a. puntuto; scelto.

pickerel, *–ĕrĕl,* s. lucchetto, m.

picket, *–ĕt,* s. picchetto, m.　　　　[nare.

pickle, *pĭk'l,* s. salamoia, f.; **–,** v. a. mari-

picklock, *–lŏk,* s. grimaldello, m.; ladro, m.

pickpocket, *–pŏkĕt,* s. tagliaborse, m.

picnic, *–nĭk,* s. pasto a bocca a borsa.

pictorial, *pĭktō'rĭăl,* a. pittoresco.

picture, *–ĕjtŭr (–chŭr),* s. pittura, f.; ritratto, m.; **–,** v. a. dipingere, rappresen-

picturesque, *–rĕsk,* a. pittoresco.　[tare.

pie, *pĭ,* s. pasticcio, m.; pica, gazza, f.

piebald, *pĭ'bŏld,* a. pezzato, nero e bianco.

piece, *pēs,* s. pezzo, m.; parte, f.; moccolo, moccolino, m.; cannone, m.; **a –**, ciascuno; **–,** v. a. rappezzare.

piecemeal, *–mēl,* a. & ad. solo, separato; pezzo a pezzo.

pied, *pĭd,* a. di vari colori.

pier, *pēr,* s. pilastro da ponti, m.; molo, m.

pierce, *pērs,* v. a. forare; penetrare; muovere.

piercingly, *–ĭnglĭ,* ad. in modo pungente.

pier-glass, *pēr'glăs,* s. specchio tra due finestre, m.

piety, *pĭ'ĕtĭ,* s. pietà, divozione, f.

pig, *pĭg,* s. porcello, m.; **–** (of lead), lastra di piombo, f.; **–,** v. n. fare i porcelli.

pigeon, *pĭj'ăn,* s. colombo, m.

pigeon-hole, *–hōl,* s. buco del colombaio, m.

pigeon-house, *–hŏŭs,* s. colombaio, m.

pig-headed, *pĭg'hĕdĕd,* a. grosso di testa; stupido.　　　　　　　[colore, m.

pigment, *pĭg'mĕnt,* s. pigmento, m.;

pigmy, *–mĭ,* s. pigmeo, nano, m.

pigsty, *–pĭg'stĭ,* s. porcile, m.

pike, *pĭk,* s. luccio, m. (pesce); picca, f.

pilaster, *pĭlăs'tŭr,* s. pilastro, m.

pile, *pĭl,* s. palo, m.; mucchio, m.; fascio, m.; edificio, m.; pelo, m., lanugine, f.; **funeral –**, rogo, m., pira, f.; **–,** v. a. ammucchiare.

piles, *pĭlz,* s. pl. emorroidi, f. pl.

pilfer, *pĭl'fŭr,* v. a. rubare, furare.

pilgrim, *pĭl'grĭm,* s. pellegrino, m.

pilgrimage, *–dj,* s. pellegrinaggio, m.

pill, *pĭl,* s. pillola, f.

pillage, *pĭl'ldj,* s. predamento, m.; **–,** v. a. saccheggiare, predare.

pillar, *pĭl'lăr,* s. colonna, f.; appoggio, m.

pillion, *pĭl'yŭn,* s. guancialetto, m.; sella da donna, f.　　　　　[mettere alla berlina.

pillory, *pĭl'lărĭ,* s. berlina, f.; **–,** v. a.

pillow, *pĭl'lō,* s. guanciale, m.　　　　[f.

pillow-case, *–kās,* s. fodera di guanciale,

pilot, *pĭ'lŏt,* s. piloto, m.; **–,** v. a. guidare; governare.　　　　　　　　　　[m.

pilotage, *–dj,* s. uffizio o salario del piloto,

pimp, *pĭmp,* s. mezzano, m.

pimpernel, *pĭm'pŭrnĕl,* s. (bot.) pimpinella, f.

pimple, *pĭm'pl,* s. pustula, bolla, f.

pimpled, *–pld,* a. pieno di pustulette.

pin, *pĭn,* s. spilla, f.; punta, f.; chiavistello, m.; caviglia, f.; stile (d' orinolo a sole), m.; birillo, m.; **–,** v. a. appuntare (con uno spillo); serrare.

pinafore, *–āfōr,* s. grembiule, m.

pin-case, *–kās,* s. scatola da spilli, f.

pincers, *pĭn'zŭrs,* s. pl. tanaglie, f.

pinch, *pĭnsh,* s. pizzico, m.; strettezza, difficoltà, f.; **–,** v. a. pizzicare; stringere; risparmiare; svellere; **–,** v. n. ridurre in istrettezza.　　　　　[m.; torsello, m.

pin-cushion, *pĭn'kŭshŭn,* s. cuscinetto,

pine, *pĭn,* s. pino, m. (albero); **–,** v. n. languire; spasimare.　　　　　　　　[f.

pine-apple, *–ăppl,* s. ananasso, m.; pina,

pinion, *pĭn'yŭn,* s. ala, f.; estremità dell' ala, f.; **–,** v. a. legare le braccia, incatenare.　　　　　　　　　　[a piccolo.

pink, *pĭngk,* s. garofano, m.; bacca, f.; **–,**

pin-money, *pĭn'mănĭ,* s. danaro lampante, m.

pinnace, *pĭn'nās,* s. scappavia, f. (barca).

pinnacle, *pĭn'năkl,* s. pinnacolo, m.; colmo, m.

pint, *pĭnt,* s. foglietta, f.; mezza bottiglia, f.

pioneer, *pĭŏnēr',* s. marraiuolo, m.; guastatore, m.　　　　　　　　　　　　[mente.

pious, *pĭ'ăs,* a. pio, divoto; **–ly,** ad. pia-

pip, *pĭp,* s. pipita, f.; **–,** v. n. garrire.

pipe, *pĭp,* s. tubo, m.; condotto, m.; pipa, f.; zampogna, f.; zufolo, m.; **–,** v. n. suonare il flauto; fischiare.

piper, *pĭ'pŭr,* s. sonator di flauto, m.

piping, *–pĭng,* a. malaticcio; (**--hot**), fervido; **–,** s. pistagna, f.

pipkin, *pĭp'kĭn,* s. pignatta, f.; pentola, f.

pippin, *pĭp'pĭn,* s. mela appiuola, f.

piquancy, *pĕ'kănsĭ,* s. asprezza, f.

piquant, *–kănt,* a. pungente, acuto; **–ly,** ad. in modo pungente.

pique, *pēk,* s. briga, f.; offesa, f.; puntiglio, m.; **–,** v. a. piccare; irritare.

piquet, *pĭkĕt',* s. picchetto, m. (gioco di carte).

piracy, *pĭ'răsĭ,* s. pirateria, ruberia, f.

pirate, *pĭ'răt,* s. pirato, m.; **–,** v. a. & n. corseggiare, rubare.

piratical, *–răt'ĭkăl,* a. piratico.

pistachio, *pĭstă'shĭō,* s. pistacchio, m.

pistol, *pĭs'tŏl*, s. pistola, f.
pistol-shot, *-shŏt*, s. colpo di pistola, m.
piston, *pĭs'tŏn*, s. pistone, m.
pit, *pĭt*, s. fossa, f.; sepolcro, m.; pianterreno, m.; –, v. a. scavare. [f.
pitapat, *-tăpăt*, s. palpitazione dil cuore,
pitch, *pĭtch*, s. pece, f.; altezza, f.; cima, f.;
grado, m.; –, v. a. impeciare; ficcare,
piantare; lanciare; (mar.) spalmare; –,
v. n. arrestarsi, fermarsi.
pitch-dark, *-dârk*, a. nero come la pece.
pitcher, *- âr*, s. brocca, f. [corista, m.
pitch-fork, *-fŏrk*, s. forcone, m.; (mus.)
piteous, *pĭt'ĕus*, a. dolente, tristo, misero;
–ly, ad. miseramente.
pitfall, *pĭt'fâl*, s. trabocchetto, m.
pith, *pĭth*, s. midollo, m., midolla, f.;
energia, f.
pithily, *-lĭ*, ad. vigorosamente.
pithiness, *-ĭnĕs*, s. vigore, m., energia, f.
pithy, *pĭth'ĭ*, a. midolloso; energico, spiritoso. [compassionevole.
pitiable, *pĭt'ĭăbl*, a. degno di compassione,
pitiful, *pĭt'ĭfŭl*, a. compassionevole, miserabile; –ly, ad. compassionevolmente.
pitifulness, *-fŭlnĕs*, s. compassione, f.;
pietà, misericordia, f. [ad. crudelmente.
pitiless, *-lĕs*, a. spietato, crudele; –ly,
pittance, *pĭt'tăns*, s. pietanza, f.
pitted, *pĭt'tĕd*, a. butterato.
pity, *pĭt'ĭ*, s. pietà, compassione, f.; –,
v. a. & n. compatire, compiangere.
pivot, *pĭv'ŏt*, s. perno, cardine, m.
pix, *pĭks*, s. pisside, f.
placable, *plā'kăbl*, a. placabile.
placard, *plăk'ârd*, s. editto, m.; bando, m.
place, *plās*, s. luogo, m.; posto, uffizio, m.;
grado, m.; –, v. a. mettere, collocare.
placid, *plăs'ĭd*, a. placido, quieto; –ly,
ad. placidamente. [letterario, m.
plagiarism, *plā'j'ârĭzm*, s. latrocinio
plagiarist, *-j'ârĭst*, plagiary, *-j'ârĭ*, s.
plagiario, m.
plague, *plāg*, s. peste, f.; contagio, m.;
pena, f.; –, v. a. infettare, appestare;
tormentare.
plaguily, *plā'gĭlĭ*, ad. affannosamente.
plaguy, *plā'gĭ*, a. affannoso, molesto.
plaice, *plās*, s. passerina, f.
plaid, *plăd*, s. ciarpa degli Scozzesi, f.
plain, *plān*, a. piano; chiaro, evidente;
franco, sincero; –ly, ad. semplicemente;
francamente; –, s. pianura, f.; campagna
rasa, f.
plain-dealing, *-dēlĭng*, s. buona fede, f.
plainness, *-nĕs*, s. livello, m.; ugualità, f.;
semplicità, f.; chiarezza, f.
plain-spoken, *-spŏkĕn*, a. che parla
apertamente.
plaint, *plānt*, s. lamento, gemito, m.
plaintiff, *plān'tĭf*, s. dimandatore, m.
plaintive, *-tĭv*, a. dolente, querulo; –ly,
ad. dolentemente. [piegare; intrecciare.
plait, *plăt*, s. piega, f.; treccia, f.; –, v. a.
plan, *plăn*, s. piano, disegno, m.; –, v. a.
progettare. [v. a. piallare; appianare.
plane, *plān*, s. pianura, f.; pialla, f.; –,

planet, *plăn'ĕt*, s. pianeta, m.
planetary, *-nĕtârĭ*, a. planetario.
plane-tree, *plăn'trē*, s. platano, m.
plank, *plăngk*, s. tavola, asse, f.; pancone,
m.; –, v. a. impalcare con tavole.
plant, *plănt*, s. pianta, f.; ramicello, m.;
–, v. a. piantare; stabilire. [m.
plantain, *plăn'tăn*, s. platano, m.; banano,
plantation, *-tă'shăn*, s. piantagione, f.;
colonia, f.
planter, *-âr*, s. piantatore, m.; colono, m.
plash, *plăsh*, s. guazzo, m.; pantano,
palude, stagno, m.
plashy, *-ĭ*, a. pantanoso, melmoso.
plaster, *plăs'târ*, s. impiastro, m.; cal-
cistruzzo, m.; –, v. a. impiastrare; in-
gessare.
plastic, *plăs'tĭk*, a. plastico.
plat, *plăt*, s. campicello, m.; –, v. a. intrecciare, tessere.
plate, *plăt*, s. piastra, f.; argenteria, f.;
lamina, lama, f.; tondo, m.; –, v. a. inargentare, indorare; ridurre in lamina.
platform, *plăt'fŏrm*, s. piattaforma, f.;
terrazza, f.; (am.) costituzione ecclesia-
stica, f.
platina, *plăt'ĭnă*, s. platino, m. (metallo).
platoon, *plătōn'*, s. (mil.) squadrone, m.;
schiera, f.; banda, f. [(di terra), m.
platter, *plăt'târ*, s. terrina, f., gran piatto
plaudit, *plă'dĭt*, s. applauso, m.
plausibility, *plâzĭbĭl'ĭtĭ*, s. plausibilità, f.
plausible, *plâ'zĭbl*, a. plausibile.
plausibily, *-zĭblĭ*, ad. in modo plausibile.
play, *plā*, s. giuoco, divertimento, m.;
spettacolo, m.; –, v. a. & n. giocare.
play-bill, *-bĭl*, s. cartello, m.
player, *-âr*, s. giocatore, m.; attore, m.
play-fellow, *-fĕlŭ*, playmate, *-măt*, s.
compagno, m.; compagno di giuoco, m.
playful, *-fŭl*, a. giocoso, scherzevole.
playfulness, *-fŭlnĕs*, s. facezia, burla, f.
play-house, *-hŏŭs*, s. teatro, m.
plaything, *-thĭng*, s. trastullo, m.; bagatella, f. [tico, m.
playwright, *-rĭt*, s. autore dramma-
plea, *plē*, s. difesa, f.; scusa, f.; pretesto,
colore, m. [v. n. litigare, piatire,
plead, *plēd*, v. a. difendere; allegare; –,
pleader, *-âr*, s. litigante, avvocato, m.;
piatitore, m.
pleading, *-ĭng*, s. il litigare, m.; –s, pl.
dibattimenti, m. pl.
pleasant, *plĕz'ânt*, a. piacevole, grato;
gaio; –ly, ad. cortesemente; gaiamente.
pleasantness, *-nĕs*, s. piacevolezza, f.
pleasantry, *-rĭ*, s.
piacevolezza, f.; cortesia, f.; gaiezza, f.
please, *plēz*, v. a. piacere; contentare.
pleasing, *-ĭng*, a. grato, gustoso.
pleasurable, *plĕsh'ârăbl*, a. piacevole,
ameno. [voglia, f.
pleasure, *plĕsh'âr*, s. piacere, diletto, m.
pleasure-boat, *-bŏt*, s. battello di piacere, m. [inglese, m.
pleasure-ground, *-grŏŭnd*, s. giardino
plebeian, *plĕbē'ân*, a. volgare; –, s. uomo
plebeo, m.

pledge, *plĕdj*, s. pegno, m., sicurtà, f.; –, v. a. impegnare, dare in pegno.

plenary, *plē'nări*, a. plenario, intero.

plenipotentiary, *plĕnĭpŏtĕn'shărĭ*, s. plenipotenziario, m. |nezza, f.

plenitude, *plĕn'ĭtŭd*, s. plenitudine, pie-

plenteous, *plĕn'tĭŭs*, **plentiful**, *–fŭl*, a. abbondevole, copioso.

plenty, *plĕn'tĭ*, s. abbondanza, f.

plethora, *plĕth'ŏră*, s. pletora, abbondanza di sangue, f.

plethoric, *plĕthŏr'ĭk*, a. pletorico.

pleurisy, *plū'rĭsĭ*, s. (med.) pleurisia, f.

pliable, *plī'ăbl*, **pliant**, *–ănt*, a. pieghevole, flessibile.   [f.

pliancy, *–ănsĭ*, s. flessibilità f.; docilità, f.

plight, *plĭt*, s. stato, m., condizione, f.; –, v. a. impegnare.

plod, *plŏd*, v. n. affaticarsi.

plodding, *–dĭng*, a. laborioso, indefesso.

plot, *plŏt*, s. complotto, m., cospirazione, trama, f.; pezzo (di terra), m.; –, v. a. concertare; –, v. n. cospirare, tramare.

plotter, *–tăr*, s. cospiratore, m.

plough, *plŏu*, s. aratro, m.; –, v. a. arare, solcare; coltivare.   [s. aratore, m.

plough-boy, *–bŏĭ*, **plough-man**, *–măn*,

plough-share, *–shăr*, s. vomere, coltro,

plover, *plŭv'ăr*, s. piviere, m.   [m.

pluck, *plŭk*, s. tirata, strappata, f.; sforzo, m.; coratella, f.; –, v. a. svellere, strappare; spennare, spiumare.

plucky, *plŭk'ĭ*, a. coraggioso, animoso.

plug, *plŭg*, s. turaccio, cavicchio, m.; stantuffo (d'una tromba), m.; –, v. a. incavigliare.

plum, *plŭm*, s. susina, prugna, f.

plumage, *plŏm'ădj*, s. piume, penne, f. pl.

plumb, *plŭm*, s. piombino, m.; –, ad. a piombo; –, v. a. piombinare.

plumbago, *–bā'gŏ*, s. piombaggine, m.

plumber, *plŭm'ăr*, s. piombaio, m.

plumb-line, *–lĭn*, s. piombino, m.

plume, *plŏm*, s. penna, f.; pennacchio, m.; –, v. a. spiumare; ornare d'nn pennacchio.

plummet, *plŭm'mĕt*, s. piombino, m.

plump, *plŭmp*, a. paffuto, grassotto; –, ad. di subito; –, v. n. gonfiare; cascare giù.   [f.

plumpness, *–nĕs*, s. grassezza, corpulenza,

plum-tree, *plŭm'trĕ*, s. prugno, susino, m.

plumy, *plŏ'mĭ*, a. coperto di piume.

plunder, *plŭn'dăr*, s. depredamento, saccheggio, m.; (am.) bagaglie, f. pl.; –, v. a. predare, rubare.   [immergersi.

plunge, *plŭnj*, v. a. immergere; –,| v. n.

plunger, *–ăr*, s. marangone, m.

plural, *plŏ'răl*, a. & s. plurale (m.).

plurality, *–lĭt'ĭ*, s. pluralità, f.

plush, *plŭsh*, s. peluzzo, m.

ply, *plĭ*, v. a. piegare; lavorare; sollecitare; –, v. n. affaticarsi; applicarsi; (mar.) bordeggiare.

pneumatic, *nŭmăt'ĭk*, a. pneumatico.

pneumonia, *–mŏ'nĭă*, s. pneumonia, f.

poach, *pŏch*, v. a. bollire (uova); cacciare furtivamente; rubare.

poacher, *–ăr*, s. cacciatore furtivo, m.

pock, *pŏk*, s. bolla del vaiuolo, f.

pocket, *pŏk'ĕt*, s. tasca, borsa, f.; scarsella, f.; –, v. a. imborsare, mettere nella borsa; (an affront) soffrire (un affronto).

pocket-book, *–bŭk*, s. libretto da tasca, taccuino, m.   [riserva, m.

pocket-money, *–mŭnĕ*, s. danaro di

pod, *pŏd*, s. guscio, m.; scorza, f.; cazzola,

poem, *pŏ'ĕm*, s. poema, m.   [f.

poesy, *pŏ'ĕsĭ*, s. poesia, f.

poet, *pŏ'ĕt*, s. poeta, m.

poetaster, *pŏ'ĕtăstăr*, s. poetastro, m.

poetess, *pŏ'ĕtĕs*, s. poetessa, f.

poetical, *pŏĕt'ĭkăl*, a. poetico; –ly, ad. poeticamente.

poetics, *pŏĕt'ĭks*, s. pl. poetica, f.

poetize, *pŏ'ĕtĭz*, v. a. comporre poesie.

poetry, *pŏ'ĕtrĭ*, s. poesia, f.   [cità, f.

poignancy, *pŏĭ'nănsĭ*, s. acutezza, morda-

poignant, *–nănt*, a. acuto, pungente; mordace, satirico.

point, *pŏĭnt*, s. punta, f.; capo, f.; promontorio, m.; punto, passo, m.; stato, m.; (rail.) baratto, m.; –, v. a. appuntare; aguzzare; puntare.   [bianco.

point-blank, *–blăngk*, ad. di punto in

pointed, *–ĕd*, a. appuntato, acuto, –ly, ad. espressamente.   [fermo, m.

pointer, *–ăr*, s. appuntatore, m.; cane da

pointless, *–lĕs*, a. spuntato. ottuso.

pointsman, *–s'măn*, s. (rail.) adetto ai baratti, m.

poise, *pŏĭz*, s. peso, m.; equilibrio, m.; –, v. a. pesare; brilanciare.

poison, *pŏĭ'zn*, s. veleno, tossico, m.; –, v. a. avvelenare.   [ruttore, m.

poisoner, *–znăr*, s. avvelenatore, m.; cor-

poisonous, *–znŭs*, a. velenoso.

poke, *pŏk*, s. tasca, borsa, f.; sacchetto, m.; –, v. a. cercare al tasto; frugare; attizzare il fuoco.   [spauracchio, m.

poker, *pŏ'kăr*, s. attizzatoio, m.; (am.)

polar, *pŏ'lăr*, a. polare.

pole, *pŏl*, s. polo, m.; pertica, f., palo, m.; timone d'una carrozza, m.

pole-axe, *–ăks*, s. azza, scure, f.

pole-cat, *–kăt*, s. puzzola, faina, f.

polemic, *pŏlĕm'ĭk*, a. & s polemico (m.); –s, s. pl. polemica, f.

pole-star, *pŏl'stăr*, s. stella polare, f.

police, *pŏlĕs'*, s. polizia, f.; polizza, f.

police-court, *–kŏrt*, s. tribunale di polizia, f.

policeman, *–măn*, s. poliziziotto, m.

policy, *pŏl'ĭsĭ*, s. politica, f.; astuzia, f.

polish, *pŏl'ĭsh*, v. a. pulire, lisciare; limare; –, v. n. divenire pulito; –, s. pulitura, f.

polished, *–ĭshd*, a. elegante; lustrato.

polite, *pŏlĭt'*, a. pulito, garbato; cortese; –ly, ad. civilmente.

politeness, *–nĕs*, s. politezza, f.

politic, *pŏl'ĭtĭk*, a. prudente.

political, pŏlĭt'ĭkăl, a. politico; **-ally,** ad. politicamente.
politician, pŏlĭtĭsh'ăn, s. politico, m.
politics, pŏl'ĭtĭks, s. pl. politica, f.
poll, pŏl, s. testa, f.; lista, f.; suffragio, m.; **-,** v. a. scapezzare; tosare; votare.
pollard, pŏl'lărd, s. albero scapezzato, m.
pollen, pŏl'lĕn, s. polline, m.
poll-tax, pŏl'tăks, s. capitazione, f.
pollute, pŏllūt', v.a. sporcare; corrompere.
polluter, -tăr, s. corruttore, m.
pollution, -lō'shŭn, s. polluzione, f.; contaminamento, m. [m.
poltroon, pŏltrōn', s. poltrone, codardo,
polygamist, pŏlĭg'ămĭst, s. poligamo, m.
polygamy, -ămĭ, s. poligamia, f.
polyglot, pŏl'ĭglŏt, a. & s. poliglotto (m.)'
polygon, -ĭgŏn, s. poligono, m.
polypus, -ĭpŭs, s. polipo, m.
polysillabic, -sĭllăb'ĭk, a. polisillabo.
polytechnic, -tĕk'nĭk, a. politecnico.
polytheist, pŏl'ĭthĕĭst, s. politeista, m.
pomade, pŏmād', **pomatum,** -mă'tŭm, s. pomata, manteca, f. [f.
pomegranate, pŏm'grănăt, s. melagrana,
pommel, pŏm'mĕl, s. pomo della spada, f.; **-,** v. a. battere; strigliare.
pomp, pŏmp, s. pompa, f., splendore, m.
pomposity, -pŏs'ĭtĭ, s. pomposità, ostentazione, f. [con pompa.
pompous, pŏm'pŭs, a. pomposo; **-ly,** ad.
pond, pŏnd, s. stagno, vivaio, m.
ponder, pŏn'dăr, v. a. & n. ponderare; considerare. [pesantemente.
ponderous, -ŭs, a. pesante; **-ly,** ad.
poniard, pŏn'yărd, s. pugnale, stiletto, m.; **-,** v. a. pugnalare.
pontiff, pŏn'tĭf, s. pontefice, m.
pontifical, -tĭf'ĭkăl, a. & s. pontificale (m. libro); **-ly,** ad. pontificalmente.
pontificate, -ĭkăt, s. pontificato, m.
pontoon, pŏntōn', s. pontone, m.
pony, pŏ'nĭ, s. ronzino, m.; 25 ghinee, f. pl.
poodle, pōō'dl, s. can barbone, m.
pooh, pŏ, i. oibò, eh via! [lago, m.
pool, pōl, s. stagno, m.; laguna, f.; piccol
poop, pōp, s. poppa (della nave), f.
poor, pŏr, a. povero; sterile; **-ly,** ad. poveramente, meschinamente, vilmente.
poor-box, -bŏks, s. cassetta pei poveri, f.
poor-house, -hŏŭs, s. spedale, m.
poor-law, -lă, s. diritto dei poveri, m.
poorness, -nĕs, s. povertà, f.
poor-rate, -răt, s. imposto pei poveri, m.
pop, pŏp, s. piccolo strepito subito, m.; **-,** v. a. porre destramente; **-,** v. n. sopravvenire all' improvviso.
Pope, pŏp, s. papa, m.
Popedom, -dŏm, s. pontificato, m.
popery, -pŏrĭ, s. papismo, m.
pop-gun, pŏp'gŭn, s. buffo, m.; cannello, m. [parigino, m.
popinjay, pŏp'ĭnjā, s. pappagallo, m.;
popish, pŏ'pĭsh, a. del papa; Cattolico Romano; **-ly,** ad. a modo di papa.

poplar, pŏp'lăr, s. pioppo, m.
poplin, pŏp'lĭn, s. poplina (stoffa di seta e lana, f.
poppy, pŏp'pĭ, s. papavero, m.
populace, pŏp'ŭlăs, s. volgo m., plebaglia, plebe, f. [polarmente.
popular, -ŭlăr, a. popolare; **-ly,** ad. po-
popularity, -lăr'ĭtĭ, s. popolarità, f.; favore pubblico, m.
popularize, pŏp'ŭlărĭz, v.a.popolarizzare.
populate, -ŭlăt, v. a. popolare.
population, -lā'shŭn, s. popolazione, f.
populous, pŏp'ŭlŭs, a. popoloso, popolato.
populousness, -nĕs, s. popolazione, f.
porcelain, pŏrs'lăn, s. porcellana, f.
porch, pŏrch, s. portico, m., piazza, f.
porcupine, pŏr'kŭpĭn, s. porco spino, m.
pore, pŏr, s. poro, m.
pork, pŏrk, s. porco, m.; carne di porco, f.
pork-butcher, -bŭchăr, s. pizzicagnolo,
porker, -ăr, s. porcello, m. [m.
porosity, pŏrŏs'ĭtĭ, s. porosità, f.
porous, pŏ'rŭs, a. poroso.
porphyry, pŏr'fĭrĭ, s. porfido, m.
porpoise, pŏr'pŭs, s. porco marino, m.
porridge, pŏr'rĭj, s. minestra, f.
porringer, pŏr'rĭnjăr, s. scodella, f.
port, pŏrt, s. porto, m.; (bill.) trucca; (mar.) cannoniera, f.; vino d'Oporto, m.
portable, -ăbl, a. portabile.
portal, pŏr'tăl, s. portone, m. [rare.
portend, pŏrtĕnd', v. a. presagire, augu-
portent, pŏr'tĕnt, s. portento, m.; mostro,
portentous, -tĕn'tŭs, a. portentoso. [m.
porter, pŏr'tăr, s. portinaio, m.; facchino, m.; lustrascarpe, m.; birra forte, f. [m.
porterage, -ărăj, s. prezzo del portare,
portfire, pŏrt'fĭr, s. accenditoio, m.; miccia, f. [lettere, m.
portfolio, -fŏ'lĭŏ, s. portafogli, porta-
portico, pŏr'tĭkŏ, s. portico, m.; piazza, f.
portion, pŏr'shŭn, s. porzione, f.; parte, f.; dote, f.; **-,** v. a. dividere, spartire; (jur.) dotare.
portliness, pŏrt'lĭnĕs, s. aria maestosa, f.
portly, -lĭ, a. maestoso, grande.
portmanteau, -măn'tŏ, s. portamantelli, m., valigia, f.
portrait(ure), pŏr'trăt(ŭr), s. ritratto, m.
portray, pŏrtrā', v. a. far ritratti, rappresentare, dipingere.
portrayer, -ăr, s. ritrattista, m. [f.
portress, pŏr'trĕs, s. portinaia, guardiana,
pose, pŏz, v. a. imbarazzare; interrogare.
poser, pŏ'zăr, s.esaminatore, m.; questione, f.; che imbarazza, che confonde.
position, pŏzĭsh'ăn, s. posizione, f.; situazione, f.; proposta, f.; tesi, f.
positive, pŏz'ĭtĭv, a. positivo, assoluto; vero, certo; **-ly,** ad. positivamente, assolutamente, certamente. [minazione, f.
positiveness, -nĕs, s. certezza, f.; deter-
posse, pŏs'sĕ, s. forza pubblica, f.
possess, pŏzzĕs', v. a. possedere; godere.
possession, -zĕsh'ăn, s. possessione, f., possesso, m.
possessive, -zĕs'sĭv, a. (gr.) possessivo.
possessor, -zĕs'săr, m. possessore, m.

posset, *pŏs′sĕt*, s. bevanda di latte e vino, f.
possibility, *–sĭbĭl′ĭtĭ*, s. possibilità, f.
possible, *pŏs′sĭbl*, a. possibile.
possibly, *–sĭblĭ*, ad. forse.
post, *pŏst*, s. corriere, m.; posto, luogo, uffizio, impiego, m.; posta, f.; –, v. a. porre, mettere; trascrivere; –, v. n. impostare (una lettera); correre la posta. [f.
postage, *–dj*, s. porto, m., spesa di posta,
postage-stamp, *–stămp*, s. francobollo, m.
post-boy, *–bŏĭ*, s. postiglione, m.
post-captain, *–kăptĭn*, s. capitano di bastimento, m.
post-card, *–kărd*, s. carta postale, f.
post-chaise, *–shāz*, s. carrozza di posta, f.
post-date, *–dāt′*, v. a. mettere una data.
poster, *–ăr*, s. cartello, m.
posterior, *pŏstē′rĭăr*, a. posteriore; dere-
posterity, *–tĕr′ĭtĭ*, s. posterità, f. [tano.
postern, *pŏs′tŭrn*, s. porticella, f.
post-haste, *pŏst′hāst*, ad. in gran fretta.
posthumous, *pŏst′ŭmŭs*, a. postumo.
postilion, *pŏstĭl′yăn*, s. postiglione, m.
posting, *pŏst′ĭng*, s. viaggio per posta, m.
postman, *–măn*, s. corriere, m.
post-mark, *–mărk*, s. bollo postale, m.
post-master, *–măstăr*, s. maestro di posta, m.
post-office, *–ŏfˡĭs*, s. uffizio della posta, m.; **letter addressed: "Post-office" or "to be kept till called for,"** lettera ferma in posta.
postpaid, *–pād*, a. affrancato.
postpone, *–pōn′*, v. a. posporre; differire; disprezzare.
postponement, *–mĕnt*, s. posposizione, f.
postscript, *pŏst′skrĭpt*, s. poscritto, m.
posture, *pŏs′tŭr (–chŭr)*, s. positura, f.; situazione, f. [m.
posy, *pō′zĭ*, s. mazzetto di fiori, m.; motto,
pot, *pŏt*, s. vaso, boccale, m.; –, v. a. mettere in vaso; insalare.
potable, *pō′tăbl*, a. potabile.
potash, *pŏt′ăsh*, s. potassa, f.
potation, *pŏtā′shŭn*, s. beveria, f.
potato, *pŏtā′tō*, s. patata, f.
pot-bellied, *pŏt′bĕlĭd*, a. panciuto.
pot-boy, *–bŏĭ*, s. garzone d' osteria, m.
potentate, *pō′tĕntāt*, s. potentato, m.
potential, *–tĕn′shăl*, a. potenziale; virtuale, efficace. [mino, f.
pot-hanger, *pŏt′hăngăr*, s. catena del ca-
pother, *pŏth′ăr*, s. tumulto, strepito, rumore, m.
pot-herb, *pŏt′hŭrb*, s. erba da mangiare, f.
pot-hook, *–hŏk*, s. catena da fuoco, f.; manico d' un vaso, m.
pot-house, *–hŏŭs*, s. taverna, f.
potion, *pō′shŭn*, s. pozione, bevanda, f.
pot-luck, *pŏt′lŭk*, s. quel che c'è, pentolino, m. [lino, m.
potman, *–măn*, s. bevitore, m.
potter, *pŏt′tăr*, s. pentolaio, m.; **–'s ware**, pl. vasellame di terra, m. [pentole, m.
pottery, *–ĭ*, s. stoviglie, f. pl ; magazzino di
pouch, *pŏŭch*, s. tasca, scarsella, f.
poulterer, *pōl′tărăr*, s. pollaiuolo, m.
poultice, *–tĭs*, s. cataplasma, m.

poultry, *–trĭ*, s. pollame, m., polli, m. pl.; **––yard**, polleria, f.
pounce, *pŏŭns*, s. polvere di pomice, f.; –, v. a. spolverizzare.
pounce-box, *–bŏks*, s. polverino, m.
pound, *pŏŭnd*, s. libbra, f.; parco, m.; **–, sterling**, lira sterlina, f.; –, v. a. pestare.
pounder, *–ăr*, s. pestello, m.; sorta di grossa pera, f.; cannone di ... libbre di portata, m.
pour, *pōr*, v. a. versare; spandere, effondere; –, v. n. scorrere; piovere strabocche-
pout, *pŏŭt*, v. n. far grugno. [volmente.
poverty, *pŏv′ărtĭ*, s. povertà, f.
powder, *pŏw′dăr*, s. polvere, f.; –, v. a. polverizzare; salare.
powder-box, *–bŏks*, s. polverino, m.
powder-chests, *–chĕsts*, s. pl. (mar.) cassoni di poppa, m. pl. [f.
powder-horn, *–hŏrn*, s. borsa da polvere,
powdery, *pŏw′dărĭ*, a. polveroso.
power, *pŏw′ăr*, s. potere, m., forza, possanza, f.; armata, f.; autorità, influenza, f.
powerful, *–fĭl*, a. potente; **–ly**, ad. potentemente; con forza.
powerless, *–lĕs*, a. impotente.
pox, *pŏks*, s. morbo gallico, m.; **chicken –**, vaiuolo benigno, m.; **small –**, bolle, f. pl. [lità d' essere praticato, f.
practicability, *prăktĭkăbĭl′ĭtĭ*, s. possibi-
practicable, *prăk′tĭkăbl*, a. praticabile, fattibile. [bile.
practically, *–kăblĭ*, ad. in modo pratica-
practical, *–tĭkăl*, a. pratico; **–ly**, ad. praticamente.
practice, *–tĭs*, s. pratica, f.; uso, costume, m.; metodo, m.; **–s**, pl. pratiche segrete, f. pl.
practise, –, v. a. & n. praticare; esercitare.
practitioner, *–tĭsh′ănăr*, s. artista, f.; pratico, m.; medico, m.
pragmatic(al), *prăgmăt′ĭk(ăl)*, a. prammatico; affaccendato; **–ly**, ad. arrogante-
prairie, *prā′rĭ*, s. prateria, f. [mente.
praise, *prāz*, s. lode, f., elogio, m.; gloria, f.; –, v. a. lodare; celebrare.
praiseworthy, *–wŭrthĭ*, a. lodevole.
prance, *prăns*, v. n. impennarsi; cavalcare con brio. [m.
prank, *prăngk*, s. beffa, f.; scappata, f.; tiro,
prate, *prāt*, v. n. cicalare, ciarlare; –, s. ciarla, ciancia, f. [f.
prattle, *prăt′tl*, v. n. ciarlare; –, s. ciarlea,
prattler, *–lăr*, s. ciarlone, m.
pray, *prā*, v. a. & n. pregare, supplicare.
prayer, *–ăr*, s. preghiera, domanda, f.; **Lord's –**, orazione domenicale, f.
prayer-book, *–bŭk*, s. libro di preghiere, m.
preach, *prēch*, v. a. & n. predicare. [m.
preacher, *–ăr*, s. predicatore, m.
preaching, *–ĭng*, s. predica, f.
preamble, *prĕăm′bl*, s. preambolo, m., prefazione, f.
prebend, *prĕb′ĕnd*, s. prebenda, f.
prebendary, *–dărĭ*, s. prebendario, m.
precarious, *prĕkā′rĭŭs*, a. precario, incerto; **–ly**, ad. in modo precario.
precariousness, *–nĕs*, s. incertezza, f.

precaution, -kŏ'shŭn, s. precauzione, f.; cautela, f.

precautionary, -ŭrĭ, a. cauto. [zare.

precede, -sēd', v. a. precedere, sopravanzare.

precedence, -sē'dĕns, s. precedenza, f.

precedent, -dĕnt, preceding, -dĭng, a. precedente.

precentor, -sĕn'tŏr, s. precentore, m.

precept, prē'sĕpt, s. precetto, m.

preceptor, -sĕp'tŭr, s. precettore, m.

precinct, prē'sĭngkt, s. precinto, circuito, m. [preziosamente.

precious, prĕsh'ŭs, a. prezioso; -ly, ad.

preciousness, -nĕs, s. preziosità, f.

precipice, prĕs'ĭpĭs, s. precipizio, m.

precipitate, -sĭp'ĭtĭt, v. a. & n. precipitare; precipitarsi; —, a. precipitato; -ly, ad. con fretta; —, s. precipitato, m.

precipitation, -tā'shŭn, s. precipitazione, temerità, f. [merario.

precipitous, -sĭp'ĭtŭs, a. precipitoso, temerario.

precise, -sīs', a. preciso, esatto; -ly, ad. precisamente, esattamente. [tezza, f.

precision, -sĭzh'ŭn, s. precisione, esattezza, f.

preclude, -klōd', v. a. precludere; impedire. [turo.

precocious, -kō'shŭs, a. precoce, prematuro.

precocity, -kŏs'ĭtĭ, s. maturità prima del tempo, f.

preconceive, prēkŏnsēv', v. a. prevedere; indovinare. [m.

preconception, -sĕp'shŭn, s. pregiudizio,

preconcert, -sŭrt', v. a. deliberare anticipatamente. [nunzio, m.

precursor, prēkŭr'sŭr, s. precursore; annunzio, m.

predatory, prĕd'ătŭrĭ, a. rapace.

predecessor, prēdĕsĕs'ŭr, s. predecessore, antecessore, m. [nare.

predestinate, prēdĕs'tĭnāt, v. a. predestinare.

predestination, -dĕstĭnā'shŭn, s. predestinazione, f.

predestine, vedi predestinate.

predicament, -dĭk'ăment, s. predicamento, m., categoria, f. [v. a. affermare.

predicate, prĕd'ĭkāt, s. predicato, m.; —,

predication, -kā'shŭn, s. affermazione, f.

predict, -dĭkt', v. a. predire.

prediction, -dĭk'shŭn, s. predizione, f.

predilection, prēdĭlĕk'shŭn, s. predilezione, f.

predispose, -dĭspōz', v. a. predisporre.

predisposition, -dĭspŏzĭsh'ŭn, s. predisposizione, f. [rità, f.; predominio, m.

predominance, prēdŏm'ĭnăns, s. superiorità, f.; predominio, m.

predominant, -ĭnănt, a. predominante.

predominate, -ĭnāt, v. n. predominare.

pre-eminence, prē ĕm'ĭnĕns, s. preminenza, f.

pre-eminent, -ĭnĕnt, a. preminente.

pre-engagement, -ĕngādj'mĕnt, s. obbligo anteriore, m. [ĝ.

pre-existence, -ĝzĭs'tĕns, s. preesistenza, f.

preface, prĕf'ds, s. prefazione, f.; —, v. a. introdurre.

prefatory, -ătŭrĭ, a. preliminare.

prefect, prē'fĕkt, s. prefetto, m.

prefecture, -fĕk'tŭr, s. prefettura, f.

prefer, prēfŭr', v. a. preferire; promuovere; proporre (una legge). [siderabile.

preferable, prĕf'ŭrăbl. a. preferibile; desiderabile.

preferably, -ăblĭ, ad. per preferenza.

preference, -ŭrĕns, s. preferenza, prelazione, f. [m.; promozione, f.

preferment, prēfŭr'mĕnt, s. avanzamento, promozione, f.

prefix, prē'fĭks, s. (gr.) prefisso, m.; —, prēfĭks', v. a. prefiggere.

pregnancy, prĕg'nănsĭ, s. pregnezza, f.

pregnant, -nănt, a. pregnante; fertile.

prejudge, prējŭdj', v. a. giudicare innanzi.

prejudice, prĕj'ŭdĭs, s. pregiudizio, m.; danno, m.; —, v. a. pregiudicare; nuocere.

prejudicial, -dĭsh'ăl, a. pregiudicevole, nocivo.

prelacy, prĕl'ăsĭ, s. prelatura, f.

prelate, prĕl'ăt, s. prelato, m.

preliminary, prēlĭm'ĭnărĭ, a. preliminare.

prelude, prĕl'ŭd, s. preludio, m.; —, prēlūd', v. a. sonare un preludio.

premature, prēmătŭr', a. prematuro; -ly, ad. prematuramente. [tempo, f.

prematureness, -nĕs, s. maturità avanti il tempo, f.

premeditate, prēmĕd'ĭtăt, v. a. premeditare. [zione, f.

premeditation, -tā'shŭn, s. premeditazione, f.

premier, prĕm'ĭŭr, s. primo ministro, m.

premise, prĕmīz', v. a. spiegare in primo luogo. [beni terreni, m. pl.

premises, prĕm'ĭsĕz, s. pl. premesse, f. pl.;

premium, prē'mĭŭm, s. premio, m.; ricompensa, f. [nisce anticipatamente.

premonitory, prēmŏn'ĭtŭrĭ, a. che ammonisce anticipatamente.

preoccupation, prēŏkkŭpā'shŭn, s. preoccupazione, prevenzione, f. [prevenire.

preoccupy, -ŏk'kŭpĭ, v. a. preoccupare,

preordain, -ŏrdān', v. a. preordinare, predestinare.

prepaid, -pād', a. affrancato. [zione, f.

preparation, prĕpără'shŭn, s. preparazione, f.

preparatory, -păr'ătŭrĭ, a. preparatorio.

prepare, prēpār', v. a. preparare; apparecchiare; —, v. n. prepararsi.

prepay, prēpā', v. a. pagare anticipatamente; francare.

prepayment, -mĕnt, s. francamento, m.

prepense, prēpĕns', a. premeditato.

preponderance, -pŏn'dŭrăns, s. preponderanza, f.

preponderate, -dŭrāt, v. a. & n. preponderare; superare. [zione, f.

preposition, prĕpŏzĭsh'ăn, s. (gr.) preposizione, f.

prepossession, prĕpŏzzĕsh'ŭn, s. preoccupazione, f.; prevenzione, f.

prepossessing, -zĕs'sĭng, a. attrattivo.

preposterous, prēpŏs'tŭrŭs, a. prepostero; assurdo; -ly, ad. a rovescio, assurdamente.

prerogative, -rŏg'ătĭv, s. prerogativa, f.

presage, prĕs'ădj, s. presagio, augurio, m.; —, prēsādj', v. a. presagire. [f.

prescience, prē'shĭĕns, s. preconoscenza, f.

prescient, -shĭĕnt, a. profetico.

prescribe, prēskrīb', v. a. & n. prescrivere; ordinare.

prescription, *–skrĭp'shŭn,* s. prescrizione, f.; ordinazione, f.

presence, *prĕz'ĕns,* s. presenza, f.; aria, f., aspetto, m.; **– of mind,** prontezza di spirito, f.   [di presenza, f.

presence-chamber, *–chămbŭr,* s. camera

present, *prĕz'ĕnt,,* a. presente; **–ly,** ad. al presente; **–,** *prĕzĕnt',* v. a. presentare, far un presente, offrire; (am.) accusare.

presentable, *prĕzĕnt'ăbl,* a. decente, convenevole, lindo, assettato.

presentation, *–tă'shŭn,* s. presentazione, f.; **––copy,** esemplare dedicatorio, m.

presentiment, *–sĕn'tĭmĕnt,* s. presentimento, m.

presentment, *–zĕnt'mĕnt,* s. presentazione, rappresentazione, f.   [f.

preservation, *–zŭrvă'shŭn,* s. preservazione, f.   [m.

preservative, *–zŭrv'ătĭv,* s. preservativo, f.

preserve, *–zŭrv',* s. conserva, f., confetti, m. pl.; **–,** v. a. preservare, conservare; confettare.   [direzione.

preside, *–sīd',* v. n. presedere; aver la

presidency, *prĕz'ĭdĕnsĭ,* s. presidenza, f.

president, *–dĕnt,* s. presidente, m.; capo, m.

press, *prĕs,* s. torchio, strettoio, m.; folla, f.; guardaroba, f.; **–,** v. a. premere, spremere, stringere; sollecitare, affrettare; importunare; **–,** v. n. affrettarsi; mettere piede; ricercare con premura.

press-gang, *–găng,* s. truppa da forzare marinari, f.

pressing, *–ĭng,* a. urgente; importuno; **–ly,** ad. istantemente, violentemente; **–,** s. pressione, f.; istanza, f.

pressure, *prĕsh'ŭr,* s. pressura, f.; oppressione, f.

presumable, *prĕzŭm'ăbl,* a. presumibile.

presume, *–zŭm',* v. a. presumere; presupporre.

presuming, *–ĭng,* a. presuntuoso.

presumption, *–zŭm'shŭn,* s. presunzione, arroganza, f.

presumptive, *–tĭv,* a. presuntivo.

presumptuous, *–tŭăs,* a. presuntuoso; **–ly,** ad. presuntuosamente.   [supporre.

presuppose, *prĕsŭppōs',* v. a. presupporre.

presupposition, *–pōzĭsh'ŭn,* s. presupposizione, f.   [renza, f.

pretence, *prĕtĕns',* s. pretesto, m.; apparenza, f.

pretend, *–tĕnd',* v. a. & n. pretendere; immaginarsi.

pretender, *–ŭr,* s. pretendente, m.

pretendingly, *–ĭnglĭ,* ad. presuntuosamente.

pretension, *–tĕn'shŭn,* s. pretensione, f.

preterite, *prĕt'ŭrĭt,* s. (gr.) preterito, m.

preternatural, *prĕtŭrnăt'ŭrăl (–chŭrăl),* a. soprannaturale.   [scusa, f.

pretext, *prĕtĕkst',* s. pretesto, colore, m.;

prettily, *prĭt'ĭlĭ,* ad. d'una maniera piacevole, acconciamente.

prettiness, *–nĕs,* s. bellezza, leggiadria, f.

pretty, *–tĭ,* a. leggiadro, vago, grazioso; **–,** ad. assai, così così; quasi.

prevail, *prĕvāl',* v. n. prevalere; avere la superiorità.   [nante.

prevailing, *–ĭng,* a. prevalente, dominante.

prevalence, *prĕv'ălĕns,* s. prevalenza, f.

prevalent, *–dlĕnt,* a. potente; efficace.

prevaricate, *prĕvăr'ĭkāt,* v. n. prevaricare; colludere.

prevarication, *–kă'shŭn,* s. prevaricazione, f.; collusione, f.

prevent, *–vĕnt',* v. a. prevenire; ovviare.

prevention, *–vĕn'shŭn,* s. preoccupazione, f.   [servativo (m.).

preventive, *–tĭv,* a. & s. preveniente; pre-

previous, *prē'vĭăs,* a. previo, precedente; **–ly,** ad. precedentemente.

prey, *prā,* s. preda, rapina, f.; **–,** v. n. predare, rubare.

price, *prĭs,* s. prezzo, valore, m.

priceless, *–lĕs,* a. inestimabile.

prick, *prĭk,* s. puntura, ferita, f.; traccia, f.; **–,** v. a. pungere; stimolare, spronare; notare (un' aria).

pricker, *–ŭr,* s. braccatore a cavallo, m.

pricking, *–ĭng,* s. pizzicore, m.

prickle, *prĭk'l,* s. punta, f.; spina, f.

prickly, *–lĭ,* a. spinoso.

pride, *prīd,* s. orgoglio, m.; superbia, vanità, f.; **–,** v. n. vantarsi.

prier, *prī'ŭr,* s. spione, spia, m.

priest, *prēst,* s. prete, m.

priestess, *–ĕs,* s. sacerdotessa, f.

priesthood, *–hŭd,* s. sacerdozio, m.

priestly, *–lĭ,* a. di prete, sacerdotale.

priest-ridden, *–rĭddn,* a. governato da preti.

prig, *prĭg,* s. saccentone, m.; pazzo, m.; **–,** v. a. truffare, furare.

priggish, *–gĭsh,* a. affettato, presuntuoso.

prim, *prĭm,* a. affettato, studiato.

primacy, *prī'măsĭ,* s. primato, m.

primarily, *–mărĭlĭ,* ad. primieramente, da prima.   • [cipale.

primary, *–mărĭ,* a. primario, primo, prin-

primate, *–măt,* s. primate, m.; capo, m.

prime, *prīm,* a. primo, principale, originale; precoce; **–ly,** ad. da prima; eccellentemente; **–,** s. principio, m.; fiore, m.; primavera, f.; **–,** v. a. mettere il polverino; preparare.

primer, *prĭm'ŭr (prī'mŭr),* s. piccolo libretto, m.; breviario, m.

primeval, *prīmē'văl,* a. primitivo.

priming, *–mĭng,* s. mettere la polvere sul focone, m.   [ad. primitivamente.

primitive, *prĭm'ĭtĭv,* a. primitivo; **–ly,**

primness, *–nĕs,* s. affettazione, f.

primogeniture, *prīmŏjĕn'ĭtŭr,* s. primogenitura, f.

prince, *prĭns,* s. principe, m.; sovrano, m.

princedom, *–dŏm,* s. principato, m.

princely, *–lĭ,* a. da principesco; **–,** ad. da principe; nobilmente.

princess, *prĭn'sĕs,* s. principessa, f.

principal, *prĭn'sĭpăl,* a. principale, essenziale; **–ly,** ad. principalmente, soprattutto; **–,** s. principale, m.; capitale, m.

principality, *–păl'ĭtĭ,* s. principato, m.; sovranità, f.

principle, *prĭn'sĭpl,* s. principio, fondamento, m.; motivo, m., causa, f.

print, *prĭnt,* s. impressione, f.; stampa, lettera, f.; giornale, m.; **out of —,** che non si trova più a comprare; **—,** v. a. imprimere; stampare.

printer, *— är,* s. stampatore, tipografo, m.; **—'s reader,** correttore, m. |f.

printing, *—ĭng,* s. impressione, f.; stampa,

printing-house, *—hōŭs,* **printing-office,** *—ŏffĭs,* s. stamperia, f.

prior, *prī'ŏr,* a. primo, precedente; **—,** s. priore, m.; superiore, m.

prioress, *—ĕs,* s. priora, f.; superiora, f.

priority, *—ŏr'ĭtĭ,* s. priorità, f.

priory, *—rĭ,* s. priorato, m.

prism, *prĭzm,* s. prisma, m.

prison, *prĭz'n,* s. prigione, f.

prisoner, *—ŏnär,* s. prigioniere, m.

pristine, *prĭs'tĭn,* a. pristino, prisco.

privacy, *prī'văsĭ,* s. segretezza, f.; ritiratezza, solitudine, f.

private, *—vät,* a. privato, particolare; segreto; **— soldier,** s. soldato semplice, m.

privateer, *—vätēr',* s. corsaro, m.

privation, *—vā'shăn,* s. privazione, f.; mancanza, f.

privilege, *prĭv'ĭlĕj,* s. privilegio, m.; **—,** v. a. privilegiare. |greto.

privily, *—ĭlĭ,* ad. privatamente; in segreto.

privity, *—ĭtĭ,* s. confidenza, f.; notizia, f.

privy, *prĭv'ĭ,* a. privato, particolare; familiare; segreto; **—,** s. cesso, m.

prize, *prĭz,* s. prezzo, m.; premio, m.; presa, f.; **—,** v. a. apprezzare, valutare.

pro, *prō,* pr. per; **— and con,** pro e contra.

probability, *prŏbăbĭl'ĭtĭ,* s. probabilità, verisimiglianza, f.

probable, *prŏb'ăbl,* a. probabile.

probably, *—ăblĭ,* ad. probabilmente.

probate, *prō'băt,* s. verificazione (d' un testamento), f. |mento, m.

probation, *—bā'shăn,* s. prova, f.; esperimento, m.

probationary, *—ärĭ,* a. per prova.

probationer, *—är,* s. scolare che fa la sua prova, f.; novizio, m. |colla tenta.

probe, *prōb,* s. tenta f.; **—,** v. a. toccare

probity, *prōb'ĭtĭ,* s. probità, sincerità, f.; integrità, f.

problem, *prŏb'lĕm,* s. problema, m.

problematic(al), *—măt'ĭk(ăl),* a. problematico; **—ly,** ad. in modo problematico.

proboscis, *prŏbŏs'sĭs,* s. proboscide, f.

procedure, *prōsēd'är,* s. procedimento, m.; progresso, m.

proceed, *—sēd',* v. n. procedere, derivare; provenire; comportarsi; **—,** s. prodotto, guadagno, m. |portamento, m.

proceeding, *—ĭng,* s. procedimento, com-

process, *prŏs'ĕs (prō'sĕs),* s. processo, m.; progresso, m.

procession, *prōsĕsh'ăn,* s. processione, f.

proclaim, *—klām',* v. a. proclamare; pubblicare; bandire.

proclamation, *prŏklămā'shăn,* s. proclama, f.; bando, m. |pensione, f.

proclivity, *prŏklĭv'ĭtĭ,* s. proclività, prò-

proconsul, *—kŏn'sŭl,* s. proconsolo, m.

procrastinate, *—krăs'tĭnăt,* v. a. procrastinare; indugiare. |zione, f.

procrastination, *—nă'shăn,* s. procrastina-

procreate, *prō'krēăt,* v. a. procreare; produrre. |il procreare, m.

procreation, *—ā'shăn,* s. procreamento, m.

proctor, *prŏk'tär,* s. procuratore, m.; fattore, m. |tore, m.

proctorship, *—shĭp,* s. uffizio di procura-

procurable, *prōkū'răbl,* a. che si può procurare, procurabile.

procuration, *prŏkūră'shăn,* s. procurazione, procura, f. |agente, m.

procurator, *—rä'tär,* s. procuratore, m.;

procure, *prōkūr',* v. a. procurare; ottenere; fare il ruffiano.

procurement, *—mĕnt,* s. procurazione, f.

procurer, *—är,* s. procuratore, m.; mezzano, m. |—ly, ad. prodigamente.

prodigal, *prŏd'ĭgăl,* a. & s. prodigo (m.);

prodigality, *—găl'ĭtĭ,* s. prodigalità, f.

prodigious, *—dĭj'ăs,* a. prodigioso; **—ly,** ad. prodigiosamente.

prodigy, *prŏd'ĭjĭ,* s. prodigio, m.

produce, *prŏd'ūs,* s. prodotto, m.; **—,** *prōdūs',* v. a. produrre; causare.

producer, *prōdū'sär,* s. produttore, m.

product, *prŏd'ŭkt,* s. prodotto, m.; effetto, m.; opera, f. |f., prodotto, m.

production, *prōdŭk'shăn,* s. produzione,

productive, *—tĭv,* a. produttivo.

productiveness, *—nĕs,* s. produttività, f.; fertilità, f. |zione, f.

profanation, *prŏfănā'shăn,* s. profana-

profane, *prōfān',* a. profano; **—ly,** ad. profanamente; **—,** v. a. profanare.

profess, *—fĕs',* v. a. & n. professare; esercitare, mantenere, seguitare. |apertamente.

professedly, *—sĕdlĭ,* ad. pubblicamente.

profession, *—fĕsh'ăn,* s. professione, f.; mestiere, m. |fessionale.

professional, *—ăl,* a. di professione, pro-

professor, *—fĕs'sär,* s. professore, m.

professorship, *—shĭp,* s. professorato, carica di professore, m.

proffer, *prŏf'fär,* v. a. proferire, offrire; proporre; **—,** s. offerta, f.

proficiency, *prōfĭsh'ĕnsĭ,* s. avanzamento, m.; progresso, m.

proficient, *—ĕnt,* a. proficiente; avanzato.

profile, *prō'fĕl,* s. profilo, m.

profit, *prŏf'ĭt,* s. profitto, guadagno, m.; vantaggio, m.; frutto, m.; **—,** v. a. avvantaggiare; essere utile; **—,** v. n. profittare; far progressi. |gioso.

profitable, *—ăbl,* a. profittevole, vantag-

profitableness, *—nĕs,* s. profitto, m.

profitably, *—ăblĭ,* ad. profittevolmente.

profitless, *—lĕs,* a. di niun profitto.

profligacy, *prŏf'lĭgăsĭ,* s. scelleratezza, f.

profligate, *—lĭgăt,* a. scellerato, malvagio; **—ly,** ad. scelleratamente.

profound, *prōfŏŭnd',* a. profondo; **—ly,** ad. profondamente; **—,** s. abisso, m.

profundity, *—fŭnd'ĭtĭ,* s. profondità, f.

profuse, *—fūs',* a. profuso; eccessivo; prodigo; **—ly,** ad. profusamente.

profusion, *–fū'zhŭn,* s. prodigalità, profusione, f.; esuberanza, f.   [tenato, m.

progenitor, *–jĕn'ĭtŭr* s. progenitore, antenato, m.

progeny, *prŏj'ĕnĭ,* s. progenie, stirpe, schiatta, f.

prognostic, *prŏgnŏs'tĭk,* s. prognostico, m.

prognosticate, *–tĭkāt,* v. a. prognosticare, predire.

prognostication, *–tĭkā'shŭn,* s. prognostico, m.   [viso, m.

programme, *prŏgrăm',* s. programma, avviso, m.

progress, *prŏg'rĕs (prŏ'grĕs),* s. progresso, processo, m.; viaggio, m.; **–,** *prŏgrĕs',* v. n. progredire, andar innanzi.   [f.

progression, *prŏgrĕsh'ŭn,* s. progressione, f.

progressive, *–sĭv,* a. progressivo; **–ly,** ad. progressivamente.

prohibit, *–hĭb'ĭt,* v. n. proibire, impedire, vietare.   [f., divieto, m.

prohibition, *–hĭbĭsh'ŭn,* s. proibizione, f.

prohibitory, *–hĭb'ĭtŭrĭ,* a. proibitivo.

project, *prŏj'ĕkt,* s. disegno, m.; soggetto, m.; **–,** *prŏjĕkt',* v. a. progettare; macchinare; **–,** v. n. aggettare; sportare.

projectile, *prŏjĕk'tĭl,* s. proietto, m.

projecting, *–jĕkt'ĭng,* a. aggettante.

projection, *–jĕk'shŭn,* s. proiezione, f.

projector, *–tŭr,* s. disegnatore, inventore, m.   [–ĕtāri, a. proletario, m.

proletarian, *–lĕtā'rĭăn,* **proletary,** *prŏl'-*

prolific, *–lĭf'ĭk,* a. prolifico, fecondo.

prolix, *prŏ'lĭks,* a. prolisso, diffuso.

prolixity, *–lĭks'ĭtĭ,* s. prolissità, f.; lunghezza, f.

prologue, *prŏ'lŏg,* s. prologo, m.

prolong, *–lŏng',* v. a. prolungare; differire.

prolongation, *–gā'shŭn,* s. prolungamento, m.; indugio, m.

promenade, *prŏmĕnād',* s. passeggiata, f., passeggio, m.; **–,** v. n. passeggiare.

prominence, *prŏm'ĭnĕns* s. prominenza, f.; risalto, m.

prominent, *–nĕnt,* a. prominente; **–ly,** ad. in modo prominente.

promiscuous, *prŏmĭs'kŭŭs,* a. promiscuo, confuso; **–ly,** ad. promiscuamente, confusamente.   [promettere.

promise, *prŏm'ĭs,* s. promessa, f.; **–,** v. a.

promissory, *–ĭssŭrĭ,* a. promissorio, di promessa.

promontory, *–ŏntŭrĭ,* s. promontorio, f.

promote, *prŏmōt'* v. a. promuovere; far fiorire.   [tettore, m.

promoter, *–mō'tŭr,* s. promotore, m.; promovente.

promotion, *–mō'shŭn,* s. promovimento, m.; avanzamento, aggrandimento, m.; esaltazione, f.

prompt, *prŏmt.* a. pronto; contante; **–ly,** ad. prontamente; **–,** v. a. suggerire, insinuare.

prompter, *–ŭr,* s. suggeritore, m.

promptitude, *–ĭtūd,* **promptness,** *–nĕs,* s. prontezza, speditezza, f.

promulgate, *prŏmŭl'gāt,* v. a. promulgare, pubblicare.   [zione, f.

promulgation, *–gā'shŭn,* s. promulgazione, f.

prone, *prŏn,* a. prono, inclinato.

proneness, *–nĕs,* s. propensione, f.; inclinazione, tendenza, f.

prong, *prŏng,* s. forchetta, forca, f.

pronoun, *prŏ'nŏŭn,* s. (gr.) pronome, m.

pronounce, *–nŏŭns',* v. a. pronunziare; dichiarare.   [zia, f.; il pronunziare, m.

pronunciation, *–nŭnsĭā'shŭn,* s. pronunzia, m.

proof, *prŏf,* s. prova, f., esperimento, m.; testimonianza, f.; **–,** a. a tutta prova; impenetrabile.   [bozza, f.

proof-sheet, *–shēt,* s. prova di stampa, f.

prop, *prŏp,* s. sostegno, puntello, m.; appoggio, m.; **–,** v. a. sostenere, puntellare.

propaganda, *prŏpăgăn'dā,* s. propaganda, f.   [gare; propagarsi.

propagate, *prŏp'āgāt,* v. a. & n. propagare.

propagation, *–gā'shŭn,* s. propagazione, f.; moltiplicazione, f.

propel, *prŏpĕl',* v. a. cacciare avanti, spingere avanti.   [lente, m.

propeller, *–ŭr,* s. vapore a vite propellente.

propensity, *–pĕns'ĭtĭ,* s. propensione, f.; tendenza, f.

proper, *prŏp'ŭr,* a. proprio; convenevole; competente; esatto; **–ly,** ad. propriamente; giustamente.

property, *–tĭ,* s. proprietà, f.; qualità, f.

prophecy, *prŏf'ĕsĭ,* s. profezia, f.

prophesy, *prŏf'ĕsī,* v. a. profetizzare; **–,** v. n. predicare.

prophet, *prŏf'ĕt,* s. profeta, m.

prophetess, *–ĕs,* s. profetessa, f.

prophetic, *prŏfĕt'ĭk,* a. profetico; **–ally,** ad. profeticamente.

propinquity, *–pĭng'kwĭtĭ,* s. propinquità, vicinanza, f.   [pizio.

propitiate, *–pĭsh'ĭāt,* v. a. rendere propizio.

propitiation, *–ĭā'shŭn,* s. propiziazione, f.

propitiatory, *–ĭātŭrĭ,* a. propiziatorio.

propitious, *–pĭsh'ŭs,* a. favorevole; **–ly,** ad. favorevolmente.

proportion, *–pŏr'zhŭn,* s. proporzione, simmetria, f.; **–,** v. a. proporzionare.

proportionable, *–ăblĭ,* **proportional,** *–ăl,* a. proporzionale.   [posta, offerta, f.

proposal, *–pō'zăl,* s. proposizione, f.; proposta, offerta, f.

propose, *–pōz',* v. a. proporre.

proposition, *prŏpŏzĭsh'ŭn,* s. proposizione, f.; offerta, f.   [mettere in campo.

propound, *prŏpŏŭnd',* v. a. proporre; mettere in campo.

proprietary, *–prī'ĕtărĭ,* **proprietor.** *–ĕtŭr,* s. proprietario, padrone, m.

proprietor, *–ĕtŭr,* s. proprietario, m.

proprietess, *–ĕtrĕs,* s. proprietaria, f.

propriety, *–ĕtĭ,* s. proprietà, f.; convenevolezza, f.

prorogation, *–rŏgā'shŭn,* s. proroga, f.

prorogue, *–rōg',* v. a. prorogare.

prosaic, *–zā'ĭk,* a. prosaico, in prosa.

proscenium, *–sē'nĭŭm,* s. proscenio, m.

proscribe, *–skrīb',* v. a. proscrivere, esiliare, bandire.   [f.

proscription, *–skrĭp'shŭn,* s. proscrizione, f.

prose, *prōz,* s. prosa, f.

prosecute, *prŏs'ĕkāt,* v. a. proseguire.

prosecution, *–kū'shŭn,* s. proseguimento, m.; continuazione, f.

prosecutor, *prŏs'ĕkūtŭr*, s. attore, m.; postulante, m.

proselyte, *prŏs'ĕlīt*, s. proselito, m.

prosody, *prŏs'ŏdĭ*, s. prosodia, f.

prospect, *prŏs'pĕkt*, s. prospettiva, f.; vista, f.; disegno, intento, m. [vido.

prospective, *-spĕk'tĭv*, a. prospettivo, pro-

prospectus, *-spĕk'tŭs*, s. programma, m.

prosper, *prŏs'pŭr*, v. a. rendere felice; —, v. n. prosperare; riuscire.

prosperity, *-pĕr'ĭtĭ*, s. prosperità, f.

prosperous, *prŏs'pŭrŭs*, a. prospero, felice; **-ly**, ad. prosperamente.

prostitute, *prŏs'tĭtūt*, s. prostituta, f.; —, v. a. prostituire. [f.

prostitution, *-tū'shŭn*, s. prostituzione,

prostrate, *prŏs'trāt*, a. prostrato; —, v. a. prostrare.

prostration, *-trā'shŭn*, s. prostrazione, f.

protect, *prŏtĕkt'*, v. a. proteggere.

protection, *-tĕk'shŭn*, s. protezione, difesa, f., riparo, appoggio, m.

protective, *-tĭv*, a. difensivo. [m.

protector, *-tŭr*, s. protettore, difensore,

protest, *prŏ'tĕst*, s. protesta, f.; protestazione, f.; —, *-tĕst'*, v. n. protestare; attestare.

Protestant, *prŏt'ĕstănt*, a. protestante; —, s. Protestante, m. & f. [stante, f.

P.otestantism, *-ĭzm*, s. religione protestante.

protestation, *-tā'shŭn*, s. protestazione, f.

protocol, *prŏ'tŏkŏl*, s. protocollo, m.

prototype, *-tĭp*, s. prototipo, m.

protract, *prŏtrăkt'*, v. a. protrarre, prolungare.

protraction, *-trăk'shŭn*, s. protrazione, f.

protrude, *-trōd'*, v. a. & n. sporgere, spingere; uscire di linea.

protuberance, *-tū'bărăns*, s. protuberanza, f., tumore, m. [mido.

protuberant, *-bărănt*, a. prominente; tu-

proud, *prŏŭd*, a. orgoglioso, superbo; **-ly**, ad. superbamente.

prove, *prōv*, v. a. provare, sperimentare; cimentare; —, v. n. divenire; accadere.

provender, *prŏv'ĕndăr*, s. foraggio, m.

proverb, *prŏv'ŭrb*, s. proverbio, detto, motto, m. [**-ly**, ad. proverbialmente.

proverbial, *prŏvŭr'bĭăl*, a. proverbiale;

provide, *-vīd'*, v. a. & n. provvedere; fornire; munire. [che.

provided, *-ĕd*, c. (– that,) a condizione

providence, *prŏv'ĭdĕns*, s. provvidenza, f.; economia, f. [ad. cautamente.

provident, *-ĭdĕnt*, a. provvidente; **-ly**,

providential, *-dĕn'shăl*, a. della provvidenza, provvidenziale; **-ly**, ad. per cura della provvidenza.

province, *prŏv'ĭns*, s. provincia, regione, f.; affare, m. [ciale (m.).

provincial, *prŏvĭn'shăl*, a. & s. provin-

provision, *-vĭzh'ŭn*, s. provvisione, f.; viveri, m. pl.; precauzione, f.; —, v. a. provvisionare.

provisional, *-ăl*, a. provvisionale; **-ly**, ad. provvisionalmente. [zione, f.

proviso, *-vī'zō*, s. condizione, f.; stipula-

provisory, *-vī'zŭrĭ*, a. provvisorio.

provocation, *prŏvŏkā'shŭn*, s. appellazione, f. [lare.

provoke, *prŏvōk'*, v. a. provocare, appellare.

provokingly, *-ĭnglĭ*, ad. in modo provocante.

provost, *prŏv'ŏst*, s. proposto, preposto, m.

prow, *prŏŭ*, s. (mar.) prora, prua, f.

prowess, *-ĕs*, s. prodessa, f., valore, m.

prowl, *prŏŭl*, v. a. cercare di rubare; saccheggiare, svaligiare. [m.

prowler, *-ŭr*, s. rubatore, m.; truffatore,

proximate, *prŏks'ĕmăt*, a. prossimo; **-ly**, ad. immediatamente.

proximity, *-ĭm'ĭtĭ*, s. prossimità, f.

proxy, *prŏks'ĭ*, s. procuratore, m.; procura, f.

prude, *prŏŭd*, s. affettazione, f. [cura, f.

prudence, *prŏ'dĕns*, s. prudenza, f.

prudent, *-dĕnt*, a. prudente, circospetto.

prudential, *-dĕn'shăl*, a. prudenziale, prudente. [denza, f. pl.

prudentials, *-shălz*, s. pl. regole di pru-

prudery, *prŏŏ'ărĭ*, s. modestia affettata, f.

prudish, *-ĭsh*, a. di modestia affettata.

prune, *prŏŭn*, s. susina secca, f.; —, v. a. dibruscare, diramare.

prunello, *prŭnĕl'lŏ*, s. prugnola, f.

pruning-hook, *prŏŭ'ĭng hŏk*, **pruning-knife**, *-nīf*, s. falcetto, m. [m.

pruriency, *prŏ'rĭĕnt*, s. prudore, pizzicore,

prurient, *-rĭĕnt*, a. pizzicante.

prussic acid, *prŭs'ĭk ăs'ĭd*, s. acido cianico, m. [(am.) leva, stanga, f.

pry, *prĭ*, v. n. spiare, investigare; —, s.

psalm, *săm*, s. salmo, m., canzone sacra, f.

Psalter, *săl'tăr*, s. Saltero, Salterio, Libro di salmi, m.

pseudonym, *sŭ'dŏnĭm*, s. pseudonimo, m.

pshaw! *shă*, i. via via! oibò! [logico.

psychologic(al), *sĭkŏlŏj'ĭk(ăl)*, a. psico-

psychology, *-kŏl'ŏjĭ*, s. psicologia, f.

puberty, *pŭ'bărtĭ*, s. pubertà, adolescenza, f. [pubertà.

pubescent, *-bĕs'ĕnt*, a. pubescente, di

public, *pŭb'lĭk*, a. pubblico, manifesto; —, s. pubblico, comune, m.; **-ly**, ad. pubblicamente. [niere, m.

publican, *-kăn*, s. pubblicano, m.; taver-

publication, *-kā'shŭn*, s. pubblicazione, f.; edizione, f.

publicist, *pŭb'lĭsĭst*, s. pubblicista, m.

publicity, *-lĭs'ĭtĭ*, s. pubblicità, notorietà, f.

publish, *pŭb'lĭsh*, v. a. pubblicare. [f.

publisher, *-ŭr*, s. pubblicatore, m.; editore, m.

pucker, *pŭk'ăr*, v. a. piegare, raggrinzare.

pudding, *pŭd'ĭng*, s. pasticcio, m.; sanguinaccio, m. [sguazzare; imbrattare.

puddle, *pŭd'dl*, s. fango, m.; —, v. a.

pudenda, *pŭdĕn'dă*, s. pl. pudende, parti vergognose, f. pl. [f.

pudicity, *-dĭs'ĭtĭ*, s. pudicizia, verecondia,

puerile, *pŭ'ărĭl*, a. fanciullesco.

puff, *pŭf*, s. soffio, m.; fungo, m.; fiocco, m.; avviso esagerato, m.; annuncio a pagamento, m.; —, v. a. soffiare, gonfiare; esaltare; —, v. n. gonfiare, sbuffare.

puffiness, *-fĭnĕs*, s. gonfiezza, f.

puffing, *–fĭng,* s. lode esagerata, f.

puff-paste, *–pāst,* s. pasta sfoglia, f.

puffy, *–fĭ,* a. gonfiato, enfiato.

pug, *pŭg,* s. scimmiotto, m.; cuor mio, m.

pugilism, *pū'jĭlĭzm,* s. pugilato, m.

pugilist, *–jĭlĭst,* s. pugilatore, m.

pugnacious, *pŭgnā'shŭs,* a. pugnace.

pug-nose, *pŭg'nōz,* s. naso schiacciato, m.

paisne, *pā'nē,* a. cadetto, inferiore. [carsi.

pule, *pūl,* v. n. pigolare, piare; rammari-

pull, *pŭl,* v. a. tirare, stracciare, svellere; remare; vogare; –, s. tirata, f.; scossa, f.

pull-back, *–băk,* s. impedimento, ostacolo,

pullet, *–lĕt,* s. pollastro, m. [m.

pulley, *–lĭ,* s. girella, f.; carrucola, f.

pulmonary, *pŭl'mŏnărĭ,* **pulmonic,** *–mŏn'ĭk,* a. polmonario.

pulp, *pŭlp,* s. polpa, f.

pulpit, *pŭl'pĭt,* s. pulpito, m.

pulpy, *–pŭl'pĭ,* a. polposo.

pulsate, *pŭl'sāt,* v. n. battere.

pulsation, *–sā'shŭn,* s. pulsazione, f.; battimento, m.

pulse, *pŭls,* s. polso, m.; legume, m.

pulverise, *pŭl'vărĭz,* v. a. polverizzare.

pulverization, *pŭlvărĭzā'shŭn,* s. polverizzamento, m.

pumice, *pŭ'mĭs,* s. pomice, f.

pump, *pŭmp,* s. tromba (da tirar acqua), f.; scarpetta, f.; –, v. a. trombare; cavar acqua; cavare con destrezza un segreto.

pumpkin, *–kĭn,* s. zucca, f.

pun, *pŭn,* s. bisticcio, equivoco, m.; –, v. n. bisticciare, equivocare.

punch, *pŭnsh,* s. punteruolo, stampo, m.; pulcinella, f.; poncio, m. (bevanda).

puncheon, *–ŭn,* s. punzone, stampo, m.

punchinello, *pŭnshĭnĕl'lō,* s. pulcinella, arlecchino, m. [tata, f.

punctilio, *pŭngktĭl'ĭō,* s. esattezza affet-

punctilious, *–ŭs,* a. troppo esatto, scrupoloso. [ad. puntualmente.

punctual, *–tŭăl,* a. puntuale, esatto; **–ly,**

punctuality, *–ăl'ĭtĭ,* s. puntualità, esattezza, f.

punctuate, *pŭngk'tŭāt,* v. punteggiare.

punctuation, *–ā'shŭn,* s. interpunzione, f.

puncture, *pŭngk'tŭr,* s. puntura, f.

pungency, *pŭn'jĕnsĭ,* s. qualità pungente, f.; acutezza, f.

pungent, *–jĕnt,* a. pungente; acuto.

punic, *pū'nĭk,* a. punico; ingannevole.

puniness, *pū'nĭnĕs,* s. piccolezza, f.

punish, *pŭn'ĭsh,* v. a. punire, gastigare.

punishable, *–ăbl,* a. degno di punizione.

punishment, *–mĕnt,* s. punizione, f.

punster, *pŭn'stŭr,* s. bisticciere, m.; motteggiatore, m. [giocare a bassetta.

punt, *pŭnt,* s. barca piatta, f.; –, v. n.

punter, *pŭn'tŭr,* s. giocatore a bassetta, m. [sano.

puny, *pū'nĭ,* a. giovane; inferiore; mal-

pup, *pŭp,* s. cagnolino, m.; –, v. n. fare i caguolini.

pupil, *pū'pĭl,* s. pupillo, scolare, m.; pupilla (del occhio), f.

pupilage, *–ăj,* s. minorità, f.; tutela, f.

pupillary, *–ărĭ,* a. pupillare.

puppet, *pŭp'pĕt,* s. burattino, bamboccio, m., bambola, f. [burattini, f.

puppet-show, *–shō,* s. commedia di

puppy, *pŭp'pĭ,* s. cagnolino, m.; sciocco, m.; –, v. n. figliare (la cagna). [f.

puppyism, *–pĭĭzm,* s. estrema affettazione,

purblind, *pŭr'blĭnd,* a. di corta vista, miope.

purchase, *pŭr'chăs,* s. acquisto, m., compra, f.; bottino, m.; –, v. a. comprare, acquistare.

purchaser, *–ăr,* s. compratore, m.

pure, *pūr,* a. puro; **–ly,** ad. puramente.

purgation, *pŭrgā'shŭn,* s. purgazione, f.

purgative, *pŭr'gătĭv,* a. purgativo; –, s. medicamento purgativo, m.

purgatory, *pŭr'gătărĭ,* s. purgatorio, m.

purge, *pŭrj,* v. a. purgare.

purification, *pūrĭfĭkā'shŭn,* s. purificazione, f. [purificarsi.

purify, *pū'rĭfĭ,* v. a. & n. purificare;

purism, *pū'rĭzm,* s. purismo, m.

purist, *pū'rĭst,* s. purista, m.

Puritan, *pū'rĭtăn,* s. puritano, m.

purity, *pū'rĭtĭ,* s. purità, f.

purl, *pŭrl,* s. smerlatura, f.; cervogia con assenzio, f.; –, v. n. mormorare.

purlieu, *pŭr'lū,* s. terreno confinante con una foresta, m.

purloin, *–lŏĭn',* v. a. involare, rubare.

purple, *pŭr'pl,* s. porpora, f.; color di porpora, m.; **–s,** pl. febbre petecchiale, f.; –, a. porporino; –, v. a. imporporare, tingere colla porpora.

purplish, *pŭr'plĭsh,* a. porporeggiante.

purport, *pŭr'pōrt,* s. contenuto (d' una scrittura), m.; senso, m.; –, v. n. intendere; significare.

purpose, *pŭr'pŭs,* s. proposito, m., intenzione, f.; soggetto, m.; effetto, m.; **on –,** a bello studio; **to no –,** in vano, inutilmente; –, v. n. proporre.

purr, *pŭr,* v. n. far le fusa, come il gatto.

purse, *pŭrs,* s. borsa, f.; –, v. a. imborsare.

purse-proud, *–prŏŭd,* a. fiero delle ricchezze.

purser, *–ăr,* s. commissario dei viveri, m.

purslain, *pŭrs'lăn,* s. (bot.) porcellana, f.

pursuance, *–sū'ăns,* s. conseguenza, f.; processo, m. [seguenza di.

pursuant, *–sū'ănt,* a. conforme; in con-

pursue, *–sū',* v. a. seguitare, perseguitare; –, v. n. continuare. [lecitazione, istanza, f.

pursuit, *–sūt',* s. persecuzione, f.; sol-

pursy, *pŭr'sĭ,* a. boiso, asmatico.

purulence, *pū'rŭlĕns,* s. purulenza, f.

purulent, *–rŭlĕnt,* a. purulento.

purvey, *pŭrvā',* v. a. & n. provvedere, procurare. [viveri, m. pl.

purveyance, *–ăns,* s. piovvisione, f.

purveyor, *–ăr,* s. provveditore, m.

push, *pŭsh,* v. a. spingere, urtare; eccitare; –, v. n. sforzarsi; –, s. urto, colpo, m.; sforzo, m.; termine, m.

pushing, _-ĭng,_ a. intraprendente.

pusillanimity, _pŭsĭllănĭm'ĭtĭ,_ s. pusillanimità, f.

pusillanimous, _-lăn'ĭmŭs,_ a. pusillanimo, m. [me.

puss, _pŭs,_ s. piccolo gatto, m.

pustule, _pŭs'tŭl,_ s. pustula, bolla, f.

put, _pŭt,_ v. a. ir. mettere, porre, collocare; aggiungere; **to — away,** riporre; **to — by,** salvare, economizzare; **to — off,** procrastinare; **to — on,** mettere, mettersi; **to — out,** estinguere; cavar (gli occhi); disturbare, confondere; **to — up with,** tollerare, soffrire; –, v. n. ir. germinare, germogliare.

putative, _pŭ'tătĭv,_ a. putativo; riputato.

putrefaction, _-trēfǎk'shŭn,_ s. putrefazione, f.

putrefy, _pŭ'trēfĭ,_ v. n. corrompersi.

putrescence, _-trēs'sĕns,_ s. putrescenza, f.

putrescent, _-sĕnt,_ **putrid,** _pŭ'trĭd,_ a. putrido, putrefatto.

putridness, _pŭ'trĭdnēs,_ s. putridezza, f.

putty, _pŭt'tĭ,_ s. cimento, m.

puzzle, _pŭz'zl,_ v. a. imbarazzare; –, v. n. essere irresoluto; –, s. imbarazzo, m.

pygmy, _pĭg'mĭ,_ s. pigmeo, m.

pyramid, _pĭr'ǎmĭd,_ s. piramide, f.

pyramidal, _-rǎm'ĭdǎl,_ a. piramidale.

pyre, _pīr,_ s. pira, f.; rogo, m,

pyrotechnics, _pĭrōtĕk'nĭks,_ s. pirotecnica, arte di far fuochi artifiziali, f.

python, _pĭ'thŏn,_ s. pitone, m. (specie di

pyx, _pĭks,_ s. pisside, f.   [boa).

Q.

quack, _kwăk,_ s. ciarlatano, m.; –, v. n. gracchiare.

quackery, _-ărĭ,_ s. ciarlataneria, f.

Quadragesima, _kwŏdrăjĕs'ĭmă,_ s. quaresima, f., digiuno di quaranta giorni, m.

quadrangle, _kwŏd'rănggl,_ s. quadrangolo, quadrato, m.   [parte, f.

quadrant, _-ănt,_ s. quadrante, m., quarta

quadrilateral, _-rĭlăt'ărăl,_ a. quadrilatero.   [f.

quadrille, _kădrĭl' (kwădrĭl'),_ s. quadriglia, f.

quadroon, _kwŏdrōn',_ s. generato da un Europeo e da una mulatta, m.   [pede, (m).

quadruped, _kwŏd'drūpĕd,_ a. & s. quadrupede, m.

quadruple, _-rŭpl,_ a. quadruplo.

quaff, _kwăf,_ v. a. & n. sbevazzare, trincare.

quagmire, _kwăg'mīr,_ s. pantano, padule, marese, m.   [guire, svenire.

quail, _kwāl,_ s. quaglia, f.; –, v. n. languaint,

quaint, _kwănt,_ a. estremamente pulito, attillato, squisito; **-ly,** ad. squisitamente.

quaintness, _-nĕs,_ s. leggiadria, f.

quake, _kwāk,_ v. n. tremare; scuotersi.

Quaker, _kwā'kăr,_ s. quacchero, m.

qualification, _kwŏlĭfĭkā'shŭn,_ s. qualificazione, qualità, f., talento, m.

qualify, _kwŏl'ĭfĭ,_ v. a. qualificare; moderare; (am.) averare con giuramento.

qualitative, _kwŏl'ĭtătĭv,_ a. qualitativo.

quality, _kwŏl'ĭtĭ,_ s. qualità, f.   [m.

qualm, _kwăm,_ s. svenimento, mal di cuore,

qualmish, _-ĭsh,_ a. che ha il mal di cuore.

quandary, _kwŏndā'rĭ,_ s. dubbio, m.

quantitative, _kwŏn'tĭtătĭv,_ a. quantitativo.

quantity, _-tĭtĭ,_ s. quantità, f.   [tivo.

quantum, _-tăm,_ s. quantità, f.; totale, m.

quarantine, _kwŏr'ăntēn,_ s. quarantina, f.

quarrel, _kwŏr'rĕl,_ s. disputa, contesa, lite, f.; –, v. n. rabbuffare.

quarreler, _-lăr,_ attaccalite, litigioso, m.

quarrelsome, _-săm,_ a. riottoso, rissoso.

quarry, _kwŏr'rĭ,_ s. petraia, f.

quarryman, _-măn,_ s. lavoratore nelle petraie, m.   [quarta, f.

quart, _kwărt,_ s. boccale, m. (misura)

quartan, _kwăr'tăn,_ s. febbre quartana, f.

quarter, _kwăr'tăr,_ s. quarto, m., quarta parte, f.; quartiere, m.; dimora, f.; grazia, f.; **– of an hour,** quarto d'ora, m.; –, v. a. squartare; alloggiare.

quarter-deck, _-dĕk,_ s. cassero d'un vascello, m.   [tre mesi.

quarterly, _-lĭ,_ ad. per quartiere; ogni

quartern, _-tărn,_ s. mezza foglietta, f. (misura).

quartet, _kwărtĕt',_ s. (mus.) quartetto, m.

quarto, _kwărt'ō,_ s. libro in quarto, m.

quash, _kwŏsh,_ v. a. conquassare, fracassare, annullare.

quaver, _kwā'văr,_ s. (mus.) croma, f.; trillo, tremore, m.; –, v. n. gorgheggiare, trillare.

quay, _kē,_ s. spiaggia, f., argine, m.

quean, _kwēn,_ s. sgualdrina, f.

queasy, _kwē'zĭ,_ a. nauseoso, disgustoso.

queen, _kwēn,_ s. regina, f.; dama (al giuoco delle carte), f.

queenly, _-lĭ,_ a. come una regina.

queer, _kwēr,_ a. strano, ridicolo; **-ly,** ad. in modo strano,   [rità, f.

queerness, _-nĕs,_ s. stranezza, f.; singolariquell,

quell, _kwĕl,_ v. a. ammaccare, raffrenare, domare; soggiogare.

quench, _kwĕnsh,_ v. a. estinguere; spengere.

quenchless, _-lĕs,_ a. inestinguibile.

querist, _kwē'rĭst,_ s. interrogatore, m.

querulous, _kwēr'ŭlăs,_ a. lamentevole; **-ly,** ad. in modo dolente.   [lagnarsi, f.

querulousness, _-nĕs,_ s. abitudine di

query, _kwē'rĭ,_ s. domanda, f., quesito, m.; –, v. a. domandare.

quest, _kwĕst,_ s. ricerca, inchiesta, f.

question, _kwĕst'yŭn,_ s. questione, domanda, f.; inchiesta, f.; tortura, f.; –, v. a. questionare; dubitare; –, v. n. far domande; informarsi.   [bioso.

questionable, _-ăbl,_ a. disputabile, dubquestioner,

questioner, _-ăr,_ s. inquisitore, m.

questor, _kwĕs'tăr,_ s. questore, m.

quibble, _kwĭb'bl,_ s. bisticcio, m.; paranomasia, alliterazione, f.; –, v. a. & n. bisticciare, fare bisticci.

quick, _kwĭk,_ a. vivo; vivace, lesto, allegro, pronto, presto; acuto, astuto, sagace; –, **-ly,** ad. prestamente, subito; –, s. vivo, m.; carne viva, f.

quicken, *kwĭk′ n,* v. a. vivificare; animare; accelerare, affrettare; –, v. n. vivificarsi.
quick-grass, *–grås,* s. gramigna, f.
quick-lime, *–lĭm,* s. calcina viva, f.
quickness, *–nĕs,* s. prestezza, attività, f.
quick-sand, *–sånd,* s. secca, f.
quickset, *–sĕt,* s. sierpaglia, f.
quick-sighted, *–sītĕd,* a. di vista acuta.
quick-silver, *–sĭlvăr,* s. argento vivo, m.
quick-silvered, *–sĭlvărd,* a. coperto d'argento vivo.   [gegno.
quick-witted, *–wĭttĕd,* a. di acuto in-
quid, *kwĭd,* a. tabacco da masticare, m.
quiddity, *–ĭtī,* s. quiddità, f.; sottigliezza,
quidnunc, *–nŭngk,* s. smargiasso, m.   [f.
quiescent, *kwĭ ĕs′ sĕnt,* a. quiescente.
quiet, *kwī′ ĕt,* a. quieto, tranquillo; **–ly,** ad. pian piano.
quietness, *–ĕtnĕs,* **quietude,** *–ĕtŭd,* s. quiete, f.; riposo, m.
quietus, *kwĭĕ′ tŭs,* s. quietanza, f.; morte, f.
quill, *kwĭl,* s. penna, f.; cannella, f.; tubo, m.; –, v. a. piegare.
quill-driver, *–drīvăr,* s. scribacchino, m.
quilt, *kwĭlt,* s. coltre, coperta (da letto), f.
quince, *kwĭns,* s. mela cotogna, f.
quince-tree, *–trē,* s. cotogno, m.
quincunx, *kwĭng′ kŭnks,* s. quinconce, m.
quinine, *kwĭn′ īn* (*kwĭnīn′*), s. chinina, f.
quinquennial, *–kwĕn′ nĭăl,* a. di cinque anni, quinquennale.
quinsy, *kwĭn′ zĭ,* s. squinanzia, angina, f.
quint, *kwĭnt,* s. quinta, f. (al giuoco di picchetto).
quintal, *kwĭn′ tăl,* s. quintale, m.
quintessence, *–tĕs′ sĕns,* s. quintessenza, f., estratto, m.
quintet, *kwĭntĕt′,* s. (mus.) quintetto, m.
quintuple, *kwĭn′ tŭpl,* a. quintuplo.
quip, *kwĭp,* s. sarcasmo, motteggio, m.
quire, *kwīr,* s. quinterno (di carta), m.
quirk, *kwărk,* s. cavillo, m.; accesso, m.; bottone, m.
quit, *kwĭt,* v. a. abbandonare, lasciare; rinunziare, far quietanza; liberare; –, a. liberato.
quite, *kwĭt,* ad. affatto, interamente.
quits, *kwĭts,* i. pace! pagati del tutto!
quittance, *kwĭt′ tăns,* s. quietanza, ricevuta, f.; ricompensa, f.
quiver, *kwĭv′ ăr,* s. faretra, f.; –, v. n. tremare; trillare; **–ed,** a. faretrato.
quiz, *kwĭz,* v. a. mistificare, ingannare.
quizzing-glass, *–ĭng glăs,* s. occhialino, m.   [strella, f.
quoit, *kŏĭt* (*kwŏĭt*), s. disco, m.; pia-
quondam, *kwŏn′ dăm,* a. un tempo.
quorum, *kwŏ′ ŭm,* s. uno de' giudici, m.
quota, *kwŏ′ tă,* s. contingente, m.; parte, f.
quotation, *–tā′ shăn,* s. citazione, allegazione, f.
quote, *kwŏt,* v. a. citare.
quoth, *kwŭth* (*kwŏth*), v. imp. – **he,** dice egli; disse egli.   [f.
quotidian, *kwŏtĭd′ ĭăn,* s. febbre quotidiana,
quotient, *kwŏ′ shĕnt,* s. (ar.) quoziente, m.

R.

rabbet, *răb′ bĕt,* s. scanalatura, incastra-tura, f.   [tura, f.
rabbi, *răb′ bī,* s. rabbino, m.
rabbit, *răb′ bĭt,* s. coniglio, m.
rabble, *răb′ bl,* s. plebe, f., popolaccio, m.
rabid, *răb′ bĭd,* a. rabbioso.
race, *rās,* s. razza, stirpe, f.; corsa, f., palio, m.; fragranza del vino, f.; –, v. n. contendere al corso.
racer, *–ăr,* s. corsiere, corridore, m.
raciness, *rā′ sĭnĕs,* s. gusto piccante (del vino), m.
rack, *răk,* s. tortura, f.; rastrelliera, f., rastrello (di cucina), m.; rocca, f.; liquore spiritoso (fatto di riso), m.; –, v. a. tormentare; travasare.
racket, *răk′ ĕt,* s. racchetta, f.; romore, m.
rack-rent, *–rĕnt,* s. affitto forzato, m.
racy, *rā′ sĭ,* a. piccante, saporoso, gustoso (del vino).
radiance, *rā′ dĭăns,* s. splendore, m.
radiant, *–dĭănt,* a. radiante.
radiate, *–dĭāt,* v. n. radiare, raggiare.
radiation, *–dĭā′ shăn,* s. radiazione, f., splendore, m.; **–ly,** ad. radicalmente.
radical, *răd′ ĭkăl,* a. & s. radicale (m.);
radicalism, *răd′ ĭkălĭzm,* s. radicalismo, m.
radish, *răd′ ĭsh,* s. rapa, f.; ravanello, m.
radius, *rā′ dĭŭs,* s. radio, m.
raffle, *răf′ fl,* s. zara, f. (giuoco); –, v. n. giuocare a zara.
raft, *răft,* s. zattera, f.   [giuocare a zara.
rafter, *răf′ tăr,* s. travicello, m.
rag, *răg,* s. cencio, straccio, m.
ragamuffin, *–ămŭf′ fĭn,* s. cencioso, birbone, m.   [arrabbiare, incollerirsi.
rage, *rādj,* s. rabbia, f., furore, m.; –, v. n.
rag-gatherer, (**--man,--picker**) *răg′-găthărăr,* (*–măn,–pĭk′ ăr*), s. cenciaiuolo, stracciaiuolo, m.
ragged, *răg′ gĕd,* a. stracciato, cencioso.
raging, *rā′ jĭng,* s. rabbia, furia, f.; **–ly,** ad. furiosamente.
raid, *rād,* s. incursione, razzia, f.
raider, *–ăr,* s. predatore, m.
rail, *rāl,* s. cancello, steccato, m.; sponda (d'un ponte), f.; balaustro, m.; (rail.) rotaia, f.; –, v. a. cancellare, chiudere con balaustrata; –, v. n. dire delle ingiurie.
railer, *–ăr,* s. oltraggiatore, m.
railing, *–lĭng,* s. cancelli, balaustri, m. pl.; oltraggio, m.
raillery, *răl′ ărĭ* (*rāl′ ărĭ*), s. beffa, baia, f.
railroad, *rāl′ rŏd,* **railway,** *–wā,* s. strada ferrata, ferrovia, f.
raiment, *rā′ mĕnt,* s. vestimento, abito, m.
rain, *rān,* s. pioggia, f.; –, v. n. piovere.
rainbow, *–bŏ,* s. arcobaleno, f.
rain-water, *–wătăr,* s. acqua piovana, f.
rainy, *rān′ ĭ,* a. piovoso.
raise, *rāz,* v. a. levare, alzare; sollevare, inalzare, eccitare.
raisin, *rā′ zn* (*rā′ zĭn*), s. uva passa, f.
rake, *rāk,* s. rastro, rastrello, m.; libertino, m.; –, v. a. rastrellare, raschiare, sar-chiellare.

rakish, *-ĭsh*, a. dissoluto, lascivo.
rally, *răl'lĭ*, v. a. raccogliere; beffare; —, v. n. raccogliersi; burlarsi.
ram, *răm*, s. montone, m.; ariete, m.; —, v. a. cacciare dentro con forza.
ramble, *răm'bl*, v. n. andare attorno; vagabondare; —, s. scorsa, f., vagabondare, m.
rambler, *-blăr*, s. vagabondo, m.
ramification, *rămĭfĭkā'shăn*, s. ramificazione, f.
ramify, *răm'ĭfĭ*, v. n. diramarsi.
rammer, *răm'măr*, s. mazzeranga, f.; bacchetta da schioppo, f. |rampicare.
ramp, *rămp*, s. salto, m.; scossa, f.; —, v. n.
rampant, *-ănt*, a. esuberante.
rampart, *răm'părt*, s. baluardo, riparo, m.
ramrod, *răm'rŏd*, s. (mil.) bacchetta (da schioppo), f. |cadente.
ramshackle, *răm'shăkl*, a. cascaticcio, rancid, *răn'sĭd*, a. rancido.
rancidness, *-nĕs*, s. rancidità, f. [zioso.
rancorous, *răng'kŭrŭs*, a. maligno, maligrancour, *-kŭr*, s. rancore, m.
random, *răn'dŏm*, s. accidente, m.; at —, a caso; inconsideratamente.
range, *rănj*, s. ordine, classe, f.; metà, f.; giro, m.; corsa, scorsa, f.; gratella (per la cucina), f.; timone (d'una carrozza), m.; —, v. a. ordinare; schierare; —, v. n. vagabondare, vagare.
rank, *răngk*, a. abbondante; rancido; stantìo; —, s. ordine, grado, m.; posto, m.; dignità, f.
rankle, *răng'kl*, v. n. putrefarsi.
rankness, *răngk'nĕs*, s. esuberanza (di crescimento), f.; rancidità, f. |dare.
ransack, *răn'săk*, v. a. saccheggiare, preransom, *-săm*, s. ricatto, m.; —, v. a. ricattare. |mente.
rant, *rănt*, v. n. parlare troppo ampollosaranter, *-ăr*, s. smaniatore, m.
rap, *răp*, s. colpo forte, m.; —, v. a. & n. bussare, picchiare, battere.
rapacious, *răpā'shŭs*, a. rapace; —ly, ad. con rapacità.
rapacity, *-păs'ĭtĭ*, s. rapacità, f.
rape, *răp*, s. rapimento, ratto, m.; raspa, f.; rapa salvatica, f.
rapid, *răp'ĭd*, a. rapido, veloce; —ly, ad. rapidamente; —s, s. pl. flusso rapido, m.
rapidity, *-pĭd'ĭtĭ*, s. rapidità, f.
rapier, *rā'pĭăr*, s. stocco, m.
rapine, *răp'ĭn*, s. rapina, f. |m.]; bugia, f.
rapper, *răp'păr*, s. martello della porta,
rapt, *răpt*, a. rapito, estatico.
rapture, *răp'tŭr (-chŭr)*, s. rapimento, m.;
rapturous, *-ŭs*, a. estatico. |estasi, f.
rare, *răr*, a. raro, straordinario; non denso; —ly, ad. raramente, di rado.
raree-show, *rā'rēshŏ*, s. mondo nuovo, piccolo spettacolo, m. |f.
rarefaction, *rărĕfăk'shăn*, s. rarefazione,
rarefy, *rā'rĕfĭ*, v. a. rarefare. |sità, f.
rarity, *rā'rĭtĭ*, s. rarità, cosa rara, curiorascal, *răs'kăl*, s. furfante, briccone, m.
rascality, *-kăl'ĭtĭ*, s. furfanteria, f. |m.
rascallion, *-kăl'yăn*, s. birbone, briccone,

rascally, *răs'kălĭ*, a. furfantesco.
rase, *vedi* **raze**.
rash, *răsh*, a. temerario, precipitoso; —ly, ad. temerariamente; —, s. eruzione, f.
rasher, *-ăr*, s. sottile fetta di prosciutto, f.
rashness, *-nĕs*, s. temerità, f.; imprudenza, sconsideratezza, f.
rasp, *răsp*, s. lima grossa, f.; —, v. a. raspare, limare; scrostare (pane).
raspberry, *răs'bĕrĭ*, s. mora di rovo, f.
rasping, *-pĭng*, s. raschiatura, f.
rat, *răt*, s. ratto, m.; disertore, m.; guastamestieri, m.; **to smell a** —, sospettare.
ratable, *rā'tăbl*, a. tassabile.
rate, *răt*, s. prezzo, valore, m.; tassa, assisa, imposizione, f.; maniera, f.; sfera, f., grado, m.; —, v. a. tassare, apprezzare, valutare; biasimare. |nauzi.
rather, *răth'ăr*, ad. piuttosto; meglio; inratification, *rătĭfĭkā'shăn*, s. ratificaratify, *răt'ĭfĭ*, v. a. ratificare. |zione, f.
ratio, *rā'shĭŏ*, s. proporzione, f.
ration, *rā'shăn*, s. razione, f.; proporzione, f.
rational, *răsh'ănăl*, a. razionale, ragionevole; —ly, ad. con ragione.
rationalism, *-ălĭzm*, s. razionalismo, m.
rationality, *-ăl'ĭtĭ*, s. razionalità, f.; ragione, f.
rats'-bane, *răts'băn*, s. arsenico, m.
rattan, *răttăn'*, s. canna d'India, f.
ratteen, *rătten'*, s. rovescio, m. (panno).
rattle, *răt'tl*, s. sonaglio, m.; strepito, fracasso, m.; —, v. a. fare strepito; riprendere; **to** — **in the throat**, gorgogliare.
rattle-snake, *-snăk*, s. caudisona, serpe a sonagli, f.
ravage, *răv'ăj*, s. strage, rovina, f., guasto, m.; —, v. a. rovinare, saccheggiare.
ravager, *-ăr*, s. predatore, m.
rave, *răv*, v. n. delirare; esser fuor di sè.
ravel, *răv'l*, v. a. imbrogliare; —, v. n. sfilacciarsi.
raven, *rā'vn*, s. corvo, corbo, m.
ravenous, *răv'ĕnŭs*, a. vorace; —ly, ad. con voracità.
ravine, *răv'ĕn*, s. borro, burrone, m.
raving, *răv'ĭng*, a. delirante; —ly, ad. freneticamente.
ravish, *răv'ĭsh*, v. a. rapire; incantare.
ravisher, *-ăr*, s. rapitore, m.; stupratore, m. |vole.
ravishingly, *-ĭnglĭ*, ad. in modo incanteravishment, *-mĕnt*, s. estasi, f.; ratto, m.
raw, *ră*, a. crudo, fresco; indigesto; novizio.
raw-boned, *-bŏnd*, a. magro, macilento.
rawness, *-nĕs*, s. l'esser crudo, m.; inray, *rā*, s. raggio, m. |esperienza, f.
raze, *răz*. v. a. scalfire; rovinare.
razor, *rā'zŭr*, s. rasoio, m.
reach, *rēch*, v. a. ir. porgere; giungere; —, v. n. arrivare; stendersi; penetrare; spettare; —, s. estensione, f.; capacità, f.; inganno, m.; autorità, f.
react, *rĕăkt'*, v. n. respingere.
reaction, *-ăk'shăn*, s. reazione, f.
read, *rĕd*, v. a. ir. leggere; studiare; **fare letture**; —, *rĕd*, a. letterato; saputo.

readable, _-ăbl_, a. leggibile.

reader, _-ăr_, s. lettore, leggitore, m.

readily, _rĕd'ĭlĭ_, ad. prontamente; volontiermente. [f.

readiness, _-nĕs_, s. prontezza, f.; diligenza.

reading, _rĕd'ĭng_, s. lettura, f.; discorso, m.

reading-room, _-rōm_, s. gabinetto di lettura, m.

re-adjust, _rĕâjŭst'_, v. a. raggiustare.

ready, _rĕd'ĭ_, a. pronto, preparato, apparecchiato, acconcio; inclinato; --, ad. già, adesso; --reckoner, s. macchina calcolatrice, f. [veramente, in realtà.

real, _rĕ'ăl_, a. reale; vero, effettivo; --ly, ad.

realisation, _-ĭză'shŭn_, s. l' effettuare, effetto, m.

realise, _rĕ'ălĭz_, v. a. effettuare. [fetto, m.

reality, _-ăl'ĭtĭ_, s. realtà, esistenza effettiva, f.; verità, f.; effetto, m.

realm, _rĕlm_, s. regno, reame, m.

ream, _rēm_, s. risma di carta, f.

re-animate, _rĕăn'ĭmăt_, v. a. rianimare.

reap, _rēp_, v. a. mietere; raccogliere.

reaper, _-ăr_, s. mietitore, m.

reaping, _-ĭng_, s. mjetitura, f. [cetto, m.

reaping-hook, _-hŏk_, s. falciuola, f., falre-appear, _rĕăppēr'_, v. n. riapparire.

rear, _rēr_, s. (mil.) retroguardia, f.; ultima classe, f.; --, v. a. levare; inalzare, ergere.

re-ascend, _rĕăssĕnd'_, v. a. & n. rimontare.

reason, _rĕ'zn_, s. ragione, f.; cagione, causa, f.; --, v. a. & n. ragionare.

reasonable, _-ăbl_, a. ragionevole.

reasonableness, _-nĕs_, s. ragione, f.; giustezza, f.

reasonably, _-ăblĭ_, ad. con ragione.

reasoner, _-ăr_, s. ragionatore, m.

reasoning, _-ĭng_, s. ragionamento, m.

re-assure, _rĕăshōr'_, v. a. assicurare di nuovo. [ribellarsi; sollevarsi.

rebel, _rĕbĕl'_, s. ribello, m.; --, v. n.

rebellion, _-bĕl'yŭn_, s. ribellione, f.

rebellious, _-bĕl'yŭs_, a. ribellante.

rebound, _rĭbŏŭnd'_, v. a. & n. rimbalzare.

rebuff, _rĭbŭf'_, v. a. ripercuotere; rifiutare; --, s. ripercussione, f.

rebuild, _-bĭld'_, v. a. ir. rifabbricare.

rebuke, _rĭbūk'_, v. a. riprendere, sgridare; --, s. rimprovero, m. [enimma, m.

rebus, _rĕ'bŭs_, s. equivoco, m.; rebus,

rebut, _rĭbŭt'_, v. a. ributtare, respingere.

recal, _-kăl'_, v. a. richiamare; --, s. richiamo, m.

recalcitrant, _-kăl'sĭtrănt_, a. ricalcitrante.

recant, _-kănt'_, v. a. ritrattare, disdire; --, v. n. ritrattarsi. [disdetta, f.

recantation, _-tă'shŭn_, s. ritrattazione,

recapitulate, _rĕkăpĭt'ŭlăt_, v. a. ricapitolare, riepilogare. [zione, f.

recapitulation, _-lă'shŭn_, s. ricapitolazione, f.

recapture, _rĕkăp'tŭr_, s. cattura ripresa, f.

recede, _rĕsēd'_, v. n. ritirarsi.

receipt, _-sēt'_, s. ricevuta, f.; ricetta, f.

receivable, _-sēv'ăbl_, a. accettabile, ammissibile. [ammettere; riscuotere.

receive, _-sēv'_, v. a. ricevere, accettare.

recent, _rĕ'sĕnt_, a. recente, nuovo; --ly, ad. recentemente. [ricovero, m.

receptacle, _rĕsĕp'tăkl_, s. ricettacolo, m.;

reception, _-sĕp'shŭn_, s. ricevuta, f.; accoglienza, f. [dine, f.

recess, _-sĕs'_, s. recesso, ritiro, m., solitu-

recession, _-sĕsh'ŭn_, s. ritiramento, m.

recipe, _rĕs'ĭpĕ_, s. prescrizione medica, f., recipe, m.

recipient, _-sĕp'ĭĕnt_, s. recipiente, m.

reciprocal, _-sĭp'rŏkăl_, a. reciproco; --ly, ad. reciprocamente. [pariglia.

reciprocate, _-sĭp'rŏkăt_, v. a. render la

reciprocity, _-prŏs'ĭtĭ_, s. scambievolezza, f.

recital, _-sī'tăl_, recitation, _-sĭtă'shŭn_, s. recitazione, f.; narrazione, f.

recitative, _rĕs'ĭtătēv_, s. (mus.) recitativo, m. [rare.

recite, _-sīt'_, v. a. recitare; raccontare, narreck, _rĕk_, v. a. & n. curare; inquietarsi.

reckless, _-lĕs_, a. negligente, trascurato.

reckon, _rĕk'n_, v. a. contare; --, v. n. pensare; calcolare. [m.

reckoning, _-nĭng_, s. conto, m., computo,

reclaim, _rĕklăm'_, v. a. richiamare; riformare; correggere.

reclaimable, _-ăbl'_, a. che si può reclamare.

recline, _-klīn'_, v. a. inclinare; riposare.

recluse, _-klōz'_, a. ritirato, richiuso; --, s. solitario, m.

reclusion, _-klōsh'ŭn_, s. ritiratezza, f.

recognisance, _-kŏg'nĭzăns_, s. scrittura d' obbligo, f.

recognise, _rĕk'ŏgnĭz_, v. a. riconoscere.

recognition, _-nĭ'shŭn_, s. ricognizione, f.; confessione, f.

recoil, _-kŏĭl'_, v. n. rinculare; venir meno.

recollect, _-kŏllĕkt'_, v. a. ricordarsi.

recollection, _-lĕk'shŭn_, s. reminiscenza, f.

recommence, _rĕkŏmmĕns'_, v. a. ricominciare. [dare.

recommend, _rĕkŏmmĕnd'_, v. a. raccoman-

recommendation, _-dă'shŭn_, s. raccomandazione, f.

recompense, _rĕk'ŏmpĕns_, s. ricompensa, rimunerazione, f.; --, v. a. ricompensare, rimunerare. [rimettere insieme.

recompose, _rĕkŏmpōz'_, v. a. ricomporre;

reconcilable, _rĕkŏnsī'lăbl_, a. riconciliabile. [metter pace.

reconcile, _rĕk'ŏnsīl_, v. a. riconciliare;

reconciliation, _-sĭlĭă'shŭn_, s. riconciliazione, f.

recondite, _rĕk'ŏndĭt_, a. recondito, astruso.

reconnoitre, _-kŏnnŏĭ'tŭr_, v. a. (mil.) riconoscere. [rare.

reconsider, _rĕkŏnsĭd'ŭr_, v. a. riconsiderare.

reconstruct, _rĕkŏnstrŭkt'_, v. a. ricostruire, riedificare.

record, _rĕk'ŏrd_, s. registro, m.; maximum di velocità, m.; --s, pl. archivi, m. pl.; --kŏrd'_, v. a. registrare, arrolare.

recorder, _-kŏrd'ŭr_, s. attuario, m.

recount, _-kŏŭnt'_, v. a. raccontare, narrare.

recourse, _-kŏrs'_, s. ricorso, ricovero, m.

recover, _-kŭv'ŭr_, v. a. ricuperare; racquistare, --, v. n. ricoverarsi.

recoverable, _-ărăbl_, a. ricuperabile.

recovery, _-ărĭ_, s. ricoveramento, m.

recreant, rĕk'rĕănt, s. codardo, f.; apostata, f. [tare, divertire.

recreate, rĕk'rĕăt, v. a. ricreare; dilet-

recreation, –krĕd'shăn, s. ricreazione, f.

recreative, rĕk'rĕătĭv, a. ricreativo.

recriminate, –krĭm'ĭnăt, v. a. incolpare (l'accusante); rimproverare. [ciproca, f.

recrimination, –nă'shăn, s. accusa re-

recruit, –krŭt', s. rinforzo, m.; soldato reclutato, m.; –, v. a. reclutare; rinforzare; supplire.

recruiting, –ĭng, s. reclutamento, m.

rectangle, rĕk'tănggl, s. rettangolo, m.

rectangular, –găldr, a. rettangolo.

rectification, –tĭfĭkă'shăn, s. rettificazione, f.; destillazione seconda, f.

rectify, rĕk'tĭfĭ, v. a. rettificare.

rectilinear, –lĭn'ĕăr, a. rettilineo.

rectitude, rĕk'tĭtŭd, s. rettitudine, f.; dirittura, probità, f.

rector, rĕk'tŭr, s. rettore, m.; curato, m.

rectorship, –shĭp, s. uffizio di rettore, m.

rectory, –tŭrĭ, s. rettoria, f.; parrocchia, f.

recumbent, rĕkăm'bĕnt, a. giacente, riposante. [ricuperare.

recuperative, –kŭ'părătĭv, a. atto a

recur, –kŭr, v. n. ricorrere. [m.

recurrence, –rĕns, s. ritorno, ricorrimento,

recurrent, –rĕnt, a. ricorrente; periodico.

recusant, rĕk'ăzănt, s. ricusante, m.; nonconformista, m.

red, rĕd, a. a. rosso; –, s. color rosso, m.

red-breast, –brĕst, s. pettirosso, m. (uccello). [l' uniforme rosso, m.

red-coat, –kŏt, s. soldato Inglese, per aver

redden, rĕd'n, v. a. & n. arrossire; divenire

reddish, –ĭsh, a. rossicio. [rosso.

redeem, rĕdĕm', v. a. redimere, riscattare.

redeemable, –ăbl, a. redimibile.

redeemer, –ăr, s. redentore, m.; il Salvatore, m.

redemption, –dĕm'shăn, s. redenzione, f.; riscatto, m.

red-handed, rĕd'hăndĕd, ad. sul fatto.

redhot, –hŏt, a. infocato.

red-lead, –lĕd, s. minio, m.

red-letter day, –lĕttăr dă, s. giorno fortunato, m.

redness, rĕd'nĕs, s. rossore, m.

redolence, rĕd'ŏlĕns, s. profumo, m.

redolent, –lĕnt, a. odoroso.

redouble, –dŭb'l, v. a. & n. raddoppiare.

redoubt, –dŏŭt, s. ridotto, fortino, m.

redoubtable, –ăbl, a. formidabile.

redound, –dŏŭnd', v. n. ridondare; ribalzare.

redress, –drĕs', v. a. riformare; correggere; rimediare; aggiustare; –, s. riparazione (del danno), f.; rimedio, m.

redresser, –ăr, s. riformatore, m.

red-tapist, rĕd'tăpĭst, s. impiegato, m.; scribacchino, m. [domare; abbassare.

reduce, rĕdŭs', v. a. ridurre; costringere,

reducible, –sĭbl, a. riducibile.

reduction, –dŭk'shăn, s. riduzione, f.

redundancy, –dăn'dănsĭ, s. superfluità, f.

redundant, –dănt, a. ridundante, superfluo. [piare.

reduplicate, –dŭ'plĭkăt, v. a. raddop-

reduplication, –kă'shăn, s. raddoppiamento, m.

re-echo, rĕĕk'ŏ, v. n. echeggiare.

reed, rĕd, s. canna, f.; giunco, m.; saetta, f.

reedy, rĕd'ĭ, a. pieno di canne.

reef, rĕf, (mar.) v. a. ammainare le vele.

reek, rĕk, s. fume, vapore, m.; –, v. n. fumare; svaporare.

reel, rĕl, s. aspo, m.; guindolo, v. a. innaspare, aggomitolare; –, v. n. vacillare.

reelection, rĕĕlĕk'shăn, s. rielezione.

re-engage, –ĕngăj', v. a. impegnare di nuovo. [m.

re-engagement, –mĕnt, s. obbligo nuovo,

re-enter, –ĕn'tŭr, v. a. rientrare.

re-establish, –ĕstăb'lĭsh, v. a. ristabilire, ristaurare. [mento, m.

re-establishment, –mĕnt, s. ristabili-

refection, rĕfĕk'shăn, s. refezione, f.; ristoro, m.

refectory, –fĕk'tărĭ, s. refettorio, m.

refer, –fĕr', v. a. riferire; rimettere; –, v. n. riferirsi, rapportarsi. [sario, m.

referee, –fărĕ', s. arbitro, m.; compromis-

reference, rĕf'ărĕns, s. relazione, f.; rapporto, m. [–, v. n. raffinarsi, purificarsi.

refine, –fĭn', v. a. raffinare, purificare;

refinement, –mĕnt, s. raffinamento, m.; eleganza, f.

refinery, –ărĭ, s. raffinatura, f.

refit, rĕfĭt', v. a. riparare; racconciare.

reflect, rĕflĕkt', v. a. ripercuotere; rimandare; –, v. n. riflettere, meditare; cascare.

reflection, –flĕk'shăn, s. riflessione, f.; riverbero, riflesso, m.

reflective, –tĭv, a. riflessivo, meditativo.

reflector, –tŭr, s. riverberatore, m.

reflex, rĕ'flĕks, a. riflesso; retroattivo.

reform, rĕfŏrm', v. a. & n. riformare, riformarsi. [s. riformazione, f.

reform, –, **reformation**, –fŏrmă'shăn,

reformatory, –fŏrm'ătărĭ, s. casa di correzione, f.

reformer, –fŏrm'ăr, s. riformatore, m.

reformist, rĕf'ŏrmĭst, s. Riformato, Protestante, m.

refract, –frăkt', v. a. rifrangere.

refraction, –frăk'shăn, s. rifrangimento, m., rifrazione, f. [f.

refractoriness, –tărĭnĕs, s. ostinazione,

refractory, –tărĭ, a. refrattario, ostinato.

refrain, –frăn', v. a. raffrenare, reprimere.

refresh, –frĕsh', v. a. rinfrescare.

refreshment, –mĕnt, s. rinfrescamento, m.

refreshment-bar, –băr, s. taverna, bettola, f.

refrigerator, –frĭj'ărătŭr, s. refrigerante, m.

refuge, rĕf'ŭj, s. rifugio, m.; asilo, m.

refugee, –fŭjĕ', s. rifuggito, m.

refund, –fŭnd', v. a. restituire; rendere.

refusal, –fŭ'zăl, s. rifiuto, m.

refuse, –fŭz', v. a. rifiutare.

refutation, –fŭtă'shăn, s. confutazione, f

refute, *–fût'*, v. a. riprovare.

regain, *–gân'*, v. a. riguadagnare.

regal, *rē'gâl*, a. reale; regio.

regale, *rēgâl'*, v. a. regalare.

regalia, *–gâ'lîâ*, s. insegne reali, f. pl.

regard, *–gârd'*, v. a. rispettare, aver riguardo; —, s. riguardo, rispetto, m., considerazione, f.   [rispetto.

regardful, *–fûl*, a. attento; **–ly,** ad. con

regardless, *–lês*, a. senza riguardo, negligente.   [sgata, f.

regatta, *–gât'tâ*, s. corsa di barche, re-

regency, *rē'jênsî*, s. reggenza, f.; governo, m.   [–, a. rigenerato.

regenerate, *rêjên'ûrât*, v. a. rigenerare;

regeneration, *–rd'shûn*, s. rigenerazione, f.

regent, *rē'jênt*, s. reggente, m.

regicide, *rêj'îsîd*, s. regicida, m.; regicidio, m.

regimen, *rêj'îmên*, s. dieta, f.   [m.

regiment, *rêj'îmênt*, s. reggimento, m.

regimentals, *–mên'tâlz*, s. pl. abito uniforme, m.

region, *rē'jûn*, s. regione, f.   [forme, m.

register, *rêj'îstûr*, s. registro, m.; **–ed letter,** s. lettera raccomandata, f.; **–,** v. a. registrare (una lettera).

registrar, *rêj'îstrâr*, s. registratore, m.; segretario, m.; uffiziale dello stato civile, m.

registration, *–trd'shûn*, s. registratura,

registry, *rêj'îstrî*, s. registratura, f. [f.

regressive, *rêgrês'sîv*, a. che ritorna.

regret, *–grêt'*, v. a. compiangere; dolersi; —, s. dolore, rincrescimento, m.

regretful, *–fûl*, a. dolente.

regular, *rêg'ûlâr*, a. regolare; ordinato; **–ly,** ad. regolarmente; —, s. religioso, m.

regularity, *–lâr'îtî*, s. regolarità, f.

regulate, *rêg'ûlât*, v. a. regolare, ordinare.

regulation, *–lâ'shûn*, s. regola, regolamento, m.

regulator, *rêg'ûlâtûr*, s. regolatore, m.; bilanciere, m.   [m.

regulus, *rêg'ûlûs*, s. metallo purificato,

rehabilitate, *rêhâbîl'îtât*, v. a. riabilitare.

rehabilitation, *–td'shûn*, s. riabilitazione, f.   [lazione, f.; prova (teatrale), f.

rehearsal, *rêhûr'sâl*, s. ripetizione, f.; re-

rehearse, *–hûrs'*, v. a. ripetere, recitare; provare (un lavoro teatrale).

reign, *rân*, s. regno, dominio, m.; —, v. n. regnare, dominare; prevalere.   [restituire.

reimburse, *rêîmbûrs'*, v. a. rimborsare;

reimbursement, *–mênt*, s. rimborso, m.

rein, *rân*, s. redine, f.; —, v. a. raffrenare.

reindeer, *rân'dêr*, s. renna, f.

re-insert, *rêînsûrt'*, v. a. inserire di nuovo.

re-instate, *rêînstât'*, v. a. ristabilire.

re-insure, *rêînshûr'*, v. a. rassicurare.

re-issue, *–îsh'shû*, s. nuova emissione, f.

reiterate, *–ît'ûrât*, v. a. reiterare; rifare.

reiteration, *–d'shûn*, s. reiterazione, f.

reject, *rêjêkt'*, v. a. rigettare; rifiutare.

rejection, *–jêk'shûn*, s. rigetto, m.; rifiuto, m.   [rallegrarsi; divertirsi.

rejoice, *–jôî'*, v. a. divertire; —, v. n.

rejoicing, *–v q*, s. rallegramento, n..

rejoin, *–ō'n'*, v. n. rigiungere; —, v. n. replicare.   [plicare.

rejoinder, *–tr*, s. replica, f.

relapse, *–lâps'*, v. n. ricadere; —, s. ricaduta, f.   [tarsi.

relate, *–lât'*, v. a. & n. recitare; rapportarsi.

related, *–lâ'têd*, a. affine.

relator, *–lâ'tûr*, s. narratore, m.

relation, *–lâ'shûn*, s. relazione, f.; affinità, f.

relationship, *–shîp*, s. parentela, f.

relative, *rêl'âtîv*, a. relativo; **–ly,** ad. relativamente; —, s. parente, m.; consanguineo, m.

relax, *–lâks'*, v. a. rilassare; mitigare; —, v. n. rilassarsi; moderarsi.

relaxation, *–d'shûn*, s. rilassamento, m.

relay, *–lâ'*, s. cambio di posta, m.

release, *–lês'*, v. a. mettere in libertà; dispensare; —, s. liberazione, f., scarico, m.

relegate, *rêl'êgât*, v. a. relegare.

relegation, *–gâ'shûn*, s. relegazione, f.; esilio, m.

relent, *–lênt'*, v. n. ammollirsi; fondersi.

relentless, *–lês*, a. inflessibile; crudele.

relevant, *rêl'êvânt*, a. soccorrevole, aiutabile.

reliable, *–lî'âbl*, a. fededegno.   [tore.

reliance, *–lî'âns*, s. confidenza, f.

relic, *rêl'îk*, s. reliquia, f.; rimembranza,

relict, *rêl'îkt*, s. vedova, f.   [f.

relief, *–lêf'*, s. sollievo, alleggiamento, m.; conforto, m.   [mitigare; aiutare.

relieve, *–lêv'*, v. a. alleviare; confortare;

relieving-officer, *–îng ôffîsûr*, s. limosiniere, m.   [pietà, f.

religion, *–lîj'ûn*, s. religione, f.; fede, f.;

religious, *–lîj'ûs*, a. religioso; **–ly,** ad. religiosamente.

religiousness, *–nês*, s. religiosità, f.

relinquish, *–lîng'kwîsh*, v. a. abbandonare, lasciare; rinunziare.

relinquishment, *–mênt*, s. abbandono, m.

relish, *rêl'îsh*, s. buono gusto, sapore, m.; diletto, m.; —, v. a. gustare, dar gusto; —, v. n. avere buon gusto; piacere.

reluctance, *–lûk'tâns*, s. ripugnanza, f.

reluctant, *–tânt*, a. ripugnante; avverso; **–ly,** ad. con ripugnanza, a contraggenio.

rely, *–lî'*, v. n. fidarsi, rimettersi in.

remain, *–mân'*, v. n. rimanere, restare; continuare; **–s,** s. pl. resti, m. pl.; ceneri, f. pl.   [m.

remainder, *–dûr*, s. resto, residuo, restante,

remand, *–mând'*, v. a. rimandare; richiamare.   [notare, osservare.

remark, *–mârk'*, s. nota, f.; —, v. a.

remarkable, *–âbl*, a. rimarchevole.

remarkably, *–âblî*, ad. in modo rimarchevole.

remediable, *–mê'dîâbl*, a. rimediabile.

remedial, *–mê'dîâl*, a. curativo.

remedy, *rêm'êdî*, s. rimedio, m.; ricorso, m.; —, v. a. rimediare.

remember, *–mêm'bûr*, v. a. far sovvenire, ridurre alla memoria; —, v. n. ricordarsi, sovvenire.   [f.

remembrance, *–brâns*, s. rimembranza,

remind, *–mînd'*, v. a. ridurre a memoria.

reminiscence, *–mînîs'sêns*, s. reminiscenza, f.   [**–ly,** ad. negligentemente.

remiss, *–mîs'*, a. rimesso, lento; pigro;

remissible, *–sĭbl,* a. remissibile, perdonabile. [allentamento, m.; perdono, m.

remission, *–mĭsh'ŭn,* s. remissione, f.; scuraggine, f.; lentezza, f.

remissness, *–mĭs'nĕs,* s. negligenza, trascuraggine, f.; lentezza, f.

remit, *–mĭt',* v. a. rimettere, rimandare; sminuire; perdonare; riferire; –, v. n. diminuirsi; mitigarsi. [f.

remittance, *–ăns,* s. rimessa (di danari),

remnant, *rĕm'nănt,* s. restante, residuo, m.; avanzo, m. [nuovo.

remodel, *rēmŏd'ĕl,* v. a. modellare di

remonstrance, *rĕmŏn'străns,* s. rimostranza, f.

remonstrate, *–strāt,* v. a. rimostrare.

remorse, *–mŏrs',* s. rimorso, m.

remorseless, *–lĕs,* a. senza rimorso, crudele. [rimotamente, lontanamente.

remote, *–mōt',* a. rimoto, lontano; **–ly,** ad.

remoteness, *–nĕs,* s. lontananza, f.; distanza, f. [montare di nuovo.

remount, *rĕmŏŭnt',* v. a. & n. rimontare.

removable, *rĕmŏv'ăbl,* a. rimovibile.

removal, *–mŏv'ăl,* s. remozione, f., rimovimento, m.; cambiamento, m.

remove, *–mŏv',* v. a. & n. rimuovere; sgomberare; mutare domicilio; –, s. partenza, f.; sloggiamento, m.

remunerate, *–mū'nărăt,* v.a. rimunerare.

remuneration, *–ā'shŭn,* s. rimunerazione, f. [rativo.

remunerative, *–mū'nărătĭv,* a. rimunerend, *rĕnd,* v. a. ir. stracciare, mettere in pezzi, lacerare.

render, *rĕn'dŭr,* v. a. rendere; traslatare.

rendezvous, *rĕn'dĕvō* (*răng'dĕvŏ*), v. a. trovarsi alla posta. [m.

renegade, *rĕn'ĕgăd,* s. rinnegato, apostata,

renew, *–nū',* v. a. rinnovare.

renewal, *–ăl,* s. rinnovellamento, m.

rennet, *rĕn'nĕt,* s. caglio, m. [gettare.

renounce, *–nŏŭns',* v. a. rinunziare; rinovate, *rĕn'ŏvăt,* v. a. rinnovare.

renovation, *–vā'shăn,* s. rinnovazione, f.

renown, *–nŏŭn',* s. rinomanza, f.

renowned, *–nŏŭnd',* a. rinomato.

rent, *rĕnt,* s. stracciatura, f.; squarcio, m.; rendita,f.; pigione (di casa ecc.), f.; –, v.a. prendere a pigione, in affitto.

rental, *–ăl,* s. conto di rendite, m.

renter, *–ŭr,* s. affittuario, m.

renunciation, *–nŭnsĭā'shăn,* s. renunzia, f. [cominciare.

reopen, *rēō'pn,* v. a. & n. riaprire; rireorganisation, *–ŏrgănĭzā'shŭn,* s. riorganizzazione, f.

reorganise, *–ŏr'gănĭz,* v.a. riorganizzare.

repair, *rĕpăr',* v. a. riparare, ristaurare; –, v. n. rendersi; –, s. riparo, m.

reparable, *rĕp'ărăbl,* a. riparabile.

reparation, *–rā'shăn,* s. riparazione, f.

repartee, *–părtē',* s. risposta pronta ed acuta, f.

repast, *–păst',* s. pasto, cibo, m.

repay, *–pă',* v. a. pagare un' altra volta; rimborsare. [borso, m.

repayment, *–mĕnt,* s. il ripagare, rim-

repeal, *–pēl',* v. a. rivocare; annullare; –, s. rivocazione, f.; annullamento, m.

repeat, *–pēt',* v. a. ripetere; replicare.

repeatedly, *–pĕ'tĕdlĭ,* ad. spesse volte, spesso. [ripetizione, m.

repeater, *–pĕ'ŭr,* s. oriuolo a ripetizione,

repel, *–pĕl',* v. a. respingere, scacciare.

repent, *–pĕnt',* v. n. pentirsi.

repentance, *–ăns,* s. pentimento, m.

repentant, *–ănt,* a. penitente.

repeople, *–pē'pl,* v. a. ripopolare.

repercussion, *rĕpărkŭsh'ŭn,* s. ripercussione, f.; riflessione, f.

repertory, *rĕp'ărtŭrĭ,* s. repertorio, m.

repetition, *–tĭsh'ŭn,* s. ripetizione, rerepine, *–pīn,* v. n. dolersi. [iterazione, f.

repining, *–ĭng,* s. dispiacere, m., noia, f.

replace, *–plăs',* v. a. collocare di nuovo; rimpiazzare.

replant, *–plănt',* v. a. ripiantare.

replantation, *rĕplăntā'shăn,* s. piantata nuova, f. [empire di nuovo.

replenish, *–plĕn'ĭsh,* v.a. riempire,

replete, *–plĕt',* a. pieno, riempito.

repletion, *–plē'shăn,* s. replezione, f.

reply, *–plī',* s. replica, f.; –, v. a. replicare, rispondere.

report, *–pōrt',* s. voce, f.; fama, f.; romore, m.; bisbiglio, m.; relazione, f.; –, v. a. rapportare, raccontare; dar conto.

reporter, *–ŭr,* s. relatore, raccontatore, m.; stenografo, m.

repose, *–pōz',* v. a.¹ & n. riposare; riposarsi sopra; fidarsi; –, s. riposo, m.

reposit, *–pŏz'ĭt,* v. a. mettere in deposito, depositare.

repository, *–ĭtŭrĭ,* s. repositorio, m.

repossess, *rĕpŏzzĕs',* v. a. rientrare in possesso. [rimproverare.

reprehend, *rĕprĕhĕnd',* v. a. riprendere,

reprehensible, *–hĕn'sĭbl,* a. riprensibile, biasimevole.

represent, *–prĕzĕnt',* v. a. rappresentare.

representation, *–tā'shăn,* s. rappresentazione, f. [–, s. rappresentante, m.

representative, *–ătĭv,* a.rappresentativo;

repress, *–prĕs',* v. a. reprimere.

repression, *–prĕsh'ŭn,* s. repressione, f.

repressive, *–prĕs'sĭv,* a. reprimente.

reprieve, *–prēv',* v. a. sospendere; –, s. respiro, m., dilazione, f.

reprimand, *rĕp'rĭmănd,* v. a. riprendere, biasimare; –, s. riprensione, f.

reprint, *–prĭnt',* v. a. ristampare; –, s. ristampa, f.

reprisals, *–prī'zălz,* s. rappresaglia, f.

reproach, *–prŏch',* s. rimprovero, m.; –, v. a. rimproverare.

reproachful, *–fŭl,* a. ingiurioso; **–ly,** ad. oltraggiosamente. [reprobo, m.

reprobate, *rĕp'rŏbăt,* v. a. riprovare; –, s.

reprobation, *–bā'shăn,* s. riprovazione, f.

reproduce, *rĕprŏdŭs',* v. a. riprodurre.

reproduction, *–dŭk'shăn,* s. riproduzione, f. [sione, f

reproof, *rĕpr'ŏf',* s. rimprovero, m., ripieu

reprove, *-prōv'*, v. a. rimproverare.
reptile, *rĕp'tĭl*, s. rettile, m.
republic, *-pŭb'lĭk*, s. repubblica, f.
republican, *-kăn*, s. repubblicano, m.
republicanism, *-kănĭzm*, s. repubblicanismo, m.   [pubblicazione, f,
republication, *rēpŭblĭkā'shăn*, s. seconda
republish, *-pŭb'lĭsh*, v. a. pubblicare di nuovo.
repudiate, *rĕpū'dĭāt*, v. n. ripudiare.
repugnance, *-pŭg'năns*, s. ripugnanza, controversia, f.   [di mala voglia.
repugnant, *-nănt*, a. ripugnante; **-ly**, ad.
repulse, *-pŭls'*, v. a. dare una repulsa;
—, s. repulsa, f.
repulsion, *-pŭl'shăn*, s. repulsa, f.
repulsive, *-pŭl'sĭv*, a. repulsivo.
repurchase, *rēpŭr'chās*, v. a. ricomprare.
reputable, *rĕp'ŭtăbl*, a. onorevole.
reputably, *-tăblĭ*, ad. onorevolmente.
reputation, *-tā'shăn*, s. riputazione, f.
repute, *-pūt'*, v. a. riputare.
request, *-kwĕst'*, s. richiesta, domanda, f.; supplica, f.; —, v. a. richiedere, pregare.
require, *-kwīr'*, v. a. domandare; ricercare.   [sogno, m.
requirement, *-mĕnt*, s. richiesta, f., bisogno, m.
requisite, *rĕk'wĭzĭt*, a. requisito, necessario; —, s. requisito, m., cosa necessaria, f.   [domanda, f.
requisition, *-zĭsh'ăn*, s. requisizione, f.;
requital, *-kwī'tăl*, s. ricompensa, f.; contraccambio, m.
requite, *-kwīt'*, v. a. ricompensare.
rescind, *-sĭnd'*, v. a. rescindere; cassare.
rescript, *rē'skrĭpt*, s. rescritto, editto, m.
rescue, *rĕs'kū*, s. liberazione, f., scampo, m.; —, v. a. liberare, scampare.
research, *-sŭrch'*, s. ricerca, f.
reseat, *rēsēt'*, v. a. rimettere.   [f.
resemblance, *rĕzĕm'blăns*, s. somiglianza,
resemble, *-zĕm'bl*, v. n. rassomigliare.
resent, *-zĕnt'*, v. n. risentirsi.
resentful, *-fŭl*, a. vendicativo; irritabile.
resentment, *-mĕnt*, s. risentimento, m.
reservation, *-zŭrvā'shăn*, s. riserva, riserba, f.; restrizione, f.   [serva, f.
reserve, *-zŭrv'*, v. a. riservare; —, s. riservedly, *-ĕdlĭ*, ad. con riserva.
reservedly, *-ĕdlĭ*, ad. con riserva.
reset, *rēsĕt'*, v. a. rimettere.
reside, *rēzīd'*, v. n. risedere, dimorare.
residence, *rĕz'ĭdĕns*, s. residenza, f.; dimora, f.
resident, *-ĭdĕnt*, a. residente, dimorante.
residuary, *-zĭd'ūărĭ*, a. restante; **-legatee**, s. legatario universale, m.
residue, *-ĭdū*, s. residuo, restante, m.
residuum, *-ŭăm*, s. (chem.) residuo, m.
resign, *-zīn'*, v. a. & n. rassegnare; cedere; deporre; disfarsi; sommettersi.
resignation, *-zĭgnā'shăn*, s. rassegnazione, f.; dimissione, f.
resin, *rĕz'ĭn*, s. resina, gomma, f.
resinous, *-ăs*, a. resinoso.
resist, *-zĭst'*, v. a. & n. resistere; opporsi.
resistance, *-ăns*, s. resistenza, f.
resolute, *rĕz'ŏlūt*, a. risoluto; **-ly**, ad. determinatamente.

resolution, *-lō'shăn*, s. risoluzione, f.
resolve, *-zŏlv'*, v. a. risolvere, determinare; —, v. n. determinarsi; liquefarsi.
resonance, *rĕz'ŏnăns*, s. risonanza, f.
resonant, *-ŏnănt*, a. risonante.
resort, *-zŏrt'*, s. concorso, m.; ricorso, rifugio, m.; —, v. n. aver ricorso; frequentare.   [tare.
resound, *-zŏănd'*, v. n. risonare.
resource, *-sŏrs'*, s. mezzo, espediente, m.
respect, *-spĕkt'*, s. rispetto, riguardo, m.; motivo, m.; stima, f.; **-s**, pl. complimenti, m. pl.; —, v. a. rispettare, riguardare; onorare, riverire.
respectability, *-ăbĭl'ĭtĭ*, s. rispettabilità, f.; condizione onorevole, f.
respectable, *-ăbl*, a. rispettabile.
respectably, *-ăblĭ*, ad. con rispetto.
respectful, *-fŭl*, a. rispettoso; sommesso; **-ly**, ad. rispettosamente.
respecting, *-ĭng*, pr. per rispetto, per conto di.   [-ly, ad. in rispetto.
respective, *-ĭv*, a. respettivo, relativo;
respirator, *rĕs'pĭrātŭr*, s. respiratore, m.
respiratory, *rĕspĭ'rătŭrĭ*, a. adatto alla respirazione.
respite, *rĕs'pĭt*, s. indugio, m.; —, v. a. sospendere, differire.   [risplendente, m.
resplendence, *-splĕn'dĕns*, s. l' essere
resplendent, *-dĕnt*, a. risplendente.
respond, *-spŏnd'*, v. n. rispondere; corrispondere.
respondent, *-ĕnt*, s. (jur.) difendente, m.
response, *-spŏns'*, s. risposta, f.; eco, m.
responsibility, *-sĭbĭl'ĭtĭ*, s. responsabilità, f.; sicurtà, f.   [mallevadore.
responsible, *-spŏn'sĭbl*, a. responsabile.
responsive, *-sĭv*, a. responsivo.
rest, *rĕst*, s. riposo, sonno, m.; resto, residuo, m.; pausa, fermata, f.; —, v. a. riposare; appoggiare; —, v. n. riposarsi; dormire.   [poso, m.
resting-place, *-ĭng plās*, s. luogo di riposo, m.
restitution, *-ĭtū'shăn*, s. restituzione, f.
restive, *rĕs'tĭv*, a. restio; ritroso.
restless, *rĕst'lĕs*, a. senza dormire; inquieto; **-ly**, ad. senza riposo; inquietamente.   [f., ristoro, m.
restoration, *-stŏrā'shăn*, s. ristorazione,
restorative, *-stŏr'ătĭv*, a. & s. ristorativo (m.).
restore, *-stŏr'*, v. a. ristorare, ristabilire.
restrain, *-strān'*, v. a. ristringere, raffrenare.   [namento, m.
restraint, *-strānt'*, s. costringimento, raffre-
restrict, *-strĭkt'*, v. a. costringere.
restriction, *-strĭk'shăn*, s. limitazione, f.
restrictive, *-strĭkt'ĭv*, a. restrittivo.   [f.
result, *-zŭlt'*, v. n. risultare; —, s. risulta,
resume, *-zūm'*, v. a. resumere; rinovellare.   [m.; ricominciamento, m.
resumption, *-zŭm'shăn*, s. ripigliamento,
resurrection, *-zŭrrĕk'shăn*, s. risurrezione, f.; **-man**, ladro di cadaveri, m.; **-pie**, pasticcio di carne, m.   [veri, m.
resurrectionist, *-ĭst*, s. rubatore di cadaveri.
resuscitate, *-sŭs'sĭtāt*, v. a. ravvivare.
retail, *rē'tāl*, s. ritaglio, m.; —, *rĕtāl'*, v. a. vendere a minuto.

retailer, _rētăl'ăr_, s. venditore a minuto, m.

retain, _-tăn'_, v. a. ritenere; tenere a mente.

retainer, _-ăr_, s. aderente, m.; persona salariata, f.; **-s,** pl. seguito, corteggio, m.

retake, _rĕtāk'_, v. a. ir. ripigliare.

retaliate, _rĕtăl'ĭăt_, v. a. rendere la pariglia.

retaliation, _-ă'shăn_, s. pariglia, f.

retard, _-tărd'_, v. a. ritardare.

retardation, _-dă'shăn_, s. ritardamento, m.

retch, _rĕch_, v. a. aver voglia di recere.

retention, _rĕtĕn'shăn_, s. ntenzione, f.; custodia, f.

retentive, _-tĭv_, a. ritentivo.

reticle, _rĕt'ĭkl_, s. rete piccola, f.

reticule, _rĕt'ĭkŭl_, s. borsa, f., sacchetto da donna, m.

retina, _rĕt'ĭnă_, s. rètina (dell' occhio), f.

retinue, _rĕt'ĭnū_, s. corteggio, m.

retire, _rĕtīr'_, v. a. & n. riúrare; ritirarsi.

retired, _-tīrd'_, a. ritirato, solitario; **- list,** s. lista delle persone pensionate, f.

retirement, _-tīr'mĕnt_, s. ritiratezza, f.; solitudine, f.

retort, _-tŏrt'_, s. storta, f.; risposta, f.; **-,** v. a. ritorcere; replicare.

retouch, _-tŭch'_, v. a. ritoccare.

retrace, _-trās'_, v. a. delineare di nuovo.

retract, _-trăkt'_, v. a. & n. ritrattare; ritrattarsi.

retreat, _-trēt'_, s. ritirata, f.; **-,** v. n. ritirarsi.

retrench, _-trĕnsh'_, v. a. & n. trincerare; trincerarsi.

retrenchment, _-mĕnt_, s. trincera, f.

retribution, _-trĭbū'shăn_, s. retribuzione, f.; ricompensa, f.

retrievable, _-trēv'ăbl_, a. che si può ricovrare.

retrieve, _-trēv'_, v. a. ricovrare, ricuperare.

retriever, _-ăr_, s. bracco, m.

retrograde, _rĕ'trŏgrăd_ (_rĕt'rŏgrăd_), a. retrogrado; **-,** v. n. retrogradare.

retrogression, _-grĕsh'ăn_, s. retrocedere, m.

retrospect, _rĕt'rŏspĕkt_, **retrospection,** _-spĕk'shăn_, s. guardare indietro, mirar indietro, m.

retrospective, _-spĕk'tĭv_, a. che guarda indietro, retrospettivo.

return, _rĕtŭrn'_, s. ritorno, m.; ricaduta, f.; ricompensa, f.; risposta, f.; **-,** v. a. rendere; restituire; ricompensare; contraccambiare; **-,** v. n. ritornare, rimettersi.

reunion, _rēăn'yăn_, s. riunione, f.

reunite, _-ănīt'_, v. a. & n. riunire; riunirsi.

reveal, _rēvēl'_, v. a. rivelare.

revel, _rĕv'ĕl_, v. n. gozzovigliare; **-,** s. gozzoviglia, f.

revelation, _-vĕlā'shăn_, s. rivelazione, f.; **Book of -,** Apocalisse, f.

reveller, _rĕv'ĕlăr_, s. gozzovigliante, m.

revelry, _rĕv'ĕlrĭ_, s. gozzoviglia, f., baccano, m.

revenge, _rēvĕnj'_, s. vendetta, f.; rivincita (al giuoco delle carte), f.; **-,** v. a. vendicare.

revengeful, _-fŭl_, a. vendicativo; **-ly,** ad. in una maniera vendicativa.

revenue, _rĕv'ĕnū_, s. rendita, entrata, f.; profitto, m.

reverberate, _-văr'bărăt_, v. a. & n. riverberare; ripercuotere.

reverberation, _-ă'shăn_, s. riverbero, m.

revere, _-vēr'_, v. a. riverire.

reverence, _rĕv'ărĕns_, v. a. riverire, onorare; **-,** s. riverenza, f.

reverend, _rĕv'ărĕnd_, a. venerando; **-,** s. abbate, curato, m.

reverent, _rĕv'ărĕnt_, **reverential,** _-ĕn'shăl_, a. riverente. [rispetto.

reverently, _-ĕntlĭ_, ad. con riverenza o sentenza, m.

reversal, _-văr'săl_, s. cambiamento di sentenza, m.

reverse, _-vărs'_, s. rovescio, m.; riverso, m.; **-,** v. a. rovesciare; abolire.

reversible, _-văr'sĭbl_, a. rivocabile; (of clothes) che si può volgere.

reversion, _-shăn_, s. reversione, f.; sopravvivanza, f. [cessione.

reversionary, _-ărĭ_, a. da godersi in succrevert, _-vărt'_, v. a. & n. ritornare.

revertible, _-ĭbl_, a. reversibile.

revictual, _rēvĭt'l_, v. a. vettovagliare.

review, _rēvū'_, s. rivista, revisione, f.; esame, m.; mostra, f.; **-,** v. a. rivedere, riconsiderare; esaminare di nuovo.

reviewer, _-ăr_, s. riveditore, giornalista, m.

revile, _-vīl'_, v. a. rimproverare; ingiuriare. [sione, f.

revise, _-vīz'_, v. a. rivedere; **-,** s. reviser, _-vī'zăr_, s. revisore, m.

revision, _-vĭzh'ăn_, s. revisione, rivista, f.

revisit, _-vĭz'ĭt_, v. a. rivisitare.

revival, _-vī'văl_, s. ravvivamento, m.; ristoramento, m.

revive, _-vīv'_, v. a. ravvivare; ristabilire; **-,** v. n. ravvivarsi.

reviver, _-vī'văr_, s. ristoratore, m.

revocable, _rĕv'ŏkăbl_, a. rivocabile.

revocation, _-kă'shăn_, s. rivocazione, f.; annullare, m.

revoke, _-vŏk'_, v. a. rivocare. [tarsi.

revolt, _-vŏlt'_, s. rivolta, f.; **-,** v. n. rivoltarsi.

revolting, _-ĭng_, a. che muove a sdegno.

revolution, _-lŏ'shăn_, s. rivoluzione, f.

revolutionary, _-ărĭ_, a., **revolutionist,** _-ĭst_, s. rivoluzionario (m.).

revolve, _-vŏlv'_, v. a rivolgere; meditare; **-,** v. n. muoversi in giro.

revolver, _-ăr_, s. rivoltella, f., revolver, m.

revolving, _-ĭng_, a. periodico.

revulsion, _-vŭl'shăn_, s. revulsione, f.; ripercotimento degli umori, m.

reward, _-wărd'_, s. ricompensa, f.; **-,** v. a. ricompensare.

rewarder, _-ăr_, s. rimuneratore, m.

rhapsody, _răp'sŏdĭ_, s. rapsodia, f.

rhetoric, _rĕt'ŏrĭk_, s. rettorica, f.

rhetorical, _-tŏr'ĭkăl_, a. rettorico, oratorio.

rhetorician, _-tŏrĭsh'ăn_, s. rettorico, m.; retore, m.

rheum, _rŏm_, s. reuma, catarro, m.

rheumatic, _-măt'ĭk_, a. reumatico. [m.

rheumatism, _rŏ'mătĭzm_, s. reumatismo, m.

rhinoceros, _rĭnŏs'ărŏs_, s. rinoceronte, f.

rhomb, _rŏm_, s. rombo, m., losanga, f.

rhomboid, _-bŏĭd_, s. romboide, m.

rhubarb, _rŏ'bărb_, s. rabarbaro, m.

rhyme, _rīm_, s. rima, f.; poesia, f.; **-,** v. n. rimare.

rhymer, *–ăr,* **rhymster,** *–stăr,* s. rimatore, poetastro, m.
rhythm, *rĭthm,* s. ritmo, m.
rhythmical, *rĭth'mĭkăl,* a. ritmico.
rib, *rĭb,* s. costola, f.; –, v. a. scanalare.
ribald, *rĭb'ăld,* s. ribaldo, libertino, m. [f.
ribaldry, *–ăldrĭ,* s. ribalderia, f.; oscenità,
ribband, *rĭb'bănd,* **ribbon,** *–ŏn,* s. nastro,
rice, *rĭs,* s. riso, m. |m., fettuccia, f.
rich, *rĭch,* a. ricco, opulento; copioso, abbondante; **–ly,** ad. riccamente.
riches, *–ĕz,* s. pl. ricchezze, f. pl.
richness, *–nĕs,* s. ricchezza, abbondanza,
rick, *rĭk,* s. cumulo, mucchio, m.   [f.
rickets, *–ĕts,* s. pl. rachitide, f.
rickety, *–ĕtĭ,* a. rachitico.
rid, *rĭd,* v. a. ir. liberare, sbrogliare.
riddance, *–dăns,* s. il sbarazzare, m.; scioglimento, m. |–, v. a. stacciare.
riddle, *rĭd'dl,* s. enimma, m.; staccio, m.;
ride, *rĭd,* v. a. & n. ir. andare a cavallo; andare in carrozza; –, s. cavalcata, f., passeggio a cavallo o in carrozza, m. [m.
rider, *rī'dăr,* s. cavalcatore, m.; cavaliere,
ridge, *rĭj,* s. cima, sommità, f.; solco, m.; spina, f.; scanalatura, f.; –, v. a. solcare; scanalare.   [v. a. rendere ridicolo.
ridicule, *rĭd'ĭkŭl,* s. cosa ridicola, f.; –,
ridiculous, *–dĭk'ŭlăs,* a. ridicolo; **–ly,** ad. ridicolosamente.
ridiculousness, *–nĕs,* s. ridicolaggine, f.
riding, *rī'dĭng,* a. viaggiante a cavallo; –, s. andare a cavallo, m.
riding-habit, *–hăbĭt,* s. abito di donna da cavalcare, abito da Amazzone, m.
riding-school, *–skŏl,* s. scuola di cavalcare.
rife, *rīf,* a. frequente, comune.   [lerizza, f.
riff-raff, *rĭf'răf,* s. robaccia, f., cattive cose, f. pl.
rifle, *rī'fl,* v. a. rubare, saccheggiare; scanalare, rigare; –, s. schioppo rigato, m.
rifleman, *–măn,* s. carabiniere, m.
rifle-pit, *–pĭt,* s. nascondiglio da cacciatore, m.
rifler, *rī'flăr,* s. predatore, m.   [tore, m.
rig, *rĭg,* v. a. addobbare; (mar.) allestire; –, s. burla, f.
rigging, *–ĭng,* s. (mar.) arredi, m. pl.
right, *rĭt,* a. dritto, diritto, destro; retto, giusto; franco; mero, puro; opportuno; **–ly,** ad. bene, giustamente; –, s. diritto, m.; giustizia, f.; ragione, f.; mano destra, f.; –, v. a. rendere giustizia; giustificare.
righteous, *–rīt'yŭs (–chŭs),* a. giusto; virtuoso; **–ly,** ad. giustamente.
righteousness, *–nĕs,* s. equità, f.; probità, f.   [ad. rigidamente.
rigid, *rĭj'ĭd,* a. rigido, severo, duro; **–ly,**
rigidity, *–jĭd'ĭtĭ,* s. rigidezza, severità, f.
rigmarole, *rĭg'mărōl,* s. ciarleria, f.
rigorous, *rĭg'ărăs,* a. rigoroso; **–ly,** ad. rigorosamente.
rigour, *rĭg'ăr,* s. rigore, m.
rill, *rĭl,* s. ruscelletto, m.
rim, *rĭm,* s. orlo, m.; margine, m.
rime, *rĭm,* s. brina, f.; brinata, f.; –, v. n.
rimy, *rī'mĭ,* a. brinato.   [far brina.
rind, *rĭnd,* s. scorza, corteccia, f.; buccia, f.
ring, *rĭng,* s. anello, m.; cerchio, m.; suono

(di campane), m.; assemblea, f.; –, v. a. ir. suonare ; –, v. n. ir. rimbombare.
ringer, *–ăr,* s. campanaio, m.
ring-finger, *–fĭnggăr,* s. dito anulare, m.
ringing, *–ĭng,* s. suono di campane, m.
ring-leader, *–lēdăr,* s. capo (di fazione),
ringlet, *–lĕt,* s. riccio, m.   [m.
ringworm, *–wŭrm,* s. empetiggine, volatica, f.
rinse, *rĭns,* v. a. sciacquare, lavare.
riot, *rī'ŏt,* s. stravizzo, rumore, tumulto, m., gozzoviglia, f.; –, v. n. gozzovigliare, tumultuare.
rioter, *–ăr,* s. scapestrato, m.; sedizioso, m.
riotous, *–ăs,* a. turbolento, sedizioso; **–ly,** ad. dissolutamente.
rip, *rĭp,* v. a. stracciare, lacerare; scucire.
ripe, *rĭp,* a. maturo; **–ly,** ad. matura-
ripen, *rī'pn,* v. a. & n. maturare. [mente.
ripeness, *–nĕs,* s. maturità, f.
ripple, *rĭp'pl,* v. n. incresparsi, ondeggiare.
rippling, *–ĭng,* s. ondeggiamento, m.
rise, *rĭz,* v. n. ir. scaturire; sorgere; levarsi; uscire; alzarsi, ascendere; rivoltarsi; fermentare; –, s. il levare, m.; elevazione, f.; origine, f.; causa, f.; (rail.) salita, f.
risible, *rĭz'ĭbl,* a. risibile, ridicolo.
rising, *rīz'ĭng,* a. levante; nascente; crescente; saliente; –, s. il levare, m.; rivolta, f.; ascesa (d' una collina), f.; ingrandimento, m.   [arrischiare.
risk, *rĭsk,* s. rischio, periglio, m.; –, v. a.
risky, *rĭsk'ĭ,* a. pericoloso.
rite, *rīt,* s. rito, m., cerimonia sacra, f.
ritual, *rĭt'ŭăl,* a. & s. rituale (m.).
rival, *rī'văl,* a. emulo; –, s. rivale, m.; –, v. a. emulare.
rivalry, *–rĭ,* s. rivalità, f.
rive, *rĭv,* v. a. & n. ir. fendere; fendersi.
river, *rĭv'ăr,* s. riviera, f., fiume, m.
rivet, *rĭv'ĕt,* s. ribaditura, f.; –, v. a. ribadire.
rivulet, *rĭv'ŭlĕt,* s. rivoletto, m.   [dire.
roach, *rōch,* s. lasca, f.
road, *rōd,* s. strada, f., cammino largo, m.
roadstead, *–stĕd,* s. rada, f.
roam, *rōm,* v. a. & n. vagare.
roan, *rōn,* a. sagginato (d' un cavallo).
roar, *rōr,* v. n. ruggire, rugghiare; –, s. rugghio, m.; gran romore, m.
roast, *rōst,* v. a. arrostire.
roastbeef, *–bĕf,* s. rusbiffe, m.
roaster, *–ăr,* s. arnese per arrostire, m.
rob, *rŏb,* v. a. rubare.
robber, *–băr,* s. ladro, pirata, m.   [m.
robbery, *–bărĭ,* s. ruberia, f., ladroneccio,
robe, *rōb,* s. veste nobile, f.; –, v. a. vestire pomposamente.   [pettirosso, m.
robin(-red-breast), *rŏb'ĭn(rĕd'brĕst),* s.
robust, *rōbŭst',* a. robusto.
robustness, *–nĕs,* s. vigore, m.
rock, *rŏk,* s. roccia, rupe, balza, f.; –, v. a. cullare; dimenare la culla; (am.) lapidare; –, v. n. barcollare.   [rocca, m.
rock-crystal, *–krĭstăl,* s. cristallo di
rocker, *rŏk'ăr,* s. che culla.
rocket, *–ĕt,* s. razzo artifiziale m.

rocking-chair, -ing chảr, s. sedia a don-
rock-oil, -ŏil, s. petrolio, m.   [dolo, f.
rock-salt, -sảlt, s. sale minerale, m.
rock-work, -wŭrk, s. sassi fitti nella
    calce, m. pl.; smalto, m.
rocky, rŏk'ĭ, a. pieno di scogli, scoglioso.
rod, rŏd, s. verga, bacchetta, frusta, sferza, f.
rodent, rŏd'ĕnt, s. animale roditore, m.
rodomontade, rŏdŏmŏntăd', s. rodomon-
    tata, f.
rodomonte, -mŏn'tĕ, s. rodomonte, smar-
    giasso m.   [uova di pesce, f. pl.
roe, rŏ, s. capriuolo, m.; capriuola, f.;
roebuck, -bŭk, s. capriolo, m.   [f.
rogation, -gă'shŭn, s. litania, f.; preghiera,
rogue, rŏg, s. furfante, furbo, ladro, m.
roguery, rŏ'gŭrĭ, s. furfanteria, f.; burla, f.
roguish, rŏ'gĭsh, a. furbesco, furbo.
roister, rŏĭs'tŭr, v. n. fare il bravaccio.
roll, rŏl, s. involgio, viluppo, m.; ruolo,
    m.; carello, m.; panicciuolo, m.; catalogo,
    m., lista, f.; -, v. a. inviluppare, in-
    volgere; -, v. n. rotolare; girare.
roller, -ăr, s. cilindro, m.; rullo, m.
rollicking, rŏl'lĭkĭng, a. gozzovigliante.
rolling-pin, rŏl'lĭng pĭn, s. spianatoio, m.
romance, rŏmăns', s. romanzo, m.; fin-
    zione, f.; -, v. n. favoleggiare; inventare.
romancer, -sŭr, romancist, -sĭst, s. ro-
    manziere, m.
romantic, -tĭk, a. romanzesco, favoloso.
Romish, rŏ'mĭsh, a. Romano, Papalino.
romp, rŏmp, s. ragazza grossolana, f.;
    -, v. n. scherzare grossolanamente.
roof, rŏf, s. tetto, m.; colmo, m.; coperta,
    f.; cielo d' una carrozza, m.; (of the
    mouth) palato, m.; -, v. a. coprire con
roofing, -ĭng, s. tetto, m.   [un tetto.
rook, rŏk, s. cornacchia, f.; barattiere, fur-
    fante, m.; (at chess) rocco, m.; -, v. a.
    truffare, ingannare.   [nacchie, m.
rookery, -ărĭ, s. luogo pieno di cor-
room, rŏm, s. spazio, m.; stanza, f.   [f.
roominess, -ĭnĕs, s. spazio, m., larghezza,
roomy, rŏ'mĭ, a. spazioso, vasto.
roost, rŏst, s. posatoio, m.; -, v. n. appol-
    laiarsi.
root, rŏt, s. radice, f.; origine, f.; voce
    primitiva, f.; -, v. n. pigliar radice;
    - out, sradicare.
rope, rŏp, s. corda, fune, f.; -, v. n. filare.
rope-dancer, -dănsŭr, s. funambolo, m.
rope-maker, -măkŭr, s. funaio, m.
rope-walk, -wăk, rope-yard, -yărd,
    s. corderia, f.
rosary, rŏ'zărĭ, s. rosaio, m.
rose, rŏz, s. rosa, f.; rosone, m.
roseate, rŏ'zĕăt, a. rosato, roseo.
rose-bed, rŏz'bĕd, s. rosaio, m.
rose-bud, -bŭd, s. gemma, f., bottone di
    rosa, m.   [m.
rosemary, -mărĭ, s. rosmarino, ramerino,
rose-tree, -trĕ, rose-bush, -bŭsh, s.
rosette, rŏzĕt', s. rosetta, f.   [rosaio, m.
rosewood, -wŭd, s. erisicetro, m.
rosin, rŏz'ĭn, s. resina, f.
rosiness, rŏ'zĭnĕs, s. color di rose, m.

rosy, rŏ'zĭ, a. roseo.   [v. n. putrefarsi.
rot, rŏt, s. moria, f.; putrefazione, f.; -,
rotate, rŏtăt', v. n. rotare, roteare.
rotation, rŏtă'shŭn, s. rotazione, f.
rotatory, rŏ'tătŭrĭ, a. rotante.
rote, rŏt, s. uso, m.; pratica, f.
rotgut, rŏt'gŭt, s. birra cattiva, f.
rotten, rŏt'n, a. infracidato, putrefatto.
rottenness, -nĕs, s. fracidezza, putrefa-
rotund, rŏtŭnd', a. ritondo.   [zione, f.
rotundity, -dĭt, s. ritondità, f.
rouble, rŏ'bl, s. rublo, m.
rouge, rŏzh, s. belletto, m.; -, v. n. im-
    bellettarsi.   [-ly, ad. rozzamente.
rough, rŭf, a. ruvido, aspro, rozzo; scabro;
rough-cast, -kăst, s. intonaco, modello
    abbozzato, m.; -, v. a. intonacare; ar-
    ricciare.   [abbozzare.
rough-draw, -dră, v. a. ir. schizzare,
roughen, rŭf'n, v. a. rendere ruvido.
rough-hew, -hŭ, v. a. ir. abbozzare,
    schizzare.
roughness, -nĕs, s. ruvidezza, rozzezza,
    asprezza, f.; zoticchezza, f.; violenza, f.
rough-shod, -shŏd, a. ferrato a ghi-
    accio.
round, rŏŭnd, a. tondo, rotondo; franco,
    candido; -, ad. da ogni banda, all' in-
    torno; -, v. a. ritondare, fare tondo; -,
    v. n. divenire tondo.
roundabout, -ăbŏŭt, a. ampio; vago; in-
    diretto; -, s. giubbone, m.
roundelay, rŏŭn'dĕlă, s. strambotto, m.
round-hand, rŏŭnd'hănd, s. caratteri
    tondi, m. pl.
round-head, -hĕd, s. puritano, m.
roundly, -lĭ, ad. rotondamente; franca-
    mente.
roundness, -nĕs, s. rotondità, f.
rouse, rŏŭz, v. a. svegliare, eccitare.
rout, rŏŭt, s. rotta, f.; -, v. a. (mil.) mettere
route, rŏt, s. via, strada, f.   [in rotta.
rove, rŏv, v. n. girare, vagare.   [m.
rover, rŏ'vŭr, s. vagabondo, m.; corsaro,
row, rŏ, s. fila, filata, f.; -, v. n. remigare.
row, rŏŭ, s. strepito, rumore, fracasso, m.
rowdy, -dĭ, s. schiamazzatore, m.
rowel, -ĕl, s. stella (dello sprone), f.
rower, rŏ'ŭr, s. rematore, m.   [barca, f.
rowing-match, -ĭng măch, s. corso in
row-lock, rŏl'ŏk, s. scarmo, m.
royal, rŏ'ĭl, a. reale; -ly, ad. realmente.
royalist, -ĭst, s. realista, m.
royalty, -tĭ, s. dignità reale, m.
rub, rŭb, v. a. fregare, strofinare; grattare;
    -, s. fregamento, m.; (fig.) ostacolo, m.
rubber, -bŭr, s. strofinaccio, m.; lima
    grossa, f.
rubber-ball, -băl, s. gomma elastica, f.
rubbish, rŭb'bĭsh, s. robe vecchie, f. pl.;
    rovine, f. pl.; marame, m.
rubicund, rŏ'bĭkŭnd, a. rubicondo.
ruble, rŏbl, s. rublo, m.
rubric, rŏ'brĭk, s. rubrica, f.   [vermiglio.
ruby, rŏ'bĭ, s. rubino, m.; -, a. rubicondo,
rudder, rŭd'dŭr, s. timone, m.
ruddiness, rŭd'dĭnĕs, s. freschezza di car-
    nagione, f.

ruddy, *-dĭ*, a. rubicondo.

rude, *rōd*, a. rozzo, grossolano, scortese, incivile; turbolento; **-ly**, ad. grossolanamente.   [insolenza, f.

rudeness, *-nĕs*, s. rozzezza, inciviltà, f.;

rudiments, *rŏ´dĭmĕnts*, s. pl. rudimenti, elementi, m. pl.   [pentirsi.

rue, *rō*, s. (bot.) ruta, f.; —, v. n. dolersi,

rueful, *rō´fŭl*, a. lamentevole, triste.

ruff, *rŭf*, s. gala, f.; collare, m.

ruffian, *rŭf´fĭăn*, a. brutale; —, s. malandrino, assassino di strada, m.

ruffianly, *-lĭ*, a. brutale, sanguinario.

ruffle, *rŭf´fl*, v. a. increspare, piegare; disordinare, disturbare; —, s. manichino, m.; tumulto, m.

rug, *rŭg*, s. pelosa coperta da letto, m.

rugged, *-gĕd*, a. ruvido, rozzo, brutale.

ruin, *rō´ĭn*, s. rovina, ruina, f.; decadenza, f.; —, v. a. rovinare; distruggere.

ruinous, *-nŭs*, a. ruinoso; **-ly**, ad. rovinosamente.

rule, *rōl*, s. regola, f.; precetto, m.; governo, m.; usanza, f.; —, v. a. & n. rigare; regolare, ordinare; governare.

ruler, *-ŭr*, s. regolo, m.; governatore, m.

rum, *rŭm*, s. rum, m.; —, a. singolare, bizzarro.

rumble, *rŭm´bl*, v. a. rombare; mormorare.

ruminate, *rō´mĭnāt*, v. n. ruminare.

rumination, *-nā´shăn*, s. meditazione, f.

rummage, *rŭm´măj*, v. a. scompigliar cercando; predare.

rummer, *-mŭr*, s. bicchiere grande, m.

rumour, *rō´mŭr*, s. rumore, m.; fama, f.; —, v. a. fare rumore.

rump, *rŭmp*, s. groppone, m.; groppa, f.

rumple, *rŭm´pl*, v. a. increspare; —, s. piega, riga, f.

run, *rŭn*, v. a. ir. traffiggere, spingere; —, v. n. ir. correre; passare; fuggire; gocciolare, colare; **to — a risk**, correr rischio, correr pericolo; **to — away**, fuggire; —, s. corsa, f.; fuga, f.; corso, m.; uso, m., voga, f.; attacco, m.

runaway, *-ăwā*, s. disertore, fuggitivo, m.

rundlet, *rŭnd´lĕt*, s. bariletto, m.   [m.

runner, *rŭn´nŭr*, s. corridore, ir.; sensale,

running, *-nĭng*, s. corrimento, corso, m.

rupture, *rŭp´tŭr (-chŭr)*, s. rottura, f.; ernia, f.; —, v. a. rompere, fracassare.

rural, *rō´răl*, a. rurale, rustico; campestre.

ruse, *rōs (rōz)*, s. astuzia, f.; stratagemma, m.

rush, *rŭsh*, s. giunco, m.; niente, m., poca cosa, f.; —, v. n. precipitarsi, lanciarsi.

rush-light, *-lĭt*, s. candela della veglia, lumicinaro, m.

rusk, *rŭsk*, s. biscotto, m.

russet, *rŭs´sĕt*, a. rossiccio.

Russia-leather, *rŭsh´ă lĕthŭr*, s. vacchetta, f., bulghero, m.   [nirsi.

rust, *rŭst*, s. ruggine, f.; —, v. n. arruggi-

rustic(al), *rŭs´tĭk(ăl)*, a. & s. rustico (m.)

rusticate, *-tĭkāt*, v. a. rendere rustico; —, v. n. starsene in villa.   [pagna, m.

rustication, *-kā´shăn*, s. vivere alla cam-

rusticity, *-tĭs´ĭtĭ*, s. rusticità, f.

rustiness, *rŭs´tĭnĕs*, s. ruggine, f.; rancidezza, f.

rustle, *rŭs´l*, v. n. ronzare; rumoreggiare

rustling, *-lĭng*, s. strepito, mormorio, m.

rusty, *rŭs´tĭ*, a. rugginoso, rancido.

rut, *rŭt*, s. frega, f.; rotaia, f.; —, v. n. andare in frega.   [**-ly**, ad. senza pietà.

ruthless, *rōth´lĕs*, a. spietato, inumano;

rye, *rī*, s. segala, f.

S.

sabbath, *săb´băth*, s. sabato, m.

sable, *sā´bl*, s. (pelle dello) zibellino, m.

sabre, *sā´bŭr*, s. sciabola, f.; —, v. a. percuotere colla sciabola, sciabolare.

sacerdotal, *săsŭrdō´tăl*, a. sacerdotale.

sack, *săk*, s. sacco, m.; vino dolce, m.; —, v. a. saccheggiare, mettere in un sacco.

sacking, *-ĭng*, s. saccheggiamento, m.; tela da sacco, f.   [Eucaristia, f.

sacrament, *săk´rămĕnt*, s. sacramento, m.;

sacramental, *-mĕntăl*, a. sacramentale; **-ly**, ad. sacramentalmente.

sacred, *sā´krĕd*, a. sacro, santo; inviolabile; **-ly**, ad. inviolabilmente.

sacredness, *-nĕs*, s. santità, f.

sacrifice, *săk´rĭfĭs*, s. sacrificio, m.; —, v. a. sacrificare; —, v. n. offrire un sacrificio.

sacrificial, *-fĭsh´ăl*, a. di sacrificio.

sacrilege, *săk´rĭlĕj*, s. sacrilegio, m.

sacrilegious, *-lĕ´jŭs*, a. sacrilego.

sad, *săd*, a. mesto, triste; cattivo, meschino; bruno; **-ly**, ad. tristemente.

sadden, *săd´n*, v. a. attristare.

saddle, *săd´l*, s. sella, f.; —, v. a. sellare.

saddle-bag, *-băg*, s. bisaccia, f.

saddle-cloth, *-klŏth*, s. gualdrappa, f.

saddle-horse, *-hŏrs*, s. cavallo da sella, f.

saddler, *săd´lŭr*, s. sellaio, m.   [m.

saddlery, *-lŭrĭ*, s. selleria, f.

sadness, *săd´nĕs*, s. tristezza, f.

safe, *sāf*, a. salvo, sicuro; felice; **-ly**, ad. salvamente; —, s. guardavivande, m., dispensa, f.; **— and sound**, sano e salvo.

safe-conduct, *-kŏn´dŭkt*, s. salvacondotto, m.

safe-guard, *-gărd*, s. salvaguardia, f.

safety, *sāf´tĭ*, s. salvezza, f.; sicurezza, f.; salute, f.   [rezza, f.

safety-valve, *-vălv*, s. valvola di sicu-

saffron, *săf´frŏn*, s. zafferano, m.; —, a. di color di zafferano.

sagacious, *săgā´shŭs*, a. sagace; astuto; **-ly**, ad. sagacemente.   [f.

sagacity, *-găs´ĭtĭ*, s. sagacità, f.; astuzia,

sage, *sāj*, s. (bot.) salvia, f.; uomo savio, m.; —, a. savio, saggio; **-ly**, ad. saviamente.

sago, *sā´gō*, s. sago, m.   [mente.

sail, *sāl*, s. vela, f.; nave, f.; ala, f.; —, v. a. & n. veleggiare, fare vela, navigare; imbarcarsi.

sailer, *-ŭr*, s. vascello, naviglio, m.

sailing, -ĭng, s. navigazione, f.; veleggia-
sailor, -ăr, s. marinaro, m. [mento, m.
saint, sănt, s. santo, m.; santa, f.
saint, -, **sainted,** -ĕd, **saintly,** -lĭ, ad. santamente. [-, per l'amor di Dio.
sake, săk, s. causa, cagione, f.; **for God's**
salable, săl'ăbl, a. da vendersi, vendibile.
salad, săl'ăd, s. insalata, f.
salad-bowl, -bŏl, s. insalatiera, f.
salad-oil, -ŏĭl, s. olio d'uliva, m. [f.
salamander, săl'ămăndăr, s. salamandra,
salary, săl'ărĭ, s. salario, m., mercede, f.
sale, săl, s. vendita, f.; incanto pubblico, m.
saleable, să'lăbl, a. vendibile. [f. pl.
sale-goods, -gŭdz, s. pl. merci di scarto,
salesman, -z'măn, s. rigattiere, m.
salient, să'lĭĕnt, a. saliente; palpitante.
saline, sălĭn', a. salino, di sale.
saliva, sălĭ'vă, s. saliva, f.
sallow, săl'lŏ, a. pallido, smorto.
sally, săl'lĭ, s. sortita, scappata, f.; escursione, f.; -, v. n. (mil.) uscir de' ripari.
salmon, săm'ăn, s. salmone, m. (pesce).
salmon-trout, -trŏŭt, s. trota del sapore del salmone, f.
saloon, sălŏn', s. sala grande, f.
salt, sălt, s. sale, m.; (fig.) senno, genio, m.; [-, a. salato; -, v. a. salare.
salt-cellar, -sĕllăr, s. saliera, f. [m.
salting-tub, -ĭng tŭb, s. bossolo del sale,
saltness, -nĕs, s. salsezza, f.
saltpetre, -pētăr, s. salnitro, nitro, m.
salt-works, -wŭrks, s. pl. salina, f.
salubrious, sălŏ'brĭŭs, a. salubre.
salubrity, -brĭtĭ, s. salubrità, sanità, f.
salutary, săl'ŭtărĭ, a. salutare.
salutation, -tă'shăn, s. salutazione, f.; saluto, m. [tare.
salute, sălŏt', s. saluto, m.; -, v. a. salu-
salvage, săl'vădj, s. premio per salvar da un naufragio, m.
salvation, -vă'shăn, s. salvamento, m.
salve, săv, s. unguento, impiastro, m. [f.
salver, săl'văr, s. vassoio, m.; sottocoppa,
salvo, săl'vŏ, s. riserbazione, f.; scusa, f.
same, săm, a. medesimo, stesso.
sameness, -nĕs, s. medesimezza, f.
sample, săm'pl, s. esemplare, modello, m.; esempio, m.; -, v. a. mostrare l'esempio.
sampler, -plăr, s. mostra, f., modello, m.
sanatory, săn'ătărĭ, a. sanitario.
sanctification, săngktĭfĭkă'shăn, s. santi-ficazione, f.
sanctify, săngk'tĭfĭ, v. a. santificare.
sanctimonious, -mŏ'nĭŭs, a. santo: ipo-crito. [f.; santità, f.
sanctimony, săngk'tĭmŏnĭ, s. santimonia,
sanction, săngk'shăn, s. sanzione, f.; -, v. a. dar sanzione.
sanctity, săngk'tĭtĭ, s. santità, f.
sanctuary, săngk'tŭărĭ, s. santuario, m.; asilo, m. [coprire di sabbia.
sand, sănd, s. arena, sabbia, f.; -, v. a.
sandal, săn'dăl, s. sandalo, pezzuola, m.
sand-bank, sănd'băngk, s. banco di rena,
sanded, -ĕd, a. sabbionoso. [m.
sand-pit, -pĭt, s. cava di sabbione, f.
sand-stone, -stŏn, s. pietra arenaria, f.

sandwich, -wĭch, s. pane bianco unto con burro e fette di carne, m.
sandy, sănd'ĭ, a. sabbioso, arenoso.
sane, săn, a. sano.
sanguinary, săng'gwĭnărĭ, a. sanguinario.
sanguine, săng'gwĭn, a. sanguigno.
sanguineness, -nĕs, s. ardore, m.
sanguineous, -gwĭn'ĕŭs, a. sanguinoso.
sanitary, săn'ĭtărĭ, a. sanitario.
sanity, -ĭtĭ, s. stato perfetto di mente, m.
sap, săp, s. succhio, sugo, m.; -, v. a. zappare.
sapient, să'pĭĕnt, a. sapiente. [m.
sapling, săp'lĭng, s. arboscello, piantone,
sapper, săp'păr, s. zappatore, m.
sapphire, săf'făr, s. zaffiro, m.
sarcasm, săr'kăzm, s. sarcasmo, m.
sarcastic(al), -kăs'tĭk(ăl), a. sarcastico; -ally, ad. satiricamente.
sarcenet, sărs'nĕt, s. taffetà, f.
sarcophagus, -kŏf'ăgăs, s. sarcofago, m.
sardine, săr'dĭn, s. sardina, f.
sash, săsh, s. cinto di seta, m., cintura, f.
sash-window, -wĭndŏ, s. finestra leva-toia o a cataratta, f.
Satan, să'tăn, s. Satana, m.
satanic(al), sătăn'ĭk(ăl), a. satanico. [m.
satchel, săch'ĕl, s. sacchetto, sacchettino,
sate, săt, **satiate,** să'shĭăt, v. a. saziare, satollare.
satellite, săt'ĕllĭt, s. satellite, m.
satiety, săt'ĭtĭ, s. sazietà, f.
satin, săt'ĭn, s. raso, m. (drappo). [f.
satinet, -nĕt, s. stoffa di seta assai leggiera,
satire, săt'ĭr, s. satira, f.
satiric(al), -tĭr'ĭk(ăl), a. satirico; -ally, ad. satiricamente.
satirist, săt'ĭrĭst, s. scrittore di satire, m.
satirize, -ĭrĭz, v. a. satireggiare. [f.
satisfaction, -ĭsfăk'shăn, s. sodisfazione,
satisfactorily, -făk'tărĭlĭ, ad. d'una ma-niera sodisfacente.
satisfactory, -tăr'ĭ, a. sodisfattorio.
satisfy, săt'ĭsfĭ, v. a. & n. sodisfare, dar sodisfazione; contentare.
satrap, să'trăp, s. satrapo, m.
saturate, săt'ŭrăt, v. a. saziare.
Saturday, săt'ŭrdă, s. sabato, m.
saturnine, săt'ŭrnĭn, a. malinconico,
satyr, săt'ĭr, s. satiro, m. [triste.
sauce, săs, s. salsa, f.; (am.) legume, m.; -, v. a. acconciare con salsa. [m.
saucer, săs'săr, s. piattello, m.; scodellino,
saucily, -sĭlĭ, ad. impertinentemente.
sauciness, -sĭnĕs, s. impudenza, f.
saucy, săs'ĭ, a. insolente.
saunter, săn'tăr, v. n. andar ramingo.
saunterer, -ăr, s. ozioso, vagabondo, m.
sausage, săs'ădj, s. salsiccia, f.
savage, săv'ădj, a. salvatico, crudele; -ly, ad. alla salvatica; -, s. selvaggio, m.
savageness, -nĕs, s. salvatichezza, f.
savanna(h), săvăn'nă, s. prateria, f.
save, săv, v. a. salvare; risparmiare; con-servare; -, pr. & ad. salvo, eccetto che, fuorchè.

save-all, *–ăl,* s. canna da accendere, f., accenditoio, m.

saveloy, *săv'ĕlŏĭ,* s. cervellata, f.

saver, *sā'văr,* s. salvatore, m.; risparmiatore, m.

saving, *–vĭng,* a. economo, parco; −, pr. salvo, eccetto; −ly, ad. con risparmio, parcamente; −s, s. pl. risparmio, m.; riserva, f.   [parmio, f.

savings-bank, *–z băngk,* s. cassa di risparmio, f.

Saviour, *săv'văr,* s. Salvatore, Redentore, m.

savour, *sā'văr,* s. sapore, m.; gusto, m.; odore, m.; −, v. a. saporare; sentire. [m.

savouriness, *–ĭnĕs,* s. sapore, buon gusto, m.

savoury, *–vărĭ,* a. saporoso.

saw, *sā,* s. sega, f.; −, v. a. segare.

saw-dust, *–dŭst,* s. segatura, f.

saw-fish, *–fĭsh,* s. sega marina, f.

saw-mill, *–mĭl,* s. mulino da segare, m.

sawyer, *–yăr,* s. segatore, m.

say, *sā,* v. a. & n. ir. dire; narrare, raccontare; −, s. detto, m.

saying, *–ĭng,* s. dizione, f.; proverbio, m.

scab, *skăb,* s. scabbia, rogna, f.; birbone, m.

scabbard, *–bărd,* s. fodero, m., guaina, f.

scabbiness, *–bĭnĕs,* s. rogna, f.

scabby, *skăb'bĭ,* s. **scabious,** *skā'bĭŭs,* a. scabbioso.

scaffold, *skăf'fŏld,* s. palco, catafalco, m.

scaffolding, *–ĭng,* s. struttura di palchi, f.; galleria, f.

scald, *skăld,* s. tigna, f.; −, v. a. scottare.

scalding-hot, *–ĭng hŏt,* a. bollente, fervente.

scale, *skăl,* s. bilancia, f.; guscio, m.; (mus.) zolfa, f.; saggiuolo, m.; **pair of −s,** s. bilancia, f.; −, v. a. scalare; −, v. n. scorticarsi.   [da scalare, f.

scaling-ladder, *skă'lĭng lăddăr,* s. scala

scallion, *skăl'yăn,* s. scalogno, m., cipollina, f.   [tagliare a festone.

scallop, *skăl'lŏp,* s. petonciano, m.; −, v.a.

scalp, *skălp,* s. pericranio, m.; −, v. a. levare via il pericranio.

scaly, *skă'lĭ,* a. scaglioso, squammoso.

scamp, *skămp,* s. mascalzone, m.

scamper, *skăm'păr,* v. n. fuggire via.

scan, *skăn,* v. a. misurare un verso, scandire; esaminare.   [famia, f.

scandal, *skăn'dăl,* s. scandalo, m.; infamia, f.

scandalise, *–dălĭz,* v. a. scandalizzare.

scandalous, *–dălŭs,* a. scandaloso, infame; −ly, ad. scandalosamente.

scant, *skănt,* a. povero, piccolo; ristretto; scarso; parco, avaro.   [mente.

scantily, *–tĭl,* ad. parcamente; meschina-

scantiness, *–ĭnĕs,* s. scarsezza, strettezza, f.; insufficienza, f.

scantling, *skăn'tlĭng,* s. pezzetta, f. [m.

scape-goat, *skāp'gŏt,* s. capro emissario,

scape-grace, *–grăs,* s. furfante, ribaldo, m.   [trizzare.

scar, *skăr,* s. cicatrice, f.; −, v. a. cica-

scarce, *skărs,* a. raro; −ly, ad. scarsamente, appena.

scarcity, *–tĭt,* s. scarsità, f.

scare, *skăr,* v. a. spaventare, far paura.

scarecrow. *–krō,* s. spauracchio, m.

scarf, *skărf,* s. ciarpa, cravatta lunga, f.

scarf-pin, *–pĭn,* s. ago della cravatta, m.

scarify, *skăr'ĭfĭ,* v. a. scarificare.

scarlatina, *skărldtĕ'nă,* s. febbre scarlattina, f.

scarlet, *skăr'lĕt,* a. & s. scarlatto (m.).

scarlet-fever, *–fevăr,* s. febbre scarlattina, f.

scarp, *skărp,* s. (mil.) scarpa, f. [tina, f.

scat, *skăt,* s. scossa di pioggia, f.

scatter, *skăt'tăr,* v.a. spandere, dispergere.

scavenger, *skăv'ĕnjăr,* s. paladino, m.

scene, *sĕn,* s. scena, f.; teatro, m.

scenery, *–ărĭ,* s. vista, f.; rappresentazione, f.; scena, f.

scenic(al), *sĕn'ĭk(ăl),* a. scenico; teatrale.

scent, *sĕnt,* s. odore, sentore, m.; odorato, m.; fiuto, m.; −, v. a. odorare; fiutare; profumare.   [d' odore, f.

scent-bottle, *–bŏtl,* s. boccetta da spirito

scentless, *–lĕs,* a. inodorabile; senza odore, m.   [fiuto.

sceptic, *skĕp'tĭk,* s. scettico, m.

sceptical, *–ăl,* a. scettico.

scepticism, *–tĭsĭzm,* s. scetticismo, m.

sceptre, *sĕp'tăr,* s. scettro, m.

schedule, *shĕd'ŭl,* s. cedola, f.; cartuccia, f.; polizza, f.

scheme, *skēm,* s. piano, disegno, m.; modello, m.; −, v. a. progettare, disegnare.

schemer, *–ăr,* s. inventore, m.

schism, *sĭzm,* s. scisma, f.; divisione, separazione, f.   [tico, m.

schismatic(al), *sĭzmăt'ĭk(ăl),* s. scisma-

scholar, *skŏl'ăr,* s. scolare, m.; letterato, m.

scholarship, *–shĭp,* s. dottrina, scienza, f.

scholastic, *skŏlăs'tĭk,* a. scolastico.

school, *skōl,* s. scuola, f.; −, v. a. insegnare.   [m.

school-boy, *–bŏĭ,* s. scolare, m.; studente,

schooling, *–ĭng,* s. insegnamento, m.

school-master, *–măstăr,* s. maestro di scuola, m.   [scuola, f.

school-mistress, *–mĭstrĕs,* s. maestra di

schooner, *skŏn'ăr,* s. goletta, f.

sciatica, *sĭ̆ī'tĭkă,* s. (med.) sciatica, f.

science, *sī'ĕns,* s. scienza, f.; dottrina, f.

scientific, *–tĭf'ĭk,* a. scientifico, dotto; −ly, ad. scientificamente.

scimitar, *sĭm'ĭtăr,* s. scimitarra, f.

scintillate, *sĭn'tĭllāt,* v. n. scintillare.

scintillation, *–lă'shăn,* s. scintillazione, f.

sciolist, *sī'ŏlĭst,* s. semidotto, m.

scion, *sī'ŏn,* s. rimessiticcio, ramicello, m.

scission, *sĭzh'ăn,* s. scissione, f.; separazione, f.

scissors, *sĭz'zărs,* s. pl. forbici, f. pl.

scoff, *skŏf,* s. scherno, m., burla, f.; −, v. a. beffare, burlare, schernire.

scoffer, *–făr,* s. schernitore, beffatore, m.

scoffingly, *–fĭnglĭ,* ad. burlescamente.

scold, *skōld,* v. a. & n. rabbuffare; contendere; −, s. riottosa, f.

sconce, *skŏns,* s. candelabro, m.

scoop, *skŏp,* s. paletta, f.; gottazza a mano, f.; −, v. a. scavare.

scope, *skŏp,* s. scopo, m.; segno, m.; disegno, m.; fine, m.; libertà, f., campo, m.

scorbutic, *skŏrbū'tĭk*, a. scorbutico.

scorch, *skŏrch*, v. a. & n. riardere; abbruciacchiare, abbronzare.

score, *skŏr*, s. conto, m.; scotto, m.; taglia, f.; ventina, f.; risguardo, rispetto, m.; ragione, f.; –, v. a. segnare, notare; mettere in conto.

scorer, *–ăr*, s. marcatore, m.

scoria, *skō'rĭā*, s. scoria, f.

scorn, *skŏrn*, s. sdegno, disprezzo, m.; –, v. a. & n. sdegnare, dispregiare.

scornful, *–fŭl*, a. sdegnoso; –ly, ad. disprègeovolmente.

scorpion, *skŏr'pĭăn*, s. scorpione, m.

scot, *skŏt*, s. scotto, m.; parte, porzione, f.

scotch, *skŏch*, s. piccol taglio, tagliuzzo, m.; –, v. a. tagliare la superfizie.

scot-free, *skŏt'frē*, a. immune, franco.

scoundrel, *skŏŭn'drĕl*, s. briccone, m.

scoundrelly, *–drĕllĭ*, a. da gagliofffo, da briccone. [f.

scoundrelism, *–drĕlĭzm*, s. scelleraggine,

scour, *skŏŭr*, v. a. & n. forbire; nettare; fregare. [–, v. a. sferzare; punire.

scourge, *skŭrj*, s. sferza, f.; gastigo, m.;

scout, *skŏŭt*, s. spia, m.; battistrada, m.; vedetta, f.; naviglio veloce, m.; –, v. n. battere le strade; fare la scoperta.

scowl, *skŏŭl*, s. guardo arcigno, m.; –, v. n. mostrar un viso arcigno.

scowlingly, *–ĭnglĭ*, ad. con viso arcigno.

scragginess, *skrăg'gĭnĕs*, s. mugrezza, f.; ruvidezza, f.

scraggy, *–gĭ*, a. macilento, scarno.

scramble, *skrăm'bl*, v. n. aggrappars; rampicare; –, s. sorta di gioco fanciullesco; disputa, f. [rimasuglio, m.

scrap, *skrăp*, s. pezzo, frammento, m.;

scrape, *skrāp*, v. a. raschiare, grattare; –, v. n. strimpellare, raspare, razzolare; –, s. difficoltà, f. [tivo sonatore, m.

scraper, *skrā'păr*, s. rastiachino, m.; cat-

scraping, *–pĭng*, s. raschiatura, f.

scratch, *skrăch*, v. a. grattare, graffiare; cancellare; –, s. graffiatura, f.

scrawl, *skrăl*, v. a. scarabocchiare; –, s. scarabocchio, m., cattiva mano, f.

scrawler, *–ăr*, s. cattivo scrittore, m.

scream, *skrēm*, screech, *skrēch*, v. n. gridar con voce acuta; –, s. grido, m.; stridore, m.

screech-owl, *skrēch'ŏwl*, s. civetta, f.

screen, *skrēn*, s. ricovero, m.; paravento, m.; vaglio da sabbia, m.; –, v. a. coprire; nascondere; proteggere; crivellare.

screw, *skrō*, s. vite, f.; female –, vite femmina, f.; male –, maschio d' una vite, m.; –, v. a. fare entrare girando; (fig.) spremere.

screw-driver, *–drĭvăr*, s. cacciavite, m.

screw-nut, *–nŭt*, s. chiocciola, f.

screw-steamer, *–stēmăr*, s. vapore a vite propellente, m. [s. scarabocchio, m.

scribble, *skrĭb'bl*, v. a. scarabocchiare; –,

scribbler, *–blăr*, s. scrittoraccio, m.

scribe, *skrĭb*, s. scriba, m.; scrivano, m.

scrimmage, *skrĭm'mŏj*, s. aggrappamento, m.; parapiglia, f.

scrip, *skrĭp*, s. bisaccia, f.; sacchetto, m.; cedola, m.

scriptural, *skrĭp'tŭrăl*, a. della scrittura sacra. [sacra, f.

Scripture, *skrĭp'tŭr (–chŭr)*, s. scrittura

scrivener, *skrĭv'ĕnăr*, s. scrivano, m.; notaro, m.; sensale, m.

scrofula, *skrŏf'ŭlă*, s. scrofola, f.

scrofulous, *–ŭlŭs*, a. scrofoloso.

scroll, *skrŏl*, s. ruolo (di carta), m.

scrub, *skrŭb*, v. a. strofinare; fregare ben bene; –, s. gagliofffo, m.; scopa, f.

scruple, *skrō'pl*, s. scrupolo, m.; –, v. n. fariscrupolo; dubbiare. [f.

scrupulosity, *–pŭlŏs'ĭtĭ*, s. scrupolosità,

scrupulous, *skrŏ'pŭlăs*, a. scrupoloso; –ly, ad. scrupolosamente. [nare.

scrutinise, *–tĭnīz*, v. a. scrutinare; esami-

scrutiny, *–tĭnĭ*, s. scrutinio, m.; ricercamento, m.

scud, *skŭd*, v. a. fuggir via.

scuffle, *skŭf'fl*, s. baruffa, f.; contesa, rissa, f.; –, v. n. abbaruffarsi; azzuffarsi, riottare.

scull, *skŭl*, s. remo, m.; –, v. a. remare.

scullery, *–lărĭ*, s. lavatoio, m.

scullion, *–yŭn*, s. guattero, m.; guattera, f.

sculptor, *skŭlp'tŭr*, s. scultore, m.

sculpture, *skŭlp'tŭr (–chŭr)*, s. scultura, f., intaglio, m.; –, v. a. scolpire, intagliare.

scum, *skŭm*, s. spuma, f.; feccia, f.; –, v. a. schiumare. [f.

scurf, *skŭrf*, s. tigna, f.; crosta (di piaga),

scurfy, *–ĭ*, a. tignoso, scabbioso.

scurrility, *skŭrrĭl'ĭtĭ*, s. scurrilità, f.

scurrilous, *skŭr'rĭlăs*, a. ingiurioso; vile, basso; –ly, ad. in modo abusivo.

scurvily, *–vĭlĭ*, ad. vilmente.

scurviness, *–vĭnĕs*, s. cattiveria, malignità, viltà, f. [ribaldo, vile.

scurvy, *–vĭ*, s. scorbuto, m.; –, a. cattivo,

scutcheon, *skŭch'ăn*, s. scudo, m.

scuttle, *skŭt'tl*, s. gran paniere, m.; –, v. n. andare qua e là.

scythe, *sĭth*, s. falce, f.

sea, *sē*, s. mare, oceano, m.; onda, f.; heavy –, mare tempestoso.

sea-board, *–bŏrd*, a. verso il mare.

sea-breeze, *–brēz*, s. vento impetuoso, m.

sea-coast, *–kŏst*, s. costa del mare, f.

sea-fight, *–fĭt*, s. combattimento navale, m.

sea-green, *–grēn*, a. colore del mare, f.

sea-gull, *–gŭl*, s. mugnaio, m. (uccello).

sea-horse, *–hŏrs*, s. cavallo marino, m.

seal, *sēl*, s. sigillo, m.; –, v. a. sigillare.

sealing-wax, *–ĭng wăks*, s. ceralacca, f.

seam, *sēm*, s. cucitura, f.; congiuntura, f.; –, v. a. cucire; giungere.

seaman, *sē'măn*, s. marinaio, m.

seamanship, *–shĭp*, s. nautica, f.

seamstress, *sēm'strĕs*, s. cucitrice, f.

seamy, *sēm'ĭ*, a. pieno di cuciture, cucito.

sea-piece, *sē'pēs*, s. marina, f.; veduta di mare, f.

sea-port, *–pŏrt*, s. porto di mare, m.

sear, *sēr*, v. a. arrossare con ferro rovente.

search, *sŭrch*, v. a. cercare, visitare; esaminare; frugare, frugacchiare; provare; —, s. inchiesta, ricerca, inquisizione, f.

search-light,—*lît*, s, riflessore elettrico, m.

sea-shore, *sĕ' shŏr*, s. costa del mare, f.

sea-sick,—*sĭk*, a. marezziato.

sea-sickness,—*sĭknĕs*, s. mal di mare, m.

sea-side, —*sĭd*, s. lido del mare, m.

season, *sĕ' zn*, s. stagione, f.; tempo opportuno, m.; condimento, m.; —, v. a. condire; accostumare; —, v. n. essere opportuno. [tuno.

seasonable, —*ăbl*, a. di stagione; opportuno.

seasonably, —*ăblî*, ad. a proposito.

seasoning, —*ĭng*, s. condimento, m.

seat, *sĕt*, s. sedia, f.; seggio, m.; situazione, f.; —, v. a. situare; collocare; stabilire.

sea-term, *sĕ' tărm*, s. termine di marina, m. [parte del mare.

seaward, —*wărd*, a. verso il mare, della

sea-weed, —*wĕd*, s. (bot.) alga, f.

sea-worthy, —*wŭrthî*, a. (of ships) nasecant, s. secante, f. [vigabile.

secant, *sĕ' kănt*, s. secante, f. [vigabile.

secede, *sĕsĕd'*, v. n. ritirarsi; separarsi.

secession, —*sĕsh' ăn*, s. separazione, f.

seclude, —*klŏd'*, v. a. escludere; eccettuare.

seclusion, —*klŏ' zhăn*, s. esclusione, f.

second, *sĕk' ŭnd*, a. secondo; —ly, ad. secondamente; —, s. secondo, m.; difensore, m.; sessantesima parte (d' un minuto, d' un grado), f.; —, v. a. secondare. [dine.

secondarily, —*ărĭlî*, ad. nel secondo ordine.

secondary, —*ărî*, a. secondario.

second-hand, —*hănd*, a. d'antiquario.

secrecy, *sĕ' krĕsî*, s. segretezza, f.

secret, —*krĕt*, a. & s. segreto (m.); —ly, ad. segretamente.

secretary, *sĕk' rĕtărĭ*, s. segretario, m.

secretaryship, —*shĭp*, s. uffizio di segretario, segretariato, m.

secrete, *sĕkrĕt'*, v. a, nascondere; separare.

secretion, —*krĕ' shăn*, s. separazione, f.

secretive, —*krĕ' tĭv*, a. misterioso.

sect, *sĕkt*, s. setta, f. [settario, m.

sectarian, —*tā' rĭăn*, **sectary,** *sĕk' tărî*, s.

section, *sĕk' shăn*, s. sezione, f.

secular, *sĕk' ŭlăr*, a. secolare; laico.

secularise, *sĕk' ŭlărĭz*, v. a. secolarizzare.

secularity, —*lăr' ĭtî*, s. cose mondane, f. pl.

secure, —*kŭr'*, a. sicuro, salvo; —ly, ad. sicuramente; —, v. a. salvare; preservare; assicurare. [malleveria, f.; difesa, f.

security, —*kŭr' ĭtî*, s. sicurtà, sicurezza, f.;

sedan, *sĕdăn'*, s. sedia portatile, f.

sedate, —*dăt'*, a. sedato, tranquillo; —ly, ad. tranquillamente.

sedateness, —*nĕs*, s. tranquillità, f.

sedative, *sĕd' ătĭv*, a. calmante.

sedentary, —*ĕntărĭ*, a. sedentario.

sedge, *sĕj*, s. giunco, m.

sediment, *sĕd' ĭmĕnt*, s. sedimento, m.; posatura, feccia, f. [f.

sedition, —*dĭsh' ăn*, s. sedizione, f.; fazione,

seditious, —*ăs*, a. sedizioso; —ly, ad. sediziosamente. [zione, f.

seditiousness, —*nĕs*, s. dispostezza a sedizione.

seduce, —*dŭs'*, v. a. sedurre; corrompere.

seducer, —*dŭ' săr*, s. seduttore, m.

seduction, —*dŭk' shăn*, s. seduzione, f.

seductive, —*tĭv*, a. seducente.

sedulous, *sĕd' ŭlăs*, a. assiduo; —ly, ad. assiduamente.

see, *sĕ*, v. a. ir. vedere; comprendere, conoscere; osservare; scoprire; —, v. n. ir. aver l' occhio; informarsi; esser attento; —, s. seggio episcopale, m.

seed, *sĕd*, s. seme, m., semenza, sementa, f.; —, v. n. granire, tallire.

seed-bed, (--garden, --plot), —*bĕd*, (--gărdn, --plŏt), s. semenzaio, m.

seedling, —*lĭng*, s. pianticella, f. [m.

seedsman, —*z'măn*, s. mercante di semi,

seed-time, —*tĭm*, s. tempo del seminare o della sementa, m. [loso.

seedy, *sĕd' î*, a. pieno di granelli, granel-

seeing, *sĕ' ĭng*, s. vedere, m.; vista, f.; — (that), c. poiché, mentre ché.

seek, *sĕk*, v. a. ir. cercare; domandare; —, v. n. ir. sforzarsi, adoperarsi.

seem, *sĕm*, v. n. parere, sembrare.

seeming, —*ĭng*, a. apparente; —ly, ad. in apparenza; —, s. apparenza, f.

seemliness, —*lĭnĕs*, s. decenza, f.

seemly, —*lî*, a. decente; convenevole.

seer, *sĕ' ăr*, s. profeta, indovino, m.

see-saw, *sĕ' să*, s. altalena, f.; —, v. n. altalenare, cullare.

seethe, *sĕth*, v. a. & n. far bollire; bollire.

segar, *sĕgăr'*, s. sigaro, m.

segment, *sĕg' mĕnt*, s. segmento, m.

seine-net, *sĕn' nĕt*, s. (mar.) scorticheria, f.

seize, *sĕz*, v. a. prendere, pigliare; sequestrare, staggire.

seizure, *sĕ' zhŭr*, s. sequestro, m.

seldom, *sĕl' dăm*, ad. raramente.

select, *sĕlĕkt'*, v. a. eleggere; —, a. scelto.

selection, —*lĕk' shăn*, s. scelta, f.

self, *sĕlf*, pn. stesso, proprio; **oneself,** *să* stesso. [di sè stesso, f.

self-command, —*kŏmmănd*, s. padronanza

self-conceit, —*kŏnsĕt*, s. presunzione, f.

self-confidence,—*kŏnfĭdĕns*,s.confidenza nel proprio merito &c., f.

self-defence, —*dĕfĕns*, s. difesa propria, f.

self-denial, —*dĕnĭăl*, s. astinenza, f.; mortificazione, f.

self-evident, —*ĕvĭdĕnt*, a. evidente.

self-interest, —*ĭntĕrĕst*, s. interesse proprio, m. [prio, m.

selfish, —*ĭsh*, a. interessato, m.

selfishness, —*ĭshnĕs*, s. proprio interesse, m.; amor proprio, m.

self-love, —*lŭv*, s. amor proprio, m.

self-opinionated, —*ŏpĭnĭănătĕd*, a. testardo. [sopra sè stesso, m.

self-possession, —*pŏzzĕshăn*, s. impero sopra sè stesso, m.

self-respect, —*rĕspĕkt*, s. stima di sè medesimo, f.

self-same, —*săm*, pn. quello stesso.

self-seeking, —*sĕkĭng*, a. egoistico.

self-styled, —*stĭld*, a. sedicente.

self-taught, —*tăt*, a. insegnato da sè stesso.

self-willed, —*wĭld*, a. ostinato.

sell, *sĕl*, v. a. ir. vendere; trafficare; —, s. inganno, m., furberia, f.

seller, —*ăr*, s. venditore, mercante, m.

selling-off, *-ĭng ŏf,* s. vendita a ribasso, f.
selvage, *sĕl'vdj,* s. orlo, m.; corda (del panno), f.   [semaforo, m.
semaphore, *sĕm'ăfŏr,* s. telegrafo marino,
semblance, *sĕm'blăns,* s. somiglianza, apparenza, f.   [f.
semibreve, *sĕm'ĭbrĕv,* s. (mus.) semibreve,
semicircle, *-sŭrkl,* s. semicircolo, m.
semicircular, *-sŭr'kŭlăr,* a. semicircolare.
semicolon, *-kŏ'lŏn,* s. punto e virgola, m.
seminary, *sĕm'ĭnări,* s. seminario, semenzaio, m.   [croma, f.
semiquaver, *-kwăvăr,* s. (mus.) semi-
semitone, *-tŏn,* s. (mus.) mezzo tuono, m.
sempstress, *vedi* seamstress.
senate, *sĕn'ăt,* s. senato, m.   [senato, f.
senate-house, *-hŏŭs,* s. assemblea del
senator, *sĕn'ătăr,* s. senatore, m.
senatorial, *-tŏ'rĭăl,* a. senatorio.
send, *sĕnd,* v. a. ir. mandare; inviare; spedire; accordare; produrre.
sender, *-ăr,* s. mandatore, inviatore, m.
seneschal, *sĕn'ĕshăl,* s. siniscalco, m.
senile, *sĕ'nĭl,* a. senile, vecchio.
senior, *sĕn'yăr,* s. seniore, m.
seniority, *-nĭŏr'ĭtĭ,* s. priorità, anzianità, f.
senna, *sĕn'nă,* s. sena, f.
sennight, *sĕn'nĭt,* s. sette giorni e notti, pl.
sensation, *sĕnsă'shăn,* s. sensazione, f.
sense, *sĕns,* s. senso, m.; sentimento, m.; intelletto, giudizio, m.; senno, m.
senseless, *-lĕs,* a. insensato; **-ly,** ad. senza giudizio.   [pazzia, f.
senselessness, *-lĕsnĕs,* s. stoltezza,
sensibility, *-sĭbĭl'ĭtĭ,* s. sensibilità, f.
sensible, *sĕn'sĭbl,* a. sensibile; giudizioso.
sensibly, *-sĭblĭ,* ad. sensibilmente.
sensitive, *-sĭtĭv,* a. sensitivo; **- plant,** s. sensitiva, f.   [sualmente.
sensual, *-shăl,* a. sensuale; **-ly,** ad. sen-
sensualist, *-ĭst,* s. uomo voluttuoso, m.
sensuality, *-shăl'ĭtĭ,* s. sensualità, f.; voluttà, libidine, f.
sentence, *sĕn'tĕns,* s. sentenza, f.; decisione, f.; motto, m.; **-,** v. a. condannare.
sententious, *-tĕn'shŭs,* a. sentenzioso; **-ly,** ad. sentenziosamente.   [opinione, f.
sentiment, *sĕn'tĭmĕnt,* s. sentimento, m.,
sentimental, *-mĕn'tăl,* a. sentimentale.
sentinel, *sĕn'tĭnĕl,* **sentry,** *-trĭ,* s. sentinella, f.   [tinella, m.
sentry-box, *sĕn'trĭ bŏks,* s. casotto di sen-
separable, *sĕp'ărăbl,* a. separabile.
separate, *sĕp'ărăt,* v. a. & n. separare; separarsi; **-,** a. separato; **-ly,** ad. a parte.
separation, *-ră'shăn,* s. separazione, f.
sepoy, *sĕ'pŏĭ,* s. soldato delle Indie orientali, m.
September, *sĕptĕm'băr,* s. settembre, m.
septennial, *-tĕn'nĭăl,* a. del età di sette anni.   [genario, m.
septuagenarian, *-tŭăjĕnă'rĭăn,* s. settua-
sepulchral, *sĕpŭl'krăl,* a. sepolcrale.
sepulchre, *sĕp'ŭlkăr,* s. sepolcro, m.
sepulture, *-ŭltŭr,* s. sepoltura, f.   [f.
sequel, *sĕ'kwĕl,* s. sequela, f.; conseguenza,
sequence, *-kwĕns,* s. seguenza, serie, f.

sequester, *sĕkwĕs'tăr,* **sequestrate,** *-trăt,* v. a. sequestrare, staggire.
sequestration, *-tră'shăn,* s. sequestro, m.
seraglio, *-răl'yŏ,* s. serraglio, m.
seraph, *sĕr'ăf,* s. serafino, m.
serenade, *sĕrĕnădâ',* s. serenata, f.; **-,** v. a. fare una serenata.   [nità.
serene, *-rĕn',* a. sereno; **-ly,** ad. con sere-
serenity, *-rĕn'ĭtĭ,* s. serenità, f.
serf, *sărf,* s. schiavo, m.
serge, *sărj,* s. rascia, saia, f. (panno).
sergeant, serjeant, *săr'jĕnt,* s. sergente, birro; avvocato, m.
serial, *sĕ'rĭăl,* s. novella *o* storia pubblicata in fascicoli periodici, f.; **-,** a. appartenente ad una serie.
series, *sĕ'rĭĕz,* s. serie, seguenza, f.
serious, *sĕ'rĭăs,* a. serio, grave; **-ly,** ad. seriamente, davvero.
sermon, *săr'mŏn,* s. sermone, m., predica,
sermonise, *-ĭz,* v. a. sermoneggiare.   [f.
serous, *sĕ'răs,* a. acqueo.
serpent, *săr'pĕnt,* s. serpe, f., serpente, m.
serpentine, *-ĭn,* a. & s. serpentino (m.).
serrated, *sĕr'rătĕd,* a. dentato.
serum, *sĕ'răm,* s. siero, m.   [serva, f.
servant, *săr'vănt,* s. servo, servitore, m.;
serve, *sărv,* v. a. servire; assistere; **-,** v. n. essere in servizio; durare; accomodarsi; esser propizio; **to - a warrant,** catturare, arrestare.
service, *săr'vĭs,* s. servizio, benefizio, m.; vantaggio, comodo, m.; impiego, m.
serviceable, *-ăbl,* a. utile, comodo; officioso.   [mente.
servile, *-vĭl,* a. servile; **-ly,** ad. servil-
servility, *-vĭl'ĭtĭ,* s. servilità, f.
servitude, *-vĭtăd,* s. servitù, schiavitù, f.
session, *sĕsh'ăn,* s. sessione, f.; assemblea de' giudici, f.
set, *sĕt,* v. a. & n. ir. mettere, collocare, porre; fissare, stabilire; affermare; tramontare; **(of the sun)** sommergersi; coagularsi, rappigliarsi; applicarsi; **to - an example,** dare esempio; **to - on fire,** incendiare; **to - apart,** mettere a parte; **to - aside,** mettere da parte; **to - down,** depositare; notare; **to - forth,** esporre; partire; **to - on,** animare, eccitare; **to - off,** partire; abbellire; **to - out,** partire; mostrare; porre in ordine; **to - up,** elevare, stabilirse; **to - about,** cominciare a fare; **to - in,** cominciare; **to - upon,** avventarsi; **-,** s. assortimento, m.; partita di giuoco, f.; guarnitura, f.; **-,** a. fisso, posto.   [m.
set-off, *-ŏf,* s. guarnizione, f., ornamento,
settee, *sĕttĕ',* s. piccolo canapè, m.
setter, *sĕt'tăr,* s. spia, f.; cane da fermo, m.; compositore, m.; **(--on)** istigatore, m.
setting, *-tĭng,* s. collocazione, f.; **- of the sun,** tramonto del sole, occaso, m.
settle, *sĕt'tl,* v. a. stabilire; fissare; ordinare, aggiustare; calmare; **-,** v. n. posarsi, rassettarsi; stanziarsi; andare a fondo; fissarsi, determinarsi; calmarsi.
settlement, *-mĕnt,* s. stabilimento, m.;

domicilio, m.; colonia, f.; patto, accordo, m.; feccia, f.
settler, *-lŭr,* s. colono, m.
set-to, *sĕt tŏ',* s. conflitto, m., disputa, f.
seven, *sĕv'n,* a. sette.
sevenfold, *-fŏld,* a. sette volte.
seventeen, *-tēn,* a. diciassette.
seventeenth, *-tēnth,* a. diciassettesimo.
seventh, *sĕv'nth,* a. settimo; **-ly,** ad. in settimo luogo.
seventieth, *-tĭēth,* a. settantesimo.
seventy, *-tĭ,* a. settanta.
sever, *sĕv'ŭr,* v. a. separare; **—,** v. n. far una separazione.
several, *-ărăl,* a. molti, diversi, parecchi; particolare; **-ly,** ad. separatamente.
severance, *-ărăns,* s. separazione, f.
severe, *sĕvēr',* a. severo, rigido, duro, austero; **-ly,** ad. severamente.
severity, *-vĕr'ĭtĭ,* s. severità, f.
sew, *sŏ,* v. a. cucire; seccare; legare alla rustica.
sewer, *-ŭr,* s. cucitrice, f.
sewer, *sū'ŭr,* s. condotto sotterraneo, m.; fogna, f.   [dezza, f.
sewerage, *-ărdj,* s. pattume, m., immon-
sewing-machine, *sŏ'ĭng măshēn,* s. macchina da cucire, f.
sex, *sĕks,* s. sesso, m.   [senne.
sexennial, *-ĕn'nĭăl,* a. di sei anni, ses-
sextant, *sĕks'tănt,* s. sestante, m.
sexton, *-tŭn,* s. beccamorti, m.; sagre-
sextuple, *-tŭpl,* a. sestuplo.   [stano, m.
sexual, *-ŭăl,* a. sessuale.   [mente.
shabbily, *shăb'bĭlĭ,* ad. poveramente, vil-
shabbiness, *-bĭnĕs,* s. mendicità, f.; bassezza, f.   [avaro.
shabby, *-bĭ,* a. stracciato; basso, vile;
shackle, *shăk'l,* v. a. mettere in ceppi; **-s,** s. pl. ceppi, m. pl.; catene, f. pl.
shad, *shăd,* s. laccia, f. (pesce).
shade, *shăd,* s. ombra, f.; oscurità, f.; ricovero, m., stuoia, f.; **—,** v. a. ombrare; (fig.) proteggere.
shadiness, *shd'dĭnĕs,* s. ombra, f.
shadow, *shăd'ŏ,* s. ombra, f.; protezione, difesa, f.; segno, emblema, m.; **—,** v. a. ombreggiare, proteggere.   [oscuro.
shadowy, *-ŏĭ,* **shady,** *shd'dĭ,* a. ombroso,
shaft, *shăft,* s. freccia, saetta, f.; dardo, m.; fusto d'una colonna, m.; timone, m.
shag, *shăg,* s. felpa, f., peluzzo, m.
shagged, *-gĕd,* **shaggy,** *-gĭ,* a. villoso, peloso; irsuto.
shagreen, *shăgrēn',* s. zigrino, m.
shake, *shăk,* v. a. ir. scuotere, agitare; crollare; **—,** v. n. ir. tremare; trillare; **to — hands,** darsi la mano; **—,** s. scossa, f., trillo, m.
shaking, *shd'kĭng,* s. scossa, f., crollo, m.
shaky, *-kĭ,* a. vacillante, rotto.
shall, *shăl,* v. def. ir. dovere.
shallop, *shăl'lŏp,* s. (mar.) barchetta, f.
shallow, *-lŏ,* a. basso, poco profondo; frivolo; **—,** s. banco, m.; guado, m.
shallowness, *-nĕs,* s. poco fondo, m.; sciochezza, f.
sham, *shăm,* a. supposto, falso, finto;

—, s. baia, burla, f.; frode, f., inganno, m.; **—,** v. a. gabbare; ingannare.   [f.
shambles, *-blz,* s. pl. macello, m., beccheria,
shambling, *-blĭng,* a. che si muove goffamente.
shame, *shăm,* s. vergogna, f.; infamia, f.; **for —,** eh via, puh! **—,** v. a. svergognare, disonorare.
shamefaced, *-făst,* a. vergognoso, confuso.
shameful, *-fŭll,* a. vergognoso; **-ly,** ad. vergognosamente.   [sfacciatamente.
shameless, *-lĕs,* a. sfacciato; **-ly,** ad.
shamelessness, *-lĕsnĕs,* s. impudenza, f.
shamois, *shăm'ŏĭ,* s. camozza, f.
shampoo, *shămpŏ',* v. a. stropicciare.
shamrock, *shăm'răk,* s. (bot.) trifoglio, m.
shank, *shăngk,* s. gamba, f.; stinco, m.; fusto, m.; verga (d' un' ancora), f.; cannuccia (di pippa), f.
shanty, *shăn'tĭ,* c. capanna, f.
shape, *shăp,* s. forma, figura, f.; modello, m.; **—,** v. a. formare, regolare; concepire.
shapeless, *-lĕs,* a. di brutta forma.
shapely, *-lĭ,* a. di bella forma.
share, *shăr,* s. parte, porzione, f.; azione, f.; sorte, m.; coltro, m.; **—,** v. a. dividere, spartire; **—,** v. n. aver parte.
share-holder, *-hŏldăr,* s. azionario, m.
sharer, *-ăr,* s. partecipante, m.
shark, *shărk,* s. pesce cane, m.
sharp, *shărp,* a. acuto, affilato; mordace, pugnente; aspro, severo, rigoroso; violento; fiero, crudele; pronto, attivo, vivace; fervido; astuto, accorto; ingegnoso; **—,** s. (mus.) bisquadro, m.
sharpen, *shăr'pn,* v. a. aguzzare, affilare.
sharper, *shărp'ăr,* s. cavaliere d' industria, scroccone, m.
sharply, *-lĭ,* ad. acutamente, severamente; aspramente; ingegnosamente.
sharpness, *-nĕs,* s. filo, m.; punta, f.; acutezza, f.; perspicacia, f.; sottigliezza d' ingegno, f.
shatter, *shăt'tŭr,* v. a. fracassare; **—,** v. n. rompersi; **—,** s. schieggia, m.
shave, *shăv,* v. a. ir. radere; tosare; far la barba; spogliare.   [m.
shaver, *shd'vŭr,* s. barbiere, m.; tosatore,
shaving, *-vĭng,* s. tosatura, f.; **-s,** pl. copponi, m. pl.
shawl, *shăl,* s. scialle, m.
she, *shē,* pn. ella, essa, quella.
sheaf, *shēf,* s. covone, m.; **—,** v. a. accovonare il grano.
shear, *shēr,* v. a. ir. tosare; **-s,** s. pl. forbicioni, m. pl., forbici, f. pl.
shearer, *-ăr,* s. tosatore, m.
shearing, *-ĭng,* s. tosatura, f.
sheath, *shēth,* s. fodero (di spada), m., guaina, f.; **—,** v. a. mettere nel fodero; coprire di steccati.
shed, *shĕd,* v. a. ir. versare; spargere, spandere; **—,** s. rimessa, capanna, f.
sheen, *shēn,* s. lustro, splendore, m.
sheep, *shēp,* s. pecora, f.; pecorone, m.; alluda, f.   [pecorile, m., mandra, f.
sheep-cot, *-kŏt,* **sheep-fold,** *-fŏld,* s.

sheepish, –ĭsh, a. timido; innocente.

sheepishness, –nĕs, s. timidità, f.; sciocchezza, f.   [m.

sheep's-eye, shĕps'ĭ, s. sguardo timido,

sheep-skin, –skĭn, s..pelle di pecora, f.

sheep-walk, –wăk, s. pascolo, m.

sheer, shēr, a. puro, chiaro; semplice; –, ad. affatto; alla prima; –, v. n. fuggire via di nascosto.   [m.; (mar.) scotta, f.

sheet, shĕt, s. lenzuolo, m.; foglio (di carta),

sheet-almanac, –ălmănăk, s. calendario di fattoria, m.   [f.

sheet-anchor, –ăngkŭr, s. àncora maestra,

sheeting, –ĭng, s. lino da lenzuola, m.

sheet-iron, –īrn, s. piastra di ferro, f.

sheet-lightning, –lītnĭng, s. fulmine largo, m.

shelf, shĕlf, s. scaffale, m., scansia, f.; secca (in mare), f.; on the –, da parte.

shell, shĕl, s. scaglia, f.; conchiglia, conca, f.; nicchio (di pesce), m.; scorza, f.; –, v. a. sgusciare, scorzare; sgranare; –, v. n. sgusciarsi, scagliarsi.

shelter, shĕl'tŭr, s. coperto, m.; rifugio, asilo, m.; sicurtà, f.; –, v. a. dare il asilo, ricevere in casa sua; proteggere.

shelterless, –lĕs, a. senza asilo.

shelve, shĕlv, v. a. pensionario; –, v. n. inclinare, essere a pendio.   [m.

shelving, –ĭng, a. declive; –, s. declivio.

shepherd, shĕp'ŭrd, s. pastore, pecoraio,

shepherdess, –ĕs, s. pastorella, f.   [m.

sherbet, shŭr'bĕt, s. sorbetto, m.

sheriff, shĕr'ĭf, s. sceriffo, m.

sherry, shĕr'rĭ, s. vino bianco (di Xeres), m.

shield, shēld, s. scudo, m.; protezione, f.; –, v. a. difendere.

shift, shĭft, s. camicia (da donna), f.; espediente, m.; scusa, f.; pretesto, m.; astuzia, f.; –, v. a. mutare; cambiare; trasportare.

shifter, –ŭr, s. truffatore, m.   [clava, f.

shillelagh, shĭllē'lă, s. rompicapo, m.,

shilling, shĭl'lĭng, s. scellino, m.

shilly-shally, shĭl'lĭ shăl'lĭ, a. irresoluto.

shin(-bone), shĭn('bōn), s. stinco, m.

shine, shīn, v. n. ir. rilucere, risplendere; brillare.   [(med.) fuoco salvatico, m.

shingle, shĭng'gl, s. assicella, f.; –s, s. pl.

shining, shī'nĭng, a. risplendente; –, s. luce, f.; splendore, m.

shiny, shīn'ĭ, a. rilucente, brillante.

ship, shĭp, s. nave, f., naviglio, vascello, m.; –, v. a. imbarcare.

ship-board, –bŏrd, s. bordo di vascello, m.

ship-boy, –bŏĭ, s. mozzo, m.   [navale, f.

ship-building, –bĭldĭng, s. architettura

shipmate, –māt, s. compagno di bordo, m.

shipment, –mĕnt, s. imbarcamento, m.

ship-owner, –ōnŭr, shipper, –pŭr, s. padrone d' una nave, m.   [flotta, f.

shipping, –pĭng, s. imbarcamento, m.;

shipshape, –shăp, a. in buon ordine.

shipwreck, –rĕk, s. naufragio, m.

shire, shīr (in comp. shŭr), s. contea, provincia, f.

shirt, shŭrt, s. camicia (da uomo), f.

shirting, –ĭng, s. tela da camicie, f.

shiver, shĭv'ŭr, v. a. sminuzzare, spezzare; –, v. n. tremare di freddo; –, s. frammento, m.; brivido, m.

shivering, –ĭng, s. brivido, m.

shoal, shōl, s. folla, moltitudine, f.; secca (in mare), f.; –, a. poco profondo; pieno di secche; –, v. n. andar in folla; esser poco profondo.

shoaly, shōl'ĭ, a. pieno di secche.

shock, shŏk, s. urto, assalto, m.; conflitto, m.; bica, f.; –, v. a. urtare; esser offensivo.

shock-head, –hĕd, s. mazzocchio, m.

shockingly, –ĭnglĭ, ad. in modo offensivo.

shoddy, shŏd'dĭ, s. filacce, f. pl.

shoe, shō, s. scarpa, f.; ferro di cavallo, m.; –, v. a. ir. calzare; ferrare (un cavallo).

shoe-black, –blăk, shoe-boy, –bŏĭ, s. lustrascarpe, m.

shoe-horn, –hŏrn, s. calzatoio, m.

shoe-lace, –lās, shoe-string, –strĭng, s. correggiuolo delle scarpe, m.

shoemaker, –mākŭr, s. calzolaio, m.

shoot, shōt, v. a. ir. lanciare, sparare, tirare; scaricare, vuotare; –, v. n. ir. germogliare, gemmare; sporgere, uscire; battere; –, s. germoglio, m.; tiro, m.

shooter, –ŭr, s. tiratore, m.; arciere, m.

shooting, –ĭng, s. caccia (con schioppo), f.; il germogliare, m.

shop, shŏp, s. bottega, f.; lavoratorio, m.

shop-bill, –bĭl, s. insegna, f.   [f.

shop-front, –frŭnt, s. finestra di bottega,

shop-keeper, –kēpŭr, s. bottegaio, m.

shop-lifter, –lĭftŭr, s. mariuolo, m.

shopman, –măn, s. garzone di bottega, m.

shop-walker, –wăkŭr, s. soprintendente d' una dogana, m.

shopwoman, –wŭmăn, s. bottegaia, f.

shore, shōr, s. costa, spiaggia, f.; lido, m.; sostegno, m.

short, shŏrt, a. corto, stretto; succinto, breve; –, ad. subito, ad un tratto; –ly, ad. in poco tempo.   [f., deficit, m.

shortcoming, –kŭmĭng, s. insufficienza,

shorten, shŏrt'n, v. a. accorciare, contrarre; abbreviare.

shorthand, –hănd, s. stenografia, f.

shorthand-writer, –rītŭr, s. stenografo, m.   [tezza, f.

shortness, shŏrt'nĕs, s. brevità, f.; cor-

short-sighted, –sītĕd, a. di corta vista.

short-sightedness, –nĕs, s. corta vista, f.   [lini, m. pl.; tiro, m.; scotto, m.

shot, shŏt, s. palla (di schioppo), f.; pal-

shoulder, shōl'dŭr, s. spalla, f., omero, m.; –, v. a. mettere sopra le spalle.

shout, shŏut, s. clamore, grido, m.; –, v. n. gridare; far applauso.

shouting, –ĭng, s. grido d'allegrezza, m.; acclamazione, f., applauso, m.

shove, shŭv, v. a. & n. spingere, urtare; assalire; –, s. colpo, m.

shovel, shŭv'l, s. pala, paletta, f.; –, v. a. gettare colla pala, ammucchiare.

show, shō, v. a. ir. mostrare, far vedere

manifestare, scoprire; provare; –, v. n. ir. parere, sembrare; –, s. mostra, f., spettacolo, m.   [–, v. n. piovere a rovescio.

shower, *shŏu'ăr*, s. rovescio, nembo, m.;

showery, *–ŭri*, a. piovoso.

showy, *shŏ'ĭ*, a. splendido; pomposo.

shred, *shrĕd*, s. ritaglio, m.; pezzo, m.; –, v. a. tagliare minuto.

shrew, *shrŏ,s.* sgridatrice, f.

shrewd, *shrŏd*, a. astuto; maligno; **–ly**, ad. astutamente.

shrewdness, *–nĕs*, s. astuzia, f.

shrewish, *shrŏ'ĭsh*, a. ritroso; **–ly**, ad. in modo garrulo.

shrewmouse, *–mŏŭs*, s. topo campestre, m.   [s. grido acuto, m.

shriek, *shrĕk*, v. n. strillare, stridere; –,

shrill, *shrĭl*, a. squillante, acuto.

shrillness, *–nĕs*, s. acutezza di voce, f.

shrimp, *shrĭmp*, s. squilla, f. (gamberetto marino); nano, m.

shrine, *shrĭn*, s. reliquiario, m.

shrink, *shrĭngk*, v. n. ir. scorciarsi, ritirarsi.   [raggrinzarsi.

shrivel, *shrĭv'l*, v. a. & n. aggrinzare;

shroud, *shrŏŭd*, s. coperta, f.; panno funebre, m.; (mar.) corda grossa, f.; –, v. a. coprire; seppellire; difendere, proteggere; –, v. n. mettersi al coperto; rifugiarsi.

Shrovetide, *shrŏv'tĭd*, s. carnevale, m.

shrub, *shrŭb*, s. arboscello, arbusto, m.; omicciattolo, m.   [busti, m.

shrubbery, *–bŭrĭ*, s. luogo piantato d' arbusti.

shrug, *shrŭg*, v. a. stringere; –, s. ristringimento delle spalle, m.

shudder, *shŭd'dăr*, v. n. tremare di paura, abbrividire; –, s. tremore, tremito, m.

shuffle, *shăf'fl*, v. a. mescolare; confondere; ingannare, truffare; usare di sotterfugi; –, v. n. sforzarsi; –, s. scompiglio, m.; furberia, f.; sotterfugio, m.

shuffling, *–flĭng*, s. sotterfugio, m.; furberia, f., artifizio, m.

shun, *shăn*, v. a. evitare; scampare.

shunt, *shănt*, s. (rail.) baratto, m.

shut, *shăt*, v. a. ir. chiudere, rinchiudere.

shutter, *–tăr*, s. paravento, m.

shuttle, *shăt'tl*, s. spola, f.

shuttlecock, *–kŏk*, s. volante, m. (gioco.)

shy, *shĭ*, a. ritroso, contegnoso; [–, v. n. aver ribrezzo, vergognarsi.

shyness, *–nĕs*, s. ritrosia, f.; peritanza, f.

sibyl, *sĭb'ĭl*, s. sibilla, f.; indovinatrice, f.

sick, *sĭk*, a. ammalato, indisposto.

sicken, *sĭk'n*, v. a. render ammalato; –, v. n. ammalarsi.

sickle, *sĭk'kl*, s. roncola, f.

sickliness, *–lĭnĕs*, s. disposizione inferma, m.   a malaticcio.   [f.

sickly, *–lĭ*, a. malaticcio.

sickness, *–nĕs*, s. malattia, f.

sick-ward, *–wărd*, s. infermeria, f.

side, *sĭd*, s. lato, canto, m.; fianco, m.; pagina, faccia (d'un libro), f.; parte, f.; fazione, f.; –, a. laterale; obliquo; –, v. n. pigliare la parte.   [denza, f.

sideboard, *–bŏrd*, s. buffetto, m., credenza.

side-face, *–făs*, s. testa del profilo, f.

---

sidelong, *–lŏng*, a. laterale; –, ad. a traverso.   [verso.

sider, *–ăr*, s. partigiano, m.

side-scene, *–sĕn*, s. scenari, m. pl.

sideways, *–wăz*, ad. a traverso, a sghembo.   [m.

siding, *sĭ'dĭng*, s. (rail.) binario laterale,

sidle, *sĭ'dl*, v. n. pendere da un lato.

siege, *sĕj*, s. assedio, m.; seggio, m.

sieve, *sĕv*, s. crivello, m.   [esaminare.

sift, *sĭft*, v. a. crivellare, investigare;

siftings, *sĭf'tĭngz*, s. pl. cruscherello, m.

sigh, *sĭ*, v. n. sospirare; –, s. sospiro, m.

sight, *sĭt*, s. vista, f.; prospettiva, f.; mira, f.; occhi, m. pl.

sightless, *–lĕs*, a. cieco.

sightly, *–lĭ*, a. di bella presenza.   [coli.

sight-seeing, *–sĕing*, s. il vedere spettacoli.

sign, *sĭn*, s. segno, m.; indizio, m.; insegna, f.; –, v. a. segnare, far segno.

signal, *sĭg'năl*, s. segnale, segno, m.; –, a. segnalato; eccellente, illustre.

signalise, *–nălĭz*, v. a. segnalare.

signal-light, *–lĭt*, s. fanale, m.

signal-man, *–măn*, s. che segnala.   [f.

signature, *sĭg'nătăr,s.*firma,f.;segnatura,

signet, *sĭg'nĕt*, s. suggello (del re), m.

significance, *–nĭf'ĭkăns*, s. importanza, f.

significant, *–kănt*, a. significante.

signification, *–kă'shŭn*, s. significazione, f., senso, m.

significative, *–nĭf'ĭkătĭv*, a. significativo.

signify, *sĭg'nĭfĭ*, v. a. significare, –, v. n. essere energico.

sign-post, *sĭn'pŏst*, s. palo d' insegna, m.

silence, *sĭ'lĕns*, s. silenzio, m.; –, v. a. imporre silenzio, far tacere.

silent, *–lĕnt*, a. taciturno; **–ly**, ad. senza, parlare, piano piano.

silex, *sĭ'lĕks*, s. selce, selice, f., ciottolo, m.

silk, *sĭlk*, s. seta, f.

silken, *sĭlk'n*, a. setoso, di seta.

silk-goods, *–gŭds*, s. pl. seterie, f. pl.

silkiness, *–ĭnĕs*, s. morbidezza, f.

silk-man,*–măn*, **silk-mercer**, *–măr'săr*, s. setaiuolo, m.   [bigatto, m.

silk-worm, *–wărm*, s. baco filugello,

silky, *sĭlk'ĭ*, a. fatto di seta; setoso.

sill, *sĭl*, s. soglio, m.

sillily, *sĭl'lĭlĭ*, ad. scioccamente.

silliness, *–lĭnĕs*, s. sciocchezza, f.

silly, *–lĭ*, a. sciocco, goffo; semplice.

silver, *sĭl'văr*, s. argento, m.; moneta d' argento, f.; –, a. d' argento; –, v. a. inargentare.

silver-smith, *–smĭth*, s. argentatore, m.

silvery, *–vărĭ*, a. argenteo, argentino.

similar, *sĭm'ĭlăr*, a. similar; **–ly**, ad. similmente.   [tŭdd,s. somiglianza, f.

similarity, *–lăr'ĭtĭ*, **similitude**, *–mĭl'*

simile, *sĭm'ĭlĕ*, s. similitudine, f.

simmer, *sĭm'măr*, v. n. bollire adagio.

simony, *sĭm'ŏnĭ*, s. simonia, f.

simper, *sĭm'păr*, v. n. sorridere scioccamente; –, s. sorriso, m.

simple, *sĭm'pl*, a. semplice; puro.   [m.

simpleton, *–tŏn*, s. semplicione, sciocco,

simplicity, –plĭs'ĭtĭ, s. semplicità, f.

simplification. –fĭkā'shŭn, s. semplificazione, f.

simplify, sĭm'plĭfĭ, v. a. semplificare.

simply, sĭm'plĭ, ad. semplicemente.

simulate, sĭm'ŭlāt, v. n. simulare.

simulation, –lā'shŭn, s. simulazione, f.

simultaneous, –mŭltā'nĕŭs, a. simultaneo; –ly, ad. tutti insieme.

sin, sĭn, s. peccato, m.; –, v. n. peccare.

since, sĭns, pr. & ad. di poi, dopo; poichè.

sincere, sĭnsēr', a. sincero; –ly, ad. sinceramente.

sincerity, –sĕr'ĭtĭ, s. sincerità, f.

sinecure, sĭ'nĕkūr, s. beneficio senza cura, sinecura, m.

sinew, sĭn'ū, s. nervo, f.; tendine, m.

sinewy, –ŭĭ, a. nervoso, vigoroso.

sinful, sĭn'fŭl, a. vizioso; –ly, ad. viziosamente.

sinfulness, –nĕs, s. corruzione, f.

sing, sĭng, v. a. ir. cantare; lodare; –, v. n. ir. cantare; garrire.

singe, sĭnj, v. a. abbruciacchiare.

singer, sĭng'ăr, s. cantatore, m.; cantatrice, f.

singing, –ĭng, s. canto, m.

single, sĭng'gl, a. solo, unico; semplice; celibe; –, v. a. separare, scegliere; segnare.

singleness, –nĕs, s. semplicità, f.; sincerità, f.

singly, –glĭ, ad. separatamente.

singular, –gŭlăr, a. singolare; –ly, ad. singolarmente; –, s. numero singolare, m.

singularity, –lăr'ĭtĭ, s. singolarità, f.

sinister, sĭn'ĭstăr, a. sinistro; cattivo; ingiusto; malizioso; infelice.

sink, sĭngk, v. a. ir. sommergere, affondare; scavare; opprimere; disfare, rovinare; –, v. n. ir. attuffarsi, andare a fondo; abbassarsi, abbattersi; succumbere; cadere, decrescere; penetrare; –, s. sentina, cloaca, f.

sinner, sĭn'năr, s. peccatore, m., peccatrice, f.

sin-offering, sĭn'ŏffăring, s. offerta espiatoria, f.

sinuosity, sĭnŭŏs'ĭtĭ, s. sinuosità, f.

sinuous, sĭn'ŭŭs, a. sinuoso, torto.

sinus, sī'năs, s. seno (di mare), m.

sip, sĭp, v. a. & n. sorseggiare, bere a sorsi; gocciare; –, s. sorso, m.

siphon, sī'făn, sifone, m.

Sir, săr, s. Signore, m.

sire, sīr, s. Sire, m.; (poet.) padre, m.

siren, sī'rĕn, s. sirena, f.

sirloin, săr'lŏĭn, s. lombata, f.

sister, sĭs'tăr, s. sorella, f.; religiosa, f.

sisterhood, –hŭd, s. qualità di sorella, f.

sister-in-law, –ĭn lā, s. cognata, f.

sisterly, –lĭ, a. di sorella.

sit, sĭt, v. n. ir. sedere; stare; esser situato; essere; riposarsi.

site, sĭt, s. situazione, f.

sitting, sĭt'ĭng, s. sedere, m.; sessione, f.

situate, sĭt'ŭāt, a. situato, posto.

situation, –ā'shŭn, s. situazione, f.; condizione, f.

six, sĭks, a. sei.

sixpence, –pĕns, s. sei soldi, m. pl.

sixteen, –tēn, a. sedici.

sixteenth, –tēnth, a. sedicesimo.

sixth, sĭksth, a. sesto; –ly, ad. in sesto

sixtieth, –tĭĕth, a. sessantesimo. [luogo.

sixty, –tĭ, a. sessanta.

size, sīz, s. grandezza, grossezza, m.; misura, m.; dimensione, f.; calibro, m.; statura, f.; condizione, f., stato, m.; colla, f.; –, v. a. incerare.

sized, sīzd, a. proporzionato.

skate, skāt, s. pattino, m.; –, v. n. sdrucciolare sopra il ghiaccio.

skating, –ĭng, s. il pattinare, m.

skating-rink, –ĭng rĭngk, s. cammino coperto per pattinare con rotelle, m.

skein, skān, s. matassa, f.

skeleton, skĕl'ĕtŏn, s. scheletro, m.

skeleton-key, –kĕ, s. chiave comune, f.

sketch, skĕch, s. schizzo, abbozzo, m.; –, v. a. schizzare, far il primo disegno.

skew, skū, a. obliquo.

skewer, –ăr, s. brocco, stecco, m.; –, v. a. appicare con stecchi. [le ruote, f.

skid, skĭd, s. forcina o scarpe da arrestare

skiff, skĭf, s. schifo, m.

skilful, skĭl'fŭl, a. versato, pratico; –ly, ad. destramente.

skilfulness, –nĕs, s. destrezza, f.

skill, skĭl, s. destrezza, abilità, arte, f.; talento, ingegno, m.; sapere, m.

skilled, skĭld, a. versato, esperto.

skillet, skĭl'lĕt, s. casserola, f.

skim, skĭm, s. schiuma, f.; –, v. a. schiumare; –, v. n. trattare o scorrere leggiermente. [care.

skin, skĭn, s. pelle, cute, f.; –, v. a. scortinare; –, v. n. scorticarsi, cicatrizzarsi.

skinned, skĭnd, a. scorticato, cicatrizzato.

skinner, skĭn'năr, s. pelliciaio, m.

skinny, –nĭ, a. magro, macilento.

skip, skĭp, s. salto, balzo, m.; –, v. a. trascorrere; omettere; –, v. n. saltare.

skirmish, skăr'mĭsh, s. scaramuccia, f.; –, v. n. scaramucciare.

skirmisher, –ăr, s. scaramucciatore, m.

skirt, skărt, s. fimbria, f.; fregio, orlo, m.; –, v. a. orlare.

skit, skĭt, s. motteggio, m.; burla, f.

skittish, –tĭsh, a. schifo, ombroso; restio, incostante; –ly, ad. schifamente.

skittle, skĭt'tl, s. birillo, m.

skulk, skŭlk, v. n. celarsi, nascondersi; far il poltrone.

skull, skŭl, s. cranio, m.

skull-cap, –kăp, s. caschetto, m., cuffia, f.

sky, skĭ, s. cielo, firmamento, m. [f.

sky-light, –lĭt, s. abbaino, m.; apertura chiusa da cancelli, f.

sky-parlor, –pärlăr, s. solaio, m.

sky-rocket, –rŏkĕt, s. razzo, m.

slab, slăb, s. tavola (di marmo), f.

slabber, –băr, v. n. sbavare; sporcare.

slack, slăk, a. sciolto, lento; negligente.

slack(en), slăk'(kn), v. a. slegare, allentare; ritardare; trascurare; stemperare; estinguere; –, v. n. rallentarsi; diminuire.

slackness, –nĕs, s. rilassamento, m.; tardità, negligenza, f.

slag, *slăg*, s. scoria, f.

slake, *slāk*, v. a. estinguere.

slam, *slăm*, v. a. chiudere con impeto; fare tutte le bazze.

slander, *slăn'där*, v. a. calunniare, diffamare; —, s. maldicenza, calunnia, f.

slanderer, *—är*, s. calunniatore, m.

slanderous, *—äs*, a. calunnioso, maldicente; **-ly**, ad. calunniosamente.

slang, *slăng*, s. parlar furbesco, m.

slant, *slănt*, v. a. volgere obliquamente.

slanting, *—ǐng*, a. traverso, obliquo.

slap, *slăp*, s. colpo, schiaffo, m., guanciata, f.; —, ad. con un colpo subito e violento; —, v. a. schiaffeggiare.

slash, *slăsh*, s. staffilata, f., taglio, m.; —, v. a. staffilare, tagliare.   [di lavagne.

slate, *slāt*, s. lavagna, f.; —, v. a. coprire

slate-pencil, *—pĕnsĭl*, s. pietra da sarti, m.

slating, *slā'tǐng*, s. tetto di lavagne, m.

slattern, *slăt'tärn*, s. donna neghittosa, f.

slatternly, *—lǐ*, ad. neghittosamente.

slaughter, *slă'tär*, s. strage, f., macello, m.; —, v. a. macellare, trucidare.

slaughterer, *—är*, s. uccisore, m.

slaughter-house, *—hŏŭs*, s. macello, ammazzatoio, m.   [carsi, stentare.

slave, *slāv*, s. schiavo, m.; —, v. n. affati-

slaver, *slā'vär*, s. bava, f.; —, v. a. fare vascello che fa la tratta dei negri, m.

slave-ship, *slāv'shĭp*, s. **slaver**, *slā'vär*, s. bava, f.; —, v. a. fare

slavery, *slā'värĭ*, schiavitù, f.   [bava.

slavish, *—vĭsh*, a. schiavesco, servile; -**ly**, ad. da schiavo, servilmente.

slavishness, *—nĕs*, s. servilità, f.

slay, *slā*, v. a. ir. uccidere, ammazzare.

slayer, *—är*, s. ammazzatore, m.

sled, *slĕd*, **sledge**, *slĕj*, **sleigh**, *slā*, s. slitta, f.   [di fabbro), m.

sledge-hammer, *—hămmär*, s. martello

sledging, *slĕj'ĭng*, **sleighing**, *slā'ĭng*, s. corso in islitta, m.

sleek, *slēk*, a. liscio, pulito; —, v. a. lisciare, pulire.   [m.

sleep, *slēp*, v. n. ir. dormire; —, s. sonno,

sleeper, *—är*, s. dormiglione, m.; (rail.) traversa, f.   [stupido.

sleepily, *—ǐlǐ*, ad. dormendo; in modo

sleepiness, *—ĭnĕs*, s. addormentamento, m.

sleepless, *—lĕs*, a. senza dormire.

sleeplessness, *—lĕsnĕs*, s. mancanza di sonno, insonnia, f.   [lismo, m.

sleep-walking, *—wăkǐng*, s. sonnambu-

sleepy, *slēp'ǐ*, a. sonnolento.

sleet, *slēt*, s. pioggia con neve, f.; —, v. n. nevicare minutamente.

sleeve, *slēv*, s. manica, f.

sleight, *slĭt*, s. astuzia, furberia, f.

slender, *slĕndär*, a. sottile, smunto, magro; parco; -**ly**, ad. poveramente.

slenderness, *—nĕs*, s. piccolezza, f.; magrezza, f.   [tagliare a fette.

slice, *slīs*, s. fetta, f.; spatola, f.; —, v. a.

slide, *slīd*, v. n. ir. sdrucciolare; scorrere; —, s. sdrucciolo, m.; sentiero liscio, m.

sliding, *—dǐng*, s. il sdrucciolare, m.; —, a. sdrucciolante, sdruccioloso.

slight, *slīt*, a. sottile, piccolo; leggiero;

—**ly**, ad. leggermente; —, s. sdegno, disprezzo, m.: —, v. a. dispregiare.

slightingly, *—tĭnglĭ*, ad. dispregevolmente.

slightness, *—nĕs*, s. radezza, f.; negligenza, trascuratezza, f.

slim, *slĭm*, a. smilzo, magro, sottile.

slime, *slĭm*, s. limo, m.; vischio, m.

sliminess, *—ĭnĕs*, s. viscosità, f.

slimy, *slī'mǐ*, a. viscoso, glutinoso.

sling, *slǐng*, s. frombola, f.; scaglia, f.; percossa, f.; —, v. a. ir. lanciare.

slink, *slǐngk*, v. a. ir. scappare; svignare.

slip, *slǐp*, v. a. mettere di nascosto; omettere; —, v. n. sdrucciolare; scappare, fuggire; —, s. passo falso, m.; errore, m.; scolo, flusso, m.

slipper, *—pär*, s. pianella, pantofola, f.

slipperiness, *—pärĭnĕs*, s. qualità sdrucciolevole, f.; incertezza, f.

slippery, *—pärĭ*, a. sdrucciolevole.

slip-shod, *—shŏd*, a. che ha le scarpe a ciabatta.

slip-slop, *—slŏp*, s. cattivo liquore, m.

slit, *slĭt*, v. a. ir. fendere, spaccare; —, s.

slobber, *slŏb'bär*, s. bava, f.   [fessura, f.

sloe, *slō*, s. (bot.) susina salvatica, f.

sloop, *slōp*, s. (mar.) schifo, m.

slop, *slŏp*, s. cattiva bevanda, f.; sciacquatura, f.; guazzo, m.

slop-basin, *—bāsn*, s. vaso in cui si versa il fondo delle tazze, m.

slope, *slōp*, s. pendio, m.; declività, f.; taglio a mezzaluna, m.; —, v. a. tagliare a sghembo.   [declive.

sloping, *slō'pĭng*, a. obliquo; pendente,

slop-pail, *slŏp'pāl*, s. secchia, f.

sloppy, *slŏp'pǐ*, a. fangoso.

sloth, *slōth*, s. pigrizia, f.; ai (animale), m.

slothful, *—fŭl*, a. ozioso.

slouch, *slŏŭch*, v. a. abbassare la testa; dondolarsi leggermente.

slough, *slŏŭ*, s. pozza, f.; fango, m.

sloughy, *slŏŭ'ǐ*, a. fangoso.   [schifo, m.

sloven, *slăv'n*, s. sporco, imbrodolato,

slovenliness, *—ĭnĕs*, s. sporcizia, f.

slovenly, *—lǐ*, a. sporco, schifo; —, ad. sporcamente.   [**-ly**, ad. lentamente.

slow, *slō*, a. lento, pigro, tardo; ottuso;

slowness, *—nĕs*, s. lentezza, tardità, f.; pigrizia, inerzia, f.

slow-worm, *—wärm*, s. ofidiano, m.

slug, *slăg*, s. infigardo, m.; lumaca, f.; verga di metallo, f.

sluggard, *—gärd*, s. pigro, m.

sluggish, *—gĭsh*, a. lento, pigro; -**ly**, ad. pigramente.   [fingardia, f.

sluggishness, *—nĕs*, s. lentezza, f.; in-

sluice, *slŏs*, s. cateratta, f.; —, v. a. sboccare; alzare la cateratta.

slum, *slăm*, s. quartiere de' poveri, m.

slumber, *slăm'bär*, s. sonno leggiero, m.; —, v. n. sonnacchiare.

slumberer, *—är*, s. sornacchio, m.

slur, *slär*, v. a. sporcare; trattare leggermente; (mus.) legare; —, s. (mus.) legatura, f.; macchia, f.

slush, *slŭsh*, s. fango, m.; grassume, m.

slut, *slŭt*, s. donna sudicia, f.

sly, *sli*, a. astuto; **on the –**, occultamente; **–ly**, ad. astutamente.

slyness, *–nĕs*, s. astuzia, f.

smack, *smăk*, s. gusto, sapore, m.; bacio, m.; –, v. a. baciare con scoppio; –, v. n. avere sapore. [sottile, f.

small, *smăl*, a. piccolo, minuto; –, s. parte

smallish, *–ish*, a. alquanto piccolo.

smallness, *–nĕs*, s. piccolezza, poca quantità, f.; tenuità, f.

small-pox, *–pŏks*, s. vainolo, m..

small-talk, *–tăk*, s. ciarleria conversc-

smalt, *smălt*, s. smalto, m. [vole, f.

smart, *smărt*, a. pungente, acuto; arguto; doloroso; spiritoso, lesto; –, s. dolore acuto, m.; –, v. n. pizzicare; fare male; soffrire. [acutamente.

smartly, *–li*, ad. vivamente, vivacemente;

smartness, *–nĕs*, s. vivacità, f.; eleganza, f.

smash, *smăsh*, v. a. rompere, spezzare; –, s. fracasso, m.

smatterer, *smăt'tărăr*, s. semidotto, letteratucolo, m.

smattering, *–tăring*, s. mediocre cognizione, f.

smear, *smēr*, v. a. sporcare, imbrattare.

smell, *smĕl*, v. a. & n. (r. & ir.) sentire; odorare, fiutare; –, s. odore, fiuto, m.

smelling-bottle, *–ing bŏttl*, s. boccetta, f.

smelt, *smĕlt*, v. a. fondere (metallo).

smelter, *–ăr*, s. fonditore, m. [f.

smelting-house, *–ing hŏŭs*, s. fonderia,

smile, *smil*, v. n. sorridere; –, s. sorriso, m.

smirk, *smărk*, v. n. sorridere.

smite, *smit*, v. a. ir. percuotere, ferire.

smith, *smĭth*, s. fabbro, m. [fabbro, f.

smithery, *–ări*, **smithy**, *–i*, s. bottega di

smitten, *smit'tn*, (p. &) a. preso, accesso.

smock, *smŏk*, s. camicia da donna, f.; gonnella, f.

smock-frock, *–frŏk*, s. giubbetta di tela, f.

smoke, *smŏk*, s. fumo, m.; vapore, m.; –, v. a. fumare, seccare la carne, m.

smoke-consumer, *–kŏnsămăr*, s. fumivoro, m.

smoke-dry, *–dri*, v. a. seccare al fumo.

smokeless, *–lĕs*, a. senza fumo.

smoker, *smŏ'kăr*, s. fumatore, m.

smoking-divan, *smŏk'ing divăn*, s. stanza da fumare, f.

smoky, *smŏ'ki*, a. fumante; fumoso.

smooth, *smŏŏth*, a. piano; liscio; dolce; affabile, soave, piacevole; **–ly**, ad. egualmente, dolcemente; –, s. (am.) prateria, f.

smoothe, *–*, v a. spianare; lisciare; adulare. [dolcezza, f.

smoothness, *–nĕs*, s. l' esser piano, m.;

smother, *smăth'ăr*, v. a. soffocare, sopprimere; –, s. fumo, m.

smoulder, *smŏl'dăr*, v. a. abbrustiare.

smudge, *smăj*, s. macchia, f.; –, v. a. annerire, insudiciare.

smug, *smăg*, a. gentile; lesto, attillato.

smuggle, *smŭg'gl*, v. a. fare contrabbandi.

smuggler, *–glăr*, s. contrabbandiere, m.

smuggling, *–gling*, s. delitto di contrabbando, m.

smut, *smăt*, s. nerezza, f.; sporchezza, f.; –, v. a. sporcare; annebbiare.

smuttiness, *–tinĕs*, s. nerezza di fumo, f.; oscurità, f.

smutty, *–ti*, a. nero, annebbiato; osceno.

snack, *snăk*, s. parte, porzione, f.

snaffle, *snăf'fl*, s. cavezzone, m.

snag, *snăg*, s. nodo, m. & f.

snail, *snăl*, s. lumaca, f.; chiocciola, f.

snake, *snăk*, s. serpe, m.

snap, *snăp*, v. a. acchiappare, pigliare; –, s. strepito, m.

snappers, *–pŭrz*, s. pl. castagnette, f. pl.

snappish, *–pish*, a. bisbetico, stizzoso; **–ly**, ad. con istizza.

snappishness, *–nĕs*, s. umore arcigno, m.

snare, *snăr*, s. laccio, m.; trappola, f.

snarl, *snărl*, v. n. grugnire, brontolare.

snarler, *snăr'lăr*, s. sgridatore, m.

snast, *snăst*, s. moccolo, m.

snatch, *snăch*, v. a. arraffare, acchiappare; –, s. accesso, m.; pezzo, m.; presa, f.

sneak, *snĕk*, v. n. rampicare; –, s. uomo basso, m.

sneer, *snĕr*, v. n. sogghignare; burlare; –, s. riso di dispregio, m.; scherno, m.

sneeringly, *–ingli*, ad. con disprezzo.

sneeze, *snĕz*, v. n. starnutire.

sniff, *snif*, v. n. respirare pel naso.

snigger, *snig'găr*, v. n. sorridere, rider sotto i baffi.

snip, *snip*, s. taglio, m.; scampolo, m.; –, v. a. troncare con forbici, mozzare.

snipe, *snip*, s. beccaccino (uccello); minchione, m. [cicare.

snivel, *sniv'l*, s. moccio, m.; –, v. n. moc-

sniveller, *–ĕlăr*, s. moccicone, m.; gridatore, m. [galuppo, m.

snob, *snŏb*, s. plebeo arricchito, m.;

snobbish, *–ish*, a. da uomo volgare.

snobbishness, *–nĕs*, s. millanteria, f.

snood, *snŏd*, s. fascia, f.; treccia di capelli, f.

snooze, *snŏz*, s. sonno leggiero, m.

snore, *snŏr*, s. il russare, m.; –, v. n. russare. [sare.

snort, *snŏrt*, v. a. sbuffare, soffiare russnout**, *snŏŭt*, s. grugno, muso, grifo, m.; proboscide d' elefante, f.

snow, *snŏ*, s. neve, f.; –, v. n. nevicare.

snow-ball, *–băl*, s. palla di neve, f.

snow-drop, *–drŏp*, s. pianterella primaverile, f. [ticcia, f.

snow-slip, *–slip*, s. lavina, f.

snowy, *snŏ'i*, a. nevoso.

snub, *snŭb*, v. a. riprendere, rabbuffare.

snub-nose, *–nŏz*, s. naso schiacciato, m.

snuff, *snŭf*, s. tabacco (in polvere), m.; lucignolo (d' una candela), m.; smoccolatura, f.; –, v. a. prendere del tabacco; –, v. n. tirare il fiato.

snuff-box, *–bŏks*, s. tabacchiera, f.

snuffers, *snŭf'fărz*, s. pl. smoccolatoie, f. pl.; **–stand**, piattello da smoccolatoie, m.

snuffle, *snŭf'l*, v. a. parlare dal naso.

snuff-taker, *–tăkăr*, s. che prende tabacco, m. [nascosto; **–ly**, ad. comodamente.

snug, *snŭg*, a. serrato, ben fatto, comodo;

so, *sŏ*, ad. così, in questa maniera; **– forth**, e così del resto. [v. n. imbeversi.

soak, *sōk*, v. a. mollare, inzuppare; **–**,

soap, *sōp*, s. sapone, m.; **–**, v. a. insaponare.

soap-ball, *–bȧl*, s. saponetta, f. [nare.

soap-boiler, *–bȯilȧr*, s. saponaio, m.

soap-bubble, *–bȧbl*, s. bolla di sapone, f.

soap-suds, *–sȧdz*, s. saponata, f.

soapy, *sōp'ȳ*, a. saponaceo. [grandi.

soar, *sōr*, v. n. alzarsi; aspirare (a cose

soaring, *–ĭng*, s. volo, m.; impulso, m.

sob, *sŏb*, v. n. singhiozzare; **–**, s. singhiozzo, m.

sober, *sō'bȧr*, a. sobrio; serio; **–ly**, ad. sobriamente; a sangue freddo.

sobriety, *–brī'ȇtȳ*, s. sobrietà, f.; gravità, f.

sociability, *–shȧblȳ'ȇtȳ*, s. sociabilità, f.

sociable, *sō'shȧbl*, a. compagnevole, socievole.

sociably, *–shȧblȳ*, ad. in modo socievole.

social, *–shȧl*, a. sociale, compagnevole; **–ly**, ad. socialmente.

socialist, *–shȧlȳst*, s. socialista, m. [f.

society, *–sī'ȇtȳ*, s. società, f.; associazione,

sock, *sŏk*, s. socco, m.; scappino, m.

socket, *sŏk'ȇt*, s. bocciuolo, m.; cassa (dell'occhio), f.; alveolo (d'un dente), m.

socle, *sō'kl*, s. zoccolo, m. [cia, f.

sod, *sŏd*, s. gleba, zolla di terra, f.; erbuc-

soda, *sō'dȧ*, s. soda, f.

soever, *sōȇv'ȧr*, pn. checchessia, qualunque.

sofa, *sō'fȧ*, s. sofà, m.

soft, *sŏft*, a. molle, dolce; delicato; tenero, morbido; benigno; effeminato; **–ly**, ad. dolcemente; pian piano. [mitigare.

soften, *sŏf'n*, v. a. ammollire, addolcire;

softening, *–ĭng*, s. mitigazione, f.

soft-hearted, *sŏft' hȧrtȇd*, a. di cuor tenero.

softness, *–nȇs*, s. mollezza, delicatezza, f.

soft-spoken, *–spōkȇn*, a. morbido, untuoso, patetico.

soil, *sŏil*, s. suolo, terreno, m.; letame, m.; macchia, bruttura, f.; **–**, v. a. sporcare.

sojourn, *sŏ'jȧrn*, v. n. soggiornare; **–**, s. soggiorno, m. [consolare.

solace, *sŏl'ȧs*, s. consolazione, f.; **–**, v. a.

solar, *sō'lȧr*, a. solare, del sole.

sold, *sōld*, s. soldo, stipendio, m. [tura, f.

solder, *sŏl'dȧr*, v. a. saldare; **–**, s. saldatura.

soldier, *sōl'jȧr*, s. soldato, m.

soldierlike, *–lĭk*, **soldierly**, *–lȳ*, a. soldatesco.

soldiery, *–jȧrȳ*, s. soldatesca, f.

sole, *sōl*, a. solo, unico; semplice; **–ly**, ad. solamente; **–**, s. pianta (del piede), suola, f.; **–**, v. a. mettere le suola.

solecism, *sŏl'ȇsȳzm*, s. solecismo, m.

solemn, *sŏl'ȇm*, a. **–ly**, ad. solennemente.

solemnity, *–lȇm'nȳtȳ*, s. solennità, f.

solemnisation, *–zd'shȧn*, s. solennizzamento, m. [celebrare.

solemnise, *sŏl'ȇmnȳz*, v. a. solennizzare;

solicit, *sŏlȳs'ȳt*, v. a. sollecitare, implorare.

solicitation, *–td'shȧn*, s. sollecitazione, f.

solicitor, *–lȳs'ȳtȧr*, s. sollecitatore, m.; (jur.) procuratore, m.

solicitous, *–lȳs'ȳtȧs*, a. sollecito, attento, diligente; **–ly**, ad. sollecitamente.

solicitude, *–lȳs'ȳtȳd*, s. sollecitudine, f.

solid, *sŏl'ȳd*, a. solido, compatto; durabile; reale; **–ly**, ad. solidamente.

solidify, *–lȳd'ȳfȳ*, v. a. solidare.

solidity, *–ȳtȳ*, s. solidità, f. [liloquio.

soliloquise, *–lȳl'ȯkwȳz*, v. n. fare un so-

soliloquy, *–lȳl'ȯkwȳ*, s. monologo, m.

solitarily, *sŏl'ȳtȧrȳlȳ*, ad. solitariamente.

solitariness, *–ȳtȧrȳnȇs*, s. vita ritirata, f.

solitary, *–ȳtȧrȳ*, a. ritirato; deserto; **–**, s. eremita, romito, m.

solitude, *–ȳtȳd*, s. solitudine, f.

solo, *sō'lō*, s. sonata a solo, f.

solstice, *sŏl'stȳs*, s. solstizio, m.

soluble, *sŏl'ȳbl*, a. solubile.

solution, *sōlȳ'shȧn*, s. soluzione, f.

solve, *sŏlv*, v. a. solvere.

solvency, *sŏl'vȇnsȳ*, s. facoltà di pagare, f.

solvent, *–vȇnt*, a. solvente.

some, *sȧm*, pn. qualche; alcuni, certi, pl.; **–body**, s. qualcheduno, qualcuno, m.; **–how**, ad. in qualche maniera; **–thing**, s. & ad. qualche cosa, f.; un poco, alquanto; **–time**, ad. un tempo, altre volte; **–times**, ad. qualchevolta; **–what**, s. & ad. qualche cosa; un poco, alquanto.

somersault, *sȧm'mȧrsȧlt*, **somerset**, *–sȇt*, s. salto del carpione, m.

somnambulism, *sŏmnȧm'bȳlȳzm*, s. sonnambulismo, m. [m.

somnambulist, *–bȳlȳst*, s. sonnambulo,

somnolence, *sŏm'nȯlȇns*, s. sonnolenza, f.

somnolent, *–lȇnt*, a. sonnolento.

son, *sȧn*, s. figlio, m.; discendente, m.: **–in-law**, genero, m.

sonata, *sōnȧ'tȧ*, s. (mus.) sonata, f.

song, *sŏng*, s. canzone, aria, f.; (**old –**) bagatella, f.

songster, *–stȧr*, s. cantatore, m.

songstress, *–strȇs*, s. cantatrice, f.

sonnet, *sŏn'nȇt*, s. sonetto, m.

sonorous, *sōnō'rȧs*, a. sonoro; **–ly**, ad. con sonorità. [tosto che.

soon, *sȯn*, ad. tosto, subito; **as – as**,

sooner, *sȯn'ȧr*, ad. più tosto.

soonest, *sȯn'ȇst*, a. & ad. il più tosto.

soot, *sȯt*, s. filiggine, caligine, f.

sooth, *sȯth*, s. verità, realtà, f.; **in good –**, veramente, in realtà.

soothe, *sȯth*, v. a. adulare; calmare.

soothsayer, *sȯth'sȧȧr*, s. indovinatore, indovino, m.

sooty, *sȯt'ȳ*, a. filigginoso.

sop, *sŏp*, s. zuppa, f., pan unto, m.

sophism, *sŏf'ȳzm*, s. sofisma, m.

sophist, *sŏf'ȳst*, s. sofista, m.

sophistic(al), *–fȳs'tȳk(ȧl)*, a. sofistico.

sophisticate, *–tȳkȧt*, v. a. sofisticare, falsificare.

sophistry, *sŏf'ȳstrȳ*, s. sofisticheria, f.

soporific, *sŏpȯrȳf'ȳk*, a. & s. sonnifero (m.).

sorcerer, *sŏr'sȧrȧr*, s. stregone, mago, m.

sorceress, *–sȧrȇs*, s. strega, maga, f.

sorcery, *–sȧrȳ*, s. stregoneria, f., ammaliamento, m.

sordid, *sŏr' dĭd*, a. sordido, sporco, avaro; −ly, ad. sordidamente, miseramente. [f.

sordidness, −*nĕs*, s. sordidezza, avarizia.

sore, *sōr*, a. doloroso; crudele; −ly, ad. gravemente; −, s. ulcera, piaga, f.

soreness, −*nĕs*, s. male, m.; dolore, m.

sorrel, *sŏr' ĕl*, a. sauro, castagno; −, s. (bot.) acetosa, f. [tivamente.

sorrily, *sŏr' rĭlĭ*, ad. meschinamente, cat-

sorrow, *sŏr' rō*, s. tristezza, afflizione, f.; −, v. n. affliggersi.

sorrowful, −*fŭl*, a. afflitto, affannato, tristo; −ly, ad. con doglia.

sorry, *sŏr' rĭ*, a. tristo, affannato.

sort, *sŏrt*, s. sorta, specie, qualità, f.; maniera, f. modo, m.; −, v. a. assortire; scerre; distinguere.

sorter, *sŏrt' ŭr*, s. scernitore, m.

sot, *sŏt*, s. minchione, babbuasso, m.

sottish, −*tĭsh*, a. sciocco, goffo; −ly, ad. scioccamente.

soul, *sōl*, s. anima, f.; spirito, m.; uomo, m.

soul-bell, −*bĕl*, s. campana della morte, f.

sound, *sōŭnd*, a. sano; solido, vigoroso, forte; −ly, ad. vigorosamente; fortemente; −, s. suono, m.; rumore, m.; tenta, f.; braccio di mare, m.; −, v. a. tentare; tastare; esaminare; −, v. n. sonare; risonare.

sounding-board, −*ĭng bōrd*, s. cassone (degli organi), m.; cielo d' un pergamo, m.

sounding-lead, −*lĕd*, (−line), s. (mar.) piombino, m.; scandaglio, m.

soundings, *sōŭnd' ĭngs*, s. pl. profondità di mare in cui si trova fondo, f.

soundness, −*nĕs*, s. salute perfetta, sanità, f.; solidità, f.; forza, f.

soup, *sōp*, s. zuppa, minestra, f.

sour, *sōŭr*, a. acido; acrigno; aspro; −ly, ad. aspramente; −, v. a. rendere acido; −, v. n. divenir acido.

source, *sōrs*, s. sorgente, f.; origine, f.

sourish, *sōŭr' ĭsh*, a. acidetto, alquanto agro. [m. pl.

sour-krout, −*krōŭt*, s. cavoli salati,

sourness, −*nĕs*, s. acidità, agrezza, f.

souse, *sōŭs*, s. salamoia, f.; −, v. a. marinare; immergere; −, ad. a un tratto.

south, *sōŭth*, s. mezzodì, meriggio, m.; −, a. meridionale. [a. meridionale.

southerly, *sŭ' thŭrlĭ*, southern, *sŭth' ŭrn*,

southernmost, *sŭth' ŭrnmōst*, a. il più meridionale. [mezzogiorno.

southward, *sōŭth' wŭrd*, ad. verso il

sou(th)wester, *sōŭ(th)wĕst' ŭr*, s. forte libeccio, m.; gran panno inoliato, m.; cappello da marinaio, m.

sovereign, *sŭv' ŭrĭn*, a. & s. sovrano (m).

sovereignly, −*lĭ*, ad. sovranamente.

sovereignty−*tĭ*, s. sovranità, f.

sow, *sŏŭ*, s. troia, scrofa, porca, f. [gere.

sow, *sō*, v. a. ir. seminare, sementare; spar-

sowing-time, −*ĭng tĭm*, s. tempo del sementare, m. [−, v. a. spaziare.

space, *spās*, s. spazio, m.; intervallo, m.;

spacious, *spā' shŭs*, a. spazioso, vasto; −ly, ad. spaziosamente.

spaciousness, −*nĕs*, s. estensione, f.

spade, *spād*, s. zappa, f.; picca, f. (alle carte). [a spanne.

span, *spăn*, s. spanna, f.; −, v. a. misurare

spangle, *spăng' gl*, s. pagliuola, f.; −, v. a. spargere di pagliuole.

spaniel, *spăn' yĕl*, s. bracco, m.

Spanish-fly, *spăn' ĭsh flĭ*, s. cantaride, canterella, f. [m.

Spanish-leather,−*lĕthŭr*, s. marrocchino,

spar, *spăr*, s. sbarra, f.; −, v. n. bisticciarsi, contendere.

spare, *spār*, v. a. risparmiare, riserbare; perdonare; −, v. n. astenersi; −, a. modico, parco, magro.

sparely, −*lĭ*, a. parcamente.

sparing, *spā' rĭng*, a. scarso, raro, economico; −ly, ad. parcamente; frugalmente.

sparingness, −*nĕs*, s. parsimonia, f.

spark, *spărk*, s. scintilla, favilla, f.; damerino, m. [giare; −, s. scintilla, f.

sparkle, *spăr' kl*, v. n. scintillare; spumeg-

sparrow, *spăr' rō*, s. passero, m.

sparrow-hawk, −*hăk*, s. sparviere, m.

sparse, *spărs*, a. & ad. sparso; radamente.

spasm, *spăzm*, s. spasimo, m.

spasmodic, −*mŏd' ĭk*, a. spasmodico.

spatter, *spăt' tŭr*, v. a. sporcare, lordare.

spatula, *spăt' ŭlă*, s. spatola, f.

spavin, *spăv' ĭn*, s. spavento, m.

spawn, *spăn*, s. fregolo, m.; uova di pesce, f. pl.; −, v. a. & n. andare in fregola.

speak, *spēk*, v. a. & n. ir. dire, parlare, conversare, favellare.

speaker, −*ăr*, s. oratore, parlatore, m.

speaking-trumpet, −*ĭng trŭmpĕt*, s. tromba parlante, f. [figgere con lancia.

spear, *spēr*, s. lancia, asta, f.; −, v. a. traf-

special, *spĕsh' ăl*, a. speciale, particolare; −ly, ad. particolarmente.

speciality, −*ăl' ĭtĭ*, specialty, *spĕsh' ăltĭ*, s. specialità, f.

specie, *spĕsh' ĭ*, s. danaro contante, m.

species, *spĕ' shĕz*, s. specie, sorta, f.

specific, *spĕsĭf' ĭk*, a. specifico.

specifically, −*ĭkălĭ*, ad. specificamente.

specification, −*kā' shŭn*, s. specificazione, f.

specify, *spĕs' ĭfĭ*, v. a. specificare. [f.

specimen, −*mĕn*, s. mostra, f.; esempio, m.

specious, *spē' shŭs*, a. specioso; −ly, ad. speciosamente. [v. a. macchiare.

speck, *spĕk*, s. macchia, f.; chiazza, f.; −,

speckle, *spĕk' kl*, v. a. macchiare; chiazzare; −, s. piccola macchia, f.

spectacle, *spĕk' tăkl*, s. spettacolo, m.; −s, pl. occhiali, m. pl.

spectator, −*tā' tŭr*, s. spettatore, m.

spectral, *spĕk' trăl*, a. da spettro.

spectre, *spĕk' tŭr*, s. spettro, fantasma, m.

spectrum, *spĕk' trŭm*, s. spettro, m.

speculate, *spĕk' ŭlāt*, v. n. speculare; considerare. [contemplazione, f.

speculation, −*lā' shŭn*, s. speculazione, f.;

speculative, *spĕk' ŭlātĭv*, a. speculativo; teoretico.

speculator, −*ŭlātŭr*, s. speculatore, m.

speculum, −*ŭlăm*, s. specchio, m.

speech, *spĕch,* s. linguaggio, m.; discorso, m.; (gr.) orazione, f.

speechify, *spĕch'ĭfĭ,* v. n. perorare.

speechless, *–lĕs,* a. muto.

speed, *spēd,* s. fretta, f.; successo, m.; –, v. a. ir. affrettare; aiutare; –, v. n. ir. affrettarsi; riuscire. [mente.

speedily, *–ĭlĭ,* s. ad. speditamente, pronta-

speedy, *spēd'ĭ,* a. spedito, pronto, snello; diligente, premuroso.

spell, *spĕl,* s. incanto, m., malia, f.; –, v. a. & n. r, & ir. compitare; incantare.

spelling, *–ĭng,* s. il compitare, m.

spelling-book, *–bŭk,* s. libretto da compitare, abbici, m.

spelter, *spĕl'tăr,* s. zelamina, f. (metallo).

spend, *spĕnd,* v. a. ir. spendere; consumare; passare; –, v. n. ir. spendersi; consumarsi.

spendthrift, *–thrĭft,* s. spendereccio, m.

spent, *spĕnt,* a. esausto, esaurito, ammortito; a – **ball,** una palla morta, f.

sperm, *spŭrm,* s. sperma, m. [m.

spermaceti, *–măsē'tĭ,* s. bianco di balena,

spew, *spū,* v. n. vomitare.

sphere, *sfēr,* s. sfera, f. [sfericamente.

spheric(al), *sfĕr'ĭk(ăl),* a. sferico; –ly, ad.

spice, *spĭs,* s. spezie, f.; spezierie, f. pl., aromati, m. pl.; (fig.) tintura, f.; –, v. a. condire con ispezierie.

spick-and-span new, *spĭk'ănd spăn nū,* a. nuovo di zecca, affatto nuovo.

spicy, *spī'sĭ,* a. aromatico

spider, *spī'dăr,* s. ragno, m. [piuolo, m.

spigot, *spĭg'ŏt,* s. zipolo, cavicchio, m.;

spike, *spīk,* s. spiga, f.; chiodo grosso, m.; –, v. a. inchiodare.

spill, *spĭl,* v. a. versare; spargere.

spin, *spĭn,* v. a. & n ir. filare; prolungare; girare. [(erba).

spinach, spinage, *spĭn'dj,* s. spinace, m.

spinal, *spī'năl,* a. spinale, di spina.

spindle, *spĭn'dl,* s. fuso, m.; albero (d' una ruota, o d' un torchio), m.

spindle-shanked (-legged), *–shăngkt (lĕgd),* a. di gambe sottili.

spine, *spīn,* s. spina, f.

spinet, *spĭn'ĕt,* s. spinetta, f.; cembalo, m.

spinner, *spĭn'năr,* s. filatore, m.; filatrice, f.

spinney, *spĭn'ĭ,* s. macchia, f. [m.

spinning-wheel, *–nĭng hwĕl,* s. filatoio,

spinster, *spĭn'stăr,* s. filatrice, f.; donzella

spiny, *spī'nĭ,* a. spinoso; difficile. [f.

spiral, *spī'răl,* a. spirale; –ly, ad. a guisa di spira. [mide, f.

spire, *spīr,* s. spira, f.; guglia, f.; piramide, f.

spirit, *spĭr'ĭt,* s. spirito, m.; animo, coraggio, ardore, m.; fantasma, m.; –, v. a. animare, incoraggiare; **to – away,** trafugare, fare scomparire.

spirited, *–ĕd,* a. animato; –ly, ad. vivacemente. [f.

spirit-lamp, *–lămp,* s. lampada a spirito.

spiritless, *–lĕs,* a. depresso, vile, abietto.

spiritual, *spĭr'ĭtăăl,* a. spirituale; –ly, ad. spiritualmente.

spiritualist, *–tăălĭst,* s. spiritualista, m.

spirituality, *–ăl'ĭtĭ,* s. spiritualità, immaterialità, f.

spirituous, *spĭr'ĭtăăs,* a. spiritoso.

spirt, *spŭrt,* v. n. zampillare; scaturire.

spit, *spĭt,* s. spiedo, schidione, m.; –, v. a. & n. ir. mettere nello spiedo; sputare.

spite, *spīt,* s. dispetto, rancore, m.; **in - of,** malgrado; –, v. a. avere in dispetto.

spiteful, *–fŭl,* a. dispettoso, malizioso; –ly, ad. dispettosamente, maliziosamente.

spitefulness, *–nĕs,* s. natura dispettosa, f.

spitfire, *spĭt'fīr,* s. donna violenta, f.

spittle, *spĭt'tl,* s· sputo, m.; saliva, f.

spittoon, *spĭttōn',* s. sputacchiera, f.

splash, *splăsh,* s. zacchera, f.; –, v. a. inzaccherare

splash-board, *–bŏrd,* s. mantelletta, f.

splay, *splā,* v. a. spallare (un cavallo).

splay-footed, *–fŭtĕd,* a. sbilenco.

spleen, *splēn,* s. milza, f.; ipocondria, f.

splendid, *splĕn'dĭd,* a. splendido, magnifico; –ly, ad. splendidamente. [f.

splendour, *–dŭr,* s. splendore, m.; pompa,

splenetic, *splĕnĕt'ĭk,* a. splenetico.

splice, *splīs,* v. a. impiombare, intrecciare.

splint, *splĭnt,* s. stecca, f.

splinter, *splĭn'tăr,* s. sverza, f.; stecca, f.; pezzo (di legno), m.; –, v. a. assicurare con istecche; –, v. n. spaccarsi.

split, *splĭt,* v. a. spaccare, fendere; –, v. n. fendersi.

spoil, *spŏĭl,* v. a. rubare, predare; guastare, desolare, rovinare; –, v. n. corrompersi, guastarsi; –, s. spoglia, preda, f.; rovina, f.

spoiler, *–ăr,* s. rubatore, guastatore, m.

spoke, *spōk,* s. razzo (di ruota), m.

spokesman, *–s'măn,* s. oratore, m.

spoliate, *spō'lĭăt,* v. a. spogliare.

spoliation, *–ĭ'shăn,* s. spogliazione, privazione, f.

sponge, *spŭnj,* s. spugna, f.; –, v. a. nettare con una spugna; scroccare.

sponge-bath, *–băth,* s. bagno inglese, m.

sponger, *–ăr,* s. parassito, m.

sponginess, *spŭn'jĭnĕs,* s. spugnosità, f.

sponging-house, *spŭnj'ĭng hŏŭs,* s. prigione de' debitori, f.

spongy, *spŭnj'ĭ,* a. spugnoso.

sponsor, *spŏn'sŭr,* s. mallevadore, m.; cauzione, f.; padrino, m.

spontaneity, *–tănē'ĭtĭ,* s. spontaneità, f.

spontaneous, *–tā'nĕăs,* a. spontaneo; –ly, ad. spontaneamente.

spool, *spōl,* s. rocchetto, cannello, m.

spoon, *spōn,* s. cucchiaio, m.

spoonful, *–fŭl,* s. cucchiaiata, f.

sporadic, *spŏrăd'ĭk,* a. sporadico.

sport, *spōrt,* s. trastullo, passatempo, m.; ludibrio, m.; caccia, f.; pesca, f.; –, v. a. divertire; –, v. n. diportarsi, spassarsi.

sportive, *–ĭv,* a. leggiadro, scherzoso.

sportiveness, *–nĕs,* s. leggiadria, f., scherzo, giuoco, divertimento, m.

sportsman, *–s'măn,* s. amatore della caccia, pesca ecc., m.

spot, *spŏt*, s. macchia, f.; pezzo, m.; luogo, m.; —, v. a. macchiare, sporcare; variegare, picchiettare. [lato

spotless, *-lĕs*, a. senza macchia, immacolato

spotted, *spŏt'tĕd*, **spotty**, *-tĭ*, a. macchiato, chiazzato.

spousal, *spŏu'zăl*, a. nuziale, matrimoniale; —, s. sposaliazio, m.

spouse, *spŏuz*, s. sposo, m.; sposa, f.

spout, *spŏt*, v. a. sgorgare, gettare; —, v. n. inveire. [s. storcimento, m.

sprain, *sprăn*, v. a. storcere, dislogare; —,

sprat, *sprăt*, s. laterino, m. (pesce).

sprawl, *sprăl*, v. n. stendersi (per terra); **spray**, *sprĕ*, s. frasca, f. [agitarsi.

spread, *sprĕd*, v. a. & n. ir. stendere, spandere, spargere; stendersi, spargersi; —, s. estensione, f.; propagazione, f.

spree, *sprĕ*, s. frascheria, f., baccano, m.

sprig, *sprĭg*, s. ramoscello, m.

sprightliness, *sprīt'lĭnĕs*, s. vivacità, allegria, f.

sprightly, *-lĭ*, a. gaio, spiritoso, svelto.

spring, *sprĭng*, v. a. ir. fare levare; scoprire; —, v. n. ir. sorgere, scaturire, sboccare; lanciare; saltare; spuntare, germogliare; procedere, derivare; —, s. salto, lancio, m.; primavera, f.; sorgente, f.; fessura, f.; molla, f.

springe, *sprĭng*, s. lacciuolo, calappio, m.

springiness, *sprĭng'nĕs*, s. elasticità, forza elastica, f.

spring-tide, *-tīd*, s. alta marea, f.

spring-water, *-wătĭr*, s. sorgente, f.

springy, *sprĭng'ĭ*, a. elastico.

sprinkle, *sprĭng'kl*, v. a. & n. aspergere, spazzare; dispergere. [spruzzo, m.

sprinkling, *-klĭng*, s. aspersione, f.;

sprite, *sprīt*, s. fantasma, m.; visione, f.

sprout, *sprŏt*, s. cavolino, m.; germoglio, broccolo, m.; —, v. n. accestire, germogliare. [latamente; —, v. n. attillarsi.

spruce, *sprōs*, a. attillato; -ly, ad. attill

spruceness, *-nĕs*, s. attillatura, f.

spume, *spūm*, s. spuma, f.; —, v. n. spumare.

spur, *spŭr*, s. sprone, m.; incentivo, stimolo, m.; fretta, f.; —, v. a. spronare; incitare, stimolare. [ficato.

spurious, *spū'rĭŭs*, s. spurio, falso, falsificato

spurn, *spŭrn*, v. a. recalcitrare; sprezzare.

sputter, *spŭt'tĭr*, v. n. sputacchiare; borbottare; barbugliare.

sputterer, *-ĭr*, s. borbottone, f.

spy, *spī*, s. spione, esploratore, m.; —, v. a. spiare, investigare.

spy-glass, *-glăs*, s. telescopio, m.

squab, *skwŏb*, a. paffuto, grosso e forte; senza penne, appena nato; —, s. sofa, letticciuolo, m. [sare; —, s. rissa, f.

squabble, *skwŏb'bl*, v. a. disputare, ris

squabbler, *-tĭr*, s. uomo rissoso, m.

squad, *skwŏd*, s. truppa di soldati, f.

squadron, *-rŏn*, s. squadra, schiera, f.; (mil.) squadrone, m.

squalid, *skwŏl'ĭd*, a. sporco, imbrattato.

squall, *skwăl*, s. turbine di vento, m.; —, v. n. gridare (come uno spaventato).

squally, *-lĭ*, a. tempestoso.

squander, *skwŏn'dăr*, v. a. scialacquare.

square, *skwăr*, a. quadro, onesto, sincecero; robusto, forte; esatto; —, s. quadro, m.; piazza, f.; squadra (strumento), f.; regolarità, f.; —, v. a. quadrare; regolare. aggiustare; —, v. n. accordarsi, convenire.

squareness, *-nĕs*, s. l' esser quadrato, m.

squash, *skwŏsh*, v. a. schiacciare.

squat, *skwŏt*, a. quatto; paffuto; —, v. n. appiattarsi, accosciarsi.

squatter, *-tăr*, s. colono, m.

squaw, *skwă*, s. femmina d' un Indiano, f.

squeak, *skwĕk*, v. n. strillare, gridare; —, s. agrido, strido, m.

squeal, *skwĕl*, v. n. gridare acutamente.

squeamish, *skwĕm'ĭsh*, a. fastidioso, troppo delicato.

squeeze, *skwĕz*, v. a. premere, spremere; stringere; —, s. compressione, f.

squib, *skwĭb*, s. scoppietto, razzo, m.

squint, *skwĭnt*, v. n. essere guercio; (—-eyed), a. bieco, guercio.

Squire, *skwĭr*, s. scudiero, m. (titolo).

squirrel, *skwĭr'rĕl*, s. scoiattolo, m.

squirt, *skwŭrt*, s. siringa, f., schizzatoio, m.; (am.) zerbino, m.; —, v. a. siringare.

stab, *stăb*, v. a. stilettare; —, s. pugnalata, stilettata, f. [f.

stability, *-bĭl'ĭt*, s. stabilità, f.; fermezza,

stable, *stă'bl*, s. stalla, f.; —, v. a. stabil

stabling, *-blĭng*, s. stallaggio, m. [lire.

stack, *stăk*, s. mucchio, cumulo, m.; —, v. a. ammucchiare.

staff, *stăf*, s. bastone, m.; scalino, m.; sostegno, m.; (mil.) stato maggiore, m.

stag, *stăg*, s. cervo, m. [f.; posta, f.

stage, *stădj*, s. teatro, m., scena, f.; osteria,

stage-box, *-bŏks*, s. palco, palchetto, m.

stager, *stă'jăr*, s. attore, m.; praticone, m.

stagger, *stăg'găr*, v. a. scuotere; allarmare; —, v. n. barcollare, titubare, star dubbioso. [shăn, s. stagnamento, m.

stagnancy, *-nănsĭ*, **stagnation**, *-nă'*

stagnant, *-nănt*, a. stagnante.

stagnate, *-nāt*, v. a. stagnare.

staid, *stăd*, a. sobrio; grave.

staidness, *-nĕs*, s. gravità, f.

stain, *stăn*, s. macchia, f.; infamia, f.; —, v. a. macchiare; diffamare.

stainer, *-ăr*, s. tintore, m. [colato.

stainless, *-lĕs*, a. senza macchia, imma

stair, *stăr*, s. grado, m.; scalino, m.; -s, pl. scala, f.

staircase, *-kăs*, s. pozzo della scala, m.

stake, *stăk*, s. palo, m.; posta (al giuoco), f.; —, v. a. munire di pali; scommettere.

stale, *stăl*, a. stantio, vecchio, attempato; —, s. orina, f.; —, v. n. orinare.

staleness, *-nĕs*, s. vecchiezza, f.; scipitaggine, scipidezza, f.

stalk, *stăk*, s. stelo, gambo, m.; stoppia (di grano ecc.), f.; torsolo (di cavolo), m.; andatura pomposa, f.; —, v. n. camminare pomposamente.

stalking-horse, *-ĭng hŏrs*, s. pretesto, m.

stall, *stăl*, s. stalla, f.; mangiatoia, f.; botteghetta, f.; mostra di bottega, f.; sedile (nel teatro), m.; —, v. a. mettere nella stalla.

stallion, *stăl'yŭn*, s. stallone, m.

stalwart, *stăl'wărt*, a. forte, robusto, valoroso.

stamen, *stăm'ĕn*, **stamina,** *—ĭnă*, s. pl. stami (de' fiori), m. pl. |tare; esitare.

stammer, *—măr*, v. n. tartagliare, balbettare.

stammerer, *—ăr*, s. tartaglione, m.

stamp, *stămp*, s. stampa, impronta, f.; impressione, f.; segno, m.; —, v. a. stampare, improntare, battere; imprimere; bollare; calpestare.

stampede, *stămpēd'*, s. sconfitta, rotta, f.

stanch, *stănsh*, v. a. & n. stagnare; stagnarsi.

stand, *stănd*, s. stazione, posta, f.; piazza, f.; stato, grado, m.; pausa, fermata, f., alto lucerniere, candelabro, m.; indugio, imbroglio, m.; difficoltà, f.; —, v. a. ir. sostenere, mantenere; difendere; —, v. n. ir. stare, fermarsi; tenersi; sussistere, dimorare; esser situato; opporsi.

standard, *—ărd*, s. stendardo, m., insegna, f.; misura, f.; modello, m.; regola, norma, f.; grado, m.; prezzo, valore, m.; sistema monetario, m.; valuta, f.

standing, *—ĭng*, a. stabilito, fisso, stagnante; permanente; **—-room,** s. spazio per istar in piedi, m.; —, s. durata, f.; posta, f., luogo, posto, m.

stand-still, *—stĭl*, s. fermata, f., riposo, m.

staple, *stā'pl*, s. emporio (di mercanzie), m.; bocchetta di toppa, f.

star, *stăr*, s. stella, f.; asterisco, m.; attore forestiere, m.; —, v. a. spargere.

starboard, *—bŏrd*, s. lato destro della nave, m.   [amidare.

starch, *stărch*, s. amido, m.; —, v. a. inetare, *stăr*, v. a. guardare fissamente; —, s. guardo fisso, m.

staringly, *—ĭnglĭ*, ad. con occhi fissi.

stark, *stărk*, a. rigido; vero, puro; —, ad. tutto, affatto.

starless, *—lĕs*, a. senza stelle.

starling, *—lĭng*, s. storno, m. (uccello); pigna (di ponte), f.

starred, *stărd*, **starry,** *stăr'rĭ*, a. stellato.

start, *stărt*, v. a. allarmare, turbare; scoprire; —, v. n. saltare, dare un salto; levarsi, partire; —, s. salto, risalto, m.; primo passo, m.; partenza (delle mosse), f.

starter, *—ăr*, s. che da le mosse, autore, m.

starting-point, **(—-post),** *—ĭng pŏĭnt,* *(—pŏst),* s. mosse, f. pl.

startle, *stăr'tl*, v. n. tremar di paura; strabiliare; —, s. salto improvviso, m.; subita impressione di paura, f.

starvation, *stărvā'shŭn,* s. morte cagionata dalla fame, f.

starve, *stărv*, v. a. far morire di fame; affamare; —, v. n. morire di fame; morire di freddo.

starveling, *—lĭng,* s. affamatuzzo, m.

state, *stăt*, s. stato, m.; grado, m.; condizione, f.; pompa, f.; dignità, f.; —, v. a. stabilire; regolare, ordinare, determinare.

stateliness, *—lĭnĕs,* s. pompa, grandezza, f.

stately, *—lĭ,* a. & ad. grande; magnifico; pomposamente.   [ziato, m.

statement, *—mĕnt,* s. racconto circonstanstatesman,*—s'măn,* s. politico, m.

statesmanship, *—shĭp,* s. politica, f.

statics, *stăt'ĭks,* s. pl. statica, f.

station. *stā'shŭn.* s. posto, m.; staggio, m.; stazione, f.; abitazione, f.; grado, m., condizione, f.; (rail.) stazione, f., atrio (della strada ferrata), m.; —, v. a. porre in un posto.   [fermo.

stationary, *—shănări,* a. stazionario

stationer, *—ăr,* s. cartolaio, m.; che vende carta, m.; librajo, m.

stationery, *—ări,* s. vendita di carta, f.

statist, *stă'tĭst,* s. politico, m.

statistic(al), *stătĭs'tĭk(ăl),* a. statistico.

statistics, *—tĭks,* s. pl. statistica, f.

statuary, *stăt'ŭărĭ,* s. scultore, m.

statue, *stăt'ŭ,* s. statua, f.

stature, *stăt'ŭr,* s. statura, f.

statute, *stăt'ŭt,* s. statuto, m., legge, f.

stave, *stāv,* v. a. sfondare (un barile), —s, s. pl. doghe (d' una botte), f. pl.

stay, *stā,* v. a. ir. ritenere, fermare; appoggiare; —, v. n. ir. stare; fermarsi; soggiornare; indugiare, aspettare; —, s. soggiorno, m.; sostegno, m.; —s, pl. busto da donna, m.   [in vece di.

stead, *stĕd,* s. luogo, m.; vece, f.; **in - of,**

steadfast, *—făst,* a. fermo, sodo, fisso; **-ly,** ad. fermamente, costantemente.

steadfastness, *—făstnĕs,* s. fermezza, f.; costanza, f.

steadily, *—ĭlĭ,* ad. con fermezza.   [f.

steadiness, *—ĭnĕs,* s. solidità, f.; fermezza,

steady, *stĕd'ĭ,* a. fermo, saldo; —, v. a. render fermo.

steak, *stāk,* s. fetta sottile di carne, f.

steal, *stēl,* v. a. & n. ir. rubare, involare.

stealth, *stĕlth,* s. furto, m.; **by —,** di soppiatto, di furto.

stealthily, *—ĭlĭ,* ad. furtivamente.

stealthy, *stĕlth'ĭ,* a. clandestino, segreto.

steam, *stĕm,* s. vapore, fumo, m.; —, v. a. cuocere a vapore; —, v. n. vaporare, fumare.

steam-bath,—*băth,* s. bagno a vapore, m.

steam-boat,—*bŏt,* s. vascello a vapore, m.

steam-boiler,—*bŏĭlăr,* s. caldaia a vapore, f.   [vapore.

steam-engine, —*ĕnjĭn,* s. macchina a

steamer, —*ăr,* s. vascello a vapore, m.

steam-power, —*pŏwăr,* s. forza di vasteed, *stĕd,* s. corsiero, m.   [pore, f.

steel, *stēl,* s. acciaio, m.; fucile, m.; —, v. a. indurare.   [l' acciaio, acciaiera, f.

steel-works, —*wŭrkz,* s. pl. fucina per

steelyard, —*yărd,* s. stadera, f.

steep, *stēp,* a. scosceso, dirupato; —, s. precipizio, m.; —, v. a. immollare; tuffare.

steeple, *stēp'l,* s. campanile, m.

steeple-chase, —*chās,* s. corso a gara sopra ostacoli, m.   [f.

steepness, *stēp'nĕs,* s. pendio, m., scesa,

steer, *stēr,* s. bue giovane, giovenco, m.; —, v. a. guidare, governare; reggere.

steerage, —*ăj,* s. timone, m.; governo, m.

steerage - passenger, –păssēnjăr, s. viaggiatore di terza classe, m.   [m.
steerage-way, –wŏd, s. solco della nave,
stellar, stĕl'lăr, a. stellare.
stem, stĕm, s. stelo, m.; gambo, m.; sprone (d' un naviglio), m.; razza, f.; –, v. a. veleggiare a ritroso.
stench, stĕnsh, s. puzza, f., fetore, m.
stencil, stĕn'sĭl, s. traforo, m.   [m.
stenographer, stĕnŏg'răfăr, s. stenografo,
stenographic, –ŏgrăf'ĭk, a. stenografico.
step, stĕp, s. passo, m.; vestigio, m.; scalino, m.; soglia, f.; –, v. n. andare, far un passo.
step-brother, –brŭthăr, s. fratellastro, m.
step-daughter, –dătăr, s. figliastra, f.
step-father, –făthăr, s. patrigno, m.
step-mother, –mŭthăr, s. matrigna, f.
stepping-stone, –ping stŏn, s. sasso da mettervi su il piede, m.
step-sister, –sĭstăr, s. sorellastra, f.
step-son, –sŭn, s. figliastro, m.
stereotype, stĕr'ĕŏtĭp, s. stereotipia, f.; –, v. a. stereotipare.
sterility, –ĭl'ĭtĭ, s. sterilità, aridità, f.
sterling, stŭr'lĭng, a. vero, puro; –, s. sterlino, m.
stern, stŭrn, a. severo, austero, torvo, brusco; –, s. (mar.) poppa, f.
sternly, –lĭ, ad. con aria torva.
stethoscope, stĕth'ŏskŏp, s. (med.) stetoscopio, m.
stevedore, stĕ'vĕdŏr, s. lustratore, m.
stew, stŭ, s. stufa, f.; –, v. a. stufare.
steward, –ărd, s. maggiordomo, maestro di casa, m.; dispensiere (d' una nave), m.
stewardship, –shĭp, s. carica di maggiordomo, f.
stew-span, stŭ'păn, s. bastardella, f.
stick, stĭk, s. bastone, m.; stecco, m.; canna, f.; –, v. a. appiccare, ficcare; spingere; –, v. n. appiccarsi, appigliarsi, fermarsi.
stickiness, –nĕs, s. viscosità, f.
stickle, stĭk'l, v. n. seguitare una parte; disputare.   [(in duello), m.
stickler, –lăr, s. partigiano, m.; secondo
sticky, stĭk'ĭ, a. viscoso, glutinoso.
stiff, stĭf, a. rigido, aspro; ostinato; fermo; costante; stentato; –ly, ad. ostinatamente.
stiffen, stĭf'fn, v. a. indurare; rendere rigido; –, v. n. diventare duro.
stiff-neck, –nĕk, s. torcicollo, m.
stiffness, –nĕs, s. rigidezza, f.; caparbietà,
stifle, stĭf'l, v. a. soffocare.   [f.
stigma, stĭg'mă, s. segno d' infamia, m.
stigmatise, –tĭz, v. a. stimatizzare.
stile, stĭl, s. barriera, f.; gnomone, m.; stilo, m.
stiletto, stĭlĕt'tŏ, s. stiletto, pugnale, m.
still, stĭl, a. quieto, tranquillo; –ly, ad. fin adesso, ancora, sempre; –, s. silenzio, m.; limbicco, m.; –, v. a. calmare; distillare.   [lare.
still-born, –bŏrn, a. morto nato.
stillness, –nĕs, s. calma, quiete, f.
stilts, stĭlts, s. pl. trampoli, m. pl.
stimulant, stĭm'dŭlănt, s. stimolante, m.
stimulate, –ŭlăt, v. a. stimolare, spronare.

stimulation, –ld'shŭn, s. stimolo, m.
stimulative, stĭm'ŭlătĭv, a. stimolativo.
stimulus, –ŭlŭs, s. stimolo, m.
sting, stĭng, s. spina, f., ago, m.; stimolo, m.; rimorso, m.; –, v. a. ir. pungere; trafiggere.
stingily, stĭn'jĭlĭ, ad. avaramente.
stinginess, –jĭnĕs, s. avarizia, f.   [f.
stinging-nettle, stĭngĭng'nĕttl, s. ortica,
stingy, stĭn'jĭ, a. avaro, taccagno, sordido, spilorcio.   [–, v. n. ir. puzzare.
stink, stĭngk, s. puzzo, fetore, m., puzza, f.;
stint, stĭnt, v. a. limitare; –, s. limite, m.
stipend, stĭ'pĕnd, s. stipendio, salario, m.
stipendiary, –pĕn'dĭărĭ, a. stipendiato.
stipulate, stĭp'dŭlt, v. n. stipulare.
stipulation, –lă'shŭn, s. stipulazione, f., contratto, m.
stir, stŭr, s. strepito, rumore, fracasso, scompiglio, m.; –, v. a. muovere; agitare, scuotere; to – up, eccitare, incitare, irritare; –, v. n. muoversi; agitarsi, scuotersi.
stirrup, stĭr'răp, s. staffa, f.   [staffa, f.
stirrup-leather, –lĕthăr, s. striscia della
stitch, stĭch, s. punto (fatto coll' ago), m.; maglia, f.; –, v. a. appuntare; cucire (un libro); pungere.
stoat, stŏt, s. puzzola, f. (insetto).
stock, stŏk, s. tronco, gambo, m.; stelo, fusto, m.; manico, m.; fondo, capitale, principale, m.; razza, schiatta, f.; cravatta, f., minchione, sciocco, m.; –, v. a. fornire, provvedere.
stockade, –kăd', s. palizzata, f.
stock-fish, –fĭsh, s. baccalà, f., stoccafisso, m.
stock-holder, –hŏldăr, s. azionario, m.
stocking, –ĭng, s. calza, f.
stock-jobber, –jŏb'băr, s. chi specula nei fondi pubblici.
stock-still, –stĭl, a. immobile.
stoic, stŏ'ĭk, s. stoico, m.
stoical, stŏ'ĭkăl, a. stoico; –ly, ad. alla stoica, stoicamente.
stoicism, –ĭsĭzm, s. stoicismo, m.
stoker, stŏ'kăr, s. fochista, m.
stole, stŏl, s. stola, f.
stomach, stŭm'ăk, s. stomaco, m.; appetito, m.; –, v. a. & n. offendersi.
stomacher, –ăkăr, s. busto da donna, m.
stomachic, stŏmăk'ĭk, a. & s. stomatico, (m.).
stone, stŏn, s. pietra, f.; nocciolo (della frutta), m.; granello (dell' uva), m.; peso (di quattordici libbre), m.; –, a. (fatto di) pietra; –, v. a. lapidare; snocciolare.
stone-blind, –blĭnd, a. cieco come una talpa.   [scarpellino, m.
stone-cutter, –kăttăr, s. tagliapietre,
stone-dead, –dĕd, a. disteso morto.
stoning, stŏn'ĭng, s. lapidazione, f.
stony, stŏn'ĭ, a. pietroso; duro.
stool, stŏl, s. sgabello, seggio, m.
stoop, stŏp, v. n. chinarsi, piegarsi; calarsi; abbassarsi; –, s. inclinazione, f., abbassamento, m.
stoopingly, –ĭnglĭ, ad. con inchino.
stop, stŏp, v. a. arrestare, ritardare, in-

dugiare; stagnare; turare; —, v. n. fermarsi, fare alto; —, s. pausa, f.; ostacolo,
stop-cock, –kŏk, s. chiave, f.   [m.
stoppage, –pdj, **stopping** –pĭng, s. impedimento, m.; ostruzione, f.; (rail.) tempo di riposo, m.
stopple, stŏp'pl, s. turacciolo, m.
stop-watch, –wŏch, s. oriuolo da corsa, m.
storage, stŏr'āj, s. magazzinaggio, m.
store, stŏr, s. abbondanza, quantità, f., viveri, m. pl.; —, v. a. munire; provvedere.
store-keeper, –kēpŭr, s. magazziniere, m.
storey, stŏ'rē, s. piano (d' una casa), m.
storied, stŏ'rĭd, a. istoriato; abbellito.
stork, stŏrk, s. cicogna, f.
storm, stŏrm, s. tempesta, burrasca, f.; assalto, m.; —, v. a. dare un assalto; —, v. n. tempestare.
stormily, –ĭlĭ, ad. tempestosamente.
stormy, stŏrm'ĭ, a. tempestoso; furioso.
story, stŏ'rĭ, s. storia, f.; favola, f.; piano (d' una casa), m.
stout, stŏŭt, a. robusto, valoroso; ostinato; –ly, ad. fortemente, bravamente; ostinatamente; —, s. cervogia forte, f.
stoutness, –nĕs, s. forza, f.; bravura, f.
stove, stŏv, s. stufa, f.   [care.
stow, stŏ, v. a. stivare; assettare; collowage, –āj, s. magazzinaggio, m.; affitto del magazzino, m.
straggle, străg'gl, v. n. vagare.
straggler, –glŭr, s. soldato ramingo, vagabondo, m.
straight, strāt, a. diritto, stretto; —, ad. direttamente, immediatamente.   [diritto.
straighten, strāt'n, v. a. dirizzare, far diritto.
straightforward, –fŏrwărd, a. franco; leale.   [rettitudine, f.
straightforwardness, –nĕs, s. onestà, rettitudine, f.
straightways, –wāz, ad. immediatamente, subito.
strain, strān, s. sforzo, m.; storcimento, m.; razza, f.; suono, m.; canzone, aria, f.; stile, m.; —, v. a. spremere, premere, stringere; colare; violentare; —, v. n.
strainer, –ŭr, s. colatoio, m.   [sforzarsi.
strait, strāt, a. stretto, angusto; intimo; rigoroso; penoso; –ly, ad. strettamente; —, s. stretto, m.; difficoltà, f.; penuria, f.
straiten, strā'tn, v.a. stringere, ristringere.
straitness, strāt'nĕs, s. strettezza, f.; difficoltà, f.; rigore, m.
strand, strănd, s. piaggia, f., lido, m.; —, v. n. dare sulle secche.
strange, strānj, a. strano, bizzarro; –ly, ad. stranamente; meravigliosamente.
strangeness, –nĕs, s. stranezza, f.; singolarità, f.   [m.
stranger, străn'jŭr, s. straniero, forestiero.
strangle, străn'gl, v. a. strangolare.   [f.
strangulation, –gŭlā'shŭn, s. strozzatura, f.; cintura, f.
strap, străp, s. correggia, striscia di cuoio, f.; cintura, f.
strapping, –pĭng, a. grande, grosso.
stratagem, străt'ăjĕm, s. stratagemma, astuzia, f.
strategic, strătĕj'ĭk, a. strategico.
strategy, străt'ĕjĭ, s. strategia, f.

stratum, strā'tŭm, s. strato, m.; letto, m.
straw, strā, s. paglia, f.; festuca, f.; niente, m.
straw-bed, –bĕd, s. pagliericcio, m.
strawberry, –bĕrrĭ, s. fragola, f.
straw-cutter, –kŭttŭr, s. tritapaglia, m.
stray, strā, a. sviato; —, s. vagabondo, m.; —, v. n. sviare, traviare.
streak, strēk, s. striscia, riga, f.; —, v. a. strisciare, rigare.
stream, strēm, s. corrente, f., ruscello, m.; —, v. n. scorrere, zampillare; gettare raggi.
streamer, –ŭr, s. pennoncello, m., banderuola, f.; fiamma, f.
street, strēt, s. strada, via, f.
street-door, –dōr, s. porta dinanzi, f.
strength, strĕngth, s. forza, f.; vigore, f.; energia, f.   [afforzare.
strengthen, strĕng'thn, v. a. fortificare, afforzare.
strenuous, strĕn'ŭŭs, a. strenuo, valoroso; attivo; –ly, ad. strenuamente, valorosamente.   [lore, m.; coraggio, m.
strenuousness, –nĕs, s. arditezza, f., valore, m.; coraggio, m.
stress, strĕs, s. importanza, f.; forza, f.; sforzo della voce, m.
stretch, strĕch, v. a. stendere, estendere, allargare; —, v. n. distendersi; sforzarsi; —, s. estensione, f., spazio, m.
stretcher, –ŭr, s. ordigno da stendere, m.
strew, strŏ, v. a. ir. spandere; spargere.
striated, strĭ'ātĕd, a. scanalato.
strict, strĭkt, a. esatto, preciso, stretto; rigoroso, severo; –ly, ad. esattamente, severamente.   [f.
strictness, –nĕs, s. esattezza, f.; severità, f.
stricture, strĭk'tŭr, s. colpo, tocco, tratto, m.; nota, f.   [—, s. passo lungo, m.
stride, strĭd, v. a. ir. stendere le gambe; —, s. passo lungo, m.
strife, strĭf, s. disputa, rissa, contesa, f.
strike, strĭk, v. a. & n. ir. percuotere; battere, colpire, ferire; toccare; spaventare; cessare da lavorare; sonare; —, s. rasiera, f.; (of workmen) bandimento, m.
striking, strĭ'kĭng, a. sorprendente; –ly, ad. meravigliosamente.
string, strĭng, s. corda, f., laccio, m.; fibra, f.; filo, m.; —, v. a. ir. mettœr le corde; render teso, stirare; infilzare.
stringent, strĭn'jĕnt, a. stringente; costrittivo; rigido.
stringy, strĭng'ĭ, a. fibroso; elastico.
strip, strĭp, s. striscia (di panno), f.; —, v. a. spogliare, privare di.   [v. a. listare.
stripe, strĭp, s. striscia, f.; colpo, m.; —,
strive, strĭv, v. n. ir. sforzarsi; dimenarsi; opporsi, fare resistenza.   [f.
striving, strĭv'ĭng, s. sforzo, m.; contesa, f.
stroke, strŏk, s. percossa, f., colpo, m.; tocco, m.; pennata, f.; —, v. a. accarezzare.
stroll, strŏl, v. n. vagare, vagabondare; —, s. scorsa, f.
strolling-player, –ĭng plăŭr, s. commediante ambulante, m. & f.
strong, strŏng, a. forte, potente; vigoroso, robusto; violento; –ly, ad. fortemente, con energia.
strong-box, –bŏks, s. forziere, m.
strong-hold, –hōld, s. fortezza, f.

strong-room, –rŏm, s. stanza d' arresto, f.
strop, strŏp, s. striscia da rasoio, f.
strophe, strŏf'ĕ, s. strofa, strofe, f.
structure, strŭk' tŭr (–chŭr), s. struttura,
f.; edifizio, m.   [combattere.
struggle, strŭg' gl, v. n. sforzarsi; agitarsi,
struggling, –glĭng, s. scossa, lotta, f.;
contesa, f.
strum, strŭm, v, n.strimpellare, sonar male.
strumpet, –pĕt, s. bagascia, f.
strut, strŭt, v. n. pavoneggiarsi; –, s.
il camminare affettato, m.
stub, stŭb, s. ceppo, tronco, m.
stubble, stŭb' bl, s. stoppia, f.
stubborn, –bŏrn, a. ostinato, pertinace;
–ly, ad. ostinatamente, pertinacemente.
stubbornness, –nĕs, s. ostinazione, pertinacia, f.   [barba.
stubbly, stŭb' lĭ, a. setoloso, ispido (d' una
stubby, –bĭ, a. corto e grosso, paffuto.
stucco, stŭk' kō, s. stucco, m.
stud, stŭd, s. borchia, f.; palo, m.; –, v. a.
guarnire di borchie.   [m.
student, stŭ' dĕnt, s. studente, m.; letterato
stud-horse, stŭd' hŏrs, s. stallone, m.
studied, stŭd' ĭd, a. studioso; letterato;
versato.   [tore), m.
studio, stŭd' ĭŏ, s. studio (di pittore, scul-
studious, stŭ' dĭŭs, a. studioso; attento;
–ly, ad. studiosamente, con diligenza.
study, stŭd' ĭ, s. studio, m.; applicazione,
diligenza, f.; gabinetto, m.; –, v. a. studiare; osservare; –, v. n. studiarsi; applicarsi.
stuff, stŭf, s. stoffa, f.; materia, f.; drappo,
m.; –, v. a. riempire, stivare; satollare;
–, v. n. mangiare con voracità.
stuffing, –fĭng, s. borra, f.
stuffy, –fĭ, a. grave, pesante (dell' aria).
stultify, stŭl' tĭfĭ, v. a. istupidire.
stumble, stŭm' bl, v. n. inciampare; errare,
fallire; –, s. passo falso, m.
stumbling-block, –blĭng blŏk, s. inciampo, m.; ostacolo, m.
stump, stŭmp, s. tronco, ceppo, toppo. m.;
moncone, m.; –, v. n. (off) andarsene.
stun, stŭn, v, a. stordire, sbalordire.
stunner, –nŭr, s. cosa sorprendente, f.
stunt, –t, v. a. impedire l' accrescimento.
stupefaction, stŭpĕfăk' shŭn, s. stupore,
m.
stupefy, stŭ' pĕfĭ, v. a. istupidire, stordire.
stupendous, –pĕn' dŭs, a. stupendo, meraviglioso.   [pidamente.
stupid, stŭ' pĭd, a. stupido; –ly, ad. stu-
stupidity, –pĭd' ĭtĭ, s. stupidità, f.
stupor, stŭ' pŏr, s. stupore, m.; intormen-
timento, m.   [natamente.
sturdily, stŭr' dĭlĭ, ad. bruscamente; osti-
sturdiness, –dĭnĕs, s. caparbietà, insolenza, f.; rigidezza, robustezza, forza, f.
sturdy, –dĭ, a. caparbio; robusto, gagliardo. forte.
sturgeon, –jŭn, s. storione, m. (pesce).
stutter, stŭt' tŭr, v. n. tartagliare; balbet-
sty, stĭ, s. porcile, m., stia, f.   [tare.
stye –, s. orzaiuolo, m.

style, stĭl, s. stile, m.; titolo, m.; forma,
f.; modo, m.; pratica, f.; –, v. a. chiamare, appellare.
stylish, stĭl' ĭsh, a. elegante; civettone.
suave, swăv, a. soave.
suavity, swăv' ĭtĭ, s. soavità, dolcezza, f.;
benignità, f.   [(m).
subaltern, sŭb' ăltŭrn, a. & s. subalterno
subdivide, –dĭvĭd', v. a. suddividere.
subdivision, –vĭzh' ŭn, s. suddivisione, f.
subdual, –dŭ' ăl, s. soggiogamento, m.
subdue, –dŭ', v. a. soggiogare, superare,
vincere; mortificare.
subject, sŭb' jĕkt, a. soggetto, suddito;
–, s. soggetto, m.; (gr.) nominativo, m.;
–, –jĕkt', v. a. soggettare, sottoporre.
subjection, –jĕk' shŭn, s. soggezione, sot-
tomessione, f.
subjoin, –jŏĭn', v. a. soggiungere.
subjugate, sŭb' jŭgăt, v. a. soggiogare.
subjugation, –gă' shŭn, s. soggiogamento,
m.   [tivo, m.
subjunctive, –jŭngk' tĭv, a. (gr.) soggiun-
sublet, –lĕt', v. a. subaffittare.
sublimate, stŭd' lĭmăt, v. a. (chem.) sublimato, m.; –, v. a. sublimare.
sublime, –lĭm', a. sublime; eccelso; –ly,
ad. in modo sublime; –, s. sublime, m.
sublimity, –lĭm' ĭtĭ, s. sublimità, eccellenza, f.   [restre.
sublunary, –lŏ' nărĭ, a. sublunare, ter-
submarine, –mărēn', a. sul fondo del mare.
submerge, –mărj', v. a. sommergere.
submersion, –mŭr' shŭn, s. sommersione,
f., allagamento, m.
submission, –mĭsh' ŭn, s. sommissione, f.
submissive, –mĭs' sĭv, a. sommissivo;
–ly, ad. umilmente.
submissiveness, –nĕs, s. sommissione, f.
submit, –mĭt', v. a. & n. sommettere;
sommettersi.   [m.
sub-officer, sŭb' ŏfĭsŭr, s. sottuffiziale,
subordinate, –ŏr' dĭnăt, a. subordinato;
inferiore; –ly, ad. subordinatamente; –,
v. a. subordinare.   [zione, f.
subordination, –nă' shŭn, s. subordina-
suborn, –ŏrn', v. a. subornare.
subornation, –nă' shŭn, s. subornazione, f.
sub-poena, –pē' nă, s. (jur.) citazione sotto
pena, f.; –, v. a. citare sotto pena.
subrogate, sŭb' rŏgăt, v. a. sostituire.
subs, sŭbz, s. pl. (fam.) sottuffiziali, m. pl.
subscribe, –skrĭb', v. a. soscrivere; segnare; –, v. n. consentire.
subscriber, –skrĭ' bŭr, s. soscrittore, m.
subscription, –skrĭp' shŭn, s. soscri-
zione, f.   [–ly, ad. sussequentemente.
subsequent, sŭb' sĕkwĕnt, a. sussequente;
subserve, –sŭrv', v. a. aiutare, secondare; servire.   [f.; utilità, f.
subserviency, –sŭr' vĭĕnsĭ, s. assistenza,
subservient, –vĭĕnt, a. ausiliario, utile.
subside, –sĭd', v. n. abbassarsi; andar a
fondo.   [m.; abbassamento, m.
subsidence, –sĭ' dĕns, s. l' andare a fondo,
subsidiary, –sĭd' ĭărĭ, a. sussidiario.
subsidise, sŭb' sĭdĭz, v. a. sovvenire.

subsidy, *–sĭdĭ*, s. sussidio, m.; soccorso (di danari), m., sovvenzione, f.

subsist, *–sĭst'*, v. n. sussistere, esistere. [f.

subsistence, *–ĕns*, s. sussistenza, esistenza.

substance, *sŭb' stăns*, s. sostanza, f.; essenza, f.; contenuto, m.

substantial, *–stăn' shăl*, a. sostanziale, essenziale, reale; forte; **-ly**, ad. sostanzialmente.   [fare esistere.

substantiate, *–shĭăt*, v. a. sostanziare,

substantive, *sŭb' stăntĭv*, s. (gr.) sostantivo, m.; **-ly**, ad. sostantivamente.

substitute, *sŭb' stĭtăt*, v. a. sostituire.

substitution, *–tŭ' shăn*, s. sostituzione, f.

substratum, *–strā' tŭm*, s. strato inferiore, m.   [scampo, m.

subterfuge, *sŭb' tŭrfāj*, s. sotterfugio,

subterranean, *–tĕrrā' nĕăn*, a. sotterraneo.

subtile, *sŭb' tĭl*, **subtle**, *săt' l*, a. sottile; fino, delicato; acuto; penetrante; **-ly**, ad. sottilmente.

subtility, *–tĭl' ĭtĭ*, **subtlety**, *săt' tĭ*, s. sottigliezza, delicatezza, astuzia, f.

subtly, *săt' lĭ*, ad. sottilmente, astutamente.

subtract, *sŭbtrăkt'*, v. a. (ar.) sottrarre.

suburb, *sŭb' ŭrb*, s. subborgo, m.

suburban, *–ăr' băn*, a. suburbano.

subvention, *–vĕn' shăn*, s. sovvenzione, f., sussidio, m.   [rovina, f.

subversion, *–vŭr' shăn*, s. sovversione,

subversive, *–sĭv*, a. sovversivo.

subvert, *–vŭrt'*, v. a. sovvertire.

subway, *sŭb' wā*, s. passaggio sotterraneo, m.

succeed, *sŭksēd'*, v. a. succedere, seguire; **-**, v. n. riuscire.

success, *–sĕs'*, s. successo, evento, m.

successful, *–fŭl*, a. fortunato, propizio; **-ly**, ad. con successo.

succession, *–sĕsh' ăn*, s. successione, f.; eredità, f.; serie, f.

successive, *–sĕs' sĭv*, a. successivo; **-ly**, ad. successivamente.

successor, *–sĕs' săr*, s. successore, m.

succinct, *–sĭngkt'*, a. succinto, conciso; **-ly**, ad. con brevità.

succour, *sŭk' kŭr*, s. soccorso, aiuto, m.; **-**, v. a. soccorrere, aiutare, assistere.

succulence, *sŭk' kŭlĕns*, s. sugosità, f.

succulent, *–kŭlĕnt*, a. sugoso.

succumb, *–kŭm'*, v. n. soccombere.

such, *sŭch*, pn. tale, simile; **- as**, quelli, quelle.   [imbevere.

suck, *sŭk*, v. a. & n. succiare; attrarre;

sucker, *–ăr*, s. succiatore, m.; cannoncello (d' una tromba), m.; germoglio, m.

sucking-pig, *–ĭng pĭg*, s. porcello di latte, m.

suckle, *sŭk' l*, v. a. nutrire con latte.

suckling, *–lĭng*, s. bambino allattato, m.; agnello di latte, m.

suction, *sŭk' shăn*, s. succhiamento, m.

sudden, *sŭd' dn*, a. subitaneo, improvviso; **-ly**, ad. subitaneamente.

suddenness, *–nĕs*, s. subitaneità, f.

sudorific, *sŭdŏrĭf' ĭk*, a. & s. (medicamento)

suds, *sŭdz*, s. lisciva, f.   [sudorifero (m.).

sue, *sū*, v. a. citare in giudizio; supplicare.

suet, *sū' ĕt*, s. grasso duro (di carne), m.

suffer, *sŭf' făr*, v. a. tollerare; permettere; **-**, v. n. soffrire, patire.

sufferable, *–ăbl*, a. sopportabile.

sufferance, *–ăns*, s. tolleranza, f.

sufferer, *–ăr*, s. sofferitore, m.

suffering, *–ĭng*, s. pena, f., dolore, m.

suffice, *sŭffīs'*, v. n. bastare.

sufficiency, *–fĭsh' ĕnsĭ*, s. sufficienza, f.; capacità, f.   [a bastanza.

sufficient, *–ĕnt*, a. sufficente; **-ly**, ad.

suffocate, *sŏf' fōkăt*, v. a. soffogare.

suffocation, *–kā' shăn*, s. soffogazione, f.

suffragan, *sŭf' frăgăn*, s. vescovo suffraganeo, m.

suffrage, *–frāj*, s. suffragio, voto, m.

suffuse, *–fāz'*, v. a. spandere, spargere.

suffusion, *–fū' zhăn*, s. suffusione, f.; spargimento, m.

sugar, *shŭg' ăr*, s. zucchero, m.; **-**, v. a. inzuccherare; render dolce.

sugar-basin, *–băsn*, s. zuccheriera, f.

sugar-cane, *–kăn*, s. canna zuccherina, f.

sugar-loaf, *–lōf*, s. pane di zucchero, m.

sugar-plum, *–plŭm*, s. confetto, zuccherino, m.   [zucchero, f. pl.

sugar-tongs, *–tŏngz*, s. pl. mollette da

sugary, *–ărĭ*, a. zuccheroso, inzuccherato.

suggest, *săjĕst'*, v. a. suggerire; insinuare.

suggestion, *–jĕst' yăn*, s. suggestione, insinuazione, f.; sollecitazione, f.

suggestive, *–jĕs' tĭv*, a. suggestivo.

suicidal, *sŭĭsī' dăl*, a. da suicidio.

suicide, *sū' ĭsīd*, s. suicidio, m.

suit, *sūt*, s. assortimento, m.; richesta, preghiera, f.; processo, m.; **-**, v. a. adattare, assortire, **-**, v. n. adattarsi, accordarsi; corrispondere.

suitable, *–ăbl*, a. convenevole, conforme.

suitableness, *–ăblnĕs*, s. convenienza, conformità, f.

suitably, *–ăblĭ*, ad. convenevolmente, conformemente.

suite, *swēt*, s. seguito, m., compagnia, f.

suitor, *sū' tăr*, s. supplicante, m.; amante, m.; litigatore, m.

sulkiness, *sŭl' kĭnĕs*, s. cattivo umore, m.

sulky, *sŭl' kĭ*, a. arcigno, torvo.

sullen, *sŭl' lĕn*, a. stizzoso, ritroso; **-ly**, ad. ostinatamente.   [caparbietà, f.

sullenness, *–nĕs*, s. cattivo umore, m.;

sully, *sŭl' lĭ*, v. a. macchiare, sporcare.

sulphur, *sŭl' fŭr*, s. zolfo, solforico, m.

sulphureous, *–fū' rĕŭs*, a. sulfureo.

sultan, *sŭl' tăn*, s. sultano, m.

sultana, *sŭltä' nă*, s. sultana, f.   [m.

sultriness, *sŭl' trĭnĕs*, s. calore soffocante,

sultry, *–trĭ*, a. fervido, fervoroso; soffocante.   [sommare, ricapitolare.

sum, *sŭm*, s. somma, f.; totale, m.; **-**, v. a.

summarily, *săm' mărĭlĭ*, ad. sommariamente.

summary, *–mărĭ*, a. & s. sommario (m.).

summer, *sŭm' măr*, s. estate, f.

summer-house, *–hŏŭs*, s. gabinetto di verdura, m.

summit, *sŭm'mĭt*, s. sommità, cima, f.

summon, *sŭm'măn*, v. a. citare, chiamáre in giudizio; intimare.   [damento, m.

summons, *–mŭnz*, s. citazione, f.; comandas

sumptuary, *sŭm'tŭărĭ*, a. suntuario.

sumptuous, *–tŭăs*, a. suntuoso; *–ly*, ad. suntuosamente.

sumptuousness, *–něs*, s. suntuosità, f.

sun, *sŭn*, s. sole, m.

sun-beam, *–bēm*, s. raggio di sole, m.

sun-burnt, *–bŭrnt*, a. bruciato dal sole, abbronzato.

Sunday, *–dā*, s. domenica, f.

sunder, *sŭn'dŭr*, v. a. separare; partire.

sun-dial, *sŭn'dĭăl*, s. orologio solare, m.

sundry, *sŭn'drĭ*, a. diversi, molti.

sun-flower, *sŭn'flŏŭr*, s. eliotropio, m.

sun-light, *–lĭt*, s. lume del sole, m.

sunny, *–nĭ*, a. esposto al sole; (fig.) felice; ridente.   [levar del sole, m.

sun-rise, *–rīz*, sun-rising, *–rīzĭng*, s.

sun-set, *–sĕt*, s. tramontare del sole, m.

sun-shade, *–shăd*, s. parasole, ombrellino, m.

sunshine, *–shĭn*, s. chiarezza del sole, f.

sunshiny, *–shĭnĭ*, a. illuminato dal sole.

sun-stroke, *–strŏk*, s. solata, f.

sup, *sŭp*, v. a. & n. bere a sorsi; cenare; *–*, s. sorso, m.

super, *sŭ'pŭr*, s. attore soprannumerario che sostiene una parte di poco rilievo, m.

superabound, *–ăbŏŭnd'*, v.a. & n. soprabbondare, sopravanzare.

superabundance, *–ăbăn'dăns*, s. soprabbondanza, f.

superabundant, *–dănt*, a. soprabbondante; *–ly*, ad. con soprabbondanza.

superadd, *–ăd'*, v. a. aggiungere di più.

superaddition, *–ăddĭsh'ăn*, s. soprappiù, m.   [vecchio.

superannuated, *ăn'nŭătĕd*, a. troppo

superannuation, *–d'shăn*, s. vecchiezza, f.; pensione, f.   [superbamente.

superb, *sŭpŭrb'*, a. superbo; *–ly*, ad.

supercargo, *sŭpărkăr'gŏ*, s. (mar.) sopraccarico, m.

supercilious, *–sĭl'ĭăs*, a. altiero, arrogante; *–ly*, ad. alticeramente, fieramente.

supererogation, *–ĕrŏgā'shăn*, s. supererogazione, f.   [bondante.

supererogatory, *–ĕrŏg'ătărĭ*, a. soprab-

superficial, *–fĭsh'ăl*, a. superficiale; *–ly*, ad. superficialmente.

superficies, *–ĭĕz*, s. superficie, f.

superfine, *sŭ'părfīn*, a. sopraffino.

superfluity, *–flŭ'ĭtĭ*, s. superfluità, f.

superfluous, *–pŭr'flŭăs*, a. superfluo, *–ly*, ad. con superfluità; inutilmente.

superhuman, *–hŭ'măn*, a. sovrumano.

superintend, *–ĭntĕnd'*, v. a. soprintendere, invigilare.   [denza, f.

superintendence, *–ĕns*, s. soprinten-

superintendent, *–ĕnt*, s. soprintendente, m.   [principale, m.

superior, *–pē'rĭăr*, a. superiore; *–*, s.

superiority, *–pĕrĭŏr'ĭtĭ*, s. superiorità, f.

superlative, *sŭpăr'lătĭv*, a. & s. superlativo (m.); *–ly*, ad. superlativamente.

supernatural, *–năt'ŭrăl (–chŭrăl)*, a. soprannaturale.   [numerario.

supernumerary, *–nŭ'mărărĭ*, a. soprannumerario

superscribe, *–skrĭb'*, v. a. soprascrivere.

superscription, *–skrĭp'shăn*, s. soprascritta, f.   [ferire; cassare, deporre.

supersede, *–sēd'*, v. a. soprassedere; dif-

superstition, *–stĭsh'ăn*, s. superstizione, f.; scrupolosità, f.

superstitious, *–ăs*, a. superstizioso; *–ly*, ad. superstiziosamente.   [sopra-

superstructive, *–strŭk'tĭv*, a. edificato

supervene, *–vēn'*, v. n. sopravvenire.

supervise, *–vīz'*, v. a. soprintendere; rivedere.   [f.

supervision, *–vĭsh'ăn*, s. soprintendenza,

supervisor, *–vĭ'zăr*, s. soprintendente, m.

supine, *sŭpīn'*, a. supino; ozioso, negligente; *–ly*, ad. negligentemente; *–*, s. *sŭ'pĭn*, (gram.) supino, m.

supineness, *–něs*, s. negligenza, f.

supper, *sŭp'pŭr*, s. cena, f.; the Lord's *–*, la santa cena, f.   [cascare.

supplant, *sŭpplănt'*, v. a. soppiantare, far

supple, *sŭp'pl*, a. flessibile; *–*, v. n. render flessibile.   [m.; aggiunta, f.

supplement, *sŭp'plĕmĕnt*, s. supplimento,

supplemental, *–mĕn'tăl*, supplementary, *–mĕn'ărĭ*, a. addizionale, supplementario.

suppleness, *sŭp'plněs*, s. flessibilità, f.

suppli(c)ant, *sŭp'plĭ(k)ănt*, s. supplicante, m.

supplicate, *–plĭkāt*, v. a. supplicare.

supplication, *–kā'shăn*, s. supplica, f.

supplicatory, *sŭp'plĭkătărĭ*, a. supplicatorio.

supplier, *–plī'ŭr*, s. che supplisce.

supply, *–plī'*, v. a. supplire; assistere, aiutare; sovvenire; *–*, s. soccorso, rinforzo, m.   [nere; appoggiare, assistere.

support, *–pŏrt'*, v. a. sopportare, soste-

supportable, *–ăbl*, a. sopportabile.

supporter, *–ăr*, s. sostegno, appoggio, f.; protettore, m.

supposable, *–pŏ'zăbl*, a. supponibile.

suppose, *–pŏz'*, v. a. supporre; credere.

supposition, *–zĭsh'ăn*, s. supposizione, f., supposto, m.; ipotesi, f.

supposititious, *–zĭtĭsh'ăs*, a. supposizio, falso..

suppress, *–prĕs'*, v. a. sopprimere.   [f.

suppression, *–prĕsh'ăn*, s. soppressione,

suppurate, *sŭp'pŭrāt*, v. n. suppurare.

suppuration, *–rā'shăn*, s. suppuramento, m.   [f., primato, m.

supremacy, *sŭprĕm'ăsĭ*, s. supremazia,

supreme, *–prēm'*, a. supremo; *–ly*, ad. supremamente.

surcease, *sŭrsēs'*, s. cessazione, f.

surcharge, *–chărj'*, v. a. sopraccaricare.

surcingle, *–sĭng'gl*, s. sopraccinghia, f.; cintola, f.

sure, *shŏr*, a. certo, sicuro, assicurato; fermo, stabile; to be *–*, senza dubbio;

–, –ly, ad. certamente, senza dubbio; sicuramente.

sureness, –nĕs, sicurezza, f.

surety, –tĭ, s. sicurezza, certezza, f.; mallevadore, m.   [mare], fpl.

surf, sŭrf, s. cavalloni, m. pl., onde (del

surface, sŭr'fās, s. superficie, f.

surfeit, sŭr'fĭt, s. indigestione, f.; sazietà, f.; disgusto, m.; –, v. a. & n. satollare, impinzare; saziarsi.

surge, sŭrj, s. onda, f.; cavallone; flutto, m.; –, v. n. fare cavalloni, gonfiarsi.

surgeon, sŭr'jŭn, s. chirurgo, m.

surgery, sŭr'jŭrĭ, s. chirurgia, f.

surgical, –jĭkăl, a. chirurgico.

surlily, sŭr'lĭlĭ, ad. burberamente.

surliness, –lĭnĕs, s. cattivo umore, m.

surly, –lĭ, a. arcigno, burbero.

surmise, –mīz', v. a. sospettare; –, s. sospetto, m.

surmount, –mōŭnt', v. a. sormontare.

surmountable, –ăbl, a. che si può sormontare.   [v. a. soprannominare.

surname, sŭr'năm, s. soprannome, m.; –,

surpass, –păs', v. a. sorpassare.

surpassing, –ĭng, a. eccellente.   [f.

surplice, sŭr'plĭs, s. cotta (d'ecclesiastico).

surplus(age), sŭr'plŭs(dj), s. sovrappiù, m.   [s. sorpresa, f.

surprise, –prīz', v. a. sorprendere; –,

surprising, –prīz'ĭng, a. meraviglioso.

surrender, –rĕn'dŭr, v. a. & n. cedere; arrendersi; –, s. rendimento, m.

surreptitious, –rĕptĭsh'ŭs, a. surrettizio; –ly, ad. surrettiziamente.

surrogate, sŭr'rŏgāt, v. a. surrogare; –, s. sostituto, m.   [chiudere intorno.

surround, –rōŭnd', v. a. circondare.

survey, –vā', v. a. osservare; esaminare; misurare il terreno; –, sŭr'vā, s. rivista, f.; agrimensura, f.

surveyor, –ŭr, s. sopritendente, m.; agrimensore, m.; ispettore, m.

survival, –vī'văl, s. sopravvivenza, f.

survive, –vīv', v. a. & n. sopravvivere.

survivor, –vī'vŭr, s. sopravvivente, m.

susceptibility, sŭssĕptĭbĭl'ĭtĭ, s. suscettibilità, f.; sensibilità, f.

susceptible, –sĕp'tĭbl, a. suscettibile.

suspect, –pĕkt', v. a. & n. sospettare; diffidare.

suspend, –pĕnd', v. a. sospendere.

suspense, –pĕns', s. dubbio, m., incertezza, f.; dilazione, f.

suspension, –pĕn'shŭn, s. sospensione, m.; interruzione, f.; – of arms, tregua, f.

suspension-bridge, –brĭj, s. ponte di catene, ponte pensile, m.

suspensory, –pĕn'sŭrĭ, s. sospensorio, m.

suspicion, –pĭsh'ŭn, s. sospetto, m.

suspicious, –ăs, s. sospettoso; –ly, ad. con sospetto.

suspiciousness, –ăsnĕs, s. sospezione, f.

sustain, –tān', v. a. sostenere, mantenere, sostentare; comportare, soffrire.

sustainable, –ăbl, a. sostenibile.

sustainer, –ŭr, s. sostegno, appoggio, m.

sustenance, sŭs'tĕnăns, s. mantenimento, m.; alimento, m.   [m.

sutler, sŭt'lŭr, s. vivandiere, m.; cantiniere,

sutling-booth, –lĭng bōth, s. bettola, f

suture, sŭ'tŭr, s. sutura, cucitura, f.

swab, swŏb, s. spazzatoio, m.

swaddle, swŏd'dl, v. a. fasciare.

swaddling-clothes, –dlĭng klōths, s. pl. fasce, f. pl., pannicelli, m. pl.

swagger, swăg'găr, v. n. bravare, vantarsi.   [monti, m.

swaggerer, –ŭr, s. bravaccio, spacca-

swain, swān, s. giovane, contadino, m.; pastorello, m.

swallow, swŏl'lō, s. rondine, f.; gola, f.; –, v. a. inghiottire, ingoiare.

swamp, swŏmp, s. pantano, palude, m.; –, v. a. sommergere.

swampy, swŏm'pĭ, a. paludoso.

swan, swŏn, s. cigno, m.

swan-skin, –skĭn, s. mollettone, m.

swap, swŏp, v. n. barattare.   [dini], m.

sward, swărd, s. tappeto verde (nei giar-

swarm, swărm, s. sciame, m.; folla, f.; formicaio, m.; –, v. n. far lo sciame; traboccare, abbondare.   [abbronzata, f.

swarthiness, swărth'ĭnĕs, s. carnagione

swarthy, –ĭ, a. abbronzato dal sole.

swash-buckler, swŏsh'bŭkklŭr, s. mangiaferro, m.

swath, swŏth, s. ciglione, m.

swathe, swăth, s. fascia, f.; –, v. n. fasciare.

away, swā, v. a. governare, dominare; –, v. n. aver potere sopra; –, s. dominio, m., autorità, f.   [ir. giurare; bestemmiare.

swear, swăr, v. a. ir. far giurare; –, v. n.

swearing, –ĭng, s. giuramento, m.

sweat, swĕt, s. sudore, m.; –, v. n. sudare; affaticarsi; traspirare.

sweep, swēp, s. spazzacamino. m.; oscillazione, f.; curvatura, f.; –, v. a. & n. ir. spazzare; toccar leggermente; oscillare.

sweeper, –ŭr, s. spazzacamino, m.; scopatore, m.

sweeping. –ĭng, a. rapido; generale; –s, s. pl. spazzatura, f.; immondizia, f.

sweep-stakes, –stāks, s. pl. tutto il denaro scommesso o vinto alla corsa dei cavalli, m.

sweepy, swēp'ĭ, a. rapido e violento.

sweet, swēt, a. dolce, soave; grato, piacevole, amabile; melodioso; –ly, ad. dolcemente; piacevolmente; –, s. dolcezza, piacevolezza, f.   [tello, f.

sweet-bread, –brĕd, s. animella di vi-

sweeten, swĕt'n, v. a. addolcire; mitigare; placare.

sweetener, –nŭr, s. mitigatore, m.

sweetheart, –hărt, s. amante, m.; innamorata, f.   [fetto, m.

sweetmeat, –mĕt, s. confettura, f., con-

sweetness, –nĕs, s. dolcezza, soavità, f.

sweet-scented, –sĕntĕd, a. profumoso.

sweet-william, –wĭlyăm, s. (bot.) garofanetto salvatico, m.

swell, swĕl, v. a. ir. gonfiare; ingrossare; aggravare; –, v. n. ir. gonfiarsi; crescere;

insuperbirsi; —, s. tumore, m.; onde, f. pl.; zerbino, m.; —, a. alla moda. [m.

swelling, *-ing*, s. gonfiamento, tumore.

swelter, *swĕl'tăr*, v. a. & n. soffocare dal caldo.   [gando.

swerve, *swărv*, v. n. sviarsi, andar va-

swift, *swĭft*, a. veloce, pronto, presto; **-ly**, ad. con rapidità; —, s. rondone (uccello), m.

swiftness, *-nĕs*, s. velocità, prestezza, f.; rapidità, f.   [—, s. lavatura, f.

swill, *swĭl*, v. n. bere molto; imbriacarsi;

swim, *swĭm*, v. a. & n. ir. passare a nuoto, nuotare; abbondare; —, s. vessica del pesce, f.   [f.; **-ly**, ad. bene bene.

swimming, *-ing*, s. nuoto, m.; vertigine,

swindle, *swĭn'dl*, v. a. ingannare, truffare.

swindler, *-dlăr*, s. truffatore, m.

swine, *swĭn*, s. porco, m.

swine-herd, *-hĕrd*, s. porcaro, porcaio, m.

swing, *swĭng*, v. a. ir. altalenare, dondolare, agitare; —, v. n. ir. dondolarsi; agitarsi; —, altalena, f.; il dondolare, m.

swinging, *swĭng'ing*, a. grande, vasto; **-ly**, ad. grandemente, vastamente.

swinish, *swĭn'ĭsh*, a. di porco, porcino;

swirl, *swărl*, v. n. gorgogliare.   [brutale.

switch, *swĭch*, s. bacchetta, verga, f.; (rail.) macchina di baratto, f.; —, v. a. sferzare.

switchback-railway, *-băk rălwă*, s. montagna russa, f.

swivel, *swĭv'vl*, s. perno, m.   [svenire.

swoon, *swŏn*, s. svenimento, m.; —, v. n.

swoop, *swŏp*, s. il piombare (d' un uccello rapace), m., **at one** —, a un tratto; —, v. a. piombare addosso.

sword, *sŏrd*, s. spada, f.

sword-cutler, *-kŭt'lăr*, s. spadaio, m.

sword-fish, *-fĭsh*, s. spada, f. (pesce).

sword-knot, *-nŏt*, s. nastro della spada, balteo, m.   [daccino, m.

swordsman, *-z'măn*, s. schermitore, spa-

Sybarite, *sĭb'ărĭt*, s. sibarita, m.

sybaritic(al), *sĭmmĕt' ĭk(ăl)*, a. voluttuoso.

sycamore, *sĭk'ămŏr*, s. sicomoro, m.

sycophant, *sĭk'ŏfănt*, s. adulatore, m.

syllabic, *sĭllăb'ĭk*, a. sillabico.

syllable, *sĭl'lăbl*, s. sillaba, f.   [rio, m.

syllabus, *sĭl'lăbŭs*, s. compendio, sommario, m.

syllogism, *sĭl'lŏjĭzm*, s. sillogismo, m.

sylph, *sĭlf*, **sylphid**, *sĭlf'ĭd*, s. spirito aereo, m.

symbol, *sĭm'bŏl*, s. simbolo, m.

symbolic(al), *-bŏl'ĭk(ăl)*, a. simbolico.

symbolise, *sĭm'bŏlĭz*, v. a. simbolizzare.

symmetrical, *sĭmmĕt'rĭkăl*, a. simmetrico.

symmetry, *sĭm'mĕtrĭ*, s. simmetria, f.

sympathetic, *-păthĕt'ĭk*, a. simpatico; **-ally**, ad. simpaticamente.

sympathise, *sĭm'păthĭz*, v. n. simpatizzare; compatire.

sympathy, *sĭm'păthĭ*, s. simpatia, f.

symphony, *sĭm'fŏnĭ*, s. sinfonia, f.

symptom, *sĭm'tăm*, s. (med.) sintomo, indizio, m.

symptomatic, *-tŏmăt'ĭk*, a. sintomatico.

synagogue, *sĭn'ăgŏg*, s. sinagoga, f.

synchronism, *sĭn'krŏnĭzm*, s. sincronismo, m.

---

syndic, *sĭn'dĭk*, s. sindaco, m.

syndicate, *-dĭkăt*, s. sindacato, m.

synod, *sĭn'ŏd*, s. sinodo, concilio, m.

synodal, *-ŏddl*, **synodic**, *-nŏd'ĭk*, a. sinodale.

synonym, *sĭn'ŏnĭm*, s. sinonimo, m.

synonymous, *-nŏn'ĭmŭs*, a. sinonimo.

synopsis, *sĭnŏp'sĭs*, s. sinopsi, f.

synoptical, *-tĭkăl*, a. sinottico.

syntax, *sĭn'tăks*, s. sintassi, f.

synthesis, *sĭn'thĕsĭs*, s. sintesi, f.

syringe, *sĭr'ĭnj*, s. siringa, f.; —, v. a. siringare, schizzare colla siringa.

system, *sĭs'tĕm*, s. sistema, metodo, m.

systematic(al), *-tĭk(ăl)*, a. sistematico, metodico; **-ally**, ad. in modo sistematico.

T.

tabby, *tăb'bĭ*, s. tabì, m. (drappo).

tabernacle, *tăb'ărnăkl*, s. tabernacolo, m.

tablature, *tăb'lătăr*, s. fresco, m., pittura a fresco, f.; intavolatura, f.

table, *tăbl*, s. tavola, f.; catalogo, m.; **– d'hôte**, tavola rotonda, f.

table-beer, *-bĕr*, s. birra piccola, f.

table-cloth, *-klŏth*, s. tovaglia, f.

table-land, *-lănd*, s. altipiano, m.

table-spoon, *-spŏn*, s. cucchiaio, m.

tablet, *tăb'lĕt*, s. tavoletta, f.; iscrizione, f.

taboo, *tăbŏ'*, v. a. interdire.

tabour, *tă'băr*, s. tamburino, m.

tabular, *tăb'ŭlăr*, a. in forma d'indice.

tacit, *tăs'ĭt*, a. tacito; sottinteso; **-ly**, ad. tacitamente.

taciturn, *-ĭtŭrn*, a. taciturno, silenzioso.

taciturnity, *-tŭrn'ĭtĭ*, s. taciturnità, f.

tack, *tăk*, s. chiodo piccolo, m., bulletta, f.; rigiro, m.; bordata, f.; —, v. a. attaccare, appiccare; (mar.) bordeggiare.

tackle, *tăk'kl*, s. cordaggio, m.; carrucola, f.

tact, *tăkt*, s. tatto, m.   [f.

tactician, *-tĭsh'ăn*, s. tattico, m.

tactics, *tăk'tĭks*, s. pl. tattica, f.

tadpole, *tăd'pŏl*, s. ranocchio, m.

taffeta, *tăf'fĕtă*, s. taffetà, m.

tag, *tăg*, s. puntale, m.; —, v. a. mettere il puntale.

tagrag and bobtail, *-răg ănd bŏbtăl*, s. canaglia, plebaglia, f.   [m.

tail, *tăl*, s. coda, f.; deretano, m.; manico,

tailor, *tăl'ăr*, s. sarto, m.

taint, *tănt*, s. macchia, f.; infezione, f.; infamia, f.; —, v. a. infettare; guastare.

taintless, *-lĕs*, a. non infetto; incorrotto.

take, *tăk*, v. a. ir. prendere, pigliare, accettare, ricevere; ammettere; credere; comprendere; **to – for**, prendere per; **to – away**, portar via; sparecchiare la tavola; **to – back**, riportare; **to – in**, ingannare, truffare; **to – off**, cavarsi, imitare; **to – up**, raccogliere; arrestare; **to – after**, ritrarre da; **to – to a person**, prendere uno a ben volere; —, v. n. ir. riuscire, aver buon successo; essere in voga; andare; immaginarsi, pensare; divenir gravida; —, s. presa, f.

take-in, *tāk'ĭn'*, s. inganno, m.

take-off, *-ŏf'*, s. caricatura, f.

taking, *tā'kĭng*, a. cortese; piacevole; —, s. presa, f.

tale, *tāl*, s. novella, favola, f.; conto, m.

tale-bearer, *-bārūr*, s. rapportatore, m.

talent, *tāl'ent*, s. talento, m.; capacità, f.

talented, *-ĕd*, a. d'ingegno, di talento.

talisman, *tāl'ĭsmăn*, s. talismano, m.

talk, *tāk*, v. n. parlare, discorrere; cicalare; —, s. conversazione, f., discorso, ragionamento, m.

talk, *tāk*, s. talco, m.

talkative, *tāk'ātĭv*, a. loquace, ciarliero.

talkativeness, *-nĕs*, s. loquacità, f.

talker, *-ūr*, s. parlatore, ciarlatore, m.; millantatore, m.

tall, *tāl*, a. grande; alto; robusto.   [f.

tallness, *-nĕs*, s. altezza, statura grande,

tallow, *tāl'lō*, s. sego, m.; —, v. a. insetallowy, *-lō'ĭ*, a. pien di sego.   [gare.

tally, *tāl'ĭ*, v. a. aggiustare, adattare.

talon, *tāl'ŏn*, s. artiglio, m., branca, f.

tamable, *tā'mābl*, a. domabile.

tamarind, *tăm'drĭnd*, s. tamarindo, m.

tamarisk, *tăm'ărĭsk*, s. tamarisco, m.

tambour, *tăm'būr*, s. tombolo, ordigno da ricamare, m.

tambourine, *-bŭrēn'*, s. tamburino, m.

tame, *tām*, a. domato, mansueto, addomesticato; sommesso; trattabile; **-ly,** ad. mansuetamente; vilmente; —, v. a. domare, addimesticare.   [viltà, f.

tameness, *-nĕs*, s. domestichezza, f.;

tamper, *tăm'pŭr*, v. n. praticare; sollecitare; impacciarsi, intrigarsi.   [(pelli).

tan, *tăn*, s. concia, f.; —, v. a. conciare

tandem, *tăn'dĕm*, a. attaccato in punta.

tangent, *tăn'jent*, s. tangente, f.

tangible, *tăn'jĭbl*, a. tangibile, toccabile.

tangle, *tăng'gl*, v. a. implicare, inlacciare.

tank, *tăngk*, s. stagno, m.; cisterna, f.

tankard, *-kŭrd*, s. boccale (col coperchio),

tanner, *tăn'nŭr*, s. conciatore, m.   [m.

tannery, *-nŭrĭ*, s. concia, f.

tantamount, *tăn'tămŏŭnt*, a. equivalente.

tanyard, *vedi* tannery.

tap, *tăp*, s. colpo leggiero, m., botta, f.; chiave di fontana, f.; —, v. a. dare un colpo leggiero, battere; spillare.

tape, *tāp*, s. nastro (di filo), m.

taper, *tā'pŭr*, s. cero, m.; candela grande (di cera), f.; —, v. n. terminarsi in punta; —, a. conico.   [arazzo, m.

tapestry, *tăp'ĕstrĭ*, s. tappezzeria, f.;

tape-worm, *tāp'wŭrm*, s. tenia, f.

tap-house, *tăp'hŏŭs*, s. birreria, f.

tar, *tār*, s. pece liquida, f.; (fig.) marinaio, m.; —, v. a. impeciare.   [mente.

tardily, *tār'dĭlĭ*, ad. tardamente, pigra-

tardiness, *-dĭnĕs*, s. tardezza, lentezza, f.

tardy, *-dĭ*, a. tardo, lento.

tare, *tār*, s. tara, f.; (bot.) loglio, m.

target, *tār'gĕt*, s. bersaglio, m.

target-practice, *-prăk'tĭs*, s. tirare al bersaglio, m.

tariff, *tār'ĭf*, s. tariffa, f.   [bersaglio, m.

tarlatan, *tār'lătăn*, s. tarlantana, f.

tarn, *tārn*, s. lago, m.; palude, f.

tarnish, *tār'nĭsh*, v. a. scolorire; —, v. n. scolorirsi.

tarpaulin, *tārpāl'ĭn*, s. tela spalmata, f.

tarragon, *tār'răgŏn*, s. (bot.) targone, m.

tarry, *tār'rĭ*, v. n. soggiornare, tardare; —, *tār'rĭ*, a. spalmato.

tart, *tārt*, a. agro, acerbo; **-ly,** ad. agramente; —, s. torta, f.

tartane, *tār'tăn*, s. tartana, f.

tartar, *tār'tŭr*, s. tartaro, m.

tartness, *tārt'nĕs*, s. agrezza, acerbità, f.

task, *tăsk*, s. lavoro assegnato, carico, m.; —, v. a. assegnare lavoro.

tassel, *tăs'sĕl*, s. nappina (di seta), f.; nastro (da aprir un libro), m.

tasselled, *tăs'sĕld*, a. ornato di fiocchi.

taste, *tāst*, s. gusto, sapore, m.; esperimento, m.; (fig.) vena, f.; —, v. a. & n. gustare, assaggiare; aver qualche gusto;

tasteful, *-fŭl*, a. saporito.   [sentire.

tasteless, *-lĕs*, a. insipido, senza sapore.

taster, *-ŭr*, s. assaggiatore, m.   [gusto.

tastily, *-tĭlĭ*, ad. saporitamente, di buon

tasty, *tāst'ĭ*, a. gustoso, saporito.

tatter, *tăt'tŭr*, s. cencio, straccio, m.

tatterdemalion, *dĕmāl'yŭn*, s. pezzente, mendico, m.

tattle, *tăt'tl*, s. ciarla, f.; —, v. n. ciarlare.

tattler, *-tlŭr*, s. ciarliero, m.

tattoo, *tăttō'*, s. (mil.) ritirata, f.; tatuaggio, m.; —, v. a. tatuare.

taunt, *tănt*, v. a. motteggiare, burlare; insultare; —, s. burla, f.; insulto, m.; rabbuffo, m.   [vole.

tauntingly, *-ĭnglĭ*, ad. in modo scherze-

taut, *tŭt*, a. (mar.) teso; stretto; fermo.

tautological, *-tŏlŏj'ĭkăl*, a. tautologico.

tautology, *-tŏl'ŏjĭ*, s. tautologia, f.

tavern, *tăv'ŭrn*, s. taverna, bettola, f.

tavern-keeper, *-kēpŭr*, s. tavernaio, m.

taw, *tă*, s. palla di marmo (da giocare), f.; —, v. a. conciare (con allume).

tawdriness, *tā'drĭnĕs*, s. sfoggio, m.

tawdry, *-drĭ*, a. fastoso, sfoggiato.

tawny, *tăn'ĭ*, a. bruno, abbronzato, fosco.

tax, *tăks*, s. tassa, imposizione, f.; —, v. a. tassare; accusare.

taxable, *-ăbl*, a. tassabile.

taxation, *-ā'shŭn*, s. tassazione, f.

tax-gatherer, *-găthŭrŭr*, s. collettore delle tasse, m.

tea, *tē*, s. tè, m.   [maestrare, istruire.

teach, *tēch*, v. a. & n. ir. insegnare, am-

teachable, *-ăbl*, a. docile.

teacher, *-ŭr*, s. insegnante, m.

teaching, *-ĭng*, s. insegnamento, m.

tea-kettle, *tē'kĕttl*, s. ràmino per il tè, m.

team, *tēm*, s. tirata, f., tiro, m.

teamster, *-stŭr*, s. chi guida un tiro.

tea-pot, *tē'pŏt*, s. tettiera, f.

tear, *tār*, v. a. ir. stracciare; svellere.

tear, *tēr*, s. lacrima, gocciola, f.

tearful, *-fŭl*, a. lacrimoso.

tearless, *-lĕs*, a. senza lacrime.

tease, *tēz*, v. a. cardare; importunare.

teasel, *tē'zl*, s. cardo, scardasso, m.

tea-service, *tĕ'sûrvĭs*, **tea-set**, *-sĕt*, **tea-things**, *-thĭngs*, s. (pl.) vasellame per il tè, m.

teat, *tĕt*, s. tetta, poppa, f. [stizza, f.

techiness, *tĕch'ĭnĕs*, s. mal umore, m.,

technical, *tĕk'nĭkăl*, a. tecnico.

technicalities, *-kăl'ĭtĭz*, s. pl. espressioni tecniche, f. pl.

technology, *-nŏl'ŏjĭ*, s. tecnologia, f.

techy, *tĕch'ĭ*, a. di mal umore, stizzoso.

tedious, *tĕ'dĭŭs*, a. tedioso, noioso; **-ly**, ad. noiosamente. [tedio, m.

tediousness, *-nĕs*, s. **tedium**, *-dĭŭm*, s.

teem, *tēm*, v. a. produrre; **–**, v. n. esser gravida. [f.

teens, *tēnz*, s. pl. età da' tredici anni a' venti,

teeth, *tēth*, pl. di **tooth**; **–**, v. n. essere nella dentizione.

teething, *tēth'ĭng*, s. dentizione, f.

teetotal, *tētō'tăl*, a. moderato, sobrio.

teetotalism, *-ĭzm*, s. frugalità, sobrietà, f.

teetotaller, *-ûr*, s. uomo sobrio, m.

teetotally, *-lĭ*, ad. (am.) totalmente.

teetotum, *-tō'tŭm*, s. trottolina, f.

telegram, *tĕl'ĕgrăm*, s. dispaccio telegrafico, telegramma, m. [v. a. telegrafare.

telegraph, *tĕl'ĕgrăf*, s. telegrafo, m.; **–**,

telegraphic, *-grăf'ĭk*, a. telegrafico.

telephone, *tĕl'ĕfōn*, s. telefono, m.

telephonic, *-fŏn'ĭk*, a. telefonico.

telescope, *tĕl'ĕskŏp*, s. telescopio, m.

telescopic, *-skŏp'ĭk*, a. telescopico.

tell, *tĕl*, v. a. & n. ir. dire; dichiarare, mostrare; numerare; dettare, comunicare; raccontare. [cassiere, computista, m.

teller, *-lûr*, s. dicitore, raccontatore, m.;

telling, *-ĭng*, a. operativo, energico.

tell-tale, *-tāl*, s. maldicente, m.

temerity, *tĕmĕr'ĭtĭ*, s. temerità, f.

temper, *tĕm'pûr*, s. tempera, f.; temperamento, umore, m.; **–**, v. a. temperare; moderare; dare la tempera. [m.

temperament, *-ămĕnt*, s. temperamento, m.

temperance, *-ăns*, s. temperanza, f.; moderazione, f.

temperate, *-ĭt*, a. temperato, moderato; sobrio; **-ly**, ad. temperatamente.

temperateness, *-ĭtnĕs*, s. moderazione, f.

temperature, *-ătûr*, s. temperie, f.; tempra, f.

tempered, *-pûrd*, a. di temperamento ...

tempest, *tĕm'pĕst*, s. tempesta, procella, f.

tempestuous, *-pĕs'tūŭs*, a. tempestoso.

Templar, *tĕm'plûr*, s. templare, m.; studente di giurisprudenza, m.

temple, *tĕmpl*, s. tempio, m.; tempia, f.

temporal, *tĕm'pŏrăl*, a. temporale; **-ly**, ad. temporalmente. [mente.

temporarily, *-rărĭlĭ*, ad. temporanea-

temporary, *-rărĭ*, s. che dura a tempo, transitorio. [poreggiare.

temporise, *tĕm'pŏrīz*, v. n. indugiare, tem-

tempt, *tĕmt*, v. a. tentare; provocare.

temptation, *tĕmtā'shŭn*, s. tentazione, f.

tempter, *-tûr*, s. tentatore, m.

temptress, *-trĕs*, s. tentatrice, f.

ten, *tĕn*, a. dieci.

tenable, *tĕn'ăbl*, a. che si può tenere.

tenacious, *tĕnā'shŭs*, a. tenace; **-ly**, ad. con tenacità.

tenacity, *-năs'ĭtĭ*, s. tenacità, viscosità, f.; ostinazione, f. [m.

tenancy, *tĕn'ănsĭ*, s. possesso temporario,

tenant, *tĕn'ănt*, s. fittaiuolo, feudatario, pigionale, m.; **–**, v. a. tenere a fitto.

tenantless, *-lĕs*, a. disabitato.

tenantry, *-rĭ*, s. corpo degli'affittuali, m.

tench, *tĕnsh*, s. tinca, f. (pesce).

tend, *tĕnd*, v. a. badare; guardare; **–**, v. n. tendere; esser diretto.

tendency, *-dĕnsĭ*, s. tendenza, f.

tender, *tĕn'dûr*, a. tenero, delicato; sensibile; **-ly**, ad. teneramente; **–**, s. offerta, f.; (rail.) tender, m.; **–**, v. a. offrire, presentare; stimare. [bilità, f.

tenderness, *-nĕs*, s. tenerezza, f.; sensi-

tendon, *tĕn'dŏn*, s. tendine, m.; nervo, m.

tendril, *tĕn'drĭl*, s. rampollo, m.

tenement, *tĕn'ĕmĕnt*, s. tenimento, m., tenuta, f.

tenet, *tĕn'ĕt*, s. dottrina, f.; opinione, f.

tenfold, *tĕn'fōld*, a. decuplo.

tennis, *tĕn'nĭs*, s. pallaccorda, f. (giuoco).

tennis-court, *-kŏrt*, s. luogo da giocare alla palla, m. [tenuto, m.; forma, f.

tenor, *tĕn'ûr*, s. tenore, m.; soggetto, con-

tense, *tĕns*, a. teso; rigido; **–**, s. (gr.) tempo, m.

tension, *tĕn'shŭn*, s. tensione, f. [giare.

tent, *tĕnt*, s. tenda, f.; **–**, v. n. campeg-

tentacle, *tĕn'tăkl*, s. tentacolo, m.

tentative, *tĕn'tătĭv*, a. tentante.

tenter, *tĕn'tûr*, s. uncino, rampino, m.

tenter-hook, *-hŏk*, s. uncino, m.

tenth, *tĕnth*, a. decimo; **–**, s. decima parte, f.; **-ly**, ad. in decimo luogo.

tenuity, *tĕnū'ĭtĭ*, s. tenuità, f.

tenure, *tĕn'ûr*, s. tenuta, dipendenza (d'un feudo), f.

tepid, *tĕp'ĭd*, a. tepido. [feudo), f.

tergiversation, *tûrjĭvŭrsā'shŭn*, s. tergiversazione, f.

term, *tûrm*, s. termine, confine, m.; espressione, locuzione, f.; condizione, f.; **–**, v. a. nominare, chiamare. [gera, f.

termagant, *tûr'măgănt*, s. sgridatrice, me-

terminate, *tûr'mĭnāt*, v. a. terminare, limitare; **–**, v. n. terminarsi.

termination, *-nā'shŭn*, s. terminazione, conclusione, f. [ferrata), m.

terminus, *tûr'mĭnŭs*, s. atrio (della strada

terrace, *tĕr'răs*, s. terrazzo, m.; **–**, v. a. terrapienare.

terrestrial, *tĕrrĕs'trĭăl*, a. terrestre.

terrible, *tĕr'rĭbl*, a. terribile.

terribly, *-rĭbĭ*, ad. terribilmente.

terrier, *tĕr'rĭûr*, s. bassetto, m.

terrific, *tĕrrĭf'ĭk*, a. spaventevole.

terrify, *tĕr'rĭfī*, v. a. atterrire, spaventare.

territorial, *-tō'rĭăl*, a. territoriale.

territory, *tĕr'rĭtŏrĭ*, s. territorio, m.; dominio, m.

terror, *tĕr'rûr*, s. terrore, spavento, m.

terrorise, *-īz*, v. a. terrorizzare, metter terrore.

terrorist, *-ĭst*, s. terrorista, m.

terse, *tŭrs*, a. terso, pulito, elegante; **–ly**, ad. elegantemente.

terseness, *–nĕs*, s. eleganza, f.

tertian, *tŭr'shăn*, s. febbre terzana, f

tesselate, *tĕs'sĕlāt*, v. a. picchiettare.

test, *tĕst*, s. coppella, f.; prova, f.; pietra del paragone, f, [ceo.

testaceous, *–tā'shŭs*, a. testaceo, crosta-

testament, *tĕs'tăment*, s. testamento, m.; scrittura sacra, f. [rio.

testamentary, *–mĕnt'ări*, a. testamenta-

testator, *–tā'tŭr*, s. testatore, m.

testatrix, *–tā'trĭks*, s. testatrice, f.

tester, *tĕs'tŭr*, s. cielo del letto, m.

testicle, *tĕs'tĭkl*, s. testicolo, m.

testifier, *tĕs'tĭfīŭr*, s. testificatore, m.

testify, *–tĭfī*, v. a. certificare.

testily, *–tĭlĭ*, ad. in modo arcigno.

testimonial, *–mō'nĭăl*, s. testimoniale, m.

testimony, *tĕs'tĭmănĭ*, s. testimonio, m., prova, f.

testiness, *tĕs'tĭnĕs*, s. cattivo umore, m.

testing, *tĕs'tĭng*, s. prova, f.

testy, *tĕs'tĭ*, a. stizzoso, ostinato.

tether, *tĕth'ŭr*, s. pastoia, f.; ritegno, m.

text, *tĕkst*, s. testo m.

textile, *tĕks'tĭl*, a. che può essere tessuto.

textual, *tĕks'tŭăl*, a. testuale.

texture, *tĕks'tŭr*, s. tessitura, f.; tessuto, m.

than, *thăn*, c. che non, anzi che.

thank, *thăngk*, v. a. ringraziare, rendere grazie; **–s**, s. pl. grazie, f. pl.

thankful, *–fŭl*, a. grato; **–ly**, ad. con gratitudine.

thankfulness, *–fŭlnĕs*, s. gratitudine, f.

thankless, *–lĕs*, a. ingrato.

thank-offering, *–ŏf'fŭrĭng*, s. rendimento di grazie, m. [di grazie, m.

thanksgiving, *–s'gĭvĭng*, s. rendimento

that, *thăt*, pn. ciò; quello, quella; quella cosa; chi, che; affinchè, acciocchè; **so –**, di maniera che. [di stoppia.

thatch, *thăch*, s. stoppia, f.; **–**, v. a. coprire

thaw, *thă*, s. sdiacciamento, m.; **–**, v. a. liquefare; **–**, v. imp. dighiacciare.

the, *thĕ (thē)*, art. il, lo; i, gli; la, le. [m.

theatre, *thĕ'ătŭr*, s. teatro, m.; spettacolo,

theatrical, *–ăt'rĭkăl*, a. teatrale, scenico.

thee, *thē*, pn. te, ti.

theft, *thĕft*, s. latrocinio, furto, m.

their, *thăr*, loro; **–s**, il loro; la loro; i loro; le loro.

theism, *thē'ĭzm*, s. teismo, m.

theist, *thē'ĭst*, s. teista, m.

them, *thĕm*, pn. loro, a loro; li, le, gli.

theme, *thēm*, s. tema, m. [sè stesse, pl.

themselves, *thĕmsĕlvz*, pn. pl. sè stessi,

then, *thĕn*, ad. allora, in quel tempo; dopo, poi; **now and –**, di quando in quando; **–**, c. dunque, perciò.

thence, *thĕns*, ad. indi, di là, da questo.

thenceforth, *–fŏrth*, ad. da indi in qua.

theocracy, *thĕŏk'răsĭ*, s. teocrazia, f., go- verno di Dio, m.

theologian, *–ŏlō'jĭăn*, s. teologo, m.

theological, *–ŏlŏj'ĭkăl*, s. teologico.

theology, *–ŏl'ŏjĭ*, s. teologia, f.

theorem, *thē'ŏrĕm*, s. teorema, m.

theoretical, *–ŏrĕt'ĭkăl*, a. teoretico; **–ly**, ad. teoricamente.

theorise, *thē'ŏrīz*, v. n. far delle teoriche.

theorist, *thē'ŏrĭst*, s. teorico, m.

theory, *thē'ŏrĭ*, s. teoria, f. [tica, f.

therapeutics, *thĕrăpū'tĭks*, s. pl. terapeu-

there, *thăr*, ad. lì, là, colà, a quel luogo; **here and –**, qua e là; **–about(s)**, in- circa, là intorno; **–after**, indi, quindi, dopo; **–at**, a ciò, a questo; **–by**, per ciò, per quel mezzo; **–fore**, perciò, dunque; **–from**, da ciò, da questo; **–in, –into**, in ciò, dentro, entro; **–of**, di ciò, di quella cosa; **–on**, sopra di ciò; **–to, –unto**, oltre a questo; **–upon**, sopra di ciò, perciò, in seguito; **–with**, con ciò, im- mediatamente, immediatamente; **–withal**, di piu, in oltre; con questo.

thermal waters, *thŭr'măl wătŭrz*, s. pl. terme, f. pl. [tro, m.

thermometer, *thŭrmŏm'ĕtŭr*, s. termome-

these, *thēz*, art. questi, queste, pl.

thesis, *thē'sĭs*, s. tesi, f.

they, *thā*, pn. eglino, essi; elleno, esse.

thick, *thĭk*, a. spesso, serrato; grosso; folto, denso; torbido; **– of hearing**, sordastro; **–, –ly**, ad. in folla, frequente- mente; **–s**, grosso, m., grossezza, f.

thicken, *thĭk'n*, v. a. spessire; condensare; **–**, v. n. spessirsi, condensarsi.

thickening, *–nĭng*, s. condensazione, f.; densità, f. [folto, m.

thicket, *–ĕt*, s. sicpaglia, f.; boschetto

thick-headed, *–hĕdĕd*, a. stupido.

thickness, *–nĕs*, s. spessezza, densità, grossezza, f.

thick-set, *–sĕt*, a. spesso, denso, folto.

thief, *thēf*, s. ladro, m.; fungo del luci- gnolo, m.

thief-catcher, *–kăchŭr*, s. birro, m.

thieve, *thēv*, v. a. rubare, involare.

thievish, *–ĭsh*, a. inclinato a rubare; **–ly**, ad. da ladro. [rubare, f.

thievishness, *–nĕs*, s. inclinazione a

thigh, *thī*, s. coscia, f.

thimble, *thĭm'bl*, s. ditale, m.

thin, *thĭn*, a. sottile, raro; magro, leggiero; chiaro; **–, –ly**, ad. in piccol numero; **–**, v. a. diradare, rarefare, attenuare; schia- rare; diramare. [la tua, i tuoi, le tue.

thine, *thīn*, pn. tuo, tua, tuoi, tue; il tuo,

thing, *thĭng*, s. cosa, f.

think, *thĭngk*, v. a. & n. ir. pensare, im- maginare; meditare, considerare; osser- vare; esaminare; immaginarsi.

thinker, *–ŭr*, s. pensatore, m.

thinking, *–ĭng*, s. giudizioso, savio; **–**, s. pensamento pensiero, m.; opinione, f.; giudizio, m. [tenuità, f.; magrezza, f.

thinness, *thĭn'nĕs*, s. radezza, rarità,

third, *thŭrd*, a. terzo; **–**, s. terza parte, f.; **–ly**, ad. nel terzo luogo.

thirst, *thŭrst*, s. sete, f.; **–**, v. n. aver sete.

thirstily, *–tĭlĭ*, ad. sitibondamente.

thirsty, *thŭrst'ĭ*, a. sitibondo; bramoso.

thirteen, *thŭr'tēn*, a. tredici.

thirteenth, *–tēnth,* a. tredicesimo.
thirtieth, *–tĕth,* a. trentesimo.
thirty, *thăr' tĕ,* a. trenta.
this, *thĭs,* pn. questo, questa; questa cosa.
thistle, *thĭs' l,* s. cardo, cardone, m.
thither, *thĭth' ăr,* ad. lì, là, a questo luogo.
thong, *thŏng,* s. striscia di cuoio, f.
thorn, *thŏrn,* s. spina, f., spino, m.; travaglio, m.
thorny, *thŏrn'ĕ,* a. spinoso; afflittivo.
thorough, *thŭr' ŏ,* pr. per traverso, a traverso; –, a. compiuto, perfetto; **–ly,** ad. interamente; perfettamente.
thoroughbred, *–brĕd,* a. di puro sangue.
thoroughfare, *–făr,* s. passaggio, m.; via pubblica, f. [piuto.
thorough-paced, *–păst,* a. perfetto, compiuto.
those, *thōz,* art. quelli, quei, quegli; quelle;
thou, *thŏŭ,* pn. tu. [colore.
though, *thŏ,* c. benchè, ancorchè, quantunque; **as –,** come se.
thought, *thăt,* s. pensiero, m.; opinione, riflessione, f.; cura, f.; intenzione, f.
thoughtful, *–fŭl,* a. pensoso, meditativo; **–ly,** ad. con viso pensoso. [fondo, m.
thoughtfulness, *–fŭlnĕs,* s. pensiero profondo, m.
thoughtless, *–lĕs,* a. spensierato, negligente; **–ly,** ad. spensieratamente, negligentemente. [tenza, f.; stolidezza, f.
thoughtlessness, *–lĕsnĕs,* s. inavvertenza, f.
thousand, *thŏŭ'zănd,* a. mille.
thousandfold, *–fōld,* a. mille volte.
thousandth, *–zăndth,* a. millesimo.
thraldom, *thrăl' dăm,* s. schiavitù, f.
thrall, *thrăl,* s. schiavo, m.
thrash, *thrăsh,* v. a. trebbiare; battere; –, v. n. affatjcarsi.
thrashing, *–ĭng,* s. trebbiatura, f.
thrashing-floor, *–flŏr,* s. aia, f.
thread, *thrĕd,* s. filo, m.; seguito (d' un discorso), m.; –, v. a. infilare, forare.
threadbare, *–băr,* a. usato, logoro.
threat, *thrĕt,* s. minaccia, f.
threaten, *thrĕt' n,* v. a. minacciare.
threatening, *–nĭng,* s. minaccia, f.
threateningly, *–nĭnglĕ,* ad. in modo minaccevole.
three, *thrē,* a. tre. [naccevole.
three-cornered, *–kŏrnărd,* a. triangolare.
three-fold, *–fōld,* a. triplice. [alberi, f.
three-master, *–măstăr,* s. nave a tre
threshold, *thrĕsh' ōld,* s. soglia, f.
thrice, *thrĭs,* ad. tre volte.
thrift, *thrĭft,* s. profitto, guadagno, m.; parsimonia, f.; frugalità, f.
thriftily, *–ĭlĕ,* ad. frugalmente. [mia, f.
thriftiness, *–ĭnĕs,* s. frugalità, f.; econo-
thriftless, *–lĕs,* a. prodigo.
thrifty, *thrĭft'ĕ,* a. frugale; economico.
thrill, *thrĭl,* s. succhiello, m.; –, v. a. forare; penetrare; –, v. n. strillare.
thrive, *thrĭv,* v. n. ir. prosperare, riuscire; crescere. [ad. con buon successo.
thriving, *thrĭ' vĭng,* a. prosperante; **–ly,**
throat, *thrŏt,* s. strozza, gola, f.
throat-band, *–bănd,* s. soggolo, m.
throb, *thrŏb,* s. palpitazione, f.; –, v. n. palpitare.
throe, *thrŏ,* s. doglia di parto, f.; agonia, f.

English and Italian,

throne, *thrōn,* s. trono, m.
throng, *thrŏng,* s. calca, folla, f.; –, v. a. serrare; –, v. n. andare in frotta; affollarsi. [strangolare.
throttle, *thrŏt' tl,* s. strozza, f.; –, v. a.
through, *thrŏ,* pr. a traverso, per; per mezzo suo; **– and –,** da banda a banda.
throughout, *–ŏŭt',* pr. fuorfuora, in ogni parte; –, ad. dappertutto.
throw, *thrŏ,* v. a. & n. ir. gettare, lanciare, tirare; –, s. colpo, getto, m.
thrum, *thrŭm,* v. a. bastonare, battere; strimpellare.
thrush, *thrăsh,* s. tordo, m.
thrust, *thrŭst,* v. a. spingere; urtare; ficcare, cacciare; forare; –, v. n. ingerirsi, affollarsi; –, s. colpo, urto, m.
thud, *thŭd,* s. colpo, m., percossa, f.
thumb, *thăm,* s. pollice, m.; –, v. a. squadernare; toccare rozzamente.
thumb-stall, *–stăl,* s. ditale, m.
thump, *thămp,* s. colpo, m., botta, f.; –, v. a. battere, bastonare.
thumping, *–ĭng,* a. grosso, grande.
thunder, *thăn' dăr,* s. tuono, m.; rumore, m.; –, v. a. fulminare; –, v. n. tonare.
thunderbolt, *–bŏlt,* s. fulmine, folgore, m.
thunderclap, *–klăp,* s. scoppio del tuono, fulmine, m.
thunder-storm, *–stŏrm,* s. temporale, m.
Thursday, *thărz' dă,* s. giovedì, m.; **Mounday –,** Giovedì santo, m.
thus, *thăs,* ad. così, in questa maniera.
thwack, *thwăk,* s. percossa, f., colpo, m.; –, v. a. percuotere; sferzare. [riare.
thwart, *thwărt,* v. a. attraversare, contrariare; –, pn. tuo, tua; tuoi, tue, pl.
thy, *thĭ,* pn. tuo, tua; tuoi, tue, pl.
thyme, *tĭm,* s. timo, m.
thyself, *thĭsĕlf',* pn. te stesso, te stessa.
tiara, *tĭă' ră,* s. tiara, f.
tick, *tĭk,* s. credito, m.; fodera (di piumaccio), f.; zecca, f. (insetto). [delle bullette.
ticket, *–ĕt,* s. bulletta, f.; –, v. a. mettere
ticking, *–ĭng,* s. traliccio, m.; tic tac, m.
tickle, *tĭk' kl,* v. a. & n. solleticare; solleticarsi.
tickling, *–ĭng,* s. solleticamento, f.
ticklish, *–klĭsh,* a. che cura il solletico delicato. [certezza, f.; difficoltà, f.
ticklishness, *–nĕs,* s. solletico, m.; **intidal,** *tĭ' dăl,* a. da marea.
tide, *tĭd,* s. marea, f., flusso del mare, m.; tempo, m., stagione, f.; –, v. n. andare a seconda della marea.
tide-waiter, *–wătăr,* s. doganiere, m.
tidily, *–lĕ,* ad. acconciamente.
tidiness, *–ĭnĕs,* s. pulitezza, f.; nettezza, f.
tidings, *tĭ' dĭngz,* s. pl. novelle, f. pl.
tidy, *tĭd' ĕ,* a. pulito, netto; destro.
tie, *tĭ,* s. legame, nodo, m.; patto, accordo, m.; –, v. a. legare; obbligare.
tier, *tēr,* s. fila, f.; filare, m.; numero, m.
tiff, *tĭf,* s. bevanda, f.; collera, stizza, f.
tiffany, *–fănĭ,* s. velo, m.; tocca, f.
tiger, *tĭ' găr,* s. tigre, f.; servo in livrea, m.
tight, *tĭt,* a. tirato, stretto; pulito, acconcio, attillato; **–ly,** ad. strettamente; attilatamente.

tighten, *tīt'n*, v. n. tirare, stringere.

tightness, *–nĕs*, s. strettezza, f.; attillatura, nettezza, f.

tigress, *tī'grĕs*, s. tigre, f.   [tegoli.

tile, *tīl*, s. tegolo, m.; –, v. a. coprire con

tiling, *–ĭng*, s. tetto coperto di tegoli, m.

till, *tĭl*, pr. & c. fino, insino; –, s. piccolo ⁂ tiratoio, m.; –, v. a. arare, coltivare.

tillage, *–lāj*, s. coltura, agricoltura, f.

tiller, *–lŭr*, s. aratore, lavoratore, m.; cassettino, m.; piccolo albero, m.; timone (d'una barca), m.

tilt, *tĭlt*, s. giostra, f., torneo, m.; tenda, coperta, f.; riparo, m.; –, v. a. coprire d'una tenda; alzare (una botte); –, v. n. armeggiare (con lancia); giostrare.

tilt-yard, *–yärd*, s. luogo da giostrare, m.

timber, *tĭm'bŭr*, s. legname, m.; trave, f.; –, v. a. digrossare il legname.

timber-work, *–wŭrk*, s. lavoro di legname, m.

timber-yard, *–yärd*, s. recinto di legname, f.

timbrel, *tĭm'brĕl*, s. tamburino, cembalo, m.

time, *tĭm*, s. tempo, m.; (mus.) cadenza, f.; **in –**, opportunamente; **from – to –**, di quando in quando; –, v. a. prendere il tempo.

time-keeper, *–kēpŭr*, s. cronometro, m.

timeliness, *–lĭnĕs*, s. opportunità, f.

timely, *–lĭ*, a. & ad. opportuno; di buon' tempo.

time-piece, *vedi* **time-keeper**.   [ora.

time-server, *–sŭrvŭr*, s. che s' accomoda a' tempi.

time-serving, *–sŭrvĭng*, s. servilità, f.

time-worn, *–wŏrn*, a. consumato dal tempo.

timid, *tĭm'ĭd*, a. timido, timoroso.

timidity, *–mĭd'ĭtĭ*, s. timidità, f.

timorous, *tĭm'ŭrŭs*, a. timoroso; **–ly**, ad. timorosamente.   [–, v. a. stagnare.

tin, *tĭn*, s. stagno, m.; latta, f. (metallo); –, v. a. dare una tintura; imbevere.

tincture, *tĭngk'tŭr*, s. tintura, tinta, f.;

tinder, *tĭn'dŭr*, s. esca, f. fomite, m. (materia infiammabile).

tinge, *tĭnj*, v. a. tingere; –, s. tinta, f.

tingle, *tĭng'gl*, v. n. tintinnire; formicolare.

tingling, *–glĭng*, s. tintinnio, m.; zufolo (d'orecchi), m.   [lini, m.

tinker, *tĭngk'ŭr*, s. rappezzatore di padelle, m.

tinkle, *tĭng'kl*, v. a. & n. far risonare; tintinnire.

tinman, *tĭn'măn*, s. lattaio, m.   [stagno.

tinner, *–nŭr*, s. chi lavora alle mine dello

tin-plate, *–plăt*, s. latta, f.; **–worker**, stagnaio, m.   [lustro falso, m.

tinsel, *tĭn'sĕl*, s. drappo orpellato, m.;

tint, *tĭnt*, s. tinta, f.; –, v. a. tingere.

tin-tack, *tĭn'tăk*, s. bulletta, f.

tiny, *tĭn'ĭ*, a. piccolo, minuto.

tip, *tĭp*, s. punta, f.; colmo, m.; –, v. a. ferrare la punta; toccare leggermente.

tippet, *–pĕt*, s. ciarpa, f.; collare, m.

tipple, *tĭp'pl*, s. bevanda, f.; –, v. n. bere poco e spesso, centellare.

tippler, *–plŭr*, s. bevitore, m.

tippling, *–plĭng*, s. ubriachezza, f.

tipsiness, *tĭp'sĭnĕs*, s. ubriachezza, ebbrezza, f.

tipstaff, *–stăf*, s. birro, m.   [brezza, f.

tipsy, *tĭp'sĭ*, a. inebriato, ebbro.

tiptoe, *tĭp'tō*, s. punta del piede, f.

tiptop, *tĭp'tŏp*, a. eccellente; migliore; –, s. sommità, f.

tirade, *tĭrād'*, s. invettiva, f.

tire, *tĭr*, s. fila, f.; acconciatura, f.; –, v. a. & n. faticare; stancarsi; noiarsi.

tiresome, *–sŭm*, a. noioso, importuno.

tiresomeness, *–nĕs*, s. noia, f.; fastidio, m.

tiring-room, *tĭ'rĭng rŏm*, s. camera da vestirsi, f.   [trecciare.

tissue, *tĭsh'ū*, s. tessuto, m.; –, v. a. intitit, *tĭt*, s. cavallino, m.; cinciallegra, f.

titbit, *–bĭt*, s. boccone delicato, m.

tithe, *tĭth*, s. decima, f.

titillate, *tĭt'ĭlāt*, v. a. solleticare.

title, *tĭt'il*, s. titolo, m.; –, v. a. titolare.

title-deed, *–dēd*, s. diritto di proprietà, m.

title-page, *–pāj*, s. frontespizio (d'un libro), m.

titmouse, *tĭt'mŏŭs*, s. cinciallegra, f.

titter, *tĭt'tŭr*, v. n. sorridere; –, s. riso ristretto, m.   [particella, f.

tittle, *tĭt'tl*, s. punto (sopra la lettera i), m.;

tittle-tattle, *–tăttl*, s. cicalamento, m.

titular, *tĭt'ŭlăr*, a. titolare.

to, *tō (tŏ)*, pr. a, al, allo, alla; ai, agli; alle; **as –**, quanto a.

toad, *tōd*, s. botta, f., rospo, m.

toad-eater, *–ētŭr*, s. parassito, m.

toad-stool, *–stŏl*, s. specie di fungo, m.

toady, *tō'dĭ*, s. scroccone, m.   [f.

toadyism, *–ĭzm*, s. adulazione, servilità,

toast, *tōst*, v. a. abbrustolire; bere alla salute, brindare; –, s. fetta di pane abbrustolata, f.; salute, f.

tobacco, *tŏbăk'kō*, s. tabacco, m.

tobacco-box, *–bŏks*, s. tabacchiera, f.

tobacconist, *–nĭst*, s. venditore di tabacco, tabaccaio, m.

tobacco-pipe, *–pĭp*, s. pipa, f.   [bacco, f.

tobacco-pouch, *–pŏŭch*, s. borsa da tabacco, f.

to-day, *tō'dā*, ad. oggi.

toddle, *tŏd'dl*, v. n. vacillare.

toddy, *tŏd'dĭ*, s. bevanda fatta di spirito, acqua e zucchero, f.

toe, *tō*, s. dito del piede, m.

together, *tŏgĕth'ŭr*, ad. insieme.

toggery, *tŏg'gŭrĭ*, s. abiti, arnesi, m. pl., masserizie, f. pl.

toil, *tōĭl*, s. pena, fatica, f.; lavoro, m.; –, v. n. affaticarsi, affannarsi.

toilet, *–ĕt*, s. tocletta, f.

toilsome, *–sŭm*, a. faticoso, penoso.

token, *tō'kn*, s. segno, m.; dono, regalo, m.

tolerable, *tŏl'ŭrăbl*, a. tollerabile; mediocre.   [così.

tolerably, *–ăblĭ*, ad. tollerabilmente, così

tolerant, *tŏl'ŭrănt*, a. tollerante.

tolerate, *–ŭrāt*, v. a. tollerare.

toleration, *–d'shŭn*, s. tolleranza, f.

toll, *tōl*, s. pedaggio, m.; –, v. n. sonare una campana a tocchi.

toll-gatherer, *–găthŭrŭr*, s. pedone, m.

tomahawk, *tŏm'ăhăk*, s. azza degli Indiani, f.

tomato, *tŏmă' tŏ*, s. pomidoro, m.

tomb, *tŏm*, s. tomba, sepoltura, f.

tomboy *tŏm' bŏĭ*, s. ragazzaccio, m.; ragaz-zaccia, f.

tomb-stone, *tŏm' stōn*, s. lapida, f.

tom-cat, *tŏm' kăt*, s. gattaccio, m.

tomfoolery, *—fŏl' ŭrĭ*, s. baggianata, f.

to-morrow, *tŏ môr' rŏ*, ad. domani.

tomtit, *tŏm' tĭt*, s. cinciallegra, f. (uccello).

ton, *tŭn*, s. tonnellata, f.

tone, *tōn*, s. tono, m.; accento, m.

tongs, *tŏngz*, s. pl. molli, f. pl.

tongue, *tŭng*, s. lingua, m.; linguaggio, m.; idioma, m.; ago d' una bilancia, m.;
to hold one's —, tacere.

tonic, *tŏn' ĭk*, a. tonico; elastico; —, s. (mus.) tonica, f.

to-night, *tŏ nīt'*, ad. stasera.   [lata, m.

tonnage, *tŭn' nâj*, s. dazio per ogni tonnel-

tonsils, *tŏn' sĭlz*, s. pl. amigdale, f. pl.

tonsure, *tŏn' shŭr*, s. tonsura, f.

too, *tŏ*, ad. troppo; anche, ancora.

tool, *tōl*, s. strumento, ordigno, arnese, m.

tooth, *tōth*, s. dente, m.: gusto, m.; —, v. a. fornire di denti; incastrare.

tooth-ache, *—āk*, s. mal di denti, m.

tooth-drawer, *—drāŭr*, s. cavadenti, m.

toothless, *—lĕs*, a. senza denti, sdentato.

tooth-pick, *—pĭk*, s. stuzzicadenti, m.

tooth-powder, *—pŭdŭr*, s. polvere per i denti, f.

toothsome, *—sŭm*, a. saporito.

top, *tŏp*, s. sommità, f.; estremità, f.; co-cuzzolo (del capo), m.; cielo (del letto), m.; —, a. sommo; migliore; —, v. a. tagliare la cima; coprire; alzare; scapezzare; smoccolare (una candela); —, v. n. alzarsi;

topaz, *tŏ' păz*, s. topazio, m.   [eccellere.

toper, *tŏ' pŭr*, s. bevitore, beone, m.

topgallant, *tŏp' găllănt*, s. (mar.) perroc-chetto, m.

topic, *tŏp' ĭk*, s. topico, m.; soggetto, m.

top-mast, *tŏp' măst*, s. (mar.) albero di gabbia, m.

topmost, *—mŏst*, a. superiore, sommo.

topographical, *tŏpŏgrăf' ĭkăl*, a. topogra-fico.

topography, *tŏpŏg' răfĭ*, s. topografia, f.

topple, *tŏp' pl*, v. n. cadere.   [sottosopra.

topsyturvy, *—stŭr' vĭ*, ad. in iscompiglio,

torch, *tŏrch*, s. torcia, f.

torch-bearer, *—bărŭr*, s. che porta la torcia innanzi, portatore di torce, m.

torch-light, *—lĭt*, s. lume di torcia, m.;
—procession, processione colle torce, f.

torment, *tŏr' mĕnt*, s. tormento, m.; pena, f.; —, *tŏrmĕnt'*, v. a. tormentare.

tornado, *tŏrnă' dŏ*, s. burrasca, f.

torpedo, *tŏrpē' dŏ*, s. torpedine, f. (pesce).

torpid, *tŏr' pĭd*, a. intorpidito.

torpor, *tŏr' pŏr*, s. torpore, stupore, m.

torrent, *tŏr' rĕnt*, s. torrente, f.

torrid, *tŏr' rĭd*, a. torrido.

tortoise, *tŏr' tĭs*, s. testuggine, f.

tortoise-shell, *—shĕl*, s. tartaruga, f.

tortuous, *tŏr' tŭŭs*, a. sinuoso.

torture, *tŏr' tŭr*, s. tortura, f.; —, v. a. dare la tortura, torturare.

torturer, *—ŭr*, s. carnefice, m.

Tory, *tŏ' rĭ*, s. tori, conservatore politico, m.

toss, *tŏs*, v. a. scuotere, agitare, gettare; palleggiare; —, s. scossa, gettata, f.; crolla-mento di capo, m.

total, *tŏ' tăl*, a. totale, tutto, intero; —ly, ad. totalmente; —, s. somma totale, f.

totality, *—tăl' ĭtĭ*, s. totalità, f.; somma totale, f.

totter, *tŏt' tŭr*, v. n. vacillare, traballare.

touch, *tŭch*, s. tocco, tatto, m.; tratto (di pennello), m.; tintura, f.; saggio, m.; prova, f.; —, v. a. toccare, tastare; —, v. n. essere vicino; appigliarsi.

touch-hole, *—hōl*, s. focone (d' un' arma da fuoco), m.

touchiness, *—ĭnĕs*, s. suscettibilità, f.

touching, *—ĭng*, a. patetico, commovente; —, prep. circa, concernente.

touch-me-not, *—mē nŏt*, s. (bot.) noli me tangere, m.   [f.

touch-stone, *—stōn*, s. pietra di paragone, f.

touch-wood, *—wŭd*, s. legno putrido, m.

touchy, *tŭch' ĭ*, a. suscettibile.   [esca).

tough, *tŭf*, a. viscoso, tenace; duro.

toughen, *tŭf n*, v. n. diventare duro.

toughness, *—nĕs*, s. durezza, f.; viscosità, f.; tenacità, f.

tour, *tŏr*, s. corsa, passeggiata, f.; giro, m.

tourist, *—ĭst*, s. viaggiatore, m.

tournament, *—nămĕnt*, tourney, *—nĭ*, s. torneo, m.

tout, *tŏŭt*, v. n. attrarre avventori.

tow, *tŏ*, s. stoppa, f.; filo della canapa m.; fune, f.; rimorchio, m.; —, v. a. rimor-

towage, *—ăj*, s. rimorchio, m.   [chiare.

toward(s), *tŏ' ărd(z)*, pr. & ad. verso, in-verso; circa.

towel, *tŏŭ' ĕl*, s. tovaglia, f.

towel-horse, *—hŏrs*, s. seccatoio, m.

tower, *tŏŭ' ŭr*, s. torre, f.; fortezza, f.; —, v. n. torreggiare; alzarsi alto.

towering, *—ĭng*, a. alto, dominante.

town, *tŏŭn*, s. città, f.

town-crier, *—krīŭr*, s. banditore, m.

town-house, *—hŏŭs*, s. casa della città, f.

townsfolk, *—z' fŏk*, s. pl. borghesi, m. pl.

township, *—shĭp*, s. corporazione o giuris-dizione d' una città, f.   [dino, m.

townsman, *—z' măn*, s. borghese, concitta-

toy, *tŏĭ*, s. bagattella, frascheria, f.; tra-stullo, m.; —, v. n. scherzare, trastullare.

toy-shop, *—shŏp*, s. bottega di balocchi, f.

trace, *trās*, s. traccia, f.; pedata, f.; —, v. n. tracciare; delineare.

track, *trăk*, s. traccia, orma, f., vestigio, m.; solco (della nave), m.; rotaia, f.; —, v. a. tracciare; seguìtare alla pesta.

trackless, *—lĕs*, a. senza traccia.

tract, *trăkt*, s. tratto, m.; spazio, m.; con-trada, f., paese, m.; trattato, m.

tractable, *trăk' tăbl*, a. trattabile, affabile.

tractableness, *—tăblnĕs*, s. trattabilità, f.; affabilità, f.; docilità, f.

tractably, *—tăblĭ*, ad. con docilità.

traction, *trăk'shăn,* s. trazione, f.

trade, *trād,* s. mestiere, m., professione, f.; traffico, commercio, m.; negozio, impiego, m.; —, v. n. trafficare, mercatare.

trader, *trā'dăr,* s. mercante, m.; vascello o bastimento mercantile, m.

tradesman, *trādz'măn,* s. botteghaio, m.

trades-union, *–ŭn'yŭn,* s. società degli operai, f.

trade-wind, *trād'wīnd,* s. vento etesio, m.

trading, *trā'dĭng,* a. mercantile; —, s. commercio, traffico, m.

tradition, *trădĭsh'ăn,* s. tradizione, f.

traditional, *–ăl,* a. tradizionale; **-ly,** ad. secondo la tradizione.

traduce, *–dūs',* v. a. censurare; calunniare; accusare; propagare.

traffic, *trăf'fĭk,* s. traffico, negozio, m.; —, v. n. trafficare, mercanteggiare. [m.

trafficker, *–ăr,* s. trafficante, mercante.

tragedian, *trădjē'dĭăn,* s. attore tragico, m.

tragedy, *trăj'ēdē,* s. tragedia, f.

tragic(al), *–ĭk(ăl),* a. tragico; **-ly,** ad. tragicamente. [bile, f.

tragicalness, *–ălnĕs,* s. calamità deplora-

tragi-comedy, *–kŏm'ēdē,* s. tragicommedia, f.

tragi-comical, *–kŏm'ĭkăl,* a. tragicomico.

trail, *trāl,* s. pesta, traccia, f.; strascino, m.; —, v. a. & n. strascinare, strascicare.

train, *trān,* s. seguito, m.; corteggio, m.; traino, m.; serie, connessione, f.; traccia (di polvere), f.; metodo, m.; artifizio, m.; (rail.) treno di vetture a vapore, m.; —, v. a. strascinare, tirare; allettare; educare, allevare, disciplinare.

train-bands, *–bănds,* s. pl. milizia, f.

trainer, *–ăr,* s. istruttore, m.

training (up), *–ĭng (ŭp),* s. istruzione, f., il disciplinare, m.; esercizio, m.

train-oil, *–ŏl,* s. olio di balena, m.

trait, *trā,* s. tratto, m.

traitor, *trā'tŭr,* s. traditore, m.

traitorous, *–ŭs,* a. proditorio, perfido; **-ly,** ad. da traditore.

traitress, *trā'trĕs,* s. traditrice, f.

trammel, *trăm'mĕl,* s. tramaglio, m. (rete); —, v. a. pigliare alla rete; intercettare.

tramp, *trămp,* s. vagabondo, m.; strepito del andare, m. [care.

trample, *trăm'pl,* v. n. calpestare, conculcare.

trampling, *–plĭng,* s. calpestio, m.

tram-way, *trăm'wā,* s. ferrata o strada ferrata a cavalli, f.

trance, *trăns,* s. estasi, f., rapimento, m.

tranquil, *trăng'kwĭl,* a. tranquillo; **-ly,** ad. tranquillamente.

tranquillise, *–kwĭlīz,* v. a. tranquillare.

tranquillity, *–kwĭl'ĭtē,* s. tranquillità, f.

transact, *trănsăkt',* v. a. negoziare, trattare, maneggiare.

transaction, *–ăk'shăn,* s. transazione, negoziazione, f.; **-s,** pl. memorie, f. pl.

transcend, *–sĕnd',* v. a. trascendere, eccedere, superare. [lenza, f.

transcendency, *trănssĕn'dĕnsē,* s. eccellenza, f.

transcendent, *–dĕnt,* a. trascendente; **-ally,** ad. in modo sopreminente.

transcribe, *–skrīb',* v. n. trascrivere, copiare.

transcriber, *–skrī'băr,* s. copista, m.

transcript, *trăn'skrĭpt,* s. copia, f. [m.

transcription, *–skrĭp'shăn,* s. trascrivere,

transept, *trăn'sĕpt,* s. navata, f.

transfer, *–făr',* v. a. trasferire, trasportare; —, *trăns'făr,* s. trasportamento, m.; cessione, f. [tabile.

transferable, *–ăbl,* a. trasferibile, trasportabile.

transfiguration, *–fĭgūră'shăn,* s. trasfigurazione, f.

transfigure, *–fĭg'ŭr,* v. a. trasfigurare.

transfix, *–fĭks',* v. a. trafiggere.

transform, *–fŏrm',* v. a. & n. trasformare; trasformarsi. [zione, f.

transformation, *–măshăn,* s. trasformazione, f.

transgress, *–grĕs',* v. a. & n. trasgredire; violare. [sione, f.

transgression, *–grĕsh'ăn,* s. trasgressione, f.

transgressor, *–grĕs'săr,* s. trasgressore, m.

transient, *trăn'shĕnt,* a. transitorio; passeggiero, m.; **-ly,** ad. in modo transitorio.

transit, *trăn'sĭt,* s. transito, m.; passaggio, m. [sizione, f.

transition, *–zĭsh'ăn,* s. passaggio, m., transizione, f.

transitive, *trăns'ĭtĭv,* a. transitivo. [f.

transitoriness, *–ĭtărĭnĕs,* s. transitorietà, f.

transitory, *–ĭtărĭ,* a. transitorio, passeggiero.

translatable, *–lā'tăbl,* a. trasferibile.

translate, *–lāt',* v. a. traslatare; tradurre.

translation, *–lā'shăn,* s. traslazione, f.; traduzione, f. [duttore, m.

translator, *–lā'tăr,* s. traslatore, m.; traduttore, m.

translucent, *–lū'sĕnt,* a. trasparente, diafano.

transmarine, *–mărēn',* a. oltremarino.

transmigration, *–mĭgrā'shăn,* s. trasmigrazione, f. [f.

transmission, *–mĭsh'ăn,* s. trasmissione, f.

transmit, *–mĭt',* v. a. trasmettere.

transmutation, *–mŭtā'shăn,* s. trasmutazione, f.

transmute, *–mŭt',* v. a. trasmutare.

transom, *trăn'sŏm,* s. traversa, f.

transparency, *–pā'rĕnsē,* s. trasparenza, f.

transparent, *–rĕnt,* a. trasparente.

transpire, *–spīr',* v. n. traspirare.

transplant, *–plănt',* v. a. trapiantare.

transplantation, *–lā'shăn,* s. trapiantamento, m.

transport, *trăns'pŏrt,* s. trasporto, m.; nave di carico, f.; —, *trănspŏrt',* v. a. trasportare; trasferire.

transportation, *–lā'shăn,* s. trasporto, m.

transporting, *–pŏrt'ĭng,* a. estatico.

transpose, *–pōz',* v. a. trasporre.

transposition, *–pōzĭsh'ăn,* s. trasposizione, f.

transubstantiation, *–sŭbstănshĭā'shăn,* s. transustanziazione, f.

transverse, *–vărs',* a. trasverso; **-ly,** ad. trasversalmente. [v. a. trappolare.

trap, *trăp,* s. trappola, f.; trama, f.; —,

trap-door, *–dŏr,* s. trappola, f.

trapeze, *trăpēz'*, s. trapezio, m.

trappings, *–pingz*, s. pl. gualdrappe, f. pl.

trash, *trăsh*, s. robaccia, f.; bagatella, f.

trashy, *trăsh'ĭ*, a. spregevole, da nulla.

travail, *trăv'ĕl*, v. n. dolori di parto, m. pl.

travel, *trăv'ĕl*, s. viaggio, m.; –, v. n. viaggiare.

traveller, *–ĕllăr*, s. viaggiatore, passaggiere, m.

travelling, *–ĭng*, s. viaggio, m.

traverse, *trăv'ărs*, v. a. traversare.

travesty, *trăv'ĕstĭ*, s. travestimento, m., traduzione burlesca, f.; –, v. a. travestire.

trawler, *trăl'ăr*, s. bastimento da pesca, m.

tray, *trā*, s. trogolo, m.

treacherous, *trĕch'ărŭs*, a. traditore; –ly, ad. traditoriamente.

treachery, *–ărĭ*, s. tradimento m.

treacle, *trĕ'kl*, s. teriaca, triaca, f.

tread, *trĕd*, v. a. ir. calpestare, calcare; tracciare; –, v. n. ir. camminare; –, s. passo, m.; (of birds) fecondazione, f.

treadle, *trĕd'l*, s. (of eggs) sperma, f.

treason, *trē'zn*, s. tradimento, m.; high –, delitto di lesa maestà, m.

treasonable, *–ăbl*, a. traditoresco.

treasure, *trĕzh'ăr*, s. tesoro, m.; –, v. a. tesaurizzare, ammassare ricchezze.

treasurer, *–ăr*, s. tesoriere, m. [riere, f.

treasurership, *–shĭp*, s. carica di tesoriere

treasury, *trĕzh'ărĭ*, s. tesoreria, f.

treat, *trēt*, s. pasto, banchetto. m., festa, f.; –, v. a. dar un pasto; trattare; –, v. n. razionare; –, s. banchetto, m., festa, f.

treatise, *trēt'ĭz*, s. trattato, m.

treatment, *–mĕnt*, s. trattamento, m.

treaty, *trēt'ĭ*, s. trattato, m.

treble, *trĕb'l*, a. triplice; –, s. (mus.) soprano, m.; –, v. a. & n. triplicare; diventare triplo.

trebly, *trĕb'lĭ*, ad. triplicemente. [m.

tree, *trē*, s. albero, m.; arcione della sella, f.

trefoil, *trē'fŏĭl*, s. (bot.) trifoglio, m.

trellis, *trĕl'lĭs*, s. graticciata, f.

tremble, *trĕm'bl*, v. n. tremare; temere.

trembling, *–blĭng*, s. tremore, m.; (mus.) trillo, tremulo, m.

tremblingly, *–lĭ*, ad. tutto tremante.

tremendous, *trĕmĕn'dŭs*, a. terribile; –ly, ad. terribilmente. [mito, m.

tremor, *trē'mŏr* (*trĕm'ŏr*), s. tremore, tremulousness, *trĕm'ulŭs*, a. tremulo.

tremulousness, *–nĕs*, s. tremito, m.; sventolamento, m.

trench, *trĕnsh*, s. fosso, m.; (mil.) trincea, f.; –, v. a. tagliare; scavare.

trenchant, *trĕn'shănt*, a. tagliente, trinciante. [f.

trencher, *trĕnsh'ăr*, s. tagliere, m.; tavola,

trencher-man, *–măn*, s. gran mangiatore, m.; parassito, m. [trapanare.

trepan, *trĕpăn'*, s. trapano, m.; –, v. a.

trespass, *trĕs'păs*, s. trasgressione, offesa, f.; delitto, m.; –, v. n. trasgredire; offendere, violare. [fensore, m.

trespasser, *–săr*, s. trasgressore, m.; offensore

tress, *trĕs*, s. treccia di capelli, f.

tressed, *trĕst*, a. annodato in treccia. [m.

trestle, *trĕs'sl*, s. cavalletto, m.; trespolo,

trial, *trī'ăl*, s. saggio, esame, m.; prova, f.; processo, m.

triangle, *trī'ăngl*, s. triangolo, m.

triangular, *–ăng'gŭlăr*, a. triangolare.

tribe, *trĭb*, s. tribù, f.; razza, stirpe, f.

tribulation, *trĭbŭlā'shŭn*, s. tribolazione, afflizione, f.

tribunal, *trĭbū'năl*, s. tribunale, m. [f.

tribune, *trĭb'ūn*, s. tribuno, m.

tributary, *trĭb'ūtărĭ*, a. & s. tributario (m.); dipendente (m.).

tribute, *trĭb'ūt*, s. tributo, m.

trice, *trīs*, s. momento, istante, m.

trick, *trĭk*, s. furberia, f.; artifizio, giuoco di mano, m.; bazza, f. (alle carte); –, v. a. burlare; ingannare; ornare.

trickery, *–ărĭ*, s. artifizio, m.

trickle, *trĭk'l*, v. n. cascare a gocciole, gocciolare, stillare.

trickster, *–stăr*, s. furbo, m.

tricoloured, *trī'kŭlărd*, a. tricolore.

trident, *trī'dĕnt*, s. tridente, m.

triennial, *trīĕn'nĭăl*, a. triennale.

trifle, *trī'fl*, s. bagatella, baia, f.; –, v. n. scherzare; beffare.

trifler, *–flăr*, s. bagattelliere, m.

trifling, *–flĭng*, a. frivolo, da nulla.

trigger, *trĭg'găr*, s. scarpa da arrestar o fermar le ruote, f.; grilletto (d' uno schioppo), m. [metria, f.

trigonometry, *trĭgŏnŏm'ĕtrĭ*, s. trigonometria, f.

trilateral, *trīlăt'ărăl*, a. di tre lati.

trill, *trĭl*, s. (mus.) trillo, m.; –, v. a. & n. trillare.

trim, *trĭm*, a. attillato, ben fatto; –, s. abbigliamento, abito, ornamento, m.; –, v. a. guarnire; radere; (trees) potare; –, v. n. temporeggiare, esitare.

trimly, *–lĭ*, ad. acconciamente.

trimmer, *–măr*, s. voltacasacca, m.

trimming, *–mĭng*, s. guarnimento, ornamento, m. pl.

Trinity, *trĭn'ĭtĭ*, s. Trinità, f.

trinket, *trĭng'kĕt*, s. bagatella, f.

trio, *trī'ŏ*, s. (mus.) trio, m.

trip, *trĭp*, s. inciampo, m.; errore, m.; piccolo viaggio, m.; –, v. a. soppiantare, dar il gambetto; –, v. n. inciampare, sdrucciolare; saltellare; fare un piccolo viaggio.

tripartite, *trĭpăr'tĭt*, a. tripartito.

tripe, *trīp*, s. intestini, m. pl.

triple, *trĭp'l*, a. triplo; –, v. a. triplicare.

triplet, *trĭp'lĕt*, s. (poet.) ternario, m.

tripod, *trī'pŏd*, s. tripode, treppiè, m.

tripping, *trĭp'pĭng*, a. agile; leggiero, snello; –, s. inciampo, m.; danza leggiera, f.

trireme, *trī'rēm*, s. trireme, f. [giera, f.

trisect, *trīsĕkt'*, v. a. dividere in tre parti.

trisyllable, *trīsĭl'lăbl*, s. parola trisillaba, f. [ad. trivialmente.

trite, *trīt*, a. usitato; trito, comune; –ly,

triteness, *–nĕs*, s. trivialità, f.

triturate, *trĭt'ŭrāt*, v. a. triturare.

triumph, *trī'ŭmf*, s. trionfo, m.; –, v. n. trionfare.

triumphal, *–ŭm'făl*, a. trionfale.

triumphant, *–ăm'fănt,* a. trionfante; **–ly,** ad. con trionfo, trionfalmente.

triumvir, *–ăm'vyr,* s. triumviro, m.

triumvirate, *–ăm'vērăt,* s. triumvirato, m.

trivial, *trĭv'ĭăl,* a. triviale, volgare; **–ly,** ad. trivialmente.

triviality, *–ăl'ĭtĭ,* s. trivialità, f.

troll, *trōl,* v. n. andare qua e là; voltolarsi.

trollop, *trŏl'lŏp,* s. donna sporca, f.

troop, *trŏp,* s. truppa, frotta, f.; compagnia, f.; **–,** v. n. adunarsi.

trooper, *–ăr,* s. soldato a cavallo, m.

trophy, *trŏ'fĭ,* s. trofeo, m.; trionfo, m.

tropic, *trŏp'ĭk,* s. tropico, m.

tropical, *–ăl,* a. metaforico.

trot, *trŏt,* s. trotto, m.; **–,** v. n. trottare.

trotter, *–tăr,* s. trottatore, m.; **–s,** pl. zampucci (di pecora), m. pl.

trouble, *trŭb'l,* s. disturbamento, m.; inquietudine, f.; pena, f., afflizione, f., cordoglio, m.; **–,** v. a. disturbare.

troublesome, *–sŭm,* a. noioso, affannoso penoso; importuno. [pena, f.

troublesomeness, *–nĕs,* s. importunità, f.;

troublous, *trŭb'lŭs,* a. tumultuoso; confuso; importuno.

trough, *trŏf,* s. trogolo, m.; madia, f.

trousering, *trŏŭ'zŭrĭng,* s. stoffa per farne calzoni, f.

trousers, *–zŭrz,* s. pl. calzoni lunghi, m. pl.

trout, *trŏŭt,* s. trota, f. (pesce).

trowel, *trŏŭ'ĕl,* s. mestola da muratori, f.

truant, *trŏ'ănt,* a. infingardo, ozioso; **–,** s. vagabondo, m.

truce, *trŏs,* s. tregua, f.; sospensione, f.

truck, *trŭk,* s. baratto, cambio, m.; carretta, f., carro da trasporto, m.; **–,** v. n. barattare. [sommettersi.

truckle, *trŭk'l,* s. piccola ruota, f.

truckle-bed, *–bĕd,* s. letticciuolo sulle rotelle, m. [petto feroce, m.

truculence, *trŭk'ŭlĕns,* s. ferocia, f.; as-

truculent, *–ălĕnt,* a. feroce; crudele.

trudge, *trŭj,* v. n. andare attorno; affaticarsi, stancarsi.

true, *trŏ,* vero, certo; sincero; esatto.

true-born, *–bŏrn,* a. legittimo.

true-bred, *–brĕd,* a. di buona razza.

true-hearted, *–hărtĕd,* a. franco, sincero.

true-love, *–lăv,* s. uva di volpe, f.

truffle, *trŭf'l,* s. tartufo nero, m.

truism, *trŏ'ĭzm,* s. verità evidente, f.

truly, *trŏ'lĭ,* ad. veramente, sinceramente.

trump, *trămp,* s. tromba, f.; trionfo (alle carte delle minchiate), m.; **–,** v. a. prendere con un trionfo (al giuoco delle carte);
to – up, inventare.

trumpery, *–ărĭ,* s. bagattella, f.; falsità, f.

trumpet, *trăm'pĕt,* s. tromba, f.: **–,** v. a. sonare la tromba; pubblicare; divulgare.

trumpeter, *–ăr,* s. trombettiere, m.

truncate, *trăng'kăt,* v. a. troncare, mozzare, stroppiare. [m.

truncheon, *trăn'shŭn,* s. bastone, frugone,

trundle, *trăn'dl,* s. carriuola, f.; cilindro, m.; **–,** v. n. rotolare.

trunk, *trăngk,* s. tronco, m.; busto, m.; forziere, baule, m.; proboscide, f. [f.

trunk-line, *–lĭn,* s. (rail.)linea principale,

trunk-maker, *–măkăr,* s. valigiaio, m.

trunnion, *trăn'yăn,* s. orecchione (di cannone), m.

truss, *trŭs,* s. fascio, fardello, m.; bracchiere, m.; **–,** v. a. imballare; ripiegare.

trust, *trŭst,* s. fiducia, fede, confidenza. f.; deposito, m.; credito, m.; **–,** v. a. fidare, confidare, far credenza; **–,** v. n. fidarsi; far capitale; sperare. [tore, m.

trustee, *trŭstĕ',* s. depositario, m.; cura-

trustful, *–fŭl,* a. fedele.

trustily, *–tĭ,* ad. fedelmente.

trustiness, *–ĭnĕs,* s. fedeltà, f.; lealtà, f.

trustworthy, *–wărthĭ,* a. degno di confidenza, fidato.

trusty, *trŭst'ĭ,* a. fedele; fidato, sicuro.

truth, *trŏth,* s. vero, m., verità, f.; fedeltà, f.; **in –,** davvero. [ad. veracemente.

truthful, *–fŭl,* a. verace, ingenuo; **–ly,**

truthfulness, *–nĕs,* s. veracità, f.

try, *trĭ,* v. a. provare, far la prova, far il saggio, cimentare, sperimentare; cercare, scalzare; esaminare; tentare; sforzarsi.

trying, *–ĭng,* a. crudele; penoso; critico.

tube, *tŭb,* s. tubo, sinfone, m.

tubercle, *tŭ'bărkl,* s. tubercolo, m.

tuberose, *tŭ'bărōs,* s. (bot.) tuberoso, m.

tubular, *tŭ'bŭlăr,* a. tubulare.

tuck, *tŭk,* s. stocco, m.; spada lunga e stretta, f.; rete, f.; **–,** v. a. succingere, tucker,

tucker, *–ăr,* s. gala, f. [levar su.

Tuesday, *tăz'dă,* s. martedì, m.

tuft, *tŭft,* s. ciuffetto, m.; fiocco, m.; cresta, f.; mazzo di piume, m.

tufted, *–ĕd,* a. velluto; cristato.

tug, *tăg,* s. tirata, f., sforzo, m.; rimorchiatore, m.; **–,** v. a. tirare, strappare; **–,** v. n. affaticarsi. [f.

tuition, *tŭĭsh'ăn,* s. cura, tutela, f.; difesa,

tulip, *tŭ'lĭp,* s. tulipano, m.

tumble, *tăm'bl,* v. a. rotolare; rovesciare; **–,** v. n. cascare, cadere; voltolarsi, dimenarsi; far capitomboli; **–,** s. caduta, f.; capitombolo, m. [ciotolone, m.

tumbler, *–blăr,* s. saltatore, ballerino, m.;

tumbrel, *tăm'brĕl,* s. carretta, f., carro, m.

tumour, *tŭ'măr,* s. tumore, m.

tumult, *tŭ'mălt,* s. tumulto, rumore, m.

tumultuous, *–măl'tŭăs,* a. tumultuoso; **–ly,** ad. tumultuosamente. [m.

tun, *tăn,* s. botte, f.; tonnellata, f.; beone,

tune, *tŭn,* s. tono, accordo, suono, m.; umore, aria, f.; **–,** v. a. accordare.

tuneful, *–fŭl,* a. armonioso, melodioso.

tuneless, *–lĕs,* a. discordante.

tunic, *tŭ'nĭk,* s. tunica, f. [cordo, m.

tuning, *tŭ'nĭng,* s. accordatura, f.; ac-

tuning-fork, *–fŏrk,* s. (mus.) diapason, m.

tunnel, *tŭn'nĕl,* s. fumaiuolo, m.; galleria sotterranea, f.; **–,** v. a. far una galleria sotterranea. [lerie sotterranee

tunnelling, *–lĭng,* s. costruzione di gal-

tunny, *tăn'nĭ,* s. tonno, m. (pesce).

turban, *tăr'băn,* s. turbante, m.

turbid, *tûr'bĭd*, a. torbido, fangoso.
turbot, *tûr'bŏt*, s. rombo, m. (pesce).
turbulence, *tûr'bûlĕns*, s. turbolenza, perturbazione, f.
turbulent, *—lĕnt*, a. turbolento, sedizioso.
tureen, *tûrēn'*, s. zuppiera, f.
turf, *tûrf*, s. erbuccia, f.; piota, f.; corsa di cavalli, f.; ippodromo, m.; —, v. a. coprire d'erbuccia.
turgid, *tûr'jĭd*, a. turgido, enfiato.
turkey, *tûr'kĭ*, s. gallo d'India, tacchino, m.; --hen, gallina d'India, f.
turmoil, *tûr'mŏĭl*, s. tumulto, strepito, m.
turn, *tûrn*, s. giro, rigiro, m.; girata, passeggiata, f.; tiro, m.; tornio, m.; servizio, uffizio, m.; cangiamento, m.; —, v. a. voltare, volgere; cambiare; fare al tornio; formare; tradurre; esaminare; —, v. n. andar in giro, voltarsi, muoversi; mutarsi, cambiarsi; frastornare; diventare; convertirsi.
turncoat, *—kŏt*, s. rinnegato, m.
turncock, *—kŏk*, s. fontaniere, m.
turner, *tûrn'ăr*, s. tornitore, m.
turning, *—ĭng*, s. giro, m.; circuito, m.
turning-in, *—ĭng ĭn*, s. ripiegatura, f.
turning-lathe, *—lăth*, s. tornio, m.
turnip, *tûr'nĭp*, s. rapa, f. [m.
turnkey, *tûrn'kĭ*, s. servitore del carceriere, m.
turn-off, *tûrn ŏf'*, s. diramazione, f.
turn-out, *—ŏut'*, s. equipaggio, m.; (rail.) baratto, m.; cessazione del lavoro, f. [m.
turnpike, *—pĭk*, s. arganello, m.; steccato, m.
turn-plate, *—plăt*, s. (rail.) piattaforma, f.
turnscrew, *—skrŏ*, s. cacciavite, m.
turn-spit, *—spĭt*, s. girarrosto, m.
turn-stile, *—stĭl*, s. cancello, m.
turpentine, *tûr'pĕntĭn*, s. trementina, f.
turpitude, *tûr'pĭtûd*, s. turpitudine, f.; infamia, f. [preziosa).
turquoise, *tûrkŏĭz'*, s. turchina, f. (pietra
turret, *tûr'rĕt*, s. torricella, f.
turreted, *—ĕd*, a. fatto a modo di torre.
turtle, *tûr'tl*, s. testuggine (di mare), f.
turtle-dove, *—dăv*, s. tortorella, f.
tush, *tûsh*, i. oibò!
tusk, *tûsk*, s. zanna (di cignale), f.
tusked, *tûskt*, a. zannuto.
tussle, *tûs'sl*, s. lotta, contesa, f.
tut, *tût*, i. oibò! via via!
tutelage, *tû'tĕlăj*, s. tutela, f.; minorità, f.
tutelar, *tû'tĕlăr*, a. tutelare.
tutor, *tû'tăr*, s. tutore, m.; precettore, m.; —, v. a. insegnare; correggere, riprendere.
tutoress, *—ĕs*, s. tutrice, f.; insegnatrice, f.
twaddle, *twŏd'dl*, v. n. cicalare.
twain, *twăn*, a. due.
twang, *twăng*, s. suono acuto, m.; cattivo accento, m.; —, v. n. rendere un suono acuto.
tweezers, *twē'zŭrs*, s. pl. mollette, f.
twelfth, *twĕlfth*, a. duodecimo.
Twelfth-Night, *—nĭt*, s. Epifania, f.
twelve, *twĕlv*, a. dodici, m.
twelve-month, *—mûnth*, s. anno, m.
twentieth, *twĕn'tĭĕth*, a. ventesimo.
twenty, *twĕn'tĭ*, a. venti, m.
twice, *twĭs*, ad. due volte, doppiamente.

twig, *twĭg*, s. vermena, f.; bacchetta, f.
twilight, *twĭ'lĭt*, s. crepuscolo, m.; barlume, m.
twill, *twĭl*, s. stoffa a spiga, f.
twin, *twĭn*, s. gemello, binato, m.
twine, *twĭn*, v. a. intralciare, torcere; —, v. n. attortigliarsi; —, s. filo, spago, m.; intrecciamento, m.
twinge, *twĭnj*, s. dolore acuto, m.; tormento, m.; —, v. n. pizzicare; tormentare.
twinkle, *twĭng'kl*, v. n. scintillare; battere gli occhi.
twinkling, *—klĭng*, s. il scintillare, m.; batter d'occhio, m. [giramento, m.
twirl, *twûrl*, v. a. voltare, girare; —, s.
twist, *twĭst*, v. a. torcere; intrecciare; —, v. n. avvolgersi; intrecciarsi; —, s. filo, m., corda, f.; tessitura, f.: nervatura, f.; fame, f.; (of tobacco) carota, f.
twit, *twĭt*, v. a. rimproverare.
twitch, *twĭch*, v. a. tirare; pizzicare; —, s. pizzico, m.
twitter, *twĭt'tăr*, v. n. beffare, gorgheggiare; —, s. moto subitaneo, m.; garrito, m.
two, *tŏ*, a. due. [m.
twofold, *—fŏld*, a. & ad. (al) doppio.
tympan(um), *tĭm'păn(ăm)*, s. timpano (dell'orecchio), m. [m.
type, *tĭp*, s. tipo, m.; carattere da stampa, m.
typhoid, *tĭ'fŏĭd*, a. tifoideo.
typhus, *tĭ'fŭs*, s. tifo, m.
typic(al), *tĭp'ĭk(ăl)*, a. tipico, simbolico.
typographer, *tĭpŏg'răfăr*, s. tipografo, m.; stampatore, m. [grafico.
typographic(al), *—pŏgrăf'ĭk(ăl)*, a. tipografico.
typography, *—pŏg'răfĭ*, s. tipografia, f.
tyrannic(al), *tĭrăn'nĭk(ăl)*, a. tirannico; -ly, ad. tirannicamente.
tyrannise, *tĭr'ănĭz*, v. a. tiranneggiare.
tyranny, *tĭr'ănĭ*, s. tirannia, f.
tyrant, *tĭ'rănt*, s. tiranno, m.
tyro, *tĭ'rŏ*, s. novizio, principiante, m.

U.

ubiquitous, *ŭbĭk'wĭtŭs*, a. esistente in ogni luogo.
ubiquity, *—wĭtĭ*, s. ubiquità, f.
udder, *ŭd'dăr*, s. mammella (di vacca ecc.), f. [f.
ugliness, *ŭg'lĭnĕs*, s. laidezza, deformità,
ugly, *ŭg'lĭ*, a. laido, deforme.
ulcer, *ŭl'săr*, s. ulcera, f.
ulcerate, *—sărăt*, v. n. ulcerare.
ulceration, *—d'shăn*, s. ulcerazione, f.
ulcerous, *—sărŭs*, a. ulceroso.
ulterior, *ŭltē'rĭăr*, a. ulteriore.
ultimate, *ŭl'tĭmăt*, a. ultimo; -ly, ad. finalmente. [ultimato, ultimatum, m.
ultimatum, *—mă'tăm*, s. ultima offerta, f.;
ultramarine, *ŭltrămărēn'*, a. d'oltre mare, oltremarino; —, s. oltramarino, m.
ultramontane, *—mŏn'tăn*, a. & s. oltramontano (m.).
umber, *ŭm'băr*, s. terra d'ombra, f.

umbrage, *ăm' brăj,* s. ombra, f.; pretesto, colore, m., scusa, f.

umbrageous, *-brā' jŭs,* a. ombroso.

umbrella, *ămbrĕl' lă,* s. ombrello, m.

umpire, *ăm' pīr,* s. arbitro, m.

unabashed, *ănăbăsht',* a. non confuso.

unabated, *-ābā' tĕd,* a. non temperato.

unable, *ăn' ăbl,* a. incapace.

unacceptable, *-ăksĕp' tăbl,* a. spiacevole.

unaccompanied, *-ăkkŭm' pănĭd,* a. senza compagnia, solo.

unaccomplished, *-ăkkŏm' plĭsht,* a. incompiuto, imperfetto.   [cabile; bizzarro.

unaccountable, *-ăkkŏŭnt' ăbl,* a. inespli-

unaccountably, *-ăblĭ,* ad. in modo inesplicabile.   [creditato.

unaccredited, *-ăkkrĕd' ĭtĕd,* a. non ac-

unaccustomed, *-ăkkŭs' tŭmd,* a. insolito, non comune.   [sciuto, non confessato.

unacknowledged, *-ăknŏl' ĕjd,* a. scono-

unacquainted, *-ăkkwānt' ĕd,* a. ignorante, non versato, ignaro.

unadorned, *-ădŏrnd',* a. non ornato.

unadulterated, *-ădăl' tărătĕd,* a. puro, non misto.

unadvisable, *-ădvī' zăbl,* a. imprudente.

unadvised, *-ădvī' zd,* a. sconsigliato, mal avvisato; imprudente; **-ly,** *-zĕdlĭ,* ad. imprudentemente, inconsideratamente.

unaffected, *-ăffĕkt' ĕd,* a. senza affettazione, semplice; **-ly,** ad. naturalmente.

unaided, *-ād' ĕd,* a. senza aiuto.   [lega.

unalloyed, *-ăllōĭd',* a. (of metals) senza

unalterable, *-ăl' tărăbl,* a. inalterabile, immutabile.   [bato.

unaltered, *-tărd,* a. non alterato o turbato.

unambitious, *-ămbĭsh' ŭs,* a. senza ambizione.

unanimity, *ănănĭm' ĭtĭ,* s. unanimità, f.

unanimous, *ŭnăn' ĭmăs,* a. unanime; **-ly,** ad. unanimemente.

unanswerable, *ănăn' sărăbl,* a. incontestabile, incontrastabile.

unanswered, *-sărd,* a. senza risposta.

unapproachable, *-ăpprōch' ăbl,* a. inaccessibile.

unarmed, *-ărmd',* a. senza armi, inerme.

unasked, *-ăskt',* a. non domandato, non richiesto.

unassailable, *-ăssāl' ăbl,* a. inattaccabile.

unassisted, *-ăssīst' ĕd,* a. senza aiuto.

unassuming, *-ăssū' mīng,* a. modesto.

unattached, *-ăttăcht',* a. indipendente; disponibile.   [può ottenere.

unattainable, *-ăttăn' ăbl,* a. che non si

unattempted, *-ăttĕm' tĕd,* a. non tentato.

unattended, *-ăttĕnd' ĕd,* a. senza seguito.

unauthorised, *-ă' thărīzd,* a. non autorizzato.   [-ing, a. inutile; vano.

unavailable, *-ăvāl' ăbl,* **unavailing,** *-ăvā'lĭng,* a. inevitabile.

unavoidable, *-ăvŏĭd' ăbl,* a. inevitabile.

unavoidably, *-ăblĭ,* ad. inevitabilmente.

unaware, *-ăwār',* a. ignaro.

unawares, *-ăwārz',* ad. all'improvviso.

unbar, *-băr',* v. a. levare la sbarra.

unbearable, *-băr' ăbl,* a. insopportabile.

unbecoming, *-bĕkŭm' īng,* a. sconvenevole, indecente; **-ly,** ad. indecentemente.

unbefriended, *-bĕfrĕnd' ĕd,* a. senza amici.

unbelief, *-bĕlēf',* s. incredulità, f.

unbeliever, *-lēv' ăr,* s. miscredente, m.; infedele, m.

unbend, *-bĕnd',* v. a. ir. rallentare.

unbending, *-ĭng,* a. inflessibile.

unbiassed, *-bī' ăst,* a. senza pregiudizi.

unbidden, *-bĭd' dn,* a. non comandato; non invitato; spontaneo.

unbind, *-bīnd',* v. a. ir. sciogliere, slegare.

unbleached, *-blēcht',* a. non imbiancato.

unblemished, *-blĕm' ĭsht,* a. immacolato, puro.

unblest, *-blĕst',* a. maledetto, riprovato.

unblushing, *-blŭsh' ĭng,* a. sfrontato.

unbolt, *-bŏlt',* v. a. scatenacciare.

unborn, *-bŏrn',* a. non ancora nato.

unbosom, *-bŏ' zŭm,* v. a. aprire il suo cuore.

unbound, *-bŏŭnd',* a. sciolto, slegato.

unbounded, *-ĕd,* a. illimitato, infinito, immenso; **-ly,** ad. infinitamente.

unbridle, *-brī' dl,* v. a. sbrigliare, levare la briglia; **-d,** a. sfrenato, licenzioso.

unbroken, *-brŏ' kn,* a. non rotto; indomito.

unbuckle, *-băk' kl,* v. a. sfibbiare.

unburden, *-băr' dn,* v. a. scaricare, alleggerire.   [sepolto.

unburied, *-bĕr' ĭd,* a. non seppellito, insepolto.

unbutton, *-băt' tn,* v. a. sbottonare.

uncage, *-kāj',* v. a. liberare.

uncalled-for, *-kāld' fŏr,* a. non richiesto; sconvenevole.   [tinuo.

unceasing, *-sĕs' īng,* a. incessante, continuo.

uncertain, *-săr' tīn,* a. incerto.

uncertainty, *-tĭ,* s. incertezza, f.

unchain, *-chān',* v. a. scatenare.

unchangeable, *-chānj' ăbl,* a. immutabile.

unchangeableness, *-nĕs,* s. immutabilità, f.   [mente.

unchangeably, *-ăblĭ,* ad. immutabilmente.

unchanged, *-chănjd',* a. inalterato.

unchanging, *-chănj' īng,* a. invariabile, costante.   [tatevole.

uncharitable, *-chăr' ĭtăbl,* a. non caritatevole.

uncharitableness, *-nĕs,* s. mancanza di carità, f.

uncharitably, *-ĭtăblĭ,* ad. senza carità.

unchaste, *-chăst',* a. non casto.

unchecked, *-chĕkt',* a. non ristretto, illimitato.   [cristiano.

unchristian, *-krĭst' yăn,* a. indegno d'un

uncivil, *-sĭv' ĭl,* a. incivile, scortese.

uncivilised, *-īzd,* a. grossolano, rozzo.

unclad, *-klăd',* a. svestito, ignudo.

unclaimed, *-klāmd',* a. non richiamato.

unclasp, *-klăsp',* v. a. sfibbiare.

uncle, *ăng' kl,* s. zio, m.; (cant) che impresta col pegno.

unclean, *-klēn',* a. immondo, sporco; impudico; **-ly,** ad. sporcamente.

uncleanliness, *-klēn' lĭnĕs,* **uncleanness,** *-klēn' nĕs,* s. immondizia, bruttura, f.; impudicizia, f.

unclose, *-klōz',* v. a. schiudere.

unclouded, *-klŏŭd' ĕd,* a. senza nuvole, sereno.

uncock, –kŏk', v. a. sbendare, allentare.
uncoil, –kŏil', v. a. svolgere.
uncoloured, –kŭl'ŭrd, a. non colorito.
uncombed, –kōmd', a. non pettinato.
uncomely, –kŭm'lĭ, a. sconvenevole, indecente, inelegante.
uncomfortable, –kŭm'fŭrtăbl, a. inconsolabile; sconsolato; misero.
uncomfortableness, –nĕs, s. disagio, m.; tristezza, tristizia, f.   [mente.
uncomfortably, –ăblĭ, ad. malagevol-
uncommon, –kŏm'mŏn, a. raro, straordinario; –ly, ad. raramente, straordinariamente.
uncommonness, –nĕs, s. rarità, f.
uncompromising, –kŏm'prŏmīzĭng, a. irreconciliabile ;   [gligenza, f.
unconcern, –kŏnsĕrn', s. indifferenza; negligenza, f.
unconcerned, –sĕrnd', a. indifferente.
unconditional, –kŏndĭsh'ŭnăl, a. senza condizione, assoluto;   [libero.
unconfined, –kŏnfīnd', a. illimitato.
unconfirmed, –kŏnfŭrmd', a. non confermato, incerto;   [incoerente.
unconnected, –kŏnnĕk'tĕd, a. sconnesso.
unconquerable, –kŏng'kŭrăbl, a. insuperabile, invincibile.
unconquered, –kŭrd, a. invitto, indomito.
unconscionable, –kŏn'shănăbl, a. irragionevole.   [mente.
unconscionably, –ăblĭ, ad. irragionevol-
unconscious, –kŏn'shŭs, a. inconscio; ignorante.   [contraddizione.
uncontradicted, –kŏntrădĭk'tĕd, a. senza
uncontrollable, –kŏntrŏl'ăbl, a. indomabile; incontrovertibile.
uncontrolled, –kŏntrŏld', a. sfrenato.
unconvinced, –kŏnvĭnst', a. non convinto.   [suasivo.
unconvincing, –vĭn'sĭng, a. non persuasivo.
uncork, –kŏrk', v. a. cavare il turacciolo.
uncorrected, –kŏrrĕk'tĕd, a. senza essere corretto.   [integro.
uncorrupted, –kŏrrŭp'tĕd, a. incorrotto,
uncouple, –kŭp'l, v. a. sciogliere.
uncouth, –kōth', a. straordinario; rozzo; –ly, ad. stranamente; rozzamente.
uncouthness, –nĕs, s. rusticità, goffaggine, f.; bizzarria, f.
uncover, –kŭv'ŭr, v. a. scoprire; svelare.
uncrown, –krōŭn', v. a. levar la corona, privare del trono.
unction, ăngk'shŭn, s. unzione, f.
unctuous, ăngk'tŭŭs, a. untuoso, olioso.
uncultivated, –kŭl'tĭvătĕd, a. non coltivato, incolto.   [zioso.
uncurbed, –kŭrbd', a. indomito; licenuncurl, –kŭrl', v. a. disfare i ricci.
uncut, –kŭt', a. non tagliato, intero.
undamaged, –dăm'ĭjd, a. non danneggiato, non guasto.
undaunted, –dănt'ĕd, a. intrepido.
undeceive, –dēsēv', v. a. disingannare, cavare d'inganno.
undecided, –dēsī'dĕd, a. indeciso.
undecipherable, –dēsī'fărăblă, a. inintelligibile.   [senza difesa.
undefended, –dēfĕnd'ĕd, a. non difeso,

undefiled, –dēfīld', a. intemerato, immacolato, puro.   [bile.
undefinable, –ăndēfī'năbl, a. non definiundefined, –dēfīnd', a. indefinito, non circoscritto.
undeniable, –dănī'ăbl, a. incontrastabile.
undeniably, –ăblĭ, ad. incontrastabilmente.   [basso; (di) meno.
under, ăn'dŭr, pr. & ad. sotto; dopo; abunderbid, –bĭd', v. a. ir. offrire meno del giusto valore.   [tario, m.
underclerk, ăn'dŭrklărk, s. sottosegreunderclothing, ăn'dŭrklōthĭng, s. sottoveste, f.
undercut, ăn'dŭrkŭt, s. torso di manzo, m.
underdone, –dŭn', a. non ben cotto.
undergo, –gō', v. a. ir. soffrire; sostenere.
undergraduate, –grăd'ŭăt, s. baccelliere, m.   [raneo, m.
underground, ăn'dŭrgrŏŭnd, s. sotterundergrowth, ăn'dŭrgrōth, s. bosco ceduo, m.   [–, ad. sottomano.
underhand, –hănd', a. clandestino, segreto;
underlet, –lĕt', v. a. subaffittare.
underlie, –lī', v. n. giacere sotto.   [sotto.
underline, –līn', v. a. interlineare; scrivere
underling, ăn'dŭrlĭng, s. piccol agente, m.; partigiano vile, m.   [gere.
undermine, –mīn', v. a. minare, distrugundermost, ăn'dŭrmōst, a. più basso.
underneath, –nĕth', pr. di sotto, sotto.
under-part, ăn'dŭr pärt, s. parte subordinata, f.
underrate, –rāt', v. a. vilipendere.
under-secretary, ăn'dŭr sĕk'rĕtărĭ, s. sottosegretario, m.
undersell, –sĕl', v. a. ir. vendere per meno.
understand, –stănd', v. a. ir. intendere, comprendere; esser informato.
understanding, –stăn'dĭng, a. intelligente, saputo; –, s. intelletto, m.; intendimento, m.; intelligenza, f.; corrispondenza, f.
understate, –stāt', v. a. sminuire.
understrapper, ăn'dŭrstrăppŭr, s. piccol agente, m.
undertake, tăk', v. a. ir. intraprendere; impegnarsi; –, v. n. ir. impacciarsi.
undertaker, –tā'kăr, s. intraprenditore, m.; agente, m.
undertaking, –tā'kĭng, s. impresa, f.
undertone, –dŭrtōn, s. tono basso, m.
undervalue, –văl'ū, v. a. disprezzare, vilipendere.
underwood, ăn'dŭrwŭd, s. bosco ceduo, m., arbusti piccoli, m. pl.
underwork, ăn'dŭrwŭrk, s. affari di poco momento, m. pl.; –, v. a. ir. contramminare, spiantare.
underwrite, –rīt', v. a. ir. sottoscrivere; assicurare (uno naviglio).   [tore, m.
underwriter, ăn'dŭrrītŭr, s. assicuraundeserved, –dēzĕrvd', a. immeritevole; –ly, ad. immeritamente.
undeserving, –dēzĕr'vĭng, a. non meritevole, indegno.   [involuntario.
undesigned, –dēzīnd', a. senza intento;

undesirable, *–dĕz′ĭ rảbl,* a. da non deside-
rarsi.   [incerto.

undetermined, *–dĕtŭr′mĭnd,* a. indeciso;

undeviating, *–dĕ′vĭdĭng,* a. diritto;
fermo, regolare.

undigested, *–dĭjĕs′tĕd,* a. indigesto.

undiminished, *–dĭmĭn′ĭsht,* a. non diminuito.   [dizioso.

undiscerning, *–dĭzzŭrn′ĭng,* a. non giu-

undisciplined, *–dĭs′sĭplĭnd,* a. indisci-
plinato.   [rato; sincero, franco, schietto.

undisguised, *–dĭsgīzd′,* a. non masche-

undismayed, *–dĭsmād′,* a. intrepido.

undisposed, *–dĭspōzd′,* a. non ancora
disposto.

undisputed, *–dĭspū′tĕd,* a. incontrastato.

undisturbed, *–dĭstŭrbd′,* a. tranquillo,
placido.

undivided, *–dĭvī′dĕd,* a. indiviso, intero.

undo, *–dŏ′,* v. a. ir. disfare; sciorre.

undone, *–dŭn′,* a. non fatto; rovinato,
perduto.   [–ly, ad. indubitatamente.

undoubted, *–dŏŭt′ĕd,* a. undubitato, certo;

undress, *ŭn′drĕs,* s. abito di camera, m.;
divisa d'un soldato, f.; –, *ŭndrĕs′,* v. a.
svestire; spogliare.

undue, *–dŭ′,* a. indebito, ingiusto.

undulate, *ŭn′dŭlāt,* v. n. ondeggiare.

undulation, *–lā′shŭn,* s. ondulazione, f.

unduly, *–dŭ′lĭ,* ad. indebitamente; impropriamente.

undutiful, *–dŭ′tĭfŭl,* a. disubbidiente, irriverente; –ly, ad. disubbidientemente.

undutifulness, *–nĕs,* s. disubbidienza,
irriverenza, f.

undying, *–dĭ′ĭng,* a. immortale.

unearned, *–ŭrnd′,* a. non guadagnato.

unearth, *–ŭrth′,* v. a. disseppellire.

unearthly, *–lĭ,* a. non terrestre.

uneasily, *–ĕ′zĭlĭ,* ad. disagiatamente; inquietamente.

uneasiness, *–ĕ′zĭnĕs,* s. disagio, m., incomodità, f.; inquietudine, f.

uneasy, *–ĕ′zĭ,* a. disagiato, incomodo;
agitato; penoso.

unedifying, *–ĕd′ĭfĭĭng,* a. poco edificante.

uneducated, *–ĕd′ŭkātĕd,* a. non educato.

unemployed, *–ĕmplŏĭd′,* a. disoccupato,
sfaccendato.   [zato; non ipotecato.

unencumbered, *–ĕnkŭm′bŭrd,* a. sbaraz-

unenlightened, *–ĭlt′nd,* a. non illuminato; ignorante.   [ricreativo.

unentertaining, *–ĭntŭrtān′ĭng,* a. poco

unenviable, *–ĕn′vĭăbl,* a. non da portare
invidia.   [inegualmente.

unequal, *–ĕ′kwảl,* a. ineguale; –ly, ad.

unequalled, *–ĕ′kwảld,* a. incomparabile.

unerring, *–ŭr′rĭng,* a. infallibile; –ly,
ad. infallibilmente.

uneven, *–ĕ′vn,* a. ineguale; capriccioso;
–ly, ad. inegualmente.

unevenness, *–nĕs,* s. inegualità, f.

unexampled, *–ĕgzăm′pld,* a. senza esempio.   [sogetto ad alcuna obiezione.

unexceptionable, *–ĕksĕp′shảndbl,* a. non

unexpected, *–ĕkspĕk′tĕd,* a. inaspettato,
inopinato; –ly, ad. inopinatamente.

unexpectedness, *–nĕs,* s. caso subito, m.

unexplored, *–ĕksplōrd′,* a. non esplorato;
non esaminato.

unfading, *–fā′dĭng,* a. sempre florido.

unfailing, *–fāl′ĭng,* a. infallibile, sicuro.

unfair, *–fār′,* a. ingiusto, disonesto; –ly,
ad. ingiustamente.

unfairness, *–nĕs,* s. ingiustizia, f.

unfaithful, *–fāth′fŭl,* a. perfido.

unfaithfulness, *–nĕs,* s. perfidia, infedeltà, f.   [franco.

unfaltering, *–fāl′tŭrĭng,* a. ardito,

unfamiliar, *–fămĭl′yăr,* a. non comune,
straordinario.

unfashionable, *–făsh′ănăbl,* **unfashion-
ably,** *–ăblĭ,* a. non alla moda.

unfasten, *–făs′n,* v. a. disfare, disunire,
sciogliere.

unfatherly, *–fătʰ′ŭrlĭ,* a. non paterno.

unfathomable, *–fătʰ′ămăbl,* **un-
fathomed,** *–ămd,* a. senza fondo; impenetrabile.   [vole.

unvafourable, *–fā′vŭrảbl,* a. sfavore-

unfavourably, *–ăblĭ,* ad. sfavorevolmente.

unfed, *–fĕd′,* a. non pasciuto.

unfeeling, *–fēl′ĭng,* a. insensibile.

unfeigned, *–fānd′, (–făn′ĕd),* a. non finto;
sincero; –ly, ad. sinceramente.

unfelt, *–fĕlt′,* a. non sentito; insensibile.

unfenced, *–fĕnst′,* a. senza siepe.

unfilial, *–fĭl′ĭảl,* a. indegno d'un figliuolo.

unfinished, *–fĭn′ĭsht,* a. non finito, imperfetto.

unfit, *–fĭt′,* a. inetto, incapace, improprio,
sconvenevole; –ly, ad. impropriamente;
–, v. a. rendere incapace.   [volezza, f.

unfitness, *–nĕs,* s. incapacità, f.; sconve-

unfitting, *–tĭng,* a. sconvenevole.

unfix, *–fĭks′,* v. a. slegare, distaccare; liquefare.

unfixed, *–fĭkst′,* a. non fisso; errante.

unfledged, *–flĕjd′,* a. senza piume, im-
plume.

unfold, *–fōld′,* v. a. spiegare, sviluppare;
fare uscire le pecore dall' ovile.

unforeseen, *–fōrsēn′,* a. non previsto;
inopinato.   [bile.

unforgiving, *–fōrgĭv′ĭng,* a. implaca-

unfortunate, *–fōr′tănăt,* a. sfortunato,
infelice; –ly, ad. sfortunatamente.

unfounded, *–fōŭnd′ĕd,* a. senza fondo.

unfrequent, *–frē′kwĕnt,* a. infrequente;
–ly, ad. raramente.   [quentato.

unfrequented, *–frēkwĕnt′ĕd,* a. non fre-

unfriended, *–frēnd′ĕd,* a. senza amici;
non protetto.   [volenza, f.

unfriendliness, *–lĭnĕs,* s. poca bene-

unfriendly, *–lĭ,* a. non amichevole, scortese.   [tese.

unfrock, *–frŏk′,* v. a. spogliare.

unfruitful, *–frŏt′fŭl,* a. infruttuoso, infecondo.   [dità, f.

unfruitfulness, *–nĕs,* s. sterilità, infecon-

unfurl, *–fŭrl′,* v. a. spandere, spiegare.

unfurnished, *ŭnfŭr′nĭshd,* a. senza mobili; spogliato.   [acconciamente.

ungainly, *–gān′lĭ,* a. sconcio; –, ad. dis-

ungenerous, *–jĕn′ărŭs,* a. ignobile; illiberale.

ungentle, *–jĕn′tl,* a. duro, rigoroso.

ungentlemanly, –mănlĭ, a. incivile, illiberale.

ungodliness, –gŏd'lĭnĕs, s. empietà, f.

ungodly, –gŏd'lĭ, a. empio.

ungovernable, –gŭv'ărnăbl, a. indomabile; sfrenato. [zioso.

ungoverned, –ărnd, a. sfrenato, lizen-

ungraceful, –grăs'ful, a. sgraziato; –ly, ad. sgraziatamente. [sgrammaticato.

ungrammatical, –grămmăt'ĭkăl, a.

ungrateful, –grăt'fŭl, a. ingrato; noioso; –ly, ad. ingratamente.

ungratefulness, –nĕs, s. ingratitudine, f.

ungrounded, –grŏănd'ĕd, a. malfondato.

ungrudgingly, –grăj'ĭnglĭ, ad. di buon cuore. [negligente.

unguarded, –gărd'ĕd, a. senza difesa;

unhallowed, –hăl'lŏd, a. profano.

unhand, –hănd', v. a. lasciare andare le mani.

unhandsome, –hănd'săm, a. laido, deforme; –ly, ad. bruttamente, malamente.

unhandy, –hăn'dĭ, a. goffo, sgraziato.

unhappily, –hăp'pĭlĭ, ad. infelicemente.

unhappiness, –pĭnĕs, s. infelicità, f.

unhappy, –pĭ, a. infelice. [piagato.

unharmed, –hărmd', a. non guastato, non

unharness, –hăr'nĕs, v. a. levare gli arnesi. [sanità, f.: aria cattiva, f.

unhealthiness, –hĕlth'ĭnĕs, s. mala

unhealthy, –hĕlth'ĭ, a. malaticcio; insalubre. [straordinario.

unheard (of), –hărd (ŏv), a. inaudito,

unheeded, –hĕd'ĕd, a. negletto; di poca importanza. [a. negligente, incauto.

unheedful, –fŭl, a. unheeding, –ĭng,

unhesitating, –hĕz'ĭtātĭng, a. risoluto; –ly, ad. senza esitare. [ordinare.

unhinge, –hĭnj', v. a. sgangherare; dis-

unholy, –hŏ'lĭ, a. empio, profano.

unhonoured, –ŏn'ŭrd, a. non onorato.

unhook, –hŏk', v. a. spiccare dall' uncino; sfibbare.

unhoped, –hŏpt', a. inespettato.

unhorse, –hŏrs', v. a. scavalcare; levare di sella.

unhurt, –hŭrt', a. non ferito, salvo.

unicorn, ŭ'nĭkŏrn, s. liocorno, m.

uniform, ŭ'nĭfŏrm, a. uniforme; –, s. uniforme (de' soldati), f.; –ly, ad. uniformemente.

uniformity, –fŏr'mĭtĭ, s. uniformità, f.

unimaginable, ănĭmăj'ĭnăbl, a. non immaginabile. [inalterato; buono.

unimpaired, –ĭmpărd', a. non diminuito,

unimpeachable, –ĭmpĕch'ăbl, a. incontrastabile. [importanza.

unimportant, –ĭmpŏrt'ănt, a. che non è d'

uninformed, –ĭnfŏrmd', a. non istrutto, ignorante. [bile.

uninhabitable, –ĭnhăb'ĭtăbl, a. non abita-

uninhabited, –ĭtĕd, a. deserto, disabitato.

uninjured, –ĭn'jŭrd, a. illeso, non offeso; senza danno. [ignorante.

uninstructed, –ĭnstrŭkt'ĕd, a. non istrutto,

uninstructive, –ĭv, a. non istruttivo.

unintelligible, –ĭntĕl'lĭjĭbl, a. inintelligibile.

unintelligibly, –jĭblĭ, ad. in modo inintelligibile.

unintended, –ĭntĕnd'ĕd, unintentional, –tĕn'shănăl, a. non premeditato. [sato.

uninterested, –ĭn'tărĕstĕd, a. disinteres-

uninteresting, –ĕstĭng, a. non interessante.

uninterrupted, –ĭntărrŭp'tĕd, a. non interrotto, continuo; –ly, ad. senza interruzione.

uninvited, –ĭnvĭ'tĕd, a. non invitato.

union, ŭ'nĭăn (ăn'yăn), s. unione, f.

Unionist, –ĭst, s. chi promuove l'unità dell' amministrazione, unionista, m.

union-jack, –jăk, s. bandiera inglese, f.

unique, ŭnĕk', a. unico, solo.

unison, ŭ'nĭsăn, s. unisono, accordo, m.

unit, ŭ'nĭt, s. unità, f. [niano, m.

Unitarian, ănĭtā'rĭăn, s. Unitario, Soci-

unite, ănĭt', y. a. unire; –. v. n. unirsi.

unitedly, –tĕdlĭ, ad. congiuntamente, insieme. [uniformità, f.

unity, ŭ'nĭtĭ, s. unità, f.; concordia, f.;

universal, ănĭvăr'săl, a. & s. universale (m.); –ly, ad. universalmente.

universality, –săl'ĭtĭ, s. universalità, f.

universe, ŭ'nĭvărs, s. universo, m.

university, –văr'sĭtĭ, s. università, f.: collegio, m.; –man, universitario, m.

unjust, ănjŭst', a. ingiusto; –ly, ad. ingiustamente. [bile, illecito.

unjustifiable, –jăs'tĭfĭlăbl, a. inammissi-

unjustifiably, –ăblĭ, ad. illecitamente.

unkempt, –kĕmt', a. arruffato, non pettinato.

unkind, –kĭnd', a. non benevolo; incivile; –ly, a. & ad. non favorevole; incivilmente.

unkindness, –nĕs, s. malignità, f.; scortesia, f. [mente.

unknowingly, –nŏ'ĭnglĭ, ad. ignorante-

unknown, –nŏn', a. incognito.

unlace, ănlăs', v. a. slacciare.

unlawful, –lă'fŭl, a. illegittimo, illecito; –ly, ad. illegittimamente. [m.

unlawfulness, –nĕs, s. stato illegittimo.

unlearn, –lărn, v. a. disimparare.

unlearned, –lărn'ĕd, a. illetterato.

unleavened, –lĕv'nd, a. non fermentato.

unless, –lĕs', c. eccetto, se non.

unlettered, –lĕt'tărd, a. non letterato.

unlicensed, –lĭ'sĕnst, a. senza licenza.

unlike, –lĭk', a. differente; improbabile.

unlikelihood, –lĭhŭd, s. improbabilità, f.

unlikely, –lĭk'lĭ, a. improbabile; –, ad. improbabilmente. [ad. senza limiti.

unlimited, –lĭm'ĭtĕd, a. illimitato; –ly,

unload, –lŏd', v. a. ir. scaricare, alleg-

unlock, –lŏk', v. a. schiavare. [gerire.

unlooked-for, –lŏkt'fŏr, a. inopinato.

unloose, –lŏs', v. a. sciorre, slegare, disfare, sciogliere. [tuna.

unluckily, –lŭk'ĭlĭ, ad. per mala for-

unlucky, –lŭk'ĭ, a. sfortunato, sinistro.

unmake, –măk', v. a. ir. disfare; mettere in pezzi. [dare; disarmare (un vascello).

unman, –măn', v. a. effeminare; degra-

unmanageable, –măn'djăbl, a. intrattabile.

unmanly, –măn'lĭ, a. indegno d' un uomo.

unmannered, –măn'nŭrd, a. incivile, scortese; rozzo, ruvido. [solano.

unmannerly, –nŭrlĭ, a. incivile, grossolano.

unmarried, –măr'rĭd, a. senza marito, smaritata; senza moglie, smogliato.

unmarry, –măr'rĭ, v. a. annullare il matrimonio. [v. n. smascherarsi.

unmask, –măsk', v. a. smascherare; –,

unmastered, –măs'tŭrd, a. indomito; invincibile. [significante.

unmeaning, –mēn'ĭng, a. senza senso, insignificante.

unmeant, –mĕnt', a. non proposto.

unmeasured, –mĕzh'ŭrd, a. smisurato, immenso.

unmeet, –mēt', a. non conveniente.

unmentionable, –mĕn'shăndbl, a. da non menzionarsi.

unmerciful, –măr'sĭfŭl, a. spietato; inumano, crudele; –ly, ad. spietatamente; inumanamente. [ingiusto.

unmerited, –mĕr'ĭtĕd, a. non meritato.

unmindful, –mīnd'fŭl, a. negligente, trascurato. [chiaro.

unmistakable, –mĭstāk'ăbl, a. evidente,

unmistakably, –ăblĭ, ad. evidentemente.

unmixed, –mĭkst', a. non misto, puro.

unmolested, –mŏlĕst'ĕd, a. non molestato.

unmounted, –mŏŭnt'ĕd, a. smontato; appiè.

unmoved, –mōvd', a. immoto, fermo.

unnatural, –nă'tŭrăl (–chŭrăl), a. snaturato; –ly, ad. contra natura; crudelmente. [cessità, inutilmente.

unnecessarily, –nĕs'ĕsărĭlĭ, ad. senza ne-

unnecessary, –ĕsărĭ, a. non necessario, inutile; soverchio. [tire.

unnerve, –nŭrv', v. a. snervare, indebolire.

unnoticed, –nŏ'tĭst, a. inosservato.

unnumbered, –nŭm'bŭrd, a. innumerabile. [probabile.

unobjectionable, –ŏbjĕk'shănăbl, a. irre-

unobserved, –ŏbzŭrvd', a. non osservato, negletto. [esser ottenuto.

unobtainable, –ŏbtān'ăbl, a. che non può

unobtrusive, –ŏbtrŏ'sĭv, a. modesto.

unoccupied, –ŏk'kŭpĭd, a. non occupato, senza possessore; incolto, sodo.

unoffending, –ŏffĕnd'ĭng, a. innocente.

unofficial, –ŏffĭsh'ăl, a. inofficioso.

unpack, –păk', v. a. sballare; spiegare.

unpaid, –pād', a. non pagato.

unpalatable, –păl'ătăbl, a. nauseoso, spiacevole. [bile.

unparalleled, –păr'ălĕld, a. incompar-

unpardonable, –păr'dnăbl, a. imperdonabile. [mente.

unpardonably, –ăblĭ, ad. irremissibil-

unparliamentary, –părlĭmĕnt'ărĭ, a. contrario all' uso del parlamento.

unperceived, –părsēvd', a. non osservato.

unpin, –pĭn', v. a. togliere via gli spilli.

unpitying, –pĭt'ĭĭng, a. non compassionevole. [ad. spiacevolmente.

unpleasant, –plĕz'ănt, a. spiacevole; –ly,

unpleasantness, –nĕs, s. spiacevolezza, f.

unpolished, –pŏl'ĭsht, a. non ripulito, rozzo, ruvido. [nato, intenerato.

unpolluted, –pŏllō'tĕd, a. non contami-

unpopular, –pŏp'ŭlăr, a. non popolare.

unpractised, –prăk'tĭst, a. non praticato; inesperto. [esempio.

unprecedented, –prĕs'ĕdĕntĕd, a. senza

unprejudiced, –prĕj'ŭdĭst, a. non preoccupato. [premeditato.

unpremeditated, –prĕmĕd'ĭtĕd, a. non

unprepared, ănprēpărd', a. impreparato.

unpretending, ănprĕtĕn'dĭng, a. poco ambizioso, non presuntuoso. [cipi.

unprincipled, –prĭn'sĭpld, a. senza prin-

unproductive, –prŏdŭk'tĭv, a. improduttivo. [vole; inutile, vano.

unprofitable, –prŏf'ĭtăbl, a. non profitte-

unprofitableness, –nĕs, s. inutilità, f.

unprofitably, –ăblĭ, ad. senza profitto; inutilmente. [porzionato.

unpropitious, –prŏpĭsh'ăs, a. non propizio, non favorevole.

unproportioned, –prŏpŏr'shănd, a. sproporzionato. [esperimentato.

unprotected, –prŏtĕkt'ĕd, a. non protetto, senza aiuto.

unproved, –prŏvd', a. non provato, non esperimentato.

unprovided, –prŏvĭ'dĕd, a. sprovvisto, destituto. [cauto, non divulgato.

unpublished, –pŭb'lĭsht, a. non pubbli-

unpunctual, –păngk'tŭăl, a. inesatto.

unpunished, –pŭn'ĭsht, a. impunito.

unquenchable, –kwĕnsh'ăbl, a. inestinguibile. [trastabile.

unquestionable, –kwĕst'yănăbl, a. incon-

unquestionably, –ăblĭ, ad. indubitabilmente. [dato; indubitato.

unquestioned, –yănd, a. non domandato.

unquiet, –kwī'ĕt, a. inquieto, agitato.

unravel, –răv'l, v. a. sviluppare, dichiarare, schiarire.

unread, –rĕd', a. non letto; ignorante.

unready, –rĕd'ĭ, a. non parato; pesante; restio.

unreal, –rĕ'ăl, a. non reale, senza realità.

unreasonable, –rĕ'znăbl, a. irragionevole.

unreasonableness, –nĕs, s. poca ragione, f. [mente.

unreasonably, –ăblĭ, ad. irragionevol-

unregarded, –rĕgărd'ĕd, a. negletto, disprezzato. [inesorabile.

unrelenting, –rĕlĕnt'ĭng, a. inflessibile.

unrelieved, –rĕlĭvd', a. non soccorso.

unremedied, –rĕm'ĕdĭd, a. irrimediabile.

unremitting, –rĕmĭt'tĭng, a. incessante.

unrepentant, –rĕpĕnt'ănt, a. impenitente.

unreserved, –rĕzŭrvd', a. senza riserva, franco; –ly, ad. francamente. [f.

unreservedness, –vĕdnĕs, s. franchezza,

unresisting, –rĕzĭst'ĭng, a. non resistente.

unrestrained, –rĕstrănd', a. non ritenuto, non limitato. [inulto.

unrevenged, –rĕvĕnjd', a. invendicato,

unriddle, –rĭd'dl, v. a. spiegare, dichiarare. [giusto; –ly, ad. ingiustamente.

unrighteous, –rĭt'yăs (–rĭt'chăs), a. in-

unrighteousness, –nĕs, s. iniquità, f.

unripe(ned), –rĭp'(ănd), a. immaturo, verde, crudo.

unripeness, –nĕs, s. immaturità, f.

unrivalled, –rĭ'văld, a. senza rivale, impareggiabile.

unroll, -rṓl', v. a. sviluppare; svolgere.

unroof, -rṓf', v. a. levar via il tetto.

unruffle, -rŭf'fl, v. n. calmarsi; —d, calmo.　[bolenza, f.

unruliness, -rṓ'lĭnĕs, s. sregolatezza, turbolenza, f.

unruly, ŭnrṓ'lĭ, a. sregolato, turbolento.

unsaddle, -săd'dl, v. a. levare la sella.

unsafe, -sāf', a. non sicuro, pericoloso; —ly, ad. pericolosamente.

unsaleable, -sāl'ābl, a. non vendibile.

unsatisfactorily, -sătĭsfăk'tărĭlĭ, ad. in modo non soddisfacente.

unsatisfactory, -tărĭ, a. non soddisfattorio.　[scontento.

unsatisfied, -săt'ĭsfīd, a. non soddisfatto.

unsavouriness, -sā'vărĭnĕs, s. insipidezza, f.　[vole.

unsavoury, -vārĭ, a. insipido; stomachevole.

unsay, -sā', v. a. & ir. disdirsi; ritrattarsi, negare.　[dotto.

unschooled, -skṓld', a. non educato, non istrutto.

unscrew, -skrṓ', v. a. svitare.

unseasonable, -sē'znăbl, a. intempestivo, improprio.　[venienza, f.

unseasonableness, -nĕs, s. sconvenienza, f.

unseasonably, -ăblĭ, ad. fuor di stagione.

unseasoned, -sē'znd, a. non condito.

unseat, -sēt', v. a. detronizzare; scavalcare.

unseemliness, -sēm'lĭnĕs, s. indecenza, f.

unseemly, -lĭ, a. indecente.

unseen, -sēn', a. non veduto; invisibile.

unselfish, -sĕlf'ĭsh, a. disinteressato, senza interesse.

unserviceable, -săr'vĭsăbl, a. inutile.

unsettle, -sĕt'tl, v. a. render incerto; disordinare.　[luto; incostante.

unsettled, -sĕt'tld, a. non fisso; irresoluto; incostante.

unshaken, -shā'kn, a. non smosso, fermo, costante.　[sguainare.

unsheath, -shēth', v. n. cavar dalla guaina,

unsheltered, -shĕl'tărd, a. non protetto, senza difesa.

unship, -shĭp', v. a. sbarcare.

unshod, -shŏd', a. senza scarpe; sferrato.

unshorn, -shŏrn', a. non tosato.

unshrinking, -shrĭngk'ĭng, a. intimidito, intrepido.

unsightliness, -sīt'lĭnĕs, s. deformità, laidezza, f.　[deforme.

unsightly, -lĭ, a. spiacevole alla vista.

unskilful, -skĭl'fŭl, a. inesperto; —ly, ad. disadattamente.

unskilfulness, -nĕs, s. disadattezza, f.

unskilled, -skĭld', a. inesperto.

unslaked, -slākt', a. estinto.

unsociable, -sō'shăbl, a. insociabile.

unsold, -sōld', a. non venduto.

unsoldierlike, -sōl'jărlĭk, **unsoldierly**, -lĭ, a. non da soldato.

unsought, -săt', a. non ricercato.

unsound, -sŏŭnd', a. malsano, malaticcio; non onesto.　[mancanza di solidità, f.

unsoundness, -nĕs, s. miscredenza, f.;

unsparing, -spăr'ĭng, a. non sordido, liberale, generoso.　[esprimibile.

unspeakable, -spēk'ăbl, a. ineffabile, in-

unspeakably, -ăblĭ, ad. in modo ineffabile.

unspotted, -spŏt'tĕd, a. immacolato.

unstable, -stā'bl, a. instabile, incostante.

unsteadily, -stĕd'ĭlĭ, ad. incostantemente.

unsteadiness, -ĭnĕs, s. incostanza, leggerezza, f.　[luto, leggiero.

unsteady, -stĕd'ĭ, a. incostante; irresoluto.

unstudied, -stŭd'ĭd, a. non istudiato, non premeditato.

unsubdued, -săbdūd', a. indomito.

unsubstantial, -săbstăn'shăl, a. non sostanziale, poco solido.

unsuccessful, -săksĕs'fŭl, a. malauroso, infelice; —ly, ad. senza successo.

unsuccessfulness, -nĕs, s. cattivo successo, m.　[decente; incongruo.

unsuitable, -sū'tăbl, a. sconvenevole, in-

unsuitableness, -nĕs, s. sconvenevolezza, incongruità, f.

unsuited, -sū'tĕd, a. sconvenevole; mal assortito.　[puro.

unsullied, -săl'lĭd, a. immacolato; intatto,

unsupplied, -săpplīd', a. sprovveduto, sfornito.　[nuto.

unsupported, -săppŏrt'ĕd, a. non soste-

unsuspected, -săspĕkt'ĕd, a. non sospetto.

unsuspicious, -săspĭsh'ŭs, a. non sospettoso.　[non corrotto.

untainted, -tānt'ĕd, a. non macchiato,

untamable, -tā'măbl, a. indomabile; intrattabile.

untamed, -tāmd', a. indomito.

untarnished, -tär'nĭsht, a. senza macchia.

untasted, -tāst'ĕd, a. non gustato, non assaggiato.　[ignorante.

untaught, -tăt', a. non ammaestrato;

unteachable, -tēch'ăbl, a. indocile.

untenable, -tĕn'ăbl, a. da non tenersi, non difendibile.　[non abitato.

untenanted, -tĕn'ăntĕd, a. non affittato, non abitato.

unthankful, -thăngk'fŭl, a. ingrato; —ly, ad. ingratamente.

unthankfulness, -nĕs, s. ingratitudine, f.

unthinking, -thĭngk'ĭng, a. spensierato, indiscreto; trascurato.

unthought (of), -thŏt' (ŏv), a. inopinato.

untidiness, -tĭ'dĭnĕs, s. inopportunità, f.

untidy, -dĭ, a. non pulito, non ornato.

untie, -tĭ', v. a. slegare, snodare, sciogliere.　[gliere.

until, -tĭl', c. infino, sino.

untilled, -tĭld', a. incolto.

untimely, -tĭm'lĭ, a. intempestivo, inopportuno; —, ad. intempestivamente.

untiring, -tĭr'ĭng, a. infaticabile.

unto, ŭn'tŏ, pr. & ad. a, ad, in; per.

untold, -tōld', a. non detto, non contato.

untouched, -tŭcht', a. intatto, non toccato.

untoward, -tō'ărd, a. ostinato, perverso; disadatto, sgraziato; —ly, ad. sinistramente, infelicemente.

untowardness, -nĕs, s. ostinazione, caponeria, f.

untrained, -trānd', a. non disciplinato.

untranslatable, -trănslā'tăbl, a. intraducibile.

untravelled, *–trăv′ĕld.* a. non viaggiato.

untried, *–trīd′,* a. non provato, non tentato.

untrod(den), *–trŏd′(n),* a. non calpestato.

untroubled, *–trŭb′ld,* a. non perturbato.

untrue, *–trō′,* a. falso; sleale.

untrustworthy, *–trăst′wûrthĭ,* a. indegno di confidenza.   [f.

untruth, *–trōth′,* s. falsità, f.; menzogna,

untutored, *–tū′tûrd,* a. senza istruzione, ignorante.   [storcere, sviluppare.

untwine, *–twīn′,* **untwist,** *–twĭst′,* v. a.

unused, *–ūzd′,* a. inusitato.

unusual, *–ū′zhŭl,* a. inusitato; straordinario, raro; **–ly,** ad. raramente.

unutterable, *–ăt′tûrăbl,* a. ineffabile.

unvalued, *–văl′ūd,* a. non stimato, disprezzato, negletto.

unvaried, *–vā′rĭd,* a. non variato.

unvarnished, *–văr′nĭsht,* a. non verniciato; semplice.

unvarying, *–vā′rĭĭng,* a. invariato.

unveil, *ŭnvāl′,* v. a. svelare; scoprire.

unversed, *–vûrst′,* a. non versato, inesperto.

unawakened, *–wā′knd,* a. addormentato.

unwalled, *–wăld′,* a. senza mura.

unwarily, *–wā′rĭlĭ,* ad. imprudentemente, inconsideratamente.

unwarlike, *–wăr′lĭk,* a. non guerriero.

unwarrantable, *–wŏr′răntăbl,* a. da non giustificarsi.

unwarranted, *–răntĕd,* a. non assicurato, non accertato.   [rato.

unwary, *–wā′rĭ,* a. imprudente, sconsiderato.

unwashed, *–wŏsht′,* a. non lavato, sporco.

unwatered, *–wā′tûrd,* a. non adacquato, non irrigato.

unweakened, *–wēk′nd,* a. indebolito.

unwearied, *–wēr′ĭd,* a. infaticabile.

unwelcome, *–wĕl′kăm,* a. non ben venuto; spiacevole.   [civo.

unwell, *–wĕl′,* a. malaticcio.

unwholesome, *–hōl′săm,* a. malsano, nocivo.

unwieldy, *–wēld′ĭ,* a. pesante, lento, grave.

unwilling, *–wĭl′ĭĭng,* a. ripugnante; mal disposto; **–ly,** ad. mal volentieri.

unwillingness, *–nĕs,* s. ripugnanza, f.

unwind, *–wīnd′,* v. a. ir. distrigare; svolgere.   [dente.

unwise, *–wīz′,* a. poco accorto, imprudente.

unwished(-for), *–wĭsht′(fŏr),* a. non desiderato.   [moni.

unwitnessed, *–wĭt′nĕst,* a. senza testimoni.

unwittingly, *–wĭt′tĭnglĭ,* a. senza saperlo.

unwonted, *–wŏn′tĕd,* a. insolito.

unworthily, *–wûr′thĭlĭ,* ad. indegnamente.

unworthiness, *–thĭnĕs,* s. indegnità, f.

unworthy, *–thĭ,* a. indegno.   [bile.

unyielding, *–yēld′ĭng,* a. restio; inflessibile.

unyoke, *–yōk′,* v. a. sciorre dal giogo.

up, *ŭp,* ad. & pr. su, in su, da basso in alto, in alto; sopra; **– !** levatevi!

upbear, *–bār′,* v. a. ir. sostenere in alto; sopportare.   [facciare.

upbraid, *–brād′,* v. a. rimproverare, rinfacciare.

upbraidingly, *–ĭnglĭ,* ad. in modo riprensibile.

upheaval, *–hē′văl,* s. alzamento, f.; levata, f.

uphill, *ŭp′hĭl,* a. difficile; penoso; **–,** s. salita, f.   [nere; proteggere, favorire.

uphold, *–hōld′,* v. a. ir. sostenere; mante-

upholder, *–ûr,* s. fautore, m.; somministratore, m.   [m.

upholsterer, *–hŏl′stărûr,* s. tappezziere,

upholstery, *–stărĭ,* s. tappezzeria, f.

upland, *ŭp′lănd,* s. paese montagnoso, m.; **–,** a. montagnoso; alto.

uplift, *–lĭft′,* v. a. alzare, elevare.

upon, *ŭpŏn′,* pr. su, sopra; per.

upper, *ŭp′pûr,* a. superiore, più alto, di sopra.

upper-hand, *–hănd,* s. superiorità, f.

uppermost, *–mŏst,* a. superiore; predominante; **to be –,** restare superiore.

upraise, *–rāz′,* v. a. elevare; esaltare.

upright, *ŭp′rĭt,* a. eretto, ritto; giusto; sincero, onesto; **–ly,** ad. dirittamente; giustamente; sinceramente, onestamente.

uprightness, *ŭp′rĭtnĕs,* s. dirittezza, f.; sincerità, onestà, f.   [casso, m.

uproar, *ŭp′rōr,* s. tumulto, rumore, fracasso, m.

uproot, *–rōt′,* v. n. sradicare.

upset, *–sĕt′,* v. a. ir. rovesciare.

upshot, *ŭp′shŏt,* s. esito, m.; evento, successo, m.; fine, f.

upside down, *ŭp′sĭd dŏŭn′,* ad. sossopra.

upstart, *ŭp′stărt,* s. villano rifatto, m.

up-train, *ŭp′trān,* s. convoglio della strada ferrata diretto verso Londra, m.

upward, *ŭp′wûrd,* a. alzato; **–s,** ad. in su, in alto.

urbanity, *ûrbăn′ŭtĭ,* s. urbanità, f.

urchin, *ûr′chĭn,* s. riccio, m.; bambino restio, m.

urethra, *ûrē′thră,* s. uretra, f.   [care.

urge, *ûrj,* v. a. sollecitare, eccitare, provocare.   [mente.

urgency, *ûr′jĕnsĭ,* s. urgenza, necessità urgente, f.

urgent, *–jĕnt,* a. urgente; **–ly,** ad. istantemente.

urinal, *ū′rĭnăl,* s. orinale, m.

urinary, *ū′rĭnărĭ,* a. dell' orina.

urine, *ū′rĭn,* s. orina, f.

urn, *ûrn,* s. urna, f.

us, *ŭs,* pn. noi, per noi, ci.

usable, *ū′zăbl,* a. atto, abile.

usage, *ū′zăj,* s. uso, m.; trattamento, m.

usance, *ū′zăns,* s. uso, m., usanza, f.

use, *ūs,* s. uso, servigio, m.; utilità, f., costume, m.; pratica, f.; **–,** v. a. usare, adoperare, servirsi; frequentare; praticare; **–,** v. n. solere, esser solito.

used, *ūzd,* a. usato; accostumato, solito.

useful, *ūs′fŭl,* a. utile, profittevole; **–ly,** ad. utilmente, profittevolmente.

usefulness, *–nĕs,* s. utilità, f.

useless, *–lĕs,* a. inutile.

uselessness, *–nĕs,* s. inutilità, f.

usher, *ŭsh′ûr,* s. bracciere, m.; sottomaestro, m.; usciere, portinaio, m.; **–,** v. a. introdurre; precedere.

usual, *ū′zhŭl,* a. comune, ordinario; **–ly,** ad. ordinariamente.

usurer, *ū′zhŭrûr . . .* usuraio, m.

usurious, *ŭzhŏ'riŭs,* a. usurario.
usurp, *ŭzŭrp',* v. a. usurpare.
usurpation, *–pd'shŭn,* s. usurpazione, f.
usury, *ŭ'zhŭrĭ,* s. usura, f. [m.
utensil, *ŭtĕn'sĭl,* s. utensile, m.; strumento,
uterine, *ŭ'tĕrĭn,* a. uterino.
utilise, *ŭ'tĭlĭz,* v. a. utilizzare.
utility, *ŭtĭl'ĭtĭ,* s. utilità, f.; profitto, m.
utmost, *ŭt'mŏst,* a. estremo, ultimo.
utter, *ŭt'tăr,* a. esteriore, estremo; tutto, intero; –, v. a. proferire, pronunziare; manifestare.
utterance, *–ŭns,* s. il pronunziare, m.; espressione, f.; vendita, f.
utterly, *–lĭ,* ad. affatto, interamente.
uvula, *ŭ'vŭlŭ,* s. ugola, f.
uxorious, *ŭgzŏ'riŭs,* a. di moglie.

V.

vacancy, *vă'kănsĭ,* s. vuoto, m.; vacanza, f., riposo, m.
vacant, *vă'kănt,* a. vacante; vuoto, vacuo.
vacate, *văkāt',* v. a. vuotare; annullare, cassare.
vacation, *văkā'shŭn,* s. vacanza, f.
vaccinate, *văk'sĭnāt,* v. a. vaccinare.
vaccination, *–nă'shŭn,* s. vaccinazione, f.
vacillate, *văs'ĭllāt,* v. n. vacillare.
vacillation, *–lă'shŭn,* s. vacillazione, f.
vacuity, *văkū'ĭtĭ,* s. spazio vacuo, m.
vacuous, *văk'ūŭs,* a. voto, vacuo.
vacuum, *văk'ūŭm,* s. vacuo, m.
vagabond, *văg'ăbŏnd,* a. & s. vagabondo (m.). [m.
vagary, *văgā'rĭ,* s. fantasia, f.; capriccio,
vagrancy, *vā'grănsĭ,* s. vita vagabonda, f.
vagrant, *vā'grănt,* a. vagabondo, vagante.
vague, *vāg,* a. vago, vagabondo.
vails, *vālz,* s. pl. profitti, m. pl.
vain, *văn,* a. vano, frivolo; orgoglioso, altiero; **–show,** s. millanteria, f.
vainglorious, *–glŏ'riŭs,* a. orgoglioso.
vainglory, *–rĭ,* s. vanagloria, f.; orgoglio, m.
valance, *vă'lăns,* s. pendaglio, m. [m.
vale, *vāl,* s. valle, vallata, f.
valediction, *vălĕdĭk'shŭn,* s. addio, m.
valedictory, *–dĭk'tărĭ,* a. di addio.
valentine, *vă'lĕntīn,* s. letterina anonima mandata o ricevuta nel giorno di S. Valentino (14 febbraio), f.
valerian, *vălē'riăn,* s. (bot.) valeriana, f.
valet, *văl'ĕt (văl'ā),* s. servo, servitore, m.
valetudinarian, *vălĕtūdĭnā'riăn,* a. infermiccio, malaticcio.
valiant, *văl'yănt,* a. valoroso, coraggioso; **–ly,** ad. valorosamente.
valid, *văl'ĭd,* a. valido; efficace.
validity, *–lĭd'ĭtĭ,* s. validità, f.; forza, f., valore, m.
valley, *văl'lĭ,* s. valle, vallata, f.
valorous, *văl'ărŭs,* a. valoroso.
valour, *văl'ŭr,* s. valore, m.; forza, f.
valuable, *văl'ūăbl,* a. prezioso; **–s,** s. pl. cose di gran prezzo, f. pl.

valuation, *–ā'shŭn,* s. valuta, f.; stima, f.
value, *văl'ū,* s. valore, m., valuta, f.; stima, f.; –, v. a. valutare; stimare, apprezzare.
valueless, *–lĕs,* a. di nessun valore.
valve, *vălv,* s. valvola, f.
vamose, *vămōs' (vă'mōs),* v. n. (am.) scappare.
vamp, *vămp,* v. a. rappezzare.
vampire, *văm'pīr,* s. vampiro, m.
van, *văn,* s. vanguardia, f.; vaglio, m.; vagone, m.
vandalism, *văn'dălĭzm,* s. vandalismo, m.
vane, *văn,* s. girella, banderuola, f.
vanguard, *văn'gărd,* s. (mil.) vanguardia, f.
vanille, *vănĭl'lă,* s. vainiglia, f. [f.
vanish, *văn'ĭsh,* v. n. svanire, sparire; **–ing line,** s. orizzonte, m.
vanity, *văn'ĭtĭ,* s. vanità, f. [mare.
vanquish, *văng'kwĭsh,* v. a. vincere; domare.
vantage(-ground), *văn'tăj (grăănd),* s. vantaggio, profitto, m. [pido.
vapid, *văp'ĭd,* a. vapido, svaporato, insipido.
vapidness, *–nĕs,* s. vapidezza, insipidezza, f.
vaporous, *vă'pŭrŭs,* a. vaporoso. [t.
vapour, *vā'pŭr,* s. vapore, m.; esalazione, f.
variable, *vā'riăbl,* a. variabile, incostante.
variableness, *–nĕs,* s. variazione, f.; mutabilità, instabilità, f.
variably, *–ăblĭ,* ad. variamente.
variance, *vā'riăns,* s. differenza, dissensione, f.; lite, f.
variation, *vărĭā'shŭn,* s. variazione, f.
varicose vein, *vărĭkōs vān,* s. varice, f.
variegate, *vā'rĭēgāt,* v. a. varicare; screziare.
variegation, *–gā'shŭn,* s. varietà di colori, f.
variety, *vărī'ĭtĭ,* s. varietà, f.
various, *vā'riŭs,* a. vario, diverso; differente; **–ly,** ad. diversamente.
varnish, *vār'nĭsh,* s. vernice, f.; –, v. a. verniciare, inverniciare.
varnishing, *–ĭng,* s. verniciatura, .
vary, *vā'rĭ,* v. a. variare, mutare, diversificare; –, v. n. variarsi; differire.
vase, *vāz (văz),* s. vaso, m.
vassal, *văs'săl,* s. vassallo, m.
vassalage, *–ăj,* s. vassallaggio, m.
vast, *văst,* a. vasto, immenso; **–ly,** ad. vastamente; eccessivamente.
vastness, *–nĕs,* s. vastità, immensità, f.; grandezza, ampiezza, f.
vat, *văt,* s. tino, m., tinozza, f.
vault, *vălt,* s. volta, f.; cantina, f.; arco, m.; –, v. a. voltare; –, v. n. saltare, volteggiare.
vaulting, *–ĭng,* s. volteggio, m.
vaunt, *vănt,* v. n. vantarsi, gloriarsi.
vaunter, *–tăr,* s. vantatore, millantatore, spaccone, spaccamonti, m.
veal, *vēl,* s. vitello, m.; carne di vitello, f.
veer, *vēr,* v. n. cangiarsi; voltarsi.
vegetable, *vĕj'ĕtăbl,* a. vegetativo; –, s. vegetale, m.; **–s,** s. pl. erbaggi, m. pl.
vegetable-garden, *–gărdn,* s. orto, m.
vegetate, *vĕj'ĕtāt,* v. n. vegetare.
vegetation, *–tă'shŭn,* s. vegetazione, f.

vegetative, *vĕj'ĕtātĭv,* a. vegetativo.
vehemence(-cy), *vē'ēmĕns(ĭ),* s. veemenza, violenza, f.　　　　　[veementemente.
vehement, *vē'ēmĕnt,* a. veemente; **-ly,** ad.
vehicle, *vē'ĭkl,* s. veicolo, m., vettura, f.
veil, *vāl,* s. velo, m.; pretesto, m., maschera, f.; **–,** v. a. velare; celare.
vein, *vān,* s. vena, f.; cavità, f.; umore, filone, m.; **–,** v. a. screziare, marezzare.
veined, *vānd,* **veiny,** *vān'ĭ,* a. venoso, pieno di vene.　　　　　　[cora, f.
vellum, *vĕl'lŭm,* s. pergamena, cartapecora.
velocipede, *vĕlŏs'ĭpĕd,* s. velocipede, m.
velocity, *–ŭtĭ,* s. velocità, celerità, f.
velvet, *vĕl'vĕt,* s. velluto, m.; **–,** a. di velluto, vellutato; (fig.) molle, delicato.
velveteen, *–tēn',* s. velluto a spiga, m.
velvet-pile, *vĕl'vĕt pīl,* s. stoffa vellutata di lana, f.
venal, *vē'nŭl,* a. venale, mercenario.
venality, *–nāl'ĭtĭ,* s. venalità, f.
vend, *vĕnd,* y. a. vendere.
veneer, *vĕnēr',* v. a. intarsiare.
veneering, *–ĭng,* s. intarsiatura, f.
venerable, *vĕn'ărăbl,* a. venerabile, venerando.
venerably, *–ăblĭ,* ad. venerabilmente.
venerate, *vĕn'ărāt,* v. a. venerare; onorare.
veneration, *–ā'shăn,* s. venerazione, f.
venereal, *vĕnē'rĕăl,* a. venereo.
vengeance, *vĕn'jăns,* s. vendetta, f.; punizione, f.
venial, *vē'nĭăl,* a. veniale.
venison, *vĕn'ĭzn,* s. selvaggina, f.
venom, *vĕn'ŏm,* s. veleno, m.
venomous, *–ŭs,* a. velenoso.
venomousness, *–nĕs,* s. velenosità, f.
vent, *vĕnt,* s. vento, m.; aria, f.; fessura, f.; vendita, f., spaccio, m.; **–,** v. a. sventare; fiutare, esalare; divulgare, palesare, esternare.
vent-hole, *–hōl,* s. spiraglio, m.　　[nare.
ventilate, *vĕn'tĭlāt,* y. a. ventilare; esaminare.
ventilation, *–lā'shăn,* s. ventilazione, f.
ventilator, *vĕn'tĭlātăr,* s. ventilatore, m.
ventricle, *vĕn'trĭkl,* s. ventricolo, m.
ventriloquism, *vĕntrĭl'ŏkwĭzm,* s. arte di ventriloquo, f.
ventriloquist, *–ŏkwĭst,* s. ventriloquo, m.
venture, *vĕn'tŭr (–chŭr),* s. ventura, f.; rischio, m.; sorte, m.; **at a –,** alla ventura, per sorte; v. a. & n. arrischiare; arrischiarsi.　　[rischiato; pericoloso.
venturesome, *–sŭm,* a. ardito, arventurous,
venturous, *vĕn'tŭrŭs,* a. ardito; **-ly,** ad. alla ventura.
venturousness, *–nĕs,* s. arditezza, f.
veracious, *vĕrā'shŭs,* a. verace; veridico.
veracity, *–răs'ĭtĭ,* s. veracità, f.; sincerità.
veranda(h), *vĕrăn'dă,* s. veranda, f.　　[f.
verb, *vărb,* s. (gr.) verbo, m.
verbal, *–ăl,* a. verbale; litterale; **-ly,** ad. verbalmente; litteralmente.
verbatim, *–bā'tĭm,* ad. parola per parola.
verbose, *–bōs',* a. verboso, prolisso.　　[f.
verbosity, *–bŏs'ĭtĭ,* s. verbosità, loquacità,

verdant, *vär'dănt,* a. verdeggiante.　　[f.
verdict, *vär'dĭkt,* s. giudizio, m., sentenza,
verdigris, *vär'dĭgrĭs,* s. verderame, m.
verdure, *vär'dŭr,* s. verdume, m.
verge, *vărj,* s. verga, bacchetta, f.; estremità, f.; giurisdizione, f.; **–,** v. a. inclinare, piegare; tendere.
verger, *vär'jăr,* s. mazziere, m.
verification, *vĕrĭfĭkā'shăn,* s. verificazione, f.; prova, f.
verify, *vĕr'ĭfī,* v. a. verificare.
verily, *vĕr'ĭlĭ,* ad. in verità.
verjuice, *vär'jŭs,* s. agresto, m.
vermicular, *vărmĭk'ŭlăr,* a. vermicolare.
vermifuge, *vär'mĭfūj,* s. medicina antelmintica, f.　　　　　[colorire di vermiglio.
vermilion, *–mĭl'yăn,* s. cinabro, m.; **–,** v. a.
vermin, *vär'mĭn,* s. vermi, vermini, m. pl.
vernacular, *–năk'ŭlăr,* a. vernacolo, nativo.　　　　　　　　[verile.
vernal, *vär'năl,* a. di primavera, prima-
versatile, *vär'sătĭl,* a. versatile; flessibile
versatility, *–tĭl'ĭtĭ,* s. versatilità, f.
verse, *vărs,* s. verso, versetto, m.
versed, *vărst,* a. versato.　　　　　[zione, f.
versification, *–sĭfĭkā'shăn,* s. versifica-
versify, *vär'sĭfī,* v. n. versificare.
version, *vär'shăn,* s. versione, f.
verst, *vărst,* s. versta, f., miglio di Russia.
versus, *vär'sŭs,* pr. contra, verso.
vertebra, *vär'tĕbră,* s. vertebra, f.
vertebral, *–tĕbrăl,* a. vertebrale.
vertex, *vär'tĕks,* a. vertice, m.; cima, f.
vertical, *vär'tĭkăl,* a. verticale; **-ly,** ad. verticalmente.　　　　　　　　[m.
vertigo, *–tĭ'gŏ,* s. vertigine, f., capogiro,
very, *vĕr'ĭ,* a. vero; mero, pretto; medesimo, stesso; **–,** ad. molto; assai.
vesicle, *vĕs'ĭkl,* s. vescichetta, f.
vespers, *vĕs'părz,* s. pl. vespero, m. (uffizio divino).
vessel, *vĕs'sĕl,* s. vaso, m.; vascello, m.
vest, *vĕst,* s. camiciuola, sottoveste, f.; **–,** v. a. investire, porre in possesso.
vesta, *vĕs'tă,* s. zolfanello, m.
Vestal, *vĕs'tăl,* s. vestale, f.; verginella, f.
vestige, *vĕs'tĭj,* s. vestigio, m., traccia, f.
vestment, *vĕst'mĕnt,* s. vestimento, abito, f.
vestry, *vĕs'trĭ,* s. sagrestia, f.　　　　[m.
vesture, *vĕs'tŭr (–chŭr),* s. vestimento, m.;
vetch, *vĕch,* s. veccia, f.　　　[vestitura, f.
veterinary, *vĕt'ĕrĭnărĭ,* a. veterinario.
veto, *vĕ'tŏ,* s. veto, m.
vex, *vĕks,* v. a. vessare, molestare.
vexation, *–ā'shăn,* s. affanno, m., sollecitudine, f.
vexatious, *–ā'shŭs,* a. affannoso, incomodo; **-ly,** ad. affannosamente.
viaduct, *vī'dăkt,* s. viadotto, m.
vial, *vī'ăl,* s. fiala, caraffa, f.
viands, *vī'ăndz,* s. vivanda, f.; cibo, m.
viaticum, *vīăt'ĭkăm,* s. viatico, m.
vibrate, *vī'brăt,* v. n. vibrare.
vibration, *–brā'shăn,* s. vibrazione, f.
vicar, *vĭk'ăr,* s. vicario, m.; pievano, m.; sostituto, m.
vicarage, *–ăj,* s. vicariato, m.

vicarious, *vĭkă′rĭăs*, a. da vicario; sostituto.

vice, *vĭs*, s. vizio, m.; colpa, f.; vite, f.; tanaglia, morsa, f.; buffone, zanni, m.

viceroy, *vī′rŏĭ*, s. vicerè, m. |f.

vicinity, *vĭsĭn′ĭtĭ*, s. vicinità, prossimità,

vicious, *vĭsh′ăs*, a. vizioso; **-ly**, ad. viziosamente.

viciousness, *-nĕs*, s. corruttela, f.

vicissitude, *vĭsĭs′stŭd*, s. vicissitudine, f.

victim, *vĭk′tĭm*, s. vittima, f.

victimise, *-ĭz*, v. a. sacrificare.

victor, *vĭk′tăr*, s. vincitore, m.

victorious, *-tŏ′rĭăs*, a. vittorioso; **-ly**, ad. vittoriosamente.

victory, *vĭk′tărĭ*, s. vittoria, f.

victual, *vĭt′l*, v. a. vettovagliare.

victualler, *-lăr*, s. provveditore (di vettovaglie), m.

victuals, *vĭk′lz*, s. pl. vettovaglie, f. pl.

vicunia, *vĭkŏn′yă*, s. vigogna, f.

videlicet, *vĭdĕl′ĭsĕt*, ad. cioè, vale a dire.

vie, *vī*, v. n. contendere, contestare.

view, *vū*, s. vista, veduta, f.; aspetto, m.; prospettiva, f.; esame, m.; traccia (di cervo), f.; -, v. a. vedere, riguardare, osservare, considerare; esaminare.

vigil, *vĭj′ĭl*, s. vigilia, f.

vigilance, *-ăns*, s. vigilanza, f.

vigilant, *-ănt*, a. vigilante, attento.

vigorous, *vĭg′ărăs*, a. vigoroso, robusto; **-ly**, ad. vigorosamente.   [energia, f.

vigour, *vĭg′ăr*, s. vigore, robustezza, f.;

vile, *vīl*, a. vile, abietto; **-ly**, ad. vilmente.

vileness, *-nĕs*, s. viltà, bassezza, f.

vilify, *vĭl′ĭfī*, v. a. vilipendere, dispregiare.

villa, *vĭl′lă*, s. casa di campagna, villa, f.

village, *vĭl′ldj*, s. villaggio, m.

villager, *-ăr*, s. contadino, villano, m.

villain, *vĭl′lăn*, s. briccone, furfante, m.

villanous, *-lănăs*, a. villano, basso, cattivo, infame; **-ly**, ad. bassamente, infamemente.

villany, *-lănĭ*, s. villania, indegnità, f.

vindicate, *vĭn′dĭkăt*, v. a. vendicare; difendere.   [f.; difesa, f.

vindication, *-kă′shăn*, s. giustificazione,

vindictive, *-dĭk′tĭv*, a. vendicativo.

vine, *vīn*, s. vite, vigna, f.

vine-arbour, *-ărbăr*, s. pergola, f.

vine-branch, *-brănsh*, s. pampano, m.

vine-dresser, *-drĕssăr*, s. vignaiuolo, m.

vine-estate, *-ĕstăt*, s. vigneto, m.

vinegar, *vĭn′ĕgăr*, s. aceto, m.

vine-growing, *vĭn′grōĭng*, s. coltura delle

vine-stick, *-stĭk*, s. palo, m.   [viti, f.

vine-stock, *-stŏk*, s. ceppo, m.

vineyard, *vĭn′yărd*, s. vigneto, m.

vinous, *vīn′ăs*, a. vinoso.

vintage, *vĭn′tăj*, s. vendemmia, f.

vintager, *-tăjăr*, s. vendemmiatore, m.

vintner, *vĭnt′năr*, s. taverniere, m.

viol, *vī′ŏl*, s. (mus.) viola, f.

violate, *vī′ŏlăt*, v. a. violare.

violation, *-lă′shăn*, s. violazione, f.

violence, *vī′ŏlĕns*, s. violenza, f.

violent, *-ŏlĕnt*, a. violento; **-ly**, ad. con violenza.

English and Italian.

violet, *vī′ŏlĭt*, s. viola, violetta, f.

violin, *vī′ŏlĭn*, s. violino, m.

violinist, *-ĭst*, s. sonatore di violino, m.

viper, *vī′păr*, s. vipera, f.   [vipereo.

viperine, *vī′părĭn*, viperous, *-părăs*, a.

virago, *vĭră′gŏ*, s. virago, f.

virgin, *văr′jĭn*, s. vergine, f.; -, a. virgineo.

virginal, *-ăl*, a. verginale.   [f

virginity, *-jĭn′ĭtĭ*, s. verginità, f.; purità,

virile, *vĭr′ĭl* (*-īl*), a. virile, mascolino.

virility, *-rĭl′ĭtĭ*, s. virilità, f.

virtu, *văr′tŭ*, s. gusto, m.; amore, m.

virtual, *văr′tŭăl*, a. virtuale; **-ly**, ad. virtualmente.

virtue, *văr′tū*, s. virtù, f.; efficacia, f.; forza, f., vigore, m., possanza, f.

virtuous, *-tŭăs*, s. virtuoso; **-ly**, ad. virtuosamente.

virulence, *vĭr′ūlĕns*, s. virulenza, f.

virulent, *-lĕnt*, a. virulento; **-ly**, ad. in modo maligno.

virus, *vī′răs*, s. marcia, f., marciume, m.

visage, *vĭz′dj*, s. viso, m., faccia, f.

viscera, *vĭs′sĕră*, s. pl. viscere, m.

viscosity, *-kŏs′ĭtĭ*, s. viscosità, f.

viscount, *vī′kŏŭnt*, s. visconte, m.

viscountess, *-ĕs*, s. viscontessa, f.

viscous, *vĭs′kăs*, a. viscoso, glutinoso.

visibility, *vĭzĭbĭl′ĭtĭ*, s. visibilità, f.

visible, *vĭz′ĭbl*, a. visibile.

visibly, *-ĭblĭ*, ad. visibilmente.

vision, *vĭzh′ăn*, s. visione, apparizione, f.

visionary, *-ărĭ*, a. & s. visionario (m.).

visit, *vĭz′ĭt*, s. visita, f.; -, v. a. visitare; far visita.

visitant, *-ănt*, s. visitante, m.; visitatore, m.   [f.

visitation, *-tă′shăn*, s. visitazione, visita,

visiting, *-ĭtĭng*, s. visitamento, m.

visitor, *-ĭtăr*, s. visitatore, m.

visor, *vĭz′ăr*, s. maschera, f.; visiera (d'un elmo), f.

visored, *-ărd*, a. mascherato.

vista, *vĭs′tă*, a. vista, f.; prospettiva, f.

vital, *vī′tăl*, a. vitale; essenziale: **-s**, s. pl. parti vitali, f. pl.

vitality, *-tăl′ĭtĭ*, s. vitalità, f.

vitiate, *vĭsh′ĭăt*, v. a. viziare; corrompere.

vitreous, *vĭt′rĭăs*, a. vitreo, di vetro.

vitrify, *vĭt′rĭfī*, v. a. & v. n. vetrificare; vetrificarsi.

vitriol, *vĭt′rĭŏl*, s. vetriolo, m.

vituperate, *vĭtū′părăt*, v. a. vituperare, biasimare.

vivacious, *vĭvă′shăs*, a. vivace; svegliato.

vivacity, *-văs′ĭtĭ*, s. vivacità, f.

vivid, *vĭv′ĭd*, a. vivace; **-ly**, ad. vivamente.

vividness, *-nĕs*, s. vivacità, f. [zione, f.

vivification, *-vĭfĭkă′shăn*, s. vivifica-

vivify, *vĭv′ĭfī*, v. a. vivificare; animare.

viviparous, *vĭvĭp′ărăs*, a. viviparo.   [f.

vivisection, *vĭvĭsĕk′shăn*, s. vivisezione,

vivisectionist, *-ĭst*, s. vivisettore, m.

vixen, *vĭks′n*, s. volpe femmina, f.; garri-

vixenish, *-nĭsh*, a. da furia.   [trice, f.

viz, *vĭz*, ad. cioè, vale a dire.

vizier, *vĭz'yăr*, s. visire, m.   [m.
vocabulary, *vŏkăb'ŭlărĭ*, s. vocabolario,
vocal, *vō'kăl*, a. vocale.
vocalist, *–ĭst*, s. cantatore, m.; cantatrice,
vocation, *–kā shŭn*, s. vocazione, f. [m.
vocative, *vŏk'ătĭv*, s. (gr.) caso vocetivo,
vociferate, *vŏsĭf'ĕrāt*, v. n. vociferare.
vociferation, *–ā shŭn*, s. vociferazione, f.
vociferous, *–sĭf'ĕrŭs*, a. vociferante; ro-
moroso.
vogue, *vōg*, s. voga, f.; moda, f.
voice, *vōĭs*, s. voce, f.; suffragio, m.
void, *vōĭd*, a. voto, vacuo, nullo; privo di;
–, s. vacuità, f.; –, v. a. votare; abbandonare.
volatile, *vŏl'ătĭl*, a. volatile; volubile.
volatilise, *vŏl'ătĭlĭz*, v. a. volatilizzare.
volatility, *–tĭl'ĭtĭ*, s. volatilità, f.
volcanic, *vŏlkăn'ĭk*, a. vulcanico.
volcano, *vŏlkā'nō*, s. vulcano, m.
vole, *vōl*, s. tutte le mani (al giuoco delle
carte), f. pl.   [f.
volition, *vŏlĭsh'ăn*, s. volizione, f.; volontà,
volley, *vŏl'lĭ*, s. salva (di moschettate);
brigata, f.; acclamazione, f., grido, m.
volt, *vōlt*, s. volta, f.
volubility, *vŏlūbĭl'ĭtĭ*, s. volubilità, f.
voluble, *vŏl'ŭbl*, a. volubile; leggiero;
presto.
volubly, *–ăblĭ*, ad. volubilmente.
volume, *vŏl'ŭm*, s. volume, m.; libro, m.
voluminous, *–ū'mĭnŭs*, a. voluminoso.
voluntarily, *vŏl'ăntărĭlĭ*, ad. volontaria-
mente.
voluntary, *–ăntărĭ*, a. volontario; –, s.
(mus.) capriccio, m., fantasia, f.
volunteer, *–tēr'*, s. (soldato) volontario,
m.; –, v. a. farsi soldato volontario; arrolarsi.   [tuoso, m.
voluptuary, *vŏlŭp'tūărĭ*, s. uomo volut-
voluptuous, *–tŭăs*, a. voluttuoso; –ly,
ad. voluttuosamente.
voluptuousness, *–nĕs*, s. voluttà, f.
volute, *vŏlūt'*, s. voluta, f.
vomica, *vŏm'ĭkă*, s. postema suppurata, f.
vomit, *vŏm'ĭt*, s. vomito, m.; –, v. a.
vomitare, recere.
voracious, *vŏră'shŭs*, a. vorace; –ly, ad.
voracemente.
voracity, *–răs'ĭtĭ*, s. voracità, f.
vortex, *vŏr'tĕks*, s. vortice, m.; gorgo, m.
votary, *vŏ'tărĭ*, s. devoto, m.; amante,
m.; partigiano, m.; –, a. votivo.
vote, *vōt*, s. voto, suffragio, m.; –, v. a. & n.
dare il suo suffragio; eleggere.
voter, *vŏ'tăr*, s. votante, m.
votive, *vŏ'tĭv*, a. votivo.   [asserire.
vouch, *vŏŭch*, v. a. affermare, accertare;
voucher, *–ăr*, s. sicurtà, f.; testimonianza,
f.   [degnarsi.
vouchsafe, *–sāf'*, v. a. accordare; –, v. n.
vow, *vŏŭ*, s. voto, m.; –, v. a. votare; dedicare; –, v. n. fare un voto; giurare.
vowel, *vŏŭ'ĕl*, s. vocale, f.
voyage, *vŏĭ'dj*, s. viaggio (per mare), m.;
–, v. n. fare viaggio per mare.
vulcanite, *vŭl'kănĭt*, s. (geol.) vulcanite, f.

vulgar, *vŭl'găr*, a. volgare; –ly, ad. volgarmente; –, s. volgo, m.
vulgarise, *vŭl'gărĭz*, v. a. render volgare,
volgarizzare.
vulgarism, *–ĭzm*, s. espressione volgare, f.
vulgarity, *–găr'ĭtĭ*, s. volgarità, bassezza, f.
vulnerable, *vŭl'nărăbl*, a. vulnerabile.
vulnerary, *vŭl'nărărĭ*, s. rimedio vul-
nerario, m.
vulpine, *vŭl'pĭn*, a. volpino; astuto.
vulture, *vŭl'tŭr (–chŭr)*, s. avvoltoio, m.
vulturine, *–ĭn*, a. d'avvoltoio; vorace.
vying, *vĭ'ĭng*, gara, f.; emulazione, f.

W.

wad, *wŏd*, s. fascio (di paglia &c.); stoppaccio, m.; –, v. a. mettere lo stoppaccio.
wadding, *–dĭng*, s. bambagia, borra (di
lana &c.), f.
waddle, *wŏd'dl*, v. n. guadare.
wade, *wŏd*, v. n. guadare.
wafer, *wŏ'făr*, s. cialda, f.; ostia da sigil-
waffle, *wŏf'fl*, s. cialda, f.   [lare, f.
waft, *wŏft*, v. a. condurre per; convogliare;
far cenno, segnare; –, v. n. galleggiare;
–, s. (mar.) segnale, m.
wag, *wăg*, v. a. scuotere, agitare leggermente; –, s. burlone, m.
wage, *wădj*, v. a. muovere guerra.
wager, *wă'jăr*, s. scommessa, f.; –, v. a.
fare una scommessa, scommettere.
wages, *wă'jĭz*, s. pl. salario, m.   [m.
waggery, *wăg'gărĭ*, s. trastullo, scherzo,
waggish, *–gĭsh*, a. scherzevole.
waggishness, *–nĕs*, s. scherzo, sollazzo,
m.   [versi.
waggle, *wăg'gl*, v. n. dimenarsi, muo-
waggon, *wăg'gŏn*, s. carro, m., carretta,
f.; (rail.) vagone, m.
waggoner, *–ăr*, s. carrettiere, m.
wagtail, *wăg'tăl*, s. cutrettola, f.
waif, *wŏf*, s. cosa perduta, f.
wail, *wăl*, s. lamento, compianto, m.
wain, *wăn*, s. carretta, f.; **Charles'**–,
Orsa maggiore, f.
wainscot, *wăn'skŏt*, s. tavolato, m.; palco,
m.; –, v. a. intavolare; soffittare.
waist, *wăst*, s. cintura, f.; parte più stretta
del corpo, f.
waistcoat, *–kŏt (wĕs'kŏt)*, s. sottoveste, f.
wait, *wăt*, v. a. & n. aspettare; attendere;
dimorare; –, s. aguato, m., insidia, f.
waiter, *–ăr*, s. servo, garzone di caffè, m.
waiting, *–ĭng*, s. aspettamento, m., guardia, f.
waiting-room, *–rŏm*, s. sala d'aspetto, f.
waiting-woman, *–wŭmăn (––maid)*, s.
cameriera, f.
waitress, *wăt'rĕs*, s. serva, f.
waits, *wăts*, s. pl. sonatori, m. pl.
waive, *wăv*, v. a. abbandonare.
wake, *wăk*, v. a. & n. ir. destare; vegliare;
–, s. vigilia, f.; solco (della nave), m.
wakeful, *–fŭl*, a. vigilante, sveglio.

wakefulness, –nĕs, s. insonnia, f.
waken, wā'kn, v. a. & n. svegliare; svegliarsi.
waking, wāk'ĭng, s. svegliamento, m.
wale, wāl, s. cimossa, f.; striscia, f.
walk, wāk, v. a. & n. andare, camminare; passeggiare; –, s. passeggiata, f.; viale,
walking, –ĭng, s. passeggiata, f. [m.
walking-stick, –stĭk, s. bastone, m.
wall, wāl, s. muro, m., muraglia, f.; parete, f.; –, v. a. circondare con un muro.
wall-creeper, –krēpăr, s. picchio, m. (uccello).
wallet, wŏl'lĕt, s. valigia, bisaccia, f. [m.
wall-flower, wŏl'flōăr, s. garofano giallo,
wall-fruit, –frōt, s. frutto di spalliera, m.
wallow, wŏl'lō, v. n. voltolarsi (nel fango).
walnut, wāl'nŭt, s. noce, f.
walnut-tree, –trē, s. noce, m.
walrus, wŏl'rŭs, s. leone marino, m.
waltz, wāltz, s. valz, m.; –, v. n. ballare
wan, wŏn, a. pallido, smorto. [il valz.
wand, wŏnd, s. verga, f.; bacchetta magica, f. [bondare.
wander, wŏn'dăr, v. a. & n. vagare, vaga-
wanderer, –ăr, s. vagabondo, m. [m.
wandering, –ĭng, s. scorsa, f.; sviamento,
wane, wān, v. n. scemarsi; declinare; –, s. scemo (della luna), m.; decadenza, f.
wanness, wŏn'nĕs, s. pallidezza, f.; macilenză, magrezza, f.
want, wŏnt, s. mancanza, deficienza, f.; bisogno, m.; –, v. a. avere bisogno di; –, v. n. mancare.
wanting, –ĭng, a. manchevole.
wanton, wŏn'tŏn, a. scherzevole; libidinoso, lascivo; –, s. persona lasciva, f.; –, v. n. scherzare, gozzovigliare, pazzeggiare. [vamente.
wantonly, –lĕ, ad. scherzevolmente; lasci-
wantonness, –nĕs, s. scherzo, trastullo, m.; lascivia, impudicizia, f.
war, wăr, s. guerra, f.; –, v. n. far guerra, guerreggiare.
warble, wăr'bl, v. n. gorgheggiare; trillare.
warbling, wăr'blĭng, s. garrito (degli uccelli), m.
ward, wărd, s. guardia, f.; quartiere, m.; pupillo, m.; tutela, f.; –, v. a. guardare, parare; eludere; difendere.
warden, wărd'ĕn, s. custode, guardiano, m.; governatore, m.; carceriere, m.
warder, –ăr, s. guardia, f.; guardiano, m.
wardmote, –mōt, s. assemblea de' magistrati del rione, f.
wardrobe, –rōb, s. guardaroba, f.
wardship, –shĭp, s. tutela, f.
ware, wăr, s. mercanzia, merce, f.
warehouse, –hŏŭs, s. magazzino, m.
warehouse-keeper, –kēpăr, s. magazziniere, m. [f.
warfare, wăr'făr, s. vita militare, f.; guerra,
warily, wā'rĭlĕ, ad. prudentemente.
wariness, wā'rĭnĕs, s. cautela, prudenza, f.
warlike, wăr'lĭk, a. bellicoso. [f.
warlock, –lŏk, s. stregone, m.
warm, wărm, a. caldo; furioso; **–ly,** ad.

caldamente; passionatamente; –, v. a. scaldare.
warming-pan, –ĭng păn, s. scaldaletto, m.
warmth, wărmth, s. caldezza, f.; zelo, m.
warn, wărn, v. a. ammonire; avvertire, avvisare. [congedo, m.
warning, –ĭng, s. avvertimento, avviso, m.;
warp, wărp, s. ordito, m.; –, v. a. ordire; stornare; –, v. n. piegarsi, incurvarsi.
warrant, wŏr'rănt, s. ordine, m., permissione, f.; brevetto, patente, m.; –, v. a. assicurare, accertare, mallevare.
warrantable, –ăbl, a. giustificabile, difendibile.
warranty, –răntĭ, s. sicurtà, f.
warren, wŏr'rĕn, s. conigliera, f.
warrior, wŏr'rĭăr, s. guerriero, m.
wart, wărt, s. verruca, f.
wary, wā'rĭ, a. prudente, cauto.
wash, wŏsh, s. lavatura, f.; lisciva, f.; imbratto, m.; palude, m.; collirio, m.; –, v. a. & n. lavare; lavarsi. [daia, f.
washer-woman, –ăr wŭmăn, s. lavan-
washhand-basin, –hănd băsn, s. bacino, f.
washhouse, –hŏŭs, s. lavatoio, m. [m.
washing, –ĭng, s. lavamento, m.
washy, wŏsh'ĭ, a. umido, inumidito.
wasp, wŏsp, s. vespa, f.
waspish, –ĭsh, a. fastidioso, stizzoso.
wassail, wŏs'sĕl, s. festa, f.; bibita composta di mele, zucchero e birra, f.
waste, wăst, v. a. guastare, distruggere; scialacquare; consumare, diminuire; –, v. n. consumarsi; –, s. distruzione, f.; profusione, f.; consunzione, f.; terra deserta, f. [–ly, ad. prodigamente.
wasteful, –fŭl, a. distruttivo; prodigo;
wastefulness, –fŭlnĕs, s. prodigalità, f.
waste-paper, –păpăr, s. carta straccia, f.
waster, wăst'ăr, s. prodigo, m. [f.
watch, wŏch, s. veglia, guardia, f.; sentinella, f.; oriuolo, m.; –, v. a. vegliare; stare attento, spiare; –, v. n. stare alle vedette. [m.; guardia, f.
watcher, –ăr, s. che veglia; osservatore,
watch-fire, –fĭr, s. fuoco di guardia, m.
watchful, –fŭl, a. vigilante; **–ly,** ad. con cura; vigilantemente.
watchfulness, –fŭlnĕs, s. vigilanza, f.
watching, –ĭng, s. veglia, f.
watch-light, –lĭt, s. fanale, m.
watchmaker, –mākăr, s. orologiaro, m.
watch-man, –măn, s. guardia notturna, f. [nella, m.
watch-tower, –tŏăr, s. casotto da senti-
watch-word, –wărd, s. parola, f.; contrassegno, m.
water, wā'tăr, s. acqua, f.; lustro (di diamante), m.; –, v. a. adacquare, bagnare; abbeverare (un cavallo); marezzare; –, v. n. (mar.) fare acqua.
waterage, –dj, s. trasporto per acqua, m.
water-closet, –klŏzĕt, s. comodo, m.
water-colours, –kŭlŏrz, s. pl. acquerella, f.; guazzo, m. [m.
water-cresses, –krĕssĕz, s. pl. crescione,
water-cure, –kŭr, s. cura delle acque, f.

waterfall, *-fâl,* s. cateratta, cascata d' acqua, f.   [abbeverare, m.
watering, *-ĭng,* s. adacquamento, m.; il
watering-place, *-ĭng plăs,* s. abbeveratoio, m.
watering-pot, *-pŏt,* s. annaffiatoio, m.
waterman, *-măn,* s. barcaiuolo, m.
water-spont, *-spŏŭt,* s. getto d' acqua,
f.; tromba, f.   [prova d' acqua.
water-tight, *-tĭt,* a. impermeabile, a
watery, *wâ'tărĭ,* a. acqueo.
wattle, *wŏt'tl,* s. barba di gallo, f.; graticcio, m.; –, v. a. ingraticolare.
wave, *wăv,* s. flutto, m.; onda, f.; –, v. n.
ondeggiare; fluttuare.
waver, *wâ'văr,* v. n. vacillare, titubare.
wavering, *-ărĭng,* a. irresoluto; –, s.
irresoluzione, f.
wavy, *wâ'vĭ,* a. ondeggiante.
wax, *wăks,* s. cera, f.; –, v. a. incerare;
–, v. n. crescere; divenire.
waxen, *wăks'n,* a. di cera; incerato.
wax-taper, *-tăpăr,* s. cero, m., torcia,
candela grande, f.
wax-work, *-wărk,* s. modello in cera, m.
waxy, *wăks'ĭ,* a. ceroso.
way, *wâ,* s. via, strada, f.; cammino, m.;
passaggio, m.; maniera, f.; espediente, m.;
to give –, allentarsi; cedere; **in the –,**
d' incomodo.
wayfarer, *-fărăr,* s. viaggiatore, m.
waylay, *-lâ* (*wâlâ'*), v. a. insidiare.
ways and means, *-z ănd mênz,* s. pl. le
vie e i mezzi.
wayside, *-sĭd,* s. lato della strada, m.
wayward, *-wârd,* a. ostinato, ritroso.
wayworn, *-wôrn,* a. stanco dal viaggio.
we, *wê,* pn. pl. noi.   [mente.
weak, *wêk,* a. debole; **-ly,** ad. debol-
weaken, *wêk'n,* v. a. debilitare.
weakening, *-nĭng,* s. debilitamento, m.
weakling, *-lĭng,* s. persona gracile, f.
weakness, *-nês,* s. debolezza, f.; debole
weal, *wêl,* s. bene, m., prosperità, f. [m.
wealth, *wêlth,* s. ricchezze, f. pl., beni, m.
wealthily, *-ĭlĭ,* ad. riccamente.   [pl.
wealthiness, *-ĭnês,* s. opulenza, f.
wealthy, *wêlth'ĭ,* a. opulento, ricco.
wean, *wên,* v. a. divezzare, spoppare.
weapon, *wêp'n,* s. arme, f.
wear, *wâr,* v. a. ir. usare; portare; consumare; –, v. n. ir. usarsi; –, s. servizio,
uso, m.
wearabl *-âbl,* a. portabile.
weariness, *wê'rĭnês,* s. fatica, f.; stanchezza, f.; fastidio, m.   [samente.
wearisome, *-săm,* a. noioso; **-ly,** ad. noio-
weary, *wê'rĭ,* a. lasso, affaticato; noiato;
–, v. a. straccare, noiare.
weasel, *wê'zĕl,* s. donnola, mustella, f.
weather, *wêth'ăr,* s. disposizione dell'
aria, f.; –, v. a. sopportare. [dagli animi.
weather-beaten, *-bêtn,* a. affievolito
weather-cock, *-kŏk,* s. banderuola, f.
weave, *wêv,* v. a. ir. tessere; intrecciare.
weaver, *-ăr,* s. tessitore, m.
weaving, *-ĭng,* s. tessitura, f.

web, *wĕb,* s. tela, f.; tessitura, f.; membrana, f.
webbed, *wĕbd,* a. coperto d' una pellicola.
wed, *wĕd,* v. a. sposare; –, v. n. ammogliarsi.   [f. pl.
wedding, *-dĭng,* s. sposalizio, m., nozze,
wedge, *wĕj,* s. conio, m.; verga (d' oro
ecc.), f.; –, v. a. serrare, premere.
wedlock, *wĕd'lŏk,* s. matrimonio, m.
Wednesday, *wênz'dâ,* s. mercoledì, m.
wee, *wê,* a. piccolo.
weed, *wĕd,* s. mal' erba, f.; abito lugubre,
m.; –, v. a. sarchiare.
weeding-hook, *-ĭng hŏk,* s. sarchio, m.
weedy, *wĕd'ĭ,* a. pieno di mal' erbe.
week, *wĕk,* s. settimana, f.
week-day, *-dâ,* s. giorno di lavoro, m.
weekly, *-lĭ,* a. & ad. settimanale; ogni o
per settimana.   [mare.
weep, *wĕp,* v. a. & n. ir. piangere, lacri-
weeper, *-ăr,* s. lacrimante, m.
weeping-willow, *-ĭng wĭllŏ,* s. salcio
piangente, m.   [(verme), m.
weevil, *wĕ'vĭl,* s. punteruolo, gorgoglione
weft, *wĕft,* s. tessuto, m., tessitura, f.!
weigh, *wâ,* v. a. & n. pesare; considerare;
esaminare.
weight, *wât,* s. peso, m.; gravezza, f.
weightily, *-ĭlĭ,* ad. pesantemente; gravemente.   [f.; importanza, f.
weightiness, *-ĭnês,* s. peso, m., gravezza,
weighty, *wât'ĭ,* a. pesante; importante.
weir, *wêr,* s. nassa, f.; chiusa, f.
welcome, *wĕl'kăm,* a. ben venuto; piacevole; **– I** i. siate ben venuto! –, s. buona
accoglienza, f.; –, v. a. fare buona accoglienza.
weld, *wĕld,* v. a. battere il ferro caldo.
welfare, *wĕl'făr,* s. salute, prosperità, f.
well, *wĕl,* s. pozzo, m., sorgente, fontana,
f.; **-s,** pl. acque minerali, f. pl.
well, –, a. in buona salute; felice; –, ad.
bene; molto; **as – as,** tanto bene che.
well-being, *-bêĭng,* s. prosperità, felicità, f.
well-bred, *-brĕd,* a. ben allevato.
well-doing, *-dŏĭng,* s. il far bene, m.
well-met, *-mĕt,* i. mi rallegro di vedervi!
well-to-do, *-tŏ dŏ,* a. a bell' agio.
well-wisher, *-wĭshăr,* s. che desidera
bene, m.; amico, m.   [orlare.
welt, *wĕlt,* s. orlo, m.; margine, f.; –, v. a.
welter, *wĕl'tăr,* v. n. voltolarsi; impan-
tanarsi.   [m.
wen, *wên,* s. tumore calloso, m.; gozzaia.
wench, *wênsh,* s. zitella, ragazza, f.
wend, *wĕnd,* v. n. andare, volgersi.
west, *wĕst,* s. occidente, occaso, m.; –, s.
all' occaso.   [dentale, d' occidente.
westerly, *-ărlĭ,* western, *-ărn,* a. occi-
westward, *-wărd,* ad. verso ponente.
wet, *wĕt,* a. umido, bagnato; –, s. umidità, f.; mollezza, f.; –, v. a. unettare,
adacquare.
wether, *wêth'ăr,* s. montone, m.
wetness, *wĕt'nês,* s. umidità, f.
wetnurse, *-nărs,* s. balia, allevatrice, f.
whack, *hwăk,* v. a. colpo forte; percossa,
whale, *hwâl,* s. balena, f.

whale-bone, –bôn, s. osso di balena, m.

whaler, –ăr, s. pescatore di balene, m.

wharf, hwărf, s. porto, m.; molo, m.

wharfage, –ǎj, s. diritto del ripaggio, n..

wharfinger, –înjăr, s. guardiano d' un molo, m. [sia; quale, quanto.

what, hwŏt, pn. che, che cosa; checches-

what(so)ever, –(sŏ)ĕv'ăr, pn. qualunque, qual si sia; qualche.

wheal, hwĕl, s. bolla, f.

wheat, hwĕt, s. frumento, m., biada, f.

wheaten, hwĕt'n, a. di grano.

wheedle, hwĕ dl, v. a. allettare, lusingare.

wheel, hwĕl, s. ruota, f.; –, v. a. voltolare, rotolare; –, v. n. voltarsi, aggirarsi.

wheel-barrow, –bărrŏ, s. carriuola, f., carrettino, m., carriola, f.

wheeler, –ăr, wheel-horse, –hŏrs, s. cavallo delle stanghe, m. [carradore, m.

wheel-wright, –rît, s. facitore di ruote,

wheeze, hwēz, v. n. respirare, rifiatare faticosamente o con difficoltà.

whelm, hwĕlm, v. a. coprire; sommergere.

whelp, hwĕlp, s. cagnolino, m.; –, v. n. fare i cagnolini.

when, hwĕn, ad. quando; mentre.

whence, hwĕns, ad. onde, donde.

whence(so)ever, –(sŏ)ĕv'ăr, ad. don-dechè. [ogni volta che.

when(so)ever, hwĕn(sŏ)ĕv'ăr, ad. quando,

where, hwăr, ad. dove; any–, ovunque; every –, dappertutto; –about, laddove; –as, in luogo che; perchè, stante che; –at, al che, del che; –by, per il quale, per cui; –fore, per la qual causa, perciò; –from, donde; –in, in che, nel quale; dove; –into, nel quale; –of, del quale; delle quali; –on, sopra di che, sul che, sul quale; –so, –soever, in qualunque luogo; –to, –unto, al che, al quale; –upon, nel che, in questo mentre; –ever, ovunque; –with, –withal, con che, con quale.

wherry, hwĕr'rî, s. barchetta, f.

whet, hwĕt, v. a. aguzzare; (fig.) eccitare.

whether, hwĕth'ăr, c. se, sia che; –, pn. quale, quale de' due.

whetstone, hwĕt'stŏn, s. cote, f.

whey, hwâ, s. siero, m.

which, hwîch, pn. che, il quale, la quale.

which(so)ever, –(sŏ)ĕv'ăr, pn. qualunque.

whiff, hwĭf, s. fiato, soffiamento, m.

Whig, hwîg, s. liberale inglese, m. [f.

while, hwîl, s. spazio di tempo, m.; volta, f.

while, –, whilst, hwîlst, c. mentre che.

whim, hwîm, s. capriccio, m., fantasia, f.

whimper, –păr, v. n. gemere, dolersi.

whimsical, –sîkăl, a. capriccioso, fan-tastico. [lagnarsi; –, s. lamento, m.

whine, hwîn, v. n. dolersi, rammaricarsi,

whinny, hwîn'nî, v. n. nitrire.

whip, hwîp, s. sferza, f.; –, v. a. sferzare, uscir subitamente. [riorità, f.

whip-hand, –hănd, s. vantaggio, m., supe-

whipper-in, –păr în, s. (in Parliament) capofila, m. [m.

whipple-tree, hwîp'pl trĕ, s. bilancino,

whirl, hwărl, s. vortice, turbine, m.; –, v. a. & n. girare con impeto; aggirarsi.

whirligig, hwăr'lîgîg, s. zurlo, m., trot-tola, f.

whirlpool, hwărl'pŏl, s. voragine, f.

whirlwind, –wînd, s. turbine, m.

whisk, hwîsk, s. spazzola, f. [f.

whisker, –ăr, s. mustacchio, m.; basetta,

whisky, hwîs'kî, s. acquavite tratta dall'orzo, f. [sarture.

whisper, hwîs'păr, v. n. bisbigliare, su-

whisperer, –ăr, s. sussurrone, m.

whispering, –îng, s. bisbiglio, m.

whist, hwîst, s. giuoco di carte, m.

whistle, hwîs'sl, s. fischio, m.; –, v. a. & n. zufolare, fischiare.

whit, hwît, s. tantino, punto, m.

white, hwît, a. bianco; puro; –, s. color bianco, m.; albume (d' un' uovo), m.

white-bait, –băt, s. pl. ghiozzi, m. pl.

white-gold, –gŏld, s. platina, f.

white-heat, –hĕt, s. incandescenza, f.

white-hot, –hŏt, a. incandescente.

white-lead, –lĕd, s. cerussa, f.

whiten, hwît'tn, v. a. & n. imbiancare.

whiteness, hwît'nĕs, s. bianchezza, f.; pallidezza, f. [intonacare; colorire.

white-wash, –wŏsh, s. liscio, m.; –, v. a.

whither, hwîth'ăr, ad. dove, ove.

whithersoever, –sŏĕv'ăr, ad. dovunque, ovunque.

whiting, hwî'tîng, s. merluzzo, m. (pesce).

whitish, hwît'îsh, a. biancastro.

whitlow, hwît'lŏ, s. panereccio, m.

Whitsuntide, hwît'săntîd, s. stagione della pentecoste, f.

whittle, hwît'tl, v. a. tagliuzzare.

whiz, hwîz, v. n. sibilare; –, s. fischio, m.

who, hŏ, pn. chi, il quale. [sibilo, m.

who(so)ever, –(sŏ)ĕv'ăr, pn. qualunque.

whole, hŏl, a. tutto, intero, totale; –, s. tutto, m. [f.

wholesale, –săl, s. vendita all' ingrosso,

wholesome, –săm, a. sano; salubre; –ly, ad. sanamente.

wholesomeness, –sămnĕs, s. salubrità, f.

wholly, hŏl'lî, ad. interamente.

whom, hŏm, pn. che. [qualunque.

whom(so)ever, –(sŏ)ĕv'ăr, pn. chiunque,

whoop, hwŏp, v. a. gridare; –, s. grido, m. [ferina, f.

whooping-cough, –îng kŏf, s. tosse

whore, hŏr', s. bagascia, f.

whose, hŏz, pn. di cui, di chi, a chi, da chi.

who(so)ever, –(sŏ)ĕv'ăr, pn. chiunque,

why, hwî, ad. perchè, ma. [qualunque.

wick, wîk, s. stoppino, lucignolo, m.

wicked, wîk'ĕd, a. cattivo, maligno; –ly, ad. malamente.

wickedness, –ĕdnĕs, s. malvagità, f.

wicker, wîk'ăr, s.& a. vinco (m.); di vinco.

wicket, –ĕt, s. portello, m.

wide, wîd, a. & ad. largo, ampio, vasto; affatto; –ly, ad. largamente; molto.

wideawake, –ăwâk, s. cappello a cencio con tesa ampia, m.; –, a. astuto.

widen, wî'dn, v. a. & n. allargare, di-stendere.

wideness, *wĭd'nĕs,* s. larghezza, f.
widgeon, *wĭj'ŭn,* s. folaga, f. (uccello).
widow, *wĭd'ō,* s. vedova, f.; —, v. a. privare del marito.
widower, *-ăr,* s. vedovo, m.
widowhood, *-hŭd,* s. vedovanza, f.
width, *wĭdth,* s. larghezza, ampiezza, f.
wield, *wēld,* v. a. maneggiare, trattare; governare; brandire, sventolare.
wieldy, *wēld'ĭ,* a. maneggevole.
wife, *wĭf,* s. moglie, sposa, f.
wifely, *-lĭ,* a. da buona moglie.
wig, *wĭg,* s. parrucca, f.
wig-block, *-blŏk,* s. testa di legno, m.
wight, *wĭt,* s. uomo, m.; creatura, f.
wig-maker, *wĭk'mākăr,* s. parrucchiere, m.   [f.
wigwam, *-wăm,* s. capanna indiana.
wild, *wĭld,* a. salvatico; deserto; intrattabile, indomito, feroce; **-ly,** ad. salvaticamente; follemente; —, s. deserto, m.
wilderness, *wĭl'dărnĕs,* s. deserto, m., solitudine, f.   [sarpigine, f.
wildfire, *wĭld'fīr,* s. fuoco greco, m.
wilding, *wĭld'ĭng,* s. corbezzola, f.
wildness, *-nĕs,* s. salvatichezza, f.; ferocia, f.
wile, *wĭl,* s. furberia, sottigliezza, f.
wilful, *wĭl'fŭl,* a. caparbio, ostinato; **-ly,** ad. ostinatamente.
wilfulness, *-nĕs,* s. ostinazione, f.
wilily, *wĭ'lĭlĭ,* ad. fraudolentemente. [f.
wiliness, *-lĭnĕs,* s. astuzia, sottigliezza.
will, *wĭl,* s. volontà, f.; testamento, m.; —, v. a. ir. volere.   [ad. volontiermente.
willing, *-lĭng,* a. inclinato, pronto; **-ly,**
willingness, *-nĕs,* s. buona volontà, f.
willow, *wĭl'lō,* s. salcio, salice, m.
wily, *wĭ'lĭ,* a. astuto, fino.
wimble, *wĭm'bl,* s. succhiello, m.
wimple, *wĭm'pl,* s. velo, m.
win, *wĭn,* v. a. ir. guadagnare; acquistare.
wince, *wĭns,* v. n. calcitrare, tirare de' calci.
winch, *wĭnsh,* s. manovello, f.
wind, *wĭnd,* s. vento, m.; alito, m.; vanità, f.
wind, *wĭnd,* v. a. ir. voltare; variare, mutare; serpeggiare; altorcigliare, avvolgere, inviluppare; aggomito'are; fiutare; annasare; —, v. n. ir. attorcigliarsi, avvolgersi.
winded, *wĭn'dĕd,* a. trafelato.
winder, *wĭn'dăr,* s. arcolaio, m.
windiness, *wĭn'dĭnĕs,* s. ventosità, flatuosità, f.   [sinuosità, f.
winding, *wĭnd'ĭng,* s. giramento, m.;
winding-sheet, *-shēt,* s. paliotto di morto.
windlass, *wĭnd'lăs,* s. organo, m. [m.
wind-mill, *-mĭl,* s. mulino a vento, m.
window, *wĭn'dō,* s. finestra, f.
wind-pipe, *wĭnd'pĭp,* s. trachea, f.
windward, *-wărd,* ad. contro vento.
windy, *wĭnd'ĭ,* a. ventoso; vano.
wine, *wĭn,* s. vino, m.   [m.
wine-bibber, *-bĭbbăr,* s. beone, briacone.
wine-glass, *-glăs,* s. bicchiere, m.
wine-grower, *-grōăr,* s. vignaiuolo, m.
wine-press, *-prĕs,* s. torchio, m.

wine-taster, *-tāstăr,* s. assiggiatore, m.
wing, *wĭng,* s. ala, f.; ventaglio, m.: —, v. a. mozzare le ale; volare via.
winged, *wĭngd,* a. alato; rapido.
wink, *wĭngk,* s. cenno, m.; segno, m.; —, v. a. chiudere gli occhi; accennare cogli occhi.   [cenno, m.
winking, *-ĭng,* s. battere gli occhi, m.;
winner, *wĭn'năr,* s. guadagnatore, m.
winning, *-nĭng,* a. attraente, allettativo; —, s. guadagno, profitto, m.   [vagliare.
winnow, *-nō,* v. a. ventilare, sventolare,
winsome, *-săm,* a. avvenente, grazioso.
winter, *wĭn'tăr,* s. inverno, m.; —, v. n. passare l' inverno, svernare.
winterly, *-lĭ,* **wintery,** *-ĭ,* **wintry,** *wĭn'trĭ,* a. invernale, d' inverno.   [m.
wipe, *wĭp,* s. colpo, bottone, m.; inganno,
wipe, —, v. a. asciugare; nettare; —, s. colpo, m.; nettamento, m.
wire, *wĭr,* s. filo di qualche metallo, m.
wiredraw, *-drā,* v. a. ir. filare un metallo; (fig.) tirare a lungo.
wire-puller, *-pŭllăr,* s. ciarlatano, m.; intrigante, m.   [macchinazioni, f. pl.
wire-pulling, *-pŭling,* s. rigiri, m. pl.,
wiry, *wĭ'rĭ,* a. fatto di filo di metallo.
wisdom, *wĭs'dŏm,* s. sapienza, prudenza, f.
wisdom-teeth, *-tēth,* s. pl. denti del giudizio, m. pl.
wise, *wĭz,* a. saggio, savio; circospetto; —, s. maniera, f., modo, m.   [m.
wiseacre, *-ākăr,* s. sciocco, minchione,
wisely, *-lĭ,* ad. saviamente, cautamente.
wish, *wĭsh,* v. a. & n. desiderare, bramare; volere; —, s. desiderio, m., voglia, f.
wishful, *-fŭl,* a. desideroso; **-ly,** ad. ardentemente.   [m.
wisp, *wĭsp,* s. strofinacciolo, m.; cercine,
wistful, *wĭst'fŭl,* a. attento; pensoso; **-ly,** ad. attentamente.   [cioè, vale a dire.
wit, *wĭt,* s. ingegno, m.; intelletto, m.; **to-,**
witch, *wĭch,* s. strega, maga, f.
witchcraft, *-krăft,* s. ammaliamento, m.,
with, *wĭth,* pr. con; da, di, a.   [malia, f.
withal, *-āl',* pr. & ad. infra, tra; anche, ancora.
withdraw, *-drā',* v. a. ir. ritirare; levare; —, v. n. ir. ritirarsi, andarsene.
withe, *wĭth,* s. ramicello di salcio, m.
wither, *wĭth'ăr,* v. a. far seccare; —, v. n. sfiorire; disseccarsi.   [pedire; arrestare.
withold, *-hōld',* v. a. ir. ritenere, im-
withholder, *-ăr,* s. ritenitore, detentore, m.
within, *-ĭn',* pr. in, fra, dentro; —, ad. interiormente; a casa.
without, *-ŏūt',* pr. fuor, fuori; senza; —, ad. & c. a meno che, se non che.   [porsi.
withstand, *-stānd',* v. a. ir. resistere, op-
withy, *wĭth'ĭ,* (with'ĭ), s. vinco, vinciglio, m.
witless, *wĭt'lĕs,* a. sciocco, scimunito.
witling, *-lĭng,* s. saccentuzzo, m.
witness, *-nĕs,* s. testimonio, m., testimonianza, f.; —, v. a. & n. testificare, attestare.   [testare.
witted, *-tĕd,* a. d' ingegno.
wittily, *-tĭlĭ,* ad. ingegnosamente.   [f.
wittiness, *-tĭnĕs,* s. acutezza d' ingegno,

wittingly, –tĭnglĭ, ad. a bello studio.
witty, –tĭ, a. ingegnoso, spiritoso.
wizard, wĭz'ãrd, s. indovino, mago, m.
woad, wŏd, s. guado, m.
woe, wō, s. dolore, m.; miseria, f.
woeful, –fŭl, a. mesto; **–ly,** ad. dogliosa-
  mente.
wolf, wŭlf, s. lupo, m.; **she –,** lupa, f.
wolfish, –ĭsh, a. di lupo; goloso.
woman, wŭm'ãn, s. femmina, donna, f.
woman-hater, –hātãr, s. odiatore delle
  donne, m.   [donna, f.
womanhood, –hŭd, s. condizione di
womanish, –ĭsh, a. feminile; effeminato.
womankind, –kĭnd, s. femminile sesso,
  m.; donne, f. pl.
womanly, –lĭ, a. di donna, donnesco.
womb, wŏm, s. matrice, f., utero, m.
wonder, wŭn'dãr, s. meraviglia, f.; stupore, m.; – v. n. meravigliarsi; stupirsi.
wonderful, –fŭl, a. meraviglioso, straordinario; **–ly,** ad. meravigliosamente.
wondrous, wŭn'drŭs, a. meraviglioso.
won't, wŏnt, abbrev. di **"will not."**
wont, wŏnt, s. uso, m.; usanza, f.
wonted, –ĕd, a. accostumato, solito.
woo, wō, v. a. fare all' amore, amoreggiare.
wood, wŭd, s. legno, bosco, m., selva, f.
wood-bine, –bĭn, s. madreselva, f.
wood-cock, –kŏk, s. beccaccia, f. (uccello).
wood-cut, –kŭt, s. stampa di legno, f.
wood-cutter, –kŭttãr, s. intagliatore in
  legno, m.
wooded, –ĕd, a. fornito di legna.
wooden, wŭd'n, a. (fatto) di legno.
wood-house, –hŏŭs, s. legnaia, f.
wood-land, –lãnd, s. paese boscoso, m.
wood-louse, –lŏŭs, s. centogambe, m.
woodman, –mãn, s. boscaiuolo, guardaboschi, m.
wood-pecker, –pĕk'ãr, s. picchio, m.
woody, wŭd'ĭ, a. boscoso, selvoso.
wooer, wō'ãr, s. innamorato, m.
woof, wŏf, s. trama, f.; tessitura, f.
wool, wŭl, s. lana, f.
wool-comber, –kōmãr, s. scardassiere, m.
wool-gathering, –gãthãring, a. **to go
  a –,** essere distratto.
woollen, –lĕn, a. (fatto) di lana.
woolly, –lĭ, a. lanoso, peloso.
wool-pack, –pãk, s. sacco di lana, m.
word, wŭrd, s. parola, f.; termine, m.; **to
  give** or **pass one's –,** dar la sua
  parola; **te keep one's –,** mantener la
  parola; **to have –s,** aver una disputa;
  to be as good as one's –, essere di
  parola; **to take one at his –,** prendere
  uno in parola; **to take one's – for,**
  credere alla parola di uno; **to send – to,**
  far dire a, far sapere; **to bring –,** portar
  notizia; **to eat one's –,** disdirsi; **upon
  one's –,** sulla sua parola; **for –,** parola
  per parola; **–,** v. a. esprimere, scrivere.
wordiness, –nĕs, s. verbosità, f.
wording, –ĭng, s. (gr.) costruzione, f.
wordy, wŭrd'ĭ, a. verboso.

work, wŭrk, s. lavoro, travaglio, m.;
  opera, f.; faccenda, f.; fatica, pena, f.;
  effetto, m.; –, v. a. & n r. & ir. lavorare,
  operare, effettuare; fabbricare; fare; fermentare, bollire.
worker, –ãr, s. lavoratore, lavorante, m.
work-house, –hŏŭs, s. casa di correzione,
  f.   [lavoro, m.
working-day, –ĭng dã, s. giorno di
workman, –mãn, s. operaio, lavoratore, m.
workmanship, –mãnshĭp, s. manifattura,
  f.; arte dell' artefice, f.
workshop, –shŏp, s. lavoratorio, m.
workwoman, –wŭmãn, s. artigiana, la-
  voratrice, f.   [terra, vita, f.
world, wŭrld, s. mondo, m.; universo, m.;
worldliness, –lĭnĕs, s. mondanità, f.;
  avarizia, f.
worldling, –lĭng, s. uomo interessato, m.
worldly, –lĭ, a. mondano; vano.
worm, wŭrm, s. verme, m.; chiocciola
  d'una vite, f.; –, v. a. & n. minare; lovo-
  rare secretamente.
worm-eaten, –ĕtn, a. bucato, tarlato.
worm-hole, –hŏl, s. intarlamento, m.
worm-wood, –wŭd, s. assenzio, m.
worry, wŭr'rĭ, v. a. tormentare; opprimere.
worse, wŭrs, a. & ad. peggiore; in modo
  peggiore, peggio.
worship, wŭr'shĭp, s. culto divino, m.;
  adorazione, f.; **your –,** vostra riverenza
  (titolo); –, v. a. adorare.
worshipful, –fŭl, a. reverendo.
worshipping, –pĭng, s. adorazione, f.
worst, wŭrst, a. il più cattivo, il peggiore;
  –, s. peggiore, peggio, m., estremità, f.;
  –, v. a. superare; vincere.   [filata, f.
worsted, wŭr'stĕd, (wŭs'tĕd), s. lana
wort, wŭrt, s. specie di cavolo, m.; mosto,
  m.   [prezzo, valore, m.; valuta, f.
worth, wŭrth, a. degno, meritante; –, s.
worthily, wŭr'thĭlĭ, ad. degnamente, meritamente.   [dignità, f.
worthiness, –thĭnĕs, s. merito, m.;
worthless, wŭrth'lĕs, a. indegno, di poco
  valore.   [viltà, f.
worthlessness, –nĕs, s. indegnità, f.;
worthy, wŭr'thĭ, a. degno, meritevole; –,
  s. uomo illustre, m.
would-be, wŭld'bĕ, a. pretendente.
wound, wŏŭnd, s. ferita, piaga, f.
wove(n), wŏv(n), a. velino.
wraith, rāth, s. apparizione d'un morto, f.
wrangle, rãng'gl, v. n. rissare, disputare;
  –, s. rissa, f.   [tore, m.
wrangler, –glãr, s. contenditore, garri-
wrangling, –glĭng, s. rissa, f., litigio, m.
wrap, rãp, v. a. involgere, inviluppare.
wrapper, –pãr, s. coperta, f.; inviluppo,
  m.; abito da camera, m.; accapatoio, m.;
  piccolo scialle, m.
wrath, rãth, s. collera, stizza, f.
wrathful, –fŭl, a. iroso, collerico, stizzoso.
wrathfully, –lĭ, ad. irosamente, stizzosa-
  mente.
wreak, rēk, v. a. vendicare; sfogare.
wreath, rēth, s. corona, ghirlanda, f.; **–,**

rẽth, v. a. attorcigliare, intrecciare; coronare.

wreck, rĕk, s. naufragio; bastimento naufragato, m.; distruzione, f., –, v. a. & n. rovinare; naufragare.

wren, rĕn, s. reatino, lui, m. (uccello).

wrench, rĕnsh, v. a. slogare, storcere; rompere a forza; –, s. storcimento, m.

wrest, rĕst, v. a. storcere, stravolgere; strappare; levare via con violenza.

wrestle, rĕs'l, v. n. lottare; contendere.

wrestling, –lĭng, s. lotta, f.

wretch, rĕch, s. misero, m.

wretched, –ĕd, a. misero povero, meschino. |nità, bassezza, f.

wretchedness, –ĕdnĕs, s. miseria, meschi-

wriggle, rĭg'gl, v. n. dimenarsi; piegarsi.

wright, rĭt, s. artigiano, lavorante, m.

wring, rĭng, v. a. ir. torcere, storcere; premere; strappare, levare via.

wrinkle, –rĭng'kl, s. ruga, grinza, f.; –, v. a. piegare, rugare; –, v. n. piegarsi.

wrist, rĭst, s. giuntura della mano, f.

wrist-band, –bănd, **wristlet**, –lĕt, s. polsino, m. |f.

writ, rĭt, s. ordine in iscritto, f.; citazione,

write, rĭt, v. a. ir. scrivere; comporre.

writer, rĭ'tŭr, s. scrittore, autore, m.; copista, m.

writhe, rĭth, v. a. torcere; –, v. n. soffrire.

writing, rĭ'tĭng, s. scrittura, f.; scritto, m.

writing-book, –bŭk, s. quaderno, m.

writing-desk, –dĕsk, s. scrittoio, tavolino, m. |scrittura, m.

writing-master, –măstŭr, s. maestro di

writing-paper, –pāpŭr, s. carta da scrivere, f.

wrong, rŏng, a. falso; indiretto; –, ad. a torto; ingiustamente; –, s. torto, m.; errore, m.; ingiustizia, f.; –, v. a. fare torto, oltraggiare.

wrongful, –fŭl, a. ingiusto, ingiurioso; –ly, ad. a torto; ingiustamente.

wroth, vedi **wrath**.

wrought, rŏt, a. lavorato, elaborato.

wry, rĭ, a. storto, bistorto, curvo; sgembo.

wry-face, –fās, s. smorfia, f.

wry-neck, –nĕk, s. torcicollo, m. (uccello).

wryness, –nĕs, s. contorsione, f.; deviazione, f.

X.

xebec, zĕ'bĕk, s. (mar.) sciabecco, m.

xylographer, zĭlŏg'răfŭr, s. xilografo, m.

xylographic, –lŏgrăf'ĭk, a. xilografico.

xylography, –lŏg'răfĭ, s. xilografia, f.

Y.

yacht, yŏt, s. (mar.) lachetto, m., saettia, f.

yachting, –ĭng, s. il viaggiare in un yacht per diporto.

yam, yăm, s. ignamo, m.

yankee, yănk'ĭ, s. soprannome dato agli Americani, m.

yard, yărd, s. cortile, m.; verga (misura di tre piedi), f.; antenna (d'una nave), f.

yarn, yărn, s. stame, m., lana filata, f.

yarrow, yăr'rŏ, s. millefoglie, f.

yawl, yŏl, s. barchetta, f., battello, m.

yawn, yăn, v. n. sbadigliare.

yclept, ĕklĕpt', a. chiamato, nominato.

ye, yē, pn. voi; vi.

yea, yā, ad. (bibl.) sì, in verità.

yean, yēn, v. a. far agnelli.

year, yēr, s. anno, m.

year-book, –bŭk, s. annali, m. pl.

yearling, –lĭng, a. che non ha che un anno. |ogni anno.

yearly, –lĭ, a. annuale, d'un anno; –ly, ad.

yearn, yărn, v. n. esser molto affannato.

yearning, –ĭng, s. compassione, f.

yeast, yēst, s. lievito, m.

yell, yĕl, v. n. ululare, abbaiare; –, s. urlamento, m.

yellow, yĕl'lŏ, a. & s. giallo (m.); –s, s. pl. itterizia, f.

yellow-boy, –bŏĭ, s. (cant) ghinea, f.

yellowish, –ĭsh, a. gialliccio.

yellowness, –nĕs, s. giallezza, f., color giallo, m.

yelp, yĕlp, v. n. abbaiare, squittire.

yelping, –ĭng, s. gagnolio, m.

yeoman, yŏ'măn, s. contadino ricco, m.; guardia a piedi, f.

yeomanry, –rĭ, s. guardie a piedi, f. pl.; contadini, m. pl.

yes, yĕs, ad. sì; veramente, in vero.

yesterday, yĕs'tŭrdă, a. ieri.

yet, yĕt, c. nondimeno, nulladimeno; –, ad. ancora, più innanzi.

yew, yŏ, s. tasso, m. (albero).

yield, yēld, v. a. rendere, produrre; fruttare; permettere, accordare; –, v. n. rendersi, sottomettersi; soccombere; –, s. prodotto, m. |sommessione, f.

yielding, –ĭng, a. condiscendente; –, s.

yoke, yŏk, s. giogo, m.; paio, m.; coppia, f.; –, v. a. accoppiare al giogo; soggiogare.

yoke-elm, –ĕlm, s. carpine, m. (albero).

yolk, yŏk, s. tuorlo, rosso dell'uovo, m.

yon(der), yŏn(dŭr), ad. là, in vista.

yore, yŏr, of –, in times of –, ad. altre volte, anticamente.

you, yŏ, pn. voi, vi, si. |perto.

young, yŭng, a. giovane, giovine; ines-

youngish, yŭn'gĭsh, a. alquanto giovine.

youngster, yŭng'stŭr, s. giovinotto, m.

your, yŏr, pn. vostro, vostra; vostri, vostre.

yours, yŏrz, pn. il vostro, la vostra, i vostri; "Yours sincerely," vostro divotissimo servitore (divo serve).

yourself, –sĕlf', pn. voi stesso.

youth, yŏth, **you hfulness**, –fŭlnĕs, s. gioventù, f.

youthful, –fŭl, a. giovanile; –ly, ad. giovanilmente.

Z.

zaffre, *zăf'făr*, s. zaffrone, m.
zany, *ză'nĭ*, s. zanni, buffone, m.
zeal, *zĕl*, s. zelo, ardore, m.
zealot, *zĕl'ăt*, s. zelatore, m.
zealotry, *–rĭ*, s. fanatismo, m.
zealous, *–ăs*, a. zelante; **-ly**, ad. con zelo.
zebra, *zĕ'bră*, s. zebra, f.
zenith, *zĕn'ĭth*. s. zenit, m.; colmo, m.
zephyr, *zĕf'ăr*, s. zeffiro, m.
zero, *zĕ'rŏ*, s. zero, m.; niente, nulla, m.

zest, *zĕst*, s. frullo, m.; pezzetto (di scorza), gusto, m.
zigzag, *zĭg'zăg*, s. serpeggiamento, m.
zinc, *zĭngk*, s. zinco, m.
zinc-plating, *–plătĭng*, s. il coprire di zinco, m.
zip, *zĭp*, v. n. sibilare, fischiare.
zodiac, *zŏ'dĭăk*, s. zodiaco, m.
zone, *zŏn*, s. zona, f.; fascia, cintura, f
zoological, *zŏŏlŏj'ĭkăl*, a. zoologico.
zoologist, *zŏŏl'ŏjĭst*, s. zoologo, m.
zoology, *zŏŏl'ŏjĭ*, s. zoologia, f.
zoophite, *zŏ'ŏfĭt*, s. piantanimale, m.
zounds, *zŏŭndz*, i. poffareddio!

List of the most remarkable geographical names, that differ in the two languages.

Abyssinia, *ăbĭssĭn'ĭă,* Abissinia, f.

Adrianople, *ădrĭănŏ'pl,* Adrianopoli, m.

Adriatic Sea, *ădrĭăt'ĭk sĕ,* Adriatico, m.

Africa, *ăf'rĭkă,* Affrica, f.

African, *ăf'rĭkăn,* Affricano, m.

Aix la Chapelle, *ăks' lă shăpĕl',* Aquisgrana, f.

Alexandria, *ălĕgzăn'drĭă,* Alessandria, f.

Algerian, *ălgē'rĭăn,* a. di Algeri.

Algiers, *ăljērz',* Algeri, f.

Alps, *ălps,* Alpi, m. pl.

Alsace, *ăl'săs,* Alsazia, f.

Alsatian, *ălsă'shĭăn,* Alsaziano, m.

American, *ămĕr'ĭkăn,* s. & a. Americano (m.).

Andalusia, *ăndălŏ'zhă,* Andalusia, f.

Antwerp, *ănt'wŭrp,* Anversa, f.

Apennines, *ăp'pĕnnīnz,* pl. Appennini, m. pl.

Arab, *ăr'ăb,* **Arabian,** *ără'bĭăn,* s. Arabo, m.; –, a. arabico.

Arabia, *ără'bĭă,* Arabia, f.

Aragonese, *ărăgŏnēz',* s. & a. Aragonese (m.).

Archipelago, *ărkĭpĕl'ăgŏ,* Arcipelago, m.

Armenian, *ărmē'nĭăn,* s. & a. Armeno (m.).

Asia, *ā'shĭă (ā'zhă),* Asia, f.

Asiatic, *ăshĭăt'ĭk,* a. asiatico.

Athenian, *ăthē'nĭăn,* s. & a. Ateniese (m.).

Athens, *ăth'ĕnz,* Atene, f.

Atlantic, *ătlăn'tĭk,* Atlantico, m.

Augsburg, *ăgs'bŭrg,* Augusta, f.

Austrian, *ăs'trĭăn,* s. & a. Austriaco (m.).

Azores, *ăsŏrz',* Azzorre, f. pl.

Baden, *bā'd'n,* Bada, Badena, f.

Bahamas, *băhă'măz,* Isole di Baama, f. pl.

Baltic Sea, *băltĭk sĕ,* Mar Baltico, m.

Barbadoes, *bărbă'dōz,* pl. Barbade, f. pl.

Barbary, *bär'bărĭ,* Barbaria, f.

Basel, *bā'zĕl (băl),* Basilea, f.

Batavian, *bătă'vĭăn,* s. & a. Batavo (m.).

Bavaria, *băvā'rĭă,* Baviera, f.

Bavarian, *băvā'rĭăn,* s. & a. Bayarese (m.).

Belgian, *bĕl'jĭăn,* a. belgico; –, s. Belga, m.

Belgium, *bĕl'jăm,* Belgio, m.

Bengal, *bĕngăl',* Bengala, f.

Berlin, *bŭr'lĭn (bărlĭn'),* Berlino, m.

Berlinian, *bărlĭn'ĭăn,* a. berlinese.

Bern, *bĕrn,* Berna, f.

Bethlehem, *bĕth'lĕĕm,* Bettlemme, f.

Biscay, *bĭs'kĭ,* Biscaglia, f.

Bœotia, *bĕŏ'shĭă,* Beozia, f.

Bohemia, *bŏhē'mĭă,* Boemia, f.

Bohemian, *bŏhē'mĭăn,* s. & a. Boemo (m.).

Bosphorus, *bŏs'fŏrăs,* Bosforo, m.

Brandenburg, *brăn'dĕnbărg,* Brandeburgo, m.

Brandenburger, *-bărgăr,* Brandeburghese, m.

Brazil, *brăzĭl',* Brasile, m.

Brazilian, *brăzĭl'ĭăn,* s. & a. Brasiliano (m.).

Bremen, *brā'mĕn,* Brema, f.

Britain (Great), *brĭt'ĭn,* Gran Brettagna, f.

Britany, *brĭt'ănĭ,* Brettagna, f.

British, *brĭt'ĭsh,* a. britannico; – **Channel,** la Manica, f.

Briton, *brĭt'ăn,* Britanno, m.

Brunswic(k), *brŭnz'wĭk,* Brunsvig, m.

Brussels, *brŭs'sĕlz,* Brusselle, f.

Bulgarian, *bŭlgā'rĭăn,* a. bulgaro.

Burgundian, *bŭrgăn'dĭăn,* a. della Borgogna.

Burgundy, *bär'găndĭ,* Borgogna, f.

Byzantium, *bĭzăn'shĭăm,* Bisanzio, m.

Cadiz, *kā'dĭz,* Cadice, f.

Caffraria, *kăfrā'rĭă,* Cafreria, f.

Calabrian, *kălă'brĭăn,* s. & a. Calabrese (m.).

Calais, *kăl'ĭs,* Calè, f.

Calmuck, *kăl'măk,* Calmucco, m.

Canary Islands, *kănā'rĭ ĭ'lăndz,* Canarie, f. pl.

Candian, *kăn'dĭăn,* s. & a. Candiotto (m.).

Carinthia, *kărĭn'thĭă,* Carinzia, f.

Carpathians, *kărpā'thĭănz,* Carpazi, m. pl.

Carthagena, *kărthăjē'nă,* Cartagena, f.

Cashmere, *kăshmēr',* Casimiro, m.

Caspian Sea, *kăs'pĭăn sĕ,* Caspio, m.

Castile, *kăstēl',* Castiglia, f.

Catalonia, *kătălŏ'nĭă,* Catalogna, f.

Caucasus, *kă'kăsăs,* Caucaso, m.

Ceylon, *sĕ'lŏn,* Ceilan, m.
China, *chī'nă,* China, f.
Chinese, *chīnēz',* s. & a. Chinese (m.).
Circassian, *sŭrkăs'shăn,* Circasso (m.).
Constantinople, *kŏnstăn tīnō'pl,* Costantinopoli, f.
Copenhagen, *kōpĕnhā'gĕn,* Copenaghen, f. [m.
Corinth, *kŏr'ĭnth,* Corinto, m.
Cornwall, *kŏrn'wŏl,* Cornovaglia, f.
Corsican, *kŏr'sĭkăn,* s. & a. Corso (m.). [m.
Cossack, *kŏs'săk,* Cosacco, m.
Courland, *kŏr'lănd,* Curlandia, f. [f.
Cracow, *krā'kō,* Cracovia, f.
Cretan, *krē'tăn,* Cretese, m.
Crimea, *krīmē'ă,* Crimea, f.
Croatia, *krōā'shĭă,* Croazia, f.
Croatian, *—shĭăn,* s. & a. Croato (m.).
Cyprus, *sī'prŭs,* Cipro, m.

Dalmatia, *dălmā'shĭă,* Dalmazia, f.
Dalmatian, *dălmā'shăn,* s. & a. Dalmata (m.).
Damascus, *dămăs'kŭs,* Damasco, m.
Dane, *dān,* Danese, m.
Danish, *dān'ĭsh,* a. danese.
Danube, *dăn'ŭb,* Danubio, m.
Dauphinate, *dā'fĭnăt,* **Dauphiny,** *—fĭnĭ,* Delfinato, m.
Delphos, *dĕl'fŭs,* Delfo, m.
Denmark, *dĕn'mărk,* Danimarca, f. [f.
Dresden, *drĕs'dn,* Dresda, f.
Dunkirk, *dŭn'kŭrk,* Duncherque, f.
Dutch, *dŭch,* a. olandese.
Dutchman, *dŭtch'man,* 'Olandese, m.

East-Indies, *ēst īn'dĭz,* Indie orientali, f. pl.
Edinburgh, *ĕd'ĭnbŭrŏ,* Edimburgo, f.
Egypt, *ē'jĭpt,* Egitto, m.
Egyptian, *ējĭp'shăn,* s. & a. Egiziano (m.).
England, *ĭng'glănd,* Inghilterra, f.
English, *ĭng'glĭsh,* a. inglese; **— Channel,** *— chăn'nĕl,* la Manica.
Englishman, *—măn,* Inglese, m.
Epirus, *ēpē'rŭs,* Epiro, m.

Euphrates, *ūfrā'tēz,* Eufrate, m.
Europe, *ū'rŏp,* Europa, f.
European, *ūrŏ'pĕăn,* s. & a. Europeo (m.).

Finland, *fĭn'lănd,* Finlandia, f.
Finlander, *—dăr,* Finlandese, m.
Flanders, *flăn'dărz,* Fiandra, f.
Fleming, *flĕm'ĭng,* Fiammingo, m.
Flemish, *flĕm'ĭsh,* a. fiammingo.
Florence, *flŏr'ĕns,* Firenze, f.
Florentine, *flŏr'ĕntīn,* s. & a. Fiorentino (m.).
Flushing, *flăsh'ĭng,* Flessinga, f.
Frankfort, *frănk'fŏrt,* Francoforte, m.
French, *frĕnsh,* a. francese.
Frenchman, *—măn,* Francese, m.
Friburg, *frē'bŭrg,* Friburgo, m.
Friesland, *frēz'lănd,* Frisia, f.
Frieslander, *—dăr,* Frisio, m.
Frozen Ocean, *frō'zn ŏ'shăn,* Oceano Settentrionale, m.

Galicia, *gălĭsh'ĭă,* Gallizia, f.
Galilee, *găl'ĭlē,* Galilea, f.
Ganges, *găn'jēz,* Gange, m.
Gascony, *găs'kŏnĭ,* Guascogna, f. [f.
Geneva, *jĕnē'vă,* Ginevra, f.
Genevese, *—vēz',* s. & a. Ginevrino (m.).
Genoa, *jĕn'ŏă,* Genova, f.
Genoese, *jĕnŏēz',* s. & a. Genovese (m.).
German, *jŭr'măn,* s. & a. Tedesco (m.).
Germany, *jŭr'mănĭ,* Germania, f.
Ghent, *gĕnt,* Gand, m.
Gibraltar, *jĭbrăl'tăr,* Gibilterra, f.
Grecian, *grē'shăn,* a. greco.
Greece, *grēs,* Grecia, f.
Greek, *grēk,* s. & a. Greco (m.).
Greenland, *grēn'lănd,* Groenlandia, f.
Greenlander, *—dăr,* s. Groenlandese, m.
Groningen, *grŏn'ĭngĕn,* Groninga, f.

Guelderland, *gĕl'dărlănd,* Gheldria, f.
Guinea, *gĭn'nĭ,* Guinea, f.

Hague (the), *hāg,* Aja, f.
Hamburg, *hăm'bŭrg,* Amburgo, f.
Havannah, *hăvăn'nă,* Avana, f.
Helvetia, *hĕlvē'shĭă,* Svizzera, f.
Herzegovina, *hĕrzĕgŏvē'nă,* Erzegovina, f.
Hesse, *hĕs,* Assia, f.
Hessian, *hĕsh'ĭăn,* s. & a. Assiaco (m.).
Holland, *hŏl'lănd,* Olanda, f. [m.
Hollander, *—dăr,* Olandese, m.
Hungarian, *hăngā'rĭăn,* s. Ungherese, m.; —, a. ungarico.
Hungary, *hăng'gărĭ,* Ungheria, f.

Iceland, *īs'lănd,* Islanda, f.
Icelander, *—dăr,* Islandese, m. [ria, f.
Illyricum, *ĭllē'rĭkŭm,* Illiria, f.
Indian, *ĭn'dĭăn,* s. &a. Indiano (m.).
Indies, *ĭn'dĭz,* pl. Indie, f. pl.
Ireland, *īr'lănd,* Irlanda, f.
Irish, *ī'rĭsh,* a. irlandese.
Irishman, *ī'rĭshmăn,* Irlandese, m.
Italian, *ĭtăl'ĭăn,* s. & a. Italiano (m.).
Italy, *ĭt'ălĭ,* Italia, f.

Jamaica, *jămā'kă,* Giamaica. f. [m.
Japan, *jăpăn',* Giappone, m.
Japanese, *jăpănēz',* s. & a. Giapponese (m.) [m.
Jordan, *jŏr'dăn,* Giordano, m.
Judea, *jŏdē'ă,* Giudea, f.

Lapland, *lap'lănd,* Lapponia, f.
Laplander, *—dăr,* Lappone, Lapponese, m. [f.
Leghorn, *lĕg'ŏrn,* Livorno, f.
Leipsic, *līp'sĭk,* Lipsia, f.
Lisbon, *lĭz'bŏn,* Lisbona, f.
Lisle, *lēl,* Lilla, f.
Lombardy, *lŏm'bărdĭ,* Lombardia, f.
London, *lăn'dn,* Londra, f.
Low-Countries, *lō'kăntrēz,* Paesi Bassi, m. pl.

Luxemburg, *lŭks'ĕmbŭrg,* Lussemburgo, m.
Lyons, *li'ănz,* Lione, f.

Macedonian, *măsĕdŏ'nĭăn,* s. & a. Macedone (m.). |f.
Madeira, *mădĕ'ră,* Madera,
Maltese, *măltēz',* a. maltese. |f.
Mantua, *măn'tŭă,* Mantoa, rea, f.
Mediterranean, *mĕdĭter- ră'nĭăn,* il Mediterraneo, m.
Mentz, *mĕnts,* Magonza, f.
Mexico, *mĕks'ĭkŏ,* Messico, m.
Moluccas, *mŏlŭk'kăz,* Mo- lucche, f. pl.
Mongol, *mŏn'gŏl,* s. & a. Mongolo (m.).
Moor, *mōr,* Moro, m.
Moorish, *mōr'ĭsh,* a. moro.
Moravian, *mŏră'vĭăn,* s. & a. Moravo (m.).
Morocco, *mŏrŏk'kŏ,* Ma- rocco, m.
Moscovy, *mŏs'kŏvĭ,* Mos- covia, f.
Moscow, *mŏs'kŏ,* Mosca, f.
Mulatto, *mŭlăt'ŏ,* s. **Mulat- tress,** *–trĕs,* Mulatto, m., Mulatta, f.
Munich, *mū'nĭk,* Monaco, f.

Naples, *nā'plz,* Napoli, f.
Neapolitan, *nĕăpŏl'ĭtăn,* s. & a. Napoletano (m.).
Netherlands, *nĕ'thăr- lăndz,* pl. Paesi Bassi, m.pl.
Neuchatel, *nŭshătĕl',* Neo- burgo, m.
Newfoundland, *nū'fănd- lănd,* Terra-Nuova, f.
Nice, *nĕs,* Nizza, f.
Nile, *nīl,* Nilo, m.
Nimeguen, *nĭmĕ'gĕn,* Ni- mega, f.
Norman, *nŏr'măn,* s. & a. Normanno (m.).
Normandy, *nŏr'măndĭ,* Normandia, f. |f.
Norway, *nŏr'wē,* Norvegia,
Norwegian, *nŏrwē'jăn,* s. & a. Norvegese (m.).
Nubian, *nū'bĭăn,* s. & a. Nubio (m.).
Nuremberg, *nū'rĕmbĕrg,* Norimberga, f.

Olympus, *ŏlĭm'pŭs,* Olim- po, m.
Orkneys (the), *ŏrk'nĭz,* pl. Orcadi, f. pl.

Pacific, *păsĭf'ĭk,* Mar Paci- fico, m.
Padua, *păd'ŭă,* Padova, f.
Paris, *păr'ĭs,* Parigi, f.
Parisian, *părĕ'ŝĭăn,* s. & a. Parigino (m.).
Parnassus, *părnăs'sŭs,* Parnasso, m.
Peloponnesus, *pĕlŏpŏnĕ'- sŭs,* Peloponneso, m., Mo- rea, f.
Persian, *pŭr'shĭăn,* s. & a. Persiano (m.).
Petersburg, *pĕ'tĕrsbŭrg,* Pietroburgo, f.
Piedmont, *pĕd'mŏnt,* Pie- monte, m.
Piedmontese, *–ēz',* s. & a. Piemontese (m.).
Poland, *pŏ'lănd,* Polonia, f.
Pole, *pōl,* Polonese, m.
Polish, *pŏ'lĭsh,* a. polonese, polacco.
Pontus, *pŏn'tŭs,* Ponto, m.
Portugal, *pŏr'tŭgăl,* Porto- gallo, m.
Portuguese, *pŏr'tŭgēz,* s. & a. Portoghese (m.).
Prussia, *prŭs'shĭă,* Prus- sia, f.
Prussian, *–n,* s. & a. Prus- siano (m.).
Pyrenean Mountains, *pĕrĕnē'ăn mŏŭn'tĭns,* Monti Pirenei, m. pl.

Rhine, *rīn,* Reno, m.
Roman, *rŏ'măn,* s. & a. Romano (m.).
Roumania, *rŏmā'nĭă,* Ru- mania, f.
Roumanian, *–n,* s. & a. Rumeno (m.).
Russia, *rŭs'shĭă,* Russia, f.
Russian, *–n,* s. & a. Russo (m.).

Saltzburg, *sălts'bŭrg,* Sali- sburgo, m.
Samoid, *săm'ŏĭd,* a. sa- moiade. |moiedo, m.
Samoied, *săm'ŏ'ĭĕd,* Sa- **Sardinia,** *sărdĭn'ĭă,* Sar- degna, f.
Sardinian, *–n,* s. & a. Sardo (m.).
Saracen, *săr'ăsĕn',* s. & a. Saraceno, Saracino (m.).
Savoy, *să'vŏĕ,* Savoia, f.
Saxon, *săks'ŏn,* s. & a. Sassone (m.). |f.
Saxony, *săks'ŏnĭ,* Sassonia,
Scheld, *skĕlt,* Schelda, f.
Sclav, *sklăv,* **Sclavonian,** s. & a. Schiavone (m.).

Sclavonia, *slăvŏ'nĭă,* Schiavonia, f.
Scotch, *skŏch,* a. scozzese.
Scotland, *skŏt'lănd,* Sco- zia, f.
Scotsman, *skŏts'măn,* Scoz- zese, m.
Scottish, *skŏt'tĭsh,* a. scoz- zese.
Seine, *sān,* Senna, f.
Sevilla, *sĕvĭl'yă,* Siviglia, f.
Sicily, *sĭs'ĭlĭ,* Sicilia, f.
Sicilian, *sĭsĭl'yăn,* s. & a. Siciliano (m.).
Silesia, *sĭlē'zhă,* Slesia, f.
Silesian, *sĭlē'zhăn,* s. & a. Slesiano (m.).
Sound (the), *sŏŭnd,* Sund, m.
Spain, *spān,* Spagna, f.
Spaniard, *spăn'yărd,* Spagnuolo, m.
Spanish, *spăn'ĭsh,* a. spa- gnuolo.
Spartan, *spăr'tăn,* Spar- tano, m.
Stirian, *stĭ'rĭăn,* s. & a. Stiriano (m.).
Suabia, *swă'bĭă,* Svevia, f.
Suabian, *–n,* s. & a. Sveve (m.).
Swede, *swēd,* Svedese, m.
Sweden, *swē'dĕn,* Sveziu, f.
Swedish, *swē'dĭsh,* a. sve- dese.
Swiss, *swĭs,* s. & a. Sviz- zero (m.).
Switzerland, *swĭt'zăr- lănd,* Svizzera, f.
Syracuse, *sĭr'ăkŭs,* Sira- cusa, f.

Tagus, *tă'gŭs,* Tago, m.
Tartar, *tăr'tăr,* s. & a. Tar- taro (m.). |f.
Tartary, *tăr'tărĭ,* Tartaria,
Thames, *tĕmz,* Tamigi, m.
Thermopylae, *thĕrmŏ'- pĭlē,* pl. Termopili, pl.
Thessalonica, *thĕssălŏ'- nĭkă,* Salonicco, m.
Thessaly, *thĕs'ălĭ,* Tes- saglia, f.
Thrace, *thrās,* Tracia, f.
Thuringia, *thūrĭn'jĭă,* Tu- ringia, f.
Tiber, *tī'bĕr,* Tevere, m.
Tigris, *tī'grĭs,* Tigri, m.
Tirolese, *tĭrŏlēz',* s. & a. Tirolese (m.).
Trent, *trĕnt,* Trento, m.
Treves, *trĕvz,* Treviri, f.
Troy, *trŏĕ,* Troia, f.
Turk, *tŭrk,* s., **Turkish,** *tŭr'kĭsh,* a. turco.

Turkey, *tŭr' kĭ,* Turchia, f.
Tuscany, *tŭs' kănĭ,* Toscana, f.
Tyrolese, *vedi* **Tirolese.**

United States, *ănĭ' tĕd stăts,* pl. Stati Uniti, m. pl.

Vaucluse, *vŏ' klŭz,* s. Valchiusa, f.
Venetian, *vĕnĭsh' ăn,* s. & a. Veneziano (m.).

Venice, *vĕn' ĭs,* Venezia, f.
Vesuvius, *vĕzŭ' vĭŭs,* Vesuvio, m.
Viennese, *vĭ ĕnnēz',* s. & a. Viennese (m.).
Vistula, *vĭs' tŭlă,* Vistola, f.

Wales, *wălz,* Galles, m.
Wallachia, *vedi* **Valachia.**
Warsaw, *wăr' sŏ,* Varsavia, f.

Welsh, *wĕlsh,* a. di Galles.
West-Indies, *wĕst ĭn' dĕz,* pl. Indie occidentali, pl.
Westphalian, *wĕstfă' lĭăn,* s. & a. Vestfalo (m.).

York, *yŏrk,* Iorck, f.

Zeeland, *zĕ' lănd,* Selandia, f.
Zurich, *zŭr' ĭk,* Zurigo, m.

List of the most usual christian names, that differ in the two languages.

Adolphus, *ădŏl´fŭs,* Adolfo.
Alfred, *ăl´frĕd,* Alfredo.
Alice, *ăl´ĭs,* Alice.
Ambrose, *ăm´brōz,* Ambrogio.
Andrew, *ăn´drō,* Andrea.
Ann, Anne, *ăn,* Anna.
Anthony, *ăn´tŏnĭ,* Antonio.
Arnold, *ăr´nŏld,* Arnoldo.
Arthur, *ăr´thŭr,* Arturo.
Augustine, *ăgŭs´tĭn,* Agostino. [gusto.
Augustus, *ăgŭs´tŭs,* Au-

Bartholomew, *bărthŏl´ŏmū,* Bartolommeo.
Ben, *bĕn,* invece di: **Benjamin.** [detto.
Benedict, *bĕn´ĕdĭkt,* Benedetto.
Benjamin, *bĕn´jămĭn,* Benjamino.
Bertha, *bĕr´thă,* Berta.
Bess, *bĕs,* **Bessy,** *–sĭ,*
Betsey, *bĕt´sĭ,* invece di: **Elizabeth.**
Biddy, *bĭd´dĭ,* invece di: **Brigitta.**
Bill, *bĭl,* **Billy,** *–lĭ,* invece di: **William.**
Blanche, *blănsh,* Bianca.
Bob, *bŏb,* **Bobby,** *–bĭ,* invece di: **Robert.**
Bridget, *brĭj´ĕt,* Brigida.

Carry, *kăr´rĭ,* **Caddy,** *kăd´dĭ,* invece di: **Caroline.**
Catherine, *kăth´ĕrĭn,* Caterina.
Cecily, *sĕs´ĭlĭ,* Cecilia.
Charles, *chărlz,* Carlo.
Christopher, *krĭs´tŏfŭr,* Cristoforo.
Clara, *klā´ră,* Chiara.
Constance, *kŏn´stăns,* Costanza.
Constantine, *kŏn´stăntĭn,* Costantino.

Dan, *dăn,* invece di: **Daniel.**
Dick, *dĭk,* **Dicky,** *–ĭ,* invece di: **Richard.**
Doll, *dŏl,* **Dolly,** *–lĭ,* invece di: **Dorothy.**
Dominic, *dŏm´ĭnĭk,* Domenico.
Dorothy, *dŏr´ŏthĭ,* Dorotea.

Edmund, *ĕd´mŭnd,* Edmondo.
Edward, *ĕd´wŭrd,* Edoardo.
Eleanor, *ĕl´ĕnŏr,* Eleonora.
Elias, *ĕlī´ăs,* Elia.
Elizabeth, *ĕlĭz´ăbĕth,* Elisabetta.
Emily, *ĕm´ĭlĭ,* Emilia.

Fabian, *fā´bĭăn,* Fabiano.
Fanny, *făn´nĭ,* invece di: **Frances,** Franceschina.
Frances, *frăn´sĕs,* Francesca.
Francis, *frăn´sĭs,* **Frank,** *frăngk,* Francesco.

Geoffrey, *jĕf´frĭ,* Goffredo.
George, *jŏrj,* Giorgio.
Giles, *jīlz,* Giulio.
Godfrey, *gŏd´frĭ,* Goffredo.
Gregory, *grĕg´ŏrĭ,* Gregorio. [stavo.
Gustavus, *gŭstā´vŭs,* Gu-

Hal, *hăl,* invece di: **Henry.**
Hannah, *hăn´nă,* Anna.
Harriet, *hăr´rĭĕt,* Enrichetta. [Henry.
Harry, *hăr´rĭ,* invece di:
Helen, *hĕl´ĕn,* **Helena,** *hĕl´ĕnă,* Elena.
Henrietta, *hĕnrĭĕt´tă,* Enrichetta. [rigo.
Henry, *hĕn´rĭ,* Enrico, Ar-

Hilary, *hĭl´ărĭ,* Ilario.
Hodge, *hŏj,* invece di: **Roger.**
Hugh, *hū,* Ugone. [frio.
Humphrey, *hŭm´frĭ,* Ono-

Ignatius, *ĭgnā´shŭs,* Ignazio.

Jack, *jăk,* invece di: **John.**
Jacob, *jā´kŏb,* Jacopo.
James, *jāmz,* Giacomo.
Jane, *jăn,* Giovanna.
Jasper, *jăs´pŭr,* Gasparo.
Jeff, *jĕf,* invece di: **Geoffrey.**
Jem, *jĕm,* **Jim,** *jĭm,* **Jimmy,** *–mĭ,* invece di: **James.**
Jenny, *jĕn´nĭ,* Giovannina.
Jeremy, *jĕr´ĕmĭ,* Geremia.
Jerry, *jĕr´rĭ,* invece di: **Jeremy.** [seph.
Jo, Joe, *jō,* invece di: **Joseph.**
Joan, *jōn,* *jō´ăn,* Giovanna.
John, *jŏn,* Giovanni.
Johnny, *jŏn´nĭ,* invece di: **John.**
Joseph, *jō´zĕf,* Giuseppe.
Josephine, *jō´zĕfĭn,* Giuseppina.
Julia, *jū´lĭă,* Giulia.
Julian, *jū´lĭăn,* Giuliano.
Julius, *jū´lĭŭs,* Giulio.

Kate, *kăt,* **Kit,** *kĭt,* **Kitty,** *–ĭ,* invece di: **Catherine.**

Laurence, *lă´rĕns,* Lorenzo.
Lewis, *lō´ĭs,* Luigi.
Lizzy, *lĭz´zĭ,* Lisetta.
Loo, *lō,* invece di: **Louisa.**
Louise, *lōĕz´,* **Louisa,** *lōē´ză,* Luigia.
Lucian, *lō´shăn,* Luciano.
Lucy, *lō´sĭ,* Lucia.

Magdalen, *măg' dălĕn,* Maddalena.

Madge, *măj,* **Margery,** *măr' jĕrĭ,* **Meg,** *mĕg,* invece di: **Margaret.**

Margaret, *măr' gărĕt,* Margherita.

Mark, *mărk,* Marco.

Mary, *mā' rĭ,* Maria.

Mat, *măt,* invece di: **Matthew.**

Matthew, *mă' thŭ,* Matteo.

Michael, *mī' kĕl,* Michele.

Moll, *mŏl,* **Molly,** *–lĭ,* Mariuccia, Marietta.

Nan, *năn,* invece di: **Anne.**

Nancy, *năn' sĭ,* Annina.

Ned, *nĕd,* **Neddy,** *–dĭ,* invece di: **Edward.**

Nell, *nĕl,* **Nelly,** *–lĭ,* invece di: **Helen.**

Nick, *nĭk,* invece di: **Nicholas,** Niccolò.

Noah, *nō' ă,* Noa.

Otho, *ŏ' thŏ,* Ottone.

Patty, *păt' tĭ,* invece di: **Matilda.**

Peg, *pĕg,* **Peggy,** *–gĭ,* invece di: **Margaret.**

Peter, *pē' tŭr,* Pietro.

Phil, *fĭl,* invece di: **Philip,** Filippo.

Poll, *pŏl,* **Polly,** *pŏl' lĭ,* invece di: **Mary.**

Ralph, *răf (rălf),* Rodolfo.

Raymond, *rā' mŭnd,* Raimondo.

Reynold, *rĕn' ŏld,* Rinaldo.

Richard, *rĭch' ărd,* Riccardo.

Robin, *rŏb' ĭn,* invece di: **Robert,** Roberto.

Roger, *rŏj' ŭr,* Ruggero.

Roland, **Rowland,** *rŏ' lănd,* Orlando.

Sal, *săl,* **Sally,** *–lĭ,* invece di: **Sarah.** [muel.

Sam, *săm,* invece di: **Samuel.**

Sandy, *săn' dĭ,* **Sawney,** *să' nĭ,* invece di: **Alexander,** Alessandro.

Sarah, *sā' ră,* Sara.

Sebastian, *sĕbăs' tyăn,* Sebastiano.

Sigismund, *sĭj' ĭsmănd,* Sigismondo. [mone.

Solomon, *sŏl' ŏmŏn,* Salo-

Sophia, *sŏfī' ă,* **Sophy,** *sŏ'-fĭ,* Sofia.

Stephen, *stē' vĕn,* Stefano.

Susan, *sū' zăn,* Susanna.

Ted, *tĕd,* **Teddy,** *–dĭ,* invece di: **Edward.**

Theobald, *thē' ŏbăld,* Teobaldo.

Theresa, *tĕrē' ză,* Teresa.

Tim, *tĭm,* invece di: **Timothy.** [teo.

Timothy, *tĭm' ŏthĭ,* Timo-

Tobias, *tŏbī' ăs,* **Toby,** *tŏ'-bĭ,* Tobia.

Tom, *tŏm,* **Tommy,** *–mĭ,* invece di: **Thomas,** Tommaso. [thony.

Tony, *tŏ' nĭ,* invece di: **Anthony.**

Ulric, *ŭl' rĭk,* Ulderico.

Ursula, *ŭr' sŭlă,* Orsola.

Valentine, *văl' ĕntīn,* Valentino.

Walter, *wăl' tŭr,* Gualtieri.

Will, *wĭl,* **Willy,** *–lĭ,* invece di: **William.**

William, *wĭl' yăm,* Guglielmo.

Zachary, *zăk' ărĭ,* Zaccaria.

Table of the Irregular Verbs *).

Present.	Imperfect.	Participle.	Present.	Imperfect.	Participle.
abide	abode	abode	**drive**	drove	driven
am	was	been	**dwell**	dwelt *	dwelt *
arise	arose	arisen	**eat**	ate, eat	eaten
awake	awoke *	awaked	**engrave**	engraved	engraven *
backbite	backbit	backbitten	**fall**	fell	fallen
bear	bore (bare)	borne, born	**feed**	fed	fed
beat	beat	beat, beaten	**feel**	felt	felt
become	became	become	**fight**	fought	fought
befall	befell	befallen	**find**	found	found
beget	begot	begot, be-gotten	**flee**	fled	fled
			fling	flung	flung
begin	began	begun	**fly**	flew	flown
begird	begirt *	begirt	**forbear**	forbore	forborne
behold	beheld	beheld	**forbid**	forbade, forbid	forbidden, for-bid
bend	bent *	bent *			
bereave	bereft *	bereft *	**forecast**	forecast	forecast
beseech	besought	besought	**forego**	forewent	foregone
beset	beset	beset	**foreknow**	foreknew	foreknown
bestride	bestrode	bestrid, be-stridden	**forelay**	forelaid	forelaid
			forerun	foreran	forerun
betake	betook	betaken	**foresee**	foresaw	foreseen
bid	bid, bade	bid, bidden	**foreshow**	foreshowed	foreshown *
bind	bound	bound	**foretell**	foretold	foretold
bite	bit	bit, bitten	**forget**	forgot	forgot, for-gotten
bleed	bled	bled			
blow	blew	blown	**forgive**	forgave	forgiven
break	broke (brake)	broken	**forsake**	forsook	forsaken
breed	bred	bred	**forswear**	forswore	forsworn
bring	brought	brought	**freeze**	froze	frozen
build	built *	built *	**get**	got	got, gotten
burn	burnt *	burnt *	**gild**	gilt *	gilt *
burst	burst	burst	**gird**	girt *	girt *
buy	bought	bought	**give**	gave	given
can	could	—	**go**	went	gone
cast	cast	cast	**grave**	graved	graven *
catch	caught	caught	**grind**	ground	ground
chide	chid	chid, chidden	**grow**	grew	grown
choose	chose	chosen	**hang**	hung *	hung *
cleave	clove, cleft	cleft, cloven	**have**	had	had
cling	clung	clung	**hear**	heard	heard
clothe	clad *	clad *	**heave**	hove *	hove *
come	came	come	**hew**	hewed	hewn *
cost	cost	cost	**hide**	hid	hid, hidden
creep	crept	crept	**hit**	hit	hit
crow	crew *	crowed	**hold**	held	held (holden)
cut	cut	cut	**hurt**	hurt	hurt
dare	durst *	dared	**inlay**	inlaid	inlaid
deal	dealt	dealt	**interweave**	interwove	interwoven
dig	dug *	dug *	**keep**	kept	kept
dip	dipt *	dipt *	**kneel**	knelt *	knelt *
do	did	done	**knit**	knit *	knit *
draw	drew	drawn	**know**	knew	known
dream	dreamt *	dreamt *	**lade**	laded	laden *
drink	drank	drunk	**lay**	laid	laid

*) L'asterisco che il verbo se congiua anche regolarmente.

Present.	Imperfect.	Participle.	Present.	Imperfect.	Participle.
lead	led	led	overhear	overheard	overheard
lean	leant ✕	leant ✕	overlade	overladed	overladen ✕
leap	leapt ✕	leapt ✕	overlay	overlaid	overlaid
learn	learnt ✕	learnt ✕	overload	overloaded	overladen ✕
leave	left	left	overpay	overpaid	overpaid
lend	lent	lent	override	overrode, overrid	overrid, over- ridden
let	let	let			
lie (giacere)	lay	lain	overrun	overran	overrun
light	lit ✕	lit ✕	oversee	oversaw	overseen
load	loaded	laden ✕	overset	overset	overset
lose	lost	lost	overshoot	overshot	overshot
make	made	made	oversleep	overslept	overslept
may	might	—	over- spread	overspread	overspread
mean	meant	meant			
meet	met	met	overtake	overtook	overtaken
methinks	methought	—	overthrow	overthrew	overthrown
miscast	miscast	miscast	partake	partook	partaken
misdo	misdid	misdone	pay	paid	paid
misgive	misgave	misgiven	pen (stabbiare)	pent	pent
mishear	misheard	misheard			
mislay	mislaid	mislaid	put	put	put
mislead	misled	misled	quit	quit ✕	quit ✕
missend	missent	missent	read	read	read
misshape	misshaped	misshapen ✕	rebuild	rebuilt ✕	rebuilt ✕
misspeak	misspoke	misspoken	recast	recast	recast
misspell	misspelt ✕	misspelt ✕	remake	remade	remade
misspend	misspent	misspent	rend	rent	rent
mistake	mistook	mistaken	repay	repaid	repaid
misteach	mistaught	mistaught	retake	retook	retaken
misunder- stand	misunder- stood	misunder- stood	rid	rid	rid
miswrite	miswrote	miswritten	ride	rode, rid	rid, ridden
mow	mowed	mown ✕	ring	rung, rang	rung
must	must	—	rise	rose	risen
ought	ought	—	rive	rived	riven
outbid	outbid	outbid, out- bidden	run	ran	run
			saw	sawed	sawn ✕
			say	said	said
outdo	outdid	outdone	see	saw	seen
outfly	outflew	outflown	seek	sought	sought
outgive	outgave	outgiven	sell	sold	sold
outgo	outwent	outgone	send	sent	sent
outgrow	outgrew	outgrown	set	set	set
outride	outrode, outrid	outrid, out- ridden	shake	shook	shaken
			shall	should	—
outrun	outran	outrun	shape	shaped	shapen ✕
outsell	outsold	outsold	shave	shaved	shaven ✕
outshine	outshone	outshone	shear	sheared, shore	shorn ✕
outshoot	outshot	outshot	shed	shed	shed
outspread	outspread	outspread	shine	shone	shone
outstride	outstrid, out- strode	outstrid, out- stridden	shoe	shod	shod
			shoot	shot	shot
outswear	outswore	outsworn	show, shew	showed	shown ✕
outwear	outwore	outworn	shred	shred	shred
outwork	outwrought ✕	outwrought ✕	shrink	shrunk, shrank	shrunk, shrunken
overbear	overbore	overborne			
overbid	overbid	overbid, over- bidden	shut	shut	shut
			sing	sang, sung	sung
overbuy	overbought	overbought	sink	sank, sunk	sunk, sunken
overcast	overcast	overcast	sit	sat	sat
overcome	overcame	overcome	slay	slew	slain
overdo	overdid	overdone	sleep	slept	slept
overdraw	overdrew	overdrawn	slide	slid	slid, slidden
overdrive	overdrove	overdriven	sling	slung	slung
overeat	overate	overeat, over- eaten	slink	slunk	slunk
			slit	slit	slit ✕
overgo	overwent	overgone	smell	smelt ✕	smelt ✕
overhang	overhung ✕	overhung ✕	smite	smote	smitten

English and Italian.

Present.	Imperfect.	Participle.	Present.	Imperfect.	Participle.
sow	sowed	sown ✻	**underdo**	underdid	underdone
speak	spoke	spoken	**undergo**	underwent	undergone
speed	sped	sped	**underlay**	underlaid	underlaid
spell	spelt ✻	spelt ✻	**underlet**	underlet	underlet
spend	spent	spent	**underrun**	underran, un-derrun	underrun
spill	spilt ✻	spilt ✻			
spin	spun	spun	**undersell**	undersold	undersold
spit	spit, spat	spit	**understand**	understood	understood
split	split	split	**undertake**	undertook	undertaken
spread	spread	spread	**underwork**	under-wrought ✻	under-wrought ✻
spring	sprang, sprung	sprung			
			under-write	underwrote	underwritten
stand	stood	stood			
steal	stole	stolen	**undo**	undid	undone
stick	stuck	stuck	**ungird**	ungirt ✻	ungirt ✻
sting	stung	stung	**unlade**	unladed	unladen ✻
stink	stank, stunk	stunk	**unload**	unloaded	unloaden ✻
strew	strewed	strown ✻	**unsay**	unsaid	unsaid
stride	strode	strid, stridden	**unstring**	unstrung	unstrung
strike	struck	struck, (stricken)	**unwind**	unwound	unwound
			upbear	upbore	upborne
string	strung	strung	**updraw**	updrew	updrawn
strive	strove	striven	**uphold**	upheld	upheld (up-holden)
strow	strewed	strewed, strown			
			uprise	uprose	uprisen
swear	swore	sworn	**upset**	upset	upset
sweat	sweat ✻	sweat ✻	**wax**	waxed	waxen ✻
sweep	swept	swept	**waylay**	waylaid	waylaid
swell	swelled	swollen	**wear**	wore	worn
swim	swam, swum	swum	**weave**	wove	wove, woven
swing	swung	swung	**weep**	wept	wept
take	took	taken	**will**	would	—
teach	taught	taught	**win**	won	won
tear	tore	torn	**wind**	wound	wound
tell	told	told	**wiredraw**	wiredrew	wiredrawn
think	thought	thought	**withdraw**	withdrew	withdrawn
thrive	throve ✻	thriven ✻	**withhold**	withheld	withheld (withholden)
throw	threw	thrown			
thrust	thrust	thrust	**withstand**	withstood	withstood
tread	trod	trod, trodden	**work**	wrought ✻	wrought ✻
unbend	unbent ✻	unbent ✻	**wring**	wrung ✻	wrung ✻
underbid	underbid, un-derbade	underbid, un-derbidden	**write**	wrote	written